BENCHMARK SERIES

MICROSOFT® 365

WORD

LEVELS 1 & 2

NITA RUTKOSKY

AUDREY ROGGENKAMP
Pierce College Puyallup
Puyallup, Washington

IAN RUTKOSKY
Pierce College Puyallup
Puyallup, Washington

PARADIGM EDUCATION SOLUTIONS
A DIVISION OF KENDALL HUNT
Dubuque

Cover Photo Credit: © antishock/Shutterstock.com
Interior Photo Credits: Follow the Indexes.

ISBN 978-1-7924-6949-7

4050 Westmark Drive
Dubuque, IA 52004-1840
Email: ordernow@kendallhunt.com
Website: ParadigmEducation.com

Published in the United States of America

BRIEF CONTENTS

CONTENTS

Word Level 2

PREFACE

Benchmark Series, *Microsoft 365: Word,* Levels 1 & 2, prepares students to work with this popular word processing software for business or personal use. Incorporating an accelerated, step-by-step, project-based approach, this courseware helps students build competency in effectively preparing and formatting as well as enhancing and customizing documents using Word.

A Solution Designed for Student Success

The **Benchmark Series** is powered by Paradigm's Cirrus™ 2.0 platform, which provides a complete solution for learning how to use Microsoft 365 applications. This courseware develops students' skills and knowledge through a learning pathway that includes a series of training, practice, and assessment activities.

With the **Benchmark Series** and Cirrus, students can

- access course content anytime, anywhere through a live internet connection
- use a PC, Mac, or Chromebook
- complete all course activities in a single, seamless environment
- work live in the application without having to install anything
- view Watch and Learn Lessons that demonstrate exactly how to perform chapter activities
- receive immediate, personalized feedback to identify and self-correct errors
- complete Guide and Practice Tutorials to gain training and measured practice that is skill-specific, guided, and interactive
- and more!

ACHIEVING PROFICIENCY

Benchmark Series, *Microsoft 365: Word,* Levels 1 & 2, is designed for students who want to create professional-looking documents for school, work, and personal communication needs. No previous experience with word processing software is required. After successfully completing this course, students will be able to demonstrate the following performance objectives.

- Plan, research, write, revise, and publish documents to meet specific needs.
- Given a workplace scenario requiring a written solution, assess the communication purpose and then prepare the materials that achieve the goal efficiently and effectively.
- Create and edit letters, flyers, announcements, and reports that include headers, footers, references, tables of contents and figures, and hyperlinks.
- Use advanced formatting and editing features as well as building blocks and fields to create and edit a range of document types.
- Add and customize images, text boxes, charts, icons, 3D models, and other elements and objects to enhance written communication.
- Merge documents using a data source file and a main document.
- Manage shared documents that include comments and track changes, check and edit documents for accessibility, and apply document protection features.

Well-designed pedagogy is important, but students learn technology skills through practice and problem solving. Technology provides opportunities for interactive learning as well as excellent ways to quickly and accurately assess student performance. To this end, this course is supported with Cirrus™ 2.0, Paradigm's cloud-based training and assessment platform. Details about Cirrus as well as its integrated student courseware and instructor resources can be found on pages xv–xvii.

PROVEN INSTRUCTIONAL DESIGN

The **Benchmark Series** has long served as a standard of excellence in software instruction. Elements of the series function individually and collectively to create an inviting, comprehensive learning environment that leads to full proficiency in computer applications. The following visual tour highlights the structure and features that comprise the highly popular **Benchmark** model.

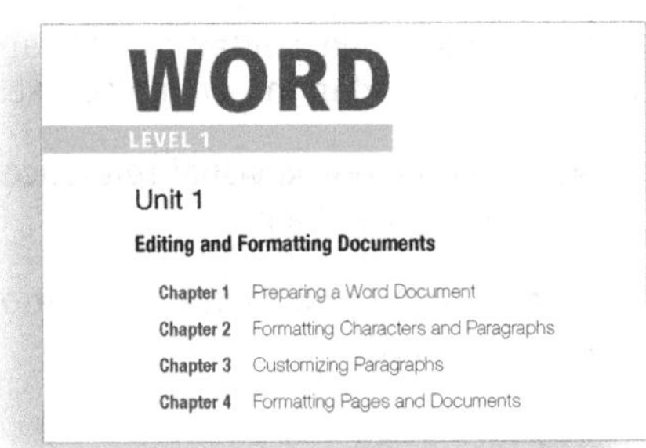
WORD
LEVEL 1
Unit 1
Editing and Formatting Documents
Chapter 1 Preparing a Word Document
Chapter 2 Formatting Characters and Paragraphs
Chapter 3 Customizing Paragraphs
Chapter 4 Formatting Pages and Documents

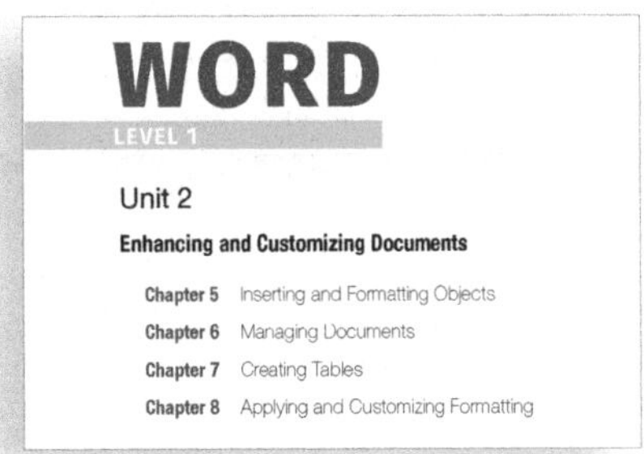
WORD
LEVEL 1
Unit 2
Enhancing and Customizing Documents
Chapter 5 Inserting and Formatting Objects
Chapter 6 Managing Documents
Chapter 7 Creating Tables
Chapter 8 Applying and Customizing Formatting

Unit openers display the unit's four chapter titles.

Chapter Openers Present Performance Objectives

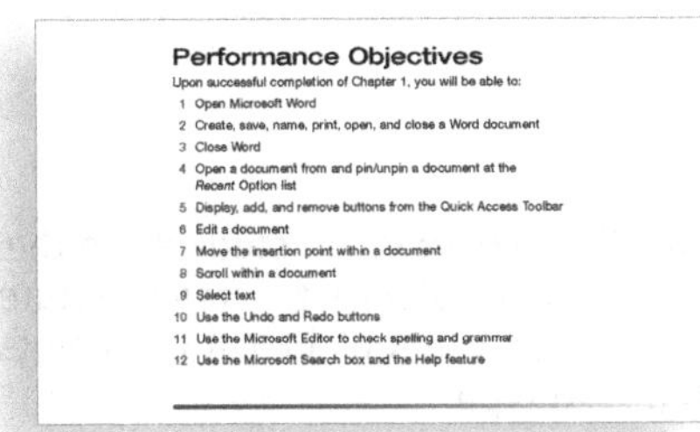
Performance Objectives
Upon successful completion of Chapter 1, you will be able to:
1 Open Microsoft Word
2 Create, save, name, print, open, and close a Word document
3 Close Word
4 Open a document from and pin/unpin a document at the *Recent* Option list
5 Display, add, and remove buttons from the Quick Access Toolbar
6 Edit a document
7 Move the insertion point within a document
8 Scroll within a document
9 Select text
10 Use the Undo and Redo buttons
11 Use the Microsoft Editor to check spelling and grammar
12 Use the Microsoft Search box and the Help feature

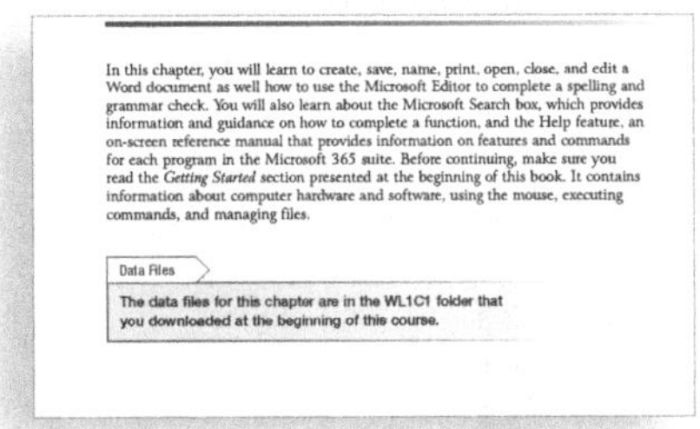
In this chapter, you will learn to create, save, name, print, open, close, and edit a Word document as well how to use the Microsoft Editor to complete a spelling and grammar check. You will also learn about the Microsoft Search box, which provides information and guidance on how to complete a function, and the Help feature, an on-screen reference manual that provides information on features and commands for each program in the Microsoft 365 suite. Before continuing, make sure you read the *Getting Started* section presented at the beginning of this book. It contains information about computer hardware and software, using the mouse, executing commands, and managing files.

Data Files
The data files for this chapter are in the WL1C1 folder that you downloaded at the beginning of this course.

Chapter openers present the performance objectives and an overview of the skills taught.

Data files are provided for each chapter. A prominent note reminds students to copy the appropriate chapter data folder and make it active.

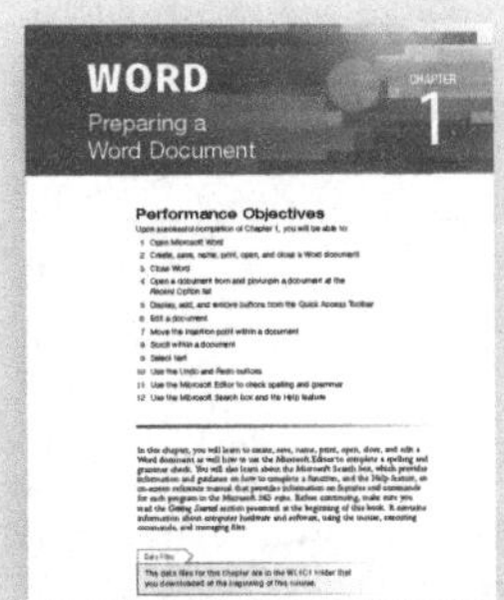

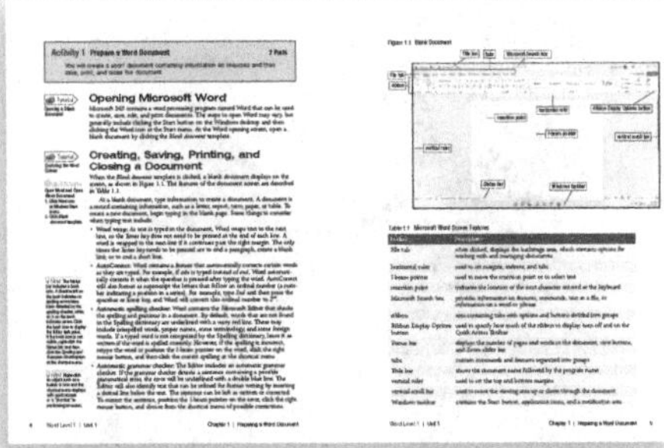

Opening Microsoft Word
Creating, Saving, Printing, and Closing a Document

Activities Build Skill Mastery within Realistic Context

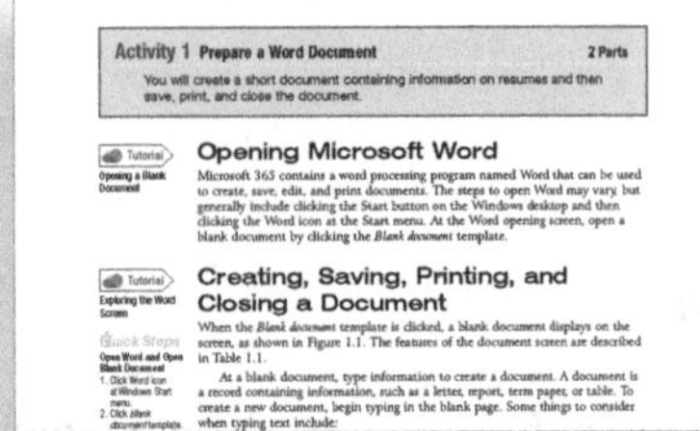

Multipart activities provide a framework for instruction and practice on software features. An activity overview identifies tasks to accomplish and key features to use in completing the work.

Typically, a file remains open throughout all parts of the activity. Students save their work incrementally. At the end of the activity, students save, preview, and then close the file.

Between activity parts, the text presents instruction on the features and skills necessary to accomplish the next portion of the activity.

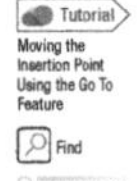

Tutorials provide interactive, guided training and measured practice and are accessed in the online course.

Button images provide a quick, visual reference to the buttons introduced in the chapter.

Hints offer useful tips on how to use application features efficiently and effectively.

Quick Steps in the margins allow fast reference and review.

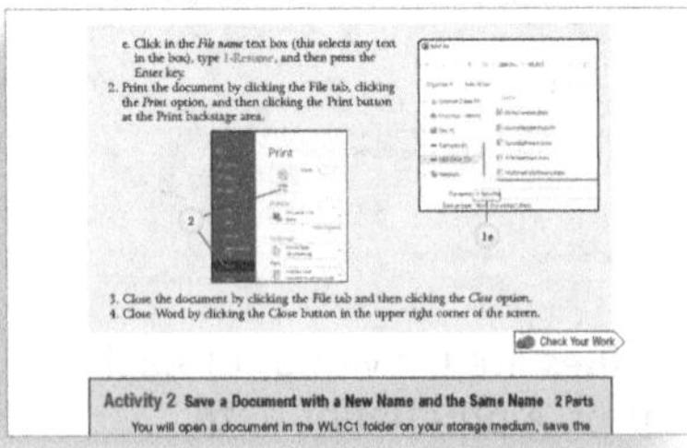

Step-by-step instructions guide students to the desired outcome for each activity part. Screen captures illustrate what the screen should look like at key points. Magenta identifies text to type.

Check Your Work images and demonstration videos are available in the online course.

Chapter Review and Assessment Reinforces Learning

Chapter Summary

- By default, a Word document contains 1-inch top, bottom, left, and right margins. Change margins with preset margin settings at the Margins button drop-down list or with options at the Page Setup dialog box with the Margins tab selected.
- The default page layout is portrait orientation. It can be changed to landscape orientation with the Orientation button in the Page Setup group on the Layout tab.
- The default paper size is 8.5 inches wide by 11 inches tall. It can be changed with options at the Size button drop-down list or options at the Page Setup dialog box with the Paper tab selected.
- A page break that Word inserts automatically is a *soft page break*. A page break inserted manually is a *hard page break*. Insert a hard page break using the Page Break button in the Pages group on the Insert tab or by pressing Ctrl + Enter.
- Insert a predesigned and formatted cover page by clicking the Cover Page button in the Pages group on the Insert tab and then clicking an option at the drop-down list.
- Insert predesigned and formatted page numbers by clicking the Page Number button in the Header & Footer group on the Insert tab, specifying the location of the page number, and then clicking a page numbering option.
- Insert predesigned headers and footers in a document with the Header button and the Footer button in the Header & Footer group on the Insert tab.
- A watermark is a lightened image that displays behind the text in a document. Use the Watermark button in the Page Background group on the Design tab to

A **Chapter Summary** reviews the purpose and execution of key software features.

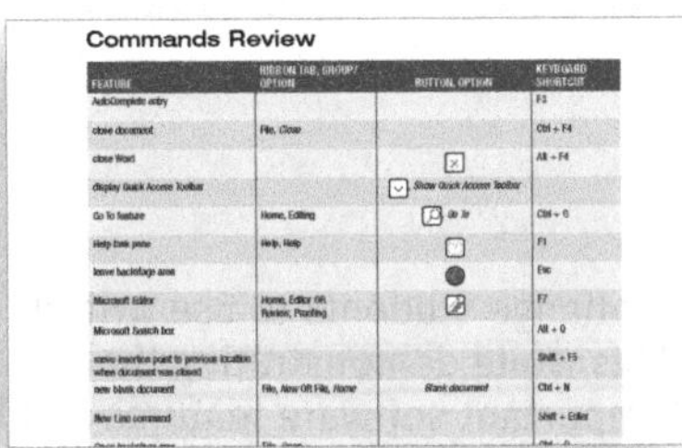

Commands Review

FEATURE	RIBBON TAB, GROUP/ OPTION	BUTTON, OPTION	KEYBOARD SHORTCUT
AutoComplete entry			F3
close document	File, *Close*		Ctrl + F4
close Word			Alt + F4
display Quick Access Toolbar		*Show Quick Access Toolbar*	
Go To feature	Home, Editing	*Go To*	Ctrl + G
Help task pane	Help, Help		F1
leave backstage area			Esc
Microsoft Editor	Home, Editor OR Review, Proofing		F7
Microsoft Search box			Alt + Q
move insertion point to previous location when document was closed			Shift + F5
new blank document	File, *New* OR File, *Home*	*Blank document*	Ctrl + N
New Line command			Shift + Enter

Commands Review tables list features taught in the chapter along with ribbon location, button names, and keyboard shortcuts.

Skills Assessment

Assessment 1

Edit a Document on Resume Writing

1. Open Word and then open **WriteResume.docx**.
2. Save the document with the name **1-WriteResume**.
3. Move the insertion point to the end of the document and then type the text shown in Figure 1.9. When typing the text, use the New Line command, Shift + Enter, to end the lines after *Created by Marie Solberg* and *Monday, October 7, 2024*.
4. Make the following changes to the document:
   a. Delete the first occurrence of the word *currently* in the first sentence of the first paragraph.
   b. Select the word *important* in the first sentence in the first paragraph and then type essential.
   c. Type and hard-hitting between the words *concise* and *written* in the second sentence of the second paragraph.
   d. Delete the words *over and over,* (including the comma and the space after the comma) in the third sentence in the second paragraph.
   e. Select and then delete the second sentence of the third paragraph (the sentence that begins *So do not take*).
   f. Move the insertion point to the beginning of the third paragraph and then press the backspace key to join the third paragraph with the second paragraph.

Skills Assessment exercises evaluate the ability to apply chapter skills and concepts in solving realistic problems.

Visual Benchmark

Create a Report about Active Listening Skills

1. Open **ActiveListen.docx** and then save it with the name **2-ActiveListen**.
2. Apply the following formatting to the document so it appears as shown in Figure 2.11:
   a. Select the document and then change the font to 12-point Cambria and the font color to standard dark blue.
   b. Set the title in 16-point Candara bold and center the title.
   c. Set the headings in 14-point Candara bold.
   d. Change the paragraph spacing after the title and headings to 6 points.
   e. Underline the text as shown in the figure.
   f. Create a hanging indent for the paragraphs as shown in the figure. (Do not create the hanging paragraphs using the Tab key.)
3. Save, preview, and then close **2-ActiveListen.docx**.

Figure 2.11 Visual Benchmark

ACTIVE LISTENING SKILLS

Becoming an Active Listener

Visual Benchmark activities are culminating assessments designed to demonstrate mastery of application features and problem-solving abilities.

Case Study

Part 1

You are the administrative assistant at a mid-sized service-oriented business. Employees frequently use Microsoft Word to create contracts to use with customers. Your boss, Mr. Brewster, wants these saved to a folder named *Contracts* in the Documents folder on your company's shared drive. Mr. Brewster has asked you to create a document for employees with step-by-step instructions for naming and saving contracts. Save your completed document with the name **1-Saving**. Preview and then close the document.

Part 2

Mr. Brewster would like to have a document describing basic Word commands and keyboard shortcuts to help employees work more efficiently in Microsoft Word. He has asked you to prepare a document containing the following information:

- A brief explanation of how to use the Go To feature to move the insertion point to a specific page
- Keyboard shortcuts to move the insertion point to the beginning and end of a line and the beginning and end of a document
- Keyboard commands to delete text from the insertion point to the beginning of a word and from the insertion point to the end of a word
- Steps to select a word and a paragraph using the mouse
- A keyboard shortcut to select the entire document

Save the completed document with the name **1-WordCommands**. Preview and then close the document.

Case Study activities require analyzing a workplace scenario and then planning and executing multipart project. Students may use the search and Help features to locate additional information required to complete the Case Study.

Unit Performance Assessments

Performance assessments for each four-chapter unit provide cross-disciplinary, comprehensive practice.

Data Files

The data files for this unit work are in the WL1U2 folder that you downloaded at the beginning of this course.

Assessing Proficiency

In this unit, you have learned to format and customize objects to enhance the appearance of documents; manage documents; print envelopes and labels; create documents using templates; create and edit tables; visually represent data in SmartArt graphics and charts; create custom numbering and bullet formatting; and customize a document using AutoCorrect options and custom themes.

Assessment 1

Format a Bioinformatics Document

1. Open **Bioinformatics.docx** and then save it with the name **U2-Bioinformatics**.
2. Move the insertion point to the end of the document and then insert the file named **GenomeMapping.docx**.
3. Press Ctrl + Home to move the insertion point to the beginning of the document and then insert the Motion Quote text box with the following

Assessing Proficiency activities check mastery of application functions and features.

Writing Activities

The following activities give you the opportunity to practice your writing skills and demonstrate your understanding of some of the important Word features you have mastered in this unit. Use correct grammar, appropriate word choices, and clear sentence construction.

Activity 1

Create a Letterhead and Compose a Letter

You are the executive assistant to the owner of Clearline Manufacturing, who has asked you to create a letterhead for the company. Use information of your choosing for the letterhead that includes the company name, address, email address, web address, and telephone number. Include an image in the letterhead. Five possible choices are available in your WL1U2 folder, and each image file name begins with *Manufacture*. Save the completed letterhead document as a template in your WL1U2 folder and name the template **CMLtrhdTemplate**. Close the template document.

Use File Explorer to open a document based on the **CMLtrhdTemplate.dotx** template. Write a letter to the president of the board of directors, Mrs. Nancy Logan (you determine her address), that includes the following:

- Explain that the director of the Human Resources Department has created a new employee handbook and that it will be made available to all new employees. Also mention that the attorney for Clearline Manufacturing has

Writing Activities challenge students to use written communication skills while demonstrating their understanding of important software features and functions.

- Apply title and/or heading styles to the title and headings in the document.
- Add a cover page of your choosing to the document and insert the appropriate information in the cover page placeholders.
- Any additional formatting that improves the appearance of the document.

Save, preview, and then close **U2-CMHandbook.docx**.

Internet Research

Create a Flyer on an Incentive Program

The owner of Blue Earth Adventures is offering an incentive to motivate adventure consultants to increase adventure bookings. The incentive is a sales contest with the grand prize of a one-week paid vacation to Cancun, Mexico. The owner has asked you to create a flyer that will be posted on the office bulletin board and that includes information about the incentive program and Cancun. Create this flyer using information about Cancun that you find on the internet. Consider using one (or more) of the images (**Cancun01.jpg**, **Cancun02.jpg**, **Cancun03.jpg**, and **Cancun04.jpg**) in your WL1U2 folder. Include any other information or objects to add visual interest to the flyer. Save the completed flyer with the name **U2-CancunFlyer**. Preview and then close **U2-CancunFlyer.docx**.

Internet Research assignments reinforce the importance of research and information processing skills along with proficiency in the Word environment.

Include any other information or objects to add visual interest to the flyer. Save the completed flyer with the name **U2-CancunFlyer**. Preview and then close **U2-CancunFlyer.docx**.

Job Study

Develop Recycling Program Communications

The chief operating officer of Harrington Engineering has just approved your draft of the company's new recycling policy, the file named **RecyclingPolicy.docx**. Open the file, edit the draft, and prepare a final copy of the policy, along with a memo to all employees describing the new guidelines. To support the company's energy resources conservation effort, you will send hard copies of the new policy to the president of the Somerset Recycling Program and to the directors of the Somerset Chamber of Commerce.

Using the concepts and techniques you learned in this unit, prepare the following documents:

- Format the recycling policy manual, including a cover page, appropriate headers and footers, and page numbers. Add at least one graphic where appropriate. Format the document using styles and a style set. Save the manual with the name **U2-RecyclingManual**. Preview the manual.
- Download a memo template at the New backstage area and then create a memo from Susan Gerhardt, Chief Operating Officer of Harrington Engineering, to all employees that introduces the new recycling program.

A **Job Study** activity included in the Unit 2 assessments presents a capstone activity requiring critical thinking and problem solving.

DRIVE STUDENT SUCCESS WITH CIRRUS

The **Benchmark Series**, powered by Paradigm's Cirrus platform, integrates seamlessly with Blackboard, Canvas, D2L, and Moodle. Students and educators can access all course material anytime, anywhere through a live internet connection. Cirrus delivers students the same learning experience whether they are using a PC, Mac, or Chromebook.

Course content is digitally delivered in a series of scheduled assignments that report to a grade book, thus tracking student progress and achievement through Cirrus's complete solution.

Dynamic Training, Practice, and Assessment

Cirrus course content for the **Benchmark Series** includes interactive assignments to guide student learning and engaging practice and assessment activities to reinforce and assess skills mastery.

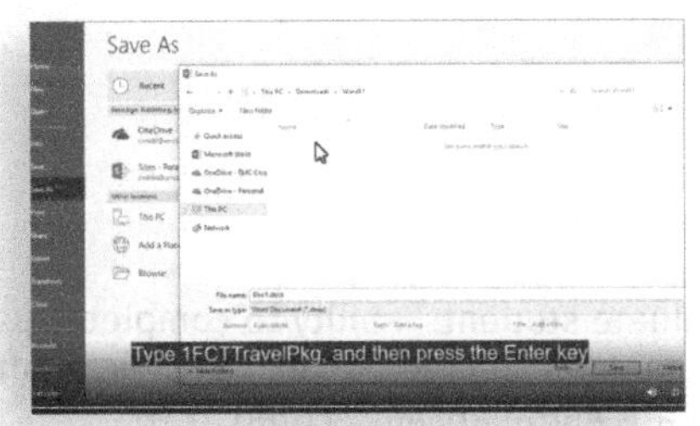

Watch and Learn Lessons explain how to perform each chapter activity part, including short demonstration videos for students to view and content for them to read. Performance objectives, chapter summaries, and Commands Review tables are also included with each lesson.

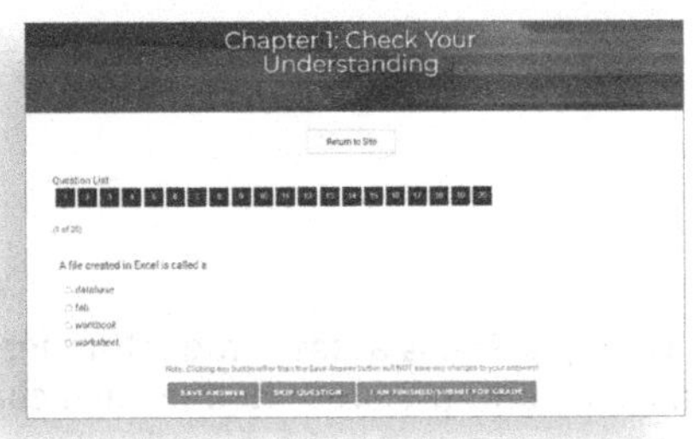

Check Your Understanding Quizzes allow students to check their understanding of the chapter concepts.

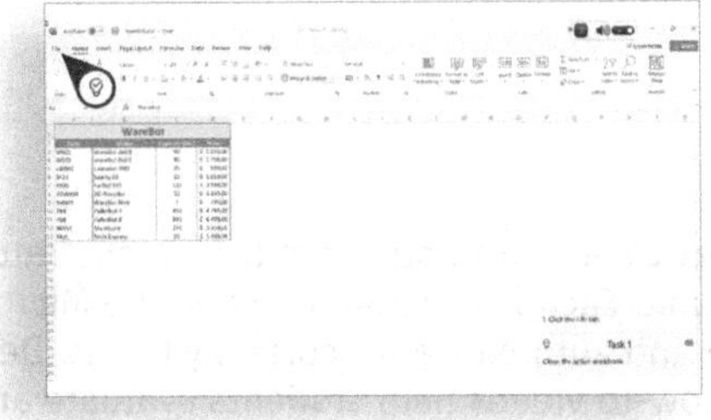

Guide and Practice Tutorials provide interactive, guided training and measured practice.

Chapter Practice and Assessment

Practice and assessment activities for each chapter reinforce and assess student learning.

Hands On Activities provide students the opportunity to practice their skills by completing chapter and end-of-chapter activities on the virtual desktop. Students upload their answers through Cirrus for instructor evaluation.

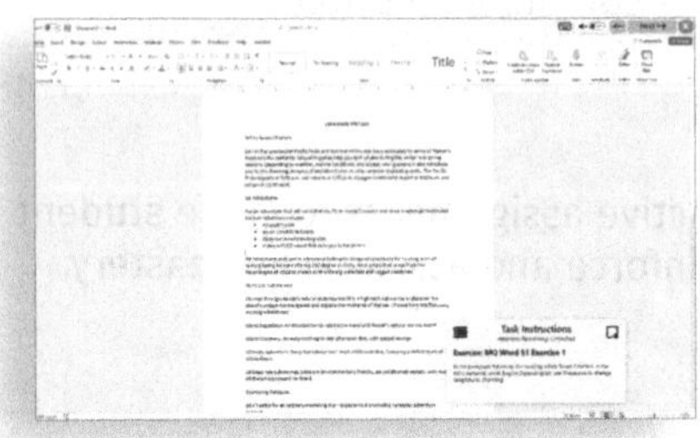

Exercises and Projects provide opportunities to practice and demonstrate skills learned in each chapter. Each is completed live in the Microsoft 365 application and is automatically scored by Cirrus. Detailed feedback and how-to videos help students evaluate and improve their performance.

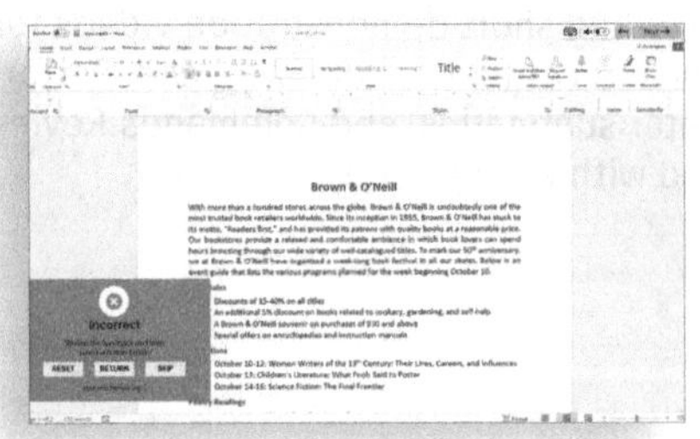

Skills Exams evaluate students' ability to complete specific tasks. Skills Exams are completed live in the Microsoft 365 application and are automatically scored.

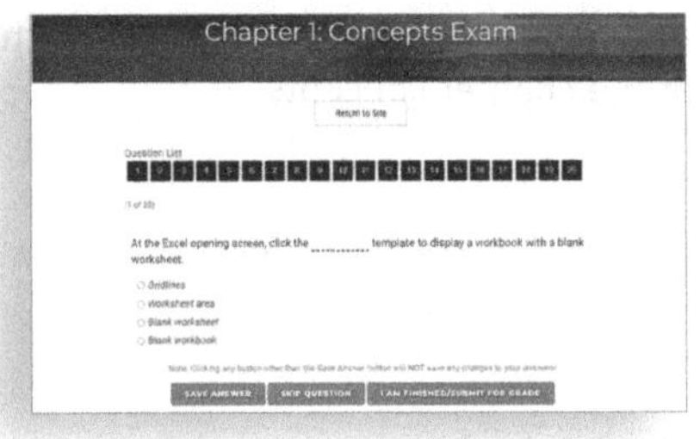

Multiple-choice **Concepts Exams** assess student understanding of key commands and concepts presented in each chapter.

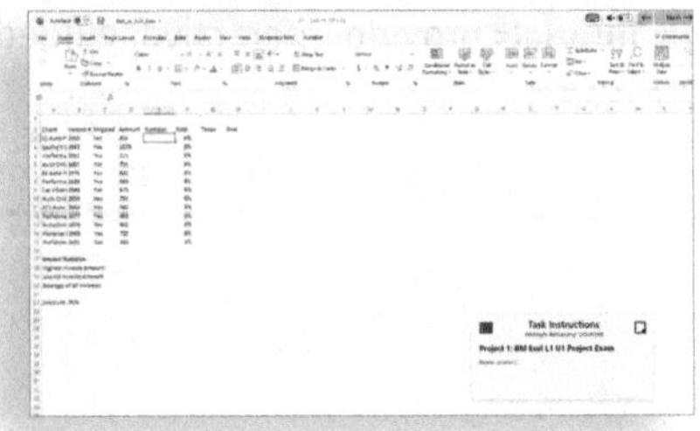

Unit-Level Project Exams allow students to demonstrate skills learned in the unit. Each is completed live in the Microsoft 365 application and automatically scored by Cirrus. Detailed feedback and how-to videos help students evaluate and improve their performance.

SUPPORT EVERY STEP OF THE WAY

Instructor Resources

Cirrus tracks students' step-by-step interactions as they move through each activity, giving instructors visibility into their progress. The Instructor Resources for the **Benchmark Series** include the following support:

- Planning resources, such as syllabus suggestions, course performance objectives, chapter-based performance objectives, and student completion time estimates
- Delivery resources, such as teaching tips, suggestions for using Cirrus demonstration elements in the classroom, and discussion questions
- Assessment resources, including live and annotated PDF model answers for chapter work and review and assessment activities, rubrics for evaluating student work, Knowledge Check completion exercises, chapter-based concept exam item banks, and new capstone projects that allow students to demonstrate their creativity and skills mastery

Faculty Preparation and Technical Assistance

Paradigm is committed to providing educators and students with unparalleled service and support. To prepare everyone for the first day of class and to deliver a smooth and successful experience throughout the course, Paradigm provides the following:

- training for educators teaching with the **Benchmark Series** and Cirrus course customization
- technical support based in the United States
- live chat for questions and assistance
- integration with an institution's learning management system

Visit **pescirrus.com** to access support from Paradigm.

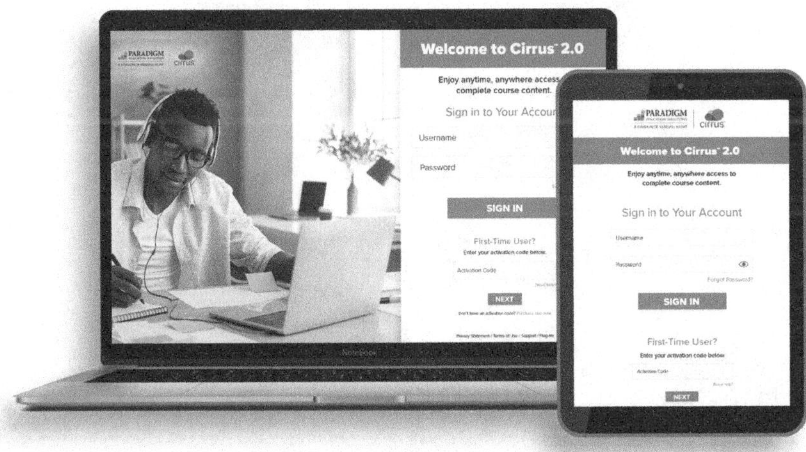

ABOUT THE AUTHORS

Nita Rutkosky began her career teaching business education at Pierce College in Puyallup, Washington, in 1978 and holds a master's degree in occupational education. In her years as an instructor, she taught many courses in software applications to students in postsecondary information technology certificate and degree programs. Since 1987, Nita has been a leading author of courseware for computer applications training and instruction. Her current titles include Paradigm's popular Benchmark Series and Marquee Series. She is a contributor to the Cirrus online content for Microsoft 365 application courses and has also written textbooks for keyboarding, desktop publishing, computing in the medical office, and essential skills for digital literacy.

Audrey Roggenkamp holds a master's degree in adult education and curriculum and has been an adjunct instructor in the Business Information Technology department at Pierce College in Puyallup, Washington, since 2005. Audrey has also been a content provider for Paradigm Education Solutions since 2005. In addition to contributing to the Cirrus online content for Microsoft 365 application courses, Audrey co-authors Paradigm's Benchmark Series, Marquee Series, and Signature Series. Her other available titles include *Keyboarding & Applications I and II* and *Using Computers in the Medical Office: Word, PowerPoint, and Excel.*

Ian Rutkosky has a master's degree in business administration and has been an adjunct instructor in the Business Information Technology department at Pierce College in Puyallup, Washington, since 2010. In addition to joining the author team for the Benchmark Series and Marquee Series, he has co-authored titles on medical office computing and digital literacy and has served as a co-author and consultant for Paradigm's Cirrus training and assessment platform.

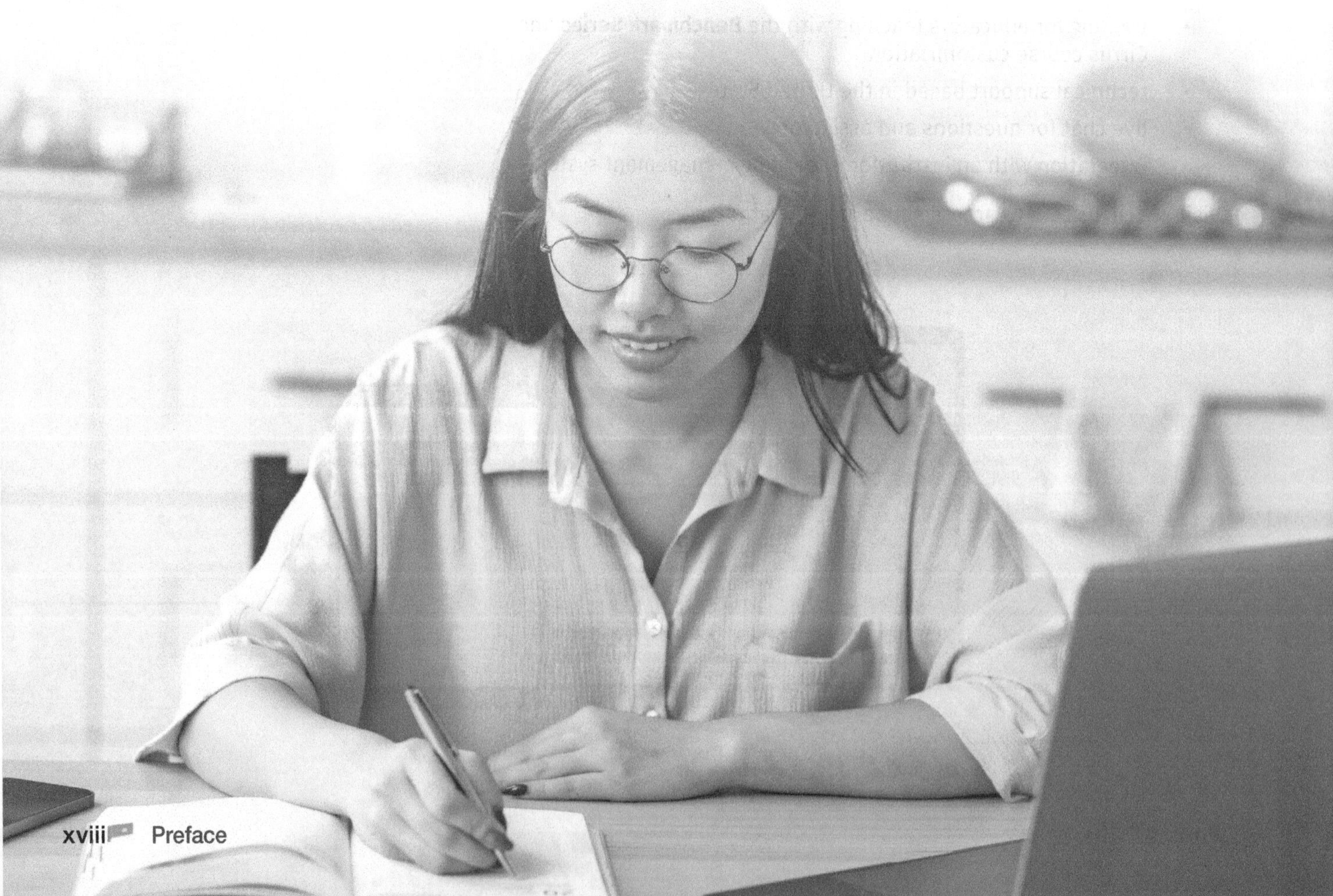

ACKNOWLEDGMENTS

The authors and publisher would like to thank the following individuals for their valuable feedback and recommendations.

Julia Basham
Southern State Community College

DeAnne (Dee) Bowersock
Ohio Business College—Sandusky Campus

Heidi Drake
Miller-Motte College of Charleston, SC

Joyce King
Bay College

Marlene Lucas
Westmoreland County Community College

Thomas Mays
Miami University

Mary Kim McDaniel
Wallace Community College—Dothan Campus

Lori McLaughlin
Richmond Community College

Kevin A. Parrett
Elizabethtown Community and Technical College

Crystal Pounds
Colby Community College

Lois Robinson
Reid State Technical College

Kyle Saunders
Bridgerland Technical College

Jane Scott
Spokane, WA

Dennis Sigur
Dillard University

Larrhea Sims
Gadsden State Community College

Melinda Shirey
Fresno City College

Angie Tatro
Pratt Community College

Jennifer Younger
North Central Kansas Technical College

Cirrus Survey Participants

Penny Aldridge
Wallace State Community College

Mary Anderson
Morris Brown College

Terry Ayers
Wallace State Community College

Julia Basham
Southern State Community College

Lani Bogoevska
Interactive College of Technology

DeAnne Bowersock
Ohio Business College—Sandusky Campus

Jeff Brabant
Miles Community College

Robin Bracisiewicz
Miller-Motte College

Tamra Brown
Western Technical College

Hanna Chapman
Chatfield College

Tondrika Dilligard
Miller-Motte College

Heidi Drake
Miller-Motte College

Chuck Durante
Lake-Sumter State College

Laura Fish
Coastal Pines Technical College

Omekia Harrison
Trenholm State Community College

Dr. Regina Henry
Strayer University

Edward Hunter
Skagit Valley College

Mark Kelly
Wallace Community College—Dothan Campus

Joyce King
Bay College

Marlene Lucas
Westmoreland County Community College

Tiffanie Maule
Pierce College

Tom Mays
Miami University

Kim McDaniel
Wallace Community College—Dothan Campus

Lori McLaughlin
Richmond Community College

Kevin Parrett
Elizabethtown Community and Technical College

Raymond Pierce
Wallace State Community College

Crystal Pounds
Colby Community College

Michael Quintieri
Miller-Motte Technical College

Bobbie Rathjens
North Central Michigan College

Lois Robinson
Reid State Technical College

Chris Sargent
Lake-Sumter State College

Kyle Saunders
Bridgerland Technical College

Melinda Shirey
Fresno City College

Dennis Sigur
Dillard University

Larrhea Sims
Gadsden State Community College

David Strickland
Miller-Motte College

Angie Tatro
Pratt Community College

Erica Teague
Gwinnett Technical College

Kershena Thomas
Miller-Motte College

Jonathan Weiss
Ocean County College

Veronica West-Williams
Miller-Motte College

Shawnette L. Williams
Manhattan Area Technical College

Jennifer Younger
North Central Kansas Technical College

GETTING STARTED

Microsoft 365 is a suite of applications for personal computers and other devices. Four applications within the suite include Word, a word processor; Excel, an electronic spreadsheet; Access, a database management system; and PowerPoint, a presentation application used to design and present slide shows. Microsoft 365 is a subscription service that delivers continually updated versions of the applications within the suite. Specific features and functionality of Microsoft 365 vary depending on the user's account, computer setup, and other factors. The Benchmark courseware was developed using features available in Microsoft 365. You may find that with your computer and version of Microsoft 365, the appearance of the application and the steps needed to complete an activity vary slightly from what is presented in the courseware.

Identifying Computer Hardware

The Microsoft 365 suite can run on several types of computer equipment, referred to as *hardware*. You will need access to a laptop or a desktop computer system that includes a PC/tower, monitor, keyboard, printer, drives, and mouse. If you are not sure what equipment you will be operating, check with your instructor. The computer system shown in Figure G.1 consists of six components. Each component is discussed separately in the material that follows.

Figure G.1 Computer System

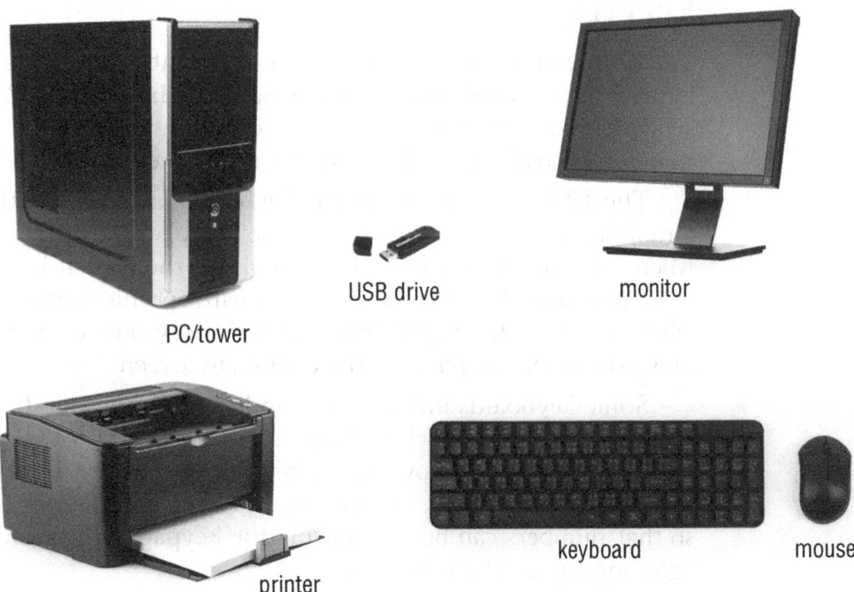

Figure G.2 System Unit Ports

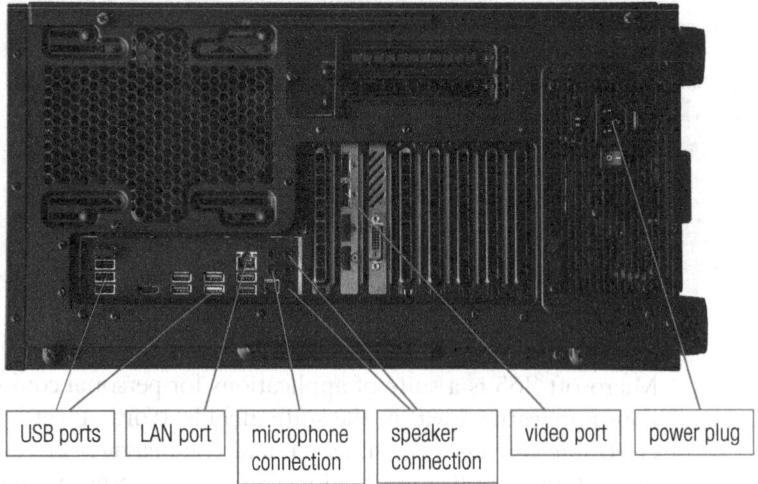

System Unit (PC/Tower)

Traditional desktop computing systems include a system unit known as the *PC (personal computer)* or *tower*. This is the brain of the computer, where all processing occurs. It contains a Central Processing Unit (CPU), hard drives, and video cards plugged into a motherboard. Input and output ports are used for attaching peripheral equipment such as a keyboard, monitor, printer, and so on, as shown in Figure G.2. When a user provides input, the PC computes it and outputs the results.

Monitor

Hint Monitor size is measured diagonally and is generally the distance from the bottom left corner to the top right corner of the monitor.

A computer monitor looks like a television screen. It displays the visual information output by the computer. Monitor size can vary, and the quality of display for monitors varies depending on the type of monitor and the level of resolution.

Keyboard

The keyboard is used to input information into the computer. The number and location of the keys on a keyboard can vary. In addition to letters, numbers, and symbols, most computer keyboards contain function keys, arrow keys, and a numeric keypad. Figure G.3 shows a typical keyboard.

The 12 keys at the top of the keyboard, labeled with the letter *F* followed by a number, are called *function keys*. Use these keys to perform functions within the Microsoft 365 applications. To the right of the regular keys is a group of special or dedicated keys. These keys are labeled with specific functions that will be performed when you press the key. Below the special keys are arrow keys. Use these keys to move the insertion point in the document screen.

Some keyboards include mode indicator lights to indicate that a particular mode, such as Caps Lock or Num Lock, has been turned on. Pressing the Caps Lock key disables the lowercase alphabet so that text is typed in all caps, while pressing the Num Lock key disables the special functions on the numeric keypad so that numbers can be typed using the keypad. When you select these modes, a light appears on the keyboard.

Figure G.3 Keyboard

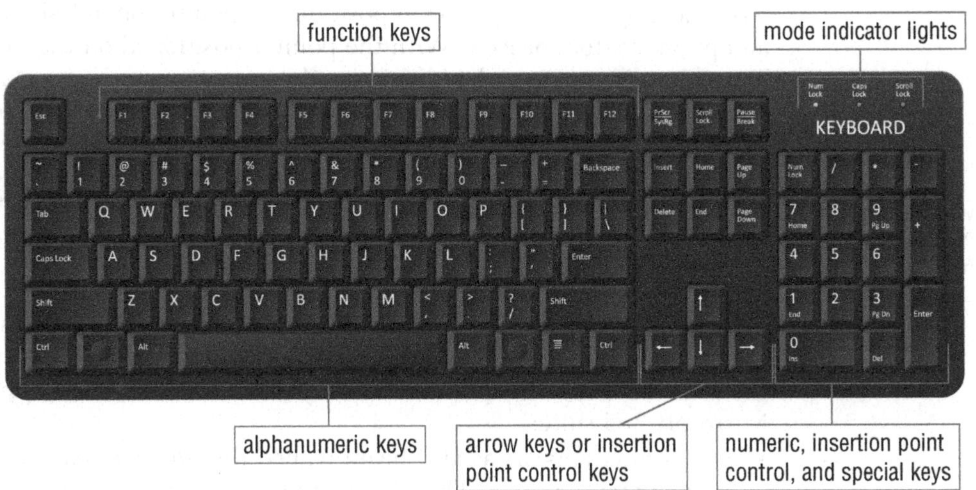

Drives and Ports

An internal hard drive is a disk drive that is located inside the PC and that stores data. External hard drives may be connected via USB ports for additional storage. Ports are the "plugs" on the PC, and are used to connect devices to the computer, such as the keyboard and mouse, the monitor, speakers, USB flash drives and so on. Most PCs will have a few USB ports, at least one display port, audio ports, and possibly an ethernet port (used to physically connect to the internet or a network).

Printer

An electronic version of a file is known as a *soft copy*. If you want to create a hard copy of a file, you need to print it. To print documents, you will need to access a printer, which will probably be either a laser printer or an ink-jet printer. A laser printer uses a laser beam combined with heat and pressure to print documents, while an ink-jet printer prints a document by spraying a fine mist of ink on the page.

Mouse

Most functions and commands in the Microsoft 365 suite are designed to be performed using a mouse or a similar pointing device. A mouse is an input device that sits on a flat surface next to the computer. You can operate a mouse with your left or right hand. Moving the mouse on the flat surface causes a corresponding pointer to move on the screen, and clicking the left or right mouse buttons allows you to select various objects and commands.

Using the Mouse The applications in the Microsoft 365 suite can be operated with the keyboard and a mouse. The mouse generally has two buttons on top, which you press to execute specific functions and commands. A mouse may also contain a wheel, which can be used to scroll in a window or as a third button. To use the mouse, rest it on a flat surface or a mouse pad. Put your hand over it with your palm resting on top of the mouse and your index finger resting on the left mouse button. As you move your hand, and thus the mouse, a corresponding pointer moves on the screen.

When using the mouse, you should understand four terms—*point*, *click*, *double-click*, and *drag*. To *point* means to position the pointer on a desired item, such as an option, button, or icon. With the pointer positioned on the item, *click* the left mouse button once to select the item. (In some cases you may *right-click*, which means to click the right mouse button, but generally, *click* refers to the left button.) To complete two steps at one time, such as choosing and then executing a function, *double-click* the left mouse button by tapping it twice in quick succession. The term *drag* means to click and hold down the left mouse button, move the pointer to a specific location, and then release the button. Clicking and dragging is used, for instance, when moving a file from one location to another.

Hint Instructions in this course use the verb *click* to refer to tapping the left mouse button and the verb *press* to refer to pressing a key on the keyboard.

Using the Pointer The pointer will look different depending on where you have positioned it and what function you are performing. The following are some of the ways the pointer can appear when you are working in an application in the Microsoft 365 suite:

- The pointer appears as an I-beam (called the *I-beam pointer*) when you are inserting text in a file. The I-beam pointer can be used to move the insertion point or to select text.

- The pointer appears as an arrow pointing up and to the left when it is moved to the Title bar, ribbon, Status bar or an option in a dialog box, among other locations.

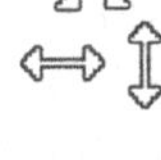

- The pointer becomes a double-headed arrow (either pointing left and right, pointing up and down, or pointing diagonally) when you perform certain functions such as changing the size of an object.

- In certain situations, such as when you move an object or image, the pointer displays with a four-headed arrow attached. The four-headed arrow means that you can move the object left, right, up, or down.

- When a request is being processed or when an application is being loaded, the pointer may appear as a moving circle. The moving circle means "please wait." When the process is completed, the circle is replaced with a normal pointer.

- When the pointer displays as a hand with a pointing index finger, it indicates that more information is available about an item. The pointer also displays as a hand with a pointing index finger when you hover over a hyperlink.

Touchpad

If you are working on a laptop computer, you may be using a touchpad instead of a mouse. A *touchpad* allows you to move the pointer by moving your finger across a surface at the base of the keyboard (as shown in Figure G.4). You click and right-click by using your thumb to press the buttons located at the bottom of the touchpad. Some touchpads have special features such as scrolling or clicking something by tapping the surface of the touchpad instead of pressing a button with a thumb.

Figure G.4 Touchpad

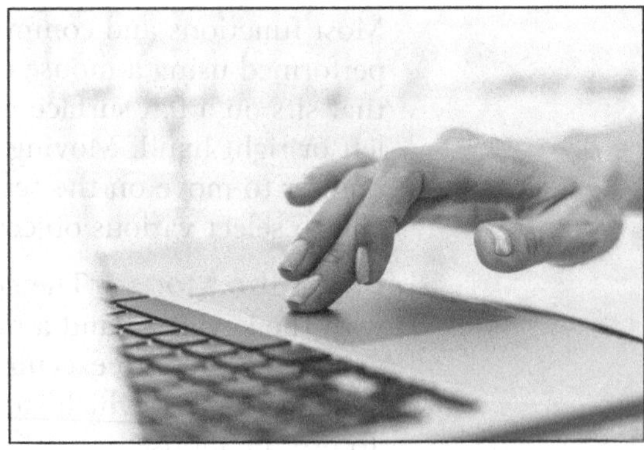

Touchscreen

Smartphones, tablets, and touch monitors all use touchscreen technology (as shown in Figure G.5), which allows users to directly interact with the objects on the screen by touching them with fingers, thumbs, or a stylus. Multiple fingers or both thumbs can be used on most touchscreens, giving users the ability to zoom, rotate, and manipulate items on the screen. While many activities in this textbook can be completed using a device with a touchscreen, a mouse or touchpad might be required to complete a few activities.

Figure G.5 Touchscreen

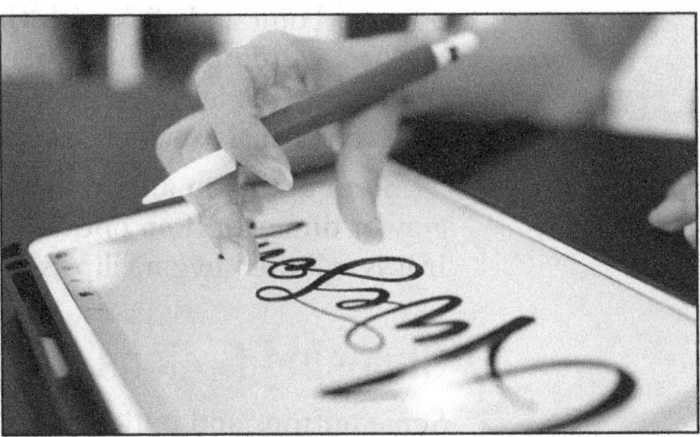

Choosing Commands

A *command* is an instruction that tells an application to complete a certain task. When an application such as Word or PowerPoint is open, the *ribbon* at the top of the window displays buttons and options for commands. To select a command with the mouse, point to it and then click the left mouse button.

Notice that the ribbon is organized into tabs, including File, Home, Insert, and so on. When the File tab is clicked, a *backstage area* opens with options such as opening or saving a file. Clicking any of the other tabs will display a variety of commands and options on the ribbon.

Using Keyboard Shortcuts and Accelerator Keys

As an alternative to using the mouse, keyboard shortcuts can be used for many commands. Shortcuts generally require two or more keys. For instance, in Word, press and hold down the Ctrl key while pressing P to display the Print backstage area, or press Ctrl + O to display the Open backstage area. A complete list of keyboard shortcuts can be found by searching the Help files in a Microsoft 365 application.

Microsoft 365 also provides shortcuts known as *accelerator keys* for every command or action on the ribbon. These accelerator keys are especially helpful for users with motor or visual disabilities or for power users who find it faster to use the keyboard than click with the mouse. To identify accelerator keys, press the Alt key on the keyboard. KeyTips display on the ribbon, as shown in Figure G.6. Press the keys indicated to execute the desired command. For example, to display a list of margin options, press the Alt key, press the P key on the keyboard to display the Layout tab, and then press the letter M on the keyboard.

Figure G.6 Word Home Tab KeyTips

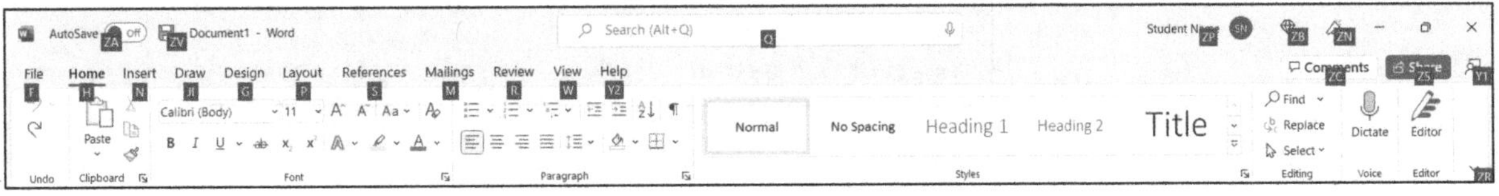

Choosing Commands from a Drop-Down List

Some buttons include arrows that can be clicked to display a drop-down list of options. Point and click with the mouse to choose an option from the list. Some options in a drop-down list may have a letter that is underlined. This indicates that typing the letter will select the option. For instance, to select the option *Insert Table*, type the letter I on the keyboard.

If an option in a drop-down list is not available to be selected, it will appear gray or dimmed. If an option is preceded by a check mark, it is currently active. If it is followed by an ellipsis (...), clicking the option will open a dialog box.

Choosing Options from a Dialog Box or Task Pane

Some buttons and options open a *dialog box* or a task pane containing options for applying formatting or otherwise modifying the data in a file. For example, the Font dialog box shown in Figure G.7 contains options for modifying the font and adding effects. The dialog box contains two tabs—the Font tab and the Advanced tab. The tab that displays in the front is the active tab. Click a tab to make it active or press Ctrl + Tab on the keyboard. Alternately, press the Alt key and then type the letter that is underlined in the tab name.

To choose an option from a dialog box using the mouse, position the arrow pointer on the option and then click the left mouse button. To move forward from option to option using the keyboard, you can press the Tab key. Press Shift + Tab to move back to a previous option. If the option displays with an underlined letter,

Figure G.7 Word Font Dialog Box

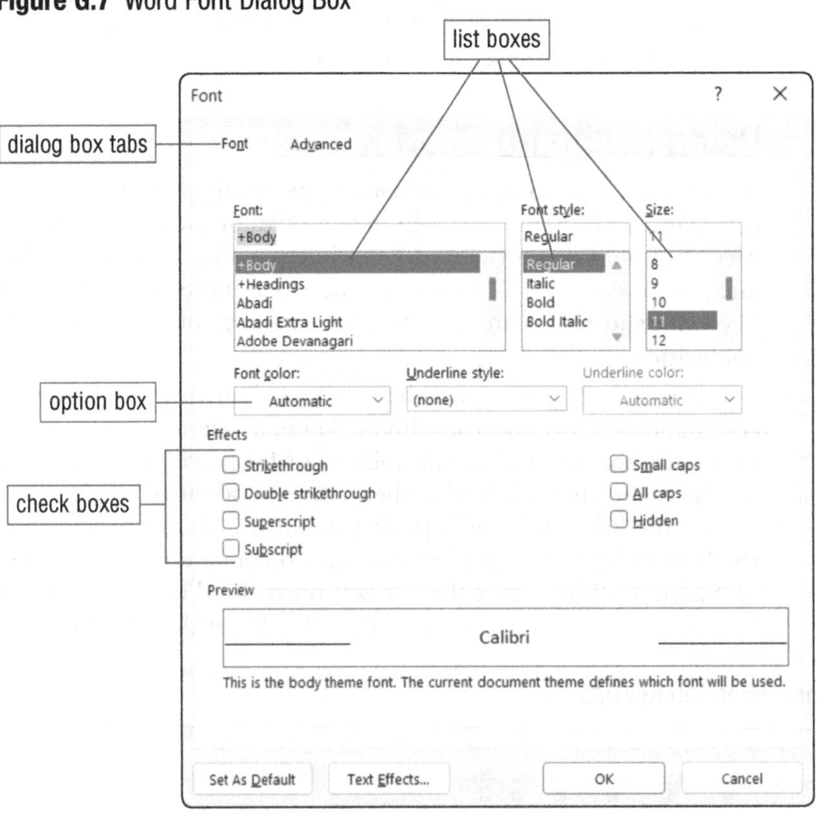

you can choose it by pressing the Alt key and the underlined letter. When an option is selected, it is highlighted in blue or surrounded by a dotted or dashed box called a *marquee*. A dialog box contains one or more of the following elements: list boxes, option boxes, check boxes, text boxes, command buttons, radio buttons, and measurement boxes.

List Boxes and Option Boxes The fonts available at the Font dialog box, shown in Figure G.7 (on the previous page), are contained in a *list box*. Click an option in the list to select it. If the list is long, click the up or down arrows in the *scroll bar* at the right side of the box to scroll through all the options. Alternately, press the up or down arrow keys on the keyboard to move through the list, and press the Enter key when the desired option is selected.

Option boxes contain a drop-down list or gallery of options that opens when the arrow in the box is clicked. An example is the *Font color* option box at the Font dialog box shown in Figure G.7. To display the different color options, click the arrow at the right side of the box. If you are using the keyboard, press Alt + C.

Check Boxes Some options can be selected using a check box, such as the effect options at the dialog box in Figure G.7. If a check mark appears in the box, the option is active (turned on). If the check box does not contain a check mark, the option is inactive (turned off). Click a check box to make the option active or inactive. If you are using the keyboard, press Alt + the underlined letter of the option.

Text Boxes Some options in a dialog box require you to enter text. For example, see the Find and Replace dialog box shown in Figure G.8. In a text box, type or edit text with the keyboard, using the left and right arrow keys to move the insertion point without deleting text and use the Delete key or Backspace key to delete text.

Command Buttons The buttons at the bottom of the dialog box shown in Figure G.8 are called *command buttons*. Use a command button to execute or cancel a command. Some command buttons display with an ellipsis (...), which means another dialog box will open if you click that button. To choose a command button, click with the mouse or press the Tab key until the command button is surrounded by a marquee and then press the Enter key.

Figure G.8 Excel Find and Replace Dialog Box

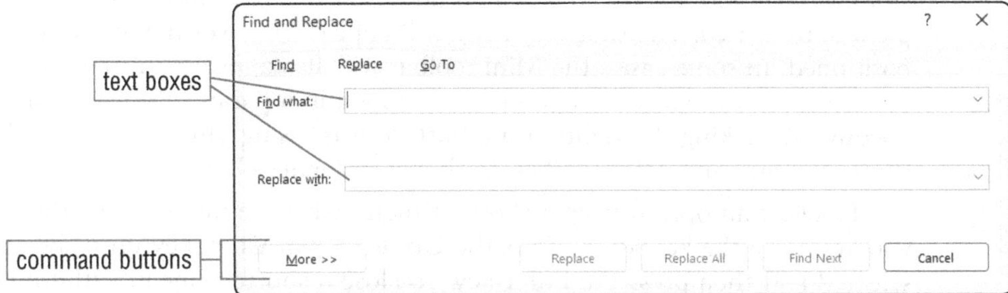

Figure G.9 Word Insert Table Dialog Box

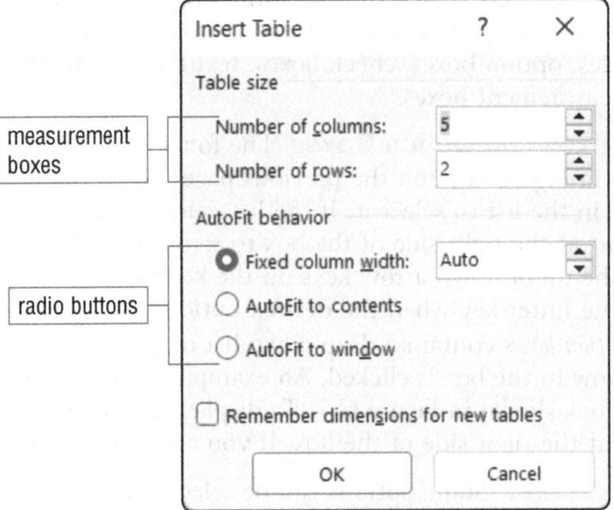

Radio Buttons The Insert Table dialog box shown in Figure G.9 contains an example of *radio buttons* (also referred to as *option buttons*). Only one radio button can be selected at any time. When the button is selected, it is filled with a dark circle. Click a button to select it, or press and hold down the Alt key, press the underlined letter of the option, and then release the Alt key.

Measurement Boxes A *measurement box* contains an amount that can be increased or decreased. An example is shown in Figure G.9. To increase or decrease the number in a measurement box, click the up or down arrow at the right side of the box. Using the keyboard, press and hold down the Alt key and then press the underlined letter for the option, press the Up Arrow key on the keyboard to increase the number or the Down Arrow key to decrease the number, and then release the Alt key.

Choosing Commands with Shortcut Menus

Microsoft 365 applications include shortcut menus that contain commands related to different items. To display a shortcut menu, point to the item for which you want to view more options with the pointer and then click the *right* mouse button, or press Shift + F10. The shortcut menu will appear wherever the insertion point is positioned. In some cases, the Mini toolbar will also appear with the shortcut menu. For example, if the insertion point is positioned in a paragraph of text in a Word document, clicking the right mouse button or pressing Shift + F10 will display the shortcut menu and Mini toolbar, as shown in Figure G.10.

To select an option from a shortcut menu with the mouse, click the option. If you are using the keyboard, press the Up or Down Arrow key until the option is selected and then press the Enter key. To close a shortcut menu without choosing an option, click outside the menu or press the Esc key.

Figure G.10 Shortcut Menu and Mini Toolbar

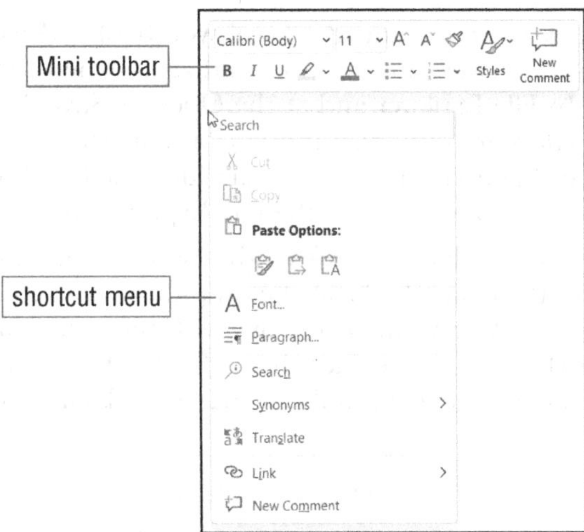

Working with Multiple Applications

As you learn the various applications in the Microsoft 365 suite, you will notice many similarities between them. For example, the steps to save, close, and print are virtually the same whether you are working in Word, Excel, or PowerPoint. This consistency greatly enhances your ability to transfer knowledge learned in one application to another within the suite. Another benefit to using Microsoft 365 is the ability to integrate content from one application with another. For example, you can open Word and create a document, open Excel and create a worksheet, and then copy a worksheet from the workbook into Word.

The Windows taskbar at the bottom of the screen displays buttons representing all the applications that are currently open. For example, Figure G.11 shows the taskbar with Word, Excel, Access, and PowerPoint open. To move from one application to another, click the button on the taskbar representing the desired application.

Maintaining Files and Folders

Windows includes a file management feature named File Explorer that can be used to maintain files and folders. To open File Explorer, click the folder icon on the Windows taskbar. Use File Explorer to complete tasks such as copying, moving, renaming, and deleting files and folders and creating new folders. Some file management tasks can also be completed within Word, Excel, PowerPoint, or Access by clicking File and then *Open* or *Save As* and then clicking the *Browse* option to browse folders and files in a dialog box.

Directions and activities in this course assume that you are managing files and folders stored on a USB flash drive or on your computer's hard drive. If you are using your OneDrive account or another cloud-based storage service, some of the file and folder management tasks may vary.

Figure G.11 Windows Taskbar with Word, Excel, Access, and PowerPoint Open

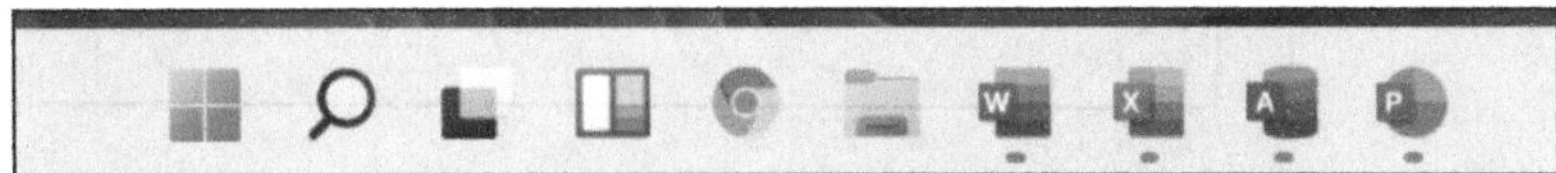

Creating and Naming a Folder

Files (such as Word documents, Excel workbooks, PowerPoint presentations, and Access databases) are easier to find again when they are grouped logically in folders. In File Explorer and at the Open or Save As dialog box, the names of files and folders are displayed in the Content pane. Each file has an icon showing what type of file it is, while folders are identified with the icon of a folder. See Figure G.12 for an example of the File Explorer window.

Create a new folder by clicking the New button at the top of the File Explorer window and then click *Folder* at the drop-down list or click the New folder button in a dialog box. A new folder displays with the name *New folder* highlighted. Type a name for the folder to replace the highlighted text, and then press the Enter key. Folder names can include numbers, spaces, and some symbols.

Selecting and Opening Files and Folders

Select files or folders in a window or dialog box to be managed. To select one file or folder, simply click on it. To select several adjacent files or folders, click the first file or folder, hold down the Shift key, and then click the last file or folder. To select files or folders that are not adjacent, click the first file or folder, hold down the Ctrl key, click any other files or folders, and then release the Ctrl key. To deselect, click anywhere in the window or dialog box.

When a file or folder is selected, the path to the folder displays in the Address bar. If the folder is located on an external storage device, the drive letter and name may display in the path. A right-pointing arrow displays to the right of each folder name in the Address bar. Click the arrow to view a list of subfolders within a folder.

Double-click a file or folder in the Content pane to open it. You can also select one or more files or folders, right-click, and then click the *Open* option at the shortcut menu.

Figure G.12 File Explorer Window

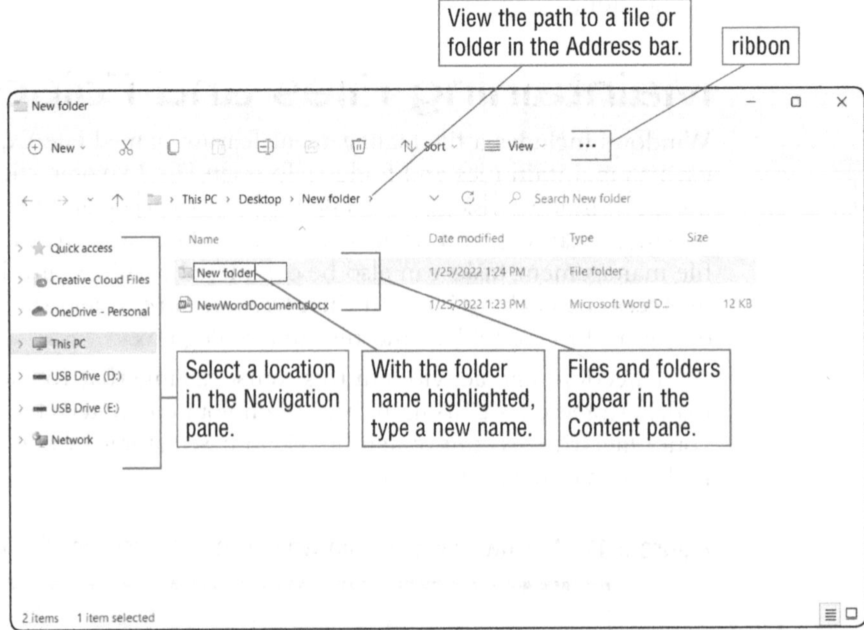

Deleting Files and Folders

Deleting files and folders is part of file maintenance. To delete a file or folder, select it and then press the Delete key. Alternatively, use the Delete button on the ribbon of the File Explorer window, or click the Organize button and then *Delete* at the dialog box. You can also right-click a file or folder and then choose the *Delete* option at the shortcut menu.

Files and folders deleted from the hard drive of the computer are automatically sent to the Recycle Bin, where they can easily be restored if necessary. If a file or folder is stored in another location, such as an external drive or online location, it may be permanently deleted. In this case, a message may appear asking for confirmation. To confirm that the file or folder should be deleted, click Yes.

To view the contents of the Recycle Bin, display the Windows desktop and then double-click the *Recycle Bin* icon. Deleted items in the Recycle Bin can be restored to their original locations, or the Recycle Bin can be emptied to free up space on the hard drive.

Moving and Copying Files and Folders

A file or folder may need to be moved or copied to another location. In File Explorer, select the file or folder and then click the Copy button on the ribbon, use the keyboard shortcut Ctrl + C, or right-click the file and select *Copy* at the shortcut menu. Navigate to the destination folder and then click the Paste button on the ribbon, use the keyboard shortcut Ctrl + V, or right-click and select *Paste*. If a copy is pasted to the same folder as the original, it will appear with the word *Copy* added to its name. To copy files at the Open or Save As dialog box, use the Organize button drop-down list or right-click to access the shortcut menu.

To move a file or folder, follow the same steps, but click the Cut button instead of the Copy button on the ribbon of the File Explorer window, select *Cut* instead of *Copy* or press Ctrl + X instead of Ctrl + C. Files can also be dragged from one location to another. To do this, open two File Explorer windows. Click a file or folder and drag it to the other window while holding down the left mouse button.

Renaming Files and Folders

To rename a file or folder in File Explorer, click its name to highlight it and then type a new name, or right-click the file or folder and then select *Rename* at the shortcut menu. You can also select the file or folder and then click the Rename button on the File Explorer ribbon or click *Rename* from the Organize button drop-down list at the Open or Save As dialog box. Type in a new name and then press the Enter key.

Viewing Files and Folders

Change how files and folders display in the Content pane in File Explorer by clicking the View button on the ribbon and then clicking one of the view options at the drop-down list. View files and folders as extra large, large, medium, or small icons; as tiles; in a list; or with details or information about the file or folder content. At the Open or Save As dialog box, click the Change your view button arrow and a list displays with similar options for viewing folders and files. Click to select an option in the list or click the Change your view button to see different views.

Displaying File Extensions Each file has a file extension that identifies the application and what type of file it is. Excel files have the extension *.xlsx;* Word files end with *.docx,* and so on. By default, file extensions are turned off. To view file extensions, open File Explorer, click the View button on the ribbon, point to *Show* at the drop-down list, and then click *File name extensions* at the side menu. The *File name extensions* option will display with a check mark next to it when file extensions are turned on. Click the option again to stop viewing file extensions.

Displaying All Files The Open or Save As dialog box in a Microsoft 365 application may display only files specific to that application. For example, the Open or Save As dialog box in Word may only display Word documents. Viewing all files at the Open dialog box can be helpful in determining what files are available. Turn on the display of all files at the Open dialog box by clicking the file type button arrow at the right side of the *File Name* text box and then clicking *All Files (*.*)* at the drop-down list.

Managing Files at the Info Backstage Area

The Info backstage area in Word, Excel, and PowerPoint provides buttons for managing files such as uploading and sharing a file, copying a path, and opening File Explorer with the current folder active. To use the buttons at the Info backstage area, open Word, Excel, or PowerPoint and then open a file. Click the File tab and then click the *Info* option. If a file is opened from the computer's hard drive or an external drive, four buttons display near the top of the Info backstage area as shown in Figure G.13.

Figure G.13 Info Backstage Buttons

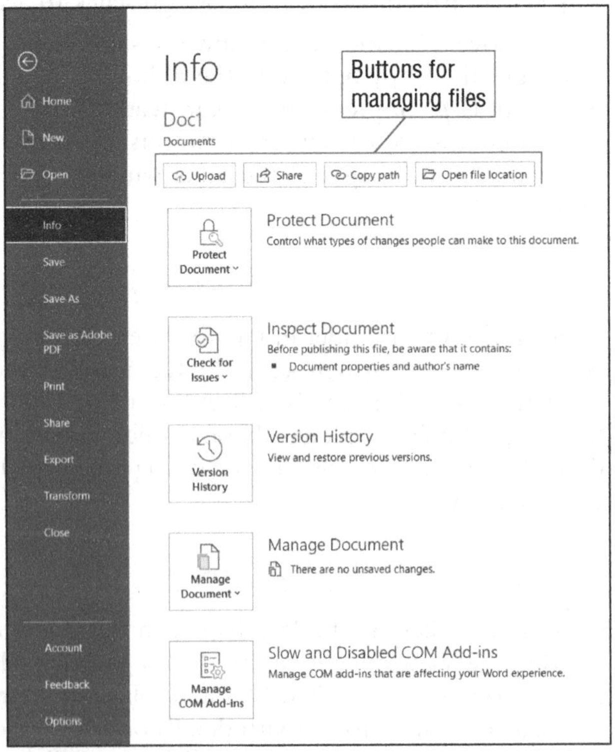

Click the Upload button to upload the open file to a shared location such as a OneDrive account. Click the Share button and a window displays indicating that the file must be saved to OneDrive before it can be shared and provides an option that, when clicked, will save the file to OneDrive. Click the Copy path button and a copy of the path for the current file is saved in a temporary location. This path can be pasted into another file, an email, or any other location where you want to keep track of the file's path. Click the Open file location button and File Explorer opens with the current folder active.

If you open Word, Excel, or PowerPoint and then open a file from OneDrive, three buttons display—Share, Copy path, and Open file location. Click the Share button to display a window with options for sharing the file with others and specifying whether the file can be viewed and edited, or only viewed. Click the Copy path button to save a copy of the path for the current file. Click the Open file location button to open File Explorer with the current folder active.

Customizing Settings

Before beginning computer activities in this textbook, you may need to customize your monitor's settings and change the DPI display setting. Activities in the course assume that the monitor display is set at 1920 × 1080 pixels and the DPI set at 125%. If you are unable to make changes to the monitor's resolution or the DPI settings, the activities can still be completed successfully. Some references in the text might not perfectly match what you see on your screen, so you may not be able to perform certain steps exactly as written. For example, an item in a drop-down gallery might appear in a different column or row than what is indicated in the step instructions.

Before you begin learning applications in the Microsoft 365 suite, take a moment to check the display settings on the computer you are using. Your monitor's display settings are important because the ribbon in the Microsoft 365 suite adjusts to the screen resolution setting of your computer monitor. A computer monitor set at a high resolution will have the ability to show more buttons on the ribbon than will a monitor set to a low resolution. The illustrations in this textbook were created with a screen resolution display set at 1920 × 1080 pixels, as shown in Figure G.14.

Figure G.14 Word Ribbon Set at 1920 x 1080 Screen Resolution

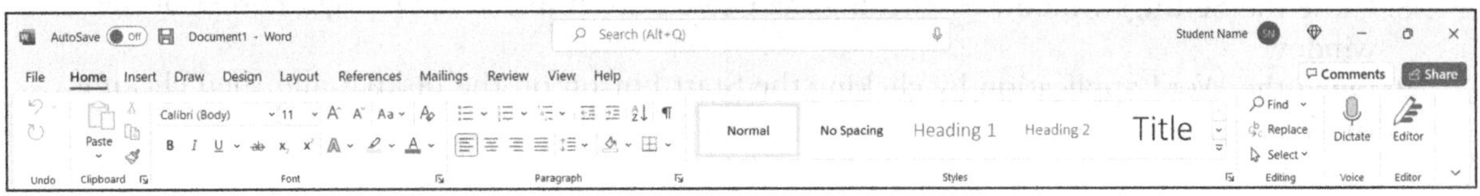

Activity 1 Adjusting Monitor Display and Changing Office Theme

Note: The resolution settings and Office theme may be locked on lab computers. Also, some laptop screens and small monitors may not be able to display in a 1920 × 1080 resolution or change the DPI setting.

1. At the Windows desktop, right-click in a blank area of the screen.
2. At the shortcut menu, click the *Display settings* option.
3. At the Settings window with *System* > *Display* at the top of the window, scroll down and look at the current setting in the *Display resolution* option box. If your screen is already set to 1920 × 1080, skip ahead to Step 5.
4. Click the *Display resolution* option box and then click the *1920 × 1080* option. ***Note: Depending on the privileges you are given on a school machine, you may not be able to complete Steps 4–5. If necessary, check with your instructor for alternative instructions.***
5. Click the Keep changes button at the message box asking if you want to keep the display settings.
6. At the Settings window, look at the percentage in which the size of text, apps, and other items currently display (also known as the DPI setting) in the *Scale* option box. For example, items on your screen may display at 100%. If the percentage is 125%, skip to Step 8.
7. Click the Scale option box arrow and then click the *125%* option at the drop-down list.

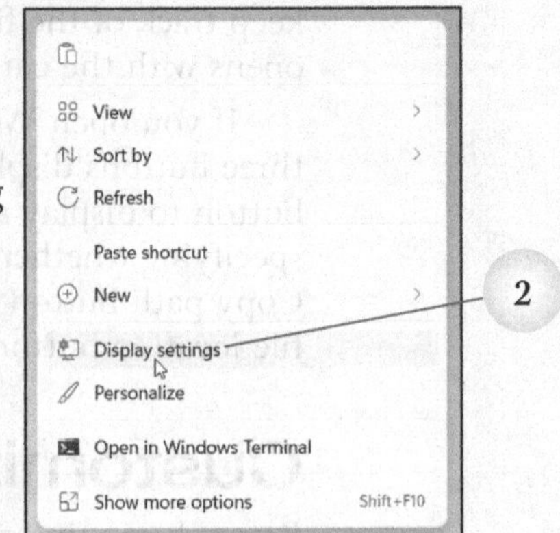

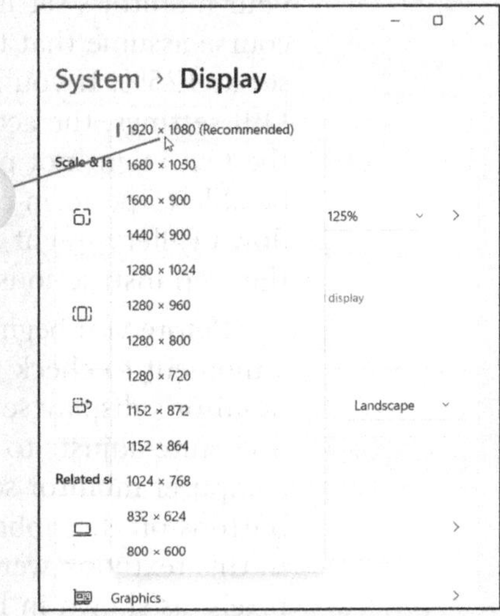

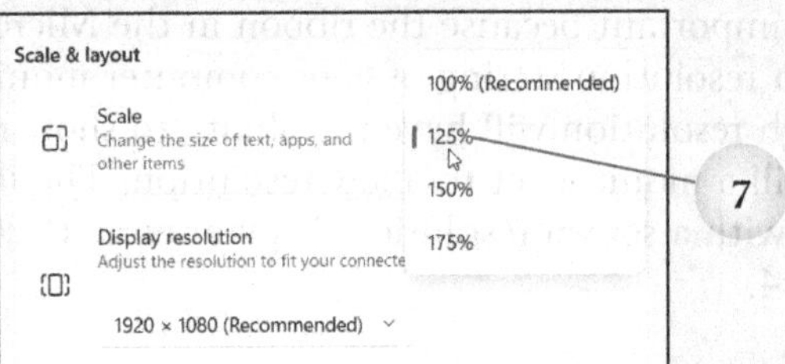

8. Close the Settings window by clicking the Close button in the upper right corner of the window.
9. Open the Word application by clicking the Start button on the taskbar and then clicking the Word icon.

10. At the opening Word screen, click the *Account* option (located near the bottom of the left panel).
11. At the Account backstage area, make sure *Use system setting* displays in the *Office Theme* option box. If it does not, click the *Office Theme* option box arrow and then click *Use system setting* at the drop-down list. If *Use system setting* is not available, click *White* at the drop-down list.
12. Close Word by clicking the Close button in the upper right corner of the screen.

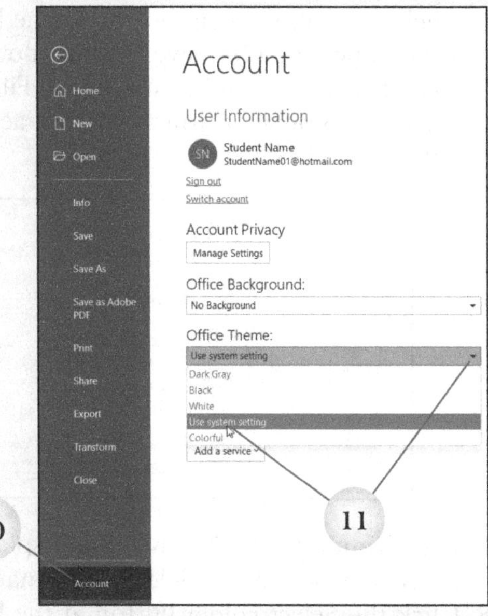

Retrieving and Copying Data Files

While working through the activities in this course, you will often be using data files as starting points. These files are provided through your Cirrus online course, and your instructor may post them in another location such as your school's network drive. You can download all the files at once (described in the activity below), or download only the files needed for a specific chapter.

Activity 2 **Downloading Files to a USB Flash Drive**

Note: In this activity, you will download data files from your Cirrus online course. Make sure you have an active internet connection before starting this activity. Check with your instructor if you do not have access to your Cirrus online course.

1. Insert your USB flash drive into an available USB port.
2. Navigate to the Course Resources section of your Cirrus online course. ***Note: The steps in this activity assume you are using the Chrome browser. If you are using a different browser, the following steps may vary.***
3. Read the acknowledgment statement about the use of the data files and then click the <u>I Accept</u> hyperlink. A zip file containing the data files will automatically begin downloading from the Cirrus website.

> If you are a PC user running Windows 11 with Microsoft 365/2021 installed on your computer and you wish to access the data files outside of the Cirrus environment, please click I Accept.
>
> **I Accept | Help with the Data Files**

3

4. Click the DataFiles.zip button in the lower left corner of the screen once the files have finished downloading.
5. Click the Extract all button on the File Explorer ribbon.
6. Click the Browse button at the Extract Compressed (Zipped) Folders window.
7. Click your USB flash drive that displays in the Navigation pane at the left side of the Select a destination folder.
8. Click the Select Folder button at the bottom right corner of the Select a destination folder.
9. Click the Extract button.

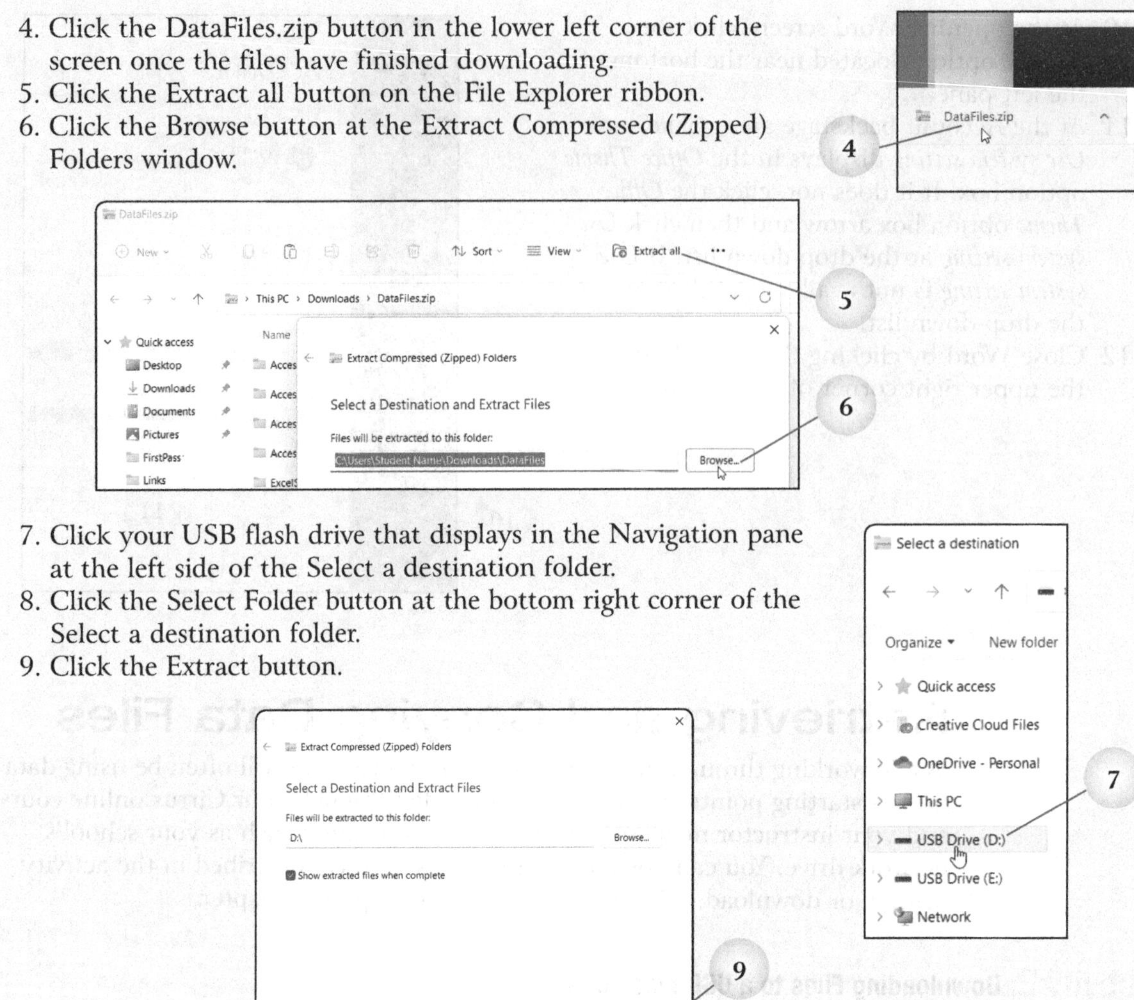

10. Close the File Explorer window by clicking the Close button in the upper right corner of the window.

WORD

LEVEL 1

Unit 1

Editing and Formatting Documents

WORD

CHAPTER 1

Preparing a Word Document

Performance Objectives

Upon successful completion of Chapter 1, you will be able to:

1. Open Microsoft Word
2. Create, save, name, print, open, and close a Word document
3. Close Word
4. Open a document from and pin/unpin a document at the *Recent* Option list
5. Display, add, and remove buttons from the Quick Access Toolbar
6. Edit a document
7. Move the insertion point within a document
8. Scroll within a document
9. Select text
10. Use the Undo and Redo buttons
11. Use the Microsoft Editor to check spelling and grammar
12. Use the Microsoft Search box and the Help feature

In this chapter, you will learn to create, save, name, print, open, close, and edit a Word document as well how to use the Microsoft Editor to complete a spelling and grammar check. You will also learn about the Microsoft Search box, which provides information and guidance on how to complete a function, and the Help feature, an on-screen reference manual that provides information on features and commands for each program in the Microsoft 365 suite. Before continuing, make sure you read the *Getting Started* section presented at the beginning of this book. It contains information about computer hardware and software, using the mouse, executing commands, and managing files.

Data Files

The data files for this chapter are in the WL1C1 folder that you downloaded at the beginning of this course.

Activity 1 Prepare a Word Document **2 Parts**

You will create a short document containing information on resumes and then save, print, and close the document.

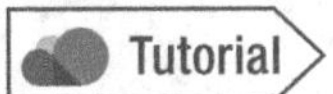

Opening a Blank Document

Opening Microsoft Word

Microsoft 365 contains a word processing program named Word that can be used to create, save, edit, and print documents. The steps to open Word may vary, but generally include clicking the Start button on the Windows desktop and then clicking the Word icon at the Start menu. At the Word opening screen, open a blank document by clicking the *Blank document* template.

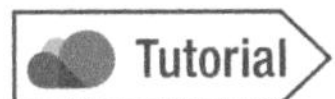

Exploring the Word Screen

Quick Steps

Open Word and Open Blank Document

1. Click Word icon at Windows Start menu.
2. Click *Blank document* template.

Creating, Saving, Printing, and Closing a Document

When the *Blank document* template is clicked, a blank document displays on the screen, as shown in Figure 1.1. The features of the document screen are described in Table 1.1.

At a blank document, type information to create a document. A document is a record containing information, such as a letter, report, term paper, or table. To create a new document, begin typing in the blank page. Some things to consider when typing text include:

- **Word wrap:** As text is typed in the document, Word wraps text to the next line, so the Enter key does not need to be pressed at the end of each line. A word is wrapped to the next line if it continues past the right margin. The only times the Enter key needs to be pressed are to end a paragraph, create a blank line, or to end a short line.
- **AutoCorrect:** Word contains a feature that automatically corrects certain words as they are typed. For example, if *adn* is typed instead of *and*, Word automatically corrects it when the spacebar is pressed after typing the word. AutoCorrect will also format as superscript the letters that follow an ordinal number (a number indicating a position in a series). For example, type *2nd* and then press the spacebar or Enter key, and Word will convert this ordinal number to 2nd.
- **Automatic spelling checker:** Word contains the Microsoft Editor that checks the spelling and grammar in a document. By default, words that are not found in the Spelling dictionary are underlined with a wavy red line. These may include misspelled words, proper names, some terminology, and some foreign words. If a typed word is not recognized by the Spelling dictionary, leave it as written if the word is spelled correctly. However, if the spelling is incorrect, retype the word or position the I-beam pointer on the word, click the right mouse button, and then click the correct spelling at the shortcut menu.
- **Automatic grammar checker:** The Editor includes an automatic grammar checker. If the grammar checker detects a sentence containing a possible grammatical error, the error will be underlined with a double blue line. The Editor will also identify text that can be refined for format writing by inserting a dotted line below the text. The sentence can be left as written or corrected. To correct the sentence, position the I-beam pointer on the error, click the right mouse button, and choose from the shortcut menu of possible corrections.

Hint The Status bar includes a book icon. A check mark on the book indicates no spelling errors have been detected by the spelling checker, while an X on the book indicates errors. Click the book icon to display the Editor task pane. If the book icon is not visible, right-click the Status bar and then click the *Spelling and Grammar Check* option at the shortcut menu.

Hint Right-click an object such as a button or icon and the shortcut menu displays with quick access or a "shortcut" to performing an action.

Figure 1.1 Blank Document

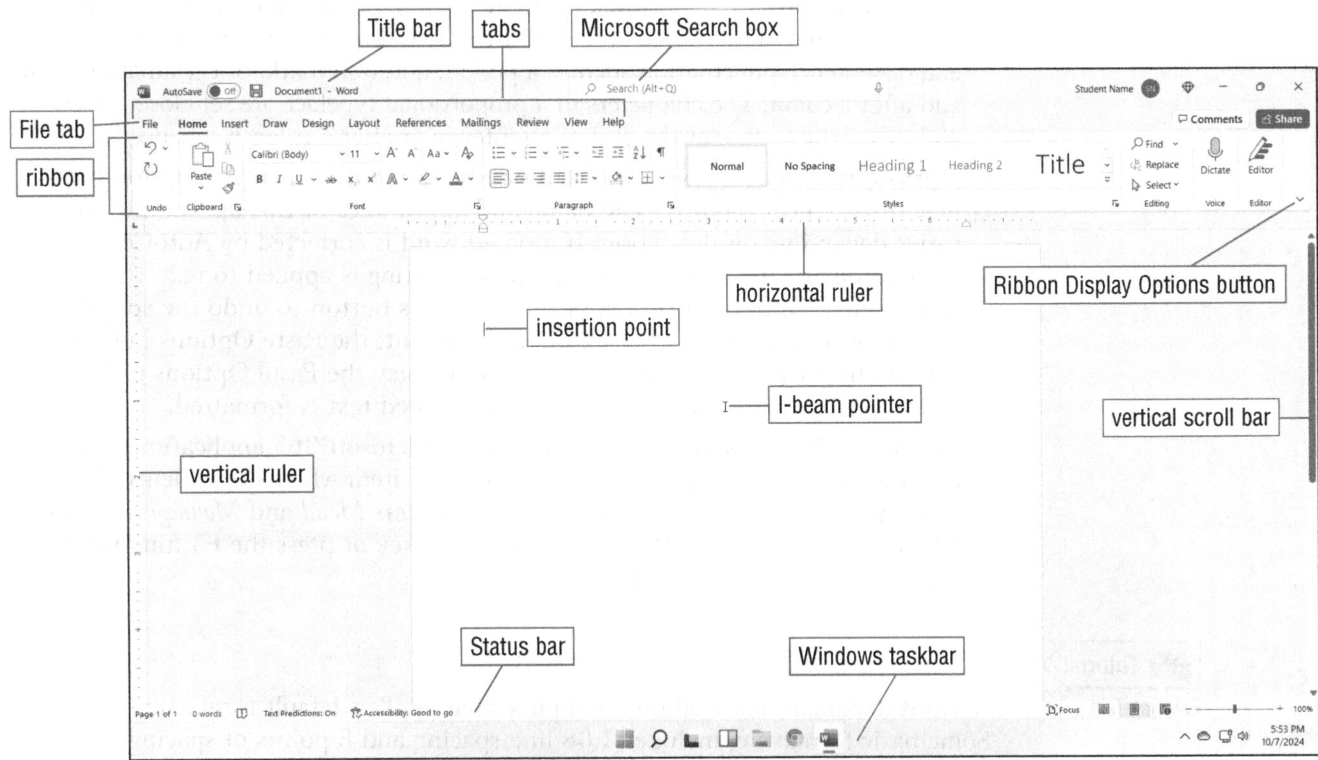

Table 1.1 Microsoft Word Screen Features

Feature	Description
File tab	when clicked, displays the backstage area, which contains options for working with and managing documents
horizontal ruler	used to set margins, indents, and tabs
I-beam pointer	used to move the insertion point or to select text
insertion point	indicates the location of the next character entered at the keyboard
Microsoft Search box	provides information on features, commands, text in a file, or information on a word or phrase
ribbon	area containing tabs with options and buttons divided into groups
Ribbon Display Options button	used to specify how much of the ribbon to display; turn off and on the Quick Access Toolbar
Status bar	displays the number of pages and words in the document, view buttons, and Zoom slider bar
tabs	contain commands and features organized into groups
Title bar	shows the document name followed by the program name
vertical ruler	used to set the top and bottom margins
vertical scroll bar	used to move the viewing area up or down through the document
Windows taskbar	contains the Start button, application icons, and a notification area

- **Spacing punctuation:** The default typeface in Word is Calibri, which is a proportional typeface. (You will learn more about typefaces in Chapter 2.) When typing text in a proportional typeface, use only one space (rather than two) after end-of-sentence punctuation such as a period, question mark, or exclamation point and after a colon. The characters in a proportional typeface are set closer together, and extra white space at the end of a sentence or after a colon is not needed.
- **Option buttons:** As text is inserted or edited in a document, an option button may display near the text. The name and appearance of this option button varies depending on the action. If a typed word is corrected by AutoCorrect, if an automatic list is created, or if autoformatting is applied to text, the AutoCorrect Options button appears. Click this button to undo the specific automatic action. If text is pasted in a document, the Paste Options button appears near the text. Click this button to display the Paste Options gallery, which has buttons for controlling how the pasted text is formatted.
- **AutoComplete:** Microsoft Word and other Microsoft 365 applications include an AutoComplete feature that inserts an entire item when a few identifying characters are typed. For example, type the letters *Mond* and *Monday* displays in a ScreenTip above the letters. Press the Enter key or press the F3 function key and Word inserts *Monday* in the document.

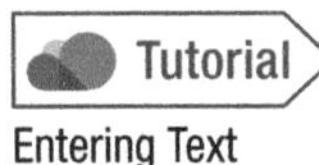

Entering Text

Using the New Line Command

A Word document is based on a template that applies default formatting. Some basic formatting includes 1.08 line spacing and 8 points of spacing after a paragraph. Each time the Enter key is pressed, a new paragraph begins and 8 points of spacing is inserted after the paragraph. To move the insertion point down to the next line without including the additional 8 points of spacing, use the New Line command, Shift + Enter.

Activity 1a Creating a Document — Part 1 of 2

1. Open Word by clicking the Word icon at the Windows Start menu.
2. At the Word opening screen, click the *Blank document* template. (These steps may vary. Check with your instructor for specific instructions.)
3. At a blank document, type the information shown in Figure 1.2 with the following specifications:
   a. Correct any spelling or grammatical errors identified by the Editor as they occur.
   b. Press the spacebar once after end-of-sentence punctuation.
   c. After typing *Created:* press Shift + Enter to move the insertion point to the next line without adding 8 points of additional spacing.
   d. To insert the word *Thursday* at the end of the document, type Thur and then press the F3 function key. (This is an example of the AutoComplete feature. Depending on your system, the AutoComplete feature may not function as indicated.)
   e. To insert the word *December*, type Dece and then press the Enter key. (This is another example of the AutoComplete feature.)
   f. Press Shift + Enter after typing *December 9, 2024*.
   g. When typing the last line (the line containing the ordinal numbers), type the ordinal number text and AutoCorrect will automatically convert the letters in the ordinal number to a superscript.
4. When you are finished typing the text, press the Enter key. (Keep the document open for the next activity.)

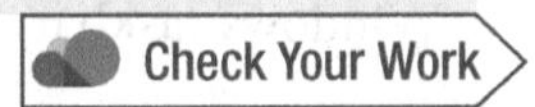

Figure 1.2 Activity 1a

The traditional chronological resume lists your work experience in reverse-chronological order (starting with your current or most recent position). The functional style deemphasizes the "where" and "when" of your career and instead groups similar experiences, talents, and qualifications regardless of when they occurred.

Like the chronological resume, the hybrid resume includes specifics about where you worked, when you worked there, and what your job titles were. Like a functional resume, a hybrid resume emphasizes your most relevant qualifications in an expanded summary section, in several "career highlights" bullet points at the top of your resume, or in activity summaries.

Created:
Thursday, December 9, 2024
Note: The two paragraphs will become the 2nd and 3rd paragraphs in the 5th section.

Tutorial

Saving with a New Name

Save

Quick Steps

Save Document

1. Click File tab.
2. Click *Save As* option.
3. Click *Browse* option.
4. Type document name in *File name* text box.
5. Press Enter key.

Hint Save a document approximately every 15 minutes or when interrupted.

Saving a Document

If a document will be used in the future, it must be saved. To save a new document, click the File tab and then click the *Save* or the *Save As* option. The Save As backstage area displays, as shown in Figure 1.3. Click the *Browse* option to open the Save As dialog box, shown in Figure 1.4. (Pressing the F12 function key will also open this dialog box.) At the dialog box, navigate to the location where the file is to be saved, type a file name, and then press the Enter key or click the Save button. Continue saving periodically whenever edits are made by clicking the Save button on the Title bar or with the keyboard shortcut Ctrl + S.

To save a new version of a document while keeping the original, click the File tab and then click the *Save As* option to display the Save As backstage area. (Do not click *Save*, or changes will be saved to the existing file.) At the Save As backstage area, click the *Browse* option to display the Save As dialog box. Type a new name for the document, select a location where the document is to be saved, and then press the Enter key or click the Save button.

Figure 1.3 Save As Backstage Area

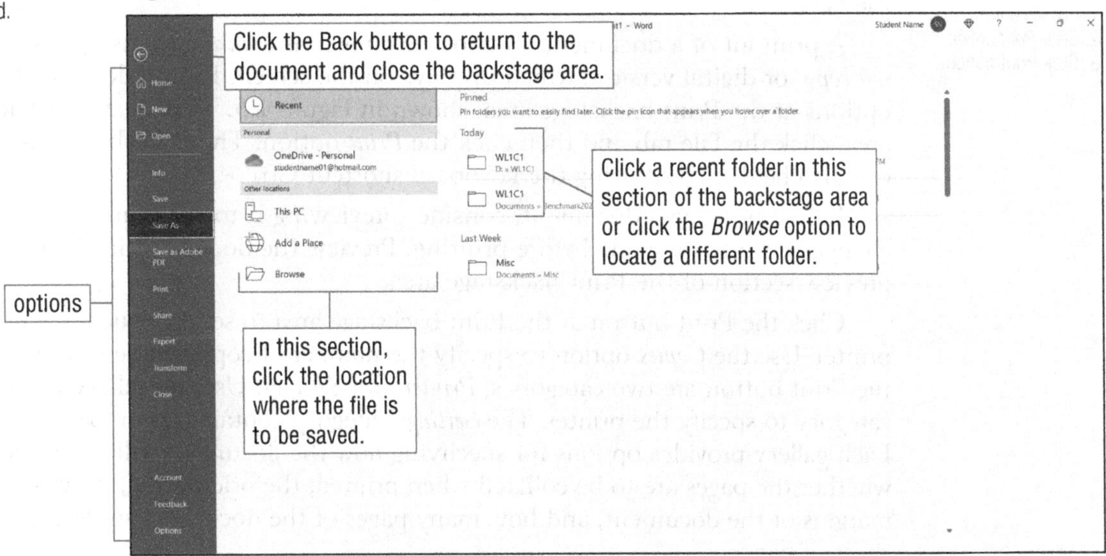

Figure 1.4 Save As Dialog Box

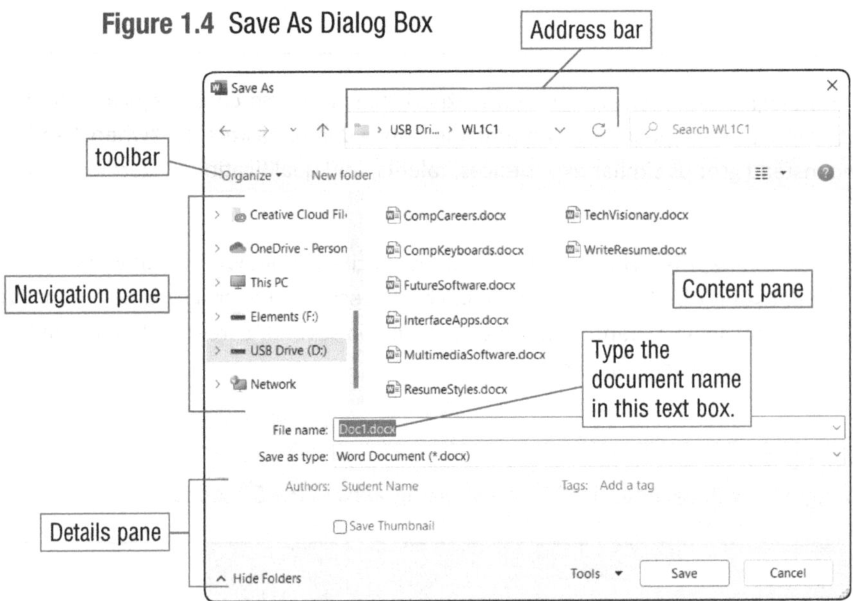

Naming a Document

Hint Word will not allow you to save two documents with the same name in the same folder. This is true even if you make one name uppercase and one lowercase.

Document names created in Word and other applications in the Microsoft 365 suite can be up to 255 characters in length, including the drive letter and any folder names, and they may include spaces. File names cannot include any of the following characters:

forward slash (/)	less-than symbol (<)	quotation marks (“ ”)
backslash (\)	asterisk (*)	colon (:)
greater-than symbol (>)	question mark (?)	pipe symbol (|)

Printing a Document

Quick Steps

Print Document

1. Click File tab.
2. Click *Print* option.
3. Click Print button.

Printing a Document

Click the File tab and the backstage area displays. The buttons and options at the backstage area change depending on the option selected at the left side of the backstage area. To leave the backstage area without completing an action, click the Back button in the upper left corner of the backstage area, or press the Esc key on the keyboard.

A printout of a document on paper is known as a *hard copy*, as opposed to the *soft copy*, or digital version, which displays on the screen. Print a document with options at the Print backstage area, shown in Figure 1.5. To display this backstage area, click the File tab and then click the *Print* option. The Print backstage area can also be displayed using the keyboard shortcut Ctrl + P.

Before printing a document, consider previewing it to determine if any changes need to be made before printing. Preview the document in the print preview section of the Print backstage area.

Click the Print button at the Print backstage area to send the document to the printer. Use the *Copies* option to specify the number of copies to be printed. Below the Print button are two categories: *Printer* and *Settings*. Use the gallery in the *Printer* category to specify the printer. The *Settings* category contains a number of galleries. Each gallery provides options for specifying how the document will print, including whether the pages are to be collated when printed; the orientation, page size, and margins of the document; and how many pages of the document are to print on a sheet of paper.

Figure 1.5 Print Backstage Area

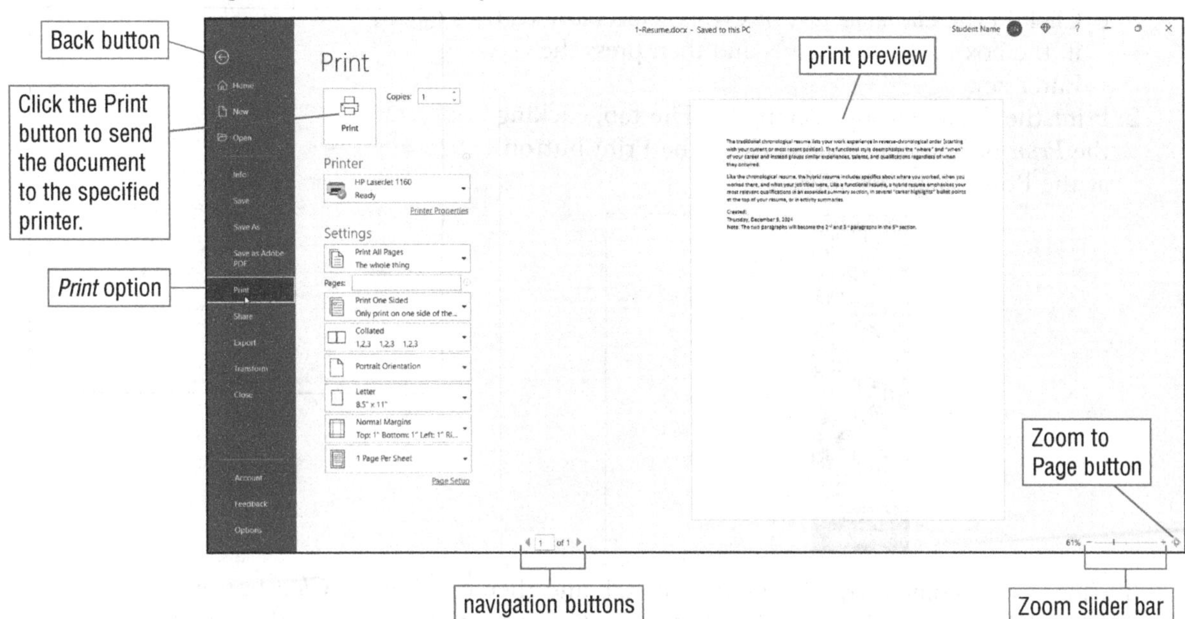

Closing a Document and Closing Word

Quick Steps

Close Document
1. Click File tab.
2. Click *Close* option.

Close Word
Click the Close button.

Closing a Document and Closing Word

When a document is saved, it is saved to the specified location and also remains on the screen. To remove the document from the screen, click the File tab and then click the *Close* option or use the keyboard shortcut Ctrl + F4. When a document is closed, it is removed and a blank screen displays. At this screen, open a previously saved document, create a new document, or close Word. To close Word, click the Close button in the upper right corner of the screen. The keyboard shortcut Alt + F4 also closes Word.

Activity 1b Saving, Printing, and Closing a Document and Closing Word — Part 2 of 2

1. Save the document you created for Activity 1a and name it **1-Resume** (*1-* for Chapter 1 and *Resume* because the document is about resumes) by completing the following steps:
   a. Click the File tab.

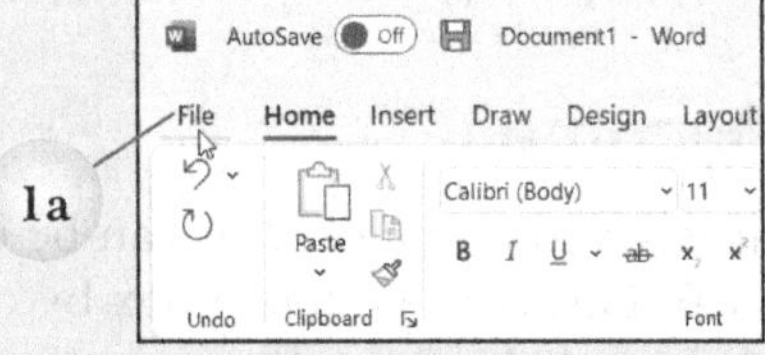

   b. Click the *Save As* option.
   c. At the Save As backstage area, click the *Browse* option.
   d. At the Save As dialog box, if necessary, navigate to the WL1C1 folder on your storage medium.

e. Click in the *File name* text box (this selects any text in the box), type 1-Resume, and then press the Enter key.

2. Print the document by clicking the File tab, clicking the *Print* option, and then clicking the Print button at the Print backstage area.

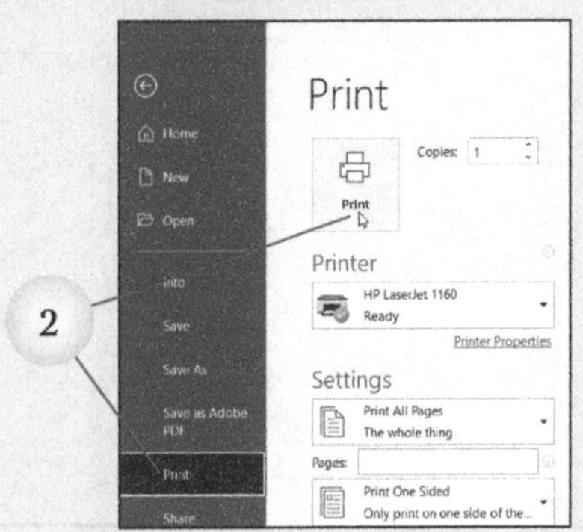

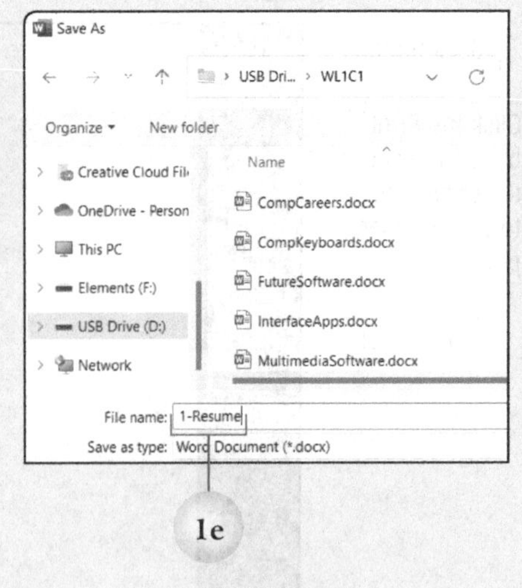

3. Close the document by clicking the File tab and then clicking the *Close* option.
4. Close Word by clicking the Close button in the upper right corner of the screen.

Activity 2 Save a Document with a New Name and the Same Name 2 Parts

You will open a document in the WL1C1 folder on your storage medium, save the document with a new name, add text, and then save the document with the same name. You will also display and add buttons to the Quick Access Toolbar, and then print and close the document.

Creating a New Document

Quick Steps

Create New Document
1. Click File tab.
2. Click *Blank document* template.

When a document is closed, a blank screen displays. To create a new document, click the File tab, click the *New* option, and then click the *Blank document* template. A new document can also be opened with the keyboard shortcut Ctrl + N. Additional templates can be found by clicking the File tab and then clicking the *Home* or *New* option. Double-click the *Single spaced (blank)* template to open a new document with single spacing and no added space after paragraphs.

Opening a Document

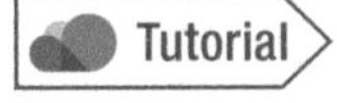

Opening a Document at the Open Dialog Box

Opening a Document from a Removable Disk

After a document is saved and closed, it can be opened at the Open dialog box, shown in Figure 1.6. Display the dialog box by clicking the File tab, clicking the *Open* option, and then clicking the *Browse* option at the backstage area. Other methods for displaying the Open backstage area include using the keyboard shortcut Ctrl + O and clicking the More documents hyperlink in the lower right corner of the Word opening screen and the Home backstage area.

Figure 1.6 Open Dialog Box

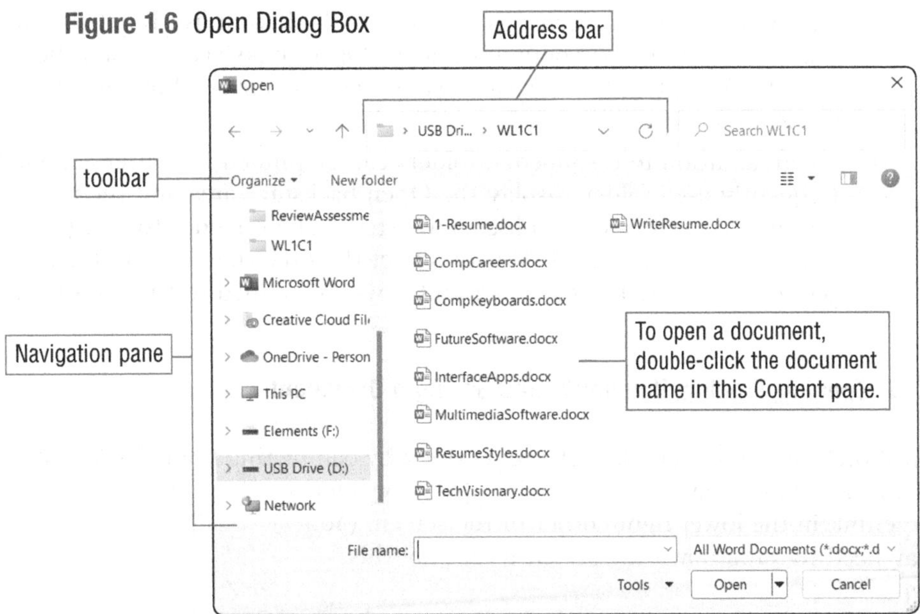

Quick Steps

Open Document

1. Click File tab.
2. Click *Open* option.
3. Click *Browse* option.
4. Double-click document name.

At the Open backstage area, click the *Browse* option and the Open dialog box displays. Go directly to the Open dialog box without displaying the Open backstage area by pressing Ctrl + F12. At the Open dialog box, navigate to the desired location (such as the drive containing your storage medium), open the folder containing the document, and then double-click the document name in the Content pane.

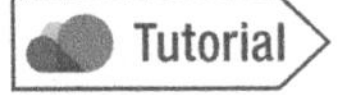

Opening a Document from the *Recent* Option List

Opening a Document from the *Recent* Option List

At the Open backstage area with the *Recent* option selected, the names of the most recently opened documents are listed. By default, Word lists the names of the 50 most recently opened documents and groups them into categories such as *Today*, *Yesterday*, and perhaps another category such as *This Week*. To open a document from the *Recent* option list, scroll down the list and then click the document name. The Word opening screen and the Home backstage area also provide a list of the names of the most recently opened documents. Click a document name in the Recent list to open the document.

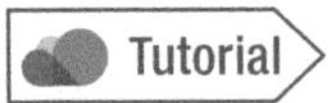

Pinning and Unpinning a Document at the *Recent* Option List

Pinning and Unpinning Documents and Folders

If a document is opened on a regular basis, consider pinning it so it can be found more easily. At the Open backstage area, hover the pointer over the document name in the *Recent* option list and then click the pin icon that appears. The document will now appear at the top of the list in the *Pinned* category. A document can also be pinned at the Home backstage area. Click the pin icon next to a document name, and the document will display in the *Pinned* tab. More than one document can be pinned to a list.

To unpin a document from the *Recent* option list at the Open backstage area or the Pinned list at the Home backstage area, click the pin icon to the right of the document name (the pin displays with a circle containing a slash).

Another method for pinning and unpinning documents is to use the shortcut menu. Right-click a document name and then click the *Pin to list* or *Unpin from list* option. The shortcut menu also includes the *Remove from list* option, which removes a document from the *Recent* option list and the Recent list. Right-click a pinned document in the *Recent* option list at the Open backstage area and the shortcut menu includes the option *Clear unpinned items*, which removes all unpinned documents from the *Recent* option list.

In addition to documents, folders can be pinned for easier access. To pin a frequently used folder, display the Open backstage area and then click the *Folders* option. Recently opened folders are listed and grouped into categories such as *Today*, *Yesterday*, and *Last Week* to reflect the time they were last accessed. Click the pin icon to the right of a folder and it will be pinned to the top of the list.

Activity 2a Opening, Pinning, Unpinning, and Saving a Document — Part 1 of 2

1. Open Word and then open **CompCareers.docx** by completing the following steps:
   a. At the Word opening screen, click the More documents hyperlink in the lower right corner of the screen. (You may need to scroll down the screen to display this hyperlink.)
   b. At the Open backstage area, click the *Browse* option.
   c. At the Open dialog box, navigate to the external drive containing your storage medium.
   d. Double-click the ***WL1C1*** folder in the Content pane.
   e. Double-click ***CompCareers.docx*** in the Content pane.
2. Close **CompCareers.docx**.
3. Press Ctrl + F12 to display the Open dialog box and then double-click ***FutureSoftware.docx*** in the Content pane to open the document.
4. Close **FutureSoftware.docx**.
5. Pin **CompCareers.docx** to the *Recent* option list by completing the following steps:
   a. Click the File tab and then click the *Open* option.
   b. At the Open backstage area, hover the pointer over **CompCareers.docx** in the *Recent* option list and then click the pin icon to the right of the document. (The **CompCareers.docx** file will now appear in the *Pinned* category at the top of the list.)

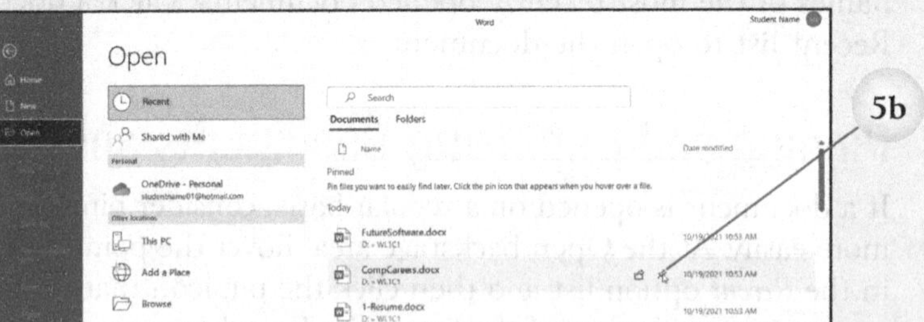

6. Click **CompCareers.docx** in the *Pinned* category at the top of the *Recent* option list to open the document.
7. Unpin **CompCareers.docx** from the *Recent* option list by completing the following steps:
   a. Click the File tab and then click the *Open* option.
   b. At the Open backstage area, hover the pointer over the **CompCareers.docx** document in the *Pinned* category in the *Recent* option list and then click the pin (displays with a circle containing a slash). (This removes the file from the *Pinned* category.)
   c. Click the Back button to return to the document.

8. With **CompCareers.docx** open, save the document with a new name by completing the following steps:
   a. Click the File tab and then click the *Save As* option.
   b. At the Save As backstage area, click the *Browse* option.
   c. At the Save As dialog box, if necessary, navigate to the WL1C1 folder on your storage medium.
   d. Press the Home key on your keyboard to move the insertion point to the beginning of the file name and then type 1-.
   e. Press the Enter key.

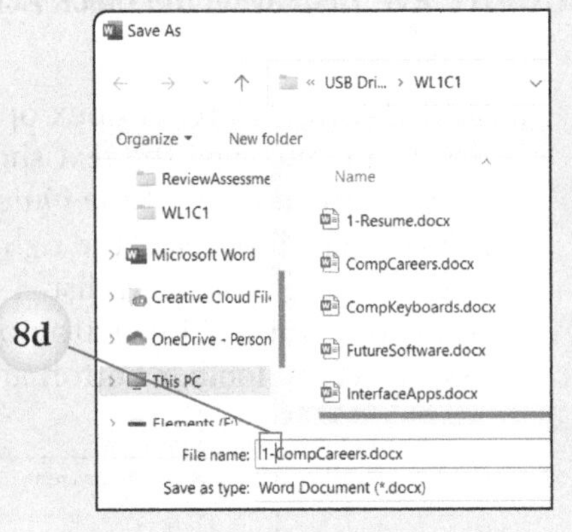

Saving with the Same Name

Quick Steps

Save Document with Same Name

Click Save button on Title bar.
OR
1. Click File tab.
2. Click *Save* option.
OR
Press Ctrl + S.

Saving Changes to a Document

After making changes to a document, save the changes before closing the file. Consider saving on a periodic basis to ensure that no changes are lost if the application crashes or freezes or if power is interrupted. Unless keeping an older version of the document is important, changes can be saved using the same file name. Save a document with the same name using the Save button on the Title bar, the *Save* option at the backstage area, or with the keyboard shortcut Ctrl + S.

Note: If a document is stored in a cloud location such as Microsoft OneDrive or SharePoint Online, any changes to it will be saved automatically with the AutoSave feature. AutoSave can be turned on or off by clicking the toggle switch in the upper left corner of the Word screen.

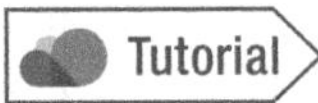

Using the Quick Access Toolbar

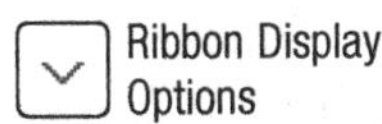

Ribbon Display Options

Quick Steps

Displaying the Quick Access Toolbar

1. Click Ribbon Display Options button.
2. Click *Show Quick Access Toolbar*.

Using the Quick Access Toolbar

The Quick Access Toolbar is a customizable toolbar that provides easy access to common functions such as opening, saving, and printing a document. Turn on the display of the Quick Access Toolbar by clicking the Ribbon Display Options button at the right side of the ribbon (displays with a down-pointing arrow) and then clicking *Show Quick Access Toolbar* at the drop-down list.

To insert a button on the Quick Access Toolbar, click the Customize Quick Access Toolbar button at the right side of the toolbar and then click the specific button name at the drop-down list. A button can also be inserted on the Quick Access Toolbar by right-clicking the button and then clicking *Add to Quick Access Toolbar* at the shortcut menu that displays. (Right-clicking a button displays the shortcut menu with options for performing an action.) To remove a button from the toolbar, right-click the button and then click *Remove from Quick Access Toolbar* at the shortcut menu.

Specify whether the toolbar displays above or below the ribbon with options at the Customize Quick Access Toolbar button drop-down list. Turn off the display of the Quick Access Toolbar by clicking the Ribbon Display Options button and then clicking *Hide Quick Access Toolbar* at the drop-down list.

Activity 2b Displaying the Quick Access Toolbar; Saving a Document with Same Name Part 2 of 2

1. With **1-CompCareers.docx** open and the insertion point positioned at the beginning of the document, type the text shown in Figure 1.7.
2. Turn on the display of the Quick Access Toolbar by clicking the Ribbon Display Options button that displays at the right side of the ribbon and then clicking *Show Quick Access Toolbar* at the drop-down list.
3. Insert the Quick Print button on the Quick Access Toolbar by clicking the Customize Quick Access Toolbar button and then clicking *Quick Print* at the drop-down list.

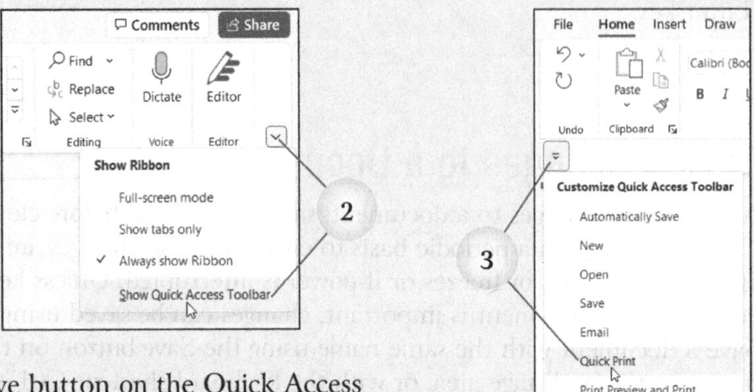

4. Insert the Save button on the Quick Access Toolbar by clicking the Customize Quick Access Toolbar button and then clicking *Save* at the drop-down list.
5. Save the changes you made in Step 1 by clicking the Save button on the Quick Access Toolbar.
6. Print the document by clicking the Quick Print button on the Quick Access Toolbar.
7. Move the Quick Access Toolbar above the ribbon by clicking the Customize Quick Access Toolbar button and then clicking *Show Above the Ribbon* at the drop-down list.
8. Move the Quick Access Toolbar back below the ribbon by clicking the Customize Quick Access Toolbar button and then clicking *Show Below the Ribbon* at the drop-down list.
9. Close the document by pressing Ctrl + F4.
10. If necessary, turn off the display of the Quick Access Toolbar by clicking the Ribbon Display Options button and then clicking *Hide Quick Access Toolbar* at the drop-down list.

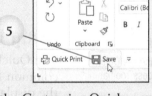

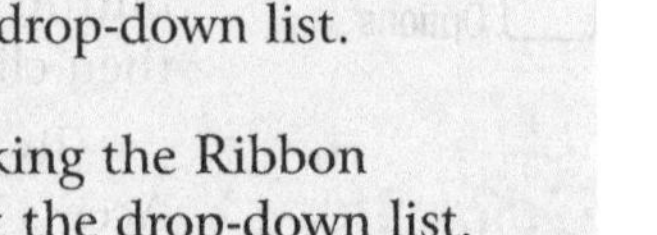

Check Your Work

Figure 1.7 Activity 2b

> The majority of new jobs being created in the United States today involve daily work with computers. Computer-related careers include technical support jobs, sales and training, programming and applications development, network and database administration, and computer engineering.

Activity 3 Scroll and Browse in a Document **2 Parts**

You will open a previously created document, save it with a new name, and then use scrolling and browsing techniques to move the insertion point to specific locations in the document.

Scrolling

Editing a Document

When a document is being edited, text may need to be inserted or deleted. To edit a document, use the mouse, the keyboard, or a combination of the two to move the insertion point to specific locations in the document. To move the insertion point using the mouse, position the I-beam pointer where the insertion point is to be positioned and then click the left mouse button.

Scrolling in a document changes the text display, but does not move the insertion point. Use the mouse with the vertical scroll bar, at the right side of the screen, to scroll through text in a document. Click the up scroll arrow at the top of the vertical scroll bar to scroll up through the document, and click the down scroll arrow to scroll down through the document.

The scroll bar contains a scroll box that indicates the location of the text in the document screen in relation to the remainder of the document. To scroll up one screen at a time, position the pointer above the scroll box (but below the up scroll arrow) and then click the left mouse button. Position the pointer below the scroll box and click the left button to scroll down a screen. Click and hold down the left mouse button and the action becomes continuous.

Another method for scrolling is to position the pointer on the scroll box, click and hold down the left mouse button, and then drag the scroll box along the scroll bar to reposition text in the document screen. As the scroll box is dragged along the vertical scroll bar in a longer document, page numbers are shown in a box at the right side of the document screen.

Activity 3a Scrolling in a Document **Part 1 of 2**

1. Open **InterfaceApps.docx** (from the WL1C1 folder you copied to your storage medium).
2. Save the document with the new name **1-InterfaceApps** to your WL1C1 folder.
3. Position the I-beam pointer at the beginning of the first paragraph and then click the left mouse button.
4. Click the down scroll arrow on the vertical scroll bar several times. (This scrolls down lines of text in the document.) With the pointer on the down scroll arrow, click and hold down the left mouse button and keep it down until you reach the end of the document.
5. Position the pointer on the up scroll arrow and then click and hold down the left mouse button until you reach the beginning of the document.
6. Position the pointer below the scroll box and then click the left mouse button. Continue clicking the mouse button (with the pointer positioned below the scroll box) until you reach the end of the document.
7. Position the pointer on the scroll box in the vertical scroll bar. Click and hold down the left mouse button, drag the scroll box to the top of the vertical scroll bar, and then release the mouse button. (Notice that the document page numbers are shown in a box at the right side of the document screen.)
8. Click in the title at the beginning of the document. (This moves the insertion point to the location of the pointer.)

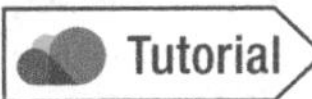

Moving the Insertion Point Using the Go To Feature

Hint Press Ctrl + G to display the Find and Replace dialog box with the Go To tab selected.

Moving the Insertion Point to a Specific Line or Page

Word includes a Go To feature that moves the insertion point to a specific location in a document, such as a line or page. To use the feature, click the Find button arrow in the Editing group on the Home tab and then click *Go To* at the drop-down list. At the Find and Replace dialog box with the Go To tab selected, move the insertion point to a specific page by typing the page number in the *Enter page number* text box and then pressing the Enter key. Move to a specific line by clicking the *Line* option in the *Go to what* list box, typing the line number in the *Enter line number* text box, and then pressing the Enter key. Click the Close button to close the dialog box.

Moving the Insertion Point and Inserting and Deleting Text

Moving the Insertion Point with the Keyboard

To move the insertion point with the keyboard, use the arrow keys to the right of the regular keyboard or use the arrow keys on the numeric keypad. When using the arrow keys on the numeric keypad, make sure Num Lock is off. Use the arrow keys together with other keys to move the insertion point to various locations in the document, as shown in Table 1.2.

When moving the insertion point, Word considers a word to be any series of characters between spaces. A paragraph is any text that is followed by a single press of the Enter key. A page is text that is separated by a soft or hard page break.

Table 1.2 Insertion Point Movement Commands

To move insertion point	Press
one character left	Left Arrow
one character right	Right Arrow
one line up	Up Arrow
one line down	Down Arrow
one word left	Ctrl + Left Arrow
one word right	Ctrl + Right Arrow
to beginning of line	Home
to end of line	End
to beginning of current paragraph	Ctrl + Up Arrow
to beginning of next paragraph	Ctrl + Down Arrow
up one screen	Page Up
down one screen	Page Down
to top of previous page	Ctrl + Page Up
to top of next page	Ctrl + Page Down
to beginning of document	Ctrl + Home
to end of document	Ctrl + End

Resuming Reading or Editing in a Document

If a previously saved document is opened, pressing Shift + F5 will move the insertion point to the position it was last located when the document was closed.

When a multiple-page document is reopened, Word remembers the page where the insertion point was last positioned. A "Welcome back!" message appears at the right side of the screen near the vertical scroll bar, identifying the page where the insertion point was last located. Click the message and the insertion point is positioned at the top of that page.

Activity 3b Moving the Insertion Point in a Document — Part 2 of 2

1. With **1-InterfaceApps.docx** open, move the insertion point to line 15 and then to page 3 by completing the following steps:
   a. Click the Find button arrow in the Editing group on the Home tab and then click *Go To* at the drop-down list.
   b. At the Find and Replace dialog box with the Go To tab selected, click *Line* in the *Go to what* list box.
   c. Click in the *Enter line number* text box, type 15, and then press the Enter key.
   d. Click *Page* in the *Go to what* list box.
   e. Click in the *Enter page number* text box, type 3, and then press the Enter key.
   f. Click the Close button to close the Find and Replace dialog box.

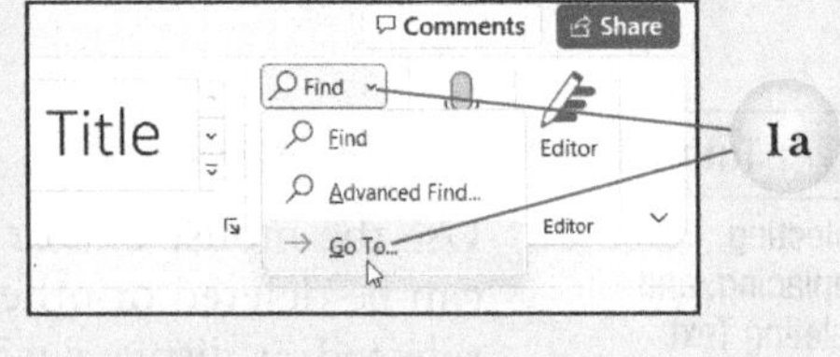

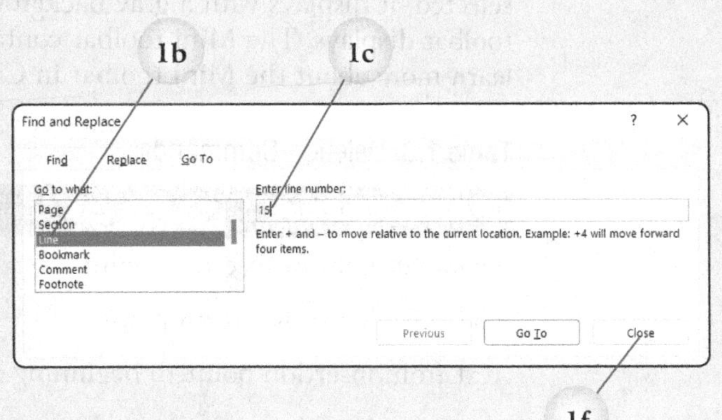

2. Close the document.
3. Open the document by clicking the File tab and then clicking the document name *1-InterfaceApps.docx* in the Recent list.
4. Move the pointer to the right side of the screen to display the "Welcome back!" message. Hover the pointer over the message and then click the left mouse button. (This positions the insertion point at the top of the third page—the page the insertion point was positioned when you closed the document.)

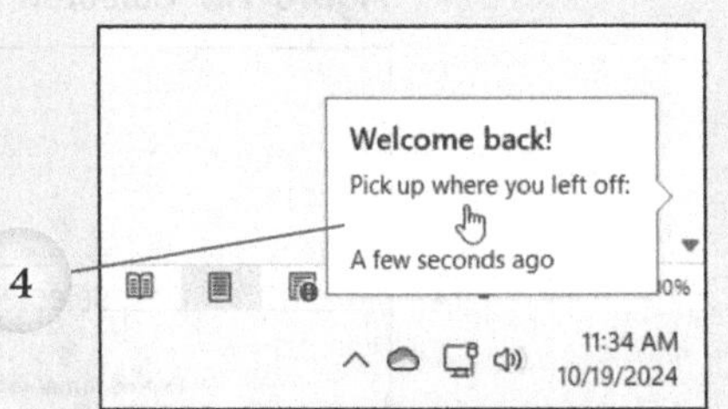

5. Press Ctrl + Home to move the insertion point to the beginning of the document.
6. Practice using the keyboard commands shown in Table 1.2 to move the insertion point within the document.
7. Preview the document at the Print backstage area by clicking the File tab and then clicking the *Print* option. At the Print backstage area, view the document at the right side of the screen and then click the Back button (displays with a left-pointing arrow) in the upper left corner of the backstage area to return to the document.
8. Close **1-InterfaceApps.docx**.

Activity 4 Insert and Delete Text — 2 Parts

You will open a previously created document, save it with a new name, and then make editing changes to the document. The editing changes include selecting, inserting, and deleting text and undoing and redoing edits.

Inserting and Deleting Text

Editing a document may include inserting and/or deleting text. To insert text in a document, position the insertion point at the location text is to be typed and then type the text. Existing characters move to the right as text is typed. A number of options are available for deleting text. Some deletion commands are shown in Table 1.3.

Selecting, Replacing, and Deleting Text

Selecting Text

Use the mouse and/or keyboard to select a specific amount of text. Selected text can be deleted or other Word functions can be performed on it. When text is selected, it displays with a gray background, as shown in Figure 1.8, and the Mini toolbar displays. The Mini toolbar contains buttons for common tasks. (You will learn more about the Mini toolbar in Chapter 2.)

Table 1.3 Deletion Commands

To delete	Press
character right of insertion point	Delete key
character left of insertion point	Backspace key
text from insertion point to beginning of word	Ctrl + Backspace
text from insertion point to end of word	Ctrl + Delete

Figure 1.8 Selected Text and Mini Toolbar

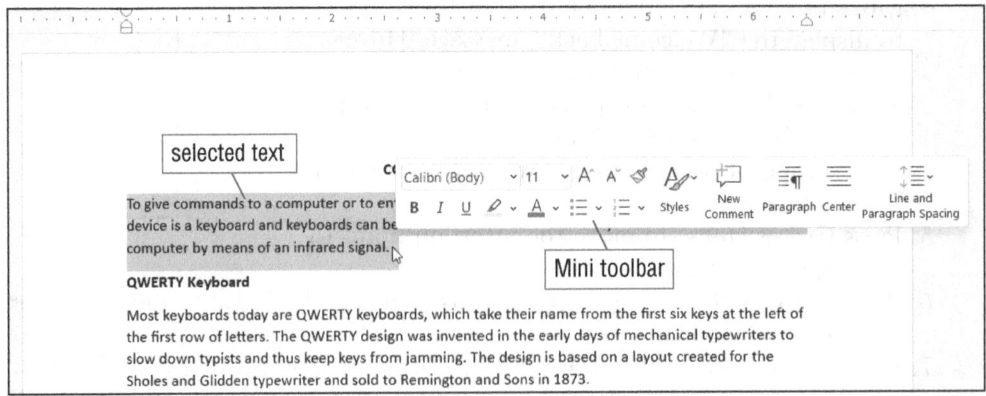

Hint If text is selected, any character you type replaces the selected text.

Selecting Text with the Mouse Use the mouse to select a word, line, sentence, paragraph, or entire document. Table 1.4 indicates the steps to follow to select various amounts of text.

One way to select text is by clicking in the selection bar. The selection bar is the space at the left side of the document screen between the left edge of the page and the text. When the pointer is positioned in the selection bar, the pointer turns into an arrow pointing up and to the right (instead of to the left). Click once to select a line of text, twice to select a paragraph, and three times to select all the text in the document.

Another way to select text is by using the I-beam pointer. Position the pointer on the first character of the text to be selected, click and hold down the left mouse button, drag the I-beam pointer to the last character of the text to be selected, and then release the mouse button. Alternately, position the insertion point where the selection is to begin, press and hold down the Shift key, click the I-beam pointer at the end of the selection, and then release the Shift key. To cancel a selection, simply click in the document screen.

Hint Hold down the Alt key while dragging with the mouse to select text vertically.

Select text vertically in a document by pressing and holding down the Alt key while dragging with the mouse. This is especially useful when selecting a group of text, such as text set in columns.

Selecting Text with the Keyboard To select text using the keyboard, turn on the Selection mode by pressing the F8 function key. With the Selection mode activated, use the arrow keys to select text. To cancel the selection, press the Esc key and then press any arrow key. The Status bar can be customized to indicate that the Selection mode is activated. To do this, right-click on the Status bar and then click *Selection Mode* at the pop-up list. When the F8 function key is pressed to turn on the Selection mode, the words *Extend Selection* display on the Status bar. Text can also be selected with the commands shown in Table 1.5.

Table 1.4 Selecting Text with the Mouse

To select	Complete these steps using the mouse
a word	Double-click the word.
a line of text	Click in the selection bar to the left of the line.
multiple lines of text	Drag in the selection bar to the left of the lines.
a sentence	Press and hold down the Ctrl key and then click in the sentence.
a paragraph	Double-click in the selection bar next to the paragraph, or triple-click in the paragraph.
multiple paragraphs	Drag in the selection bar.
an entire document	Triple-click in the selection bar, or click the Select button in Editing group and then click *Select All*.

Table 1.5 Selecting Text with the Keyboard

To select	Press
one character to right	Shift + Right Arrow
one character to left	Shift + Left Arrow
to end of word	Ctrl + Shift + Right Arrow
to beginning of word	Ctrl + Shift + Left Arrow
to end of line	Shift + End
to beginning of line	Shift + Home
one line up	Shift + Up Arrow
one line down	Shift + Down Arrow
to beginning of paragraph	Ctrl + Shift + Up Arrow
to end of paragraph	Ctrl + Shift + Down Arrow
one screen up	Shift + Page Up
one screen down	Shift + Page Down
to end of document	Ctrl + Shift + End
to beginning of document	Ctrl + Shift + Home
entire document	Ctrl + A

Activity 4a Editing a Document

Part 1 of 2

1. Open **CompKeyboards.docx**. (This document is in the WL1C1 folder you copied to your storage medium.)
2. Save the document with the new name **1-CompKeyboards**.
3. Change the word *give* in the first sentence of the first paragraph to *enter* by double-clicking *give* and then typing enter.
4. Change the second *to* in the first sentence to *into* by double-clicking *to* and then typing into.

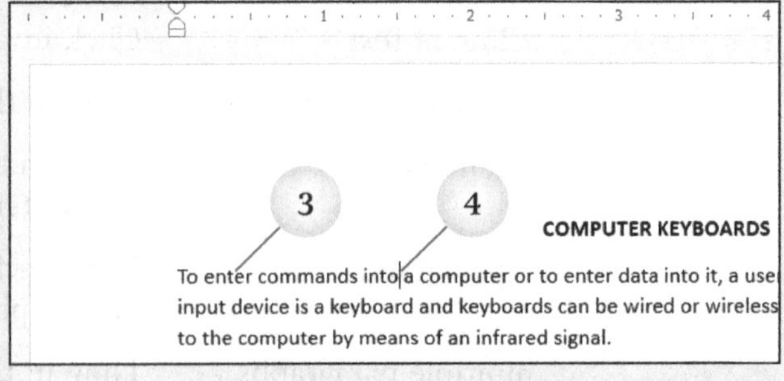

5. Select the words *means of* in the last sentence in the first paragraph and then press the Delete key to delete the selected text.
6. Select and then delete the last sentence in the *QWERTY Keyboard* section by completing the following steps:
   a. Position the I-beam pointer anywhere in the last sentence in the *QWERTY Keyboard* section.
   b. Press and hold down the Ctrl key, click the left mouse button, and then release the Ctrl key.
   c. Press the Delete key.

7. Delete the heading *QWERTY Keyboard* using the Selection mode by completing the following steps:
   a. Position the insertion point immediately left of the *Q* in *QWERTY*.
   b. Press the F8 function key to turn on the Selection mode.
   c. Press the Down Arrow key.
   d. Press the Delete key.
8. Complete steps similar to those in Step 7 to delete the heading *DVORAK Keyboard*.
9. Begin a new paragraph with the sentence that reads *Keyboards have different physical appearances* by completing the following steps:
   a. Position the insertion point immediately left of the *K* in *Keyboards* (the first word of the fifth sentence in the last paragraph).
   b. Press the Enter key.
10. Save **1-CompKeyboards.docx**.

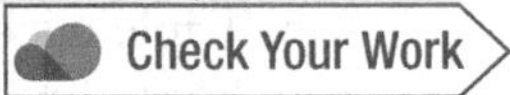

Using Undo and Redo

Undo

Redo

Hint You cannot undo a save.

Hint Use the keyboard shortcut Ctrl + Z to undo an action.

Hint Use the keyboard shortcut Ctrl + Y to redo an action.

Using the Undo and Redo Buttons

Undo typing, formatting, or another action by clicking the Undo button in the Undo group on the Home tab. For example, type text and then click the Undo button and the text is removed. Or apply formatting to text and then click the Undo button and the formatting is removed.

Click the Redo button in the Undo group on the Home tab to reverse the original action. For example, apply formatting such as underlining to text and then click the Undo button and the underlining is removed. Click the Redo button and the underlining formatting is reapplied to the text. Many Word actions can be undone or redone. Some actions, however, such as printing and saving, cannot be undone or redone.

Word maintains actions in temporary memory. To undo an action performed earlier, click the Undo button arrow. This causes a drop-down list to display. To make a selection from this drop-down list, click the desired action; the action, along with any actions listed above it in the drop-down list, is undone.

Activity 4b Undoing and Redoing Deletions

Part 2 of 2

1. With **1-CompKeyboards.docx** open, delete the last sentence in the last paragraph using the mouse by completing the following steps:
   a. Position the I-beam pointer anywhere in the sentence that begins *All keyboards have modifier keys*.
   b. Press and hold down the Ctrl key, click the left mouse button, and then release the Ctrl key.

install software on a QWERTY keyboard that emulates a DVORAK keyboard. The ability to emulate other keyboards is convenient especially when working with foreign languages.

Keyboards have different physical appearances. Many keyboards have a separate numeric keypad, like that of a calculator, containing numbers and mathematical operators. Some keyboards are sloped and "broken" into two pieces to reduce strain. All keyboards have modifier keys that enable the user to change the symbol or character entered when a given key is pressed.

1a-1b

   c. Press the Delete key.
2. Delete the last paragraph by completing the following steps:
   a. Position the I-beam pointer anywhere in the last paragraph (the paragraph that begins *Keyboards have different physical appearances*).
   b. Triple-click the left mouse button.
   c. Press the Delete key.
3. Undo the deletion by clicking the Undo button in the Undo group on the Home tab.
4. Redo the deletion by clicking the Redo button in the Undo group on the Home tab.
5. Select the first sentence in the second paragraph and then delete it.
6. Select the first paragraph in the document and then delete it.
7. Undo the two deletions by completing the following steps:
   a. Click the Undo button arrow.
   b. Click the second *Clear* listed in the drop-down list. (This will redisplay the first paragraph and the first sentence in the second paragraph. The sentence will be selected.)

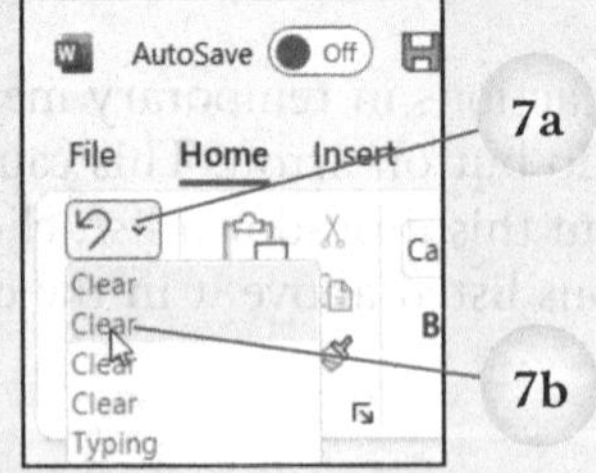

8. Click outside the sentence to deselect it.
9. Save, preview, and then close **1-CompKeyboards.docx**.

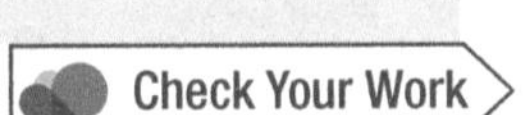

Activity 5 Complete a Spelling and Grammar Check — 1 Part

You will open a previously created document, save it with a new name, and then use the Editor to check the spelling and grammar in the document.

Using the Editor to Check Spelling and Grammar

Check Spelling and Grammar

1. Click Editor button.
2. Click Editor Score box.
3. Change or ignore errors.
4. Click OK.
5. Click Close button.

Hint Press the F7 function key to display the Editor task pane.

Using the Editor to Check Spelling and Grammar in a Document

Thoughtful and well-written documents are free of errors in spelling and grammar. The Microsoft Editor is a service available in Word that checks a document for spelling and grammar errors and offers suggested corrections. It may also suggest refinements for clarity and conciseness in the writing.

The Editor can find and offer corrections for misspelled words, duplicate words, and irregular capitalizations. To check spelling, it compares the words in the document with the words in its dictionary. If it finds a match, it passes over the word. If the word is not found in its dictionary, it offers possible corrections. Editor will also check a document for grammar issues, such as incorrect use of words, and offer refinement suggestions to improve the writing in the document, such as clarity, conciseness, formality, and punctuation. Editor cannot find all errors so it does not eliminate the need for proofreading.

To complete a spelling and grammar check, click the Editor button in the Editor group on the Home tab, click the Review tab and then click the Editor button in the Proofing group, or press the F7 function key. The Editor task pane opens at the right side of the screen and an Editor Score box displays near the top of the task pane. This box contains a percentage score that represents the number and type of suggestions to be reviewed based on the document length. Below the Editor Score box is an option box with options for specifying the formal level of the document. Click the option box arrow and three options displays. Choose the *Formal* option for an official and highly professional document, choose the *Professional* option for a general business document, or choose *Casual* for a casual or creative document.

The Editor task pane also contains options in the *Corrections* section identifying the number of possible spelling errors and grammar errors and a *Refinements* section identifying the number of areas that may need refining. Click the Editor Score box to search and display spelling and grammar errors as they are encountered. Click the *Spelling* option in the *Corrections* section to review all possible spelling errors and click the *Grammar* option to review all possible grammar errors.

Click the Editor Score box at the Editor task pane and the first spelling or grammar error is selected. The *Suggestions* list box contains one or more possible corrections. Click a suggestion to make the correction in the document. Or, click the arrow to the right of a suggestion for more options, as described in Table 1.6. If none of the suggestions seems right and the word is correct as typed, use the other options in the task pane to ignore the error or add the word to the spelling dictionary. Refer to Table 1.7 for descriptions of the options in the Editor task pane.

Table 1.6 Suggestion Drop-Down List Options

Option	Function
Read Aloud	reads the suggested correction aloud (speaker necessary)
Spell Out	spells the suggested correction aloud (speaker necessary)
Change All	changes all instances of the error to the suggested correction
Add to AutoCorrect	makes a suggested correction automatic by adding it as an option in AutoCorrect

Table 1.7 Editor Task Pane Options

Option	Function
Ignore Once	ignores the selected error
Ignore All	ignores the error and all other occurrences of it in the document
Add to Dictionary	adds the word to the spelling checker dictionary
Delete Repeated Word	deletes one of two repeated words
Stop checking for this	ignores a suspected grammar error and no longer checks for this type of error in the document

If Word detects a grammar error, the text containing the error is selected and possible corrections are provided in the Editor task pane *Suggestions* list box. Depending on the error, some of the options described in Table 1.7 may be available and a grammar rule will be provided near the top of the task pane. Click the down arrow at the right of the grammar rule and information about the rule displays along with suggestions on how to correct the error.

When checking the spelling and grammar in a document, temporarily leave the Editor task pane by clicking in the document. To resume the spelling and grammar check, click the resume button (the name may vary) in the task pane.

Activity 5 Checking the Spelling and Grammar in a Document

Part 1 of 1

1. Open **TechVisionary.docx** and save it with the name **1-TechVisionary**.
2. Click the Editor button in the Editor group on the Home tab (located at the right side of the ribbon).

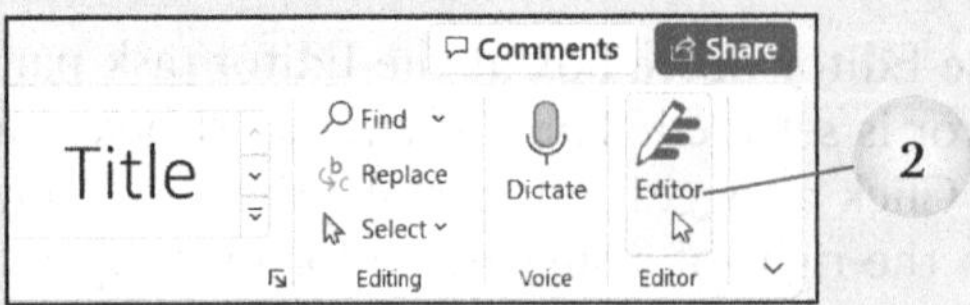

3. The Editor task pane opens and identifies the total number of possible spelling and grammar errors along with information in the *Corrections* section. Change the document's formal level by clicking the *Formal writing* option box and then clicking *Professional* at the drop-down list.
4. Click the Editor Score button near the top of the task pane.

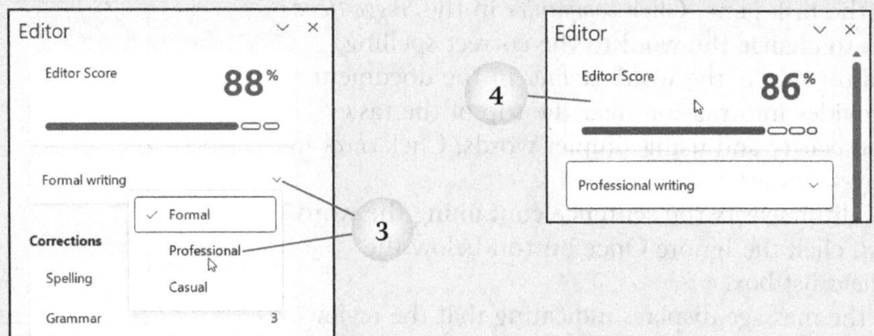

5. The Editor selects the word *chalenged* in the document and provides the correct spelling in the *Suggestions* list box in the task pane. Click *challenged* in the *Suggestions* list box to change the word to the correct spelling.
6. The Editor selects the word *too* in the document and provides the word *to* in the *Suggestions* list box. Click the down arrow to the right of the text *Possible Word Choice Error* near the top of the task pane, read the information provided about a possible word choice error, and then click the up arrow to remove the information.
7. Click *to* in the *Suggestions* list box to correct the grammar error.

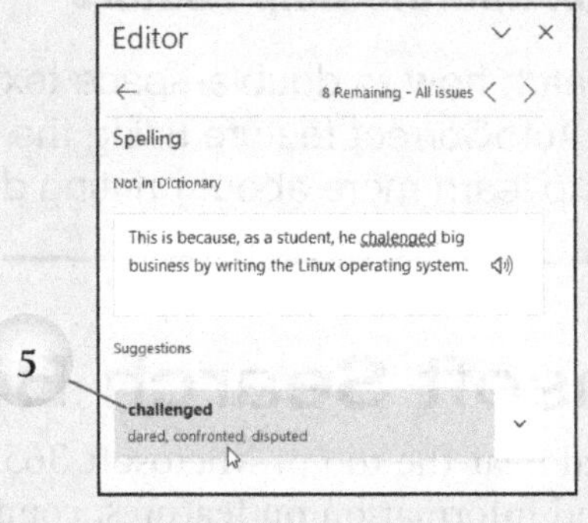

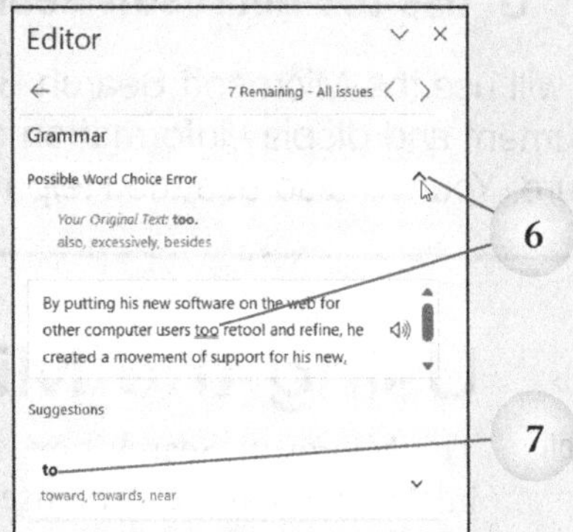

8. If the Editor selects the sentence containing the words *a viable*, click the Ignore Once button below the *Suggestions* list box.
9. The Editor selects the words *operating* and *system*, noting that two spaces appear between the words. The *Suggestions* list box provides an option with the words *operating system* with only one space between the words. Click the option in the *Suggestions* list box to correct the error.

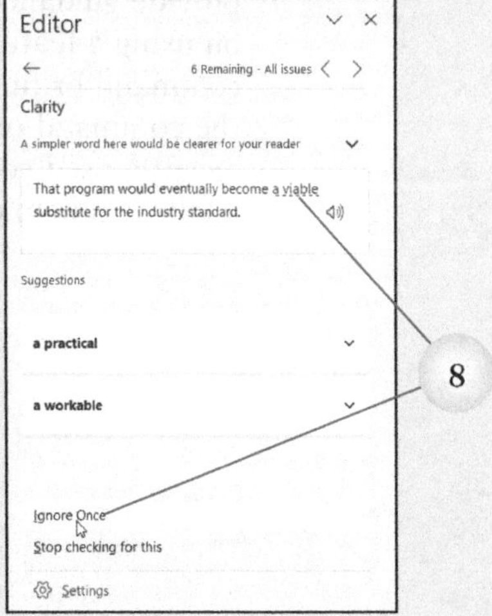

10. The Editor selects the word *the*, which is used two times in a row. Click the *Delete Repeated Word* option in the task pane to delete the second *the*.
11. The Editor selects the word *company's* in the document and provides a grammar suggestion in the *Suggestions* list box in the task pane. Click *companies* in the *Suggestions* list box to change the word to the correct spelling.
12. The Editor selects the word *monitor* in the document and provides information near the top of the task pane on clarity and using simpler words. Click *check* in the *Suggestions* list box.
13. If the Editor selects the sentence containing the word *operated*, click the Ignore Once button below the *Suggestions* list box.
14. When the message displays indicating that the reviewing of the Editor's suggestions is finished, click OK.
15. Close the Editor task pane by clicking the Close button in the upper right corner of the task pane.
16. Save, preview, and then close **1-TechVisionary.docx**.

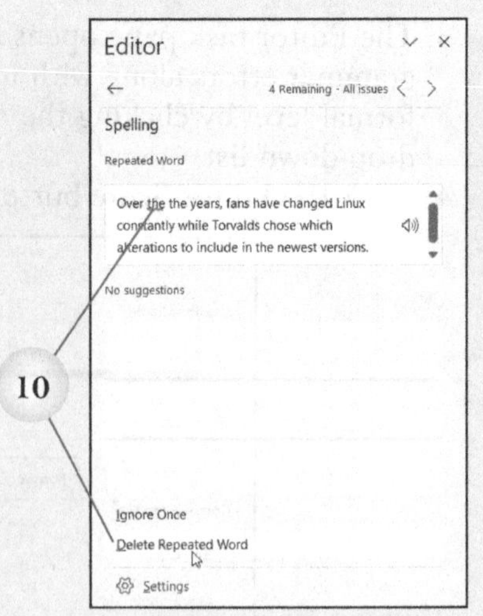

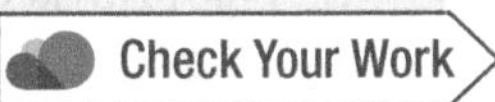

Activity 6 Use the Microsoft Search Box and the Help Feature — 2 Parts

You will use the Microsoft Search Box to learn how to double-space text in a document and display information on the AutoCorrect feature using the Help feature. You will also use the Help feature to learn more about printing documents.

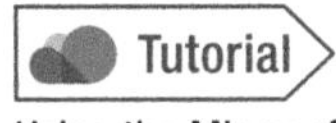

Using the Microsoft Search Box

Using the Microsoft Search Box

The Microsoft Search box is located near the top of Microsoft 365 applications in Windows and can be used to find information on features, commands, text in a file, or information on a word or phrase. The search box can also be used to provide guidance on using a particular feature. To find information or get guidance on using a feature, click in the search box (or press Alt + Q) and then type a command or function. A drop-down list displays with options for completing the command or function. The drop-down list may also contain the most recently used commands, suggested actions based on the current task, how to get additional help on using the command or function, and any recently opened files.

Activity 6a Using the Microsoft Search Box

1. Open **MultimediaSoftware.docx** and then save it with the name **1-MultimediaSoftware.**
2. Press Ctrl + A to select all text in the document.
3. Use the Microsoft Search box to learn how to double-space the text in the document by completing the following steps:
   a. Click in the Microsoft Search box located near the top of the screen.
   b. Type double space.
   c. Click the *2.0 Line and Paragraph Spacing* option in the *Best Action* section. (This double-spaces the selected text in the document.)
   d. Click in the document to deselect the text.

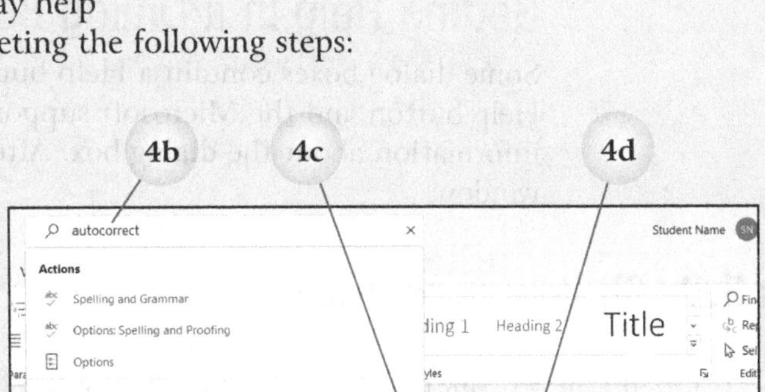

4. Use the Microsoft Search box to display help information on AutoCorrect by completing the following steps:
   a. Click in the Microsoft Search box.
   b. Type autocorrect.
   c. Hover the pointer over the arrow that displays to the right of the *"autocorrect"* option in the *Get Help* section.
   d. At the side menu that displays, click the first option (an article on AutoCorrect). This displays the Help task pane with the article information.
   e. Read the information in the Help task pane and then close the task pane by clicking the the Close button in the upper right corner of the task pane.

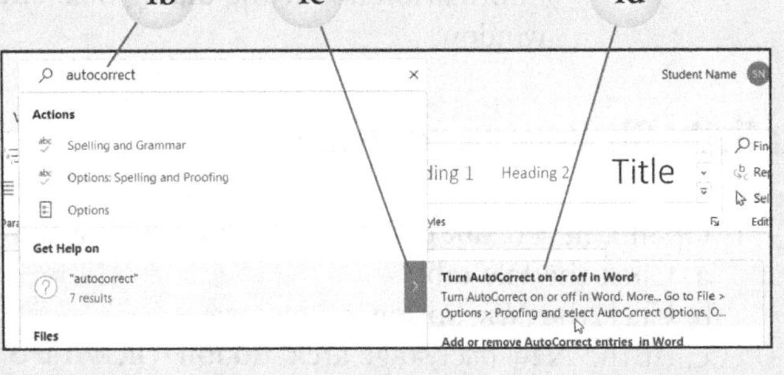

5. Save, preview, and then close **1-MultimediaSoftware.docx.**

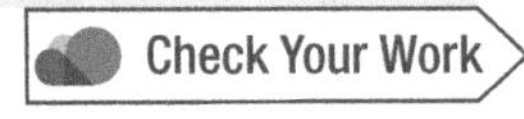

Using the Help Feature

Using the Help Feature

The Help feature is an on-screen reference manual containing information about Word features and commands. The Help feature in Word is similar to the Help features in Excel, PowerPoint, and Access. Get help by using the Microsoft Search box, at the Help task pane, or at the Microsoft support website. Display the Help task pane by pressing the F1 function key or clicking the Help tab and then clicking the Help button.

Help

At the Help task pane, type a topic, feature, or question in the search text box and then press the Enter key. Articles related to the search text are shown in the task pane. Click an article to display the article information in the task pane.

Getting Help from a ScreenTip

Hover the pointer over a certain button, such as the Format Painter button or Font Color button, and the ScreenTip displays with a Help icon and the Tell me more hyperlinked text. Click Tell me more or press the F1 function key and the Help task pane displays with information about the button feature.

Getting Help at the Backstage Area

Click the File tab in Word to display the backstage area. A Microsoft Word Help button, labeled with a question mark (?), appears in the upper right corner of the backstage area. The Help button is also available at many of the other backstage areas. Click the Help button and the Microsoft support website opens in a browser window with information about the backstage area. After reading the information, close the browser window and return to Word.

Getting Help in a Dialog Box

Some dialog boxes contain a Help button. Open a dialog box and then click the Help button and the Microsoft support website opens in a browser window with information about the dialog box. After reading the information, close the browser window.

Activity 6b Using the Help Feature — Part 2 of 2

1. Open a new blank document by completing the following steps:
   a. Click the File tab.
   b. Click the *New* option.
   c. At the New backstage area, double-click the *Single spaced (blank)* template. (You may need to scroll down the screen to display this template.)

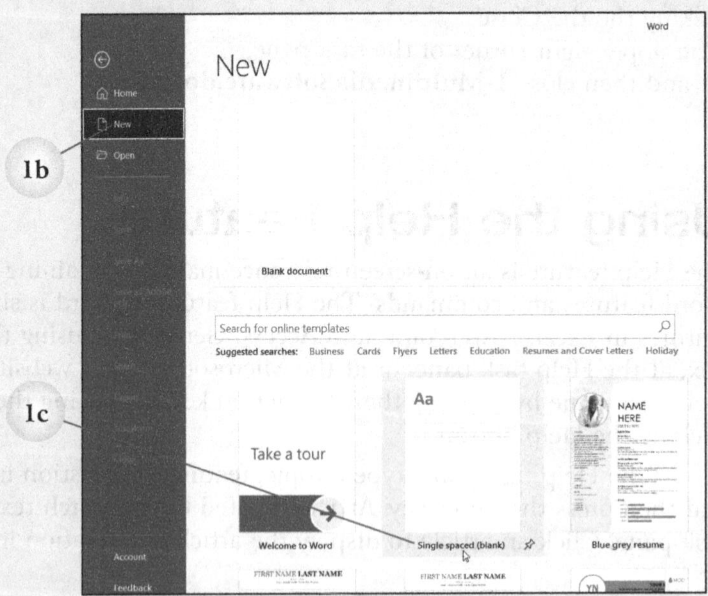

2. Press the F1 function key to display the Help task pane.

3. Type print a document in the task pane search text box and then press the Enter key.
4. When the list of articles displays, click the Print a document in Word hyperlinked article. (You may need to scroll down the task pane to find this article.)
5. Read the information in the task pane about printing a document.
6. Click the Close button to close the Help task pane.
7. Hover the pointer over the Format Painter button in the Clipboard group on the Home tab.
8. Click the Tell me more hyperlinked text at the bottom of the ScreenTip.
9. Read the information in the Help task pane about the Format Painter feature.
10. Click the Help task pane Close button.
11. Click the File tab.
12. Click the Microsoft Word Help button in the upper right corner of the backstage area.

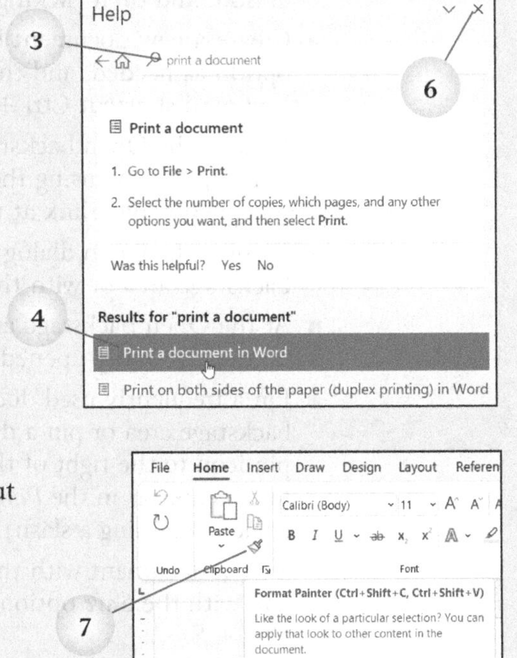

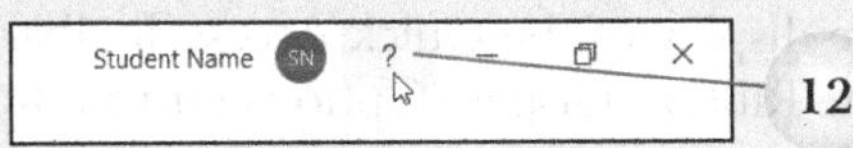

13. Look at the information at the Microsoft support website and then close the browser window.
14. Click the Back button to return to the document.
15. Close the blank document.

Chapter Summary

- Refer to Figure 1.1 and Table 1.1 (on page 5) for an example and a list of key Word screen features respectively.
- Click the File tab and the backstage area displays, containing options for working with and managing documents.
- Document names can contain a maximum of 255 characters, including the drive letter and folder names, and they may include spaces.
- The ribbon contains tabs with options and buttons divided into groups.
- The insertion point displays as a blinking vertical line and indicates the position of the next character to be entered in the document.
- Print a hard copy of a document by clicking the File tab, clicking the *Print* option, and then clicking the Print button.
- Close a document by clicking the File tab and then clicking the *Close* option or with the keyboard shortcut Ctrl + F4.
- Close Word by clicking the Close button in the upper right corner of the screen or with the keyboard shortcut Alt + F4.

- Create a new single-spaced document by clicking the File tab, clicking the *New* option, and then clicking the *Single spaced (blank)* template.
- Create a new document by clicking the File tab, clicking the *Home* or *New* option as needed, and then clicking the *Blank document* template or by using the keyboard shortcut Ctrl + N.
- Display the Open backstage area by clicking the File tab and then clicking the *Open* option; by using the keyboard shortcut Ctrl + O; or by clicking the More documents hyperlink at the Home backstage area or the Word opening screen.
- Display the Open dialog box by clicking the *Browse* option at the Open backstage area or with the keyboard shortcut Ctrl + F12.
- At the Open backstage area with the *Recent* option selected, the names of the 50 most recently opened documents display.
- Pin a frequently used document or folder to the *Recent* option list at the Open backstage area or pin a document at the Home backstage area by clicking the pin icon to the right of the document or folder name. Pinned documents and folders appear in the *Pinned* category. Click the pin icon again (displays with a circle containing a slash) to unpin a document or folder from the list.
- Save a document with the same name by clicking the Save button on the Title bar, with the *Save* option at the backstage area, or with the keyboard shortcut Ctrl + S.
- The Quick Access Toolbar is a customizable toolbar that provides easy access to common functions. Turn on the display of the Quick Access Toolbar with the *Show Quick Access Toolbar* option at the Ribbon Display Options button drop-down list.
- Add a button to the Quick Access Toolbar by clicking the Customize Quick Access Toolbar button at the right side of the toolbar and then clicking the button name at the drop-down list.
- Remove a button from the Quick Access Toolbar by right-clicking the button and then clicking *Remove from Quick Access Toolbar* at the shortcut menu.
- The scroll box on the vertical scroll bar indicates the location of the text in the document screen in relation to the entire of the document.
- The insertion point can be moved throughout the document using the mouse, the keyboard, or a combination of the two.
- The insertion point can be moved by character, word, screen, or page and from the first to the last character in a document. Refer to Table 1.2 (on page 16) for keyboard insertion point movement commands.
- Delete text by character, word, line, several lines, or partial page using specific keys or by selecting text using the mouse or the keyboard. Refer to Table 1.3 (on page 18) for deletion commands.
- A specific amount of text can be selected using the mouse and/or the keyboard. Refer to Table 1.4 (on page 19) for information on selecting with the mouse, and refer to Table 1.5 (on page 20) for information on selecting with the keyboard.
- Use the Undo button on the Home tab to undo an action such as typing, deleting, or formatting text. Use the Redo button to redo something that has been undone with the Undo button.
- Word contains the Microsoft Editor that checks for spelling and grammar errors in the document. Corrections are suggested in the Editor task pane. Refer to Table 1.6 and Table 1.7 (on page 24) for a description of options at the Editor task pane.

- Use the Microsoft Search box, located near the top of the screen, to find information on features, commands, text in a file, or information on a word or phrase.
- Word's Help feature is an on-screen reference manual containing information on Word features and commands. Press the F1 function key to display the Help task pane or click the Help tab and then click the Help button.
- Hover the pointer over a certain button and the ScreenTip displays with a Help icon and the Tell me more hyperlinked text. Click this hyperlinked text to display the Help task pane, which contains information about the button feature.
- Some dialog boxes and the backstage area contain a Help button that links to the Microsoft support website to provide more information about functions and features.

Commands Review

FEATURE	RIBBON TAB, GROUP/ OPTION	BUTTON, OPTION	KEYBOARD SHORTCUT
AutoComplete entry			F3
close document	File, *Close*		Ctrl + F4
close Word			Alt + F4
display Quick Access Toolbar		, *Show Quick Access Toolbar*	
Go To feature	Home, Editing	, *Go To*	Ctrl + G
Help task pane	Help, Help		F1
leave backstage area			Esc
Microsoft Editor	Home, Editor OR Review, Proofing		F7
Microsoft Search box			Alt + Q
move insertion point to previous location when document was closed			Shift + F5
new blank document	File, *New* OR File, *Home*	*Blank document*	Ctrl + N
New Line command			Shift + Enter
Open backstage area	File, *Open*		Ctrl + O
Open dialog box	File, *Open*	*Browse*	Ctrl + F12
Print backstage area	File, *Print*		Ctrl + P
redo action	Undo, Home		Ctrl + Y
save	File, *Save*		Ctrl + S
Save As backstage area	File, *Save As*		
Save As dialog box	File, *Save As*	*Browse*	F12
Selection mode			F8
undo action	Undo, Home		Ctrl + Z

Review and Assessment

CHAPTER 1

Skills Assessment

Assessment 1

Edit a Document on Resume Writing

1. Open Word and then open **WriteResume.docx**.
2. Save the document with the name **1-WriteResume**.
3. Move the insertion point to the end of the document and then type the text shown in Figure 1.9. When typing the text, use the New Line command, Shift + Enter, to end the lines after *Created by Marie Solberg* and *Monday, October 7, 2024*.
4. Make the following changes to the document:
   a. Delete the first occurrence of the word *currently* in the first sentence of the first paragraph.
   b. Select the word *important* in the first sentence in the first paragraph and then type essential.
   c. Type and hard-hitting between the words *concise* and *written* in the second sentence of the second paragraph.
   d. Delete the words *over and over,* (including the comma and the space after the comma) in the third sentence in the second paragraph.
   e. Select and then delete the second sentence of the third paragraph (the sentence that begins *So do not take*).
   f. Move the insertion point to the beginning of the third paragraph and then press the backspace key to join the third paragraph with the second paragraph.
   g. Delete the name *Marie Solberg* and then type your first and last names.
5. Save, preview, and then close **1-WriteResume.docx**.

Figure 1.9 Assessment 1

Created by Marie Solberg
Monday, October 7, 2024
Note: Please insert this information between the 2nd and 3rd sections.

Assessment 2

Check the Spelling and Grammar of a Resume Style Document

1. Open **ResumeStyles.docx**.
2. Save the document with the name **1-ResumeStyles**.
3. Use the Editor to complete a spelling and grammar check on the document and correct the errors.
4. Type the sentence Different approaches work for different people. between the first and second sentences in the first paragraph of text below the title *RESUMES*.
5. Move the insertion point to the end of the document (on the blank line following the last paragraph of text), type your first and last names, press Shift + Enter, and then type the current date.
6. Save, preview, and then close **1-ResumeStyles.docx**.

Assessment 3

Create a Document Describing Keyboard Shortcuts

1. Press the F1 function key to display the Help task pane.
2. Type keyboard shortcuts in the search text box and then press the Enter key.
3. At the Help task pane, click the Keyboard shortcuts in Word hyperlink. (If this article is not available, choose a similar article that describes Word keyboard shortcuts.)
4. Read through the information in the Help task pane.
5. Open a new blank single-spaced document.
6. Create a document with the following specifications:
   a. Type Keyboard Shortcuts as the title.
   b. Describe four keyboard shortcuts by providing a brief description of how each shortcut is used.
   c. Click in the title *Keyboard Shortcuts* and then use the Microsoft Search box to center the title.
7. Save the document with the name **1-KeyboardShortcuts**.
8. Preview and then close **1-KeyboardShortcuts.docx**.

Visual Benchmark

Create a Cover Letter

1. At a new blank document, type the cover letter shown in Figure 1.10, following the directions in red. (A cover letter is a business letter written to accompany a resume. It may be sent electronically or through the mail. When sent through the mail, a cover letter should include the postal address of the writer and the addressee in block paragraph format, as shown in Figure 1.10.)
2. Save the completed letter with the name **1-CoverLtr**.
3. Preview and then close **1-CoverLtr.docx**.

Figure 1.10 Visual Benchmark

(press Enter three times)

4520 South Park Street *(press Shift + Enter)*
Newark, NJ 07122 *(press Shift + Enter)*
Current Date *(press Enter two times)*

Ms. Sylvia Hammond *(press Shift + Enter)*
Sales Director, Eastern Division *(press Shift + Enter)*
Grand Style Products *(press Shift + Enter)*
1205 Sixth Street *(press Shift + Enter)*
Newark, NJ 07102 *(press Enter)*

Dear Ms. Hammond: *(press Enter)*

Thank you for agreeing to meet with me next Wednesday. Based on our initial conversation, I believe that my ability to sell solutions rather than products is a good fit for your needs as you seek to expand your visibility in the region. *(press Enter)*

As noted in the enclosed resume, I have led an underperforming product division to generating 33 percent of total revenue (up from 5 percent) at our location. We now deliver, from a single location, 25 percent of total sales for our 20-site company. Having completed this turnaround over the last 5 years, I'm eager for new challenges that will enable me to use my proven skills in sales, marketing, and program/event planning to contribute to a company's bottom line. *(press Enter)*

I have been thinking about the challenges you described in building your presence at the retail level, and I have some good ideas to share at our meeting. I am excited about the future of Grand Style Products and eager to contribute to the company's growth. *(press Enter)*

Sincerely, *(press Enter two times)*

Student Name *(press Enter)*

Enclosure

Case Study

Part 1

You are the administrative assistant at a mid-sized service-oriented business. Employees frequently use Microsoft Word to create contracts to use with customers. Your boss, Mr. Brewster, wants these saved to a folder named *Contracts* in the Documents folder on your company's shared drive. Mr. Brewster has asked you to create a document for employees with step-by-step instructions for naming and saving contracts. Save your completed document with the name **1-Saving**. Preview and then close the document.

Part 2

Mr. Brewster would like to have a document describing basic Word commands and keyboard shortcuts to help employees work more efficiently in Microsoft Word. He has asked you to prepare a document containing the following information:

- A brief explanation of how to use the Go To feature to move the insertion point to a specific page
- Keyboard shortcuts to move the insertion point to the beginning and end of a line and the beginning and end of a document
- Keyboard commands to delete text from the insertion point to the beginning of a word and from the insertion point to the end of a word
- Steps to select a word and a paragraph using the mouse
- A keyboard shortcut to select the entire document

Save the completed document with the name **1-WordCommands**. Preview and then close the document.

Part 3

According to Mr. Brewster, the company is considering updating its computers to Microsoft 365. He has asked you to go to the Microsoft home page at microsoft.com and then use the Search feature to find information on Microsoft 365 plans for use in business. Determine what applications and services are included and pricing for each plan. When you find the information, type a document that contains information on two different Microsoft 365 plans. Save the document with the name **1-Microsoft365**. Preview and then close the document.

WORD

CHAPTER 2

Formatting Characters and Paragraphs

Performance Objectives

Upon successful completion of Chapter 2, you will be able to:

1 Change the font and font size and choose font effects
2 Format selected text with buttons on the Mini toolbar
3 Apply styles from style sets
4 Apply themes
5 Customize styles and themes
6 Change the alignment of text in paragraphs
7 Indent text in paragraphs
8 Increase and decrease spacing before and after paragraphs
9 Repeat the last action
10 Automate formatting with Format Painter
11 Change line spacing
12 Reveal and compare formatting

The appearance of a document on the screen and when printed is called the *format*. A Word document is based on a template that applies default formatting. Some of the default formats include 11-point Calibri font, line spacing of 1.08, 8 points of spacing after each paragraph, and left-aligned text. In this chapter, you will learn about changing the typeface, type size, and typestyle as well as applying font effects such as bold and italic. You will also learn to format paragraphs by changing text alignment and line spacing, indenting text, and applying formatting with Format Painter.

Data Files

The data files for this chapter are in the WL1C2 folder that you downloaded at the beginning of this course.

Activity 1 **Apply Font Formatting to Characters in a Document** **4 Parts**

You will open a document containing a glossary of terms and then format the document by changing the font and the font size; adding bold, italics, and underlining; and applying font effects.

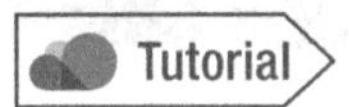

Applying Font Formatting Using the Font Group

Applying Font Formatting

One of the most visible aspects of a document's format is the font. Font formatting can be applied to the individual characters of text, including letters, numbers, and symbols. Applying font formatting can draw the reader's attention to specific parts of a document, make information accessible to the reader by formatting items such as headings, highlight key words, and emphasize important information.

A font consists of three elements: typeface, type size, and typestyle. By default, a Word document is formatted with the Calibri typeface in 11-point size. The typestyle is roman type; that is, regular and not bold or italic. This default may need to be changed to another font for such reasons as altering the mood of the document, enhancing its visual appeal, and increasing its readability.

Hint Change the default font by selecting the font at the Font dialog box and then clicking the Set As Default button.

The Font group on the Home tab, shown in Figure 2.1, contains a number of options and buttons for applying font formatting to characters in a document. The top row contains options for changing the font and font size as well as buttons for increasing and decreasing the size of the font and changing the text case. The bottom row contains buttons for applying typestyles such as bold, italic, and underline and for applying text effects, highlighting, and color. Use the Clear All Formatting button in the top row of the Font group to remove all formatting applied to characters and paragraphs in the text. To remove only character formatting, select text and then use the keyboard shortcut Ctrl + spacebar.

Hint Use a serif typeface for text-intensive documents.

A typeface is a set of characters with a common design and shape and can be decorative or plain and either monospaced or proportional. Word refers to a typeface as a *font*. A monospaced typeface allots the same amount of horizontal space for each character, while a proportional typeface allots varying amounts of space for different characters. Typefaces are divided into two main categories: serif and sans serif. A serif is a small line at the end of a character stroke. Consider using a serif typeface for text-intensive documents because the serifs help move the reader's eyes across the page. Use a sans serif typeface for headings, headlines, and advertisements. Some popular typefaces are shown in Table 2.1.

Figure 2.1 Font Group Option Boxes and Buttons

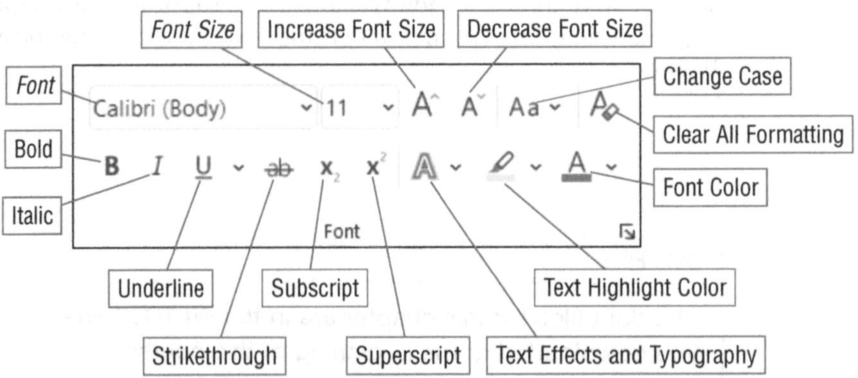

Table 2.1 Categories of Typefaces

Serif Typefaces	Sans Serif Typefaces	Monospaced Typefaces
Cambria	Calibri	Consolas
Constantia	Candara	Courier New
Times New Roman	Corbel	Lucida Console
Bookman Old Style	Arial	MS Gothic

Hint Press Ctrl +] to increase font size by 1 point and press Ctrl + [to decrease font size by 1 point.

Type is generally set in proportional size. The size of proportional type is measured vertically in units called *points*. A point is approximately 1/72 of an inch—the higher the point size, the larger the characters. Within a typeface, characters may have varying styles, including regular, bold, italic, bold italic, and underlined.

Use the *Font* option box in the Font group to change the font. Select the text in the document, click the *Font* option box arrow, and then click a font option at the drop-down gallery. Another method for changing the font is to click the current font name in the *Font* option box to select it and then type the new font name. Change the font size by clicking the *Font Size* option box arrow and then clicking the font size at the drop-down gallery. Or, click the current font size in the *Font Size* option box to select it and then type the new font size number.

To see a live preview of the text in different fonts and sizes before changing the formatting in the document, select the text and then display the *Font* or *Font Size* drop-down gallery. Hover the pointer over different font options to see how the selected text displays in each font or size.

Activity 1a Changing the Font and Font Size

Part 1 of 4

1. Open **CompTerms.docx** and then save it with the name **2-CompTerms**.
2. Change the typeface to Cambria by completing the following steps:
   a. Select all text in the document by clicking the Select button in the Editing group and then clicking *Select All* at the drop-down list. (You can also select the entire document by pressing Ctrl + A.)
   b. Click the *Font* option box arrow, scroll down the drop-down gallery until *Cambria* displays, and then hover the pointer over *Cambria*. This displays a live preview of the text set in Cambria.
   c. Click the *Cambria* option.

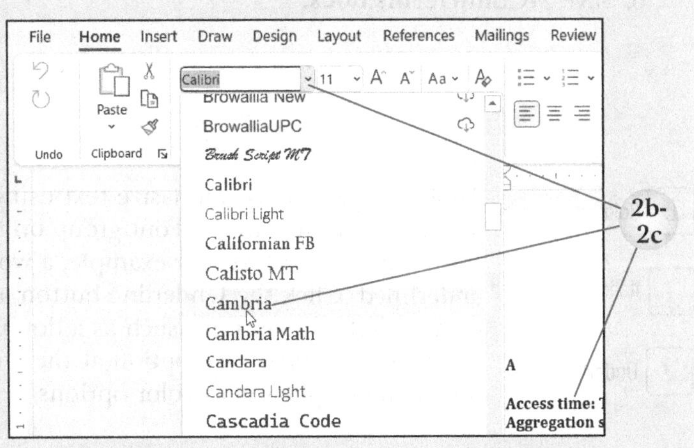

3. Change the type size to 14 points by completing the following steps:
   a. With the text in the document still selected, click the *Font Size* option box arrow.
   b. At the drop-down gallery, hover the pointer over *14* and look at the live preview of the text with 14 points applied.
   c. Click the *14* option.

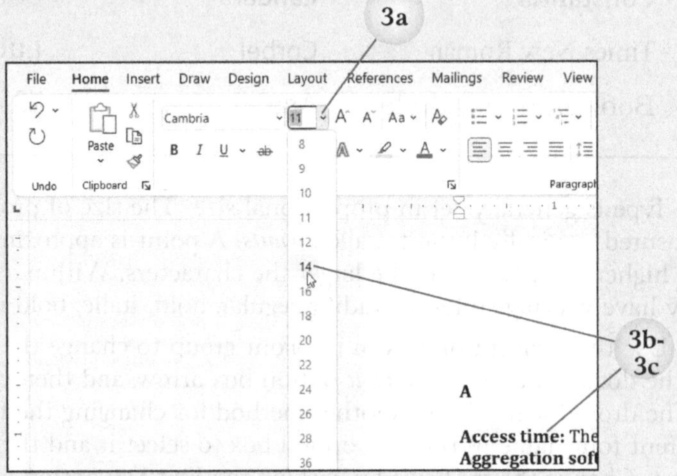

4. Change the type size and typeface by completing the following steps:
   a. Click the Decrease Font Size button in the Font group three times. (This decreases the size to 10 points.)
   b. Click the Increase Font Size button two times. (This increases the size to 12 points.)
   c. Click the *Font* option box arrow, scroll down the drop-down gallery, and then click *Constantia*. (The most recently used fonts are listed at the beginning of the gallery, followed by a listing of all fonts.)
5. Deselect the text by clicking anywhere in the document.
6. Save **2-CompTerms.docx**.

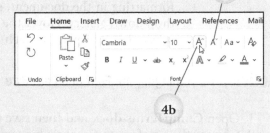

Check Your Work

Choosing a Typestyle

B Bold

I Italic

U Underline

Apply a typestyle to emphasize text using the Bold, Italic, and Underline buttons in the bottom row in the Font group on the Home tab. More than one typestyle can be applied to text. For example, a word may be set as bold italic and also underlined. Click the Underline button arrow and a drop-down gallery displays with underlining options, such as a double line, dashed line, and thicker underline. Click the *Underline Color* option at the Underline button drop-down gallery and a side menu displays with color options.

Activity 1b Applying Font Formatting to Characters as You Type

1. With **2-CompTerms.docx** open, press Ctrl + Home to move the insertion point to the beginning of the document.
2. Type a heading for the document by completing the following steps:
   a. Click the Bold button in the Font group. (This turns on bold formatting.)
   b. Click the Underline button in the Font group. (This turns on underline formatting.)
   c. Type Glossary of Terms.

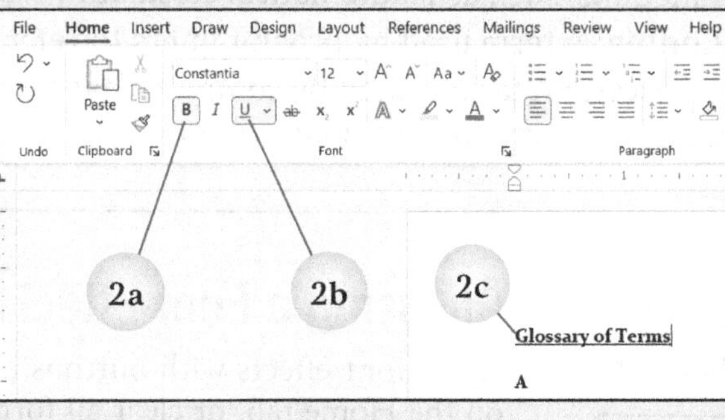

3. Press Ctrl + End to move the insertion point to the end of the document.
4. Type the text shown in Figure 2.2 with the following specifications:
   a. While typing, make the appropriate text bold, as shown in the figure, by completing the following steps:
      1) Click the Bold button. (This turns on bold formatting.)
      2) Type the text.
      3) Click the Bold button. (This turns off bold formatting.)
   b. Press the Enter key two times after typing the *C* heading.
   c. While typing, italicize the appropriate text, as shown in the figure, by completing the following steps:
      1) Click the Italic button in the Font group.
      2) Type the text.
      3) Click the Italic button.
5. After typing the text, press the Enter key two times and then press Ctrl + Home to move the insertion point to the beginning of the document.
6. Change the underlining below the title by completing the following steps:
   a. Select the title *Glossary of Terms*.
   b. Click the Underline button arrow and then click the third underline option from the top of the drop-down gallery (*Thick underline*).

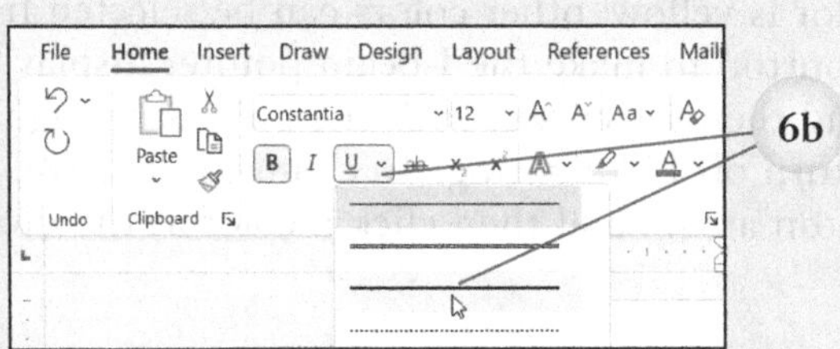

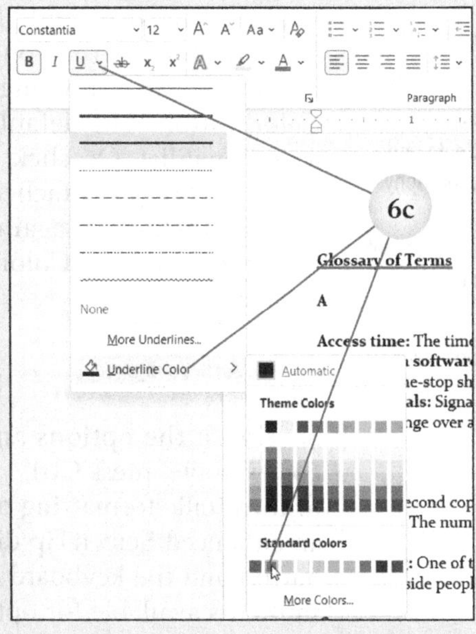

   c. Click the Underline button arrow, point to the *Underline Color* option, and then click the *Red* color (second color option in the *Standard Colors* section).
7. With the title still selected, change the font size to 14 points.
8. Save **2-CompTerms.docx**.

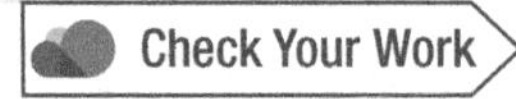

Figure 2.2 Activity 1b

> C
>
> **Chip:** A thin wafer of *silicon* containing electronic circuitry that performs various functions, such as mathematical calculations, storage, and controlling computer devices.
> **Coding:** A term used by programmers to refer to the act of writing source code.
> **Crackers:** A term coined by computer hackers for those who intentionally enter (or hack) computer systems to damage them.

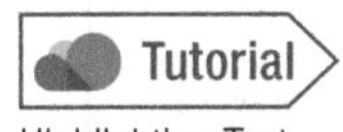
Highlighting Text

Applying Text Effects Using the Ribbon

Choosing a Font Effect

Apply font effects with buttons in the top and bottom rows in the Font group on the Home tab, or clear all formatting from selected text with the Clear All Formatting button. Change the case of text with the Change Case button drop-down list. Click the Change Case button in the top row in the Font group and then click one of the options in the drop-down list: *Sentence case*, *lowercase*, *UPPERCASE*, *Capitalize Each Word*, and *tOGGLE cASE*. The case of selected text can also be changed with the keyboard shortcut Shift + F3. Each time Shift + F3 is pressed, the selected text displays in the next case option in the list.

The bottom row in the Font group contains buttons for applying font effects. Use the Strikethrough button to draw a line through selected text. This has a practical application in some legal documents in which deleted text must be retained in the document. Use the Subscript button to create text that is lowered slightly below the line, as in the chemical formula H_2O. Use the Superscript button to create text that is raised slightly above the text line, as in the mathematical equation four to the third power (written as 4^3).

Click the Text Effects and Typography button in the bottom row and a drop-down gallery displays with predesigned effect options along with outline, shadow, reflection, and glow text effects. The Text Highlight Color and Font Color buttons in the Font group are used to highlight text or change the color of the font. To apply highlighting, select text and then click the Text Highlight Color button. The default color is yellow; other colors can be selected from the drop-down list. Or, click the button to make the I-beam pointer display with a highlighter pen attached, and then select text with the pointer to highlight it. Click the button again to turn off highlighting. To change font color, select text, click the Font Color button arrow, and then click a color at the drop-down gallery.

Applying Formatting Using Keyboard Shortcuts

Several of the options and buttons in the Font group have keyboard shortcuts. For example, press Ctrl + B to turn bold formatting on or off and press Ctrl + I to turn italic formatting on or off. Position the pointer on an option or button and an enhanced ScreenTip displays with the name and description of the option or button and the keyboard shortcut, if it has one. Table 2.2 identifies the keyboard shortcuts available for options and buttons in the Font group.

Table 2.2 Font Group Option and Button Keyboard Shortcuts

Font Group Option/Button	Keyboard Shortcut
Font	Ctrl + Shift + F
Font Size	Ctrl + Shift + P
Increase Font Size	Ctrl + Shift + > OR Ctrl +]
Decrease Font Size	Ctrl + Shift + < OR Ctrl + [
Bold	Ctrl + B
Italic	Ctrl + I
Underline	Ctrl + U
Subscript	Ctrl + =
Superscript	Ctrl + Shift + +
Change Case	Shift + F3

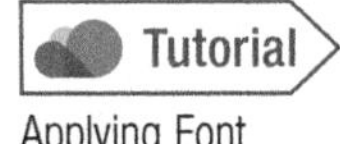

Applying Font Formatting Using the Mini Toolbar

Formatting with the Mini Toolbar

When text is selected, the Mini toolbar displays above the selected text, as shown in Figure 2.3. Click a button on the Mini toolbar to apply formatting to the selected text. When the pointer is moved away from the Mini toolbar, the toolbar disappears.

Figure 2.3 Mini Toolbar

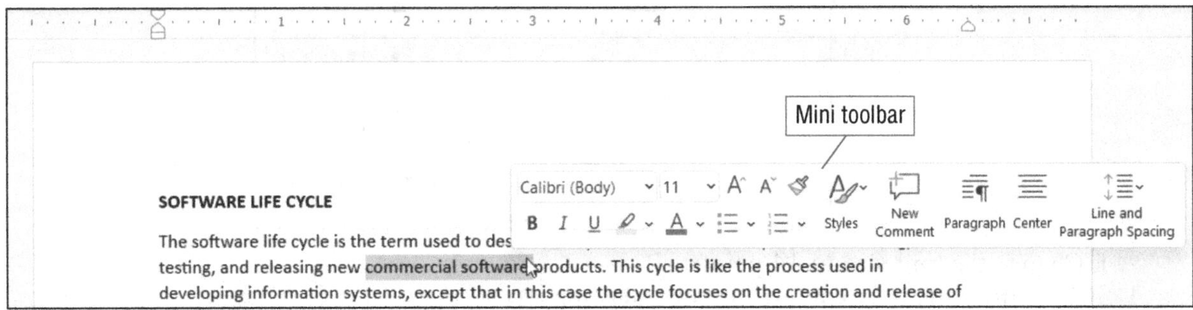

Activity 1c Applying Font Effects

Part 3 of 4

1. With **2-CompTerms.docx** open, move the insertion point to the beginning of the term *Chip*, press the Enter key, and then press the Up Arrow key.
2. Type the text shown in Figure 2.4 on page 45. Create each superscript number by clicking the Superscript button, typing the number, and then clicking the Superscript button.

3. Remove formatting and then change the case and size of the text, and apply text effects to the title by completing the following steps:
   a. Select the title *Glossary of Terms*.
   b. Remove all formatting from the title by clicking the Clear All Formatting button in the Font group.
   c. Click the Change Case button in the Font group and then click *UPPERCASE* at the drop-down list.
   d. Click the Text Effects and Typography button in the Font group and then click the option in the second column, second row (the option with blue gradient fill and reflection).
   e. Apply a dark blue outline text effect to the selected title by clicking the Text Effects and Typography button, pointing to *Outline*, and then clicking the *Dark Blue* color (ninth color option in the *Standard Colors* section).

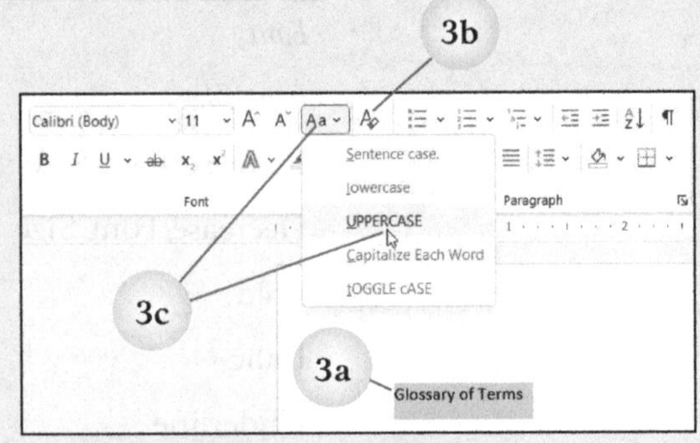

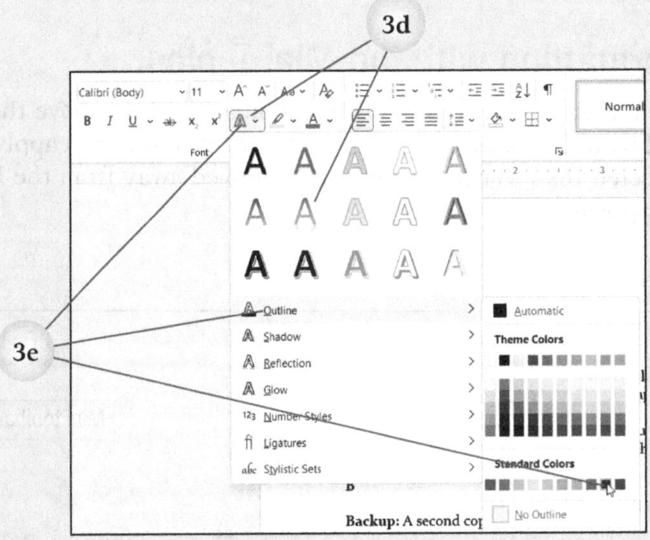

   f. Change the font size to 14 points.
4. Strike through text by completing the following steps:
   a. In the *Crackers* definition, select the phrase *or hack* and the parentheses around it.
   b. Click the Strikethrough button in the Font group.

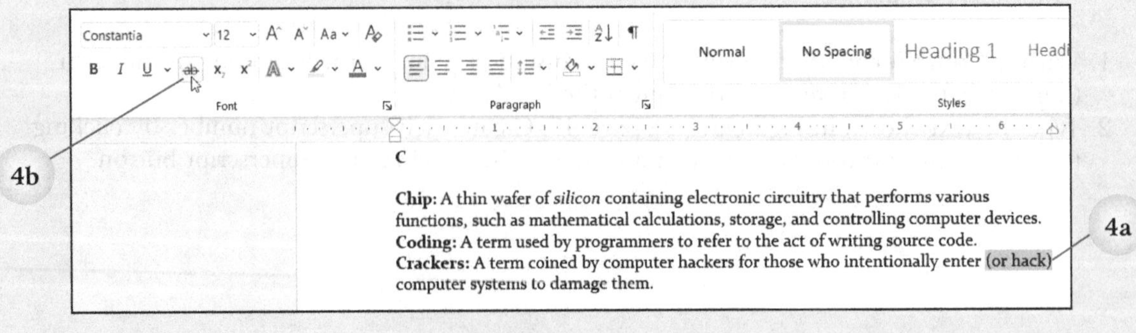

5. Change the font color for the entire document by completing the following steps:
   a. Press Ctrl + A to select the entire document.
   b. Click the Font Color button arrow.
   c. Click the *Dark Red* color (first color option in the *Standard Colors* section) at the drop-down gallery.
   d. Click in the document to deselect text.

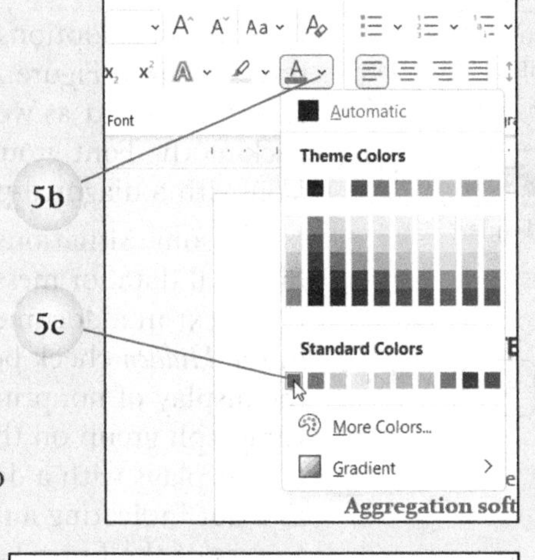

6. Highlight text in the document by completing the following steps:
   a. Select the term *Beta testing* and the definition that follows.
   b. Click the Text Highlight Color button in the Font group. (This applies yellow text highlighting color to the selected text.)
   c. Click the Text Highlight Color button arrow and then click the *Turquoise* color (third column, first row) at the drop-down palette. (This turns on highlighting and the pointer displays as an I-beam pointer with a highlighter pen attached.)
   d. Select the term *Coding* and the definition that follows.
   e. Click the Text Highlight Color button arrow and then click the *Yellow* color (first column, first row) at the drop-down gallery.
   f. Click the Text Highlight Color button to turn off highlighting.

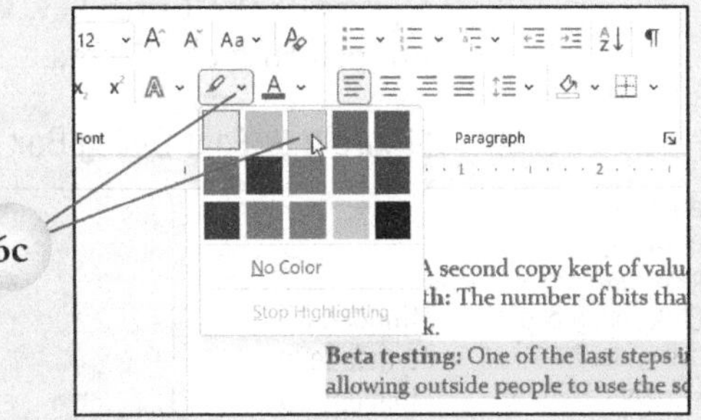

7. Apply italic formatting using the Mini toolbar by completing the following steps:
   a. In the definition for *Aggregation software*, select the phrase *one-stop shopping* (When you select the text, the Mini toolbar displays.)
   b. Click the Italic button on the Mini toolbar.
   c. In the definition for *Bandwidth*, select the word *bits* and then click the Italic button on the Mini toolbar.
8. Save **2-CompTerms.docx**.

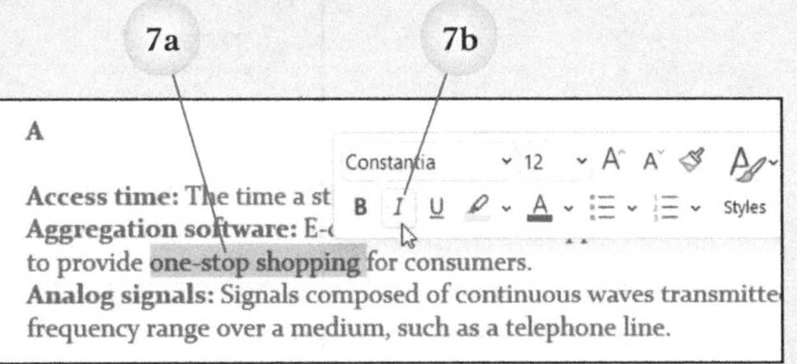

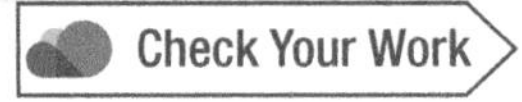

Figure 2.4 Activity 1c

Chinese abacus: Pebbles strung on a rod inside a frame. Pebbles in the upper part of an abacus correspond to 5×10^0, or 5, for the first column; 5×10^1, or 50, for the second column; 5×10^2, or 500, for the third column; and so on.

Applying Font Formatting Using the Font Dialog Box

Hiding Text

Applying Font Formatting Using the Font Dialog Box

In addition to options and buttons in the Font group, options at the Font dialog box, shown in Figure 2.5, can be used to change the typeface, type size, and typestyle of text as well as apply font effects. Display the Font dialog box by clicking the Font group dialog box launcher. The dialog box launcher is a small icon with a diagonal-pointing arrow in the lower right corner of the Font group.

Show/Hide ¶

In some situations, sensitive data in a document such as personal information, financial data, or messages to specific people may need to be hidden from view. Hide text in a document by selecting the text and then inserting a check mark in the *Hidden* check box at the Font dialog box. To display hidden data, turn on the display of nonprinting characters by clicking the Show/Hide ¶ button in the Paragraph group on the Home tab. With the Show/Hide ¶ button active, hidden text displays with a dotted underline. Other nonprinting symbols displays such as a dot indicating a press of the spacebar and the paragraph symbol ¶ indicating a press of the Enter key. Click the Show/Hide ¶ to turn off the display of nonprinting characters.

Quick Steps

Change Font at Font Dialog Box

1. Select text.
2. Click Font group dialog box launcher.
3. Choose options at dialog box.
4. Click OK.

Figure 2.5 Font Dialog Box

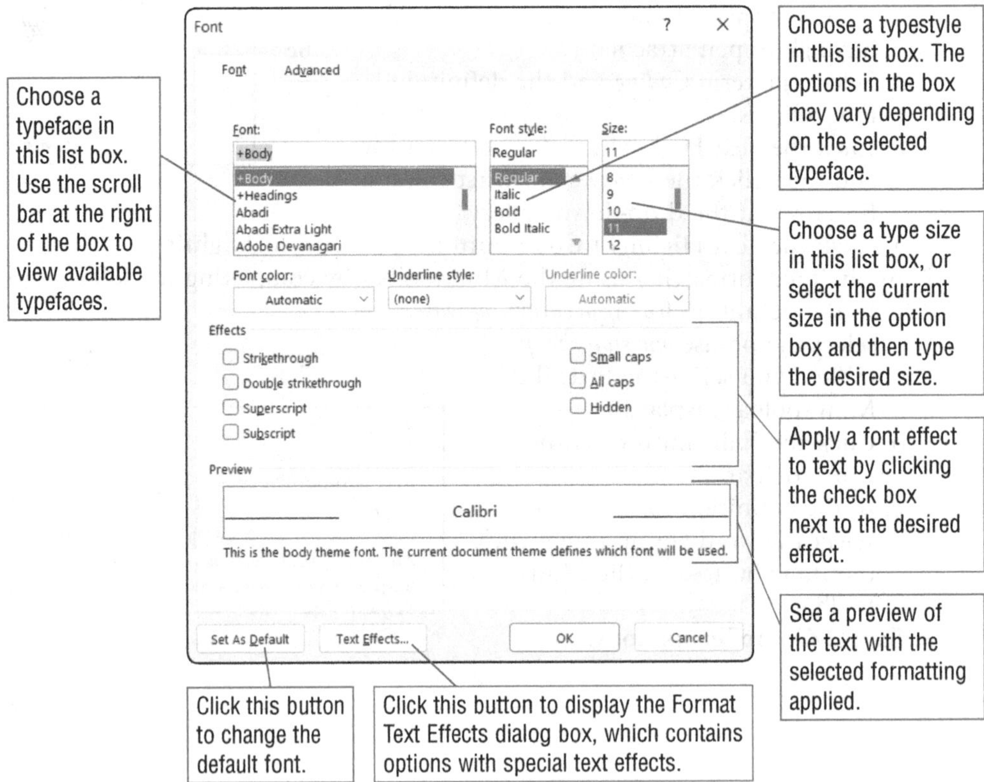

Activity 1d Changing the Font at the Font Dialog Box

Part 4 of 4

1. With **2-CompTerms.docx** open, press Ctrl + End to move the insertion point to the end of the document (a double space below the last line of text).
2. Type Created by Susan Ashby and then press the Enter key.
3. Type Wednesday, February 21, 2024.

4. Change the font for the entire document to 13-point Candara in standard dark blue color by completing the following steps:
   a. Press Ctrl + A to select the entire document.
   b. Click the Font group dialog box launcher.
   c. At the Font dialog box, type can in the *Font* option box (this displays fonts that begin with *can*) and then click *Candara* in the *Font* list box.
   d. Click in the *Size* option box and then type 13.
   e. Click the *Font color* option box arrow and then click the *Dark Blue* color (ninth color option in the *Standard Colors* section).
   f. Click OK to close the dialog box.

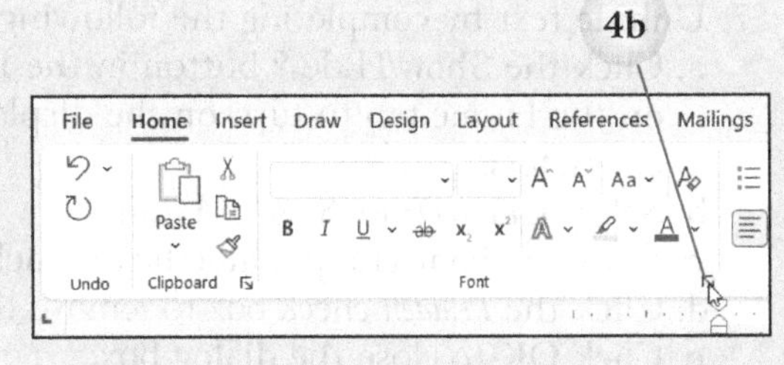

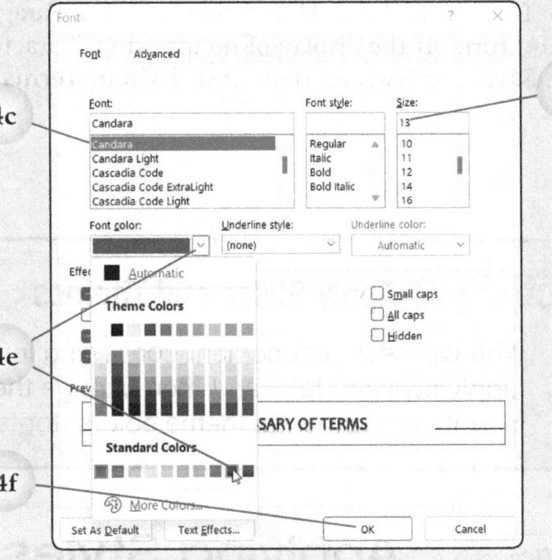

5. Double-underline text by completing the following steps:
   a. Select *Wednesday, February 21, 2024*.
   b. Click the Font group dialog box launcher.
   c. At the Font dialog box, click the *Underline style* option box arrow and then click the double-line option at the drop-down list.
   d. Click OK to close the dialog box.

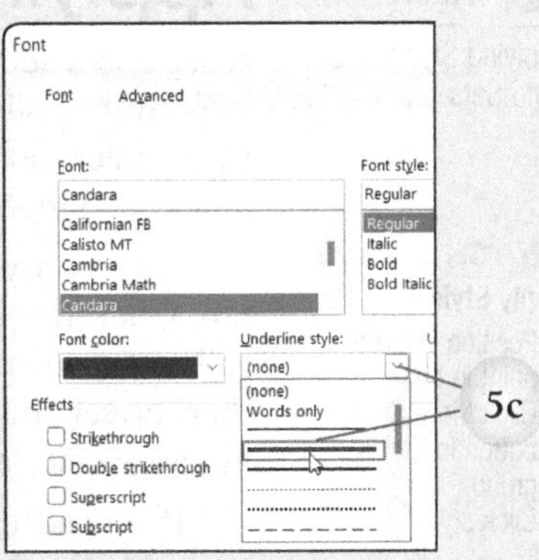

6. Change text to small caps and hide text by completing the following steps:
   a. Select the text *Created by Susan Ashby* and *Wednesday, February 21, 2024*.
   b. Display the Font dialog box.
   c. Click the *Small caps* check box in the *Effects* section. (This inserts a check mark in the check box.)
   d. Click the *Hidden* check box to insert a check mark.
   e. Click OK to close the dialog box.

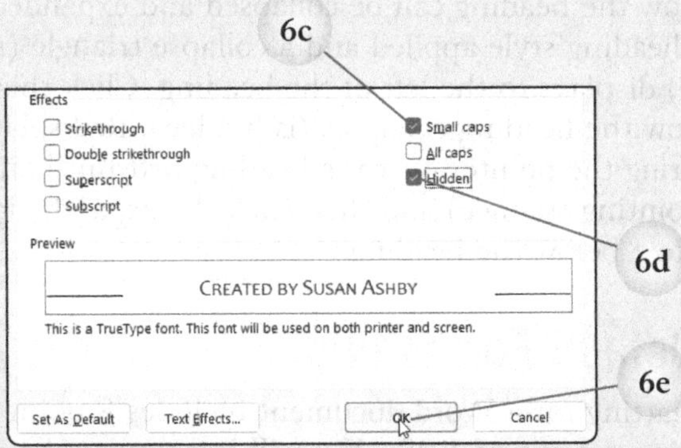

7. Unhide text by completing the following steps:
   a. Click the Show/Hide ¶ button in the Paragraph group on the Home tab to turn on the display of nonprinting characters.
   b. Select *CREATED BY SUSAN ASHBY.*
   c. Click the Font group dialog box launcher.
   d. Click the *Hidden* check box to remove the check mark.
   e. Click OK to close the dialog box.
   f. Click the Show/Hide ¶ button in the Paragraph group to turn off the display of nonprinting characters.
8. Save, preview, and then close **2-CompTerms.docx**.

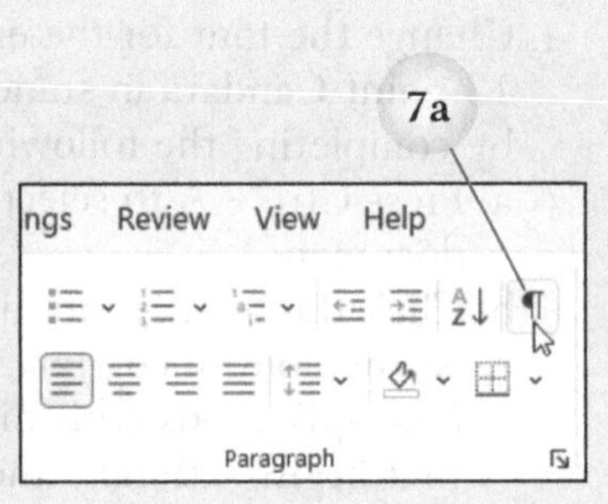

Activity 2 Apply Styles and Themes — 3 Parts

You will open a document containing information on the life cycle of software, apply styles to text, and then change the style set. You will also apply a theme and then change the theme colors, fonts, and paragraph spacing.

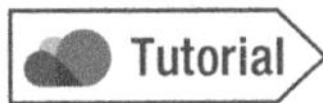

Applying Styles and Style Sets

Quick Steps

Apply Style
1. Position insertion point in text.
2. Click More Styles button in Styles group.
3. Click style.

Applying Styles from a Style Set

A style is a set of predefined formats that can be applied to a document to make it look more polished and professional and provide a structure that can be discerned by a screen reader. When styles are applied, the look of a document can be quickly changed by choosing a different style set.

Word provides a set of predesigned styles in the Styles group on the Home tab. Click the More Styles button (the arrow button at the right side of the gallery) to display all the style options. Position the insertion point in the text and then hover the pointer over the options in the gallery to see how the text will look in various styles and then click a style to apply it.

If a heading style (such as Heading 1, Heading 2, and so on) is applied to text, the text below the heading can be collapsed and expanded. Hover the pointer over text with a heading style applied and a collapse triangle (right- and down-pointing triangle) displays to the left of the heading. Click this collapse triangle and any text below the heading collapses (is hidden). Redisplay the text below a heading by hovering the pointer over the heading text until an expand triangle displays (right-pointing triangle) and then click the expand triangle. This expands (redisplays) the text below the heading.

Removing Default Formatting

The default formatting for a Word document includes 8 points of spacing after paragraphs and line spacing of 1.08. (You will learn more about these formatting options later in this chapter.) This default formatting, as well as any character formatting applied to text in the document, can be removed by applying the No Spacing style to the text. This style is in the styles gallery in the Styles group.

Changing the Style Set

Quick Steps
Change Style Set
1. Click Design tab.
2. Click style set.

To quickly change the look of an entire document, choose a new style set. Style sets can be found in a gallery on the Design tab in the Document Formatting group. Each set contains a different combination of title, heading, and paragraph styles. To apply a new style set, click the Design tab and then click the style set in the style sets gallery in the Document Formatting group.

Activity 2a Applying Styles and Changing the Style Set

Part 1 of 3

1. Open **SoftwareCycle.docx** and then save it with the name **2-SoftwareCycle**.
2. Position the insertion point anywhere in the title *SOFTWARE LIFE CYCLE* and then click the *Heading 1* style in the Styles group.

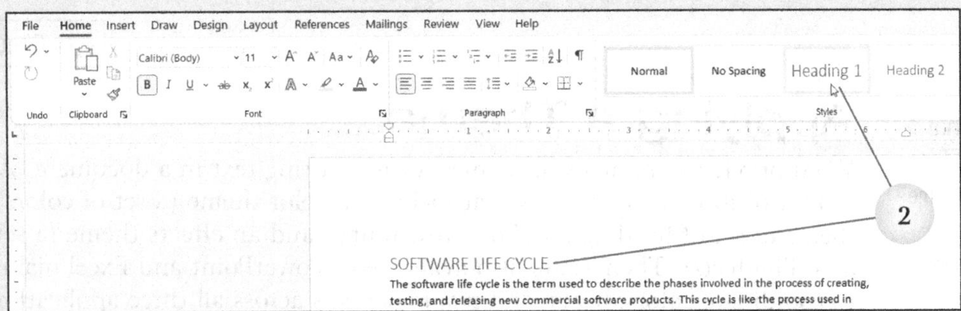

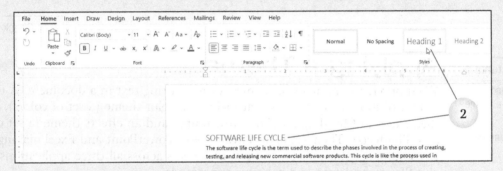

3. Position the insertion point anywhere in the heading *Proposal and Planning* and then click the *Heading 2* style in the styles gallery.

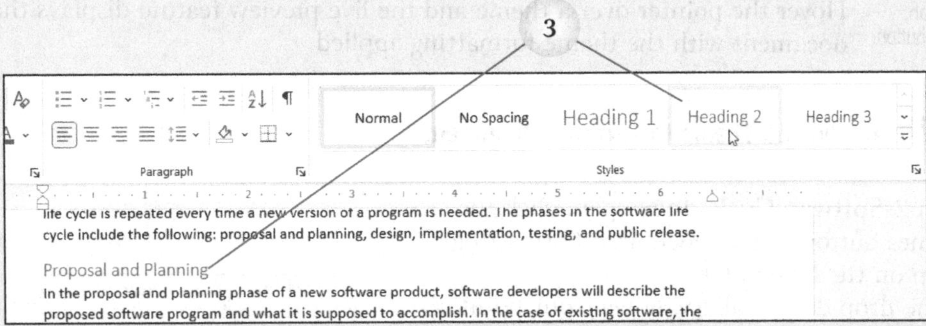

4. Position the insertion point anywhere in the heading *Design* and then click the *Heading 2* style in the styles gallery.
5. Apply the Heading 2 style to the remaining headings (*Implementation*, *Testing*, and *Public Release and Support*).
6. Collapse and expand text below the heading with the Heading 1 style applied by completing the following steps:
   a. Hover the pointer over the heading *SOFTWARE LIFE CYCLE* until a collapse triangle displays at the left of the heading and then click the triangle. (This collapses all the text below the heading.)
   b. Click the expand triangle at the left of the heading *SOFTWARE LIFE CYCLE*. (This redisplays the text in the document.)

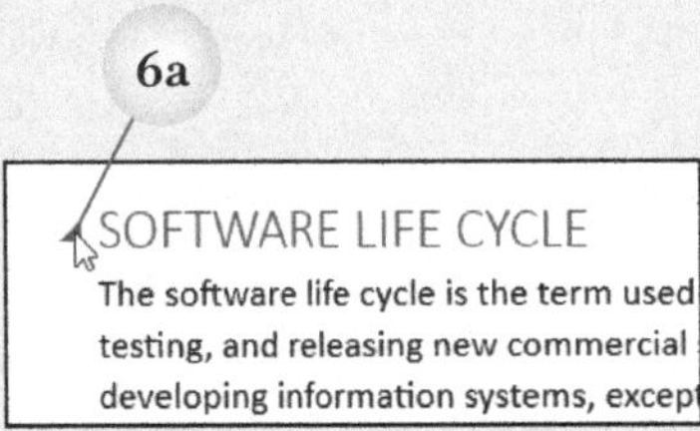

7. Click the Design tab.
8. Click the *Casual* style set in the style sets gallery in the Document Formatting group (the ninth option in the style set; this location may vary). (Notice how the Heading 1 and Heading 2 formatting changes.)

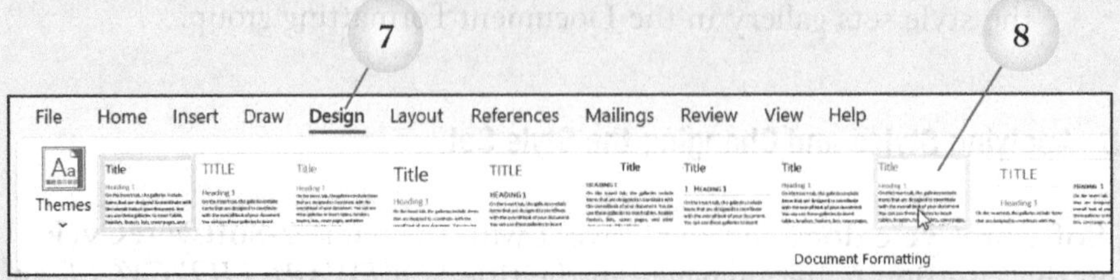

9. Save and then preview **2-SoftwareCycle.docx**.

Applying and Modifying a Theme

Applying a Theme

Word provides a number of themes for formatting text in a document. A theme is a set of formatting choices that includes a color theme (a set of colors), a font theme (a set of heading and body text fonts), and an effects theme (a set of line and fill effects). Themes are also available in PowerPoint and Excel making it easy to coordinate colors, fonts, and graphic effects across all three applications and give files a consistent and cohesive appearance.

Quick Steps

Apply Theme

1. Click Design tab.
2. Click Themes button.
3. Click theme.

To apply a theme, click the Design tab, click the Themes button in the Document Formatting group, and then click the theme at the drop-down gallery. Hover the pointer over a theme and the live preview feature displays the document with the theme formatting applied.

Activity 2b Applying a Theme to Text in a Document — Part 2 of 3

1. With **2-SoftwareCycle.docx** open, click the Themes button in the Document Formatting group on the Design tab.
2. At the drop-down gallery, hover your pointer over several different themes and notice how the text formatting changes in your document.
3. Click the *Organic* theme.
4. Save and then preview **2-SoftwareCycle.docx**.

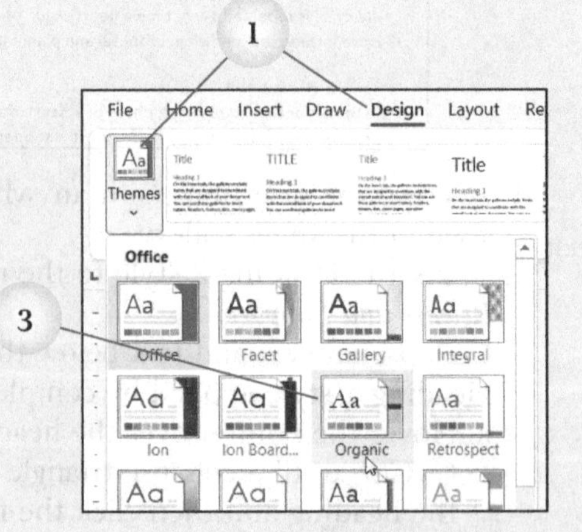

Check Your Work

Modifying a Theme

Quick Steps

Change Theme Color
1. Click Design tab.
2. Click Colors button.
3. Click theme color option.

Change Theme Fonts
1. Click Design tab.
2. Click Fonts button.
3. Click theme font option.

Change Paragraph Spacing
1. Click Design tab.
2. Click Paragraph Spacing button.
3. Click paragraph spacing option.

Theme Colors

Theme Fonts

Theme Effects

Paragraph Spacing

The color and font of a style or theme can be modified using buttons in the Document Formatting group on the Design tab. Click the Colors button and a drop-down gallery displays with various color schemes. Click the Fonts button in this group and a drop-down gallery displays with font choices. Each font group in the drop-down gallery contains two choices. The first choice is the font that is applied to headings, and the second choice is applied to body text in the document. If a document contains graphics with lines and fills, a specific theme effect can be applied with options at the Effects button drop-down gallery.

The buttons in the Document Formatting group provide a visual representation of the current theme. If the theme colors are changed, the small color squares in the Themes button and the larger squares in the Colors button reflect the change. Change the theme fonts and the *A*s on the Themes button and the uppercase *A* on the Fonts button reflect the change. If the theme effects are changed, the circle in the Effects button reflects the change.

The Paragraph Spacing button in the Document Formatting group on the Design tab contains predesigned paragraph spacing options. To change paragraph spacing, click the Paragraph Spacing button and then click an option at the drop-down gallery. Hover the pointer over an option at the drop-down gallery and after a moment a ScreenTip displays with information about the formatting applied by the option. For example, hover the pointer over the *Compact* option at the side menu and a ScreenTip displays indicating that selecting the *Compact* option will change the spacing before paragraphs to 0 points, the spacing after paragraphs to 4 points, and the line spacing to single line spacing.

Activity 2c Modifying a Theme

Part 3 of 3

1. With **2-SoftwareCycle.docx** open, click the Colors button in the Document Formatting group on the Design tab and then click the *Red Orange* option at the drop-down gallery. (Notice how the colors in the title and headings change.)
2. Click the Fonts button and then click the *Corbel* option. (Notice how the document text font changes.)

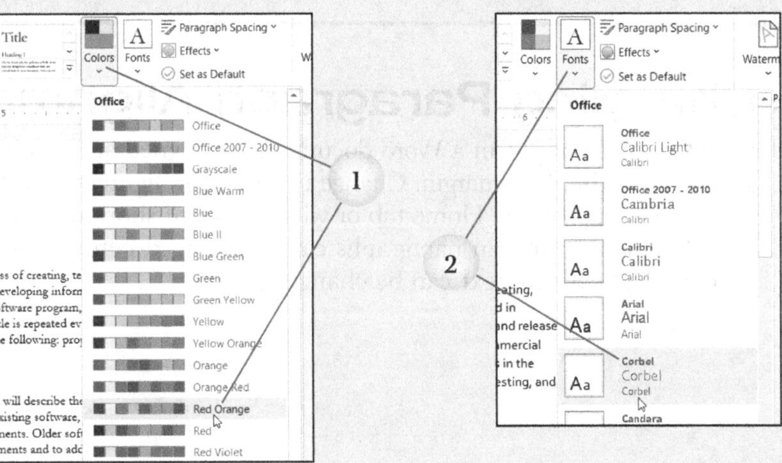

3. Click the Paragraph Spacing button and then, one at a time, hover the pointer over each paragraph spacing option, beginning with *Compact*. For each option, read the ScreenTip that explains the paragraph spacing applied by the option.
4. Click the *Double* option.

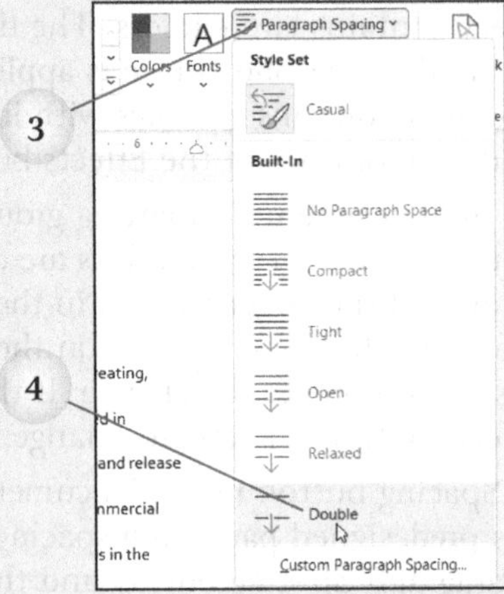

5. Scroll through the document and notice the paragraph spacing.
6. Change the paragraph spacing by clicking the Paragraph Spacing button and then clicking the *Compact* option.
7. Save, preview, and then close **2-SoftwareCycle.docx**.

Activity 3 Apply Paragraph Formatting and Use Format Painter 5 Parts

You will open a report on intellectual property and fair use issues and then format the report by changing the alignment and indent of text in paragraphs, changing spacing before and after paragraphs of text, and repeating the last formatting command. You will also format headings using Format Painter and change the line spacing of text.

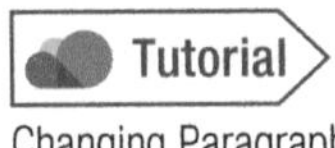

Changing Paragraph Alignment

Changing Paragraph Alignment

By default, paragraphs in a Word document are aligned at the left margin and are ragged at the right margin. Change this default alignment with buttons in the Paragraph group on the Home tab or with keyboard shortcuts, as shown in Table 2.3. The alignment of text in paragraphs can be changed before text is typed, or the alignment of existing text can be changed.

Table 2.3 Paragraph Alignment Buttons and Keyboard Shortcuts

To align text	Paragraph Group Button	Keyboard Shortcut
At the left margin		Ctrl + L
Between margins		Ctrl + E
At the right margin		Ctrl + R
At the left and right margins		Ctrl + J

Changing Paragraph Alignment as Text Is Typed

Center

Align Right

Align Left

If the alignment is changed before text is typed, the alignment formatting is inserted in the paragraph mark. Type text and press the Enter key and the paragraph formatting is continued. For example, click the Center button in the Paragraph group on the Home tab, type text for the first paragraph, and then press the Enter key; the center alignment formatting is still active and the insertion point is centered between the left and right margins. To display the paragraph symbols in a document, click the Show/Hide ¶ button in the Paragraph group. With the Show/Hide ¶ button active (displays with a gray background), nonprinting formatting symbols display.

Changing Paragraph Alignment of Existing Text

Hint Align text to help the reader follow the message of a document and to make the layout look appealing.

To change the alignment of existing text in a paragraph, position the insertion point anywhere within the paragraph. The entire paragraph does not need to be selected. To change the alignment of several adjacent paragraphs in a document, select a portion of the first paragraph through a portion of the last paragraph. All the text in the paragraphs does not need to be selected.

To return paragraph alignment to the default (left-aligned), click the Align Left button in the Paragraph group. All paragraph formatting can also be returned to the default with the keyboard shortcut Ctrl + Q. This keyboard shortcut removes paragraph formatting from selected text. To remove all formatting from selected text, including character and paragraph formatting, click the Clear All Formatting button in the Font group.

Changing Alignment at the Paragraph Dialog Box

Quick Steps

Change Paragraph Alignment

Click alignment button in Paragraph group on Home tab.

OR

1. Click Paragraph group dialog box launcher.
2. Click *Alignment* option box arrow.
3. Click alignment option.
4. Click OK.

Along with buttons in the Paragraph group on the Home tab and keyboard shortcuts, options in the *Alignment* option box at the Paragraph dialog box, shown in Figure 2.6, can be used to change paragraph alignment. Display this dialog box by clicking the Paragraph group dialog box launcher. At the Paragraph dialog box, click the *Alignment* option box arrow. At the drop-down list, click the alignment option and then click OK to close the dialog box.

Figure 2.6 Paragraph Dialog Box with the Indents and Spacing Tab Selected

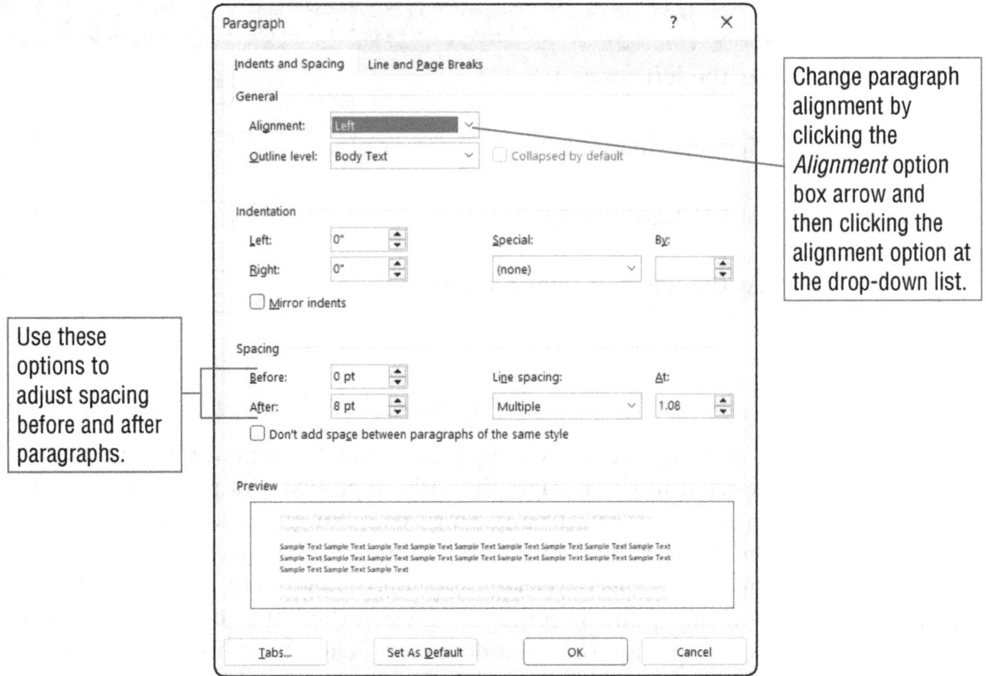

Activity 3a Changing Paragraph Alignment

Part 1 of 5

1. Open **IntelProp.docx** and then save it with the name **2-IntelProp**.
2. Press Ctrl + A to select the entire document and then change the paragraph alignment to justified by clicking the Justify button in the Paragraph group.
3. With the text still selected use the Paragraph dialog box to change paragraph alignment by completing the following steps:
   a. Click the Paragraph group dialog box launcher.

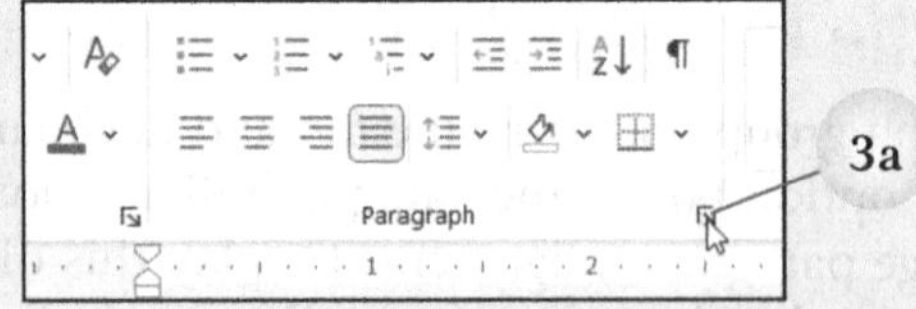

   b. At the Paragraph dialog box with the Indents and Spacing tab selected, click the *Alignment* option box arrow and then click the *Left* option at the drop-down list.
   c. Click OK to close the dialog box.
   d. Deselect the text.

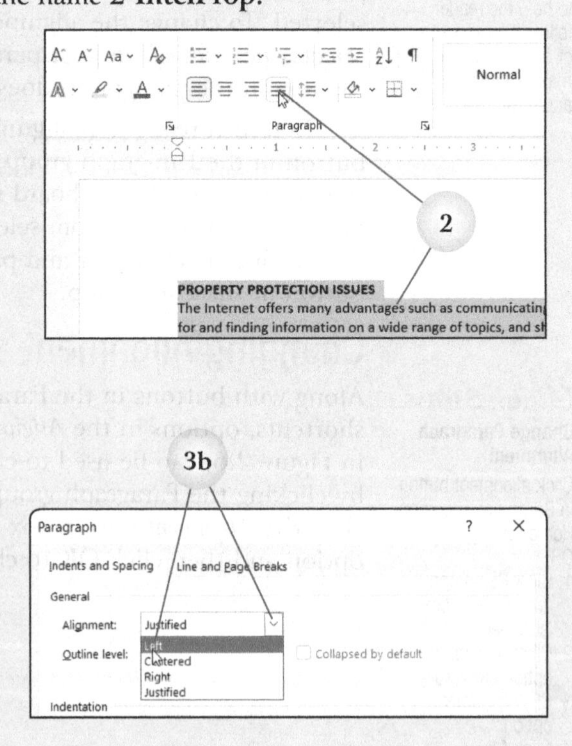

4. Change paragraph alignment by completing the following steps:
   a. Press Ctrl + End to move the insertion point to the end of the document and then position the insertion point anywhere in the text *Prepared by Clarissa Markham*.
   b. Click the Paragraph group dialog box launcher.
   c. At the Paragraph dialog box with the Indents and Spacing tab selected, click the *Alignment* option box arrow and then click the *Right* option at the drop-down list.
   d. Click OK to close the dialog box. (The line of text containing the name *Clarissa Markham* and the line of text containing the name *Joshua Streeter* are both aligned at the right because the New Line command, Shift + Enter, was used to separate the lines of text without creating a new paragraph.)
5. Save **2-IntelProp.docx**.

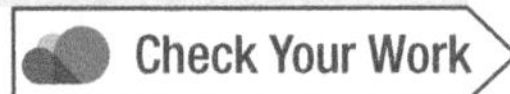

Indenting Text

Quick Steps

Indent Text

Drag indent marker(s) on horizontal ruler.
OR
Press keyboard shortcut keys.
OR
1. Click Paragraph group dialog box launcher.
2. Insert measurement in *Left*, *Right*, and/or *By* measurement box.
3. Click OK.

Indenting Text in Paragraphs

The first line of a paragraph is commonly indented to show paragraph breaks in a document. Paragraphs may also be indented from the left and right margins to set them off from the rest of the text. For instance, a long quotation or a bulleted or numbered list may be indented in this manner.

To indent text from the left margin, the right margin, or both margins, use the indent buttons in the Paragraph group on the Layout tab, keyboard shortcuts, options from the Paragraph dialog box, markers on the horizontal ruler, or the Alignment button above the vertical ruler. Figure 2.7 identifies indent markers on the horizontal ruler as well as the Alignment button. Refer to Table 2.4 for methods for indenting text in a document. If the horizontal ruler is not visible, display the ruler by clicking the View tab and then clicking the *Ruler* check box in the Show group to insert a check mark.

Figure 2.7 Horizontal Ruler and Indent Markers

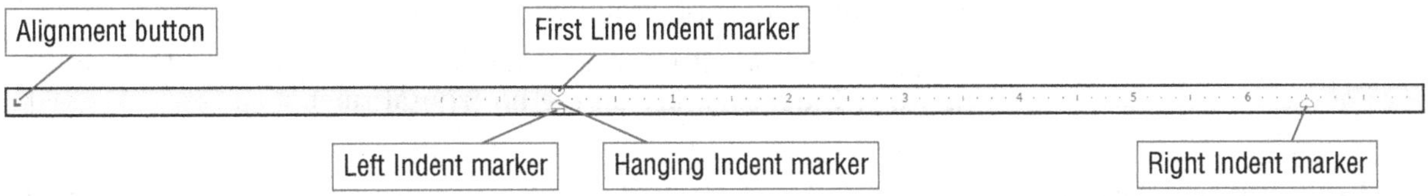

Table 2.4 Methods for Indenting Text

Indent	Methods for Indenting
First line of paragraph	• Press the Tab key. • Display the Paragraph dialog box, click the *Special* option box arrow, click *First line*, and then click OK. • Drag the First Line Indent marker on the horizontal ruler. • Click the Alignment button above the vertical ruler until the First Line Indent symbol displays and then click the horizontal ruler at the desired location.

Continues

Table 2.4 Methods for Indenting Text—*Continued*

Indent	Methods for Indenting
Text from left margin	• Click the Increase Indent button in the Paragraph group on the Home tab to increase the indent or click the Decrease Indent button to decrease the indent. • Insert a measurement in the *Indent Left* measurement box in the Paragraph group on the Layout tab. • Press Ctrl + M to increase the indent or press Ctrl + Shift + M to decrease the indent. • Display the Paragraph dialog box, type the indent measurement in the *Left* measurement box, and then click OK. • Drag the Left Indent marker on the horizontal ruler.
Text from right margin	• Insert a measurement in the *Indent Right* measurement box in the Paragraph group on the Layout tab. • Display the Paragraph dialog box, type the indent measurement in the *Right* measurement box, and then click OK. • Drag the Right Indent marker on the horizontal ruler.
All lines of text except first (called a *hanging indent*)	• Press Ctrl + T. (Press Ctrl + Shift + T to remove a hanging indent.) • Display the Paragraph dialog box, click the *Special* option box arrow, click *Hanging*, and then click OK. • Click the Alignment button, left of the horizontal ruler and above the vertical ruler, until the Hanging Indent symbol displays and then click the horizontal ruler at the desired location. • Drag the Hanging Indent marker on the horizontal ruler.
Text from both left and right margins	• Display the Paragraph dialog box, type the indent measurement in the *Left* measurement box, type the indent measurement in the *Right* measurement box, and then click OK. • Insert measurements in the *Indent Right* and *Indent Left* measurement boxes in the Paragraph group on the Layout tab. • Drag the Left Indent marker on the horizontal ruler and then drag the Right Indent marker on the horizontal ruler.

Activity 3b Indenting Text

Part 2 of 5

1. With **2-IntelProp.docx** open, indent the first line of text in each paragraph by completing the following steps:
   a. Select the text in the document after the title *PROPERTY PROTECTION ISSUES* and before the heading *Intellectual Property*.
   b. Make sure the horizontal ruler is visible. (If it is not, click the View tab and then click the *Ruler* check box in the Show group to insert a check mark.)
   c. Position the pointer on the First Line Indent marker on the horizontal ruler, click and hold down the left mouse button, drag the marker to the 0.5-inch mark, and then release the mouse button.

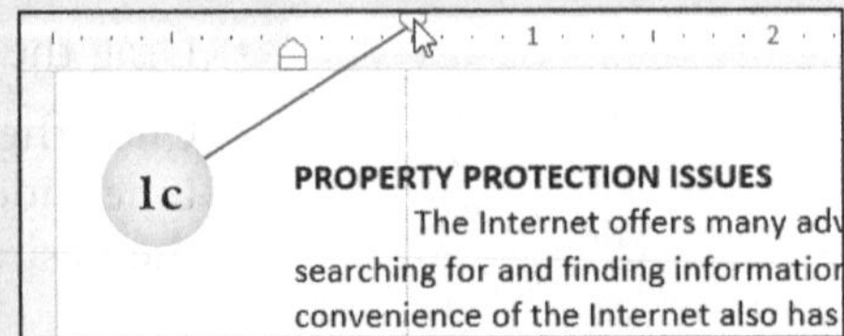

d. Select the text in the *Intellectual Property* section and then drag the First Line Indent marker on the horizontal ruler to the 0.5-inch mark.
e. Select the text in the *Fair Use* section, click the Alignment button above the vertical ruler until the First Line Indent symbol displays, and then click the horizontal ruler at the 0.5-inch mark.

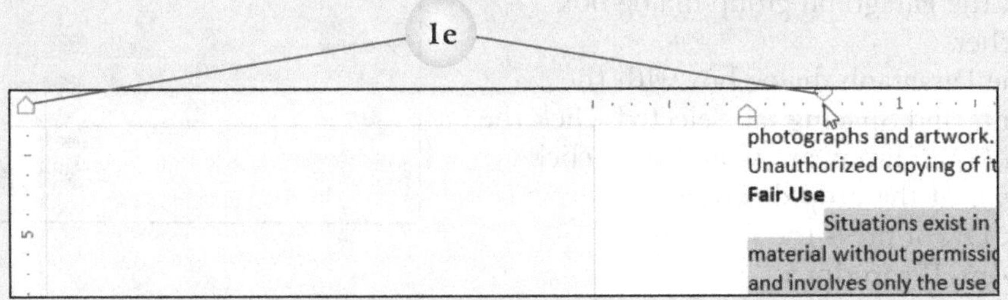

f. Position the insertion point anywhere in the paragraph of text below the heading *Intellectual Property Protection*, make sure the First Line Indent symbol displays on the Alignment button, and then click the 0.5-inch mark on the horizontal ruler.

2. Since the text in the second paragraph in the *Fair Use* section is a quote, indent the text from the left and right margins by completing the following steps:
   a. Position the insertion point anywhere in the second paragraph in the *Fair Use* section (the paragraph that begins *[A] copyrighted work, including such*).
   b. Click the Paragraph group dialog box launcher.
   c. At the Paragraph dialog box with the Indents and Spacing tab selected, select the current measurement in the *Left* measurement box and then type 0.5.
   d. Select the current measurement in the *Right* measurement box and then type 0.5.
   e. Click the *Special* option box arrow and then click *(none)* at the drop-down list.
   f. Click OK.

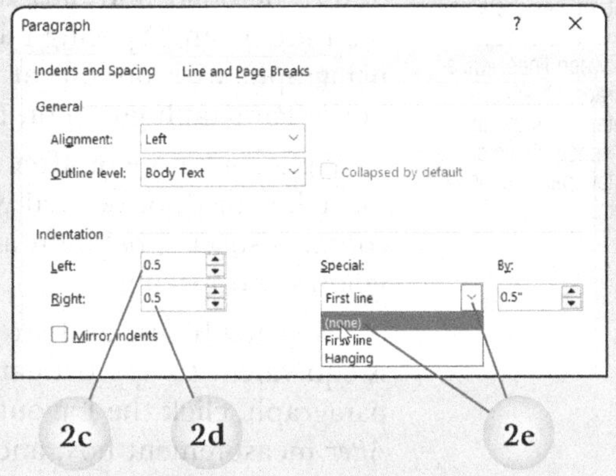

3. Create a hanging indent for the first paragraph in the *REFERENCES* section by positioning the insertion point anywhere in the first paragraph below the heading *REFERENCES* (on the third page) and then pressing Ctrl + T.
4. Create a hanging indent for the second paragraph in the *REFERENCES* section by completing the following steps:
   a. Position the insertion point anywhere in the second paragraph in the *REFERENCES* section.
   b. Click the Alignment button until the Hanging Indent symbol displays.
   c. Click the 0.5-inch mark on the horizontal ruler.

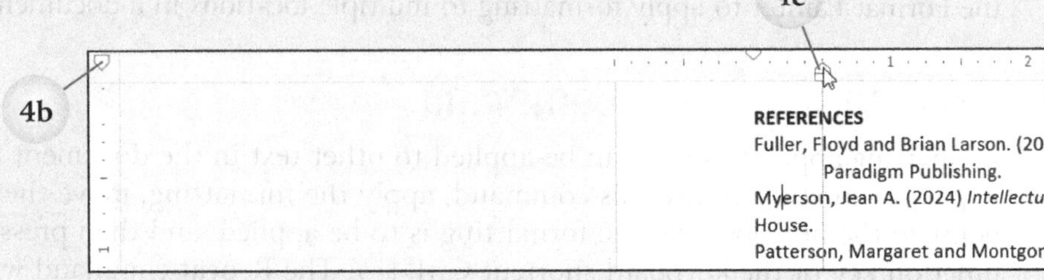

5. Create a hanging indent for the third and fourth paragraphs by completing the following steps:
   a. Select a portion of the third and fourth paragraphs.
   b. Click the Paragraph group dialog box launcher.
   c. At the Paragraph dialog box with the Indents and Spacing tab selected, click the *Special* option box arrow and then click *Hanging* at the drop-down list.
   d. Click OK or press the Enter key.
6. Save **2-IntelProp.docx**.

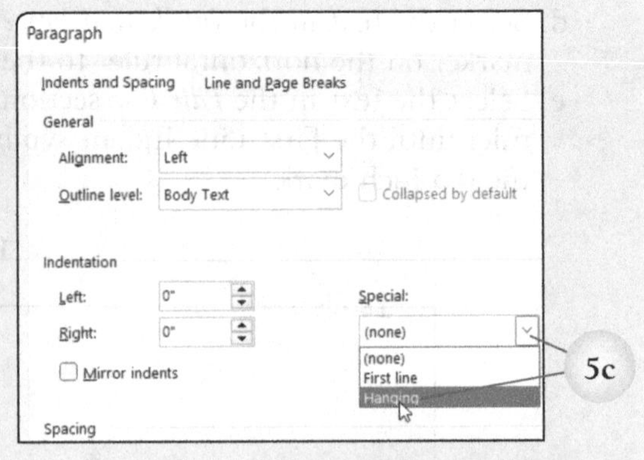

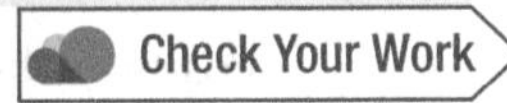

Spacing Before and After Paragraphs

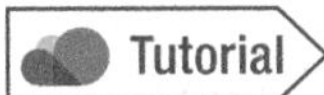

Changing Spacing Before and After Paragraphs

Hint Line spacing determines the amount of vertical space between lines, while paragraph spacing determines the amount of space above or below paragraphs of text.

By default, Word applies 8 points of additional spacing after a paragraph. This spacing can be removed or it can be increased or decreased, and spacing can be inserted above the paragraph. To change spacing before or after a paragraph, use the *Before* and *After* measurement boxes in the Paragraph group on the Layout tab, or use the *Before* and *After* measurement boxes at the Paragraph dialog box with the Indents and Spacing tab selected. Spacing can also be added before and after paragraphs with options at the Line and Paragraph Spacing button drop-down list in the Paragraph group on the Home tab.

Spacing before or after a paragraph is part of the paragraph and will be moved, copied, or deleted with the paragraph. If a paragraph, such as a heading, contains spacing before it and the paragraph falls at the top of a page, Word ignores the spacing.

Spacing before and after paragraphs is added in points. One vertical inch is equivalent to approximately 72 points. To add spacing before or after a paragraph, click the Layout tab, select the current measurement in the *Before* or *After* measurement box, and then type the number of points. The up or down arrows at the *Before* and *After* measurement boxes can also be clicked to increase or decrease the amount of spacing.

Automating Formatting

Applying consistent formatting in a document, especially a multiple-page document, can be time consuming. Word provides options for applying formatting automatically. Use the Repeat command to repeat the last action, such as applying formatting, or the Format Painter to apply formatting to multiple locations in a document.

Repeating the Last Command

Repeating the Last Command

Quick Steps

Repeat Last Action
Press F4.
OR
Press Ctrl + Y.

Formatting applied to text can be applied to other text in the document using the Repeat command. To use this command, apply the formatting, move the insertion point to the next location the formatting is to be applied, and then press the F4 function key or the keyboard shortcut Ctrl + Y. The Repeat command will repeat only the last command executed.

Activity 3c Changing Spacing Before and After Paragraphs and Repeating the Last Command

Part 3 of 5

1. With **2-IntelProp.docx** open, add 6 points of spacing before and after each paragraph in the document by completing the following steps:
   a. Select the entire document.
   b. Click the Layout tab.
   c. Click the *Before* measurement box up arrow in the Paragraph group. (This inserts *6 pt* in the box.)
   d. Click the *After* measurement box up arrow two times. (This inserts *6 pt* in the box.)
2. Add an additional 6 points of spacing above the headings by completing the following steps:
   a. Position the insertion point anywhere in the heading *Intellectual Property* and then click the *Before* measurement box up arrow. (This changes the measurement to *12 pt*.)

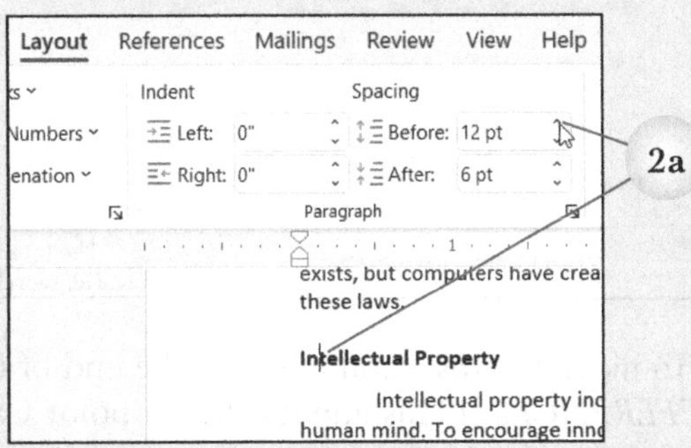

   b. Position the insertion point anywhere in the heading *Fair Use* and then press the F4 function key. (F4 is the Repeat command.)
   c. Position the insertion point anywhere in the heading *Intellectual Property Protection* and then press the F4 function key.
   d. Position the insertion point anywhere in the heading *REFERENCES* and then press Ctrl + Y. (Ctrl + Y is also the Repeat command.) (When a heading displays at the beginning of a page, the spacing above is ignored.)
3. Save **2-IntelProp.docx**.

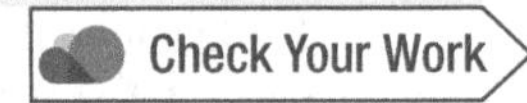

Formatting with Format Painter

Quick Steps

Format with Format Painter

1. Click in formatted text.
2. Click Format Painter button.
3. Select text.

Formatting with Format Painter

The Home tab contains a button for copying formatting, which displays in the Clipboard group with a paintbrush. To use this button, called Format Painter, position the insertion point anywhere in text containing the desired formatting, click the Format Painter button, and then select the text to which the formatting is to be applied. When the Format Painter button is clicked, the I-beam pointer displays with a paintbrush attached. To apply the formatting a single time, click the Format Painter button. To apply the formatting in more than one location in the document, double-click the Format Painter button and then select the text to which the formatting is to be applied. When finished, click the Format Painter button to turn it off. The Format Painter button can also be turned off by pressing the Esc key.

Activity 3d Formatting Headings with Format Painter

Part 4 of 5

1. With **2-IntelProp.docx** open, click the Home tab.
2. Select the entire document and then change the font to 12-point Cambria.
3. Select the title *PROPERTY PROTECTION ISSUES*, click the Center button in the Paragraph group, and then change the font to 16-point Candara.
4. Apply 16-point Candara and center-alignment formatting to the heading *REFERENCES* by completing the following steps:
   a. Click in the title *PROPERTY PROTECTION ISSUES*.
   b. Click the Format Painter button in the Clipboard group.

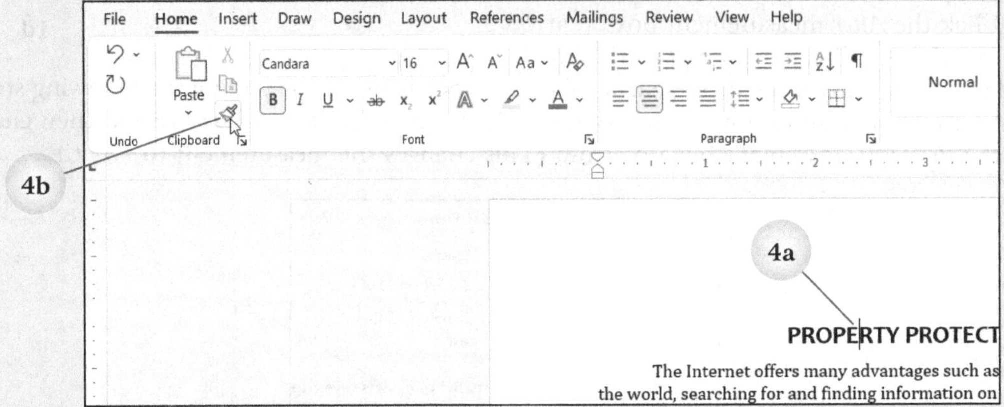

   c. Press Ctrl + End to move the insertion point to the end of the document and then click in the heading *REFERENCES*. (This applies the 16-point Candara formatting and centers the text.)
5. Select the heading *Intellectual Property* and then change the font to 14-point Candara.
6. Use the Format Painter button to apply 14-point Candara formatting to the other headings by completing the following steps:
   a. Position the insertion point anywhere in the heading *Intellectual Property*.
   b. Double-click the Format Painter button in the Clipboard group.
   c. Using the mouse, select the heading *Fair Use*.
   d. Using the mouse, select the heading *Intellectual Property Protection*.
   e. Click the Format Painter button in the Clipboard group. (This turns off the feature and deactivates the button.)
   f. Deselect the heading.
7. Save **2-IntelProp.docx**.

Changing Line Spacing

Changing Line Spacing

The default line spacing for a document is 1.08. (The line spacing for the IntelProp file, which you opened at the beginning of Activity 3, had been changed to single line spacing.) In certain situations, Word automatically adjusts the line spacing. For example, if a large character or object, such as a graphic, is inserted into a line, Word increases the line spacing of that line. The line spacing for a paragraph, section, or an entire document can be changed.

Quick Steps

Change Line Spacing

1. Click Line and Paragraph Spacing button.
2. Click option.

OR

Press keyboard shortcut command.

OR

1. Click Paragraph group dialog box launcher.
2. Click *Line spacing* option box arrow.
3. Click line spacing option.
4. Click OK.

OR

1. Click Paragraph group dialog box launcher.
2. Type line measurement in *At* measurement box.
3. Click OK.

Change line spacing using the Line and Paragraph Spacing button in the Paragraph group on the Home tab, keyboard shortcuts, or options in the Paragraph dialog box. Table 2.5 shows the keyboard shortcuts to change line spacing.

Line spacing can also be changed at the Paragraph dialog box with the *Line spacing* option or the *At* measurement box. Click the *Line spacing* option box arrow and a drop-down list displays with a variety of spacing options, such as *Single*, *1.5 lines*, and *Double*. A specific line spacing measurement can be entered in the *At* measurement box. For example, to change the line spacing to 1.75 lines, type *1.75* in the *At* measurement box.

Table 2.5 Line Spacing Keyboard Shortcuts

Press	To change line spacing to
Ctrl + 1	single line spacing (1.0)
Ctrl + 2	double line spacing (2.0)
Ctrl + 5	1.5 line spacing

Activity 3e Changing Line Spacing

Part 5 of 5

1. With **2-IntelProp.docx** open, change the line spacing for all paragraphs to double spacing by completing the following steps:
   a. Select the entire document.
   b. Click the Line and Paragraph Spacing button in the Paragraph group on the Home tab.
   c. Click *2.0* at the drop-down list.
2. With the entire document still selected, press Ctrl + 5. (This changes the line spacing to 1.5 lines.)
3. Change the line spacing to 1.2 lines at the Paragraph dialog box by completing the following steps:
   a. With the entire document still selected, click the Paragraph group dialog box launcher.
   b. At the Paragraph dialog box, make sure the Indents and Spacing tab is selected, click in the *At* measurement box, and then type 1.2. (This measurement box is to the right of the *Line spacing* option box.)
   c. Click OK or press the Enter key.
   d. Deselect the text.
4. Save, preview, and then close **2-IntelProp.docx**.

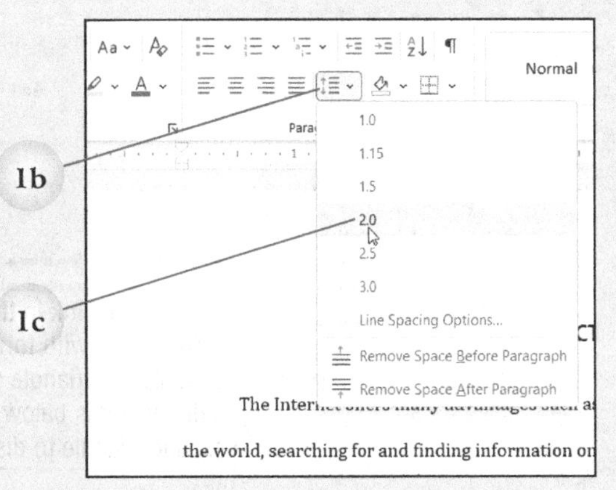

Check Your Work

Activity 4 Reveal and Compare Formatting in a Document — 2 Parts

You will open a document containing two computer-related problems to solve, reveal the formatting, compare the formatting, and make formatting changes.

Revealing and Comparing Formatting

Display formatting applied to specific text in a document at the Reveal Formatting task pane, shown in Figure 2.8. The Reveal Formatting task pane displays font, paragraph, and section formatting applied to text where the insertion point is positioned or to selected text. Display the Reveal Formatting task pane with the keyboard shortcut Shift + F1. Generally, a collapse triangle (a solid right-and-down-pointing triangle) precedes *Font* and *Paragraph* and an expand triangle (a hollow right-pointing triangle) precedes *Section* in the *Formatting of selected text* list box in the Reveal Formatting task pane. Click the collapse triangle to hide any items below a heading and click the expand triangle to reveal items. Some of the items below headings in the *Formatting of selected text* list box are hyperlinks. Click a hyperlink and a dialog box displays with the specific option.

Figure 2.8 Reveal Formatting Task Pane

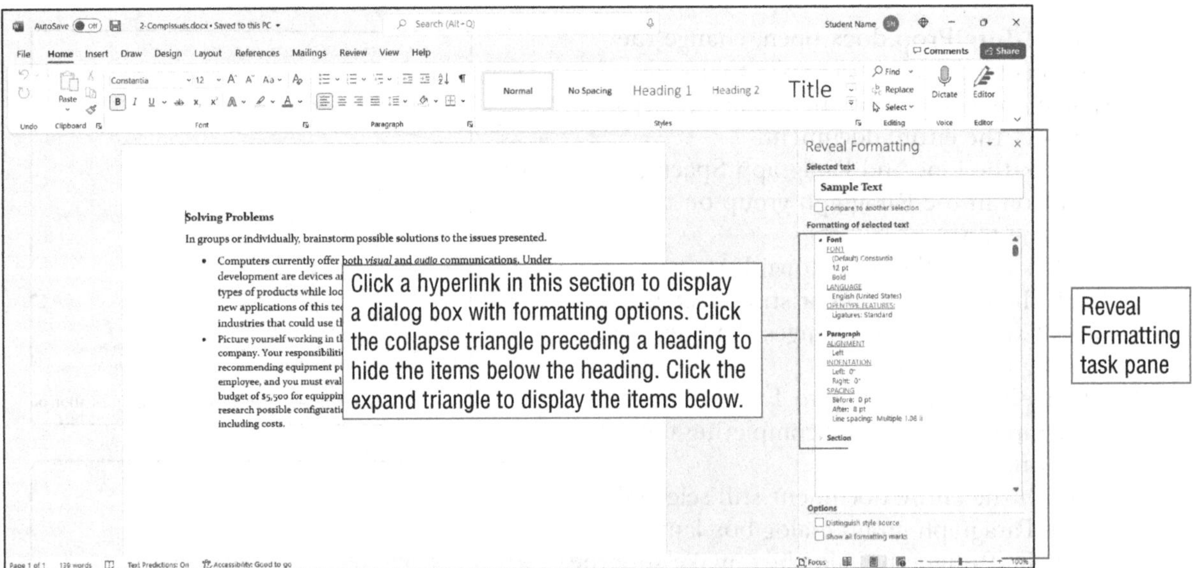
Click a hyperlink in this section to display a dialog box with formatting options. Click the collapse triangle preceding a heading to hide the items below the heading. Click the expand triangle to display the items below.
Reveal Formatting task pane
Reveal Formatting
Sample Text
Solving Problems
In groups or individually, brainstorm possible solutions to the issues presented.

Activity 4a Revealing Formatting — Part 1 of 2

1. Open **CompIssues.docx** and then save it with the name **2-CompIssues.**
2. Press Shift + F1 to display the Reveal Formatting task pane.
3. Click in the heading *Solving Problems* and then notice the formatting information in the Reveal Formatting task pane.
4. Click in the bulleted paragraph and then notice the formatting information in the Reveal Formatting task pane.
5. Leave **2-CompIssues.docx** open for the next activity.

Quick Steps

Compare Formatting

1. Press Shift + F1 to display Reveal Formatting task pane.
2. Click or select text.
3. Click *Compare to another selection* check box.
4. Click or select text.

Along with displaying formatting applied to text, the Reveal Formatting task pane can be used to compare formatting in two text selections to determine what is different. To compare formatting, select the first instance of formatting to be compared, click the *Compare to another selection* check box, and then select the second instance of formatting to be compared. Any differences between the two selections display in the *Formatting differences* list box.

Activity 4b Comparing Formatting

Part 2 of 2

1. With **2-CompIssues.docx** open, make sure the Reveal Formatting task pane is visible. If it is not, turn it on by pressing Shift + F1.
2. Select the first bulleted paragraph (the paragraph that begins *Computers currently offer both*).
3. Click the *Compare to another selection* check box to insert a check mark.
4. Select the second bulleted paragraph (the paragraph that begins *Picture yourself working in the*).
5. Determine the formatting differences by reading the information in the *Formatting differences* list box. (The list box shows *12 pt -> 11 pt* below the FONT hyperlink, indicating that the difference is point size.)
6. Format the second bulleted paragraph so it is set in 12-point size.
7. Click the *Compare to another selection* check box to remove the check mark.
8. Select the word *visual*, which is used in the first sentence in the first bulleted paragraph.
9. Click the *Compare to another selection* check box to insert a check mark.
10. Select the word *audio*, which is used in the first sentence of the first bulleted paragraph.
11. Determine the formatting differences by reading the information in the *Formatting differences* list box.
12. Format the word *audio* so it matches the formatting of the word *visual*.
13. Click the *Compare to another selection* check box to remove the check mark.
14. Close the Reveal Formatting task pane by clicking the Close button in the upper right corner of the task pane.
15. Save, preview, and then close **2-CompIssues.docx**.

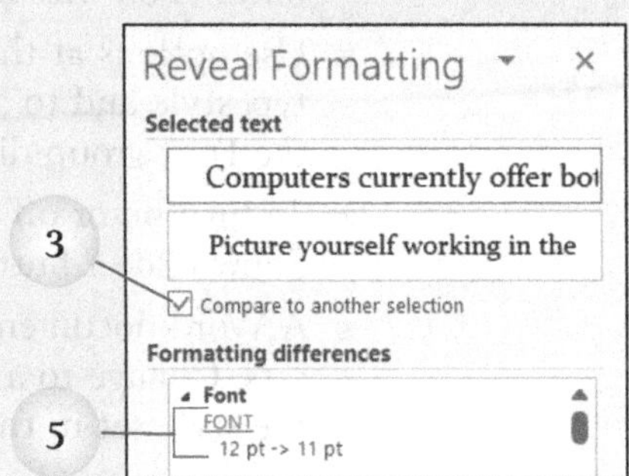

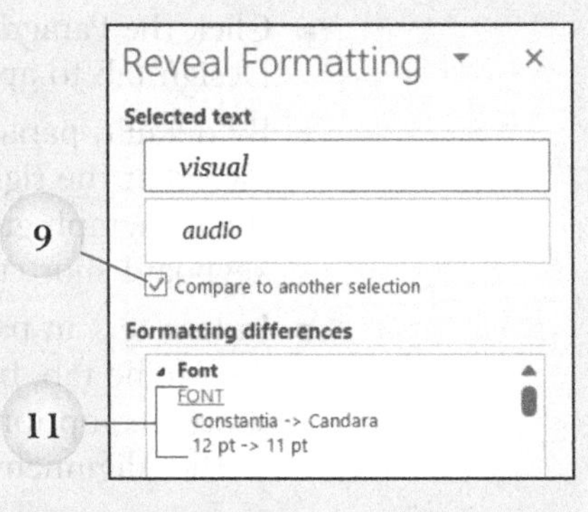

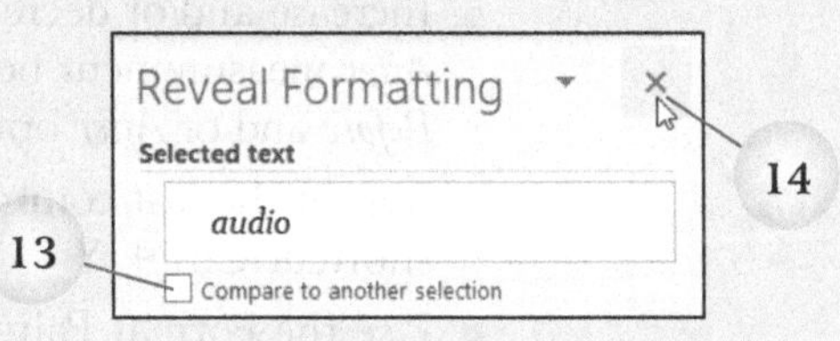

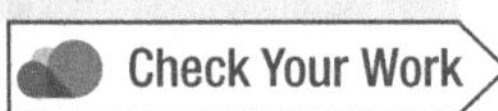

Chapter Summary

- A font consists of three elements: typeface, type size, and typestyle.
- A typeface (font) is a set of characters with a common design and shape. Typefaces are monospaced, allotting the same amount of horizontal space for each character, or proportional, allotting varying amounts of space for different characters. Typefaces are divided into two main categories: serif and sans serif.
- Type size is measured in points; the higher the point size, the larger the characters.
- A typestyle is a variation of style within a certain typeface, such as bold, italic, or underline. Apply typestyles with buttons in the Font group on the Home tab.
- Apply font effects, such as superscript, subscript, and strikethrough formatting, with buttons in the second row in the Font group on the Home tab.
- The Mini toolbar automatically displays above selected text. Use options and buttons on this toolbar to apply formatting to the selected text.
- Use options at the Font dialog box to change the typeface, type size, and typestyle and to apply specific font effects. Display this dialog box by clicking the Font group dialog box launcher in the Font group on the Home tab.
- To turn on or off the display of nonprinting characters and hidden text, click the Show/Hide ¶ button in the Paragraph group on the Home tab.
- A Word document contains a number of predesigned formats grouped into style sets. Change to a different style set by clicking the Design tab and then clicking the style set in the style set gallery in the Document Formatting group.
- Apply a theme and change theme colors, fonts, and effects with buttons in the Document Formatting group on the Design tab.
- Click the Paragraph Spacing button in the Document Formatting group on the Design tab to apply a predesigned paragraph spacing option to text.
- By default, paragraphs in a Word document are aligned at the left margin and ragged at the right margin. Change this default alignment with buttons in the Paragraph group on the Home tab, at the Paragraph dialog box, or with keyboard shortcuts.
- Indent text in paragraphs with indent buttons in the Paragraph group on the Home tab, buttons in the Paragraph group on the Layout tab, keyboard shortcuts, options at the Paragraph dialog box, markers on the horizontal ruler, or the Alignment button above the vertical ruler.
- Increase and/or decrease spacing before and after paragraphs using the *Before* and *After* measurement boxes in the Paragraph group on the Layout tab or using the *Before* and/or *After* options at the Paragraph dialog box.
- Repeat the last command by pressing the F4 function key or the keyboard shortcut Ctrl + Y.
- Use the Format Painter button in the Clipboard group on the Home tab to copy formatting already applied to text to different locations in the document.
- Change line spacing with the Line and Paragraph Spacing button in the Paragraph group on the Home tab, keyboard shortcuts, or options at the Paragraph dialog box.
- Display the Reveal Formatting task pane with the keyboard shortcut Shift + F1. Use the *Compare to another selection* option in the task pane to compare formatting of two text selections to determine what is different.

Commands Review

FEATURE	RIBBON TAB, GROUP	BUTTON	KEYBOARD SHORTCUT
bold text	Home, Font		Ctrl + B
center-align text	Home, Paragraph		Ctrl + E
change case of text	Home, Font		Shift + F3
clear all formatting	Home, Font		
clear character formatting			Ctrl + spacebar
clear paragraph formatting			Ctrl + Q
decrease font size	Home, Font		Ctrl + Shift + < OR Ctrl + [
decrease indent	Home, Paragraph		
display or hide nonprinting characters	Home, Paragraph		Ctrl + Shift + *
font	Home, Font		
font color	Home, Font		
Font dialog box	Home, Font		Ctrl + D
font size	Home, Font		
Format Painter	Home, Clipboard		
highlight text	Home, Font		
increase font size	Home, Font		Ctrl + Shift + > OR Ctrl +]
increase indent	Home, Paragraph		
italicize text	Home, Font		Ctrl + I
justify text	Home, Paragraph		Ctrl + J
left-align text	Home, Paragraph		Ctrl + L
line spacing	Home, Paragraph		Ctrl + 1 (single) Ctrl + 2 (double) Ctrl + 5 (1.5)

Continues

FEATURE	RIBBON TAB, GROUP	BUTTON	KEYBOARD SHORTCUT
Paragraph dialog box	Home, Paragraph		
paragraph spacing	Design, Document Formatting		
repeat last action			F4 or Ctrl + Y
Reveal Formatting task pane			Shift + F1
right-align text	Home, Paragraph		Ctrl + R
spacing after paragraph	Layout, Paragraph		
spacing before paragraph	Layout, Paragraph		
strikethrough text	Home, Font	ab	
subscript text	Home, Font	X_2	Ctrl + =
superscript text	Home, Font	X^2	Ctrl + Shift + +
text effects and typography	Home, Font	A	
theme colors	Design, Document Formatting		
theme effects	Design, Document Formatting		
theme fonts	Design, Document Formatting	A	
themes	Design, Document Formatting	Aa	
underline text	Home, Font	U	Ctrl + U

Review and Assessment

CHAPTER 2

Skills Assessment

Assessment 1 — Apply Character Formatting to a Lease Agreement Document

1. Open **LeaseAgrmnt.docx** and then save it with the name **2-LeaseAgrmnt**.
2. Press Ctrl + End to move the insertion point to the end of the document, press the Enter key, and then type the text shown in Figure 2.9. Bold, italicize, and underline text as shown.
3. Select the entire document and then change the font to Candara and the font size to 12 points.
4. Select and then bold *THIS LEASE AGREEMENT* in the first paragraph.
5. Select and then italicize *12 o'clock midnight* in the *Term* section.
6. Select the title *LEASE AGREEMENT* and then change the font to 16-point Corbel and the font color to standard dark blue. (The title should remain bold.)
7. Select the heading *Term*, change the font to 14-point Corbel, and then apply small caps formatting. (The heading should remain bold.)
8. Use Format Painter to change the formatting to small caps in 14-point Corbel bold for the remaining headings (*Rent*, *Damage Deposit*, *Use of Premises*, *Condition of Premises*, *Damage to Premises*, and *Inspection of Premises*).
9. Save, preview, and then close **2-LeaseAgrmnt.docx**.

Figure 2.9 Assessment 1

Inspection of Premises

Lessor shall have the right to exhibit the Premises and to display a *for rent* sign on the Premises at any time within forty-five days before the expiration of this Lease.

Assessment 2 Apply Styles, a Style Set, and a Modified Theme in a Document on New Zealand

1. Open **NewZealand.docx** and then save it with the name **2-NewZealand**.
2. Apply the Heading 1 style to the title *NEW ZEALAND*.
3. Apply the Heading 2 style to the headings in the document (*Culture*, *Nature*, and *Sailing Nation*).
4. Apply the Lines (Stylish) style set.
5. Apply the Banded theme.
6. Apply the Orange theme colors.
7. Apply the Candara theme fonts.
8. Apply the Open paragraph spacing.
9. Highlight in yellow the text *New Zealand has it all!* at the end of the first paragraph of text below the title.
10. Save, preview, and then close **2-NewZealand.docx**.

Assessment 3 Apply Character and Paragraph Formatting to an Employee Privacy Document

1. Open **WorkPrivacy.docx** and then save it with the name **2-WorkPrivacy**.
2. Select the text from the beginning of the first paragraph to the end of the document (including the blank line following the last paragraph) and then make the following changes:
   a. Change the line spacing to 1.5 lines.
   b. Change the spacing after paragraphs to 0 points.
   c. Indent the first line of each paragraph 0.5 inch.
   d. Change the paragraph alignment to justified.
3. Move the insertion point to the end of the document, drag the First Line Indent marker on the horizontal ruler back to 0 inches, and then type the text shown in Figure 2.10. (Create a hanging indent as shown in the figure without using the Tab key.)
4. Select the entire document and then change the font to Constantia.
5. Select the title *WORKPLACE PRIVACY* and then apply the following formatting:
   a. Center the title.
   b. Change the font to 14-point Calibri.
   c. Click the Text Effects and Typography button and then click the option in the second column, first row (blue fill and shadow).
6. Use the Format Painter to apply the same formatting to the title *BIBLIOGRAPHY* that you applied to the title *WORKPLACE PRIVACY*.
7. Save, preview, and then close **2-WorkPrivacy.docx**.

Figure 2.10 Assessment 3

BIBLIOGRAPHY

Nye, H. G. (2024). *Privacy in the workplace*, 2nd edition (pp. 103-112). Denver, CO: Goodwin Publishing Group.

Visual Benchmark

Create a Report about Active Listening Skills

1. Open **ActiveListen.docx** and then save it with the name **2-ActiveListen**.
2. Apply the following formatting to the document so it appears as shown in Figure 2.11:
   a. Select the document and then change the font to 12-point Cambria and the font color to standard dark blue.
   b. Set the title in 16-point Candara bold and center the title.
   c. Set the headings in 14-point Candara bold.
   d. Change the paragraph spacing after the title and headings to 6 points.
   e. Underline the text as shown in the figure.
   f. Create a hanging indent for the paragraphs as shown in the figure. (Do not create the hanging paragraphs using the Tab key.)
3. Save, preview, and then close **2-ActiveListen.docx**.

Figure 2.11 Visual Benchmark

ACTIVE LISTENING SKILLS

Listening is a two-way activity. When the audience pays attention, the speaker gains confidence, knowing that their message is being received and appreciated. At the same time, alert listeners obtain information, hear an amusing or interesting story, and otherwise benefit from the speaker's presentation.

Become an Active Listener

Active listeners pay attention to the speaker and to what is being said. They are respectful of the speaker and eager to be informed or entertained. In contrast, *passive listeners* "tune out" the presentation and may even display rudeness by not paying attention to the speaker. Here are ways in which you can become an active listener:

Listen with a purpose: Stay focused on what the speaker is saying, and you will gain useful information or hear a suspenseful story narrated well. Try to avoid letting your attention wander.

Be courteous: Consider that the speaker spent time preparing for the presentation and thus deserves your respect.

Take brief notes: If the speaker is providing information, take brief notes on the main ideas. Doing so will help you understand and remember what is being said. If you have questions or would like to hear more about a particular point, ask the speaker for clarification after the presentation.

Practice Active Listening Skills in Conversation

Most people have had the experience of being in a one-way conversation, in which one person does all the talking and the others just listen. In fact, this is not a conversation, which is an exchange of information and ideas. In a true conversation, everyone has a chance to be heard. Do not monopolize conversation. Give the other person or persons an opportunity to talk. Pay attention when others are speaking and show your interest in what is being said by making eye contact and asking questions. Avoid interrupting, since this shows your disinterest and suggests that what you have to say is more important.

Case Study

Part 1

You work for the local chamber of commerce and are responsible for assisting the office manager, Teresa Alexander. Ms. Alexander would like to maintain consistency in articles submitted for publication in the monthly chamber newsletter. She wants you to explore various decorative and plain fonts. She would like you to choose two handwriting fonts, two decorative fonts, and two plain fonts and then prepare a document containing an example of each font. Save the document with the name **2-Fonts**. Preview and then close the document.

Part 2

Ms. Alexander has asked you to write a short article for the chamber newsletter. In the article, you are to describe an upcoming event at your school or in your community. Effectively use at least two of the fonts you selected in Case Study Part 1. Save the document with the name **2-Article**. Preview and then close the document.

Part 3

Ms. Alexander will be posting the newsletter to the chamber's website and would like you to explain how to save a Word document as a web page. Display the Save As dialog box and then determine how to save a document as a filtered web page using the *Save as type* option box. Create a Word document with step-by-step instructions. Save the document with the name **2-WebPage**. Close the document. Open **2-Article.docx**, the document you created in Case Study Part 2, and then save the document as a filtered web page.

WORD

CHAPTER 3

Customizing Paragraphs

Performance Objectives

Upon successful completion of Chapter 3, you will be able to:

1 Apply numbered and bulleted formatting to text
2 Apply paragraph borders and shading
3 Sort paragraphs of text
4 Set, clear, and move tabs on the horizontal ruler and at the Tabs dialog box
5 Cut, copy, and paste text in a document
6 Use the Paste Options button to specify how text is pasted in a document
7 Use the Clipboard task pane to copy and paste text within and between documents

---

As you learned in Chapter 2, Word contains a variety of options for formatting text in paragraphs. In this chapter, you will learn how to apply numbered and bulleted formatting as well as borders and shading. You will also learn how to sort paragraphs of text in alphabetical, numerical, and date order and to set and modify tabs on the horizontal ruler and at the Tabs dialog box. Editing some documents might include selecting and then deleting, moving, or copying text. You can perform these types of editing tasks with buttons in the Clipboard group on the Home tab or with keyboard shortcuts.

Data Files

The data files for this chapter are in the WL1C3 folder that you downloaded at the beginning of this course.

Activity 1 Format a Document on Computer Technology 3 Parts

You will open a document containing information on computer technology, type numbered and bulleted text in the document, and apply numbered and bulleted formatting to paragraphs in the document.

Applying Numbering and Bullets

Numbering

Bullets

When typing a list of items, use numbers to indicate the sequence or importance of the items and use bullets when the order of the items is not important. Word provides buttons for automatically numbering or bulleting text. Use the Numbering button in the Paragraph group on the Home tab to insert numbers before specific paragraphs and use the Bullets button to insert bullets.

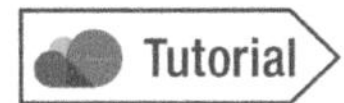

Creating Numbered Lists

Quick Steps

Type Numbered Paragraphs

1. Type 1.
2. Press spacebar.
3. Type text.
4. Press Enter key.

Hint Define a new numbering format by clicking the Numbering button arrow and then clicking *Define New Number Format*.

Creating Numbered Lists

To type a numbered list, type *1.* and then press the spacebar, and Word indents the number 0.25 inch from the left margin. Text typed after the number will be indented 0.5 inch. When the Enter key is pressed to end the first item, the next number, *2.*, is automatically inserted at the beginning of the next paragraph. Continue typing items and Word inserts the next number in the list. To insert a line break without inserting a number, press Shift + Enter.

To turn off numbering, press the Enter key two times or click the Numbering button in the Paragraph group on the Home tab. To turn numbering back on, simply type the next number in the list (and the period) followed by a space. Word will automatically indent the number and the text. (Numbered and bulleted formatting can be removed from a paragraph with the keyboard shortcut Ctrl + Q. Remove all formatting from selected text by clicking the Clear All Formatting button in the Font group on the Home tab.)

When the AutoFormat feature inserts numbering and indents text, the AutoCorrect Options button displays. Click this button and a drop-down list displays with options for undoing and/or stopping the automatic numbering.

Activity 1a Creating a Numbered List Part 1 of 3

1. Open **TechInfo.docx** and then save it with the name **3-TechInfo**.
2. Press Ctrl + End to move the insertion point to the end of the document and then type the text shown in Figure 3.1. Apply bold formatting and center the title *Technology Career Questions*. When typing the numbered paragraphs, complete the following steps:
   a. Type 1. and then press the spacebar. (The *1.* is indented 0.25 inch from the left margin and typed text is indented 0.5 inch from the left margin. Also, the AutoCorrect Options button displays. Use this button if you want to undo or stop automatic numbering.)
   b. Type the paragraph of text and then press the Enter key. (This moves the insertion point down to the next paragraph and inserts an indented number *2* followed by a period.)
   c. Continue typing the remaining text. (Remember, you do not need to type the paragraph number and period—they are automatically inserted. The last numbered item will wrap differently on your screen than shown in Figure 3.1.)
   d. After typing the last question, press the Enter key two times. (This turns off paragraph numbering.)
3. Save **3-TechInfo.docx**.

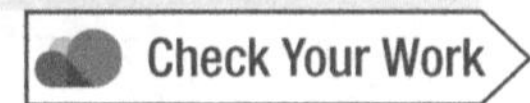

Check Your Work

Figure 3.1 Activity 1a

Technology Career Questions

1. What is your ideal technical job?
2. Which job suits your personality?
3. Which is your first-choice certificate?
4. How does the technical job market look in your state right now?

Automatic numbering is turned on by default. Turn off automatic numbering at the AutoCorrect dialog box with the AutoFormat As You Type tab selected, as shown in Figure 3.2. To display this dialog box, click the File tab and then click *Options*. At the Word Options dialog box, click the *Proofing* option in the left panel and then click the AutoCorrect Options button in the *AutoCorrect options* section of the dialog box. At the AutoCorrect dialog box, click the AutoFormat As You Type tab and then click the *Automatic numbered lists* check box to remove the check mark. Click OK to close the AutoCorrect dialog box and then click OK to close the Word Options dialog box.

Quick Steps

Create Numbered List

1. Select text.
2. Click Numbering button.

To create a numbered list, click the Numbering button in the Paragraph group on the Home tab. Type text and it will be formatted as a numbered list. Click the button again to turn off numbering, or select existing text and then click the Numbering button to apply numbered formatting.

Figure 3.2 AutoCorrect Dialog Box with the AutoFormat As You Type Tab Selected

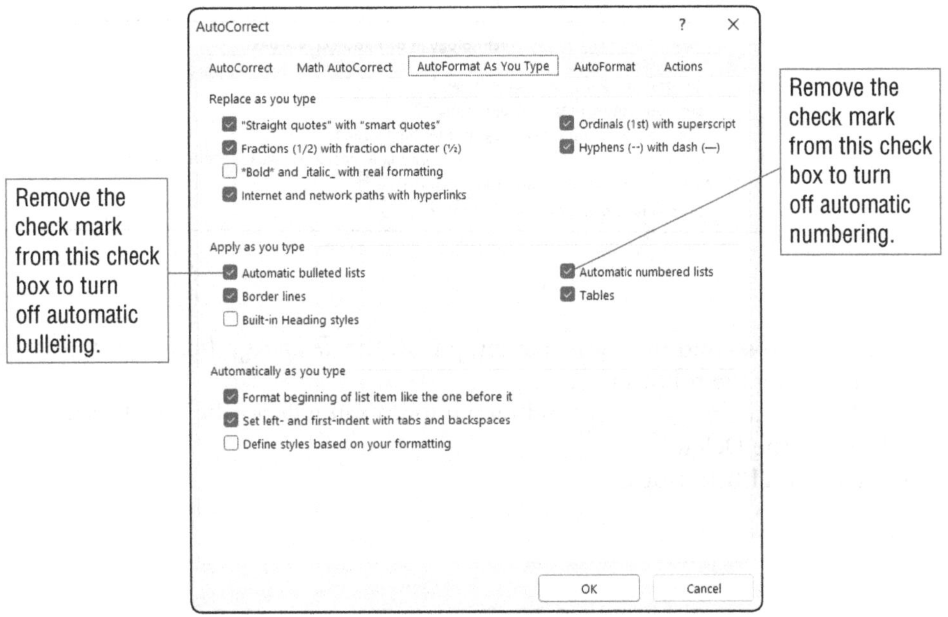

Activity 1b Applying Numbered Formatting

1. With **3-TechInfo.dox** open, apply numbers to paragraphs by completing the following steps:
   a. Select the five paragraphs of text in the *Technology Information Questions* section.
   b. Click the Numbering button in the Paragraph group on the Home tab.

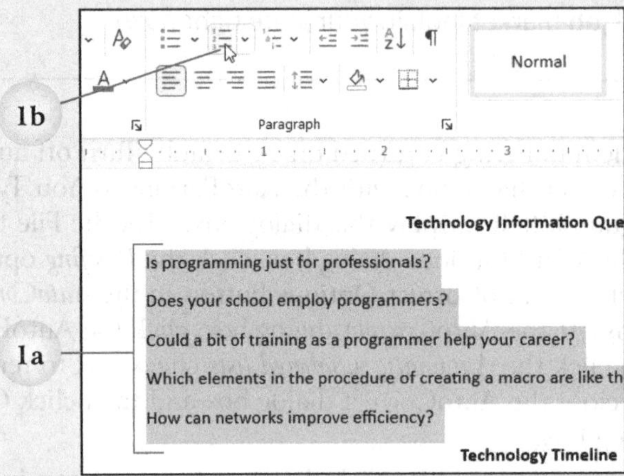

2. Add text between paragraphs 4 and 5 in the *Technology Information Questions* section by completing the following steps:
   a. Position the insertion point immediately right of the question mark at the end of the fourth paragraph.
   b. Press the Enter key.
   c. Type What kinds of networks are used in your area?

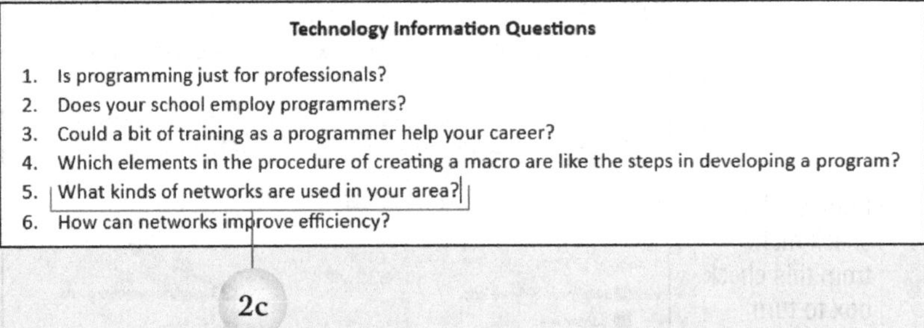

3. Delete the second question (paragraph) in the *Technology Information Questions* section by completing the following steps:
   a. Select the text of the second paragraph. (You will not be able to select the number.)
   b. Press the Delete key.
4. Save **3-TechInfo.docx**.

Creating Bulleted Lists

Quick Steps

Type Bulleted List

1. Type *, >, or - symbol.
2. Press spacebar.
3. Type text.
4. Press Enter key.

Create Bulleted List

1. Select text.
2. Click Bullets button.

Creating Bulleted Lists

In addition to automatically numbering paragraphs, Word's AutoFormat feature creates bulleted lists. A bulleted list with a hanging indent is automatically created when a paragraph begins with the symbol *, >, or -. Type one of the symbols and then press the spacebar and the AutoFormat feature inserts a bullet 0.25 inch from the left margin and indents the text following the bullet another 0.25 inch. Change the indent of bulleted text by pressing the Tab key to demote text or pressing Shift + Tab to promote text. Word uses different bullets for demoted text.

Bulleted formatting can be turned on or applied to existing text with the Bullets button in the Paragraph group on the Home tab. Click the Bullets button to turn on bulleting, type text, and then click the button again to turn off bulleting. Or select existing text and then click the Bullets button to apply bulleted formatting. When the AutoFormat feature inserts bullets and indents text, the AutoCorrect Options button displays. This button contains options for undoing and/or stopping the automatic bulleting. The automatic bulleting feature can be turned off at the AutoCorrect dialog box with the AutoFormat As You Type tab selected.

Activity 1c Creating a Bulleted List and Applying Bulleted Formatting

Part 3 of 3

1. With **3-TechInfo.docx** open, press Ctrl + End to move the insertion point to the end of the document.
2. Turn on bold formatting, change to center alignments, and then type Technology Visionaries as shown in Figure 3.3.
3. Press the Enter key, turn off bold formatting, and change to left alignment.
4. Type a greater-than symbol (>), press the spacebar, type the text of the first bulleted item in Figure 3.3, and then press the Enter key.
5. Press the Tab key (which demotes the bullet to a hollow circle) and then type the remaining bulleted text, pressing the Enter key after each entry. After typing the last bulleted item, press the Enter key three times to turn off automatic bulleting.
6. Promote *Robert Noyce* by positioning the insertion point at the beginning of *Robert Noyce* and then pressing Shift + Tab.
7. Format the paragraphs of text in the *Technology Timeline* section as a bulleted list by completing the following steps:
   a. Select the paragraphs of text in the *Technology Timeline* section.
   b. Click the Bullets button in the Paragraph group. (Word will insert the same arrow bullets that you inserted in Step 4. Word keeps the same bullet formatting until you choose a different bullet style.)
8. Save, preview, and then close **3-TechInfo.docx**.

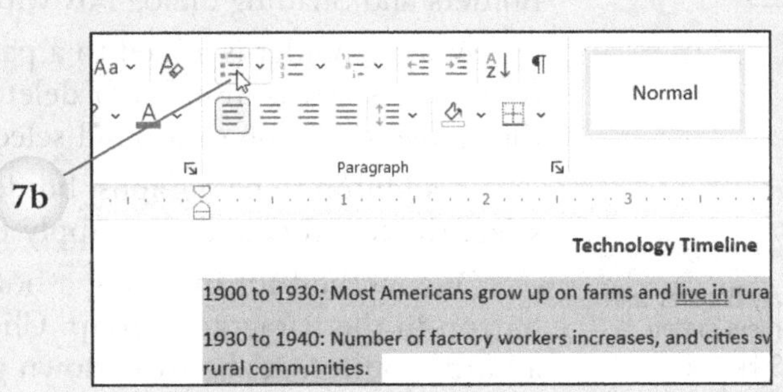
Normal
Paragraph
7b
Technology Timeline
1900 to 1930: Most Americans grow up on farms and live in rura
1930 to 1940: Number of factory workers increases, and cities s
rural communities.

Check Your Work

Figure 3.3 Activity 1c

Technology Visionaries

- Jack Kilby
  - Inventor of the handheld calculator
  - Credited with designing the first integrated circuit
  - Robert Noyce
  - Co-founder of Intel
  - Developed an integrated circuit using silicon

Activity 2 Customize a Document on Chapter Questions — 3 Parts

You will open a document containing chapter questions and then apply border and shading formatting to text.

Adding Emphasis to Paragraphs

To call attention to or to highlight specific text in a document, consider adding emphasis to the text by applying paragraph borders and/or shading. Apply borders with the Borders button in the Paragraph group on the Home tab and shading with the Shading button. Additional border and shading options are available at the Borders and Shading dialog box.

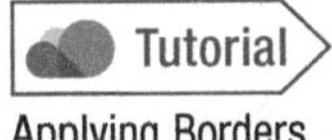

Applying Borders

Borders

Applying Paragraph Borders

Every paragraph in a Word document contains an invisible frame, and a border can be applied to the frame around the paragraph. Apply a border to specific sides of the paragraph frame or to all sides. Add borders to paragraphs using the Borders button in the Paragraph group on the Home tab or using options at the Borders and Shading dialog box with the Border tab selected.

When a border is added to a paragraph of text, the border expands and contracts as text is inserted or deleted from the paragraph. Insert a border around the active paragraph or around selected paragraphs.

In addition to paragraphs, borders can be applied to specific text. To do this, select the text first and then apply the border(s).

Quick Steps

Apply Borders with Borders Button

1. Select text.
2. Click Borders button arrow.
3. Click border option at drop-down gallery.

One method for inserting a border is to use options from the Borders button in the Paragraph group. Click the Borders button arrow and then choose a border option at the drop-down gallery. For example, to insert a border at the bottom of the paragraph, click the *Bottom Border* option. Clicking an option will add the border to the paragraph where the insertion point is located. To add a border to more than one paragraph, select the paragraphs first and then click the option.

Activity 2a Applying Borders to Paragraphs of Text

Part 1 of 3

1. Open **Questions.docx** and then save it with the name **3-Questions**.
2. Insert an outside border to specific text by completing the following steps:
   a. Select text from the heading *Chapter 1 Questions* through the four bulleted paragraphs.
   b. Click the Borders button arrow in the Paragraph group on the Home tab.
   c. Click the *Outside Borders* option at the drop-down gallery.
3. Select text from the heading *Chapter 2 Questions* through the five bulleted paragraphs and then click the Borders button (The button will apply the border option that was previously selected.)
4. Save **3-Questions.docx**.

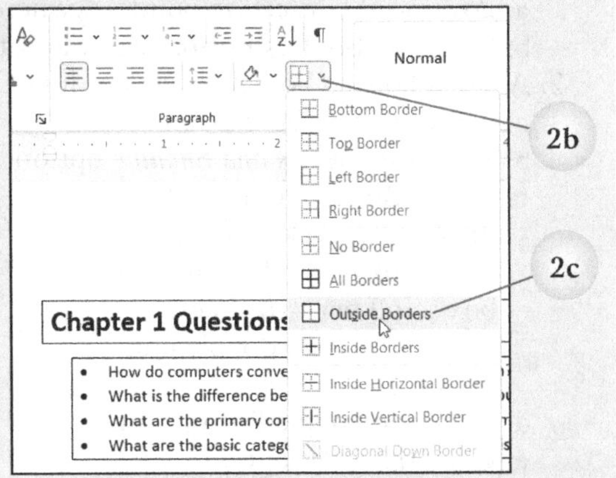

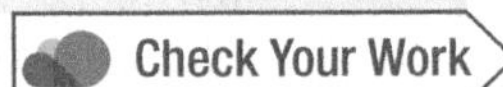

Quick Steps

Apply Borders at Borders and Shading Dialog Box

1. Select text.
2. Click Borders button arrow.
3. Click *Borders and Shading* option.
4. Choose options in dialog box.
5. Click OK.

To further customize paragraph borders, use options at the Borders and Shading dialog box with the Borders tab selected, as shown in Figure 3.4. Display this dialog box by clicking the Borders button arrow and then clicking *Borders and Shading* at the drop-down list. At the Borders and Shading dialog box, specify the border setting, style, color, and width.

Figure 3.4 Borders and Shading Dialog Box with the Borders Tab Selected

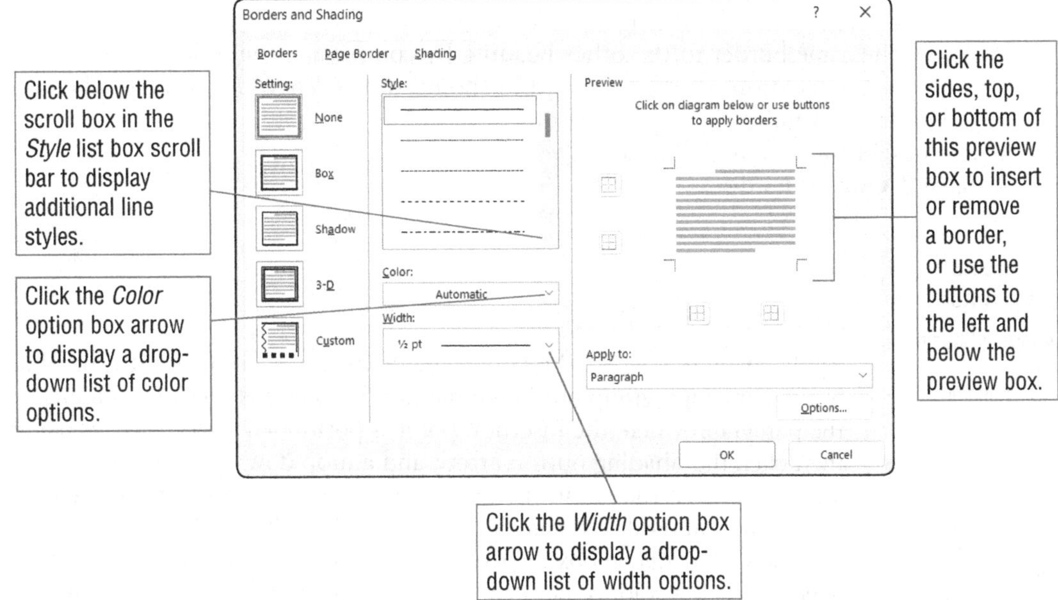

Activity 2b Applying Borders at the Borders and Shading Dialog Box

Part 2 of 3

1. With **3-Questions.docx** open, remove the borders around the heading *Chapter 1 Questions* by completing the following steps:
   a. Position the insertion point anywhere in the heading *Chapter 1 Questions*.
   b. Click the Borders button arrow and then click *No Border* at the drop-down gallery.
2. Apply a bottom border to the heading *Chapter 1 Questions* by completing the following steps:
   a. Click the Borders button arrow.
   b. Click the *Borders and Shading* option.
   c. At the Borders and Shading dialog box, click below the scroll box in the *Style* list box scroll bar two times. (This displays a double-line option.)
   d. Click the double-line option.
   e. Click the *Color* option box arrow.
   f. Click the *Blue* color (eighth color option in the *Standard Colors* section).
   g. Click the *Width* option box arrow.
   h. Click the *3/4 pt* option at the drop-down list.
   i. Click the *None* option in the *Setting* section.
   j. Click the bottom border of the box in the *Preview* section.
   k. Click OK to close the dialog box and apply the border.

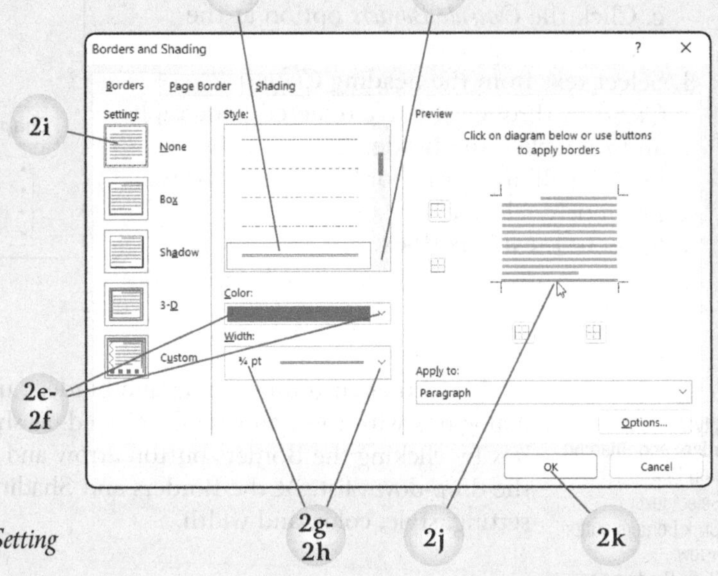

3. Apply the same border to the other heading by completing the following steps:
   a. With the insertion point positioned in the heading *Chapter 1 Questions*, click the Format Painter button.
   b. Click in the heading *Chapter 2 Questions*.
4. Save **3-Questions.docx**.

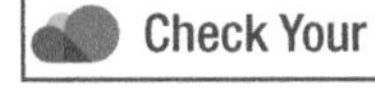

Applying Shading

Shading

Quick Steps

Apply Shading
1. Select text.
2. Click Shading button.

OR
1. Click Borders button arrow.
2. Click *Borders and Shading* option.
3. Click Shading tab.
4. Choose options in dialog box.
5. Click OK.

Applying Shading

Apply shading to selected text or paragraphs in a document with the Shading button in the Paragraph group on the Home tab. If no text is selected, shading is applied to the paragraph where the insertion point is positioned. Select text or paragraphs and then click the Shading button arrow, and a drop-down gallery displays. Shading colors are presented in themes in the drop-down gallery. Use one of the theme colors or click one of the standard colors at the bottom of the gallery. Click the *More Colors* option and the Colors dialog box displays. At the Colors dialog box with the Standard tab selected, click a color or click the Custom tab and then specify a custom color.

Shading can also be applied using options at the Borders and Shading dialog box. Display this dialog box by clicking the Borders button arrow and then clicking the *Borders and Shading* option. At the Borders and Shading dialog box, click the Shading tab. Use options in the dialog box to specify a fill color, choose a pattern style, and specify a color for the dots that make up the pattern.

Activity 2c Applying Paragraph Shading

1. With **3-Questions.docx** open, apply shading to the paragraph containing the heading *Chapter 1 Questions* by completing the following steps:
   a. Click in the heading *Chapter 1 Questions*.
   b. Click the Shading button arrow.
   c. Click the *Blue, Accent 5, Lighter 80%* option (ninth column, second row in the *Theme Colors* section).

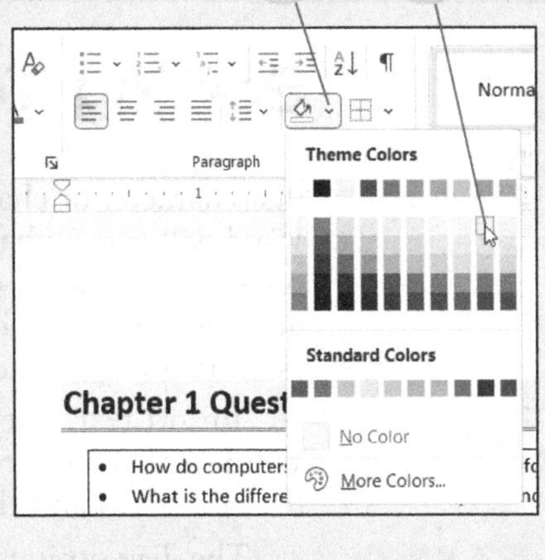

2. Apply the same blue shading to the other heading by completing the following steps:
   a. With the insertion point positioned in the heading *Chapter 1 Questions*, click the Format Painter button.
   b. Click in the heading *Chapter 2 Questions*.
3. Apply shading to selected paragraphs with options at the Borders and Shading dialog box by completing the following steps:
   a. Select the four bulleted paragraphs below the heading *Chapter 1 Questions*.
   b. Click the Borders button arrow.
   c. Click the *Borders and Shading* option.
   d. At the Borders and Shading dialog box, click the Shading tab.
   e. Click the *Fill* option box arrow.
   f. Click the *Gold, Accent 4, Lighter 80%* option (eighth column, second row in the *Theme Colors* section).
   g. Click the *Style* option box arrow.
   h. Click the *5%* option.
   i. Click the *Color* option box arrow.
   j. Click the *Blue, Accent 5, Lighter 60%* option (ninth column, third row in the *Theme Colors* section).
   k. Click OK to close the dialog box.

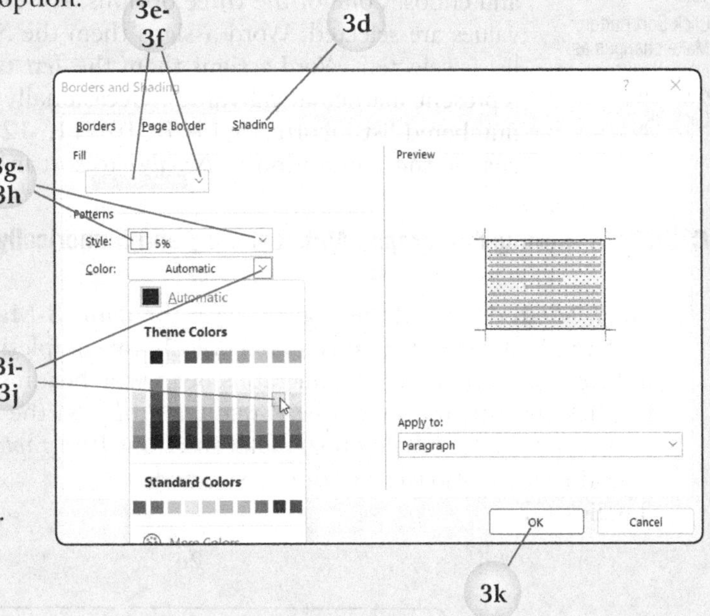

4. Apply the same shading to the bulleted paragraphs below the heading *Chapter 2 Questions* by completing the following steps:
   a. Click in the bulleted paragraphs below the heading *Chapter 1 Questions*.
   b. Click the Format Painter button.
   c. Select the five bulleted paragraphs below the heading *Chapter 2 Questions*.
5. Save, preview, and then close **3-Questions.docx**.

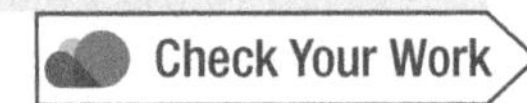

Activity 3 Sort Text in a Document on Maui — 1 Part

You will open a document on Maui and then sort several different paragraphs of text alphabetically and numerically.

Tutorial

Sorting Text in Paragraphs

Sorting Text in Paragraphs

Paragraphs can be sorted alphabetically, numerically, or by date, based on the first character or characters in each paragraph. If the first character is a letter, Word will sort alphabetically from A to Z or from Z to A. This can be useful for such things as a list of names or a glossary of terms. Paragraphs that begin with a number, such as a dollar amount or measurement, can be arranged numerically in ascending or descending order.

Sort

To sort text, select the specific paragraphs to be sorted. (If text is not selected, Word sorts the entire document.) Click the Sort button in the Paragraph group on the Home tab and the Sort Text dialog box displays. At this dialog box, click OK.

Quick Steps

Sort Paragraphs of Text

1. Click Sort button.
2. Make changes as needed at Sort Text dialog box.
3. Click OK.

The *Type* option at the Sort Text dialog box provides the options *Text*, *Number*, or *Date* depending on the text selected. Word attempts to determine the data type and chooses one of the three options. For example, if numbers with mathematical values are selected, Word assigns them the *Number* type. However, if a numbered list is selected, Word assigns them the *Text* type since the numbers do not represent mathematical values. Occasionally this will result in Word reorganizing a numbered list incorrectly (as 1., 10., 11., 12., 2., for example). If this occurs, change the *Type* option to *Number* to sort in correct numerical order.

Activity 3 Sorting Paragraphs Alphabetically and Numerically — Part 1 of 1

1. Open **Maui.docx** and then save it with the name **3-Maui**.
2. Sort the bulleted paragraphs alphabetically by completing the following steps:
   a. Select the five bulleted paragraphs below the heading *Maui Activities*.
   b. Click the Sort button in the Paragraph group on the Home tab.
   c. At the Sort Text dialog box, make sure that *Paragraphs* displays in the *Sort by* option box and that the *Ascending* option is selected.
   d. Click OK.

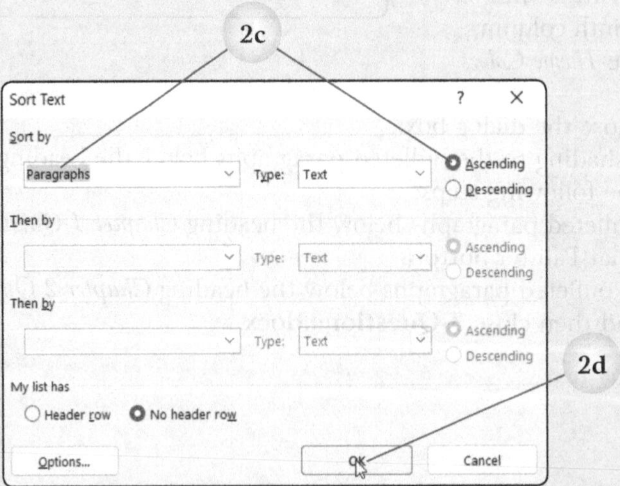

3. Sort the numbered paragraphs by completing the following steps:
   a. Select the ten numbered paragraphs below the heading *Maui Sites*.
   b. Click the Sort button in the Paragraph group.
   c. At the Sort Text dialog box, click the *Type* option box arrow and then click *Number* at the drop-down list.
   d. Click OK.
4. Sort the prices below the heading *Adventure Deals* in descending numerical order by completing the following steps:
   a. Select the paragraphs below the heading *Adventure Deals*.
   b. Click the Sort button in the Paragraph group.
   c. Click the *Type* option box arrow and then click *Number* at the drop-down list.
   d. Click the *Descending* option.
   e. Click OK.
5. Save, preview, and then close **3-Maui.docx**.

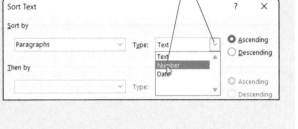

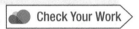

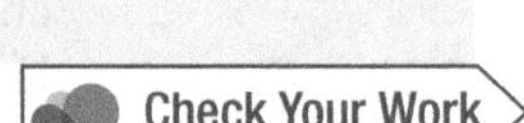

Activity 4 Prepare a Document on Workshops and Training Dates **4 Parts**

You will set and move tabs on the horizontal ruler and at the Tabs dialog box and type tabbed text about workshops, training dates, and a table of contents.

Setting and Modifying Tabs

Blocks of text can be organized by setting tabs to separate the text and to give the text a more uniform appearance. Tabs allow text to be aligned at different points in the document. When typing blocks of text, only press the Tab key one time between the blocks. The default setting for tabs in Word is a left tab set every 0.5 inch. When the Tab key is pressed, the insertion point moves to the right 0.5 inch. In some situations, these default tabs are appropriate; in others, custom tabs may be needed. Tabs can be set on the horizontal ruler or at the Tabs dialog box.

Setting and Modifying Tabs on the Horizontal Ruler

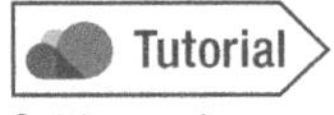

Setting and Modifying Tabs on the Horizontal Ruler

Quick Steps

Set Tabs on Horizontal Ruler

1. Click Alignment button above vertical ruler.
2. Click tab locations on horizontal ruler.

Use the horizontal ruler to set, move, and delete tabs. If the ruler is not visible, click the View tab and then click the *Ruler* check box in the Show group to insert a check mark. By default, tabs are set every 0.5 inch on the horizontal ruler. To set a new tab, first click the Alignment button to the left of the ruler and above the vertical ruler to specify how text will be aligned on the tab. The types of tabs that can be set on the ruler are left, center, right, decimal, and bar. These tab types are represented with the symbols shown in Table 3.1. Text is aligned at the left edge of a left tab, in the middle of a center tab, at the right edge of a right tab, and at the decimal point with a decimal tab. Setting a bar tab causes a vertical bar (line) to be inserted in the document at the point where the tab is set. Refer to Figure 3.7 on page 86 to see an example of a document with a bar tab.

Table 3.1 Alignment Button Tab Symbols

Alignment Button Symbol	Type of Tab
∟	left
⊥	center
⅃	right
⊥.	decimal
|	bar

Hint When setting tabs on the horizontal ruler, a dotted guideline displays to help align them.

Hint Position the insertion point in any paragraph of text, and tabs for the paragraph appear on the horizontal ruler.

When the Alignment button displays the correct tab symbol, position the pointer on the ruler where the tab should be set, and then click the left button to set the tab. When a new tab is set, any default tabs to the left of it are automatically deleted by Word. If the tab symbol on the Alignment button is changed, the symbol remains in place until it is changed again or Word is closed. If Word is closed and then reopened, the Alignment button displays with the left tab symbol.

To set a tab at a specific measurement on the horizontal ruler, press and hold down the Alt key, position the pointer at the desired position, and then click and hold down the left mouse button. This displays two measurements in the white portion of the horizontal ruler. The first measurement is the location of the pointer on the ruler in relation to the left margin. The second measurement is the distance from the pointer to the right margin. With the left mouse button held down, position the tab symbol at the desired location and then release the mouse button followed by the Alt key.

Tabs can be used to type text in columns. Type text and then press the Tab key to create a new column. At the end of a line, press the Enter key or press Shift + Enter. If the Enter key is used to end each line, all lines of text in columns will need to be selected to make paragraph formatting changes. To make changes to columns of text with line breaks inserted using Shift + Enter, the insertion point needs to be positioned in only one location in the columns of text.

Activity 4a Setting Left, Center, and Right Tabs on the Horizontal Ruler — Part 1 of 4

1. Press Ctrl + N to open a new blank document.
2. Type WORKSHOPS and apply bold formatting and center alignment, as shown in Figure 3.5.
3. Press the Enter key and then change the paragraph alignment back to left and turn off bold formatting.
4. Set a left tab at the 0.5-inch mark, a center tab at the 3.25-inch mark, and a right tab at the 6-inch mark by completing the following steps:
   a. Click the Show/Hide ¶ button in the Paragraph group on the Home tab to turn on the display of nonprinting characters.
   b. Make sure the horizontal ruler is visible. (If it is not, click the View tab and then click the *Ruler* check box in the Show group to insert a check mark.)

c. Make sure the left tab symbol displays in the Alignment button above the vertical ruler.
d. Position the pointer on the 0.5-inch mark on the horizontal ruler and then click the left mouse button.

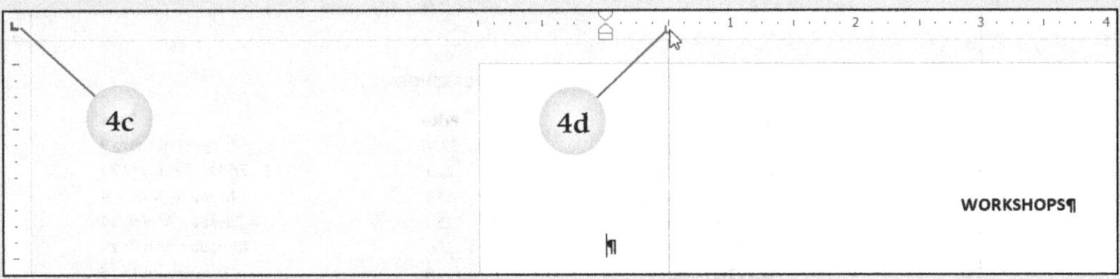

e. Position the pointer on the Alignment button and then click the left mouse button until the center tab symbol displays (see Table 3.1).
f. Position the pointer on the 3.25-inch mark on the horizontal ruler. Press and hold down the Alt key and then click and hold down the left mouse button. Make sure the first measurement on the horizontal ruler displays as approximately *3.25″* and then release the mouse button followed by the Alt key. (If *3.25″* does not display, consider increasing the zoom.)

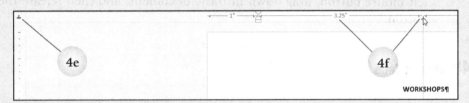

g. Position the pointer on the Alignment button and then click the left mouse button until the right tab symbol displays (see Table 3.1).
h. Position the pointer below the 6-inch mark on the horizontal ruler. Press and hold down the Alt key and then click and hold down the left mouse button. Make sure the first measurement on the horizontal ruler displays as approximately *6″* and then release the mouse button followed by the Alt key.

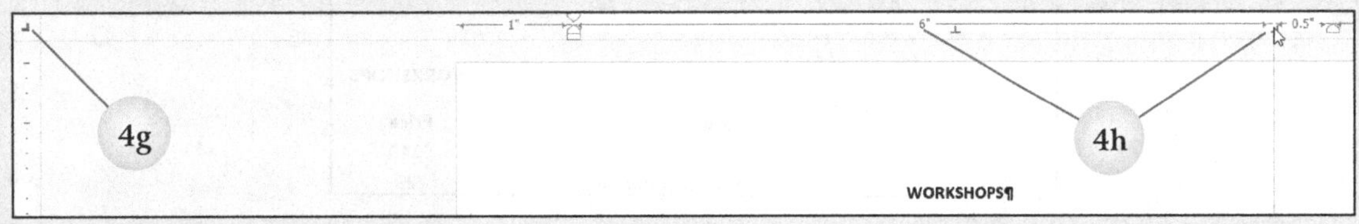

5. Type the text in columns, as shown in Figure 3.5 on page 84. Press the Tab key before typing each column entry and press Shift + Enter after typing each entry in the third column. Apply bold formatting to column headings, as shown in the figure.
6. After typing the final entry in the last column entry, press the Enter key two times.
7. Press Ctrl + Q to remove paragraph formatting (tab settings) below the columns from the current paragraph.
8. Click the Show/Hide ¶ button to turn off the display of nonprinting characters.
9. Save the document with the name **3-Tabs**.

Figure 3.5 Activity 4a

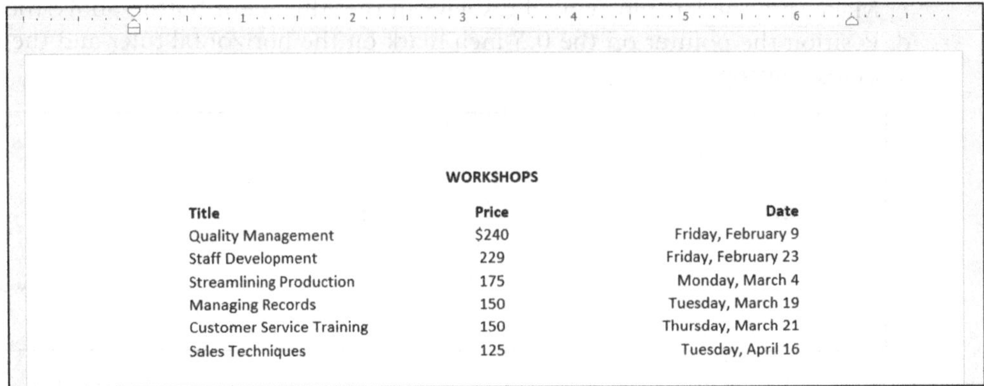

WORKSHOPS

Title	Price	Date
Quality Management	$240	Friday, February 9
Staff Development	229	Friday, February 23
Streamlining Production	175	Monday, March 4
Managing Records	150	Tuesday, March 19
Customer Service Training	150	Thursday, March 21
Sales Techniques	125	Tuesday, April 16

After a tab has been set on the horizontal ruler, it can be moved to a new location. To move a tab, position the pointer on the tab symbol on the ruler, click and hold down the left mouse button, drag the symbol to the new location on the ruler, and then release the mouse button. To delete a tab from the ruler, position the pointer on the tab symbol to be deleted, click and hold down the left mouse button, drag down into the document, and then release the mouse button.

Activity 4b Moving Tabs

Part 2 of 4

1. With **3-Tabs.docx** open, position the insertion point anywhere in the first entry in the tabbed text.
2. Position the pointer on the left tab symbol at the 0.5-inch mark on the horizontal ruler, click and hold down the left mouse button, drag the left tab symbol to the 1-inch mark on the ruler, and then release the mouse button. ***Hint:* *Use the Alt key to help you position the tab symbol precisely.***

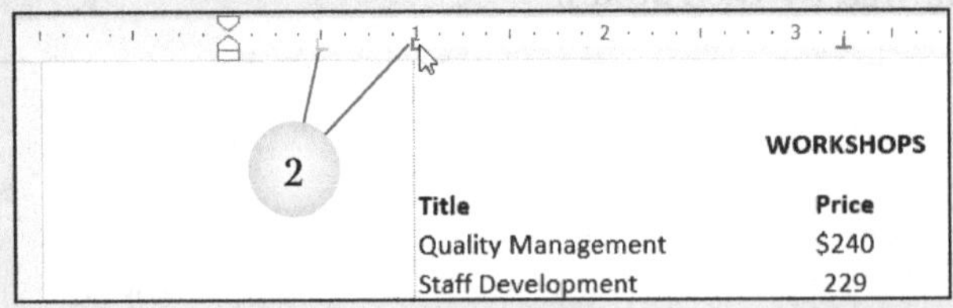

3. Position the pointer on the right tab symbol at the 6-inch mark on the horizontal ruler, click and hold down the left mouse button, drag the right tab symbol to the 5.5-inch mark on the ruler, and then release the mouse button. ***Hint:* *Use the Alt key to help you position the tab symbol precisely.***
4. Save **3-Tabs.docx**.

Check Your Work

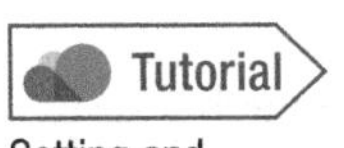

Setting and Clearing Tabs at the Tabs Dialog Box

Quick Steps

Set Tabs at Tabs Dialog Box

1. Click Paragraph group dialog box launcher.
2. Click Tabs button.
3. Specify tab positions, alignments, and leader options.
4. Click OK.

Setting and Modifying Tabs at the Tabs Dialog Box

Use the Tabs dialog box, shown in Figure 3.6, to set tabs at specific measurements and clear one tab or all tabs. To display the Tabs dialog box, click the Paragraph group dialog box launcher. At the Paragraph dialog box, click the Tabs button in the lower left corner of the dialog box.

A left, right, center, decimal, or bar tab can be set at the Tabs dialog box. (For an example of a bar tab, refer to Figure 3.7 on page 86.) To set a tab, click the type of tab in the *Alignment* section of the dialog box, type the tab measurement in the *Tab stop position* text box, and then click the Set button. To clear an individual tab at the Tabs dialog box, select or enter the tab position and then click the Clear button. To clear all tabs, click the Clear All button.

Figure 3.6 Tabs Dialog Box

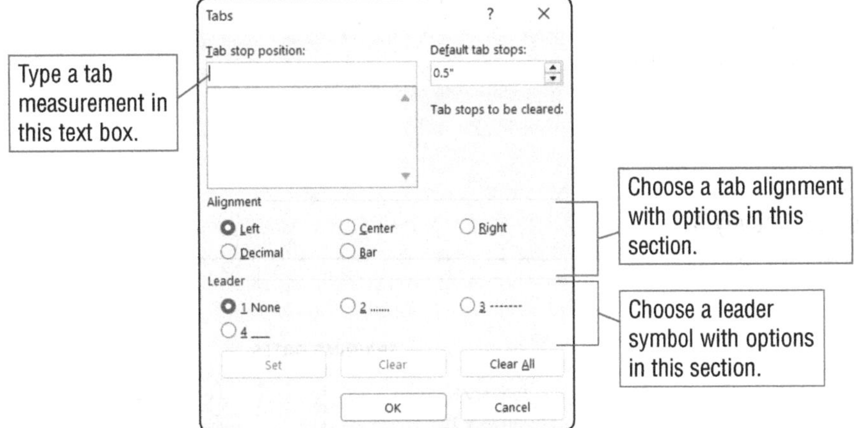

Activity 4c Setting Left Tabs and a Bar Tab at the Tabs Dialog Box

Part 3 of 4

1. With **3-Tabs.docx** open, press Ctrl + End to move the insertion point to the end of the document.
2. Type the title TRAINING DATES and apply bold formatting and center alignment, as shown in Figure 3.7. Press the Enter key, return the paragraph alignment to left, and then turn off bold formatting.
3. Display the Tabs dialog box and then set left tabs and a bar tab by completing the following steps:
   a. Click the Paragraph group dialog box launcher.
   b. At the Paragraph dialog box, click the Tabs button in the lower left corner of the dialog box.
   c. Make sure *Left* is selected in the *Alignment* section of the dialog box.
   d. Type 1.75 in the *Tab stop position* text box.
   e. Click the Set button.
   f. Type 4 in the *Tab stop position* text box and then click the Set button.
   g. Type 3.25 in the *Tab stop position* text box, click *Bar* in the *Alignment* section, and then click the Set button.
   h. Click OK to close the Tabs dialog box.

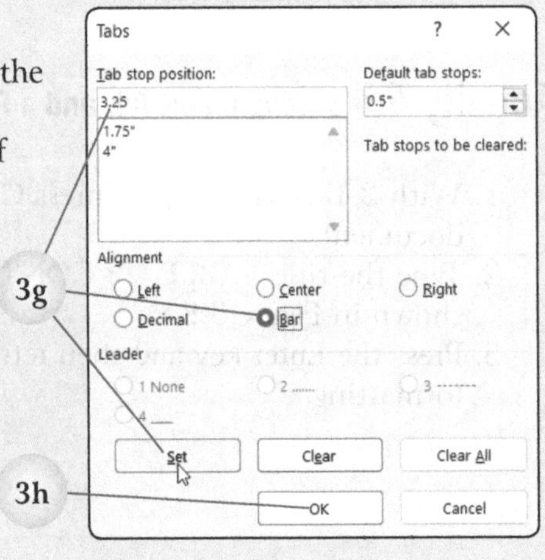

4. Type the text in columns, as shown in Figure 3.7. Press the Tab key before typing each column entry and press Shift + Enter to end each line. After typing *February 26*, press the Enter key.
5. Clear tabs below the columns from the current paragraph by completing the following steps:
   a. Click the Paragraph group dialog box launcher.
   b. At the Paragraph dialog box, click the Tabs button.
   c. At the Tabs dialog box, click the Clear All button.
   d. Click OK.
6. Press the Enter key.
7. Remove the 8 points of spacing after the last entry in the text by completing the following steps:
   a. Position the insertion point anywhere in the *January 29* entry.
   b. Click the Line and Paragraph Spacing button in the Paragraph group on the Home tab.
   c. Click the *Remove Space After Paragraph* option.
8. Save **3-Tabs.docx**.

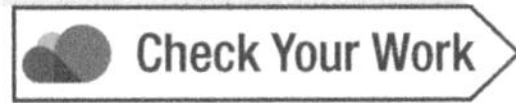

Figure 3.7 Activity 4c

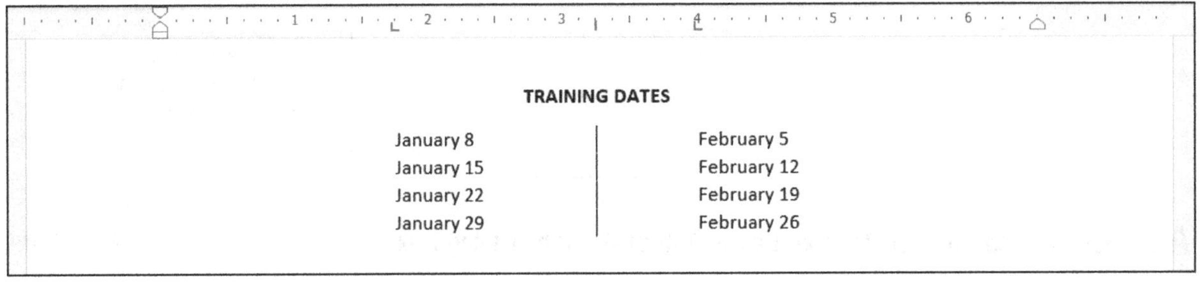

Four types of tabs (left, right, center, and decimal) can be set with leaders at the Tabs dialog box. Leaders are useful in a table of contents or other material where the reader's eyes should be directed across the page. Figure 3.8 shows an example of leaders. Leaders can be periods (.), hyphens (-), or underlines (_). To add leaders to a tab, click the type of leader in the *Leader* section of the Tabs dialog box.

Activity 4d Setting a Left Tab and a Right Tab with Period Leaders — Part 4 of 4

1. With **3-Tabs.docx** open, press Ctrl + End to move the insertion point to the end of the document.
2. Type the title TABLE OF CONTENTS and apply bold formatting and center alignment, as shown in Figure 3.8.
3. Press the Enter key and then return the paragraph alignment to left and turn off bold formatting.

4. Set a left tab and then a right tab with period leaders by completing the following steps:
   a. Click the Paragraph group dialog box launcher.
   b. Click the Tabs button.
   c. At the Tabs dialog box, make sure *Left* is selected in the *Alignment* section of the dialog box.
   d. With the insertion point positioned in the *Tab stop position* text box, type 1 and then click the Set button.
   e. Type 5.5 in the *Tab stop position* text box.
   f. Click *Right* in the *Alignment* section.
   g. Click *2* ...... in the *Leader* section and then click the Set button.
   h. Click OK to close the dialog box.

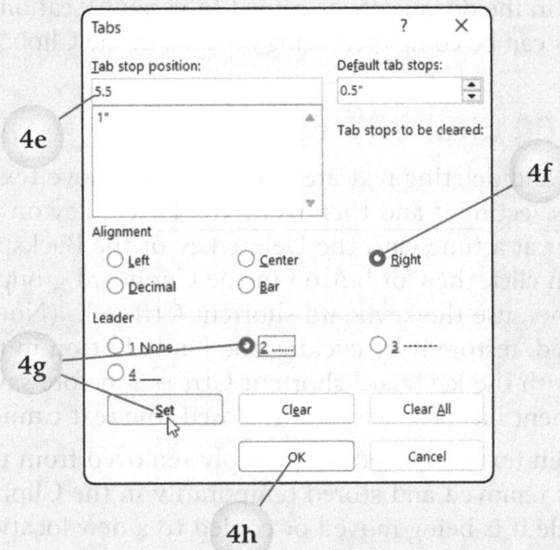

5. Type the text in columns, as shown in Figure 3.8. Press the Tab key before typing each column entry and press Shift + Enter to end each line.
6. Save, preview, and then close **3-Tabs.docx**.

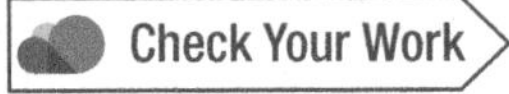

Figure 3.8 Activity 4d

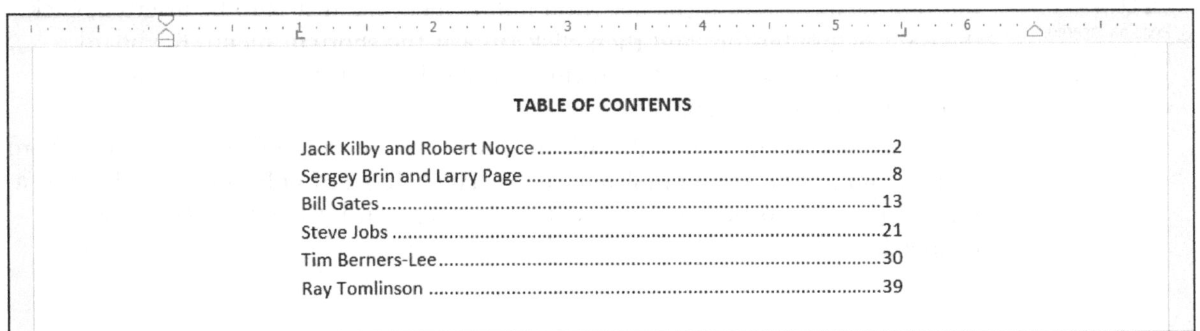

TABLE OF CONTENTS

Jack Kilby and Robert Noyce 2
Sergey Brin and Larry Page 8
Bill Gates 13
Steve Jobs 21
Tim Berners-Lee 30
Ray Tomlinson 39

Activity 5 Move and Copy Text in a Document on Volcanoes 2 Parts

You will open a document containing information on volcanoes and then cut, copy, and paste text in the document.

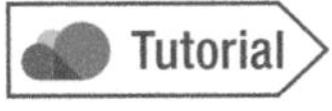

Cutting, Copying, and Pasting Text

Cutting, Copying, and Pasting Text

When editing a document, specific text may need to be deleted, moved to a different location in the document, or copied to various locations in the document. These activities can be completed using buttons in the Clipboard group on the Home tab.

Deleting and Cutting Text

Cut

Cutting and deleting text are two ways to remove text from a document. Delete text by selecting it and then using the Delete key on the keyboard, or delete one character at a time with the Delete key or the Backspace key. To cut text, select it and then click the Cut button in the Clipboard group on the Home tab, or select it and then use the keyboard shortcut Ctrl + X. (Note: If text is accidentally cut or deleted, restore it by clicking the Undo button in the Undo group on the Home tab or with the keyboard shortcut Ctrl + Z before saving or closing the file. After a document has been saved and closed, the text cannot be restored.)

Hint The Clipboard content is deleted when the computer is turned off. Text you want to save permanently should be saved as a separate document.

When text is deleted, it is simply removed from the document. When text is cut, it is removed and stored temporarily in the Clipboard. The Clipboard holds text while it is being moved or copied to a new location in the document or to a different document.

Cutting and Pasting Text

Paste

Quick Steps

Move Selected Text

1. Select text.
2. Click Cut button or use Ctrl + X.
3. Position insertion point.
4. Click Paste button or use Ctrl + V.

To move text to a different location in the document, select the text, click the Cut button, position the insertion point at the location the text is to be inserted, and then click the Paste button in the Clipboard group.

Selected text can also be moved using the shortcut menu. To do this, select the text and then position the insertion point inside the selected text until it turns into an arrow pointer. Click the right mouse button and then click *Cut* at the shortcut menu. Position the insertion point where the text is to be inserted, click the right mouse button, and then click *Paste* at the shortcut menu. Keyboard shortcuts are also available for cutting and pasting text. Use Ctrl + X to cut text and Ctrl + V to paste text.

When text is cut from a document, it will remain in the Clipboard while Word is open and can be pasted multiple times. The Clipboard holds only one item at a time. If another portion of text is cut to the Clipboard, the first selection will be removed.

Quick Steps

Move Text with Mouse

1. Select text.
2. Position pointer in selected text.
3. Click and hold down left mouse button and drag to new location.
4. Release left mouse button.

Moving Text by Dragging with the Mouse

The mouse can be used to move text. To do this, select text to be moved and then click and drag the selection with the pointer. As the text is being dragged, the pointer will display as an arrow with a small gray box attached. Move to the location the selected text is to be inserted, and then release the button. If the selected text is inserted in the wrong location, click the Undo button immediately.

Activity 5a Cutting and Dragging Selected Text

Part 1 of 2

1. Open **Volcanoes.docx** and then save it with the name **3-Volcanoes.**
2. Move a paragraph by completing the following steps:
   a. Select the paragraph that begins with *Eruption Stage*.
   b. Click the Cut button in the Clipboard group on the Home tab.
   c. Position the insertion point at the beginning of the paragraph that begins with *Cooling Stage*.
   d. Click the Paste button (make sure you click the Paste button and not the Paste button arrow) in the Clipboard group on the Home tab.

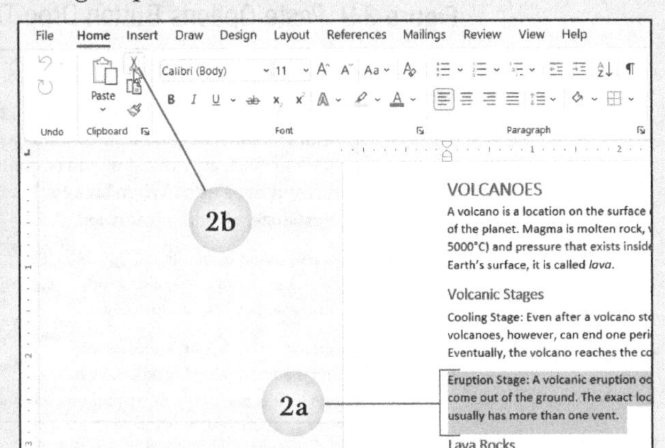

3. Following steps similar to those in Step 2, move the paragraph that begins with *Basalt* before the paragraph that begins with *Andesite*.
4. Move a paragraph using the mouse by completing the following steps:
   a. Use the mouse to select the paragraph that begins with *Shield Volcanoes*.
   b. Move the I-beam pointer inside the selected text until it displays as an arrow pointer.
   c. Click and hold down the left mouse button, drag the arrow pointer (which displays with a small gray box attached) so that the insertion point (which displays as a black vertical bar) is positioned at the beginning of the paragraph that begins with *Composite Volcanoes* and then release the mouse button.

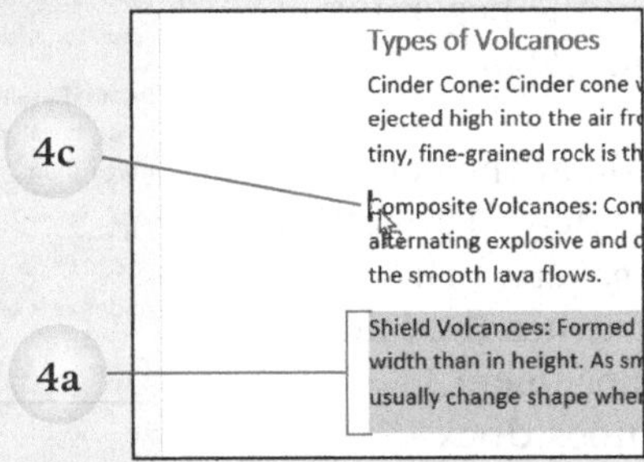

5. Deselect the text.
6. Save **3-Volcanoes.docx**.

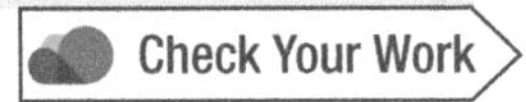

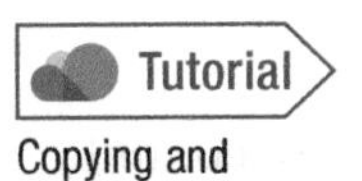

Copying and Pasting Text and Formatting

(Ctrl) Paste Options

Using the Paste Options Button

When text is pasted in a document, the Paste Options button displays in the lower right corner of the text. Click this button (or press the Ctrl key on the keyboard) and the Paste Options gallery displays, as shown in Figure 3.9. The gallery can also be displayed by clicking the Paste button arrow in the Clipboard group.

The Paste Options gallery contains buttons for specifying the formatting of pasted text.(The number of buttons may vary depending on what is cut or copied.) The first button, Keep Source Formatting, is the default and pastes the text with the original formatting. Click the second button, Merge Formatting, and pasted text will take on the formatting of the text where it is pasted. Click the third button, Keep Text Only, to paste only the text and not the text formatting. Hover the pointer over a button in the gallery and the live preview displays the text in the document as it will appear when pasted.

Figure 3.9 Paste Options Button Drop-Down Gallery

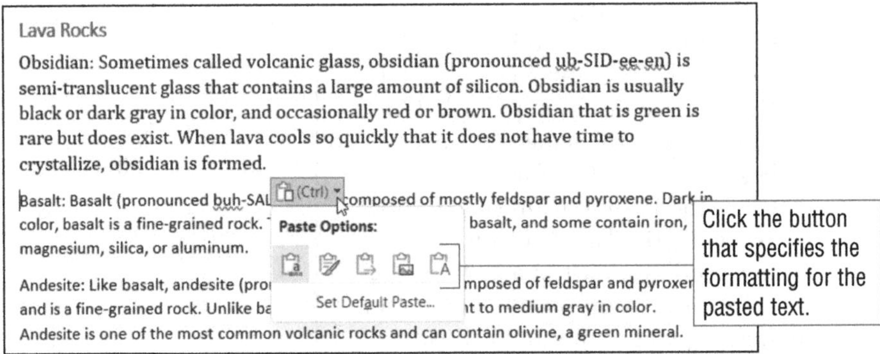

Activity 5b Using the Paste Options Button

Part 2 of 2

1. With **3-Volcanoes.docx** open, open **LavaRocks.docx**.
2. In the **LavaRocks.docx** document, select the paragraph of text that begins with *Obsidian* and then click the Cut button in the Clipboard group on the Home tab.
3. Close the **LavaRocks.docx** document without saving it.
4. Position the insertion point at the beginning of the paragraph that begins with *Basalt*.
5. Click the Paste button.
6. Click the Paste Options button at the end of the paragraph and then click the Merge Formatting button in the Paste Options gallery. (This changes the font so that it matches the font of the other paragraphs in the document.)
7. Save and then close **3-Volcanoes.docx**.

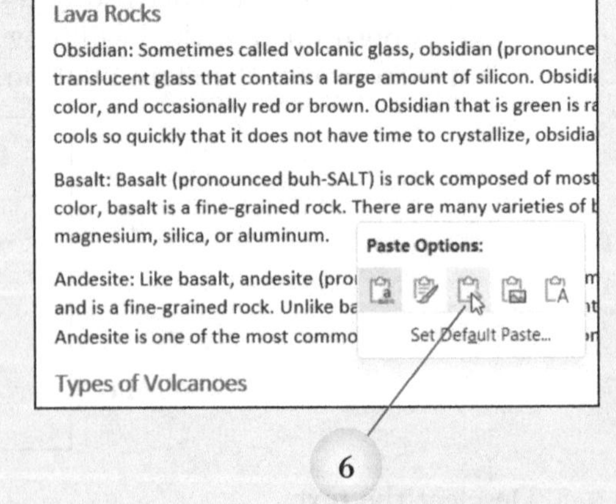

Check Your Work

Activity 6 Copy Text in a Staff Meeting Announcement 1 Part

You will copy and paste text in a document announcing a staff meeting for the Technical Support Team.

Copying and Pasting Text

Quick Steps

Copy Selected Text

1. Select text.
2. Click Copy button or use Ctrl + C.
3. Position insertion point.
4. Click Paste button or use Ctrl + V.

Use copy and paste to copy text from one document and paste it into another. Or, paste copied text into one document multiple times to insert duplicate portions of text without needing to retype it. Copy selected text and then paste it in a different location using the Copy and Paste buttons in the Clipboard group on the Home tab or the keyboard shortcuts Ctrl + C and Ctrl + V.

Text can also be copied and pasted using the mouse. To do this, select the text and then click inside the selected text. Hold down the left mouse button and also press and hold down the Ctrl key while dragging the selected text with the mouse. While text is being dragged, the pointer displays with a small gray box and a box containing a plus [+] symbol and a black vertical bar moves with the pointer. Position the black bar in the desired location, release the mouse button, and then release the Ctrl key to paste the text.

Activity 6 Copying Text Part 1 of 1

1. Open **StaffMtg.docx** and then save it with the name **3-StaffMtg**.
2. Copy the text in the document to the end of the document by completing the following steps:
   a. Select all the text in the document and include one blank line below the text. ***Hint: Click the Show/Hide ¶ button to turn on the display of nonprinting characters. When you select the text, select one of the paragraph markers below the text.***
   b. Click the Copy button in the Clipboard group on the Home tab.
   c. Press Ctrl + End to move the insertion point to the end of the document.
   d. Click the Paste button.
3. Paste the text again at the end of the document. To do this, click the Paste button. (This inserts a copy of the text from the Clipboard.)
4. Select all the text in the document using the mouse and include one blank line below the text.
5. Move the I-beam pointer inside the selected text until it becomes an arrow pointer.
6. Click and hold down the Ctrl key and then the left mouse button. Drag the arrow pointer (which displays with a box containing a plus symbol) so the vertical black bar is positioned at the end of the document, release the mouse button, and then release the Ctrl key.
7. Deselect the text.
8. Make sure all the text fits on one page. If not, consider deleting any extra blank lines.
9. Save, preview, and then close **3-StaffMtg.docx**.

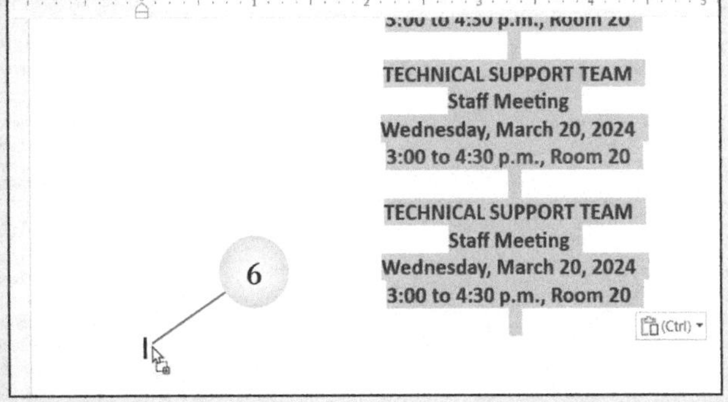

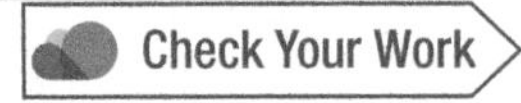

Activity 7 Create a Contract Negotiations Document — 1 Part

You will use the Clipboard task pane to copy and paste paragraphs to and from separate documents to create a contract negotiations document.

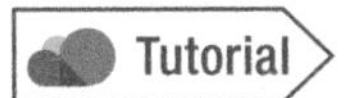

Using the Clipboard Task Pane

Quick Steps

Use the Clipboard

1. Click Clipboard group task pane launcher.
2. Select and copy or cut text.
3. Position insertion point.
4. Click option in Clipboard task pane.

Hint You can copy or cut items to the Clipboard from various Microsoft 365 applications and then paste them into any Microsoft 365 file.

Using the Clipboard Task Pane

Use the Clipboard task pane to collect up to 24 different items, such as text, images, and objects, and then paste the items multiple times and in multiple locations in Word as well as other applications, such as Excel, PowerPoint, and Access. The Clipboard allows cutting and copying multiple items without limiting pasting to only the last item cut or copied.

To display the Clipboard task pane, click the Clipboard group task pane launcher in the lower right corner of the Clipboard group on the Home tab. The Clipboard task pane displays at the left side of the screen in a manner similar to what is shown in Figure 3.10.

Select the item to be copied and then click the Copy button or Cut button in the Clipboard group. Continue selecting items and clicking the Copy or Cut button. To insert an item from the Clipboard task pane into the document, position the insertion point in the desired location and then click the option in the Clipboard task pane representing the item. Click the Paste All button to paste all the items in the Clipboard task pane into the document. If the copied or cut item is text, the first 50 characters display in the list box on the Clipboard task pane. When all the items are inserted, click the Clear All button to clear all items from the task pane.

Figure 3.10 Clipboard Task Pane

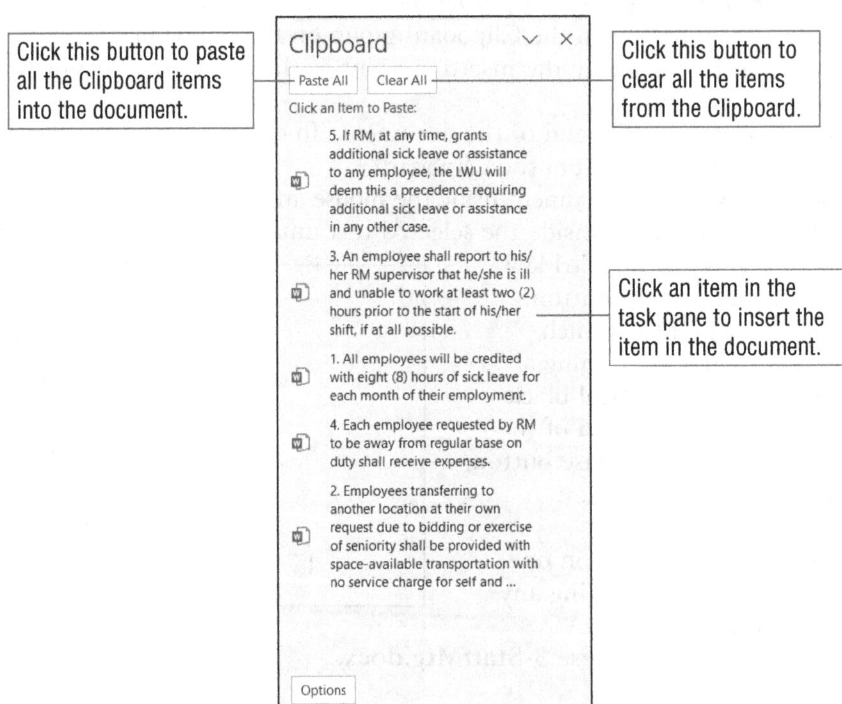

Activity 7 Collecting and Pasting Paragraphs of Text

1. Open **ContractItems.docx**.
2. Display the Clipboard task pane by clicking the Clipboard group task pane launcher in the bottom right corner of the Clipboard group on the Home tab. (If the Clipboard task pane list box contains any items, click the Clear All button at the top of the Clipboard task pane.)

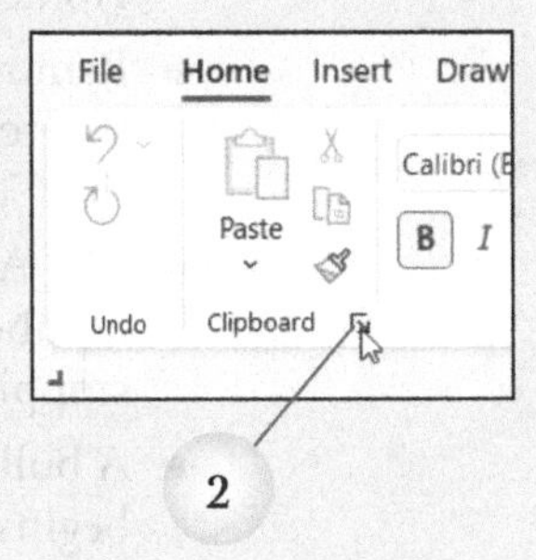

3. Select paragraph 1 in the document (the *1.* is not selected) and then click the Copy button.
4. Select paragraph 3 in the document (the *3.* is not selected) and then click the Copy button.
5. Close **ContractItems.docx**.
6. Paste the paragraphs by completing the following steps:
   a. Press Ctrl + N to open a new blank document. (If the Clipboard task pane does not display, click the Clipboard group task pane launcher.)
   b. Type CONTRACT NEGOTIATION ITEMS and apply bold formatting and center alignment.
   c. Press the Enter key, turn off bold formatting, and return the paragraph alignment to left.
   d. Click the Paste All button in the Clipboard task pane to paste both paragraphs in the document.
   e. Click the Clear All button in the Clipboard task pane.

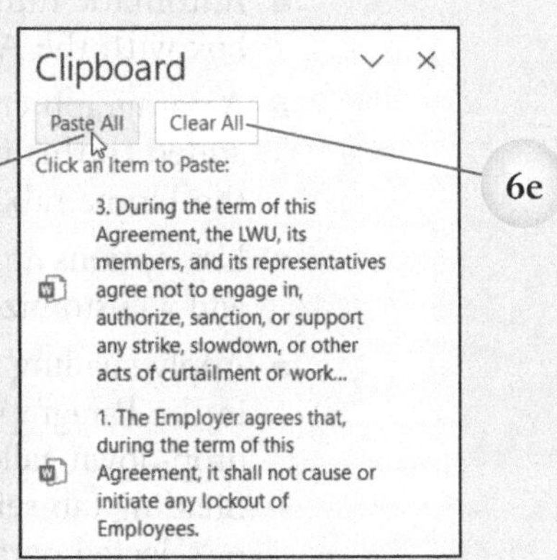

7. Open **UnionContract.docx**.
8. Select and then copy each of the following paragraphs:
   a. Paragraph 2 in the *Transfers and Moving Expenses* section.
   b. Paragraph 4 in the *Transfers and Moving Expenses* section.
   c. Paragraph 1 in the *Sick Leave* section.
   d. Paragraph 3 in the *Sick Leave* section.
   e. Paragraph 5 in the *Sick Leave* section.
9. Close **UnionContract.docx**.
10. Make sure the insertion point is positioned at the end of the document on a new line and then paste the paragraphs by completing the following steps:
    a. Click the button in the Clipboard task pane representing paragraph 2. (When the paragraph is inserted in the document, the paragraph number changes to *3.*)
    b. Click the button in the Clipboard task pane representing paragraph 4.
    c. Click the button in the Clipboard task pane representing paragraph 3.
    d. Click the button in the Clipboard task pane representing paragraph 5.

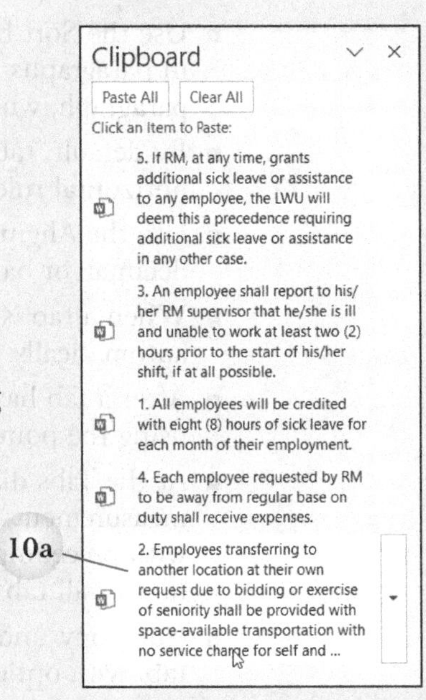

11. Click the Clear All button.
12. Close the Clipboard task pane.
13. Save the document with the name **3-NegotiateItems**.
14. Preview and then close **3-NegotiateItems.docx**.

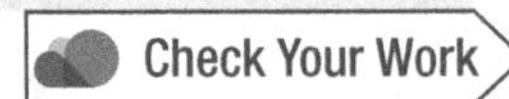

Chapter Summary

- Number paragraphs using the Numbering button in the Paragraph group on the Home tab and insert bullets before paragraphs using the Bullets button.
- Remove all paragraph formatting from a paragraph by using the keyboard shortcut Ctrl + Q. Remove all character and paragraph formatting by clicking the Clear All Formatting button in the Font group.
- The AutoCorrect Options button displays when the AutoFormat feature inserts numbers or bullets. Click this button to display options for undoing and/or stopping automatic numbering or bulleting.
- A bulleted list with a hanging indent is automatically created when a paragraph begins with *, >, or -. The type of bullet inserted depends on the type of character entered.
- Automatic numbering and bulleting can be turned off at the AutoCorrect dialog box with the AutoFormat As You Type tab selected.
- A paragraph created in Word contains an invisible frame and a border can be added to this frame. Click the Borders button arrow in the Paragraph group on the Home tab to display a drop-down gallery of border options.
- Use options at the Borders and Shading dialog box with the Borders tab selected to add a customized border to a paragraph, selected paragraphs, or selected text.
- Apply shading to selected text or paragraphs by clicking the Shading button arrow in the Paragraph group on the Home tab and then clicking a color option at the drop-down gallery. Use options at the Borders and Shading dialog box with the Shading tab selected to add shading and/or a pattern to selected text, a paragraph, or selected paragraphs.
- Use the Sort button in the Paragraph group on the Home tab to sort text in paragraphs alphabetically or numerically by the first character of each paragraph, which can be a number, symbol, or letter.
- By default, tabs are set every 0.5 inch. Tab settings can be changed on the horizontal ruler or at the Tabs dialog box.
- Use the Alignment button above the vertical ruler to select a left, right, center, decimal, or bar tab.
- When a tab is set on the horizontal ruler, any default tabs to the left are automatically deleted.
- After a tab has been set on the horizontal ruler, it can be moved or deleted using the pointer.
- At the Tabs dialog box, any of the five types of tabs can be set at a specific measurement. Four types of tabs (left, right, center, and decimal) can be set with preceding leaders, which can be periods, hyphens, or underlines. Individual tabs or all tabs can be cleared at the Tabs dialog box.
- Cut, copy, and paste text using buttons in the Clipboard group on the Home tab, with options at the shortcut menu, or with keyboard shortcuts.
- When selected text is pasted, the Paste Options button displays in the lower right corner of the text. Click the button and the Paste Options gallery displays with buttons for specifying how text and formatting is pasted in the document.
- With the Clipboard task pane, up to 24 items can be cut or copied and then pasted in various locations in a document or other document.
- Display the Clipboard task pane by clicking the Clipboard group task pane launcher in the Clipboard group on the Home tab.

Commands Review

FEATURE	RIBBON TAB, GROUP	BUTTON, OPTION	KEYBOARD SHORTCUT
borders	Home, Paragraph		
Borders and Shading dialog box	Home, Paragraph	, *Borders and Shading*	
bullets	Home, Paragraph		
clear all formatting	Home, Font		
clear paragraph formatting			Ctrl + Q
Clipboard task pane	Home, Clipboard		
copy text	Home, Clipboard		Ctrl + C
cut text	Home, Clipboard		Ctrl + X
numbering	Home, Paragraph		
Paragraph dialog box	Home, Paragraph		
paste text	Home, Clipboard		Ctrl + V
shading	Home, Paragraph		
Sort Text dialog box	Home, Paragraph		
Tabs dialog box	Home, Paragraph	, Tabs	

CHAPTER 3

Review and Assessment

Skills Assessment

Assessment 1

Format and Sort an Adventure Tours Document

1. Open **Tours.docx** and then save it with the name **3-Tours**.
2. Move the insertion point to the end of the document and then type the text shown in Figure 3.11. (Type the > symbol and press the spacebar for the first item and the symbol will be formatted as an arrow bullet, and the bullet for each remaining item will be inserted automatically as you type.)
3. Select the four paragraphs below the heading *Tour Specials* and then apply numbered formatting.
4. Type the following paragraph of text between paragraphs 3 and 4 below the heading *Tour Specials*: 7-day tours beginning at $1,779 per person. ***Note: The new paragraph will be the fourth item in the numbered list.***
5. Select the nine paragraphs below the heading *European Tours* and then apply bulleted formatting. (Arrow bullets will be applied to the paragraphs.)
6. With the nine paragraphs still selected, sort the paragraphs in ascending order.
7. Move the insertion point to the beginning of the document and then apply the Shaded style set. (Click the Design tab to display style sets; you will need click the more style sets button to display this style set.)
8. Apply the Slice theme. (Click the Design tab to display the Theme button.)
9. Select the nine paragraphs below the heading *European Tours* and then apply Dark Green, Accent 4, Lighter 80% paragraph shading (eighth column, second row in the *Theme Colors* section) to the selected paragraphs.
10. Apply the same Dark Green, Accent 4, Lighter 80% paragraph shading to the five numbered paragraphs below the heading *TOUR SPECIALS* and the three bulleted paragraphs below the heading *TOP TOURS*.
11. Save, preview, and then close **3-Tours.docx**.

Figure 3.11 Assessment 1

➢ Taste of Italy
➢ Hallmarks of Europe
➢ Best of England

Assessment 2

Type Tabbed Text and Apply Formatting to a Computer Software Document

1. Open **ProdSoftware.docx** and then save it with the name **3-ProdSoftware**.
2. Move the insertion point to the end of the document and then set left tabs at the 0.75-inch, 2.75-inch, and 4.5-inch marks on the horizontal ruler. Type the text in Figure 3.12 at the tabs you set. Use the New Line command, Shift + Enter, after typing each line of text in columns (except the last line).
3. Apply the Retrospect theme.
4. Select the productivity software categories in the *Productivity Software* section (from *Word processing* through *Computer-aided design*) and then sort the text alphabetically.
5. With the text still selected, apply bulleted formatting. (Solid circle bullets will be applied to the text.)
6. Select the personal-use software categories in the *Personal-Use Software* section (from *Personal finance software* through *Games and entertainment software*) and then sort the text alphabetically in ascending order.
7. With the text still selected, apply bulleted formatting.
8. Apply to the heading *Productivity Software* a single-line top border and Olive Green, Text 2, Lighter 80% paragraph shading (fourth column, second row in the *Theme Colors* section).
9. Apply the same single-line top border and olive green shading to the other two headings (*Personal-Use Software* and *Software Training Schedule*).
10. Position the insertion point in the first line of tabbed text and then move the tab symbols on the horizontal ruler as follows:
    a. Move the tab at the 0.75-inch mark to the 1-inch mark.
    b. Move the tab at the 4.5-inch mark to the 4-inch mark.
11. Save, preview, and then close **3-ProdSoftware.docx**.

Figure 3.12 Assessment 2

Word	April 16	8:30 to 11:30 a.m.
PowerPoint	April 18	1:00 to 3:30 p.m.
Excel	May 14	8:30 to 11:30 a.m.
Access	May 16	1:00 to 3:30 p.m.

Assessment 3

Type and Format a Table of Contents Document

1. At a new blank document, type the document shown in Figure 3.13 with the following specifications:
    a. Change the font to 11-point Cambria.
    b. Apply bold formatting and center alignment to the title as shown.
    c. Before typing the tabbed text, display the Tabs dialog box. Set a left tab at the 1-inch mark and the 1.5-inch mark and a right tab with period leaders at the 5.5-inch mark.
    d. When typing the text, press the Enter key to end each line of text.
2. Save the document with the name **3-TofC**.
3. Preview **3-TofC.docx**.
4. Select the tabbed text and then make changes as follows. (Because you pressed the Enter key instead of Shift + Enter at the end of each line of text, you need to select all the tabbed text before moving the tabs.)

a. Delete the left tab symbol at the 1.5-inch mark.
b. Set a new left tab at the 0.5-inch mark.
c. Move the right tab at the 5.5-inch mark to the 6-inch mark.

5. Insert single-line borders above and below the title *TABLE OF CONTENTS*.
6. Apply Orange, Accent 2, Lighter 80% paragraph shading (sixth column, second row in the *Theme Colors* section) to the title *TABLE OF CONTENTS*.
7. Save, preview, and then close **3-TofC.docx**.

Figure 3.13 Assessment 3

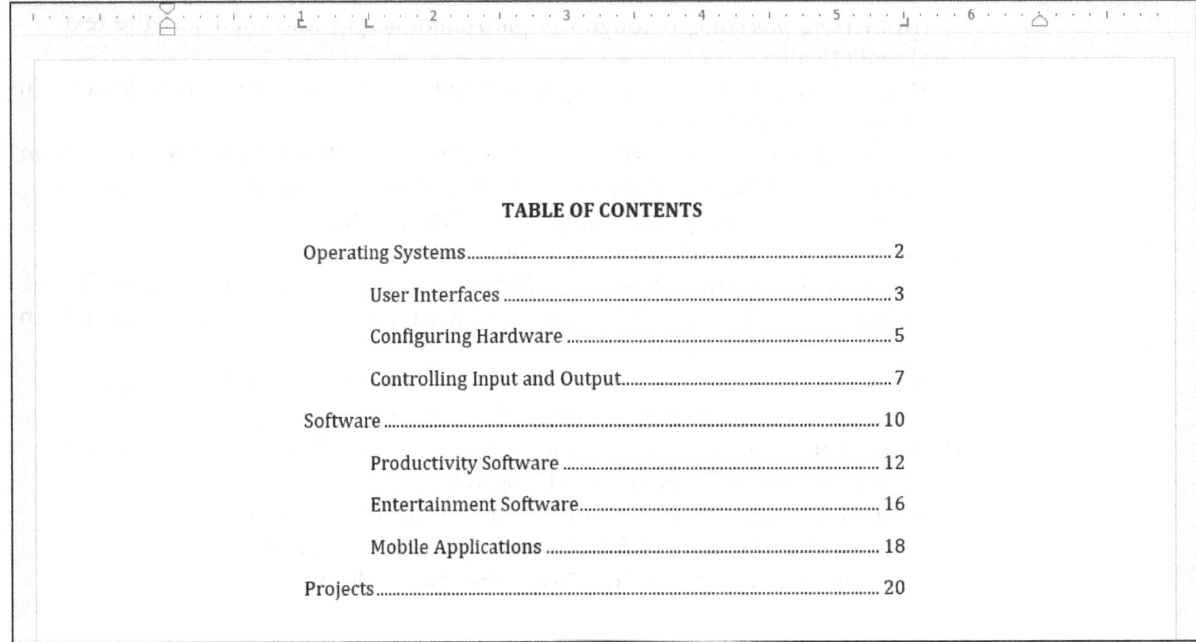

TABLE OF CONTENTS

Operating Systems	2
User Interfaces	3
Configuring Hardware	5
Controlling Input and Output	7
Software	10
Productivity Software	12
Entertainment Software	16
Mobile Applications	18
Projects	20

Assessment 4 Format a Building Construction Agreement Document

1. Open **ConstructAgrmnt.docx** and then save it with the name **3-ConstructAgrmnt**.
2. Select and then delete the paragraph that begins *SUPERVISION OF WORK*.
3. Move the paragraph that begins *FINANCE AGREEMENT* before the paragraph that begins *START OF CONSTRUCTION*.
4. Open **AgrmntItems.docx**.
5. Display the Clipboard task pane and then clear all the contents, if necessary.
6. Select and then copy the first paragraph.
7. Select and then copy the second paragraph.
8. Select and then copy the third paragraph.
9. Close **AgrmntItems.docx**.
10. With **3-ConstructAgrmnt.docx** open, display the Clipboard task pane.
11. Position the insertion point at the beginning of the *CHANGES AND ALTERATIONS* paragraph and then paste the *SUPERVISION* paragraph and merge the formatting.
12. Position the insertion point at the beginning of the *POSSESSION OF RESIDENCE* paragraph and then paste the *PAY REVIEW* paragraph and merge the formatting.
13. Clear all items from the Clipboard and then close the Clipboard task pane.
14. Save, preview, and then close **3-ConstructAgrmnt.docx**.

Assessment 5

Hyphenate Words in a Report

1. In some Word documents, especially documents with left and right margins wider than 1 inch, the right margin may appear quite ragged. If the paragraph alignment is changed to justified alignment, the right margin will appear even, but extra space will be added between words throughout the line. In these situations, hyphenating long words that fall at the ends of text lines provides the document with a more balanced look. Click the Layout tab and then explore the options available in the Hyphenation button drop-down list in the Page Setup group. Figure out how to automatically hyphenate words in a document and how to limit the number of consecutive hyphens using an option at the Hyphenation dialog box.
2. Open **Costumes.docx** and then save it with the name **3-Costumes**.
3. Automatically hyphenate words in the document, limiting the number of consecutive hyphens to two. ***Hint: Display the Hyphenation dialog box by clicking the Hyphenation button in the Page Setup group on the Layout tab and then clicking*** **Hyphenation Options*****.***
4. Save, preview, and then close **3-Costumes.docx**.

Visual Benchmark

Create a Resume

1. Open **Resume.docx** and then save it with the name **3-Resume**.
2. Apply character and paragraph formatting to the resume so it appears as shown in Figure 3.14.
3. Save, preview, and then close **3-Resume.docx**.

Figure 3.14 Visual Benchmark

DEVON CHAMBERS

344 North Anderson Road * Oklahoma City, OK 73177 * (404) 555-3228

PROFILE

Business manager with successful track record at entrepreneurial start-up and strong project management skills. Keen ability to motivate and supervise employees, a strong hands-on experience with customer service, marketing, and operations. Highly organized and motivated professional looking to leverage strengths in leadership and organizational skills in a project coordinator role.

PROFESSIONAL EXPERIENCE

Midwest Deli, Oklahoma City, OK .... 07/21 to present
Assistant Manager

- Coordinated the opening of a new business, which included budgeting start-up costs, establishing relationships with vendors, ordering supplies, purchasing and installing equipment, and marketing the business to the community
- Manage business personnel, which includes recruitment, interviewing, hiring, training, motivating staff, and resolving conflicts
- Manage daily business operations through customer satisfaction, quality control, employee scheduling, process improvement, and product inventory maintenance

Marin Associates, Shawnee, OK.. 06/19 to 06/21
Projects Coordinator

- Developed and maintained a secure office network and installed and repaired computers
- Provided support for hardware and software issues
- Directed agency projects such as equipment purchases, office reorganization, and building maintenance and repair

Moore Insurance Agency, Shawnee, OK.. 04/17 to 05/19
Administrative Assistant

- Prepared documents and forms for staff and clients
- Organized and maintained paper and electronic files and scheduled meetings and appointments
- Disseminated information using the telephone, mail services, websites, and email

EDUCATION

Associate of Arts, Business 2021
Oklahoma City Community College

TECHNOLOGY SKILLS

- Proficient in Microsoft Word, Excel, and PowerPoint
- Knowledgeable in current and previous versions of the Windows operating system
- Experience with networking, firewalls, and security systems

REFERENCES

Professional and personal references available upon request.

Case Study

Part 1

You are the assistant to Gina Coletti, manager of La Dolce Vita, an Italian restaurant. She has been working on updating and formatting the lunch menu. She has asked you to complete the menu by opening **Menu.docx**, determining how the appetizer section is formatted, and then applying the same formatting to the sections *Soups and Salads*; *Sandwiches, Calzones, and Burgers*; and *Individual Pizzas*. Save the document with the name **3-Menu**. Preview and then close the document.

Part 2

Ms. Coletti has reviewed the completed menu and is pleased with it, but she wants to add a border around the entire page to increase visual interest. Open **3-Menu.docx** and then save it with the name **3-MenuPgBorder**. Display the Borders and Shading dialog box with the Page Border tab selected and then experiment with the options available. Apply an appropriate page border to the menu. (Consider applying an art image border.) Save, preview, and then close **3-MenuPgBorder.docx**.

Part 3

Each week, the restaurant offers daily specials. Ms. Coletti has asked you to create a new menu for specials using the text in **MenuSpecials.docx**. She has asked you to format the specials menu in a similar manner as the main menu, but to change some elements to make it unique. Make the formatting changes, and then apply the same page border to the specials menu document that you applied to the main menu document. Save the document with the name **3-MenuSpecials**. Preview and then close the document.

Part 4

You have been asked by the head chef to research a new recipe for an Italian dish. Using the internet, find a recipe that interests you and then prepare a Word document containing the recipe steps and ingredients. Bullet the items in the list of ingredients and number the steps in the recipe preparation. Save the document with the name **3-Recipe**. Preview and then close the document.

WORD

Formatting Pages and Documents

CHAPTER 4

Performance Objectives

Upon successful completion of Chapter 4, you will be able to:

1. Change margins, page orientation, and paper size
2. Format pages at the Page Setup dialog box
3. Insert a page break, blank page, and cover page
4. Insert and remove page numbers
5. Insert and edit predesigned headers and footers
6. Insert a watermark, page background color, and page border
7. Insert section breaks
8. Create and format text in columns
9. Hyphenate words automatically and manually
10. Create a drop cap
11. Use the Click and Type feature
12. Vertically align text
13. Find and replace text

Word provides a number of options for changing the layout of a document, such as adjusting page margins, orientation, and paper size. Word also includes features that can be inserted in a document, such as a page break, blank page, cover page, and watermark, as well as page numbers, headers, footers, page color, and page borders. You will learn about these features in this chapter along with other page and document formatting options, such as inserting section breaks, formatting text into columns, hyphenating words, creating a drop cap, and vertically aligning text. You will also learn how to find and replace text in a document.

Data Files

The data files for this chapter are in the WL1C4 folder that you downloaded at the beginning of this course.

Activity 1 Format a Document on Photography — 2 Parts

You will open a document containing information on photography and then change the margins, page orientation, and paper size.

Changing Page Setup

The Page Setup group on the Layout tab contains a number of options for changing the layout of pages in a document. Use options in the Page Setup group to perform such actions as changing margins, orientation, and paper size and inserting page breaks. The Pages group on the Insert tab contains three buttons for inserting a cover page, blank page, or page break.

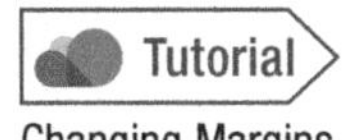

Changing Margins

Changing Margins

A page in a Word document, by default, has a one-inch top, bottom, left, and right margin. Situations may occur where these margins may need to be increased to allow space for binding a document, room in the margins for making notes or inserting objects, or decreased to allow for more text on the page.

Margins

Change page margins with options at the Margins button drop-down list, as shown in Figure 4.1. To display this drop-down list, click the Layout tab and then click the Margins button in the Page Setup group. To change the margins, click one of the preset margins in the drop-down list. Be aware that most printers require a minimum margin (between ¼ and ⅜ inch) because they cannot print to the edge of the page.

Quick Steps

Change Margins

1. Click Layout tab.
2. Click Margins button.
3. Click margin option.

Change Page Orientation

1. Click Layout tab.
2. Click Orientation button.
3. Click *Portrait* or *Landscape*.

Change Paper Size

1. Click Layout tab.
2. Click Size button.
3. Click paper size.

Figure 4.1 Margins Button Drop-Down List

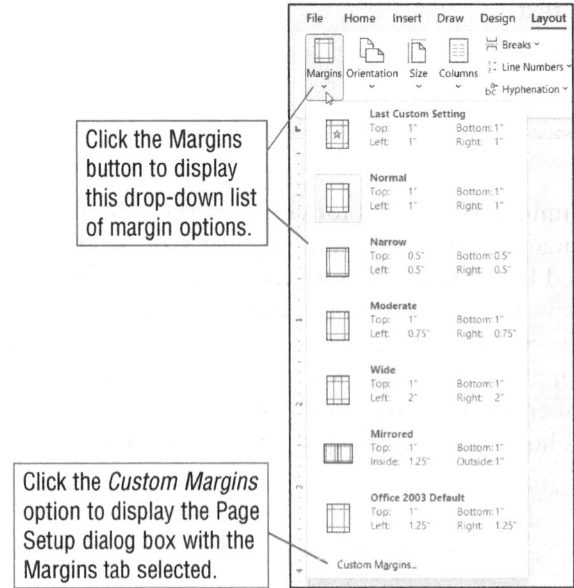

Changing Page Orientation

Changing Page Orientation

Click the Orientation button in the Page Setup group on the Layout tab and two options display: *Portrait* and *Landscape*. At the portrait orientation, which is the default, the page is 8.5 inches wide and 11 inches tall. At the landscape orientation, the page is 11 inches wide and 8.5 inches tall. Change the page orientation and the page margins automatically shift: The left and right margin measurements become the top and bottom margin measurements.

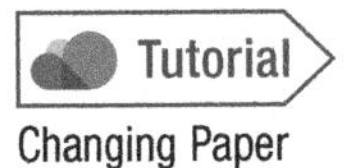

Changing Paper Size

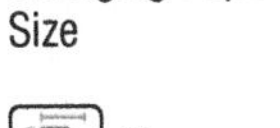

Changing Paper Size

By default, Word formats documents for printing on standard letter-sized paper that is 8.5 inches wide and 11 inches tall. Change this default setting with options at the Size button drop-down list. Display this drop-down list by clicking the Size button in the Page Setup group on the Layout tab.

Activity 1a Changing Margins, Page Orientation, and Paper Size — Part 1 of 2

1. Open **Photography.docx** and then save it with the name **4-Photography**.
2. Click the Layout tab.
3. Click the Margins button in the Page Setup group and then click the *Narrow* option.

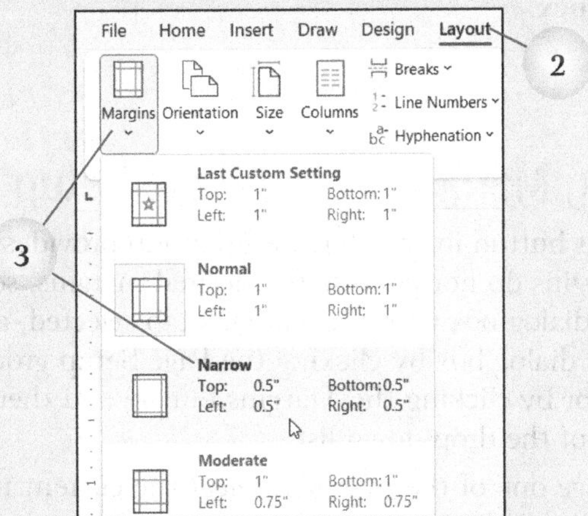

4. Click the Orientation button in the Page Setup group and then click *Landscape* at the drop-down list.

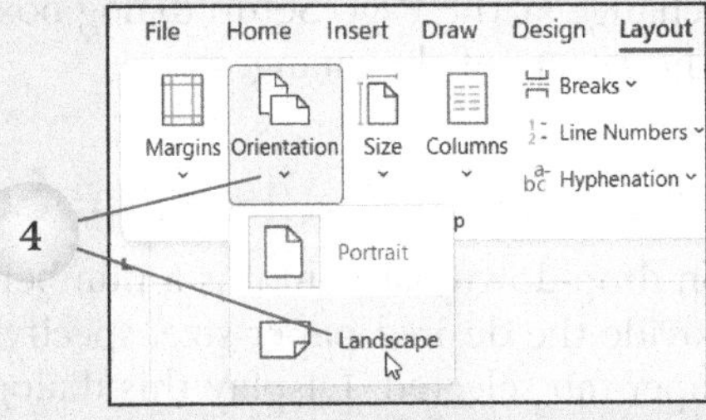

5. Scroll through the document and notice how the text displays on the page in landscape orientation.
6. Click the Orientation button in the Page Setup group and then click *Portrait* at the drop-down list. (This changes the orientation back to the default.)

7. Click the Size button in the Page Setup group and then click the *Executive* option (*7.25" × 10.5"*). Paper size options may vary. If this option is not available, choose an option with a similar paper size.

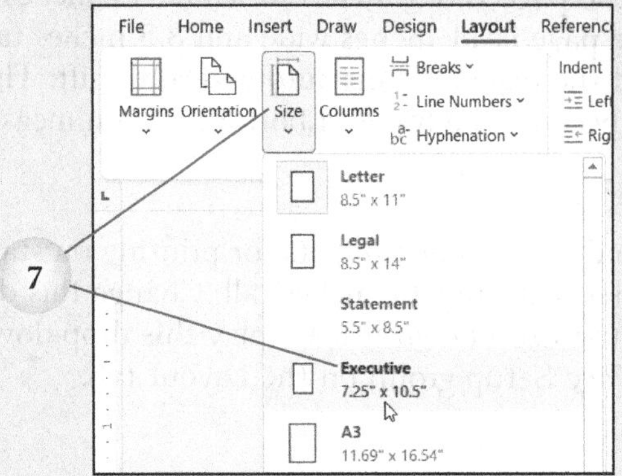

8. Scroll through the document and notice how the text displays on the page.
9. Click the Size button and then click *Legal* (*8.5" × 14"*).
10. Scroll through the document and notice how the text displays on the page.
11. Click the Size button and then click *Letter* (*8.5" × 11"*). (This returns the size back to the default.)
12. Save **4-Photography.docx**.

Changing Margins at the Page Setup Dialog Box

Quick Steps

Change Margins at Page Setup Dialog Box

1. Click Layout tab.
2. Click Page Setup group dialog box launcher.

OR

1. Click Layout tab.
2. Click Margins button.
3. Click *Custom Margins*.
4. Specify margins.
5. Click OK.

Change Paper Size at Page Setup Dialog Box

1. Click Layout tab.
2. Click Size button.
3. Click *More Paper Sizes*.
4. Specify size.
5. Click OK.

The Margins button in the Page Setup group provides a number of preset margins. If these margins do not provide the desired margins, set specific margins at the Page Setup dialog box with the Margins tab selected, as shown in Figure 4.2. Display this dialog box by clicking the Page Setup group dialog box launcher on the Layout tab or by clicking the Margins button and then clicking *Custom Margins* at the bottom of the drop-down list.

To change one of the margins, select the current measurement in the *Top*, *Bottom*, *Left*, or *Right* measurement box and then type the new measurement, or click the measurement box up arrow to increase the measurement or the measurement box down arrow to decrease the measurement. As the margin measurements change at the Page Setup dialog box, the sample page in the *Preview* section shows the effects of the changes.

Changing Paper Size at the Page Setup Dialog Box

The Size button drop-down list contains a number of preset paper sizes. If these sizes do not provide the desired paper size, specify a size at the Page Setup dialog box with the Paper tab selected. Display this dialog box by clicking the Size button in the Page Setup group and then clicking *More Paper Sizes* at the bottom of the drop-down list.

Figure 4.2 Page Setup Dialog Box with the Margins Tab Selected

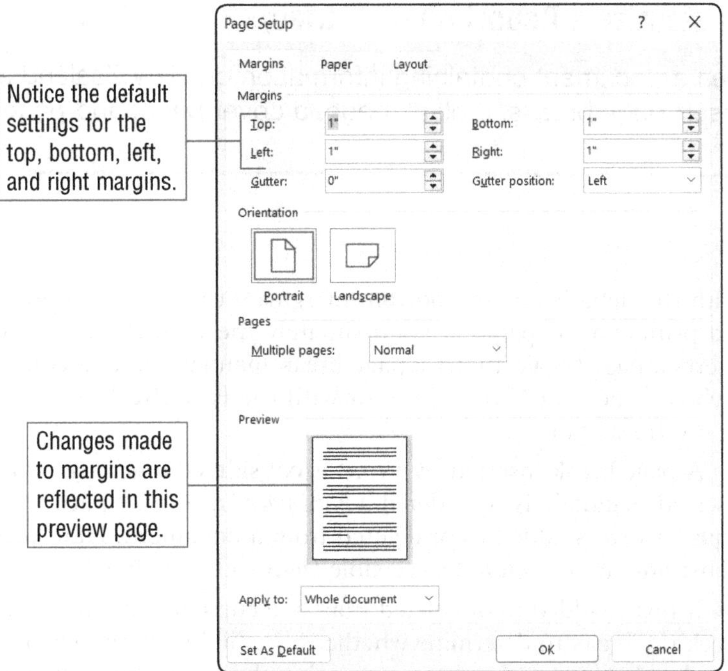

Activity 1b Changing Margins and Paper Size at the Page Setup Dialog Box

Part 2 of 2

1. With **4-Photography.docx** open, make sure the Layout tab is selected.
2. Click the Page Setup group dialog box launcher.
3. At the Page Setup dialog box with the Margins tab selected, click the *Top* measurement box up arrow until *0.7"* displays.
4. Click the *Bottom* measurement box up arrow until *0.7"* displays.
5. Select the current measurement in the *Left* measurement box and then type 0.75.
6. Select the current measurement in the *Right* measurement box and then type 0.75.
7. Click OK to close the dialog box.
8. Click the Size button in the Page Setup group and then click *More Paper Sizes* at the drop-down list.
9. At the Page Setup dialog box with the Paper tab selected, click the *Paper size* option box arrow and then click *Legal* at the drop-down list.
10. Click OK to close the dialog box.
11. Scroll through the document and notice how the text displays on the page.
12. Click the Size button in the Page Setup group and then click *Letter* at the drop-down list.
13. Save, preview, and then close **4-Photography.docx**.

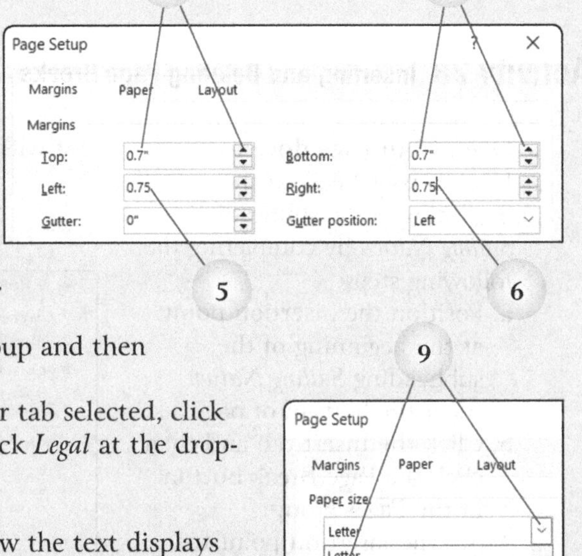

Check Your Work

Activity 2 Customize a Report on Countries 3 Parts

You will open a document containing information on New Zealand and Australia and then insert page breaks, a blank page, a cover page, and page numbers.

Inserting and Deleting a Page Break

Page Break

Inserting and Deleting a Page Break

With the default top and bottom margins set at 1 inch, approximately 9 inches of text prints on the page. At approximately the 10-inch mark, Word automatically inserts a page break. Insert a page break manually in a document with the keyboard shortcut Ctrl + Enter or with the Page Break button in the Pages group on the Insert tab.

A page break inserted by Word is considered a *soft page break* and a page break inserted manually is considered a *hard page break*. Soft page breaks automatically adjust if text is added to or deleted from a document. Hard page breaks do not adjust and are therefore less flexible than soft page breaks.

Quick Steps

Insert Page Break
1. Click Insert tab.
2. Click Page Break button.

OR

Press Ctrl + Enter.

Show/Hide ¶

If text is added to or deleted from a document containing a hard page break, check the break to determine whether it is still in a desirable location. Display a hard page break, along with other nonprinting characters, by clicking the Show/Hide ¶ button in the Paragraph group on the Home tab. A hard page break displays as a row of dots with the words *Page Break* in the center. To delete a hard page break, position the insertion point at the beginning of the page break and then press the Delete key or double-click the words *Page Break* and then press the Delete key. If the display of nonprinting characters is turned off, delete a hard page break by positioning the insertion point immediately below the page break and then pressing the Backspace key.

Activity 2a Inserting and Deleting Page Breaks Part 1 of 3

1. Open **Countries.docx** and then save it with the name **4-Countries**.
2. Insert a page break at the beginning of the subheading *Sailing Nation* by completing the following steps:
   a. Position the insertion point at the beginning of the subheading *Sailing Nation* (near the bottom of page 1).
   b. Click the Insert tab and then click the Page Break button in the Pages group.

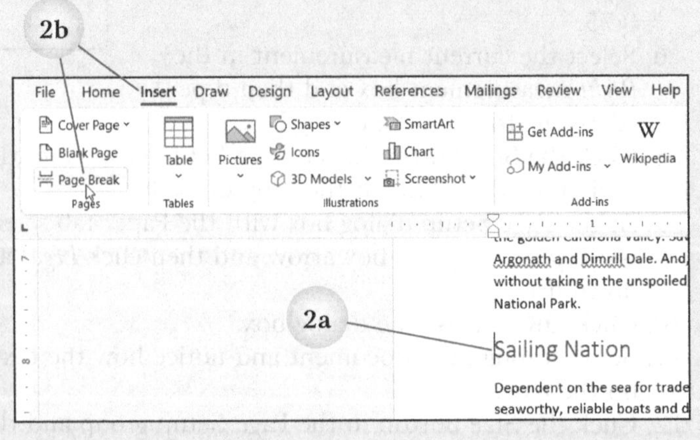

3. Move the insertion point to the beginning of the heading *AUSTRALIA* (on the second page) and then insert a page break by pressing Ctrl + Enter.

4. Delete a page break by completing the following steps:
   a. Move the insertion point to the end of the second paragraph in the *Nature* section (at the end of page 1).
   b. Click the Home tab.
   c. Turn on the display of nonprinting characters by clicking the Show/Hide ¶ button in the Paragraph group.
   d. Position the insertion point at the beginning of the page break.
   e. Press the Delete key two times.
   f. Click the Show/Hide ¶ button to turn off the display of nonprinting characters.
5. Save **4-Countries.docx**.

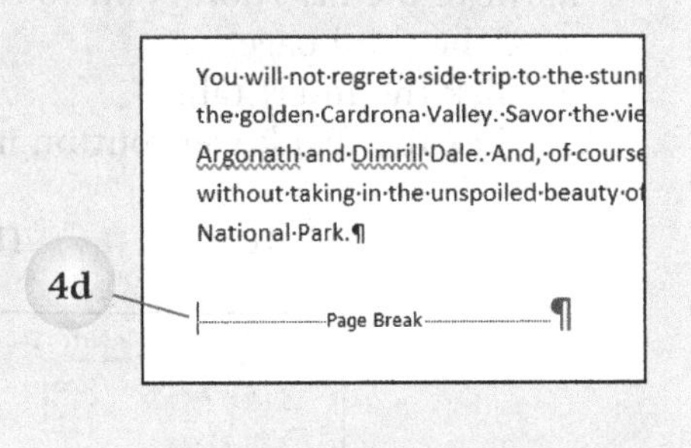

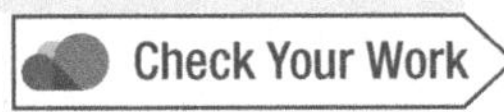

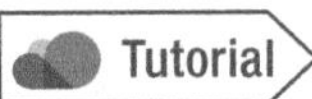

Inserting and Removing a Blank Page

Blank Page

Inserting and Removing a Blank Page

Click the Blank Page button in the Pages group on the Insert tab to insert a blank page at the position of the insertion point. This might be useful in a document where a blank page is needed for an illustration, graphic, or figure. When a blank page is inserted, Word inserts a page break and then inserts another page break to create the blank page. To remove a blank page, turn on the display of nonprinting characters and then delete the page breaks.

Tutorial

Inserting and Removing a Cover Page

Cover Page

Inserting and Removing a Cover Page

An educational paper, such as a report, thesis, or dissertation or a scientific or professional paper, may include a cover page that introduces the document by including a title, subtitle, image, abstract, or other elements. Word provides several predesigned cover pages. Click the Cover Page button in the Pages group on the Insert tab and a drop-down list displays with visual representations of the cover pages. Scroll through the list and then click a cover page option.

A predesigned cover page contains location placeholders, in which specific text is entered. For example, a cover page might contain the placeholder *[Document title]*. Click the placeholder to select it and then type the title of the document. Delete a placeholder by clicking to select it, clicking the placeholder tab, and then pressing the Delete key. Remove a cover page by clicking the Cover Page button and then clicking *Remove Current Cover Page* at the drop-down list.

Quick Steps

Insert Blank Page
1. Click Insert tab.
2. Click Blank Page button.

Insert Cover Page
1. Click Insert tab.
2. Click Cover Page button.
3. Click cover page option.

Hint Adding a cover page gives a document a polished and professional look.

Activity 2b Inserting and Removing a Blank Page and Inserting a Cover Page

1. With **4-Countries.docx** open, create a blank page by completing the following steps:
   a. Move the insertion point to the beginning of the heading *AUSTRALIA* at the beginning of the third page.
   b. Click the Insert tab.
   c. Click the Blank Page button in the Pages group.

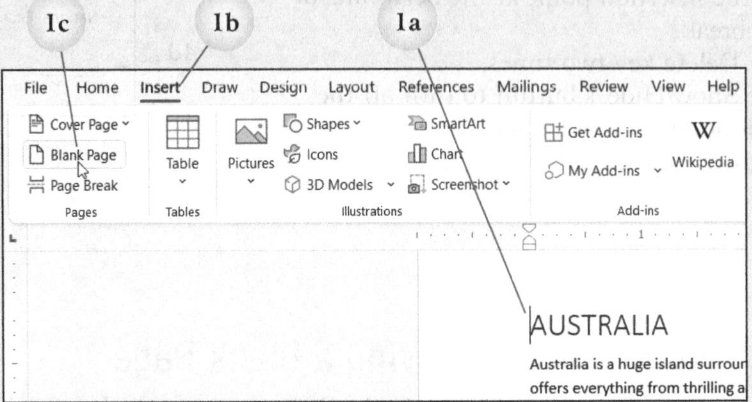

2. Insert a cover page by completing the following steps:
   a. Press Ctrl + Home to move the insertion point to the beginning of the document.
   b. Click the Cover Page button in the Pages group.
   c. Scroll down the drop-down list and then click the *Banded* option.

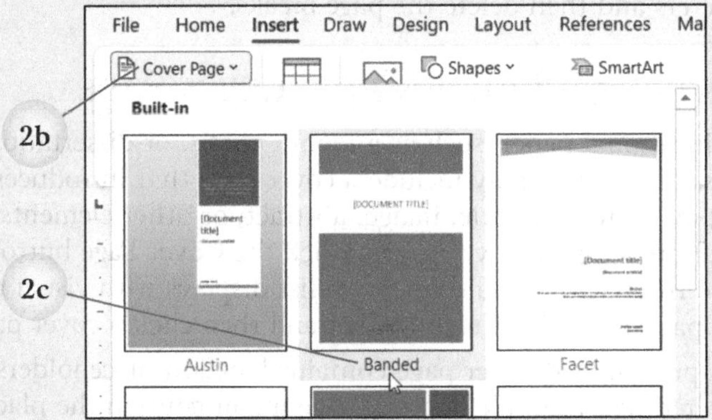

   d. Click the *[DOCUMENT TITLE]* placeholder and then type south pacific countries. (The text you type will display in uppercase letters.)

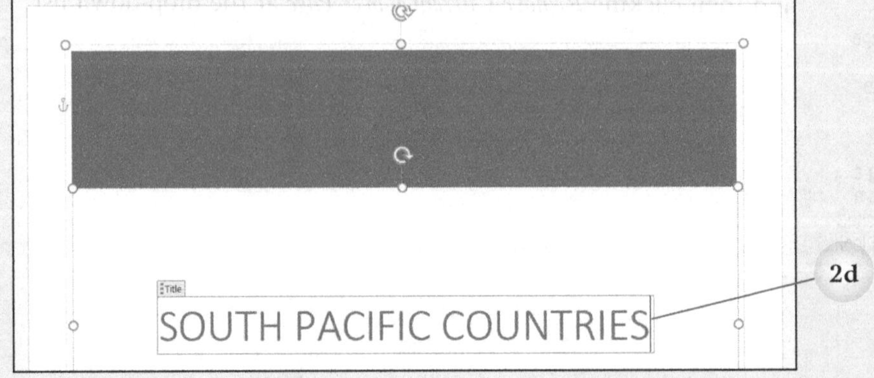

e. Click the *[COMPANY NAME]* placeholder and then type premier college. (The text you type will display in uppercase letters.) (If a name appears in the placeholder, select the name and then type premier college.)
f. Select the name above the company name and then type your first and last names. If instead of a name, the *[Author name]* placeholder displays above the company name, click the placeholder and then type your first and last names.

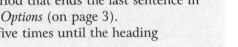

3. Delete the [Company address] placeholder by completing the following steps:
   a. Click the *[Company address]* placeholder.
   b. Click the *Address* placeholder tab.
   c. Press the Delete key.

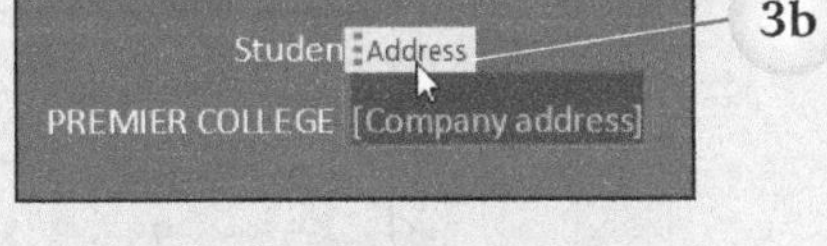

4. Remove the blank page you inserted in Step 1 by completing the following steps:
   a. Move the insertion point immediately right of the period that ends the last sentence in the paragraph of text below the subheading *Transport Options* (on page 3).
   b. Press the Delete key on the keyboard approximately five times until the heading *AUSTRALIA* displays on page 3.
5. Save **4-Countries.docx**.

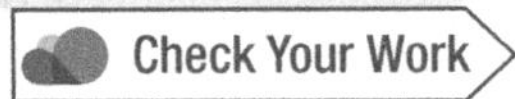

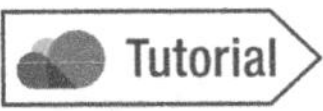

Inserting and Removing Page Numbers

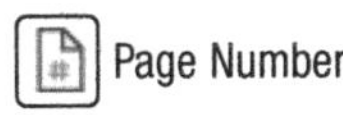

Quick Steps
Insert Page Numbers
1. Click Insert tab.
2. Click Page Number button.
3. Click number option.

Inserting and Removing Page Numbers

Word by default does not include page numbers on pages. Consider inserting page numbers in a document to help readers find specific parts of a document, know the size of the complete text by checking the last page number, and to allow for citations of particular pages.

To insert page numbers in a document, click the Page Number button in the Header & Footer group on the Insert tab. A drop-down list displays with options for placing page numbers in the top margin of the page (in the Header pane), in the bottom margin of the page (in the Footer pane), in a page margin (either in a Header or Footer pane), or at the location of the insertion point. Click or point to an option and a drop-down list will appear showing several predesigned page number formats. Scroll through the list and then click an option.

Choose a page number option other than *Current Position*, and the Header and Footer panes open. Changes can be made to the page numbering format in the Header pane or Footer pane. To do this, select the page number and then apply formatting, such as a different font size, style, or color. A page number inserted in a document with the *Current Position* option is positioned in the document, not in the Header or Footer pane. Format the page number like any other text in the document.

After formatting page numbers inserted in the Header or Footer pane, click the Close Header and Footer button, or simply double-click anywhere in the document outside the Header or Footer pane. Remove page numbers from the document by clicking the Page Number button in the Header & Footer group and then clicking *Remove Page Numbers* at the drop-down list.

Activity 2c Inserting and Removing Predesigned Page Numbers

Part 3 of 3

1. With **4-Countries.docx** open, insert page numbers by completing the following steps:
   a. Move the insertion point so it is positioned anywhere in the heading *NEW ZEALAND*.
   b. If necessary, click the Insert tab.
   c. Click the Page Number button in the Header & Footer group and then point to *Top of Page*.
   d. Scroll through the drop-down list and then click the *Brackets 2* option.

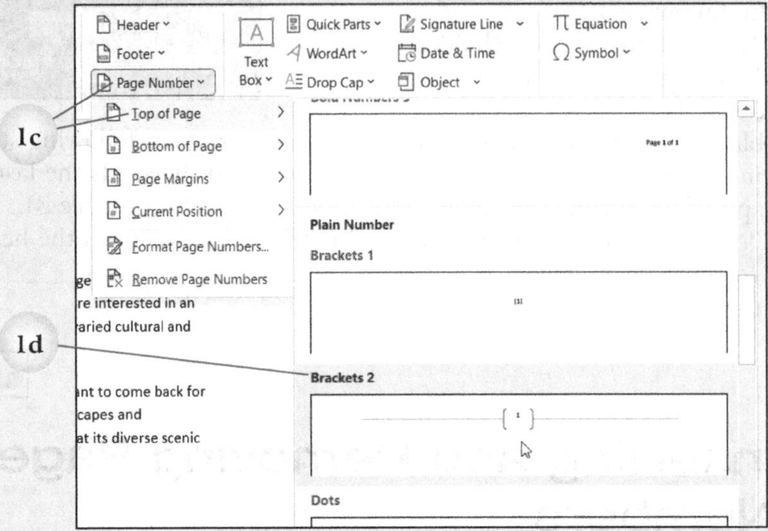

   e. Click the Close Header and Footer button in the Close group on the Header & Footer tab.
2. Scroll through the document and notice the page numbers at the top of each page except the cover page. (The cover page and text are divided by a page break. Word does not include the cover page when numbering pages.)
3. Remove the page numbering by clicking the Insert tab, clicking the Page Number button, and then clicking *Remove Page Numbers* at the drop-down list.
4. Click the Page Number button, point to *Bottom of Page*, scroll down the drop-down list, and then click the *Accent Bar 2* option.

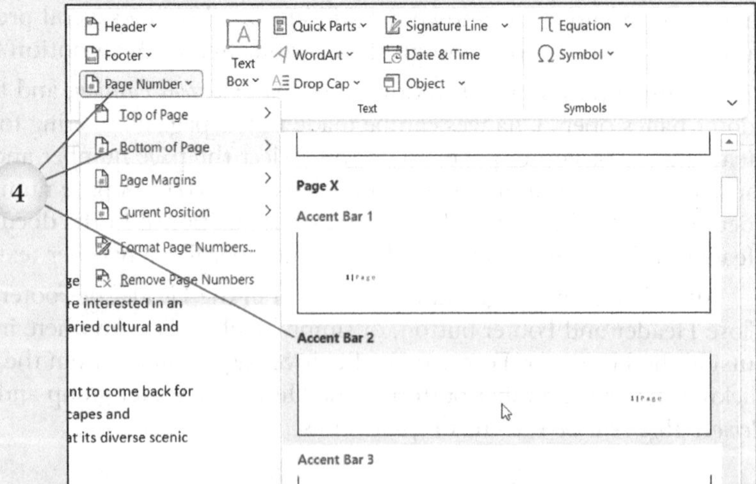

5. Click the Close Header and Footer button.
6. Save, preview, and then close **4-Countries.docx**.

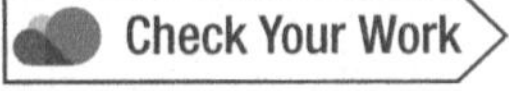

Activity 3 Add Elements to a Report on the Writing Process — 3 Parts

You will open a document containing information on the process of writing effectively, insert a predesigned header and footer, remove a header, and format and delete header and footer elements.

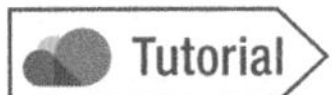

Tutorial

Inserting and Removing a Predesigned Header and Footer

Inserting Predesigned Headers and Footers

As mentioned in the last section, text that appears in the top margin of a page is called a *header* and text that appears in the bottom margin of a page is referred to as a *footer*. Headers and footers are common in manuscripts, textbooks, reports, and other publications. They typically include page numbers and other information, such as the author's name, the title of the publication, and/or the chapter title.

Header

Quick Steps

Insert Predesigned Header or Footer

1. Click Insert tab.
2. Click Header button or Footer button.
3. Click header or footer option.
4. Type text in specific placeholders in header or footer.
5. Click Close Header and Footer button.

Insert a predesigned header in a document by clicking the Insert tab and then clicking the Header button in the Header & Footer group. This displays the Header button drop-down list. At this drop-down list, click a predesigned header option and the header is inserted in the document.

A predesigned header or footer may contain location placeholders, such as [Document title] or [Type here]. Click in the placeholder text to select it and type the title of the document or other personalized text. Delete a placeholder by clicking to select it and then pressing the Delete key. If the placeholder contains a tab, delete the placeholder by clicking the placeholder tab and then pressing the Delete key.

To return to the document after inserting a header or footer, double-click in the document outside the Header or Footer pane or click the Close Header and Footer button.

Activity 3a Inserting a Predesigned Header — Part 1 of 3

1. Open **WritingProcess.docx** and then save it with the name **4-WritingProcess**.
2. With the insertion point positioned at the beginning of the document, insert a header by completing the following steps:
   a. If necessary, click the Insert tab.
   b. Click the Header button in the Header & Footer group.
   c. Scroll to the bottom of the drop-down list and then click the *Sideline* option.

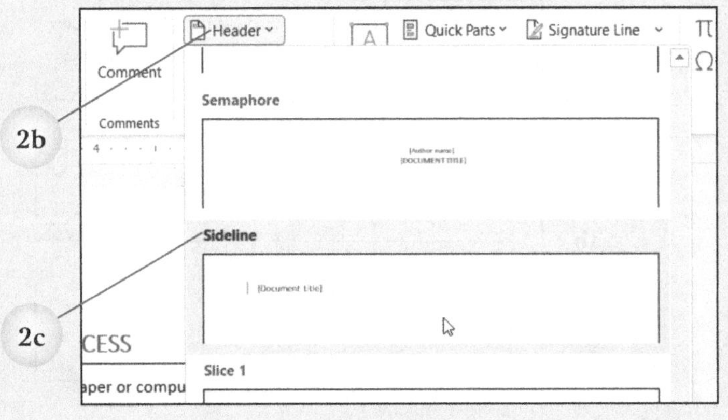

d. Click the *[Document title]* placeholder and then type The Writing Process.
e. Double-click in the document text. (This makes the document text active and dims the header.)
5. Scroll through the document to see how the header will print.
6. Save and then preview **4-WritingProcess.docx**.

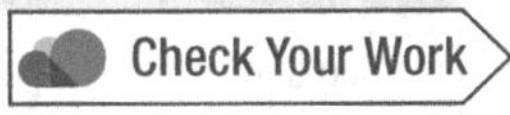

Insert a predesigned footer in the same manner as a header. Click the Footer button in the Header & Footer group on the Insert tab and a drop-down list displays that is similar to the Header button drop-down list. Click a footer and the predesigned footer is inserted in the document.

Removing a Header or Footer

Remove a header from a document by clicking the Insert tab and then clicking the Header button in the Header & Footer group. At the drop-down list, click the *Remove Header* option. Complete similar steps to remove a footer.

Activity 3b Removing a Header and Inserting a Predesigned Footer — Part 2 of 3

1. With **4-WritingProcess.docx** open, press Ctrl + Home to move the insertion point to the beginning of the document.
2. Remove the header by clicking the Insert tab, clicking the Header button in the Header & Footer group, and then clicking the *Remove Header* option at the drop-down list.
3. Insert a footer in the document by completing the following steps:
   a. Click the Footer button in the Header & Footer group.
   b. Scroll down the drop-down list and then click *Ion (Light)*.

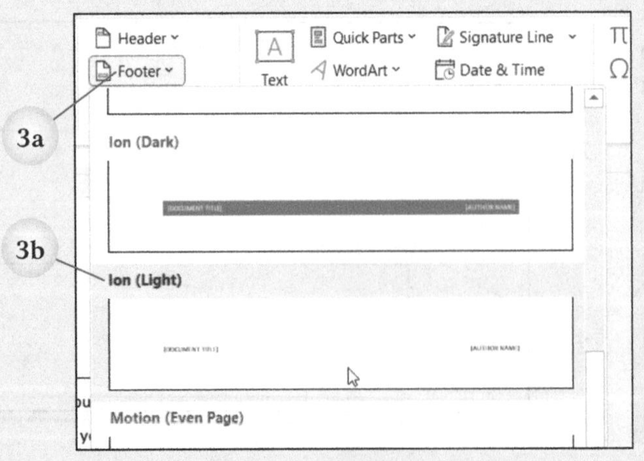

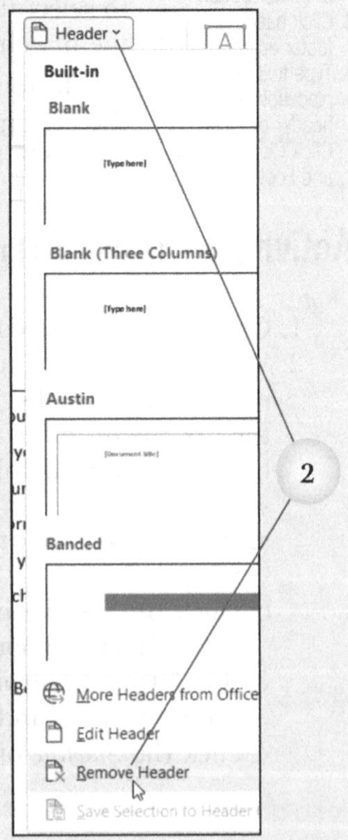

c. Notice that Word inserted the document title at the left side of the footer. (Word remembered the document title you entered in the header.) Word also inserted your name at the right side of the footer. If the document title does not appear, click the *[DOCUMENT TITLE]* placeholder and then type THE WRITING PROCESS. If your name does not appear, click the *[AUTHOR NAME]* placeholder and then type your first and last names.

d. Click the Close Header and Footer button to close the Footer pane and return to the document.

4. Scroll through the document to see how the footer will print.
5. Save and then preview **4-WritingProcess.docx**.

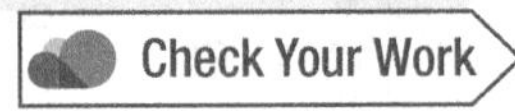

Editing a Predesigned Header or Footer

Predesigned headers and footers contain elements such as page numbers, a title, and an author's name. The formatting of an element can be changed by clicking the element and then applying formatting. Delete an element from a header or footer by selecting the element and then pressing the Delete key.

Activity 3c Formatting and Deleting Header and Footer Elements — Part 3 of 3

1. With **4-WritingProcess.docx** open, remove the footer by clicking the Insert tab, clicking the Footer button, and then clicking *Remove Footer* at the drop-down list.
2. Insert and then format a header by completing the following steps:
   a. Click the Header button in the Header & Footer group on the Insert tab, scroll down the drop-down list, and then click *Grid*. (This header inserts the document title and a date placeholder.)
   b. Delete the date placeholder by clicking the *[Date]* placeholder, clicking the placeholder tab, and then pressing the Delete key.
   c. Click the Close Header and Footer button.
3. Insert and then format a footer by completing the following steps:
   a. Click the Insert tab.
   b. Click the Footer button, scroll down the drop-down list, and then click *Retrospect*.
   c. Select the name in the author placeholder at the left side of the footer and then type your first and last names.
   d. Select your name and the page number, apply bold formatting, and then change the font size to 10 points.
   e. Double-click in the document text.
4. Scroll through the document to see how the header and footer will print.
5. Save, preview, and then close **4-WritingProcess.docx**.

Activity 4 Format a Report on Desirable Employee Qualities — 2 Parts

You will open a document containing information on desirable employee qualities and then insert a watermark, change the page background color, and insert a page border.

Quick Steps

Insert Watermark
1. Click Design tab.
2. Click Watermark button.
3. Click watermark option.

Apply Page Background Color
1. Click Design tab.
2. Click Page Color button.
3. Click color option.

Formatting the Page Background

The Page Background group on the Design tab contains three buttons for customizing the page background. Click the Watermark button and choose a predesigned watermark from options at the drop-down list. If a document will be shared electronically or published online, consider adding a page background color with the Page Color button. Use the Page Borders button to apply a border to the background of a page. Customize the style of the page border by using options in the Borders and Shading dialog box.

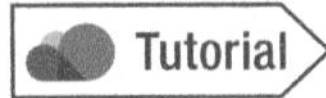

Inserting and Removing a Watermark

Watermark

Inserting a Watermark

A watermark is a lightened image that displays behind the text in a document. Use a watermark to add visual appeal or to identify a document as a draft, sample, or confidential document. Word provides a number of predesigned watermarks. View watermark options by clicking the Watermark button in the Page Background group on the Design tab. Scroll through the list and then click an option.

Applying a Page Background Color

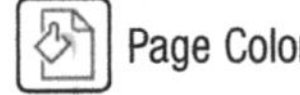

Page Color

Applying a Page Background Color

Use the Page Color button in the Page Background group on the Design tab to apply a background color to a document. This background color is intended for documents that will be viewed on-screen or online, as color is visible on the screen but does not print. Insert a page color by clicking the Page Color button and then clicking a color at the drop-down color palette.

Activity 4a Inserting and Removing a Watermark and Applying a Page Background Color — Part 1 of 2

1. Open **EmpQualities.docx** and then save it with the name **4-EmpQualities**.
2. Insert a watermark by completing the following steps:
   a. With the insertion point positioned at the beginning of the document, click the Design tab.
   b. Click the Watermark button in the Page Background group.
   c. At the drop-down list, click the *CONFIDENTIAL 1* option.
3. Scroll through the document and notice how the watermark displays behind the text.

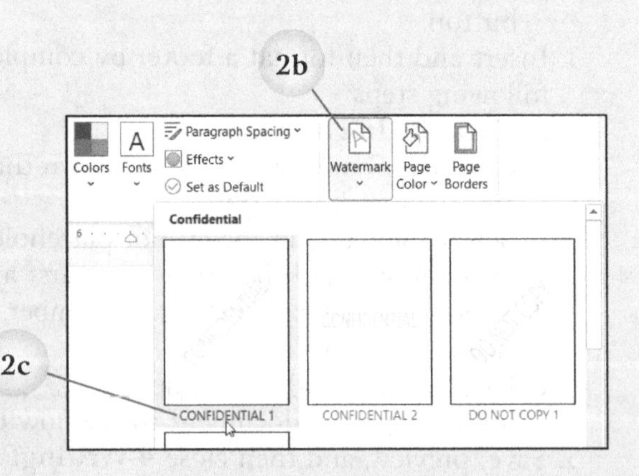

4. Remove the watermark and insert a different one by completing the following steps:
   a. Click the Watermark button and then click *Remove Watermark* at the drop-down list.
   b. Click the Watermark button and then click the *DO NOT COPY 1* option at the drop-down list.
5. Scroll through the document and notice how the watermark displays.
6. Move the insertion point to the beginning of the document.
7. Click the Page Color button in the Page Background group and then click the *Gray, Accent 3, Lighter 80%* option (seventh column, second row in the *Theme Colors* section).
8. Save **4-EmpQualities.docx**.

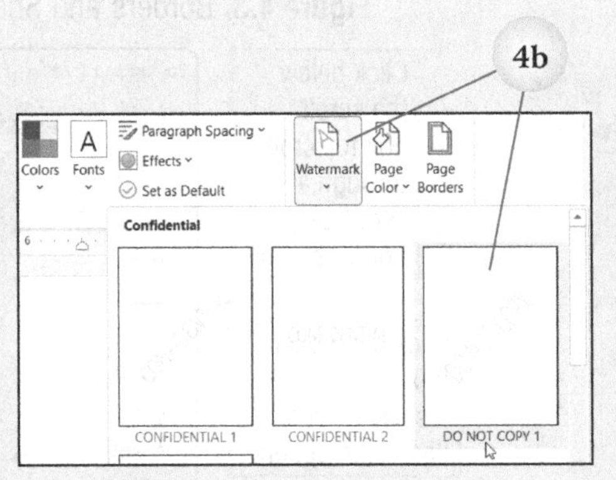

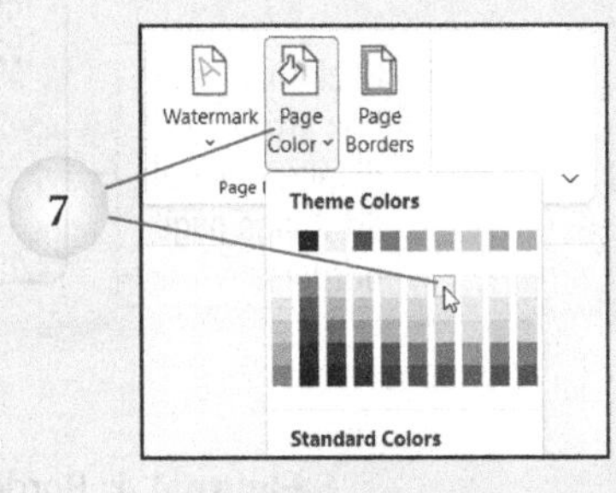

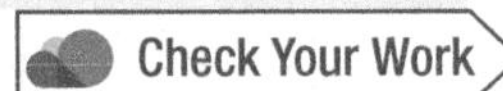

Inserting a Page Border

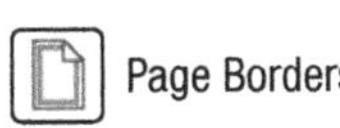

Quick Steps

Insert Page Border

1. Click Design tab.
2. Click Page Borders button.
3. Specify options at dialog box.
4. Click OK.

Inserting a Page Border

To improve the visual interest of a document, make the text stand out, or to make a document look finished, consider inserting a page border. When a page border is inserted in a multiple-page document, it prints on each page. To insert a page border, click the Page Borders button in the Page Background group on the Design tab. This displays the Borders and Shading dialog box with the Page Border tab selected, as shown in Figure 4.3 on the next page. At this dialog box, specify the border style, color, and width.

The dialog box contains an option for inserting a page border containing an art image. To display the images available, click the *Art* option box arrow and then scroll through the drop-down list. Click an image to insert the art image page border in the document.

Changing Page Border Options

By default, a page border appears and prints 24 points from the top, left, right, and bottom edges of the page. Some printers, particularly inkjet printers, have a nonprinting area around the outside edges of the page that can interfere with the printing of a border. Before printing a document with a page border, click the File tab and then click the *Print* option. Look at the preview of the page at the right side of the Print backstage area and determine whether the entire border is visible. If a portion of the border is not visible in the preview page (generally at the bottom and right sides of the page), consider changing measurements at the Border and Shading Options dialog box, shown in Figure 4.4 on the next page.

Figure 4.3 Borders and Shading Dialog Box with the Page Border Tab Selected

Click below the scroll box to scroll through a list of page border styles.

Click this option box arrow to display a list of line width options.

Click this option box arrow to display a list of art image page borders.

Preview the page border in this section.

Click this option box arrow to display a palette of page border colors.

Click this button to display the Border and Shading Options dialog box.

Figure 4.4 Border and Shading Options Dialog Box

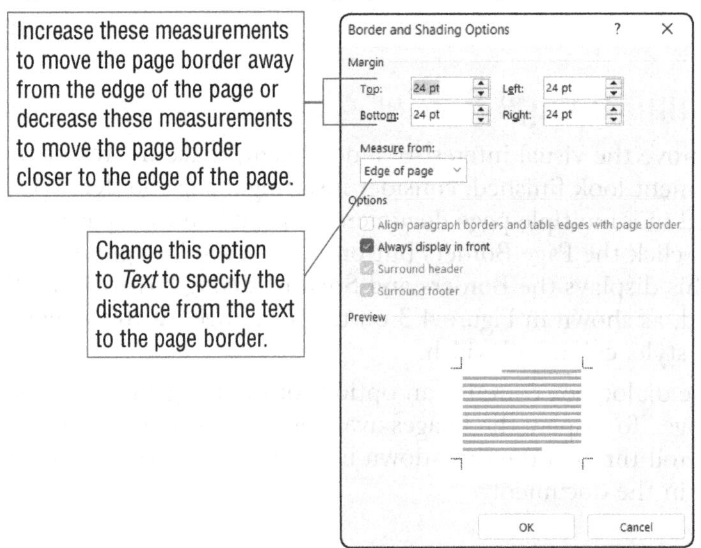

Display the Border and Shading Options dialog box by clicking the Design tab and then clicking the Page Borders button. At the Borders and Shading dialog box with the Page Border tab selected, click the Options button in the lower right corner of the dialog box. The options at the Border and Shading Options dialog box change depending on whether the Borders tab or the Page Border tab is selected when the Options button is clicked.

If a printer contains a nonprinting area and the entire page border will not print, consider increasing the spacing from the page border to the edge of the page. Do this with the *Top*, *Left*, *Bottom*, and/or *Right* measurement boxes. The *Measure from* option box has a default setting of *Edge of page*. To fit the border more closely around the text of the document, choose the *Text* option in the option box. This option sets the top and bottom margins at *1 pt* and the side margins at *4 pt*. These measurements can be increased or decreased by clicking the arrows in the measurement boxes.

Change the *Measure from* option to *Text* and the *Surround header* and *Surround footer* options become available and the check boxes contain check marks. With check marks in the check boxes, header and footer text is positioned inside the page border. To specify that header and footer text should be positioned outside the page border, remove the check marks from the check boxes.

Activity 4b Inserting a Page Border

Part 2 of 2

1. With **4-EmpQualities.docx** open, remove the page color by clicking the Page Color button in the Page Background group on the Design tab and then clicking the *No Color* option.
2. Insert a page border by completing the following steps:
   a. Click the Page Borders button in the Page Background group on the Design tab.
   b. At the Borders and Shading dialog box with the Page Border tab selected, click the *Box* option in the *Setting* section.
   c. Scroll down the list of line styles in the *Style* list box to the last line style and then click the third line from the end.
   d. Click the *Color* option box arrow and then click the *Orange, Accent 2* option (sixth column, first row in the *Theme Colors* section).
   e. Click OK to close the dialog box.

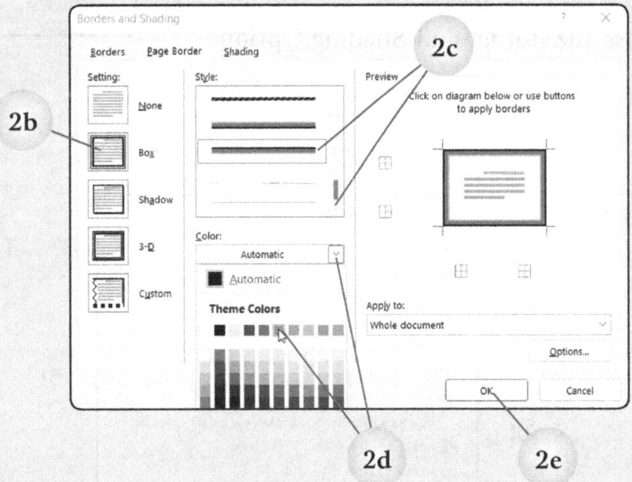

3. Increase the spacing from the page border to the edges of the page by completing the following steps:
   a. Click the Page Borders button.
   b. At the Borders and Shading dialog box with the Page Border tab selected, click the Options button in the lower right corner.
   c. At the Border and Shading Options dialog box, click the *Top* measurement box up arrow until *31 pt* displays. (This is the maximum measurement allowed.)
   d. Increase the measurements in the *Left, Bottom,* and *Right* measurement boxes to *31 pt*.
   e. Click OK to close the Border and Shading Options dialog box.
   f. Click OK to close the Borders and Shading dialog box.

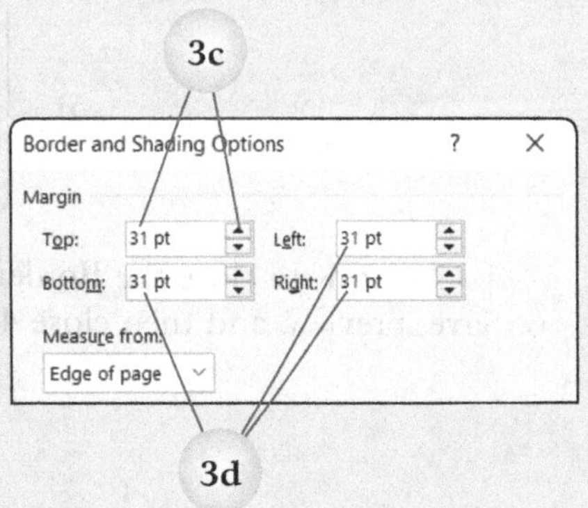

4. Save and then preview **4-EmpQualities.docx**.
5. Insert an art image page border and change the page border spacing options by completing the following steps:
   a. Click the Page Borders button.
   b. Click the *Art* option box arrow and then click the border image shown at the right (approximately one-third of the way down the drop-down list).
   c. Click the Options button in the lower right corner of the Borders and Shading dialog box.
   d. At the Border and Shading Options dialog box, click the *Measure from* option box arrow and then click *Text* at the drop-down list.
   e. Click the *Top* measurement box up arrow until *4 pt* displays.
   f. Increase the measurement in the *Bottom* measurement box to *4 pt* and the measurements in the *Left* and *Right* measurement boxes to *10 pt*.
   g. Click the *Surround header* check box to remove the check mark.
   h. Click the *Surround footer* check box to remove the check mark.
   i. Click OK to close the Border and Shading Options dialog box.

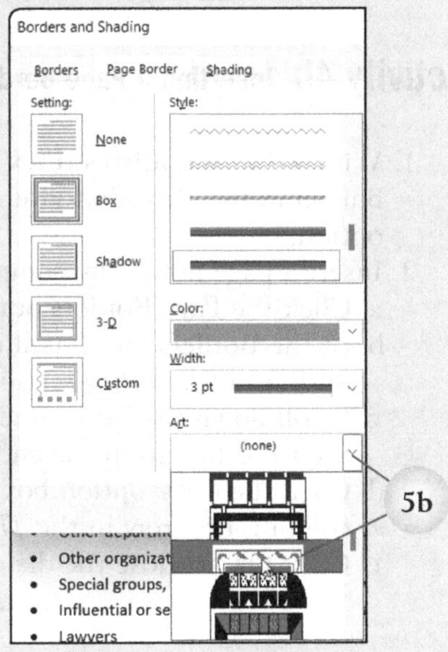

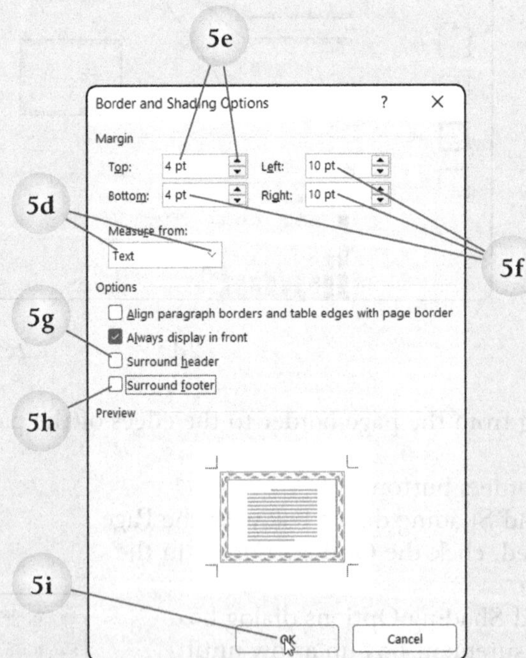

   j. Click OK to close the Borders and Shading dialog box.
6. Save, preview, and then close **4-EmpQualities.docx**.

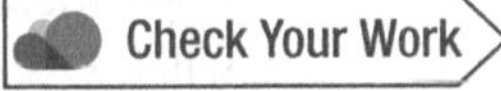

Activity 5 Format a Document on Singapore — 6 Parts

In a document on Singapore, you will format text into columns, improve the readability by hyphenating long words, and improve the visual interest by inserting a drop cap.

Inserting and Deleting a Section Break

Quick Steps

Insert Section Break

1. Click Layout tab.
2. Click Breaks button.
3. Click section break option.

Hint When you delete a section break, the text that follows takes on the formatting of the text preceding the break.

Inserting a Section Break

Some documents may have several sections of text that need to be formatted in different ways. To help make formatting easier, insert section breaks. Formatting changes that are made to one section—such as narrower margins, a paragraph border, colored text, and so on—will only apply to that section and not to the rest of the document.

Insert a section break in a document by clicking the Breaks button in the Page Setup group on the Layout tab. Choose from four types of section breaks in the drop-down list: *Next Page*, *Continuous*, *Even Page*, and *Odd Page*. Click *New Page* to insert a section break and start a new section on the next page. Click *Continuous* to insert a section break and start a new section on the same page. Click *Even Page* or *Odd Page* to insert a section break and then start a new section on either the next even or the next odd page.

To see the locations of section breaks in a document, click the Show/Hide ¶ button on the Home tab to turn on the display of nonprinting characters. A section break is shown in the document as a double row of dots with the words *Section Break* in the middle. Word will identify the type of section break. For example, if a continuous section break is inserted, the words *Section Break (Continuous)* display in the middle of the row of dots. To delete a section break, click the Show/Hide ¶ button to turn on the display of nonprinting characters, click on the section break, and then press the Delete key.

Activity 5a Inserting a Continuous Section Break — Part 1 of 6

1. Open **Singapore.docx** and then save it with the name **4-Singapore**.
2. Insert a continuous section break by completing the following steps:
   a. Move the insertion point to the beginning of the heading *Climate*.
   b. Click the Layout tab.
   c. Click the Breaks button in the Page Setup group and then click *Continuous* in the *Section Breaks* section of the drop-down list.
3. Click the Home tab, click the Show/Hide ¶ button in the Paragraph group, and then notice the section break at the end of the first paragraph of text.
4. Click the Show/Hide ¶ button to turn off the display of nonprinting characters.

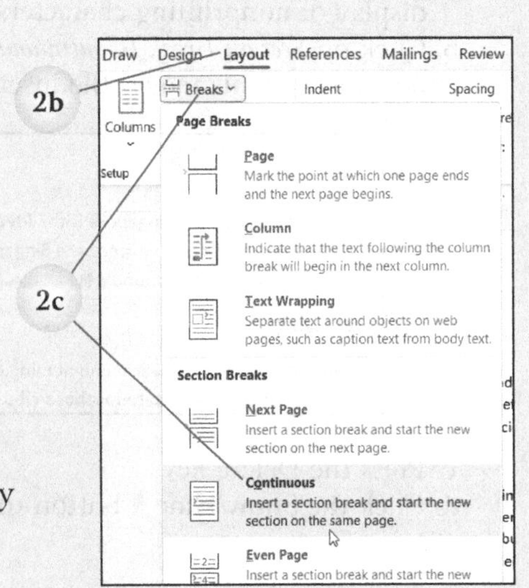

5. With the insertion point positioned at the beginning of the heading *Climate*, change the left and right margins to 1.5 inches. (The margin changes affect only the text after the continuous section break.)
6. Save and then preview **4-Singapore.docx**.

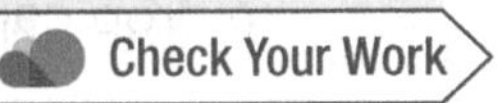

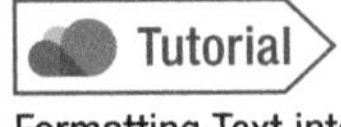

Formatting Text into Columns

Formatting Text into Columns

When preparing a document containing text, an important point to consider is its readability. *Readability* refers to the ease with which a person can read and understand groups of words. The line length of text in a document can enhance or detract from its readability. If the line length is too long, the reader may lose his or her place and have a difficult time moving to the next line below.

To improve the readability of a document, consider formatting the text in columns. One common type is the newspaper column, which is typically used for text in newspapers, newsletters, and magazines.

Quick Steps

Create Columns

1. Click Layout tab.
2. Click Columns button.
3. Click number of columns.

Format text in one, two, or three columns with the Columns button in the Page Setup group on the Layout tab. To customize the column width and spacing, click the *More Columns* option to display the Columns dialog box. Adjust the measurement to create columns of varying widths. A document can include as many columns as will fit on the page. Word determines how many columns can be included based on the page width, the margin widths, and the size and spacing of the columns. Columns should be at least 0.5 inch in width.

Activity 5b Formatting Text into Columns — Part 2 of 6

1. With **4-Singapore.docx** open, make sure the insertion point is positioned below the section break and then change the left and right margins back to 1 inch.
2. Delete the section break by completing the following steps:
   a. Click the Show/Hide ¶ button in the Paragraph group on the Home tab to turn on the display of nonprinting characters.
   b. Click on *Section Break (Continuous)* at the end of the first paragraph below the title in the document. (This moves the insertion point to the beginning of the section break.)

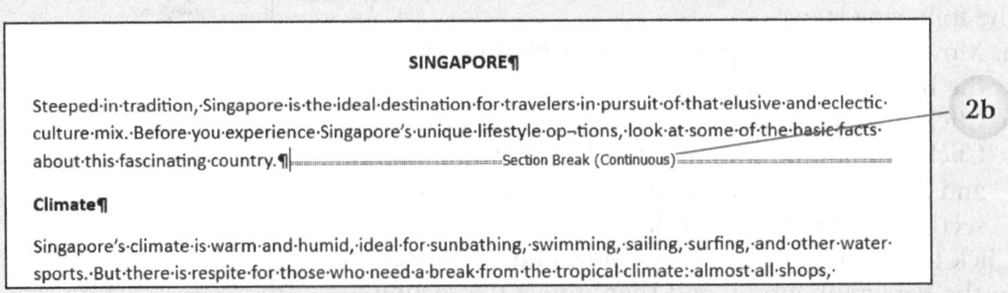

SINGAPORE¶

Steeped·in·tradition,·Singapore·is·the·ideal·destination·for·travelers·in·pursuit·of·that·elusive·and·eclectic· culture·mix.·Before·you·experience·Singapore's·unique·lifestyle·op¬tions,·look·at·some·of·the·basic·facts· about·this·fascinating·country.¶ Section Break (Continuous)

Climate¶

Singapore's·climate·is·warm·and·humid,·ideal·for·sunbathing,·swimming,·sailing,·surfing,·and·other·water· sports.·But·there·is·respite·for·those·who·need·a·break·from·the·tropical·climate:·almost·all·shops,·

   c. Press the Delete key.
   d. Click the Show/Hide ¶ button to turn off the display of nonprinting characters.

3. Move the insertion point to the beginning of the first paragraph of text below the title and then insert a continuous section break.
4. Format the text into columns by completing the following steps:
   a. Make sure the insertion point is positioned below the section break.
   b. If necessary, click the Layout tab.
   c. Click the Columns button in the Page Setup group.
   d. Click *Two* at the drop-down list.
5. Save **4-Singapore.docx**.

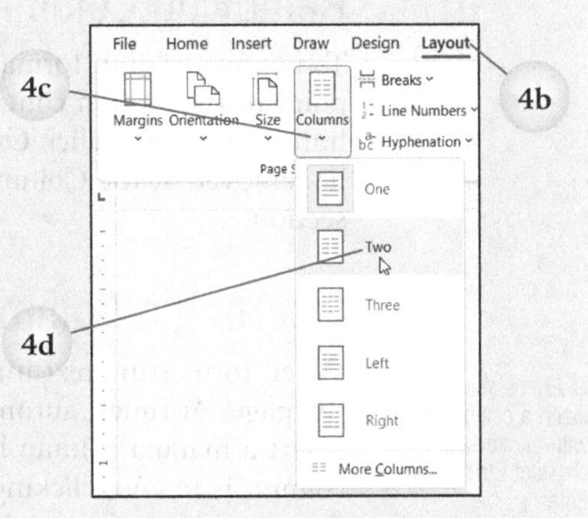

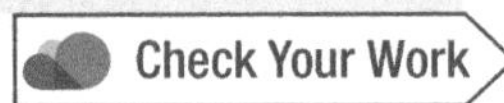

Creating Columns with the Columns Dialog Box

Quick Steps

Create Columns at Columns Dialog Box

1. Click Layout tab.
2. Click Columns button.
3. Click *More Columns*.
4. Specify column options.
5. Click OK.

Use the Columns dialog box to create newspaper columns that are equal or unequal in width. To display the Columns dialog box, shown in Figure 4.5, click the Columns button in the Page Setup group on the Layout tab and then click *More Columns* at the drop-down list.

With options at the Columns dialog box, specify the style and number of columns, enter specific column measurements, create unequal columns, and insert a line between columns. By default, column formatting is applied to the whole document. This can be changed to *This point forward* at the *Apply to* option box at the bottom of the Columns dialog box. With the *This point forward* option, a section break is inserted and the column formatting is applied to text from the location of the insertion point to the end of the document or until another column format is encountered. The *Preview* section of the dialog box shows an example of how the columns will appear in the document.

Figure 4.5 Columns Dialog Box

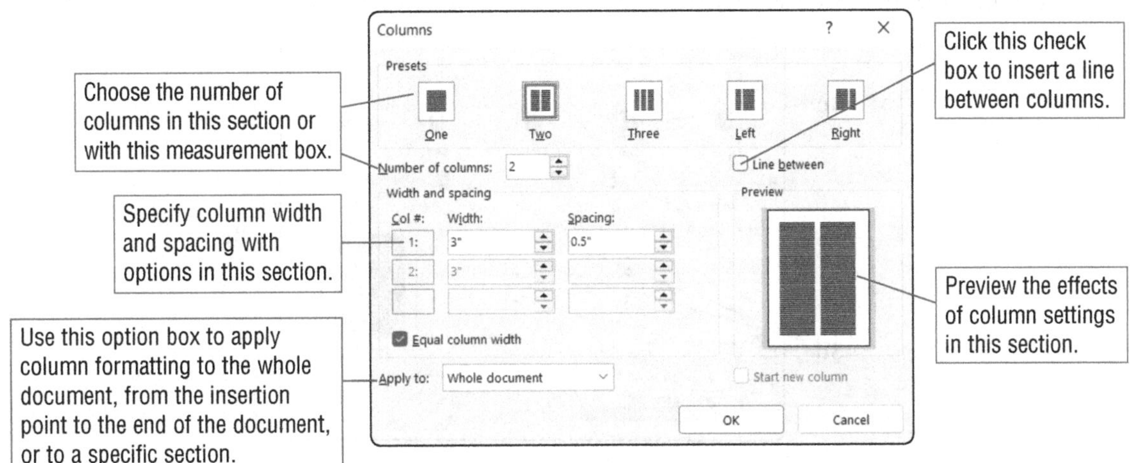

Removing Column Formatting

To remove column formatting using the Columns button, position the insertion point in the section containing columns, click the Layout tab, click the Columns button, and then click *One* at the drop-down list. Column formatting can also be removed at the Columns dialog box by selecting the *One* option in the *Presets* section.

Inserting a Column Break

Hint You can also insert a column break with the keyboard shortcut Ctrl + Shift + Enter.

When formatting text into columns, Word automatically breaks the columns to fit the page. At times, automatic column breaks may appear in undesirable locations. Insert a manual column break by positioning the insertion point where the column is to end, clicking the Layout tab, clicking the Breaks button in the Page Setup group, and then clicking *Column* at the drop-down list.

Activity 5c Formatting Text into Columns at the Columns Dialog Box

Part 3 of 6

1. With **4-Singapore.docx** open, delete the section break by completing the following steps:
   a. If necessary, click the Home tab.
   b. Click the Show/Hide ¶ button in the Paragraph group to turn on the display of nonprinting characters.
   c. Click on *Section Break (Continuous)* and then press the Delete key.
   d. Click the Show/Hide ¶ button to turn off the display of nonprinting characters.
2. Remove column formatting by clicking the Layout tab, clicking the Columns button, and then clicking *One* at the drop-down list.
3. Format the text into columns by completing the following steps:
   a. If necessary, position the insertion point at the beginning of the first paragraph of text below the title.
   b. Click the Columns button and then click *More Columns* at the drop-down list.
   c. At the Columns dialog box, click *Two* in the *Presets* section.
   d. Click the *Spacing* measurement box down arrow until *0.3"* displays.
   e. Click the *Line between* check box to insert a check mark.
   f. Click the *Apply to* option box arrow and then click *This point forward* at the drop-down list.
   g. Click OK to close the dialog box.

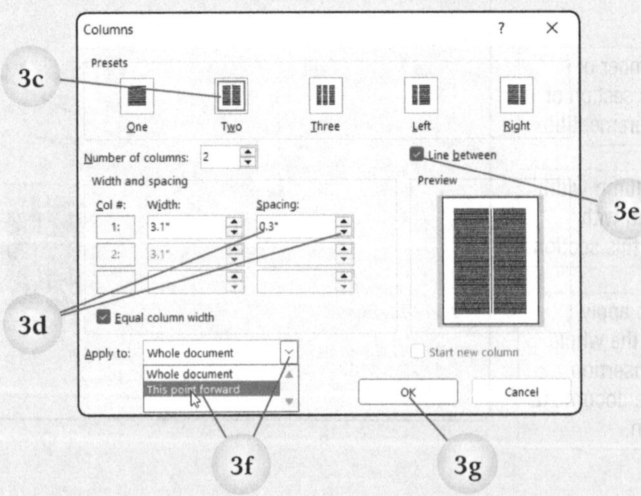

4. Insert a column break by completing the following steps:
   a. Position the insertion point at the beginning of the heading *Entertainment* (at the bottom of the first column).
   b. Click the Breaks button in the Page Setup group and then click *Column* at the drop-down list.
5. Save and then preview **4-Singapore.docx**.

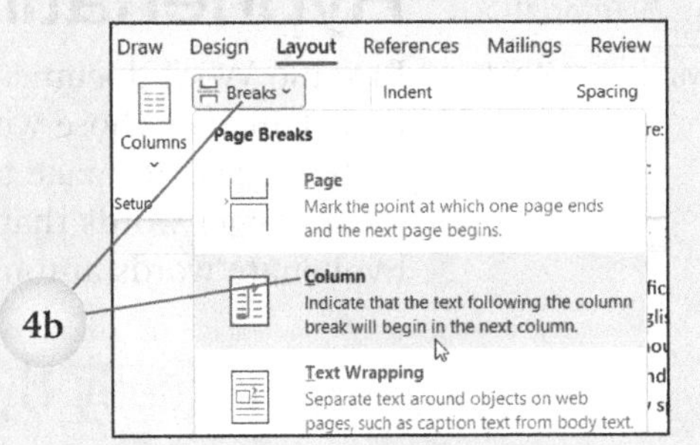

Balancing Columns on a Page

In a document containing text formatted into columns, Word automatically lines up (balances) the last lines of text at the bottoms of the columns, except on the last page. Text in the last column of the last page may end far short of the bottom of the page, and the page will look unbalanced. Balance columns by inserting a continuous section break at the end of the text.

Activity 5d Formatting and Balancing Columns of Text

Part 4 of 6

1. With **4-Singapore.docx** open, delete the column break by positioning the insertion point at the beginning of the heading *Entertainment*, if necessary, and then pressing the Backspace key.
2. Select the entire document and then change the font to 12-point Constantia.
3. Move the insertion point to the end of the document and then balance the columns by clicking the Layout tab, clicking the Breaks button in the Page Setup group, and then clicking *Continuous* at the drop-down list.

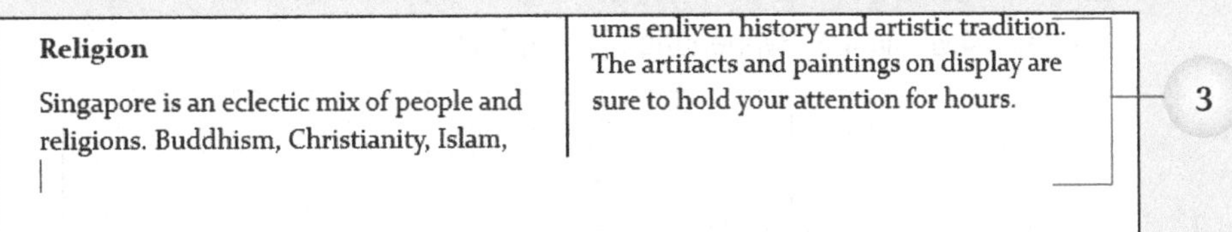

4. Apply the Green, Accent 6, Lighter 60% paragraph shading (last column, third row) to the title *SINGAPORE*.
5. Apply the Green, Accent 6, Lighter 80% paragraph shading (last column, second row) to each heading in the document.
6. Insert page numbers that print at the bottom center of each page using the *Plain Number 2* option.
7. Double-click in the document to make it active.
8. Save **4-Singapore.docx**.

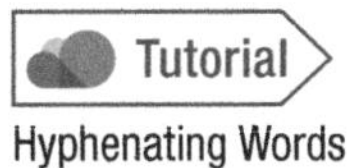
Hyphenating Words

Hyphenating Words

In some Word documents, especially those with left and right margins wider than 1 inch or those with text set in columns, the right margin may appear quite ragged. To make the margin neater and more uniform, use hyphens to break longer words that fall at the ends of lines. Use the hyphenation feature to hyphenate words automatically or manually.

Automatically Hyphenating Words

Hyphenation

Hint Avoid dividing words at the ends of more than two consecutive lines.

To automatically hyphenate words in a document, click the Layout tab, click the Hyphenation button in the Page Setup group, and then click *Automatic* at the drop-down list. Scroll through the document and check to see whether hyphens were added in appropriate locations within the words. To undo hyphenation, immediately click the Undo button in the Undo group on the Home tab.

Manually Hyphenating Words

Quick Steps

Automatically Hyphenate Document
1. Click Layout tab.
2. Click Hyphenation button.
3. Click *Automatic*.

Manually Hyphenate Document
1. Click Layout tab.
2. Click Hyphenation button.
3. Click *Manual*.
4. Click Yes or No to hyphenate indicated words.
5. When complete, click OK.

To control where hyphens appear in words during hyphenation, choose manual hyphenation. To do this, click the Layout tab, click the Hyphenation button in the Page Setup group, and then click *Manual* at the drop-down list. This displays the Manual Hyphenation dialog box, as shown in Figure 4.6. (The word in the *Hyphenate at* text box will vary.)

At this dialog box, click Yes to hyphenate the word as indicated in the *Hyphenate at* text box, click No if the word should not be hyphenated, or click Cancel to cancel hyphenation. The hyphen can be repositioned in the word in the *Hyphenate at* text box. Word shows the word with syllable breaks indicated by hyphens and a blinking black bar indicates the location where the manual hyphen will be inserted. To hyphenate a word at a different place, click and drag the blinking black bar to the position desired and then click Yes. Continue clicking Yes or No at the Manual Hyphenation dialog box.

Figure 4.6 Manual Hyphenation Dialog Box

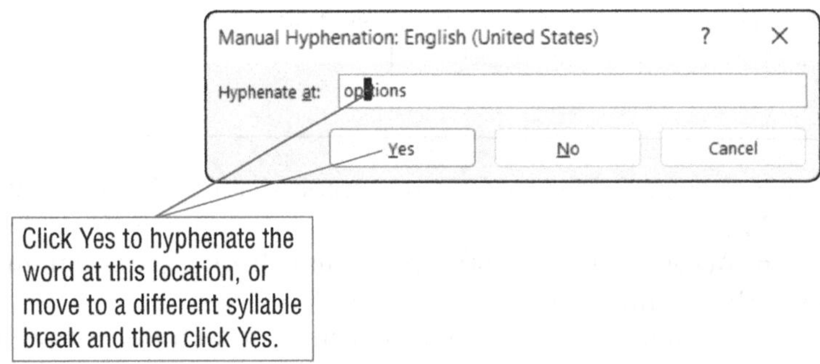

Click Yes to hyphenate the word at this location, or move to a different syllable break and then click Yes.

Activity 5e Automatically and Manually Hyphenating Words

1. With **4-Singapore.docx** open, hyphenate words automatically by completing the following steps:
   a. Press Ctrl + Home.
   b. Click the Layout tab.
   c. Click the Hyphenation button in the Page Setup group and then click *Automatic* at the drop-down list.

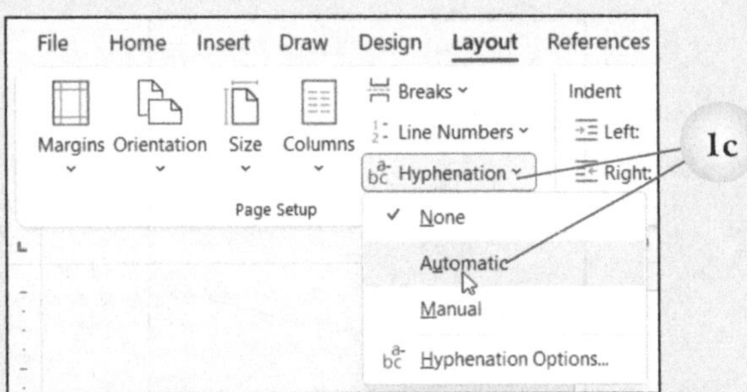

2. Scroll through the document and notice the hyphenation.
3. Click the Home tab and then click the Undo button to remove the hyphens.
4. Manually hyphenate words by completing the following steps:
   a. Click the Layout tab, click the Hyphenation button in the Page Setup group, and then click *Manual* at the drop-down list.
   b. At the Manual Hyphenation dialog box, make one of the following choices (proper names and capitalized text should not be hyphenated):
      - Click Yes to hyphenate the word as indicated in the *Hyphenate at* text box.
      - Click and drag the hyphen in the word to break the word on a different syllable and then click Yes.
      - Click No if the word should not be hyphenated.
   c. Continue clicking Yes or No at the Manual Hyphenation dialog box.
   d. At the message indicating that hyphenation is complete, click OK.
5. Save **4-Singapore.docx**.

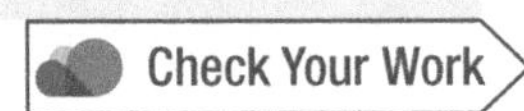

Creating and Removing a Drop Cap

Quick Steps

Create Drop Cap
1. Click Insert tab.
2. Click Drop Cap button.
3. Click drop cap option.

Creating a Drop Cap

Use a drop cap to enhance the appearance of text. A drop cap is the first letter of the first word of a paragraph that is set into the paragraph with formatting that differentiates it from the rest of the paragraph. Drop caps can be used to identify the beginnings of major sections or parts of a document.

Create a drop cap with the Drop Cap button in the Text group on the Insert tab. The drop cap can be set in the paragraph or in the margin. At the Drop Cap dialog box, specify a font, the number of lines the letter should drop, and the distance the letter should be positioned from the text of the paragraph. Add a drop cap to the entire first word of a paragraph by selecting the word and then clicking the Drop Cap button.

Activity 5f Inserting a Drop Cap

1. With **4-Singapore.docx** open, create a drop cap by completing the following steps:
   a. Position the insertion point in the first word of the first paragraph below the title (the word *Steeped*).
   b. Click the Insert tab.
   c. Click the Drop Cap button in the Text group.
   d. Click *In margin* at the drop-down gallery.

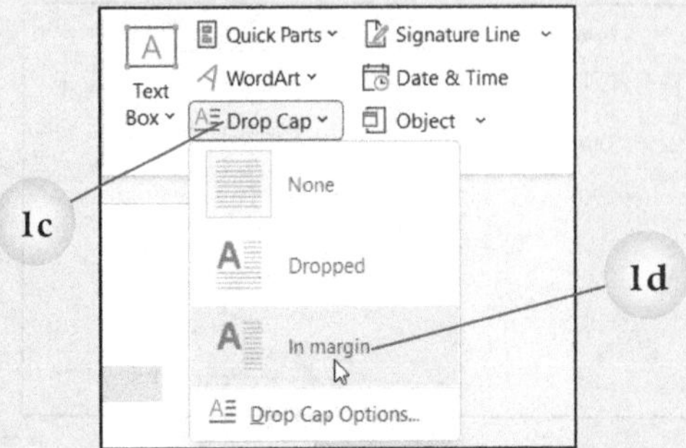

2. Looking at the drop cap, you decide that you do not like it positioned in the margin and want it to be a little smaller. To change the drop cap, complete the following steps:
   a. With the *S* in the word *Steeped* selected, click the Drop Cap button and then click *None* at the drop-down gallery.
   b. Click the Drop Cap button and then click *Drop Cap Options* at the drop-down gallery.
   c. At the Drop Cap dialog box, click *Dropped* in the *Position* section.
   d. Click the *Font* option box arrow, scroll up the drop-down list, and then click *Cambria*.
   e. Click the *Lines to drop* measurement box down arrow to change the number to *2*.
   f. Click OK to close the dialog box.
   g. Click outside the drop cap to deselect it.
3. Save, preview, and then close **4-Singapore.docx**.

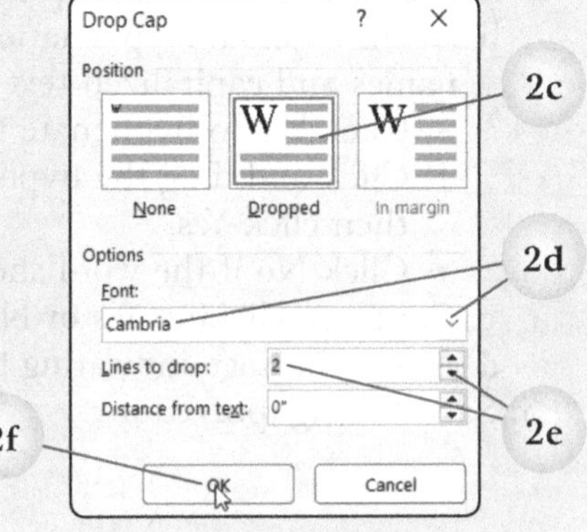

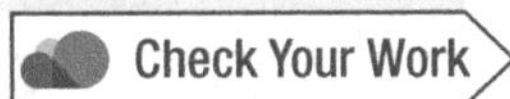

Activity 6 Create an Announcement about Supervisor Training

2 Parts

You will create an announcement about upcoming supervisor training and use the Click and Type feature to center and right-align text. You also will vertically center the text on the page.

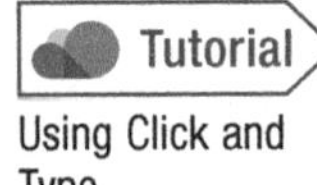

Using Click and Type

Using the Click and Type Feature

Word contains a Click and Type feature that allows text to be aligned left, right, or center beginning at a specific point in the document. This feature can be used to position text as it is being typed rather than typing the text and then selecting and formatting the text, which requires multiple steps.

Quick Steps

Use Click and Type

1. Hover mouse at left margin, between left and right margins, or at right margin.
2. When horizontal lines display next to pointer, double-click left mouse button.

To use the Click and Type feature, open a new blank document and move the pointer slowly over the page, going from left to right. The pointer will appear as an I-beam with horizontal lines representing the text alignment. Near the left margin, the horizontal lines are left-aligned. In the center of the page, the lines are centered. At the right margin, the horizontal lines are right-aligned. Double-click in the document and begin typing. Text should automatically align to match the horizontal lines indicated on the I-beam pointer. (Note: Make sure the horizontal lines display near the pointer before double-clicking the mouse button. Double-clicking when the alignment lines are not shown will insert a tab instead of changing the text alignment.)

Activity 6a Using Click and Type — Part 1 of 2

1. Press Ctrl + N to open a blank document and then create the centered text shown in Figure 4.7 by completing the following steps:
   a. Position the I-beam pointer between the left and right margins at about the 3.25-inch mark on the horizontal ruler and at the top of the vertical ruler.
   b. When the center-alignment lines display below the I-beam pointer, double-click the left mouse button.

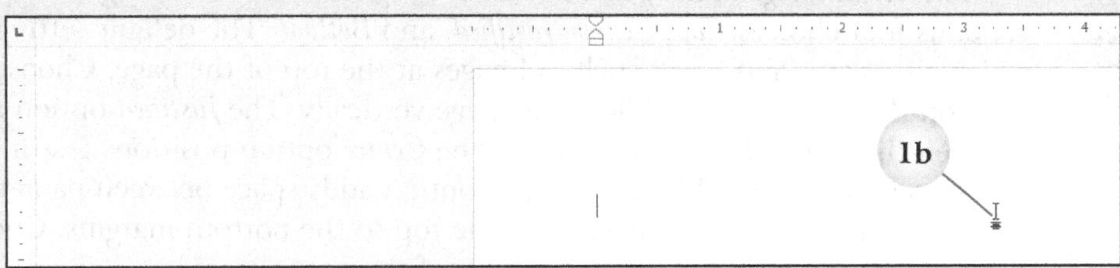

   c. Type the centered text shown in Figure 4.7. Press Shift + Enter to end each line except the last line.
2. Change to right alignment by completing the following steps:
   a. Position the I-beam pointer near the right margin at approximately the 1.25-inch mark on the vertical ruler until the right-alignment lines display at the left of the I-beam pointer.

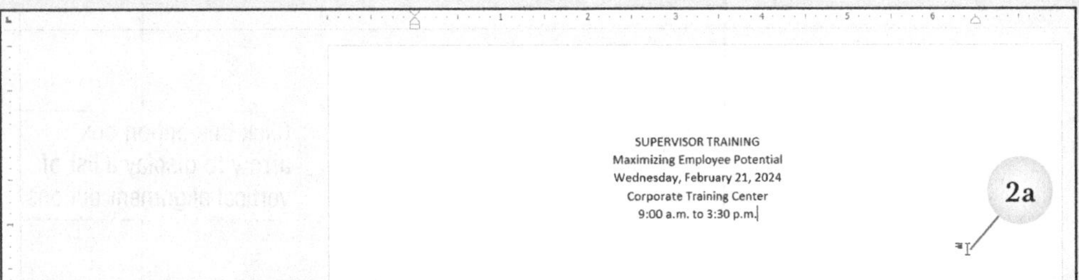

   b. Double-click the left mouse button.
   c. Type the right-aligned text shown in Figure 4.7. Press Shift + Enter to end the first line.
3. Select the centered text and then change the font to 14-point Candara bold and the line spacing to double spacing.
4. Select the right-aligned text, change the font to 10-point Candara bold, and then deselect the text.
5. Save the document with the name **4-Training**.

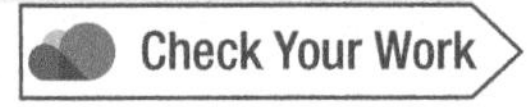

Figure 4.7 Activity 6a

SUPERVISOR TRAINING
Maximizing Employee Potential
Wednesday, February 21, 2024
Corporate Training Center
9:00 a.m. to 3:30 p.m.

Sponsored by
Cell Systems

Changing Vertical Alignment

Changing Vertical Alignment

Text or items in a Word document are aligned at the top of the page by default. Change this alignment with the *Vertical alignment* option box at the Page Setup dialog box with the Layout tab selected, as shown in Figure 4.8. Display this dialog box by clicking the Layout tab, clicking the Page Setup group dialog box launcher, and then clicking the Layout tab at the Page Setup dialog box.

Quick Steps

Vertically Align Text

1. Click Layout tab.
2. Click Page Setup group dialog box launcher.
3. Click Layout tab.
4. Click *Vertical alignment* option box.
5. Click alignment.
6. Click OK.

The *Vertical alignment* option box in the *Page* section of the Page Setup dialog box contains four choices: *Top*, *Center*, *Justified*, and *Bottom*. The default setting is *Top*, which aligns text and items such as images at the top of the page. Choose *Center* to position the text in the middle of the page vertically. The *Justified* option aligns text between the top and bottom margins. The *Center* option positions text in the middle of the page vertically, while the *Justified* option adds space between paragraphs of text (not within) to fill the page from the top to the bottom margins. Choose the *Bottom* option to align text at the bottom of the page.

Figure 4.8 Page Setup Dialog Box with the Layout Tab Selected

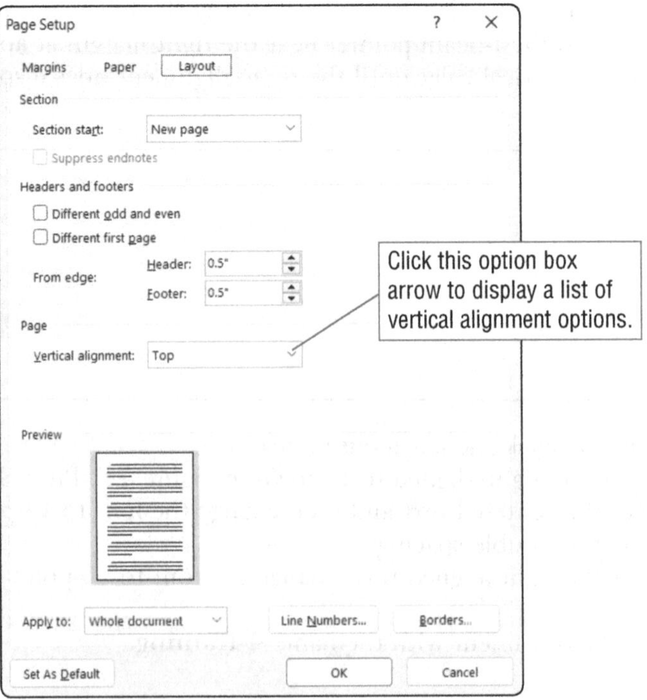

Activity 6b Vertically Centering Text

Part 2 of 2

1. With **4-Training.docx** open, click the Layout tab and then click the Page Setup group dialog box launcher.
2. At the Page Setup dialog box, click the Layout tab.
3. Click the *Vertical alignment* option box arrow in the *Page* section and then click *Center* at the drop-down list.
4. Click OK to close the dialog box.
5. Save, preview, and then close **4-Training.docx**.

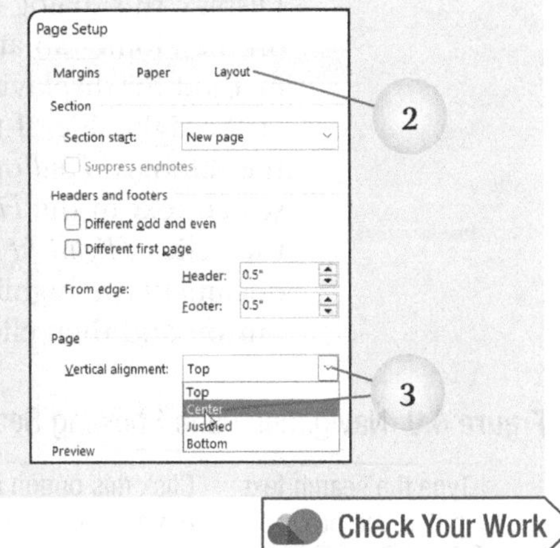

Check Your Work

Activity 7 Format a Lease Agreement

3 Parts

You will open a lease agreement, search for specific text, and then search for specific text and replace it with other text.

Editing Text with Find and Replace

Find

Replace

The Editing group on the Home tab contains the Find button and the Replace button. Use the Find button to search for specific text in a document and use the Replace button to search for and then replace specific text.

Finding Text

Tutorial

Finding Text Using the Navigation Pane

Tutorial

Finding Text Using the Find and Replace Dialog Box

Quick Steps

Find Text

1. Click Find button.
2. Type search text.
3. Click Next button.

Click the Find button in the Editing group on the Home tab (or press the keyboard shortcut Ctrl + F) and the Navigation pane displays at the left side of the screen with the Results tab selected. With this tab selected, type *search text* in the search text box and any occurrence of the text in the document is highlighted. A fragment of the text surrounding the search text is shown in a thumbnail in the Navigation pane. For example, when searching for *Lessee* in **4-LeaseAgrmnt.docx** in Activity 7a (on page 133), the screen displays as shown in Figure 4.9. Any occurrence of *Lessee* displays highlighted in yellow in the document and the Navigation pane shows thumbnails of the text surrounding the occurrences of *Lessee*.

Click a text thumbnail in the Navigation pane and the occurrence of the search text is selected in the document. Hover the pointer over a text thumbnail in the Navigation pane and the page number location displays in a small box near the pointer. Move to the next occurrence of the search text by clicking the Next button (contains a down arrow) below and to the right of the search text box. Click the Previous button (contains an up arrow) to move to the previous occurrence of the search text.

Click the down arrow at the right side of the search text box and a drop-down list displays. It shows options for displaying dialog boxes, such as the Find Options dialog box and the Find and Replace dialog box. It also shows options for specifying what should be found in the document, such as figures, tables, and equations.

The search text in a document can be highlighted with options at the Find and Replace dialog box with the Find tab selected as shown in Figure 4.10. Display this dialog box by clicking the Find button arrow in the Editing group on the Home tab and then clicking *Advanced Find* at the drop-down list. Another method for displaying the Find and Replace dialog box is to click the down arrow at the right side of the search text box in the Navigation pane and then click the *Advanced Find* option at the drop-down list. To highlight found text, type the search text in the *Find what* text box, click the Reading Highlight button, and then click *Highlight All* at the drop-down list. All occurrences of the text in the document are highlighted. To remove highlighting, click the Reading Highlight button and then click *Clear Highlighting* at the drop-down list.

Figure 4.9 Navigation Pane Showing Search Results

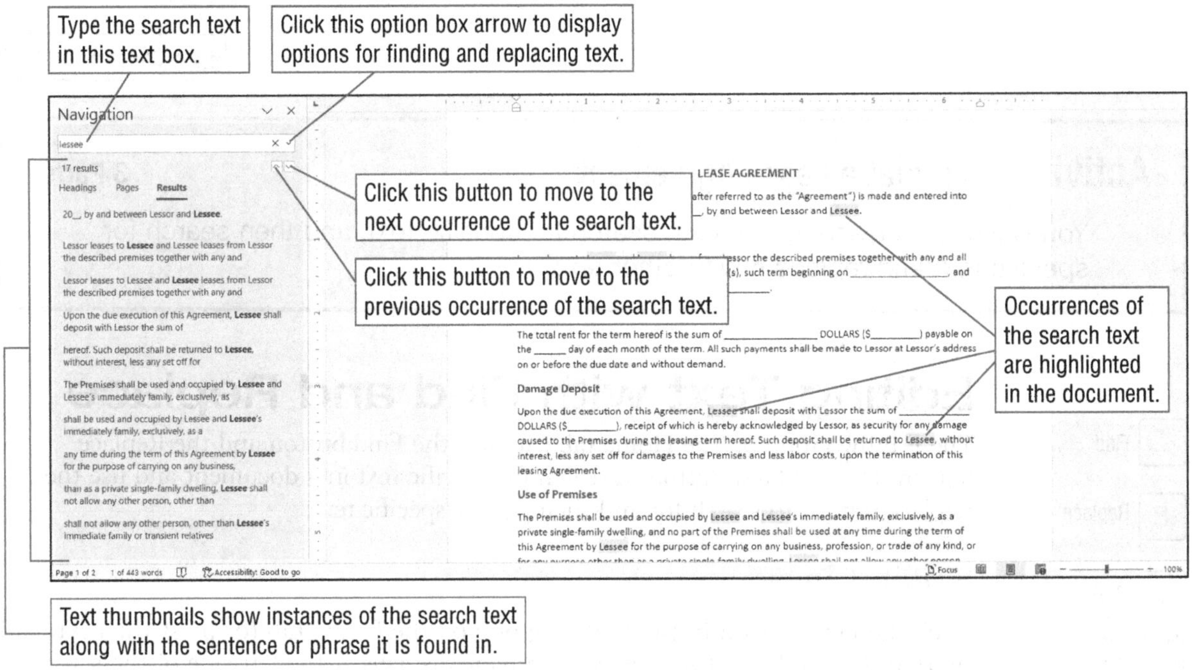

Type the search text in this text box.

Click this option box arrow to display options for finding and replacing text.

Click this button to move to the next occurrence of the search text.

Click this button to move to the previous occurrence of the search text.

Occurrences of the search text are highlighted in the document.

Text thumbnails show instances of the search text along with the sentence or phrase it is found in.

Figure 4.10 Find and Replace Dialog Box with Find Tab Selected

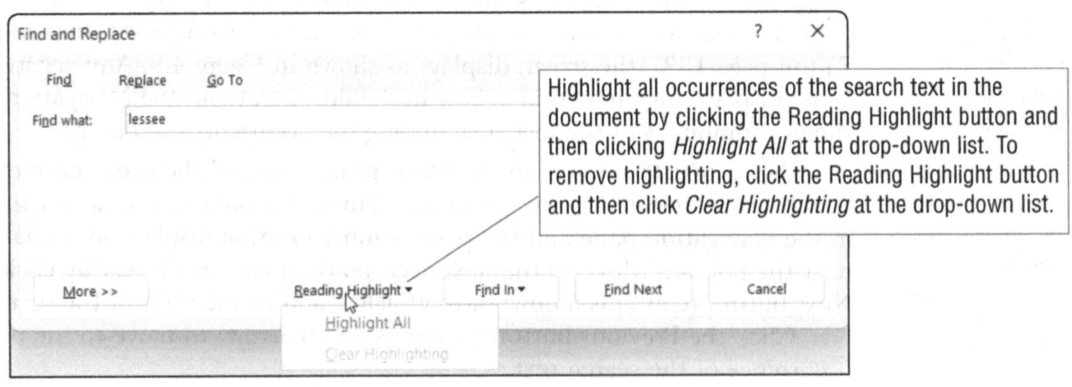
Find and Replace
Find
Replace
Go To
Find what:
lessee
Highlight all occurrences of the search text in the document by clicking the Reading Highlight button and then clicking Highlight All at the drop-down list. To remove highlighting, click the Reading Highlight button and then click Clear Highlighting at the drop-down list.
More >>
Reading Highlight
Find In
Find Next
Cancel
Highlight All
Clear Highlighting

Activity 7a Finding and Highlighting Text

1. Open **LeaseAgrmnt.docx** and then save it with the name **4-LeaseAgrmnt.**
2. Find all occurrences of *lessee* by completing the following steps:
   a. Click the Find button in the Editing group on the Home tab.
   b. If necessary, click the Results tab in the Navigation pane.
   c. Type lessee in the search text box in the Navigation pane.
   d. After a moment, all occurrences of *lessee* in the document are highlighted and text thumbnails display in the Navigation pane. Click a couple of the text thumbnails in the Navigation pane to select the text in the document.
   e. Click the Previous button (contains an up arrow) to select the previous occurrence of *lessee* in the document.

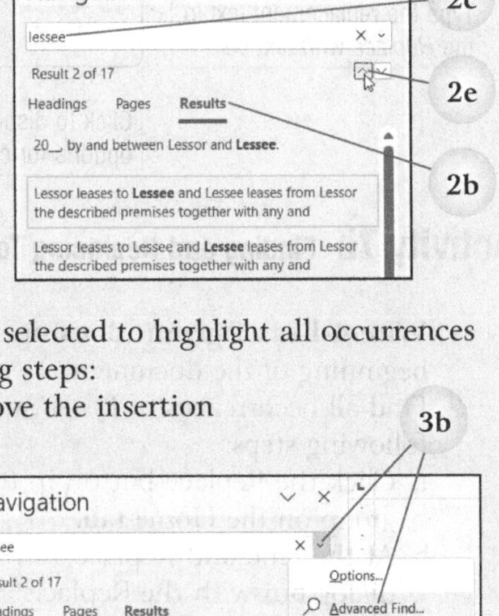

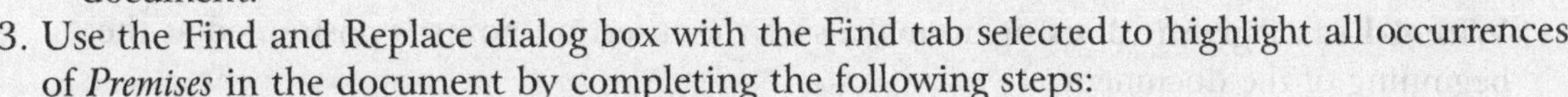

3. Use the Find and Replace dialog box with the Find tab selected to highlight all occurrences of *Premises* in the document by completing the following steps:
   a. Click in the document and press Ctrl + Home to move the insertion point to the beginning of the document.
   b. Click the search option box arrow in the Navigation pane and then click *Advanced Find* at the drop-down list.
   c. At the Find and Replace dialog box with the Find tab selected (and *lessee* selected in the *Find what* text box), type Premises.
   d. Click the Reading Highlight button and then click *Highlight All* at the drop-down list.
   e. Click in the document to make it active and then scroll through the document and notice the occurrences of highlighted text.
   f. Click in the dialog box to make it active.
   g. Click the Reading Highlight button and then click *Clear Highlighting* at the drop-down list.
   h. Click the Close button to close the Find and Replace dialog box.
4. Close the Navigation pane by clicking the Close button in the upper right corner of the pane.

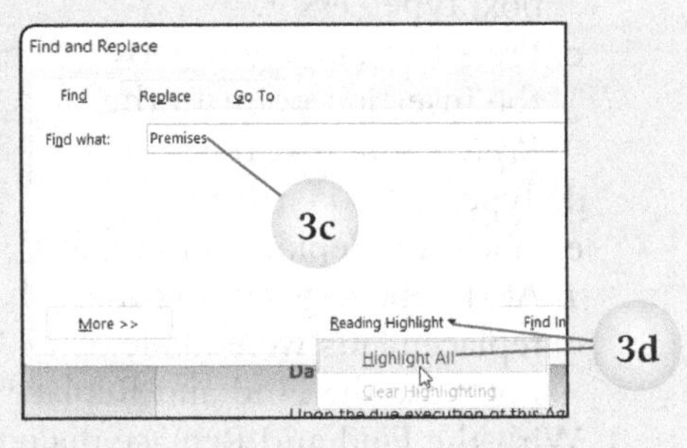

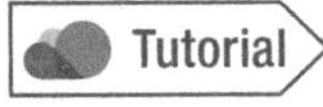

Finding and Replacing Text

Quick Steps

Find and Replace Text

1. Click Replace button.
2. Type search text.
3. Press Tab key.
4. Type replacement text.
5. Click Replace or Replace All button.

Finding and Replacing Text

To find and replace text, click the Replace button in the Editing group on the Home tab or use the keyboard shortcut Ctrl + H. This displays the Find and Replace dialog box with the Replace tab selected, as shown in Figure 4.11. Type the search text in the *Find what* text box, press the Tab key, and then type the replacement text in the *Replace with* text box.

The Find and Replace dialog box contains several command buttons. Click the Find Next button to tell Word to find the next occurrence of the text. Click the Replace button to replace the text and find the next occurrence. If all occurrences of the text in the *Find what* text box are to be replaced with the text in the *Replace with* text box, click the Replace All button.

Hint If the Find and Replace dialog box is in the way of specific text, drag it to a different location.

Figure 4.11 Find and Replace Dialog Box with the Replace Tab Selected

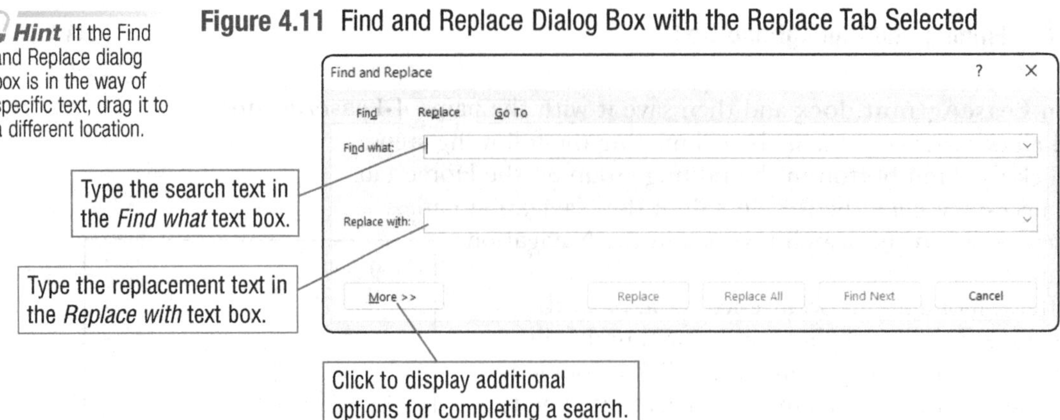

Activity 7b Finding and Replacing Text

Part 2 of 3

1. With **4-LeaseAgrmnt.docx** open, make sure the insertion point is positioned at the beginning of the document.
2. Find all occurrences of *Lessor* and replace them with *Tracy Hartford* by completing the following steps:
   a. Click the Replace button in the Editing group on the Home tab.
   b. At the Find and Replace dialog box with the Replace tab selected and *Premises* selected in the *Find what* text box, type Lessor.
   c. Press the Tab key to move the insertion point to the *Replace with* text box.
   d. Type Tracy Hartford.
   e. Click the Replace All button.
   f. At the message stating that 11 replacements were made, click OK. (Do not close the Find and Replace dialog box.)

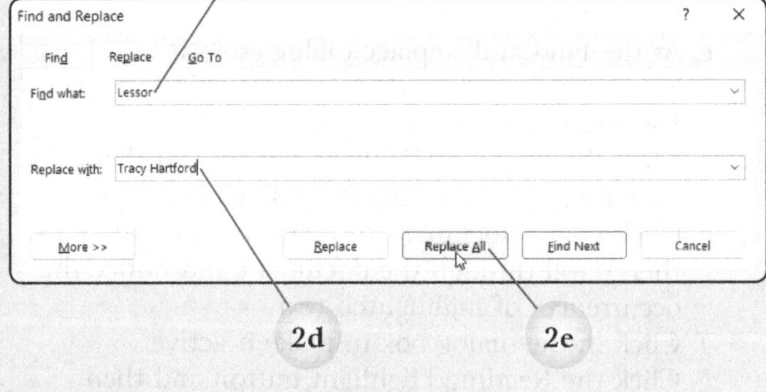

3. With the Find and Replace dialog box still open, complete steps similar to those in Step 2 to find all occurrences of *Lessee* and replace them with *Michael Iwami*.
4. Click the Close button to close the Find and Replace dialog box.
5. Save **4-LeaseAgrmnt.docx**.

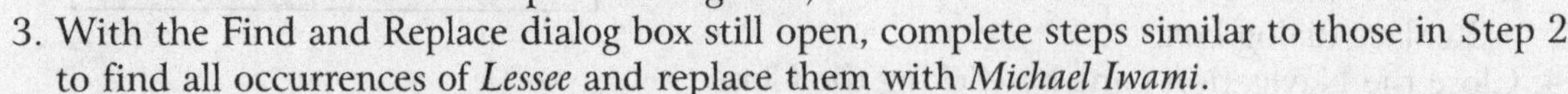

Specifying Search Options

The Find and Replace dialog box provides more options for completing a search. To display these options, click the More button in the lower left corner of the dialog box. This causes the Find and Replace dialog box to expand, as shown in Figure 4.12. Search Options in the dialog box are described in Table 4.1. Click check boxes to select options for customizing the search, and then click the Less button (previously the More button) to hide the options and shrink the dialog box again. If a mistake was made when replacing text, close the Find and Replace dialog box and then click the Undo button in the Undo group on the Home tab.

Figure 4.12 Expanded Find and Replace Dialog Box

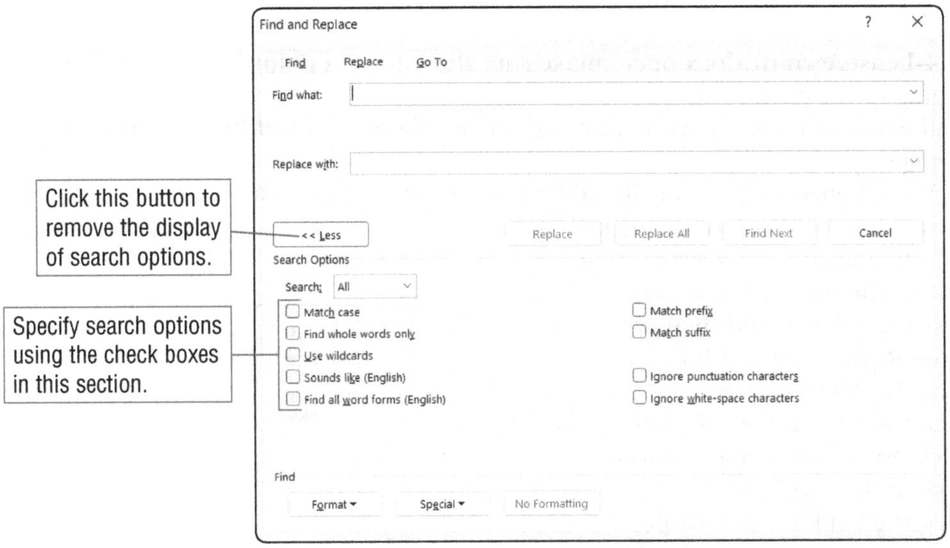

Table 4.1 Options at the Expanded Find and Replace Dialog Box

Choose this option	To
Match case	Exactly match the case of the search text. For example, search for *Book* and select the *Match case* option and Word will stop at *Book* but not *book* or *BOOK*.
Find whole words only	Find a whole word, not a part of a word. For example, search for *her* without selecting *Find whole words only* and Word will stop at *there*, *here*, *hers*, and so on.
Use wildcards	Use special characters as wildcards to search for specific text.
Sounds like (English)	Match words that sound alike but are spelled differently, such as *know* and *no*.
Find all word forms (English)	Find all forms of the word entered in the *Find what* text box. For example, enter *hold* and Word will stop at *held* and *holding*.
Match prefix	Find only those words that begin with the letters in the *Find what* text box. For example, enter *per* and Word will stop at words such as *perform* and *perfect* but skip words such as *super* and *hyperlink*.
Match suffix	Find only those words that end with the letters in the *Find what* text box. For example, enter *ly* and Word will stop at words such as *accurately* and *quietly* but skip words such as *catalyst* and *lyre*.
Ignore punctuation characters	Ignore punctuation within characters. For example, enter *US* in the *Find what* text box and Word will stop at *U.S.*
Ignore white-space characters	Ignore spaces between letters. For example, enter *F B I* in the *Find what* text box and Word will stop at *FBI*.

Activity 7c Finding and Replacing Word Forms and Suffixes

1. With **4-LeaseAgrmnt.docx** open, make sure the insertion point is positioned at the beginning of the document.
2. Find all word forms of the word *lease* and replace them with *rent* by completing the following steps:
   a. Click the Replace button in the Editing group on the Home tab.
   b. At the Find and Replace dialog box with the Replace tab selected, type lease in the *Find what* text box.
   c. Press the Tab key and then type rent in the *Replace with* text box.
   d. Click the More button.
   e. Click the *Find all word forms (English)* check box. (This inserts a check mark in the check box.)
   f. Click the Replace All button.
   g. At the message stating that the Replace All button is not recommended when the *Find all word forms* check box is selected, click OK.
   h. At the message stating that six replacements were made, click OK.
   i. Click the *Find all word forms* check box to remove the check mark.

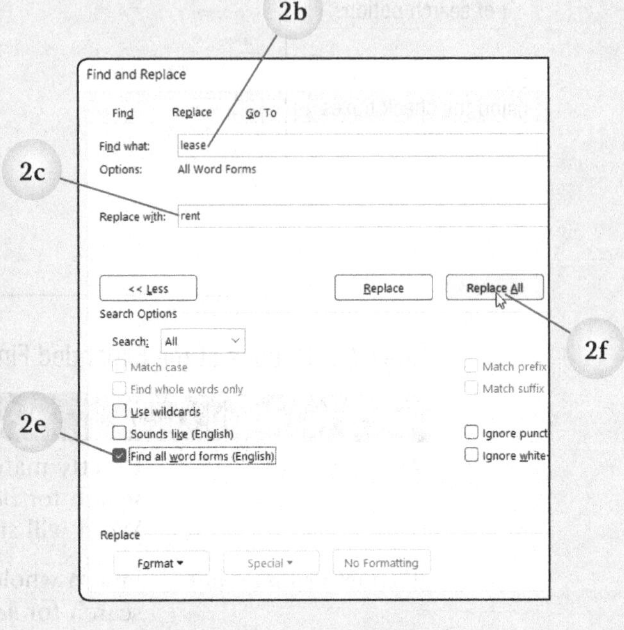

3. Find the word *less* and replace it with the word *minus* and specify that you want Word to find only those words that end in *less* by completing the following steps:
   a. At the expanded Find and Replace dialog box, select the text in the *Find what* text box and then type less.
   b. Select the text in the *Replace with* text box and then type minus.
   c. Click the *Match suffix* check box to insert a check mark (telling Word to find only words that end in *less*).
   d. Click the Replace All button.
   e. Click OK at the message stating that two replacements were made.
   f. Click the *Match suffix* check box to remove the check mark.
   g. Click the Less button.
   h. Close the Find and Replace dialog box.

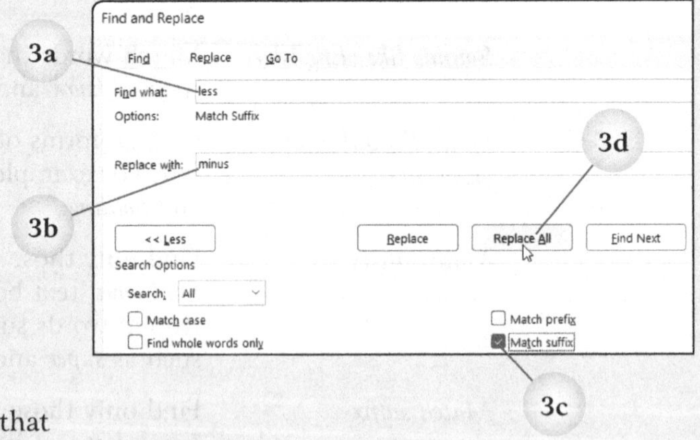

4. Save, preview, and then close **4-LeaseAgrmnt.docx**.

Chapter Summary

- By default, a Word document contains 1-inch top, bottom, left, and right margins. Change margins with preset margin settings at the Margins button drop-down list or with options at the Page Setup dialog box with the Margins tab selected.
- The default page layout is portrait orientation. It can be changed to landscape orientation with the Orientation button in the Page Setup group on the Layout tab.
- The default paper size is 8.5 inches wide by 11 inches tall. It can be changed with options at the Size button drop-down list or options at the Page Setup dialog box with the Paper tab selected.
- A page break that Word inserts automatically is a *soft page break*. A page break inserted manually is a *hard page break*. Insert a hard page break using the Page Break button in the Pages group on the Insert tab or by pressing Ctrl + Enter.
- Insert a predesigned and formatted cover page by clicking the Cover Page button in the Pages group on the Insert tab and then clicking an option at the drop-down list.
- Insert predesigned and formatted page numbers by clicking the Page Number button in the Header & Footer group on the Insert tab, specifying the location of the page number, and then clicking a page numbering option.
- Insert predesigned headers and footers in a document with the Header button and the Footer button in the Header & Footer group on the Insert tab.
- A watermark is a lightened image that displays behind the text in a document. Use the Watermark button in the Page Background group on the Design tab to insert a watermark.
- Insert a page background color in a document with the Page Color button in the Page Background group on the Design tab. The page background color is designed for viewing a document onscreen and does not print.
- Click the Page Borders button in the Page Background group on the Design tab and the Borders and Shading dialog box with the Page Border tab selected displays. Use options at this dialog box to insert a page border or an art image page border in a document.
- Apply formatting to a portion of a document by inserting a continuous section break or a section break that begins a new page. Turn on the display of nonprinting characters to display section breaks.
- Set text in columns to improve the readability of documents, such as newsletters and reports. Format text in columns using the Columns button in the Page Setup group on the Layout tab or with options at the Columns dialog box.
- Remove column formatting with the Columns button in the Page Setup group on the Layout tab or at the Columns dialog box.
- Insert a column break by clicking the Layout tab, clicking the Breaks button, and then clicking the *Column* option. Balance column text on the last page of a document by inserting a continuous section break at the end of the text.
- Improve the appearance of text by hyphenating long words that fall at the ends of lines. Use the hyphenation feature to hyphenate words automatically or manually. Click the Hyphenation button in the Page Setup group on the Layout tab to display a drop-down list with hyphenation options.
- To enhance the appearance of text, use drop caps to identify the beginnings of major sections or paragraphs. Create drop caps with the Drop Cap button in the Text group on the Insert tab.

- Use the Click and Type feature to center, right-align, and left-align text.
- Vertically align text in a document with the *Vertical alignment* option box at the Page Setup dialog box with the Layout tab selected.
- Use the Find button in the Editing group on the Home tab to search for specific text. Use the Replace button to search for specific text and replace it with other text.
- At the Find and Replace dialog box, click the Find Next button to find the next occurrence of the text. Click the Replace button to replace the text and find the next occurrence or click the Replace All button to replace all occurrences of the text.
- Click the More button at the Find and Replace dialog box to display additional search options.

Commands Review

FEATURE	RIBBON TAB, GROUP	BUTTON, OPTION	KEYBOARD SHORTCUT
blank page	Insert, Pages		
Border and Shading Options dialog box	Design, Page Background	, Options	
Borders and Shading dialog box with Page Border tab selected	Design, Page Background		
column break	Layout, Page Setup	, *Column*	Ctrl + Shift + Enter
columns	Layout, Page Setup		
Columns dialog box	Layout, Page Setup	, *More Column*	
continuous section break	Layout, Page Setup	, *Continuous*	
cover page	Insert, Pages		
drop cap	Insert, Text		
Find and Replace dialog box with Find tab selected	Home, Editing	, *Advanced Find*	
Find and Replace dialog box with Replace tab selected	Home, Editing		Ctrl + H
footer	Insert, Header & Footer		
header	Insert, Header & Footer		
hyphenate words automatically	Layout, Page Setup	, *Automatic*	
Manual Hyphenation dialog box	Layout, Page Setup	, *Manual*	
margins	Layout, Page Setup		
Navigation pane	Home, Editing		Ctrl + F
orientation	Layout, Page Setup		
page background color	Design, Page Background		
page break	Insert, Pages		Ctrl + Enter
page numbers	Insert, Header & Footer		
Page Setup dialog box with Margins tab selected	Layout, Page Setup	, *Custom Margins* OR	
Page Setup dialog box with Paper tab selected	Layout, Page Setup	, *More Paper Sizes*	
paper size	Layout, Page Setup		
watermark	Design, Page Background		

Review and Assessment

CHAPTER 4

Skills Assessment

Assessment 1

Format a Cover Letter Document and Insert a Cover Page

1. Open **CoverLetter.docx** and then save it with the name **4-CoverLetter**.
2. Change the left and right margins to 1.25 inches.
3. Move the insertion point to the beginning of the heading *Writing Cover Letters to People You Know* and then insert a blank page.
4. Insert a page break at the beginning of the heading *Writing Cover Letters to People You Do Not Know*.
5. Move the insertion point to the beginning of the document, insert the Filigree cover page, and then insert the following text in the specified fields:
   a. Type job search strategies in the *[DOCUMENT TITLE]* placeholder.
   b. Type Writing a Cover Letter in the *[Document subtitle]* placeholder.
   c. Type the current date in the *[DATE]* placeholder.
   d. Type career finders in the *[COMPANY NAME]* placeholder.
   e. Delete the *[Company address]* placeholder.
6. Move the insertion point to anywhere in the subtitle *WRITING A COVER LETTER* (on the page after the cover page) and then insert the Brackets 1 page numbering at the bottom of the page. (The page numbering will not appear on the cover page.)
7. Make the document active and turn on the display of nonprinting characters.
8. Move the insertion point to the blank line below the first paragraph of text (and above the page break) and then press the Delete key six times. (This deletes the page break on the first page and the page break creating a blank page 2, as well as extra blank lines.) Turn off the display of nonprinting characters.
9. Save, preview, and then close **4-CoverLetter.docx**.

Assessment 2

Format a Photography Report into Columns

1. Open **PhotoReport.docx** and then save it with the name **4-PhotoReport**.
2. Format the text from the first paragraph of text below the title to the end of the document into two columns with a line between and with 0.4 inch between columns.
3. Create a drop cap with the first letter of the first paragraph below the title. Specify that the drop cap is in the paragraph rather than the margin and is dropped two lines.
4. Move the insertion point to the end of the document and then insert a continuous section break to balance the columns on the second page.
5. Manually hyphenate the document. (Do not hyphenate headings and names.)
6. Save, preview, and then close **4-PhotoReport.docx**.

Assessment 3 Format an Intellectual Property Report and Insert Headers and Footers

1. Open **ProtectIssues.docx** and then save it with the name **4-ProtectIssues**.
2. Change the top margin to 1.5 inches.
3. Change the page layout to landscape orientation.
4. With the insertion point positioned at the beginning of the document, insert the Retrospect footer. Select the name at the left side of the footer and then type your first and last names.
5. Save the document and then preview only page 1.
6. Change the page layout back to portrait orientation.
7. Apply the Moderate page margins.
8. Remove the footer.
9. Insert the Ion (Dark) header.
10. Insert the Ion (Dark) footer. Type property protection issues as the title and make sure your first and last names display at the right side of the footer.
11. Select the footer text (document name and your name), apply bold formatting, and then change the font size to 8 points.
12. Insert the DRAFT 1 watermark in the document.
13. Apply the Green, Accent 6, Lighter 80% page color (last column, second row in the *Theme Colors* section).
14. Save and then preview **4-ProtectIssues.docx**.
15. With the document still open, change the paper size to Legal (8.5 inches by 14 inches).
16. Save the document with Save As and name it **4-ProtectIssues-Legal**.
17. Check with your instructor to determine if you can print legal-sized documents. If so, print page 1 of the document.
18. Save, preview, and then close **4-ProtectIssues-Legal.docx**.

Assessment 4 Format a Real Estate Agreement

1. Open **REAgrmnt.docx** and then save it with the name **4-REAgrmnt**.
2. Find all occurrences of *BUYER* (matching the case) and replace them with *James Berman*.
3. Find all occurrences of *SELLER* (matching the case) and replace them with *Mona Trammell*.
4. Find all word forms of the word *buy* and replace them with *purchase*.
5. Insert Plain Number 2 page numbering at the bottom center of the page.
6. Insert a page border with the following specifications:
   - Choose the first double-line border in the *Style* list box.
   - Change the color of the page border to the standard dark red color (first color in the *Standard Colors* section).
   - Change the width of the page border to 1 1/2 points.
7. Display the Border and Shading Options dialog box for the page border and then change the top, left, bottom, and right measurements to 30 points. ***Hint: Display the Border and Shading Options dialog box by clicking the Options button at the Borders and Shading dialog box with the Page Border tab selected.***
8. Save, preview, and then close **4-REAgrmnt.docx**.

Visual Benchmark

Format a Resume Styles Report

1. Open **Resumes.docx** and then save it with the name **4-Resumes**.
2. Format the document so it appears as shown in Figure 4.13 with the following specifications:
   a. Change the top margin to 1.5 inches.
   b. Change the line spacing for the entire document to 1.5 lines.
   c. Apply the Heading 1 style to the title and the Heading 2 style to the headings.
   d. Apply the Lines (Simple) style set.
   e. Apply the Savon theme.
   f. Apply the Blue Green theme colors.
   g. Change the paragraph spacing after the title to 9 points. Apply 6 points of paragraph spacing after the three headings.
   h. Insert the Austin cover page. Insert text in the placeholders and delete the Abstract placeholder as shown in the figure. (If a name appears in the author placeholder, delete it and then type your first and last names.)
   i. Insert the Ion (Dark) header and the Ion (Dark) footer.
3. Save, preview, and then close **4-Resumes.docx**.

Figure 4.13 Visual Benchmark

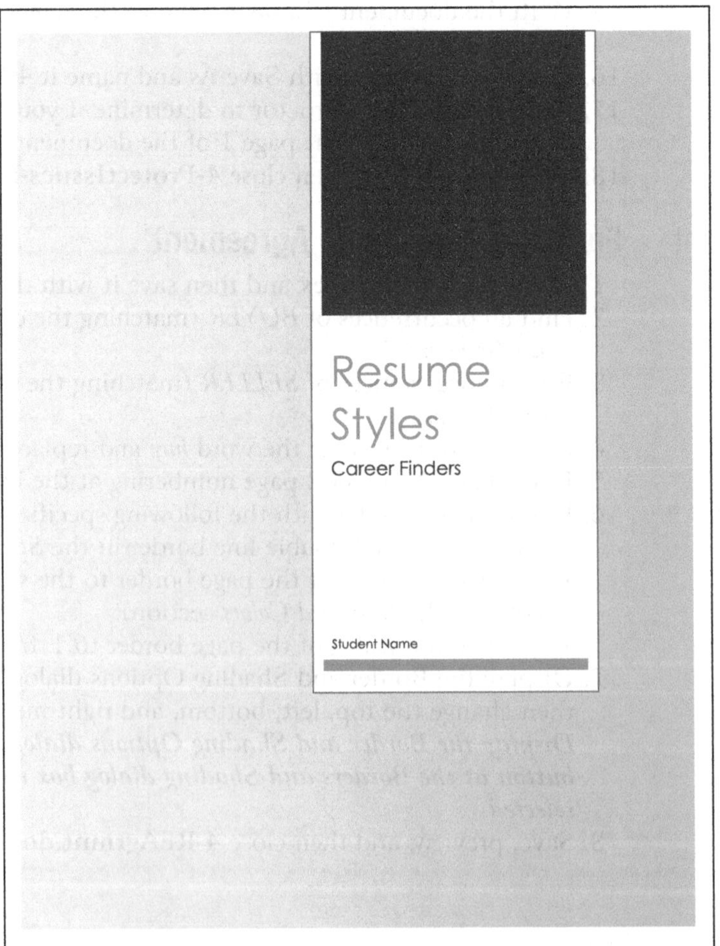

Continues

Figure 4.13 Visual Benchmark—*Continued*

1

RESUME STYLES

You can write a resume several different ways. The three most popular resume styles include: chronological resumes, functional resumes, and hybrid resumes. To these three we will add the structured interview resume. Although not used often, this resume format enables people to set out the benefits that they offer an employer in a conversational style. It's inviting to read and enables you to convey a lot of targeted information. It is particularly useful if you are able to anticipate the types of questions that will be asked at an interview. By presenting your resume in this way, you provide the employer with an expectation of how you might perform in an interview, giving the employer a reason to consider your application further.

The Chronological Resume

This resume style is the one most commonly used. It lists the individual's training and jobs by the date he or she started each of them. Typically, people list their most recent training or jobs first and proceed backward to the things they did in the past. This is called "reverse chronological" order. The components of this resume include:

- Personal contact information
- Employment history, including names of employers, dates of employment, positions held, and achievements
- Educational qualifications
- Professional development

The Functional Resume

This is the style that emphasizes an individual's skills and achiev
the applicant does not have a degree or has educational qu
that are not relevant to the job being sought. This style might c
had many different jobs with no clear pattern or progression, c
several gaps.

RESUME STYLES

2

The Hybrid Resume

This is an increasingly popular approach that combines the best of both the chronological resume and the functional resume. A hybrid resume retains much of the fixed order of the chronological resume, but it includes more emphasis on skills and achievements—sometimes in a separate section. The hybrid approach is the one that we recommend to most people. It provides more opportunity for job seekers to explain how they stand out from the crowd. Now that many resumes are uploaded electronically without a cover letter attached, a hybrid resume that emphasizes your skills and achievements may be the best choice for marketing yourself to prospective employers.

RESUME STYLES STUDENT NAME

Case Study

Part 1

You work for Citizens for Consumer Safety, a nonprofit organization that provides information on household safety. Your supervisor, Melinda Johansson, has asked you to format a document on smoke detectors. She will use the document as an informational handout during a presentation on smoke detectors. Open **SmokeDetectors.docx** and then save it with the name **4-SmokeDetectors-1**. Apply a style set, apply appropriate styles to the title and headings, and then apply a theme and theme colors to the document. Ms. Johansson has asked you to change the page layout to landscape orientation and to change the left and right margins to 1.5 inches. She wants to allow extra space at the left and right margins so audience members can write notes in these areas. Use the Help feature or experiment with the options on the Header & Footer tab and figure out how to put page numbers on every page but the first page. Insert page numbers in the document that print at the top right of every page except the first page. Save, preview, and then close **4-SmokeDetectors-1.docx**.

Part 2

After reviewing the formatted document on smoke detectors, Ms. Johansson has decided that she would like it to print in the default orientation (portrait) and that she would like to see different theme and style choices. She has also decided that the term *smoke alarm* should be replaced with *smoke detector*. She has asked you to open and then make changes to the original document. Open **SmokeDetectors.docx** and then save it with the name **4-SmokeDetectors-2**. Apply styles to the title and headings and apply a theme and theme colors to the document (other than the one you chose for Part 1). Search for all occurrences of *Smoke Alarm* and replace them with *Smoke Detector* matching the case. Search for all occurrences of *smoke alarm* and replace them with *smoke detector* without matching the case. Insert a cover page of your choosing and then insert the appropriate information on the page. Use the current date and your name as the author and delete all unused placeholders. Make any other formatting changes to improve the appearance and layout of the document. Save, preview, and then close **4-SmokeDetectors-2.docx**.

Part 3

Ms. Johansson has asked you to prepare a document on infant car seats and infant car seat safety to be available for distribution at a local community center. Find websites that provide information on child and infant car seats and car seat safety. Using the information you find, write a report that covers at least the following topics:

- Description of types of infant car seats (such as rear-facing, convertible, forward-facing, built-in, and booster)
- Safety rules and guidelines for safe installation
- Websites that sell infant car seats, along with price ranges for specific models
- Websites that provide safety information

Format the report using styles and a theme and include a cover page and headers and/or footers. Save the completed document with the name **4-CarSeats**. Preview and then close the document.

WORD LEVEL 1

Unit 1 Performance Assessment

Data Files

The data files for this unit work are in the WL1U1 folder that you downloaded at the beginning of this course.

Assessing Proficiency

In this unit, you have learned to create, edit, save, and print Word documents. You have also learned to format characters, paragraphs, pages, and documents.

Assessment 1

Format a Document on Website Design

1. Open **Website.docx** and then save it with the name **U1-Website**.
2. Use the Editor to complete a spelling and grammar check on the document.
3. Select the text from the paragraph that begins *Make your home page work for you.* through the end of the document and then apply bulleted formatting.
4. Select and then apply bold formatting to the first sentence of each bulleted paragraph.
5. Apply a single-line bottom border to the document title and apply Gold, Accent 4, Lighter 80% paragraph shading (eighth column, second row in the *Theme Colors* section) to the title.
6. Save and then preview **U1-Website.docx**.
7. Change the top, left, and right margins to 1.5 inches.
8. Select the bulleted paragraphs, change the paragraph alignment to justified, and then apply numbered formatting.
9. Select the entire document and then change the font to 12-point Cambria.
10. Insert the text shown in Figure U1.1 after paragraph number 2. (The number *3.* should automatically be inserted preceding the text you type.)
11. Save, preview, and then close **U1-Website.docx**.

Figure U1.1 Assessment 1

> **Avoid a cluttered look.** In design, less is more. Strive for a clean look to your pages, using ample margins and white space.

Assessment 2 Format an Accumulated Returns Document

1. Open **TotalReturns.docx** and then save it with the name **U1-TotalReturns**.
2. Select the entire document and then make the following changes:
   a. Apply the No Spacing style.
   b. Change the line spacing to 1.5 lines.
   c. Change the font to 12-point Cambria.
   d. Apply 6 points of spacing after paragraphs.
3. Select the title *TOTAL RETURN CHARTS*, change the font to 14-point Corbel bold, change the alignment to centered, and apply Blue-Gray, Text 2, Lighter 80% paragraph shading (fourth column, second row in the *Theme Colors* section).
4. Apply bold formatting to the following text that appears at the beginnings of the second through the fifth paragraphs:
   Average annual total return:
   Annual total return:
   Accumulation units:
   Accumulative rates:
5. Select the paragraphs of text in the body of the document (all paragraphs except the title) and then change the paragraph alignment to justified.
6. Select the paragraphs that begin with the bolded words, sort the paragraphs in ascending order, and then indent the text 0.5 inch from the left margin.
7. Insert a watermark that prints *DRAFT* diagonally across the page.
8. Save, preview, and then close **U1-TotalReturns.docx**.

Assessment 3 Format a Technology Visionaries Report

1. Open **TechVisionaries.docx** and then save it with the name **U1-TechVisionaries**.
2. Apply the Heading 1 style to the titles *TECHNOLOGY VISIONARIES* and *REFERENCES*.
3. Apply the Heading 2 style to the headings in the document (*Konrad Zuse*, *William Hewlett and David Packard*, *Gordon E. Moore*, and *Jack S. Kilby*).
4. Apply the Centered style set.
5. Apply the Tight paragraph spacing.
6. Apply the Frame theme and then change the theme fonts to Candara.
7. Change the paragraph spacing after each heading from 2 points to 6 points.
8. Create a hanging indent for the paragraphs of text below the title *REFERENCES*.
9. Insert page numbers that print at the bottom center of each page.
10. Save, preview, and then close **U1-TechVisionaries.docx**.

Assessment 4 Set Tabs and Type Income by Division Text in Columns

1. At a new blank document, type the text shown in Figure U1.2 with the following specifications:
   a. Apply bold formatting to and center the title as shown.
   b. You determine the tab settings for the text in columns.
   c. Select the entire document and then change the font to 12-point Arial.
2. Save the document with the name **U1-Income**.
3. Preview and then close **U1-Income.docx**.

Figure U1.2 Assessment 4

INCOME BY DIVISION			
	2022	**2023**	**2024**
Public Relations	$14,375	$16,340	$16,200
Database Services	9,205	15,055	13,725
Graphic Design	18,400	21,790	19,600
Technical Support	5,780	7,325	9,600

Assessment 5

Set Tabs and Type Table of Contents Text

1. At a blank document, type the text shown in Figure U1.3 with the following specifications:
   a. Apply bold formatting to and center the title as shown.
   b. You determine the tab settings for the text in columns.
   c. Select the entire document, change the font to 12-point Cambria, and then change the line spacing to 1.5 lines.
2. Save the document with the name **U1-TofC**.
3. Preview and then close **U1-TofC.docx**.

Figure U1.3 Assessment 5

TABLE OF CONTENTS

Ancient Astronomy..3

Laws of Nature 7

Modern Astronomy...12

Our Solar System..23

Laws of Planetary Motion 31

Earth and Sky...45

Assessment 

Format a Union Agreement Contract

1. Open **LaborContract.docx** and then save it with the name **U1-LaborContract**.
2. Find *AERO MANUFACTURING* and replace all occurrences with *KEIL CORPORATION.*
3. Find *AM* (matching the case) and replace all occurrences with *KC*.
4. Find *LABOR WORKERS' UNION* and replace all occurrences with *SERVICE EMPLOYEES' UNION.*
5. Find *LWU* and replace all occurrences with *SEU*.
6. Select the entire document and then change to 1.15 line spacing.
7. Select the numbered paragraphs in the section *Transfers and Moving Expenses* and change them to bulleted paragraphs.

8. Select the numbered paragraphs in the section *Sick Leave* and change them to bulleted paragraphs.
9. Change to landscape orientation and change the top margin to 1.5 inches.
10. Save and then preview **U1-LaborContract.docx**.
11. Change the top margin back to 1 inch and then change back to portrait orientation.
12. Insert the Whisp cover page and then insert the current date in the date placeholder, the title *Union Agreement* as the document title, and *Keil Corporation* as the document subtitle. Select the author placeholder (or the name) at the bottom of the cover page and then type your first and last names. Delete the company name placeholder.
13. Move the insertion point to the page after the cover page, insert the Ion (Dark) footer, and then make sure *UNION AGREEMENT* displays in the title placeholder and your name displays in the author placeholder. If not, type UNION AGREEMENT in the title placeholder and your first and last names in the author placeholder.
14. Save, preview, and then close **U1-LaborContract.docx**.

Assessment 7 Copy and Paste Text in a Health Plan Document

1. Open **KeyLifePlan.docx** and then save it with the name **U1-KeyLifePlan**.
2. Open **PlanOptions.docx** and then display the Clipboard task pane. Make sure the Clipboard is empty.
3. Select the heading *Plan Highlights* and the six paragraphs of text below it and then copy the selected text to the Clipboard.
4. Select the heading *Plan Options* and the two paragraphs of text below it and then copy the selected text to the Clipboard.
5. Select the heading *Quality Assessment* and the six paragraphs of text below it (located at the end of the document) and then copy the selected text to the Clipboard.
6. Close **PlanOptions.docx**.
7. With **U1-KeyLifePlan.docx** open, display the Clipboard task pane.
8. Move the insertion point to the beginning of the heading *Provider Network*, paste the *Plan Options* item from the Clipboard, and merge the formatting.
9. With the insertion point positioned at the beginning of the heading *Provider Network*, paste the *Plan Highlights* item from the Clipboard and merge the formatting.
10. Move the insertion point to the beginning of the heading *Plan Options*, paste the *Quality Assessment* item from the Clipboard, and merge the formatting.
11. Clear the Clipboard and then close it.
12. Apply the Heading 1 style to the title *KEY LIFE HEALTH PLAN*.
13. Apply the Heading 2 style to the four headings in the document.
14. Change the top margin to 1.5 inches.
15. Apply the Lines (Simple) style set.
16. Apply the Compact paragraph spacing.
17. Apply the Red Orange theme colors.
18. Insert a double-line page border in the standard dark red color.
19. Insert the Slice 1 header.
20. Insert the Slice footer and type your first and last names in the author placeholder.
21. Insert a page break at the beginning of the heading *Plan Highlights*.
22. Save, preview, and then close **U1-KeyLifePlan.docx**.

Assessment 8

Format a Bioinformatics Document

1. Open **Bioinformatics.docx** and then save it with the name **U1-Bioinformatics**.
2. Change the line spacing for the entire document to 1.5 spacing.
3. Insert a continuous section break at the beginning of the first paragraph of text (the paragraph that begins *Bioinformatics is the mixed application*).
4. Format the text below the section break into two columns.
5. Balance the columns on the second page.
6. Create a drop cap with the first letter of the first word *Bioinformatics* that begins the first paragraph of text. Specify that the drop cap is in the paragraph and not the margin and make the drop cap two lines in height.
7. Manually hyphenate the words in the document.
8. Insert page numbers at the bottoms of the pages using the Thin Line page numbering option. (The Thin Line page number option is located in the *Plain Number* section of the Page Number button side menu.)
9. Save, preview, and then close **U1-Bioinformatics.docx**.

Assessment 9

Create and Format a Resume

1. Open **Resume.docx** and then save it with the name **U1-Resume**.
2. Apply the following formatting so your document appears as shown in Figure U1.4:
   a. Change the font for the entire document to Candara.
   b. Change the top margin measurement to 1.25 inches.
   c. Apply character and paragraph formatting as shown (including bold formatting, paragraph alignment, bulleted formatting, borders and shading formatting, and adding leaders to the right tab in the *PROFESSIONAL EXPERIENCE* section, as shown in the figure).
3. Save, preview, and then close **U1-Resume.docx**.

Figure U1.4 Assessment 9

KIERNAN O'MALLEY

1533 Baylor Street East, Auburn, WA 98020 (253) 555-3912

NETWORK ADMINISTRATION PROFESSIONAL
Pursuing **CCNA Cloud certification** and **Network+** credentials
Proficient in Microsoft Office applications in Windows environment

EDUCATION

Information Systems (IS), Western Washington University, Bellingham, WA......................2024
Medical Specialist, Seattle University, Seattle, WA .... 2020 to 2023
Medical Terminology, Green River Community College, Auburn, WA..................................2019

APPLIED RESEARCH PROJECTS

Completed **Applied Research Projects (ARPs)**, in conjunction with IS degree requirements, covering all aspects of design and management of organizational technical resources, as follows:

- **Organizational Culture and Leadership** (2024): Evaluated the organizational culture of Bellevue Surgery Center's endoscopy unit and operating room (OR) to ensure that the mission and vision statements were being appropriately applied at the staff level.
- **Human Resources (HR) Management** (2024): Established a comprehensive orientation package for the Bellevue Surgery Center's clinical staff.
- **Strategic Management and Planning** (2023): Conducted internal/external environmental assessments in order to identify an approach for Bellevue Surgery Center to expand its OR facilities.
- **Financial Accounting** (2023): Created a quarterly operating budget for the Bellevue Surgery Center and implemented an expenditure tracking system.
- **Database Management Systems** (2022): Created an inventory-control system that optimizes inventory maintenance in a cost-effective manner.
- **Statistics and Research Analysis** (2022): Generated graphics to illustrate the Valley Hospital's assisted-reproduction success rate.
- **Management Support System** (2021): Identified solutions to resolve inventory-control vulnerabilities at minimal cost for Valley Hospital.

PROFESSIONAL EXPERIENCE

CERTIFIED SURGICAL TECHNOLOGIST

Bellevue Surgery Center, Bellevue, WA..2022 to present
Valley Hospital, Renton, WA ....2020 to 2021
Kenmore Ambulatory Surgery Center, Kenmore, WA ....2018 to 2020
South Sound Medical Center, Auburn, WA... 2017 to 2018

Writing Activities

The following activities give you the opportunity to practice your writing skills and to demonstrate your understanding of some of the important Word features you have mastered in this unit. Use correct grammar, appropriate word choices, and clear sentence construction. Follow the steps in Figure U1.5 to improve your writing skills.

Activity 1

Write Paragraph on Button Functions

Explore the three buttons in the Editing group on the Home tab. Learn what functions are performed by each button. At a blank document, write a paragraph describing the functions performed by each button. After writing the paragraph, add steps on how to find text using the Navigation pane. Save the completed document with the name **U1-EditingGroupButtons**. Preview and then close **U1-EditingGroupButtons.docx**.

Activity 2

Write Information on Advanced Word Options

Use Word's Help feature and the search text *word options advanced* to learn how to customize display options at the Word Options dialog box with the *Advanced* option selected. After learning about the display options, create a document that describes the steps to change the display of the *Show this number of Recent Documents* option to *10*. Assume that the steps begin at a blank document. Describe the steps to turn on the *Quickly access this number of Recent Documents* option and change the number to *6*. Again, assume that the steps begin at a blank document. Add any additional information, such as a title, heading, and/or explanatory text, that helps the reader understand the contents of the document. Save the completed document with the name **U1-DisplayOptions**. Preview and then close **U1-DisplayOptions.docx**.

Internet Research

Research Business Desktop Computer Systems

You hold a part-time job at the local chamber of commerce, where you assist the office manager, Rianna Woods. Ms. Woods will be purchasing new desktop computers for the office staff. She has asked you to research using the internet and identify at least three PCs that can be purchased, and she wants you to put your research and recommendations in writing. Ms. Woods is looking for solid, reliable, economical, and powerful desktop computers with good warranties and service plans. She has given you a budget of $900 per unit.

Search the internet for three desktop PC systems from three different manufacturers. Consider price, specifications (processor speed, amount of RAM, hard drive space, and monitor type and size), performance, warranties, and service plans when choosing the systems. Include your research findings with your report.

Using Word, write a brief report in which you summarize the capabilities and qualities of each of the three computer systems you recommend. Include a final paragraph detailing which system you suggest for purchase and why. If possible, incorporate user opinions and/or reviews about the system to support your decision. Format your report using the concepts and techniques you learned in Unit 1. Save the report with the name **U1-InternetResearch**. Preview and then close the document.

Figure U1.5 The Writing Process

The Writing Process

Plan Gather ideas, select which information to include, and choose the order in which to present the information.

Checkpoints
- What is the purpose?
- What information does the reader need to reach your intended conclusion?

Write Following the information plan and keeping the reader in mind, draft the document using clear, direct sentences that say what you mean.

Checkpoints
- What subpoints support each main thought?
- How can you connect paragraphs so the reader moves smoothly from one idea to the next?

Revise Improve what is written by changing, deleting, rearranging, or adding words, sentences, and paragraphs.

Checkpoints
- Is the meaning clear?
- Do the ideas follow a logical order?
- Have you included any unnecessary information?
- Have you built your sentences around strong nouns and verbs?

Edit Check spelling, sentence construction, word use, punctuation, and capitalization.

Checkpoints
- Can you spot any redundancies or clichés?
- Can you reduce any phrases to effective words (for example, change *the fact that* to *because*)?
- Have you used commas only where there is a strong reason for doing so?
- Did you proofread the document for errors that your spelling checker cannot identify?

Publish Prepare a final copy that can be reproduced and shared with others.

Checkpoints
- Which design elements, such as bold formatting and different fonts, will help highlight important ideas or sections?
- Will charts or other graphics help clarify meaning?

WORD

LEVEL 1

Unit 2

Enhancing and Customizing Documents

WORD

Inserting and Formatting Objects

CHAPTER 5

Performance Objectives

Upon successful completion of Chapter 5, you will be able to:

1 Insert symbols, special characters, and the date and time

2 Insert, format, and customize images, text boxes, shapes, and WordArt

3 Insert and customize a screenshot

4 Insert, format, and modify a SmartArt graphic

Documents in Word may include special characters and symbols as well as the current date and time. The visual interest of a document can be enhanced by graphics, such as images, text boxes, shapes, WordArt, and screenshots. Word's SmartArt feature can be used to insert a graphic, such as a diagram or organizational chart. This chapter covers how to insert and customize these elements using buttons in the Illustrations group, the Text group, and the Symbols group on the Insert tab.

Data Files

The data files for this chapter are in the WL1C5 folder that you downloaded at the beginning of this course.

Activity 1 Format a Document on Computer Input Devices 2 Parts

In a document on computer input devices, you will insert a special character, symbols, and the date and time.

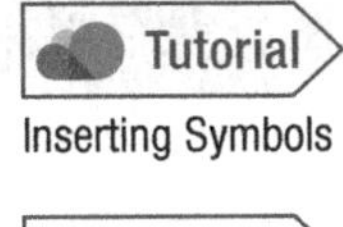

Tutorial

Inserting Symbols

Tutorial

Inserting Special Characters

Symbol

Quick Steps

Insert Symbol

1. Click Insert tab.
2. Click Symbol button.
3. Click symbol.

OR

1. Click Insert tab.
2. Click Symbol button.
3. Click *More Symbols.*
4. Double-click symbol.
5. Click Close.

Quick Steps

Insert Special Character

1. Click Insert tab.
2. Click Symbol button.
3. Click *More Symbols.*
4. Click Special Characters tab.
5. Double-click special character.
6. Click Close.

Inserting Symbols and Special Characters

Use the Symbol button on the Insert tab to insert special symbols in a document. Click the button and a drop-down list displays the most recently inserted symbols. Click one of the symbols in the list to insert it in the document or click the *More Symbols* option to display the Symbol dialog box, as shown in Figure 5.1. Double-click a symbol to insert it, or click it once and then click the Insert button. Click Close to exit the dialog box. Another method for selecting a symbol at the Symbol dialog box is to type the symbol code in the *Character code* text box. Click a symbol in the dialog box and the character code displays in the *Character code* text box. If a symbol is used on a regular basis, remembering the character code can be useful for inserting the symbol in a document.

At the Symbol dialog box with the Symbols tab selected, the font can be changed with the *Font* option box. When the font is changed, different symbols display in the dialog box. Click the Special Characters tab at the Symbol dialog box and a list of special characters displays along with keyboard shortcuts for creating them.

Figure 5.1 Symbol Dialog Box with the Symbols Tab Selected

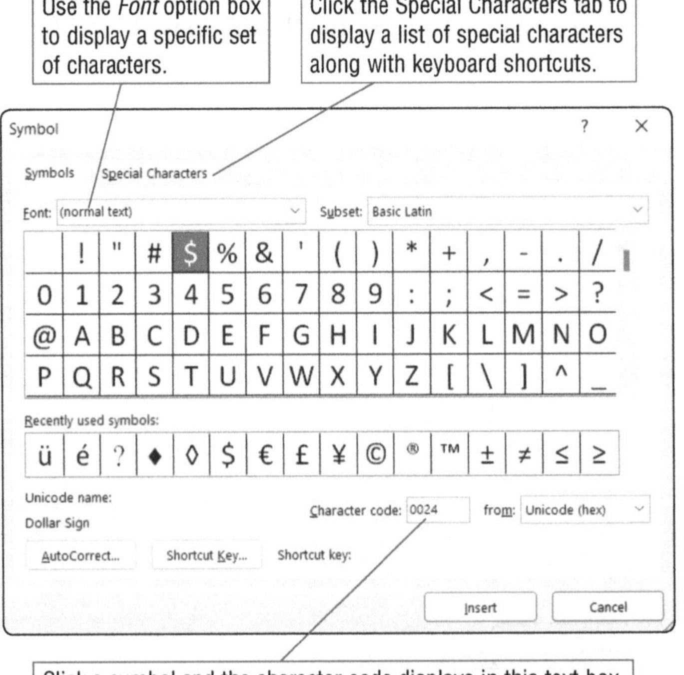
Use the *Font* option box to display a specific set of characters.
Click the Special Characters tab to display a list of special characters along with keyboard shortcuts.
Symbol
Symbols
Special Characters
Font: (normal text)
Subset: Basic Latin
Recently used symbols:
Unicode name:
Dollar Sign
Character code: 0024
from: Unicode (hex)
AutoCorrect...
Shortcut Key...
Shortcut key:
Insert
Cancel
Click a symbol and the character code displays in this text box. If you know the symbol character code, type it in the text box.

Activity 1a Inserting Symbols and Special Characters

Part 1 of 2

1. Open **InputDevices.docx** and then save it with the name **5-InputDevices**.
2. Press Ctrl + End to move the insertion point to the end of the document.
3. Type Prepared by: and then press the spacebar.
4. Type the first name Matthew and then press the spacebar.
5. Insert the last name *Viña* by completing the following steps:
   a. Type Vi.
   b. Click the Insert tab.
   c. Click the Symbol button in the Symbols group.
   d. Click *More Symbols* at the drop-down list.
   e. At the Symbol dialog box, make sure *(normal text)* appears in the *Font* option box and then double-click the *ñ* symbol (located in approximately the twelfth row).
   f. Click the Close button.
   g. Type a.
6. Press Shift + Enter.
7. Insert the keyboard symbol (⌨) by completing the following steps:
   a. Click the Symbol button and then click *More Symbols*.
   b. At the Symbol dialog box, click the *Font* option box arrow and then click *Wingdings* at the drop-down list. (You will need to scroll down the list to see this option.)
   c. Select the current number in the *Character code* text box and then type 55.
   d. Click the Insert button and then click the Close button.
8. Type SoftCell Technologies.
9. Insert the registered trademark symbol (®) by completing the following steps:
   a. Click the Symbol button and then click *More Symbols*.
   b. At the Symbol dialog box, click the Special Characters tab.
   c. Double-click the ® symbol (tenth option from the top).
   d. Click the Close button.
   e. Press Shift + Enter.
10. Select the keyboard symbol (⌨) and then change the font size to 18 points.
11. Save and then preview **5-InputDevices.docx**.

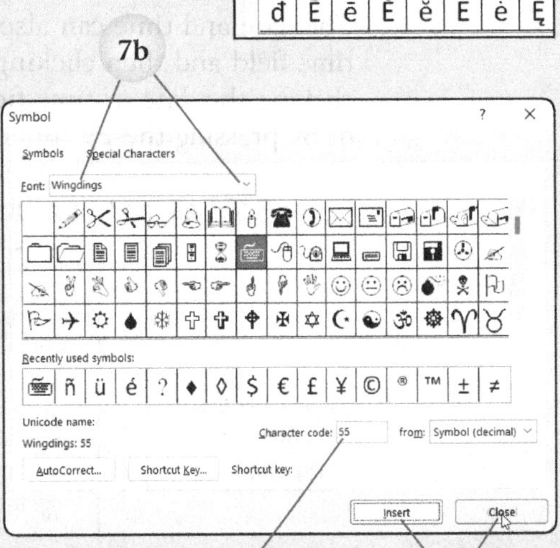

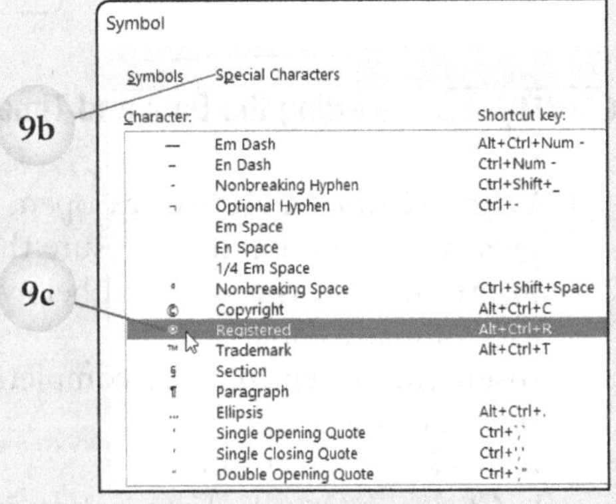

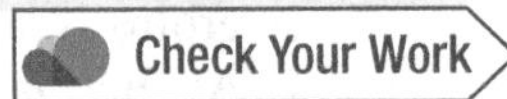

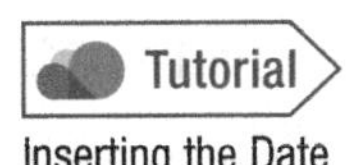

Inserting the Date and Time

Quick Steps

Insert Date and Time

1. Click Insert tab.
2. Click Date & Time button.
3. Click option in list box.
4. Click OK.

Inserting the Date and Time

Use the Date & Time button in the Text group on the Insert tab to insert the current date and time in a document. Click this button and the Date and Time dialog box displays, as shown in Figure 5.2. (Your date will vary from what you see in the figure.) At the Date and Time dialog box, click the desired date and/or time format in the *Available formats* list box.

If the *Update automatically* check box does not contain a check mark, the date and/or time are inserted in the document as text that can be edited in the normal manner. The date and/or time can also be inserted as a field. The advantage to using a field is that the date and time are updated when a document is reopened. Insert a check mark in the *Update automatically* check box to insert the date and/or time as a field. The date can also be inserted as a field using the keyboard shortcut Alt + Shift + D, and the time can be inserted as a field with the keyboard shortcut Alt + Shift + T.

A date or time field will automatically update when a document is reopened. The date and time can also be updated in the document by clicking the date or time field and then clicking the Update tab that appears above the field, by right-clicking the date or time field and then clicking *Update Field* at the shortcut menu, or by pressing the F9 function key.

Figure 5.2 Date and Time Dialog Box

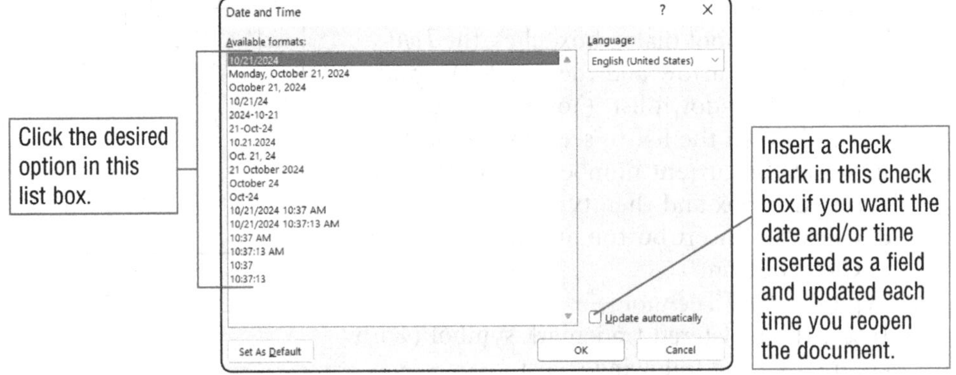

Activity 1b Inserting the Date and Time

Part 2 of 2

1. With **5-InputDevices.docx** open, press Ctrl + End and make sure the insertion point is positioned below the company name.
2. Insert the current date by completing the following steps:
   a. Click the Insert tab.
   b. Click the Date & Time button in the Text group.
   c. At the Date and Time dialog box, click the third option from the top in the *Available formats* list box. (Your date and time will vary from what you see in the image at the right.)
   d. If necessary, click in the *Update automatically* check box to insert a check mark.
   e. Click OK to close the dialog box.

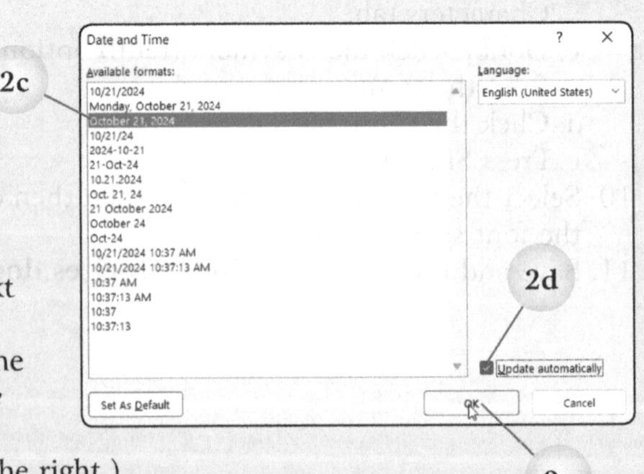

3. Press Shift + Enter.
4. Insert the current time by pressing Alt + Shift + T.
5. Save **5-InputDevices.docx.**
6. Update the time by clicking the time and then pressing the F9 function key.
7. Save, preview, and then close **5-InputDevices.docx.**

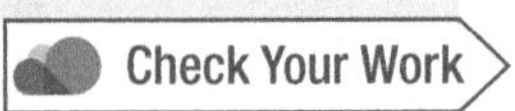

Activity 2 Insert Images in a Tour Document — 2 Parts

You will open a document with information on an Australian tour and add visual interest to the document by inserting and formatting images.

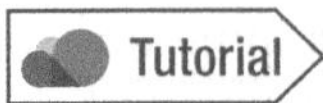

Inserting, Sizing, and Positioning an Image

Inserting and Formatting an Image

Insert an image, such as a photo or clip art, in a Word document with buttons in the Illustrations group on the Insert tab. Use the Pictures button in the Illustrations group to insert an image from a folder on the computer's hard drive or removable drive or an online source. Insert an image in a document to illustrate important information and to add visual interest.

Inserting an Image

Click the Pictures button in the Illustrations group on the Insert tab and a drop-down list displays with options for searching for images on the computer's hard drive or external storage medium, displaying a window with stock images (images available from Microsoft), or opening the Online Pictures window containing categories of images.

Click the *This Device* option at the Pictures button drop-down list and the Insert Picture dialog box displays. At this dialog box, navigate to the folder containing the desired image and then double-click the image to insert it in the document. Click the *Stock Images* option at the drop-down list and a window opens with royalty-free images that can be used in Microsoft 365 applications. To insert a stock image, click a category, and then double-click an image. Or, type key words in the search text box and then press the Enter key to find a specific type of image.

Click the *Online Pictures* option at the Pictures button drop-down list and the Online Pictures window displays. At this window, type the search term or topic in the search text box and then press the Enter key. Images that match the search text are shown in the window. Insert the image by clicking the image and then clicking the Insert button or by double-clicking the image. Be aware that many of the images available online are copyrighted. Before using an image in a document that will be shared publicly, make sure the image is either in the public domain (and thus not copyrighted) or determine how to get permission to use the image.

Sizing and Cropping an Image

When an image is inserted in a document, the Picture Format tab is active. The Size group on the Picture Format tab contains buttons for changing the size of an image and cropping an image. Change the size of an image by typing a measurement in the *Shape Height* and/or *Shape Width* measurement boxes or by clicking the up or down arrows in the measurement box.

Images in Word can also be sized using the mouse. Click an image to select it and circular sizing handles display around the image. Position the pointer on a sizing handle until the pointer turns into a double-headed arrow and then click and hold down the left mouse button. Drag the sizing handle in or out to decrease or increase the size of the image and then release the mouse button. Use the middle sizing handles at the left and right sides of the image to make the image wider or thinner. Use the middle sizing handles at the top and bottom of the image to make the image taller or shorter. Use the sizing handles at the corners of the image to change both the width and height at the same time.

Crop

Use the Crop button in the Size group to remove any unnecessary parts of an image. Click the Crop button and crop handles display around the image. Position the pointer on a crop handle and the pointer displays as a crop tool. Drag a crop handle to remove parts of the image.

Arranging an Image

The Arrange group on the Picture Format tab contains buttons for positioning, aligning, and rotating images. The group also contains buttons for wrapping text around an image and specifying if an image should appear in front of or behind text or other items.

Wrap Text

Layout Options

Use the Wrap Text button in the Arrange group to specify how text or other objects in the document should wrap around a selected image. The Wrap Text button drop-down list contains options for specifying square or tight wrapping, wrapping text above or below the image, and positioning the image behind or in front of text. The Layout Options button can also be used to specify text wrapping. When an image is selected, the Layout Options button displays outside the upper right corner of the image. Click the Layout Options button and then click a wrapping option at the drop-down list. Another method for specifying text wrapping is to right-click an image, point to *Wrap Text* at the shortcut menu, and click a text wrapping option at the side menu.

Position

Move an image to a specific location on the page with options at the Position button drop-down gallery in the Arrange group. Choose an option from this gallery and the image is moved to the specified location and square text wrapping is applied to it.

Rotate Objects

Rotate an image by positioning the pointer on the rotation handle, a circular arrow that appears above a selected image. The pointer will display with a black circular arrow attached. Click and hold down the left mouse button, drag in the desired direction, and then release the mouse button. An image can also be rotated or flipped with options at the Rotate Objects button drop-down gallery in the Arrange group.

Moving an Image

In addition to the Position button in the Arrange group on the Picture Format tab, an image can be moved using the mouse. Before moving an image with the mouse, specify how text should wrap around the image. After specifying text wrapping, position the pointer on the image until the pointer displays with a four-headed arrow attached. Click and hold down the left mouse button, drag the image to the new location, and then release the mouse button.

As an image is moved to the top, left, right, or bottom margin or to the center of the document, green alignment guides display. Use these guides to help

position the image on the page. If alignment guides do not display, turn them on by clicking the Align button in the Arrange group and then clicking *Use Alignment Guides* at the drop-down list. In addition to alignment guides, gridlines can be turned on to help position an image precisely. Turn on the display of gridlines by clicking the Align button and then clicking *View Gridlines*.

Activity 2a Inserting and Customizing an Image

Part 1 of 2

1. Open **Tour.docx** and then save it with the name **5-Tour.**
2. Insert an image by completing the following steps:
   a. Click the Insert tab, click the Pictures button in the Illustrations group, and then click the *This Device* option at the drop-down list.
   b. At the Insert Picture dialog box, navigate to your WL1C5 folder.
   c. Double-click the ***Uluru.jpg*** image file in the Content pane.

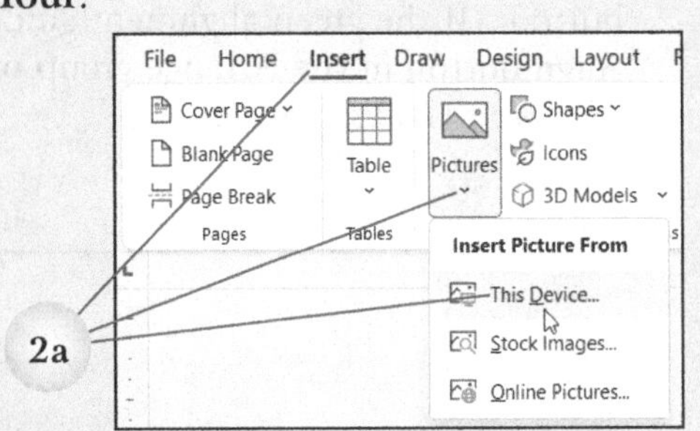

3. Crop the image by completing the following steps:
   a. Click the Crop button in the Size group on the Picture Format tab.
   b. Position the pointer on the bottom middle crop handle (which appears as a short black line) until the pointer turns into the crop tool (which appears as a small black T).
   c. Click and hold down the left mouse button, drag up to just below the rock (as shown at the right), and then release the mouse button.
   d. Click the Crop button in the Size group to turn the feature off.

4. Change the size of the image by clicking in the *Shape Height* measurement box in the Size group, typing 3, and then pressing the Enter key.
5. Specify text wrapping by clicking the Wrap Text button in the Arrange group and then clicking *Tight* at the drop-down list.
6. Change to a different text wrapping by completing the following steps:
   a. Click the Layout Options button outside the upper right corner of the image.
   b. Click the *Behind Text* option at the side menu (second column, second row in the *With Text Wrapping* section).
   c. Close the side menu by clicking the Close button in the upper right corner of the side menu.

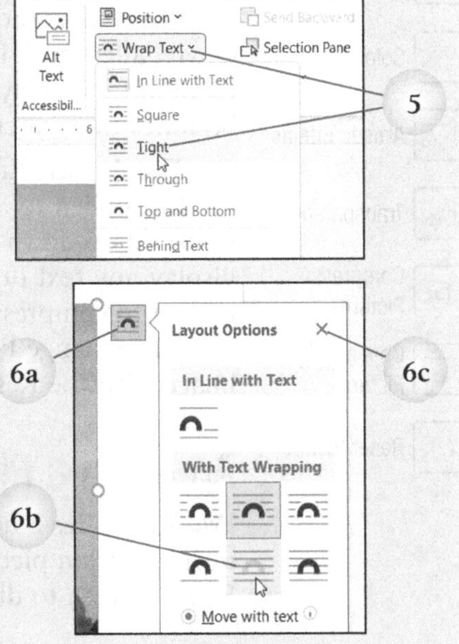

7. Rotate the image by clicking the Rotate Objects button in the Arrange group and then clicking *Flip Horizontal* at the drop-down gallery.

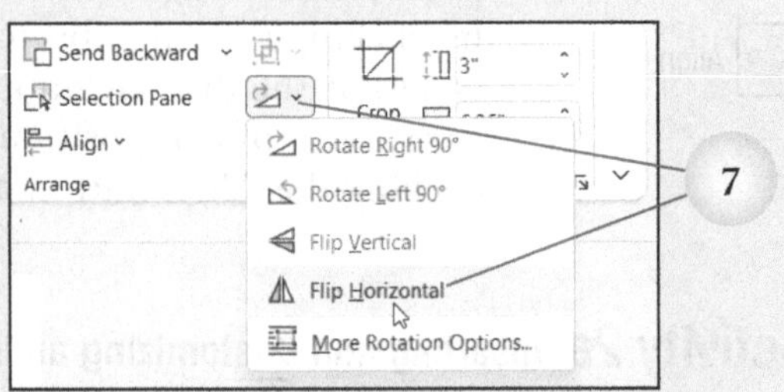

8. Position the pointer on the border of the selected image until the pointer displays with a four-headed arrow attached. Click and hold down the left mouse button, drag the image up and slightly to the right until you see green alignment guides at the top margin and the center of the page, and then release the mouse button. (If the green alignment guides do not display, turn on the guides by clicking the Align button in the Arrange group on the Picture Format tab and then clicking the *Use Alignment Guides* option.)

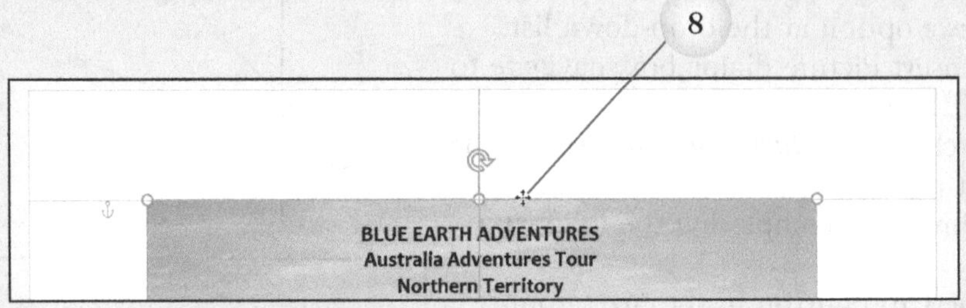

9. Save and then preview **5-Tour.docx**.

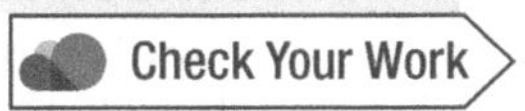

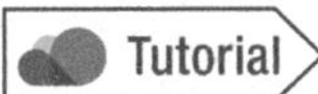

Formatting an Image

Adjusting an Image

The Adjust group on the Picture Format tab contains buttons for adjusting the background, color, brightness, and contrast of an image. Click the Remove Background button to display the Background Removal tab with buttons for removing unwanted portions of an image. Soft or sharpen an image or change the brightness and/or contrast with options at the Corrections button drop-down gallery. Use options at the Color button drop-down gallery to change the image color as well as the color saturation and color tone. The Color button drop-down gallery also includes the *Set Transparent Color* option. Click this option and the pointer displays as a dropper tool. Click a color in the image and that color becomes transparent.

The Artistic Effects button drop-down gallery offers a variety of effects that can be applied to an image. Lighten an image with options at the Transparency button drop-down gallery. For example, make an image more transparent to display any text or other objects behind the image. Use the Compress Pictures button to compress the size of images in a document. Remove or replace an image with the Change Picture button and discard all formatting changes and reset an image with the Reset Picture button.

Applying a Picture Style

Word provides a number of predesigned picture styles that can be applied to an image. Click a picture style in the Picture Styles group or click the More Picture Styles button to display a drop-down gallery of picture styles.

Creating Alternative Text for an Image

When an image is inserted in a document, consider adding *alternative text.* Alternative text, also known as alt text, is a brief description of an image or object that can be read by a screen reader and helps a person with a visual impairment understand what the image or object represents. Create alternative text at the Alt Text task pane. Display this task pane by clicking the Alt Text button in the Accessibility group on the Picture Format tab or by right-clicking the image and then clicking *Edit Alt Text* at the shortcut menu. At the Alt Text task pane, type a description of the image. If the image is only decorative and not important for understanding the content of the document, insert a check mark in the *Mark as decorative* check box. An image marked as decorative will not include any description for screen readers.

Activity 2b Formatting and Adjusting Images — Part 2 of 2

1. With **5-Tour.docx** open and the image selected, apply an artistic effect by clicking the Artistic Effects button in the Adjust group and then clicking the *Watercolor Sponge* option (second column, third row).
2. Lighten the image by clicking the Transparency button in the Adjust group and then clicking the *Transparency: 30%* option (third option in the drop-down gallery).
3. After looking at the artistic effect and transparency, remove the artistic effect and transparency by clicking the Reset Picture button in the Adjust group.

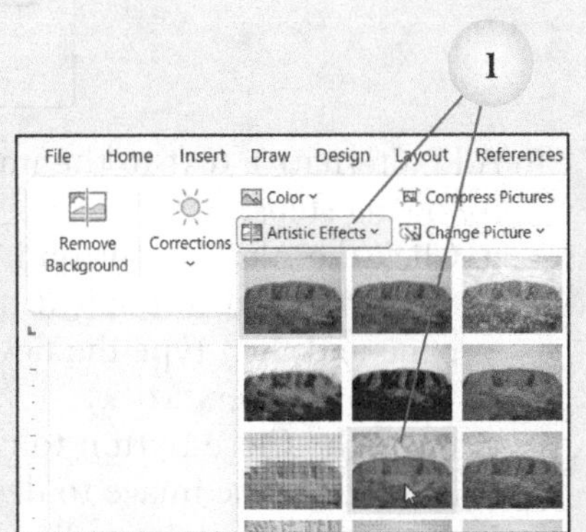

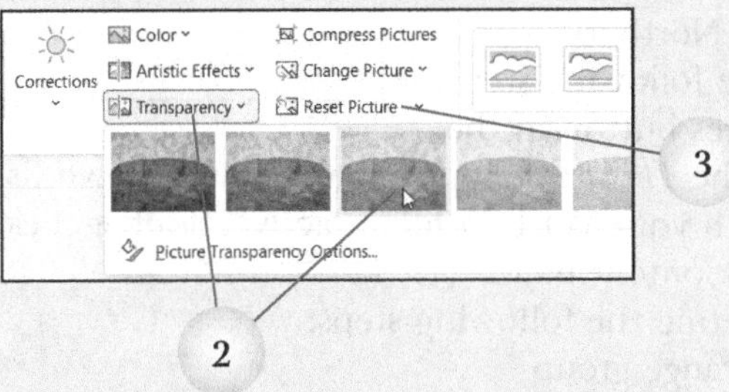

4. Sharpen the image by clicking the Corrections button in the Adjust group and then clicking the *Sharpen: 25%* option (fourth option in the *Sharpen/Soften* section).
5. Change the contrast of the image by clicking the Corrections button in the Adjust group and then clicking the *Brightness: 0% (Normal) Contrast: +40%* option (third column, bottom row in the *Brightness/Contrast* section).

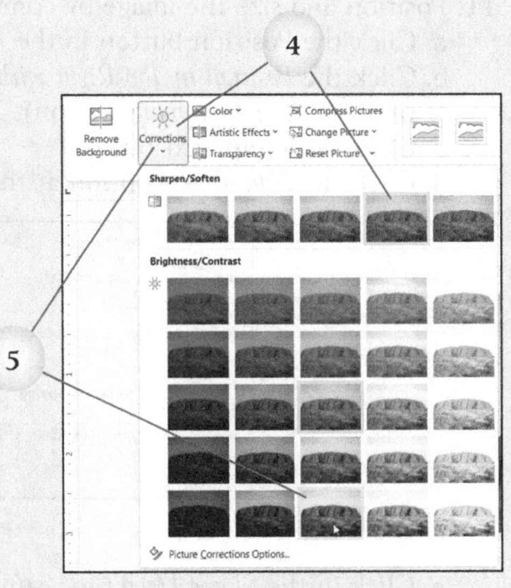

6. Compress the image by completing the following steps:
   a. Click the Compress Pictures button in the Adjust group.
   b. At the Compress Pictures dialog box, make sure check marks appear in the check boxes for both options in the *Compression options* section and then click OK.

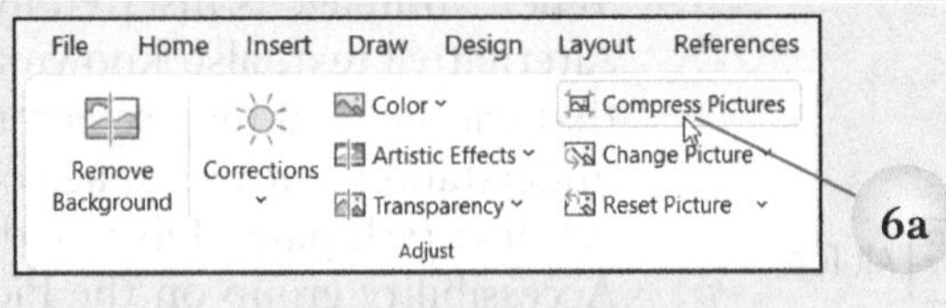

7. Apply a picture style by clicking the More Pictures Styles button in the Picture Styles group and then clicking the *Simple Frame, Black* option (second column, second row at the drop-down gallery).

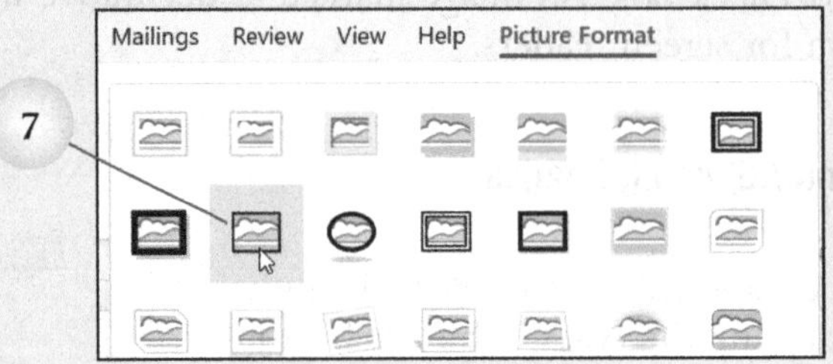

8. Add alternative text to the image by completing the following steps:
   a. Click the Alt Text button in the Accessibility group.
   b. Select the text in the text box in the Alt Text task pane and then type the description Uluru (also known as Ayers Rock).
   c. Click the Close button to close the task pane.

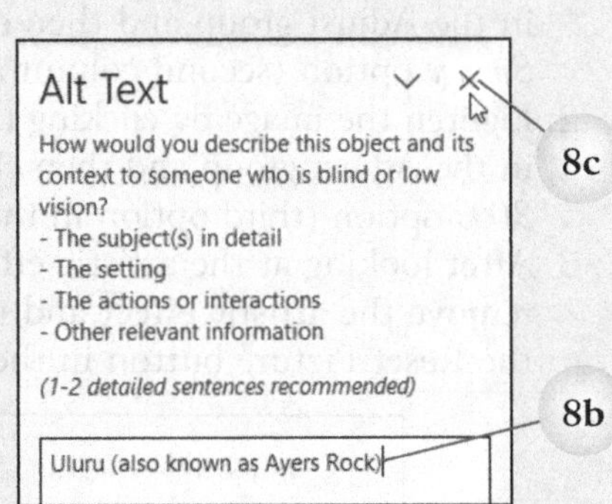

9. Click outside the image to deselect it.
10. Insert an image of Australia (with the Northern Territory identified) by completing the following steps:
    a. Click the Insert tab, click the Pictures button in the Illustrations group, and then click the *This Device* option at the drop-down list.
    b. At the Insert Picture dialog box, with your WL1C5 folder active, double-click the ***NT-Australia.png*** image file in the Content pane.
11. Position and size the image by completing the following steps:
    a. Click the Position button in the Arrange group.
    b. Click the *Position in Top Right with Square Text Wrapping* option (third column, first row in the *With Text Wrapping* section).
    c. Click the Wrap Text button.
    d. Click the *Behind Text* option at the drop-down gallery.

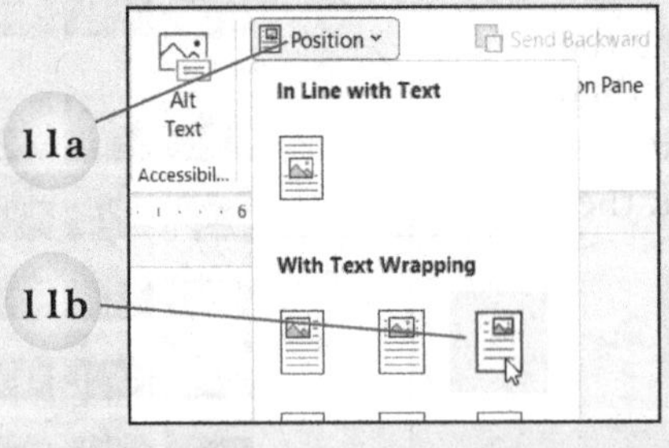

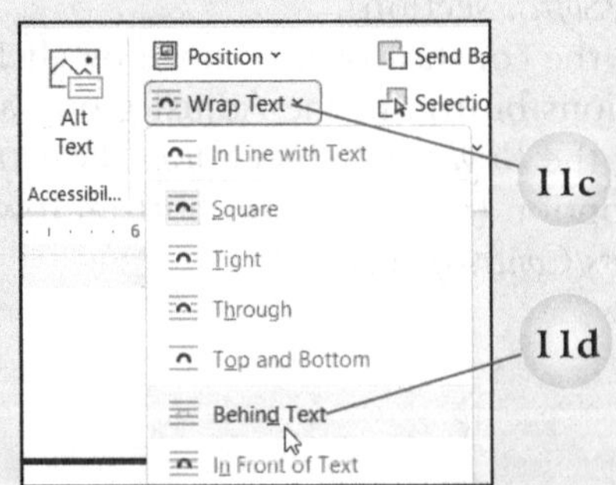

    e. Click in the *Shape Height* measurement box in the Size group, type 1, and then press the Enter key.

12. Make the white background of the image transparent by completing the following steps:
    a. Click the Color button in the Adjust group.
    b. Click the *Set Transparent Color* option at the bottom of the drop-down list. (The pointer turns into a dropper tool.)
    c. Position the dropper tool on any white portion of the image and then click the left mouse button.
13. Click the Color button and then click the *Orange, Accent color 2 Dark* option (third column, second row in the *Recolor* section).
14. Insert an airplane image by clicking the Insert tab, clicking the Pictures button, clicking the *This Device* option, and then double-clicking the ***Airplane.jpg*** image file in your WL1C5 folder.
15. With the airplane image selected, remove the background by completing the following steps:
    a. Click the Remove Background button in the Adjust group on the Picture Format tab.
    b. Click the Mark Areas to Remove button. (The pointer changes to a pen.)
    c. Position the pointer (pen) in the white area above the wing at the left side of the airplane, press and hold down the left mouse button, drag around the white area above the airplane to below the wing at the right side of the airplane (do not drag through any portion of the airplane), and then release the mouse button. (The white background the pointer passes through should be removed.)
    d. Use the pointer to drag in the remaining white background just above the wing and below the body of the airplane (Do not drag through any portion of the airplane.)
    e. If you are not satisfied with the background removal, click the Discard All Changes button and start again. If you are satisfied with the background removal, click the Keep Changes button.

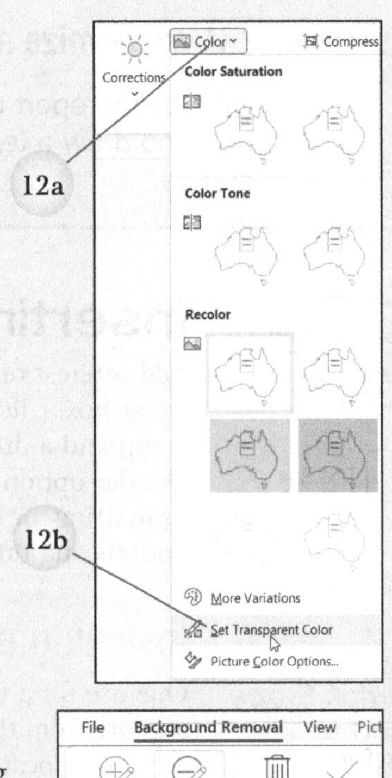

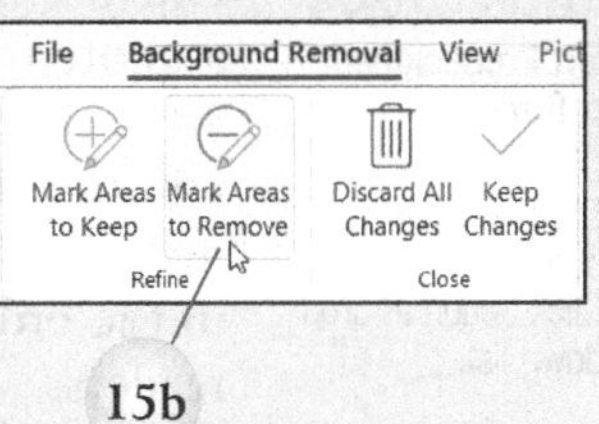

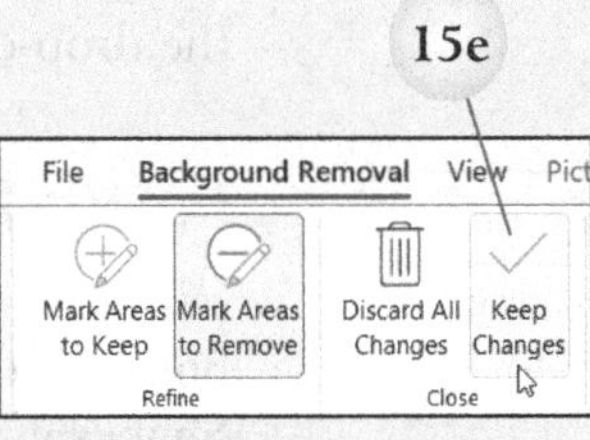

16. Position the airplane by clicking the Position button and then clicking the *Position in Top Left with Square Text Wrapping* option (first column, top row in the *With Text Wrapping* section).
17. Specify text wrapping by clicking the Wrap Text button and then clicking the *Behind Text* option.
18. Change the image width by clicking in the *Shape Width* measurement box, typing 2.1, and then pressing the Enter key.
19. Save, preview, and then close **5-Tour.docx**.

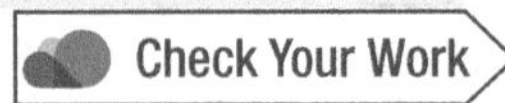

Activity 3 Customize a Report on Robots — 2 Parts

You will open a report on robots and then add a pull quote using a predesigned text box and draw a text box and type information about an upcoming conference.

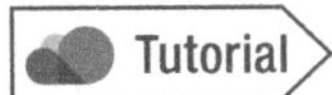

Inserting a Text Box

Inserting and Formatting a Text Box

Add interest or create a location in a document for text by inserting or drawing a text box. Click the Insert tab and then click the Text Box button in the Text group and a drop-down list displays with predesigned text boxes and the *Draw Text Box* option. Choose one of the predesigned text boxes, which already contain formatting, or draw a text box and then customize or apply formatting to it with options and buttons on the Shape Format tab.

Inserting a Predesigned Text Box

Quick Steps

Insert Predesigned Text Box

1. Click Insert tab.
2. Click Text Box button.
3. Click option at drop-down list.

One use for a text box in a document is to insert a pull quote. A pull quote is a quote from the text that is "pulled out" and enlarged and positioned in an attractive location on the page. Some advantages of using pull quotes are that they reinforce important concepts, summarize the message, and break up text blocks to make them easier to read. If a document contains multiple pull quotes, keep them in the order in which they appear in the text to ensure clear comprehension by readers.

A text box for a pull quote can be drawn in a document or a predesigned text box can be inserted in the document. To insert a predesigned text box, click the Insert tab, click the Text Box button, and then click the predesigned text box at the drop-down list.

Formatting a Text Box

Formatting a Text Box

When a text box is selected, the Shape Format tab is active. This tab contains buttons for formatting and customizing the text box. Use options in the Insert Shapes group to insert a shape in the text box or in another location in the document. Apply predesigned styles to a text box and change the shape fill, outline, and effects with options in the Shape Styles group. Change the formatting of the text in the text box with options in the WordArt Styles group. Click the More WordArt Styles button in the WordArt Styles group and then click a style at the drop-down gallery. Further customize the formatting of text in the text box with the Text Fill, Text Outline, and Text Effects buttons in the Text group. Use options in the Arrange group to position the text box on the page, specify text wrapping in relation to the text box, align the text box with other objects in the document, and rotate the text box. Specify the text box size with the *Shape Height* and *Shape Width* measurement boxes in the Size group.

Activity 3a Inserting and Formatting a Predesigned Text Box

Part 1 of 2

1. Open **Robots.docx** and then save it with the name **5-Robots.**
2. Insert a predesigned text box by completing the following steps:
   a. Click the Insert tab.
   b. Click the Text Box button in the Text group.
   c. Scroll down the drop-down list and then click the *Ion Quote (Dark)* option.
3. Type the following text in the text box:
   "The task of creating a humanlike body has proven incredibly difficult."
4. Delete the line and the source placeholder in the text box by pressing the F8 function key (which turns on the Selection mode), pressing Ctrl + End (which selects text from the location of the insertion point to the end of the text box), and then pressing the Delete key.
5. With the Shape Format tab active, click the More Shape Styles button in the Shape Styles group and then click the *Subtle Effect - Blue, Accent 5* option (sixth column, fourth row in the *Theme Styles* section).
6. Click the Shape Effects button in the Shape Styles group, point to *Shadow*, and then click the *Offset: Bottom Right* option (first column, first row in the *Outer* section).

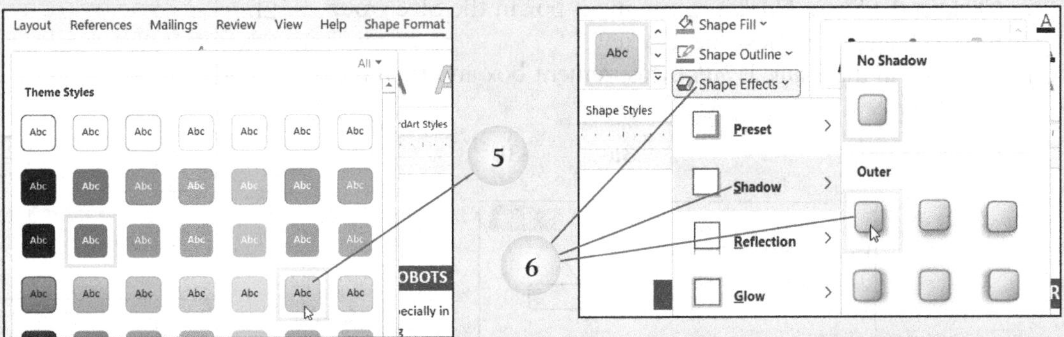

7. Position the pointer on the border of the selected text box until the pointer turns into a four-headed arrow and then drag the text box so it is positioned as shown below.

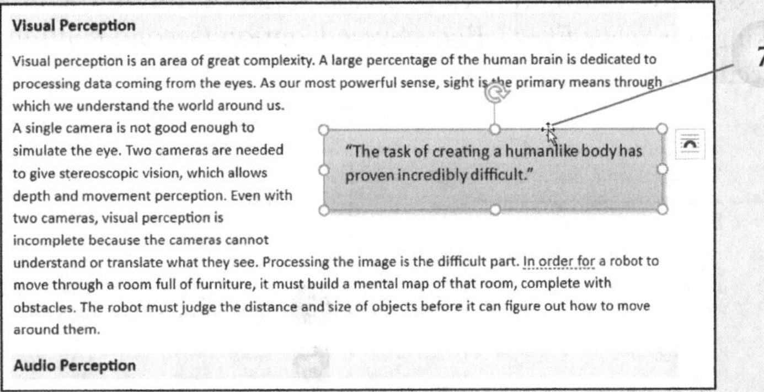

Visual Perception

Visual perception is an area of great complexity. A large percentage of the human brain is dedicated to processing data coming from the eyes. As our most powerful sense, sight is the primary means through which we understand the world around us.

A single camera is not good enough to simulate the eye. Two cameras are needed to give stereoscopic vision, which allows depth and movement perception. Even with two cameras, visual perception is incomplete because the cameras cannot understand or translate what they see. Processing the image is the difficult part. In order for a robot to move through a room full of furniture, it must build a mental map of that room, complete with obstacles. The robot must judge the distance and size of objects before it can figure out how to move around them.

"The task of creating a humanlike body has proven incredibly difficult."

Audio Perception

8. Click outside the text box to deselect it.
9. Save **5-Robots.docx.**

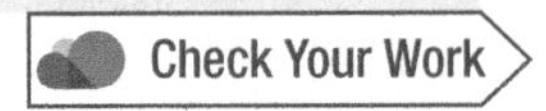

Drawing a Text Box

Quick Steps

Draw Text Box

1. Click Insert tab.
2. Click Text Box button.
3. Click *Draw Text Box*.
4. Click or drag in document to create box.

To draw a text box rather than inserting a predesigned one, click the Insert tab, click the Text Box button in the Text group, and then click *Draw Text Box* at the drop-down list. With the pointer displaying as crosshairs (a plus [+] symbol), click in the document to insert the text box or position the crosshairs in the document and then drag to create the text box with the desired size and dimensions. When a text box is selected, the Shape Format tab is active. Use buttons on this tab to format a drawn text box in the same manner as a built-in text box.

Activity 3b Inserting and Formatting a Text Box

Part 2 of 2

1. With **5-Robots.docx** open, press Ctrl + End to move the insertion point to the end of the document.
2. Insert a text box by completing the following steps:
   a. Click the Insert tab.
   b. Click the Text Box button and then click the *Draw Text Box* option.
   c. Position the pointer (displays as crosshairs) on the insertion point and then click the left mouse button. (This inserts the text box in the document.)
3. Change the text box height and width by completing the following steps:
   a. Click in the *Shape Height* measurement box in the Size group, type 1.2, and then press the Tab key.
   b. Type 4.5 in the *Shape Width* measurement box and then press the Enter key.

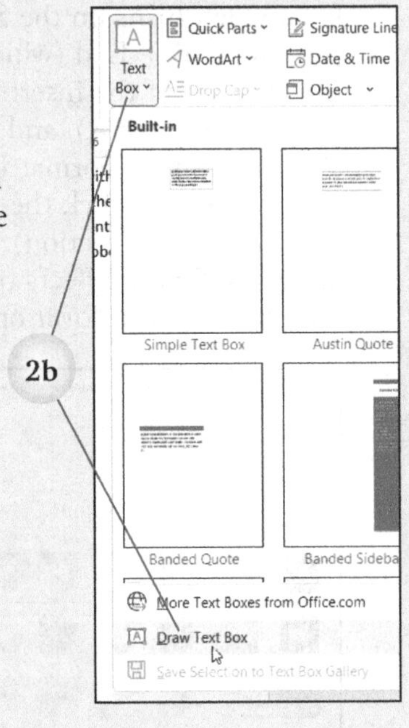

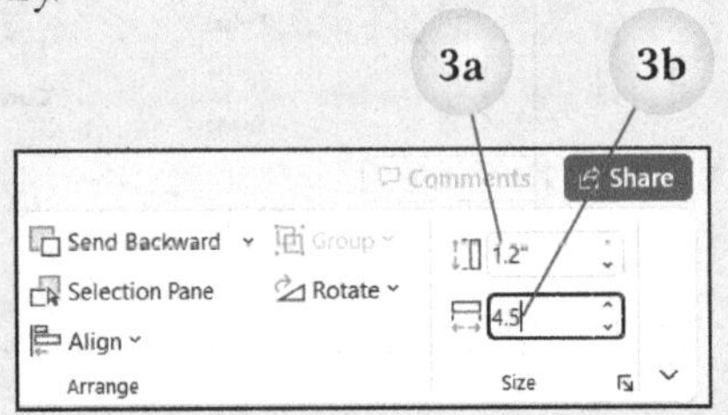

4. Center the text box by clicking the Align button in the Arrange group and then clicking *Align Center* at the drop-down list.
5. Apply a shape style by clicking the More Shape Styles button in the Shape Styles group and then clicking the *Subtle Effect - Blue, Accent 1* option (second column, fourth row in the *Theme Styles* section).

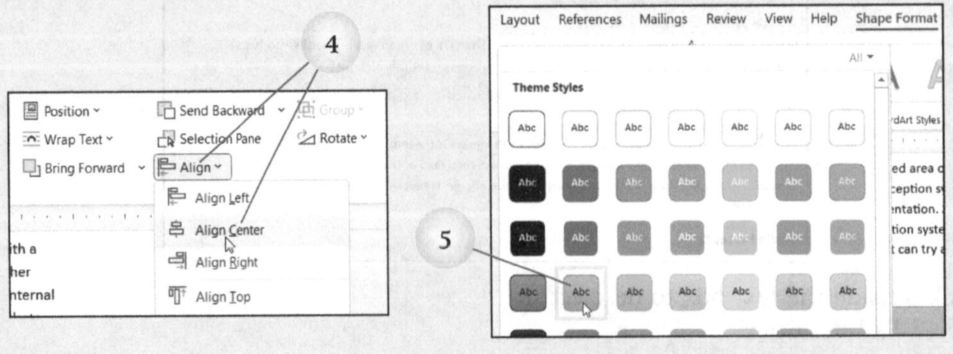

6. Apply a bevel shape effect by clicking the Shape Effects button, pointing to the *Bevel* option, and then clicking the *Soft Round* option at the side menu (second column, second row in the *Bevel* section).
7. Apply a 3-D shape effect by clicking the Shape Effects button, pointing to *3-D Rotation*, and then clicking the *Perspective: Above* option (first column, second row in the *Perspective* section).

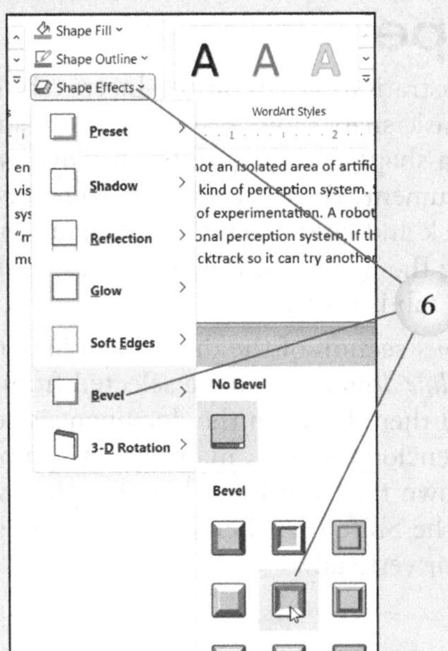

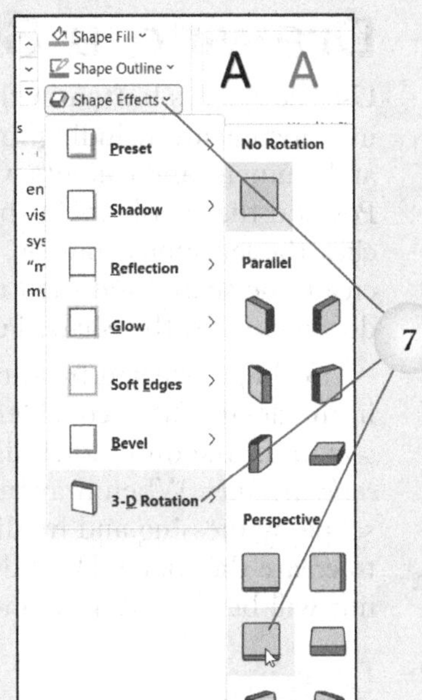

8. Insert and format text in the text box by completing the following steps:
   a. Press the Enter key two times. (The insertion point should be positioned in the text box.)
   b. Click the Home tab.
   c. Change the font size to 14 points, apply bold formatting, and change the font color to Dark Blue (ninth color option in the *Standard Colors* section).
   d. Click the Center button in the Paragraph group.
   e. Type International Conference on Artificial Intelligence Summer 2025.
   f. Click outside the text box to deselect it. (Your text box should appear as shown below.)

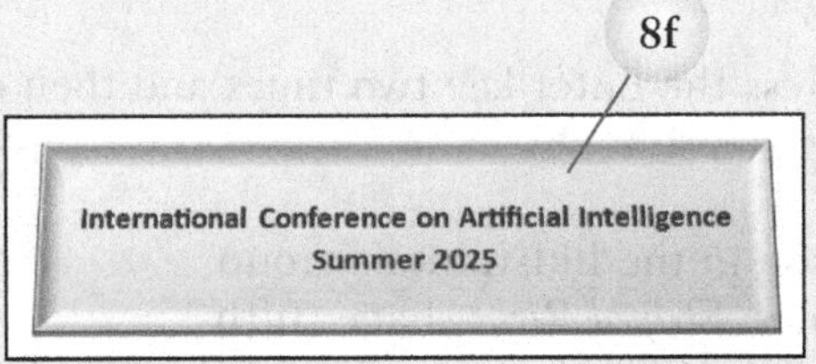

9. Save, preview, and then close **5-Robots.docx**.

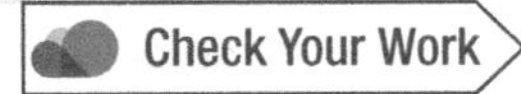

Activity 4 Prepare a Company Flyer **2 Parts**

You will create a company flyer document and increase the visual interest in the document by inserting and customizing shapes and WordArt.

Inserting, Sizing, and Positioning a Shape and Line

Formatting a Shape and Line

Shapes

Quick Steps

Draw Shape

1. Click Insert tab.
2. Click Shapes button.
3. Click shape.
4. Click or drag in document to create shape.

Hint To draw a square, choose the Rectangle shape and then press and hold down the Shift key while drawing.

Drawing a Shape

Use the Shapes button in the Illustrations group on the Insert tab to draw shapes in a document, including lines, basic shapes, block arrows, flow chart shapes, stars and banners, and callouts. Click a shape and the pointer displays as crosshairs. Position the crosshairs in the document where the shape is to be inserted and then click the left mouse button or click and hold down the left mouse button, drag to create the shape, and then release the mouse button. The shape is inserted in the document and the Shape Format tab is active.

A shape selected from the *Lines* section of the drop-down list and then drawn in the document is considered a *line drawing*. A shape selected from another section of the drop-down list and then drawn in the document is considered an *enclosed object*. When drawing an enclosed object, maintain the proportions of the shape by pressing and holding down the Shift key while dragging with the mouse to create the shape. Hold down the Shift key when drawing a straight line and the line will be aligned horizontally or vertically.

Copying a Shape

To copy a shape, select the shape and then click the Copy button in the Clipboard group on the Home tab. Position the insertion point at the location the copied shape is to be inserted and then click the Paste button. A selected shape can also be copied by right-clicking the shape and then clicking *Copy* at the shortcut menu. Position the insertion point where the shape is to be copied, right-click, and then click *Paste* at the shortcut menu. Another method for copying shapes is to press and hold down the Ctrl key while dragging a copy of the shape to the new location.

Activity 4a Drawing and Copying Arrow Shapes **Part 1 of 2**

1. At a blank document, press the Enter key two times and then draw an arrow shape by completing the following steps:
   a. Click the Insert tab.
   b. Click the Shapes button in the Illustrations group and then click the *Arrow: Striped Right* shape (fifth column, second row in the *Block Arrows* section).
   c. Position the pointer (which displays as crosshairs) on the insertion point and then click the left mouse button. (This inserts the arrow shape in the document and makes the Shape Format tab active.)
2. Format the arrow by completing the following steps:
   a. Click in the *Shape Height* measurement box in the Size group, type 2.4, and then press the Tab key.
   b. Type 4.5 in the *Shape Width* measurement box and then press the Enter key.

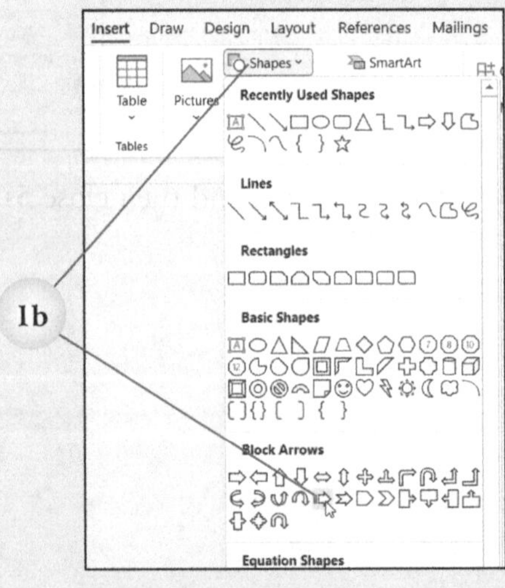

c. Horizontally align the arrow by clicking the Align button in the Arrange group and then clicking *Distribute Horizontally* at the drop-down list.

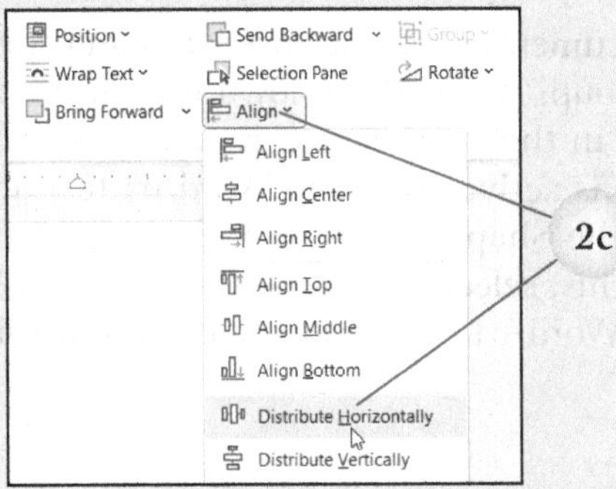

d. Click the More Shape Styles button in the Shape Styles group and then click the *Intense Effect - Green, Accent 6* option (last option in the *Theme Styles* section at the drop-down gallery).

e. Click the Shape Effects button in the Shape Styles group, point to *Bevel*, and then click the *Angle* option (first column, second row in the *Bevel* section).

f. Click the Shape Outline button arrow in the Shape Styles group and then click the *Dark Blue* color (ninth color option in the *Standard Colors* section).

3. Copy the arrow by completing the following steps:
   a. With the pointer positioned in the arrow (pointer displays with a four-headed arrow attached), press and hold down the Ctrl key and click and hold down the left mouse button. Drag down until the copied arrow appears just below the top arrow, release the mouse button, and then release the Ctrl key.
   b. Copy the selected arrow by pressing and holding down the Ctrl key and clicking and holding down the left mouse button, dragging the copied arrow just below the second arrow, and then releasing the Ctrl key and the mouse button.
4. Flip the middle arrow by completing the following steps:
   a. Click the middle arrow to select it.
   b. Click the Rotate button in the Arrange group on the Shape Format tab and then click the *Flip Horizontal* option at the drop-down gallery.

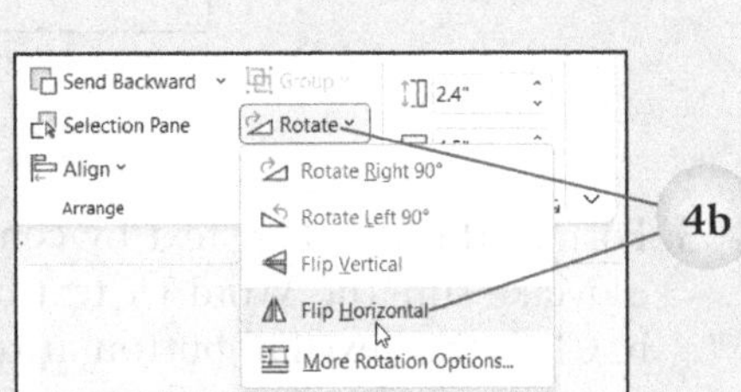

5. Insert the text *Financial* in the top arrow by completing the following steps:
   a. Click the top arrow to select it.
   b. Type Financial.
   c. Select *Financial*.
   d. Click the Home tab.
   e. Change the font size to 16 points, apply bold formatting, and change the font color to Dark Blue (ninth color option in the *Standard Colors* section).
6. Complete steps similar to those in Step 5 to insert the word *Direction* in the middle arrow.
7. Complete steps similar to those in Step 5 to insert the word *Retirement* in the bottom arrow.
8. Save the document with the name **5-FinConsult**.

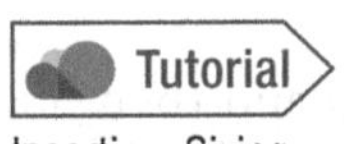
Inserting, Sizing, and Positioning WordArt

Formatting WordArt

WordArt

Quick Steps

Create WordArt Text

1. Click Insert tab.
2. Click WordArt button.
3. Click option.
4. Type WordArt text.

Creating and Formatting WordArt

Use the WordArt feature to distort or modify text to conform to a variety of shapes. This is useful for creating company logos, letterheads, flyer titles, and headings.

To insert WordArt in a document, click the Insert tab and then click the WordArt button in the Text group. At the drop-down list, click an option and a WordArt text box is inserted in the document containing the words *Your text here* and the Shape Format tab is active. Type the WordArt text and then format the WordArt with options on the Shape Format tab. Existing text can also be formatted as WordArt. To do this, select the text, click the WordArt button on the Insert tab, and then click the WordArt option at the drop-down list.

Activity 4b Inserting and Modifying WordArt

Part 2 of 2

1. With **5-FinConsult.docx** open, press Ctrl + Home to move the insertion point to the beginning of the document.
2. Insert WordArt text by completing the following steps:
   a. Type Miller Financial Services and then select *Miller Financial Services*.
   b. Click the Insert tab.
   c. Click the WordArt button in the Text group and then click the option in the third column, first row (orange fill and outline).

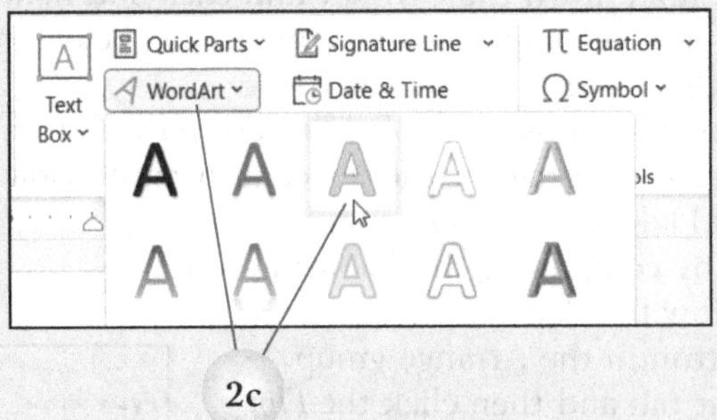

3. Format the WordArt text by completing the following steps:
   a. Make sure the WordArt text border displays as a solid line.
   b. Click the Text Fill button arrow in the WordArt Styles group on the Shape Format tab and then click the *Light Green* color (fifth color option in the *Standard Colors* section).
   c. Click the Text Outline button arrow in the WordArt Styles group and then click the *Green, Accent 6, Darker 50%* option (last option in the *Theme Colors* section).

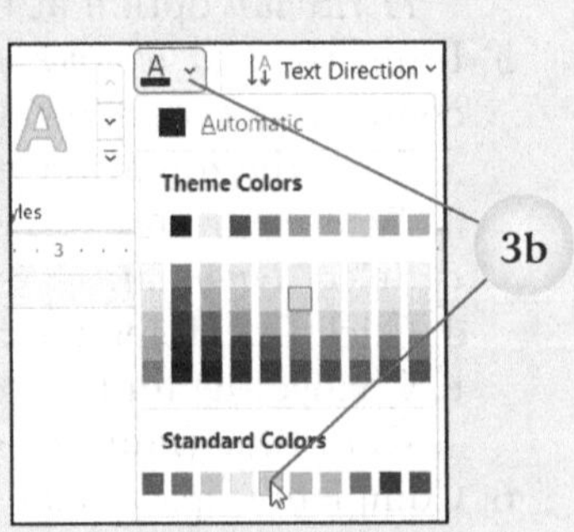

d. Click the Text Effects button in the WordArt Styles group, point to *Glow*, and then click the *Glow: 5 point; Blue, Accent color 1* option (first column, first row in the *Glow Variations* section).

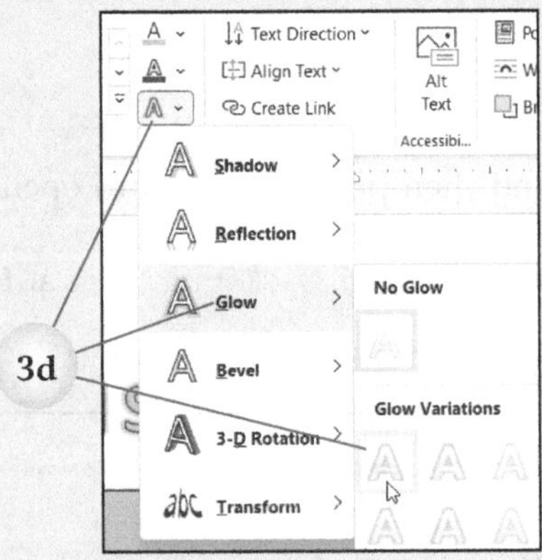

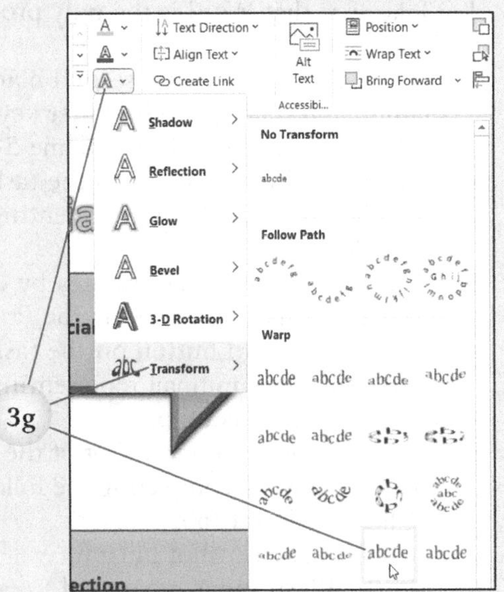

e. Click in the *Shape Height* measurement box in the Size group, type 1, and then press the Tab key.

f. Type 6 in the *Shape Width* measurement box in the Size group and then press the Enter key.

g. Click the Text Effects button in the WordArt Styles group, point to *Transform*, and then click the *Warp Up* option (third column, fourth row in the *Warp* section).

h. Click the Position button in the Arrange group and then click the *Position in Top Center with Square Text Wrapping* option (second column, first row in the *With Text Wrapping* section).

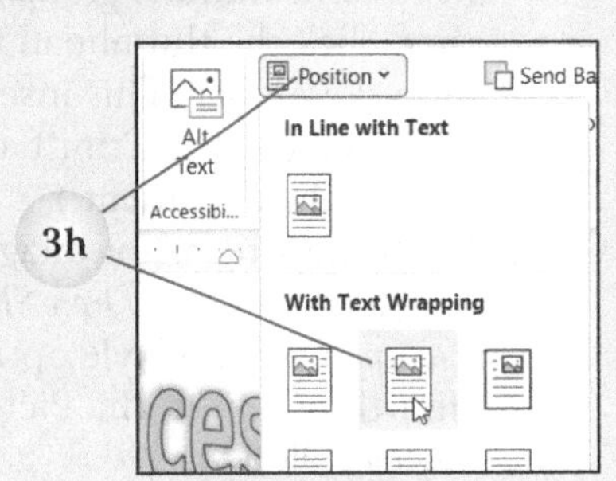

4. Click outside the WordArt to deselect it.
5. Move the arrows as needed to ensure they do not overlap the WordArt or each other and that they all fit on one page.
6. Save, preview, and then close **5-FinConsult.docx**.

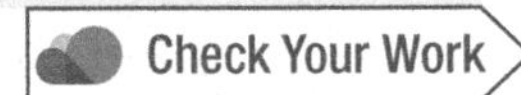

Activity 5 Insert and Format Screenshots — 2 Parts

You will create a document with screenshots of the Print and Info backstage areas and create another document with screen clippings of sample cover pages.

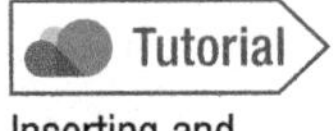

Inserting and Formatting Screenshot and Screen Clipping Images

Inserting a Screenshot

The Illustrations group on the Insert tab contains a Screenshot button, which captures a screen or part of a screen as an image. To capture the entire screen, open a new document, click the Insert tab, click the Screenshot button in the Illustrations group, and then click the screen thumbnail at the drop-down list. (The currently active document does not appear as a thumbnail at the drop-down list—only other documents or files that are open.) Click the specific thumbnail at the drop-down list and a screenshot is inserted as an image in the open document. Once the screenshot is inserted in the document, the Picture Format tab is active. Use buttons on this tab to customize the screenshot image.

Activity 5a Inserting and Formatting Screenshots

Part 1 of 2

1. Make sure that Word is the only program open and then press Ctrl + N to open a blank document.
2. Press Ctrl + N to open a second blank document, type Print Backstage Area at the left margin, and then press the Enter key.
3. Save the document with the name **5-BackstageAreas**.
4. Point to the Word button on the taskbar and then click the thumbnail representing the blank document.
5. Display the Print backstage area by clicking the File tab and then clicking the *Print* option.
6. Point to the Word button on the taskbar and then click the thumbnail representing **5-BackstageAreas.docx**. 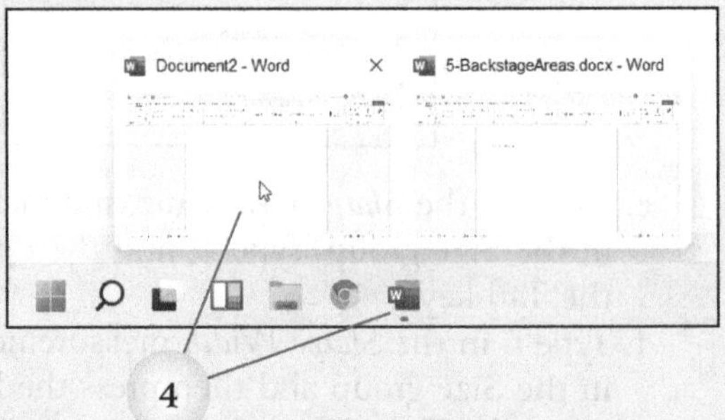
7. Insert and format a screenshot of the Print backstage area by completing the following steps:
   a. Click the Insert tab.
   b. Click the Screenshot button in the Illustrations group and then click the thumbnail in the drop-down list. (This inserts a screenshot of the Print backstage area in the document.)
   c. With the screenshot image selected, click the *Drop Shadow Rectangle* picture style option (fourth option in the Picture Styles gallery).
   d. Select the measurement in the *Shape Width* measurement box, type 5.5, and then press the Enter key. 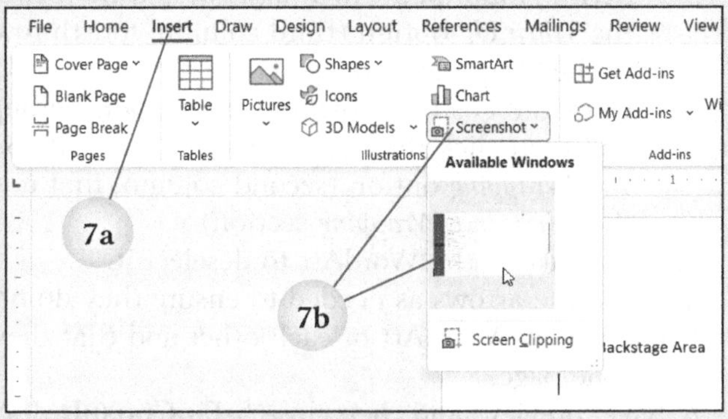
8. Press Ctrl + End and then press the Enter key. (The insertion point should be positioned below the screenshot image and at the left margin. You may need to press the Enter key again so that the insertion point is positioned at the left margin.)
9. Type Info Backstage Area at the left margin and then press the Enter key.
10. Point to the Word button on the taskbar and then click the thumbnail representing the blank document (with the Print backstage area displayed).
11. At the backstage area, click the *Info* option. (This displays the Info backstage area.)
12. Point to the Word button on the taskbar and then click the thumbnail representing **5-BackstageAreas.docx**.
13. Insert and format a screenshot of the Info backstage area by completing steps similar to those in Step 7.
14. Press Ctrl + Home to move the insertion point to the beginning of the document.
15. Save, preview, and then close **5-BackstageAreas.docx**.
16. At the Info backstage area, press the Esc key to redisplay the blank document.
17. Close the blank document.

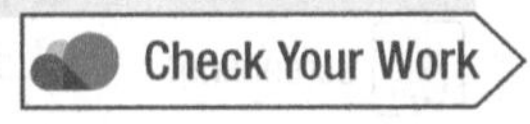

To create a screenshot of only part of the image on the screen, use the *Screen Clipping* option at the Screenshot button drop-down list. Click this option and the other open document, file, or Windows Start screen or desktop displays in a dimmed manner and the pointer displays as crosshairs. Using the mouse, draw a border around the specific area of the screen to be captured. The area identified is inserted in the other document as an image, the image is selected, and the Picture Format tab is active.

Activity 5b Inserting and Formatting a Screen Clipping

Part 2 of 2

1. Open **NSSLtrhd.docx** and then save it with the name **5-NSSCoverPages**.
2. Type the text Sample Cover Pages and then press the Enter key two times.
3. Select the text you just typed, change the font to 18-point Copperplate Gothic Bold, and then center the text.
4. Press Ctrl + End to move the insertion point below the text.
5. Open **NSSCoverPg01.docx** and then change the zoom to 50% by clicking approximately five times on the Zoom Out button at the left of the Zoom slider bar on the Status bar.
6. Point to the Word button on the taskbar and then click the thumbnail representing **5-NSSCoverPages.docx**.
7. Insert and format a screen clipping image by completing the following steps:
   a. Click the Insert tab.
   b. Click the Screenshot button and then click the *Screen Clipping* option.
   c. When **NSSCoverPg01.docx** displays in a dimmed manner, position the mouse crosshairs in the upper left corner of the cover page, click and hold down the left mouse button, drag down to the lower right corner of the cover page, and then release the mouse button. (See the image below and to the right.)
   d. With the cover page screen clipping image inserted in **5-NSSCoverPages.docx**, make sure the image is selected. (The sizing handles should appear around the cover page image.)
   e. Click the Wrap Text button in the Arrange group on the Picture Format tab and then click *Square* at the drop-down gallery.
   f. Select the current measurement in the *Shape Width* measurement box, type 3, and then press the Enter key.
   g. Click the Picture Border button arrow and then click the *Black, Text 1* option (second column, first row in the *Theme Colors* section).
8. Point to the Word button on the Taskbar and then click the thumbnail representing **NSSCoverPg01.docx**.

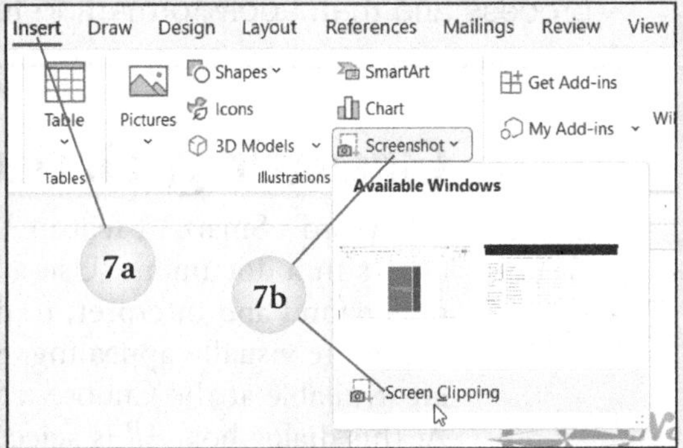

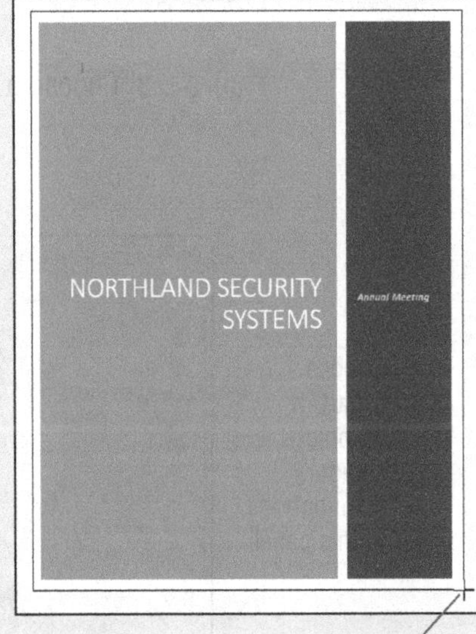

9. Close **NSSCoverPg01.docx**.
10. Open **NSSCoverPg02.docx** and then, if necessary, change the zoom to 50%.
11. Point to the Word button on the Taskbar and then click the thumbnail representing **5-NSSCoverPages.docx**.
12. Insert and format a screen clipping image of the cover page by completing steps similar to those in Step 7.
13. Using the mouse, position the two cover page screenshot images side by side in the document.
14. Save, preview, and then close **5-NSSCoverPages.docx**.
15. With **NSSCoverPg02.docx** the active document, change the zoom to 100% and then close the document.

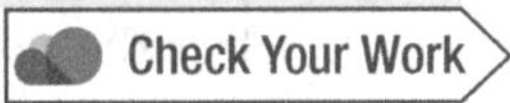

Activity 6 Prepare and Format a SmartArt Graphic — 2 Parts

You will prepare SmartArt process graphics that identify steps in the production process and then apply formatting to enhance the graphics.

Creating SmartArt

Hint Use SmartArt to communicate your message and ideas in a visual manner.

Use Word's SmartArt feature to insert graphics, such as diagrams and organizational charts in a document. Use a SmartArt graphic to make information easier to understand and interpret, to draw attention to important information, or to make text more visually appealing. SmartArt offers a variety of predesigned graphics that are available at the Choose a SmartArt Graphic dialog box, as shown in Figure 5.3. At this dialog box, *All* is selected by default in the left panel and all the available predesigned SmartArt graphics are shown in the middle panel.

Figure 5.3 Choose a SmartArt Graphic Dialog Box

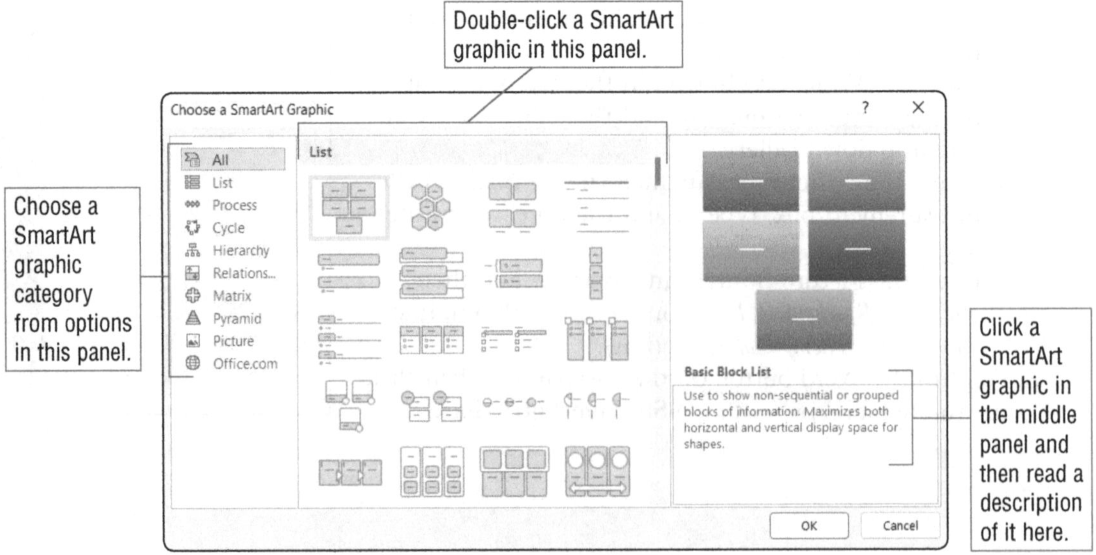

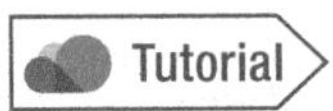

Inserting, Sizing, and Positioning SmartArt

Quick Steps

Insert SmartArt Graphic

1. Click Insert tab.
2. Click SmartArt button.
3. Double-click graphic.

Inserting a SmartArt Graphic

To insert a SmartArt graphic, click the Insert tab and then click the SmartArt button in the Illustrations group to open the Choose a SmartArt Graphic dialog box (see Figure 5.3). Predesigned SmartArt graphics are shown in the middle panel of the dialog box. Use the scroll bar at the right side of the middle panel to scroll down the list of choices. Click a graphic in the middle panel and its name displays in the right panel along with a description. SmartArt includes graphics for presenting a list of data; showing processes, cycles, and relationships; and presenting data in a matrix or pyramid. Double-click a graphic in the middle panel of the dialog box (or click the graphic and then click OK) and the graphic is inserted in the document.

When a SmartArt graphic is inserted in a document, a Text pane may appear at the left of the graphic. Type text in the Text pane or type directly in the graphic.

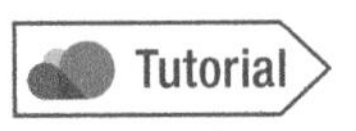

Formatting a SmartArt Graphic

Hint Limit the number of shapes and amount of text in your SmartArt graphic.

Formatting a SmartArt Graphic

Apply formatting to a SmartArt graphic with options at the SmartArt Design tab. This tab becomes active when the graphic is inserted in the document. Use options and buttons on this tab to add objects, change the graphic layout, apply a style to the graphic, and reset the graphic to the original formatting.

Formatting can also be applied to a SmartArt graphic with options on the SmartArt Format tab. Use options and buttons on this tab to change the sizes and shapes of objects in the graphic; apply shape styles and WordArt styles; change the shape fill, outline, and effects; and arrange and size the graphic.

Activity 6a Inserting and Formatting SmartArt Graphics — Part 1 of 2

1. At a blank document, insert the SmartArt graphic shown in Figure 5.4 by completing the following steps:
   a. Click the Insert tab.
   b. Click the SmartArt button in the Illustrations group.
   c. At the Choose a SmartArt Graphic dialog box, click *Process* in the left panel and then double-click the *Alternating Flow* graphic (second column, second row).
   d. If the Text pane does not display at the left of the graphic, click the Text Pane button in the Create Graphic group on the SmartArt Design tab to display it.
   e. With the insertion point positioned after the top bullet in the Text pane, type Design.
   f. Click the *[Text]* placeholder below *Design* and then type Mock-up.
   g. Continue clicking occurrences of the *[Text]* placeholder and typing text so the Text pane displays as shown at the right.
   h. Close the Text pane by clicking the Close button in the upper right corner of the pane. (You can also click the Text Pane button in the Create Graphic group.)

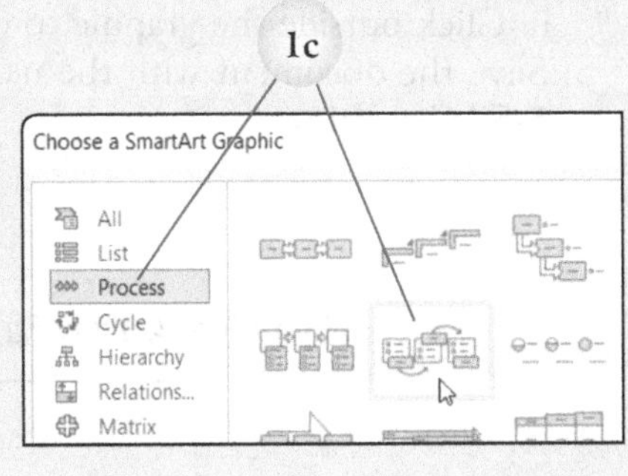

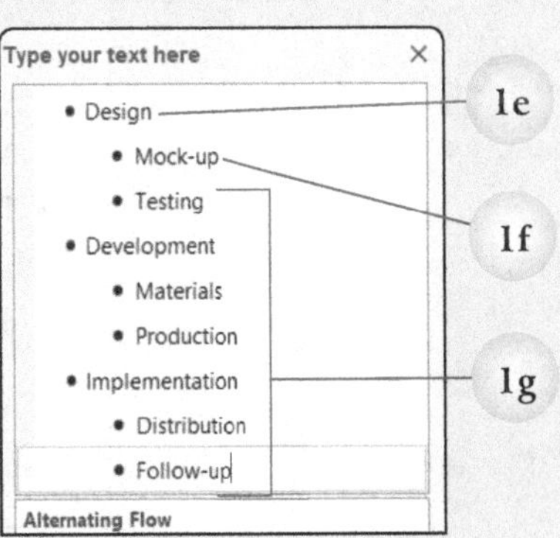

2. Change the graphic colors by clicking the Change Colors button in the SmartArt Styles group and then clicking the *Colorful Range - Accent Colors 5 to 6* option (last option in the *Colorful* section).
3. Apply a style by clicking the More SmartArt Styles button in the SmartArt Styles group and then clicking the *Inset* option (second option in the *3-D* section).

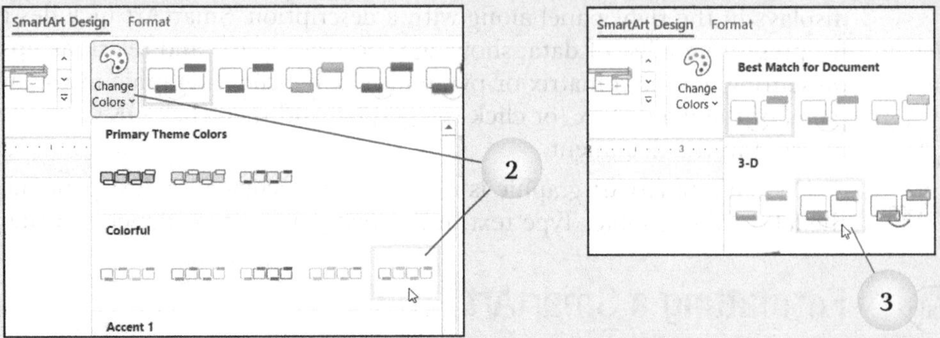

4. Copy the graphic and then change the layout by completing the following steps:
   a. Click inside the SmartArt graphic border but outside any shapes.
   b. Click the Home tab and then click the Copy button in the Clipboard group.
   c. Press Ctrl + End, press the Enter key, and then press Ctrl + Enter to insert a page break.
   d. Click the Paste button in the Clipboard group.
   e. Click inside the copied SmartArt graphic border but outside any shapes.
   f. Click the SmartArt Design tab.
   g. Click the More Layouts button in the Layouts group and then click the *Continuous Block Process* layout (second column, second row).
   h. Click outside the graphic to deselect it.
5. Save the document with the name **5-SAGraphics**.

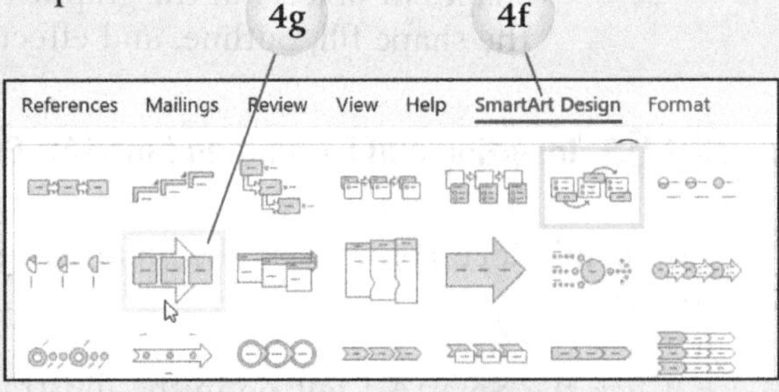

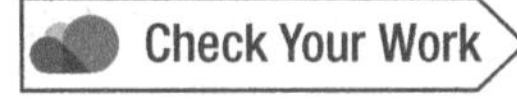

Figure 5.4 Activity 6a

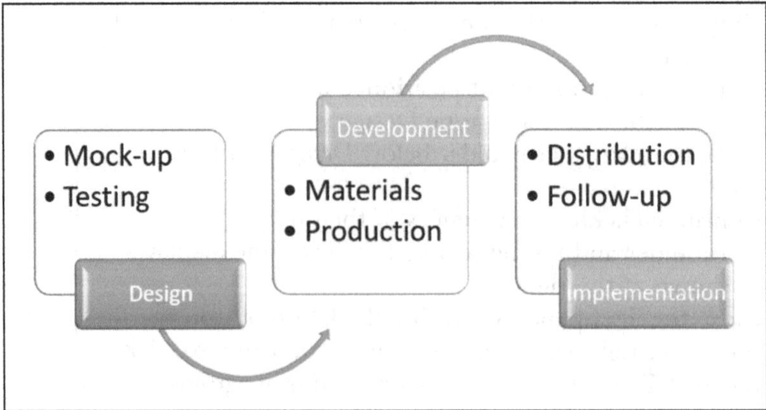

Arranging and Moving a SmartArt Graphic

Position

Wrap Text

Position a SmartArt graphic by clicking the Position button in the Arrange group on the SmartArt Format tab. Apply text wrapping to a SmartArt graphic using options in the Arrange group, with the Layout Options button, or by right-clicking the graphic and clicking *Wrap Text* at the shortcut menu.

Move a SmartArt graphic by positioning the pointer on the graphic until the pointer displays with a four-headed arrow attached, clicking and holding down the left mouse button, and then dragging the graphic to the new location. The SmartArt graphic or shapes within it can also be moved using the up, down, left, and right arrow keys on the keyboard.

Activity 6b Formatting SmartArt Graphics

Part 2 of 2

1. With **5-SAGraphics.docx** open, format shapes by completing the following steps:
   a. Click the SmartArt graphic on the first page to select it (a border surrounds the graphic).
   b. Click the SmartArt Format tab.
   c. In the SmartArt graphic, click the rectangle shape containing the word *Design*.
   d. Press and hold down the Shift key and then click the shape containing the word *Development*.
   e. With the Shift key still held down, click the shape containing the word *Implementation* and then release the Shift key. (All three shapes should now be selected.)
   f. Click the Change Shape button in the Shapes group.
   g. Click the *Arrow: Pentagon* arrow shape (seventh column, second row in the *Block Arrows* section).
   h. With the shapes still selected, click the Larger button in the Shapes group.
   i. With the shapes still selected, click the Shape Outline button arrow in the Shape Styles group and then click the *Dark Blue* color (ninth color option in the *Standard Colors* section).

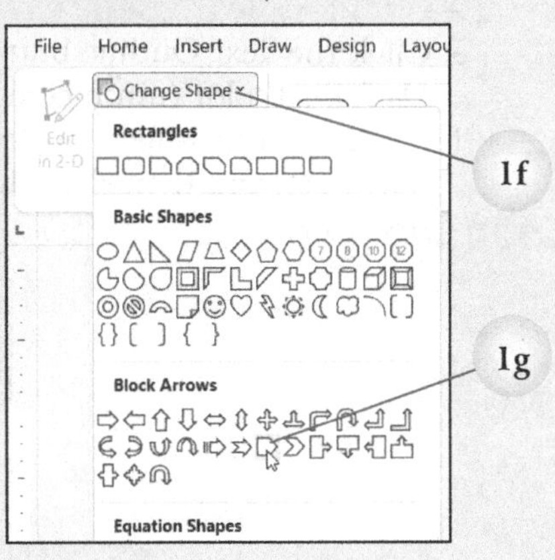

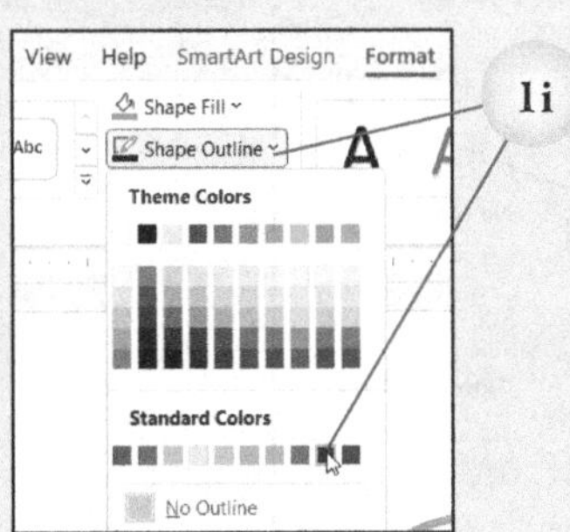

   j. Click inside the SmartArt graphic border but outside any shapes. (This deselects the shapes, but keeps the graphic selected.)
2. Click the Size button, click in the *Height* measurement box in, type 4, and then press the Enter key.

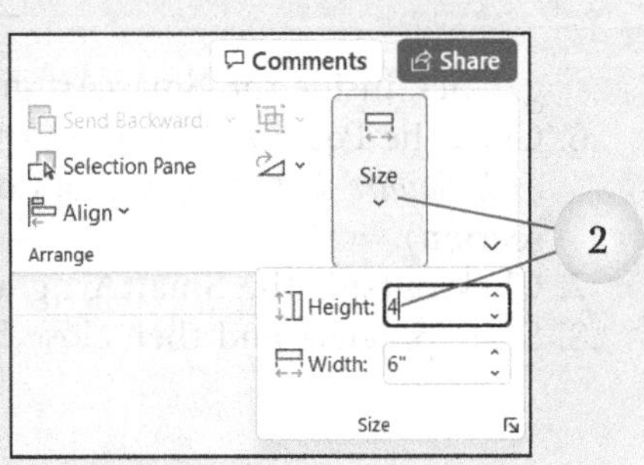

3. Click the Position button and then click the *Position in Middle Center with Square Text Wrapping* option (second column, second row in the *With Text Wrapping* section).
4. Click outside the SmartArt graphic to deselect it.
5. Format the bottom SmartArt graphic by completing the following steps:
   a. Press Ctrl + End to move to the end of the document and then click in the bottom SmartArt graphic to select it.
   b. Press and hold down the Shift key and then click each of the three shapes.
   c. Click the More WordArt Styles button in the WordArt Styles group on the SmartArt Format tab.
   d. Click the option in the first column, first row (black fill, shadow).

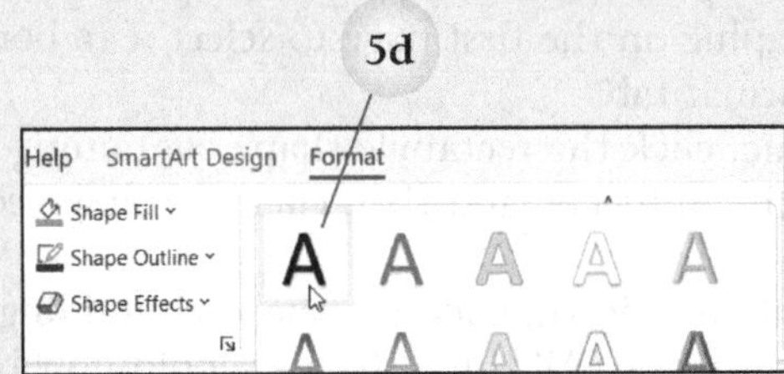

   e. Click the Text Outline button arrow in the WordArt Styles group and then click the *Dark Blue* color (ninth color option in the *Standard Colors* section).
   f. Click the Text Effects button in the WordArt Styles group, point to *Glow* at the drop-down list, and then click the *Glow: 5 point; Orange, Accent color 2* option (second column, first row).

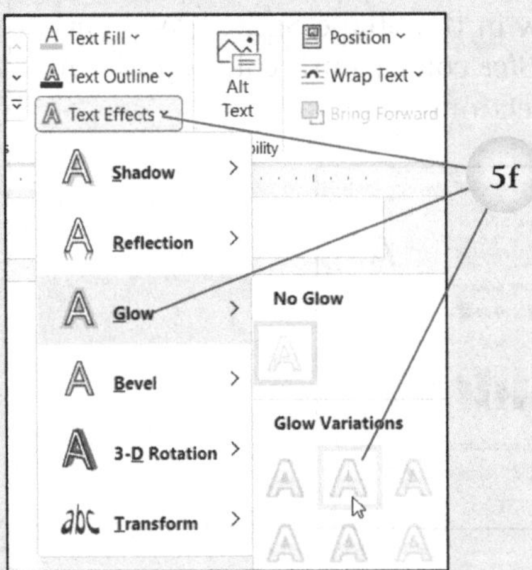

   g. Click inside the SmartArt graphic border but outside any shapes.
6. Click the Position button in the Arrange group and then click the *Position in Middle Center with Square Text Wrapping* option (second column, second row in the *With Text Wrapping* section).
7. Click outside the SmartArt graphic to deselect it.
8. Save, preview, and then close **5-SAGraphics.docx**.

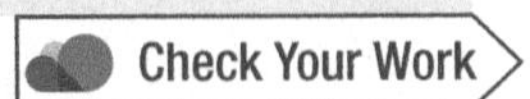

Activity 7 Prepare and Format a Company Organizational Chart 1 Part

You will prepare an organizational chart for a company and then apply formatting to enhance the appearance of the chart.

Creating an Organizational Chart with SmartArt

Quick Steps

Insert Organizational Chart

1. Click Insert tab.
2. Click SmartArt button.
3. Click *Hierarchy*.
4. Double-click organizational chart.

To visually illustrate hierarchical data, consider using a SmartArt option to create an organizational chart. To display organizational chart SmartArt options, click the Insert tab and then click the SmartArt button in the Illustrations group. At the Choose a SmartArt Graphic dialog box, click *Hierarchy* in the left panel. Organizational chart options display in the middle panel of the dialog box. Double-click an organizational chart and the chart is inserted in the document. Type text in a SmartArt graphic by selecting the shape and then typing text in it or type text in the Text pane at the left of the graphic. Format a SmartArt organizational chart with options and buttons on the SmartArt Design tab and the SmartArt Format tab, and with the Layout Options button.

Activity 7 Creating and Formatting a SmartArt Organizational Chart Part 1 of 1

1. At a blank document, create the SmartArt organizational chart shown in Figure 5.5. To begin, click the Insert tab.
2. Click the SmartArt button in the Illustrations group.
3. At the Choose a SmartArt Graphic dialog box, click *Hierarchy* in the left panel of the dialog box and then double-click the *Organization Chart* option (first option in the middle panel).

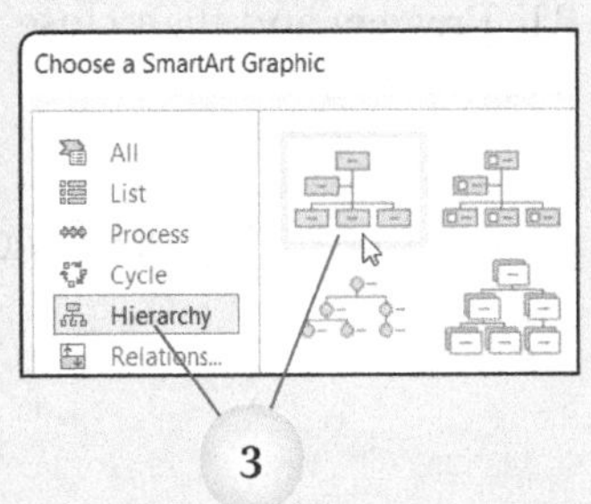

4. If the Text pane displays at the left of the organizational chart, close it by clicking the Text Pane button in the Create Graphic group.
5. Delete one of the boxes in the organizational chart by clicking the border of the box in the lower right corner to select it and then pressing the Delete key. (Make sure that the selection border surrounding the box is a solid line and not a dashed line. If a dashed line appears, click the box border again. This should change the border to a solid line.)
6. With the bottom right box selected, click the Add Shape button arrow in the Create Graphic group and then click the *Add Shape Below* option.

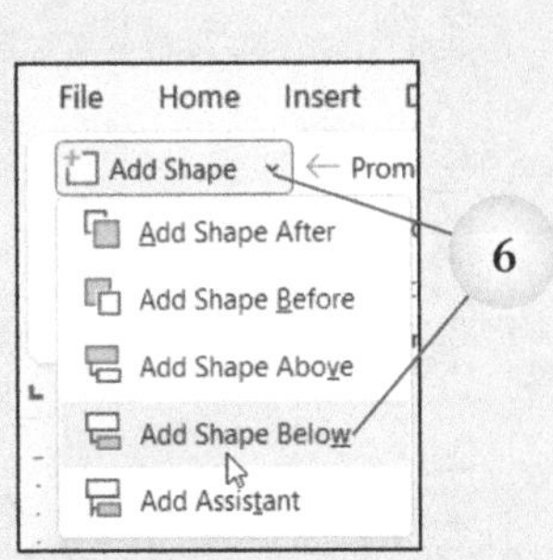

7. Click the *[Text]* placeholder in the top box, type Blaine Willis, press Shift + Enter, and then type President. Click in each of the remaining boxes and type the text as shown in Figure 5.5. (Press Shift + Enter after typing each name.)
8. Click the More SmartArt Styles button in the SmartArt Styles group and then click the *Inset* style (second option in the *3-D* section).
9. Click the Change Colors button and then click the *Colorful Range - Accent Colors 4 to 5* option (fourth option in the *Colorful* section).

10. Click the SmartArt Format tab.
11. Click the text pane control (displays with a left-pointing arrow) at the left side of the graphic border. (This displays the Text pane.)
12. Using the mouse, select all the text in the Text pane.
13. Click the Change Shape button in the Shapes group and then click the *Rectangle: Top Corners Rounded* option (eighth option in the *Rectangles* section).

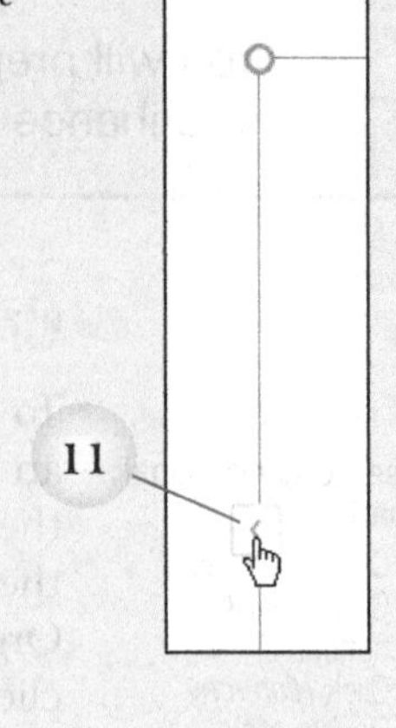

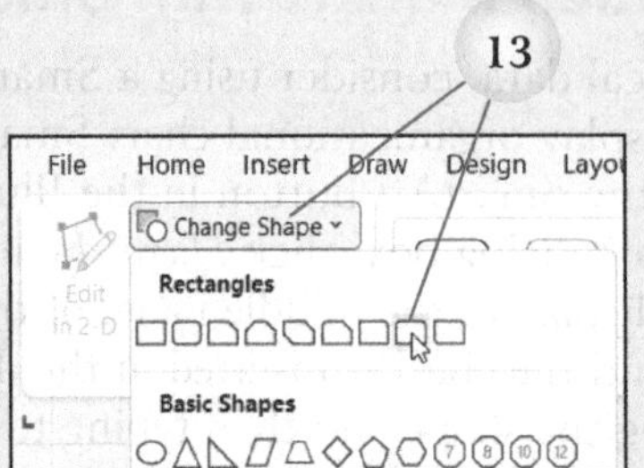

14. Click the Shape Outline button arrow in the Shape Styles group and then click the *Dark Blue* color (ninth color option in the *Standard Colors* section).
15. Close the Text pane.
16. Click inside the organizational chart border but outside any shapes.
17. Click the Size button, click in the *Height* measurement box, and then type 4.
18. Click in the *Width* measurement box, type 6.5, and then press the Enter key.
19. Click outside the organizational chart to deselect it.
20. Save the document with the name **5-OrgChart**.
21. Preview and then close **5-OrgChart.docx**.

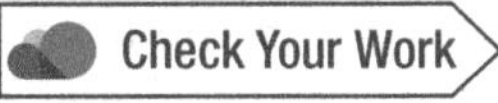

Figure 5.5 Activity 7

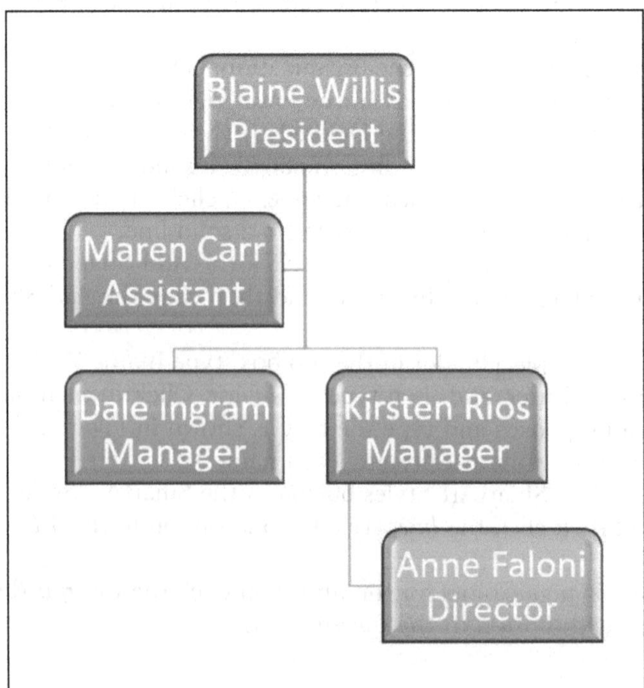

Chapter Summary

- Insert symbols with options at the Symbol dialog box with the Symbols tab selected, and insert special characters with options at the Symbol dialog box with the Special Characters tab selected.
- Click the Date & Time button in the Text group on the Insert tab to display the Date and Time dialog box. Insert the date or time with options at this dialog box or with keyboard shortcuts. If the date or time is inserted as a field, update the field by clicking the Update tab or pressing the F9 function key.
- Insert an image, such as a photo or clip art, with the Pictures button in the Illustrations group on the Insert tab.
- To insert an image from a folder on the computer's hard drive or removable storage medium, click the Insert tab, click the Pictures button in the Illustrations group, and then click the *This Device* option at the drop-down list. At the Insert Picture dialog box, navigate to the specific folder and then double-click the image file.
- To insert a stock image available from Microsoft 365, click the Insert tab, click the Pictures button, and then click *Stock Images* at the drop-down list. At the window that displays, chose an image, click a category and then chose an image, or search for a specific image and then click the image. Click the Insert button and then close the Close button to close the window. You can also double-click an image and then click the Close button to close the stock images window.
- To insert an online image, click the Insert tab, click the Pictures button, and then click *Online Pictures* at the drop-down list. At the Online Pictures window, type the search text or topic and then press the Enter key. Click an image to select it and then click the Insert button.
- Use the *Shape Height* and *Shape Width* measurement boxes in the Size group on the Picture Format tab to change the size of an image. The size of an image can also be changed with the sizing handles around a selected image.
- Use the Crop button in the Size group to remove unnecessary parts of an image. To crop an image, click the Crop button and then use the crop handles to specify what part of the image should be cropped.
- The Arrange group on the Picture Format tab contains buttons for positioning, aligning, and rotating text.
- Use the Wrap Text button in the Arrange group to specify how text or other objects should wrap around a selected image. The Layout Options button that displays outside the upper right corner of a selected image can also be used to specify text wrapping.
- Move an image using options at the Position button drop-down gallery on the Picture Format tab or by choosing a text wrapping style and then moving the image by dragging it with the mouse.
- Rotate a selected image using the pointer on the rotation handle (circular arrow) that appears above the image.
- The Adjust group on the Picture Format tab contains buttons for adjusting the background, color, brightness, and contrast of an image. An artistic effect can be applied to a selected image using the Artistic Effects button in the Adjust group. Use the *Set Transparent Color* option at the Color button drop-down gallery to make a color transparent in the selected image. Adjust the transparency of an image with options at the Transparency button drop-down gallery.

- Apply a predesigned picture style to a selected image with styles in the Picture Styles group on the Picture Format tab.
- Create alternative text to describe images in a document for readers with visual impairments. Type a description of an image at the Alt Text task pane. Display this task pane by clicking the Alt Text button on the Picture Format tab or right-clicking an image and then clicking *Edit Alt Text* at the shortcut menu.
- Click the Text Box button in the Text group on the Insert tab to display a drop-down list of predesigned text boxes (text boxes that already contain formatting) that can be inserted in a document.
- Draw a text box by clicking the Text Box button in the Text group on the Insert tab, clicking the *Draw Text Box* option at the drop-down list, and then clicking or dragging in the document.
- Customize a text box with options on the Shape Format tab.
- Draw shapes in a document by clicking the Shapes button in the Illustrations group on the Insert tab, clicking a shape at the drop-down list, and then clicking or dragging in the document to draw the shape. Customize a shape with options on the Shape Format tab.
- Copy a selected shape by clicking the Copy button in the Clipboard group on the Home tab, positioning the insertion point in the new location, and then clicking the Paste button. Another method for copying a selected shape is to press and hold down the Ctrl key while dragging the selected shape.
- Use WordArt to distort or modify text to conform to a variety of shapes. Customize WordArt with options on the Shape Format tab.
- Use the Screenshot button in the Illustrations group on the Insert tab to capture part or all of a window visible on the screen. Use buttons on the Picture Format tab to customize a screenshot image.
- Use the SmartArt feature to insert predesigned graphics and organizational charts in a document. Click the SmartArt button in the Illustrations group on the Insert tab to display the Choose a SmartArt Graphic dialog box containing a variety of graphics.
- Format a SmartArt graphic with options and buttons on the SmartArt Design tab and the SmartArt Format tab.
- Position a SmartArt graphic by clicking the Position button in the Arrange group on the SmartArt Format tab and then clicking a position option at the drop-down gallery.
- Specify how text or other objects should wrap around a SmartArt graphic with options at the Wrap Text button drop-down gallery. The Layout Options button that appears outside the upper right corner of the selected SmartArt graphic can also be used to specify text wrapping.
- Move a selected SmartArt graphic by dragging it with the mouse or using the up, down, left, and right arrow keys on the keyboard. Before moving a SmartArt graphic, apply text wrapping.
- Use a SmartArt option to create an organizational chart, which is a visual illustration of hierarchical data.

Commands Review

FEATURE	RIBBON TAB, GROUP	BUTTON, OPTION	KEYBOARD SHORTCUT
Alt Text task pane	Picture Format, Accessibility		
Choose a SmartArt Graphic dialog box	Insert, Illustrations		
Date and Time dialog box	Insert, Text		
insert date as field			Alt + Shift + D
Insert Picture dialog box	Insert, Illustrations	, *This Device*	
insert time as field			Alt + Shift + T
predesigned text box	Insert, Text		
screenshot	Insert, Illustrations		
shapes	Insert, Illustrations		
Symbol dialog box	Insert, Symbols	, *More Symbols*	
text box	Insert, Text		
update field			F9
WordArt	Insert, Text		

CHAPTER 5

Review and Assessment

Skills Assessment

Assessment 1

Add Visual Interest to a Report on Intellectual Property

1. Open **ProtectIssues.docx** and then save it with the name **5-ProtectIssues**.
2. Insert the **Hackers.png** image file from your WL1C5 folder. (Do this at the Insert Picture dialog box. Display this dialog box by clicking the Insert tab, clicking the Pictures button, and then clicking the *This Device* option at the drop-down list.)
3. Format the image with the following specifications:
   a. Change the height to 1 inch.
   b. Change the color of the image to Blue, Accent color 1 Light (second column, third row in the *Recolor* section).
   c. Correct the contrast to Brightness: 0% (Normal) Contrast: +20% (third column, fourth row in the *Brightness/Contrast* section).
   d. Change the position of the image to Position in Middle Left with Square Text Wrapping (first column, second row in the *With Text Wrapping* section).
   e. Use the Rotate Objects button in the Arrange group to flip the image horizontally.
4. Move the insertion point to the beginning of the paragraph immediately below the heading *Intellectual Property Protection* (on the second page). Insert the Austin Quote text box and then make the following customizations:
   a. Type the following text in the text box: "Plagiarism may be punished by law, and in many educational institutions it can result in suspension or even expulsion."
   b. Select the text and then change the font size to 11 points.
   c. Change the width of the text box to 2.8 inches.
   d. Change the position of the text box to Position in Top Center with Square Text Wrapping (second column, first row in the *With Text Wrapping* section).
5. Move the insertion point to the end of the document, insert the Plaque shape (tenth column, second row in the *Basic Shapes* section) at the location of the insertion point, and then make the following customizations:
   a. Change the shape height to 1.4 inches and the shape width to 3.9 inches.
   b. Use the Align button in the Arrange group to distribute the shape horizontally.
   c. Apply the Subtle Effect - Blue, Accent 1 shape style (second column, fourth row).
   d. Type the text Felicité Compagnie inside the shape. Insert the *é* symbol at the Symbol dialog box with the *(normal text)* font selected.
   e. Use options at the Date and Time dialog box to insert the current date below *Felicité Compagnie* and the current time below the date. Make sure the date and time will not update automatically.
   f. Select the text in the shape, change the font size to 14 points, and then apply bold formatting.
6. Save, preview, and then close **5-ProtectIssues.docx**.

Assessment 2

Create a Sales Meeting Announcement

1. At a blank document, press the Enter key two times and then create WordArt with the following specifications:
   a. Insert WordArt with the option in the first column, third row of the WordArt button drop-down list (black fill, white outline, blue hard shadow) and then type Inlet Corporation in the WordArt text box.
   b. Change the width of the WordArt text box to 6.5 inches.
   c. Use the *Transform* option from the Text Effects button in the WordArt Styles group to apply the Chevron: Up text effect (first column, second row in the *Warp* section) to the WordArt text.
2. Press Ctrl + End and then press the Enter key three times. Change the font to 18-point Candara, apply bold formatting, change to center alignment, and then type the following text, pressing the Enter key after each line of text except the fourth line:

   National Sales Meeting
   Pacific Division
   Ocean View Resort
   May 13 through May 15, 2024
3. Insert the **Ocean.jpg** image file from your WL1C5 folder and then make the following changes to the image:
   a. Crop approximately 1 inch off the bottom of the image.
   b. Apply the Brightness: 0% (Normal) Contrast: +20% correction (third column, fourth row in the *Brightness/Contrast* section).
   c. Apply the Compound Frame, Black picture style (fourth column, second row in the Picture Styles gallery).
   d. Change the position of the image to Position in Top Center with Square Text Wrapping (second column, first row in the *With Text Wrapping* section).
   e. Change text wrapping to Behind Text.
4. Save the announcement document with the name **5-SalesMtg**.
5. Preview and then close **5-SalesMtg.docx**.

Assessment 3

Create an Announcement

1. Open **FirstAidCourse.docx** and then save it with the name **5-FirstAidCourse**.
2. Format the announcement as shown in Figure 5.6. Insert the **FirstAid.png** image file from your WL1C5 folder with the following specifications:
   a. Change the text wrapping to Tight.
   b. Change the image color to Blue, Accent color 5 Light (sixth column, third row in the *Recolor* section).
   c. Correct the brightness and contrast to Brightness: 0% (Normal) Contrast: +40% (third column, bottom row in the *Brightness/Contrast* section).
   d. Size and move the image as shown in the figure.
3. Apply paragraph shading, insert the page border, and add period leaders to the right tab, as shown in Figure 5.6.
4. Save, preview, and then close **5-FirstAidCourse.docx**. (If printing the document and some of the page border does not print, consider increasing the measurements at the Border and Shading Options dialog box.)

Figure 5.6 Assessment 3

First Aid at Work

The Safety Committee is offering a two-day first aid course for employees. The objective of the course is to equip employees with the essential knowledge and practical experience to enable them to carry out first aid in the workplace. Course content includes health and safety administration, handling an incident and developing an action plan, recognizing and treating injuries and illnesses, and cardio-pulmonary resuscitation (CPR).

Dates .... March 4 and 5

Times .... 9:00 a.m. to 4:30 p.m.

Location .... Administration Building

Room .... Conference Room 200

Registration is available from February 12 until the course begins on March 4. Before registering, please check with your immediate supervisor to ensure that you can be excused from your normal duties for the two days.

For more information, contact Maxwell Singh at extension 3505.

Assessment 4

Insert Screen Clippings in a Memo

1. Open **FirstAidMemo.docx** and then save it with the name **5-FirstAidMemo**.
2. Insert and format screen clippings so that your document appears as shown in Figure 5.7. Use the document **FirstAidAnnounce.docx** to create the first screen clipping, and use the document **5-FirstAidCourse.docx** you created in Assessment 3 for the second screen clipping. ***Hint: Decrease the display percentage of the document so the entire document is visible on the screen.***
3. Move the insertion point below the screen clipping images and then insert the text as shown in the figure. Insert your initials in place of the *XX*.
4. Save, preview, and then close **5-FirstAidMemo.docx**.

Figure 5.7 Assessment 4

DATE: January 10, 2024

TO: Carmen Singleton

FROM: Maxwell Singh

SUBJECT: FIRST AID COURSE ANNOUNCEMENTS

As you requested, I have created two announcements for the first aid course in March. Please review the two announcements shown below and let me know which one you prefer.

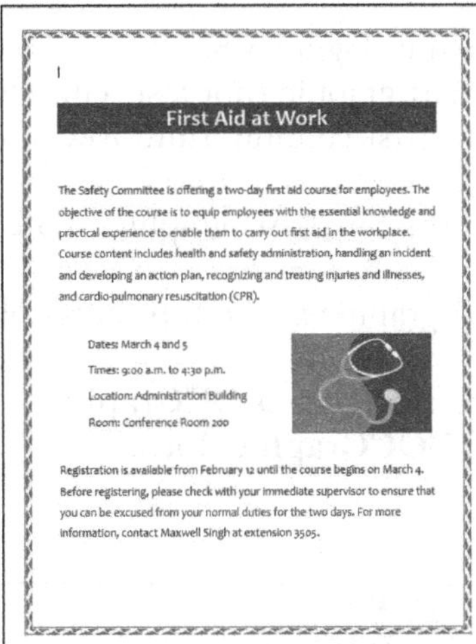

First Aid at Work

The Safety Committee is offering a two-day first aid course for employees. The objective of the course is to equip employees with the essential knowledge and practical experience to enable them to carry out first aid in the workplace. Course content includes health and safety administration, handling an incident and developing an action plan, recognizing and treating injuries and illnesses, and cardio-pulmonary resuscitation (CPR).

Dates: March 4 and 5

Times: 9:00 a.m. to 4:30 p.m.

Location: Administration Building

Room: Conference Room 200

Registration is available from February 12 until the course begins on March 4. Before registering, please check with your immediate supervisor to ensure that you can be excused from your normal duties for the two days. For more information, contact Maxwell Singh at extension 3505.

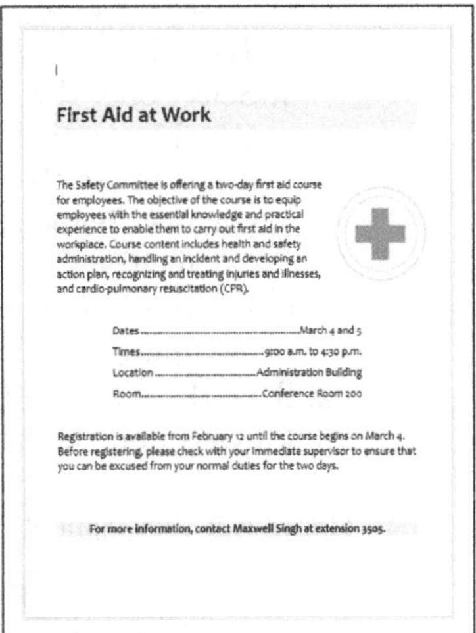

First Aid at Work

The Safety Committee is offering a two-day first aid course for employees. The objective of the course is to equip employees with the essential knowledge and practical experience to enable them to carry out first aid in the workplace. Course content includes health and safety administration, handling an incident and developing an action plan, recognizing and treating injuries and illnesses, and cardio-pulmonary resuscitation (CPR).

Dates....................March 4 and 5

Times....................9:00 a.m. to 4:30 p.m.

Location....................Administration Building

Room....................Conference Room 200

Registration is available from February 12 until the course begins on March 4. Before registering, please check with your immediate supervisor to ensure that you can be excused from your normal duties for the two days.

For more information, contact Maxwell Singh at extension 3505.

XX
5-FirstAidMemo.docx

Assessment 5 Create and Format a Company SmartArt Graphic

1. At a blank document, create the SmartArt graphic shown in Figure 5.8 with the following specifications:
   a. Use the Titled Matrix SmartArt graphic (second option in the *Matrix* group).
   b. Apply the Colorful - Accent Colors SmartArt style (first option in the *Colorful* section).
   c. Apply the Polished SmartArt style (first option in the *3-D* section).
   d. With the middle shape selected, apply the Intense Effect - Green, Accent 6 shape style. (Click the SmartArt Format tab, click the More Shape Styles button in the Shape Styles group, and then click the last option in the *Theme Styles* section.)
   e. Type all the text shown in Figure 5.8.
   f. Select only the SmartArt graphic (not a specific shape) and then apply the WordArt option in the first column, third row of the WordArt button drop-down list to the text.
   g. Change the height of the SmartArt graphic to 3.2 inches and the width to 5.3 inches.
   h. Position the SmartArt graphic at the top center of the page with square text wrapping.
2. Save the document with the name **5-OCGraphic**.
3. Preview and then close **5-OCGraphic.docx**.

Figure 5.8 Assessment 5

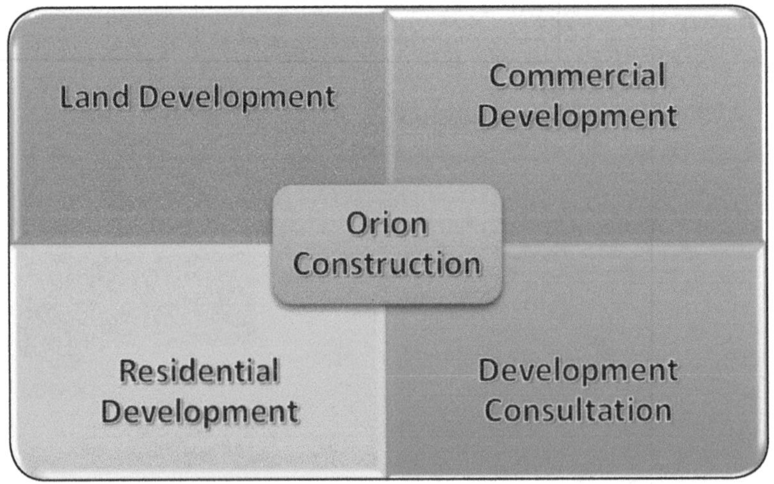

Assessment 6 Create and Format a Company Organizational Chart

1. At a blank document, create the organizational chart shown in Figure 5.9 with the following specifications:
   a. Use the Hierarchy SmartArt graphic (second column, second row with *Hierarchy* selected in the left panel).
   b. With the top text box selected, add a shape above it.
   c. Select the text box at the right in the third row and then add a shape below it.
   d. Type the text shown in the organizational chart in Figure 5.4.
   e. Apply the Colorful Range - Accent Colors 3 to 4 SmartArt style (third option in the *Colorful* section).
   f. Increase the height to 4.5 inches and the width to 6.5 inches.
   g. Position the organizational chart in the middle of the page with square text wrapping.
2. Save the document with the name **5-CoOrgChart**.
3. Preview and then close **5-CoOrgChart.docx**.

Figure 5.9 Assessment 6

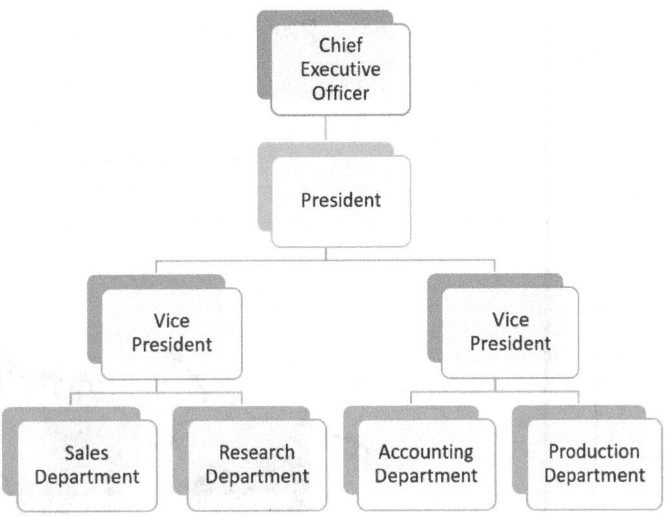

Visual Benchmark

Activity 1 Create a Flyer

1. Create the flyer shown in Figure 5.10 with the following specifications:
   - Create the title *Pugs on Parade!* as WordArt using the option in the first column, first row in the WordArt button drop-down list. Change the width to 6.5 inches, apply the Warp Up transform effect (third column, fourth row in the *Warp* section), and then change the text fill color to standard dark red.
   - Create the shape containing the text *Admission is free!* using the Explosion: 8 Points shape (first column, first row in the *Stars and Banners* section of the Shapes button drop-down list).
   - Insert the **Pug.jpg** image file from your WL1C5 folder. Change the text wrapping for the image to Behind Text and then size and position the image as shown in the figure.

- Create the line above the last line of text as a top border. Change the color to standard dark red and the width to 3 points.
- Make any other changes so your document appears similar to Figure 5.10.

2. Save the document with the name **5-PugFlyer**.
3. Preview and then close **5-PugFlyer.docx**.

Figure 5.10 Visual Benchmark 1

Pugs on Parade!

Come join us for the sixth annual "Pugs on Parade" party, Saturday, July 27, at Mercer Way Park from 1:00 to 3:30 p.m.

Admission is free!

Prizes awarded for the best costumes.

Activity 2

Format a Report

1. Open **Resume.docx** and then save it with the name **5-Resume**.
2. Format the report so it appears as shown in Figure 5.11 with the following specifications:
   a. Insert the WordArt text *Résumé Writing* with the following specifications:
      - Use the option in the first column, third row of the WordArt button drop-down list.
      - Type the text Résumé Writing and insert the *é* symbol using the Symbol dialog box.
      - Change the position to Position in Top Center with Square Text Wrapping.
      - Change the width of the WordArt to 5.5 inches.
      - Apply the Warp Up transform text effect (third column, fourth row in the *Warp* section).

   b. Insert the pull quote with the following specifications:
      - Use the Motion Quote text box.
      - Type the text shown in the pull quote text box in Figure 5.11. (Use the Symbol dialog box to insert the two *é* symbols in the word *résumé*.)
      - Select the text box and then change the font size of the text to 11 points.
      - Change the width of the text box to 2.3 inches.
      - Position the text box in the middle center with square text wrapping.

   c. Insert the cake image with the following specifications:
      - Insert the **Cake.png** image file from your WL1C5 folder.
      - Change the width to 1.2 inches.
      - Change the text wrapping to Tight.
      - Position the cake image as shown in Figure 5.11.
3. Save, preview, and then close **5-Resume.docx**.

Activity 3

Create and Format a SmartArt Graphic

1. At a blank document, create the document shown in Figure 5.12 (on page 195). Create and format the SmartArt graphic as shown in the figure. ***Hint: Use the* Step Up Process *graphic*.** Change the width of the SmartArt graphic to 6.5 inches. (Bold the white text with the dark blue paragraph shading. When formatting the SmartArt, you will need to change the colors of each shape separately.)
2. Save the completed document with the name **5-SalesGraphic**.
3. Preview and then close **5-SalesGraphic.docx**.

Figure 5.11 Visual Benchmark 2

Résumé Writing

To produce the best "fitting" résumé, you need to know about yourself, and you need to know about the job you are applying for. Before you do anything else, ask yourself why you are preparing a résumé. The answer to this question is going to vary from one person to the next, and here are our top ten reasons for writing a résumé:

1. You have seen a job that appeals to you advertised in the paper.
2. You want to market yourself to win a contract or a proposal or be elected to a committee or organization.
3. You have seen a job that appeals to you on an internet job site.
4. Your friends or family told you of a job opening at a local company.
5. You want to work for the local company and thought that sending a résumé to them might get their attention.
6. You have seen a job advertised internally at work.
7. You are going for a promotion.
8. You are feeling fed up and writing down all your achievements will cheer you up and might motivate you to look for a better job.
9. You are thinking "Oh, so that's a résumé! I suppose I ought to try to remember what I've been doing with my life."
10. Your company is about to be downsized and you want to update your résumé to be ready for any good opportunities.

All these certainly are good reasons to write a résumé, but the résumé serves many different purposes. One way of seeing the different purposes is to ask yourself who is going to read the résumé in each case.

Résumés 1 through 5 will be read by potential employers who probably do not know you. Résumés 6 and 7 are likely to be read by your boss or other people who know you. Résumés 8 through 10 are really for your own benefit and should not be considered as suitable for sending out to employers.

The Right Mix

Think about the list of reasons again. How else can you divide up these reasons? An important difference is that, in some cases, you will have a good idea of what the employer is looking for because you have a job advertisement in front of you and can tailor your résumé accordingly. For others, you have no idea what the reader might want to see.

"Updating your résumé from time to time is a good idea so you do not forget important details..."

Updating your résumé from time to time is a good idea so you do not forget important details but remember that the result of such a process will not be a winning résumé. It will be a useful list of tasks and achievements.

Writing a résumé is like baking a cake. You need all the right ingredients: flour, butter, eggs, and so on. It is what you do with the ingredients that makes the difference between a great résumé (or cake) and failure.

Keeping your résumé up-to-date is like keeping a stock of ingredients in the pantry—it is potentially very useful, but do not imagine that is the end of it!

Figure 5.12 Visual Benchmark 3

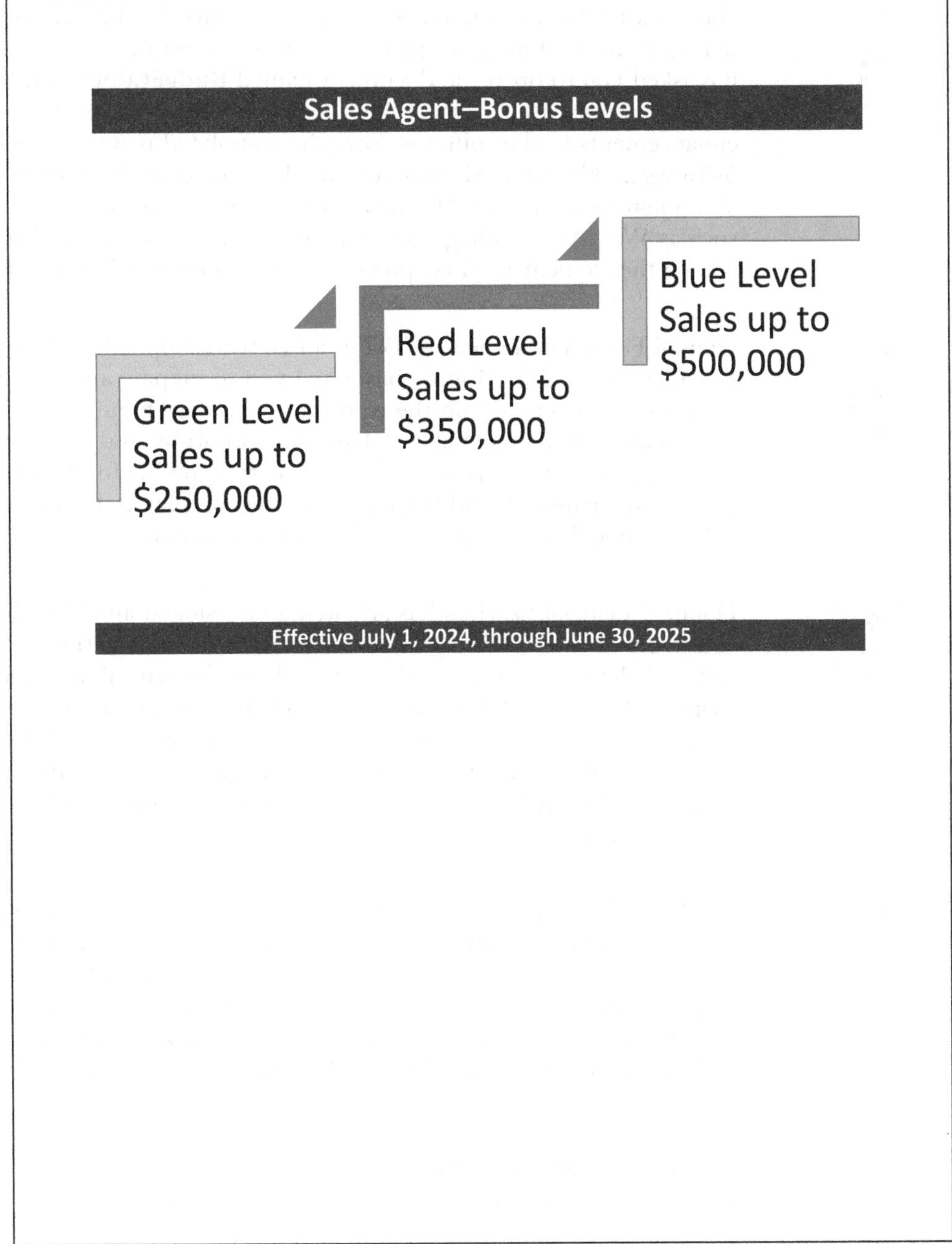

Case Study

Part 1

You work for Honoré Financial Services and have been asked by the office manager, Jason Monroe, to prepare an information newsletter. Mr. Monroe has asked you to open the document named **Budget.docx** and then format it into columns. You are to decide the number of columns and any additional enhancements to the columns. Save the completed newsletter, naming it **5-Budget**. When Mr. Monroe reviews the newsletter, he decides that it needs additional visual appeal. He wants you to insert visual elements in the newsletter, such as WordArt, an image, a predesigned text box, and/or a drop cap. After adding the element(s), save, preview, and then close **5-Budget.docx**.

Part 2

Honoré Financial Services will offer a free workshop titled *Planning for Financial Success*. Mr. Monroe has asked you to prepare an announcement containing information on the workshop. You determine what to include in the announcement, such as the date, time, location, and so forth. Enhance the announcement by inserting an image and by applying formatting such as font, paragraph alignment, and borders. Save the completed document with the name **5-Announce**. Preview and then close the document.

Part 3

Honoré Financial Services has adopted a new slogan and Mr. Monroe has asked you to create a shape with the new slogan inside it. Experiment with the shadow and 3-D shape effects available on the Shape Format tab and then create a shape and enhance it with shadow and/or 3-D effects. Insert the new Honoré Financial Services slogan, *Retirement Planning Made Easy*, in the shape. Include any additional enhancements to improve the visual interest of the shape and slogan. Save the completed document with the name **5-Slogan**. Preview and then close the document.

Part 4

Mr. Monroe has asked you to prepare an organization chart that will become part of the company profile. Create a SmartArt organizational chart using the position titles shown in Figure 5.13. Use the order and structure in Figure 5.13 to guide the layout of the SmartArt chart. Format the organizational chart to enhance the appearance. Save the completed organizational chart document with the name **5-HFSOrgChart**. Preview and then close the document.

Figure 5.13 Case Study, Part 4

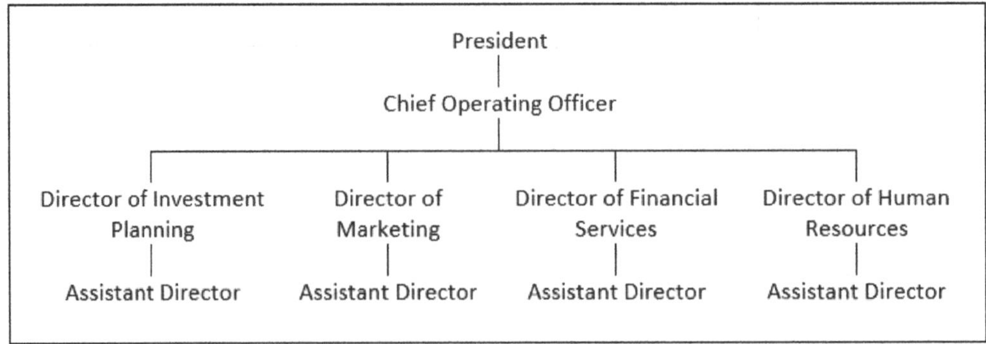

Part 5

Mr. Monroe has asked you to prepare a document containing information on teaching children how to budget. Use the internet to find websites and articles that provide information on this topic. Write a synopsis of the information and include at least four suggestions for teaching children to manage their money. Format the text into newspaper columns. Add additional enhancements to improve the appearance of the document. Save the completed document with the name **5-ChildBudget**. Preview and then close the document.

WORD

CHAPTER

6

Managing Documents

Performance Objectives

Upon successful completion of Chapter 6, you will be able to:

1. Change the view of a document
2. Use learning tools to aid reading fluency and comprehension
3. Change page movement, display percentage, and ribbon display options
4. Hide and show white space
5. Split a window, view documents side by side, and open a new window
6. Insert a file into an open document
7. Preview and print specific text and pages in a document
8. Prepare and print envelopes and labels
9. Create a document using a template
10. Save documents in different file formats
11. Save a template and open a template using File Explorer

Word provides a number of options for managing documents, including customizing the document view, using learning tools, changing the display and display percentage, and changing ribbon display options. Managing documents can also include working with windows and performing such actions as arranging windows, splitting windows, viewing documents side by side, and opening a new window. In this chapter, you will learn these techniques, as well as saving documents in different file formats and saving and opening a template. You will also learn how to create and print envelopes and labels.

Data Files

The data files for this chapter are in the WL1C6 folder that you downloaded at the beginning of this course.

Activity 1 Change Views and Display and Use Immersive Options in a Report on Navigating and Searching the Web — 3 Parts

You will open a document on navigating and searching the web, change the document view, use immersive reader options, change page movement to side to side, change display percentages, and hide and show white space at the tops and bottoms of pages.

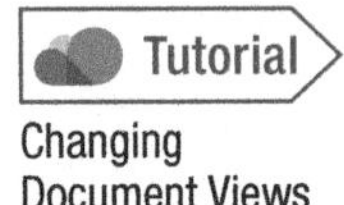

Changing Document Views

Changing the Document View

By default, a Word document displays in Print Layout view. This view displays the document on the screen as it will appear when printed. Other views are available, such as Draft and Read Mode. Change views with buttons in the view area on the Status bar (see Figure 6.1) or with options on the View tab.

Displaying a Document in Draft View

Change to Draft view and the document displays in a format for efficient editing and formatting. In this view, margins and other features such as headers and footers do not appear on the screen. Change to Draft view by clicking the View tab and then clicking the Draft button in the Views group.

Displaying a Document in Web Layout View

Web Layout

To see what a document would look like as a web page, click the Web Layout button on the View tab or click the Web Layout button on the Status bar. In Web Layout view, the document margins are wider; this can be useful for viewing objects such as tables and graphics.

Displaying a Document in Read Mode View

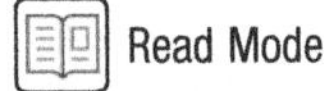

Read Mode view displays a document in a format for easy viewing and reading. Change to Read Mode view by clicking the Read Mode button in the view area on the Status bar or by clicking the View tab and then clicking the Read Mode button in the Views group. Navigate in Read Mode view using the keys on the keyboard, as shown in Table 6.1. Another way to navigate in Read Mode is to click the Next and Previous arrow buttons at the right and left sides of the screen to page forward and backward through the document.

The File, Tools, and View tabs appear in the upper left corner of the screen in Read Mode view. Click the File tab to display the backstage area. Click the Tools tab and a drop-down list displays with options for finding specific text in the document, searching for information on the internet, and translating text in the document.

Figure 6.1 View Buttons and the Zoom Slider Bar

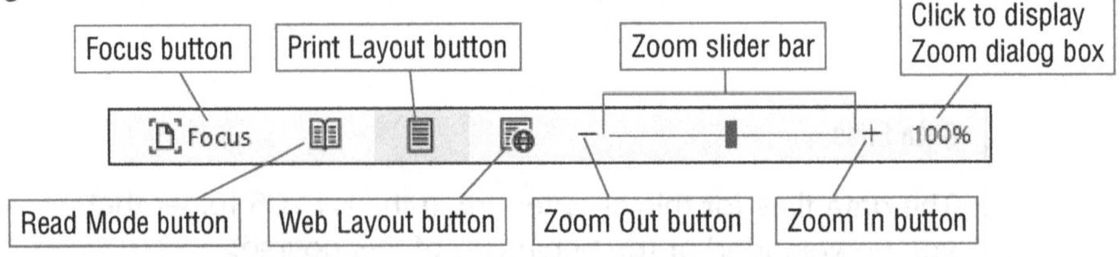

Table 6.1 Keyboard Commands in Read Mode View

Press this key	To complete this action
Page Down key, Right Arrow key, or spacebar	display next two pages
Page Up key, Left Arrow key, or Backspace key	display previous two pages
Home	display first page in document
End	display last page in document
Esc	return to previous view

Click the View tab to customize Read Mode view. Use View tab options to switch to Focus Mode, display the Navigation pane to navigate to specific locations in the document, or to show comments inserted in the document. The View tab also includes options for making text more readable by changing column width, page color, and page layout; showing syllable breaks; increasing spacing between characters, words, and lines; and hearing text read aloud. These options are also available on the Immersive Reader tab, described on the next page.

If a document contains an object such as a table, SmartArt graphic, image, or shape, zoom in on the object in Read Mode view by double-clicking it. The display size of the object increases and a button containing a magnifying glass with a plus symbol inside (🔍) appears just outside the upper right corner of the object. Click the magnifying glass to zoom in and out. Click outside the object to exit the zoom view. To close Read Mode view and return to the previous view, press the Esc key or click the View tab and then click *Edit Document* at the drop-down list.

Activity 1a Changing Views

Part 1 of 3

1. Open **WebReport.docx** and then save it with the name **6-WebReport**.
2. Display the document in Draft view by clicking the View tab and then clicking the Draft button in the Views group.

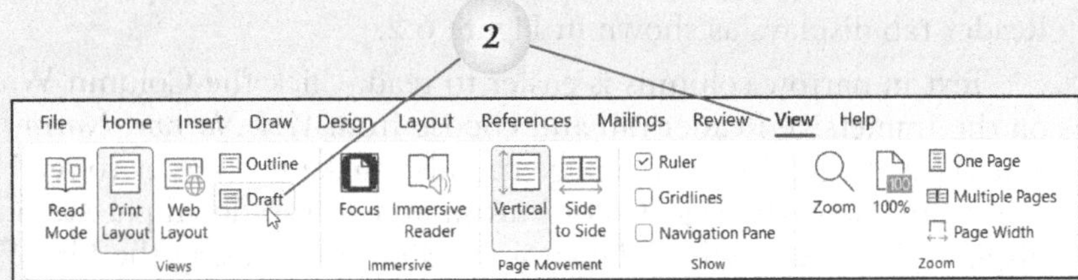

3. Click the Web Layout button in the Views group to display the document as it would appear if published as a web page.
4. Display the document in Read Mode view by clicking the Read Mode button in the view area on the Status bar.

5. If a speaker is connected to your computer, have the text read out loud by clicking the View tab and then clicking the *Read Aloud* option at the drop-down list. After listening for a short period of time, turn off the reading by clicking the View tab and then clicking the *Read Aloud* option.
6. Increase the display size of the table at the right side of the screen by double-clicking the table. (If the table is not visible, click the Next button at the right side of the screen to view the next page.)
7. Click the button containing a magnifying glass with a plus symbol that displays outside the upper right corner of the table. (This increases the zoom.)

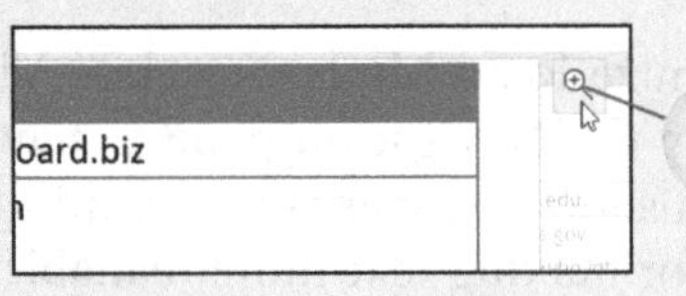

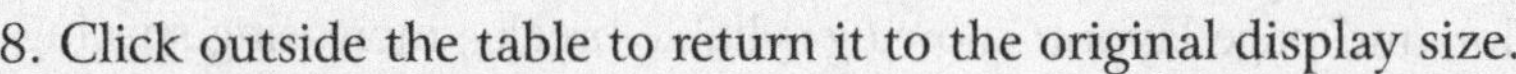

8. Click outside the table to return it to the original display size.
9. Practice navigating in Read Mode view using the actions shown in Table 6.1 (except the last action).
10. Press the Esc key to return to the Print Layout view.

Using Immersive Options

Using Immersive Options

Focus

Immersive Reader

The Immersive group on the View tab contains a Focus button and an Immersive Reader button. Click the Focus button to switch to Focus Mode and only the document displays without the distraction of other screen features. Edit a document in Focus Mode in the normal manner. Move the insertion point to the top of the screen and the ribbon displays. To close Focus Mode, press the Esc key or move the insertion point to the top of the screen and then click the Focus button on the View tab. Another option for switching to Focus Mode is to click the Focus button on the Status bar.

The same learning tools available in Read Mode view can also be found on the Immersive Reader tab, along with additional options. Click the View tab and then click the Immersive Reader button in the Immersive group and the Immersive Reader tab displays as shown in Figure 6.2.

Column Width

Page Color

Line Focus

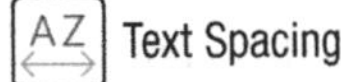
Text Spacing

Syllables

Text in narrow columns is easier to read. Click the Column Width button on the Immersive Reader tab and choose from *Very Narrow*, *Narrow*, *Moderate*, and *Wide*. Adding color to a page can also make text easier to read and reduce eye strain. Click the Page Color button and a drop-down palette of color choices displays. Improve focus and comprehension by choosing the Line Focus button to read text one, three, or five lines at a time. Click the Text Spacing button to make text easier to read by increasing space between words, characters, and lines. Click the Syllables button to display syllable breaks in words, making words easier to recognize and pronounce.

Read Aloud

If audio output is available, click the Read Aloud button to hear the text read. Each word is highlighted as it is being read. A playback toolbar displays with buttons for controlling the narration, as shown in Figure 6.3. Turn off reading by clicking the Stop button on the playback toolbar or by clicking the Read Aloud button again. The Read Aloud button is also available in the Speech group on the Review tab.

Figure 6.2 Immersive Reader Tab

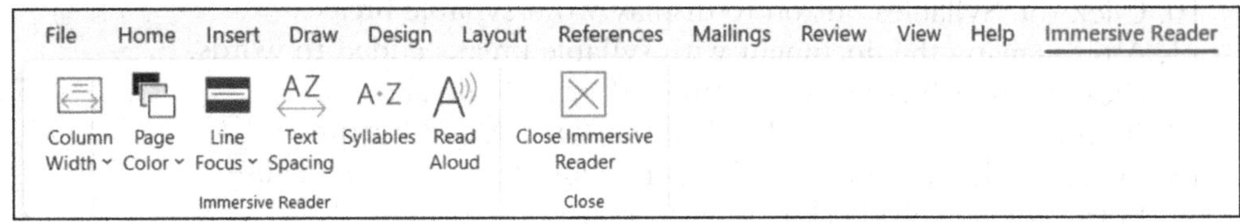

Figure 6.3 Playback Toolbar

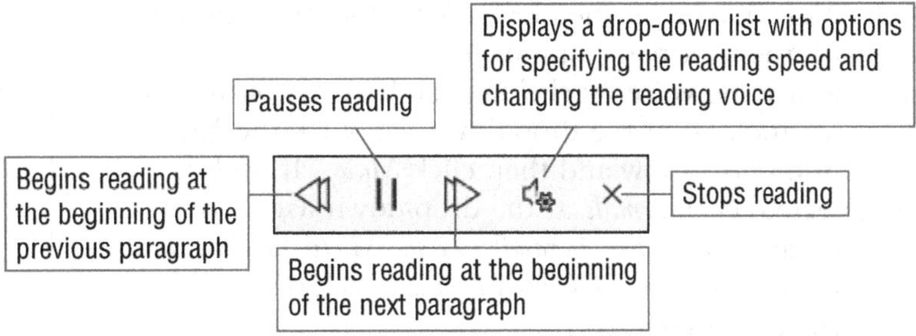

Activity 1b Using Immersive Reader Option

Part 2 of 3

1. With **6-WebReport.docx** open, display the document in Focus Mode by clicking the View tab and then clicking the Focus button in the Immersive group. Return to the Print Layout view by moving the pointer to the top of the screen and then clicking the Focus button.
2. Display the Immersive Reader tab by clicking the View tab, if necessary, and then clicking the Immersive Reader button in the Immersive group.
3. Change column width by clicking the Column Width button on the Immersive Reader tab and then clicking *Moderate* at the drop-down list.
4. Change page background color by clicking the Page Color button and then clicking the *Light Gray* option (last column, first row in the color palette).
5. Focus on only a few lines in the document by clicking the Line Focus button and then clicking *Five Lines* at the drop-down list.

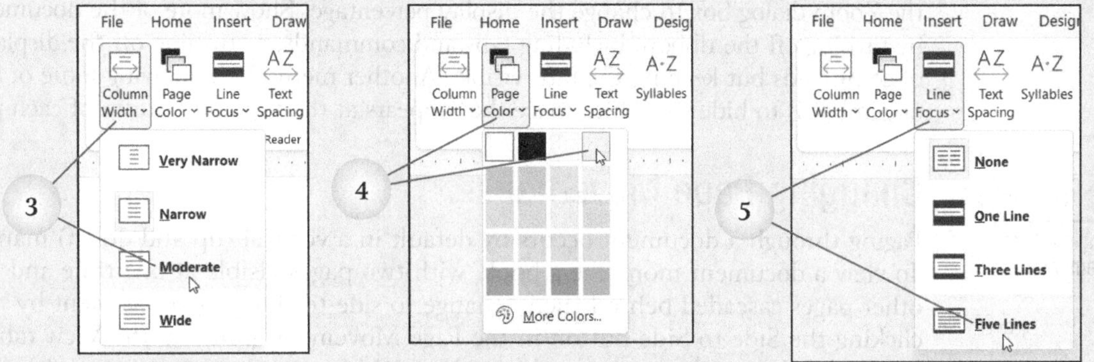

6. Click the down arrow at the right side of the screen to scroll down five lines in the document.
7. Remove the line focus by clicking the Line Focus button and then clicking *None* at the drop-down list.
8. If the Text Spacing button is active (displays with a gray background), click the button to remove spacing between characters.
9. After viewing the document with extra spacing, click the Text Spacing button to turn off text spacing.

10. Click the Syllables button to display word syllable breaks.
11. After viewing the document with syllable breaks added to words, click the Syllables button to turn off syllable breaks.
12. If audio output is available, click the Read Aloud button.
13. Listen to the reading for a short time and then click the Pause button on the playback toolbar to pause the reading.
14. Click the Play button (previously the Pause button) to resume the reading.
15. Click the Next button on the playback toolbar to begin the reading with the next paragraph of text.
16. Change the reading voice by clicking the Settings button on the playback toolbar. At the drop-down list, click the *Voice Selection* option box arrow and then click *Male*. (If *Male* is already selected, click *Female* at the drop-down list. If your choices are names such as *Microsoft David*, *Microsoft Zira*, and *Microsoft Mark* instead of *Male* and *Female*, click one of the names at the drop-down list.)
17. After listening to the reading by a male voice, return to the female voice by clicking the Settings button, clicking the *Voice Selection* option box arrow, and then clicking *Female*.
18. Click the Stop button on the playback toolbar to turn off reading.
19. Remove the page color by clicking the Page Color button and then clicking the *None* option (first column, first row) at the color palette.
20. Close the Immersive Reader tab by clicking the Close Immersive Reader button on the Immersive Reader tab.

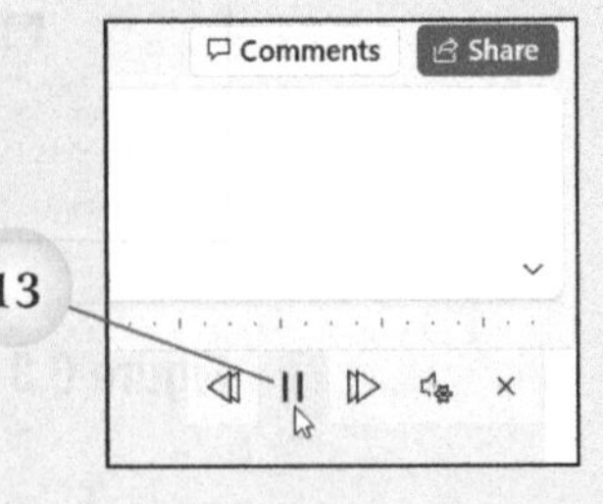

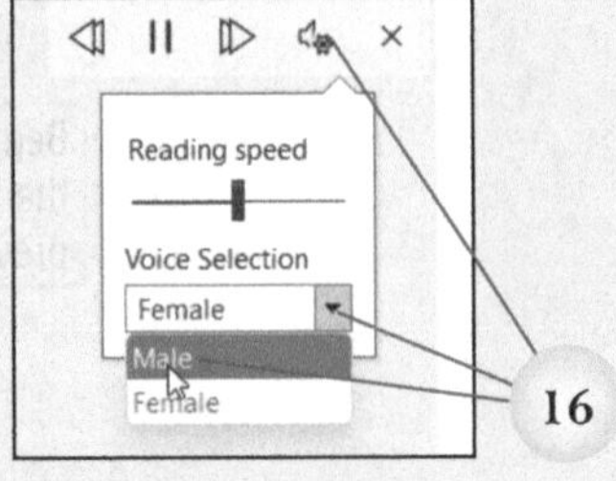

Changing the Document Display

Word includes a number of options for changing the way a document displays on the screen. Show pages in a document like pages in a book with the Side to Side button in the Page Movement group on the View tab. Use options on the Zoom slider bar or the Zoom dialog box to change the display percentage. Show more of the document by turning off the ribbon, including tabs and commands, or turning off the display of commands but keeping the tabs visible. Another method for showing more of a document is to hide the white space that appears at the top and bottom of each page.

Changing Page Movement

Changing Page Movement

Paging through a document occurs by default in a vertical (up and down) manner. To view a document more like a book, with two pages visible at one time and other pages cascaded behind them, change to side-to-side page movement by clicking the Side to Side button in the Page Movement group on the View tab. Figure 6.4 shows how pages appear in the 6-WebReport.docx document with the Side to Side button active.

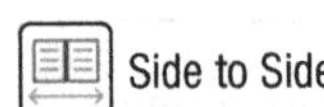

Scroll through pages on a touch screen using a finger to flip through pages. If the computer screen is not a touch screen, use the horizontal scroll bar or the mouse wheel to scroll through pages. To use the horizontal scroll bar, click the Next button (right-pointing triangle) at the right side of the scroll bar to display the next page or click the Previous button (left-pointing triangle) at the left side of the scroll bar to display the previous page; drag the scroll box on the scroll bar; or click to the left or right of the scroll box. The mouse wheel can also be used to scroll through pages.

Figure 6.4 Side-to-Side Page Movement

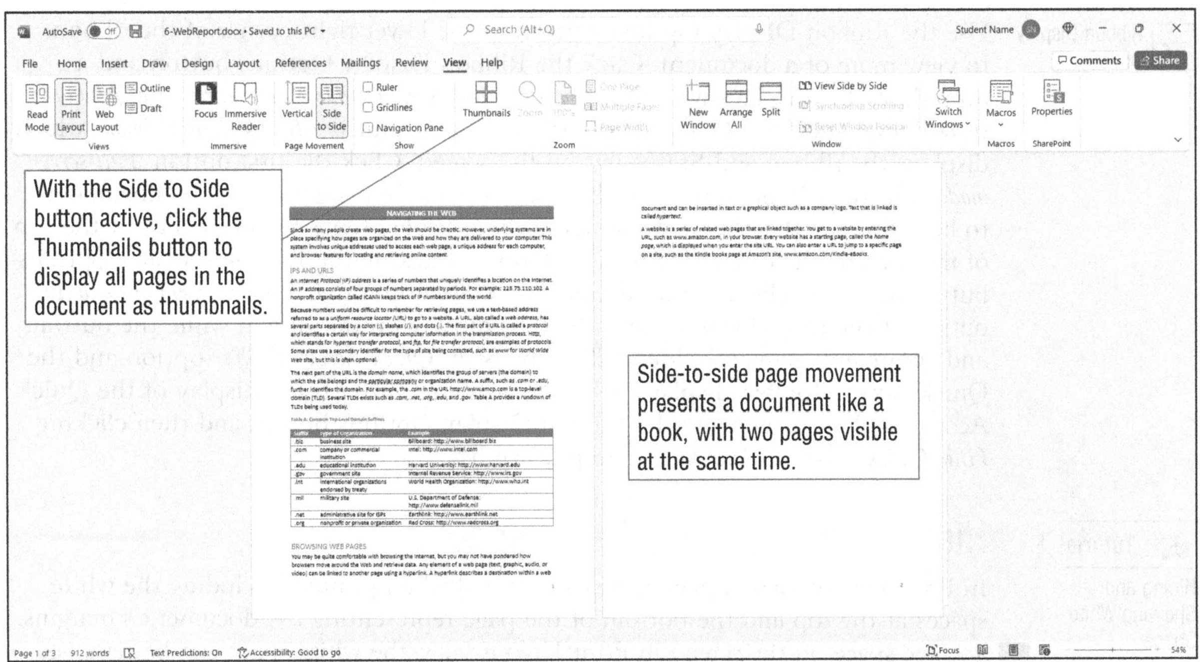

With the Side to Side button active, click the Thumbnails button to display all pages in the document as thumbnails.
Side-to-side page movement presents a document like a book, with two pages visible at the same time.

Thumbnails

When the Side to Side button is active, the Thumbnails button appears in the Zoom group on the View tab and other options in the Zoom group are unavailable. Click the Thumbnails button and all pages in the document display as thumbnails. Click a thumbnail to move the insertion point to the beginning of the page represented by the thumbnail and that page along with the next or previous page displays side to side. Another method for displaying page thumbnails is to hold down the Ctrl key while moving the mouse wheel. Return to the default vertical page movement by clicking the Vertical button in the Page Movement group on the View tab.

Vertical

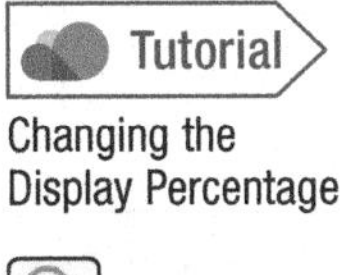
Tutorial

Changing the Display Percentage

Changing the Display Percentage

By default, a document displays at 100%. This display percentage can be changed with the Zoom slider bar at the right side of the Status bar and with options in the Zoom group on the View tab. To change the display percentage with the Zoom slider bar, drag the button on the bar to increase or decrease the percentage. Click the Zoom Out button at the left of the slider bar to decrease the display percentage or click the Zoom In button to increase the display percentage.

Zoom

100%

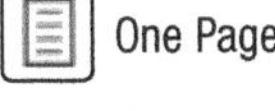
One Page

Multiple Pages

Page Width

Click the Zoom button in the Zoom group on the View tab to display the Zoom dialog box, which contains options for changing the display percentage. If the display percentage has been changed, return to the default by clicking the 100% button in the Zoom group on the View tab. Click the One Page button to display the entire page on the screen and click the Multiple Pages button to display multiple pages on the screen. Click the Page Width button and the document expands across the screen.

Hint Click the percentage at the right of the Zoom slider bar to display the Zoom dialog box.

Changing Ribbon Display Options

Use the Ribbon Display Options button in the lower right corner of the ribbon to view more of a document. Click the Ribbon Display Options button and a drop-down list displays with four options: *Full-screen mode*, *Show tabs only*, *Always show Ribbon* and *Show Quick Access Toolbar*. The default is *Always show Ribbon*, which displays the ribbon and Status bar on the screen. Click the first option, *Full-screen mode*, and the ribbon and Status bar are hidden, allowing more of the document to be visible on the screen. To temporarily redisplay these features, click at the top of the screen. Turn these features back on by clicking the Ribbon Display Options button and then clicking the *Always show Ribbon* option. Click the *Show tabs only* option at the drop-down list and the tabs display on the ribbon while the buttons and commands remain hidden. Click the *Show Quick Access Toolbar* option and the Quick Access Toolbar displays below the ribbon. Turn off the display of the Quick Access Toolbar by clicking the Ribbon Display Options button and then clicking *Hide Quick Access Toolbar* at the drop-down list.

Hiding and Showing White Space

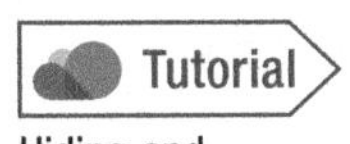

Hiding and Showing White Space

In Print Layout view, a page appears as it will when printed, including the white spaces at the top and the bottom of the page representing the document's margins. To save space on the screen in Print Layout view, the white space can be removed from view by positioning the pointer at the top edge or bottom edge of a page or between pages until the pointer displays as the Hide White Space icon and then double-clicking the left mouse button. To redisplay the white space, position the pointer on the thin gray line separating pages until the pointer turns into the Show White Space icon and then double-click the left mouse button.

Activity 1c Changing Views, Changing Display, and Hiding/Showing White Space — Part 3 of 3

1. With **6-WebReport.docx** open, press Ctrl + Home to move the insertion point to the beginning of the document.
2. Change to side-to-side page movement by clicking the View tab and then clicking the Side to Side button in the Page Movement group. (This displays pages 1 and 2 side by side.)
3. Click the Next button at the right side of the horizontal scroll bar to display pages 2 and 3.
4. Display page thumbnails by clicking the Thumbnails button in the Zoom group.
5. Click the page 1 thumbnail.

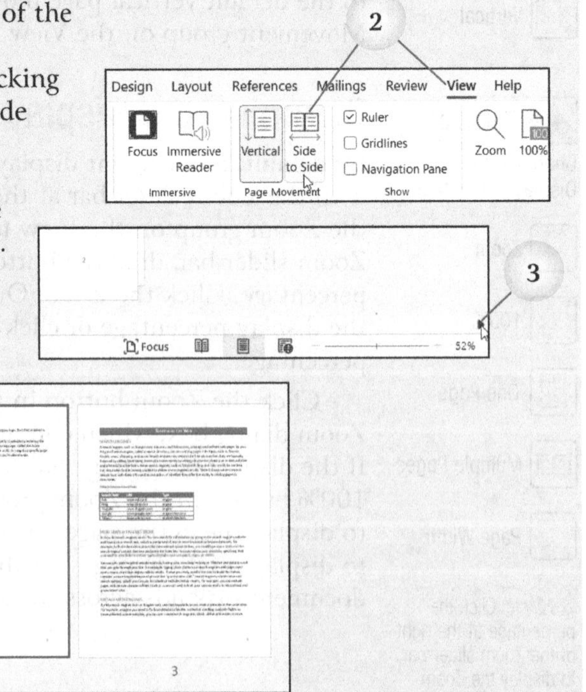

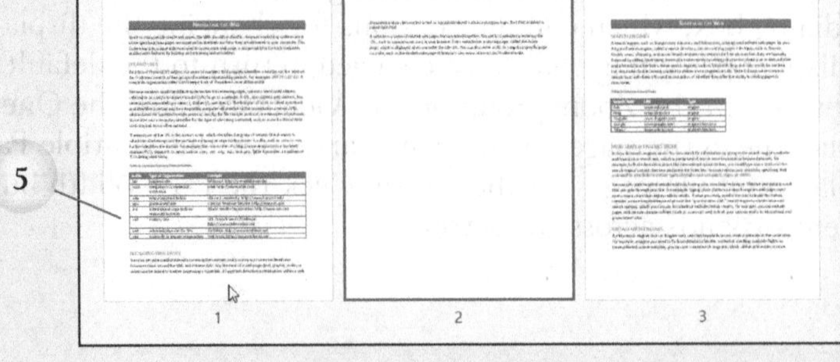

6. Return to the default page movement by clicking the Vertical button in the Page Movement group.
7. Click the Zoom button in the Zoom group on the View tab.
8. At the Zoom dialog box, click the *75%* option and then click OK.

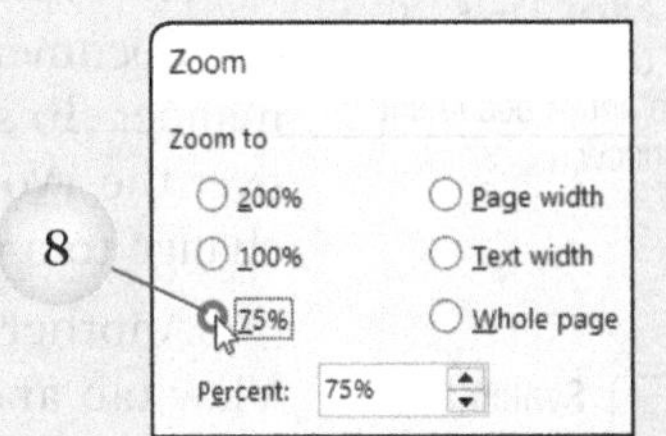

9. Return the display percentage to the default by clicking the 100% button in the Zoom group.
10. Click the Ribbon Display Options button in the lower right corner of the ribbon and then click *Full-screen mode* at the drop-down list.

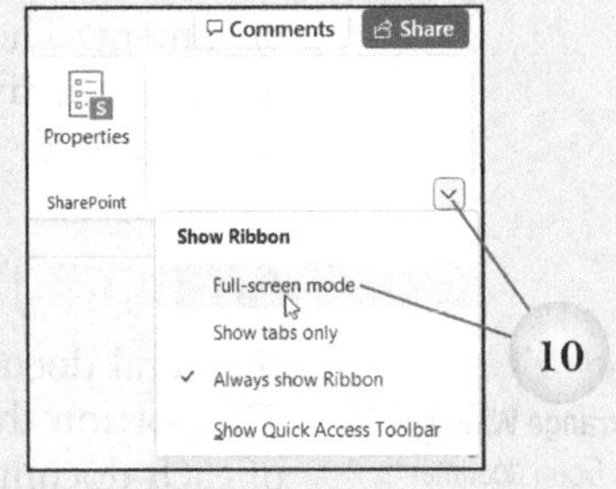

11. Press the Page Down key until the end of the document displays.
12. Click at the top of the screen to temporarily redisplay the ribbon and Status bar.
13. Click the Ribbon Display Options button and then click *Show tabs only* at the drop-down list.
14. Double-click the Home tab to redisplay the ribbon.
15. Press Ctrl + Home to move the insertion point to the beginning of the document.
16. Hide the white spaces at the tops and bottoms of pages by positioning the pointer at the top edge of the page until the pointer turns into the Hide White Space icon and then double-clicking the left mouse button.

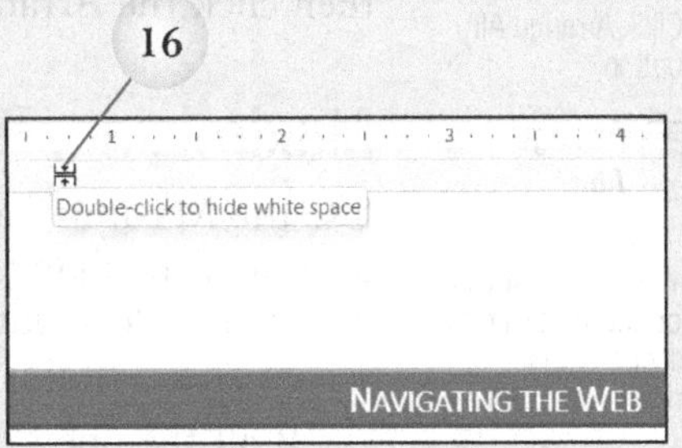

17. Scroll through the document and notice the appearance of pages.
18. Redisplay the white spaces at the tops and bottoms of pages by positioning the pointer on any thin gray line separating pages until the pointer turns into the Show White Space icon and then double-clicking the left mouse button.

18 browsers move around the Web and retrieve d video) can be linked to another page using a hy document an Double-click to show white space ap called *hypertext.*

19. Close **6-WebReport.docx**.

Activity 2 Manage Multiple Documents — 7 Parts

You will open multiple documents and then arrange, maximize, restore, and minimize windows; move selected text between split windows; compare formatting of documents side by side; and print specific text, pages, and multiple copies.

Working with Windows

Hint Press Ctrl + F6 to switch between open documents.

Working with Windows

Multiple documents can be opened in Word, the insertion point can be moved between documents, and information can be moved or copied from one document and pasted into another. When a new document is opened, it displays on top of any previously opened document. With multiple documents open, the window containing each document can be resized to see all or a portion of it on the screen.

Hint Press Ctrl + W or Ctrl + F4 to close the active document window.

A Word button appears on the taskbar when a document is open. If more than one document is open, another button will appear behind the first in a cascading manner. To see all documents that are currently open in Word, hover the pointer over the Word button. A thumbnail of each document will appear. To make a change to a document, click the thumbnail that represents the document.

Switch Windows

Another method for determining what documents are open is to click the View tab and then click the Switch Windows button in the Window group. The document name in the list with the check mark in front of it is the active document. The active document contains the insertion point. To make a different document active, click the document name. To switch to another document using the keyboard, type the number shown in front of the document.

Arranging Windows

Quick Steps

Arrange Windows

1. Open documents.
2. Click View tab.
3. Click Arrange All button.

Arrange All

If several documents are open, they can be arranged so a portion of each appears. The portion that appears includes the title (if present) and the opening paragraph of each document. To arrange a group of open documents, click the View tab and then click the Arrange All button in the Window group.

Maximizing, Restoring, and Minimizing Documents

Hint The keyboard shortcut to maximize a document is Ctrl + F10.

Use the Maximize and Minimize buttons in the upper right corner of the active document to change the size of a document window. The two buttons are at the left of the Close button. (The Close button is in the upper right corner of the screen and contains an X.)

Maximize

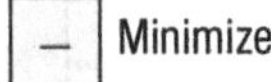
Minimize

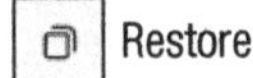
Restore

If all the open documents are arranged on the screen, clicking the Maximize button in the active document causes that document to expand to fill the screen. Any other open windows will be hidden behind it. In addition, the Maximize button changes to the Restore button. To return the active document back to its original size, click the Restore button. Click the Minimize button in the active document and the document is reduced to a button on the taskbar. To maximize a document that has been minimized, hover the pointer over the taskbar button and click the thumbnail of the document.

Activity 2a Arranging, Maximizing, Restoring, and Minimizing Windows **Part 1 of 7**

Note: If you are using Word on a network system that contains a virus checker, you may not be able to open multiple documents at once. Continue by opening each document individually.

1. Open the following documents: **AptLease.docx**, **IntelProp.docx**, **NSS.docx**, and **Visionaries.docx**. (To open all the documents at one time, display the Open dialog box, hold down the Ctrl key, click each document name, release the Ctrl key, and then click the Open button.)
2. Arrange the windows by clicking the View tab and then clicking the Arrange All button in the Window group.
3. Make **AptLease.docx** the active document by clicking the Switch Windows button in the Window group on the View tab of the document at the top of your screen and then clicking ***AptLease.docx*** at the drop-down list.
4. Close **AptLease.docx**.
5. Make **IntelProp.docx** active and then close it.

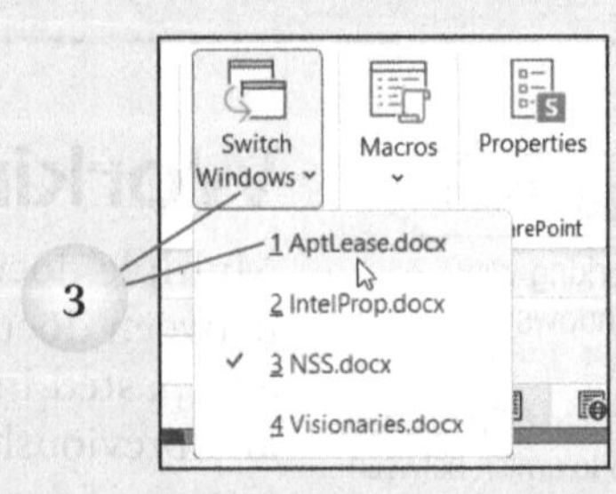

6. Make **Visionaries.docx** active and minimize it by clicking the Minimize button in the upper right corner of the active window.
7. Maximize **NSS.docx** by clicking the Maximize button immediately left of the Close button.
8. Close **NSS.docx**.
9. Restore **Visionaries.docx** by clicking the button on the taskbar that represents the document.
10. Maximize **Visionaries.docx**.

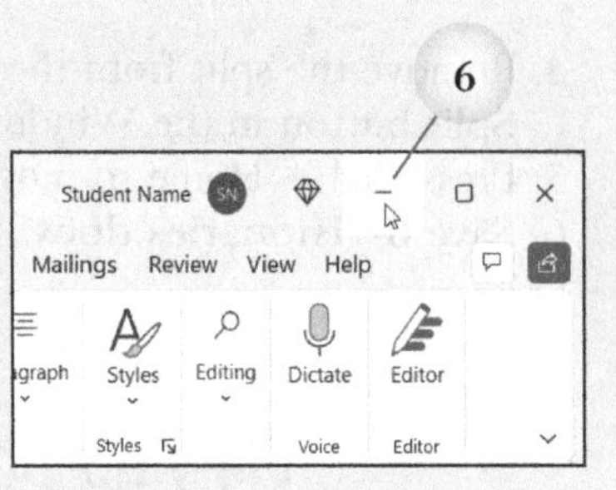

Splitting a Window

Quick Steps

Split Window

1. Open document.
2. Click View tab.
3. Click Split button.

Split

Hint The keyboard shortcut to split a window is Alt + Ctrl + S.

Remove Split

A window can be split into two panes so that two different parts of a document can be seen at once. For example, show an outline for a report in one pane and the part of the report to be edited in the other pane. The original window is split into two panes that extend horizontally across the screen.

Split a window by clicking the View tab and then clicking the Split button in the Window group. This splits the window in two with a split bar and another horizontal ruler. The location of the split bar can be changed by positioning the pointer on the split bar until the pointer displays as an up-and-down-pointing arrow with two small lines in the middle, holding down the left mouse button, dragging to the new location, and then releasing the mouse button.

When a window is split, the insertion point is positioned in the bottom pane. To move the insertion point to the other pane with the mouse, position the I-beam pointer in the other pane and then click the left mouse button. To remove the split bar from the document, click the View tab and then click the Remove Split button in the Window group. The split bar can also be double-clicked or dragged to the top or bottom of the screen.

Activity 2b Moving Selected Text between Split Windows — Part 2 of 7

1. With **Visionaries.docx** open, save the document with the name **6-Visionaries**.
2. Click the View tab and then click the Split button in the Window group.
3. Move the *William Hewlett and David Packard* section just above the *Gordon E. Moore* section by completing the following steps:
   a. Click in the top pane and then click the Home tab.
   b. Select the heading *William Hewlett and David Packard* and the three paragraphs below the heading.
   c. Click the Cut button in the Clipboard group on the Home tab.
   d. Click in the bottom pane, scroll down the document, and then position the insertion point at the beginning of the heading *Gordon E. Moore*.
   e. Click the Paste button in the Clipboard group on the Home tab.

4. Remove the split from the window by clicking the View tab and then clicking the Remove Split button in the Window group.
5. Press Ctrl + Home to move the insertion point to the beginning of the document.
6. Save **6-Visionaries.docx**.

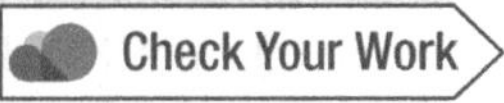

Viewing Documents Side by Side

View Documents Side by Side
1. Open two documents.
2. Click View tab.
3. Click View Side by Side button.

The contents of two documents can be compared on screen by opening both documents, clicking the View tab, and then clicking the View Side by Side button in the Window group. The documents are arranged on the screen side by side, as shown in Figure 6.5. By default, synchronous scrolling is active. With this feature active, scrolling in one document causes the same scrolling in the other document. This feature is useful for comparing the text, formatting, or other features between documents. To scroll in one document and not the other, click the Synchronous Scrolling button in the Window group to turn it off.

Figure 6.5 Viewing Documents Side by Side

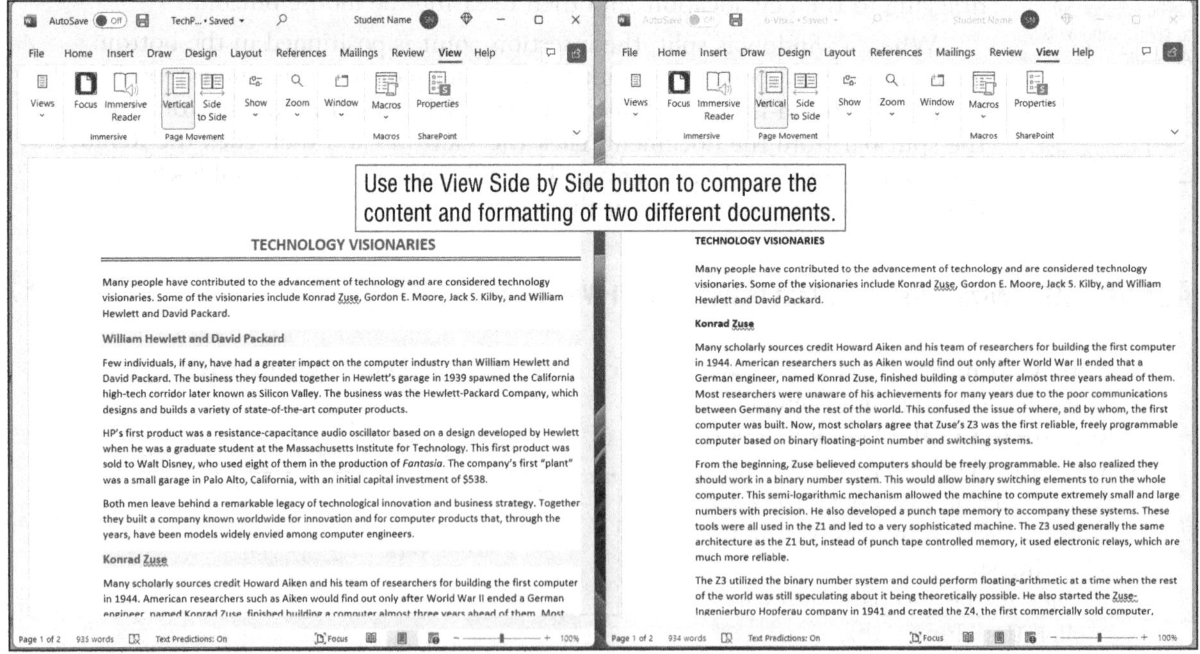

Activity 2c Viewing Documents Side by Side

Part 3 of 7

1. With **6-Visionaries.docx** open, open **TechPioneers.docx**.
2. Click the View tab and then click the View Side by Side button in the Window group.

3. Scroll through both documents simultaneously. Notice the difference between the two documents. (The titles and headings are set in different alignment, font color and size, and/or shading.) Format the title and headings in **6-Visionaries.docx** so that they match the formatting in **TechPioneers.docx**. ***Hint: Use the Format Painter button to copy the formatting.***
4. Turn off synchronous scrolling by clicking the View tab in the active document, clicking the Window button, and then clicking the Synchronous Scrolling button at the drop-down list.

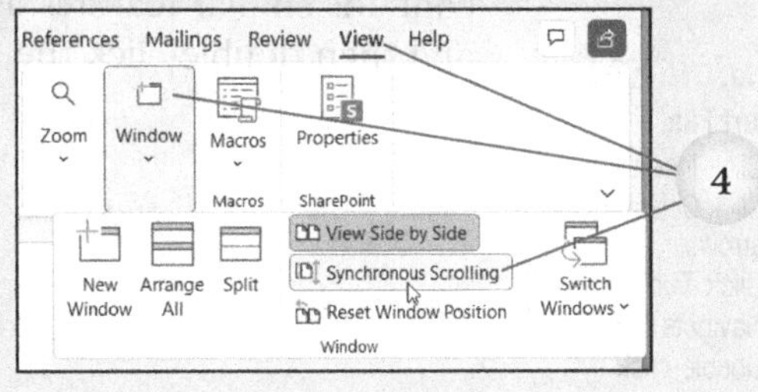

5. Click in the document and then scroll through the document and notice that no scrolling occurs in the other document.
6. Make **TechPioneers.docx** the active document and then close it.
7. Save **6-Visionaries.docx**.

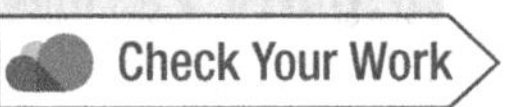

Opening a New Window

Quick Steps

Open New Window

1. Open document.
2. Click View tab.
3. Click New Window button.

A second copy of a document can be opened in a new window so that two copies of the same document may be viewed side by side. To do this, first open a document and then click the New Window button in the Window group on the View tab. When a new window is opened, the document name in the Title bar is followed by *- 2*. The document name in the original window is followed by *- 1*. Any change made to the document in one window is reflected in the document in the other window, as both windows display the exact same file.

Activity 2d Opening a New Window — Part 4 of 7

1. With **6-Visionaries.docx** open, open a second copy of the document in a new window by clicking the New Window button in the Window group on the View tab. (Notice that the document name in the Title bar displays followed by *- 2*.)
2. Click the View tab and then click the View Side by Side button in the Window group.
3. Click the Window button on the View tab and then click the Synchronous Scrolling button to turn off synchronous scrolling.
4. Click in the **6-Visionaries.docx - 2** window to make the document active. Look at the first paragraph of text and notice the order in which the names are listed in the last sentence of the paragraph (Konrad Zuse, Gordon E. Moore, Jack S. Kilby, and William Hewlett and David Packard).
5. Click in the **6-Visionaries.docx - 1** window and then cut and paste the headings and text so that each name and text following the name appears in the order listed in the first paragraph.
6. Click the Save button on the Title bar.
7. Close the second copy of the document by clicking the Word button on the taskbar and then clicking the Close button in the upper right corner of the **6-Visionaries.docx - 2** thumbnail (above the Word button on the taskbar).
8. With **6-Visionaries.docx** active, scroll to the bottom of the first page and make sure the title *Jack S. Kilby* displays on the same page as the paragraph of text that follows.
9. Save **6-Visionaries.docx**.

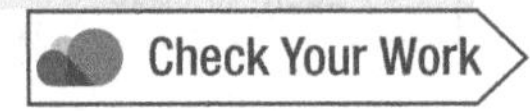

Inserting a File

Object

Quick Steps

Insert File

1. Click Insert tab.
2. Click Object button arrow.
3. Click *Text from File*.
4. Navigate to folder.
5. Double-click document.

Inserting a File into a Document

The contents of one document can be inserted into another using the Object button in the Text group on the Insert tab. Click the Object button arrow and then click *Text from File* and the Insert File dialog box displays. This dialog box contains similar features as the Open dialog box. Navigate to the specific folder and then double-click the document to be inserted in the open document.

Activity 2e Inserting a File

Part 5 of 7

1. With **6-Visionaries.docx** open, move the insertion point to the blank line above the title *REFERENCES*.
2. Insert a file into the open document by completing the following steps:
   a. Click the Insert tab.
   b. Click the Object button arrow in the Text group and then click *Text from File* at the drop-down list.
   c. At the Insert File dialog box, navigate to your WL1C6 folder and then double-click *Torvalds.docx*.
3. Save **6-Visionaries.docx**.

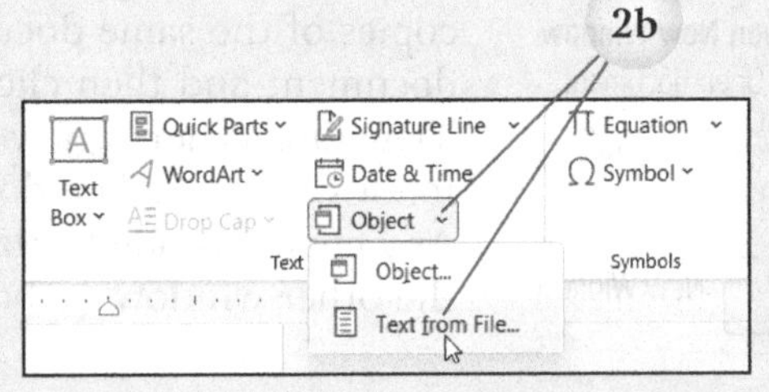

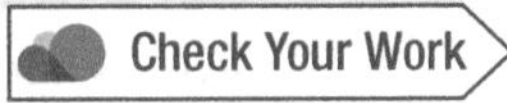

Previewing and Printing

Hint The Print backstage area can also be displayed with the keyboard shortcut Ctrl + P.

Previewing and Printing

Use options at the Print backstage area, shown in Figure 6.6, to specify what is to be printed and to preview pages before printing them. To display the Print backstage area, click the File tab and then click the *Print* option. If the Quick Access Toolbar displays, the Print Preview and Print button can be added to the toolbar so that, when clicked, the Print backstage area displays. Display the Quick Access Toolbar by clicking the Ribbon Display Options button at the right side of the ribbon and then clicking *Show Quick Access Toolbar*. Insert the button on the Quick Access Toolbar by clicking the Customize Quick Access Toolbar button at the right side of the toolbar and then clicking *Print Preview and Print* at the drop-down list.

Previewing Pages

Zoom to Page

At the Print backstage area, a preview of the current page is shown (see Figure 6.6). Click the Next Page button to view the next page in the document preview, and click the Previous Page button to display the previous page. Use the Zoom slider bar to increase or decrease the size of the page and click the Zoom to Page button to fit the entire page in the viewing area.

Figure 6.6 Print Backstage Area

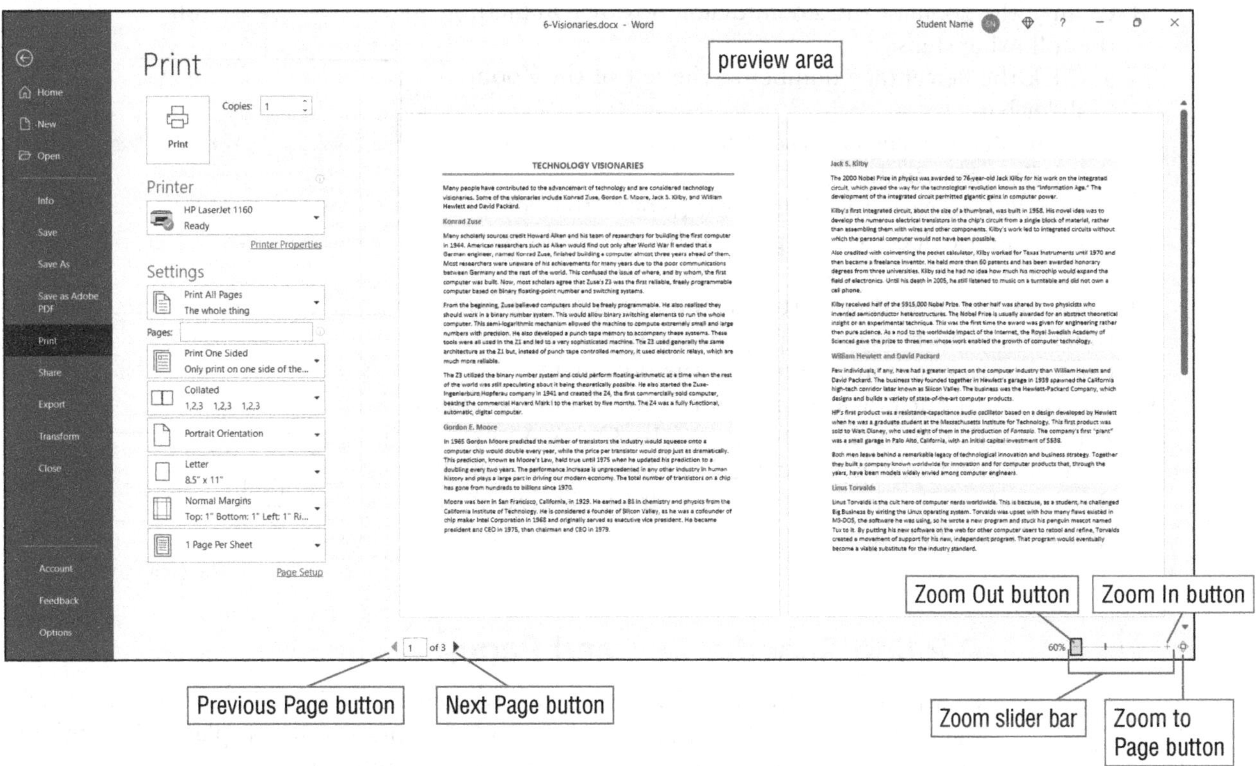

Activity 2f Previewing Pages

Part 6 of 7

1. With **6-Visionaries.docx** open, press Ctrl + Home to move the insertion point to the beginning of the document.
2. If necessary, turn on the display of the Quick Access Toolbar by clicking the Ribbon Display Options button and then clicking *Show Quick Access Toolbar* at the drop-down list.
3. Insert the Print Preview and Print button on the Quick Access Toolbar by clicking the Customize Quick Access Toolbar button and then clicking *Print Preview and Print* at the drop-down list.
4. Preview the document by clicking the Print Preview and Print button on the Quick Access Toolbar.
5. Click the Zoom In button (plus [+] symbol) at the right of the Zoom slider bar two times. (This increases the size of the preview page.)
6. At the Print backstage area, click the Next Page button below and to the left of the preview page. (This displays page 2 in the preview area.)

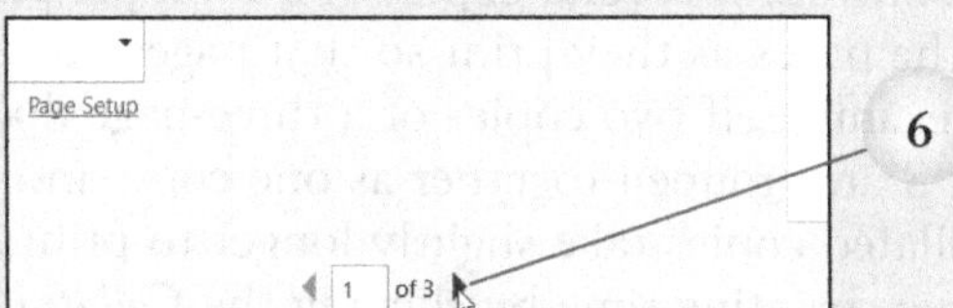

7. Click the Zoom Out button (minus [–] symbol) at the left of the Zoom slider bar until two pages of the document display in the preview area.

8. Change the zoom at the Zoom dialog box by completing the following steps:
   a. Click the percentage number at the left of the Zoom slider bar.
   b. At the Zoom dialog box, click the *Many pages* option in the *Zoom to* section.
   c. Click OK to close the dialog box. (Notice that all the pages in the document appear as thumbnails in the preview area.)
9. Click the Zoom to Page button at the right of the Zoom slider bar. (This returns the page to the default size.)
10. Click the Back button to return to the document.
11. Remove the Print Preview and Print button from the Quick Access Toolbar by clicking the Customize Quick Access Toolbar button and then clicking *Print Preview and Print* at the drop-down list. If necessary, turn off the display of the Quick Access Toolbar.

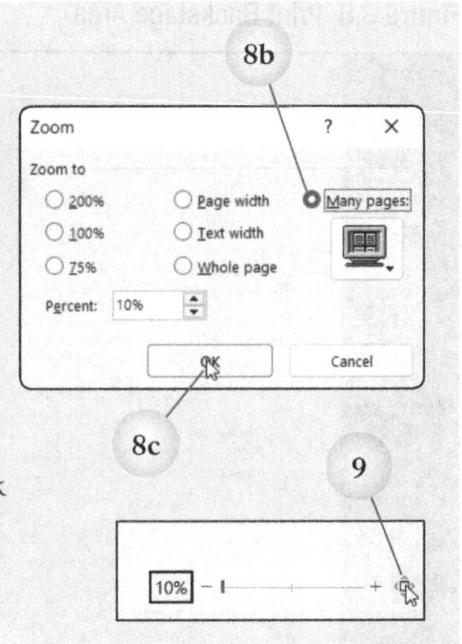

Printing Specific Text and Pages

Hint Save a document before printing it.

Control what prints in a document with options at the Print backstage area. Click the first gallery in the *Settings* category and a drop-down list displays with options for printing. All pages in the document may be printed; or, print only selected text, the current page, or a custom range of pages.

Print a portion of a document by selecting the text and then choosing the *Print Selection* option at the Print backstage area. With this option, only the selected text prints. (If no text is selected, this option is dimmed.) Click the *Print Current Page* option to print only the page on which the insertion point is located. Use the *Custom Print* option to identify a specific page, multiple pages, or a range of pages to print. To print specific pages, use a comma (,) to indicate *and* and use a hyphen (-) to indicate *through*. For example, to print pages 2 and 5, type 2,5 in the *Pages* text box and to print pages 6 through 10, type 6-10.

With the other galleries available in the *Settings* category of the Print backstage area, specify whether to print on one or both sides of the page, change the page orientation (portrait or landscape), specify how the pages are collated, choose a paper size, and specify document margins. The last gallery contains options for printing 1, 2, 4, 6, 8, or 16 pages of a multiple-page document on one sheet of paper. This gallery also contains the *Scale to Paper Size* option. Click this option and then use the side menu to choose the paper size to scale the document.

To print more than one copy of a document, use the *Copies* measurement box to the right of the Print button. If several copies of a multiple-page document are printed, Word collates the pages as they print so that pages appear in sequential order in each copy. For example, if two copies of a three-page document are printed, pages 1, 2, and 3 are grouped together as one copy, and then the pages print a second time. Collated copies take slightly longer to print. If copies do not need to be collated, reduce printing time by clicking the *Collated* gallery in the Print backstage area and then clicking the *Uncollated* option.

To send a document directly to the printer without displaying the Print backstage area, consider adding the Quick Print button to the Quick Access Toolbar. To do this, display the Quick Access Toolbar, click the Customize Quick Access Toolbar button and then click *Quick Print* at the drop-down gallery. Click the Quick Print button and all the pages of the active document will print.

Activity 2g Printing Specific Text and Pages

Part 7 of 7

1. With **6-Visionaries.docx** open, print selected text by completing the following steps:
   a. Select the heading *Konrad Zuse* and the three paragraphs of text that follows it.
   b. Click the File tab and then click the *Print* option.
   c. At the Print backstage area, click the first gallery in the *Settings* category (displays with *Print All Pages*) and then click *Print Selection* at the drop-down list.
   d. Click the Print button.
2. Change the margins and page orientation and then print only the first page by completing the following steps:
   a. Press Ctrl + Home to move the insertion point to the beginning of the document.
   b. Click the File tab and then click the *Print* option.
   c. At the Print backstage area, click the fourth gallery (displays with *Portrait Orientation)* in the *Settings* category and then click *Landscape Orientation* at the drop-down list.
   d. Click the sixth gallery (displays with *Normal Margins*) in the *Settings* category and then click *Narrow* at the drop-down list.
   e. Click the first gallery (displays with *Print All Pages*) in the *Settings* category and then click *Print Current Page* at the drop-down list.
   f. Click the Print button. (The first page of the document prints in landscape orientation with 0.5-inch margins.)

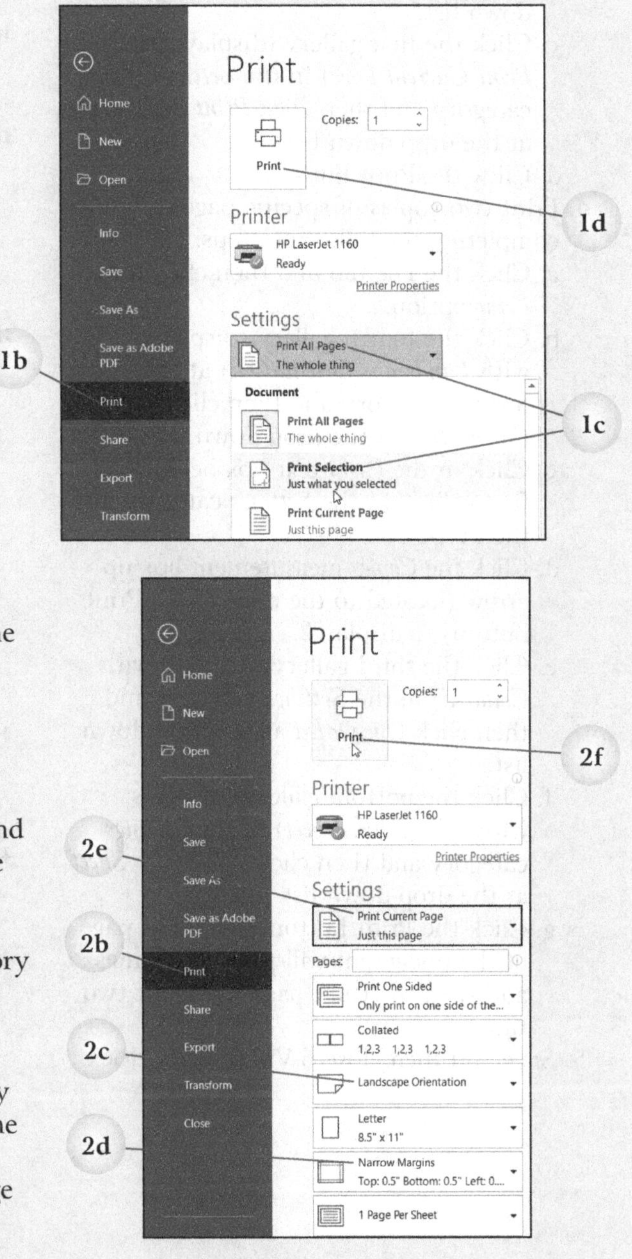

3. Print all the pages as thumbnails on one page by completing the following steps:
   a. Click the File tab and then click the *Print* option.
   b. At the Print backstage area, click the bottom gallery (displays with *1 Page Per Sheet*) in the *Settings* category and then click *4 Pages Per Sheet* at the drop-down list.
   c. Click the first gallery (displays with *Print Current Page*) in the *Settings* category and then click *Print All Pages* at the drop-down list.
   d. Click the Print button.
4. Print two copies of specific pages by completing the following steps:
   a. Click the File tab and then click the *Print* option.
   b. Click the fourth gallery (displays with *Landscape Orientation*) at the *Settings* category and then click *Portrait Orientation* in the drop-down list.
   c. Click in the *Pages* text box below the first gallery in the *Settings* category and then type 1,3.
   d. Click the *Copies* measurement box up arrow (located to the right of the Print button) to display 2.
   e. Click the third gallery (displays with *Collated*) in the *Settings* category and then click *Uncollated* at the drop-down list.
   f. Click the bottom gallery (displays with *4 Pages Per Sheet*) in the *Settings* category and then click *1 Page Per Sheet* at the drop-down list.
   g. Click the Print button. (The first page of the document will print two times and then the third page will print two times.)
5. Save and then close **6-Visionaries.docx**.

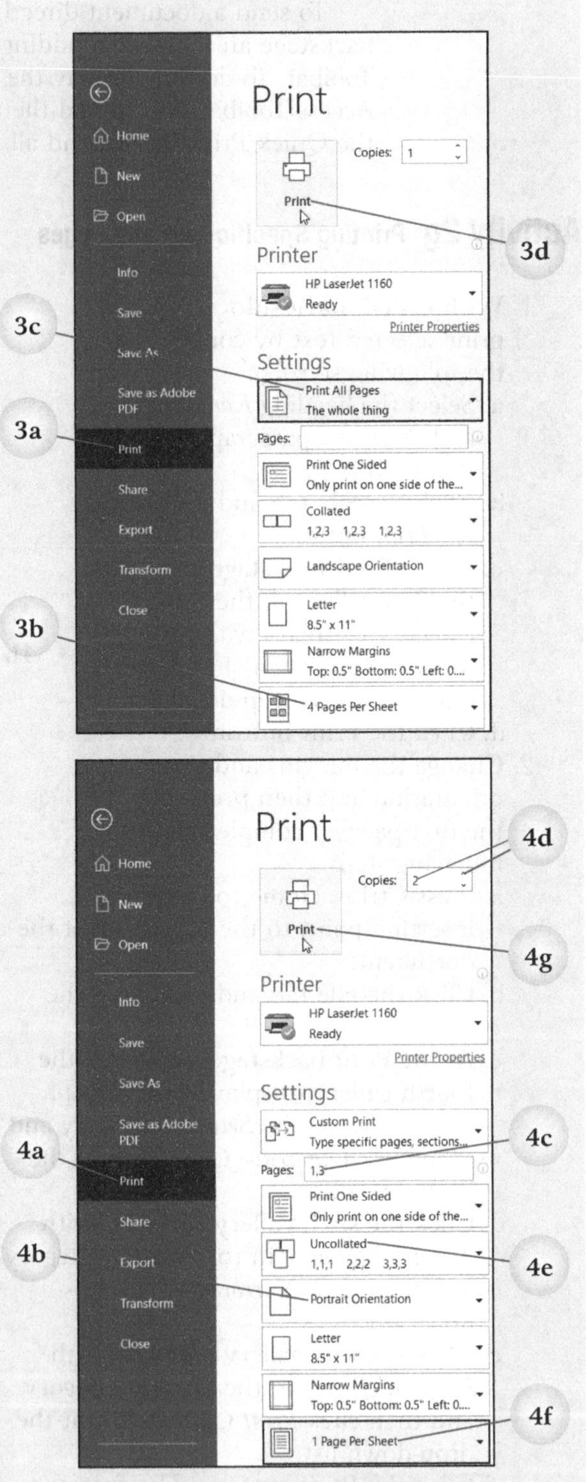

Check Your Work

Activity 3 Prepare Envelopes **2 Parts**

You will create an envelope document and type the return address and delivery address using envelope addressing guidelines issued by the United States Postal Service. You will also open a letter document and then prepare an envelope using the inside address on the business letter.

Preparing an Envelope

Envelopes

Preparing Envelopes

Word automates the creation of envelopes with options at the Envelopes and Labels dialog box with the Envelopes tab selected, as shown in Figure 6.7. Display this dialog box by clicking the Mailings tab and then clicking the Envelopes button in the Create group. At the dialog box, type the delivery address in the *Delivery address* text box and the return address in the *Return address* text box. Print the envelope immediately by clicking the Print button, or prepare the envelope to be printed along with a letter or other document by clicking the Add to document button.

Quick Steps

Prepare Envelope

1. Click Mailings tab.
2. Click Envelopes button.
3. Type delivery address.
4. Click in *Return address* text box.
5. Type return address.
6. Click Add to Document button or Print button.

When a return address is entered in the dialog box, Word will display the question *Do you want to save the new return address as the default return address?* At this question, click Yes to save the current return address for future envelopes or click No if the return address should not be used as the default. To omit a return address, insert a check mark in the *Omit* check box.

The Envelopes and Labels dialog box contains a *Preview* sample box and a *Feed* sample box. The *Preview* sample box shows how the envelope will appear when printed and the *Feed* sample box shows how the envelope should be fed into the printer.

Figure 6.7 Envelopes and Labels Dialog Box with the Envelopes Tab Selected

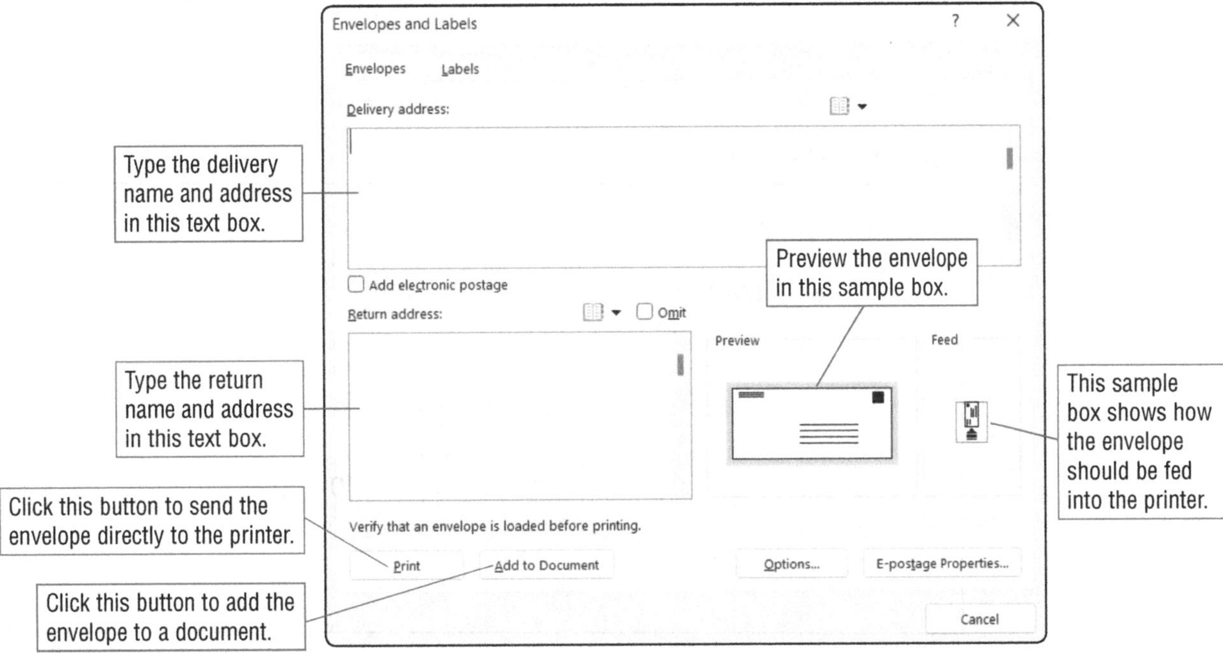

When addressing envelopes, consider following general guidelines issued by the United States Postal Service (USPS). The USPS guidelines suggest using all capital letters with no commas or periods for return and delivery addresses. Figure 6.8 shows envelope addresses that follow the USPS guidelines. Use abbreviations for street suffixes (such as *ST* for *Street* and *AVE* for *Avenue*). For a complete list of address abbreviations, visit the USPS.com website and then search for *Official USPS Abbreviations.*

Activity 3a Preparing an Envelope

Part 1 of 2

1. At a blank document, create an envelope document with the delivery address and return address shown in Figure 6.8. Begin by clicking the Mailings tab.
2. Click the Envelopes button in the Create group.
3. At the Envelopes and Labels dialog box with the Envelopes tab selected, type the delivery address shown in Figure 6.8 (the one containing the name *GREGORY LINCOLN*). (Press the Enter key to end each line in the name and address.)
4. Click in the *Return address* text box. (If any text displays in the *Return address* text box, select and then delete it.)
5. Type the return address shown in Figure 6.8 (the one containing the name *WENDY STEINBERG*). (Press the Enter key to end each line in the name and address.)
6. Click the Add to Document button.
7. At the message *Do you want to save the new return address as the default return address?*, click No.
8. Save the document with the name **6-Env**.
9. Preview and then close **6-Env.docx**.

Check Your Work

Figure 6.8 Activity 3a

WENDY STEINBERG
4532 S 52 ST
BOSTON MA 21002-2334

GREGORY LINCOLN
4455 SIXTH AVE
BOSTON MA 21100-4409

After typing a letter in Word, prepare an envelope to mail the letter by clicking the Envelopes button. Word automatically inserts the first address in the document in the *Delivery address* text box. (Note: Each line of the address must end with a press of the Enter key, and not Shift + Enter, for Word to recognize it.)

Alternately, select the delivery address in the letter document and then click the Envelopes button. When using this method, the address will be formatted exactly as it appears in the letter and may not conform to the USPS guidelines; however, these guidelines are only suggestions, not requirements.

Activity 3b Creating an Envelope in an Existing Document — Part 2 of 2

1. Open **LAProgram.docx**.
2. Click the Mailings tab.
3. Click the Envelopes button in the Create group.
4. At the Envelopes and Labels dialog box (with the Envelopes tab selected), make sure the delivery address appears properly in the *Delivery address* text box.
5. If any text appears in the *Return address* text box, insert a check mark in the *Omit* check box (located to the right of the *Return address* option). (This tells Word not to print the return address on the envelope.)
6. Click the Print button.
7. Close **LAProgram.docx** without saving the changes.

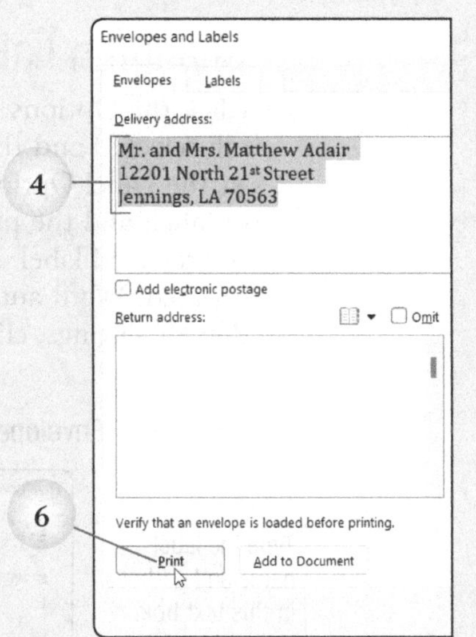

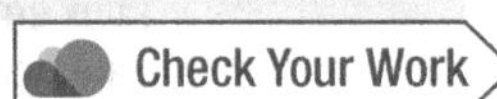

Activity 4 Prepare Labels — 2 Parts

You will create mailing labels containing different names and addresses, labels with the same name and address, and labels with an image.

Preparing Labels

Use Word's Labels feature to print text on mailing labels, file folder labels, and other types of labels. Word formats text for a variety of brands and sizes of labels that can be purchased at most office supply stores. Use the Labels feature to create a sheet of mailing labels with a different name and address on each label or with the same name and address or image on each label.

Creating Mailing Labels with Different Names and Addresses

Creating Mailing Labels with Different Names and Addresses

To create a sheet of mailing labels with a different name and address on each label, click the Labels button in the Create group on the Mailings tab. At the Envelopes and Labels dialog box with the Labels tab selected, as shown in Figure 6.9, leave the *Address* text box empty and then click the New Document button to insert the labels in a new document. The insertion point is positioned in the first label. Type the name and address in the label and then press the Tab key one or two times (depending on the label) to move the insertion point to the next label. Pressing Shift + Tab will move the insertion point to the preceding label.

Changing Label Options

Click the Options button at the Envelopes and Labels dialog box with the Labels tab selected and the Label Options dialog box displays, as shown in Figure 6.10. At the Label Options dialog box, choose the type of printer, the type and brand of label, and the product number. This dialog box also provides information about the selected label, such as type, height, width, and paper size. When a label is selected, Word automatically determines the label margins. To customize these default settings, click the Details button at the Label Options dialog box.

Figure 6.9 Envelopes and Labels Dialog Box with the Labels Tab Selected

Figure 6.10 Label Options Dialog Box

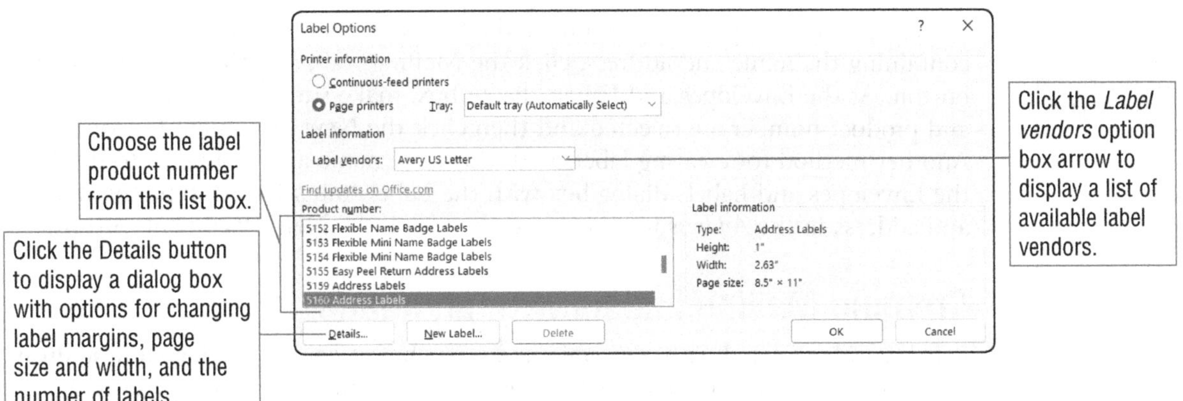

Activity 4a Creating Mailing Labels with Different Names and Addresses

Part 1 of 2

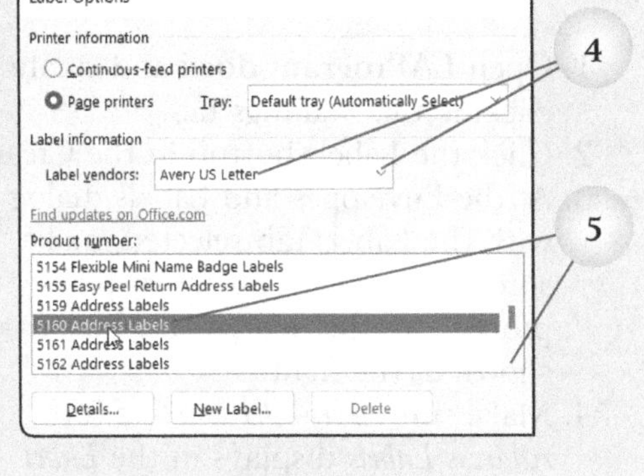

1. At a blank document, click the Mailings tab.
2. Click the Labels button in the Create group.
3. At the Envelopes and Labels dialog box with the Labels tab selected, click the Options button.
4. At the Label Options dialog box, click the *Label vendors* option box arrow and then click *Avery US Letter* at the drop-down list. (You may need to scroll down the list to see this option.)
5. Scroll down the *Product number* list box and then click *5160 Address Labels*.
6. Click OK or press the Enter key.
7. At the Envelopes and Labels dialog box, click the New Document button.
8. At the document screen, type the first name and address shown in Figure 6.11 in the first label.
9. Press the Tab key two times to move the insertion point to the next label and then type the second name and address shown in Figure 6.11.
10. Continue in this manner until all the names and addresses shown in Figure 6.11 have been typed. (After typing the third name and address, you only need to press the Tab key once to move the insertion point to the first label in the second row.)
11. Save the document with the name **6-Labels**.
12. Preview and then close **6-Labels.docx**.
13. Close the blank document without saving changes.

Check Your Work

Figure 6.11 Activity 4a

DAVID LOWRY 12033 S 152 ST HOUSTON TX 77340	MARCELLA SANTOS 394 APPLE BLOSSOM DR FRIENDSWOOD TX 77533	KEVIN DORSEY 26302 PRAIRIE DR HOUSTON TX 77316
AL AND DONNA SASAKI 1392 PIONEER DR BAYTOWN TX 77903	JACKIE RHYNER 29039 107 AVE E HOUSTON TX 77302	MARK AND TINA ELLIS 607 FORD AVE HOUSTON TX 77307

Creating Mailing Labels with the Same Name and Address and an Image

Creating Mailing Labels with the Same Name and Address

To create labels with the same name and address on each label, open a document containing the name and address, click the Mailings tab, and then click the Labels button. At the Envelopes and Labels dialog box, make sure the desired label vendor and product number are selected and then click the New Document button. Another method for creating labels with the same name and address is to display the Envelopes and Labels dialog box with the Labels tab selected, type the name and address in the *Address* text box, and then click the New Document button.

Creating Mailing Labels with an Image

Labels can be created with a graphic image, such as a company's logo and address and/or slogan. To create labels with an image, insert the image in a document, select the image, click the Mailings tab, and then click the Labels button. At the Envelopes and Labels dialog box, make sure the correct vendor and product number are selected and then click the New Document button.

Activity 4b Creating Mailing Labels with the Same Name and Address and an Image — Part 2 of 2

1. Open **LAProgram.docx** and create mailing labels with the delivery address. Begin by clicking the Mailings tab.
2. Click the Labels button in the Create group.
3. At the Envelopes and Labels dialog box with the Labels tab selected, make sure the delivery address displays properly in the *Address* text box, as shown at the right.
4. Make sure *Avery US Letter, 5160 Address Labels* displays in the *Label* section; if not, refer to Steps 3 through 6 of Activity 4a to select the label type.
5. Click the New Document button.
6. Save the mailing label document with the name **6-LAProgram**.
7. Preview and then close **6-LAProgram.docx**.
8. Close **LAProgram.docx**.

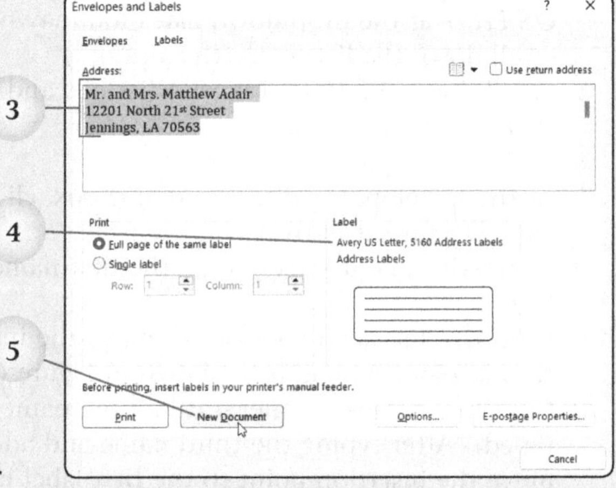

9. At a blank document, insert an image by completing the following steps:
   a. Click the Insert tab, click the Pictures button in the Illustrations group, and then click the *This Device* option at the drop-down list.
   b. At the Insert Picture dialog box, navigate to your WL1C6 folder and then double-click the ***BGCLabels.png*** image file.
10. With the image selected in the document, click the Mailings tab and then click the Labels button.
11. At the Envelopes and Labels dialog box, make sure *Avery US Letter, 5160 Address Labels* displays in the *Label* section and then click the New Document button.
12. Save the document with the name **6-BGCLabels**.
13. Preview and then close **6-BGCLabels.docx**.
14. Close the document containing the image without saving changes.

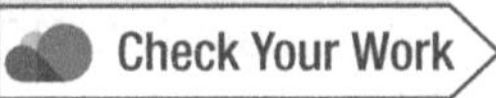

Activity 5 Create a Business Letter Using a Template — 1 Part

You will use a letter template provided by Word to create a business letter.

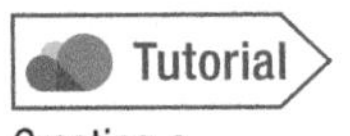

Creating a Document Using a Template

Quick Steps

Create Document Using Template

1. Click File tab.
2. Click *New* option.
3. Click or double-click template.

OR

1. Click File tab.
2. Click *New* option.
3. Click in search text box.
4. Type search text.
5. Press Enter.
6. Double-click template.

Creating a Document Using a Template

Word includes a number of document templates that are formatted for specific uses. Each Word document is based on a template document and the Normal template is the default. Choose from other available Word templates to create a variety of documents with special formatting, such as letters, calendars, and certificates.

View available templates by clicking the File tab and then clicking the *New* option. Thumbnails of various templates display in the New backstage area, as shown in Figure 6.12. Open one of the templates by double-clicking it. This opens a new document based on the template.

In addition to the templates that are shown at the New backstage area, templates can be downloaded from the internet. To do this, click in the search text box, type the search text or category, and then press the Enter key. Templates that match the search text or category display in the New backstage area. Click the template and then click the Create button or double-click the template. This downloads the template and opens a document based on it. Placeholders or content controls may appear in the document as suggested locations for personalized text. Click the placeholder or content control and then type text to personalize the document.

If a template is used on a regular basis, consider pinning it to the New backstage area. To do this, search for the template, hover the pointer over it, and then click the pin (Pin to list) to the right of the template name. To unpin a template, click the pin (Unpin from list).

Figure 6.12 New Backstage Area

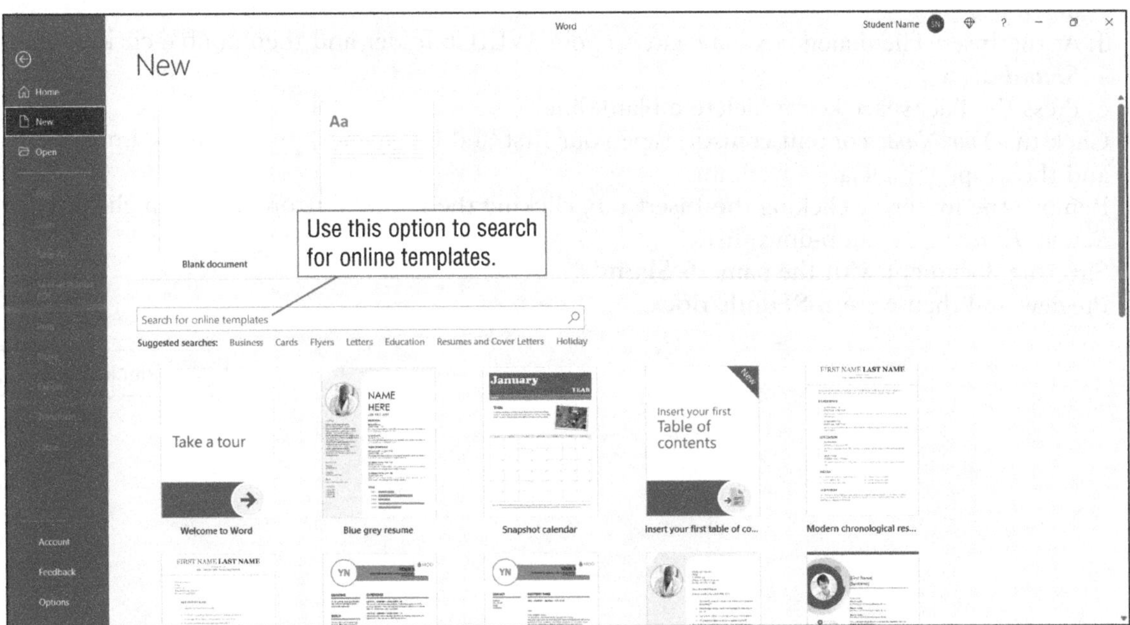

Activity 5 Creating a Business Letter Using a Template

Part 1 of 1

1. Click the File tab and then click the *New* option.
2. At the New backstage area, click in the search text box, type business letter simple design and then press the Enter key.
3. Double-click the *Business letter (simple design)* template. (If this template is not available, open **BusinessLetter.docx** from your WL1C6 folder.)

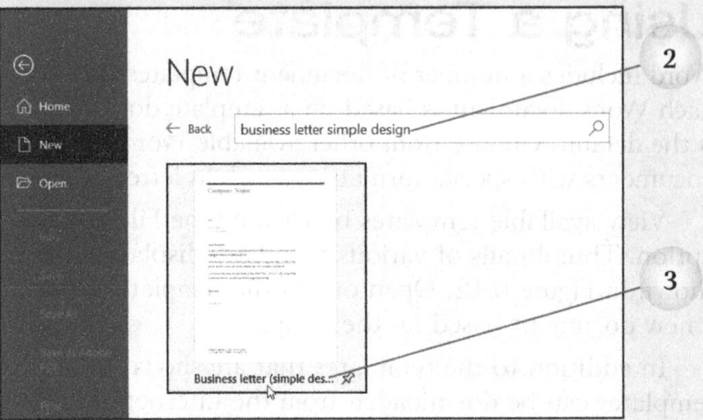

4. When the business letter document displays on the screen, click the *Company Name* content control and then type Sorenson Funds. (Clicking anywhere in the *Company Name* content control selects the entire control.)
5. Click the *Date* content control and then type the current date.
6. Click the *Street Address City, ST ZIP Code* content control. Type Ms. Jennifer Gonzalez, press the Enter key, type 12990 Boyd Street, press the Enter key, and then type Baltimore, MD 20375.
7. Click the *Recipient* content control and then type Ms. Gonzalez.
8. Insert a file in the document by completing the following steps:
   a. Click in the three paragraphs of text in the body of the letter and then press the Delete key.
   b. Click the Insert tab.
   c. Click the Object button arrow in the Text group and then click *Text from File* at the drop-down list.
   d. At the Insert File dialog box, navigate to your WL1C6 folder and then double-click ***SFunds.docx***.
   e. Press the Backspace key to delete a blank line.
9. Click the *Your Name* content control, type your first and last names, press Shift + Enter, and then type Financial Consultant.
10. Remove the footer by clicking the Insert tab, clicking the Footer button, and then clicking *Remove Footer* at the drop-down list.
11. Save the document with the name **6-SFunds**.
12. Preview and then close **6-SFunds.docx**.

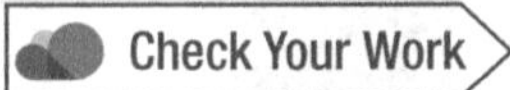

Activity 6 Save Documents in Different File Formats **2 Parts**

You will save an apartment lease agreement document in different file formats, including Word 97-2003 and plain text. You will also save a company document as a PDF file and then edit the file in Word.

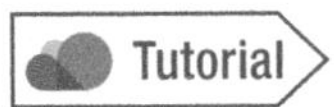

Saving in a Different Format

Quick Steps

Save in Different Format at Save As Dialog Box

1. Press F12 to display Save As dialog box.
2. Type document name.
3. Click *Save as type* option box.
4. Click format.
5. Click Save button.

Saving in a Different Format

When a document is saved, it is saved as a Word document with the file extension *.docx*. If the document is to be shared with someone who is using a different word processing program or a different version of Word, consider saving the document in another format. Save a document in a different file format by clicking the File tab and then clicking the *Export* option. At the Export backstage area, click the *Change File Type* option. Available file types display as shown in Figure 6.13. Save the Word document with the default file format, in a previous version of Word, in the OpenDocument Text format, or as a template. The OpenDocument Text format is an XML-based file format free from licensing and restrictions. It was designed to make word processing, spreadsheet, and presentation files easier to share across applications.

If a document is being sent to a user who does not have access to Microsoft Word, consider saving the document in plain text or rich text file format. Use the *Plain Text* (**.txt*) option to save the document with all the formatting stripped, which is good for universal file exchange. Use the *Rich Text Format* (**.rtf*) option to save the document and preserve most of the formatting, including bold, italic, underline, bullets, and fonts. With the *Single File Web Page* (**.mht, *.mhtml*) option, a document can be saved as a single-page web document. Double-click the *Save as Another File Type* option and the Save As dialog box opens. Use the *Save as type* option box to specify the file format.

In addition to displaying the Save As dialog box through the Export backstage area, the dialog box can be displayed by clicking the File tab, clicking the *Save As* option, and then clicking the *Browse* option. (Pressing the F12 function key will also display the Save As dialog box.) Click the *Save as type* option box at the Save As dialog box and a drop-down list displays containing all the available file formats for saving a document. Click the specific format and then click the Save button.

Figure 6.13 Export Backstage Area with the *Change File Type* Option Selected

Click the *Change File Type* option to display options for saving a file in a different format.

Click the file type and then click the Save As button.

Activity 6a Saving in Different File Formats

Part 1 of 2

1. Open **AptLease.docx** and then save it in Word 97-2003 format by completing the following steps:
   a. Click the File tab and then click the *Export* option.
   b. At the Export backstage area, click the *Change File Type* option.
   c. Click the *Word 97-2003 Document (*.doc)* option in the *Document File Types* section.
   d. Click the Save As button.

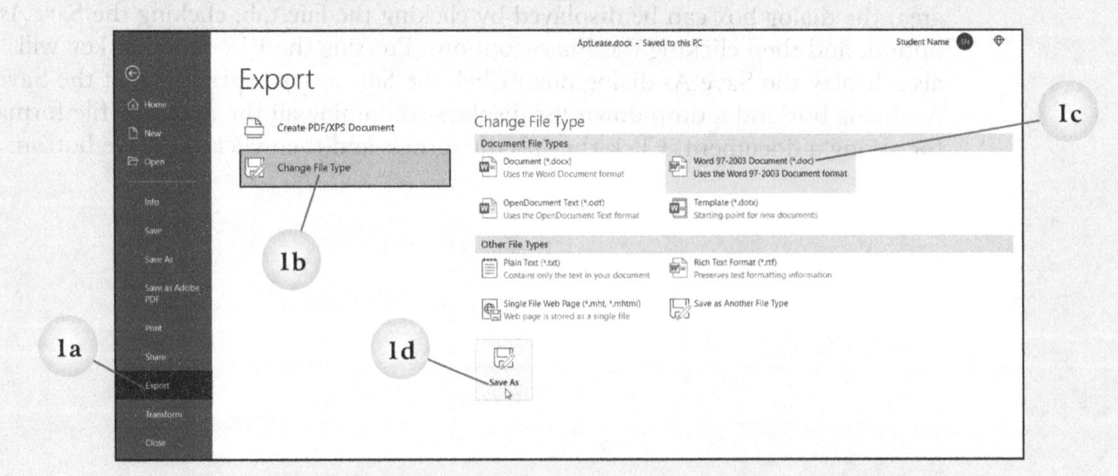

e. At the Save As dialog box with the *Save as type* option changed to *Word 97-2003 Document (*.doc)*, type 6-AptLease-Word97-2003 in the *File name* text box and then press the Enter key.

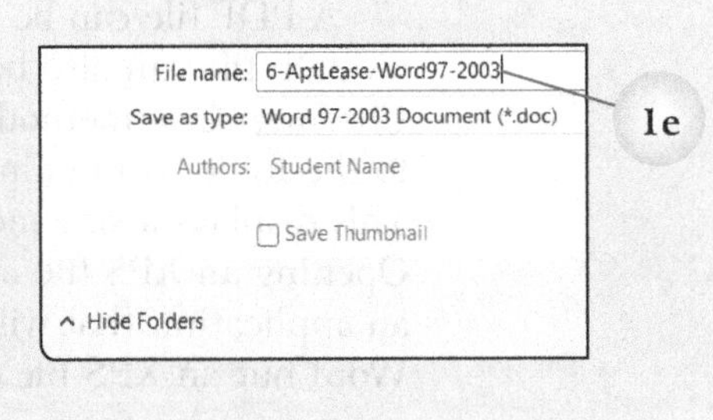

2. At the document, notice *Compatibility Mode* after the document name.
3. Click the Design tab and notice that the Themes, Colors, and Fonts buttons are dimmed. (This is because the themes features were not available in Word 97 through 2003.)
4. Close **6-AptLease-Word97-2003.doc**.
5. Open **AptLease.docx**.
6. Save the document in OpenDocument Text format at the Save As dialog box by completing the following steps:
   a. Press the F12 function key to display the Save As dialog box.
   b. At the Save As dialog box, type 6-AptLease-OpenDocTxt in the *File name* text box.
   c. Click the *Save as type* option box.
   d. Click *OpenDocument Text (*.odt)* at the drop-down list.
   e. Click the Save button.
   f. At the message that displays, click the Yes button.

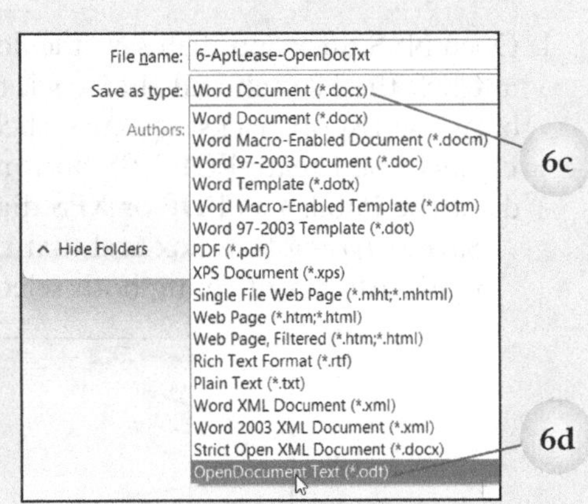

7. Close **6-AptLease-OpenDocTxt.odt**.
8. Display the Open dialog box and, if necessary, display all the files. To do this, click the file type button at the right of the *File name* text box and then click *All Files (*.*)* at the drop-down list.

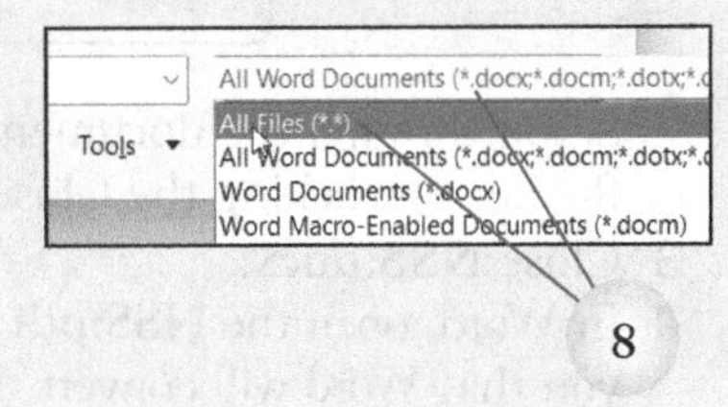

9. Double-click ***6-AptLease-OpenDocTxt.odt***. (Notice that the document has retained the formatting.)
10. Close **6-AptLease-OpenDocTxt.odt**.

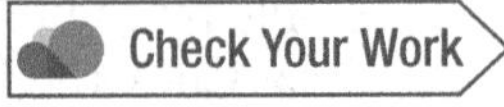

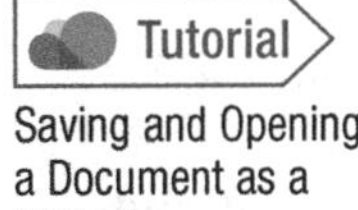

Saving and Opening a Document as a PDF File

Quick Steps

Save a PDF File or in XPS Format

1. Click File tab.
2. Click *Export* option.
3. Click Create PDF/XPS button.
4. At Publish as PDF or XPS dialog box, specify PDF or XPS format.
5. Click Publish button.

A Word document can be saved as a PDF file or in the XPS file format. PDF stands for *portable document format* and is a file format that preserves fonts, formatting, and images in a printer-friendly version that looks the same on most computers. A person who receives a Word file saved as a PDF file does not need to have the Word application on their computer to open, read, and print the file. Exchanging PDF files is a popular method for collaborating, since this file type has cross-platform compatibility, allowing users to open PDF files on both Macintosh and Windows-based computers, as well as different brands of tablets and smartphones. The XML paper specification (XPS) format, which was developed by Microsoft, is a fixed-layout format with all the formatting preserved (similar to PDF).

To save a document as a PDF file or in XPS format, click the File tab, click the *Export* option, and then click the Create PDF/XPS button. This displays the Publish as PDF or XPS dialog box with the *PDF (*.pdf)* option selected in the *Save as type* option box. To save the document in XPS format, click the *Save as type* option box and then click *XPS Document (*.xps)* at the drop-down list. At the Save As dialog box, type a name in the *File name* text box and then click the Publish button.

A PDF file can be opened in Adobe Acrobat Reader, Microsoft Edge, or Word. (A PDF file can also be opened in other available web browsers, such as Google Chrome.) One method for opening a PDF file is to open File Explorer, navigate to the folder containing the file, right-click the file, and then point to *Open with*. This displays a side menu with the programs that can be used to open the file. Opening an XPS file may require opening the Microsoft Store and searching for an application that will open the file. A PDF file can be opened and edited in Word but an XPS file cannot.

Activity 6b Saving as a PDF File and Editing a PDF File in Word — Part 2 of 2

1. Open **NSS.docx** and then save the document as a PDF file by completing the following steps:
   a. Click the File tab and then click the *Export* option.
   b. At the Export backstage area, click the *Create PDF/XPS Document* option.
   c. Click the Create PDF/XPS button.
   d. At the Publish as PDF or XPS dialog box, make sure that *PDF (*.pdf)* is selected in the *Save as type* option box and that the *Open file after publishing* check box contains a check mark. After confirming both selections, click the Publish button.

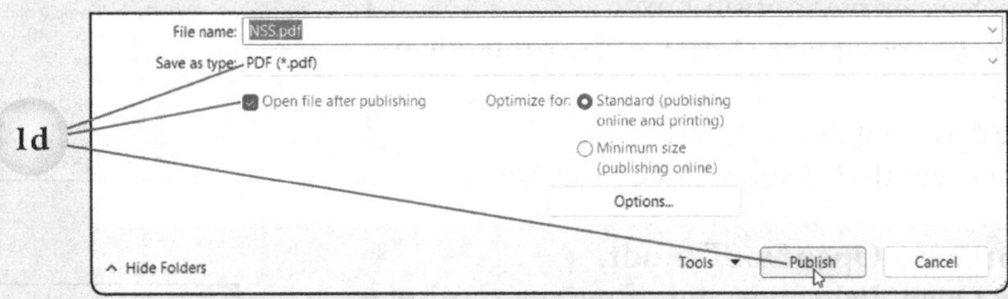

2. Scroll through the document in Adobe Acrobat Reader and then close Adobe Acrobat Reader by clicking the Close button in the upper right corner of the window.
3. Close **NSS.docx**.
4. In Word, open the **NSS.pdf** PDF file you saved to your WL1C6 folder. At the message telling you that Word will convert the file to an editable Word document, click OK.
5. Notice that the formatting of the text is slightly different from the original formatting. Edit the file by completing the following steps:
   a. Click the Design tab and then click the *Lines (Distinctive)* style set.
   b. Delete the text *We are* in the text below the first heading and replace it with Northland Security Systems is.
6. Save the file with Save As with the name **6-NSS**. (The file will be saved as a Word file.)
7. Preview and then close **6-NSS.docx**.
8. Make a screen capture of the Open dialog box and then paste it in a Word document and print the document by completing the following steps:
   a. Display the Open dialog box.
   b. Press and hold down the Alt key, press the Print Screen button on your keyboard, and then release the Alt key.
   c. Close the Open dialog box and close the Open backstage area.
   d. Press Ctrl + N to open a blank document.
   e. Click the Paste button.
9. Save the document with the name **6-ScreenCapture**.
10. Preview and then close **6-ScreenCapture.docx**.

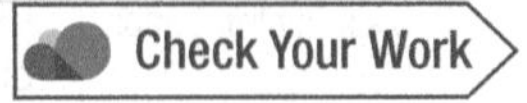

Activity 7 Save and Open a Document Based on a Template — 2 Parts

You will open a summons document, save it as a template, use it to create a summons, and then find and replace text within the document. You will also save the summons document as a template in your WL1C6 folder and then use File Explorer to locate the template and open a new document based on it.

Saving and Using a Template

Saving a Template

Using a template to create a document has several advantages. A template provides consistency and uniformity in documents, reduces document preparation time, offers increased flexibility, and templates are easy to update. Save a template by changing the *Save as type* option at the Save As dialog box to *Word Template (*.dotx)*.

Saving a Template in the Custom Office Templates Folder

When the *Save as type* option is changed to *Word Template (*.dotx)*, Word will save the document as a template in the Custom Office Templates folder. To use the template, click the File tab and then click the *New* option. At the New backstage area, click the *Personal* option. This displays custom templates in the New backstage area. Double-click a template to open a new document based on that template.

Activity 7a Saving and Opening a Document Based on a Template — Part 1 of 2

1. Open **Summons.docx** and then save it as a template in the Custom Office Templates folder by completing the following steps:
   a. Press the F12 function key to display the Save As dialog box.
   b. At the Save As dialog box, click the *Save as type* option box and then click *Word Template (*.dotx)* at the drop-down list. (When the *Save as type* option is changed to *Word Template (*.dotx)*, Word automatically makes Custom Office Templates the active folder.)
   c. Select the name in the *File name* text box, type your last name followed by Summons, and then press the Enter key.

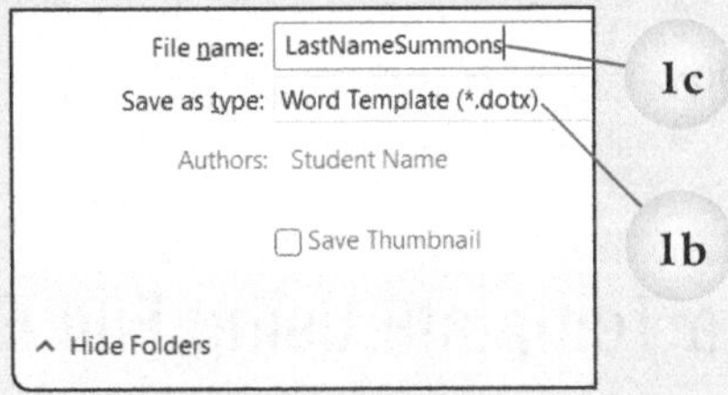

2. Close the summons template.

3. Open a document based on the summons template by completing the following steps:
   a. Click the File tab and then click the *New* option.
   b. At the New backstage area, click the *Personal* option.
   c. Click the summons template that is preceded by your last name.

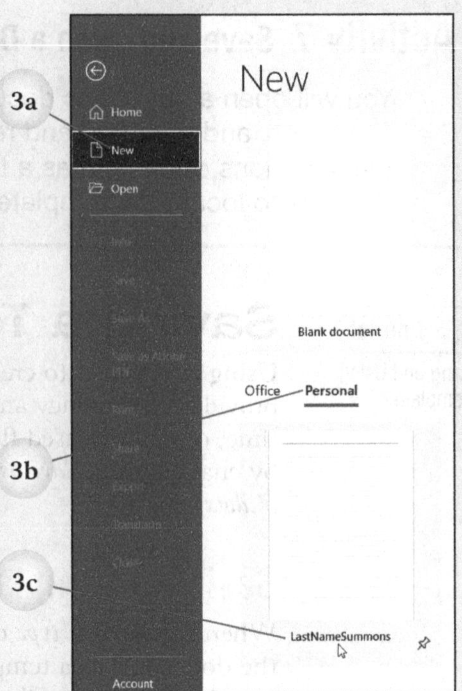

4. With the summons document open, find and replace text as follows:
   a. Find *NAME1* and replace all occurrences with *AMY GARCIA*.
   b. Find *NAME2* and replace all occurrences with *NEIL CARLIN*.
   c. Find *NUMBER* and replace with *C-98002*.
5. Save the document in your WL1C6 folder with the name **6-SummonsGarcia**.
6. Preview and then close **6-SummonsGarcia.docx**.
7. Delete the summons template from the hard drive by completing the following steps:
   a. Press Ctrl + F12 to display the Open dialog box.
   b. At the Open dialog box, click the *Documents* folder in the Navigation pane.
   c. Double-click the *Custom Office Templates* folder in the Content pane.
   d. Click the summons template that begins with your last name.
   e. Click the Organize button and then click *Delete* at the drop-down list.

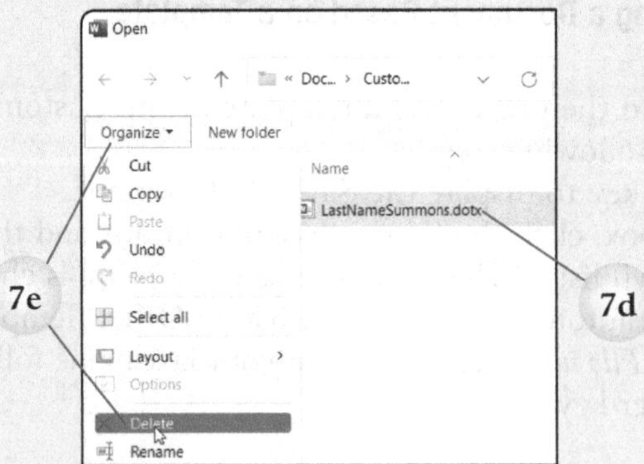

8. Close the Open dialog box.

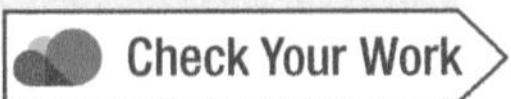

Opening a Template Using File Explorer

In Word, opening a document based on a template is accomplished through the New backstage area with the *Personal* option selected. If a template is saved in a location other than the Custom Office Templates folder, File Explorer can be used to open a document based on the template. To do this, click the File Explorer button on the taskbar, navigate to the folder containing the template, and then double-click the template. This will open a new document based on the template.

Activity 7b Using File Explorer to Open a Document Based on a Template

1. Open **Summons.docx** and then save it as a template in your WL1C6 folder by completing the following steps:
   a. Click the File tab and then click the *Export* option.
   b. At the Export backstage area, click the *Change File Type* option.
   c. Click the *Template (*.dotx)* option in the *Document File Types* section.
   d. Click the Save As button.

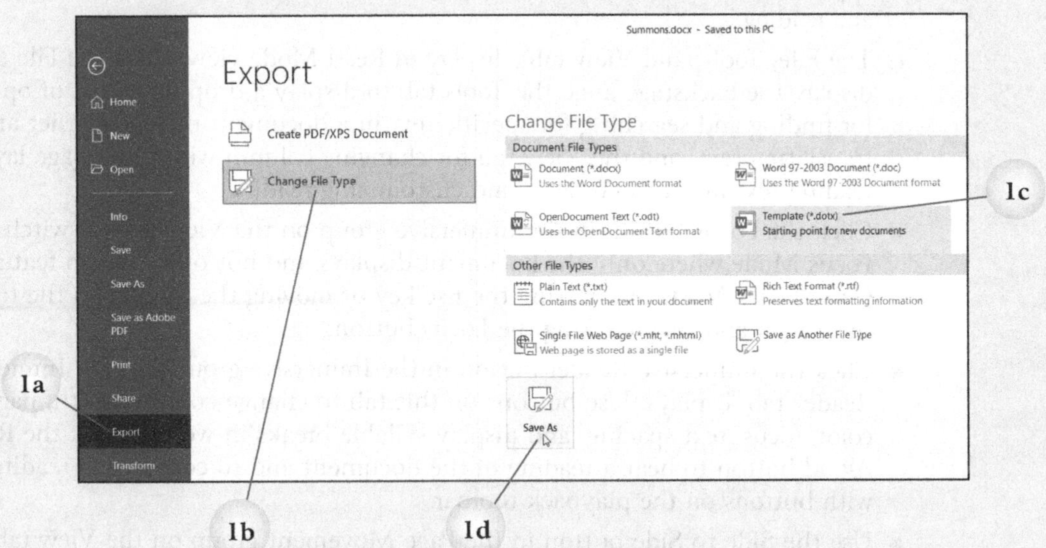

   e. At the Save As dialog box with *Word Template (*.dotx)* in the *Save as type* option box, type 6-SummonsTemplate in the *File name* text box.
   f. Navigate to your WL1C6 folder and then click the Save button.
2. Close the summons template.
3. Open a document based on the summons template using File Explorer by completing the following steps:
   a. Click the File Explorer button on the taskbar. (The taskbar displays along the bottom of the screen.)
   b. Navigate to your WL1C6 folder and then double-click ***6-SummonsTemplate.dotx***.
4. With the summons document open, find and replace text as follows:
   a. Find *NAME1* and replace all occurrences with *CASEY NYE*.
   b. Find *NAME2* and replace all occurrences with *SANDRA IVERS*.
   c. Find *NUMBER* and replace with *C-99743*.
5. Save the document in your WL1C6 folder with the name **6-SummonsNye**.
6. Preview and then close **6-SummonsNye.docx**.

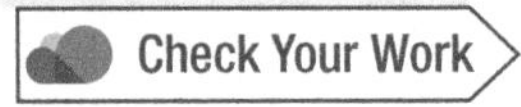

Chapter Summary

- Change the document view with buttons in the view area on the Status bar or with options in the Views group on the View tab.
- Print Layout is the default view but this can be changed to other views, such as Draft view, Web Layout view and Read Mode view.
- Draft view displays the document in a format for efficient editing and formatting. Change to Web Layout view to display a document as it would appear online. Read Mode view displays a document in a format for easy viewing and reading.
- The File, Tools, and View tabs display in Read Mode view. Click the File tab to display the backstage area, the Tools tab to display a drop-down list of options for finding and searching for specific text in a document or the internet and translating text, and the View tab for changing column width and page layout, reading text in the document, and customizing reading.
- Click the Focus button in the Immersive group on the View tab to switch to Focus Mode where only the document displays and not other screen features. Close Focus Mode by pressing the Esc key or moving the pointer to the top of the screen and then clicking the Focus button.
- Click the Immersive Reader button in the Immersive group and the Immersive Reader tab displays. Use buttons on this tab to change column width, page color, focus, text spacing, and display syllable breaks in words. Click the Read Aloud button to hear a reading of the document and to control the reading with buttons on the playback toolbar.
- Use the Side to Side button in the Page Movement group on the View tab to change page movement in a document from the default of vertical to side to side, where two pages are shown at one time. On a screen without touch screen capabilities, scroll through the side to side pages using the horizontal scroll bar or the mouse wheel. Click the Vertical button on the View tab to return to the default page movement.
- Use the Zoom slider bar or buttons in the Zoom group on the View tab to change the display percentage.
- Use options at the Ribbon Display Options button drop-down list to specify if the Quick Access Toolbar, ribbon, and Status bar should be visible or hidden.
- Save space on the screen by hiding white space at the top and bottom of pages. Hide white space using the Hide White Space icon, which appears when the pointer is positioned at the top or bottom edge of a page. Redisplay white space using the Show White Space icon, which appears when the pointer is positioned on the thin gray line separating pages.
- Move among open documents by hovering the pointer over the Word button on the taskbar and then clicking the thumbnail of the document or by clicking the View tab, clicking the Switch Windows button in the Window group, and then clicking the document name.
- View portions of all open documents by clicking the View tab and then clicking the Arrange All button in the Window group.
- Use the Minimize, Restore, and Maximize buttons in the upper right corner of the active window to reduce or increase the size of the window.
- Divide a window into two panes by clicking the View tab and then clicking the Split button in the Window group.

- View the contents of two open documents side by side by clicking the View tab and then clicking the View Side by Side button in the Window group.
- Open a new window containing the same document by clicking the View tab and then clicking the New Window button in the Window group.
- Insert a document into the open document by clicking the Insert tab, clicking the Object button arrow, and then clicking *Text from File* at the drop-down list. At the Insert File dialog box, double-click the document.
- Preview a document at the Print backstage area. Scroll through the pages in the document with the Next Page and the Previous Page buttons, which are below the preview page. Use the Zoom slider bar to increase or decrease the display size of the preview page.
- Use options at the Print backstage area to customize a print job by changing the page orientation, size, and margins; specify how many pages to print on one page; indicate the number of copies and whether to collate the pages; and specify the printer.
- Prepare and print an envelope at the Envelopes and Labels dialog box with the Envelopes tab selected.
- If the Envelopes and Labels dialog box is opened in a document containing a name and address (with each line ending with a press of the Enter key), that information is automatically inserted in the *Delivery address* text box in the dialog box.
- Use Word's labels feature to print text on mailing labels, file labels, and other types of labels. Create labels at the Envelopes and Labels dialog box with the Labels tab selected.
- Available templates are shown in the New backstage area. Double-click a template to open a document based on it. Search for templates online by typing the search text or category in the search text box and then pressing the Enter key.
- Click the *Change File Type* option at the Export backstage area and options display for saving the document in a different file format. Documents can also be saved in different file formats with the *Save as type* option box at the Save As dialog box.
- Save a document as a PDF file or in XPS format at the Publish as PDF or XPS dialog box. Display this dialog box by clicking the *Create PDF/XPS Document* option at the Export backstage area and then clicking the Create PDF/XPS button. A PDF file can be opened and edited in Word.
- Change the *Save as type* option at the Save As dialog box to *Word Template (*.dotx)* and the Custom Office Templates folder becomes the active folder. A template saved in this folder is available at the New backstage area with the *Personal* option selected. Open a document based on a template at the New backstage area with the *Personal* option selected.
- If a template is saved in a location other than the Custom Office Templates folder, File Explorer can be used to open a document based on the template.

Commands Review

FEATURE	RIBBON TAB, GROUP/OPTION	BUTTON, OPTION	KEYBOARD SHORTCUT
arrange documents	View, Window		
Draft view	View, Views		
Envelopes and Labels dialog box with Envelopes tab selected	Mailings, Create		
Envelopes and Labels dialog box with Labels tab selected	Mailings, Create		
Export backstage area	File, *Export*		
Focus mode	View, Immersive		
Immersive Reader	View, Immersive		
Insert File dialog box	Insert, Text	, *Text from File*	
maximize document			Ctrl + F10
minimize document			
New backstage area	File, *New*		
new window	View, Window		
Print backstage area	File, *Print*		Ctrl + P
Read Mode view	View, Views		
restore document to previous size			
side to side page movement	View, Page Movement		
split window	View, Window		Alt + Ctrl + S
switch windows	View, Window		
synchronous scrolling	View, Window		
vertical page movement	View, Page Movement		
view documents side by side	View, Window		
Web Layout view	View, Views		

Review and Assessment

CHAPTER 6

Skills Assessment

Assessment 1 Manage Documents

1. Open **OMSHandbook.docx**.
2. Change to Draft view.
3. Change to Read Mode view and then return to the document. ***Hint: To return to the document, click the View tab and then click the*** **Edit Document** ***option.***
4. Display the Immersive Reader tab and then make the following changes:
   a. Change the column width to Wide.
   b. Change the page color to Sepia (third column, first row).
   c. If a speaker is connected to your computer, start the reading of the document.
   d. Use buttons on the playback toolbar to skip to the next paragraph, skip to the previous paragraph, change the reading voice to the male voice, and then change back to female voice.
   e. Close Immersive Reader.
5. Change the page movement to side to side, display page thumbnails, remove the display of thumbnails, and then change page movement back to vertical.
6. Close **OMSHandbook.docx**.
7. Open **StaffMtg.docx**, **Agreement.docx**, and **Robots.docx**.
8. Make **Agreement.docx** the active document.
9. Make **StaffMtg.docx** the active document.
10. Arrange all the windows.
11. Make **Robots.docx** the active document and then minimize it.
12. Minimize the remaining documents.
13. Restore **StaffMtg.docx**.
14. Restore **Agreement.docx**.
15. Restore **Robots.docx**.
16. Maximize and then close **StaffMtg.docx** and then maximize and close **Robots.docx**.
17. Maximize **Agreement.docx** and then save the document with the name **6-Agreement**.
18. Open **AptLease.docx**.
19. View **6-Agreement.docx** and **AptLease.docx** side by side.
20. Scroll through both documents simultaneously and notice the formatting differences between the titles, headings, and fonts in the two documents. Change the font and apply shading to only the title and headings in **6-Agreement.docx** to match the font and shading of the title and headings in **AptLease.docx**.
21. Make **AptLease.docx** active and then close it.
22. Save **6-Agreement.docx**.
23. Move the insertion point to the end of the document and then insert the document **Terms.docx**.

24. Apply formatting to the inserted text so it matches the formatting of the previous text in **6-Agreement.docx**.
25. Move the insertion point to the end of the document and then insert the document **Signature.docx**.
26. Save, preview, and then close **6-Agreement.docx**.

Assessment 2 Prepare an Envelope

1. At a blank document, prepare an envelope with the text shown in Figure 6.14.
2. Save the envelope document with the name **6-EnvMiller**.
3. Preview and then close **6-EnvMiller.docx**.

Figure 6.14 Assessment 2

DR ROSEANNE HOLT
21330 CEDAR DR
LOGAN UT 84598

GENE MILLER
4559 CORRIN AVE
SMITHFIELD UT 84521

Assessment 3 Prepare Mailing Labels

1. Prepare mailing labels with the names and addresses shown in Figure 6.15. Use a label option of your choosing. (You may need to check with your instructor before choosing an option.) When entering a street number such as *147TH*, Word will convert the *th* to superscript letters when you press the spacebar after typing *147TH*. To remove the superscript formatting, immediately click the Undo button in the Undo group on the Home tab.
2. Save the document with the name **6-LabelsOhio**.
3. Preview and then close **6-LabelsOhio.docx**.
4. At the blank document screen, close the document without saving changes.

Figure 6.15 Assessment 3

SUSAN LUTOVSKY 1402 MELLINGER DR FAIRHOPE OH 43209	JIM AND PAT KEIL 413 JACKSON ST AVONDALE OH 43887	IRENE HAGEN 12930 147TH AVE E CANTON OH 43296
VINCE KILEY 14005 288TH ST CANTON OH 43287	LEONARD KRUEGER 13290 N 120TH ST CANTON OH 43291	HELGA GUNDSTROM PO BOX 3112 AVONDALE OH 43887

Assessment 4

Prepare an Award Certificate

1. Display the New backstage area, search for *formal award certificate*, and then download the *Formal award certificate* template. (If the template is not available at the New backstage area, open the **Certificate.docx** document from your WL1C6 folder.) Insert the following information in the specified fields:

Recipient Name	Curtis Sayers
Program / Project Name	Community Outreach / Micro Loans
Month, Day, Year	(insert current month, day, year)
SIGNED, Signature Name, Title	Emerson Day, President
Company Logo	(insert the image file **GoldStar.png**)

2. Save the document with the name **6-Certificate**.
3. Preview and then close **6-Certificate.docx**.

Assessment 5

Save a Document as a Web Page

1. Experiment with the *Save as type* option box at the Save As dialog box and figure out how to save a document as a single-file web page.
2. Open **NSS.docx**, display the Save As dialog box, and then change the *Save as type* option to *Single File Web Page (*.mht;*.mhtml)*. Click the Change Title button in the Save As dialog box. At the Enter Text dialog box, type Northland Security Systems in the *Page title* text box and then click OK to close the dialog box. Click the Save button in the Save As dialog box.
3. Close the **NSS.mht** web page file.
4. **Optional:** If possible, open your web browser and then open the **NSS.mht** web page file. You may need to check with your instructor to determine the specific steps on opening the web browser and opening the file.
5. Close your web browser.

Assessment

Prepare Personal Mailing Labels

1. At a blank document, type your name and address and then apply formatting to enhance the appearance of the text. (You determine the font, font size, and font color.)
2. Create labels with your name and address. (You determine the label vendor and product number.)
3. Save the label document with the name **6-PersonalLabels**.
4. Preview and then close **6-PersonalLabels.docx**.
5. Close the document containing your name and address without saving the changes.

Assessment 7

Save a Template; Open a Document Based on the Template

1. Open **Labels.docx** and then save it in the *Word Template (*.dotx)* format in your WL1C6 folder and name the template **6-LabelsTemplate**.
2. Close **6-LabelsTemplate.dotx**.
3. Open File Explorer and then open a document based on the **6-LabelsTemplate.dotx** template document.
4. Click in the *Name* content control and then type Jack Stiles. (When you click in the Street Address content control in the next step, Word will automatically update the name on all labels.)
5. Click in the *Street Address* content control and then type 4493 Second Street. (When you click in the City, ST ZIP Code content control in the next step, Word will automatically update the street address on all labels.)
6. Click in the *City, ST ZIP Code* content control and then type Stowe, VT 05661.
7. Click anywhere in the label document and Word will automatically update the city, state, and zip code in all labels.
8. Save the completed document with the name **6-StilesLabels**.
9. Preview and then close **6-StilesLabels.docx**.

Assessment 8

Download and Complete an Award Certificate

1. Display the New backstage area and then search for and download an award template of your choosing. (Type award in the search text box and then download an award template that interests you.)
2. Insert the appropriate information in the award placeholders or content controls.
3. Save the completed award and name the document **6-Award**.
4. Preview and then close **6-Award.docx**.

Visual Benchmark

Activity 1

Prepare Custom Labels

1. You can create a sheet of labels with the same information in each label by typing the information in the *Address* text box at the Envelopes and Labels dialog box. Or you can type the information, select it, and then create the label. Using this technique, create the sheet of labels shown in Figure 6.16 with the following specifications:
   - Open **NSSLabels.docx**.
   - Set the text in 12-point Magneto.
   - Select the entire document and then create the labels using the Avery US Letter label vendor and the 5161 product number.
2. Save the labels document with the name **6-NSSLabels**.
3. Preview and then close **6-NSSLabels.docx**.
4. Close **NSSLabels.docx** without saving it.

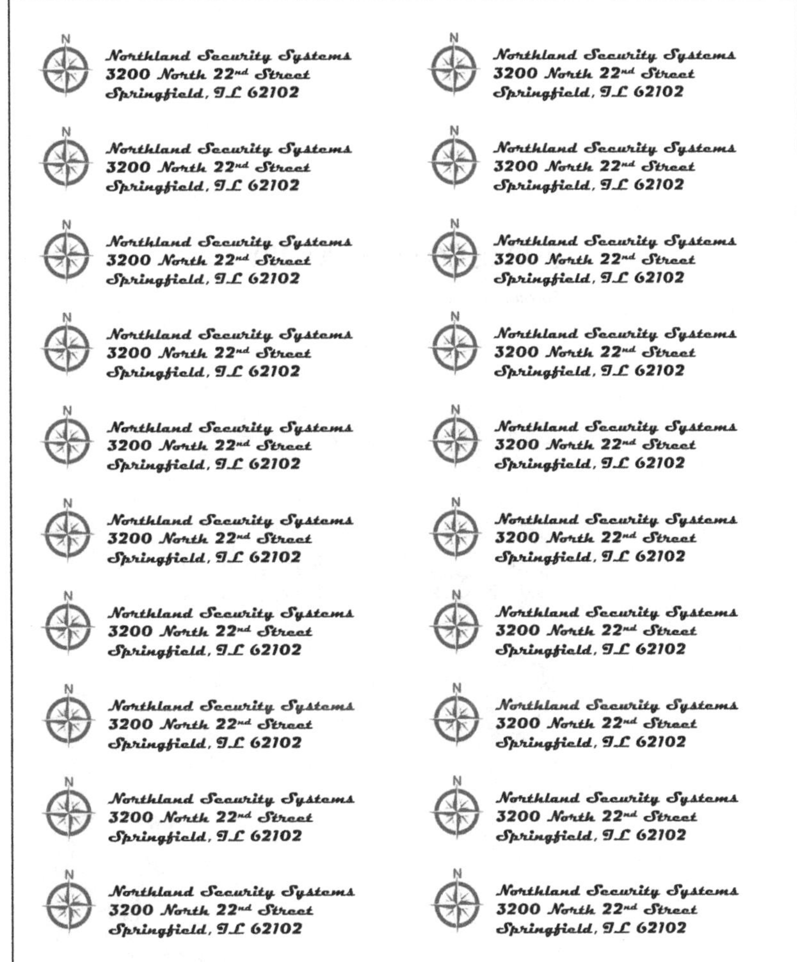

Figure 6.16 Visual Benchmark 1

Activity 2

Create an Invitation

1. Open File Explorer and then open a document based on the template **GalaTemplate.dotx** located in your WL1C6 folder.
2. Type the text in the appropriate content controls as shown in Figure 6.17.
3. Change the color of the text *Annual Garden Gala* to Blue (eighth color in the *Standard Colors* section).
4. Change the color of the date and time text to Green, Accent 6, Darker 25% (last column, fifth row in the *Theme Colors* section).
5. Insert the **Flowers.png** image file from your WL1C6 folder with the following specifications:
   - Change the text wrapping to behind the text.
   - Set the light background as transparent. ***Hint: Use the* Set Transparent Color *option from the Color button on the Picture Format tab.***
   - Size and position the image so it appears as shown in Figure 6.17.
6. Save the invitation with the name **6-Gala**.
7. Save the invitation document as a PDF file with the same name.
8. Open the **6-Gala.pdf** file in Adobe Acrobat Reader, review the file, and then close Adobe Acrobat Reader.
9. Save, preview, and then close **6-Gala.docx**.

Figure 6.17 Visual Benchmark 2

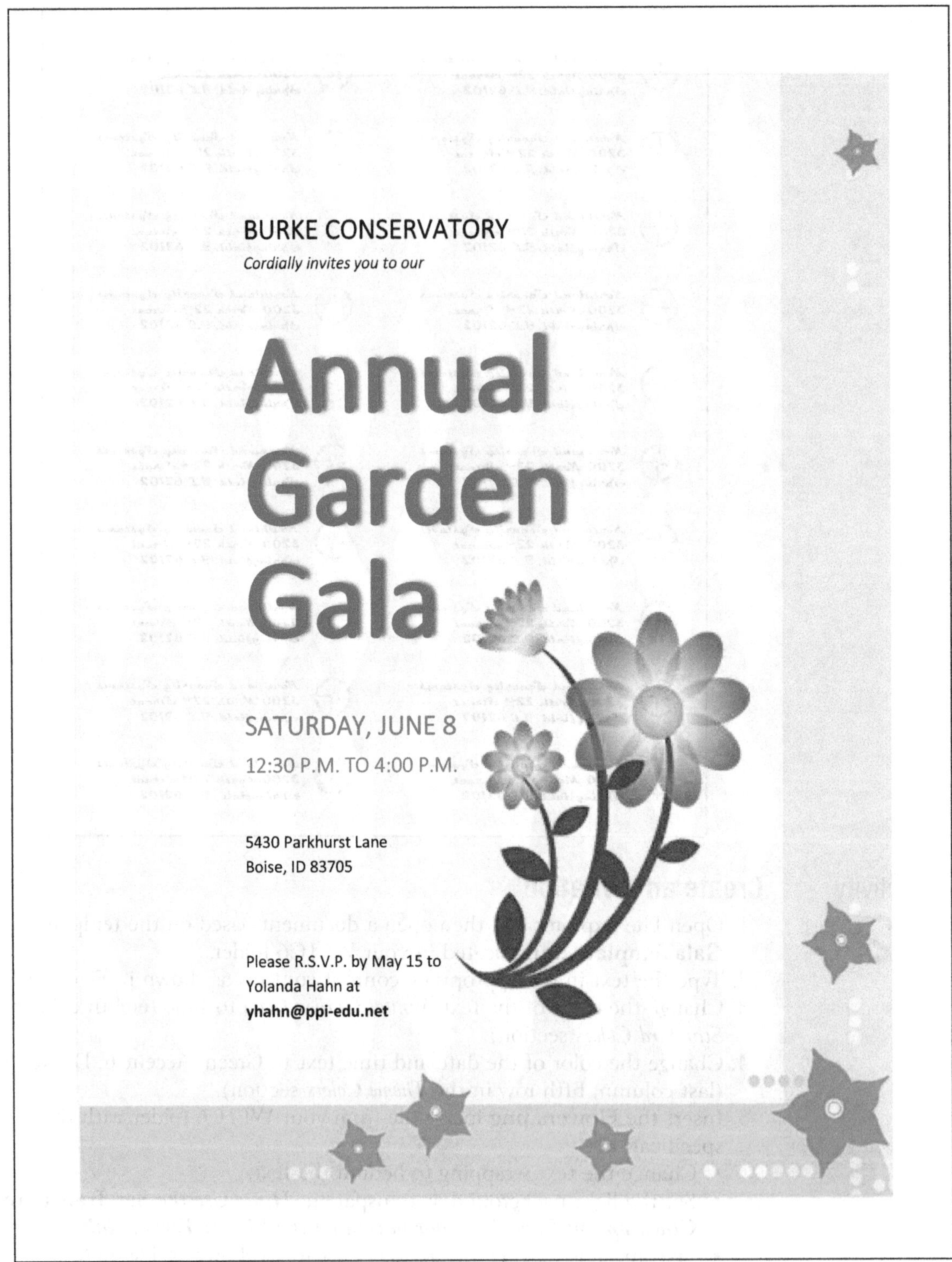

Case Study

Part 1

You are the office manager for a real estate company, Macadam Realty, and have been asked by the senior sales associate, Lucy Hendricks, to prepare mailing labels for the company. Include on the labels the company name, Macadam Realty, and the address, 100 Third Street, Suite 210, Denver, CO 80803. Use a decorative font for the name and address and make the *M* in *Macadam* and the *R* in *Realty* larger and more pronounced than the surrounding text. Save the completed document with the name **6-RELabels**. Preview and then close **6-RELabels.docx**.

Part 2

One of your responsibilities at Macadam Realty is to format contract forms. Open **REConAgrmnt.docx** and then save it with the name **6-REConAgrmnt**. Ms. Hendricks has asked you to insert signature information at the end of the document using the file named **RESig.docx**. With **6-REConAgrmnt.docx** still open, open **REBuildAgrmnt.docx**. Format **6-REConAgrmnt.docx** so it is formatted in a manner similar to **REBuildAgrmnt.docx**. Consider the following when specifying formatting: fonts, font sizes, font formatting, and paragraph shading. Save and then close **6-REConAgrmnt.docx**. Close **REBuildAgrmnt.docx**.

Part 3

Ms. Hendricks has asked you to insert document properties in **REBuildAgrmnt.docx** and **6-REConAgrmnt.docx**. Use the Help feature to learn how to insert document properties. With the information you learn from the Help feature, open each document separately, display the Info backstage area, click the Show All Properties hyperlink (you may need to scroll down the backstage area to locate this hyperlink), and then insert document properties in the following fields (you determine the information to type): *Title*, *Subject*, *Company*, and *Category*. Print the document properties for each document. (Change the first gallery in the *Settings* category in the Print backstage area to *Document Info*.) Save each document with the original name and then close the documents.

Part 4

A client of the real estate company, Anna Hurley, is considering purchasing several rental properties and has asked for information on how to locate real estate rental forms. Using the internet, locate at least three websites that offer real estate rental forms. Write a letter to Anna Hurley at 2300 South Poplar Street, Denver, CO 80205. In the letter, list the websites you found and include information on which site you thought offered the most resources. Also include in the letter that Macadam Realty is very interested in helping her locate and purchase rental properties. Save the document with the name **6-RELtr**. Create an envelope for the letter and add it to the letter document. Save, preview, and then close **6-RELtr.docx**. (If printing, you may need to manually feed the envelope into the printer.)

WORD

CHAPTER 7

Creating Tables

Performance Objectives

Upon successful completion of Chapter 7, you will be able to:

1 Create a table
2 Change the table design
3 Select cells in a table
4 Change the table layout
5 Convert text to a table and a table to text
6 Draw a table
7 Insert a Quick Table
8 Perform calculations on data in a table
9 Insert an Excel spreadsheet

Use the Tables feature in Word to organize data in tables with any number of columns and rows. The data can consist of text, values, and/or mathematical formulas. Presenting information in a table can show patterns and relationships and help with data comprehension.

This chapter will introduce the steps for creating a table in Word using the Table button drop-down grid and options at the Insert Table dialog box. You will also learn to draw a table in a document and apply formatting to tables using buttons and options on the Table Design and Table Layout tabs. Finally, you will learn to perform calculations in a table and practice inserting an Excel spreadsheet into a Word document to display text and numerical data.

Data Files

The data files for this chapter are in the WL1C7 folder that you downloaded at the beginning of this course.

Activity 1 Create and Format Tables with Company Information 8 Parts

You will create a table containing contact information and another containing information on employee benefit plans offered by a company. You will then change the design and layout of each table.

Creating a Table

Creating a Table

Create a table in a document to organize and provide a visual grouping of data and make the data easier to read and interpret. Tables are grids containing boxes of information called *cells*. Each cell is the intersection between a row and a column. A cell can contain text, characters, numbers, data, graphics, or formulas.

Table

Quick Steps

Create Table

1. Click Insert tab.
2. Click Table button.
3. Point to create number of columns and rows.
4. Click mouse button.

OR

1. Click Insert tab.
2. Click Table button.
3. Click *Insert Table*.
4. Specify number of columns and rows.
5. Click OK.

Hint You can create a table within a table, creating a *nested* table.

Insert a table in a document by clicking the Insert tab and then clicking the Table button in the Tables group. Move the pointer down and to the right in the drop-down grid to select the number of rows and columns to include in the table. A table can also be created with options at the Insert Table dialog box. Display this dialog box by clicking the Table button in the Tables group on the Insert tab and then clicking *Insert Table* at the drop-down list.

Figure 7.1 shows an example of a table with four columns and four rows. Various parts of the table are identified in the figure. These include the gridlines, move table column markers, table move handle, and resize handle. In a table, nonprinting characters identify the ends of cells and the ends of rows. To view these characters, click the Show/Hide ¶ button in the Paragraph group on the Home tab. The end-of-cell marker appears inside each cell and the end-of-row marker appears at the end of each row of cells. These markers are identified in Figure 7.1.

Columns in a table are generally referred to using the letters A–Z, while rows are numbered. When a table is inserted in a document, the insertion point is positioned in the first cell in the upper left corner of the table. This is referred to as cell A1, as it is located in column A, row 1. Cell B1 is to the right of A1, and cell A2 is directly below it.

When the insertion point is positioned in a cell in the table, move table column markers display on the horizontal ruler. These markers represent the ends of columns and can be moved to change the widths of columns. Figure 7.1 identifies move table column markers.

Figure 7.1 Table with Nonprinting Characters Displayed

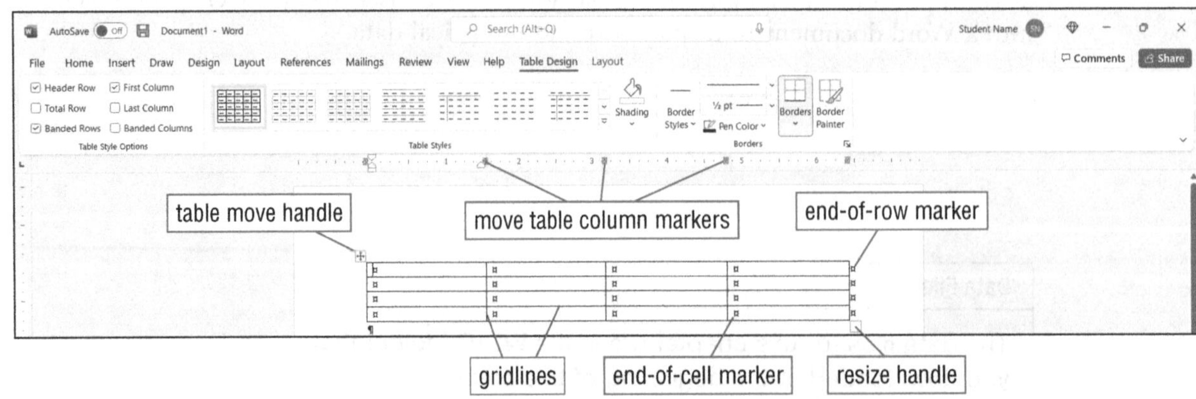

Entering Text in Cells

Hint Pressing the Tab key in a table moves the insertion point to the next cell. Pressing Ctrl + Tab moves the insertion point to the next tab within a cell.

With the insertion point positioned in a cell, type or edit text. Point and click with the mouse to move the insertion point from cell to cell, or press the Tab key to move to the next cell and Shift + Tab to move to the preceding cell.

Text typed in a cell automatically wraps to the next line to fit the width of the column. The Enter key can also be pressed to move to the next line within a cell. The cell expands vertically to accommodate the text, and all cells in that row also expand. Pressing the Tab key in a table causes the insertion point to move to the next cell in the table. To move the insertion point to a tab within a cell, press Ctrl + Tab. If the insertion point is in the last cell of the table, pressing the Tab key adds another row to the table. Insert a page break within a table by pressing Ctrl + Enter. The page break is inserted between rows, not within a row.

Moving the Insertion Point within a Table

To use the mouse to move the insertion point to a different cell within the table, click in the specific cell. To use the keyboard to move the insertion point to a different cell within the table, refer to the information shown in Table 7.1.

Table 7.1 Insertion Point Movement within a Table Using the Keyboard

To move the insertion point	Press
to next cell	Tab
to preceding cell	Shift + Tab
forward one character	Right Arrow key
backward one character	Left Arrow key
to previous row	Up Arrow key
to next row	Down Arrow key
to first cell in row	Alt + Home
to last cell in row	Alt + End
to top cell in column	Alt + Page Up
to bottom cell in column	Alt + Page Down

Activity 1a Creating a Table

Part 1 of 8

1. At a blank document, turn on bold formatting and then type the title CONTACT INFORMATION, as shown in Figure 7.2.
2. Turn off bold formatting and then press the Enter key.
3. Create the table shown in Figure 7.2 by completing the following steps:
   a. Click the Insert tab.
   b. Click the Table button in the Tables group.
   c. Move the pointer down and to the right in the drop-down grid until the label above the grid displays as *3x5 Table* and then click the left mouse button.

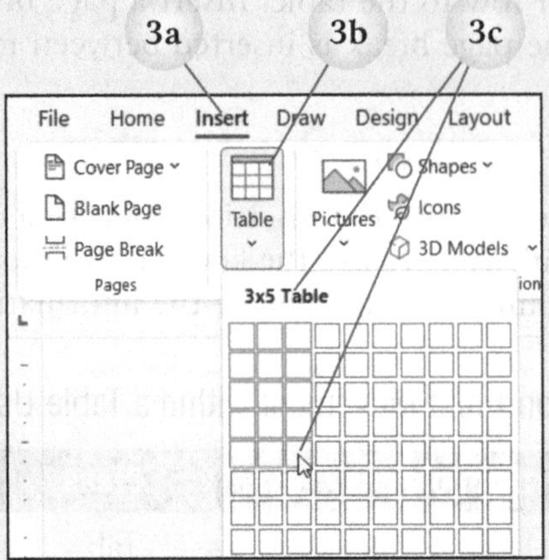

4. Type the text in the cells as indicated in Figure 7.2. Press the Tab key to move to the next cell and press Shift + Tab to move to the preceding cell. (If you accidentally press the Enter key within a cell, immediately press the Backspace key. Do not press the Tab key after typing the text in the last cell. If you do, another row is inserted in the table. If this happens, immediately click the Undo button in the Undo group on the Home tab or press Ctrl + Z.)
5. Save the table document with the name **7-Tables**.

Figure 7.2 Activity 1a

CONTACT INFORMATION

Maggie Rivera	First Trust Bank	(203) 555-3440
Les Cromwell	Madison Trust	(602) 555-4900
Cecilia Nordyke	American Financial	(509) 555-3995
Regina Stahl	United Fidelity	(301) 555-1201
Justin White	Key One Savings	(360) 555-8963

Using the Insert Table Dialog Box

A table can also be created with options at the Insert Table dialog box, shown in Figure 7.3. To display this dialog box, click the Insert tab, click the Table button in the Tables group, and then click *Insert Table*. At the Insert Table dialog box, enter the number of columns and the number of rows and then click OK.

Figure 7.3 Insert Table Dialog Box

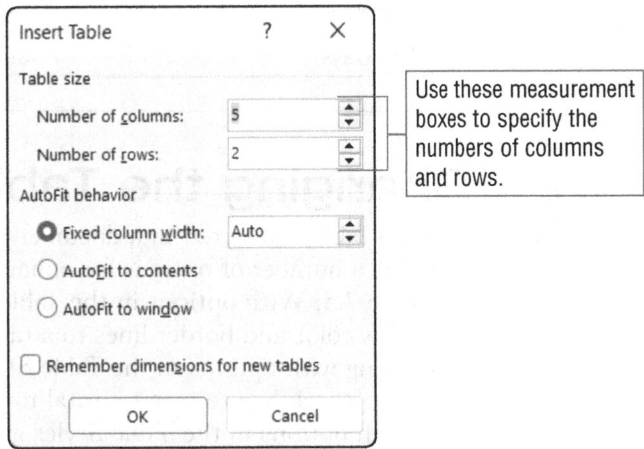

Activity 1b Creating a Table with the Insert Table Dialog Box

Part 2 of 8

1. With **7-Tables.docx** open, press Ctrl + End to move the insertion point below the table.
2. Press the Enter key two times.
3. Turn on bold formatting and then type the title OPTIONAL PLAN PREMIUM RATES, as shown in Figure 7.4.
4. Turn off bold formatting and then press the Enter key.
5. Click the Insert tab, click the Table button in the Tables group, and then click *Insert Table* at the drop-down list.
6. At the Insert Table dialog box, type 3 in the *Number of columns* measurement box. (The insertion point is automatically positioned in this measurement box.)
7. Press the Tab key (this moves the insertion point to the *Number of rows* measurement box) and then type 5.
8. Click OK.
9. Type the text in the cells as indicated in Figure 7.4. Press the Tab key to move to the next cell and press Shift + Tab to move to the preceding cell. To indent the text in cells B2 through B5 and cells C2 through C5, press Ctrl + Tab to move the insertion point to a tab within a cell and then type the text.
10. Save **7-Tables.docx**.

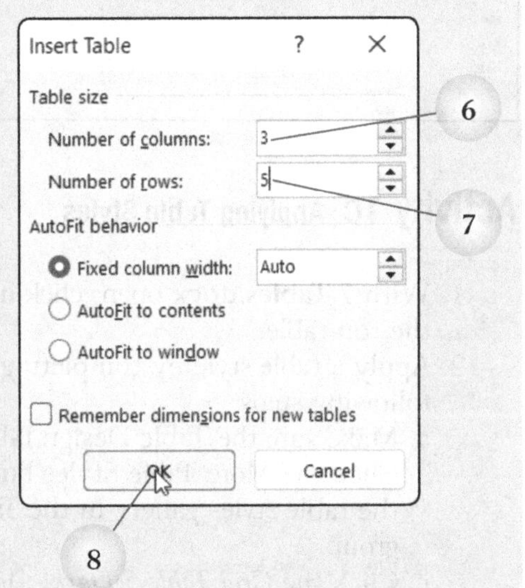

Check Your Work

Figure 7.4 Activity 1b

OPTIONAL PLAN PREMIUM RATES

Waiting Period	Basic Plan Employees	Plan Gold Employees
60 days	0.67%	0.79%
90 days	0.49%	0.59%
120 days	0.30%	0.35%
180 days	0.23%	0.26%

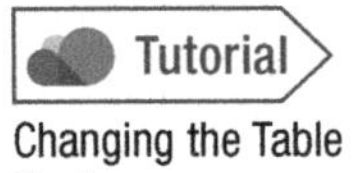

Changing the Table Design

Changing the Table Design

When a table is inserted in a document, the Table Design tab is active. This tab contains a number of options for enhancing the appearance of the table, as shown in Figure 7.5. With options in the Table Styles group, apply a predesigned style that adds color and border lines to a table and shading to cells. Customize the formatting with options in the Table Style Options group. For example, click the *Total Row* check box to insert a total row in the table. Apply a predesigned table style with options in the Table Styles group.

Border Styles

Border Painter

Use options in the Borders group to change the look of cell borders in a table. Click the Border Styles button to display a drop-down list of available styles. Use other buttons in the Borders group to change the line style, width, and color and to add or remove borders. Apply the same border style to other cells with the Border Painter button.

Figure 7.5 Table Design Tab

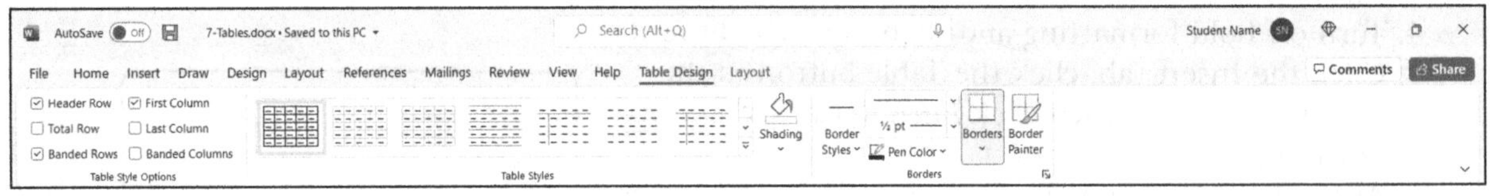

Activity 1c Applying Table Styles

Part 3 of 8

1. With **7-Tables.docx** open, click in any cell in the top table.
2. Apply a table style by completing the following steps:
   a. Make sure the Table Design tab is active.
   b. Click the More Table Styles button in the table styles gallery in the Table Styles group.
   c. Click the *Grid Table 5 Dark - Accent 5* table style (sixth column, fifth row in the *Grid Tables* section).

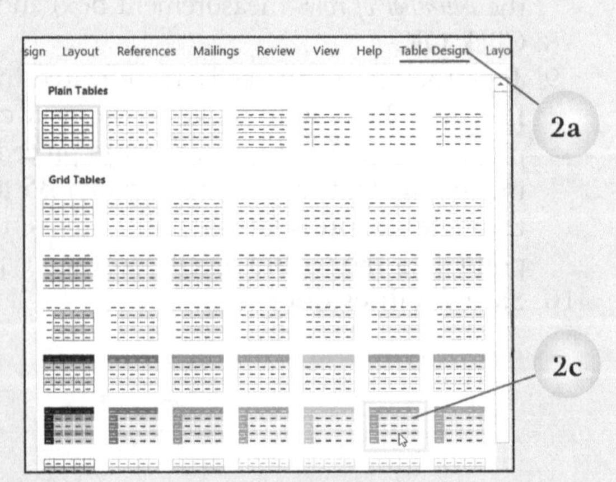

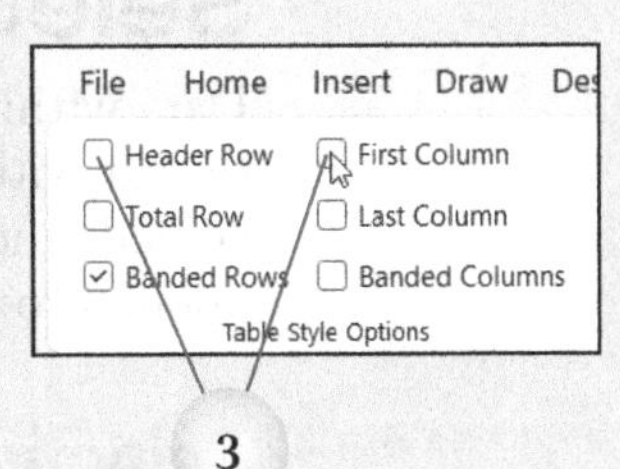

3. After looking at the table, you realize that the first row is not a header row and the first column should not be formatted differently from the other columns. To format the first row and the first column in the same manner as the other rows and columns, click the *Header Row* check box and the *First Column* check box in the Table Style Options group to remove the check marks.
4. Click in any cell in the bottom table and then apply the List Table 6 Colorful - Accent 5 table style (sixth column, sixth row in the *List Tables* section).
5. Add color borders to the top table by completing the following steps:
   a. Click in any cell in the top table.
   b. Click the Pen Color button arrow in the Borders group on the Table Design tab and then click the *Orange, Accent 2, Darker 50%* color option (sixth column, last row in the *Theme Colors* section).
   c. Click the *Line Weight* option box arrow in the Borders group and then click *1 ½ pt* in the drop-down list. (When you choose a line weight, the Border Painter button is automatically activated.)

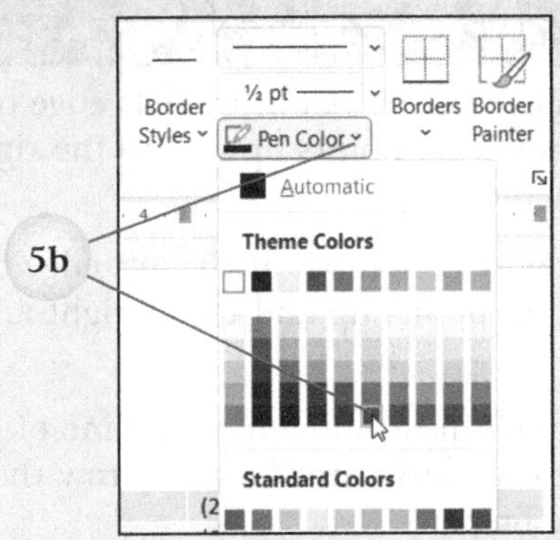

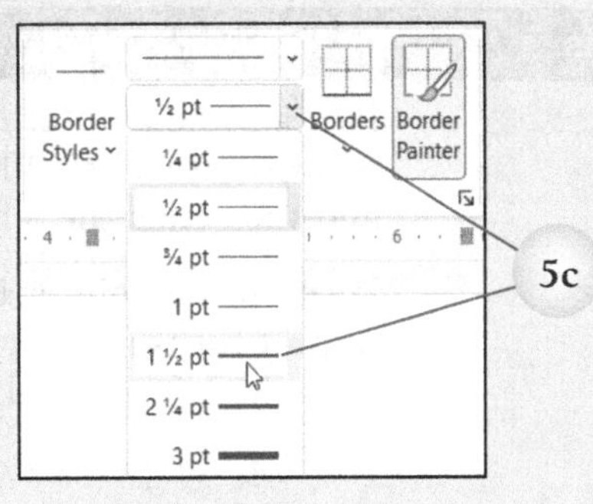

   d. Using the mouse (the pointer appears as a pen), drag along all four sides of the table. (As you drag with the mouse, a thick brown line is inserted. If you make a mistake or the line does not appear as you intended, click the Undo button and then continue drawing along each side of the table.)
6. Click the Border Styles button arrow and then click the *Double solid lines, 1/2 pt, Accent 2* option (third column, third row in the *Theme Borders* section).
7. Drag along all four sides of the bottom table.
8. Click the Border Painter button to turn off the feature.
9. Save **7-Tables.docx**.

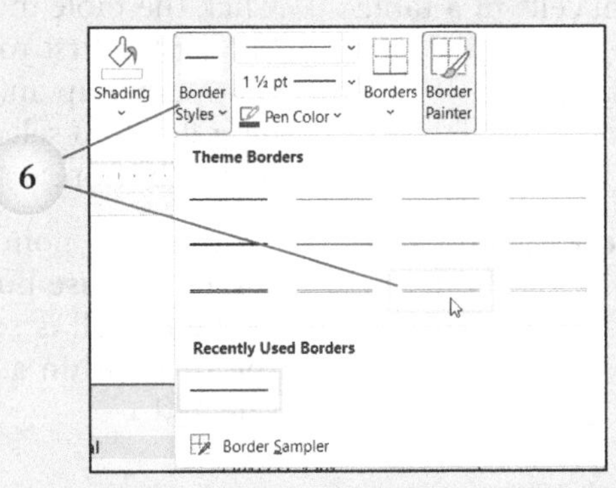

Check Your Work

Selecting Cells

Data within a table can be formatted in several ways. For example, the alignment of text within cells or rows can be changed, rows or columns can be moved or copied, and character formatting, such as bold, italic, and underlining, can be applied to text. To make changes to a cell, row, or column, first select the cells.

Selecting in a Table with the Mouse

Use the pointer to select a cell, row, or column or to select an entire table. Table 7.2 describes methods for selecting in a table with the mouse. To select a cell, position the pointer in the *cell selection bar*, an invisible strip just inside the left edge of a cell. The pointer turns into a small black arrow pointing up and to the right. Click to select the cell. Each row in a table contains a *row selection bar*, which is the space just outside the left edge of the table. Position the pointer in the row selection bar and the pointer turns into a white arrow that points up and to the right. Click to select the row.

Table 7.2 Selecting in a Table with the Mouse

To select this	Do this
cell	Position the pointer in the cell selection bar at the left edge of the cell until it turns into a small black arrow that points up and to the right and then click the left mouse button.
row	Position the pointer in the row selection bar at the left edge of the table until it turns into an arrow that points up and to the right and then click the left mouse button.
column	Position the pointer on the uppermost horizontal gridline of the table in the appropriate column until it turns into a small black arrow that points down and then click the left mouse button.
adjacent cells	Position the pointer in the first cell to be selected, click and hold down the left mouse button, drag the pointer to the last cell to be selected, and then release the mouse button.
all cells in a table	Click the table move handle or position the pointer in the row selection bar for the first row at the left edge of the table until it turns into an arrow that points up and to the right, click and hold down the left mouse button, drag down to select all the rows in the table, and then release the left mouse button.
text within a cell	Position the pointer at the beginning of the text, click and hold down the left mouse button, and then drag the mouse across the text. (When a cell is selected, its background color changes to gray. When the text within a cell is selected, only those lines containing text are selected.)

Selecting in a Table with the Keyboard

In addition to the mouse, the keyboard can be used to select specific cells within a table. Table 7.3 shows the commands for selecting specific elements of a table.

To select only the text within a cell, rather than the entire cell, position the insertion point in front of text in a cell and then press the F8 function key to turn on the Extend mode. Move the insertion point with an arrow key to select one character at a time, being careful not to select the entire cell. When a cell is selected, its background color changes to gray. When the text within a cell is selected, only those lines containing text are selected.

Table 7.3 Selecting in a Table with the Keyboard

To select	Press
next cell's contents	Tab
preceding cell's contents	Shift + Tab
entire table	Alt + 5 (on numeric keypad with Num Lock off)
adjacent cells	Press and hold down the Shift key and then press an arrow key repeatedly.
column	Position the insertion point in the top cell of the column, press and hold down the Shift key, and then press and hold down the Down Arrow key until the column is selected.

Activity 1d Selecting, Moving, and Formatting Cells in a Table — Part 4 of 8

1. With **7-Tables.docx** open, move two rows in the top table by completing the following steps:
   a. Position the pointer in the row selection bar at the left edge of the row containing the name *Cecilia Nordyke* until the pointer turns into an arrow that points up and to the right, click and hold down the left mouse button, and then drag down to select two rows (the *Cecilia Nordyke* row and the *Regina Stahl* row).

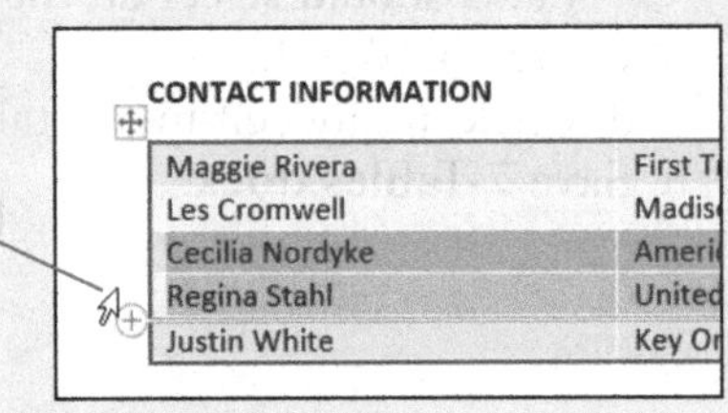

   b. Click the Home tab and then click the Cut button in the Clipboard group.
   c. Position the insertion point at the beginning of the name *Les Cromwell* and then click the Paste button in the Clipboard group.
2. Move the third column in the bottom table by completing the following steps:
   a. Position the pointer on the top border of the third column in the bottom table until the pointer turns into a short black arrow that points down and then click the left mouse button. (This selects the entire column.)
   b. Click the Cut button.
   c. With the insertion point positioned at the beginning of the text *Basic Plan Employees*, click the Paste button. (Moving the column removed the right border.)
   d. Insert the right border by clicking the Table Design tab, clicking the Border Styles button arrow, and then clicking the *Double solid lines, 1/2 pt, Accent 2* option at the drop-down list (third column, third row in the *Theme Borders* section).

e. Drag along the right border of the bottom table.
f. Click the Border Painter button to turn off the feature.

3. Apply shading to a row by completing the following steps:
   a. Position the pointer in the row selection bar at the left edge of the first row in the bottom table until the pointer turns into an arrow that points up and to the right and then click the left mouse button. (This selects the entire first row of the bottom table.)
   b. Click the Shading button arrow in the Table Styles group on the Table Design tab and then click the *Orange, Accent 2, Lighter 80%* color option (sixth column, second row in the *Theme Colors* section).

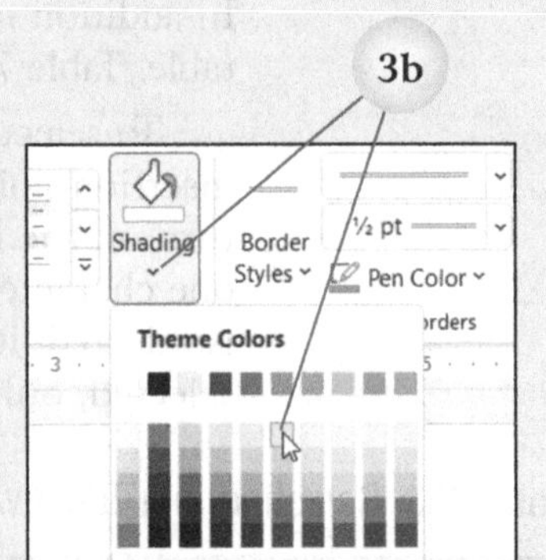

4. Apply a border line to the right sides of two columns by completing the following steps:
   a. Position the pointer on the top border of the first column in the bottom table until the pointer turns into a short black arrow that points down and then click the left mouse button.
   b. Click the *Line Style* option box arrow and then click the top line option (a single line).
   c. Click the Borders button arrow and then click *Right Border* at the drop-down list.
   d. Select the second column in the bottom table.
   e. Click the Borders button arrow and then click *Right Border* at the drop-down list.

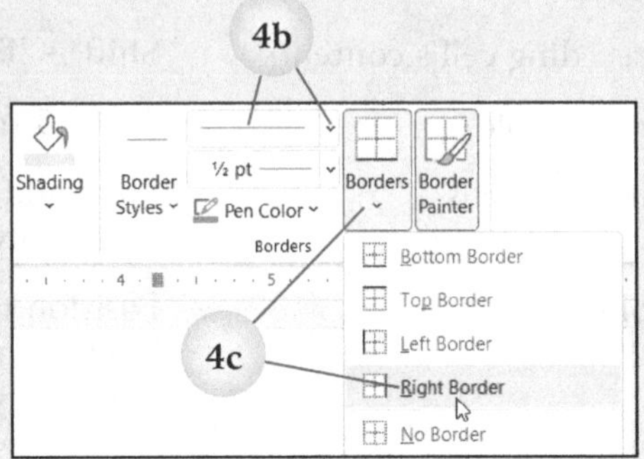

5. Apply italic formatting to a column by completing the following steps:
   a. Click in the first cell of the first row in the top table.
   b. Press and hold down the Shift key and then press the Down Arrow key four times. (This should select all the cells in the first column.)
   c. Press Ctrl + I.
   d. Click in any cell in the table to deselect the column.
6. Save **7-Tables.docx**.

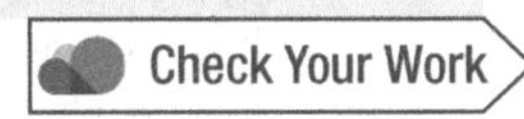

Changing the Table Layout

Changing the Table Layout

To further customize a table, consider changing the layout by inserting or deleting columns and rows and specifying how text should align in cells. Change the table layout with options on the Table Layout tab, shown in Figure 7.6. Use options and buttons on the tab to select specific cells, delete and insert rows and columns, merge and split cells, specify cell height and width, sort data in cells, and insert formulas.

Figure 7.6 Table Layout Tab

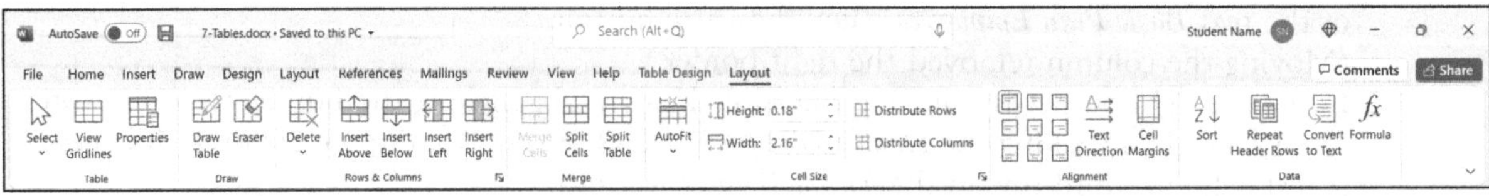

Selecting with the Select Button

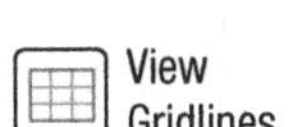

Along with selecting cells with the keyboard and mouse, specific cells can be selected with the Select button in the Table group on the Table Layout tab. Position the insertion point in the specific cell, column, or row and then click the Select button. At the drop-down list, specify what is to be selected: the entire table or a column, row, or cell.

Viewing Gridlines

Hint Some table layout options are available at a shortcut menu that can be viewed by right-clicking in a table.

By default, the cells in a table are bordered by a grid of thin black horizontal and vertical lines. These borders can be modified or removed using options on the Table Design tab, as shown on page 248. If the design of a table is changed so that the table does not contain visible borders, seeing the boundaries of each cell when entering data can be difficult. In this case, turn on the display of nonprinting gridlines to be used as a reference when working with the table. These gridlines appear as dashed lines on the screen, but they will not print. Turn on or off the display of nonprinting dashed gridlines with the View Gridlines button in the Table group on the Table Layout tab.

View Gridlines

Inserting and Deleting Rows and Columns

Insert or delete a row or a column with buttons in the Rows & Columns group on the Table Layout tab. Click a button in the group to insert the row or column above, below, to the left, or to the right. To delete a cell, a row, a column, or the entire table, click the Delete button and then click the option identifying what is to be deleted. The shortcut menu can also be used to insert or delete a row or column. To use the shortcut menu to insert a row or column, right-click in a cell, point to the *Insert* option, and then click an insert option at the side menu. To delete a row or column, right-click in a cell and then click the *Delete Cells* option. This displays the Delete Cells dialog box with options for deleting cells, a row, or a column.

In addition to using options on the Table Layout tab, rows or columns can be inserted using an Insert Control. Display the Insert Control for a row by positioning the pointer just outside the left border of the table at the left edge of the row border. When the Insert Control displays (a plus symbol in a circle and a border line), click the control and a row is inserted below the Insert Control border line. To insert a column, position the pointer above the column border line until the Insert Control displays and then click the control. This inserts a new column immediately left of the Insert Control border line.

Activity 1e Selecting, Inserting, and Deleting Columns and Rows — Part 5 of 8

1. Make sure **7-Tables.docx** is open.
2. The table style applied to the bottom table removed row border gridlines. If you do not see dashed row border gridlines in the bottom table, turn on the display of nonprinting gridlines by positioning your insertion point in the table, clicking the Table Layout tab, and then clicking the View Gridlines button in the Table group. (The button should appear with a gray background, indicating it is active. Skip this step if the button is already active.)
3. Select a column and apply formatting by completing the following steps:
   a. Click in any cell in the first column in the top table.

b. Make sure the Table Layout tab is active, click the Select button in the Table group, and then click *Select Column* at the drop-down list.

c. With the first column selected, press Ctrl + I to remove italic formatting and then press Ctrl + B to apply bold formatting.

File Home Insert Draw Design
Select View Gridlines Properties Draw Table Eraser
Draw
Select Cell
Select Column
Select Row
Select Table
3b

4. Select a row and apply formatting by completing the following steps:
   a. Click in any cell in the first row in the bottom table.
   b. Click the Select button in the Table group and then click *Select Row* at the drop-down list.
   c. With the first row selected in the bottom table, press Ctrl + I to apply italic formatting.
5. Insert a new row in the bottom table and type text in the new cells by completing the following steps:
   a. Click in the cell containing the text *60 days*.
   b. Click the Insert Above button in the Rows & Columns group.
   c. Type 30 days in the first cell of the new row. Press the Tab key, press Ctrl + Tab, and then type 0.85% in the second cell of the new row. Press the Tab key, press Ctrl + Tab, and then type 0.81% in the third cell of the new row.

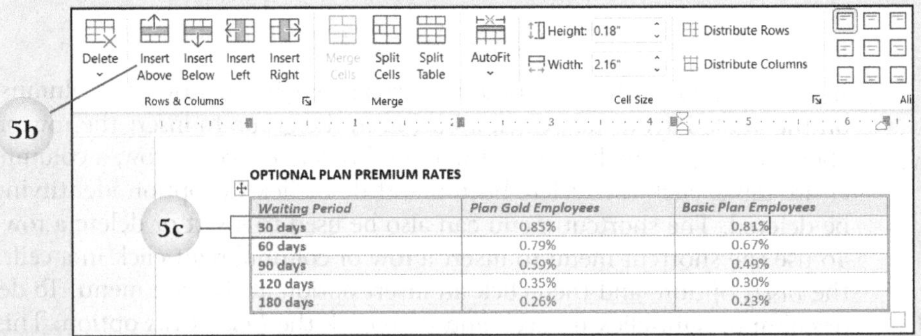

OPTIONAL PLAN PREMIUM RATES

Waiting Period	*Plan Gold Employees*	*Basic Plan Employees*
30 days	0.85%	0.81%
60 days	0.79%	0.67%
90 days	0.59%	0.49%
120 days	0.35%	0.30%
180 days	0.26%	0.23%

6. Insert two new rows in the top table by completing the following steps:
   a. Select the two rows of cells that begin with the names *Cecilia Nordyke* and *Regina Stahl*.
   b. Click the Insert Below button in the Rows & Columns group.
   c. Click in any cell of the top table to deselect the new rows.
7. Insert a new row in the top table by positioning the pointer at the left edge of the table next to the border line below *Regina Stahl* until the Insert Control displays and then clicking the Insert Control.

CONTACT INFORMATION
Maggie Rivera
Cecilia Nordyke
Regina Stahl
Les Cromwell
Justin White
7

8. Type the following text in the new cells:

Teresa Getty	Meridian Bank	(503) 555-9800
Michael Vazquez	New Horizon Bank	(702) 555-2435
Samantha Roth	Cascade Mutual	(206) 555-6788

Maggie Rivera	First Trust Bank	(203) 555-3440
Cecilia Nordyke	American Financial	(509) 555-3995
Regina Stahl	United Fidelity	(301) 555-1201
Teresa Getty	Meridian Bank	(503) 555-9800
Michael Vazquez	New Horizon Bank	(702) 555-2435
Samantha Roth	Cascade Mutual	(206) 555-6788
Les Cromwell	Madison Trust	(602) 555-4900
Justin White	Key One Savings	(360) 555-8963

8

9. Delete a row by completing the following steps:
   a. Click in the cell containing the name *Les Cromwell*.
   b. Click the Delete button in the Rows & Columns group and then click *Delete Rows* at the drop-down list.

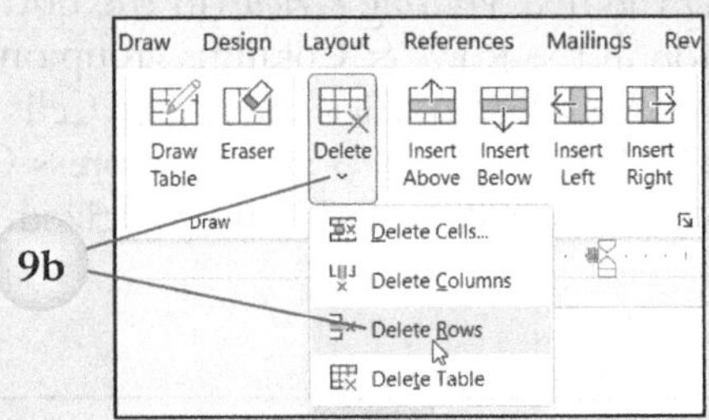

10. Insert a new column in the top table by positioning the pointer immediately above the border line between the first and second columns until the Insert Control displays and then clicking the Insert Control.

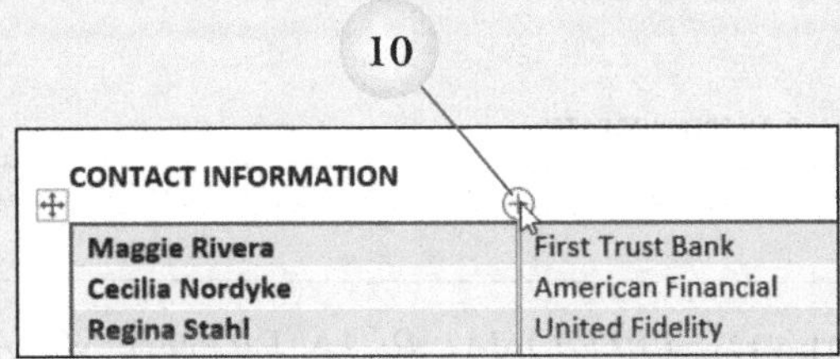

11. Type the following text in the new cells:
    B1 = Vice President
    B2 = Loan Officer
    B3 = Account Manager
    B4 = Branch Manager
    B5 = President
    B6 = Vice President
    B7 = Regional Manager

CONTACT INFORMATION

Maggie Rivera	Vice President	First Tru
Cecilia Nordyke	Loan Officer	America
Regina Stahl	Account Manager	United F
Teresa Getty	Branch Manager	Meridia
Michael Vazquez	President	New Ho
Samantha Roth	Vice President	Cascade
Justin White	Regional Manager	Key One

12. Save **7-Tables.docx**.

Merging and Splitting Cells and Tables

Split Table

Click the Merge Cells button in the Merge group on the Table Layout tab to merge selected cells and click the Split Cells button to split the currently active cell. Click the Split Cells button and the Split Cells dialog box displays with options for specifying the number of columns or rows into which the active cell should be split. To split one table into two tables, position the insertion point in a cell in the row that will be the first row in the new table and then click the Split Table button.

Activity 1f Merging and Splitting Cells and Splitting a Table

Part 6 of 8

1. With **7-Tables.docx** open, insert a new row and merge cells in the row by completing the following steps:
   a. Click in the cell containing the text *Waiting Period* (in the bottom table).
   b. Click the Insert Above button in the Rows & Columns group on the Table Layout tab.
   c. With all the cells in the new row selected, click the Merge Cells button in the Merge group.
   d. Type OPTIONAL PLAN PREMIUM RATES and then press Ctrl + E to center-align the text in the cell. (The text you type will be bold and italicized.)

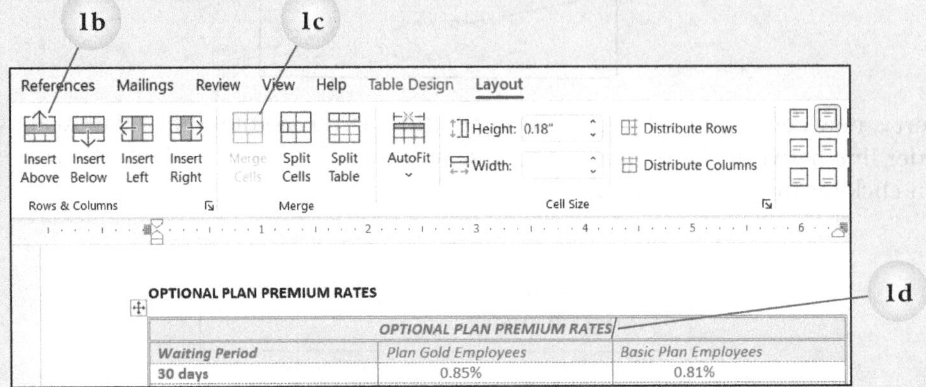

2. Select and then delete the text *OPTIONAL PLAN PREMIUM RATES* above the bottom table.
3. Insert rows and text in the top table and merge cells by completing the following steps:
   a. Click in the cell containing the text *Maggie Rivera*.
   b. Click the Table Layout tab.
   c. Click the Insert Above button two times. (This inserts two rows at the top of the table.)
   d. With the cells in the top row selected, click the Merge Cells button.
   e. Type CONTACT INFORMATION, NORTH and then press Ctrl + E to center-align the text in the cell.
   f. Type the following text in the four cells in the new second row.

      Name Title Company Telephone

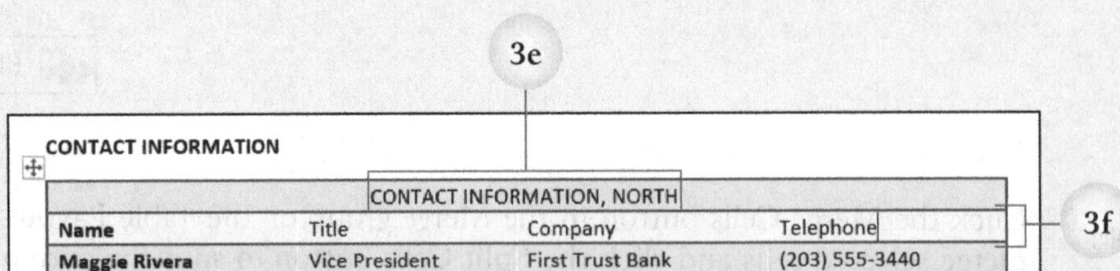

4. Apply heading formatting to the new top row by completing the following steps:
   a. Click the Table Design tab.
   b. Click the *Header Row* check box in the Table Style Options group to insert a check mark.
5. Select and then delete the text *CONTACT INFORMATION* above the top table.
6. Split a cell by completing the following steps:
   a. Click in the cell containing the telephone number *(301) 555-1201*.
   b. Click the Table Layout tab.
   c. Click the Split Cells button in the Merge group.
   d. At the Split Cells dialog box, click OK. (The telephone number will wrap to a new line. You will change this in the next activity.)
   e. Click in the new cell.

f. Type x453 in the new cell. If AutoCorrect automatically capitalizes the *x*, hover the pointer over the *X* until the AutoCorrect Options button displays. Click the AutoCorrect Options button and then click *Undo Automatic Capitalization* or click *Stop Auto-capitalizing First Letter of Table Cells.*

Telephone	
(203) 555-3440	
(509) 555-3995	
(301) 555-1201	x453
(503) 555-9800	

6f

7. Split the cell containing the telephone number *(206) 555-6788* and then type x2310 in the new cell. (If necessary, make the *x* lowercase.)
8. Split the top table into two tables by completing the following steps:
   a. Click in the cell containing the name *Teresa Getty*.
   b. Click the Split Table button in the Merge group.
   c. Click in the cell containing the name *Teresa Getty* (in the first row of the new table).
   d. Click the Insert Above button in the Rows & Columns group on the Table Layout tab.
   e. With the new row selected, click the Merge Cells button.
   f. Type CONTACT INFORMATION, SOUTH in the new row and then press Ctrl + E to center-align the text.
9. Save and then preview **7-Tables.docx**.
10. Delete the middle table by completing the following steps:
    a. Click in any cell in the middle table.
    b. Click the Table Layout tab.
    c. Click the Delete button in the Rows & Columns group and then click *Delete Table* at the drop-down list.
11. Draw a dark-orange border at the bottom of the top table by completing the following steps:
    a. Click in any cell in the top table and then click the Table Design tab.
    b. Click the *Line Weight* option box arrow in the Borders group and then click *1 ½ pt* at the drop-down list. (This activates the Border Painter button.)
    c. Click the Pen Color button and then click the *Orange, Accent 2, Darker, 50%* color option (sixth column, bottom row in the *Theme Colors* section).
    d. Using the mouse, drag along the bottom border of the top table.
    e. Click the Border Painter button to turn off the feature.
12. Save **7-Tables.docx**.

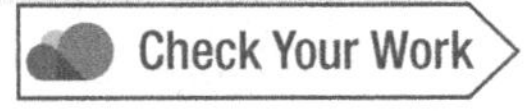
Check Your Work

Customizing Cell Size

Tutorial

Customizing Cells in a Table

Distribute Rows

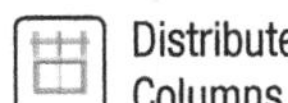
Distribute Columns

When a table is created, the column widths are equal and the row heights are equal. Both can be customized with buttons in the Cell Size group on the Table Layout tab. Use the *Table Row Height* measurement box to increase or decrease the heights of rows and use the *Table Column Width* measurement box to increase or decrease the widths of columns. The Distribute Rows button will make all the selected rows the same height and the Distribute Columns button will make all the selected columns the same width.

Column width can also be changed using the move table column markers on the horizontal ruler or using the table gridlines. To change column width using the horizontal ruler, position the pointer on a move table column marker until it turns into a left-and-right-pointing arrow and then drag the marker on the horizontal ruler to the specific position. Press and hold down the Shift key while dragging a table column marker and the horizontal ruler remains stationary while the table column marker moves. Press and hold down the Alt key while dragging a table column marker and measurements display on the horizontal ruler. To change column width using gridlines, position the pointer on the gridline separating columns until the insertion point turns into a left-and-right-pointing arrow with a vertical double-line in the middle and then drag the gridline to the new position. Press and hold down the Alt key while dragging the gridline and column measurements display on the horizontal ruler.

Adjust row height in a manner similar to adjusting column width. Drag the adjust table row marker on the vertical ruler or drag the gridline separating rows. Press and hold down the Alt key while dragging the adjust table row marker or the row gridline and measurements display on the vertical ruler.

AutoFit

Use the AutoFit button in the Cell Size group to make the column widths in a table automatically fit the contents. To do this, position the insertion point in any cell in the table, click the AutoFit button in the Cell Size group, and then click *AutoFit Contents* at the drop-down list.

Activity 1g Changing Column Width and Row Height

Part 7 of 8

1. With **7-Tables.docx** open, change the width of the first column in the top table by completing the following steps:
   a. Click in the cell containing the name *Maggie Rivera*.
   b. Position the pointer on the Move Table Column marker just right of the 1.5-inch mark on the horizontal ruler until the pointer turns into a left-and-right-pointing arrow.
   c. Press and hold down the Shift key and then click and hold down the left mouse button.
   d. Drag the marker to the 1.25-inch mark, release the mouse button, and then release the Shift key.

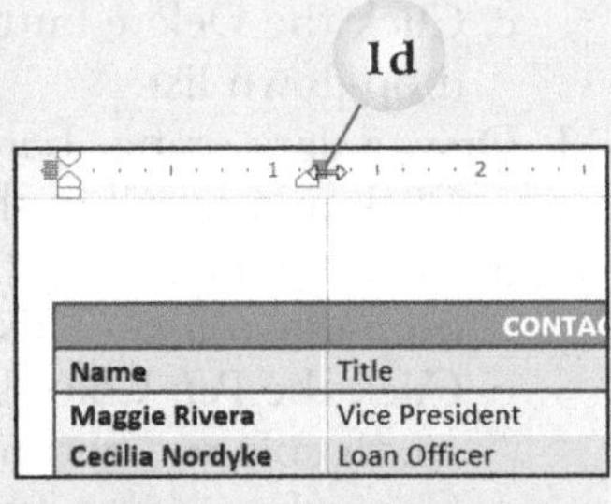

2. Complete steps similar to those in Step 1 to drag the move table column marker just right of the 3-inch mark on the horizontal ruler to the 2.75-inch mark. (Make sure the text *Account Manager* in the second column does not wrap to the next line. If it does, slightly increase the width of the column.)
3. Change the width of the third column in the top table by completing the following steps:
   a. Position the pointer on the gridline separating the third and fourth columns until the pointer turns into a left-and-right-pointing arrow with a vertical double-line in the middle.
   b. Press and hold down the Alt key, click and hold down the left mouse button, drag the gridline to the left until the measurement for the third column on the horizontal ruler displays as *1.31"*, and then release the mouse button followed by the Alt key.

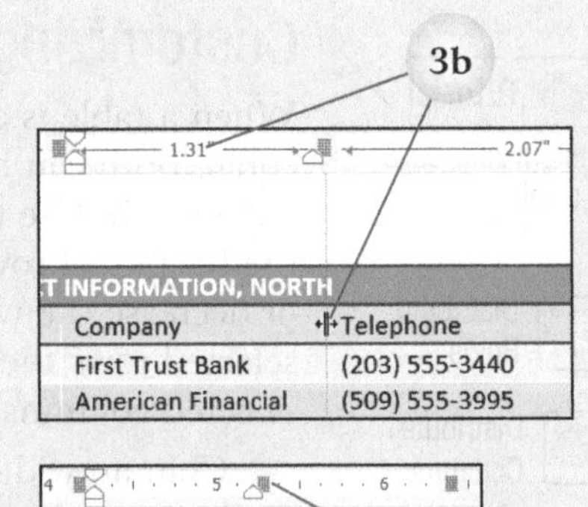

4. Position the pointer on the gridline that separates the telephone number *(301) 555-1201* from the extension *x453* and then drag the gridline to the 5.25-inch mark on the horizontal ruler. (Make sure the phone number does not wrap down to the next line.)
5. Drag the right border of the top table to the 5.75-inch mark on the horizontal ruler.

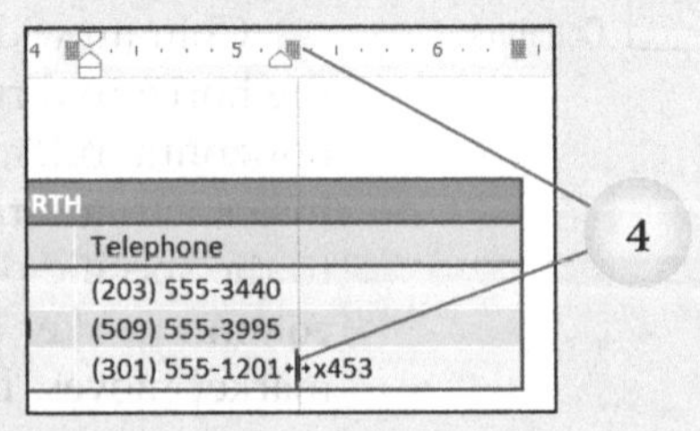

6. Automatically fit the columns in the bottom table by completing the following steps:
   a. Click in any cell in the bottom table.
   b. Click the AutoFit button in the Cell Size group on the Table Layout tab and then click *AutoFit Contents* at the drop-down list.

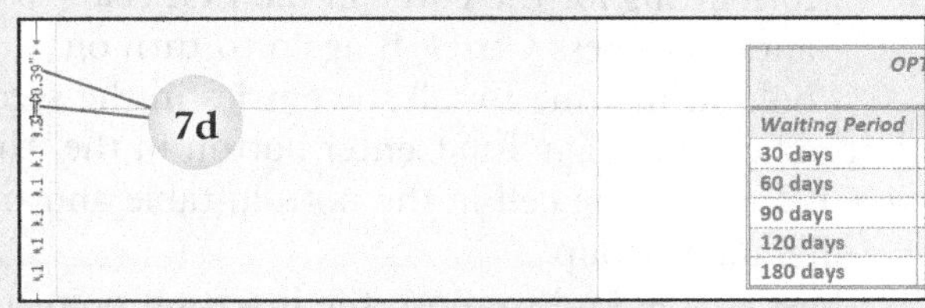

7. Increase the height of the first row in the bottom table by completing the following steps:
   a. Make sure the insertion point is positioned in one of the cells in the bottom table.
   b. Position the pointer on the top adjust table row marker on the vertical ruler.
   c. Press and hold down the Alt key and then click and hold down the left mouse button.
   d. Drag the Adjust Table Row marker down until the first row measurement on the vertical ruler displays as *0.39"*, release the mouse button, and then release the Alt key.

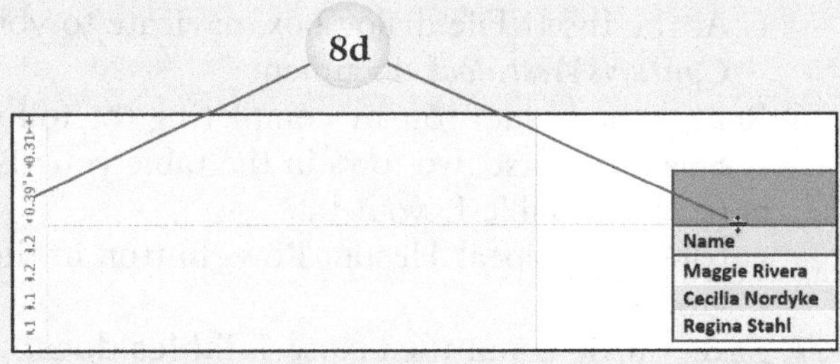

8. Increase the height of the first row in the top table by completing the following steps:
   a. Click in any cell in the top table.
   b. Position the pointer on the gridline at the bottom of the top row until the pointer turns into an up-and-down-pointing arrow with a vertical double-line in the middle.
   c. Click and hold down the left mouse button and then press and hold down the Alt key.
   d. Drag the gridline down until the first row measurement on the vertical ruler displays as *0.39"*, release the mouse button, and then release the Alt key.

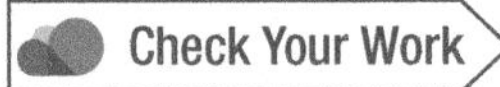

9. Save **7-Tables.docx**.

Check Your Work

Changing Cell Alignment

The Alignment group on the Table Layout tab contains a number of buttons for specifying the horizontal and vertical alignment of text in cells. Each button contains a visual representation of the alignment. Hover the pointer over a button to display a ScreenTip with the button name and description.

Repeating a Header Row

Quick Steps

Repeat Header Row

1. Click in header row or select rows.
2. Click Table Layout tab.
3. Click Repeat Header Rows button.

Repeat Header Rows

If a table continues over two or more pages, consider adding the header row at the beginning of each page for easier reference while reading. To repeat a header row, click in the first row (header row) and then click the Repeat Header Rows button in the Data group on the Table Layout tab. To repeat more than one header row, select the rows and then click the Repeat Header Rows button.

Activity 1h Aligning Text in Cells and Repeating Header Rows Part 8 of 8

1. With **7-Tables.docx** open, click in the top cell in the top table (the cell containing the title *CONTACT INFORMATION, NORTH*).
2. Click the Align Center button in the Alignment group on the Table Layout tab.
3. Format and align the text in the second row in the top table by completing the following steps:
   a. Select the second row.
   b. Press Ctrl + B to turn off bold formatting for the entry in the first cell and then press Ctrl + B again to turn on bold formatting for all the entries in the second row.
   c. Click the Align Top Center button in the Alignment group.
4. Click in the top cell in the bottom table and then click the Align Center button in the Alignment group.
5. Press Ctrl + End to move the insertion point to the end of the document, press the Enter key four times, and then insert a table into the current document by completing the following steps:
   a. Click the Insert tab.
   b. Click the Object button arrow in the Text group and then click *Text from File* at the drop-down list.
   c. At the Insert File dialog box, navigate to your WL1C7 folder and then double-click the ***ContactsWest.docx*** document.
6. Repeat the header row by completing the following steps:
   a. Select the first two rows in the table you just inserted.
   b. Click the Table Layout tab.
   c. Click the Repeat Header Rows button in the Data group.
7. Save, preview, and then close **7-Tables.docx**.

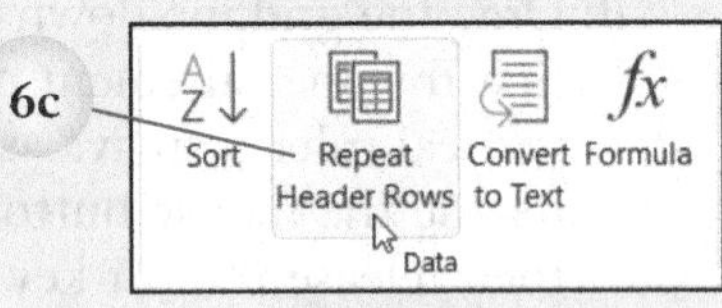

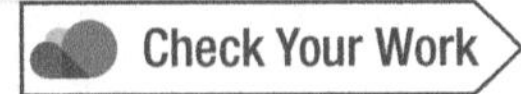

Activity 2 Create and Format Tables with Employee Information 6 Parts

You will create and format a table containing information on the names and departments of employees of Tri-State Products, two tables containing additional information on employees, and a calendar quick table.

Changing Cell Margin Measurements

Cell Margins

By default, the cells in a table contain specific margin measurements. The top and bottom margins in a cell have a default measurement of 0 inch and the left and right margins have a default measurement of 0.08 inch. Change these default measurements with options at the Table Options dialog box, shown in Figure 7.7. Display this dialog box by clicking the Cell Margins button in the Alignment group on the Table Layout tab. Use the measurement boxes in the *Default cell margins* section to change the top, bottom, left, and/or right cell margin measurements.

Figure 7.7 Table Options Dialog Box

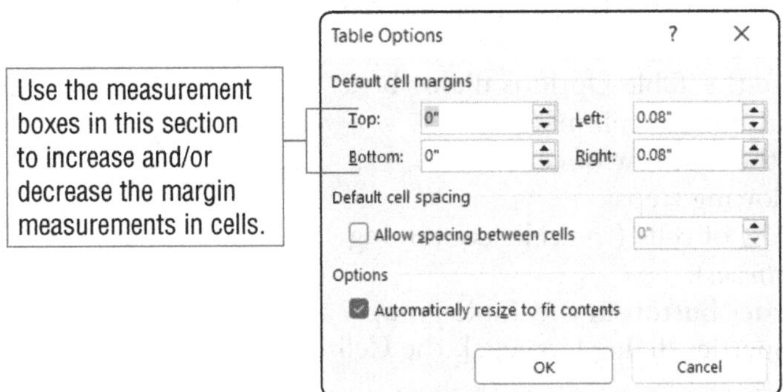

Changes to cell margins will affect all the cells in a table. To change the cell margin measurements for one cell or selected cells, position the insertion point in the cell or select the cells and then click the Properties button in the Table group on the Table Layout tab (or click the Cell Size group dialog box launcher). At the Table Properties dialog box, click the Cell tab and then the Options button in the lower right corner of the dialog box. This displays the Cell Options dialog box, shown in Figure 7.8.

Before setting the new cell margin measurements, remove the check mark from the *Same as the whole table* check box. With the check mark removed, the cell margin options become available. Specify the new cell margin measurements and then click OK to close the dialog box.

Figure 7.8 Cell Options Dialog Box

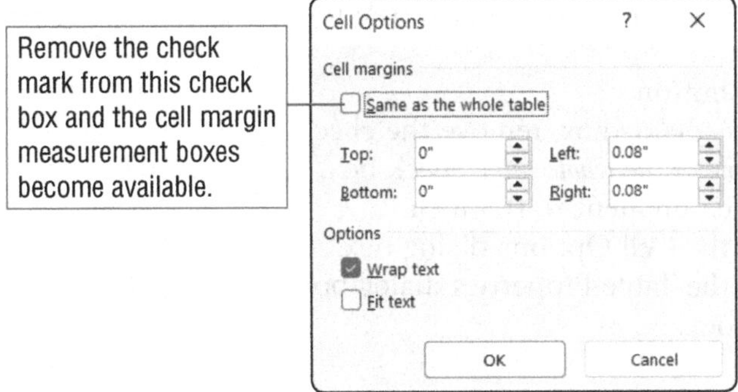

Activity 2a Changing Cell Margin Measurements

Part 1 of 6

1. Open **TSPTables.docx** and then save it with the name **7-TSPTables**.
2. Change the top and bottom cell margin measurements for all the cells in the table by completing the following steps:
   a. Position the insertion point in any cell in the table and then click the Table Layout tab.
   b. Click the Cell Margins button in the Alignment group.

c. At the Table Options dialog box, change the *Top* and *Bottom* measurements to 0.05 inch.
d. Click OK to close the Table Options dialog box.

3. Change the top and bottom cell margin measurements for the first row of cells by completing the following steps:
   a. Select the first row of cells (the cells containing *Name* and *Department*).
   b. Click the Properties button in the Table group.
   c. At the Table Properties dialog box, click the Cell tab.
   d. Click the Options button in the lower right corner of the dialog box.
   e. At the Cell Options dialog box, click the *Same as the whole table* check box to remove the check mark.
   f. Change the *Top* and *Bottom* measurements to 0.1 inch.
   g. Click OK to close the Cell Options dialog box.
   h. Click OK to close the Table Properties dialog box.
4. Change the left cell margin measurement for specific cells by completing the following steps:
   a. Select all the rows in the table *except* the top row.
   b. Click the Cell Size group dialog box launcher.
   c. At the Table Properties dialog box, make sure the Cell tab is active.
   d. Click the Options button.
   e. At the Cell Options dialog box, remove the check mark from the *Same as the whole table* check box.
   f. Change the *Left* measurement to 0.3 inch.
   g. Click OK to close the Cell Options dialog box.
   h. Click OK to close the Table Properties dialog box.
5. Save **7-TSPTables.docx**.

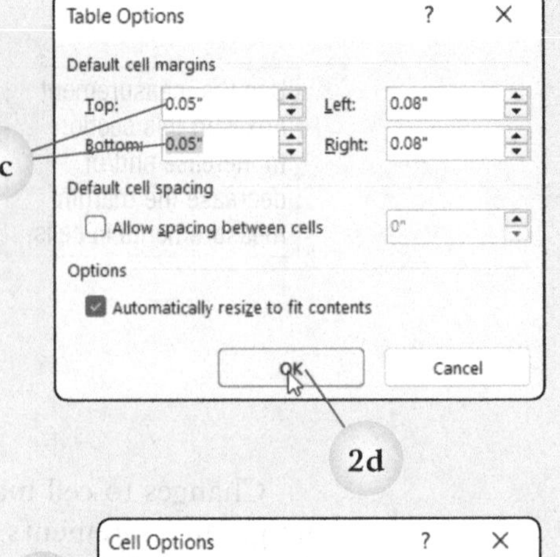

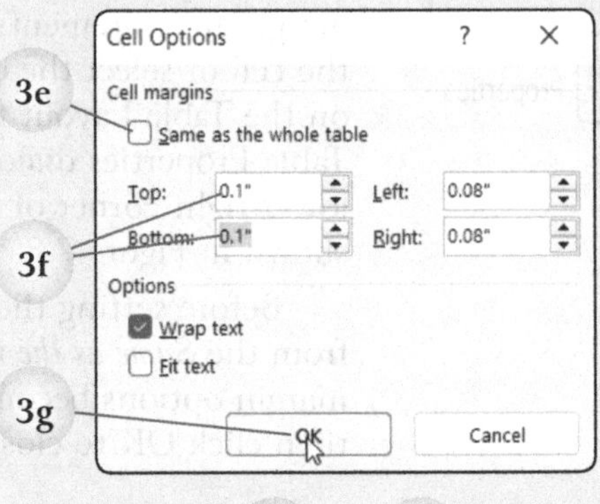

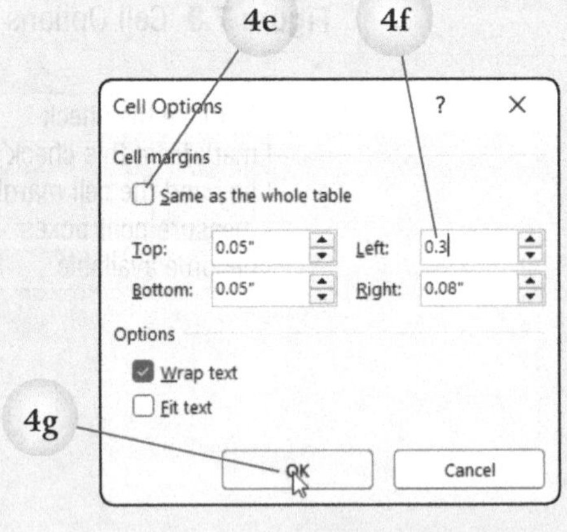

Check Your Work

Changing Text Direction in a Cell

Change the direction of text in a cell using the Text Direction button in the Alignment group on the Table Layout tab. Each time the Text Direction button is clicked, the text in the cell rotates 90 degrees.

Changing Table Alignment and Dimensions

By default, a table aligns at the left margin. Change this alignment with options at the Table Properties dialog box with the Table tab selected, as shown in Figure 7.9. To change the alignment, click the specific alignment option in the *Alignment* section of the dialog box. Change table dimensions by clicking the

Preferred width check box to insert a check mark. This makes active both the width measurement box and the *Measure in* option box. Type a width measurement in the measurement box and specify whether the measurement type is inches or a percentage with the *Measurement in* option box.

Figure 7.9 Table Properties Dialog Box with the Table Tab Selected

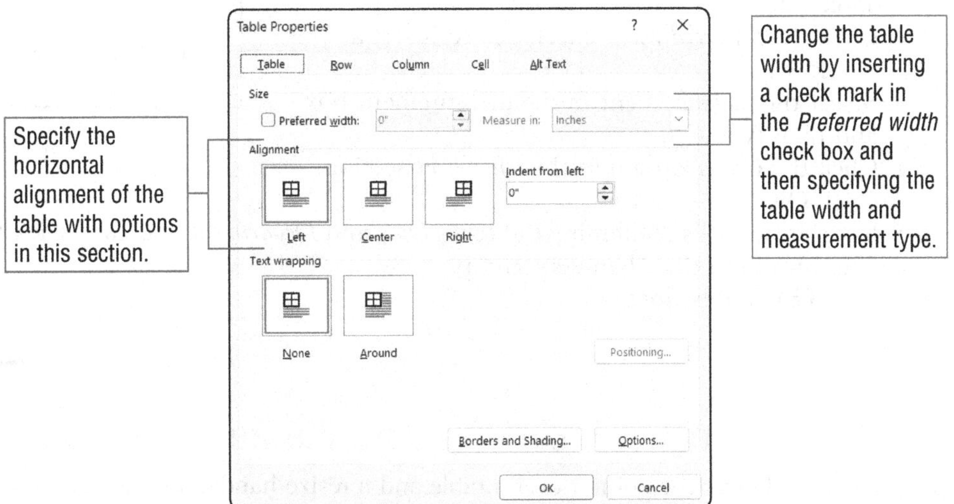

Activity 2b Changing Size and Cell Alignment and Text Direction

Part 2 of 6

1. With **7-TSPTables.docx** open, insert a new column and change text direction by completing the following steps:
   a. Click in any cell in the first column.
   b. Click the Insert Left button in the Rows & Columns group on the Table Layout tab.
   c. With the cells in the new column selected, click the Merge Cells button in the Merge group.
   d. Type Tri-State Products.
   e. Click the Align Center button in the Alignment group.
   f. Click two times on the Text Direction button in the Alignment group.

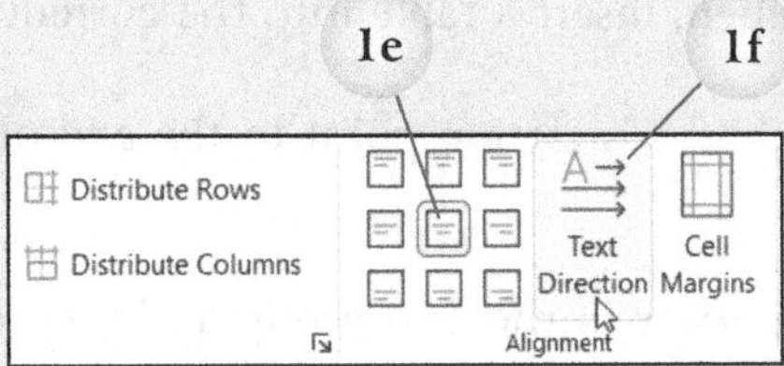

   g. With *Tri-State Products* selected, click the Home tab and then increase the font size to 16 points.
2. Automatically fit the contents by completing the following steps:
   a. Click in any cell in the table.
   b. Click the Table Layout tab.
   c. Click the AutoFit button in the Cell Size group and then click *AutoFit Contents* at the drop-down list.

3. Change the table width and alignment by completing the following steps:
   a. Click the Properties button in the Table group on the Table Layout tab.
   b. At the Table Properties dialog box, click the Table tab.
   c. Click the *Preferred width* check box to insert a check mark.
   d. Select the measurement in the measurement box and then type 4.5.
   e. Click the *Center* option in the *Alignment* section.
   f. Click OK.

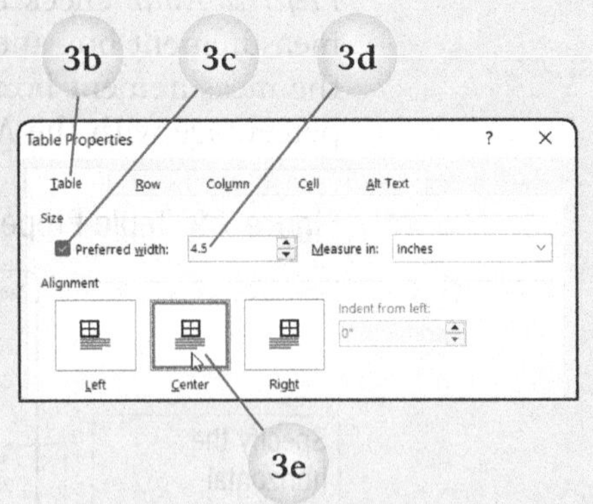

4. Select the two cells containing the text *Name* and *Department* and then click the Align Center button in the Alignment group.
5. Save **7-TSPTables.docx**.

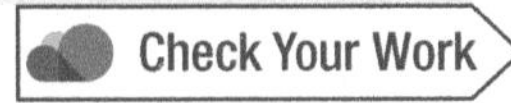

Changing Table Size with the Resize Handle

Hover the pointer over a table and a resize handle displays in the lower right corner. The resize handle displays as a small white square. Drag this resize handle to increase and/or decrease the size and proportion of the table.

Quick Steps

Move Table

1. Position pointer on table move handle until pointer displays with four-headed arrow attached.
2. Click and hold down left mouse button.
3. Drag table to new location.
4. Release mouse button.

Moving a Table

Position the pointer in a table and a table move handle displays in the upper left corner. Use this handle to move the table within the document. To move a table, position the pointer on the table move handle until the pointer displays with a four-headed arrow attached, click and hold down the left mouse button, drag the table to the new location, and then release the mouse button.

Activity 2c Resizing and Moving Tables — Part 3 of 6

1. With **7-TSPTables.docx** open, insert a table into the current document by completing the following steps:
   a. Press Ctrl + End to move the insertion point to the end of the document and then press the Enter key.
   b. Click the Insert tab.
   c. Click the Object button arrow in the Text group and then click *Text from File* at the drop-down list.
   d. At the Insert File dialog box, navigate to your WL1C7 folder and then double-click the ***TSPEmps.docx*** document.
2. Automatically fit the bottom table by completing the following steps:
   a. Click in any cell in the bottom table.
   b. Click the Table Layout tab.
   c. Click the AutoFit button in the Cell Size group and then click *AutoFit Contents* at the drop-down list.

3. Format the bottom table by completing the following steps:
   a. Click the Table Design tab.
   b. Click the More Table Styles button in the table styles gallery, scroll down the gallery, and then click the *List Table 4 - Accent 6* table style (last column, fourth row in the *List Tables* section).
   c. Click the *First Column* check box in the Table Style Options group to remove the check mark.
   d. Select the first and second rows, click the Table Layout tab, and then click the Align Center button in the Alignment group.
   e. Select the second row and then press Ctrl + B to apply bold formatting.

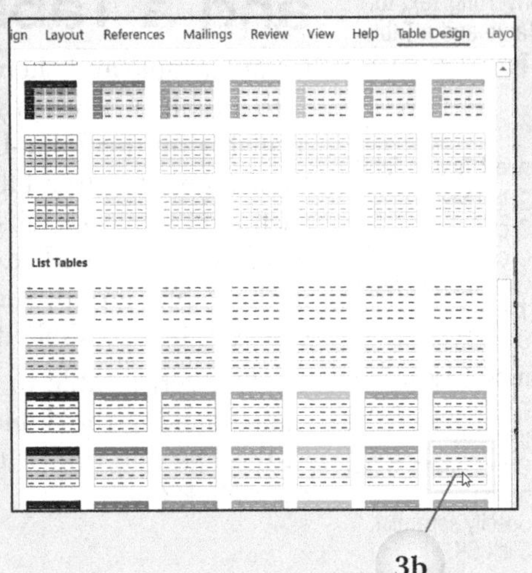

3b

4. Size the bottom table by completing the following steps:
   a. Position the pointer on the resize handle in the lower right corner of the bottom table.
   b. Click and hold down the left mouse button, drag down and to the right until the width and height of the table increase approximately 1 inch, and then release the mouse button.

TRI-STATE PRODUCTS		
Name	**Employee #**	**Department**
Whitaker, Christine	1432-323-09	Financial Services
Higgins, Dennis	1230-933-21	Public Relations
Coffey, Richard	1321-843-22	Research and Development
Lee, Yong	1411-322-76	Human Resources
Fleishmann, Jim	1246-432-90	Public Relations
Schaffer, Mitchell	1388-340-44	Purchasing
Porter, Robbie	1122-361-38	Public Relations
Buchanan, Lillian	1432-857-87	Research and Development
Kensington, Jacob	1112-473-31	Human Resources

4a-4b

5. Move the bottom table by completing the following steps:
   a. Move the pointer over the bottom table and then position the pointer on the table move handle that appears just outside the upper left corner of the table until the pointer displays with a four-headed arrow attached.
   b. Click and hold down the left mouse button, drag the table so it is positioned equally between the left and right margins, and then release the mouse button.

5a-5b

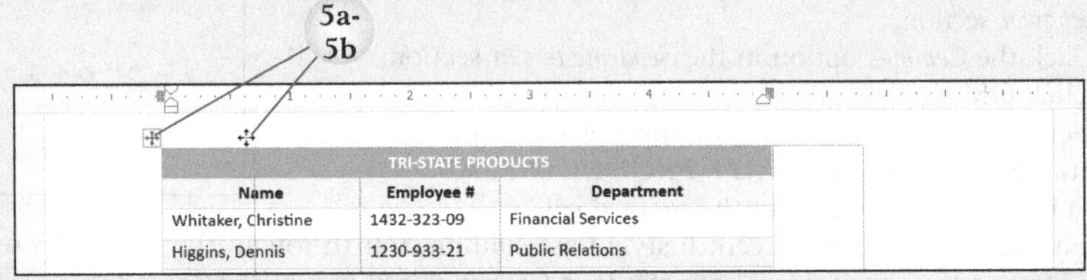

TRI-STATE PRODUCTS		
Name	**Employee #**	**Department**
Whitaker, Christine	1432-323-09	Financial Services
Higgins, Dennis	1230-933-21	Public Relations

6. Select the cells in the column below the heading *Employee #* and then click the Align Top Center button in the Alignment group.
7. Save **7-TSPTables.docx**.

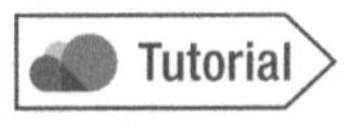

Converting Text to a Table and a Table to Text

Quick Steps

Convert Text to Table
1. Select text.
2. Click Insert tab.
3. Click Table button.
4. Click *Convert Text to Table*.
5. Click OK.

Convert Table to Text
1. Click Table Layout tab.
2. Click Convert to Text button.
3. Specify separator.
4. Click OK.

Convert to Text

Converting Text to a Table and a Table to Text

Create a table and then enter text in the cells or create the text and then convert it to a table. Converting text to a table provides formatting and layout options available on the Table Design tab and the Table Layout tab. When typing the text to be converted to a table, separate units of information using separator characters, such as commas or tabs. These characters identify where the text is divided into columns. To convert text, select the text, click the Insert tab, click the Table button in the Tables group, and then click *Convert Text to Table* at the drop-down list. At the Convert Text to Table dialog box, specify the separator and then click OK.

Convert a table to text by positioning the insertion point in any cell of the table, clicking the Table Layout tab, and then clicking the Convert to Text button in the Data group. At the Convert Table To dialog box, specify the separator and then click OK.

Activity 2d Converting Text to a Table — Part 4 of 6

1. With **7-TSPTables.docx** open, press Ctrl + End to move the insertion point to the end of the document. (If the insertion point does not display below the second table, press the Enter key until the insertion point displays below the table.)
2. Insert the document named **TSPExecs.docx** into the current document.
3. Convert the text to a table by completing the following steps:
   a. Select the text you just inserted.
   b. Make sure the Insert tab is active.
   c. Click the Table button in the Tables group and then click *Convert Text to Table* at the drop-down list.
   d. At the Convert Text to Table dialog box, type 2 in the *Number of columns* measurement box.
   e. Click the *AutoFit to contents* option in the *AutoFit behavior* section.
   f. Click the *Commas* option in the *Separate text at* section.
   g. Click OK.

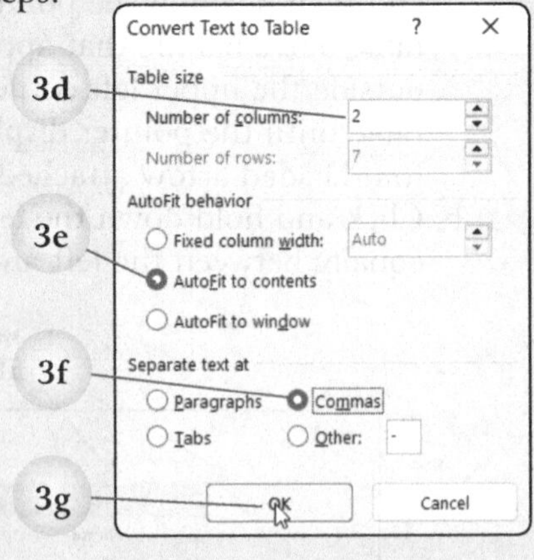

4. Select and merge the cells in the top row (the row containing the title *TRI-STATE PRODUCTS*) and then center-align the text in the merged cell.
5. Apply the List Table 4 - Accent 6 style (last column, fourth row in the *List Tables* section) and remove the check mark from the *First Column* check box in the Table Style Options group on the Table Design tab.
6. Drag the table so it is centered below the table above it.
7. Apply the List Table 4 - Accent 6 style to the top table. Increase the widths of the columns so the text *Tri-State Products* is visible and the text in the second and third columns displays on one line.
8. Drag the table so it is centered above the middle table. Make sure the three tables fit on one page.

9. Click in the middle table and then convert the table to text by completing the following steps:
   a. Click the Table Layout tab and then click the Convert to Text button in the Data group.
   b. At the Convert Table To dialog box, make sure *Tabs* is selected and then click OK.
10. Preview **7-TSPTables.docx**.
11. Click the Undo button to return the text to a table.
12. Save **7-TSPTables.docx**.

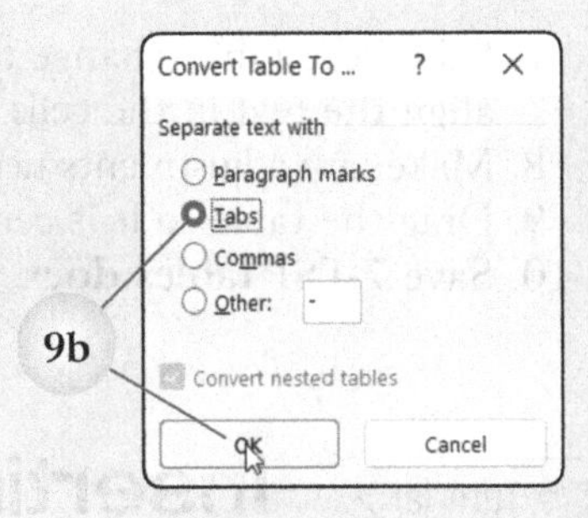

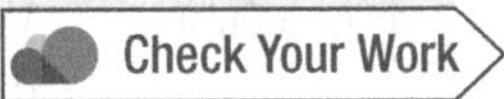

Drawing a Table

In Activity 1, options in the Borders group on the Table Design tab were used to draw borders around an existing table. These options can also be used to draw an entire table. To draw a table, click the Insert tab, click the Table button in the Tables group, and then click *Draw Table* at the drop-down list. Or click the Draw Table button in the Draw group on the Table Layout tab; this turns the pointer into a pen. Drag the pen pointer in the document to create the table. To correct an error when drawing a table, click the Eraser button in the Draw group on the Table Layout tab (which changes the pointer to an eraser) and then drag over any border lines to be erased. Clicking the Undo button will also undo the most recent action. To turn off the draw feature, click the Draw Table button in the Draw group or press the Esc key on the keyboard.

Activity 2e Drawing and Formatting a Table — Part 5 of 6

1. With **7-TSPTables.docx** open, select and then delete three rows in the middle table from the row that begins with the name *Lee, Yong* through the row that begins with the name *Schaffer, Mitchell*.
2. Move the insertion point to the end of the document (outside any table) and then press the Enter key. (Make sure the insertion point is positioned below the third table.)
3. Click the Insert tab, click the Table button, and then click the *Draw Table* option at the drop-down list. (This turns the insertion point into a pen.)
4. Using the mouse, drag in the document (below the bottom table) to create the table shown at the right, drawing the outside border first. If you make a mistake, click the Undo button. You can also click the Eraser button in the Draw group on the Table Layout tab and drag over a border line to erase it. Click the Draw Table button in the Draw group to turn off the draw feature.

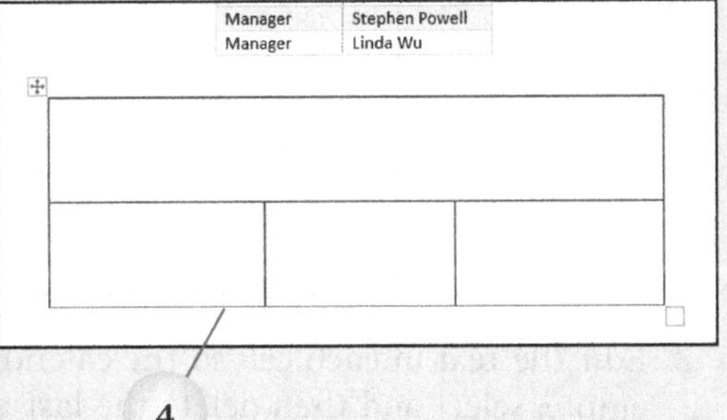

5. After drawing the table, type Tri-State Products in the top cell, Washington Division in the cell at the left, Oregon Division in the middle bottom cell, and California Division in the cell at the right.
6. Apply the Grid Table 4 - Accent 6 table style (last column, fourth row in the *Grid Tables* section).

7. Select the table, change the font size to 12 points, apply bold formatting, and then center-align the text in the cells using the Align Center button in the Alignment group.
8. Make any adjustments needed to the border lines so the text in each cell is on one line.
9. Drag the table so it is centered and positioned below the bottom table.
10. Save **7-TSPTables.docx**.

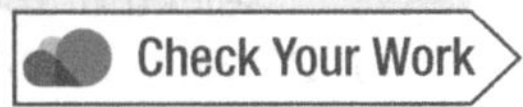

Inserting a Quick Table

Inserting a Quick Table

Word includes a Quick Tables feature for inserting predesigned tables in a document. To insert a quick table, click the Insert tab, click the Table button in the Tables group, point to *Quick Tables*, and then click a table at the side menu. Additional formatting can be applied to a quick table with options on the Table Design tab and the Table Layout tab.

Activity 2f Inserting a Quick Table — Part 6 of 6

1. With **7-TSPTables.docx** open, press Ctrl + End to move the insertion point to the end of the document and then press Ctrl + Enter to insert a page break.
2. Insert a quick table by clicking the Insert tab, clicking the Table button, pointing to *Quick Tables*, and then clicking the *Calendar 3* option at the side menu.

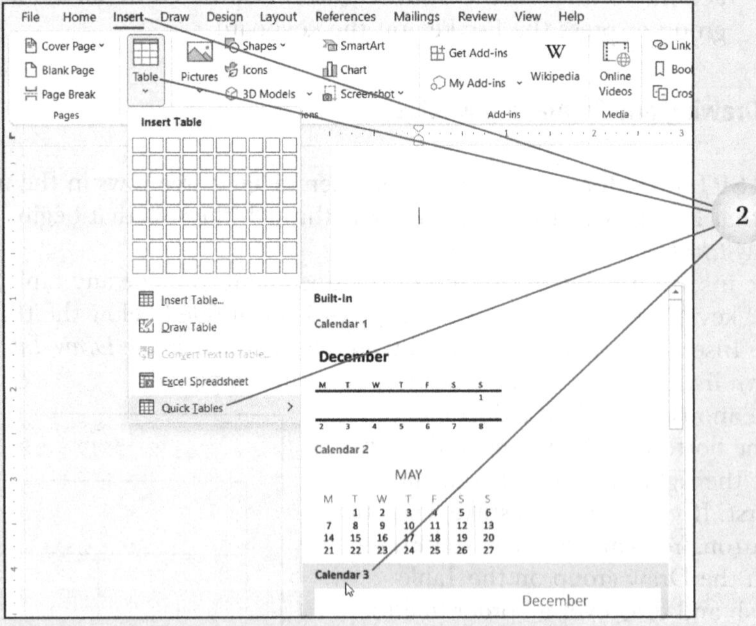

3. Edit the text in each cell so the calendar reflects the current month. (If the bottom row is empty, select and then delete the last and second to last rows.)
4. Select the entire table by clicking the Table Layout tab, clicking the Select button in the Table group, and then clicking the *Select Table* option. With the table selected, change the font to Copperplate Gothic Light.
5. Drag the table so it is centered between the left and right margins.
6. Save, preview, and then close **7-TSPTables.docx**.

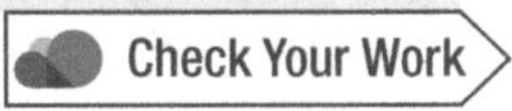

Activity 3 Calculate Sales Data — 1 Part

You will insert formulas in a Tri-State Products sales table to calculate total sales, average sales, and top sales.

Performing Calculations in a Table

Formula

Quick Steps

Insert Formula in Table

1. Click in cell.
2. Click Table Layout tab.
3. Click Formula button.
4. Type formula in Formula dialog box.
5. Click OK.

Hint Use the Update Field keyboard shortcut, F9, to update the selected field.

Performing Calculations in a Table

Use the Formula button in the Data group on the Table Layout tab to insert formulas that perform calculations on data in a table. The numbers in cells can be added, subtracted, multiplied, and divided. Other calculations can be performed, such as determining averages, counting items, and identifying minimum and maximum values. For more complex calculations, consider using an Excel worksheet.

To perform a calculation on the data in a table, position the insertion point in the cell where the result of the calculation is to be inserted and then click the Formula button in the Data group on the Table Layout tab. This displays the Formula dialog box, as shown in Figure 7.10. At this dialog box, accept the default formula in the *Formula* text box or type a calculation and then click OK.

Four basic operators are available for writing a formula, including the plus symbol (+) for addition, the minus symbol (–) for subtraction, the asterisk (*) for multiplication, and the forward slash (/) for division. If a calculation contains two or more operators, Word performs the operations from left to right. To change the order of operations, put parentheses around the part of the calculation to be performed first.

In the default formula, the SUM part of the formula is called a *function*. Word also provides other functions for inserting formulas. These functions are available in the *Paste function* option box in the Formula dialog box. For example, use the AVERAGE function to average numbers in cells.

Specify the numbering format with the *Number format* option box in the Formula dialog box. For example, when calculating amounts of money, specify the number of digits that should follow the decimal point.

If changes are made to a formula, the result of the formula needs to be updated. To do this, right-click the formula result and then click *Update Field* at the shortcut menu. Another method is to click the formula result and then press the F9 function key, which is the Update Field keyboard shortcut. To update the results of all the formulas in a table, select the entire table and then press the F9 function key.

Figure 7.10 Formula Dialog Box

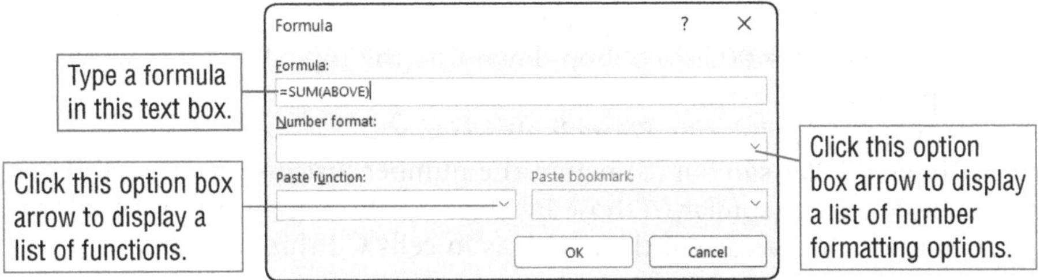

Activity 3 Inserting and Recalculating Formulas

Part 1 of 1

1. Open **TSPSalesTable.docx** and then save it with the name **7-TSPSalesTable.**
2. Insert a formula in the table by completing the following steps:
   a. Click in cell B9. (Cell B9 is the empty cell immediately below the cell containing the amount *$375,630.*)
   b. Click the Table Layout tab.
   c. Click the Formula button in the Data group.
   d. At the Formula dialog box, make sure *=SUM(ABOVE)* appears in the *Formula* text box.
   e. Click the *Number format* option box arrow and then click *#,##0* at the drop-down list (the top option in the list).
   f. Click OK to close the Formula dialog box.

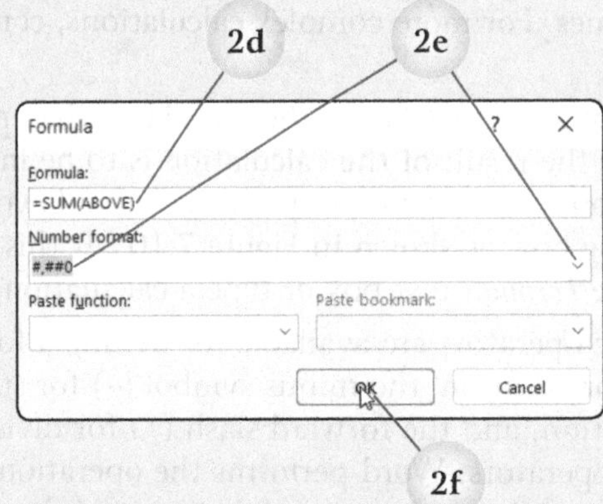

   g. In the table, type a dollar symbol ($) before the number just inserted in cell B9.
3. Complete steps similar to those in Steps 2c through 2g to insert a formula in cell C9. (Cell C9 is the empty cell immediately below the cell containing the amount *$399,120.*)
4. Insert a formula that calculates the average of amounts by completing the following steps:
   a. Click in cell B10. (Cell B10 is the empty cell immediately right of the cell containing the word *Average.*)
   b. Click the Formula button in the Data group.
   c. At the Formula dialog box, delete the formula in the *Formula* text box *except* for the equals (=) sign.
   d. With the insertion point positioned immediately right of the equals sign, click the *Paste function* option box arrow and then click *AVERAGE* at the drop-down list.
   e. With the insertion point positioned between the left and right parentheses, type B2:B8. (When typing cell designations in a formula, you can type either uppercase or lowercase letters.)
   f. Click the *Number format* option box arrow and then click *#,##0* at the drop-down list (the top option in the list).

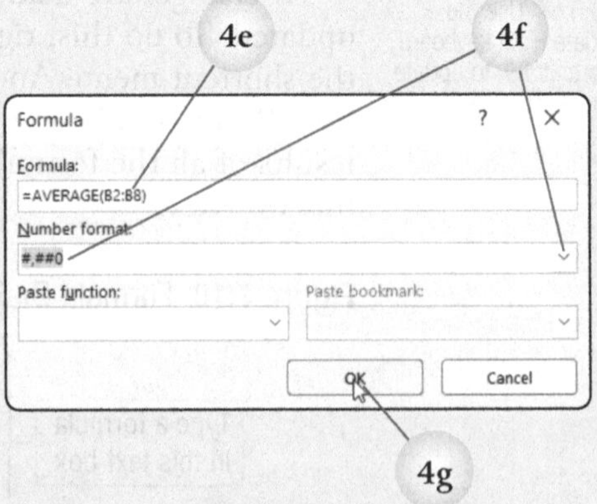

   g. Click OK to close the Formula dialog box.
   h. Type a dollar symbol ($) before the number just inserted in cell B10.
5. Complete steps similar to those in Steps 4b through 4h to insert a formula in cell C10 that calculates the average of the amounts in cells C2 through C8.

6. Insert a formula that calculates the maximum number by completing the following steps:
   a. Click in cell B11. (Cell B11 is the empty cell immediately right of the cell containing the words *Top Sales*.)
   b. Click the Formula button in the Data group.
   c. At the Formula dialog box, delete the formula in the *Formula* text box *except* for the equals sign.
   d. With the insertion point positioned immediately right of the equals sign, click the *Paste function* option box arrow and then click *MAX* at the drop-down list. (You will need to scroll down the list to locate the *MAX* option.)
   e. With the insertion point positioned between the left and right parentheses, type B2:B8.
   f. Click the *Number format* option box arrow and then click *#,##0* at the drop-down list.
   g. Click OK to close the Formula dialog box.
   h. Type a dollar symbol ($) before the number just inserted in cell B11.
7. Complete steps similar to those in Steps 6b through 6h to insert the maximum number in cell C11.
8. Save and then preview **7-TSPSalesTable.docx**.
9. Change the amount in cell B2 from *$543,241* to *$765,700*.
10. Recalculate all the formulas in the table by completing the following steps:
    a. Make sure the Table Layout tab is active and then click the Select button in the Table group.
    b. Click the *Select Table* option.
    c. Press the F9 function key.
11. Save, preview, and then close **7-TSPSalesTable.docx**.

Activity 4 Insert an Excel Worksheet — 1 Part

You will insert an Excel worksheet in a blank document, decrease the number of rows and columns in the worksheet, insert data from a Word document, and calculate data in the worksheet.

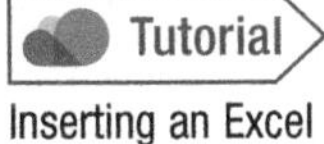

Inserting an Excel Spreadsheet

Inserting an Excel Spreadsheet

An Excel spreadsheet (usually referred to as a *worksheet*) can be inserted into a Word document, which provides some Excel functions for modifying and formatting the data. To insert an Excel worksheet, click the Insert tab, click the Table button in the Tables group, and then click the *Excel Spreadsheet* option at the drop-down list. This inserts a worksheet in the document with seven columns and ten rows visible. Increase or decrease the number of visible cells by dragging the sizing handles around the worksheet. Use buttons on the Excel ribbon tabs to format the worksheet. Click outside the worksheet and the Excel ribbon tabs are removed. Double-click the table to redisplay the Excel ribbon tabs.

Activity 4 Inserting and Formatting an Excel Worksheet

Part 1 of 1

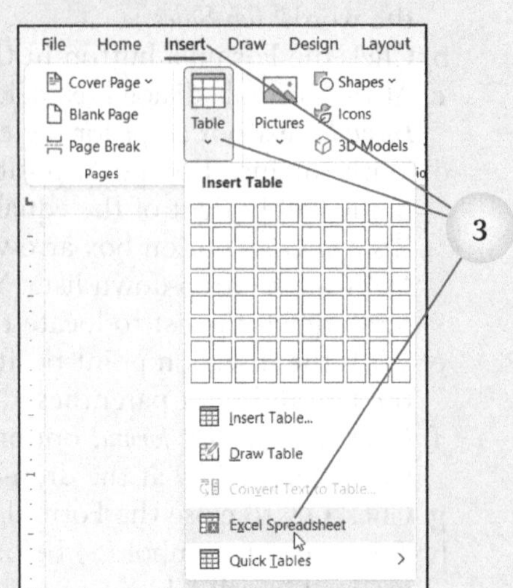

1. Open **SalesIncrease.docx**.
2. Press Ctrl + N to open a blank document.
3. Insert an Excel spreadsheet into the blank document by clicking the Insert tab, clicking the Table button in the Tables group, and then clicking *Excel Spreadsheet* at the drop-down list.
4. Decrease the size of the worksheet by completing the following steps:
   a. Position the pointer on the sizing handle (small black square) in the lower right corner of the worksheet until the pointer displays as a black, diagonal, two-headed arrow.
   b. Click and hold down the left mouse button, drag up and to the left, and then release the mouse button. Continue dragging the sizing handles until only columns A, B, and C and rows 1 through 7 are visible.
5. Copy a table into the Excel worksheet by completing the following steps:
   a. Position the pointer on the Word button on the taskbar and then click the *SalesIncrease.docx* thumbnail.
   b. Position the pointer over the table and then click the table move handle (small square containing a four-headed arrow) in the upper left corner of the table. (This selects all the cells in the table.)
   c. Click the Copy button in the Clipboard group on the Home tab.
   d. Close **SalesIncrease.docx**.
   e. With the first cell in the worksheet active, click the Paste button in the Clipboard group.

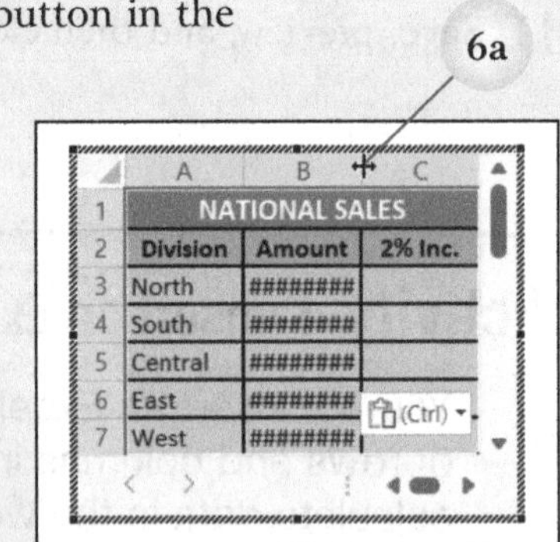

6. Format the worksheet and insert a formula by completing the following steps:
   a. Increase the width of the second column by positioning the pointer on the column boundary between columns B and C and double-clicking the left mouse button.
   b. Click in cell C3, type the formula =B3*1.02, and then press the Enter key.
7. Copy the formula in cell C3 to the range C4:C7 by completing the following steps:
   a. Position the pointer (white plus symbol) in cell C3, click and hold down the left mouse button, drag into cell C7, and then release the mouse button.
   b. Click the Fill button in the Editing group on the Home tab and then click *Down* at the drop-down list.
8. Click outside the worksheet to remove the Excel ribbon tabs.
9. Save the document with the name **7-Worksheet**.
10. Preview and then close **7-Worksheet.docx**.

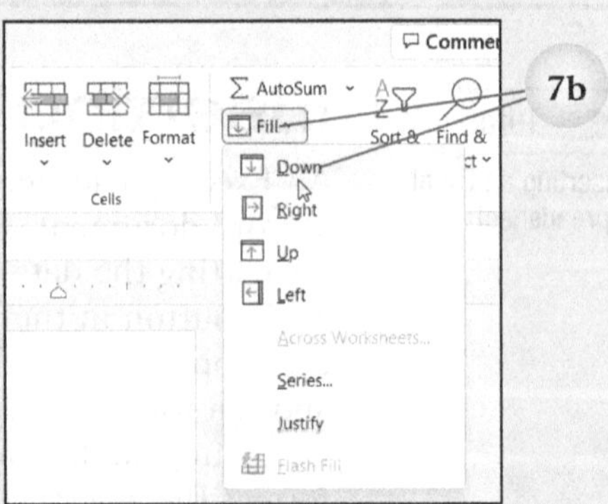

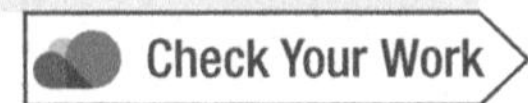

Chapter Summary

- Create a table in a document to organize and provide a visual grouping of data and make the data easier to read and interpret.
- Use the Tables feature to create a table with columns and rows of information. Create a table with the Table button in the Tables group on the Insert tab or with options at the Insert Table dialog box.
- A cell is the intersection between a row and a column. The lines that form the cells of the table are called *gridlines*.
- Press the Tab key to move the insertion point to the next cell or press Shift + Tab to move the insertion point to the preceding cell.
- Press Ctrl + Tab to move the insertion point to a tab within a cell.
- Move the insertion point to cells in a table using the mouse by clicking in a cell or using the keyboard commands shown in Table 7.1.
- Change the table design with options and buttons on the Table Design tab.
- Refer to Table 7.2 for a list of mouse commands for selecting specific cells in a table and Table 7.3 for a list of keyboard commands for selecting specific cells in a table.
- Change the layout of a table with options and buttons on the Table Layout tab.
- Select a table, column, row, or cell using the Select button in the Table group on the Table Layout tab.
- Turn on and off the display of gridlines by clicking the View Gridlines button in the Table group on the Table Layout tab.
- Insert and delete columns and rows with buttons in the Rows & Columns group on the Table Layout tab.
- Merge selected cells with the Merge Cells button and split cells with the Split Cells button, both in the Merge group on the Table Layout tab.
- Change the column width and row height using the height and width measurement boxes in the Cell Size group on the Table Layout tab; by dragging move table column markers on the horizontal ruler, adjust table row markers on the vertical ruler, or gridlines in the table; or using the AutoFit button in the Cell Size group.
- Change the alignment of text in cells with buttons in the Alignment group on the Table Layout tab.
- If a table spans two pages or more, a header row can be inserted at the beginning of each page. To do this, click in the header row or select the header rows and then click the Repeat Header Rows button in the Data group on the Table Layout tab.
- Change cell margins with options in the Table Options dialog box.
- Change text direction in a cell with the Text Direction button in the Alignment group on the Table Layout tab.
- Change the table dimensions and alignment with options at the Table Properties dialog box with the Table tab selected.
- Use the resize handle to change the size of the table and the table move handle to move the table.
- Convert text to a table with the *Convert Text to Table* option at the Table button drop-down list. Convert a table to text with the Convert to Text button in the Data group on the Table Layout tab.

- Draw a table in a document by clicking the Insert tab, clicking the Table button in the Tables group, and then clicking *Draw Table* at the drop-down list. Using the mouse, drag in the document to create the table.
- Quick tables are predesigned tables that can be inserted in a document by clicking the Insert tab, clicking the Table button in the Tables group, pointing to *Quick Tables*, and then clicking a table at the side menu.
- Perform calculations on data in a table by clicking the Formula button in the Data group on the Table Layout tab and then specifying the formula and number format at the Formula dialog box.
- Insert an Excel spreadsheet (worksheet) into a Word document to provide Excel functions by clicking the Insert tab, clicking the Table button in the Tables group, and then clicking *Excel Spreadsheet* at the drop-down list.

Commands Review

FEATURE	RIBBON TAB, GROUP	BUTTON, OPTION
AutoFit table contents	Table Layout, Cell Size	, *AutoFit Contents*
cell alignment	Table Layout, Alignment	
convert table to text	Table Layout, Data	
convert text to table	Insert, Tables	, *Convert Text to Table*
delete column	Table Layout, Rows & Columns	, *Delete Columns*
delete row	Table Layout, Rows & Columns	, *Delete Rows*
distribute columns	Table Layout, Cell Size	
distribute rows	Table Layout, Cell Size	
draw table	Insert, Tables	, *Draw Table*
Formula dialog box	Table Layout, Data	fx
insert column left	Table Layout, Rows & Columns	
insert column right	Table Layout, Rows & Columns	
Insert Excel spreadsheet	Insert, Tables	, *Excel Spreadsheet*
insert row above	Table Layout, Rows & Columns	
insert row below	Table Layout, Rows & Columns	
Insert Table dialog box	Insert, Tables	, *Insert Table*
merge cells	Table Layout, Merge	
Quick Table	Insert, Tables	, *Quick Tables*
repeat header row	Table Layout, Data	
Split Cells dialog box	Table Layout, Merge	
table	Insert, Tables	
Table Options dialog box	Table Layout, Alignment	
text direction	Table Layout, Alignment	
view gridlines	Table Layout, Table	

Review and Assessment

CHAPTER 7

Skills Assessment

Assessment 1 Create, Format, and Modify a Training Schedule Table

1. At a blank document, create a table with four columns and five rows.
2. Type text in the cells as shown in Figure 7.11.
3. Insert a new column at the right side of the table and then type the following text in the new cells:

   Trainer
   Marsden
   Trujillo
   Yong
   Stein

4. Change the widths of the columns to the following measurements:

   First column = 0.8 inch
   Second column = 1.2 inches
   Third column = 0.7 inch
   Fourth column = 1.3 inches
   Fifth column = 0.9 inch

5. Insert a new row above the first row and then, with the new row selected, merge the cells. Type APPLICATION TRAINING SCHEDULE in the cell and then center-align the text.
6. Select the second row (contains the text *Section*, *Training*, *Days*, and so on) and then apply bold formatting to and center-align the text.
7. Make the Table Design tab active, apply the Grid Table 4 table style (first column, fourth row in the *Grid Tables* section), and then remove the check mark from the *First Column* check box.
8. Horizontally center the table on the page. ***Hint: Do this at the Table Properties dialog box with the Table tab selected.***
9. Save the document with the name **7-SchTable**.
10. Preview and then close **7-SchTable.docx**.

Figure 7.11 Assessment 1

Section	Training	Days	Time
WD100	Word Level 1	MWF	9:00 to 10:00 a.m.
WD110	Word Level 2	TTh	1:30 to 3:00 p.m.
EX100	Excel Level 1	MTW	3:00 to 4:00 p.m.
EX110	Excel Level 2	TTh	2:00 to 3:30 p.m.

Assessment 2 Create, Format, and Modify a Property Replacement Costs Table

1. At a blank document, create a table with two columns and six rows.
2. Type the text in the cells in the table as shown in Figure 7.12. (Press the Enter key after typing the word *PROPERTY* in the first cell.)
3. Merge the cells in the top row and then change the alignment to align top center.
4. Change the alignment to align top right for the text in the cells containing money amounts and the blank cell below the last amount (cells B2 through B6).
5. Click in the *Accounts receivable* cell and then insert a row below it. Type Equipment in the new cell at the left and type $83,560 in the new cell at the right.
6. Insert a formula in cell B7 that sums the amounts in cells B2 through B6 and then change the number format to *#,##0*. Type a dollar symbol ($) before the amount in cell B7.
7. Automatically fit the contents of the cells.
8. Apply the Grid Table 4 - Accent 1 table style (second column, fourth row in the *Grid Tables* section) and remove the check mark from the *First Column* check box.
9. Click the Border Styles button arrow, click the *Double solid lines, 1/2 pt* option (first column, third row in the *Theme Borders* section), and then draw a border around all four sides of the table.
10. Save the document with the name **7-CostsTable**.
11. Preview and then close **7-CostsTable.docx**.

Figure 7.12 Assessment 2

PROPERTY REPLACEMENT COSTS	
Accounts receivable	$95,460
Business personal property	$1,367,340
Legal liability	$75,415
Earnings and expenses	$945,235
Total	

Assessment 3 Format a Table on Transportation Services

1. Open **ServicesTable.docx** and then save it with the name **7-ServicesTable**.
2. Insert a new column at the left of the table and then merge the cells. Type Metro Area in the merged cell, press the Enter key, and then type Transportation Services.
3. Select the text in the first column, change the font size to 16 points, and then click the Text Direction button two times to rotate the text. ***Hint: The Text Direction button is in the Alignment group on the Table Layout tab.***
4. Center-align (using the Align Center button) the text in the first column.
5. Change the width of the first column to 0.9 inch and the width of the third column to 1.1 inches.
6. Apply the Grid Table 5 Dark - Accent 5 table style (sixth column, fifth row in the *Grid Tables* section).

7. Horizontally center the table on the page.
8. Indent the text in the three cells below the cell containing the text *Valley Railroad*, as shown in Figure 7.13. ***Hint: Use Ctrl + Tab to create the indent in each cell.***
9. Apply italic and bold formatting to the four headings in the second column (*Langley City Transit*, *Valley Railroad*, *Mainline Bus*, and *Village Travel Card*).
10. Save, preview, and then close **7-ServicesTable.docx**.

Figure 7.13 Assessment 3

Metro Area Transportation Services	Service	Telephone
	Langley City Transit	
	Subway and bus information	(507) 555-3049
	Service status hotline	(507) 555-4123
	Travel information	(507) 555-4993
	Valley Railroad	
	Railway information	(202) 555-2300
	Status hotline	(202) 555-2343
	Travel information	(202) 555-2132
	Mainline Bus	
	Bus routes	(507) 555-6530
	Emergency hotline	(507) 555-6798
	Travel information	(507) 555-7542
	Village Travel Card	
	Village office	(507) 555-1232
	Card inquiries	(507) 555-1930

Assessment 4

Insert Formulas in a Table

1. In this chapter, you learned how to insert formulas in a table. Experiment with writing formulas (consider using the Help feature or another reference) and then open **FinAnalysis.docx**. Save the document with the name **7-FinAnalysis**.
2. Apply the Grid Table 4 - Accent 6 table style (last column, fourth row in the *Grid Tables* section) to the table and then apply other formatting so your table appears similar to the one in Figure 7.14.
3. Insert a formula in cell B13 that sums the amounts in cells B6 through B12. Apply the #,##0 format. Type a dollar symbol ($) before the amount. Complete similar steps to insert formulas and dollar symbols in cells C13, D13, and E13.
4. Insert a formula in cell B14 that subtracts the amount in B13 from the amount in B4. Apply the #,##0 format. ***Hint: The formula should look like this:* =(B4-B13)**. Type a dollar symbol before the amount. Complete similar steps to insert formulas and dollar symbols in cells C14, D14, and E14.
5. Save, preview, and then close **7-FinAnalysis.docx**.

Figure 7.14 Assessment 4

TRI-STATE PRODUCTS				
Financial Analysis				
	First Qtr.	**Second Qtr.**	**Third Qtr.**	**Fourth Qtr.**
Revenue	$1,450,348	$1,538,239	$1,634,235	$1,523,455
Expenses				
Facilities	$250,220	$323,780	$312,485	$322,655
Materials	$93,235	$102,390	$87,340	$115,320
Payroll	$354,390	$374,280	$380,120	$365,120
Benefits	$32,340	$35,039	$37,345	$36,545
Marketing	$29,575	$28,350	$30,310	$31,800
Transportation	$4,492	$5,489	$5,129	$6,349
Miscellaneous	$4,075	$3,976	$4,788	$5,120
Total				
Net Revenue				

Visual Benchmark

Activity 1

Create a Cover Letter Containing a Table

1. Click the File tab, click the *New* option, and then double-click the *Single spaced (blank)* template.
2. At the single-spaced blank document, type the letter shown in Figure 7.15. Create and format the table in the letter as shown in the figure. ***Hint: Apply the Grid Table 4 - Accent 1 table style*** (second column, fourth row in the *Grid Tables* section).
3. Save the completed document with the name **7-CoverLtr**.
4. Preview and then close **7-CoverLtr.docx**.

Activity 2

Insert and Format a Quick Table

1. At a blank document, insert the Calendar 1 quick table and then format the calendar so that it appears as shown in Figure 7.16. (You may want to turn on gridlines to see the cells in the calendar.) Consider the following when formatting the calendar:
   a. Increase the size of the calendar so that it is approximately 6.5 inches wide and 8 inches tall.
   b. Change *December* to *October 2024* and then change the font size as shown in the figure for all cells.
   c. Type the dates (1 2, 3, and so on) and the information in cells.
   d. Position the days of the week (M, T, W, and so on) in the cells as shown.
   e. Apply bold formatting and change the font color to Orange, Accent 2, Darker 50% (sixth column, bottom row in the *Theme Colors* section) for all text in the document.
   f. Insert the **FallLeaves.png** image file from your WL1C7 folder. Change the wrapping to behind text and then size and position the image as shown.
   g. Change the color of the black border lines below each week to Orange, Accent 2, Darker 50% (sixth column, bottom row in the *Theme Colors* section).
   h. Make any other formatting changes so your document looks similar to the document in Figure 7.16.
2. Save the completed document with the name **7-OctCalendar**.
3. Preview and then close **7-OctCalendar.docx**.

Figure 7.15 Visual Benchmark 1

10234 Larkspur Drive *(press Enter)*
Cheyenne, WY 82002 *(press Enter)*
July 15, 2024 *(press Enter five times)*

Dr. Theresa Sullivan *(press Enter)*
Rocky Mountain News *(press Enter)*
100 Second Avenue *(press Enter)*
Cheyenne, WY 82001 *(press Enter two times)*

Dear Dr. Sullivan: *(press Enter two times)*

Your advertised opening for a corporate communications staff writer describes interesting challenges. As you can see from the table below, my skills and experience are excellent matches for the position. *(press Enter two times)*

QUALIFICATIONS AND SKILLS	
Your Requirement	**My Experience, Skills, and Value Offered**
Two years of business writing experience	Four years of experience creating diverse business messages, from corporate communications to feature articles and radio broadcast material.
Ability to complete projects on deadline	Proven project coordination skills and tight deadline focus. My current role as producer of a daily three-hour talk-radio program requires planning, coordination, and execution of many detailed tasks, always in the face of inflexible deadlines.
Oral presentation skills	Unusually broad experience, including high-profile roles as an on-air radio presence and "the voice" for an on-hold telephone message company.
Relevant education (BA or BS)	BA in Mass Communications; one year post-graduate study in Multimedia Communications.

As you will note from the enclosed résumé, my experience encompasses corporate, print media, and multimedia environments. I offer a diverse and proven skill set that can help your company create and deliver its message to various audiences to build image, market presence, and revenue. I look forward to meeting with you to discuss the value I can offer your company. *(press Enter two times)*

Sincerely, *(press Enter four times)*

Marcus Tolliver *(press Enter two times)*

Enclosure: Résumé

Figure 7.16 Visual Benchmark 2

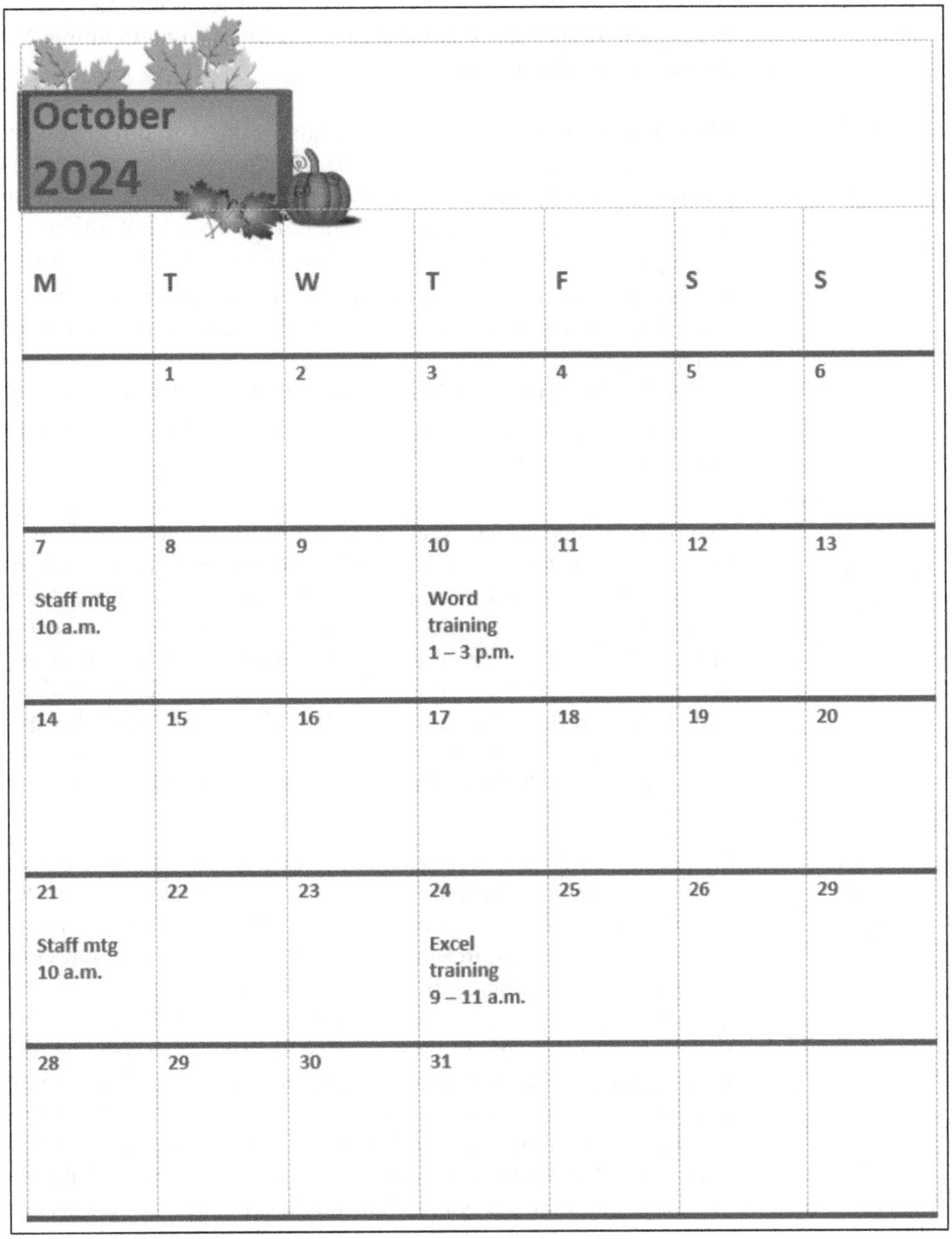

October
2024

M	T	W	T	F	S	S
	1	2	3	4	5	6
7 Staff mtg 10 a.m.	8	9	10 Word training 1 – 3 p.m.	11	12	13
14	15	16	17	18	19	20
21 Staff mtg 10 a.m.	22	23	24 Excel training 9 – 11 a.m.	25	26	29
28	29	30	31			

Case Study

Part
1

You have recently been hired as an office clerk for a landscaping business, Landmark Landscaping, which has two small offices in your city. The person who held the position before you kept track of monthly sales using Word, and the office manager would prefer that you continue using that application. Open the document **LLMoSales.docx** and then save it with the name **7-LLMoSales**. After reviewing the information, you decide that a table would be a better format for maintaining and presenting the data. Convert the data to a table and modify its appearance so that it is easy to read and understand. Insert a total row at the bottom of the table and then insert formulas to sum the totals in the columns that contain amounts. Apply formatting to the table to enhance its appearance. Determine a color theme for the table and then continue to use that color theme when preparing other documents for Landmark Landscaping. Save, preview, and then close the document.

Part 2

The office manager of Landmark Landscaping would like you to create a monthly calendar (use the current month) using a quick table. Insert the dates in the calendar and apply formatting using the color theme you determined for the company in Part 1. Consider inserting an image or any other element to enhance the appearance of the calendar. Add the following information to the calendar:

- Sales meeting on the first Tuesday of the month from 10:00 to 11:30 a.m.
- Product presentation the second Wednesday of the month from 9:00 to 10:00 a.m.
- Sales training the fourth Thursday of the month from 2:00 to 4:30 p.m.

Save the completed calendar with the name **7-LLCalendar**. Preview and then close the document.

Part 3

The office manager has asked you to find information on how to add alt text to a table to make the table accessible to people with disabilities. Use the Help feature and the search text *table properties* or the search text *table alt text* to find information on how to add alt text to a table. If a video is available in the Help task pane, watch the video along with reading any information provided in the task pane. With the information you find, open **7-LLMOSales.docx** and then add alt text to the table. Save and then close **7-LLMOSales.docx**. At a blank document, write the steps you followed to add the alt text. Save the document with the name **7-AltText**. Preview and then close the document.

Part 4

One of the landscape architects at Landmark Landscaping has asked you to prepare a table containing information on the trees that need to be ordered next month. She would also like you to include the Latin names for the trees because this information is important when ordering. Create a table that contains the common name of each tree, the Latin name, the quantity required, and the price per tree, as shown in Figure 7.17. Use the internet (or any other resource available to you) to find the Latin name of each tree listed in Figure 7.17. Create a column in the table that multiplies the number of trees to be ordered by the price and include this formula for each tree. Create a row at the bottom of the table that calculates the total order (note that totals are not required for the columns with the quantity required and the price per tree). Format and enhance the table so it is attractive and easy to read and apply colors that match the color scheme you chose in Part 1. Save the document with the name **7-LLTrees**. Preview and then close the document.

Figure 7.17 Case Study, Part 4

Douglas Fir, 15 required, $2.99 per tree
Elm, 10 required, $4.49 per tree
Western Hemlock, 10 required, $3.89 per tree
Red Maple, 8 required, $8.99 per tree
Ponderosa Pine, 5 required, $4.69 per tree

WORD

CHAPTER 8

Applying and Customizing Formatting

Performance Objectives

Upon successful completion of Chapter 8, you will be able to:

1 Create and insert custom numbers and bullets
2 Create and insert multilevel list formatting
3 Specify AutoCorrect exceptions
4 Add and delete AutoCorrect text
5 Use the AutoCorrect Options button
6 Customize AutoFormatting
7 Create custom theme colors and theme fonts
8 Save, apply, edit, and delete a custom theme
9 Reset the template theme

Word offers a number of features to apply and customize formatting and to help streamline the formatting of a document. In this chapter, you will learn how to define and insert custom numbers and bullets and to format text in a multilevel list. You will use Word's AutoCorrect and Autoformatting features and customize them for your convenience when creating documents. The Microsoft 365 suite offers design themes that provide consistent formatting and help create documents with a professional and polished look. This chapter provides instruction on how to customize a theme by modifying the color and fonts and applying theme effects.

Data Files

The data files for this chapter are in the WL1C8 folder that you downloaded at the beginning of this course.

Activity 1 Apply Number Formatting to an Agenda 2 Parts

You will open an agenda document, apply formatting that includes number formatting, and then define and apply custom numbering.

Inserting and Creating Custom Numbers and Bullets

Number paragraphs or insert bullets before paragraphs using buttons in the Paragraph group on the Home tab. Use the Numbering button to insert numbers before specific paragraphs and use the Bullets button to insert bullets. To insert custom numbering or bullets, click the button arrow and then choose from the drop-down gallery that displays.

Inserting Custom Numbers

Insert numbers as text is typed or select text and then apply a numbering format. Type *1.* and then press the spacebar and Word indents the number approximately 0.25 inch. Type text after the number and then press the Enter key and Word indents all the lines in the paragraph 0.5 inch from the left margin (called a *hanging indent*). At the beginning of the next paragraph, Word inserts the number *2* followed by a period 0.25 inch from the left margin. Continue typing items and Word numbers successive paragraphs in the list. To number existing paragraphs of text, select the paragraphs and then click the Numbering button in the Paragraph group on the Home tab.

Hint If the automatic numbering or bulleting feature is on, press Shift + Enter to insert a line break without inserting a number or bullet.

Click the Numbering button in the Paragraph group and arabic numbers (1., 2., 3., etc.) are inserted in the document. This default numbering can be changed by clicking the Numbering button arrow and then clicking an option at the drop-down gallery.

To change list levels, click the Numbering button arrow, point to the *Change List Level* option at the bottom of the drop-down gallery, and then click a list level at the side menu. Set the numbering value with options at the Set Numbering Value dialog box, shown in Figure 8.1. Display this dialog box by clicking the Numbering button arrow and then clicking the *Set Numbering Value* option at the bottom of the drop-down gallery.

Figure 8.1 Set Numbering Value Dialog Box

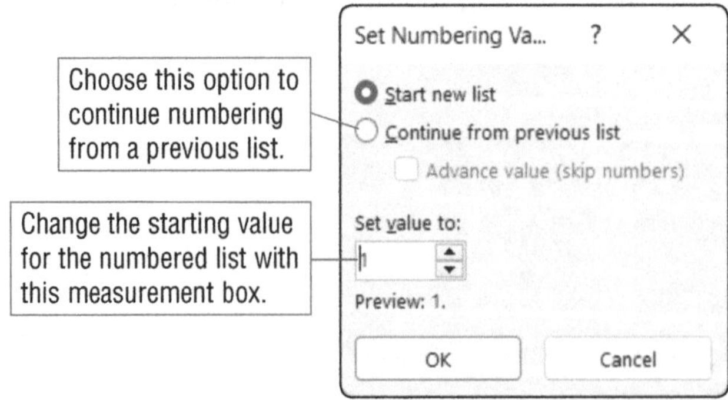

Activity 1a Inserting Custom Numbers

1. Open **FDAgenda.docx** and then save it with the name **8-FDAgenda**.
2. Restart the list numbering at 1 by completing the following steps:
   a. Select the numbered paragraphs.
   b. Click the Numbering button arrow in the Paragraph group on the Home tab and then click *Set Numbering Value* at the drop-down gallery.
   c. At the Set Numbering Value dialog box, select the number in the *Set value to* measurement box, type 1, and then press the Enter key.

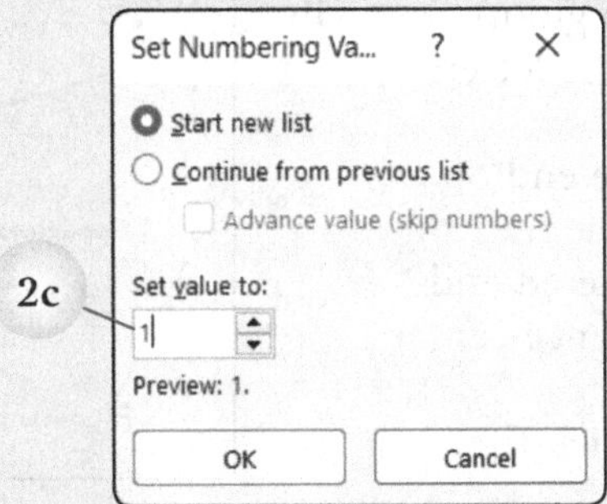

3. Change the paragraph numbers to letters by completing the following steps:
   a. With the numbered paragraphs selected, click the Numbering button arrow.
   b. At the Numbering button drop-down gallery, click the option that uses capital letters followed by a period (second column, second row in the *Numbering Library* section [this location may vary]).

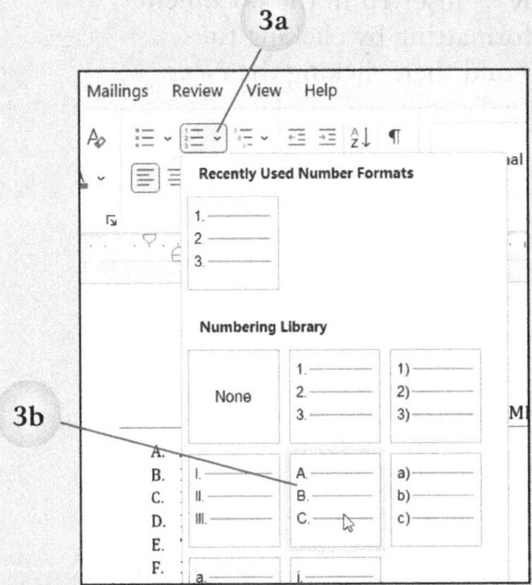

4. Add text by positioning the insertion point immediately right of the text *Introductions*, pressing the Enter key, and then typing Organizational Overview.

5. Demote the lettered list by completing the following steps:
   a. Select the lettered paragraphs.
   b. Click the Numbering button arrow, point to the *Change List Level* option, and then click the *a.* option at the side menu (*Level 2*).
6. With the paragraphs still selected, promote the list by clicking the Decrease Indent button in the Paragraph group on the Home tab. (The lowercase letters change back to capital letters.)
7. Move the insertion point to the end of the document and then type The meeting will stop for lunch, which is catered and will be held in the main conference center from 12:15 to 1:30 p.m.
8. Press the Enter key and then click the Numbering button.
9. Click the AutoCorrect Options button next to the *A.* inserted in the document and then click *Continue Numbering* at the drop-down list. (This changes the letter from *A.* to *H.*)
10. Type Future Goals, press the Enter key, type Proposals, press the Enter key, and then type Adjournment.
11. Press the Enter key and *K.* is inserted in the document. Turn off the numbering formatting by clicking the Numbering button arrow and then clicking the *None* option at the drop-down gallery.

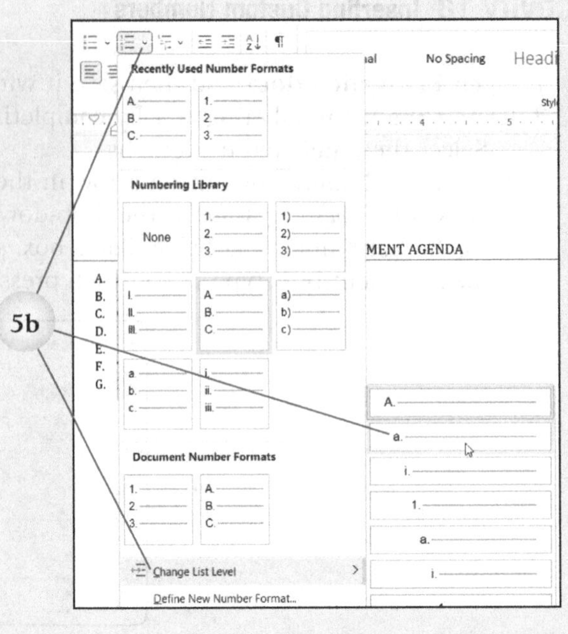

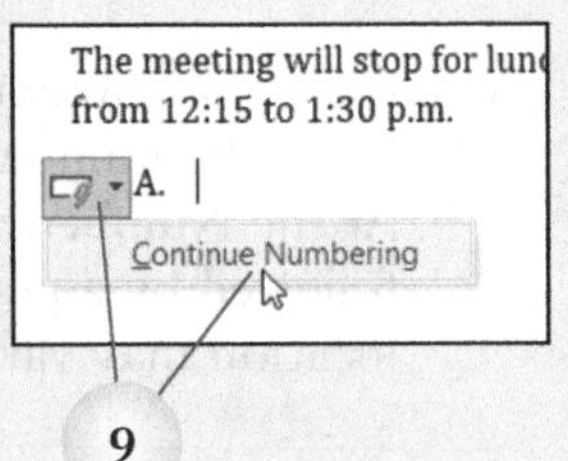

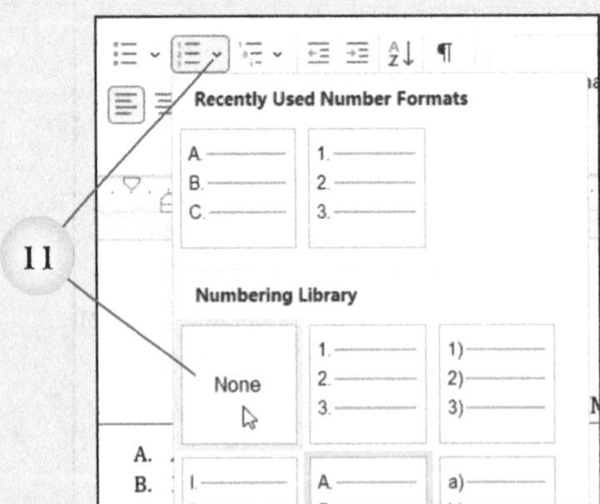

12. Decrease the paragraph indent by clicking the Decrease Indent button in the Paragraph group on the Home tab.
13. Save and then preview **8-FDAgenda.docx**.
14. Select and then delete the paragraph of text in the middle of the list (the paragraph that begins *The meeting will stop*). (All the lettered items should be listed consecutively and the same amount of space should appear between them.)
15. Save **8-FDAgenda.docx**.

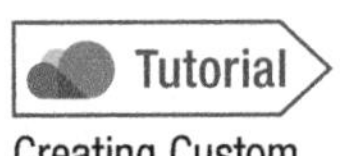

Creating Custom Numbering Formats

Quick Steps

Define New Number Format

1. Click Numbering button arrow.
2. Click *Define New Number Format.*
3. Specify format.
4. Click OK.

Creating Custom Numbering Formats

Along with default and custom numbers, custom numbering formats can be created with options at the Define New Number Format dialog box, shown in Figure 8.2. Display this dialog box by clicking the Numbering button arrow and then clicking *Define New Number Format* at the drop-down gallery. Use options at the dialog box to specify the number style, font, and alignment. Preview the formatting in the *Preview* section.

Any number format created at the Define New Number Format dialog box is automatically included in the *Numbering Library* section of the Numbering button drop-down gallery. Remove a number format from the drop-down gallery by right-clicking the format and then clicking *Remove* at the shortcut menu.

Figure 8.2 Define New Number Format Dialog Box

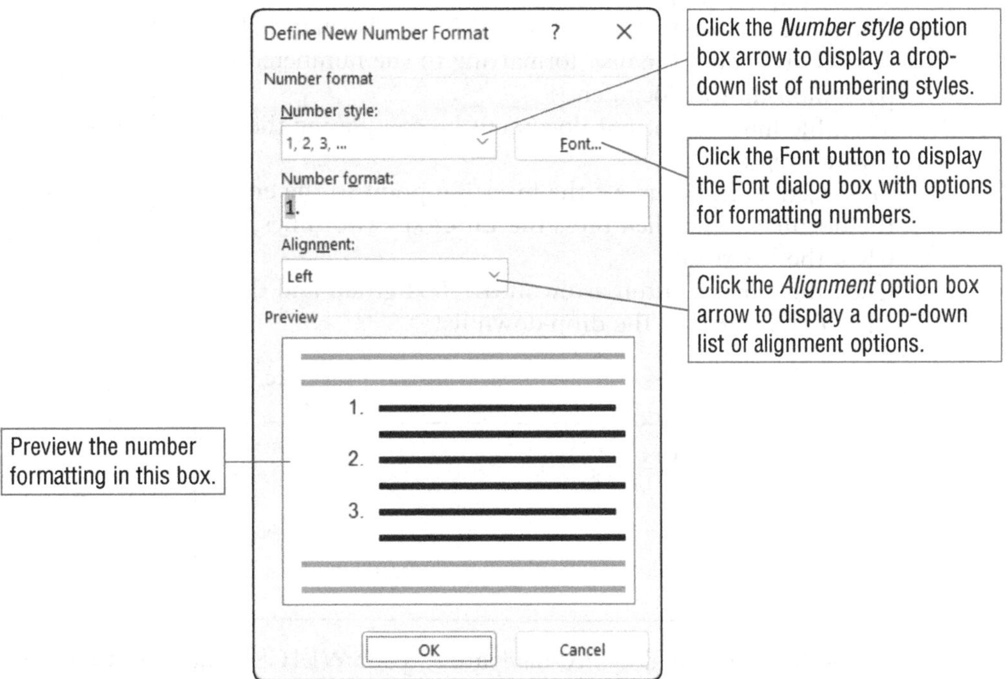

Activity 1b Creating a Numbering Format

Part 2 of 2

1. With **8-FDAgenda.docx** open, define a new numbering format by completing the following steps:
   a. With the insertion point positioned anywhere in the numbered paragraphs, click the Numbering button arrow in the Paragraph group on the Home tab.
   b. Click *Define New Number Format* at the drop-down gallery.
   c. At the Define New Number Format dialog box, click the *Number style* option box arrow and then click the *I, II, III, ...* option.
   d. Click the Font button at the right of the *Number style* list box.

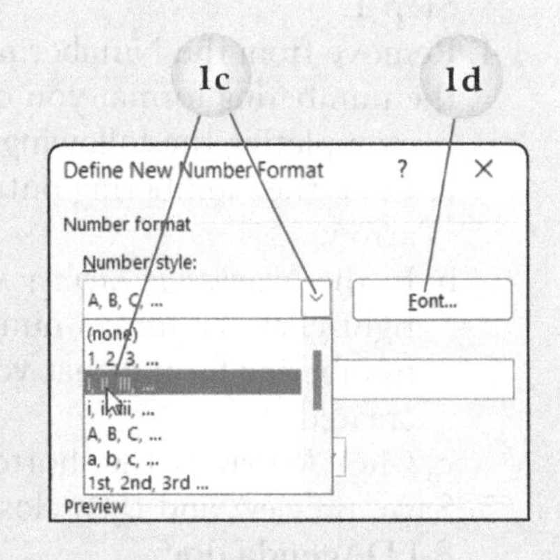

e. At the Font dialog box, scroll down the *Font* list box and then click *Calibri*.
f. Click *Bold* in the *Font style* list box.

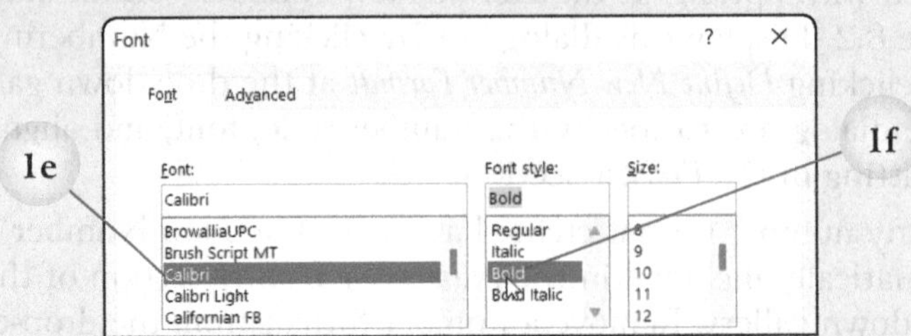

g. Click OK to close the Font dialog box.
h. Click the *Alignment* option box arrow and then click *Right* at the drop-down list.
i. Click OK to close the Define New Number Format dialog box. (This applies the new formatting to the numbered paragraphs in the document.)

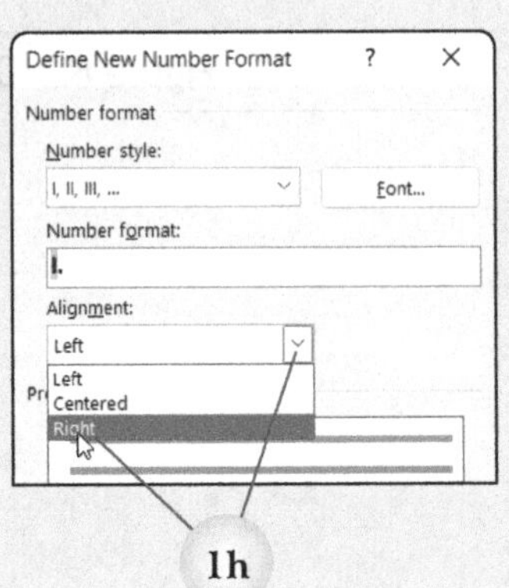

2. Insert a file into the current document by completing the following steps:
   a. Press Ctrl + End to move the insertion point to the end of the document and then press the Enter key two times.
   b. Click the Insert tab.
   c. Click the Object button arrow in the Text group and then click *Text from File* at the drop-down list.

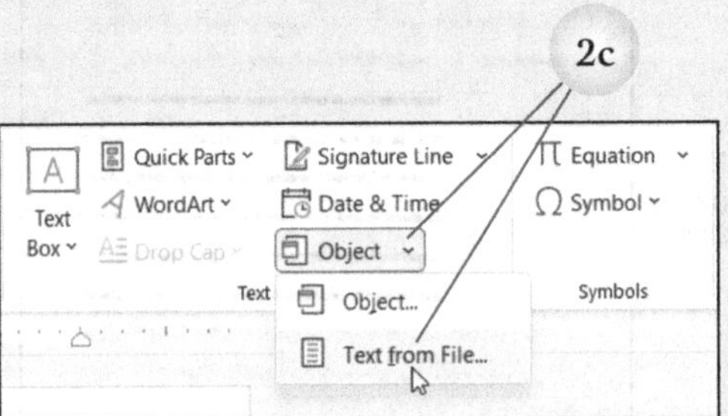

   d. At the Insert File dialog box, navigate to your WL1C8 folder and then double-click the *PDAgenda.docx* document.
3. Select the text below the title *PRODUCTION DEPARTMENT AGENDA*, click the Home tab, click the Numbering button arrow, and then click the roman numeral style created in Step 1.
4. Remove from the Numbering Library the numbering format you created by completing the following steps:
   a. Click the Numbering button arrow.
   b. In the *Numbering Library* section, right-click the roman numeral numbering format that you created.
   c. Click *Remove* at the shortcut menu.
5. Save, preview, and then close **8-FDAgenda.docx**.

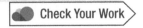

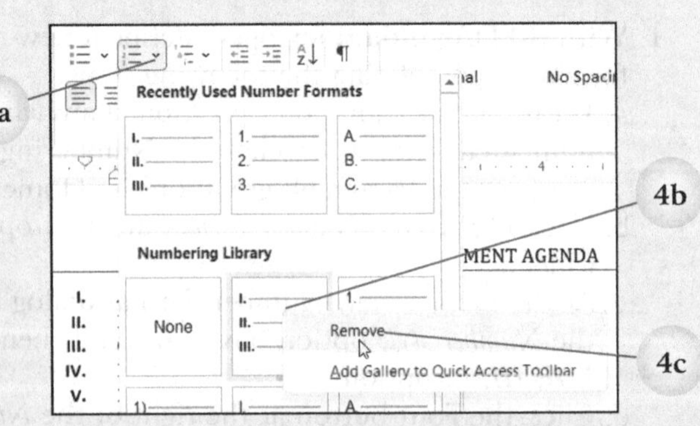

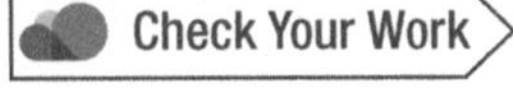

Activity 2 Apply Custom Bullets to an Adventure Document — 1 Part

You will open an adventure document and then define and insert custom picture and symbol bullets.

Creating Custom Bullets

Quick Steps

Define Custom Bullet

1. Click Bullets button arrow.
2. Click *Define New Bullet* at drop-down gallery.
3. Click Symbol button or Picture button.
4. Click symbol or picture.
5. Click OK.
6. Click OK.

Hint Create a picture bullet to add visual interest to a document.

Creating Custom Bullets

Click the Bullets button in the Paragraph group and a round bullet is inserted in the document. Insert custom bullets by clicking the Bullets button arrow and then clicking a bullet type at the drop-down gallery. This drop-down gallery displays the most recently used bullets along with an option for defining a new bullet.

Click the *Define New Bullet* option and the Define New Bullet dialog box displays, as shown in Figure 8.3. Use options at the dialog box to choose a symbol or picture bullet, change the font size of the bullet, and specify the alignment of the bullet. When creating a custom bullet, consider matching the theme or mood of the document to maintain a consistent look or create a picture bullet to add visual interest.

A custom bullet created at the Define New Bullet dialog box is automatically included in the *Bullet Library* section of the Bullets button drop-down gallery. Remove a custom bullet from the drop-down gallery by right-clicking the bullet and then clicking *Remove* at the shortcut menu.

As with the level of a numbered list, the level of a bulleted list can be changed. To do this, click the item or select the items to be changed, click the Bullets button arrow, and then point to *Change List Level*. At the side menu of bullet options that displays, click a bullet. To insert a line break in the list while the automatic bullets feature is on without inserting a bullet, press Shift + Enter. (A line break can also be inserted in a numbered list without inserting a number by pressing Shift + Enter.)

Figure 8.3 Define New Bullet Dialog Box

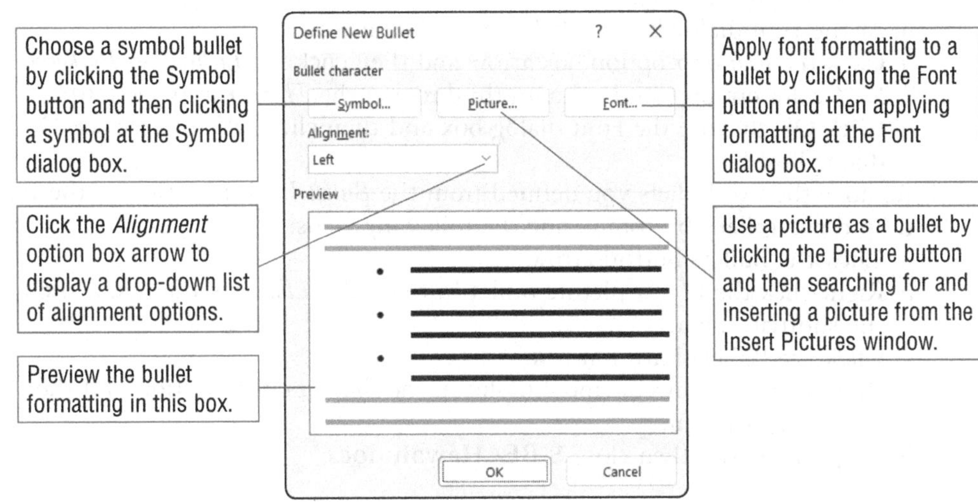
Choose a symbol bullet by clicking the Symbol button and then clicking a symbol at the Symbol dialog box.
Click the *Alignment* option box arrow to display a drop-down list of alignment options.
Preview the bullet formatting in this box.
Define New Bullet
Bullet character
Symbol...
Picture...
Font...
Alignment:
Left
Preview
OK
Cancel
Apply font formatting to a bullet by clicking the Font button and then applying formatting at the Font dialog box.
Use a picture as a bullet by clicking the Picture button and then searching for and inserting a picture from the Insert Pictures window.

Activity 2 Creating Custom Bullets

Part 1 of 1

1. Open **BEAHawaii.docx** and then save it with the name **8-BEAHawaii.**
2. Define and insert a picture bullet by completing the following steps:
   a. Select the four paragraphs of text below the heading *Rainy Day Activities*.
   b. Click the Bullets button arrow in the Paragraph group on the Home tab and then click *Define New Bullet* at the drop-down gallery.
   c. At the Define New Bullet dialog box, click the Picture button.
   d. At the Insert Pictures window, click the *Browse* option at the right of the *From a file* option, navigate to your WL1C8 folder, and then double-click the ***Flower.png*** image file.
   e. Click OK to close the Define New Bullet dialog box. (The new bullet is applied to the selected paragraphs.)

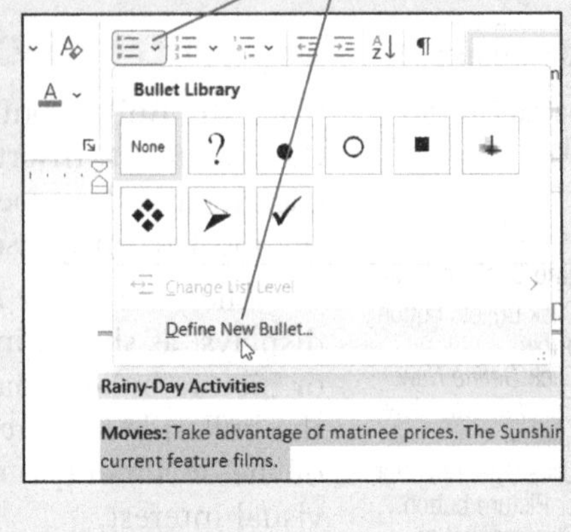

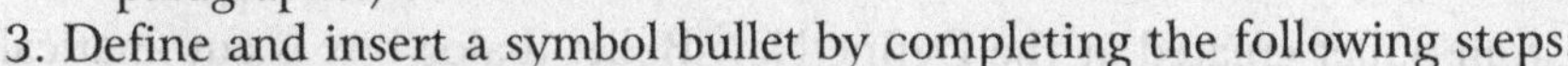

3. Define and insert a symbol bullet by completing the following steps:
   a. Select the six paragraphs below the heading *Kauai Sights*.
   b. Click the Bullets button arrow and then click *Define New Bullet* at the drop-down gallery.
   c. At the Define New Bullet dialog box, click the Symbol button.
   d. At the Symbol dialog box, click the *Font* option box arrow, scroll down the drop-down list, and then click *Wingdings*.
   e. Click the flower symbol shown at the right (character code 124).
   f. Click OK to close the Symbol dialog box.
   g. At the Define New Bullet dialog box, click the Font button.
   h. At the Font dialog box, click *11* in the *Size* list box.
   i. Click the *Font color* option box arrow and then click the *Light Blue, Background 2, Darker 25%* color option (third column, third row in the *Theme Colors* section).
   j. Click OK to close the Font dialog box and then click OK to close the Define New Bullet dialog box.
4. Remove the two bullets you defined from the *Bullet Library* section of the Bullets button drop-down gallery by completing the following steps:
   a. Click the Bullets button arrow.
   b. Right-click the flower picture bullet in the *Bullet Library* section and then click *Remove* at the shortcut menu.
   c. Click the Bullets button arrow.
   d. Right-click the flower symbol bullet in the *Bullet Library* section and then click *Remove* at the shortcut menu.
5. Save, preview, and then close **8-BEAHawaii.docx**.

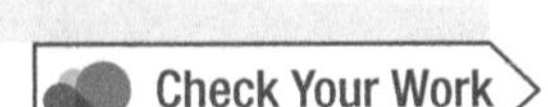

Activity 3 Apply Multilevel List Numbering to a Job Search Document

2 Parts

You will open a document containing a list of job search terms, apply multilevel list numbering to the text, and then define and apply a new multilevel list numbering style.

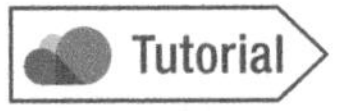

Applying Multilevel List Formatting

Multilevel List

Quick Steps

Insert Multilevel List Formatting

1. Click Multilevel List button.
2. Click style at drop-down gallery.

Applying Multilevel List Formatting

Use the Multilevel List button in the Paragraph group on the Home tab to specify the type of list formatting for paragraphs of text at the left margin, first tab, second tab, and so on. To apply predesigned multilevel list formatting to text in a document, click the Multilevel List button and then click a list style at the drop-down list.

Some options at the Multilevel List button drop-down list have labels such as *Heading 1*, *Heading 2*, and so on after the numbers. Click one of these options and Word inserts the numbering and applies the heading styles to the text.

Activity 3a Inserting Multilevel List Formatting

Part 1 of 2

1. Open **JSList.docx** and then save it with the name **8-JSList(3a)**.
2. Select the paragraphs of text below the title and then apply multilevel list formatting by completing the following steps:
   a. Click the Multilevel List button in the Paragraph group on the Home tab.
   b. At the drop-down list, click the middle option in the top row of the *List Library* section.

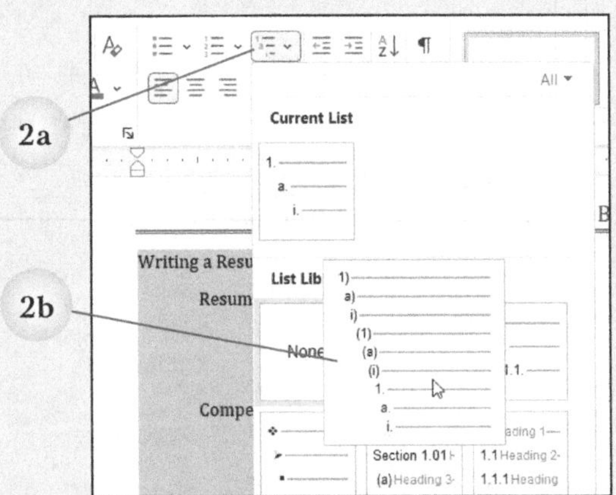

   c. Deselect the text.
3. Save, preview, and then close **8-JSList(3a).docx**.

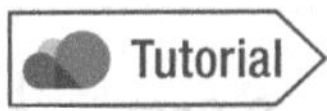

Creating a Custom Multilevel List Option

Quick Steps

Define Multilevel List

1. Click Multilevel List button.
2. Click *Define New Multilevel List.*
3. Choose level, list format, and/or position.
4. Click OK.

Hint When defining a multilevel list, you can mix numbers and bullets in the same list.

Creating a Custom Multilevel List

The Multilevel List button drop-down list contains predesigned level formatting options. If the drop-down list does not contain the type of list formatting required, create custom list formatting. To do this, click the Multilevel List button and then click the *Define New Multilevel List* option. This displays the Define new Multilevel list dialog box, shown in Figure 8.4. At this dialog box, click a level in the *Click level to modify* list box and then specify the level format, style, position, and alignment.

Typing a Multilevel List

Select text and then apply a multilevel list or apply the list and then type the text. When typing the text, press the Tab key to move to the next level or press Shift + Tab to move to the previous level.

Figure 8.4 Define New Multilevel List Dialog Box

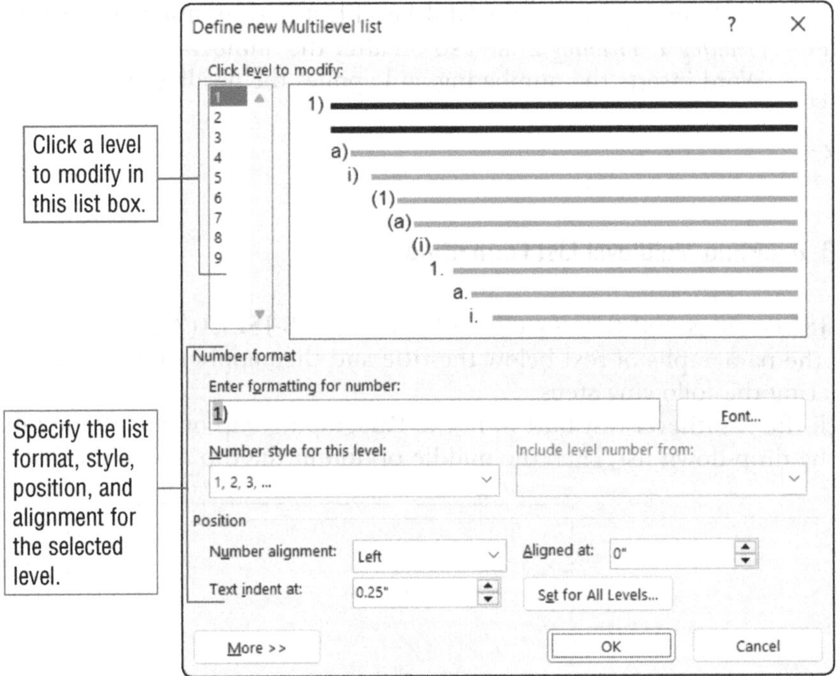

Activity 3b Creating and Applying a New Multilevel List

1. Open **JSList.docx** and then save it with the name **8-JSList(3b)**.
2. Select the paragraphs of text below the title.
3. Click the Multilevel List button in the Paragraph group on the Home tab.
4. Click the *Define New Multilevel List* option at the drop-down list.
5. At the Define new Multilevel list dialog box, make sure *1* is selected in the *Click level to modify* list box.
6. Click the *Number style for this level* option box arrow and then click *A, B, C, …* at the drop-down list.
7. Click in the *Enter formatting for number* text box, delete any text after *A*, and then type a period. (See image at the right.)
8. Click the *Aligned at* measurement box up arrow until *0.3"* displays in the measurement box.
9. Click the *Text indent at* measurement box up arrow until *0.6"* displays in the measurement box.

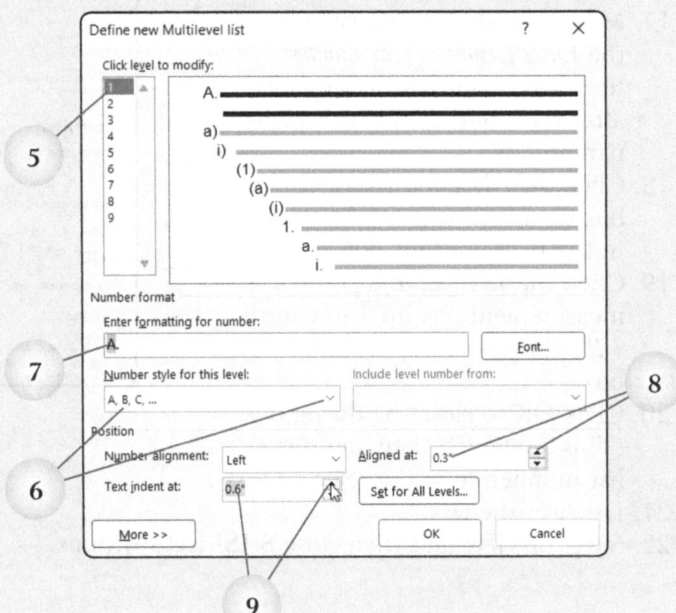

10. Click *2* in the *Click level to modify* list box.
11. Click the *Number style for this level* option box arrow and then click *1, 2, 3, …* at the drop-down list.
12. Click in the *Enter formatting for number* text box, delete any text after the *1*, and then type a period.
13. Click the *Aligned at* measurement box up arrow until *0.6"* displays in the measurement box.
14. Click the *Text indent at* measurement box up arrow until *0.9"* displays in the measurement box.

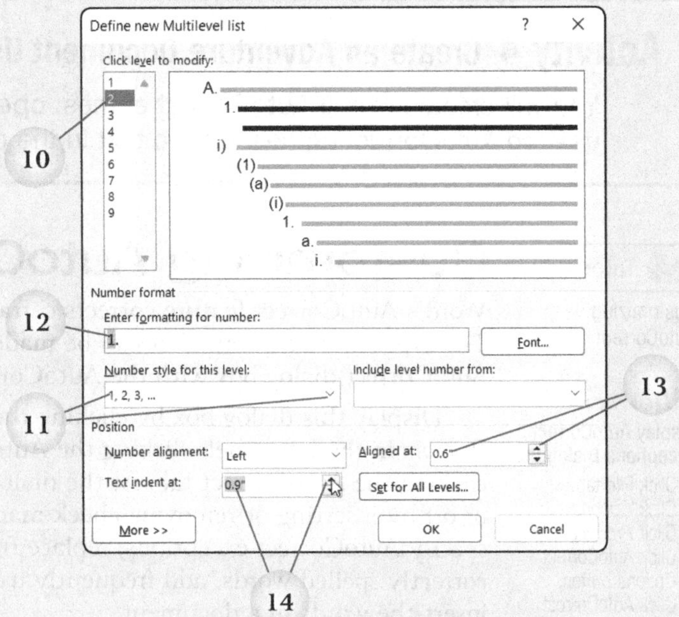

15. Click *3* in the *Click level to modify* list box.
16. Click the *Number style for this level* option box arrow and then click *a, b, c, ...* at the drop-down list.
17. Make sure that *a)* appears in the *Enter formatting for number* text box. (If not, delete any text after the *a* and then type a right parenthesis.)
18. Click the *Aligned at* measurement box up arrow until *0.9"* displays in the measurement box.
19. Click the *Text indent at* measurement box up arrow until *1.2"* displays in the measurement box.
20. Click OK to close the dialog box. (This applies the new multilevel list numbering to the selected text.)
21. Deselect the text.
22. Save, preview, and then close **8-JSList(3b).docx**.

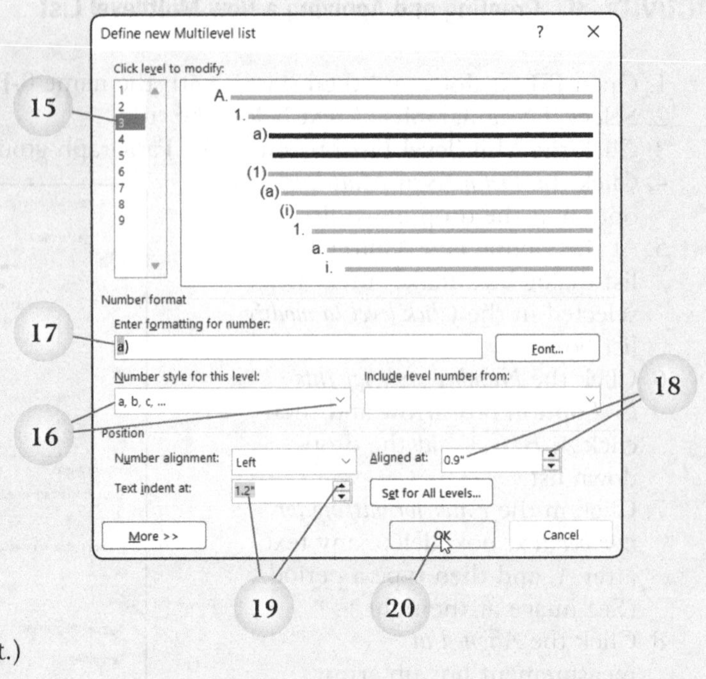

Check Your Work

Activity 4 Create an Adventure Document Using AutoCorrect — 4 Parts

You will create several AutoCorrect entries, open a letterhead document, and then use the AutoCorrect entries to type text in the document.

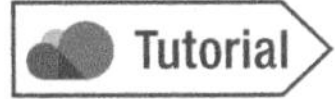
Tutorial

Customizing AutoCorrect

Quick Steps

Display AutoCorrect Exceptions Dialog Box

1. Click File tab.
2. Click *Options*.
3. Click *Proofing*.
4. Click AutoCorrect Options button.
5. Click AutoCorrect tab.
6. Click Exceptions button.

Customizing AutoCorrect

Word's AutoCorrect feature corrects certain text automatically as it is typed. The types of corrections that can be made are specified with options at the AutoCorrect dialog box with the AutoCorrect tab selected, as shown in Figure 8.5.

Display this dialog box by clicking the File tab, clicking *Options*, clicking *Proofing* in the left panel, clicking the AutoCorrect Options button, and then clicking the AutoCorrect tab. At the dialog box, turn AutoCorrect features on or off by inserting or removing check marks from the check boxes. In addition, specify AutoCorrect exceptions, replace frequently misspelled words with the correctly spelled words, add frequently used words, and specify keys to quickly insert the words in a document.

Figure 8.5 AutoCorrect Dialog Box with the AutoCorrect Tab Selected

AutoCorrect: English (United States)

AutoCorrect | Math AutoCorrect | AutoFormat As You Type | AutoFormat | Actions

Show AutoCorrect Options buttons

Correct TWo INitial CApitals

Exceptions...

Capitalize first letter of sentences

Capitalize first letter of table cells

Capitalize names of days

Correct accidental usage of cAPS LOCK key

Replace text as you type

Replace: With: Plain text Formatted text

(c)	©
(e)	€
(r)	®
(tm)	™
...	…
:(	☹
:-(	☹

Add Delete

Automatically use suggestions from the spelling checker

OK Cancel

Remove the check marks from the check boxes identifying corrections that should not be made by AutoCorrect.

Click this button to display the AutoCorrect Exceptions dialog box.

Type the text shown in the first column of this list box in a document and then press the spacebar or press the Enter key and the text is replaced by the symbol or text shown in the second column.

Specifying AutoCorrect Exceptions

The check box options at the AutoCorrect dialog box with the AutoCorrect tab selected identify the types of corrections made by AutoCorrect. Specify which corrections should not be made with options at the AutoCorrect Exceptions dialog box, shown in Figure 8.6. Display this dialog box by clicking the Exceptions button at the AutoCorrect dialog box with the AutoCorrect tab selected.

AutoCorrect usually capitalizes a word that comes after a period, since a period usually ends a sentence. This automatic capitalization may be incorrect in some cases, as when the period is used in an abbreviation. Exceptions to this general practice are shown in the AutoCorrect Exceptions dialog box with the First Letter tab selected. Many exceptions already display in the dialog box but additional exceptions can be added by typing each exception in the *Don't capitalize after* text box and then clicking the Add button.

Figure 8.6 AutoCorrect Exceptions Dialog Box

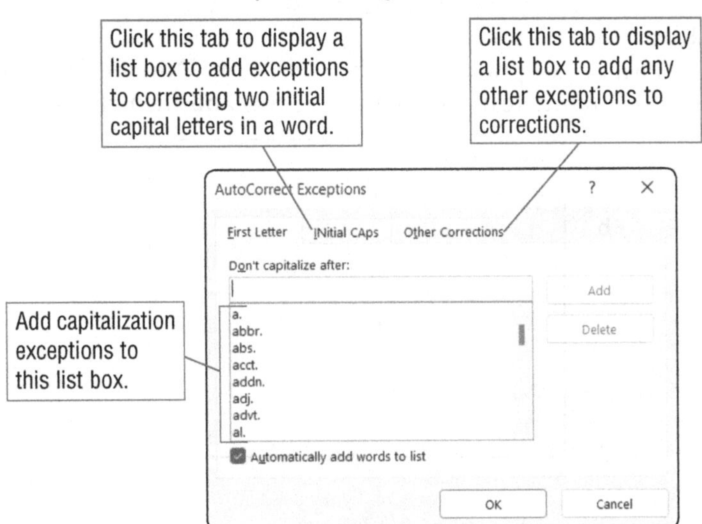
Click this tab to display a list box to add exceptions to correcting two initial capital letters in a word.
Click this tab to display a list box to add any other exceptions to corrections.
AutoCorrect Exceptions
First Letter
INitial CAps
Other Corrections
Don't capitalize after:
Add
Delete
a.
abbr.
abs.
acct.
addn.
adj.
advt.
al.
Add capitalization exceptions to this list box.
Automatically add words to list
OK
Cancel

By default, AutoCorrect corrects the use of two initial capital letters in a word. If AutoCorrect should not correct these instances, display the AutoCorrect Exceptions dialog box with the INitial CAps tab selected and then type the exception text in the *Don't correct* text box. At the AutoCorrect Exceptions dialog box with the Other Corrections tab selected, type the text that should not be corrected in the *Don't correct* text box. Delete an exception from the dialog box with any of the tabs selected by clicking the text in the list box and then clicking the Delete button.

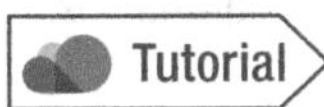

Adding and Deleting an AutoCorrect Entry

Quick Steps

Add Word to AutoCorrect

1. Click File tab.
2. Click *Options*.
3. Click *Proofing*.
4. Click AutoCorrect Options button.
5. Click AutoCorrect tab.
6. Type misspelled or abbreviated word.
7. Press Tab.
8. Type correctly spelled or complete word.
9. Click Add button.
10. Click OK.

Adding and Deleting an AutoCorrect Entry

Commonly misspelled words and/or typographical errors can be added to AutoCorrect. For example, if a user consistently types *relavent* instead of *relevant*, *relavent* can be added to the AutoCorrect dialog box with the AutoCorrect tab selected with the direction to correct it to *relevant*. The AutoCorrect dialog box also contains a few symbols that can be inserted in a document. For example, type *(c)* and AutoCorrect changes the text to © (copyright symbol). Type *(r)* and AutoCorrect changes the text to ® (registered trademark symbol). The symbols display at the beginning of the AutoCorrect dialog box list box.

An abbreviation can be added to AutoCorrect that will insert the entire word (or words) in the document when it is typed. For example, in Activity 4a, the abbreviation *fav* will be added to AutoCorrect and *Family Adventure Vacations* will be inserted when *fav* is typed followed by a press of the spacebar or Enter key. The capitalization of the abbreviation can also be controlled. For example, in Activity 4a, the abbreviation *Na* will be added to AutoCorrect and *Namibia* will be inserted when *Na* is typed and *NAMIBIA* will be inserted when *NA* is typed.

AutoCorrect text can be deleted from the AutoCorrect dialog box. To do this, display the AutoCorrect dialog box with the AutoCorrect tab selected, click the word or words in the list box, and then click the Delete button.

Activity 4a Adding Text and Specifying Exceptions to AutoCorrect **Part 1 of 4**

1. At a blank screen, click the File tab and then click *Options*.
2. At the Word Options dialog box, click *Proofing* in the left panel.
3. Click the AutoCorrect Options button in the *AutoCorrect options* section.
4. At the AutoCorrect dialog box with the AutoCorrect tab selected, add an exception to AutoCorrect by completing the following steps:
   a. Click the Exceptions button.
   b. At the AutoCorrect Exceptions dialog box, click the INitial CAps tab.
   c. Click in the *Don't correct* text box, type STudent, and then click the Add button.

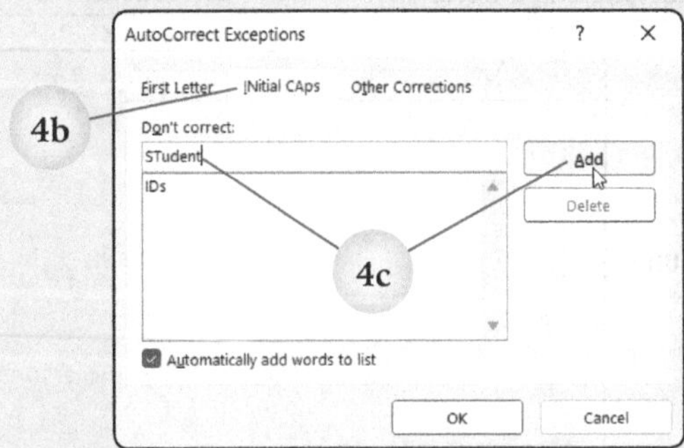

d. Click in the *Don't correct* text box, type STyle, and then click the Add button.
e. Click OK.

5. At the AutoCorrect dialog box with the AutoCorrect tab selected, click in the *Replace* text box and then type fav.
6. Press the Tab key (which moves the insertion point to the *With* text box) and then type Family Adventure Vacations.
7. Click the Add button. (This adds *fav* and *Family Adventure Vacations* to AutoCorrect and also selects *fav* in the *Replace* text box.)

8. Type Na in the *Replace* text box. (The text *fav* is automatically removed when you begin typing *Na*.)
9. Press the Tab key and then type Namibia.
10. Click the Add button.
11. With the insertion point positioned in the *Replace* text box, type vf.
12. Press the Tab key and then type Victoria Falls.
13. Click the Add button.
14. With the insertion point positioned in the *Replace* text box, type bea.
15. Press the Tab key and then type Blue Earth Adventures.
16. Click the Add button.
17. Click OK to close the AutoCorrect dialog box and then click OK to close the Word Options dialog box.
18. Open **BEALtrhd.docx** and then save it with the name **8-BEAAfrica**.
19. Type the text shown in Figure 8.7. Type the text exactly as shown (including applying bold formatting and centering *fav* at the beginning of the document). AutoCorrect will correct the words as they are typed.
20. Save **8-BEAAfrica.docx**.

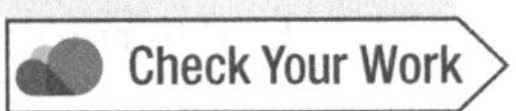

Figure 8.7 Activity 4a

> **fav**
>
> Na and vf Adventure
>
> bea is partnering with fav to provide adventurous and thrilling family vacations. Our first joint adventure is a holiday trip to Na. Na is one of the most fascinating holiday destinations in Africa and offers comfortable facilities, great food, cultural interaction, abundant wildlife, and a wide variety of activities to interest people of all ages. During the 12-day trip, you and your family will travel across Na through national parks, enjoying the beautiful and exotic scenery and watching wildlife in natural habitats.
>
> If you or your family member is a college student, contact one of our college travel adventure consultants to learn more about the newest Student Travel package titled "STudent STyle" that offers a variety of student discounts, rebates, and free travel accessories for qualifying participants.
>
> bea and fav are offering a 15 percent discount if you sign up for this once-in-a-lifetime trip to Na. This exciting adventure is limited to 20 people, so don't wait to sign up.

Undoing an AutoCorrect Correction

Using the AutoCorrect Options Button

After AutoCorrect corrects a portion of text, hover the pointer near the text and a small blue box displays below it. Move the pointer to this blue box and the AutoCorrect Options button displays. Click this button to display a drop-down list with the options to change the text back to the original version, stop automatically correcting the specific text, and display the AutoCorrect dialog box.

AutoCorrect Options

If the AutoCorrect Options button does not display, turn on the feature. To do this, display the AutoCorrect dialog box with the AutoCorrect tab selected, click the *Show AutoCorrect Options buttons* check box to insert a check mark, and then click OK to close the dialog box.

Activity 4b Using the AutoCorrect Options Button — Part 2 of 4

1. With **8-BEAAfrica.docx** open, select and then delete the last paragraph.
2. With the insertion point positioned on the blank line below the last paragraph of text (you may need to press the Enter key), type the following text. (AutoCorrect will automatically change *Ameria* to *America*, which you will change in the next step.) Through the sponsorship of Ameria Resorts, we are able to offer you a 15 percent discount for groups of 12 or more people.
3. Change the spelling of *America* back to *Ameria* by completing the following steps:
   a. Position the pointer over *America* until a blue box displays below it.
   b. Position the pointer on the blue box until the AutoCorrect Options button displays.

c. Click the AutoCorrect Options button and then click the *Change back to "Ameria"* option.
4. Save and then preview **8-BEAAfrica.docx**.

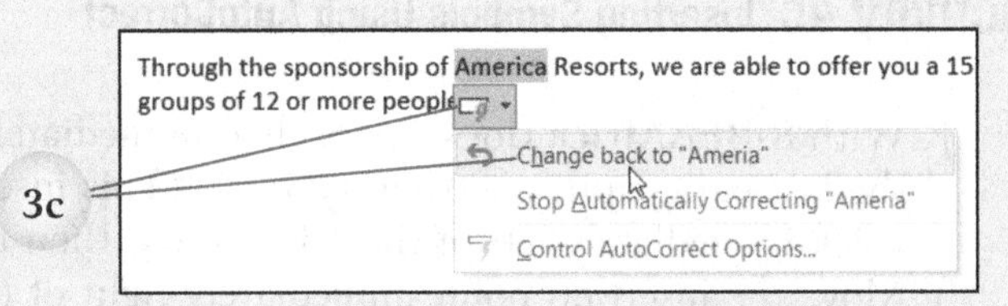

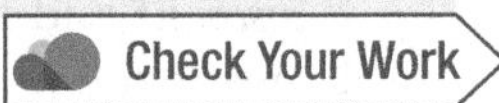

Inserting Symbols Automatically

AutoCorrect recognizes and replaces symbols as well as text. Several symbols included in AutoCorrect are shown in the AutoCorrect dialog box and are listed first in the *Replace* text box. Table 8.1 lists these symbols along with the characters to insert them.

In addition to the symbols provided by Word, other symbols can be inserted in the AutoCorrect dialog box with the AutoCorrect button in the Symbol dialog box. To insert a symbol in the AutoCorrect dialog box, click the Insert tab, click the Symbol button in the Symbols group, and then click *More Symbols* at the drop-down list. At the Symbol dialog box, click the specific symbol and then click the AutoCorrect button in the lower left corner of the dialog box. This displays the AutoCorrect dialog box with the symbol inserted in the *With* text box and the insertion point positioned in the *Replace* text box. Type the text that will insert the symbol, click the Add button, and then click OK to close the AutoCorrect dialog box. Click the Close button to close the Symbol dialog box.

Table 8.1 AutoCorrect Symbols Available at the AutoCorrect Dialog Box

Type	To insert
(c)	©
(r)	®
(tm)	™
...	. . .
:) or :-)	☺
:| or :-|	😐
:(or :-(	☹
-->	→
<--	←
==>	➔
<==	🡐
<=>	⇔

Activity 4c Inserting Symbols Using AutoCorrect

1. With **8-BEAAfrica.docx** open, click immediately right of the last *s* in *Resorts* (located in the last paragraph) and then type (r). (This inserts the registered trademark symbol.)
2. Click immediately left of the *1* in *15* and then type ==>. (This inserts the ➔ symbol.)
3. Move the insertion point immediately right of the *t* in *discount* and then type <==. (This inserts the 🡐 symbol.)
4. Insert the pound (£) currency unit symbol in AutoCorrect by completing the following steps:
   a. Click the Insert tab.
   b. Click the Symbol button and then click *More Symbols* at the drop-down list.
   c. At the Symbol dialog box, make sure that *(normal text)* displays in the *Font* option box. If it does not, click the *Font* option box arrow and then click *(normal text)* at the drop-down list (first option in the list).
   d. Scroll through the list of symbols and then click the pound (£) currency unit symbol (located in approximately the sixth or seventh row; character code *00A3*).
   e. Click the AutoCorrect button in the lower left corner of the dialog box.
   f. At the AutoCorrect dialog box, type pcu in the *Replace* text box and then click the Add button.
   g. Click OK to close the AutoCorrect dialog box.

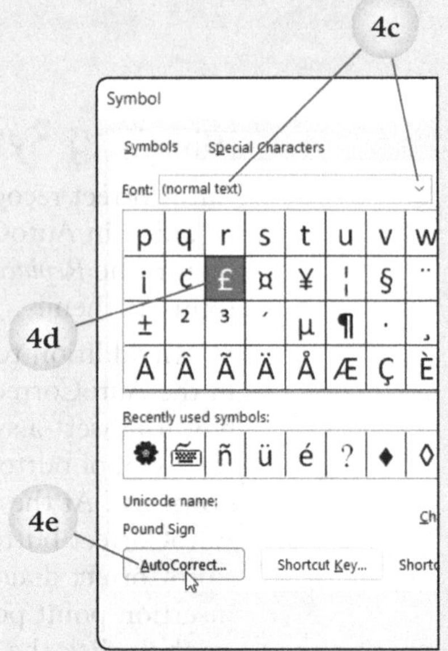

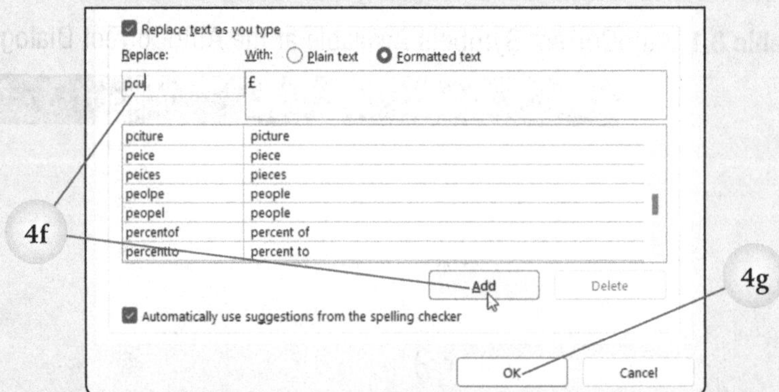

   h. Click the Close button to close the Symbol dialog box.
5. Press Ctrl + End to move the insertion point to the end of the document and then press the Enter key.
6. Type the text shown in Figure 8.8. (Press Shift + Enter or the Enter key as indicated in the figure.) Create the pound currency unit symbol by typing pcu and then pressing the spacebar. Press the Backspace key once and then type 2,999. (Complete similar steps when typing *£2,549 (UK)*.)
7. Save **8-BEAAfrica.docx**.

Figure 8.8 Activity 4c

Individual price: *(press Shift+ Enter)*
$3,999 (US) *(press Shift+ Enter)*
£2,999 (UK) *(press Enter)*

Individual price for groups of 12 or more: *(press Shift+ Enter)*
$3,399 (US) *(press Shift+ Enter)*
£2,549 (UK)

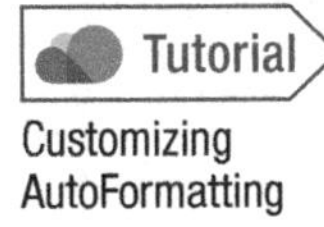

Customizing AutoFormatting

Customizing AutoFormatting

When typing text, Word provides options to automatically apply some formatting, such as changing a fraction to a fraction character (1/2 to ½), changing numbers to ordinals (1st to 1st), changing an internet or network path to a hyperlink (https://ppi-edu.net to https://ppi-edu.net), and applying bullets or numbers to text. The autoformatting options display in the AutoCorrect dialog box with the AutoFormat As You Type tab selected, as shown in Figure 8.9.

Display this dialog box by clicking the File tab and then clicking *Options*. At the Word Options dialog box, click *Proofing* in the left panel and then click the AutoCorrect Options button. At the AutoCorrect dialog box, click the AutoFormat As You Type tab. At the dialog box, remove the check marks from those options to be turned off and insert check marks for those options to be formatted automatically.

Figure 8.9 AutoCorrect Dialog Box with the AutoFormat As You Type Tab Selected

AutoCorrect ? X
AutoCorrect | Math AutoCorrect | AutoFormat As You Type | AutoFormat | Actions

Replace as you type
- [x] "Straight quotes" with "smart quotes"
- [x] Fractions (1/2) with fraction character (½)
- [ ] *Bold* and _italic_ with real formatting
- [x] Internet and network paths with hyperlinks
- [x] Ordinals (1st) with superscript
- [x] Hyphens (--) with dash (—)

Apply as you type
- [x] Automatic bulleted lists
- [x] Border lines
- [ ] Built-in Heading styles
- [x] Automatic numbered lists
- [x] Tables

Automatically as you type
- [x] Format beginning of list item like the one before it
- [x] Set left- and first-indent with tabs and backspaces
- [ ] Define styles based on your formatting

OK | Cancel

Insert check marks in the check boxes for formatting options that Word should apply automatically.

Click this tab to display options for formats that Word should apply automatically as text is being typed.

Activity 4d Changing AutoFormatting and Deleting AutoCorrect Text

1. Make sure **8-BEAAfrica.docx** is open.
2. Suppose that you need to add a couple of web addresses to a document and do not want the addresses automatically formatted as hyperlinks (since you are sending the document as hard copy rather than electronically). Turn off the autoformatting of web addresses by completing the following steps:
   a. Click the File tab and then click *Options*.
   b. At the Word Options dialog box, click *Proofing* in the left panel.
   c. Click the AutoCorrect Options button.
   d. At the AutoCorrect dialog box, click the AutoFormat As You Type tab.
   e. Click the *Internet and network paths with hyperlinks* check box to remove the check mark.

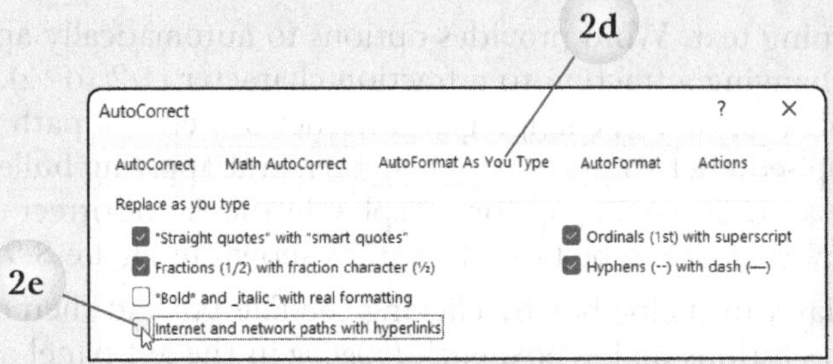

   f. Click OK to close the AutoCorrect dialog box.
   g. Click OK to close the Word Options dialog box.
3. Press Ctrl + End to move the insertion point to the end of the document, press the Enter key, and then type the text shown in Figure 8.10.
4. Turn on the autoformatting of web addresses that was turned off in Step 2 by completing Steps 2a through 2g (except in Step 2e, insert the check mark rather than remove it).
5. Delete *fav* from AutoCorrect by completing the following steps:
   a. Click the File tab and then click *Options*.
   b. At the Word Options dialog box, click *Proofing* in the left panel.
   c. Click the AutoCorrect Options button.
   d. At the AutoCorrect dialog box, click the AutoCorrect tab.
   e. Click in the *Replace* text box and then type fav. (This selects the entry in the list box.)
   f. Click the Delete button.
6. Complete steps similar to those in Steps 5e and 5f to delete the *Na*, *vf*, and *bea* AutoCorrect entries.

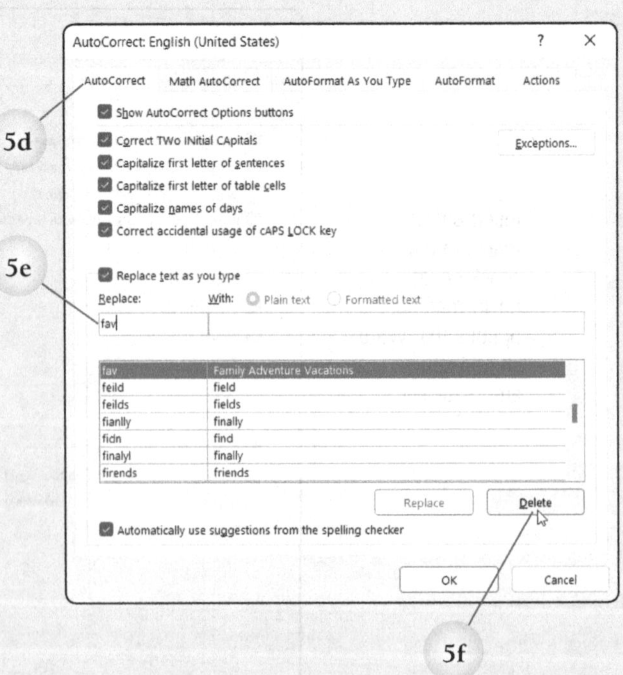

7. Delete the exceptions added to the AutoCorrect Exceptions dialog box by completing the following steps:
   a. At the AutoCorrect dialog box with the AutoCorrect tab selected, click the Exceptions button.
   b. At the AutoCorrect Exceptions dialog box, if necessary, click the INitial CAps tab.
   c. Click *STudent* in the list box and then click the Delete button.
   d. Click *STyle* in the list box and then click the Delete button.
   e. Click OK to close the AutoCorrect Exceptions dialog box.
8. Click OK to close the AutoCorrect dialog box.
9. Click OK to close the Word Options dialog box.
10. Save, preview, and then close **3-BEAAfrica.docx**.

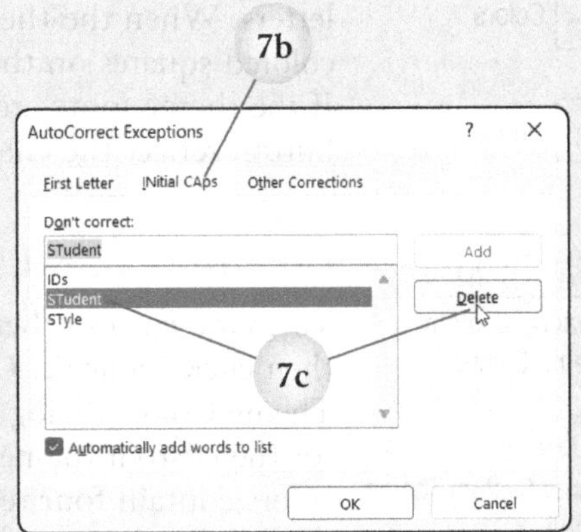

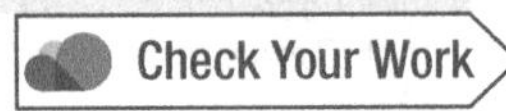

Figure 8.10 Activity 4d

For additional information on the Na adventure, as well as other exciting vacation specials, please visit our website at https://ppi-edu.net/BlueEarth or visit https://ppi-edu.net/FamAdvs.

Activity 5 Apply Custom Themes to Company Documents — 5 Parts

You will create custom theme colors and theme fonts and then apply theme effects. You will save the changes as a custom theme, apply the custom theme to a company services document and a company security document, and then delete the theme.

Customizing Themes

A document created in Word is based on the Normal template. This template provides a document with default layout, formatting, styles, and themes. The Normal template provides a number of built-in or predesigned themes. Some of these built-in themes have been used in previous chapters to apply colors, fonts, and effects to content in documents. The same built-in themes are available in Microsoft Word, Excel, Access, PowerPoint, and Outlook. Because the same themes are available across these applications, business files—such as documents, workbooks, databases, and presentations—can be branded with a consistent and professional appearance.

Hint Every document created in Word has a theme applied to it.

A theme is a combination of theme colors, theme fonts, and theme effects. Within a theme, any of these three elements can be changed with the additional buttons in the Document Formatting group on the Design tab. Apply one of the built-in themes or create a custom theme. A custom theme will display in the *Custom* section of the Themes button drop-down gallery. To create a custom theme, change the theme colors, theme fonts, and/or theme effects.

The Themes, Colors, and Fonts buttons in the Document Formatting group on the Design tab provide representations of the current theme. For example, the Themes button shows uppercase and lowercase *Aa* with colored squares below the letters. When the theme colors are changed, the changes are reflected in the small colored squares on the Themes button and the four squares on the Colors button. If the theme fonts are changed, the letters on the Themes button and the Fonts button reflect the change.

Creating Custom Theme Colors

Quick Steps

Create Custom Theme Colors

1. Click Design tab.
2. Click Colors button.
3. Click *Customize Colors.*
4. Type name for custom theme colors.
5. Change background, accent, and hyperlink colors.
6. Click Save button.

Creating Custom Theme Colors

To create custom theme colors, click the Design tab, click the Colors button, and then click *Customize Colors* at the drop-down gallery. This displays the Create New Theme Colors dialog box, similar to the one shown in Figure 8.11. Type a name for the custom theme colors in the *Name* text box and then change colors. Theme colors contain four text and background colors, six accent colors, and two hyperlink colors, as shown in the *Theme colors* section of the dialog box. Change a color in the list box by clicking the color button at the right of the color option and then clicking a color at the color palette.

After making all the changes to the colors, click the Save button. This saves the custom theme colors and also applies the color changes to the active document. Display the custom theme colors by clicking the Colors button. The custom theme colors will display at the top of the drop-down gallery in the *Custom* section.

Resetting Custom Theme Colors

If changes have been made to colors at the Create New Theme Colors dialog box, the colors can be reset by clicking the Reset button in the lower left corner of the dialog box. Clicking this button restores the colors to the default Office theme colors.

Figure 8.11 Create New Theme Colors Dialog Box

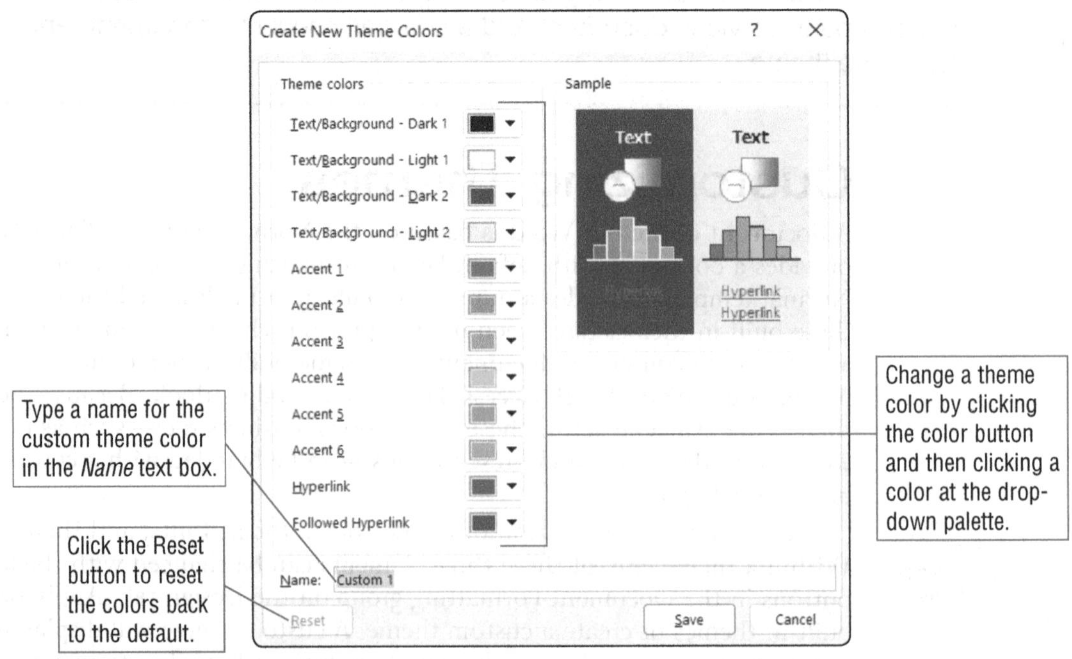

Activity 5a Creating Custom Theme Colors

Part 1 of 5

Note: If you are running Word on a computer connected to a network in a public environment, such as a school, you may need to complete all five parts of Activity 5 during the same session. Network system software may delete your custom themes when you exit Word. Check with your instructor.

1. At a blank document, click the Design tab.
2. Click the Colors button in the Document Formatting group and then click *Customize Colors* at the drop-down gallery.
3. At the Create New Theme Colors dialog box, type your first and last names in the *Name* text box.
4. Click the color button to the right of the *Text/Background - Light 1* option and then click the *Dark Red* color (first color option in the *Standard Colors* section).

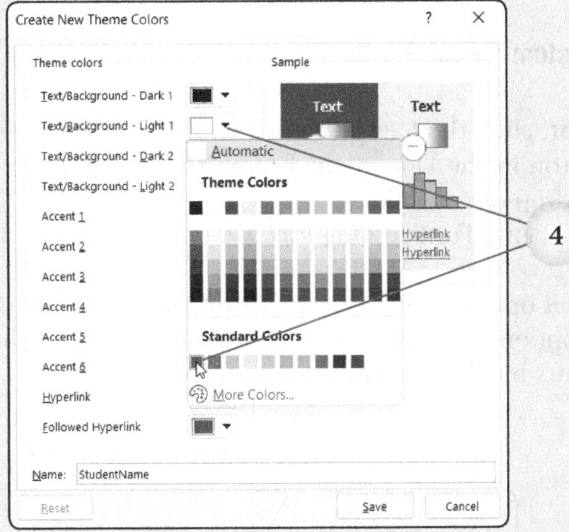

5. Click the color button to the right of the *Accent 1* option and then click the *Yellow* color (fourth color option in the *Standard Colors* section).
6. You decide that you do not like the colors you have chosen and want to start over. To do this, click the Reset button in the lower left corner of the dialog box.
7. Click the color button to the right of the *Text/Background - Dark 2* option and then click the *Blue* color (eighth color option in the *Standard Colors* section).
8. Change the color for the *Accent 1* option by completing the following steps:
   a. Click the color button to the right of the *Accent 1* option.
   b. Click the *More Colors* option below the color palette.
   c. At the Colors dialog box, click the Standard tab.
   d. Click the dark green color, as shown at the right.
   e. Click OK to close the dialog box.
9. Save the custom theme colors by clicking the Save button.
10. Close the document without saving it.

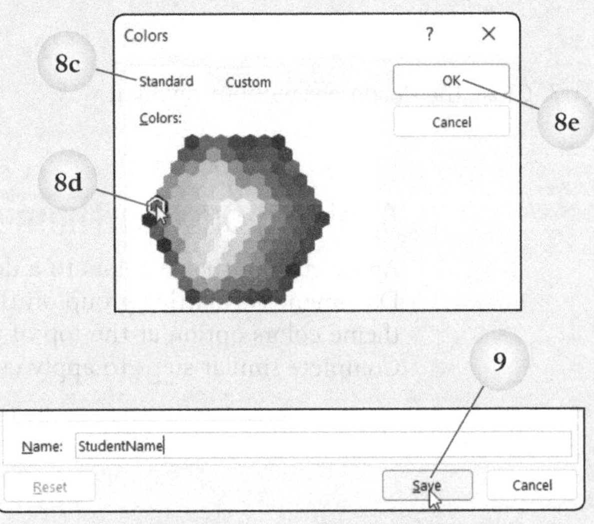

Creating Custom Theme Fonts

Quick Steps

Create Custom Theme Fonts

1. Click Design tab.
2. Click Fonts button.
3. Click *Customize Fonts*.
4. Choose fonts.
5. Type name for custom theme fonts.
6. Click Save button.

Creating Custom Theme Fonts

To create a custom theme font, click the Design tab, click the Fonts button, and then click *Customize Fonts* at the drop-down gallery. This displays the Create New Theme Fonts dialog box. At this dialog box, type a name for the custom font in the *Name* text box. Choose a font for headings and a font for body text and then click the Save button.

Activity 5b Creating Custom Theme Fonts

Part 2 of 5

1. At a blank document, click the Design tab.
2. Click the Fonts button in the Document Formatting group and then click the *Customize Fonts* option at the drop-down gallery.
3. At the Create New Theme Fonts dialog box, type your first and last names in the *Name* text box.
4. Click the *Heading font* option box arrow, scroll up the drop-down list, and then click *Arial*.
5. Click the *Body font* option box arrow, scroll down the drop-down list, and then click *Cambria*.
6. Save the custom fonts by clicking the Save button.

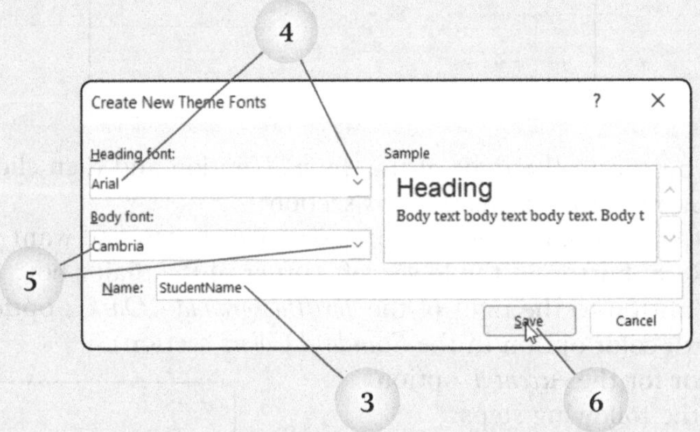

7. Close the document without saving it.

Applying Custom Theme Colors and Fonts

Apply custom theme colors to a document by clicking the Colors button in the Document Formatting group on the Design tab and then clicking the custom theme colors option at the top of the drop-down gallery in the *Custom* section. Complete similar steps to apply custom theme fonts.

Applying Theme Effects

The options in the Theme Effects button drop-down gallery apply sets of line and fill effects to the graphics in a document. Custom theme effects cannot be created, but a theme effect can be applied to a document and the formatting can then be saved in a custom theme.

Saving a Custom Document Theme

Saving a Custom Document Theme

A custom document theme containing custom theme colors, fonts, and effects can be saved. To do this, create and apply custom theme colors, fonts, and theme effects to a document, click the Themes button on the Design tab, and then click *Save Current Theme* at the drop-down gallery. This displays the Save Current Theme dialog box, which has many of the same options as the Save As dialog box. Type a name for the custom document theme in the *File name* text box and then click the Save button.

Quick Steps

Save Custom Document Theme

1. Click Design tab.
2. Click Themes button.
3. Click *Save Current Theme.*
4. Type name for theme.
5. Click Save button.

Activity 5c Applying Theme Effects and Saving a Custom Document Theme — Part 3 of 5

1. Open **NSSServices.docx** and then save it with the name **8-NSSServices.**
2. Make the following changes to the document:
   a. Apply the Title style to the company name *Northland Security Systems.*
   b. Apply the Heading 1 style to the heading *Northland Security Systems Mission*.
   c. Apply the Heading 2 style to the remaining headings, *Security Services* and *Security Software*.
   d. Apply the Word 2010 style set (the last option in the expanded style set gallery on the Design tab).
3. Apply the custom theme colors you saved by completing the following steps:
   a. Click the Colors button in the Document Formatting group on the Design tab.
   b. Click the theme colors option with your name at the top of the drop-down gallery in the *Custom* group.

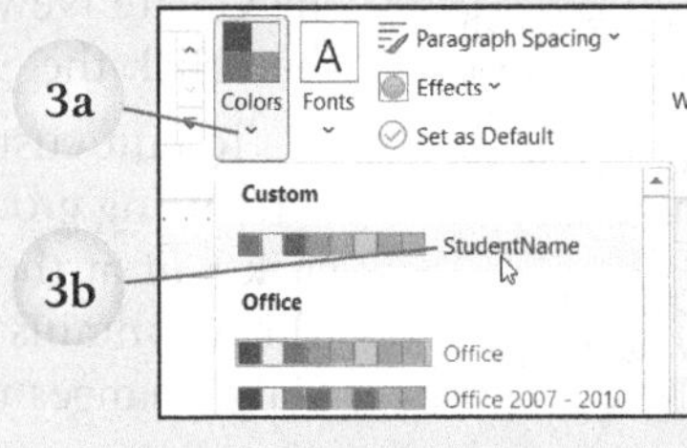

4. Apply the custom theme fonts you saved by clicking the Fonts button in the Document Formatting group and then clicking the custom theme fonts with your name.
5. Apply a theme effect by clicking the Effects button in the Document Formatting group and then clicking *Glossy* at the drop-down gallery (last option).
6. Make the following changes to the SmartArt graphic:
   a. Click the graphic to select it. (When the graphic is selected, a border displays around it.)
   b. Click the SmartArt Design tab.
   c. Click the Change Colors button and then click *Colorful Range - Accent Colors 5 to 6* (last option in the *Colorful* section).

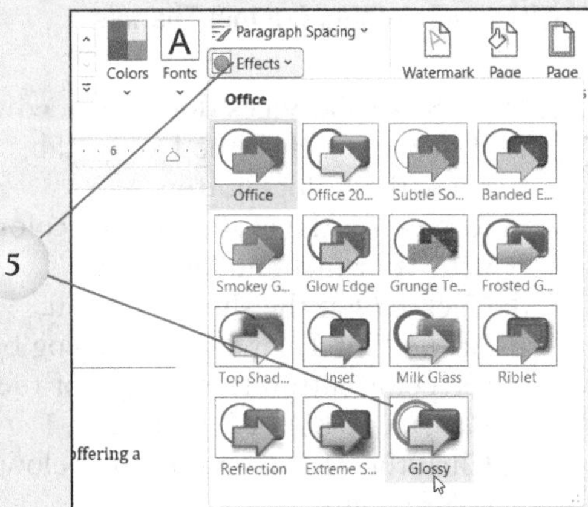

d. Click the More SmartArt Styles button in the SmartArt Styles group and then click *Cartoon* (third option in the *3-D* section).
e. Click outside the SmartArt graphic to deselect it.
7. Save the custom theme colors and fonts, as well as the Glossy theme effect, as a custom document theme by completing the following steps:
a. Click the Design tab.
b. Click the Themes button in the Document Formatting group.
c. Click the *Save Current Theme* option at the bottom of the drop-down gallery.
d. At the Save Current Theme dialog box, type your first and last names (without a space between) in the *File name* text box and then click the Save button.

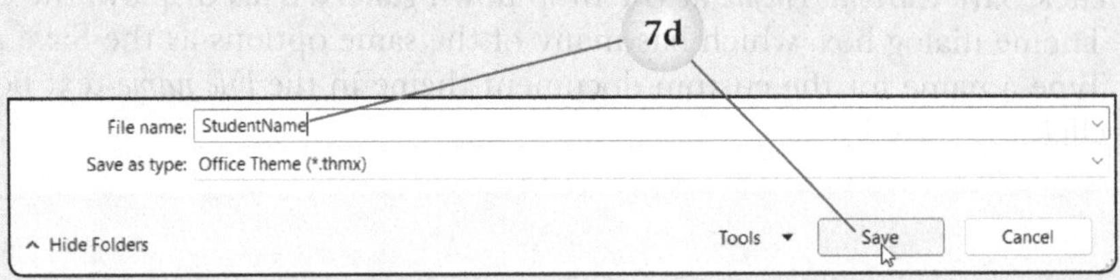

8. Save and then preview **8-NSSServices.docx**.

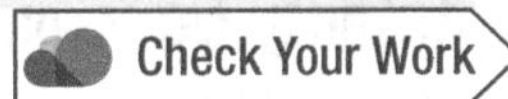

Editing a Custom Theme

Quick Steps

Edit Custom Theme Colors or Fonts

1. Click Design tab.
2. Click Colors button or Fonts button.
3. Right-click custom theme colors or fonts.
4. Click *Edit*.
5. Make changes.
6. Click Save button.

Editing Custom Themes

Custom theme colors and theme fonts can be edited. To edit custom theme colors, click the Design tab and then click the Colors button in the Document Formatting group. At the drop-down gallery of custom and built-in theme colors, right-click the custom theme colors and then click *Edit* at the shortcut menu. This displays the Edit Theme Colors dialog box, which contains the same options as the Create New Theme Colors dialog box. Make changes to the theme colors and then click the Save button.

To edit custom theme fonts, click the Fonts button in the Document Formatting group on the Design tab, right-click the custom theme fonts, and then click *Edit* at the shortcut menu. This displays the Edit Theme Fonts dialog box, which contains the same options as the Create New Theme Fonts dialog box. Make changes to the theme fonts and then click the Save button.

Activity 5d Editing Custom Themes

Part 4 of 5

1. With **8-NSSServices.docx** open, edit the theme colors by completing the following steps:
a. If necessary, click the Design tab.
b. Click the Colors button.
c. Right-click the custom theme colors named with your first and last names.
d. Click *Edit* at the shortcut menu.
e. At the Edit Theme Colors dialog box, click the color button to the right of the *Text/Background - Dark 2* option.
f. Click the *More Colors* option below the color palette.

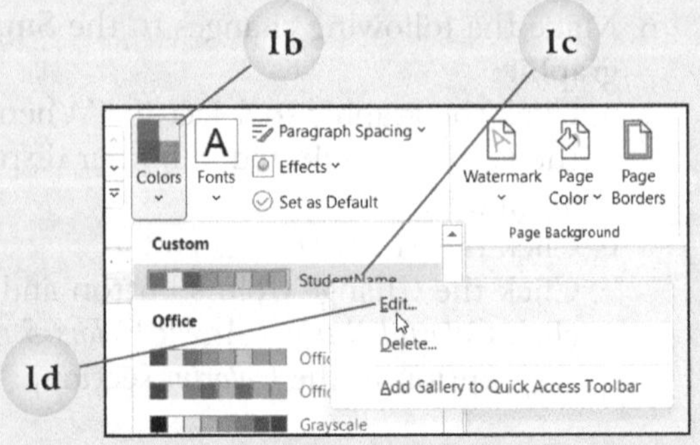

g. At the Colors dialog box, click the Standard tab.
h. Click the dark green color. (This is the same color you chose for *Accent 1* in Activity 5a.)
i. Click OK to close the dialog box.
j. Click the Save button.

2. Edit the theme fonts by completing the following steps:
   a. Click the Fonts button in the Document Formatting group.
   b. Right-click the custom theme fonts named with your first and last names and then click *Edit* at the shortcut menu.
   c. At the Edit Theme Fonts dialog box, click the *Body font* option box arrow, scroll down the drop-down list, and then click *Constantia*.
   d. Click the Save button.
3. Apply a different theme effect by clicking the Effects button and then clicking *Extreme Shadow* at the drop-down gallery (second column, last row). (This applies a shadow behind each shape.)
4. Save the changes to the custom theme by completing the following steps:
   a. Click the Themes button and then click *Save Current Theme* at the drop-down gallery.
   b. At the Save Current Theme dialog box, click the theme named with your first and last names in the content pane.
   c. Click the Save button.
   d. At the message stating that the theme already exists and asking if you want to replace it, click Yes.
5. Save, preview, and then close **8-NSSServices.docx**.

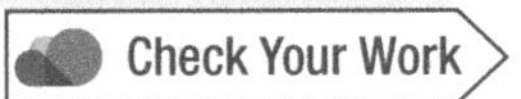
Check Your Work

Resetting a Template Theme

Quick Steps

Resetting Template Theme
1. Click Design tab.
2. Click Themes button.
3. Click *Reset to Theme from Template*.

If a built-in theme other than the Office default theme or a custom theme is applied to a document, the theme can be reset to the default by clicking the Themes button and then clicking *Reset to Theme from Template* at the drop-down gallery. If the document is based on the default template provided by Word, clicking this option resets the theme to the Office default theme.

Tutorial

Deleting a Custom Theme

Quick Steps

Delete Custom Theme Colors or Fonts
1. Click Design tab.
2. Click Colors or Fonts button.
3. Right-click custom theme.
4. Click *Delete*.
5. Click Yes.

Delete a Custom Theme
1. Click Design tab.
2. Click Themes button.
3. Right-click custom theme.
4. Click *Delete*.
5. Click Yes.

Deleting Custom Themes

Delete custom theme colors from the Colors button drop-down gallery, delete custom theme fonts from the Fonts drop-down gallery, and delete custom themes at the Themes button drop-down gallery or the Save Current Theme dialog box.

To delete custom theme colors, click the Colors button, right-click the theme to be deleted, and then click *Delete* at the shortcut menu. At the confirmation message, click Yes. To delete custom theme fonts, click the Fonts button, right-click the theme to be deleted, and then click *Delete* at the shortcut menu. At the confirmation message, click Yes.

Delete a custom theme (including custom colors, fonts, and effects) at the Themes button drop-down gallery or the Save Current Theme dialog box. To delete a custom theme from the drop-down gallery, click the Themes button, right-click the custom theme, click *Delete* at the shortcut menu, and then click Yes at the confirmation message. To delete a custom theme from the Save Current Theme dialog box, click the Themes button and then click *Save Current Theme* at the drop-down gallery. At the dialog box, click the custom theme document name, click the Organize button on the dialog box toolbar, and then click *Delete* at the drop-down list. If a confirmation message displays, click Yes.

Changing Default Settings

If formatting is applied to a document—such as a specific style set, theme, and paragraph spacing—it can be saved as the default formatting. To do this, click the Set as Default button in the Document Formatting group on the Design tab. At the message asking if the current style set and theme should be set as the default and indicating that the settings will be applied to new documents, click Yes.

Activity 5e Applying and Deleting Custom Themes — Part 5 of 5

1. Open **NSSSecurity.docx** and then save it with the name **8-NSSSecurity**.
2. Apply the Title style to the company name, apply the Heading 1 style to the two headings in the document, and then apply the Word 2010 style set.
3. Apply your custom theme by completing the following steps:
   a. If necessary, click the Design tab.
   b. Click the Themes button.
   c. Click the custom theme named with your first and last names at the top of the drop-down gallery in the *Custom* section.

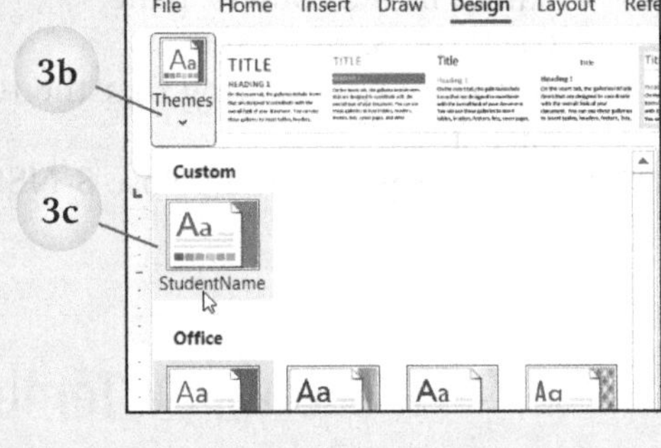

4. Save and then preview **8-NSSSecurity.docx**.
5. Reset the theme to the Office default theme by clicking the Themes button and then clicking *Reset to Theme from Template* at the drop-down gallery.
6. Save and then close **8-NSSSecurity.docx**.
7. Press Ctrl + N to display a new blank document.
8. Delete the custom theme colors by completing the following steps:
   a. Click the Design tab.
   b. Click the Colors button in the Document Formatting group.
   c. Right-click the custom theme colors named with your first and last names.
   d. Click *Delete* at the shortcut menu.
   e. At the message that displays asking if you want to delete the theme colors, click Yes.

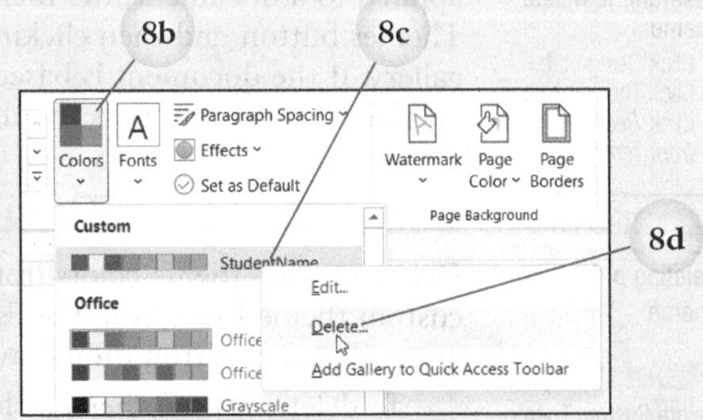

9. Complete steps similar to those in Step 8 to delete the custom theme fonts named with your first and last names.
10. Delete the custom theme by completing the following steps:
    a. Click the Themes button.
    b. Right-click the custom theme named with your first and last names.
    c. Click *Delete* at the shortcut menu.
    d. At the message asking if you want to delete the theme, click Yes.
11. Close the document without saving it.

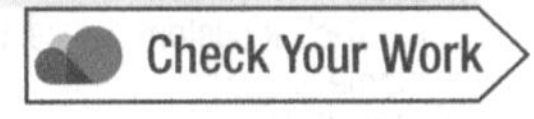

Chapter Summary

- Use the Bullets button to insert bullets before specific paragraphs of text and use the Numbering button to insert numbers.
- Insert custom numbers by clicking the Numbering button arrow and then clicking an option at the drop-down gallery.
- Set the numbering value at the Set Numbering Value dialog box. Display this dialog box by clicking the Numbering button arrow and then clicking the *Set Numbering Value* option.
- Define custom numbering formatting at the Define New Number Format dialog box. Display this dialog box by clicking the Numbering button arrow and then clicking the *Define New Number Format* option.
- Insert custom bullets by clicking the Bullets button arrow and then clicking an option at the drop-down gallery. Define new custom bullets at the Define New Bullet dialog box. Display this dialog box by clicking the Bullets button arrow and then clicking the *Define New Bullet* option.
- Apply list formatting to multilevel paragraphs of text by clicking the Multilevel List button in the Paragraph group on the Home tab. Define new custom multilevel list formatting at the Define new Multilevel list dialog box. Display this dialog box by clicking the Multilevel List button and then clicking the *Define New Multilevel List* option.
- When typing a multilevel list, press the Tab key to move to the next level and press Shift + Tab to move to the previous level.
- Words can be added to AutoCorrect at the AutoCorrect dialog box. Display this dialog box by clicking the File tab, clicking *Options*, clicking *Proofing*, clicking the AutoCorrect Options button, and then clicking the AutoCorrect tab.
- Specify exceptions to AutoCorrect at the AutoCorrect Exceptions dialog box. Display this dialog box by clicking the Exceptions button at the AutoCorrect dialog box with the AutoCorrect tab selected.
- Use the AutoCorrect Options button, which displays when the pointer is hovered over corrected text, to change corrected text back to the original spelling, stop automatically correcting specific text, or display the AutoCorrect dialog box.
- The AutoCorrect dialog box contains several symbols that can be inserted in a document by typing specific text or characters. To add more symbols, display the Symbol dialog box, click the specific symbol, and then click the AutoCorrect button.
- When typing text, control what Word formats automatically with options at the AutoCorrect dialog box with the AutoFormat As You Type tab selected.
- A Word document is based on the Normal template that provides a document with default layout, formatting, styles, and themes. The Normal template provides a number of predesigned themes that are available in the Document Formatting group on the Design tab.
- A theme is a combination of theme colors, theme fonts, and theme effects. A custom theme can be created that includes custom theme colors, theme fonts, and/or theme effects.
- Create custom theme colors with options at the Create New Theme Colors dialog box. Display this dialog box by clicking the Colors button on the Design tab and then clicking *Customize Colors* at the drop-down gallery. Click the Reset button in the dialog box to return to the default Office theme colors.

- Create custom theme fonts with options at the Create New Theme Fonts dialog box. Display this dialog box by clicking the Fonts button on the Design tab and then clicking *Customize Fonts* at the drop-down gallery.
- A theme effect is a set of lines and fill effects that can be applied to a document. Custom theme effects cannot be created, but a theme effect can be applied to a document and then saved in a custom theme.
- Save a custom theme at the Save Current Theme dialog box. Display this dialog box by clicking the Themes button on the Design tab and then clicking *Save Current Theme* at the drop-down gallery.
- Apply custom theme colors by clicking the Colors button in the Document Formatting group on the Design tab and then clicking the custom theme colors option at the top of the drop-down gallery. Complete similar steps to apply custom theme fonts.
- Edit custom theme colors by clicking the Design tab and then clicking the Colors button in the Document Formatting group. At the drop-down gallery, right-click the custom theme colors and then click *Edit* at the shortcut menu. This displays the Edit Theme Colors dialog box where changes can be made to the theme colors. Edit custom theme fonts in a similar manner.
- Click the *Reset to Theme from Template* option at the Themes button drop-down gallery to reset to the Office default theme.
- Delete a custom theme at the Themes button drop-down gallery or at the Save Current Theme dialog box.
- Formatting applied to a document can be saved as the default formatting by clicking the Set as Default button in the Document Formatting group on the Design tab.

Commands Review

FEATURE	RIBBON TAB, GROUP/OPTION	BUTTON, OPTION
AutoCorrect dialog box	File, *Options, Proofing*	AutoCorrect Options
bullets	Home, Paragraph	
Create New Theme Colors dialog box	Design, Document Formatting	*, Customize Colors*
Create New Theme Fonts dialog box	Design, Document Formatting	*, Customize Fonts*
Define New Bullet dialog box	Home, Paragraph	*, Define New Bullet*
Define new Multilevel list dialog box	Home, Paragraph	*, Define New Multilevel List*
Define New Number Format dialog box	Home, Paragraph	*, Define New Number Format*
numbering	Home, Paragraph	
Save Current Theme dialog box	Design, Document Formatting	*, Save Current Theme*

Review and Assessment

CHAPTER 8

Skills Assessment

Assessment 1 — Define and Apply Custom Bullets and Multilevel Lists to a Document

1. Open **TechTimeline.docx** and then save it with the name **8-TechTimeline**.
2. Select the questions below the heading *Early Computer Technology Questions* and then insert check mark (✓) bullets.
3. Define a computer symbol bullet in 14-point font size and then apply the symbol bullet to the 12 paragraphs of text below the heading *Technology Timeline: 1800 - 1970*. (To find the computer symbol, select the Wingdings font at the Symbol dialog box and then type 58 in the *Character code* text box.)
4. Select the paragraphs of text below the heading *Information Systems and Commerce* (on page 2), click the Multilevel List button, and then click the middle option in the top row of the *List Library* section.
5. Select the paragraphs of text below the heading *Internet* (on page 3) and then apply the same multilevel list formatting.
6. Save and then preview page 3 of **8-TechTimeline.docx**.
7. Select the paragraphs of text below the heading *Information Systems and Commerce* and then define a new multilevel list with the following specifications:
   a. Level 1 inserts arabic numbers (1, 2, 3), each followed by a period. The numbers are aligned at the left margin (at 0 inch) and the text indent is 0.25 inch.
   b. Level 2 inserts capital letters (A, B, C), each followed by a period. The letters are aligned 0.25 inch from the left margin and the text indent is 0.5 inch.
   c. Level 3 inserts arabic numbers (1, 2, 3), each followed by a right parenthesis. The numbers are aligned 0.5 inch from the left margin and the text indent is 0.75 inch.
   d. Make sure the new multilevel list formatting is applied to the selected paragraphs.
8. Select the paragraphs of text below the heading *Internet* and then apply the new multilevel list formatting.
9. Save, preview, and then close **8-TechTimeline.docx**.

Assessment 2 Format a Health Plan Document with AutoCorrect

1. Open **KLHPlan.docx** and then save it with the name **8-KLHPlan**.
2. Add the following text to AutoCorrect:
   a. Type kl in the *Replace* text box and type Key Life Health Plan in the *With* text box.
   b. Type m in the *Replace* text box and type medical in the *With* text box.
3. With the insertion point positioned at the beginning of the document, type the text shown in Figure 8.12.
4. Move the insertion point to the blank line below the first paragraph of text below the heading *Quality Assessment*. Insert a bullet symbol by typing > and then pressing the Tab key. Type Member rights, press the Enter key, and then type the following lines of text (each should be preceded by the bullet symbol):

   Preventative health care
   Provider quality standards
   Clinical care review

5. If necessary, turn off autoformatting of web addresses. ***Hint: Do this at the AutoCorrect dialog box with the AutoFormat As You Type tab selected.***
6. Move the insertion point to the end of the document and then type the text shown in Figure 8.13. ***Hint: Type (tm) to insert the trademark symbol.***
7. Make the following changes to the document:
   a. Apply the Heading 1 style to the title *Key Life Health Plan*.
   b. Apply the Heading 2 style to the heading *How the Plan Works*.
   c. Apply the Frame theme.
8. Save and then preview **8-KLHPlan.docx**.
9. Delete the two entries you made at the AutoCorrect dialog box.
10. Turn on the autoformatting of web addresses.
11. Close **8-KLHPlan.docx**.

Figure 8.12 Assessment 2

kl

How the Plan Works

When you enroll in the kl, you and each eligible family member select a plan option. A kl option includes a main m clinic, any affiliated satellite clinics, and designated hospitals. kl provides coverage for emergency m services outside the service area. If the m emergency is not life threatening, call your primary care physician to arrange for care before going to an emergency facility. If you have a life-threatening emergency, go directly to the nearest appropriate facility.

Figure 8.13 Assessment 2

Key Life Health Plan™

https://ppi-edu.net/KeyLife

Assessment 3

Create and Apply Custom Themes to a Company Document

1. At a blank document, create custom theme colors named with your initials that make the following color changes:
   a. Change the Text/Background - Dark 2 color to Orange, Accent 2, Darker 50% (sixth column, last row in the *Theme Colors* section).
   b. Change the Accent 1 color to Green, Accent 6, Darker 50% (tenth column, last row in the *Theme Colors* section).
   c. Change the Accent 4 color to Orange, Accent 2, Darker 50%.
   d. Change the Accent 6 color to Green, Accent 6, Darker 25% (tenth column, fifth row in the *Theme Colors* section).
2. Create custom theme fonts named with your initials that change the heading font to Copperplate Gothic Bold and the body font to Constantia.
3. Apply the *Riblet* effect (last column, third row in the Effects button drop-down list).
4. Save the custom document theme with the name *WL1C8* followed by your initials. ***Hint: Do this with the* Save Current Theme *option at the Themes button drop-down gallery.***
5. Close the document without saving the changes.
6. Open **DIRevenues.docx** and then save it with the name **8-DIRevenues**.
7. Move the insertion point to the end of the document and then insert the document named **DIGraphic.docx**. ***Hint: Do this with the Object button arrow on the Insert tab.***
8. Apply the WL1C8 (followed by your initials) custom document theme to the document.
9. Save, preview, and then close **8-DIRevenues.docx**.
10. Open a blank document.
11. Make a screen capture of the Colors button drop-down gallery by completing the following steps:
    a. Click the Design tab and then click the Colors button. (Make sure your custom theme colors display.)
    b. Press the Print Screen button on your keyboard.
    c. Click in the document, click the Home tab, and then click the Paste button in the Clipboard group. (This inserts the screen capture in your document.)
12. Press Ctrl + End, press the Enter key two times, and then complete steps similar to those in Step 11 to insert a screen capture of the Fonts button drop-down gallery. (Make sure your custom theme fonts display.)
13. Press Ctrl + End, press the Enter key two times, and then complete steps similar to those in Step 11 to insert a screen capture of the Themes button drop-down gallery. (Make sure your custom theme displays.)
14. If necessary, size the three images so that they fit on one page.
15. Save the document with the name **8-ScreenImages**.
16. Preview and then close **8-ScreenImages.docx**.
17. Open a blank document; delete the custom theme colors, custom theme fonts, and custom document theme you created; and then close the blank document.

Assessment 4

Customize AutoCorrect and Edit an Adventure Document

1. Open **BEAAdventures.docx** and then save it with the name **8-BEAAdventures**.
2. In this chapter, you learned how to customize AutoCorrect. Continue exploring AutoCorrect and determine how to turn off automatic bulleted lists, automatic numbered lists, and the formatting of ordinals as superscripts. Turn off these three features.
3. Position the insertion point at the beginning of the adventure *European Grand Tour*, type >, and then press the spacebar. (With the bulleted list feature turned off, the text you type should not be converted to an arrow bullet.) Type > and press the spacebar before each of the three remaining adventures.
4. Position the insertion point at the beginning of *Antarctic Exploration*, type 1., and then press the spacebar. (With the numbered list feature turned off, the text you type should not be indented.) Sequentially number the remaining three Antarctic adventures (2., 3., and 4.).
5. Move the insertion point to the end of the document and then type For more information on Antarctic adventures, please visit us at our San Diego office at 9880 43rd Street East or call 619-555-9090. (With the formatting of ordinals as superscripts turned off, the text *rd* in *43rd* will not be formatted as a superscript.)
6. Save, preview, and then close **8-BEAAdventures.docx**.
7. At the blank screen, turn on the three features you turned off in Step 2 (automatic bulleted lists, automatic numbered lists, and the formatting of ordinals as superscripts).

Visual Benchmark

Create and Format an International Correspondence Document

1. Open **IntlCorres.docx** and then save it with the name **8-IntlCorres**.
2. Apply the following formatting so your document appears similar to the document shown in Figure 8.14:
   - Change the top margin to 1.5 inches and the left and right margins to 1.25 inches.
   - Apply the Heading 1 style to the title and the Heading 2 style to the three headings.
   - Apply the Shaded style set. (You will need to click the More Style Sets button in the Document Formatting group on the Design tab to display this style set.)
   - Change the theme colors to Green.
   - Apply check mark bullets as shown in the figure.
   - Apply symbol bullets as shown in the figure. (The globe bullet is available in the Webdings font, character code 254, at the Symbol dialog box.)
   - Apply automatic numbering as shown in the figure and start numbering with 11 after the heading *CANADIAN CODES AND TERRITORIES*.
   - Apply any other formatting required to make your document similar to the document shown in Figure 8.14.
3. Save, preview, and then close **8-IntlCorres.docx**.

Figure 8.14 Visual Benchmark

INTERNATIONAL CORRESPONDENCE

With the increased number of firms conducting business worldwide, international written communication has assumed new importance. Follow these guidelines when corresponding internationally, especially with people for whom English is not the primary language:

- ✓ Use a direct writing style and clear, precise words.
- ✓ Avoid slang, jargon, and idioms.
- ✓ Develop an awareness of cultural differences that may interfere with the communication process.

INTERNATIONAL ADDRESSES

Use the company's letterhead or a business card as a guide for spelling and other information. Include the following when addressing international correspondence:

- Line 1: Addressee's Name, Title
- Line 2: Company Name
- Line 3: Street Address
- Line 4: City and Codes
- Line 5: COUNTRY NAME (capitalized)

CANADIAN CODES AND PROVINCES

1. ON – Ontario
2. QC – Quebec
3. NS – Nova Scotia
4. NB – New Brunswick
5. MB – Manitoba
6. BC – British Columbia
7. PE – Prince Edward Island
8. SK – Saskatchewan
9. AB – Alberta
10. NL – Newfoundland and Labrador

CANADIAN CODES AND TERRITORIES

11. NT – Northwest Territories
12. YT – Yukon
13. NU – Nunavut

Case Study

Part 1

You work in the Human Resources Department of Oceanside Medical Services and your supervisor has asked you to create a custom document theme. Open **OMSOrgChart.docx** and then save it with the name **8-OMSOrgChart**. Open **OMSLtrhd.docx** and look at the colors in the letterhead. Make **8-OMSOrgChart.docx** the active document, and then create and save custom theme colors that match the letterhead. Create and save custom theme fonts that apply the Arial font to the headings and the Constantia font to the body text. Apply the Glossy effect. Save the custom document theme in the Save Current Theme dialog box and then name it with your initials followed by *OMS*. Save, preview, and then close **8-OMSOrgChart.docx**. Close **OMSLtrhd.docx**.

Part 2

Open **OMSHandbook.docx** and then save it with the name **8-OMSHandbook**. Apply the custom document theme you created and saved in Part 1 (named with your initials followed by *OMS*). Apply or insert the following in the document:

- Create an AutoCorrect entry that will replace *OMS* with *Oceanside Medical Services*. Position the insertion point on the blank line below the heading *NEW EMPLOYEE ORIENTATION* (located near the bottom of the first page) and then type the text shown in Figure 8.15.
- Define a new symbol bullet (you determine the symbol) and then apply it to all the currently bulleted paragraphs in the handbook document.
- Select the lines of text on the first page beginning with *Section 1: General Information* through *Compensation Procedures* and then define and apply a new multilevel list number format that applies capital letters followed by periods to the first level and arabic numbers (1, 2, 3) followed by periods to the second level. You determine the indents.
- Insert a cover page of your choosing and insert the appropriate information in the placeholders.

Save, preview, and then close **8-OMSHandbook.docx**.

Figure 8.15 Case Study, Part 2

> The OMS New Employee Orientation Program is designed to welcome new employees into the spirit and culture of OMS, to clearly establish health care performance expectations, and to set the stage for success. New personnel are encouraged to begin their jobs with the monthly orientation in order to be introduced to the overall operations of OMS.

Part 3

At a blank document, make a screen capture (use the Print Screen button) of the Colors button drop-down gallery (in the Document Formatting group on the Design tab) and paste it in the document. (Refer to Assessment 3, Step 11.) Make a screen capture of the Fonts button drop-down gallery (in the Document Formatting group on the Design tab) and paste it in the document. Make a screen capture of the Themes button drop-down gallery and paste it in the document. Make sure all the screen capture images are visible and fit on one page. Save the document with the name **8-OMSScreenImages**. Preview and then close **8-OMSScreenImages.docx**. Open a blank document and then delete your custom theme colors, custom theme fonts, and custom document theme. Delete the *OMS* AutoCorrect entry and then close the document.

WORD LEVEL 1

Unit 2 Performance Assessment

Data Files

The data files for this unit work are in the WL1U2 folder that you downloaded at the beginning of this course.

Assessing Proficiency

In this unit, you have learned to format and customize objects to enhance the appearance of documents; manage documents; print envelopes and labels; create documents using templates; create and edit tables; visually represent data in SmartArt graphics and charts; create custom numbering and bullet formatting; and customize a document using AutoCorrect options and custom themes.

Assessment 1

Format a Bioinformatics Document

1. Open **Bioinformatics.docx** and then save it with the name **U2-Bioinformatics**.
2. Move the insertion point to the end of the document and then insert the file named **GenomeMapping.docx**.
3. Press Ctrl + Home to move the insertion point to the beginning of the document and then insert the Motion Quote text box with the following specifications:
   a. Type "Understanding our DNA is similar to understanding a number that is billions of digits long." in the text box.
   b. Select the text in the text box and then change the font size to 12 points.
   c. Change the width of the text box to 2.6 inches.
   d. Position the text box in the middle of the page with square text wrapping.
4. Insert page numbering at the bottom of the page using the Thin Line page numbering option.
5. Save, preview, and then close **U2-Bioinformatics.docx**.

Assessment 2 Create a Workshop Flyer

1. Create the flyer shown in Figure U2.1 with the following specifications:
   a. Create the WordArt with the following specifications:
      - Use the option in the fourth column, first row in the WordArt button drop-down gallery (white fill, blue outline, shadow).
      - Increase the width to 6.5 inches and the height to 1 inch.
      - Apply the Deflate text effect transform shape (second column, sixth row in the *Warp* section).
      - Position the WordArt in the top center of the page with square text wrapping.
      - Change the text fill color to Green, Accent 6, Lighter 40% (last column, fourth row in the *Theme Colors* section).

   b. Type the text shown in the figure. Change the font to 22-point Calibri, apply bold formatting, and center-align the text.
   c. Insert the **WorldGlobe.png** image file from your WL1U2 folder. Change the wrapping style to Square and size and position the image as shown in Figure U2.1.
2. Save the document with the name **U2-BEAFlyer**.
3. Preview and then close **U2-BEAFlyer.docx**.

Figure U2.1 Assessment 2

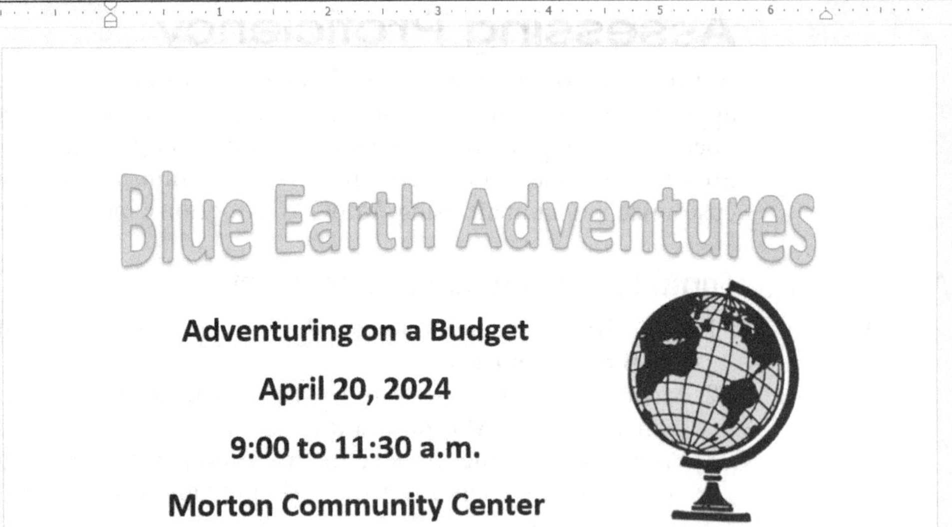

Assessment 3 Create a Staff Meeting Announcement

1. Click the File tab, click the *New* option, and then double-click the *Single spaced (blank)* template.
2. Create the announcement shown in Figure U2.2 with the following specifications:
   a. Use the Hexagon shape in the *Basic Shapes* section of the Shapes button drop-down list (ninth column, first row) to create the shape. (You determine the size of the shape.)
   b. Apply the Subtle Effect - Blue, Accent 1 shape style (second column, fourth row in the *Theme Styles* section).
   c. Apply the Divot bevel shape effect (first column, third row in the *Bevel* section).

d. Type the text in the shape as shown in Figure U2.2. Insert the *ñ* as a symbol (in the normal text font, character code 00F1) and insert the clock as a symbol (in the Wingdings font, character code 185). Set the text and clock symbol in larger font sizes.

3. Save the completed document with the name **U2-MeetNotice**.
4. Preview and then close **U2-MeetNotice.docx**.

Figure U2.2 Assessment 3

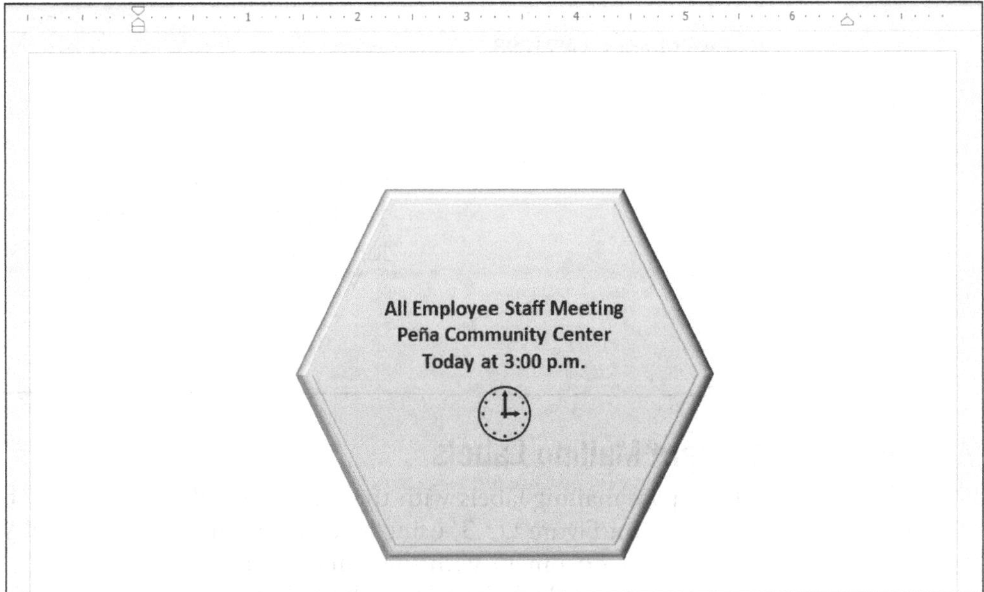

Assessment 4 Create a Snorkeling Flyer

1. At a blank document, insert the **Snorkeling.jpg** image file from your WL1U2 folder.
2. Crop off some of the bottom of the image.
3. Correct the brightness and contrast to Brightness: 0% (Normal) Contrast: +20% (third column, fourth row in the *Brightness/Contrast* section).
4. Use the Position button to position the image in the top center with square text wrapping and then use the Wrap Text button to wrap the image behind text.
5. Apply the Double Frame, Black picture style to the image.
6. Press the Enter key twice and then change to center alignment. Type the text Snorkeling Adventures on the first line; Blue Island Bay on the second line; and 1-888-555-3322 on the third line. Change the font for the text to 18-point Castellar and apply bold formatting. Make sure the text fits in the water portion of the image.
7. Save the document with the name **U2-SnorkelingFlyer**.
8. Preview and then close **U2-SnorkelingFlyer.docx**.

Assessment 5 Prepare an Envelope

1. At a blank document, prepare an envelope with the text shown in Figure U2.3.
2. Save the envelope document with the name **U2-Env**.
3. Preview and then close **U2-Env.docx**.

Figure U2.3 Assessment 5

Mrs. Eileen Hebert
15205 East 42nd Street
Lake Charles, LA 71098

Mr. Earl Robicheaux
1436 North Sheldon Street
Jennings, LA 70542

Assessment 6 Prepare Mailing Labels

1. Prepare mailing labels with the name and address for Mrs. Eileen Hebert, shown in Figure U2.3, using a label vendor and product of your choosing.
2. Save the document with the name **U2-Labels**.
3. Preview and then close **U2-Labels.docx**.

Assessment 7 Create and Format a Table with Software Training Information

1. At a blank document, create the table shown in Figure U2.4. Format the table and the text (do not apply a table style) in a manner similar to what is shown in Figure U2.4.
2. Insert a formula in cell B8 that totals the numbers in cells B4 through B7.
3. Insert a formula in cell C8 that totals the numbers in cells C4 through C7.
4. Save the document with the name **U2-TechTraining**.
5. Preview and then close **U2-TechTraining.docx**.

Figure U2.4 Assessment 7

TRI-STATE PRODUCTS		
Computer Technology Department Microsoft 365® Training		
Application	**# Enrolled**	**# Completed**
Access 365	20	15
Excel 365	62	56
PowerPoint 365	40	33
Word 365	80	72
Total		

Assessment 8 Edit and Format a Table Containing Training Scores

1. Open **TrainingScores.docx** and then save it with the name **U2-TrainingScores**.
2. Insert formulas that calculate the averages in the appropriate rows and columns. (When writing the formulas, change the *Number format* option to *0*.)
3. Autofit the contents of the table.
4. Apply a table style of your choosing.
5. Apply any other formatting to enhance the appearance of the table.
6. Save, preview, and then close **U2-TrainingScores.docx**.

Assessment 9 Create an Organizational Chart

1. Use SmartArt to create an organizational chart for the text shown in Figure U2.5 (in the order shown). Change the colors to Colorful Range - Accent Colors 4 to 5 and apply the Metallic Scene SmartArt style.
2. Save the completed document with the name **U2-OrgChart**.
3. Preview and then close **U2-OrgChart.docx**.

Figure U2.5 Assessment 9

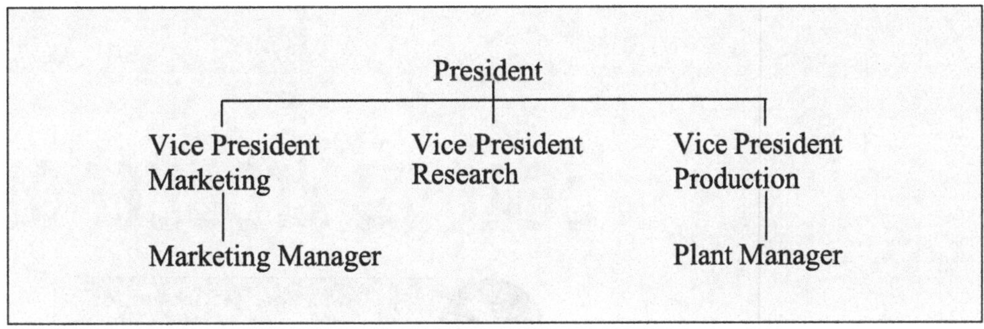

Assessment 10 Create a SmartArt Graphic

1. At a blank document, create the WordArt graphic and SmartArt graphic shown in Figure U2.6 with the following specifications:
   a. Create the WordArt text using the option in the third column, third row of the WordArt button drop-down list. Change the shape height to 1 inch and the shape width to 6 inches and then apply the Square transform text effect (first effect in the *Warp* section). Position the WordArt at the top center of the page with square text wrapping.
   b. Create the SmartArt graphic using the Vertical Picture Accent List graphic. Click the picture icon in the top circle and then insert the **SP-Seagull.png** image file from your WL1U2 folder. Insert the same image file in the other two circles. Type the text in each rectangle shape as shown in Figure U2.6. Change the colors to Colorful Range - Accent Colors 5 to 6 and apply the Cartoon SmartArt style.
2. Save the document with the name **U2-SPGraphic**.
3. Preview and then close **U2-SPGraphic.docx**.

Figure U2.6 Assessment 10

Assessment 11 Format a Stock Awards Document

1. Open **CMStocks.docx** and then save it with the name **U2-CMStocks**.
2. Apply the Title style to the title *Clearline Manufacturing*.
3. Apply the Heading 1 style to the headings *Stock Awards* and *Employee Stock Plan*.
4. Apply the Centered style set.
5. Select the bulleted paragraphs of text and then define and apply a new picture bullet using the **BlueCircle.png** image file in your WL1U2 folder.
6. Select the lines of text below the heading *Employee Stock Plan* and then apply a multilevel list (middle option in the top row of the *List Library* section of the Multilevel List button drop-down list).
7. With the text still selected, define a new multilevel list that inserts capital letters followed by periods (A., B., C.) for level 2 and arabic numbers followed by periods (1., 2., 3.) for level 3. (Make sure the new multilevel list applies to the selected text.)
8. Save, preview, and then close **U2-CMStocks.docx**.

Assessment 12 Format an Equipment Rental Agreement

1. At a blank document, create custom theme colors named with your initials that change the Text/Background - Dark 2 color to Orange, Accent 2, Darker 50% (sixth column, last row in the *Theme Colors* section) and the Accent 1 color to Green, Accent 6, Darker 25% (tenth column, fifth row in the *Theme Colors* section).
2. Create custom theme fonts named with your initials that apply the Verdana font to headings and the Cambria font to body text.
3. Save the custom document theme and name it with your initials. (Do this with the *Save Current Theme* option at the Themes button drop-down gallery).
4. Close the document without saving the changes.
5. Open **MRCForm.docx** and then save it with the name **U2-MRCForm**.
6. Add the following text to AutoCorrect:
   a. Type mrc in the *Replace* text box and type Meridian Rental Company in the *With* text box.
   b. Type erag in the *Replace* text box and type Equipment Rental Agreement in the *With* text box.
7. Move the insertion point to the blank line below the heading *Default* (on the third page) and then type the text shown in Figure U2.7. Use the Numbering feature to number each paragraph with a lowercase letter followed by a right parenthesis. (If the AutoCorrect feature capitalizes the first word after the letter and right parenthesis, use the AutoCorrect options button to return the letter to lowercase.)
8. Apply the Centered style set.
9. Apply your custom document theme to the document.
10. Delete the two entries you made at the AutoCorrect dialog box.
11. Save, preview, and then close **U2-MRCForm.docx**.
12. Open a blank document; delete the custom theme colors, custom theme fonts, and custom document theme named with your initials; and then close the document.

Figure U2.7 Assessment 12

Upon the occurrence of default, mrc may, without any further notice, exercise any one or more of the following remedies:

a) terminate this erag as to any or all items of Equipment;

b) cause Lessee to return the Equipment to mrc in the condition set forth in this erag;

c) dispose of the Equipment without affecting the obligations of Lessee as provided by this erag;

d) exercise any other rights accruing to mrc upon a default by Lessee of this erag.

Writing Activities

The following activities give you the opportunity to practice your writing skills and demonstrate your understanding of some of the important Word features you have mastered in this unit. Use correct grammar, appropriate word choices, and clear sentence construction.

Activity 1

Create a Letterhead and Compose a Letter

You are the executive assistant to the owner of Clearline Manufacturing, who has asked you to create a letterhead for the company. Use information of your choosing for the letterhead that includes the company name, address, email address, web address, and telephone number. Include an image in the letterhead. Five possible choices are available in your WL1U2 folder, and each image file name begins with *Manufacture*. Save the completed letterhead document as a template in your WL1U2 folder and name the template **CMLtrhdTemplate**. Close the template document.

Use File Explorer to open a document based on the **CMLtrhdTemplate.dotx** template. Write a letter to the president of the board of directors, Mrs. Nancy Logan (you determine her address), that includes the following:

- Explain that the director of the Human Resources Department has created a new employee handbook and that it will be made available to all new employees. Also mention that the attorney for Clearline Manufacturing has reviewed the handbook and approved its content.
- Open **CMHandbook.docx** and then use the headings to summarize the contents of the handbook in a paragraph in the letter. Explain in the letter that a draft of the handbook is enclosed.

Save the completed letter document with the name **U2-CMLetter**. Preview and then close **U2-CMLetter.docx**.

Activity
2

Create a Custom Document Theme

Create a custom document theme for formatting Clearline Manufacturing documents that includes the colors and/or fonts you chose for the company letterhead. Open **CMHandbook.docx** and then save it with the name **U2-CMHandbook**. Apply at least the following to the document:

- Apply the custom document theme you created.
- Apply title and/or heading styles to the title and headings in the document.
- Add a cover page of your choosing to the document and insert the appropriate information in the cover page placeholders.
- Any additional formatting that improves the appearance of the document.

Save, preview, and then close **U2-CMHandbook.docx**.

Internet Research

Create a Flyer on an Incentive Program

The owner of Blue Earth Adventures is offering an incentive to motivate adventure consultants to increase adventure bookings. The incentive is a sales contest with the grand prize of a one-week paid vacation to Cancun, Mexico. The owner has asked you to create a flyer that will be posted on the office bulletin board and that includes information about the incentive program and Cancun. Create this flyer using information about Cancun that you find on the internet. Consider using one (or more) of the images (**Cancun01.jpg**, **Cancun02.jpg**, **Cancun03.jpg**, and **Cancun04.jpg**) in your WL1U2 folder. Include any other information or objects to add visual interest to the flyer. Save the completed flyer with the name **U2-CancunFlyer**. Preview and then close **U2-CancunFlyer.docx**.

Job Study

Develop Recycling Program Communications

The chief operating officer of Harrington Engineering has just approved your draft of the company's new recycling policy, the file named **RecyclingPolicy.docx**. Open the file, edit the draft, and prepare a final copy of the policy, along with a memo to all employees describing the new guidelines. To support the company's energy resources conservation effort, you will send hard copies of the new policy to the president of the Somerset Recycling Program and to the directors of the Somerset Chamber of Commerce.

Using the concepts and techniques you learned in this unit, prepare the following documents:

- Format the recycling policy manual, including a cover page, appropriate headers and footers, and page numbers. Add at least one graphic where appropriate. Format the document using styles and a style set. Save the manual with the name **U2-RecyclingManual**. Preview the manual.
- Download a memo template at the New backstage area and then create a memo from Susan Gerhardt, Chief Operating Officer of Harrington Engineering, to all employees that introduces the new recycling program.

- Copy the *Procedure* section of the recycling policy manual into the memo where appropriate. Include a table listing five employees who will act as recycling coordinators at Harrington Engineering (make up the names). Add columns for the employees' department names and telephone extensions. Save the memo with the name **U2-RecylingMemo**. Preview the memo.
- Write a letter to the president of the Somerset Recycling Program, William Elizondo, indicating that Harrington Engineering has approved a new recycling policy and that a copy of the new policy is enclosed with the letter. Identify some of the new recycling guidelines in the policy. Add a notation indicating that copies with enclosures were sent to all the members of the Somerset Chamber of Commerce. Save the letter with the name **U2-RecyclingLetter**. Preview the letter.
- Create mailing labels (see Figure U2.8). Save the labels with the name **U2-RecyclingLabels**. Preview the labels.

Figure U2.8 Mailing Labels

William Elizondo Somerset Recycling Program 700 West Brighton Road Somerset, NJ 55123	Paul Schwartz Somerset Chamber of Commerce 45 Wallace Road Somerset, NJ 55123
Ashley Crighton Somerset Chamber of Commerce 45 Wallace Road Somerset, NJ 55123	Carol Davis Somerset Chamber of Commerce 45 Wallace Road Somerset, NJ 55123
Robert Knight Somerset Chamber of Commerce 45 Wallace Road Somerset, NJ 55123	

INDEX

D

E

F

G

H

I

K

L

M

N

Q

R

S

T

U

V

W

X

Z

Interior Photo Credits

All screen captures provided by the authors.

Preface

Page x: © LightField Studios/Shutterstock.com; **Page xii:** © Neyman Kseniya/Shutterstock.com; **Page xiv:** © Cameron Prins/Shutterstock.com; **Page xvii:** laptop: © Kite_rin/Shutterstock.com, tablet: © guteksk7/Shutterstock.com; **Page xviii:** © KucherAV/Shutterstock.com; **Page xix:** © Prostock-studio/Shutterstock.com

Getting Started

GS-1: clockwise from top left: © Alexander Selyunin/Shutterstock.com, © Paradigm Education Solutions, © rangizzz/Shutterstock.com, © NetPhotographer/Shutterstock.com, © Bborriss.67/Shutterstock.com; **GS-2:** © Aleksey Mnogosmyslov/Shutterstock.com; **GS-3:** © Paradigm Education Solutions; **GS-4:** © Pixels Hunter/Shutterstock.com; **GS-5:** © AngieYeoh/Shutterstock.com

Chapter 5

Page 161: photo © Kelly Rutkosky; **Page 163:** photos © Kelly Rutkosky; **Page 165:** Australia outlines: publicdomainvectors.org; **Page 188:** first aid icon: publicdomainvectors.org; **Page 189:** stethoscope: publicdomainvectors.org, first aid icon: publicdomainvectors.org; **Page 192:** photo: Audrey Roggenkamp; **Page 194:** cake: publicdomainvectors.org

Chapter 6

Page 239: compass: publicdomainvectors.org; **Page 240:** flowers: publicdomainvectors.org

Chapter 7

Page 281: fall imagery: publicdomainvectors.org

Unit 2 Performance Assessment

Page 320: globe: publicdomainvectors.org; **Page 324:** seagulls: publicdomainvectors.org

WORD

LEVEL 2

Unit 1

Formatting and Customizing Documents

WORD

Applying Advanced Formatting

CHAPTER 1

Performance Objectives

Upon successful completion of Chapter 1, you will be able to:

1 Adjust character spacing, use OpenType features, apply text effects, and change the default font
2 Insert intellectual property symbols, hyphens, dashes, and nonbreaking spaces
3 Find and replace font formatting, paragraph formatting, special characters, styles, and body and heading fonts, and use wildcard characters
4 Manage document properties
5 Inspect a document for confidentiality, accessibility, and compatibility issues

Microsoft Word is a powerful word processing program containing many features for making documents look polished, professional, and publication-ready. This chapter will introduce you to some advanced formatting that will bring your skills to the next level. Use options at the Font dialog box with the Advanced tab selected to apply advanced character formatting such as scaling, spacing, and kerning, as well as OpenType features such as ligatures, number styles, and stylistic sets. Insert special symbols such as intellectual property symbols, hyphens, and nonbreaking spaces at the Symbol dialog box or with keyboard shortcuts. To make designing a document faster and easier, use Word's Find and Replace feature to find and replace formatting, special characters, styles, and body and heading fonts. Finally, you'll learn to prepare documents for sharing by managing document properties and inspecting a document for confidentiality, accessibility, and compatibility issues.

Data Files

The data files for this chapter are in the WL2C1 folder that you downloaded at the beginning of this course.

Activity 1 Apply Advanced Character Formatting to a Letter 5 Parts

You will open a document containing a donor appreciation letter and then apply advanced character formatting to the text, including character scaling, spacing, and kerning; and apply OpenType features such as ligatures, number styles, and stylistic sets. You will also apply text effects and change the default font for all new documents.

Tutorial

Applying Advanced Character Formatting

Applying Character Formatting

The Font dialog box with the Advanced tab selected contains a number of options for improving the appearance of text in a document, stretching or shrinking text to fit in a specified area, and to create a specific mood in a document. Use options at the dialog box to adjust character spacing, apply OpenType features, and apply text effects to selected text.

Adjusting Character Spacing

Quick Steps

Adjust Character Spacing

1. Click Font group dialog box launcher.
2. Click Advanced tab.
3. Specify scaling, spacing, positioning, and/or kerning.
4. Click OK.

Each typeface is designed with a specific amount of space between characters. This character spacing can be changed with options in the *Character Spacing* section of the Font dialog box with the Advanced tab selected, as shown in Figure 1.1. Display this dialog box by clicking the Font group dialog box launcher on the Home tab and then clicking the Advanced tab at the dialog box.

Choose the *Scale* option to stretch or compress text horizontally as a percentage of the current size from 1% to 600%. Expand or condense the spacing

Figure 1.1 Font Dialog Box with the Advanced Tab Selected

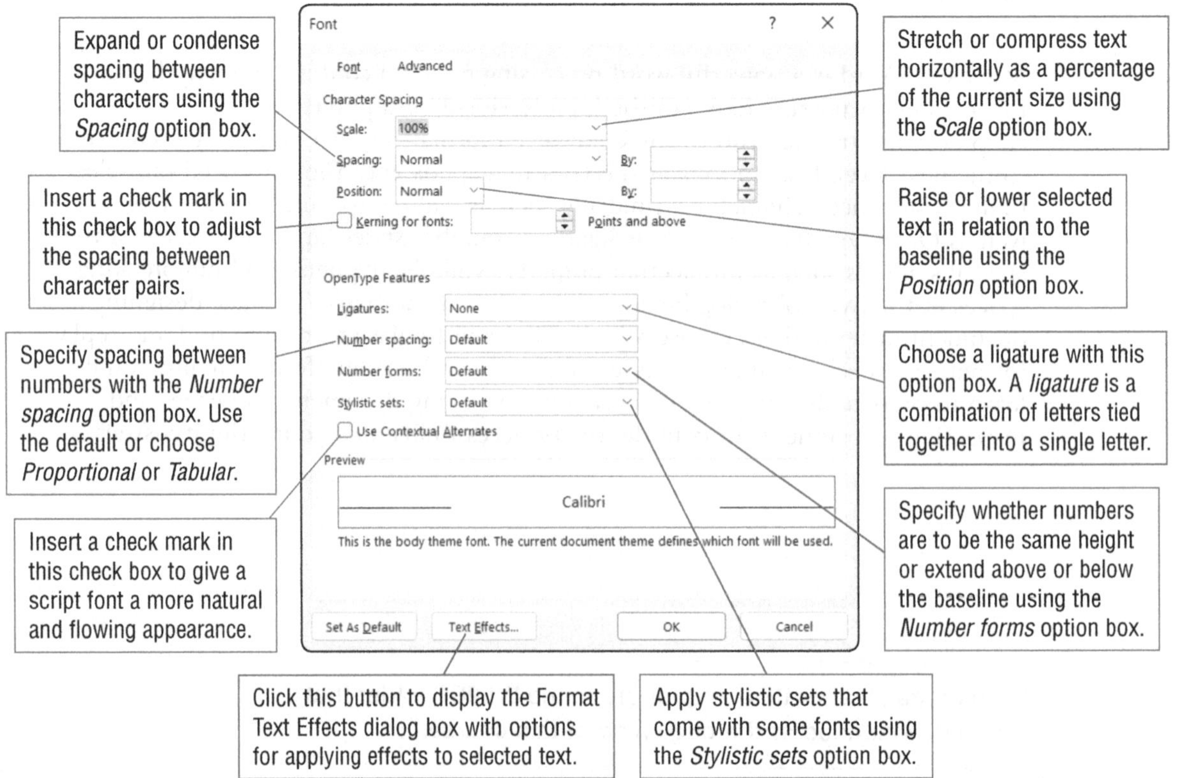
Font
Font
Advanced
Character Spacing
Scale:
100%
Spacing:
Normal
By:
Position:
Normal
By:
Kerning for fonts:
Points and above
OpenType Features
Ligatures:
None
Number spacing:
Default
Number forms:
Default
Stylistic sets:
Default
Use Contextual Alternates
Preview
Calibri
This is the body theme font. The current document theme defines which font will be used.
Set As Default
Text Effects...
OK
Cancel
Expand or condense spacing between characters using the *Spacing* option box.
Insert a check mark in this check box to adjust the spacing between character pairs.
Specify spacing between numbers with the *Number spacing* option box. Use the default or choose *Proportional* or *Tabular*.
Insert a check mark in this check box to give a script font a more natural and flowing appearance.
Stretch or compress text horizontally as a percentage of the current size using the *Scale* option box.
Raise or lower selected text in relation to the baseline using the *Position* option box.
Choose a ligature with this option box. A *ligature* is a combination of letters tied together into a single letter.
Specify whether numbers are to be the same height or extend above or below the baseline using the *Number forms* option box.
Click this button to display the Format Text Effects dialog box with options for applying effects to selected text.
Apply stylistic sets that come with some fonts using the *Stylistic sets* option box.

Hint Subtle adjustments to the scaling and spacing of characters can have a big impact on the visual display of text in a document.

Hint Apply kerning for fonts set 14 points or larger or for italic text.

between characters with the *Spacing* option box. Choose the *Expanded* or *Condensed* option and then enter a specific point size in the *By* text box. Raise or lower selected text in relation to the baseline with the *Position* option box. Choose the *Raised* or *Lowered* option and then enter the point size in the *By* text box.

Insert a check mark in the *Kerning for fonts* check box to apply kerning to selected text in a document. Kerning involves adjusting the spacing between certain character combinations by positioning two characters closer together than normal and uses the shapes and slopes of the characters to improve their appearance. Kerning allows more text to fit in a specific amount of space; kerned characters also look more natural and help the eye move along the text when reading. Consider kerning text set in larger font sizes, such as 14 points and larger, and text set in italics. Figure 1.2 displays text with and without kerning applied. Notice how the letters *Te* and *Va* are closer together in the kerned text compared with the text that is not kerned.

Turn on automatic kerning by displaying the Font dialog box with the Advanced tab selected and then inserting a check mark in the *Kerning for fonts* check box. Specify the beginning point size to be kerned in the *Points and above* measurement box.

Figure 1.2 Text with and without Kerning Applied

Tennison Valley (kerned)
Tennison Valley (not kerned)

Activity 1a Adjusting Character Spacing and Kerning Text

Part 1 of 5

1. Open **PRDonorApp.docx** and then save it with the name **1-PRDonorApp.**
2. Select the title *Donor Appreciation.*
3. With the Home tab active, click the Font group dialog box launcher.
4. At the Font dialog box, click the Advanced tab.
5. Click the *Scale* option box arrow and then click *150%* at the drop-down list.
6. Click the *Spacing* option box arrow and then click *Condensed* at the drop-down list.
7. Click the *Kerning for fonts* check box to insert a check mark.
8. Click OK to close the dialog box.
9. Select the text *Enjoy the "flavor of Tanzania" and an evening of cultural entertainment....*
10. Click the Font group dialog box launcher to display the Font dialog box with the Advanced tab selected.
11. Click the *Kerning for fonts* check box to insert a check mark.
12. Click OK to close the dialog box.
13. Save **1-PRDonorApp.docx.**

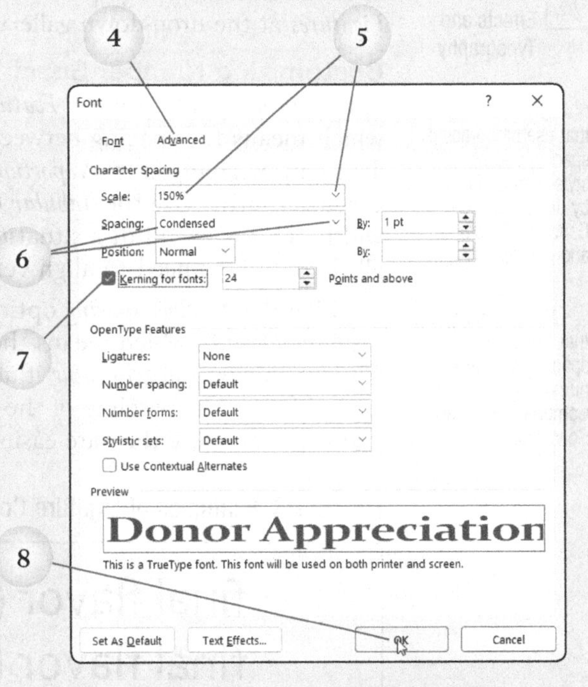

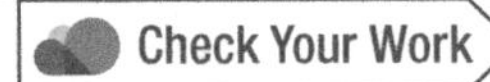

Applying OpenType Features

Quick Steps

Apply OpenType Features

1. Click Font group dialog box launcher.
2. Click Advanced tab.
3. Specify ligatures, number spacing and forms, and/or stylistic sets.
4. Click OK.

Hint Microsoft and Adobe worked cooperatively to create OpenType fonts, which are scalable fonts based on TrueType fonts.

Applying OpenType Features

The OpenType font file format was developed by Adobe and Microsoft to work on both Macintosh and Windows computers. The benefits of the OpenType format are cross-platform compatibility, which means font files can be moved between Macintosh and Windows computers; the ability to support expanded character sets and layout figures; and the capability for web page designers to create high-quality fonts for online documents. Microsoft Word offers some advanced OpenType features in the Font dialog box with the Advanced tab selected (refer to Figure 1.1 on page 4) that desktop publishers and web and graphic designers can use to enhance the appearance of text.

Using Ligatures to Combine Characters At the Font dialog box with the Advanced tab selected, *Ligatures* is the first option box in the *OpenType Features* section. A ligature is a combination of characters joined into a single letter. The OpenType standard specifies four categories of ligatures: *Standard Only*, *Standard and Contextual*, *Historical and Discretionary*, and *All*. The font designer decides which category to support and in which group to put combinations of characters.

With the *Standard Only* option selected, the standard set of ligatures that most typographers and font designers determine are appropriate for the font are applied to text. Common ligatures include letter combinations with the letter *f*, as shown in Figure 1.3. Notice how the *fi* and *fl* letter pairs are combined when ligatures are applied.

Use the other ligature options to specify *Contextual* ligatures, which are ligatures that the font designer believes are appropriate for use with the font, but are not standard. Choose the option *Historical and Discretionary* to apply ligatures that were once standard, but are no longer commonly used; use them to create a historical or "period" effect. The *All* ligatures option applies all the ligature combinations to selected text. Another method for applying ligatures to selected text is to click the Text Effects and Typography button in the Font group on the Home tab, point to *Ligatures* at the drop-down gallery and then click an option at the side menu.

Text Effects and Typography

Hint Some fonts that use proportional spacing and old style number forms by default include Candara, Constantia, and Corbel.

Hint Some fonts that use tabular spacing and lining number forms include Cambria, Calibri, and Consolas.

Customizing Number Spacing and Number Forms The *Number spacing* option box in the *OpenType Features* section will automatically display *Default*, which means the spacing between numbers is determined by the font designer. This can be changed to *Proportional*, which adjusts the spacing for numbers with varying widths. Use the *Tabular* option to specify that each number is the same width. This is useful in a situation in which the numbers are set in columns and all the numbers need to align vertically.

Like the *Number spacing* option box, the *Number forms* option box automatically displays *Default*, which means the font designer determines the number form. Change this option to *Lining* if all the numbers should be the same height and not extend below the baseline of the text. Generally, lining numbers are used in tables and forms because they are easier to read. With the *Old-style* option, the lines of

Figure 1.3 Examples of Ligature Combinations

final flavor (using ligatures)
final flavor (not using ligatures)

the numbers can extend above or below the baseline of the text. For some fonts, changing the *Number forms* option to *Old-style* results in numbers such as *3* and *5* extending below the baseline or being centered higher on the line. See Figure 1.4 for examples of number form and spacing.

The spacing and form of numbers can also be adjusted with the Text Effects and Typography button in the Font group. Click the button arrow and then hover the pointer over the *Number Styles* option in the drop-down gallery to display a side menu of options.

Figure 1.4 Number Form and Spacing

Old-style form and proportional spacing (in Candara):

123456789

Lining form and tabular spacing (in Cambria):

123456789

Activity 1b Applying a Ligature and Number Form

Part 2 of 5

1. With **1-PRDonorApp.docx** open, select the text *Enjoy the "flavor of Tanzania" and an evening of cultural entertainment….*
2. Click the Font group dialog box launcher and, if necessary, click the Advanced tab.
3. At the Font dialog box with the Advanced tab selected, click the *Ligatures* option box arrow and then click *Standard and Contextual* at the drop-down list.
4. Click OK to close the dialog box.
5. Select the text *2025 – 2026* and *$3,500,000*.
6. Click the Text Effects and Typography button in the Font group, point to *Number Styles* at the drop-down gallery, and then click *Tabular Old-style* at the side menu.
7. Save **1-PRDonorApp.docx**.

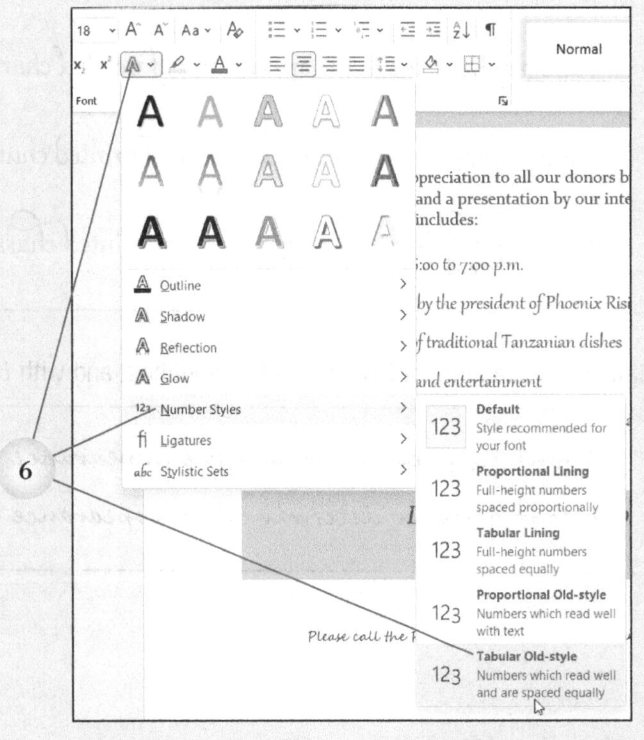

Check Your Work

Applying Stylistic Sets A font designer may include a number of stylistic sets for a specific font. A different stylistic set may apply additional formatting to the characters in a font. For example, the sentences in Figure 1.5 are set in 16-point Gabriola. Notice the slight variations in characters in some of the stylistic sets. Choose a stylistic set and see a visual representation of the characters with the stylistic set applied in the *Preview* section of the dialog box. A stylistic set can also be applied by clicking the Text Effects and Typography button in the Font group, pointing to *Stylistic Sets* at the drop-down gallery, and then clicking the stylistic set at the side menu.

Insert a check mark in the *Use Contextual Alternates* check box in the Font dialog box with the Advanced tab selected to fine-tune letter combinations based on the surrounding characters. Use this feature to give script fonts a more natural and flowing appearance. Figure 1.6 shows text set in 12-point Segoe Script. The first line of text is set with the default setting and the second line of text is set with the *Use Contextual Alternates* option selected. Notice the slight differences in letters such as *t*, *n*, *s*, and *h*.

Not all fonts are developed in the OpenType file format. Experiment with a font using the OpenType features at the Font dialog box with the Advanced tab selected to determine what features are supported by the font.

Figure 1.5 Examples of Gabriola Font Stylistic Sets

Typography refers to the appearance of printed characters on the page. **(Default set)**

Typography refers to the appearance of printed characters on the page. **(Stylistic set 4)**

Typography refers to the appearance of printed characters on the page. **(Stylistic set 5)**

Typography refers to the appearance of printed characters on the page. **(Stylistic set 6)**

Figure 1.6 Examples of Segoe Script Font without and with *Use Contextual Alternates* Selected

A font designer determines the appearance of each character in a font.

A font designer determines the appearance of each character in a font.

Activity 1c Applying a Stylistic Set and Using Contextual Alternates

Part 3 of 5

1. With **1-PRDonorApp.docx** open, select the bulleted text.
2. Display the Font dialog box with the Advanced tab selected.
3. Click the *Stylistic sets* option box arrow and then click *4* at the drop-down list.
4. Click OK to close the dialog box.
5. Select the text *Please call the Phoenix Rising office to let us know if you will be joining us.*
6. Display the Font dialog box with the Advanced tab selected.
7. Click the *Use Contextual Alternates* check box to insert a check mark.

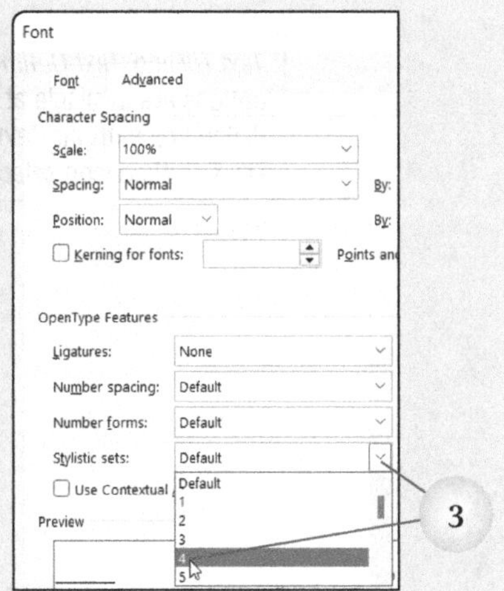

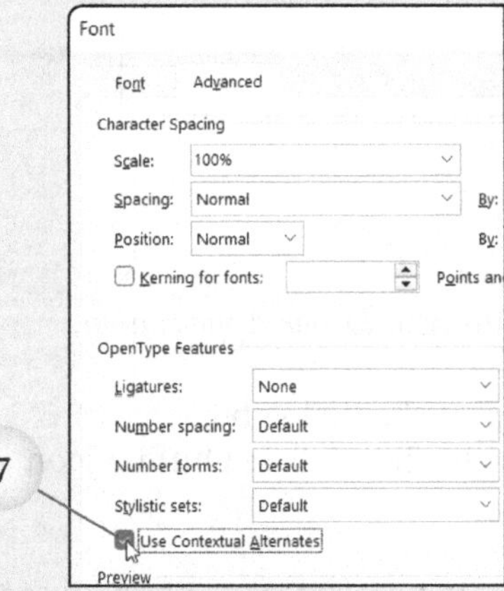

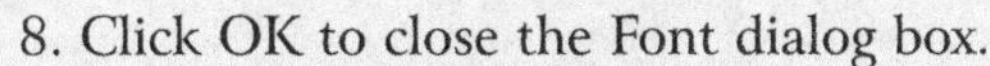

8. Click OK to close the Font dialog box.
9. Save **1-PRDonorApp.docx**.

Check Your Work

Tutorial

Applying Text Effects at the Format Text Effects Dialog Box

Quick Steps

Apply Text Effects

1. Click Font group dialog box launcher.
2. Click Text Effects button.
3. Choose options at Format Text Effects dialog box.
4. Click OK.

Applying Text Effects

Text effects can enhance the look of a document by adding color and interest. Use text effects to create attention-getting flyers and brochures. Or add effects to titles and subtitles to give reports and other documents a more professionally designed look and feel. Click the Text Effects button at the bottom of the Font dialog box with the Advanced tab selected and the Format Text Effects dialog box displays with the Text Fill & Outline icon selected, as shown in Figure 1.7. Click *Text Fill* or *Text Outline* to display the text formatting options. Click the Text Effects icon to display additional effects formatting options. Many of the options available at the dialog box also are available by clicking the Text Effects and Typography button in the Font group on the Home tab.

Figure 1.7 Format Text Effects Dialog Box

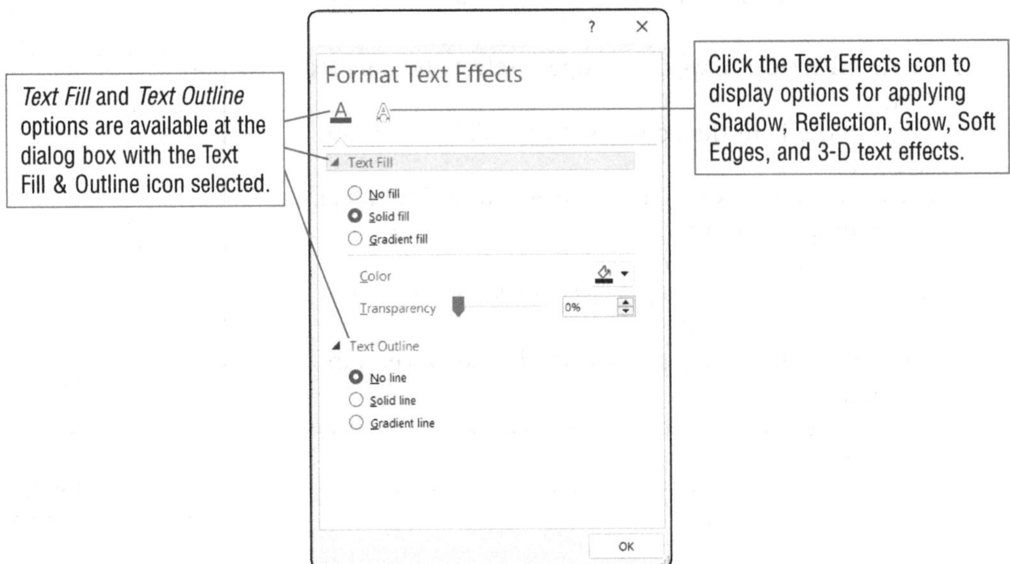

Activity 1d Applying Text Effects

Part 4 of 5

1. With **1-PRDonorApp.docx** open, select the title *Donor Appreciation*.
2. Display the Font dialog box.
3. Click the Text Effects button at the bottom of the dialog box.
4. At the Format Text Effects dialog box with the Text Fill & Outline icon selected, click *Text Fill* to expand the options.
5. Click *Gradient fill* to select the option.
6. Click the Preset gradients button and then click the *Medium Gradient - Accent 6* option (last column, third row).

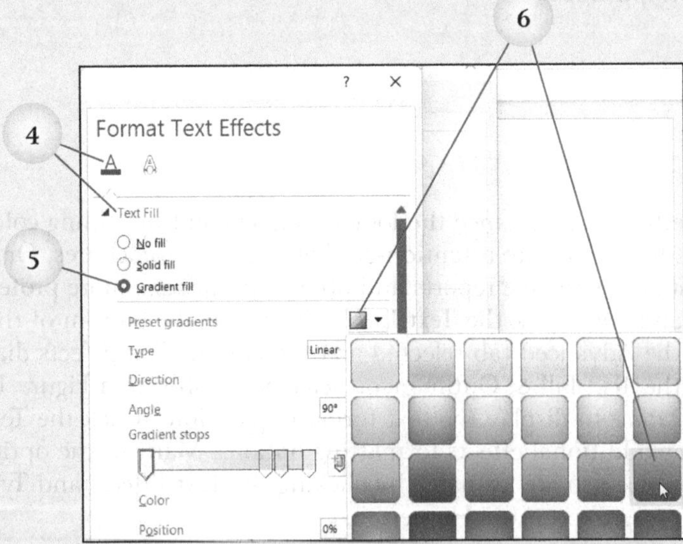

7. Click the Direction button and then click the *Linear Down* option (second column, first row).

8. Scroll down the dialog box and then click *Text Outline* to expand the options.
9. Click *Solid line* to select the option.
10. Click the Color button and then click the *Orange, Accent 6, Darker 50%* option (last column, last row in the *Theme Colors* section).

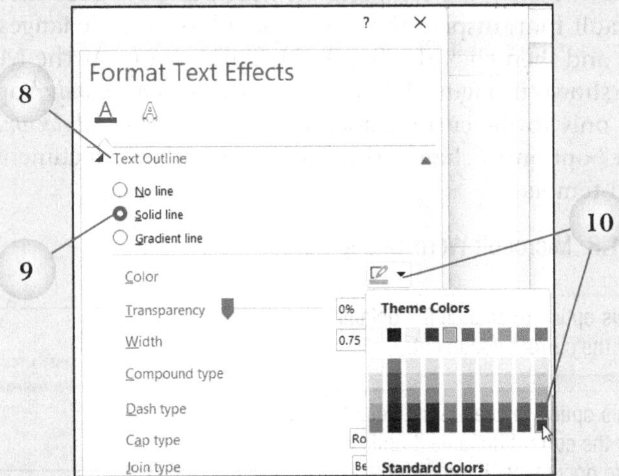

11. Click the Text Effects icon.
12. Click *Shadow* to expand the options.
13. Click the Presets button and then click the *Offset: Left* option (third column, second row in the *Outer* section).

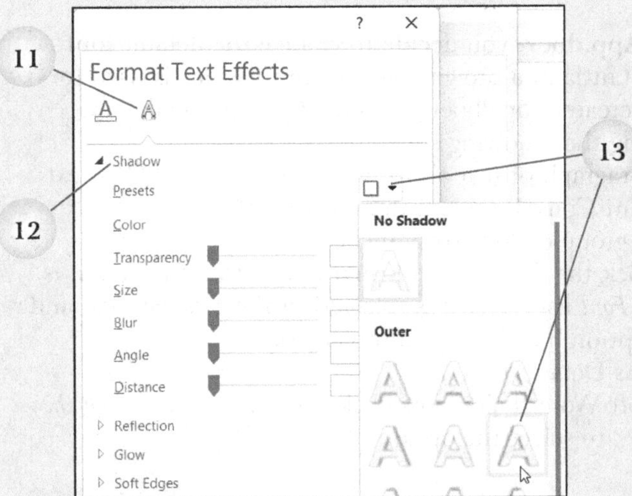

14. Click *Glow* to expand the options.
15. Click the Presets button in the *Glow* section and then click the *Glow: 5 point; Orange, Accent color 6* option (last column, first row in the *Glow Variations* section).
16. Click OK to close the Format Text Effects dialog box.
17. Click OK to close the Font dialog box and then deselect the title.
18. Save **1-PRDonorApp.docx**.

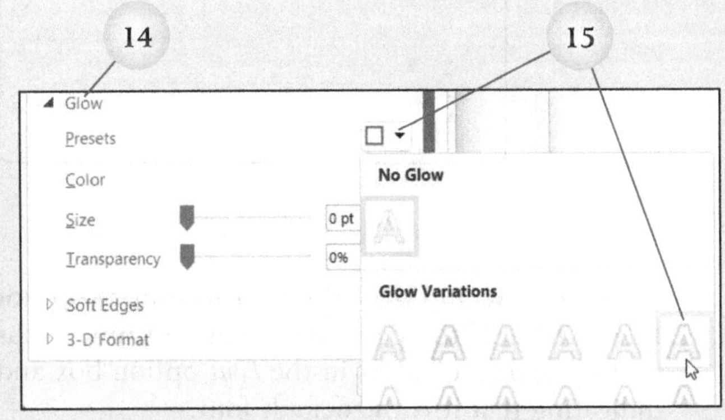

Check Your Work

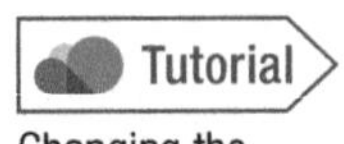

Changing the Default Font

Quick Steps

Change Default Font

1. Click Font group dialog box launcher.
2. Change font and/or effects.
3. Click Set As Default button.
4. Click *This document only?* or *All documents based on the Normal template?*
5. Click OK.

Changing the Default Font

If documents are generally created with a font other than the default, the default can be changed with the Set As Default button at the Font dialog box. The default font can be changed for the current document or it can be changed in the Normal template, which is the template on which all new documents are based. To change the default font, display the Font dialog box, make changes to the font and/or effects, and then click the Set As Default button. At the Microsoft Word dialog box, as shown in Figure 1.8, click the *This document only?* option to apply the default only to the current document or click the *All documents based on the Normal template?* option to change the default for all new documents based on the default Normal template.

Figure 1.8 Microsoft Word Dialog Box

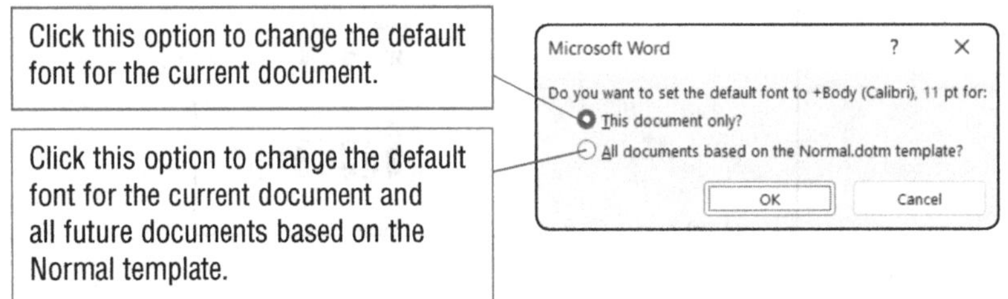

Activity 1e Changing the Default Font

Part 5 of 5

1. For **1-PRDonorApp.docx**, you decide to change the default font to 12-point Constantia in a brown color, since this font is used for most documents created for Phoenix Rising. Change the default font by completing the following steps:
   a. Click in the paragraph of text above the bulleted text. (This text is set in 12-point Constantia and in a brown color.)
   b. Click the Font group dialog box launcher.
   c. If necessary, click the Font tab and then notice that *Constantia* is selected in the *Font* list box, *12* is selected in the *Size* list box, and the *Font color* option box displays a brown color.
   d. Click the Set As Default button.
   e. At the Microsoft Word dialog box, click *All documents based on the Normal template?* to select the option.
   f. Click OK.

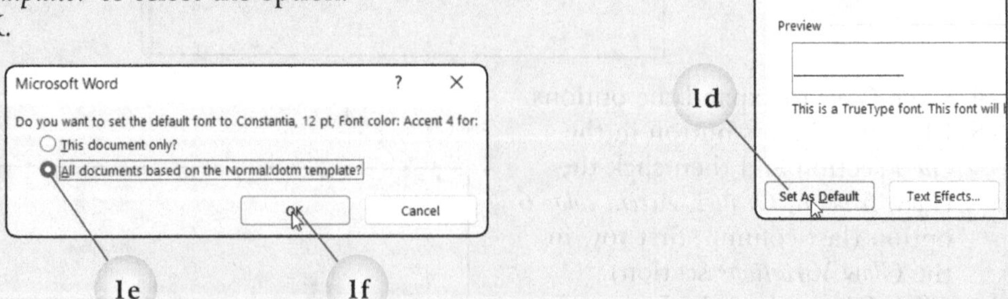

2. Save, preview, and then close **1-PRDonorApp.docx**.
3. Press Ctrl + N to open a new blank document based on the Normal template. Notice that *Constantia* displays in the *Font* option box and *12* displays in the *Font Size* option box, indicating that it is the default font.

4. Change the font back to the original default by completing the following steps:
   a. Click the Font group dialog box launcher.
   b. Scroll up the *Font* list box and then click *+Body*. (This is the original default font, which applies the Calibri font to body text in a document.)
   c. Click *11* in the *Size* list box.
   d. Click the *Font color* option box arrow and then click the *Automatic* option at the top of the drop-down list.
   e. Click the Set As Default button.
   f. At the Microsoft Word dialog box, click the *All documents based on the Normal template?* option.
   g. Click OK.
5. Close the blank document without saving changes.

Activity 2 Create a Document with Symbols and Special Characters **3 Parts**

You will create a document that includes intellectual property symbols; nonbreaking, em dash, and en dash hyphens; and nonbreaking spaces.

Inserting Symbols and Special Characters

Symbols and special characters can be inserted in a document with options at the Symbol dialog box with either the Symbols tab or Special Characters tab selected. Display this dialog box by clicking the Insert tab, clicking the Symbol button, and then clicking the *More Symbols* option. Symbols can also be inserted by typing a sequence of characters or by using keyboard shortcuts. Word creates some special characters automatically as text is typed.

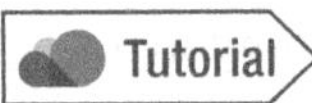

Inserting Intellectual Property Symbols

Inserting Intellectual Property Symbols

Among the symbols that can be inserted in a document are three intellectual property protection symbols: ©, ™, and ®. Insert the © symbol to identify copyrighted intellectual property indicating that someone legally owns the rights to make and distribute copies of a particular work; use the ™ symbol to specify a trademark that a company uses for a particular word, phrase, or logo that represents the business; and use the ® symbol to identify a registered trademark that has been granted by the United States Patent and Trademark Office for a word, phrase, or logo for a company's product or service.

Insert these symbols with options at the Symbol dialog box with the Special Characters tab selected, by typing a sequence of characters, or by using a keyboard shortcut. Insert a © symbol by typing (c) or pressing Alt + Ctrl + C, insert a ™ symbol by typing (tm) or pressing Alt + Ctrl + T, and insert a ® symbol by typing (r) or pressing Alt + Ctrl + R.

Activity 2a Inserting Intellectual Property Symbols

Part 1 of 3

1. At a blank document, type the text shown in Figure 1.9. Bold and center the title as shown and insert each intellectual property symbol using the appropriate sequence of characters or keyboard shortcut. To insert the sequence of characters for each symbol rather than the actual symbol, type the sequence of characters and then immediately click the Undo button. This changes the symbol back to the sequence of characters. (The text in your document will wrap differently than what is shown in the figure.)
2. Save the document with the name **1-Symbols**.

Check Your Work

Figure 1.9 Activity 2a

INTELLECTUAL PROPERTY PROTECTION

A copyright protects original works in areas such as publishing, music, literature, and drama. Use the © symbol to identify copyrighted intellectual property. Create this symbol by typing (c), by using the keyboard shortcut Alt + Ctrl + C, or by clicking the symbol at the Symbol dialog box with the Special Characters tab selected.

A trademark identifies a word, symbol, device, or name such as a brand name. Use the ™ symbol to identify a trademarked name or product. Create this symbol by typing (tm), by using the keyboard shortcut Alt + Ctrl + T, or by clicking the symbol at the Symbol dialog box with the Special Characters tab selected.

A registered trademark is a trademark that has been registered with the US Patent and Trademark Office. Use the ® symbol to identify a registered trademark. Create this symbol by typing (r), by using the keyboard shortcut Alt + Ctrl + R, or by clicking the symbol at the Symbol dialog box with the Special Characters tab selected.

Inserting Hyphens and Nonbreaking Characters

Inserting Hyphens and Dashes

A hyphen (-) is a punctuation mark used to join compound words, such as *fresh-looking* or *sister-in-law*. Use the hyphen key on the keyboard to insert such hyphens. Hyphens can also be used to divide words that fall at the ends of lines. This can create a more even-looking right margin and is especially useful when formatting text in narrow columns.

To hyphenate words that fall at the ends of lines, use the Hyphenation button in the Page Setup group on the Layout tab. This button includes options for automatically or manually hyphenating words that fall at the end of a line. If words are automatically hyphenated, Word inserts an optional hyphen, which displays only when the word is divided across two lines or if the display of nonprinting characters is turned on. If the document is changed so that the word no longer breaks on a line, the hyphen is removed. To control where hyphens appear in words during hyphenation, choose manual rather than automatic hyphenation.

Some text should not be hyphenated and divided across lines. For example, a company name such as *Knowles-Myers Corporation* should not be divided between *Knowles* and *Myers* and set on two lines. To avoid a break like this, insert a nonbreaking hyphen by clicking the *Nonbreaking Hyphen* option at the Symbol dialog box with the Special Characters tab selected or with the keyboard shortcut Ctrl + Shift + -.

An em dash (—) is used to indicate a break in thought or to highlight a term or phrase by separating it from the rest of the sentence. Em dashes are particularly useful in long sentences and sentences with multiple phrases and commas. For example, the sentence "The main focus of this document is on general-purpose, single-user computers—personal computers—that enable users to complete a variety of computing tasks." contains two em dashes: before and after the words *personal computers*.

To create an em dash in a Word document, type a word, type two hyphens, type the next word, and then press the spacebar. When the spacebar is pressed, Word automatically converts the two hyphens to an em dash. If automatic formatting of em dashes is turned off, an em dash can be inserted with the *Em Dash* option at the Symbol dialog box with the Special Characters tab selected or with the keyboard shortcut Alt + Ctrl + - (on the numeric keypad).

Hint An em dash is the width of the capital letter *M* and an en dash is the width of the capital letter *N*.

En dashes (–) are used between inclusive dates, times, and numbers to mean "through." For example, in the text *9:30–11:00 a.m.*, the numbers should be separated by an en dash rather than a regular hyphen. Word does not automatically convert hyphens to en dashes, as it does with em dashes. To create an en dash, click the *En Dash* option at the Symbol dialog box with the Special Characters tab selected or use the keyboard shortcut Ctrl + - (on the numeric keypad).

Activity 2b Inserting Hyphens and Dashes

Part 2 of 3

1. With **1-Symbols.docx** open, press Ctrl + End, press the Enter key, and then type the text shown in Figure 1.10 with the following specifications:
   a. Type an en dash between the times *9:00* and *10:30 a.m.* by pressing Ctrl + - (on the numeric keypad). If you are working on a laptop that does not have a numeric keypad, insert an en dash by clicking the Insert tab, clicking the Symbol button, and then clicking *More Symbols*. At the Symbol dialog box, click the Special Characters tab, click the *En Dash* option, click the Insert button, and then click the Close button.
   b. Create the em dashes before and after the phrase *Excel, PowerPoint, and Access* by typing hyphens (two hyphens for each em dash).
   c. Insert a nonbreaking hyphen within *Tri-State* by pressing Ctrl + Shift + -.
2. Save **1-Symbols.docx**.

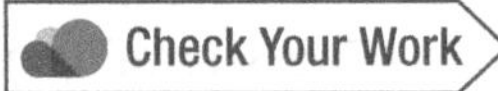

Figure 1.10 Activity 2b

SOFTWARE TRAINING

The Microsoft® 365 Word training is scheduled for Thursday, March 7, 2024, from 9:00–10:30 a.m. Additional training for other applications in the Microsoft suite—Excel, PowerPoint, and Access—will be available during the month of April. Contact the Training Department for additional information. All Tri-State employees are eligible for the training.

Inserting Nonbreaking Spaces

As text is typed in a document, Word makes decisions about where to end lines and automatically wraps text to the beginning of new lines. In some situations, a line may break between two words or phrases that should remain together. To control where text breaks across lines, consider inserting nonbreaking spaces between words that should remain together.

Insert a nonbreaking space with the *Nonbreaking Space* option at the Symbol dialog box with the Special Characters tab selected or with the keyboard shortcut Ctrl + Shift + spacebar. If nonprinting characters are turned on, a normal space displays as a dot and a nonbreaking space displays as a degree symbol.

Activity 2c Inserting Nonbreaking Spaces

Part 3 of 3

1. With **1-Symbols.docx** open, click the Show/Hide ¶ button in the Paragraph group on the Home tab.

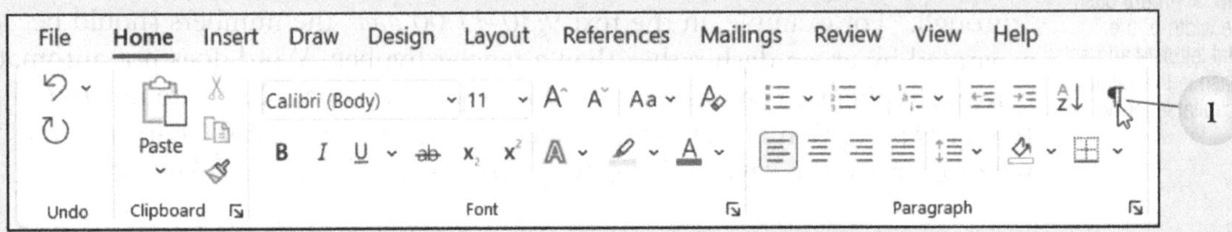

2. Press Ctrl + End, press the Enter key, and then type the text in Figure 1.11. Insert nonbreaking spaces in the keyboard shortcuts by pressing Ctrl + Shift + spacebar before and after each plus (+) symbol.
3. Turn off the display of nonprinting characters.
4. Save, preview, and then close **1-Symbols.docx**.

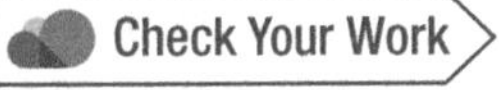

Figure 1.11 Activity 2c

KEYBOARD SHORTCUTS

Microsoft Word includes a number of keyboard shortcuts you can use to access commands. The ScreenTip for some buttons and options displays the keyboard shortcut for executing the command. Hovering the pointer over the *Font* option box on the Home tab causes the ScreenTip to display Ctrl + Shift + F as the keyboard shortcut. Additional Home tab Font group keyboard shortcuts include Ctrl + B to bold text, Ctrl + I to italicize text, and Ctrl + U to underline text. You can also press Ctrl + Shift + + to turn on superscript and press Ctrl + = to turn on subscript.

Activity 3 Use Find and Replace Options in a Lease Agreement 5 Parts

You will open a commercial lease agreement; find and replace font formatting, paragraph formatting, special characters, styles, and body and heading fonts; and then find and replace text using a wildcard character.

Using Find and Replace Options

The Find and Replace dialog box can be used to find and replace fonts, special characters, and body and heading fonts. The expanded Find and Replace dialog box contains a *Use wildcards* option. With this option selected, a wildcard character can be used to find specific text or characters in a document. Display the Find and Replace dialog box by clicking the Replace button in the Editing group on the Home tab.

Finding and Replacing Formatting

Finding and Replacing Font Formatting

Use options at the Find and Replace dialog box with the Replace tab selected to search for characters containing specific font formatting and replace them with other characters or font formatting. With the insertion point positioned in the *Find what* text box, specify the font formatting to be found in the document by clicking the More button to expand the dialog box, clicking the Format button in the lower left corner of the dialog box, and then clicking the *Font* option at the drop-down list. At the Find Font dialog box, specify the formatting to be found and then close the dialog box. Click in the *Replace with* text box and then complete similar steps to specify the replacement font formatting.

Finding and Replacing Paragraph Formatting

The Find and Replace dialog box contains options for searching for and replacing specific paragraph formatting. Identify the paragraph formatting to be found in the document by clicking in the *Find what* text box, clicking the Format button in the lower left corner of the dialog box, and then clicking *Paragraph* at the drop-down list. At the Paragraph dialog box, specify the formatting to be found and then close the dialog box. Click in the *Replace with* text box and then complete similar steps to specify the replacement paragraph formatting.

Activity 3a Finding and Replacing Font and Paragraph Formatting Part 1 of 5

1. Open **ComLease.docx** and then save it with the name **1-ComLease**.
2. Find text set in the Corbel font with dark red color and replace it with text set in Constantia with automatic color by completing the following steps:
   a. Click the Replace button in the Editing group on the Home tab.
   b. At the Find and Replace dialog box, click the More button to expand the dialog box.

c. Click in the *Find what* text box, click the Format button in the lower left corner of the dialog box, and then click *Font* at the drop-down list.
d. At the Find Font dialog box, scroll down the *Font* list box and then click *Corbel*.
e. Click the *Font color* option box arrow and then click the *Dark Red* color (first color option in the *Standard Colors* section).
f. Click OK to close the dialog box.
g. Click in the *Replace with* text box.
h. Click the Format button in the lower left corner of the dialog box and then click *Font* at the drop-down list.
i. At the Replace Font dialog box, scroll down the *Font* list box and then click *Constantia*.
j. Click the *Font color* option box arrow and then click the *Automatic* option.
k. Click OK to close the dialog box.
l. At the Find and Replace dialog box, click the Replace All button.
m. At the message indicating 40 replacements were made, click OK.

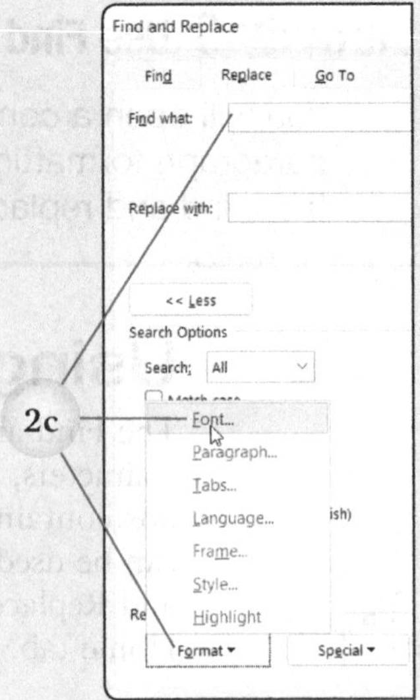

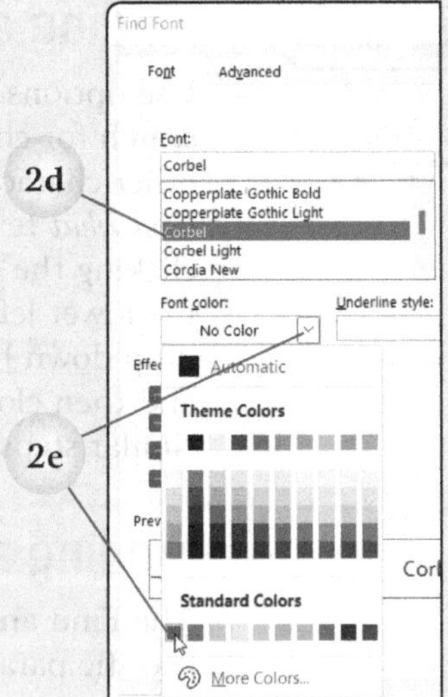

3. With the Find and Replace dialog box open, search for all first-line indents in the document and remove the indents by completing the following steps:
   a. With the insertion point positioned in the *Find what* text box, click the No Formatting button.
   b. Click the Format button and then click *Paragraph* at the drop-down list.
   c. At the Find Paragraph dialog box, click the *Special* option box arrow in the *Indentation* section and then click *First line* at the drop-down list.
   d. Click OK to close the Find Paragraph dialog box.
   e. At the Find and Replace dialog box, click in the *Replace with* text box.
   f. Click the No Formatting button.
   g. Click the Format button and then click *Paragraph* at the drop-down list.
   h. At the Replace Paragraph dialog box, click the *Special* option box arrow in the *Indentation* section and then click *(none)* at the drop-down list.
   i. Click OK to close the Replace Paragraph dialog box.
   j. Click the Replace All button.
   k. At the message indicating 7 replacements were made, click OK.

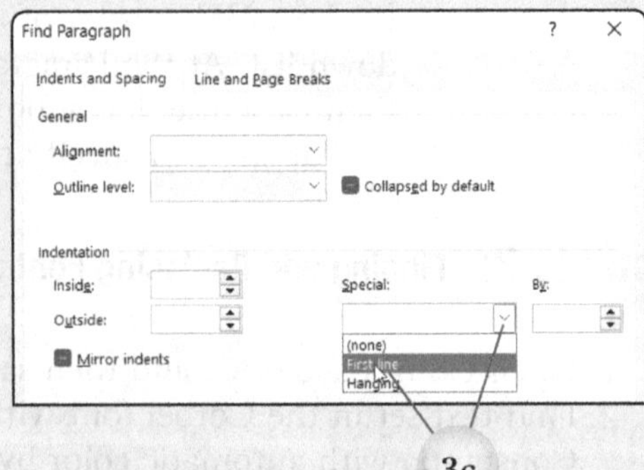

4. Close the Find and Replace dialog box.
5. Save **1-ComLease.docx**.

Check Your Work

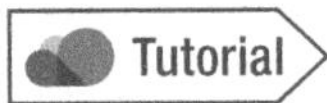

Finding and Replacing Special Characters

Quick Steps

Find and Replace Special Character

1. Click Replace button.
2. Click More button.
3. Click Special button.
4. Click character at drop-down list.
5. Click in *Replace with* text box.
6. Insert replacement character.
7. Click Replace All button.
8. Click OK.

Finding and Replacing Special Characters

Find or find and replace special characters with the Special button at the expanded Find and Replace dialog box. Click the Special button and a drop-down list displays similar to the one shown in Figure 1.12. Click a special character in the drop-down list and a code representing the character is inserted in the text box where the insertion point is positioned. For example, with the insertion point positioned in the *Find what* text box, clicking *Paragraph Mark* at the Special button drop-down list inserts the code *^p* in the text box. If a character code is known, it can be typed directly in the *Find what* or *Replace with* text box

Figure 1.12 Special Button Drop-Down List

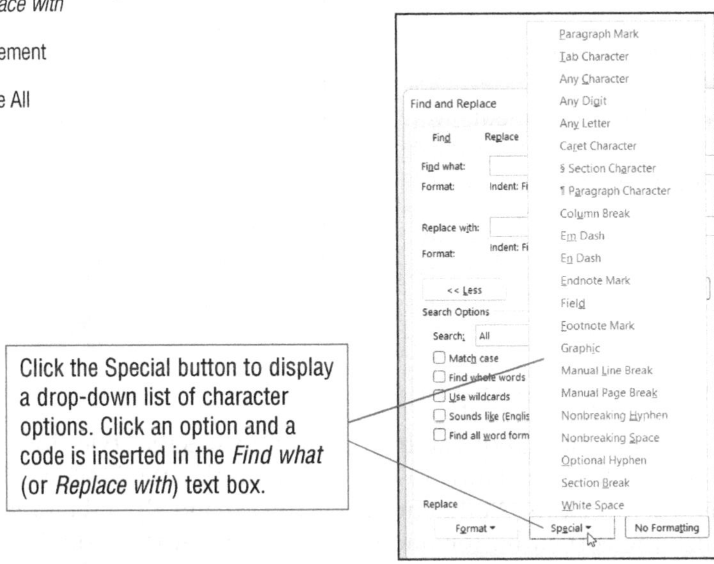

Activity 3b Finding and Replacing Special Characters

Part 2 of 5

1. With **1-ComLease.docx** open, search for and delete all continuous section breaks by completing the following steps:
   a. Click the Replace button in the Editing group on the Home tab.
   b. If necessary, expand the Find and Replace dialog box.
   c. If formatting information displays below the *Find what* text box, click the No Formatting button.
   d. Click the Special button at the bottom of the dialog box.
   e. Click *Section Break* in the drop-down list. (This inserts *^b* in the *Find what* text box.)
   f. Click in the *Replace with* text box and make sure the text box is empty. If formatting information displays below the text box, click the No Formatting button.

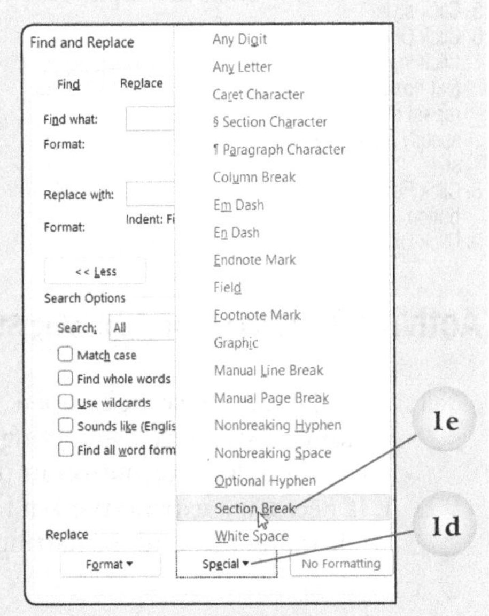

g. Click the Replace All button.
h. At the message indicating 3 replacements were made, click OK.

2. With the expanded Find and Replace dialog box open, find all occurrences of regular hyphens and replace them with nonbreaking hyphens by completing the following steps:
   a. With ^b selected in the *Find what* text box, type - (a hyphen).
   b. Press the Tab key to move the insertion point to the *Replace with* text box.
   c. Click the Special button at the bottom of the dialog box.
   d. Click *Nonbreaking Hyphen* at the drop-down list.
   e. Click the Replace All button.
   f. At the message indicating 19 replacements were made, click OK.
   g. Close the Find and Replace dialog box.
3. Save **1-ComLease.docx**.

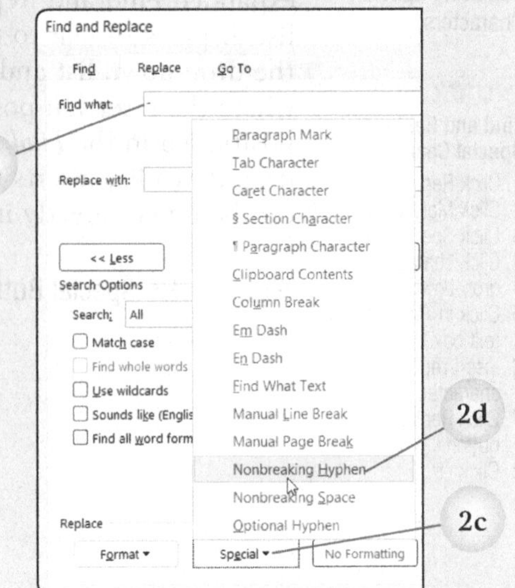

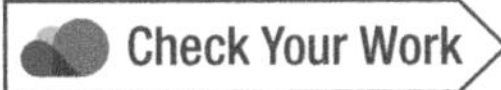

Finding and Replacing Styles

Quick Steps

Find and Replace Style
1. Click Replace button.
2. Click More button.
3. Click Format button.
4. Click *Style*.
5. Click style.
6. Click OK.
7. Click in *Replace with* text box and then repeat steps 3-6 to specify replacement style.
8. Click Replace All button.
9. Click OK.

Finding and Replacing Styles

The Find and Replace dialog box can be used to find specific styles in a document and replace them with other styles. To find styles, display the Find and Replace dialog box and then click the More button. At the expanded Find and Replace dialog box, click the Format button and then click *Style* at the drop-down list. At the Find Style dialog box, click the style in the *Find what style* list box and then click OK. Click in the *Replace with* text box at the Find and Replace dialog box, click the Format button, and then click *Style*. At the Replace Style dialog box, click the replacement style in the *Replace With Style* list box and then click OK.

Activity 3c Finding and Replacing Styles — Part 3 of 5

1. With **1-ComLease.docx** open, search for Heading 3 styles and replace them with Heading 2 styles by completing the following steps:
   a. Click the Replace button in the Editing group on the Home tab.
   b. If necessary, expand the Find and Replace dialog box.
   c. Clear any text and formatting from the *Find what* and *Replace with* text boxes.

d. With the insertion point positioned in the *Find what* text box, click the Format button and then click *Style* at the drop-down list.
e. At the Find Style dialog box, scroll down the *Find what style* list box and then click *Heading 3*.
f. Click OK to close the Find Style dialog box.

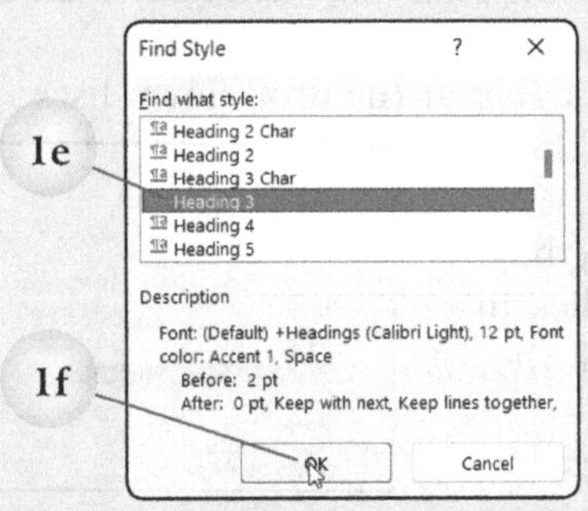

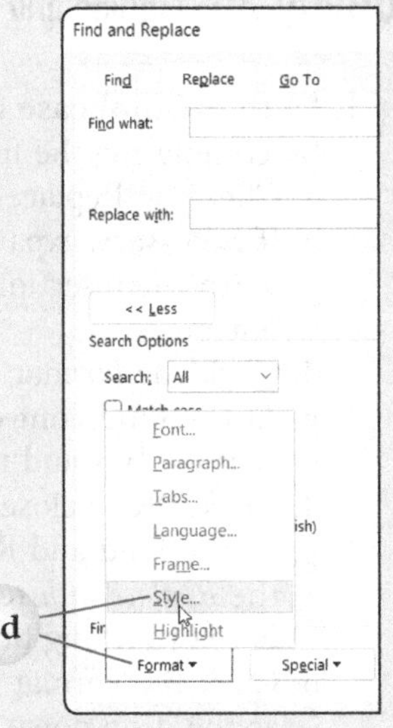

g. At the Find and Replace dialog box, click in the *Replace with* text box.
h. Click the Format button and then click *Style* at the drop-down list.
i. At the Replace Style dialog box, scroll down the *Replace With Style* list box, click *Heading 2*, and then click OK.
j. At the Find and Replace dialog box, click the Replace All button.
k. At the message indicating 6 replacements were made, click OK.
l. Click the Close button to close the Find and Replace dialog box.

2. Save **1-ComLease.docx**.

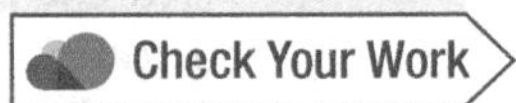

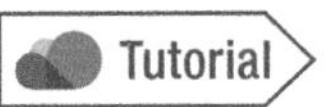

Finding and Replacing Body and Heading Fonts

Quick Steps

Find and Replace Body or Heading Font

1. Click Replace button.
2. Click More button.
3. Click Format button.
4. Click *Font*.
5. Click *+Body* or *+Headings* in *Font* list box.
6. Click OK.
7. Click in *Replace with* text box.
8. Insert replacement font.
9. Click Replace All button.
10. Click OK.

Finding and Replacing Body and Heading Fonts

By default, a Word document has the Office theme applied, which applies the Office set of colors, fonts, and effects. The theme fonts include a body font and heading font. The default settings for theme fonts are *Calibri (Body)* and *Calibri Light (Headings)*. These fonts display at the beginning of the *Font* option box drop-down gallery. If a different theme has been applied, other body and heading fonts will be used; they can be viewed at the *Font* option box drop-down gallery.

A document can be searched for one body or heading font and then replaced with a different font. To do this, display the Find and Replace dialog box with the Replace tab selected. Expand the dialog box, click the Format button, and then click *Font* at the drop-down list. At the Find Font dialog box, scroll up the *Font* list box and then click *+Body* if searching for the body font or click *+Headings* if searching for the heading font. Click in the *Replace with* text box and then complete the steps to insert the replacement font.

Activity 3d Finding and Replacing Body and Heading Fonts

1. With **1-ComLease.docx** open, search for the +Body font and replace it with Constantia by completing the following steps:
   a. Click the Replace button in the Editing group on the Home tab.
   b. If necessary, expand the Find and Replace dialog box.
   c. With the insertion point positioned in the *Find what* text box, click the No Formatting button.
   d. Click the Format button and then click *Font* at the drop-down list.
   e. At the Find Font dialog box, scroll up the *Font* list box and then click *+Body*.
   f. Click OK to close the Find Font dialog box.
   g. At the Find and Replace dialog box, click in the *Replace with* text box and then click the No Formatting button.
   h. Click the Format button and then click *Font* at the drop-down list.
   i. At the Replace Font dialog box, scroll down the *Font* list box and then click *Constantia*.
   j. Click OK to close the Replace Font dialog box.
   k. At the Find and Replace dialog box, click the Replace All button.
   l. At the message indicating 43 replacements were made, click OK.

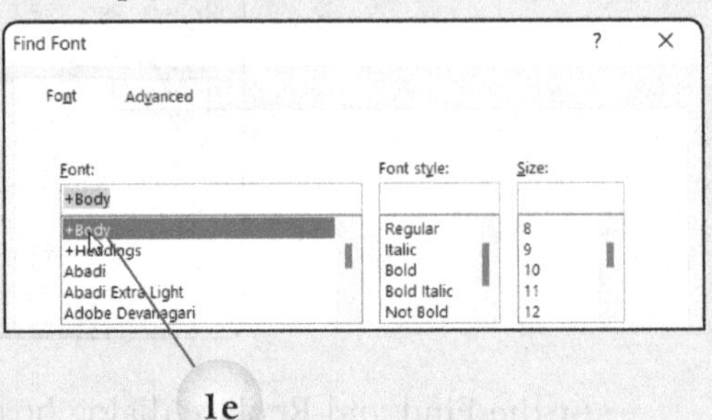

2. With the Find and Replace dialog box open, search for text set in the +Headings font and replace it with text set in 14-point Corbel bold and the standard dark blue color, and then change the paragraph alignment to center alignment by completing the following steps:
   a. With the insertion point positioned in the *Find what* text box, click the No Formatting button.
   b. Click the Format button and then click *Font* at the drop-down list.
   c. At the Find Font dialog box, click *+Headings* in the *Font* list box.
   d. Click OK to close the Find Font dialog box.
   e. At the Find and Replace dialog box, click in the *Replace with* text box.
   f. Click the No Formatting button.
   g. Click the Format button and then click *Font* at the drop-down list.
   h. At the Replace Font dialog box, scroll down and then click *Corbel* in the *Font* list box, click *Bold* in the *Font style* list box, scroll down and then click *14* in the *Size* list box, and click the *Font color* option box arrow and then click the *Dark Blue* option (ninth color option in the *Standard Colors* section).
   i. Click OK to close the Replace Font dialog box.
   j. With the insertion point positioned in the *Replace with* text box at the Find and Replace dialog box, click the Format button and then click *Paragraph* at the drop-down list.

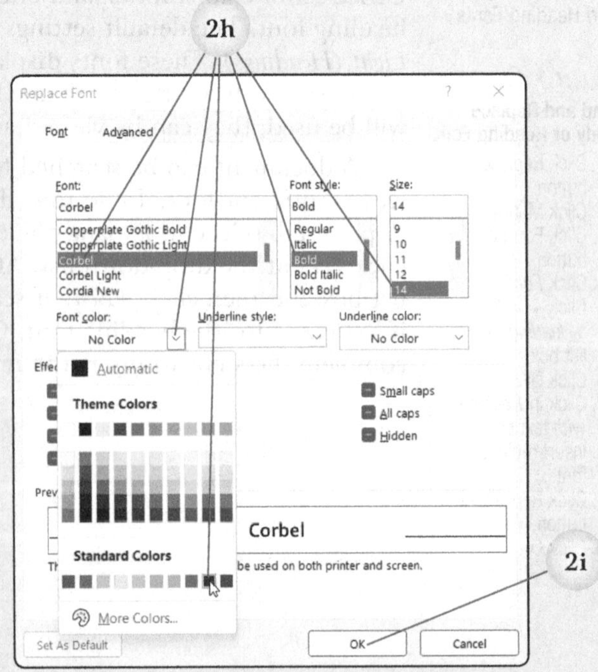

k. At the Replace Paragraph dialog box, click the *Alignment* option box arrow and then click *Centered* at the drop-down list.

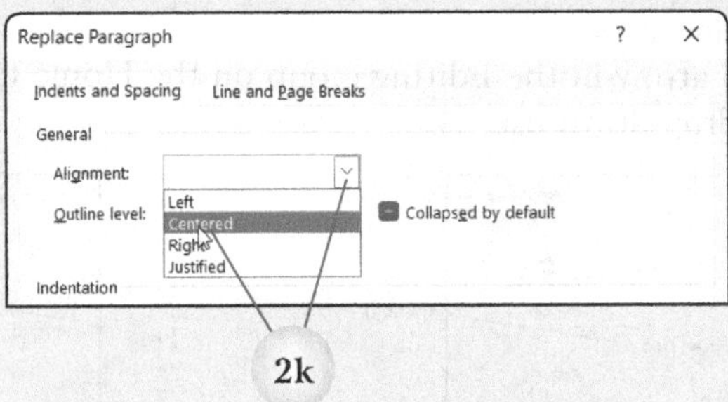

l. Click OK to close the Replace Paragraph dialog box.
m. Click the Replace All button.
n. At the message indicating 7 replacements were made, click OK.

3. Click the Less button and then close the Find and Replace dialog box.
4. Scroll through the document and notice the heading, formatting, and paragraph changes made to the document.
5. Save **1-ComLease.docx**.

Check Your Work

Tutorial

Finding and Replacing Text Using a Wildcard Character

Quick Steps

Find and Replace Text Using Wildcard Character

1. Click Replace button.
2. Click More button.
3. Click *Use wildcards* check box.
4. Click in *Find what* text box.
5. Type find text using wildcard character.
6. Click in *Replace with* text box.
7. Type replacement text.
8. Click Replace All button.
9. Click OK.

Finding and Replacing Using Wildcard Characters

The expanded Find and Replace dialog box contains a *Use wildcards* check box. Insert a check mark in this check box to use wildcard characters in a search to find or find and replace data. For example, suppose the company name *Hansen Products* also mistakenly appears in a document as *Hanson Products*. Both spellings can be found by typing *Hans?n* in the *Find what* text box. Word will find *Hansen* and *Hanson* if the *Use wildcards* check box contains a check mark. If the *Use wildcards* check box does not contain a check mark, Word will try to find the exact spelling *Hans?n* and not find either spelling in the document. Table 1.1 identifies some common wildcard characters along with the functions they perform. For information on additional wildcard characters, use the Help feature.

Table 1.1 Wildcard Characters

Wildcard Character	Function
*	Indicates any characters. For example, type le*s and Word finds *less, leases,* and *letters*.
?	Indicates one character. For example, type gr?y and Word finds *gray* and *grey*.
@	Indicates any occurrence of the previous character. For example, type cho@se and Word finds *chose* and *choose*.
<	Indicates the beginning of a word. For example, type <(med) and Word finds *medical*, *medicine*, and *media*.
>	Indicates the ending of a word. For example, type (tion)> and Word finds *election*, *deduction*, and *education*.

Activity 3e Finding and Replacing Using a Wildcard Character

1. With **1-ComLease.docx** open, use a wildcard character to search for words beginning with *leas* by completing the following steps:
   a. Click the Find button arrow in the Editing group on the Home tab and then click *Advanced Find* at the drop-down list.

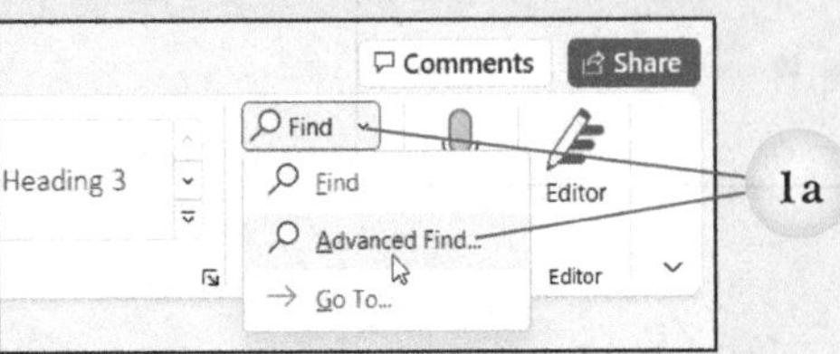

   b. At the Find and Replace dialog box, click the More button.
   c. Click the No Formatting button.
   d. Click the *Use wildcards* check box to insert a check mark.
   e. Click in the *Find what* text box and then type <(leas).
   f. Click the Find Next button to find the first occurrence of a word that begins with *leas*.
   g. Click the Find Next button four more times.
   h. Press the Esc key to end the find and close the Find and Replace dialog box.
2. The name *Arigalason* is spelled a variety of ways in the document. Use a wildcard character to search for all the versions of the name and replace them with the correct spelling by completing the following steps:
   a. Press Ctrl + Home to move the insertion point to the beginning of the document.
   b. Click the Replace button.
   c. At the Find and Replace dialog box, delete the text in the *Find what* text box and then type Ar?galas?n.
   d. Make sure that the dialog box is expanded and that the *Use wildcards* check box contains a check mark.
   e. Press the Tab key.
   f. Click the No Formatting button.
   g. Type Arigalason (the correct spelling) in the *Replace with* text box.
   h. Click the Replace All button.

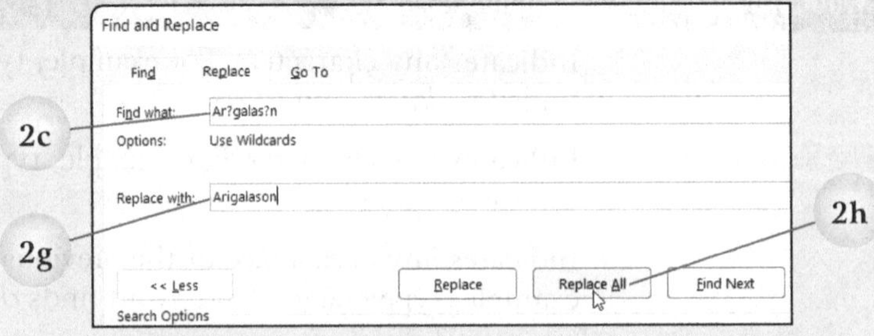

   i. At the message indicating that 23 replacements were made, click OK.
3. Close the Find and Replace dialog box.
4. Save, preview, and then close **1-ComLease.docx**.

Activity 4 Insert Properties and Inspect a Document 4 Parts

You will open a document (an advertising flyer), insert document properties, inspect the document and remove specific elements, and then check the compatibility and accessibility of the document.

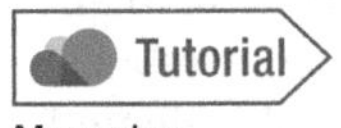

Managing Document Properties

Managing Document Properties

Every document has properties associated with it, such as the type of document, the location in which it has been saved, and when it was created, modified, and accessed. Document properties can be viewed and modified at the Info backstage area. To display information about the open document, click the File tab and then click the *Info* option. Document property information displays at the right side of the Info backstage area, as shown in Figure 1.13.

The document property information at the Info backstage area includes the file size, number of pages and words, total editing time, and any tags or comments that have been added. Some properties, such as the title, tags, or comments, may be edited. Hover over the property and a rectangular text box with a light blue border displays. Click inside the text box to type or edit information. In the *Related Dates* section, dates display for when the document was created and when it was last modified and printed. The *Related People* section includes the name of the author of the document and provides options for adding additional author names. Display additional document properties by clicking the Show All Properties hyperlink.

Figure 1.13 Info Backstage Area

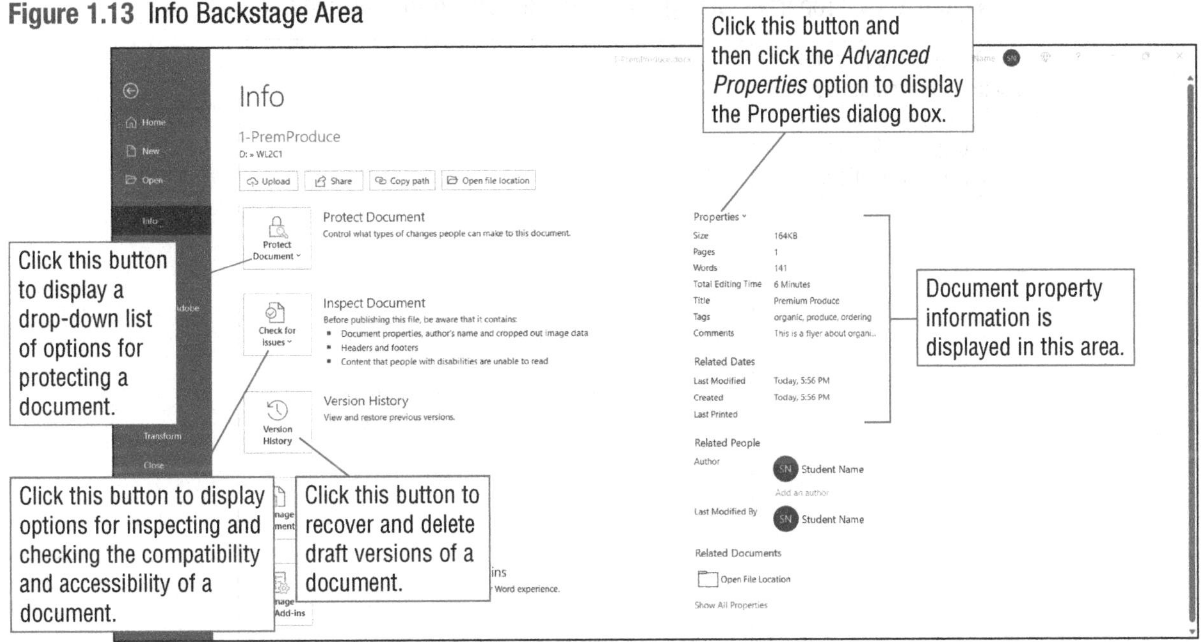

Quick Steps

Display Properties Dialog Box

1. Click File tab.
2. Click *Info* option.
3. Click Properties button.
4. Click *Advanced Properties.*

In addition to adding or updating document property information at the Info backstage area, specific information about a document can be viewed, added, edited, and customized with options at the Properties dialog box, shown in Figure 1.14. Open the dialog box by displaying the Info backstage area, clicking the Properties button, and then clicking *Advanced Properties* at the drop-down list.

The Properties dialog box with the General tab selected displays information about the document type, size, and location. Click the Summary tab to view fields such as *Title*, *Subject*, *Author*, *Company*, *Category*, *Keywords*, and *Comments*. Some fields may contain data and others may be blank. Insert, edit, or delete text in the fields. With the Statistics tab selected, information displays such as the number of pages, paragraphs, lines, words, and characters. With the Contents tab selected, the dialog box displays the document title. Click the Custom tab to add custom properties to the document. For example, a property can be added that displays the date the document was completed, information on the department in which the document was created, and much more.

Another method for displaying document properties is to display the Open dialog box, click the document in the Content pane, click the Organize button, and then click *Properties* at the drop-down list. Or right-click the file name in the Content pane and then click *Properties* at the shortcut menu. The Properties dialog box that displays contains the tabs General, Security, Details, and Previous Versions. Some of the information in this Properties dialog box is the same as the information in the Properties dialog box that is accessed through the Info backstage area, while some of the information is different. Generally, consider using the Properties dialog box accessed through the Info backstage area to add, edit, and create custom properties and use the Properties dialog box accessed through the Open dialog box to view document properties.

Figure 1.14 Properties Dialog Box with the General Tab Selected

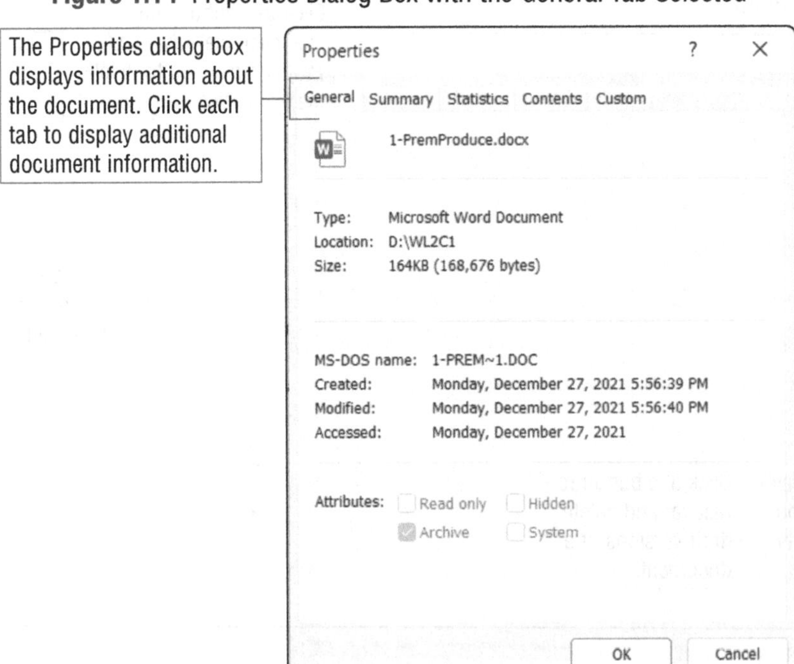

Activity 4a Inserting Document Properties

Part 1 of 4

1. Open **PremProduce.docx** and then save it with the name **1-PremProduce.**
2. Insert document properties by completing the following steps:
   a. Click the File tab and then click the *Info* option.
   b. Hover the pointer over the text *Add a title* at the right of the *Title* document property, click in the text box, and then type Premium Produce.
   c. Display the Properties dialog box by clicking the Properties button and then clicking *Advanced Properties* at the drop-down list.

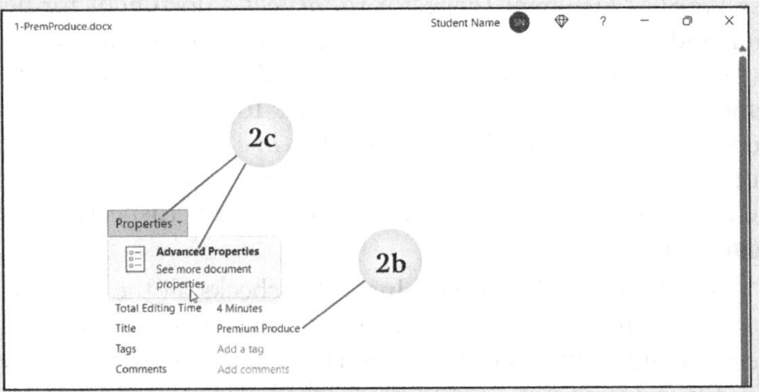

   d. At the Properties dialog box with the Summary tab selected, press the Tab key to make the *Subject* text box active and then type Organic produce.
   e. Click in the *Category* text box and then type Premium Produce flyer.
   f. Press the Tab key and then type the following words, separated by commas, in the *Keywords* text box: organic, produce, ordering.
   g. Press the Tab key and then type the following text in the *Comments* text box: This is a flyer about organic produce and the featured produce of the month.
   h. Click OK to close the dialog box.

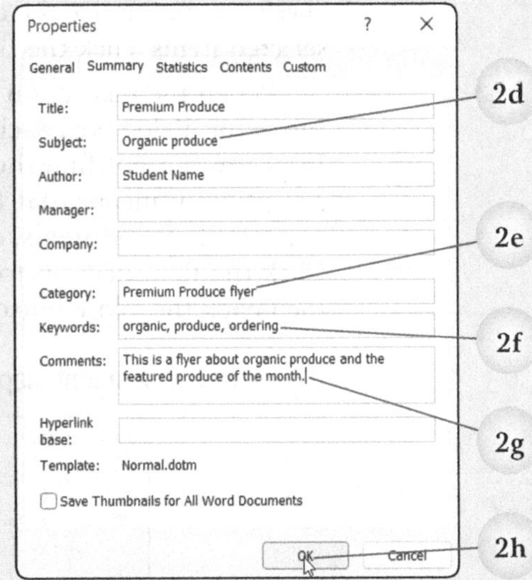

3. Click the Back button to return to the document.
4. Save **1-PremProduce.docx**.
5. Print only the document properties by completing the following steps:
   a. Click the File tab and then click the *Print* option.
   b. At the Print backstage area, click the first gallery in the *Settings* category and then click *Document Info* at the drop-down list.
   c. Click the Print button.
6. Save **1-PremProduce.docx**.

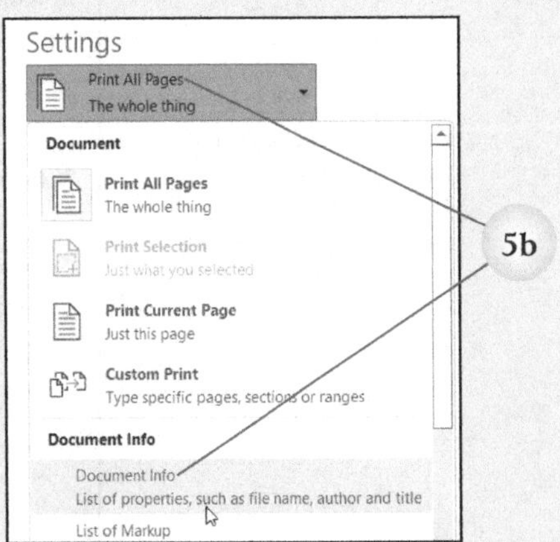

Check Your Work

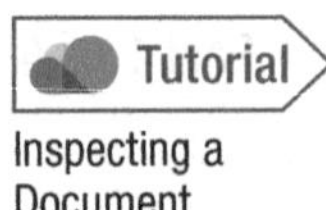

Inspecting a Document

Inspecting Documents

Use options from the Check for Issues button drop-down list at the Info backstage area to inspect a document for personal and hidden data along with compatibility and accessibility issues. Click the Check for Issues button at the Info backstage area and a drop-down list displays with the options *Inspect Document*, *Check Accessibility*, and *Check Compatibility*.

Using the Document Inspector

Check for Issues

Use Word's Document Inspector to inspect a document for personal data, hidden data, and metadata (data that describes other data, such as document properties). In certain situations, some personal or hidden data may need to be removed before a document is shared with others. To check a document for personal and hidden data, click the File tab, click the *Info* option, click the Check for Issues button at the Info backstage area, and then click the *Inspect Document* option at the drop-down list. This displays the Document Inspector dialog box, shown in Figure 1.15.

By default, the Document Inspector checks all the items listed in the dialog box. To control what items are inspected in the document, remove the check marks preceding items that should not be checked. For example, if the headers and footers in a document do not need to be checked, click the *Headers, Footers, and Watermarks* check box to remove the check mark. To scan the document to check for the selected items, click the Inspect button at the bottom of the dialog box.

When the inspection is complete, the results display in the Document Inspector dialog box. A check mark before an option indicates that the Document Inspector did not find the specific items. If an exclamation point displays before an option, it means that the items were found and a list of the items displays. To remove the found items, click the Remove All button at the right of the option. Click the Reinspect button to ensure that the specific items were removed and then click the Close button.

Figure 1.15 Document Inspector Dialog Box

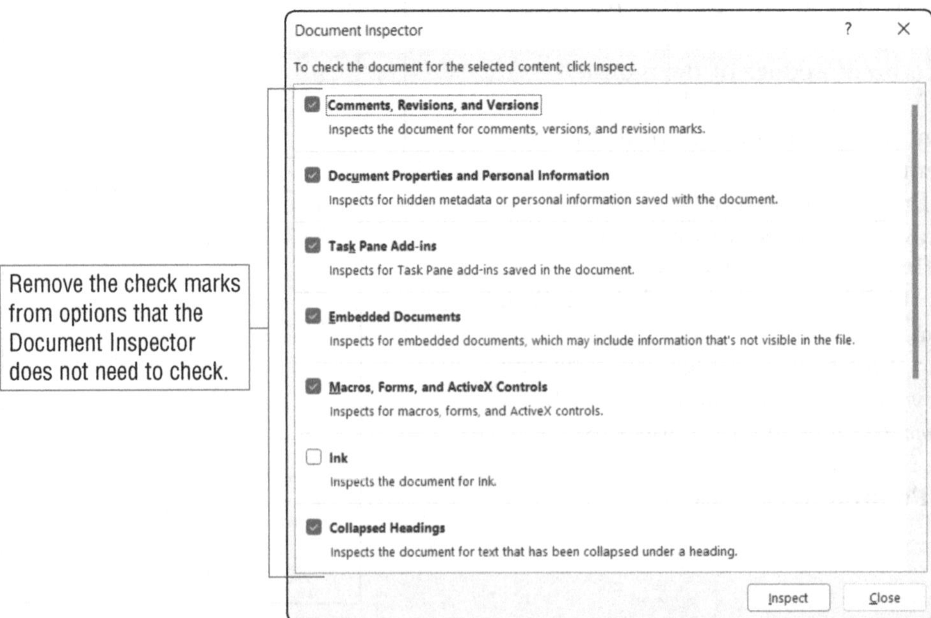

Activity 4b Inspecting a Document

1. With **1-PremProduce.docx** open, type and then hide text by completing the following steps:
   a. Press Ctrl + Home to move the insertion point to the beginning of the document and then type Before distributing the flyer, make sure the Pricing link is active.
   b. Select the text you just typed.
   c. Click the Home tab, if necessary.
   d. Click the Font group dialog box launcher.
   e. At the Font dialog box with the Font tab selected, click the *Hidden* check box in the *Effects* section to insert a check mark.
   f. Click OK to close the dialog box.

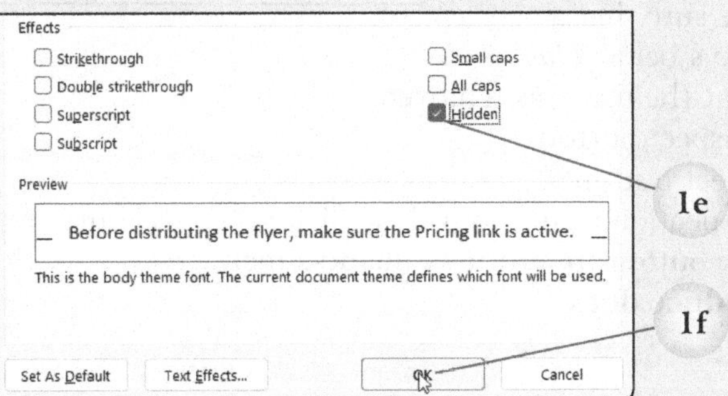

2. Click the Save button on the Title bar.
3. Inspect the document by completing the following steps (this document contains a watermark, a footer, document properties, and hidden text):
   a. Click the File tab and then click the *Info* option.
   b. Click the Check for Issues button at the Info backstage area and then click *Inspect Document* at the drop-down list.
   c. At the Document Inspector dialog box, specify not to check the document for collapsed headings by clicking the *Collapsed Headings* check box to remove the check mark.
   d. Click the Inspect button.

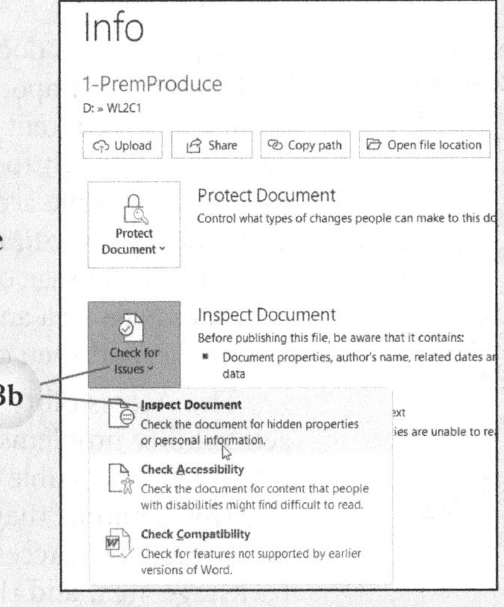

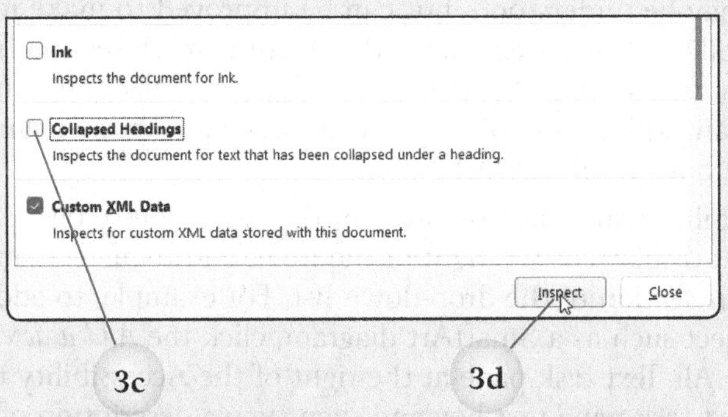

   e. Notice that the results show the document contains document properties and personal information. Scroll down the list box showing the inspection results and notice that the results show that the document also contains a header, a footer, and hidden text.

f. Remove the footer and watermark by clicking the Remove All button at the right of the *Headers, Footers, and Watermarks* section. (Make sure that a message displays below *Headers, Footers, and Watermarks* stating that the text was removed.)

g. Remove the hidden text by clicking the Remove All button at the right of the *Hidden Text* section. (Make sure that a message displays below *Hidden Text* stating that the text was removed.)

Custom XML Data
No custom XML data was found.
Headers, Footers, and Watermarks
The following items were found:
* Headers
* Footers
Headers and footers may include shapes such as watermarks.
Remove All
Invisible Content
No invisible objects found.
Hidden Text
Hidden text was found.
Remove All
Note: Some changes cannot be undone.
Reinspect
Close
3f
3g
3h

h. Click the Reinspect button.

i. Click the Inspect button.

j. Review the inspection results and then click the Close button.

k. Click the Back button to return to the document.

4. Save **1-PremProduce.docx**.

Checking for Accessibility and Compatibility Issues

Quick Steps

Check Accessibility

1. Click File tab.
2. Click *Info* option.
3. Click Check for Issues button.
4. Click *Check Accessibility.*

OR

1. Click Review tab.
2. Click Check Accessibility button.

Checking for Accessibility Issues

When preparing a document, making sure the content is accessible to people of all abilities is important. Word provides the Accessibility Checker to check a document for content that a person with disabilities (such as a visual impairment) might find difficult to read or understand using assistive technology. If a document contains a possible accessibility issue, a message will display on the Status bar such as *Accessibiltiy: Investigate*. Check the accessibility of a document by clicking the accessibility message on the Status bar or clicking the Check for Issues button at the Info backstage area and then clicking *Check Accessibility*. Another option is to click the Review tab and then click the Check Accessibility button in the Accessibility group.

The Accessibility Checker examines the document for the most common accessibility problems and sorts them into three categories: errors (content that will not be accessible); warnings (content that may be difficult to understand); and tips (content that may be understood, but can be improved to make it more accessible). The Accessibility Checker examines the document, closes the Info backstage area, and then displays the Accessibility task pane. Select an issue in one of the sections and an explanation of why it is an issue and how it can be corrected displays at the bottom of the task pane.

To correct an accessibility issue, click the item in the Accessibility task pane, click the down arrow that displays at the right of the item, and then click an option in the *Recommended Actions* section of the drop-down list. For example, to add alternative text to an object such as a SmartArt diagram, click the *Add a description* option. This displays the Alt Text task pane at the right of the Accessibility task pane. Click in the Alt Text task pane text box and then type a description of the object. If a person with a visual impairment uses a screen reader to hear a reading of the document, the screen reader will read the text in the Alt Text text box describing the item. Microsoft includes the Intelligent Services feature that will generate an alternative description for an object such as a picture or clip art. When checking accessibility, verify the generated text or create new alternative text.

Activity 4c Checking for Accessibility Issues

1. With **1-PremProduce.docx** open, conduct an accessibility check by completing the following steps:
   a. Click the File tab and then click the *Info* option.
   b. At the Info backstage area, click the Check for Issues button and then click *Check Accessibility* at the drop-down list.
   c. Notice the Accessibility task pane at the right side of the screen, which contains an *Errors* section.
   d. Click the *Missing alternative text (2)* option to expand it.
   e. Click *Picture 2* in the *Errors* section and then read the information at the bottom of the task pane describing why the error should be fixed and how to fix it.

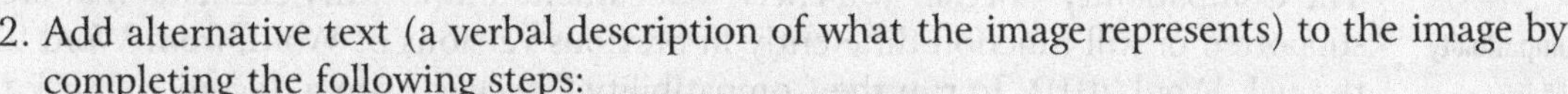

2. Add alternative text (a verbal description of what the image represents) to the image by completing the following steps:
   a. Click the down arrow at the right of *Picture 2*.
   b. Click the *Add a description* option at the drop-down list. (This displays the Alt Text task pane and the Accessibility task pane is reduced to a button at the right side of the Alt Text task pane.)
   c. At the Alt Text task pane, type Image of fruits and vegetables representing Premium Produce. in the text box.

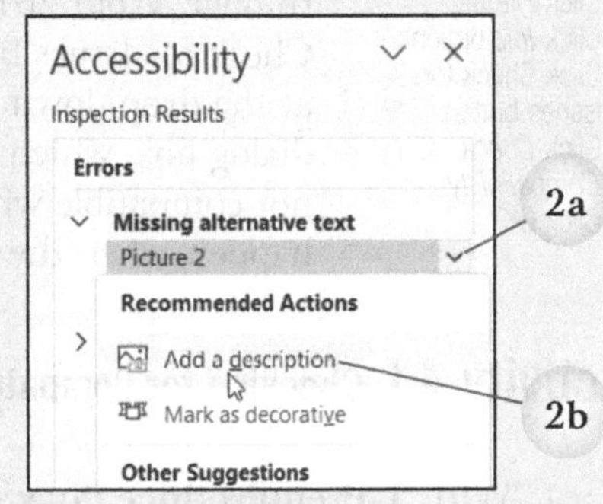

3. Expand the Accessibility task pane by clicking the Accessibility button at the right side of the Alt Text task pane.

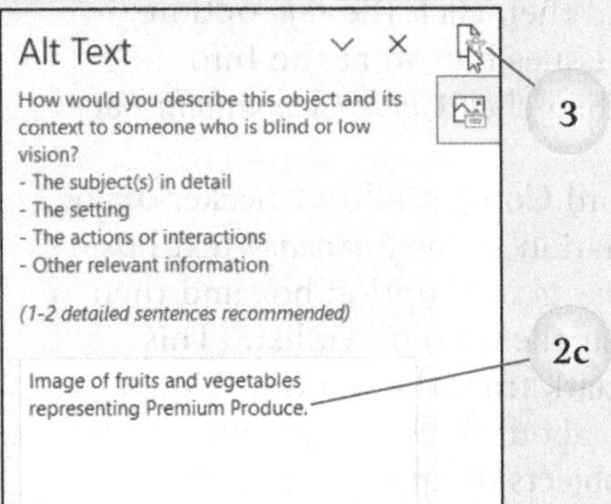

4. Hover the pointer over *Diagram 1* below *Missing alternative text*, click the down arrow at the right of the option, and then click *Add a description* at the drop-down list.
5. Type SmartArt graphic indicating no pesticides, no herbicides, and organically grown produce. in the Alt Text task pane text box.
6. Close the Alt Text task pane.
7. At the Accessibility task pane, click the *Image or object not inline* option to expand it.

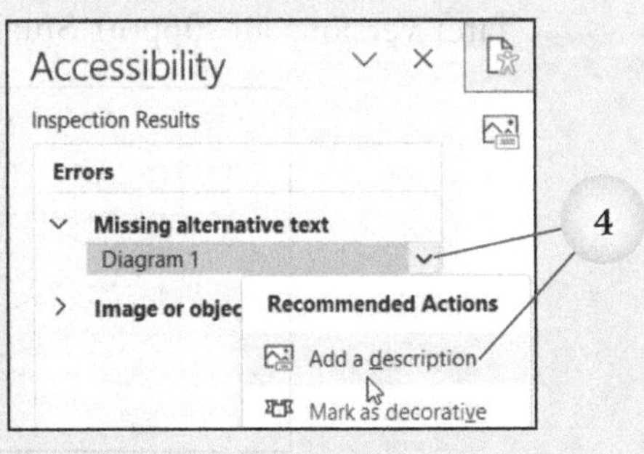

8. Hover the pointer over *Diagram 1* and then click the down arrow.
9. Click *Place this inline* at the drop-down list. (This changes the text wrapping of the SmartArt to *In Line with Text*.)
10. Close the Accessibility task pane.
11. Save **1-PremProduce.docx**.

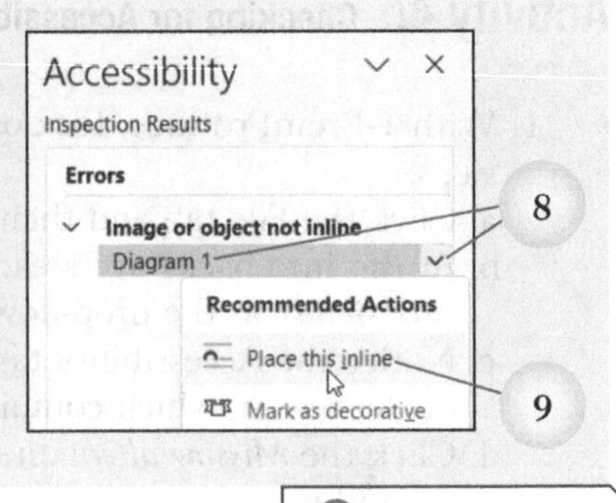

Check Your Work

Checking for Compatibility Issues

Quick Steps
Check Compatibility
1. Click File tab.
2. Click *Info* option.
3. Click Check for Issues button.
4. Click *Check Compatibility*.
5. Click OK.

The Compatibility Checker will check a document and identify elements that are not supported or will function differently in previous versions of Word, from Word 97 through Word 2010. To run the Compatibility Checker, open a document, click the Check for Issues button at the Info backstage area, and then click *Check Compatibility* at the drop-down list. This displays the Microsoft Word Compatibility Checker dialog box, which includes a summary of the elements in the document that are not compatible with previous versions of Word. This box also indicates what will happen when the document is saved and then opened in a previous version.

Activity 4d Checking for Compatibility Issues

Part 4 of 4

1. With **1-PremProduce.docx** open, check the compatibility of elements in the document by completing the following steps:
   a. Click the File tab and then click the *Info* option.
   b. Click the Check for Issues button at the Info backstage area and then click *Check Compatibility* at the drop-down list.
   c. At the Microsoft Word Compatibility Checker dialog box, read the information in the *Summary* text box.
   d. Click the *Select versions to show* option box and then click *Word 97-2003* at the drop-down list. (This removes the check mark from the option.) Notice that the information about SmartArt graphics being converted to static objects disappears from the *Summary* text box. This is because Word 2007 and later versions all support SmartArt graphics.

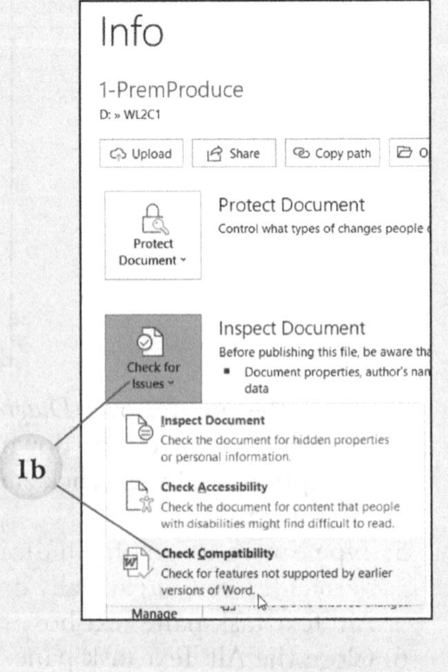

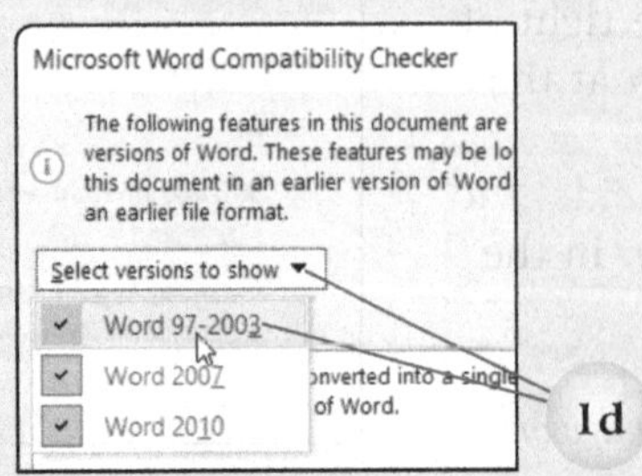

   e. Click OK to close the dialog box.

2. Save the document in Word 2003 format by completing the following steps:
   a. Press the F12 function key to display the Save As dialog box with WL2C1 the active folder.
   b. At the Save As dialog box, click the *Save as type* option box and then click *Word 97-2003 Document (*.doc)* at the drop-down list.
   c. Select the text in the *File name* text box and then type 1-PremProduce-2003format.
   d. Click the Save button.

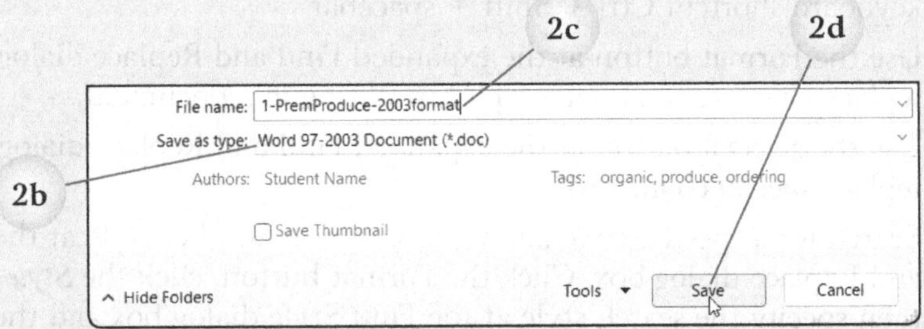

   e. Click the Continue button at the Microsoft Word Compatibility Checker dialog box.
3. Close **1-PremProduce-2003format.doc**.

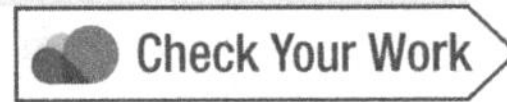

Chapter Summary

- Use options in the *Character Spacing* section of the Font dialog box with the Advanced tab selected to adjust character spacing and turn on kerning.
- The OpenType features available at the Font dialog box with the Advanced tab selected include options for choosing a ligature style, specifying number spacing and form, and applying stylistic sets.
- The Text Effects and Typography button in the Font group on the Home tab contains options for applying text effects such as outline, shadow, reflection, and glow effects as well as typography options such as number styles, ligatures, and stylistic sets.
- Click the Text Effects button at the Font dialog box to display the Format Text Effects dialog box. Use options at this dialog box to apply text fill and text outline effects to selected text.
- Change the default font with the Set As Default button at the Font dialog box. The default font can be changed for the current document or all new documents based on the Normal template.
- Use the © symbol to identify copyrighted intellectual property, use the ™ symbol to identify a trademark, and use the ® symbol to identify a registered trademark.
- Insert a nonbreaking hyphen by clicking the *Nonbreaking Hyphen* option at the Symbol dialog box with the Special Characters tab selected or by using the keyboard shortcut Ctrl + Shift + -.
- Use an em dash to indicate a break in thought or to highlight a term or phrase by separating it from the rest of the sentence. Insert an em dash by typing a word, typing two hyphens, typing the next word, and then pressing the spacebar. An em dash can also be inserted with the keyboard shortcut Alt + Ctrl + - (on the numeric keypad) or at the Symbol dialog box with the Special Characters tab selected.

- Use an en dash to indicate inclusive dates, times, and numbers. To insert an en dash, click the *En Dash* option at the Symbol dialog box with the Special Characters tab selected or use the keyboard short Ctrl + - (on the numeric keypad).
- Insert nonbreaking spaces between words that should not be separated across a line break. Insert a nonbreaking space by clicking the *Nonbreaking Space* option at the Symbol dialog box with the Special Characters tab selected or with the keyboard shortcut Ctrl + Shift + spacebar.
- Use the Format button at the expanded Find and Replace dialog box to find and replace character and paragraph formatting in a document.
- Use the Special button at the expanded Find and Replace dialog box to find and replace special characters.
- Search for a specific style and replace it with another style at the expanded Find and Replace dialog box. Click the Format button, click the *Style* option, and then specify the search style at the Find Style dialog box and the replacement style at the Replace Style dialog box.
- A Word document contains a body font and a heading font. A document can be searched to find a body or heading font and replace it with a different font.
- Wildcard characters can be used to find text in a document. To use a wildcard, display the expanded Find and Replace dialog box and then click the *Use wildcards* check box to insert a check mark.
- Document properties can be viewed and modified at the Info backstage area and at the Properties dialog box. Display the Properties dialog box by clicking the Properties button at the Info backstage area and then clicking *Advanced Properties* at the drop-down list.
- Inspect a document for personal data, hidden data, and metadata with options at the Document Inspector dialog box. Display this dialog box by clicking the Check for Issues button at the Info backstage area and then clicking *Inspect Document* at the drop-down list.
- The Accessibility Checker checks a document for content that a person with disabilities might find difficult to read or understand with the use of assistive technology. Run the Accessibility Checker by clicking the Check for Issues button at the Info backstage area and then clicking *Check Accessibility* at the drop-down list, by clicking the accessibility message on the Status bar, or by clicking the Review tab and then clicking the Check Accessibility button.
- Run the Compatibility Checker to check a document and identify elements that are not supported or that will function differently in previous versions of Word. Run the Compatibility Checker by clicking the Check for Issues button at the Info backstage area and then clicking *Check Compatibility* at the drop-down list.

Commands Review

FEATURE	RIBBON TAB, GROUP/OPTION	BUTTON, OPTION	KEYBOARD SHORTCUT
Accessibility Checker	File, *Info*	, *Check Accessibility*	
Compatibility Checker	File, *Info*	, *Check Compatibility*	
copyright symbol	Insert, Symbols	, *More Symbols*	Alt + Ctrl + C
Document Inspector dialog box	File, *Info*	, *Inspect Document*	
em dash	Insert, Symbols	, *More Symbols*	Alt + Ctrl + - (on numeric keypad)
en dash	Insert, Symbols	, *More Symbols*	Ctrl + - (on numeric keypad)
Find and Replace dialog box	Home, Editing	, *Replace*	Ctrl + H
Font dialog box	Home, Font		Ctrl + D
nonbreaking hyphen	Insert, Symbols	, *More Symbols*	Ctrl + Shift + -
nonbreaking space	Insert, Symbols	, *More Symbols*	Ctrl + Shift + spacebar
Properties dialog box	File, *Info*	Properties, *Advanced Properties*	
registered trademark symbol	Insert, Symbols	, *More Symbols*	Alt + Ctrl + R
Symbol dialog box	Insert, Symbols	, *More Symbols*	
Text Effects and Typography button	Home, Font		
trademark symbol	Insert, Symbols	, *More Symbols*	Alt + Ctrl + T

Review and Assessment

CHAPTER 1

Skills Assessment

Assessment 1
Apply Character Spacing and OpenType Features to a Donations Document

1. Open **PRDonations.docx** and then save it with the name **1-PRDonations**.
2. Select the quote text *"In every community there is work to be done. In every nation there are wounds to heal. In every heart there is the power to do it."* and then apply stylistic set 4. (Do this at the Font dialog box with the Advanced tab selected.)
3. Select the heading *Domestic Donations* and change the scale to 90% and the spacing to Expanded. (Do this at the Font dialog box with the Advanced tab selected.)
4. Apply the same formatting in Step 3 to the heading *International Donations*.
5. Select the numbers in the *Domestic Donations* section. ***Hint: To select only the numbers, position the pointer at the beginning of $450,000, press and hold down the Alt key, use the pointer to drag down and select the four numbers in the second column, and then release the Alt key.***
6. With the numbers selected, change the number spacing to Tabular spacing. (Do this at the Font dialog box with the Advanced tab selected.)
7. Select the numbers in the *International Donations* section and then change the number spacing to Tabular spacing.
8. Select the text *We are dedicated to working toward a more just and peaceful world.* and then insert a check mark in the *Use Contextual Alternates* check box at the Font dialog box with the Advanced tab selected.
9. Save, preview, and then close **1-PRDonations.docx**.

Assessment 2
Find and Replace Formatting and Use a Wildcard Character in an Employee Guide Document

1. Open **EmpGuide.docx** and then save it with the name **1-EmpGuide**.
2. Find text set in the +Headings font and replace the font with Candara.
3. Find text set in the +Body font and replace the font with Constantia.
4. Find text set in 11-point Candara and replace it with 12-point Candara italic.
5. Using a wildcard charcter, find all occurrences of *Ne?land?Davis* and replace them with *Newland-Davis*.
6. Select the title *Newland-Davis Medical* and then change the scale option to 150% and the spacing option to Expanded. (Do this at the Font dialog box with the Advanced tab selected.)
7. Save, preview, and then close **1-EmpGuide.docx**.

Assessment 3 — Replace Special Characters, Insert Document Properties, and Inspect and Check the Accessibility of a First Aid Training Flyer

1. Open **FirstAidTraining.docx** and then save it with the name **1-FirstAidTraining**.
2. Move the insertion point immediately right of *Health* in the subtitle *Sponsored by Frontline Health* and then insert a trademark symbol.
3. Search for all occurrences of hyphens and replace them with nonbreaking hyphens.
4. Search for all occurrences of em dashes and replace them with en dashes.
5. Display the Info backstage area and then type First Aid Training in the *Title* document property text box.
6. Display the Properties dialog box and then type the following in each specified document property:
   a. Subject: Training
   b. Company: Tri-State Products
   c. Keywords: first aid, training, CPR
7. Save the document and then inspect the document and remove headers, footers, and watermarks.
8. Complete an accessibility check and then insert alternative text for the picture image by typing Stethoscope image in the text box in the Alt Text task pane. Position the picture image inline with text and then close all open task panes.
9. Print only the document properties.
10. Save, preview, and then close **1-FirstAidTraining.docx**.

Assessment 4 — Check an Adventures Document for Accessibility Issues

1. Open **BEAdventures.docx** and then save it with the name **1-BEAdventures**.
2. Using the Help feature, learn more about the rules for the Accessibility Checker.
3. After reading the information, complete an accessibility check on the document. Look at the errors that appear in the Accessibility task pane and then correct each error.
4. Save and then close **1-BEAdventures.docx**.
5. Open a blank document and then type text explaining the errors that were found in **1-BEAdventures.docx** by the Accessibility Checker and what you did to correct the errors.
6. Save the completed document with the name **1-BEAAccessibility**.
7. Preview and then close **1-BEAAccessibility.docx**.

Visual Benchmark

Format an Hawaiian Adventures Document

1. Open **Hawaii.docx** and then save it with the name **1-Hawaii**.
2. Complete the steps formatting so your document appears similar to the document shown in Figure 1.16:
   - Inspect the document and remove the watermark (the watermark is in the footer) and the header.
   - Expand the spacing (by increasing the spacing point size) for the title and apply a stylistic set so your title appears similar to the title in the figure.
   - Expand the spacing (by increasing the spacing point size) and apply a stylistic set to the two headings in the document so the headings appear similar to the headings in the figure.

- Apply a stylistic set to the quote and the author of the quote near the bottom of the page.
- Select the tabbed text and then use the Text Effects and Typography button in the Font group on the Home tab to apply the tabular lining number style.
- Search for all occurrences of em dashes and replace each with a colon followed by a space.
- Search for all occurrences of hyphens and replace each with an en dash.

3. Save, preview, and then close **1-Hawaii.docx**.

Figure 1.16 Visual Benchmark

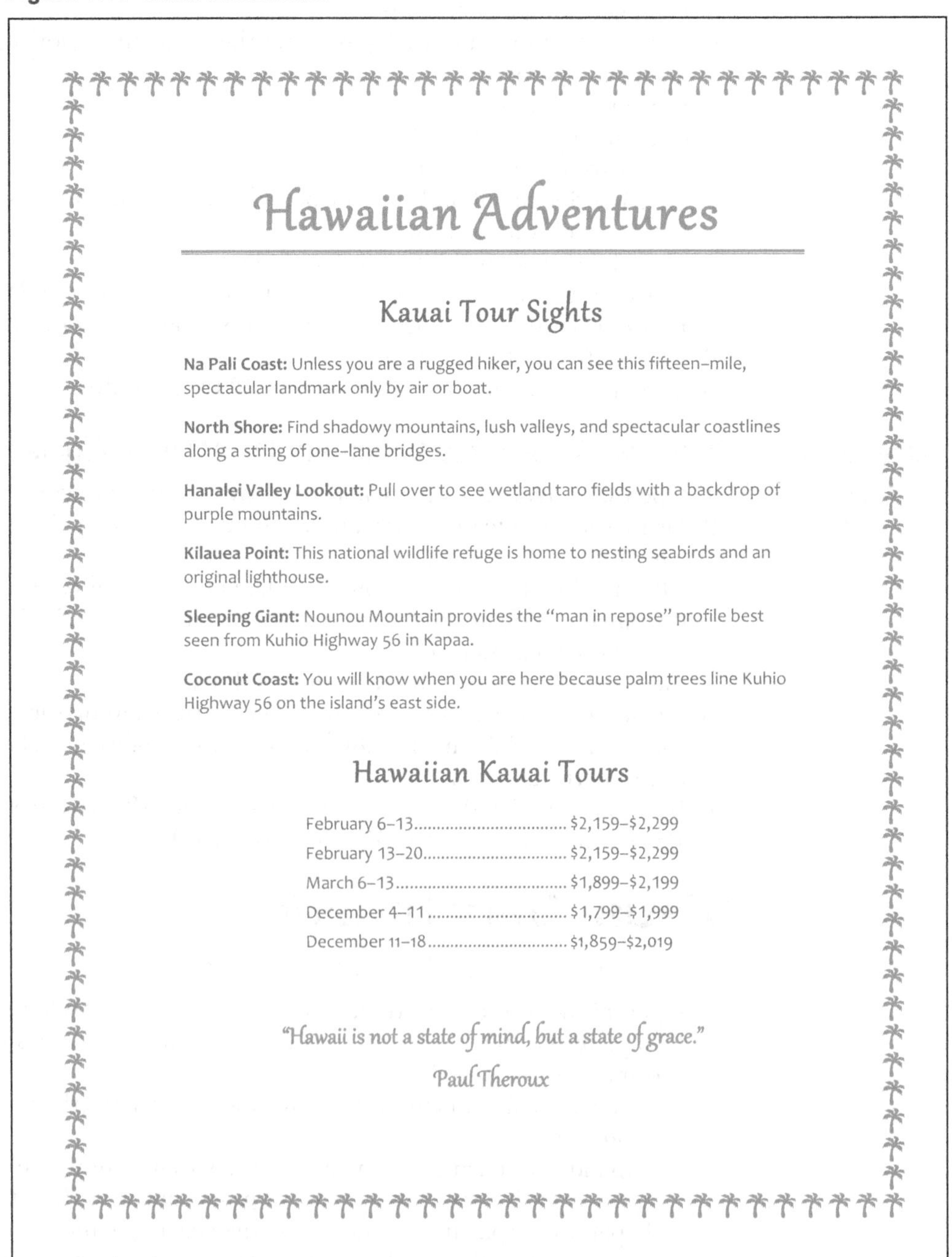

Hawaiian Adventures

Kauai Tour Sights

Na Pali Coast: Unless you are a rugged hiker, you can see this fifteen–mile, spectacular landmark only by air or boat.

North Shore: Find shadowy mountains, lush valleys, and spectacular coastlines along a string of one–lane bridges.

Hanalei Valley Lookout: Pull over to see wetland taro fields with a backdrop of purple mountains.

Kilauea Point: This national wildlife refuge is home to nesting seabirds and an original lighthouse.

Sleeping Giant: Nounou Mountain provides the "man in repose" profile best seen from Kuhio Highway 56 in Kapaa.

Coconut Coast: You will know when you are here because palm trees line Kuhio Highway 56 on the island's east side.

Hawaiian Kauai Tours

February 6–13 .... $2,159–$2,299
February 13–20 .... $2,159–$2,299
March 6–13 .... $1,899–$2,199
December 4–11 .... $1,799–$1,999
December 11–18 .... $1,859–$2,019

"Hawaii is not a state of mind, but a state of grace."
Paul Theroux

Case Study

Part 1

You are the assistant to the executive director of Phoenix Rising, a nonprofit organization. Phoenix Rising is sponsoring an affordable housing forum and you need to format a flyer for the event. Open **PRForum.docx** and then save it with the name **1-PRForum**. The information about the forum is provided in the document and your responsibility is to apply attractive and appealing formatting to the information. To provide a frame of reference for formatting, open **1-PRDonations.docx** and **1-PRDonorApp.docx** to see how those documents are formatted and then apply similar formatting to **1-PRForum.docx**. Replace any regular hyphens with en dashes and consider whether you want to have an em dash or other punctuation after *Date*, *Time*, and *Location*. Save, preview, and then close **1-PRForum.docx**. Close all open documents.

Part 2

The executive director of Phoenix Rising needs a new organizational chart. Open **PRLtrhd.docx** and then save it with the name **1-PROrgChart**. Look at the information in Figure 1.17 below and then create a SmartArt organizational chart to display the information. Provide a title for the organizational chart and apply formatting so that the title and organizational chart appear similar to the other documents you prepared in this case study. Save, preview, and then close **1-PROrgChart.docx**.

Figure 1.17 Case Study, Part 2

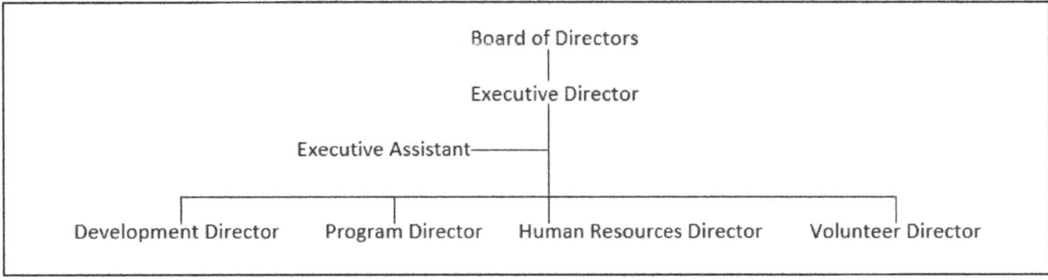

Part 3

The executive director wants to ensure that all documents you prepare for Phoenix Rising are checked for accessibility issues and has asked you to check two documents. Open **1-PRForum.docx**, run an accessibility check on the document, and fix any errors identified by the Accessibility Checker. Save and then close **1-PRForum.docx**. Open **1-PROrgChart.docx**, run an accessibility check, and fix any errors identified by the Accessibility Checker. Save and then close **1-PROrgChart.docx**. Open **PRLtrhd.docx** and then save it with the name **1-PRAccessibility.docx**. Write a letter to the executive director explaining any accessibility issues found in each document by the Accessibility Checker and the steps you took to correct them. Save, preview, and then close **1-PRAccessibility.docx**.

Part 4

To further identify a document and its contents, the executive director has asked you to provide document properties for **1-PROrgChart.docx**. Open **1-PROrgChart.docx** and then insert at least the following document properties:

- Title
- Author (use your name)
- Company
- Keywords

After inserting the document properties, save **1-PROrgChart.docx**, print only the document properties, and then close the document.

WORD

CHAPTER 2

Proofing Documents

Performance Objectives

Upon successful completion of Chapter 2, you will be able to:

1 Use the Editor to complete a spelling check and a grammar check
2 Display readability statistics
3 Create a custom dictionary, change the default dictionary, and remove a dictionary
4 Display document word, paragraph, and character counts
5 Insert line numbers
6 Display synonyms and antonyms for specific words using the thesaurus
7 Use the Search and Researcher task panes to find information on a specific topic
8 Translate text to and from different languages
9 Sort text in paragraphs, columns, and tables

Microsoft Word includes proofing tools to help you create well-written, error-free documents. These tools include the Microsoft Editor that checks spelling and grammar in a document and the thesaurus that displays words with similar or opposite meanings. If documents will be created with specific words, terms, or acronyms not found in the main spelling dictionary, a custom dictionary can be created. When completing a spelling check, the Editor will compare words in a document with the main dictionary as well as a custom dictionary. Word provides a translation feature for translating text into different languages. In Word, text in paragraphs, columns and tables can be sorted alphabetically or numerically in ascending or descending order. In this chapter, you will learn how to use the proofing tools, create a custom dictionary, translate text to and from different languages, and sort text.

Data Files

The data files for this chapter are in the WL2C2 folder that you downloaded at the beginning of this course.

Activity 1 Check Spelling in an Investment Plan Document 1 Part

You will open an investment plan document and then use the Editor to complete a spelling and grammar check.

Checking Spelling and Grammar

Editor

Word contains the Microsoft Editor that checks the spelling and grammar of a document. To use the Editor, click the Editor button at the right side of the Home tab, click the Review tab and then click the Editor button in the Proofing group, or press the F7 function key. When checking a document, the Editor flags misspelled words, potential grammar errors, and writing clarity issues and offers corrections.

The Editor's spell checking feature can find and correct misspelled words, duplicate words, and irregular capitalizations. To check spelling, it compares the words in the document with the words in its dictionary. If it finds a match, it passes over the word. The Editor will identify misspelled words (any words not found in the Editor's dictionary), typographical errors (such as transposed letters), double occurrences of a word, irregular capitalizations, some proper names and jargon or technical terms.

The Editor's grammar checking feature searches a document for errors in grammar, punctuation, and word usage and will also identify text with writing clarity or conciseness issues. Using the Editor can help create well-written documents, but does not replace the need for proofreading.

Editing during a Spelling and Grammar Check

When checking the spelling and grammar in a document, edits or corrections can be made in the document. Do this by clicking in the document outside the Editor task pane, making the change or edit, and then clicking the Resume checking all results button in the task pane.

Customizing Spelling and Grammar Checking

Customizing Spell Checking

Customize the Editor spelling checker with options at the Word Options dialog box with the *Proofing* option selected, as shown in Figure 2.1. Display this dialog box by clicking the File tab and then clicking *Options*. At the Word Options dialog box, click *Proofing* in the left panel. Use options at this dialog box to specify what the Editor should review or ignore.

Using the Editor Task Pane Reading Feature

Hint Read grammar suggestions carefully. Some may not be valid in a specific context and a problem identified by the grammar checker may not actually be an issue.

The Editor task pane includes a reading feature that will read aloud the text that displays in the Editor task pane. To hear a reading of the text, click the speaker icon to the right of the sentence. The suggested word and definition that display in the *Suggestions* list box can also be read aloud by clicking the word in the list box and then clicking the *Read Aloud* option at the drop-down list. For the reading feature to work, the computer speakers must be turned on.

Figure 2.1 Word Options Dialog Box with the *Proofing* Option Selected

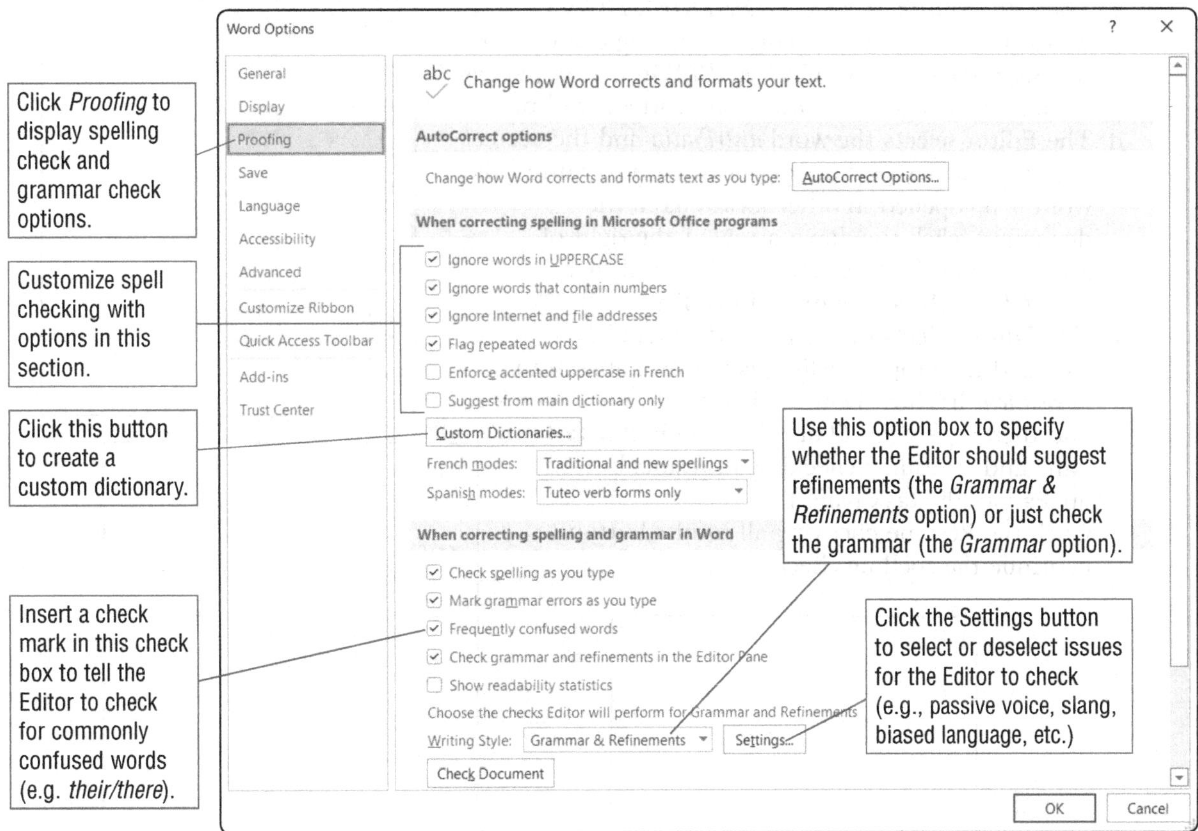

Activity 1 Spell Checking a Document with Uppercase Words

Part 1 of 1

Note: The Microsoft Editor is updated on a continuous basis so some of the steps in this activity may vary. Ignore any suggestions provided by Editor that are not specifically addressed in this activity.

1. Open **PlanDists.docx** and then save it with the name **2-PlanDists**.
2. Change a spell checking option by completing the following steps:
   a. Click the File tab.
   b. Click *Options*.
   c. At the Word Options dialog box, click the *Proofing* option in the left panel.
   d. Click the *Ignore words in UPPERCASE* check box to remove the check mark.
   e. Click OK to close the dialog box.
3. Complete a spelling check on the document by completing the following steps:
   a. Click the Editor button in the Editor group on the Home tab.
   b. At the Editor task pane, click the Editor Score box near the top of the task pane.

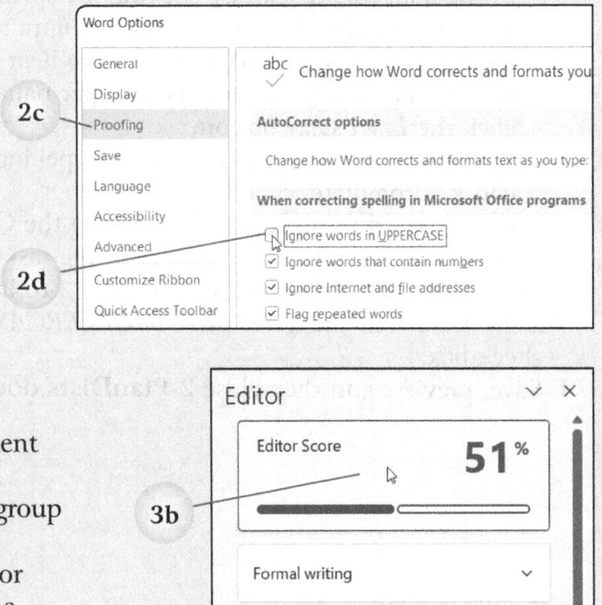

c. The Editor displays *AERLY DISTRIBUTIONS* in the Editor task pane and the correct spelling displays in the *Suggestions* list box. Click *EARLY* in the *Suggestions* list box to change the word to the correct spelling.

d. The Editor selects the word *distributin* and the correct spelling displays in the *Suggestions* list box. Since this word is misspelled in other locations in the document, click the down arrow at the right of *distribution* in the *Suggestions* list box and then click *Change All* at the drop-down list.

e. The Editor selects *eter*. The word should be *after* and the proper spelling is not available in the *Suggestions* list box. Double-click *eter* in the document and then type after. (This dims the Editor task pane and a Resume checking all results button appears in the task pane.)

f. Click the Resume checking all results button to continue the spelling check.

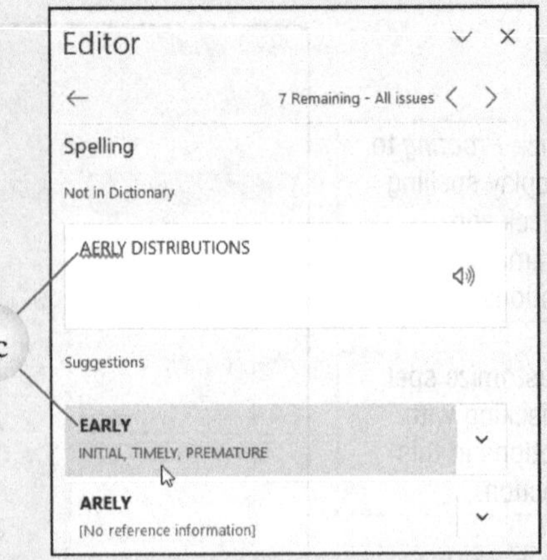

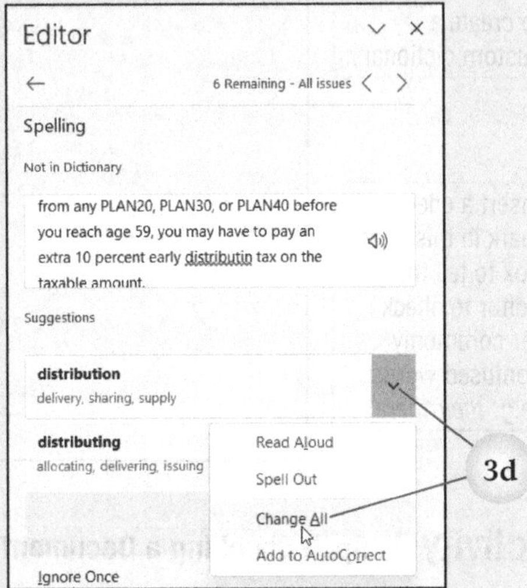

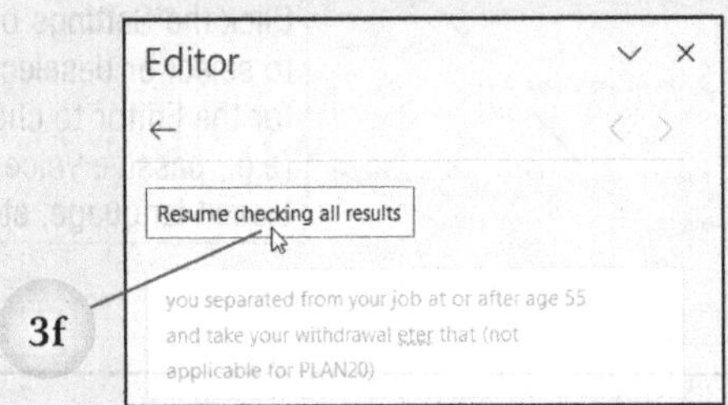

g. The spelling checker selects *to*. (This is a double word occurrence.) Click the *Delete Repeated Word* option to delete the second occurrence of *to*.

h. The spelling checker selects *Ingstrom* and displays *Logan Ingstrom* in the Editor task pane. Listen to the name being read by clicking the speaker icon at the right of the name. (Your computer speakers must be turned on for you to hear the name being read.) Ingstrom is a proper name, so click the *Ignore Once* option.

i. When the message displays that the spelling check is complete, click OK.

j. Close the Editor task pane by clicking the Close button in the upper right corner of the task pane.

4. Complete steps similar to those in Step 2 to insert a check mark in the *Ignore words in UPPERCASE* check box.
5. Save, preview, and then close **2-PlanDists.docx**.

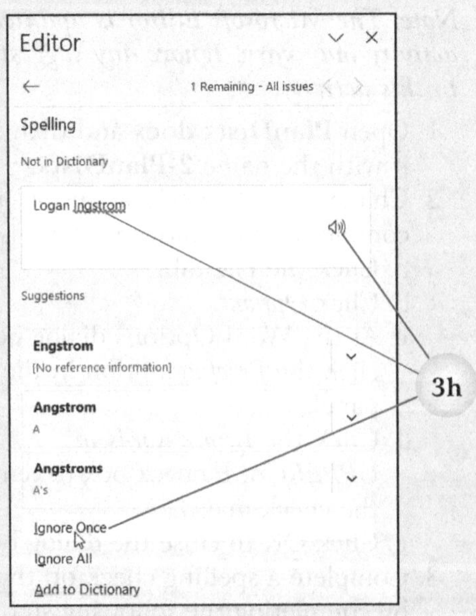

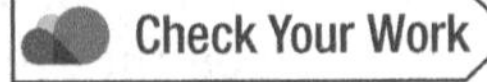

Activity 2 Change Grammar Options and Check the Grammar in a Company Letter

2 Parts

You will check the grammar in a company letter, change grammar options, and then check the document for spelling and grammar errors. You will also display readability statistics for the document.

Changing Grammar Checking Options

Quick Steps

Change Grammar Checking Options

1. Click File tab.
2. Click *Options*.
3. Click *Proofing*.
4. Change options in the dialog box.
5. Click OK.

When performing a spelling and grammar check, Word highlights text that may contain grammatical errors and displays the potential errors in the Editor task pane. By default, the grammar checker also looks for ways to refine the writing, such as by eliminating wordiness. To simply check the grammar and not look for refinements, change the option in the Word Options dialog box (see Figure 2.1 on page 43) from *Grammar & Refinements* to *Grammar*.

Click the Settings button at the Word Options dialog box with *Proofing* selected in the left panel and the Grammar Settings dialog box displays with a list of issues the Editor can consider when checking a document (e.g., errors in punctuation, misused words, biased language, and so on). Each option is preceded by a check box. If a check box contains a check mark, the option is active and the Editor will check for the issue. Scroll down the list box to see the issues available for checking in a document. Customize by inserting or removing check marks.

Activity 2a Changing Grammar Options and Checking Grammar

Part 1 of 2

1. Open **MCFLetter.docx** and save it with the name **2-MCFLetter**.
2. Look at the document and notice the dotted line below the text *all of* and *main focus* in the document indicating a possible grammar error.
3. Change the grammar option by completing the following steps:
   a. Click the File tab and then click *Options*.
   b. Click *Proofing* in the left panel.
   c. Click the *Writing Style* option box arrow and then click *Grammar* at the drop-down list.

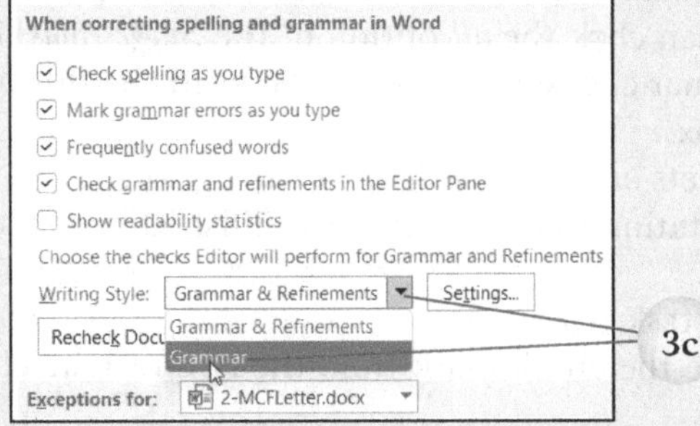

   d. Click OK.
4. At the document, notice that most of the dotted lines have been removed. This is because the *Grammar* option does not check a document for grammar issues such as wordiness and conciseness.

5. Change the grammar option back to the default and specify that the grammar checker is to check for passive voice by completing the following steps:
   a. Click the File tab and then click *Options*.
   b. Click *Proofing* in the left panel.
   c. Click the *Writing Style* option box arrow and then click *Grammar & Refinements* at the drop-down list.
   d. Click the Settings button.
   e. At the Grammar Settings dialog box, scroll down the *Options* list box to the *Clarity* section and then click the *Passive Voice* check box to insert a check mark. (Skip this step if the option already contains a check mark.)
   f. Click OK to close the Grammar Settings dialog box.
   g. Click OK to close the Word Options dialog box.

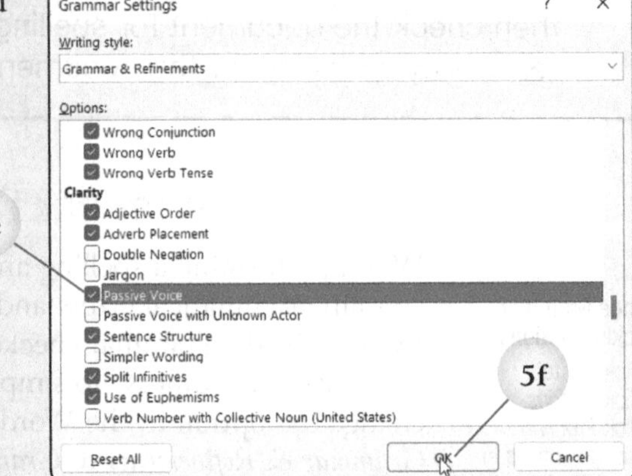

6. Check the spelling and grammar in the document by completing the following steps:
   a. Click the Editor button in the Editor group on the Home tab.
   b. At the Editor task pane, click the Editor Score box.
   c. The grammar checker selects the text *Expense charges are being lowered by McCormack Funds* and does not offer any suggestions in the *Suggestions* list box.
   d. Click the down arrow at the right of the text *Saying who or what did the action would be clearer* in the Editor task pane and then read the information that displays below the text about active voice.
   e. Click in the document and then edit the first sentence in the first paragraph so it reads as *McCormack Funds is lowering expense charges beginning May 1, 2024*.
   f. Click the Resume checking all results button in the Editor task pane.
   g. When the grammar checker selects *all of* in the document, notice the information *More concise language would be clearer for your reader* that displays below *Conciseness* in the Editor task pane and then click the *all* option in the *Suggestions* list box.
   h. When the grammar checker selects *main focus* in the document, click *focus* in the *Suggestions* list box.
   i. If the Editor selects *at*, click the *Ignore Once* option.
   j. At the message stating that the you have finished reviewing Editor's suggestion, click OK.
   k. Close the Editor task pane.

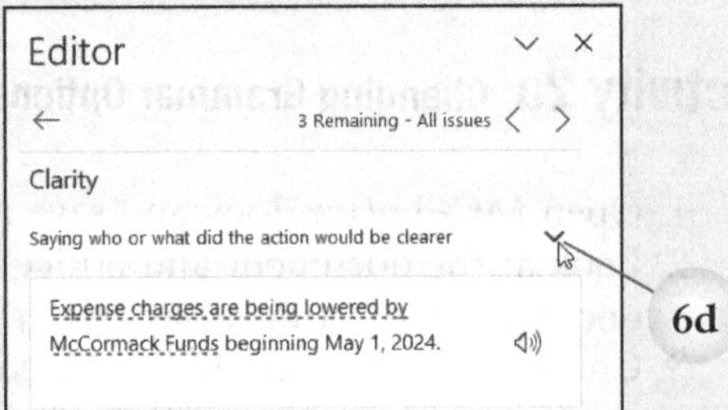

7. If necessary, remove the check mark from the *Passive Voice* check box by completing the following steps:
   a. Click the File tab and then click *Options*.
   b. Click *Proofing* in the left panel.
   c. Click the Settings button.

d. At the Grammar Settings dialog box, scroll down the *Options* list box to the *Clarity* section and then click the *Passive Voice* check box to remove the check mark.
e. Click OK to close the Grammar Settings dialog box.
f. Click OK to close the Word Options dialog box.
8. Save **2-MCFLetter.docx**.

Setting the Proofing Language

Quick Steps

Choose Proofing Language

1. Click Review tab.
2. Click Language button.
3. Click *Set Proofing Language.*
4. Click language in list box.
5. Click OK.

Microsoft provides a number of dictionaries for proofing text in various languages. To change the language used for proofing a document, click the Review tab, click the Language button in the Language group, and then click *Set Proofing Language* at the drop-down list. At the Language dialog box, click a language in the *Mark selected text as* list box. To make the selected language the default, click the Set As Default button in the lower left corner of the dialog box. Click OK to close the Language dialog box.

Displaying Readability Statistics

Quick Steps

Show Readability Statistics

1. Click File tab.
2. Click *Options.*
3. Click *Proofing.*
4. Click *Show readability statistics* check box.
5. Click OK.
6. Complete spelling and grammar check.

Readability statistics about a document can be displayed when completing a spelling and grammar check. Figure 2.2 lists the readability statistics for the document used in Activity 2b. The statistics include word, character, paragraph, and sentence counts; average number of sentences per paragraph, words per sentence, and characters per word; and readability information such as the percentage of passive sentences in the document, the Flesch Reading Ease score, and the Flesch-Kincaid Grade Level score. Control the display of readability statistics with the *Show readability statistics* check box in the Word Options dialog box with *Proofing* selected.

The Flesch Reading Ease score is based on the average number of syllables per word and the average number of words per sentence. The higher the score, the greater the number of people who will be able to understand the text in the document. Standard writing generally scores in the 60 to 70 range.

The Flesch-Kincaid Grade Level score is based on the average number of syllables per word and the average number of words per sentence. The score indicates a grade level. Standard writing is generally scored at the seventh or eighth grade level.

Figure 2.2 Readability Statistics Dialog Box

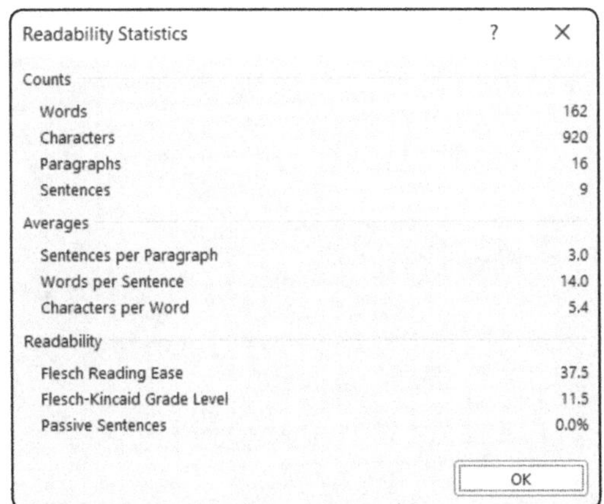

Activity 2b Displaying Readability Statistics

Part 2 of 2

1. With **2-MCFLetter.docx** open, display readability statistics about the document by completing the following steps:
   a. Click the File tab and then click *Options*.
   b. At the Word Options dialog box, click *Proofing* in the left panel.
   c. Click the *Show readability statistics* check box to insert a check mark.

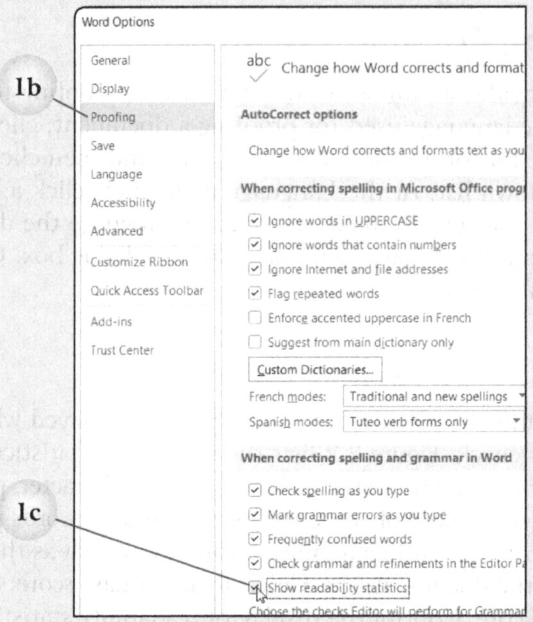

   d. Click OK to close the Word Options dialog box.
   e. At the document, click the Editor button in the Editor group on the Home tab.
   f. Look at the readability statistics that display in the Readability Statistics dialog box and then click OK to close the dialog box.
   g. Click OK at the message indicating that you have finished reviewing Editor's suggestions.
   h. If necessary, close the Editor task pane.
2. Complete steps similar to those in Steps 1a–1d to remove the check mark from the *Show readability statistics* check box.
3. Save, preview, and then close **2-MCFLetter.docx**.

Activity 3 Use Proofing Tools and Search for Information in a Document on Endangered Trees — 4 Parts

You will open an endangered trees document, create a custom dictionary, add specific terms to the custom dictionary, and then complete a spelling check. You will also display the word count, use the Thesaurus feature to replace a word with a synonym, insert line numbers, and find information on specific topics using the Search and Researcher task panes.

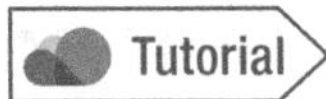

Creating and Removing a Custom Dictionary

Quick Steps

Create Custom Dictionary

1. Click File tab.
2. Click *Options.*
3. Click *Proofing.*
4. Click Custom Dictionaries button.
5. Click New button.
6. Type name for dictionary.
7. Press Enter key.

Hint When you change the custom dictionary settings in one Microsoft 365 application, the changes affect all the other applications in the suite.

Creating a Custom Dictionary

When completing a spelling check on a document, the Editor uses the main dictionary, named *RoamingCustom.dic,* to compare words. This main dictionary contains most common words, but may not include specific proper names, medical and technical terms, acronyms, or other text related to a specific field or business. If documents will be created with specific words, terms, or acronyms not found in the main dictionary, consider creating a custom dictionary. When completing a spelling check, the Editor will compare words in a document with the main dictionary as well as a custom dictionary.

To create a custom dictionary, display the Word Options dialog box with *Proofing* selected and then click the Custom Dictionaries button. This displays the Custom Dictionaries dialog box, shown in Figure 2.3. To create a new dictionary, click the New button. At the Create Custom Dictionary dialog box, type a name for the dictionary in the *File name* text box and then press the Enter key. The new dictionary name displays in the *Dictionaries* list box in the Custom Dictionaries dialog box. More than one dictionary can be used when spell checking a document. Insert a check mark in the check box next to each dictionary to be used when spell checking.

Changing the Default Dictionary

At the Custom Dictionaries dialog box, the default dictionary displays in the *Dictionaries* list box followed by *(Default).* Change this default by clicking the dictionary name in the list box and then clicking the Change Default button.

Figure 2.3 Custom Dictionaries Dialog Box

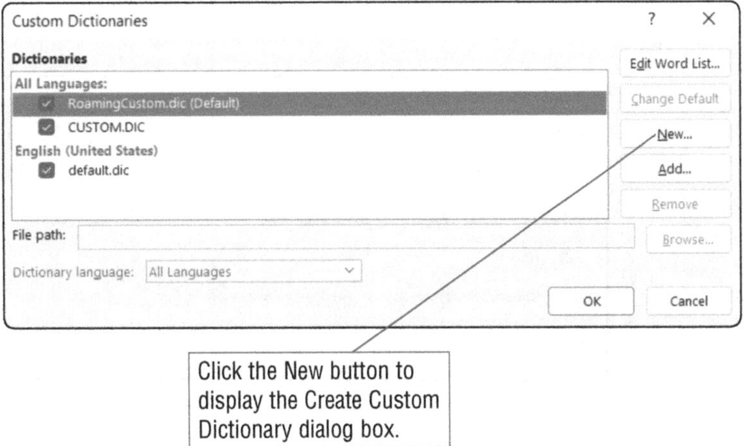

Removing a Dictionary

Quick Steps

Remove Custom Dictionary
1. Click File tab.
2. Click *Options*.
3. Click *Proofing*.
4. Click Custom Dictionaries button.
5. Click custom dictionary name.
6. Click Remove button.
7. Click OK.

Remove a custom dictionary with the Remove button at the Custom Dictionaries dialog box. To do this, display the Custom Dictionaries dialog box, click the dictionary name in the *Dictionaries* list box, and then click the Remove button. No prompt will display confirming the deletion, so make sure the correct dictionary name is selected before clicking the Remove button.

Activity 3a Creating a Custom Dictionary and Changing the Default Dictionary

Part 1 of 4

1. Open **EndangeredTrees.docx**, notice the wavy red lines indicating words not recognized by the Editor (words not in the main dictionary), and then close the document.
2. Create a custom dictionary, add words to the dictionary, and then change the default dictionary by completing the following steps:
   a. Click the File tab and then click *Options*.
   b. At the Word Options dialog box, click *Proofing* in the left panel.
   c. Click the Custom Dictionaries button.
   d. At the Custom Dictionaries, click the New button.
   e. At the Create Custom Dictionary dialog box, type your first and last names (without a space between them) in the *File name* text box and then press the Enter key.
   f. At the Custom Dictionaries dialog box, add a word to your dictionary by completing the following steps:
      1) Click the name of your dictionary in the *Dictionaries* list box.
      2) Click the Edit Word List button.

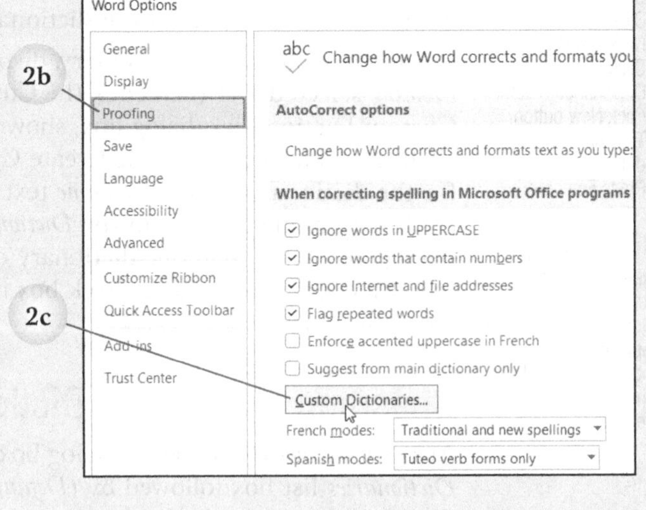

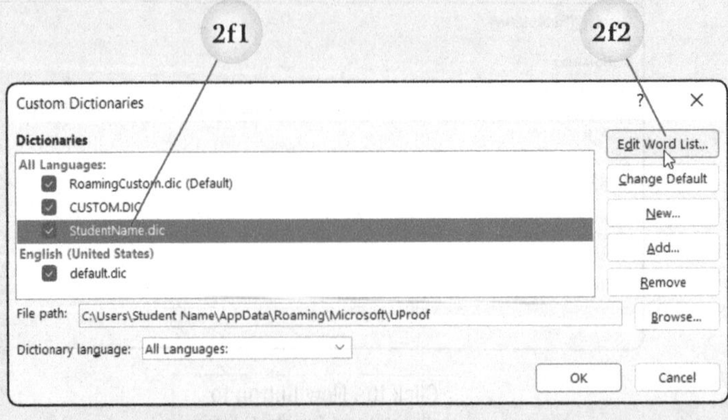

3) At the dialog box for your custom dictionary, type acerifolia in the *Word(s)* text box.
4) Click the Add button.

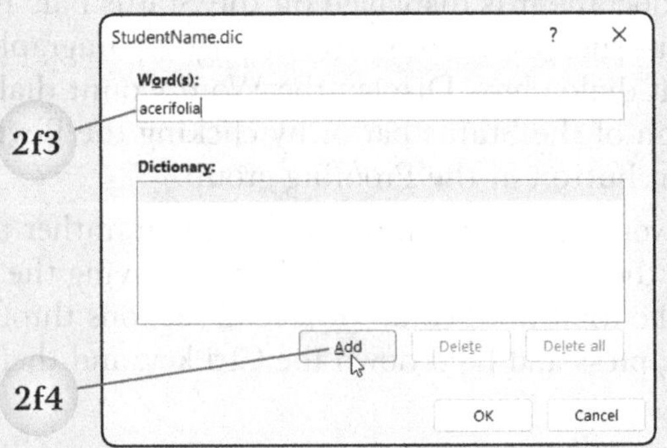

g. Add another word to the dictionary by clicking in the *Word(s)* text box, typing floridana, and then pressing the Enter key.
h. Add another word to the dictionary by clicking in the *Words(s)* text box, typing giganteum, and then pressing the Enter key.
i. Click OK to close the dialog box.
j. At the Custom Dictionaries dialog box, click the name of your dictionary in the list box and then click the Change Default button. (Notice that the word *(Default)* displays after your custom dictionary.)

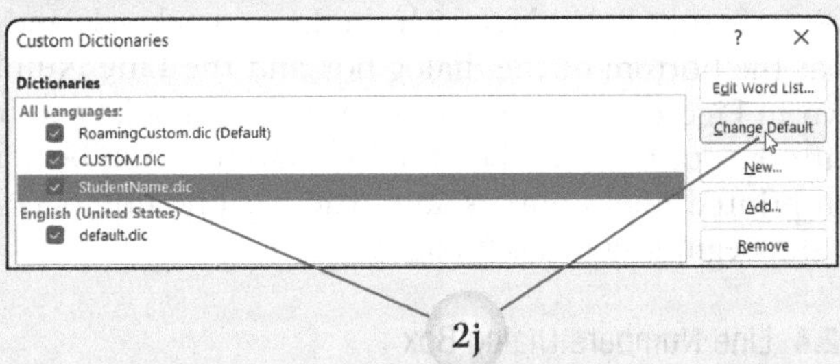

k. Click OK to close the Custom Dictionaries dialog box.
l. Click OK to close the Word Options dialog box.
3. Open **EndangeredTrees.docx** and then save it with the name **2-EndangeredTrees**.
4. Use the Editor to complete a spelling and grammar check on the document and accept all spelling and grammar suggestions. (The Editor will not stop at the words you added to your custom dictionary.)
5. Save **2-EndangeredTrees.docx**.
6. Change the default dictionary and then remove your custom dictionary by completing the following steps:
   a. Click the File tab and then click *Options*.
   b. At the Word Options dialog box, click *Proofing* in the left panel.
   c. Click the Custom Dictionaries button.
   d. At the Custom Dictionaries dialog box, click *RoamingCustom.dic* in the *Dictionaries* list box.
   e. Click the Change Default button. (This changes the default back to the RoamingCustom.dic dictionary.)
   f. Click the name of your dictionary in the *Dictionaries* list box.
   g. Click the Remove button. (If a message displays, click the Yes button.)
   h. Click OK to close the Custom Dictionaries dialog box.
   i. Click OK to close the Word Options dialog box.

Displaying Word Count

Quick Steps

Display Word Count Dialog Box

Click word count section of Status bar.
OR
1. Click Review tab.
2. Click Word Count button.

 Word Count

Displaying Word Count

Words are counted as they are typed in a document and the total number of words in a document is displayed on the Status bar. To display more information—such as the numbers of pages, paragraphs, and lines—display the Word Count dialog box. Display the Word Count dialog box by clicking the word count section of the Status bar or by clicking the Review tab and then clicking the Word Count button in the Proofing group.

Count words in a portion of the document, rather than the entire document, by selecting the portion of text and then displaying the Word Count dialog box. To determine the total word count of several sections throughout a document, select the first section, press and hold down the Ctrl key, and then select the other sections.

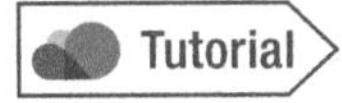

Inserting Line Numbers

 Line Numbers

Quick Steps

Insert Line Numbers

1. Click Layout tab.
2. Click Line Numbers button.
3. Click line number option.

Inserting Line Numbers

Use the Line Numbers button in the Page Setup group on the Layout tab to insert line numbers in a document. Numbering lines has practical applications for certain legal papers and reference purposes. To number lines in a document, click the Layout tab, click the Line Numbers button in the Page Setup group, and then click a line number option at the drop-down list.

To have more control over inserting line numbers in a document, click the Line Numbers button and then click *Line Numbering Options* at the drop-down list. At the Page Setup dialog box with the Layout tab selected, click the Line Numbers button at the bottom of the dialog box and the Line Numbers dialog box displays, as shown in Figure 2.4. Use options at this dialog box to insert line numbers and to specify the starting number, the location line numbers are printed, the interval between printed line numbers, and whether line numbers are consecutive or start over at the beginning of each page.

Figure 2.4 Line Numbers Dialog Box

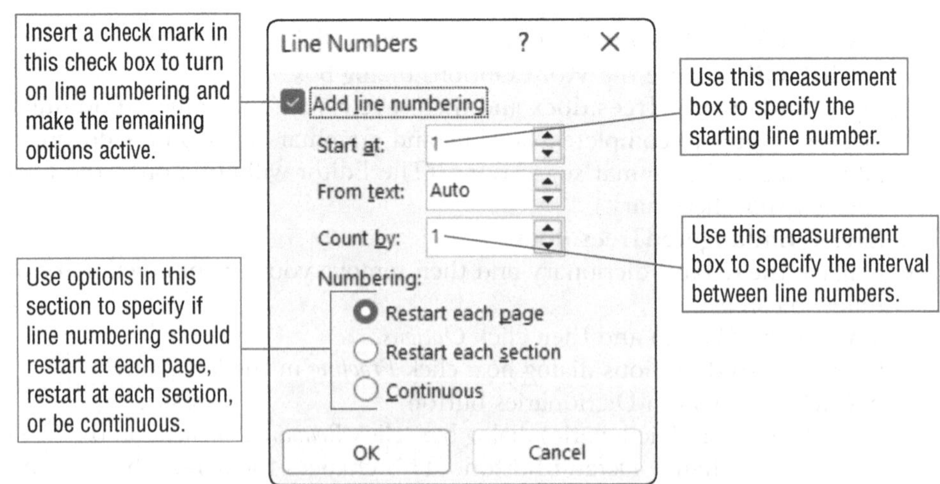

Using the Thesaurus

Using the Thesaurus

Word offers a Thesaurus feature for finding synonyms, antonyms, and related words for a particular word. Synonyms are words that have the same or nearly the same meaning. When the Thesaurus feature is used, antonyms may display for some words, which are words with opposite meanings.

Thesaurus

Quick Steps

Use Thesaurus

1. Click Review tab.
2. Click Thesaurus button.
3. Type word in search text box.
4. Press Enter key.

To use the Thesaurus feature, click the Review tab and then click the Thesaurus button in the Proofing group or use the keyboard shortcut Shift + F7. At the Thesaurus task pane, click in the search text box at the top of the task pane, type a word, and then press the Enter key or click the Start searching button (which contains a magnifying glass icon). A list of synonyms and antonyms for the typed word displays in the task pane list box. Another method for finding synonyms and antonyms is to select a word and then display the Thesaurus task pane. Figure 2.5 shows the Thesaurus task pane with synonyms and antonyms for the word *normally*.

Depending on the word typed in the search text box, words in the Thesaurus task pane list box may appear followed by *(n.)* for *noun*, *(adj.)* for *adjective*, or *(adv.)* for *adverb*. Any antonyms at the end of the list of related synonyms will be followed by *(Antonym)*. If a dictionary is installed on the computer, a definition of the selected word will appear below the task pane list box.

The Thesaurus feature provides synonyms for the selected word as well as a list of related synonyms. For example, in the Thesaurus task pane list box shown in Figure 2.5, the main synonym *usually* displays for *normally* and is preceded by a collapse triangle (a right-and-down-pointing triangle). The collapse triangle indicates that the list of related synonyms is displayed. Click the collapse triangle

Figure 2.5 Thesaurus Task Pane

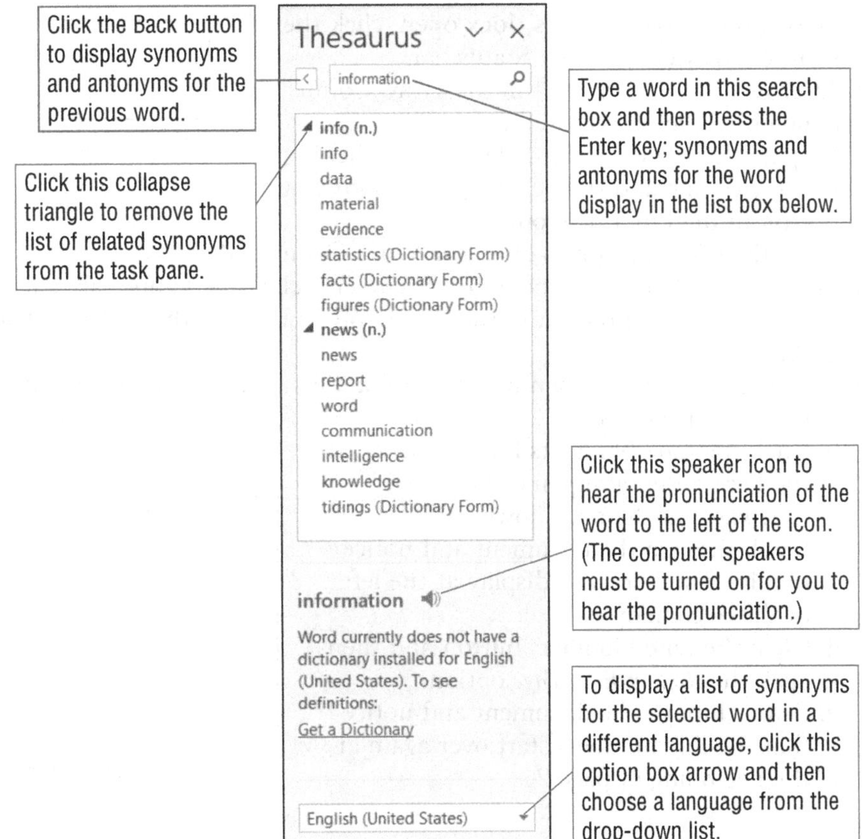

and the list of related synonyms is removed from the task pane list box and the collapse triangle changes to an expand triangle (a right-pointing triangle). Click a word in the Thesaurus task pane list box to see synonyms for it.

When reviewing synonyms and antonyms for words within a document, display the list of synonyms and antonyms for the previous word by clicking the Back button (left-pointing arrow) at the left of the search text box. Click the down-pointing triangle at the left of the Close button in the upper right corner of the task pane and a drop-down list displays with options for moving, sizing, and closing the task pane.

To replace a selected word in the document with a synonym in the Thesaurus task pane, point to the synonym in the task pane list box using the mouse. This displays a down arrow to the right of the word. Click the down arrow and then click the *Insert* option at the drop-down list.

The Thesaurus task pane, like the Editor task pane, includes a reading feature that will speak the word currently selected in the task pane. To hear the word pronounced, click the speaker icon at the right of the word below the task pane list box. (For this feature to work, the computer speakers must be turned on.)

The Thesaurus task pane also includes a language option for displaying synonyms of the selected word in a different language. To use this feature, click the option box arrow at the bottom of the task pane and then click a language at the drop-down list.

Activity 3b Displaying the Word Count, Inserting Line Numbers, and Using the Thesaurus

Part 2 of 4

1. With **2-EndangeredTrees.docx** open, click the word count section of the Status bar.
2. After reading the statistics in the Word Count dialog box, click the Close button.
3. Display the Word Count dialog box by clicking the Review tab and then clicking the Word Count button in the Proofing group.
4. Click the Close button to close the Word Count dialog box.
5. Press Ctrl + A to select the entire document, click the Home tab, click the Line and Paragraph Spacing button in the Paragraph group, and then click *2.0* at the drop-down gallery.
6. Deselect the text and then insert line numbers by completing the following steps:
   a. Click the Layout tab.
   b. Click the Line Numbers button in the Page Setup group and then click *Continuous* at the drop-down list.
   c. Scroll through the document and notice the line numbers that display at the left of the document.
   d. Click the Line Numbers button and then click the *Restart Each Page* option.
   e. Scroll through the document and notice that the line numbers start over again at the beginning of page 2.

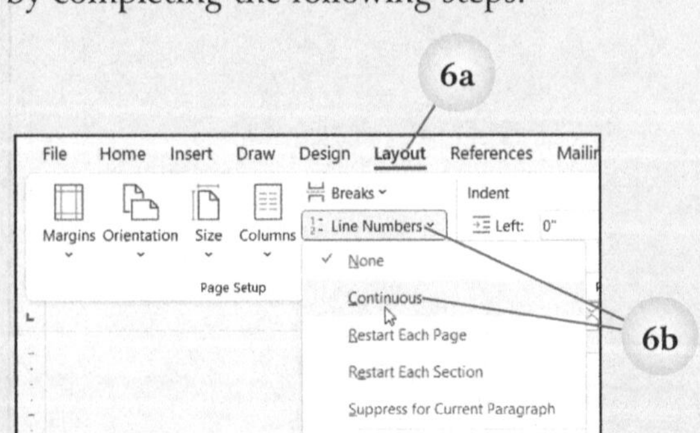

f. Click the Line Numbers button and then click *Line Numbering Options* at the drop-down list.
g. At the Page Setup dialog box, click the Line Numbers button at the bottom of the dialog box.
h. At the Line Numbers dialog box, select the current number in the *Start at* measurement box and then type 30.
i. Click the *Count by* measurement box up arrow. (This displays *2* in the measurement box.)
j. Click the *Continuous* option in the *Numbering* section.
k. Click OK to close the Line Numbers dialog box.

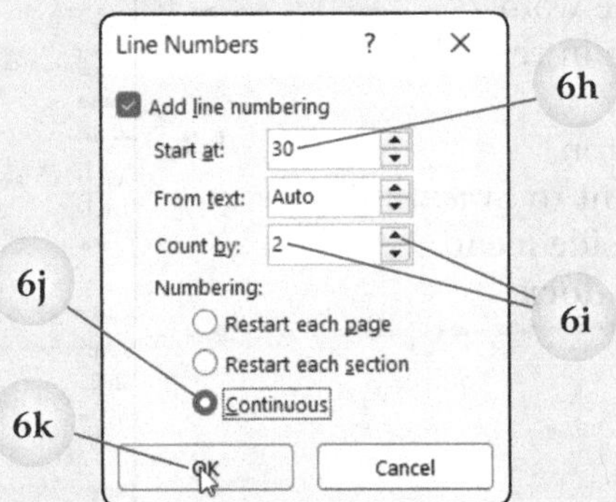

l. Click OK to close the Page Setup dialog box.
m. Scroll through the document and notice the line numbers that display at the left side of the document. The numbers start with *30* and increase by intervals of two.
n. Click the Line Numbers button and then click *None* at the drop-down list.

7. Select the document, click the Home tab, click the Line and Paragraph Spacing button in the Paragraph group, and then click *1.0* at the drop-down gallery.
8. Use the Thesaurus feature to change the word *information* in the first paragraph to *knowledge* by completing the following steps:
   a. Click in the word *information* in the second sentence of the first paragraph.
   b. Click the Review tab.
   c. Click the Thesaurus button in the Proofing group.
   d. At the Thesaurus task pane, point to *knowledge* in the task pane list box, click the down arrow at the right of the word, and then click *Insert* at the drop-down list.
   e. Close the Thesaurus task pane.

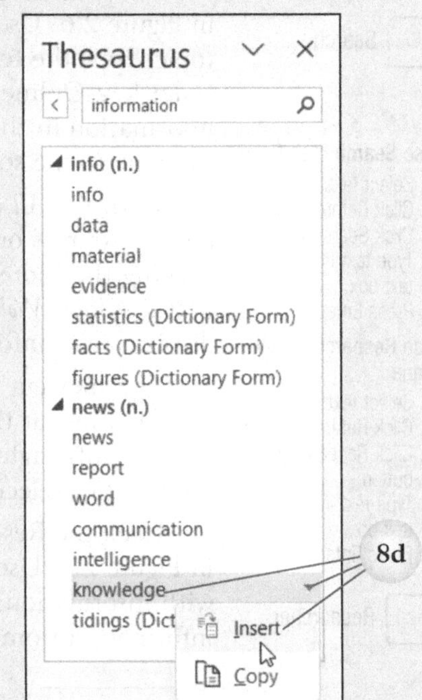

9. Follow steps similar to those in Step 8 to use the Thesaurus to replace *exact* with *precise* (located in the second sentence of the second paragraph).
10. Save **2-EndangeredTrees.docx**.

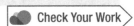

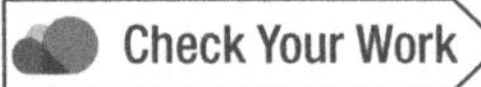

Another method for displaying synonyms of a word is to use a shortcut menu. To do this, position the pointer on the word and then click right mouse button. At the shortcut menu, point to *Synonyms* and then click a synonym at the side menu. Click the *Thesaurus* option at the bottom of the side menu to display synonyms and antonyms for the word in the Thesaurus task pane.

Activity 3c **Replacing Synonyms Using the Shortcut Menu** **Part 3 of 4**

1. With **2-EndangeredTrees.docx** open, position the pointer on the word *unique* in the first sentence in the third paragraph.
2. Click the right mouse button.
3. At the shortcut menu, point to *Synonyms* and then click *rare* at the side menu.
4. Save **2-EndangeredTrees.docx**.

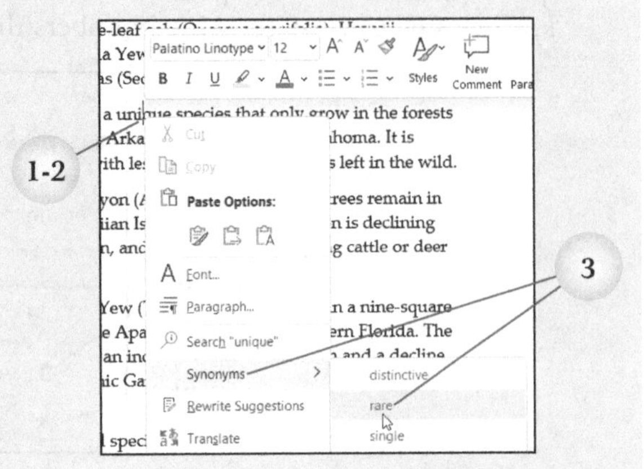

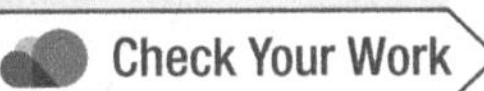

Using Research Tools

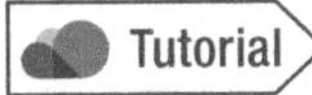

Using Research Tools

Search

Use Search Task Pane
1. Select text.
2. Click References tab.
3. Click Search button.
4. Type text in search text box.
5. Press Enter.

Use Researcher Task Pane
1. Select text.
2. Click References tab.
3. Click Researcher button.
4. Type text in search text box.
5. Press Enter.

Researcher

The Research group on the References tab contains two buttons—Search and Researcher. Click the Search button and the Search task pane displays as shown in Figure 2.6. Use the Search task pane to find information online for a specific topic. Type the text on which to search in the Search text box and then press the Enter key. Online sources containing the topic display in the task pane. Read the information in the task pane or click a hyperlink to display additional information from an online source.

With the *All* option selected in the Search task pane, the task pane will display sources on the web and media resources. Specify what to display by clicking the More button in the task pane and then clicking one of the options that display—*Web*, *Media*, or *Help*. Click the *Help* option and the Help task pane displays with information on the text in the search text box.

The shortcut menu provides another method for displaying information on a specific topic at the Search task pane. To use the shortcut menu, click in a word or select words, right-click the word(s), and then click the *Search* option (followed by the word or selected words) at the shortcut menu.

Click the Researcher button and the Researcher task pane displays as shown in Figure 2.7. Use the Researcher task pane to search for websites and journals with information on a specific topic. Type a topic in the search text box and information from journals and websites displays in the task pane.

Figure 2.6 Search Task Pane

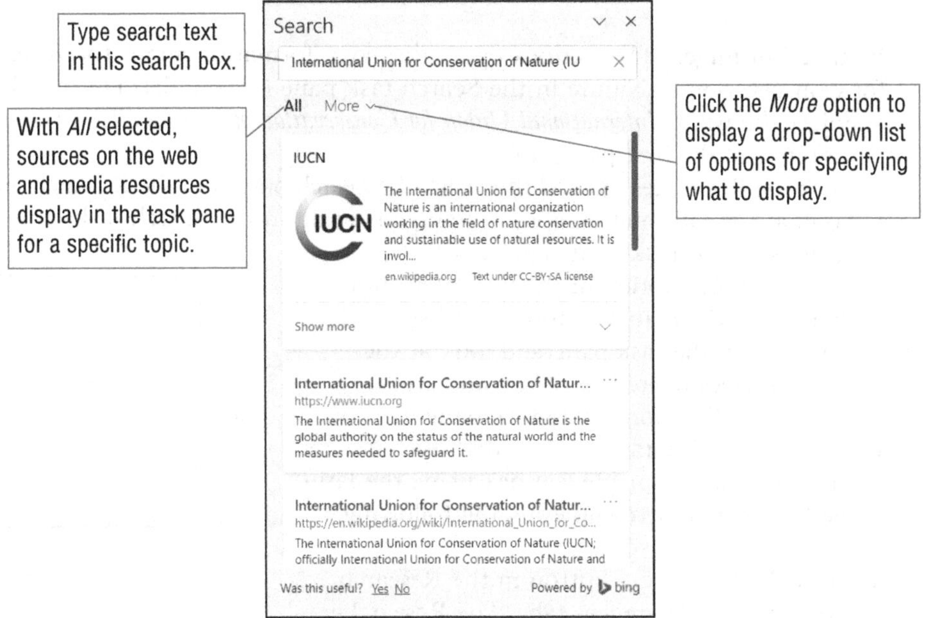

Figure 2.7 Researcher Task Pane

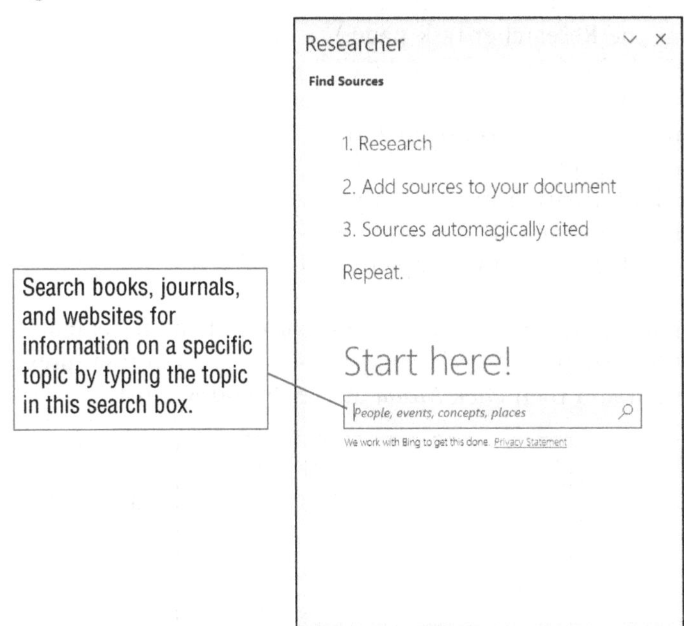

Activity 3d Using the Search and Researcher Task Panes

1. With **2-EndangeredTrees.docx** open, display information about the International Union for Conservation of Nature in the Search task pane by completing the following steps:
   a. Select the words *International Union for Conservation of Nature (IUCN)* in the first sentence of the first paragraph.
   b. Click the References tab and then click the Search button in the Research group.
   c. Look at the information about the organization in the Search task pane. (Note that options in this task pane may vary.)
   d. Click the *More* option in the task pane and then click *Media* at the drop-down list.
   e. Scroll down the task pane and look at the media images related to the organization.
   f. Click the *All* option in the task pane.

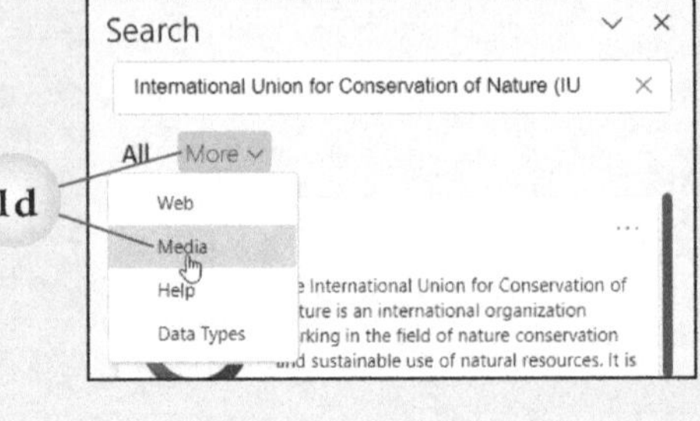

2. Use the Researcher task pane to display information on the maple-leaf oak using the latin name for the tree by completing the following steps:
   a. Click the Researcher button in the Research group on the References tab. (The Researcher task pane opens and the Search task pane is reduced to a button that display outside the upper right corner of the task pane above a button representing the Researcher task pane.)
   b. Type quercus acerifolia in the search text box and then press the Enter key.
   c. Look at the information in the task pane and then click the *Journals* option.
   d. Look at the journal information in the task pane.

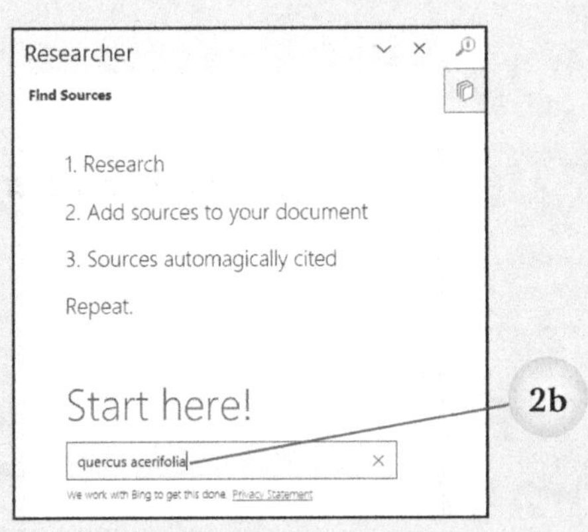

3. Display the Search task pane and then search for information on the maple-leaf oak by completing the following steps:
   a. Click the Search button outside the upper right corner of the Researcher task pane.
   b. Select the text in the search text box, type maple-leaf oak, and then press the Enter key.
   c. Click the *More* option and then click *Media* at the drop-down list.

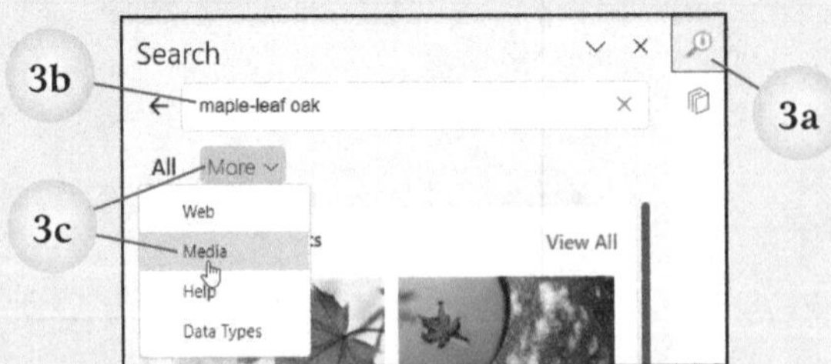

   d. Scroll down the list of images of the maple-leaf oak.
4. Close the Search task pane.
5. Close the Researcher task pane.
6. Save, preview, and then close **2-EndangeredTrees.docx**.

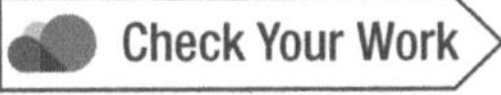

Activity 4 Translate Text in Documents 2 Parts

You will use the translation feature to translate selected text from English to Spanish and English to French. You will also translate a document from English to Spanish.

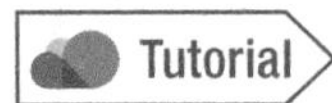

Translating Text to and from Different Languages

Translate

Translating Text to and from Different Languages

Word includes a Translate feature that will translate text to and from different languages. To use the Translate feature, click the Review tab and then click the Translate button in the Language group. At the drop-down list, click the *Translate Selection* option to translate selected text or click the *Translate Document* to translate the contents of the open document.

Translating Selected Text

Quick Steps

Translate Selected Text

1. Click Review tab.
2. Click Translate button.
3. Click *Translate Selection.*

To translate specific text in a document, click the Translate button in the Language group on the Review tab and then click the *Translate Selection* option. This opens the Translator task pane at the right side of the screen with the *Selection* option selected, similar to what is shown in Figure 2.8.

By default, the Translate feature will automatically detect the language in the document and *Auto-detect* will display in the *From* option box. A specific language can be selected by clicking the *From* option box and then clicking the language at the drop-down list. Click the *To* option box and then click the translation language at the drop-down list. Select text in the document and then click the Insert button near the bottom of the task pane. The selected text is replaced by the translated text.

Figure 2.8 Translator Task Pane

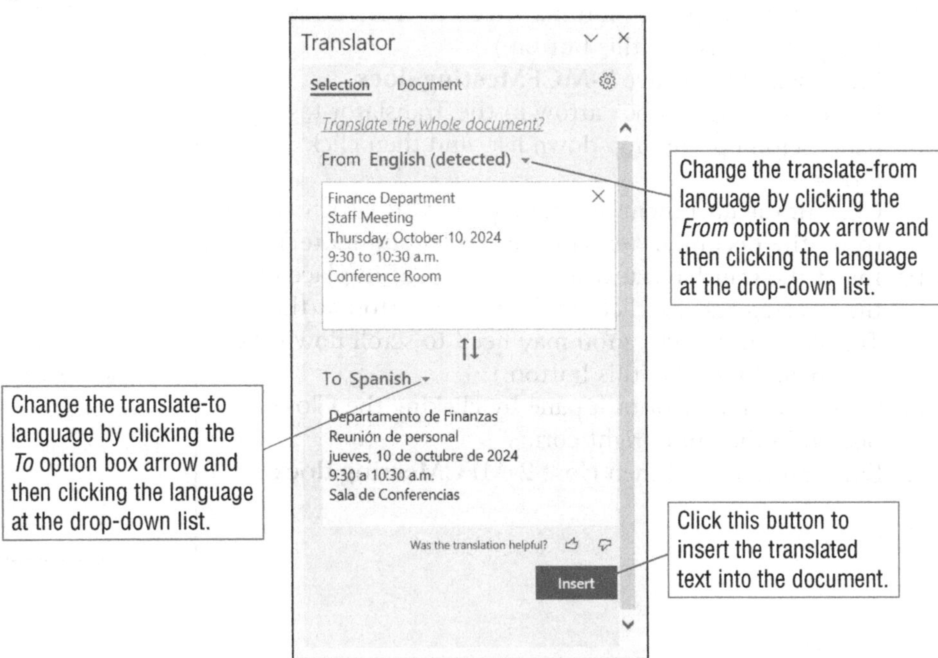

Activity 4a Translating Selected Text

Note: Check with your instructor before completing this activity to make sure you have access to the internet.

1. Open **MCFMeeting.docx** and then save it with the name **2-MCFMeeting.docx**.
2. Display the Translator task pane by clicking the Review tab, clicking the Translate button in the Language group, and then clicking *Translate Selection* at the drop-down list.

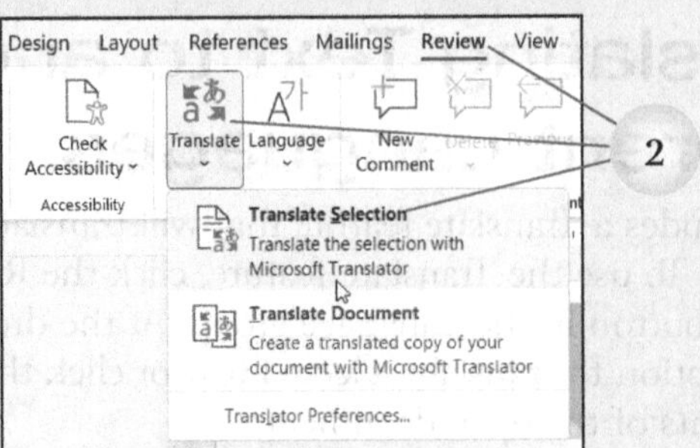

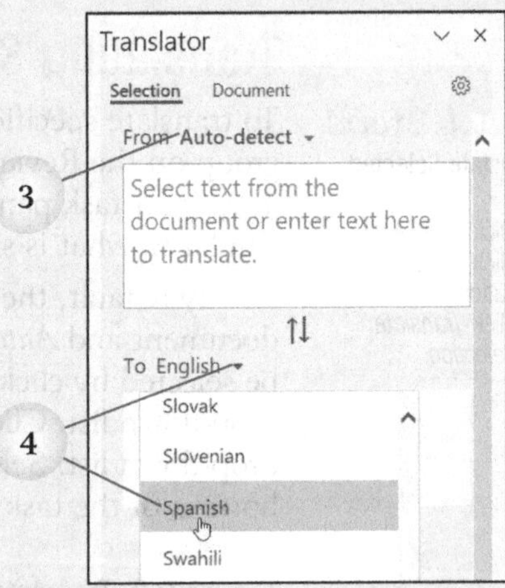

3. At the Translator task pane with the *Selection* option selected, check to make sure the *From* option box displays with *Auto-detect* (or it might also display as *English*).
4. Click the *To* option box arrow, scroll down the drop-down list, and then click *Spanish*. (The language names display in alphabetical order in the drop-down list.)
5. Click in the document and then press Ctrl + A to select the entire document (except the header and footer). Notice that the translation of the selected text displays below the *To* option box in the Translator task pane.
6. Insert the translated text in the document in place of the selected text by clicking the Insert button at the Translator task pane. (You may need to scroll down the task pane to display this button.)
7. Preview and then save **2-MCFMeeting.docx**.
8. Click the *To* option box arrow in the Translator task pane, scroll up the drop-down list, and then click *French*.
9. Click in the document and then press Ctrl + A to select the entire document (except the header and footer).
10. Insert the translated text in the document in place of the selected text by clicking the Insert button at the Translator task pane. (You may need to scroll down the task pane to display this button.)
11. Close the Translator task pane by clicking the Close button in the upper right corner.
12. Save, preview, and then close **2-MFCMeeting.docx**.

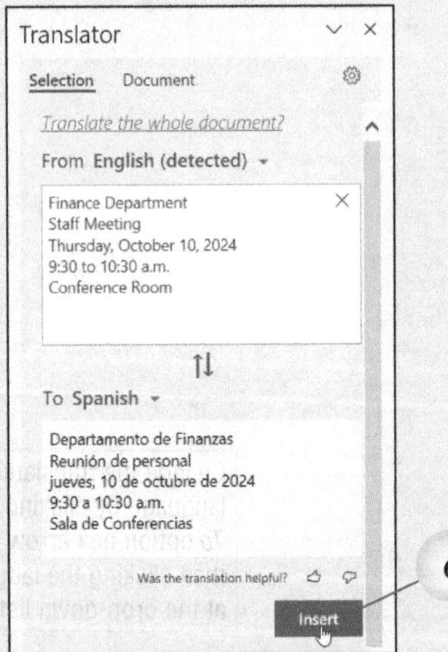

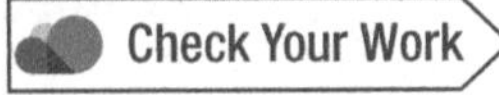

Translating a Document

Quick Steps
Translate Document
1. Click Review tab.
2. Click Translate button.
3. Click *Translate Document*.

To translate an entire document, click the Translate button in the Language group on the Review tab and then choose the *Translate Document* option. The Translator task pane opens with the *Document* option selected. Select the language to translate from and to, and then click the Translate button. A new document opens with the translated text. Click the Translate button and then click the *Translator Preferences* option to narrow the list of languages to be included in the translation list, or click the gear icon in the task pane.

Preparing a Document for Translation

Word's Translate feature is considered a machine translation because a machine, rather than a person, does the translating. While this method is fast and convenient, it is prone to errors. Before sharing a machine-translated document, ask someone familiar with the target language to proofread the text to be sure the information is properly translated. For important or sensitive information to be used in a business context, always rely on a professional translator. To optimize machine translation and reduce errors, follow these guidelines:

- Use standard, formal language. Avoid abbreviations, acronyms, slang, colloquialisms, and idioms, as these may not translate well to a different language.
- Write simple, direct sentences that express only one idea.
- Avoid ambiguities. Use articles (such as *the*) in sentences whenever possible and repeat the noun in a sentence rather than use a pronoun.
- Before translating, run a spelling and grammar check to be sure all words are spelled correctly and that proper punctuation and grammar are used.
- Apply predesigned heading styles to any headings in the document.

Activity 4b Translating a Document — Part 2 of 2

1. Open **Australia.docx** and then save it with the name **2-Australia**.
2. Display the Translator task pane by clicking the Review tab, clicking the Translate button, and then clicking *Translate Document* at the drop-down list. (If a new document opens with translated text, close the document without saving changes.)
3. At the Translator task pane with the *Document* option selected, make sure that *Auto-detect* or *English* displays in the *From* option box.
4. Click the *To* option box arrow, scroll down the drop-down list, and then click *Spanish*.
5. Click the Translate button at the Translator task pane. (This opens a new document with the translated document.)
6. Save the document with the name **2-TranslatedDoc**.
7. Preview and then close **2-TranslatedDoc.docx**.
8. At the **2-Australia.docx** document, close the Translator task pane and then close the document.

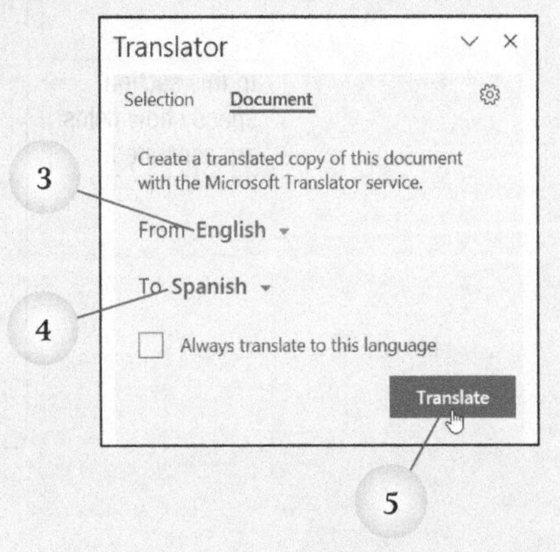

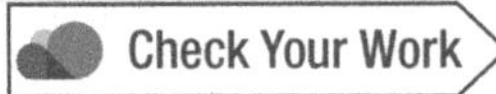

Activity 5 Sort Company Information — 3 Parts

You will open a document containing information on company employees and then sort data in paragraphs, columns, and tables.

Sorting Text

Text in a document can be sorted alphanumerically, numerically, or chronologically. In an alphanumeric sort, punctuation marks and special symbols are sorted first, followed by numbers and then text. Use options at the Sort Text dialog box to specify what is to be sorted. Text in paragraphs, columns, and tables can be sorted.

Review: Sorting Text in Paragraphs

Sort

Quick Steps

Sort Paragraphs of Text

1. Click Sort button.
2. Make changes as needed at Sort Text dialog box.
3. Click OK.

Sorting Text in Paragraphs

To sort paragraphs of text, select the text and then click the Sort button in the Paragraph group on the Home tab. This displays the Sort Text dialog box, which contains sorting options.

The *Type* option at the Sort Text dialog box will display *Text*, *Number*, or *Date* depending on the text selected. Word attempts to determine the data type and chooses one of the three options. For example, if numbers with mathematical values are selected, Word assigns them the *Number* type. However, if a numbered list is selected, Word assigns them the *Text* type since the numbers do not represent mathematical values.

By default, paragraphs of text are sorted by the first word of each paragraph. This can be changed with options at the Sort Options dialog box, shown in Figure 2.9. Display this dialog box by clicking the Options button at the Sort Text dialog box. Use the options in the *Separate fields at* section to specify how text is separated in the document. For example, to sort text by the second word of each paragraph, click the *Other* option box (this moves the insertion point into the text box to the right of the *Other* option box) and then press the spacebar.

Figure 2.9 Sort Options Dialog Box

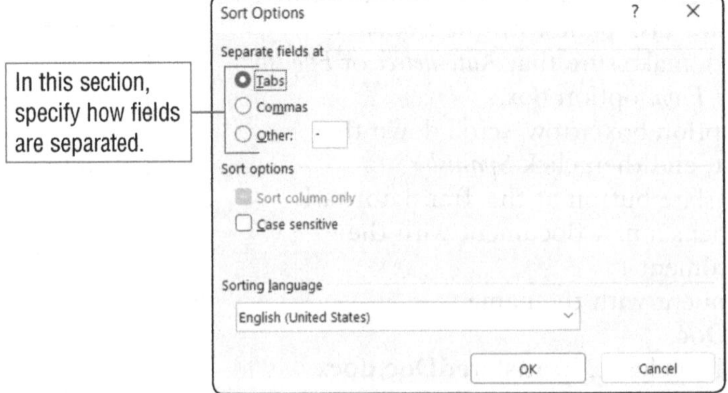

Activity 5a Sorting Text in Paragraphs

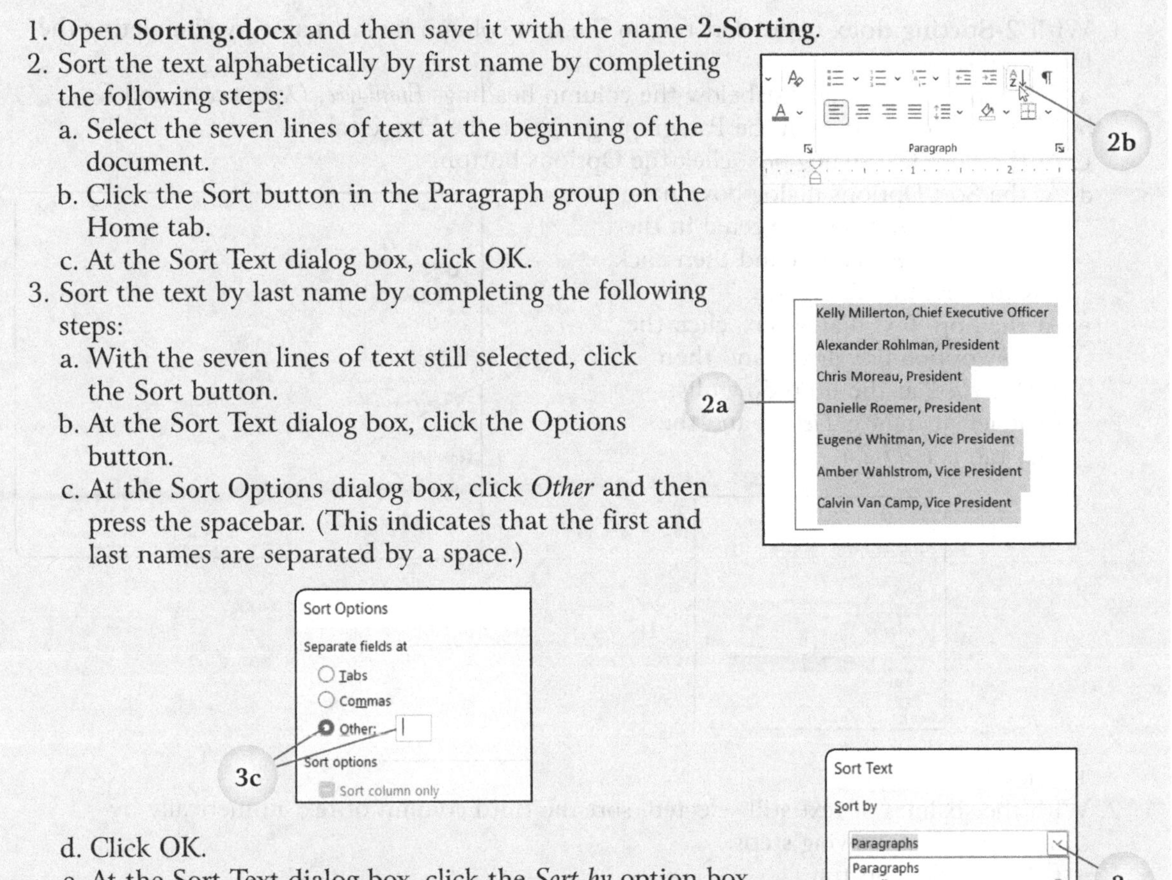

1. Open **Sorting.docx** and then save it with the name **2-Sorting**.
2. Sort the text alphabetically by first name by completing the following steps:
   a. Select the seven lines of text at the beginning of the document.
   b. Click the Sort button in the Paragraph group on the Home tab.
   c. At the Sort Text dialog box, click OK.
3. Sort the text by last name by completing the following steps:
   a. With the seven lines of text still selected, click the Sort button.
   b. At the Sort Text dialog box, click the Options button.
   c. At the Sort Options dialog box, click *Other* and then press the spacebar. (This indicates that the first and last names are separated by a space.)
   d. Click OK.
   e. At the Sort Text dialog box, click the *Sort by* option box arrow and then click *Word 2* at the drop-down list.
   f. Click OK.
4. Save **2-Sorting.docx**.

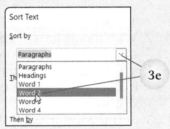

Check Your Work

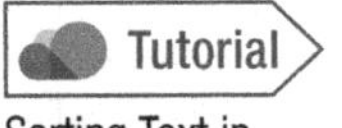
Tutorial

Sorting Text in Columns

Quick Steps

Sort Text in Columns

1. Select specific text.
2. Click Sort button.
3. Click Options button.
4. Specify *Tabs* as separator.
5. Click OK.
6. Make changes at Sort Text dialog box.
7. Click OK.

Sorting Text in Columns

To sort text set in columns, the text must be separated with tabs. When sorting text in columns, Word considers the left margin *Field 1*, text typed at the first tab *Field 2*, and so on. When sorting text in columns, make sure the columns are separated with only one tab because Word recognizes each tab as beginning a separate column. Thus, using more than one tab between columns may result in field numbers that correspond to empty columns.

Sorting on More than One Field

Text can be sorted on more than one field. For example, in Activity 5b, Step 3, the department entries will be sorted alphabetically and then the employee names will be sorted alphabetically within the departments. To do this, specify the *Department* column in the *Sort by* option box and then specify the *Employee* column in the *Then by* option box. If a document contains columns with heading text, click the *Header row* option in the *My list has* section.

Activity 5b Sorting Text in Columns

1. With **2-Sorting.docx** open, sort text in the first column by last name by completing the following steps:
   a. Select the six lines of text below the column headings *Employee*, *Department*, and *Ext*.
   b. Click the Sort button in the Paragraph group on the Home tab.
   c. At the Sort Text dialog box, click the Options button.
   d. At the Sort Options dialog box, make sure the *Tabs* option is selected in the *Separate fields at* section and then click OK to close the dialog box.
   e. At the Sort Text dialog box, click the *Sort by* option box arrow and then click *Field 2* at the drop-down list. (The left margin is *Field 1* and the first tab is *Field 2*.)

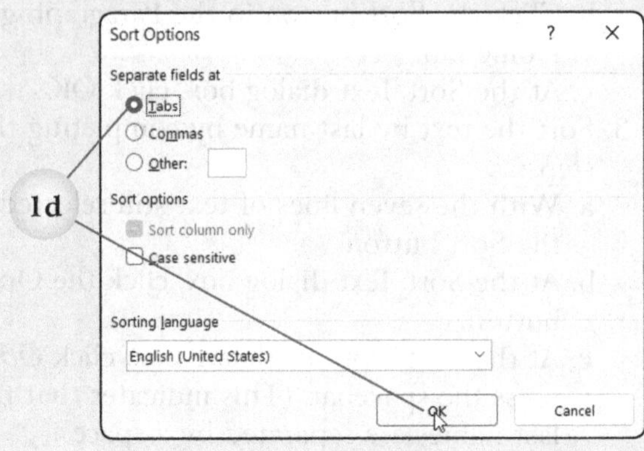

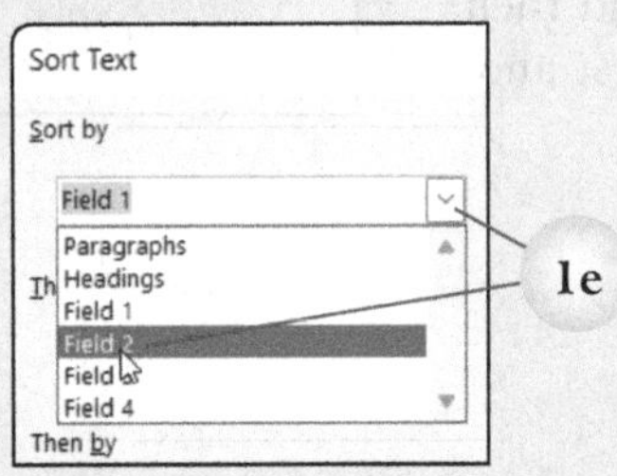

   f. Click OK.
2. With the six lines of text still selected, sort the third column of text numerically by completing the following steps:
   a. Click the Sort button.
   b. Click the *Sort by* option box arrow and then click *Field 4* at the drop-down list.
   c. Click OK.
3. Sort the text in the first two columns by completing the following steps:
   a. Select the seven lines of text set in the columns, including the headings.
   b. Click the Sort button.
   c. At the Sort Text dialog box, click the *Header row* option in the *My list has* section.
   d. If necessary, click the *Sort by* option box arrow and then click *Department*.
   e. Click the *Type* option box arrow in the *Sort by* section and then click *Text*.
   f. Click the *Then by* option box arrow and then click *Employee* at the drop-down list.
   g. Click OK.
4. Save **2-Sorting.docx**.

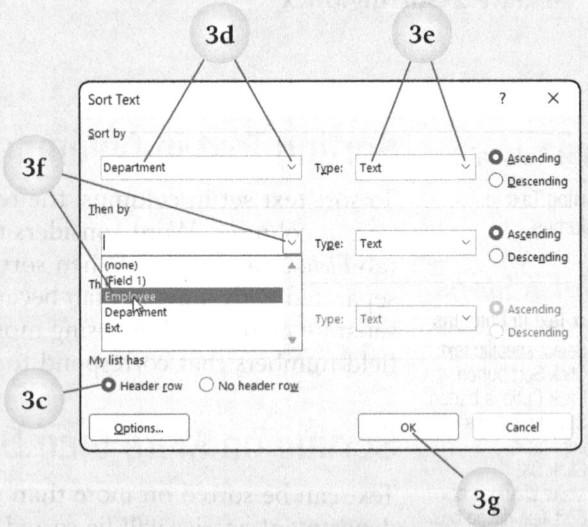

Check Your Work

Sorting Text in a Table

Sorting Text in a Table

Sorting text in columns within tables is similar to sorting columns of text separated by tabs. When sorting text in a table, the dialog box is named the Sort dialog box rather than the Sort Text dialog box. If a table contains a header, click the *Header row* option in the *My list has* section of the Sort dialog box to tell Word not to include the header row when sorting. To sort only specific cells in a table, select the cells and then complete the sort.

Quick Steps

Sort Text in Table

1. Position insertion point in table.
2. Click Sort button.
3. Make changes at Sort dialog box.
4. Click OK.

Activity 5c Sorting Text in a Table

Part 3 of 3

1. With **2-Sorting.docx** open, sort the text in the first column of the table by completing the following steps:
   a. Position the insertion point in any cell in the table.
   b. Click the Sort button.
   c. At the Sort dialog box, make sure the *Header row* option is selected in the *My list has* section.
   d. Click the *Sort by* option box arrow and then click *Sales, First Half* at the drop-down list.
   e. Make sure nothing displays in the *Then by* option box. If necessary, click the *Then by* option box arrow and then click *(none)* at the drop-down list.
   f. Click OK.
2. Sort the numbers in the third column in descending order by completing the following steps:
   a. Select all the cells in the table except the cells in the first row.
   b. Click the Sort button.
   c. Click the *Sort by* option box arrow and then click *Column 3* at the drop-down list.
   d. Click *Descending*.

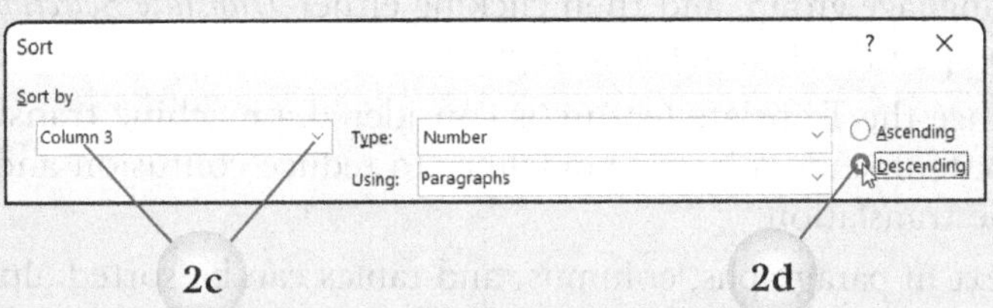

   e. Click OK.
3. Save, preview, and then close **2-Sorting.docx**.

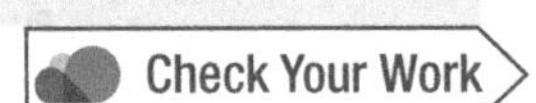

Chapter Summary

- Word's Editor contains a spelling and grammar checker. The spelling checker checks text against its dictionary and suggests corrections. The grammar checker finds errors in grammar, punctuation, and word usage.
- When checking spelling and grammar, make changes by clicking in the document outside the Editor task pane. Make the changes and then click the Resume checking all results button in the task pane.
- Customize spelling and grammar checking options at the Word Options dialog box with *Proofing* selected in the left panel.
- Change the proofing language at the Language dialog box. Display this dialog box by clicking the Review tab, clicking the Language button in the Language group, and then clicking *Set Proofing Language.*
- To display readability statistics for a document, insert a check mark in the *Show readability statistics* check box in the Word Options dialog box with *Proofing* selected and then complete a spelling and grammar check.
- Word uses the main dictionary when spell checking a document. Change the default dictionary and add or remove a custom dictionary at the Custom Dictionaries dialog box. Display this dialog box by clicking the Custom Dictionaries button at the Word Options dialog box with *Proofing* selected.
- The Word Count dialog box displays the numbers of pages, words, characters, paragraphs, and lines in a document. Display this dialog box by clicking the word count section of the Status bar or by clicking the Word Count button in the Proofing group on the Review tab.
- Number the lines in a document with options at the Line Numbers button drop-down list or the Line Numbers dialog box.
- Use the Thesaurus feature to find synonyms and antonyms for words in a document. Display synonyms and antonyms at the Thesaurus task pane or by right-clicking a word and then pointing to *Synonyms* at the shortcut menu.
- Use the Search button in the Research group on the References tab to find information online for a specific topic and use the Researcher button to search for websites and journals with information on a specific topic.
- Translate text by clicking the Review tab, clicking the Translate button in the Language group, and then clicking either *Translate Selection* or *Translate Document* to open the Translator task pane.
- Since the Translate feature is considered a machine translation, consider content standards and guidelines to reduce confusion and errors and optimize the translation.
- Text in paragraphs, columns, and tables can be sorted alphabetically, numerically, or chronologically. Sort text by clicking the Sort button in the Paragraph group on the Home tab and then using options at the Sort Text dialog box to specify what is to be sorted.
- By default, paragraphs of text are sorted by the first word of each paragraph. This can be changed with options at the Sort Options dialog box. Display the dialog box by clicking the Options button at the Sort Text dialog box. Use the options in the *Separate fields at* section of the dialog box to specify how text is separated in the document.

- When sorting text set in columns, Word considers text typed at the left margin *Field 1*, text typed at the first tab *Field 2*, and so on.
- Sort on more than one field with the *Sort by* and *Then by* options at the Sort dialog box.
- Use the *Header row* option in the *My list has* section in the Sort Text dialog box to sort all the text in rows in a table except the first row.

Commands Review

FEATURE	RIBBON TAB, GROUP	BUTTON, OPTION	KEYBOARD SHORTCUT
line numbers	Layout, Page Setup		
proofing language	Review, Language	, *Set Proofing Language*	
Researcher task pane	References, Research		
Search task pane	References, Research		
Sort Options dialog box	Home, Paragraph	, Options	
Sort Text dialog box	Home, Paragraph		
spelling and grammar checker	Review, Proofing		F7
Thesaurus task pane	Review, Proofing		Shift + F7
Translator task pane	Review, Language	, *Translate Selection* OR *Translate Document*	
Word Count dialog box	Review, Proofing		

CHAPTER 2

Review and Assessment

Skills Assessment

Assessment 1

Check Spelling and Grammar in a Document

1. Open **QuoteMarks.docx** and then save it with the name **2-QuoteMarks**.
2. Complete a spelling and grammar check on the document. (Ignore any quoted text selected by the Editor.)
3. Apply the Heading 1 style to the title of the document and the Heading 2 style to the headings in the document (which currently display with bold formatting).
4. Apply the Parallax theme.
5. Center the document title.
6. Save, preview, and then close **2-QuoteMarks.docx**.

Assessment 2

Check Spelling and Grammar and Proofread a Letter

1. Open **AirMiles.docx** and then save it with the name **2-AirMiles**.
2. Complete a spelling and grammar check on the document.
3. After completing the spelling and grammar check, proofread the letter and correct any errors not identified by the Editor. Replace the *XX* near the end of the document with your initials.
4. Select the entire document and then change the font to 12-point Candara.
5. Save, preview, and then close **2-AirMiles.docx**.

Assessment 3

Check Spelling and Grammar and Display Readability Statistics and Word Count in a Document

1. Open **KonradZuse.docx** and then save it with the name **2-KonradZuse**.
2. Turn on the display of readability statistics and then complete a spelling and grammar check on the document. (All proper names are spelled correctly.)
3. Make a note of the number of words, the Flesch Reading Ease score, and the Flesch-Kincaid Grade Level score. Type that information in the appropriate locations at the end of the document.
4. Turn off the display of readability statistics.
5. Insert continuous line numbering.
6. Save, preview, and then close **2-KonradZuse.docx**.

Assessment 4

Translate Selected Text in a Document

1. Open **PRConference.docx** and then save it with the name **2-PRConference**.
2. Select all the text in the first cell in the table (begins with *Annual Conference*).
3. Display the Translator task pane with the *Selection* option selected.
4. Specify that the text is to be translated into Spanish.
5. Click in the empty row at the bottom of the table and then insert the translated text.
6. Close the Translator task pane.
7. Save, preview, and then close **2-PRConference.docx**.

Assessment 5

Translate an Entire Document

1. Open **Announcement.docx** and then save it with the name **2-Announcement**.
2. Translate the entire document into French.
3. Save the translated document with the name **2-Announce-French**.
4. Preview and then close **2-Announce-French.docx**.
5. Close the Translator task pane and then close **2-Announcement.docx**.

Assessment 6

Sort Text in a Document

1. Open **SFSSorting.docx** and then save it with the name **2-SFSSorting**.
2. Select the nine lines of text below the heading *Executive Team* and then sort the text alphabetically by last name.
3. Sort the three columns of text below the title *New Employees* by date of hire in ascending order.
4. Sort the text in the *First Qtr.* column in the table numerically in descending order.
5. Save, preview, and then close **2-SFSSorting.docx**.

Visual Benchmark

Activity 1

Sort Data in a Document

1. Open **Natura.docx** and then save it with the name **2-Natura**.
2. Complete sorts so that your text appears as shown in Figure 2.10. ***Hint: Sort the text in the table first by the country and then by the customer name.***
3. Save, preview, and then close **2-Natura.docx**.

Activity 2

Translate Text

1. Open **CCDonations.docx** and then save it with the name **2-CCDonations**.
2. Select the paragraph of text below the heading *English:* and then translate the paragraph into Spanish and then into French. Insert the translated text into the document, as shown in Figure 2.11. (Your translations may vary from those shown in the figure.)
3. Use the Curlz MT font with bold formatting to format the heading at the beginning of each paragraph and the quote (without bold formatting) that displays near the end of the letter. Center the quote and apply the Blue font color to the quote and then apply paragraph shading as shown in the figure.
4. Save, preview, and then close **2-CCDonations.docx**.

Figure 2.10 Visual Benchmark 1

Natural products for natural beauty...

Natura Representatives

Denise Beaulieu	206-555-3901
Marcus Brown	347-555-2389
Charles Collins	202-555-9954
Dallas Conway	305-555-3492
Midori Fujita	504-555-7384
Isaac Hill	520-555-4366
Finn McDougal	312-444-0394
Paulina Menzel	346-555-2348
Hamilton Pierce	410-555-2384
Genevieve Salinger	602-555-4392

Natura Customers

Customer	Street Address	City	State/ Province	Postal Code	Country
Flying Queen	478 River Ave.	Winnipeg	MB	V4B 4A9	Canada
Rose	467 Seventh St. E.	Saskatoon	SK	S7H1A3	Canada
Swan	347 Park St.	Halifax	NS	B3H 2W2	Canada
Wave Rider	342 W. Georgia	Vancouver	BC	V6E 3H7	Canada
Beauty	89 Kiefer Creek Rd.	Ballwin	MO	63021	USA
Belle	P.O. Box 359	Belt	MT	59412	USA
Blue Fairy	307 Gold Hill Dr.	Grass Valley	CA	95945	USA
Maiden	345 Polk St.	San Francisco	CA	94109	USA
Melody	P.O. Box 789	Stromsburg	NE	68666	USA
Nautilus	45 Scarborough St.	Hartford	CT	06105	USA
Nina's Gift	784 Arizona Ave.	Santa Monica	CA	90401	USA
Red Coral	67 N. 73rd St.	Omaha	NE	68114	USA
Sailing Beauty	358 Fifth Ave.	Anchorage	AK	99501	USA
Sea Princess	876 N. Roxboro St.	Durham	NC	27701	USA
Suzanna	2331 S. Pioneer St.	Abilene	TX	79605	USA
The Dolphin	478 Dodson Dr.	East Point	GA	30344	USA
The Mermaid	782 West Fairway Pl.	Chandler	AZ	85224	USA
The Picasso	784 Parks St.	Duxbury	MA	02331	USA
Water Spirit	215 Vine St.	Cincinnati	OH	45202	USA
Woodwinds	34 Downey Ave.	Modesto	CA	95354	USA

Figure 2.11 Visual Benchmark 2

Cordova Children's Community Center

Support Your Local Community Center

English:
As you consider your donation contributions for the coming year, we ask that you consider your community by supporting the Cordova Children's Community Center. The center is a nonprofit agency providing educational and recreational activities for children. Please stop by for a visit. Our dedicated staff will be available to discuss with you the services offered by the center, how the center spends your donation dollars, and provide information on current and future activities and services.

Spanish:
Al considerar sus contribuciones de donación para el próximo año, le pedimos que considere su comunidad apoyando al Centro Comunitario infantil de Cordova. El centro es una agencia sin fines de lucro que ofrece actividades educativas y recreativas para los niños. Por favor, pase por aquí para una visita. Nuestro dedicado personal estará disponible para discutir con usted los servicios ofrecidos por el centro, cómo el centro gasta sus dólares de donación, y proporcionar información sobre las actividades y servicios actuales y futuros.

French:
Alors que vous considérez vos contributions de dons pour l'année à venir, nous vous demandons de considérer votre communauté en soutenant le Cordova Children's Community Center. Le centre est une agence à but non lucratif offrant des activités éducatives et récréatives pour les enfants. S'il vous plaît arrêtez-vous pour une visite. Notre personnel dévoué sera disponible pour discuter avec vous des services offerts par le centre, de la façon dont le centre dépense vos dons et fournir des informations sur les activités et services actuels et futurs.

"Children are our most valuable natural resource." ~ Herbert Hoover

770 Sunrise Terrace ◆ Santa Fe, NM 87509 ◆ 505-555-7700

Case Study

Part 1

You work in the executive offices at Nickell Industries and have been asked to develop a writing manual for employees. The company has not used a consistent theme when formatting documents, so you decide to choose a theme and use it when formatting all Nickell documents. Open **NIManual.docx** and then save the document with the name **2-NIManual**. Check the spelling and grammar in the document. (You determine whether to accept or ignore grammar suggestions made by the Editor.)

Make the following changes to the document:

- Insert a next page section break at the beginning of the title *Editing and Proofreading*.
- Apply styles of your choosing to the titles and headings in the document.
- Apply the theme you have chosen for company documents.
- Insert headers and/or footers.
- Create a cover page.
- Save the document.

Part 2

As you review the writing manual document you have created for Nickell Industries, you decide to highlight the points for developing sections of documents. You decide that a vertical block list SmartArt graphic will present the ideas in an easy-to-read format and provide some visual interest to the manual. Insert a page break at the end of the text in **2-NIManual.docx**, type the title *Developing a Document*, and then insert the following in the SmartArt graphic in the appropriate shapes:

Beginning
- Introduce main idea.
- Get reader's attention.
- Establish a positive tone.

Middle
- Provide detail for main idea.
- Lead reader to intended conclusion.

End
- State conclusion.
- State action reader should take.

Apply colors that follow the theme you have chosen for company documents. Save and then close the document.

Part 3

Nickell Industries does business in other countries, including Mexico. One of the executives in the Finance Department has asked you to translate into Spanish some terms that will be used to develop an invoice. Create a document that translates the following terms from English to Spanish and also include in the document the steps for translating text. Your reason for doing this is that if the executives know the steps, they can translate the text at their own computers.

- city
- telephone
- invoice
- product
- description
- total

Format the document with the theme you have chosen for company documents and add any other enhancements to improve the appearance of the document. Save the completed document with the name **2-NITranslations**. Preview and then close **2-NITranslations.docx**.

Part
4

While working on the writing manual for Nickell Industries, you decide to purchase some reference books on grammar and punctuation. Using the internet, search for books that provide information on grammar and punctuation and then choose three books. You know that the books will be purchased soon, so you decide to add the information in the writing manual document, telling readers what reference books are available. Open **2-NIManual.docx** and then include this information on a separate page at the end of the text in the document. Save, preview, and then close the document.

WORD

CHAPTER 3

Inserting Headers, Footers, and References

Performance Objectives

Upon successful completion of Chapter 3, you will be able to:

1 Insert headers and footers in documents
2 Format, edit, and remove headers and footers
3 Insert and print sections
4 Keep text together on a page
5 Insert footnotes and endnotes
6 Insert and edit sources and citations
7 Insert, modify, and format sources lists

Word provides a number of predesigned headers (text that displays and prints at the tops of pages) and footers (text that displays and prints at the bottoms of pages) that can be inserted in documents, or custom headers and footers can be created. A document can be divided into sections and different formatting can be applied to each section, such as different headers, footers, and page numbers. In this chapter, you will learn how to create custom headers and footers, how to format and print sections in a document, and how to control soft page breaks within a document. You will also learn how to reference documents and acknowledge sources using footnotes, endnotes, and source lists.

Data Files

The data files for this chapter are in the WL2C3 folder that you downloaded at the beginning of this course.

Activity 1 Insert Headers and Footers in a Computer Software Report — 8 Parts

You will open a report on computer software and then create, customize, and position headers and footers in the document. You will also create headers and footers for different pages in a document, divide a document into sections, and then create footers for specific sections.

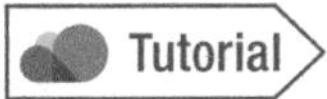

Creating a Custom Header and Footer

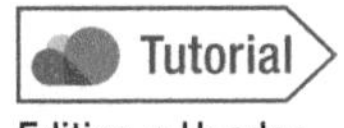

Editing a Header and Footer

Hint One method for formatting a header or footer is to select the header or footer text and then use the options on the Mini toolbar.

Inserting Headers and Footers

Text that appears in the top margin of a page is called a *header* and text that appears in the bottom margin of a page is called a *footer*. Headers and footers are commonly used in manuscripts, textbooks, reports, and other publications to display the page numbers and section or chapter titles. For example, see the footer at the bottom of this page.

Insert a predesigned header by clicking the Insert tab and then clicking the Header button in the Header & Footer group. This displays a drop-down list of header choices. Click the predesigned header and the formatted header is inserted in the document. Complete similar steps to insert a predesigned footer.

If the predesigned headers and footers do not meet specific needs, create a custom header or footer. To create a custom header, click the Insert tab, click the Header button in the Header & Footer group, and then click *Edit Header* at the drop-down list. This displays a Header pane in the document along with the Header & Footer tab, as shown in Figure 3.1. Use options on this tab to insert elements such as page numbers, and images; to navigate to other headers and footers in the document; and to position headers and footers on different pages in a document.

Inserting Elements in Headers and Footers

Use buttons in the Insert group on the Header & Footer tab to insert elements into the header or footer, such as the date and time, Quick Parts, and images. Click the Date & Time button in the Insert group and the Date and Time dialog box displays. Choose a date and time option in the *Available formats* list box of the dialog box and then click OK.

Click the Document Info button to display a drop-down list of document information fields that can be inserted into the document. Hover the pointer over the *Document Property* option in the Document Info button drop-down list to display a side menu of document properties, such as *Author*, *Comments*, and *Company*, that can be inserted in the header or footer.

Figure 3.1 Header & Footer Tab

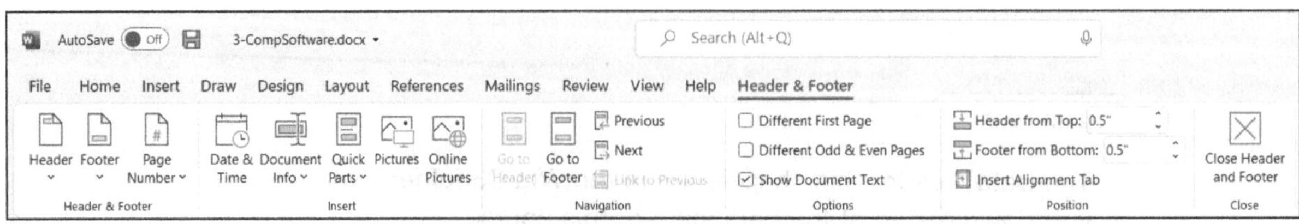

The Quick Parts button in the Insert group on the Header & Footer tab contains options for inserting document properties, fields, and other elements. Click the Pictures button to display the Insert Picture dialog box and insert an image from the computer's hard drive or removable drive. Click the Online Pictures button and the Online Pictures window opens with options for searching for and then downloading an image into the header or footer.

Activity 1a Inserting Elements in a Header and Footer

Part 1 of 8

1. Open **CompSoftware.docx** and then save it with the name **3-CompSoftware**.
2. Insert a header by completing the following steps:
   a. Click the Insert tab.
   b. Click the Header button in the Header & Footer group and then click *Edit Header* at the drop-down list.
   c. With the insertion point positioned in the Header pane, click the Pictures button in the Insert group on the Header & Footer tab.

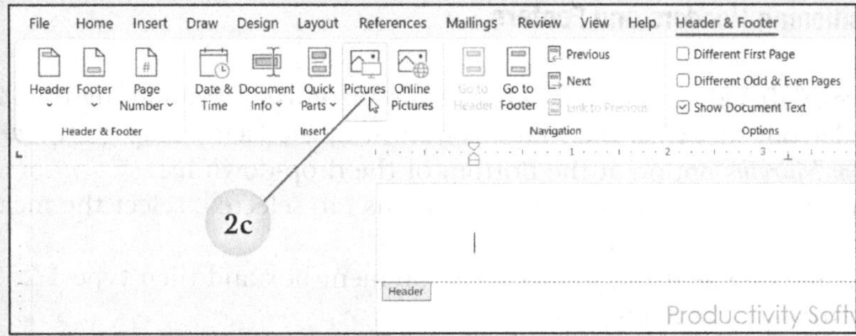

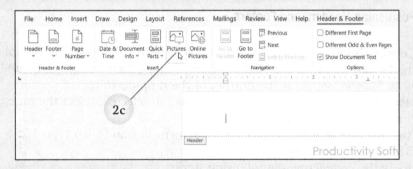

   d. At the Insert Picture dialog box, navigate to your WL2C3 folder and then double-click the ***Worldwide.png*** image file.
   e. With the image selected, click in the *Shape Height* measurement box in the Size group, type 0.5 and then press the Enter key.
   f. Click the Wrap Text button in the Arrange group and then click *Behind Text* at the drop-down list.
   g. Drag the image up approximately one-third of an inch.
   h. Click outside the image to deselect it.
   i. Press the Tab key two times. (Pressing the Tab key moves the insertion point to the right margin.)
   j. Click the Header & Footer tab and then click the Date & Time button in the Insert group.
   k. At the Date and Time dialog box, click the twelfth option from the top (the option that displays the date in numbers and the time) and then click OK to close the dialog box.
   l. Select the date and time text and then use the Mini toolbar to apply bold formatting and change the font size to 9 points.
   m. Double-click in the document to make it active. (The text in the header will display dimmed.)
3. Save **3-CompSoftware.docx**.

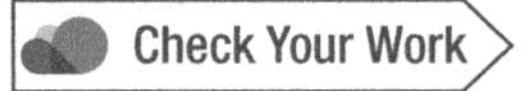

Positioning Headers and Footers

Word inserts a header 0.5 inch from the top of the page and a footer 0.5 inch from the bottom of the page. These default positions can be changed with buttons in the Position group on the Header & Footer tab. Use the *Header from Top* and the *Footer from Bottom* measurement boxes to adjust the position of the header and the footer, respectively, on the page.

By default, headers and footers contain two tab settings. A center tab is set at 3.25 inches and a right tab is set at 6.5 inches. If the document contains default left and right margin settings of 1 inch, the center tab set at 3.25 inches is the center of the document and the right tab set at 6.5 inches is at the right margin. If the default margins are changed, the default center tab may need to be changed before inserting header or footer text at the center tab. Position tabs with the Insert Alignment Tab button in the Position group. Click this button and the Alignment Tab dialog box displays. Use options at this dialog box to change tab alignment and set tabs with leaders.

Activity 1b Positioning Headers and Footers — Part 2 of 8

1. With **3-CompSoftware.docx** open, change the margins by completing the following steps:
   a. Click the Layout tab, click the Margins button in the Page Setup group, and then click the *Custom Margins* option at the bottom of the drop-down list.
   b. At the Page Setup dialog box with the Margins tab selected, select the measurement in the *Left* measurement box and then type 1.25.
   c. Select the measurement in the *Right* measurement box and then type 1.25.
   d. Click OK to close the dialog box.
2. Create a footer by completing the following steps:
   a. Click the Insert tab.
   b. Click the Footer button in the Header & Footer group and then click *Edit Footer* at the drop-down list.
   c. With the insertion point positioned in the Footer pane, type your first and last names at the left margin.
   d. Press the Tab key. (This moves the insertion point to the center tab position.)
   e. Click the Page Number button in the Header & Footer group, point to *Current Position*, and then click *Accent Bar 2* at the drop-down list.

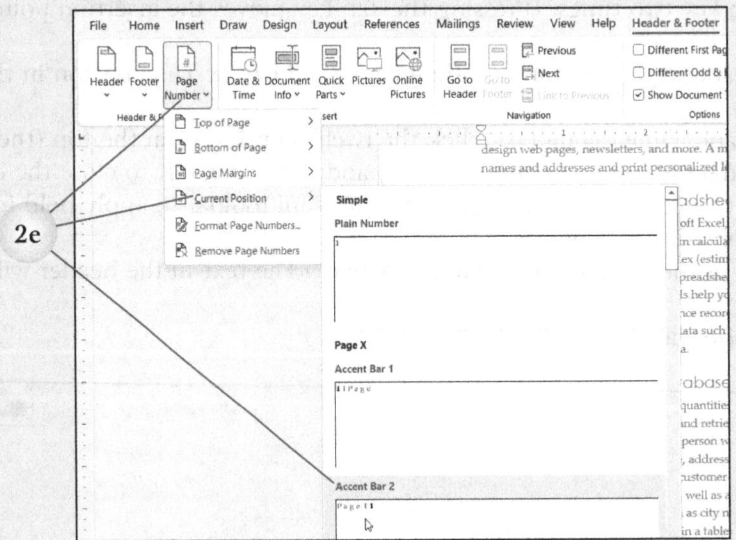

f. Press the Tab key.

g. Click the Document Info button in the Insert group and then click *File Name* at the drop-down list.

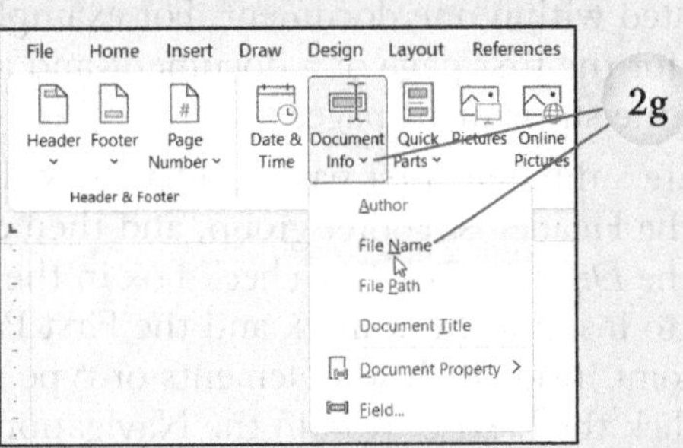

h. You notice that the center tab and right tab are slightly off, because the left and right margins in the document are set at 1.25 inches instead of 1 inch. To align the tabs correctly, drag the center tab marker to the 3-inch mark on the horizontal ruler and drag the right tab marker to the 6-inch mark on the horizontal ruler.

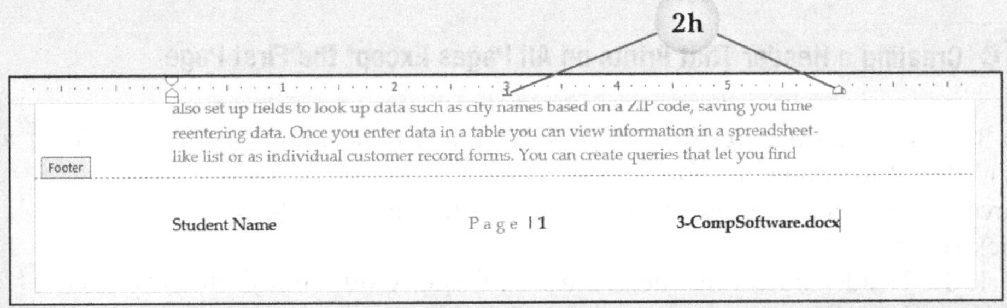

i. Select all the footer text and then apply bold formatting and change the font size to 9 points.

3. Change the position of the header and footer by completing the following steps:
   a. Click the Header & Footer tab.
   b. Click the Go to Header button in the Navigation group.
   c. Click the *Header from Top* measurement box up arrow to display *0.6"*.
   d. Click the Go to Footer button in the Navigation group.
   e. Click in the *Footer from Bottom* measurement box, type 0.6, and then press the Enter key.
   f. Click the Close Header and Footer button.

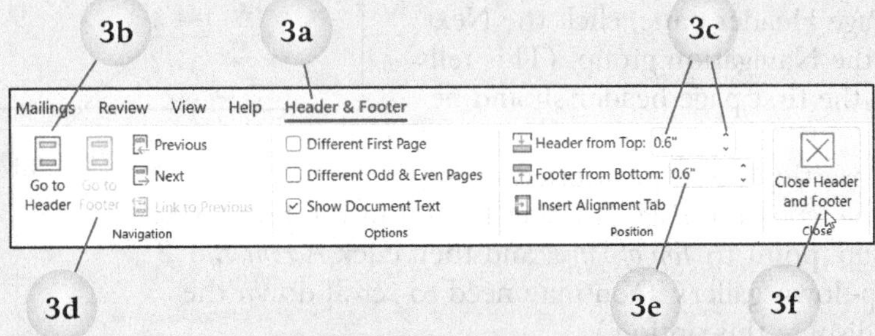

4. Save and then preview **3-CompSoftware.docx**.

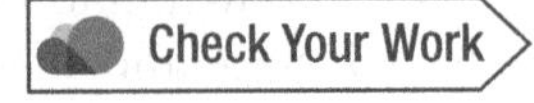

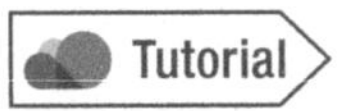

Creating a Different First Page Header and Footer

Quick Steps

Create Different First Page Header or Footer

1. Click Insert tab.
2. Click Header or Footer button.
3. Click *Edit Header* or *Edit Footer* at drop-down list.
4. Click *Different First Page* check box.
5. Insert elements and/or text.
6. Click Next button.
7. Insert elements and/or text.

Creating a Different First Page Header or Footer

A header and/or footer inserted in a document will display and print on every page in the document by default. However, different headers and footers can be created within one document. For example, a unique header or footer can be created for the first page of a document and a different header or footer can be created for the subsequent pages.

To create a different first page header, click the Insert tab, click the Header button in the Header & Footer group, and then click *Edit Header* at the drop-down list. Click the *Different First Page* check box in the Options group on the Header & Footer tab to insert a check mark and the First Page Header pane displays with the insertion point inside it. Insert elements or type text to create the first page header and then click the Next button in the Navigation group. This displays the Header pane with the insertion point positioned inside it. Insert elements and/or type text to create the header. Complete similar steps to create a different first page footer.

In some situations, the first page header or footer should be blank. This is particularly useful if a document contains a title page and the header or footer should not display and print on it.

Activity 1c Creating a Header That Prints on All Pages Except the First Page — Part 3 of 8

1. With **3-CompSoftware.docx** open, press Ctrl + A to select the entire document and then press Ctrl + 2 to change to double-line spacing.
2. Remove the header and footer by completing the following steps:
   a. Click the Insert tab.
   b. Click the Header button in the Header & Footer group and then click *Remove Header* at the drop-down list.
   c. Click the Footer button in the Header & Footer group and then click *Remove Footer* at the drop-down list.
3. Press Ctrl + Home and then create a header that prints on all pages except the first page by completing the following steps:
   a. With the Insert tab active, click the Header button in the Header & Footer group.
   b. Click *Edit Header* at the drop-down list.
   c. Click the *Different First Page* check box in the Options group on the Header & Footer tab to insert a check mark.
   d. With the insertion point positioned in the First Page Header pane, click the Next button in the Navigation group. (This tells Word that the first page header should be blank.)
   e. With the insertion point positioned in the Header pane, click the Page Number button in the Header & Footer group, point to *Top of Page*, and then click *Accent Bar 2* at the drop-down gallery. (You may need to scroll down the gallery to display this option.)
   f. Click the Close Header and Footer button.
4. Scroll through the document and notice that the header appears on the second, third, fourth, and fifth pages.
5. Save and then preview **3-CompSoftware.docx**.

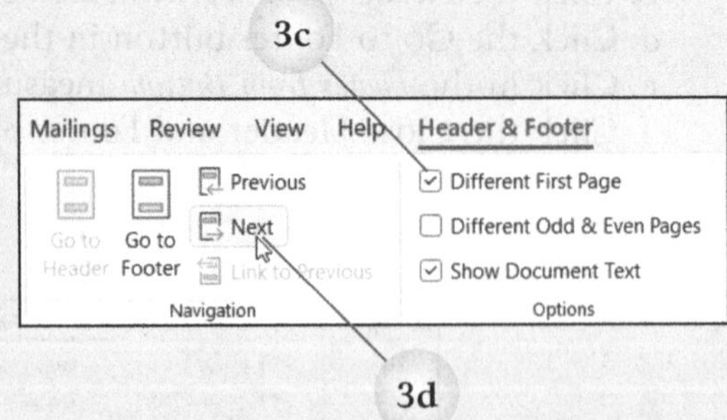

Check Your Work

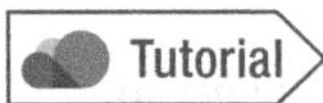

Creating Odd Page and Even Page Headers and Footers

Quick Steps

Create Odd and Even Page Headers or Footers

1. Click Insert tab.
2. Click Header or Footer button.
3. Click *Edit Header* or *Edit Footer.*
4. Click *Different Odd & Even Pages* check box.
5. Insert elements and/or text.

Creating Odd and Even Page Headers or Footers

If a document will be read in book form, consider inserting odd and even page headers or footers. When presenting pages in a document in book form with facing pages, the outside margins are the left side of the left page and the right side of the right page. Also, when a document has facing pages, the right-hand page is generally numbered with an odd number and the left-hand page is generally numbered with an even number.

Create even and odd headers or footers to insert this type of page numbering. Use the *Different Odd & Even Pages* check box in the Options group on the Header & Footer tab to create odd and even headers and/or footers.

Activity 1d Creating Odd and Even Page Footers — Part 4 of 8

1. With **3-CompSoftware.docx** open, remove the header from the document by completing the following steps:
   a. Click the Insert tab.
   b. Click the Header button in the Header & Footer group and then click *Edit Header* at the drop-down list.
   c. Click the *Different First Page* check box in the Options group to remove the check mark.
   d. Click the Header button in the Header & Footer group and then click *Remove Header* at the drop-down list. (This displays the insertion point in an empty Header pane.)
2. Create one footer that prints on odd pages and another that prints on even pages by completing the following steps:
   a. Click the Go to Footer button in the Navigation group.
   b. Click the *Different Odd & Even Pages* check box in the Options group to insert a check mark. (This displays the Odd Page Footer pane with the insertion point inside it.)
   c. Click the Page Number button in the Header & Footer group, point to *Bottom of Page*, and then click *Plain Number 3* at the drop-down list.
   d. Click the Next button in the Navigation group. (This displays the Even Page Footer pane with the insertion point inside it.)

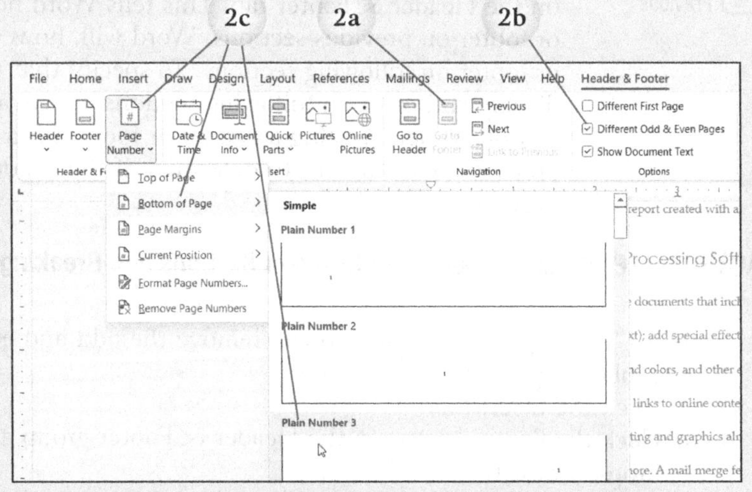

e. Click the Page Number button, point to *Current Position*, and then click *Plain Number* at the drop-down list.
f. Click the Close Header and Footer button.

3. Scroll through the document and notice the page numbers at the right sides of the odd page footers and the left sides of the even page footers.
4. Save and then preview **3-CompSoftware.docx**.

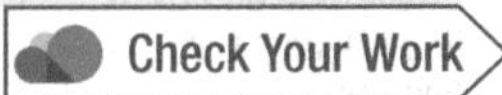

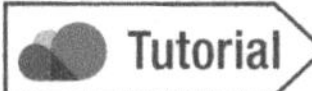

Creating a Header and Footer for Different Sections

Quick Steps

Create Headers or Footers for Different Sections

1. Insert section break.
2. Click Insert tab.
3. Click Header or Footer button.
4. Click *Edit Header* or *Edit Footer*.
5. Click Link to Previous button to deactivate.
6. Insert elements and/or text.
7. Click Next button.
8. Insert elements and/or text.

Creating a Header and Footer for Different Sections

A document can be divided into sections by inserting section breaks and then different formatting can be applied to each section. A section break can be inserted that begins a new page or a section break can be inserted that allows the sections to be formatted differently, but does not begin a new page. A section break can also be inserted that starts a new section on the next even-numbered page or the next odd-numbered page.

To insert different headers and/or footers on pages in a document, divide the document into sections. For example, if a document contains several chapters, each chapter can be a separate section and a different header and footer can be created for each section. When dividing a document into sections by chapter, insert section breaks that also begin new pages.

Breaking a Section Link

When a header or footer is created for a specific section in a document, it can be created for all the previous and following sections or only the following sections. By default, each section in a document is linked to the other sections. To display and print a header or footer only on the pages within a section and not the previous section, deactivate the Link to Previous button in the Navigation group on the Header & Footer tab. This tells Word not to display and print the header or footer on previous sections. Word will, however, display and print the header or footer on following sections. To specify that the header or footer should not display and print on following sections, create a blank header or footer at the next section. When creating a header or footer for a specific section in a document, preview the document to determine if the header or footer appears on the correct pages.

Activity 1e Creating Footers for Different Sections and Breaking a Section Link — Part 5 of 8

1. With **3-CompSoftware.docx** open, remove the odd and even page footers by completing the following steps:
   a. Click the Insert tab.
   b. Click the Footer button in the Header & Footer group and then click *Edit Footer* at the drop-down list.
   c. Click the *Different Odd & Even Pages* check box in the Options group to remove the check mark.
   d. Click the Footer button in the Header & Footer group and then click *Remove Footer* at the drop-down list.
   e. Click the Close Header and Footer button.

2. Remove the page break before the second title in the document by completing the following steps:
   a. Move the insertion point immediately right of the period that ends the paragraph in the section *Presentation Software* (near the middle of page 3).
   b. Press the Delete key two times. (The title *Graphics and Multimedia Software* should now display below the paragraph on the third page.)
3. Insert an odd page section break (a section break that starts a section on the next odd page) by completing the following steps:
   a. Position the insertion point at the beginning of the title *Graphics and Multimedia Software*.
   b. Click the Layout tab, click the Breaks button in the Page Setup group, and then click *Odd Page* at the drop-down list.

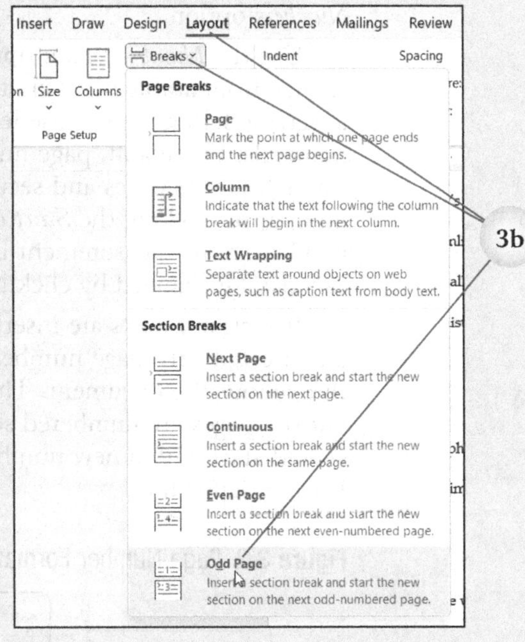

4. Create section titles and footers with page numbers for the two sections by completing the following steps:
   a. Position the insertion point at the beginning of the document.
   b. Click the Insert tab.
   c. Click the Footer button in the Header & Footer group and then click *Edit Footer* at the drop-down list.
   d. At the Footer -Section 1- pane, type Section 1 Productivity Software and then press the Tab key two times. (This moves the insertion point to the right margin.)
   e. Type Page and then press the spacebar.
   f. Click the Page Number button in the Header & Footer group, point to *Current Position*, and then click *Plain Number* at the side menu.
   g. Click the Next button in the Navigation group.
   h. Click the Link to Previous button to deactivate it. (This removes the message *Same as Previous* from the top right side of the footer pane.)
   i. In the footer, change the text *Section 1 Productivity Software* to *Section 2 Graphics and Multimedia Software*.
   j. Click the Close Header and Footer button.

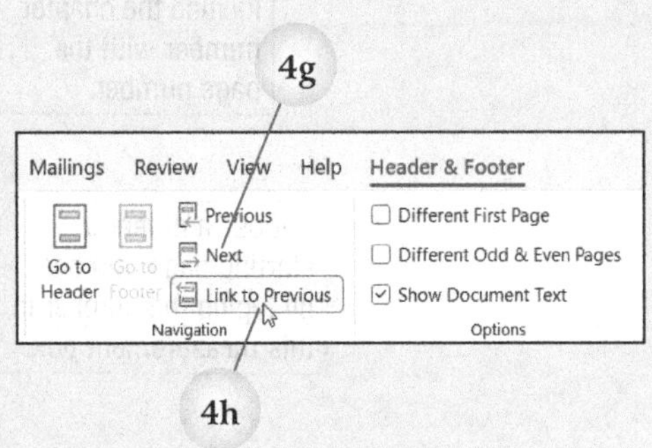

5. Scroll through the document and notice the footers and page numbers in the sections. (Note that due to the section break, there is no page 4 shown in the document. A blank page 4 will display in print preview and, if the document is printed, a blank page 4 will print.)
6. Save **3-CompSoftware.docx**.

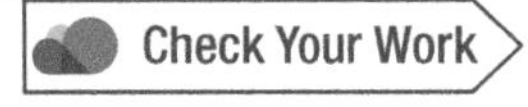

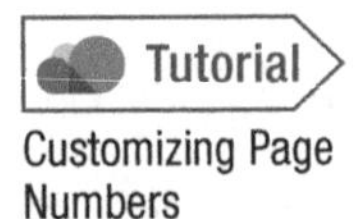

Customizing Page Numbers

Page Number

Customizing Page Numbers

By default, Word inserts arabic numbers (1, 2, 3, and so on) and numbers pages sequentially beginning with 1. These default settings can be customized with options at the Page Number Format dialog box, shown in Figure 3.2. To display this dialog box, click the Insert tab, click the Page Number button in the Header & Footer group, and then click *Format Page Numbers* at the drop-down list. Another method for displaying the dialog box is to click the Page Number button in the Header & Footer group on the Header & Footer tab and then click the *Format Page Numbers* option.

Use the *Number format* option at the Page Number Format dialog box to change from arabic numbers to arabic numbers preceded and followed by hyphens, lowercase letters, uppercase letters, lowercase roman numerals, or uppercase roman numerals. By default, page numbering begins with 1 and continues sequentially through all the pages and sections in a document. Change the beginning page number by clicking the *Start at* option and then typing the beginning page number in the measurement box. The number in the *Start at* measurement box can also be changed by clicking the measurement box up or down arrow.

If section breaks are inserted in a document and then a header and footer are inserted with page numbers for each section, the page numbers are sequential throughout the document. The document used in Activity 1f has a section break, but the pages are numbered sequentially. If the page numbering in a section should start with a new number, use the *Start at* option at the Page Number Format dialog box.

Figure 3.2 Page Number Format Dialog Box

Page Number Format ? X

Number format: 1, 2, 3, ...

Include chapter number

Chapter starts with style: Heading 1

Use separator: - (hyphen)

Examples: 1-1, 1-A

Page numbering

Continue from previous section

Start at:

OK Cancel

Insert a check mark in this check box to include the chapter number with the page number.

Click this option box arrow to choose a numbering format.

Choose a different starting page number by typing the number in this measurement box.

Activity 1f Customizing Page Numbering

Part 6 of 8

1. With **3-CompSoftware.docx** open, change the page numbers to lowercase roman numerals and change the starting page number by completing the following steps:
   a. Press Ctrl + Home.
   b. Click the Insert tab.
   c. Click the Page Number button in the Header & Footer group and then click *Format Page Numbers* at the drop-down list.
   d. At the Page Number Format dialog box, click the *Number format* option box arrow and then click *i, ii, iii, ...* at the drop-down list.
   e. Click the *Start at* option and then type 4.
   f. Click OK to close the dialog box.

Page Number Format
Number format: i, ii, iii, ...
Include chapter number
Chapter starts with style: Heading 1
Use separator: - (hyphen)
Examples: 1-1, 1-A
Page numbering
Continue from previous section
Start at: 4
OK
Cancel
1d
1e
1f

2. Scroll through the document and notice the lowercase roman numeral page numbers (beginning with *iv*) that display at the right margins at the bottoms of the pages.
3. Scroll to the bottom of the page containing the title *Graphics and Multimedia Software* and notice that the page numbers did not change. (This is because the sections were unlinked.)
4. Position the insertion point in the first paragraph of text below the title *Graphics and Multmedia Software* and then change the page numbering by completing the following steps:
   a. Click the Page Number button and then click *Format Page Numbers* at the drop-down list.
   b. At the Page Number Format dialog box, click the *Number format* option box arrow and then click *i, ii, iii, ...* at the drop-down list.
   c. Click the *Start at* option and then type 7.
   d. Click OK to close the dialog box.
5. Save and then preview **3-CompSoftware.docx**.

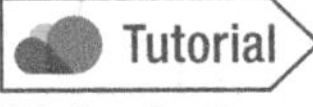

Printing Sections

Printing Sections

Print specific pages in a document by inserting page numbers in the *Pages* text box at the Print backstage area. When entering page numbers in this text box, use a hyphen to indicate a range of consecutive pages or a comma to specify nonconsecutive pages.

Quick Steps

Print Section

1. Click File tab.
2. Click *Print* option.
3. Click in *Pages* text box.
4. Type s followed by section number.
5. Click Print button.

In a document that contains sections, use the *Pages* text box at the Print backstage area to specify the section and pages within the section to be printed. For example, if a document is divided into three sections, print only section 2 by typing *s2* in the *Pages* text box. If a document contains six sections, print sections 3 through 5 by typing *s3-s5* in the *Pages* text box. Specific pages within or between sections can also be identified for printing. For example, to print pages 2 through 5 of section 4, type p2s4-p5s4; to print from page 3 of section 1 through page 5 of section 4, type p3s1-p5s4; to print page 1 of section 3, page 4 of section 5, and page 6 of section 8, type p1s3,p4s5,p6s8.

Activity 1g Changing Section Page Numbering and Printing Section Pages

Part 7 of 8

1. With **3-CompSoftware.docx** open, press Ctrl + Home to move the insertion point to the beginning of the document.
2. Change the number formats and starting page numbers for sections 1 and 2 by completing the following steps:
   a. Click the Insert tab, click the Footer button in the Header & Footer group, and then click *Edit Footer* at the drop-down list.
   b. At the Footer -Section 1- footer pane, click the Page Number button in the Header & Footer group and then click the *Format Page Numbers* option at the drop-down list.
   c. Click the *Number format* option box arrow and then click the *1, 2, 3, ...* option at the drop-down list.
   d. Select the current number in the *Start at* measurement box and then type 1.
   e. Click OK to close the dialog box.
   f. Display the section 2 footer by clicking the Next button in the Navigation group.
   g. At the Footer -Section 2- footer pane, click the Page Number button and then click the *Format Page Numbers* option at the drop-down list.
   h. At the Page Number Format dialog box, click the *Number format* option box arrow and then click the *1, 2, 3, ...* option at the drop-down list.
   i. Select the current number in the *Start at* measurement box and then type 1.
   j. Click OK to close the dialog box.
   k. Click the Close Header and Footer button.

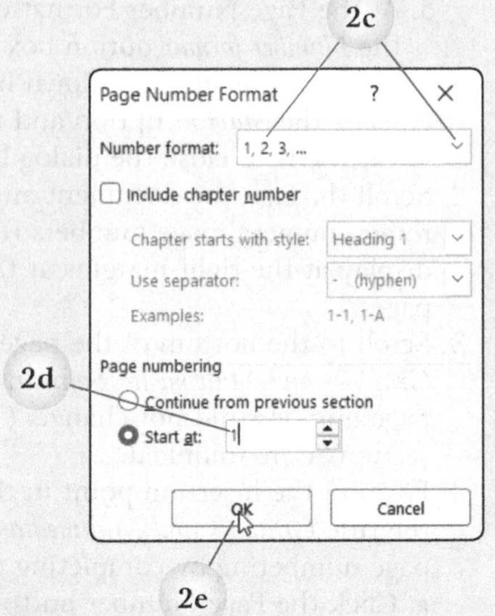

3. Print only page 1 of section 1 and page 1 of section 2 by completing the following steps:
   a. Click the File tab and then click the *Print* option.
   b. At the Print backstage area, click in the *Pages* text box in the *Settings* category and then type p1s1,p1s2.
   c. Click the Print button.
4. Save **3-CompSoftware.docx.**

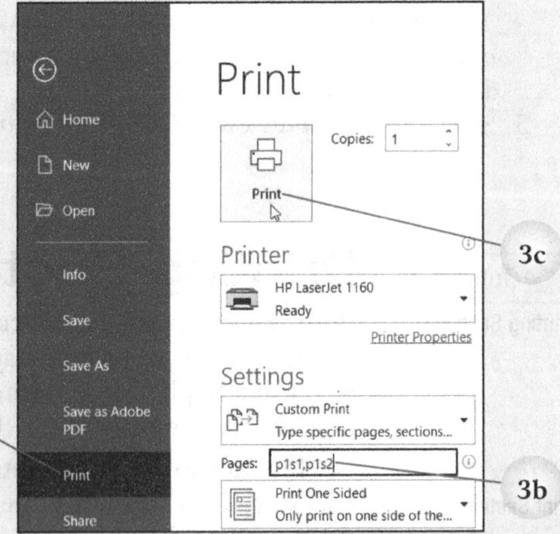

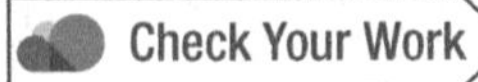

Keeping Text Together

Quick Steps

Keep Text Together

1. Click Paragraph group dialog box launcher.
2. Click Line and Page Breaks tab.
3. Click *Keep with next, Keep lines together,* and/or *Page break before.*
4. Click OK.

Hint Text formatted with the *Keep with next* option applied to it is identified with the nonprinting character ■ in the left margin.

Keeping Text Together

In a multipage document, Word automatically inserts soft page breaks, which are page breaks that adjust when data is added or deleted from the document. However, a soft page break may occur in an undesirable location. For example, a soft page break may cause a heading to display at the bottom of a page while the text related to the heading displays at the top of the next page. A soft page break may also create a widow or orphan. A widow is the last line of text in a paragraph that appears by itself at the top of a page and an orphan is the first line of text in a paragraph that appears by itself at the bottom of a page.

Use options at the Paragraph dialog box with the Line and Page Breaks tab selected, as shown in Figure 3.3, to control widows and orphans and keep a paragraph, group of paragraphs, or group of lines together. Display this dialog box by clicking the Paragraph group dialog box launcher on the Home tab and then clicking the Line and Page Breaks tab at the dialog box.

By default, the *Widow/Orphan control* option is active and Word tries to avoid creating widows and orphans when inserting soft page breaks. The other three options in the *Pagination* section of the dialog box are not active by default. Use the *Keep with next* option to keep a line together with the next line. This is useful for keeping a heading together with the first line of text below it. To keep a group of selected lines together, use the *Keep lines together* option. Use the *Page break before* option to insert a page break before selected text.

Figure 3.3 Paragraph Dialog Box with the Line and Page Breaks Tab Selected

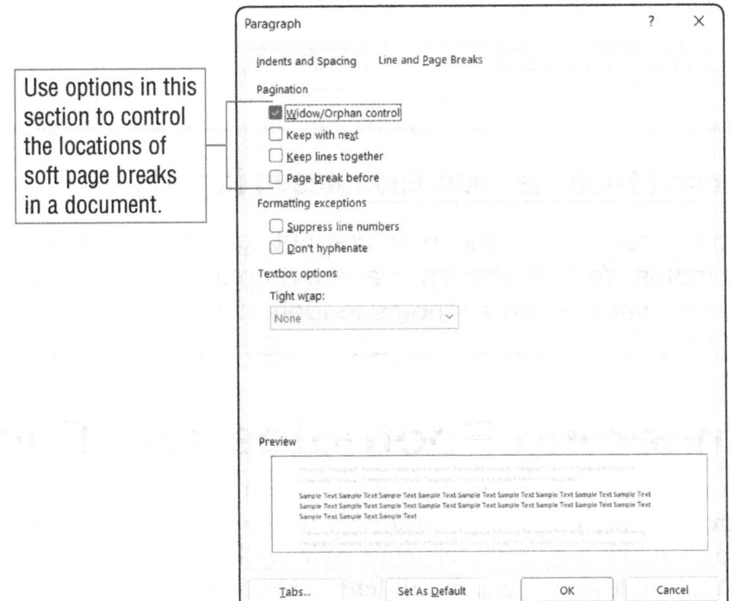

Activity 1h Keeping Text Together — Part 8 of 8

1. With **3-CompSoftware.docx** open, scroll through the document and notice that the heading *Spreadsheet Software* displays at the bottom of page 1 and the paragraph that follows the heading displays at the top of page 2. Keep the heading and paragraph together by completing the following steps:
   a. Position the insertion point in the heading *Spreadsheet Software*.
   b. Make sure the Home tab is active and then click the Paragraph group dialog box launcher.
   c. At the Paragraph dialog box, click the Line and Page Breaks tab.
   d. Click the *Keep with next* check box to insert a check mark.
   e. Click OK to close the dialog box.
2. Scroll through the document and notice the heading *Multimedia Software* near the end of the document. Insert a soft page break at the beginning of the heading by completing the following steps:
   a. Move the insertion point to the beginning of the heading *Multimedia Software*.
   b. Click the Paragraph group dialog box launcher.
   c. At the Paragraph dialog box with the Line and Page Breaks tab selected, click the *Page break before* check box to insert a check mark.
   d. Click OK to close the dialog box.
3. Save, preview, and then close **3-CompSoftware.docx**.

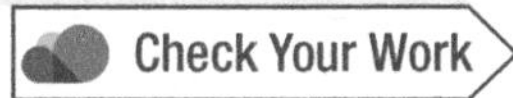

Activity 2 Insert Footnotes and Endnotes in Reports — 3 Parts

You will open a report on pioneers of computing and then insert, format, and modify footnotes. You will also open a report on technology visionaries, insert endnotes, and then convert endnotes to footnotes.

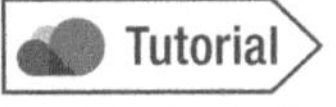

Inserting Footnotes and Endnotes

Hint Ctrl + Alt + F is the keyboard shortcut to insert a footnote and Ctrl + Alt + D is the keyboard shortcut to insert an endnote.

Inserting Footnotes and Endnotes

A research paper or report contains information from a variety of sources. To give credit to those sources, footnotes or endnotes can be inserted in a document formatted in a specific reference style, such as that of the *Chicago Manual of Style*. (You will learn more about different reference styles in the next activity.) A footnote is an explanatory note or source reference that is printed at the bottom of the page on which the corresponding information appears. An endnote is also an explanatory note or reference, but it is printed at the end of the document.

Two steps are involved in creating a footnote or endnote. First, the note reference number is inserted in the document where the corresponding information appears. Second, the note entry text is typed. Footnotes and endnotes are created in a similar manner.

Quick Steps

Insert Footnote
1. Click References tab.
2. Click Insert Footnote button.
3. Type footnote text.

Insert Endnote
1. Click References tab.
2. Click Insert Endnote button.
3. Type endnote text.

To create a footnote, position the insertion point where the reference number is to appear, click the References tab, and then click the Insert Footnote button in the Footnotes group. This inserts a number in the document along with a separator line at the bottom of the page and a superscript number below it. With the insertion point positioned immediately right of the superscript number, type the note entry text. By default, Word numbers footnotes with superscript arabic numbers and endnotes with superscript lowercase roman numerals.

Activity 2a Creating Footnotes

Part 1 of 3

1. Open **CompPioneers.docx** and then save it with the name **3-CompPioneers.**
2. Create the first footnote shown in Figure 3.4 by completing the following steps:
   a. Position the insertion point at the end of the first paragraph of text below the heading *Konrad Zuse* (immediately following the period).
   b. Click the References tab.
   c. Click the Insert Footnote button in the Footnotes group.
   d. With the insertion point positioned at the bottom of the page immediately following the superscript number, type the first footnote shown in Figure 3.4. (Italicize the text as shown in the figure.)

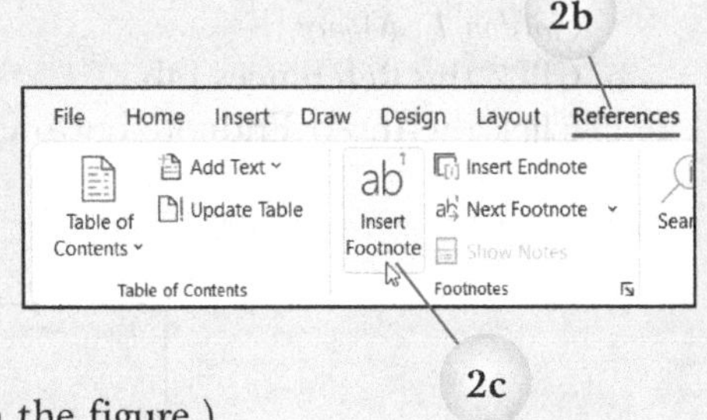

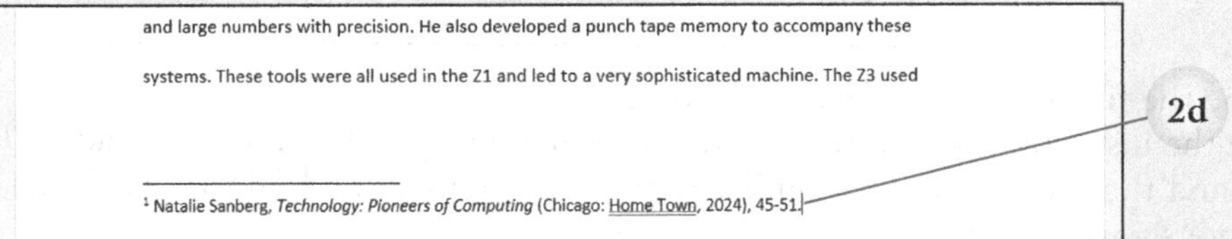

3. Move the insertion point to the end of the third paragraph below the heading *Konrad Zuse*. Using steps similar to those in Steps 2c and 2d, create the second footnote shown in Figure 3.4. (Italicize the text as shown in the figure.)
4. Move the insertion point to the end of the last paragraph below the heading *Konrad Zuse* and then create the third footnote shown in Figure 3.4.
5. Move the insertion point to the end of the third paragraph below the heading *William Hewlett and David Packard* and then create the fourth footnote shown in Figure 3.4.
6. Move the insertion point to the end of the last paragraph in the document and then create the fifth foonote shown in Figure 3.4.
7. Save, preview, and then close **3-CompPioneers.docx.**

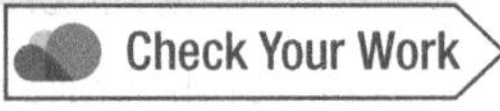

Figure 3.4 Activity 2a

Natalie Sanberg, *Technology: Pioneers of Computing* (Chicago: Home Town, 2024), 45-51.

Miguel Whitworth and Danielle Reyes, "Development of Computing," *Design Technologies* (2024): 24-26.

Sam Wells, *Biographies of Computing Pioneers* (San Francisco: Laurelhurst, 2024), 20-23.

Terrell Montgomery, *History of Computers* (Boston: Langley-Paulsen, 2024), 13-15.

Justin Evans, "Hewlett-Packard's Impact on Computing," *Computing Technologies* (2024): 7-12.

Printing Footnotes and Endnotes

When printing a document that contains footnotes, Word automatically reduces the number of text lines on a page to create space for the number of lines in the footnotes and the separator line. If the page does not contain enough space, the footnote number and entry text are moved to the next page. Word separates the footnotes from the text with a 2-inch separator line that begins at the left margin. When endnotes are created in a document, Word prints all the endnotes at the end of the document, separated from the text by a 2-inch line.

Activity 2b Creating Endnotes

Part 2 of 3

1. Open **TechVisionaries.docx** and then save it with the name **3-TechVisionaries.**
2. Create the first endnote shown in Figure 3.5 by completing the following steps:
   a. Position the insertion point at the end of the second paragraph below the heading *Gordon E. Moore*.
   b. Click the References tab.
   c. Click the Insert Endnote button in the Footnotes group.

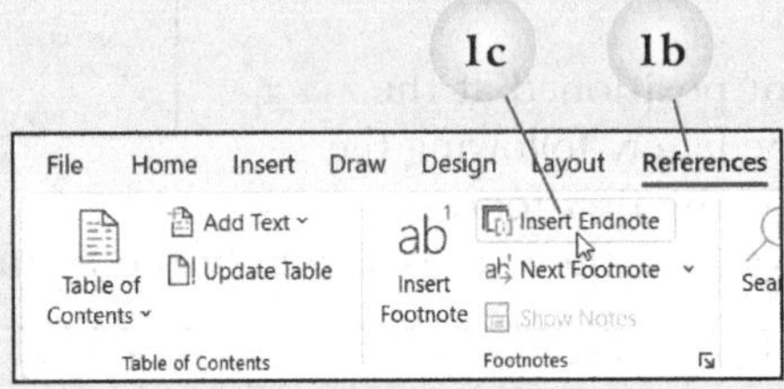

   d. Type the first endnote shown in Figure 3.5.
3. Move the insertion point to the end of the fourth paragraph below the heading *Jack S. Kilby* and then complete steps similar to those in Steps 2c and 2d to create the second endnote shown in Figure 3.5.
4. Move the insertion point to the end of the first paragraph below the heading *Linus Torvalds* and then create the third endnote shown in Figure 3.5.
5. Move the insertion point to the end of the last paragraph in the document and then create the fourth endnote shown in Figure 3.5.
6. Save **3-TechVisionaries.docx.**

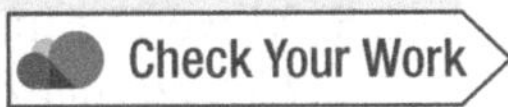

Figure 3.5 Activity 2b

Gina Shaw, *History of Computing Technologies* (Los Angeles: Gleason Rutherford Publishing, 2024): 11-14.

Ellen Littleton, "Jack Kilby: Nobel Prize Winner," *Horizon Computing* (Boston: Robison Publishing House, 2024): 23-51.

Eric Ventrella, "Computer Nerd Hero," *Computing Today* (2024): 5-10.

Joseph Daniels, "Linus Torvalds: Technology Visionary," *Connections* (2024): 13-17.

Viewing and Editing Footnotes and Endnotes

Next Footnote

Show Notes

Hint To view the entry text for a footnote or endnote where the note occurs within the document, position the pointer on the note reference number. The footnote or endnote text displays in a box above the number.

Viewing and Editing Footnotes and Endnotes

To view the footnotes in a document, click the Next Footnote button in the Footnotes group on the References tab. This moves the insertion point to the first footnote reference number following the insertion point. To view the endnotes in a document, click the Next Footnote button arrow and then click *Next Endnote* at the drop-down list. Use other options at the Next Footnote button drop-down list to view the previous footnote, next endnote, or previous endnote. Move the insertion point to specific footnote text with the Show Notes button.

If a footnote or endnote reference number is moved, copied, or deleted, all the remaining footnotes or endnotes automatically renumber. To move a footnote or endnote, select the reference number and then click the Cut button in the Clipboard group on the Home tab. Position the insertion point at the new location and then click the Paste button in the Clipboard group. To delete a footnote or endnote, select the reference number and then press the Delete key. This deletes the reference number as well as the footnote or endnote text.

Click the Footnotes group dialog box launcher and the Footnote and Endnote dialog box displays, as shown in Figure 3.6. Use options at this dialog box to convert footnotes to endnotes and endnotes to footnotes; change the locations of footnotes or endnotes; change the number formatting; start footnote or endnote numbering with a specific number, letter, or symbol; or change numbering within sections in a document.

Figure 3.6 Footnote and Endnote Dialog Box

Footnote and Endnote ? ×

Location

Footnotes: Bottom of page

Endnotes: End of document

Convert...

Footnote layout

Columns: Match section layout

Format

Number format: i, ii, iii, ...

Custom mark: Symbol...

Start at: i

Numbering: Continuous

Apply changes

Apply changes to: Whole document

Insert | Cancel | Apply

Click this button to display the Convert Notes dialog box with options for converting footnotes to endnotes or endnotes to footnotes.

Use these option boxes to specify locations for footnotes or endnotes.

Specify the formatting of the footnote or endnote number with options in this section of the dialog box.

Activity 2c Editing Endnotes, Converting Endnotes to Footnotes, and Editing Footnotes

Part 3 of 3

1. With **3-TechVisionaries.docx** open, press Ctrl + Home to move the insertion point to the beginning of the document and then edit the endnotes by completing the following steps:
   a. If necessary, click the References tab.
   b. Click the Next Footnote button arrow in the Footnotes group and then click *Next Endnote* at the drop-down list.
   c. Click the Show Notes button in the Footnotes group to display the endnote text.
   d. Change the page numbers for the Gina Shaw entry from *11-14* to *6-10*.
   e. Click the Show Notes button again to return to the reference number in the document.

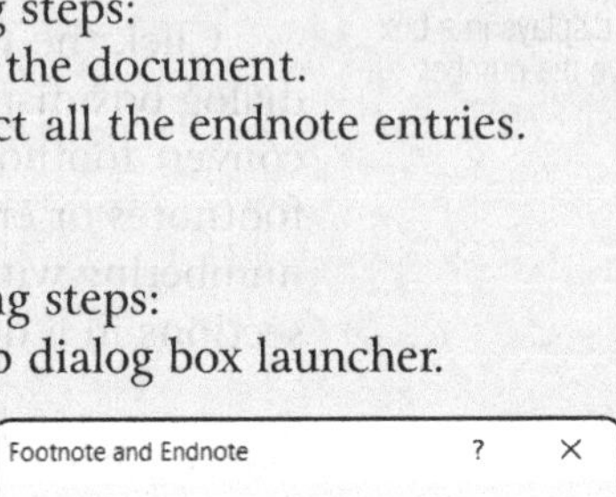

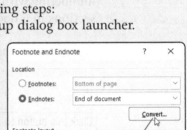

2. Press Ctrl + A to select the document (but not the endnote entry text) and then change the font to Constantia.
3. Change the font for the endnotes by completing the following steps:
   a. Press Ctrl + End to move the insertion point to the end of the document.
   b. Click in any endnote entry and then press Ctrl + A to select all the endnote entries.
   c. Change the font to Constantia.
   d. Press Ctrl + Home.
4. Convert the endnotes to footnotes by completing the following steps:
   a. Click the References tab and then click the Footnotes group dialog box launcher.
   b. At the Footnote and Endnote dialog box, click the Convert button.
   c. At the Convert Notes dialog box with the *Convert all endnotes to footnotes* option selected, click OK.
   d. Click the Close button to close the Footnote and Endnote dialog box.
5. Change the footnote number format by completing the following steps:
   a. Click the Footnotes group dialog box launcher.
   b. Click the *Footnotes* option in the *Location* section of the dialog box.
   c. Click the *Footnotes* option box arrow and then click *Below text* at the drop-down list.
   d. Click the *Number format* option box arrow in the *Format* section and then click *a, b, c, …* at the drop-down list.
   e. Change the starting number by clicking the *Start at* measurement box up arrow until *d* displays in the measurement box.
   f. Click the Apply button and then scroll through the document and notice the renumbering of the footnotes.

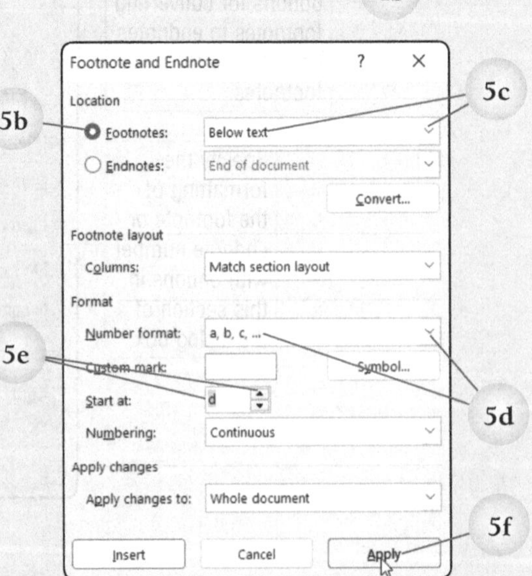

6. Change the footnote number format back to arabic numbers by completing the following steps:
   a. With the References tab active, click the Footnotes group dialog box launcher.
   b. At the Footnote and Endnote dialog box, click the *Footnotes* option in the *Location* section.

c. Click the *Number format* option box arrow in the *Format* section and then click *1, 2, 3, ...* at the drop-down list.
d. Change the starting number back to 1 by clicking the *Start at* measurement box down arrow until *1* displays in the measurement box.
e. Click the Apply button.

7. Delete the third footnote by completing the following steps:
   a. Press Ctrl + Home.
   b. Make sure the References tab is active and then click the Next Footnote button three times.
   c. Select the third footnote reference number (superscript number) and then press the Delete key.
8. Save, preview, and then close **3-TechVisionaries.docx**.

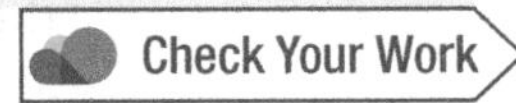

Activity 3 Cite Sources in a New Zealand Report **8 Parts**

You will open a report on New Zealand, add information and insert source citations and a bibliography, and then modify and customize citation styles.

Citing and Editing Sources

In addition to using footnotes and endnotes to credit sources in a research paper or manuscript, consider inserting in-text citations and a sources list to identify sources of quotations, facts, theories, and other borrowed or summarized material. An in-text citation acknowledges that information is being borrowed from a source. Not acknowledging someone else's words or ideas is called *plagiarizing*.

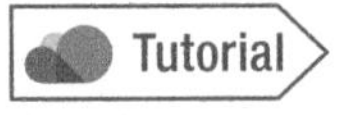

Formatting a Report in MLA Style

Formatting a Report in APA Style

Formatting a Report Using an Editorial Style

Word provides a number of commonly used editorial styles for citing references in research papers and reports, including the American Psychological Association (APA) reference style, which is generally used in the social sciences and research fields; the Modern Language Association (MLA) style, which is generally used in the humanities and English composition; and the *Chicago Manual of Style* (Chicago), which is used both in the humanities and the social sciences and is considered more complex than either APA or MLA style.

To prepare a research paper or report in APA or MLA style, format the document according to the following general guidelines:

- Use standard-sized paper (8.5 × 11 inches)
- Set 1-inch top, bottom, left, and right margins
- Format the text in a 12-point serif typeface (such as Cambria or Times New Roman)
- Double-space text
- Indent the first line of each paragraph 0.5 inch
- Insert page numbers in the header, positioned at the right margin.

When formatting a research paper or report according to MLA or APA style, follow certain guidelines for properly formatting the first page of the document. With MLA style, at the beginning of the first page, at the left margin, insert the author's name (the person writing the report), the instructor's name, the course title, and the current date. Double-space after each of the four lines. After the current date, double-space and then type and center the title of the document. Also double-space between the title and the first line of text. The text should be left-aligned and double-spaced. Finally, insert a header in the upper right corner of the document that includes the author's last name and the page number.

When using APA style, create a title page that is separate from the body of the document. On this page, include the title of the paper, the author's name, and the school's name, all double-spaced, centered, and positioned on the upper half of the page. Also include a header with the text *Running Head:* followed by the title of the paper in uppercase letters at the left margin and the page number at the right margin.

Activity 3a Formatting the First Page of a Research Paper in MLA Style

Part 1 of 8

1. Open **NewZealand.docx** and then save it with the name **3-NewZealand**.
2. Format the document in MLA style by completing the following steps:
   a. Press Ctrl + A to select the entire document.
   b. Display the Font dialog box with the Font tab selected and change the font to Cambria and the font size to 12 points. Click the Set As Default button in the lower left corner of the dialog box and then click OK at the Microsoft Word dialog box. (This changes the default setting to 12-point Cambria for the current document only.)
   c. Press Ctrl + Home to position the insertion point at the beginning of the document.
   d. Type your first and last names and then press the Enter key.
   e. Type your instructor's name and then press the Enter key.
   f. Type your course title and then press the Enter key.
   g. Type the current date.

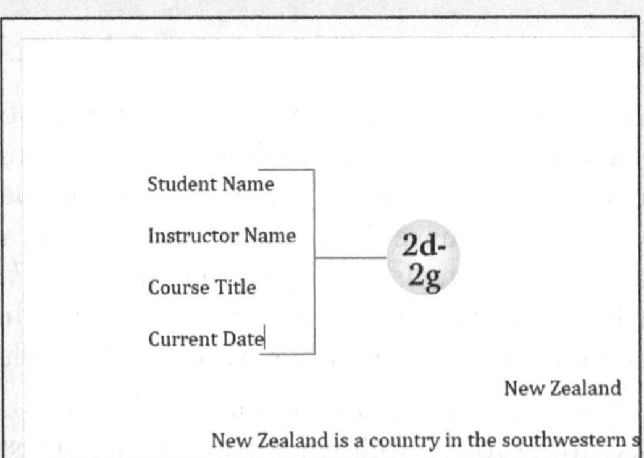

3. Insert a header in the document by completing the following steps:
   a. Click the Insert tab.
   b. Click the Header button in the Header & Footer group and then click *Edit Header* at the drop-down list.
   c. Press the Tab key two times to move the insertion point to the right margin in the Header pane.

d. Type your last name and then press the spacebar.
e. Click the Page Number button in the Header & Footer group on the Header & Footer tab, point to *Current Position*, and then click the *Plain Number* option.

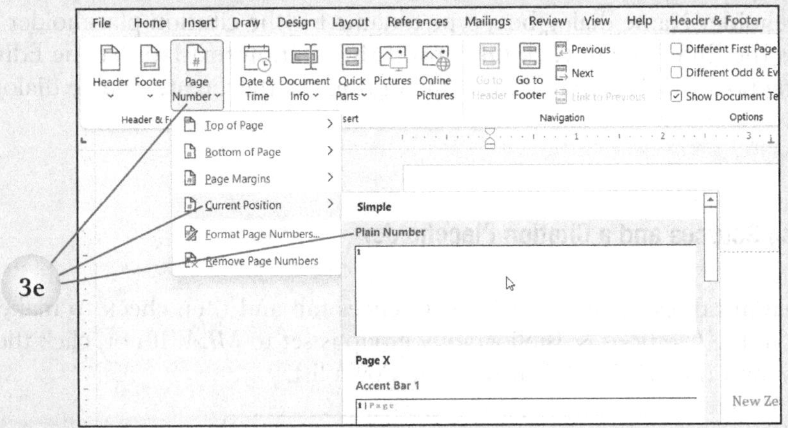

f. Double-click in the body of the document.
4. Save **3-NewZealand.docx**.

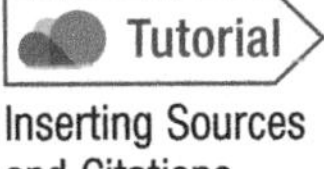

Inserting Sources and Citations

Insert Citation

Quick Steps

Insert New Citation

1. Click References tab.
2. Click Insert Citation button.
3. Click *Add New Source.*
4. Type source information.
5. Click OK.

Inserting Source Citations

When creating an in-text source citation, enter the information about the source in fields at the Create Source dialog box. To insert a citation in a document, click the References tab, click the Insert Citation button in the Citations & Bibliography group, and then click *Add New Source* at the drop-down list. At the Create Source dialog box, shown in Figure 3.7, select the type of source to be cited (such as a book, journal article, or report) and then type the bibliographic information in the required fields. To include more information than required in the displayed fields, click the *Show All Bibliography Fields* check box to insert a check mark and then type the additional bibliographic details in the extra fields. After filling in the necessary source information, click OK. The citation is automatically inserted in the document at the location of the insertion point.

Figure 3.7 Create Source Dialog Box

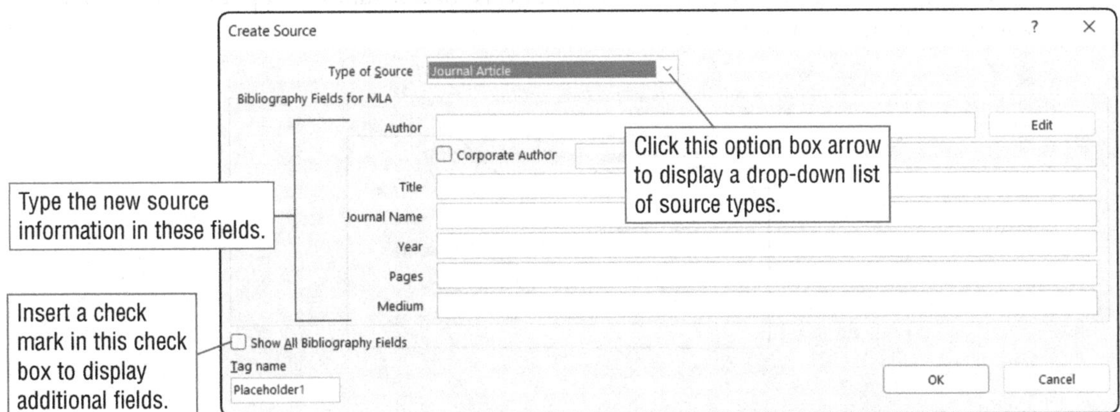

Inserting Citation Placeholders

Quick Steps

Insert Citation Placeholder

1. Click References tab.
2. Click Insert Citation button.
3. Click *Add New Placeholder*.
4. Type citation name.
5. Click OK.

If information for an in-text source citation will be inserted later, insert a citation placeholder. To do this, click the Insert Citation button in the Citations & Bibliography group and then click *Add New Placeholder* at the drop-down list. At the Placeholder Name dialog box, type a name for the citation placeholder and then press the Enter key or click OK. Insert the citation text later at the Edit Source dialog box, which contains the same options as the Create Source dialog box.

Activity 3b Inserting Sources and a Citation Placeholder — Part 2 of 8

1. With **3-NewZealand.docx** open, click the References tab and then check to make sure the *Style* option box in the Citations & Bibliography group is set to *MLA*. If not, click the *Style* option box arrow and then click *MLA* at the drop-down list.

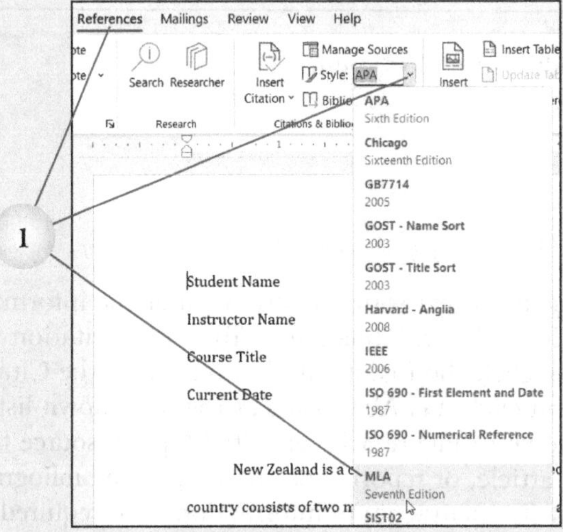

2. Select and then delete the text *(Jefferson)* at the end of the first paragraph of text (before the period that ends the sentence).
3. With the insertion point positioned between the word *city* and the period that ends the last sentence in the first paragraph, press the spacebar and then insert a citation by completing the following steps:
   a. Click the Insert Citation button in the Citations & Bibliography group and then click *Add New Source* at the drop-down list.

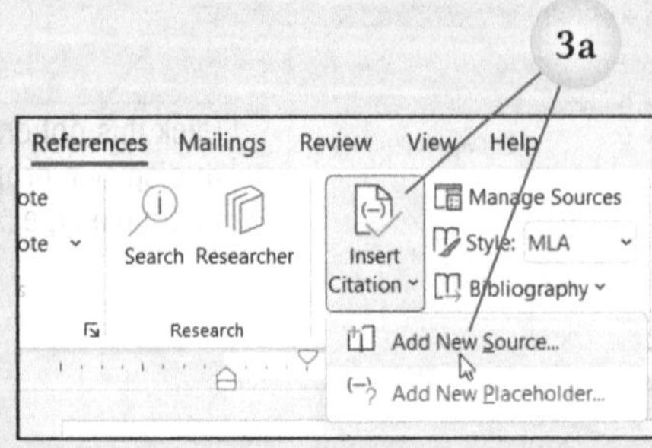

b. At the Create Source dialog box, if necessary, click the *Type of Source* option box arrow and then click *Journal Article* at the drop-down list.
c. In the *Bibliography Fields for MLA* section, click in the *Author* text box, type Gabe Jefferson, and then press the Tab key three times.
d. In the *Title* text box, type Exploring New Zealand and then press the Tab key.
e. In the *Journal Name* text box, type Island Countries and then press the Tab key.
f. In the *Year* text box, type 2024 and then press the Tab key.
g. In the *Pages* text box, type 8-10.
h. Click OK.

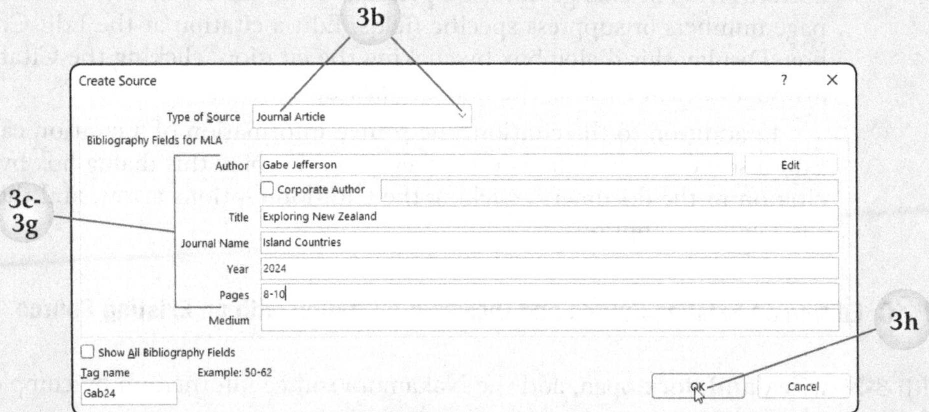

4. Select and then delete the text *(Lopez)* at the end of the third paragraph.
5. With the insertion point positioned between the word *language* and the period that ends the last sentence in the third paragraph, press the spacebar and then insert the following source information for a book. (At the Create Source dialog box, click the *Type of Source* option box arrow and then click *Book* at the drop-down list.)

Author	Rafael Lopez
Title	South Pacific Countries
Year	2024
City	Chicago
Publisher	Great Lakes

6. Select and then delete the text *(Nakamura)* in the last paragraph of text.
7. With the insertion point positioned between the word *constitution* and the period that ends the last sentence in the last paragraph of text, press the spacebar and then insert a citation placeholder by completing the following steps:
   a. Click the Insert Citation button.
   b. Click *Add New Placeholder* at the drop-down list.
   c. At the Placeholder Name dialog box, type Nakamura and then press the Enter key. (You will create the citation and fill in the source information in the next activity.)
8. Save **3-NewZealand.docx**.

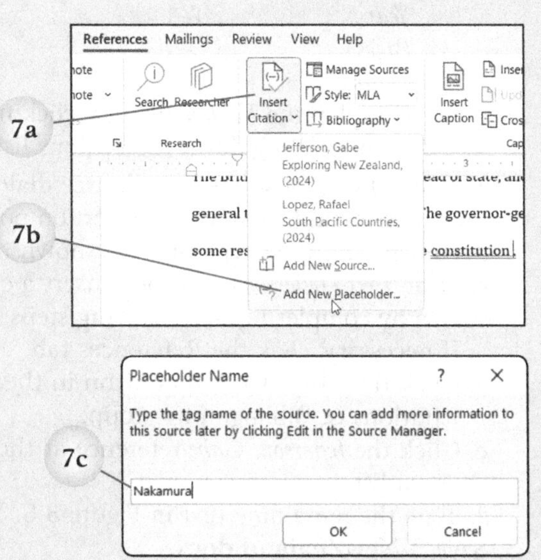

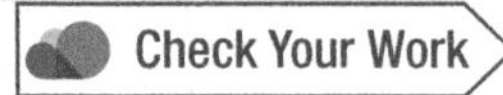

Quick Steps

Insert Citation with Existing Source

1. Click References tab.
2. Click Insert Citation button.
3. Click source.

Inserting a Citation with an Existing Source

Once source information is inserted at the Create Source dialog box, Word automatically saves it. To insert a citation in a document for source information that has already been saved, click the Insert Citation button in the Citations & Bibliography group and then click the source at the drop-down list.

Editing a Citation and Source

Editing a Citation and Source

After source information is inserted in a document, it may need to be edited to correct errors or change data. Or perhaps the citation needs to be edited to add page numbers or suppress specific fields. Edit a citation at the Edit Citation dialog box. Display this dialog box by clicking the citation, clicking the Citation Options arrow, and then clicking the *Edit Citation* option.

In addition to the citation, the source information of a citation can be edited. Edit a source at the Edit Source dialog box. Display this dialog box by clicking the citation in the document, clicking the Citation Options arrow, and then clicking the *Edit Source* option.

Activity 3c Editing an Existing Source and Inserting a Citation with an Existing Source — Part 3 of 8

1. With **3-NewZealand.docx** open, add the Nakamura source information by completing the following steps:
   a. Click the *Nakamura* citation in the document.
   b. Click the Citation Options arrow at the right side of the selected citation.
   c. Click *Edit Source* at the drop-down list.
   d. At the Edit Source dialog box, click the *Type of Source* option box arrow and then click *Journal Article*.
   e. Type the following information in the specified text boxes:

Author	Janet Nakamura
Title	New Zealand Government
Journal Name	International Governmental Organizations
Year	2024
Pages	15-28
Volume	6

   (Display the *Volume* field by clicking the *Show All Bibliography Fields* check box and then scrolling down the options list.)
   f. Click OK to close the Edit Source dialog box.

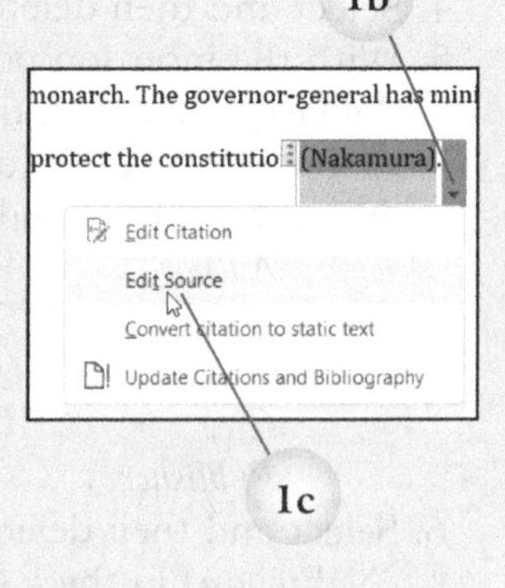

2. Press Ctrl + End to move the insertion point to the end of the document and then type the text shown in Figure 3.8 up to the citation text *(Jefferson)* and then insert a citation from an existing source by completing the following steps:
   a. If necessary, click the References tab.
   b. Click the Insert Citation button in the Citations & Bibliography group.
   c. Click the *Jefferson, Gabe* reference at the drop-down list.
   d. Type the remaining text in Figure 3.8.
3. Save **3-NewZealand.docx**.

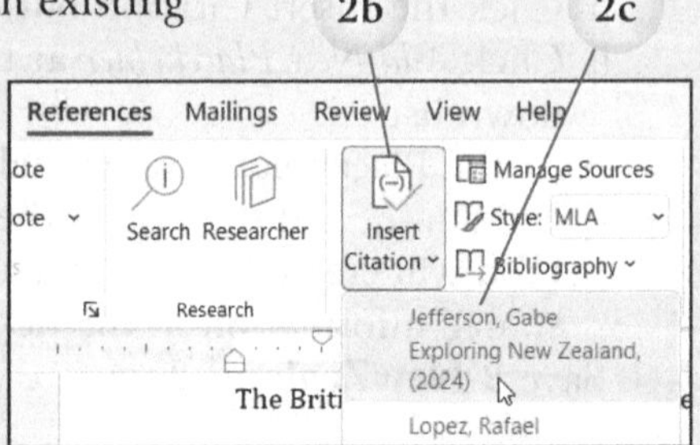

Check Your Work

Figure 3.8 Activity 3c

> An interesting fact about New Zealand is that in 1893 it was the first country to approve the right for women to vote (Jefferson). Other interesting facts are that over thirty percent of the country is a national reserve, the country has more sheep than people, it has the most southerly capital in the world, and it was the last country in the world inhabited by humans.

Quick Steps

Insert Page Number in Citation

1. Click citation to display placeholder.
2. Click Citation Options arrow.
3. Click *Edit Citation*.
4. Type page number(s).
5. Click OK.

Inserting Page Numbers in a Citation

If a direct quote from a source is included in a report, insert quotation marks around the text used from that source and insert in the citation the page number or numbers of the quoted material. To insert specific page numbers in a citation, click the citation to select the citation placeholder. Click the Citation Options arrow and then click *Edit Citation* at the drop-down list. At the Edit Citation dialog box, type the page number or numbers of the source from which the quote was borrowed and then click OK.

Managing Sources

Manage Sources

Quick Steps

Manage Sources

1. Click References tab.
2. Click Manage Sources button.
3. Edit, add, and/or delete sources.
4. Click Close.

Hint Click the Browse button in the Source Manager dialog box to select another master list.

Managing Sources

All the sources cited in the current document and in previous documents display in the Source Manager dialog box, as shown in Figure 3.9. Display this dialog box by clicking the References tab and then clicking the Manage Sources button in the Citations & Bibliography group. The *Master List* list box in the Source Manager dialog box displays all the sources that have been created in Word. The *Current List* list box displays all the sources used in the currently open document.

Use options at the Source Manager dialog box to copy a source from the master list to the current list, delete a source, edit a source, and create a new source. To copy a source from the master list to the current list, click the source in the *Master List* list box and then click the Copy button between the two list boxes. Click the Delete button to delete a source. Edit a source by clicking the source, clicking the Edit button, and then making changes at the Edit Source dialog box. Click the New button to create a new source at the Create Source dialog box.

If the *Master List* list box contains a large number of sources, search for a specific source by typing keywords in the *Search* text box. As text is typed, the list narrows to sources that match the text. After making all the changes at the Source Manager dialog box, click the Close button.

Figure 3.9 Source Manager Dialog Box

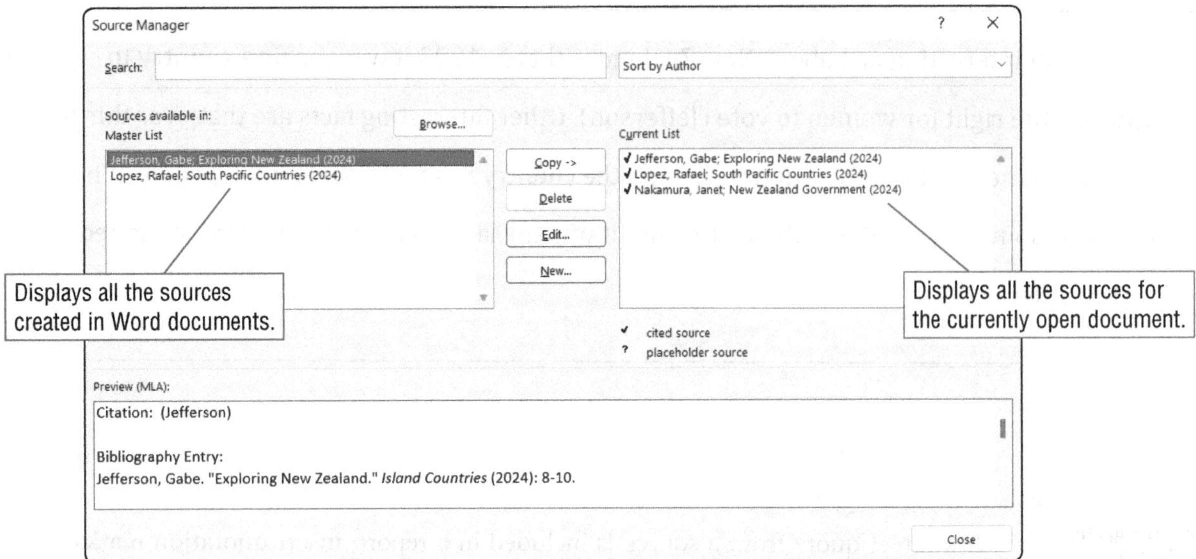

Activity 3d Managing Sources

Part 4 of 8

1. With **3-NewZealand.docx** open, edit a source by completing the following steps:
   a. If necessary, click the References tab.
   b. Click the Manage Sources button in the Citations & Bibliography group.
   c. At the Source Manager dialog box, click the *Jefferson, Gabe* source entry in the *Master List* list box.
   d. Click the Edit button.

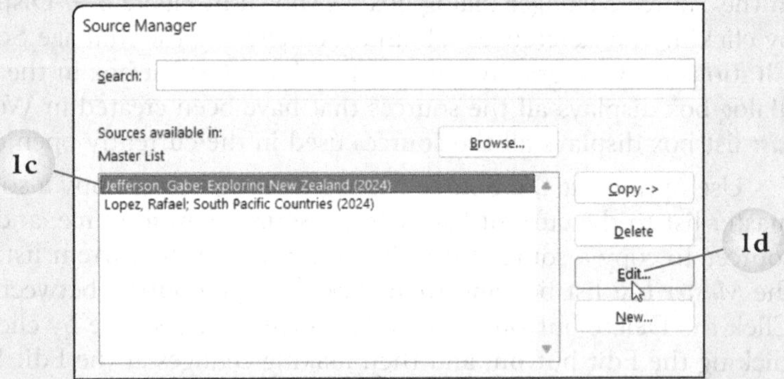

   e. At the Edit Source dialog box, delete the text in the *Author* text box and then type Gabriel Jackson.
   f. Click OK to close the Edit Source dialog box.
   g. At the message asking if you want to update both the master list and current list with the changes, click Yes.
   h. Click the Close button to close the Source Manager dialog box. (Notice that the last name changed in both of the Jefferson citations to reflect the edit.)
2. Delete a source by completing the following steps:
   a. Select and then delete the last sentence in the third paragraph in the document (the sentence beginning Te reo *is another name*), including the citation.
   b. Click the Manage Sources button.

c. At the Source Manager dialog box, click the *Lopez, Rafael* entry in the *Current List* list box. (This entry will not contain a check mark because you deleted the citation from the document.)

d. Click the Delete button.

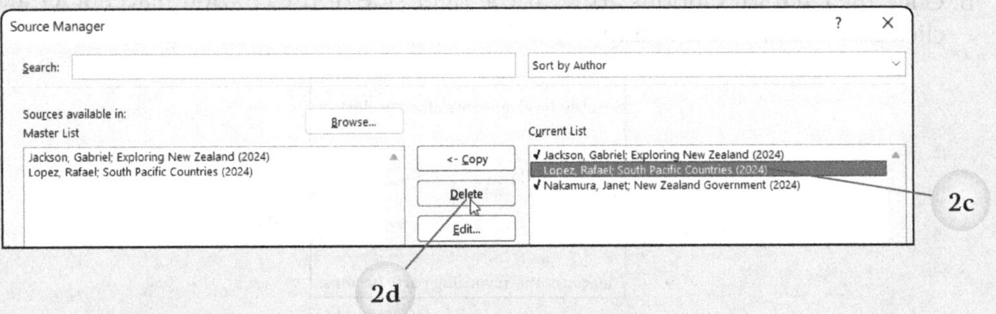

e. Click the Close button to close the Source Manager dialog box.

3. Create and insert a new source in the document by completing the following steps:
   a. Click the Manage Sources button.
   b. Click the New button in the Source Manager dialog box.
   c. Type the following book information in the Create Source dialog box. (Change the *Type of Source* option to *Book*.)

Author	Georgia Miraldi
Title	World Climates
Year	2024
City	Houston
Publisher	Rio Grande

   d. Click OK to close the Create Source dialog box.
   e. Click the Close button to close the Source Manager dialog box.
   f. Position the insertion point between the last word *snowfall* at the end of the fourth paragraph and the period that ends the sentence and then press the spacebar.
   g. Insert a citation for Georgia Miraldi by clicking the Insert Citation button in the Citations & Bibliography group and then clicking *Miraldi, Georgia* at the drop-down list.

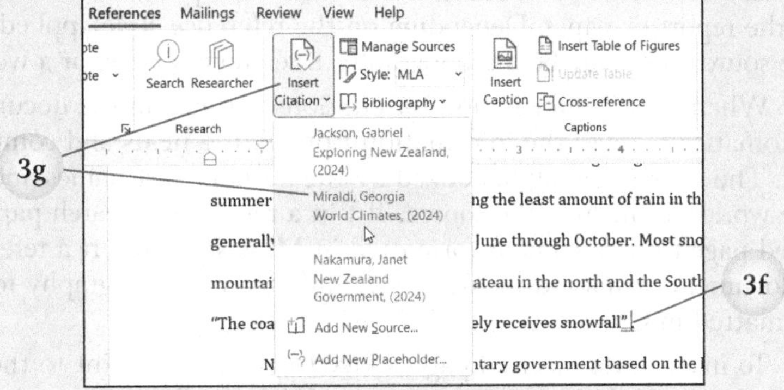

4. To correctly acknowledge the direct quote from Georgia Miraldi, the page on which the quote appears in the book needs to be added. Insert the page number in the citation by completing the following steps:
   a. Click the *Miraldi* citation in the document.
   b. Click the Citation Options arrow at the right side of the citation placeholder and then click *Edit Citation* at the drop-down list.

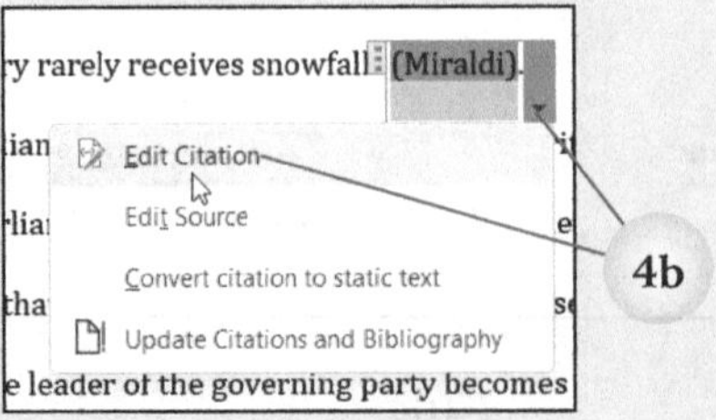

   c. At the Edit Citation dialog box, type 19 in the *Pages* text box.
   d. Click OK.

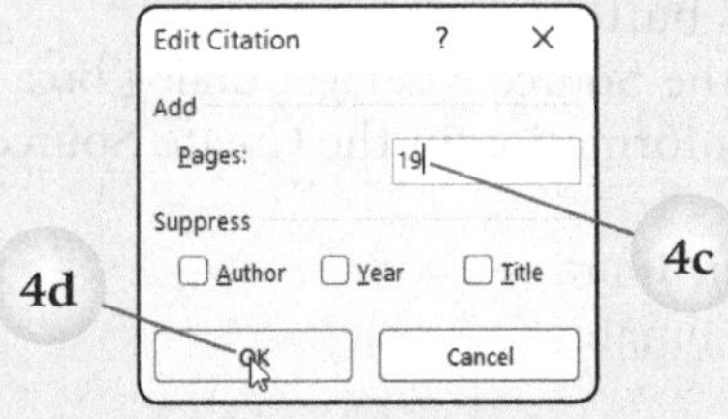

5. Save **3-NewZealand.docx.**

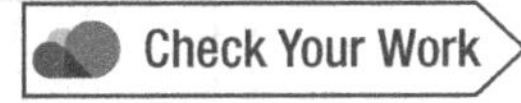

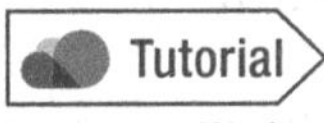

Inserting a Works Cited Page

Quick Steps

Insert Sources List

1. Insert new page at end of document.
2. Click References tab.
3. Click Bibliography button.
4. Click works cited, reference, or bibliography option.

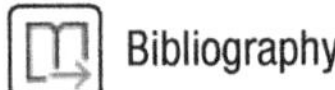

Inserting a Sources List

If citations are included in a report or research paper, a sources list needs to be inserted as a separate page at the end of the document. A sources list is an alphabetical list of the books, journal articles, reports, and other sources referenced in the report or paper. Depending on the reference style applied to the document, the sources list may be a bibliography, a references page, or a works cited page.

When source information for citations is typed in the document, Word automatically saves the information from all the fields and compiles a sources list. The sources are alphabetized by the authors' last names and/or the titles of the works. To include the sources list in a report or research paper, insert a works cited page for a document formatted in MLA style, insert a references page for a document formatted in APA style, and insert a bibliography for a document formatted in Chicago style.

To insert a works cited page, move the insertion point to the end of the document and then insert a new page. Click the References tab and make sure the *Style* option box is set to *MLA*. Click the Bibliography button in the Citations & Bibliography group and then click the *Works Cited* option. For a document formatted in the APA style, click the Bibliography button and then click the *References* option.

Activity 3e Inserting a Works Cited Page

Part 5 of 8

1. With **3-NewZealand.docx** open, insert a works cited page at the end of the document by completing these steps:
   a. Press Ctrl + End to move the insertion point to the end of the document.
   b. Press Ctrl + Enter to insert a page break.
   c. If necessary, click the References tab.
   d. Click the Bibliography button in the Citations & Bibliography group.
   e. Click the *Works Cited* option in the *Built-In* section of the drop-down list.

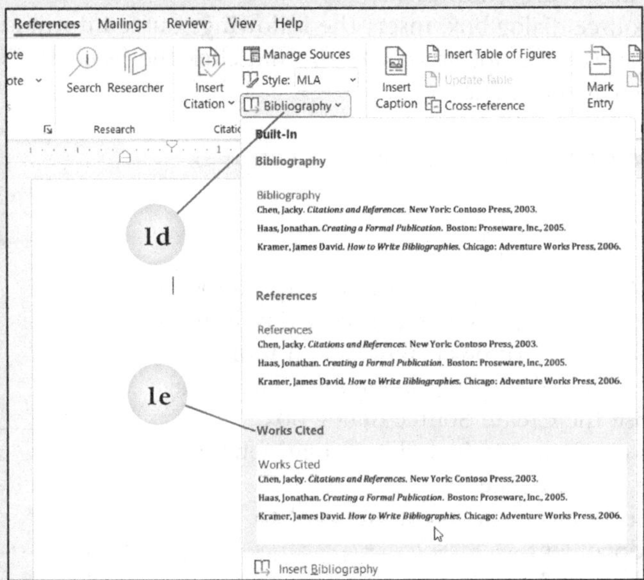

2. Format the works cited page to meet MLA requirements with the following changes:
   a. Select the *Works Cited* heading and all the entries and click the *No Spacing* style in the Styles group on the Home tab.
   b. Change the spacing to 2.0.
   c. Press Ctrl + T to format the works cited entries with a hanging indent.
   d. Center the title *Works Cited*.
3. Save **3-NewZealand.docx**.

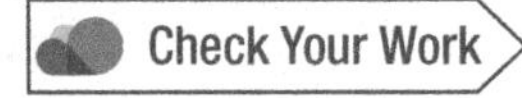

Modifying and Updating a Sources List

Quick Steps
Update Sources List
1. Click in sources list.
2. Click Update Citations and Bibliography tab.

If a new source is inserted at the Source Manager dialog box or an existing source is modified, Word automatically inserts the source information in the sources list. If a new citation requires a new source to be added, Word will not automatically update the sources list. To update the sources list, click in the list and then click the Update Citations and Bibliography tab. The updated sources list reflects any changes made to the citations and source information in the document.

Activity 3f Modifying and Updating a Works Cited Page

1. With **3-NewZealand.docx** open, create a new source and citation by completing the following steps:
   a. Position the insertion point immediately left of the period that ends the last sentence in the third paragraph of the document (after the word *Language*).
   b. Press the spacebar.
   c. If necessary, click the References tab.
   d. Click the Insert Citation button in the Citations & Bibliography group and then click *Add New Source* at the drop-down list.
   e. At the Create Source dialog box, insert the following source information for a website. (Change the *Type of Source* option to *Web site* and click the *Show All Bibliography Fields* check box to display all the fields.)

Author	Chay Suong
Name of Web Page	New Zealand Sign Language
Year	2024
Month	April
Day	21
Year Accessed	(type current year in numbers)
Month Accessed	(type current month in letters)
Day Accessed	(type current day in numbers)
URL	https://ppi-edu.net/signlanguage

   f. Click OK to close the Create Source dialog box.
2. Update the works cited page to include the new source by completing the following steps:
   a. Press Ctrl + End to move the insertion point to the end of the document.
   b. Click in the works cited text.
   c. Click the Update Citations and Bibliography tab above the heading *Works Cited*. (Notice that the updated sources list includes the Suong reference.)
3. Save **3-NewZealand.docx**.

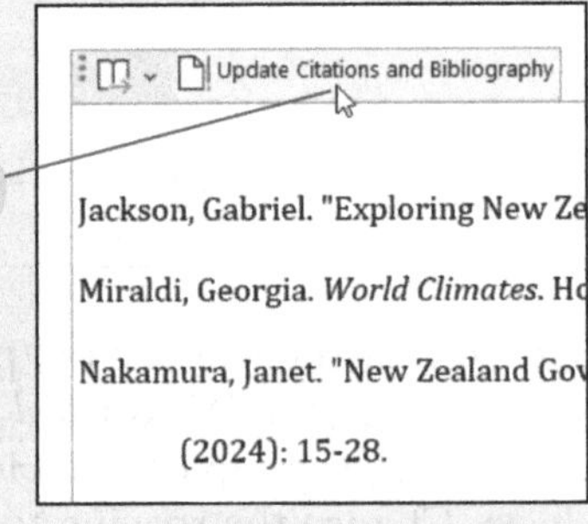

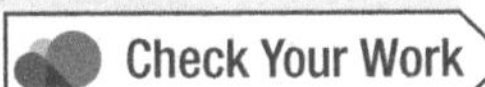

Formatting a Sources List

The formatting applied by Word to the sources list may need to be changed to meet the specific guidelines of MLA, APA, or Chicago style. For example, MLA and APA styles require the following formats for a sources list:

- Begin the sources list on a separate page after the last page of text in the report.
- Include the title *Works Cited*, *References*, or *Bibliography* at the top of the page and center it on the width of the page.
- Use the same font for the sources list as for the main document.
- Double-space between and within entries.
- Begin each entry at the left margin and format subsequent lines in each entry with a hanging indent.
- Alphabetize the entries.

The general formatting requirements for Chicago style are similar except that single spacing is applied within entries and double spacing is applied between entries.

Activity 3g Formatting a Works Cited Page

Part 7 of 8

1. With **3-NewZealand.docx** open, notice that the works cited entries are set in 12-point Cambria and a hanging indent is applied to the entries.
2. Select the four reference entries below the *Works Cited* title, click the Home tab, and then click the *No Spacing* style in the Styles group.
3. With the four entries still selected, press Ctrl + 2 to apply double spacing to the entries and then press Ctrl + T to apply a hanging indent to the entries. (Applying the *No Spacing* style in Step 2 removed the hanging indent.)
4. Save and then preview **3-NewZealand.docx**.

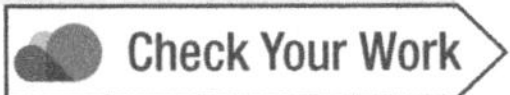

Choosing a Citation Style

Quick Steps

Change Citation Style

1. Click References tab.
2. Click *Style* option box arrow.
3. Click a style.

Different subjects and different instructors or professors may require different formats for citing references. The style for reference citations can be changed before beginning a new document or while working in an existing document. To change the style of citations in an existing document, click the References tab, click the *Style* option box arrow, and then click the style at the drop-down list.

Activity 3h Choosing a Citation Style

Part 8 of 8

1. With **3-NewZealand.docx** open, change the document and works cited page from MLA style to APA style by completing the following steps:
   a. Click the References tab.
   b. Click the *Style* option box arrow in the Citations & Bibliography group and then click *APA* at the drop-down list.

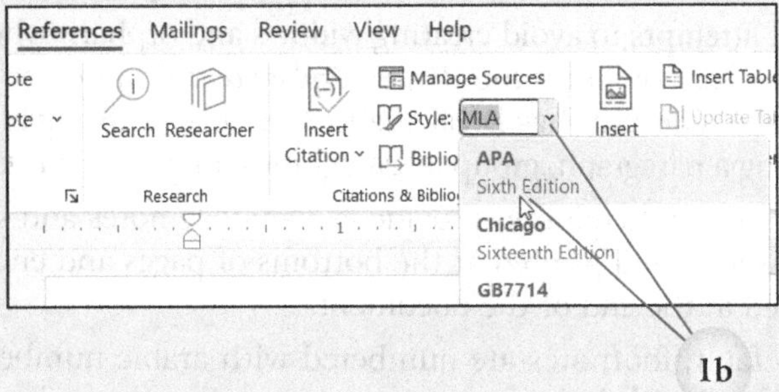

   c. Notice the changes made to the works cited entries.
   d. Scroll up the document and notice the changes to the citations.
   e. Press Ctrl + End to move the insertion point to the end of the document.
   f. Change the title *Works Cited* to *References*.
2. Save, preview, and then close **3-NewZealand.docx**.
3. Display a blank document, click the References tab, change the style to *MLA*, and then close the document without saving it.

Chapter Summary

- Text that appears in the top margin of a page is called a *header*; text that appears in the bottom margin of a page is called a *footer*. Insert predesigned headers and footers in a document or create custom headers and footers.
- To create a custom header, click the Header button in the Header & Footer group on the Insert tab and then click *Edit Header*. At the Header pane, insert elements or text. Complete similar steps to create a custom footer.
- Use buttons in the Insert group on the Header & Footer tab to insert elements such as the date and time, Quick Parts, and images into a header or footer.
- Word inserts headers and footers 0.5 inch from the edge of the page. Reposition a header or footer with buttons in the Position group on the Header & Footer tab.
- A unique header or footer can be created on the first page; a header or footer can be omitted on the first page; different headers or footers can be created for odd and even pages; or different headers or footers can be created for sections in a document. Use options in the Options group on the Header & Footer tab to specify the type of header or footer to be created.
- Each section in a document is linked to the other sections in the document. To specify that a header or footer prints only on the pages within a section and not the previous sections, click the Link to Previous button in the Navigation group on the Header & Footer tab to deactivate the button.
- Insert page numbers in a document in a header or footer or with options at the Page Number button in the Header & Footer group on the Insert tab.
- Format page numbers with options at the Page Number Format dialog box.
- To print sections or specific pages within a section, use the *Pages* text box at the Print backstage area. When specifying sections and pages, use the letter *s* before a section number and the letter *p* before a page number.
- Word attempts to avoid creating widows and orphans when inserting soft page breaks. Turn on or off the *Widow/Orphan control* option at the Paragraph dialog box with the Line and Page Breaks tab selected. This dialog box also contains options for keeping a paragraph, group of paragraphs, or group of lines together.
- Footnotes and endnotes provide explanatory notes and source citations. Footnotes are inserted and printed at the bottoms of pages and endnotes are inserted and printed at the end of the document.
- By default, footnotes are numbered with arabic numbers and endnotes are numbered with lowercase roman numerals.
- Move, copy, or delete a footnote/endnote reference number in a document and all the other footnotes/endnotes automatically renumber.
- Delete a footnote or endnote by selecting the reference number and then pressing the Delete key.
- Consider using in-text citations to acknowledge sources in a paper. Commonly used citation and reference styles include those of the American Psychological Association (APA), Modern Language Association (MLA), and *Chicago Manual of Style* (Chicago).
- Insert a citation using the Insert Citation button in the Citations & Bibliography group on the References tab. Specify source information at the Create Source dialog box.

- Insert a citation placeholder in a document if the source information will be added at a later time.
- Insert a citation in a document for source information that has already been saved by clicking the Insert Citation button in the Citations & Bibliography group and then clicking the source at the drop-down list.
- Edit a source at the Edit Source dialog box. Display this dialog box by clicking the source citation in the document, clicking the Citation Options arrow, and then clicking *Edit Source* at the drop-down list. Another option is to display the Source Manager dialog box, click the source to be edited, and then click the Edit button.
- Copy, delete, and edit sources and create new sources with options at the Source Manager dialog box. Display this dialog box by clicking the Manage Sources button in the Citations & Bibliography group on the References tab.
- Insert a sources list, such as a works cited page, references page, or bibliography, at the end of the document on a separate page. To do so, use the Bibliography button in the Citations & Bibliography group on the References tab.
- To update a sources list, click in the list and then click the Update Citations and Bibliography tab.
- The MLA and APA styles require specific formatting for a list of sources. Refer to page 104 for a list of formatting requirements.
- Change the reference style with the *Style* option box in the Citations & Bibliography group on the References tab.

Commands Review

FEATURE	RIBBON TAB, GROUP	BUTTON, OPTION	KEYBOARD SHORTCUT
bibliography	References, Citations & Bibliography		
create footer	Insert, Header & Footer	, *Edit Footer*	
create header	Insert, Header & Footer	, *Edit Header*	
citation style	References, Citations & Bibliography		
Create Source dialog box	References, Citations & Bibliography	, *Add New Source*	
endnote	References, Footnotes		Alt + Ctrl + D
footer	Insert, Header & Footer		
footnote	References, Footnotes		Alt + Ctrl + F
header	Insert, Header & Footer		
next footnote	References, Footnotes		
page number	Insert, Header & Footer		
show notes	References, Footnotes		
Source Manager dialog box	References, Citations & Bibliography		

CHAPTER 3

Review and Assessment

Skills Assessment

Assessment 1

Insert Specialized Footers in a Report

1. Open **Robots.docx** and then save it with the name **3-Robots**.
2. Keep the heading *NAVIGATION* together with the paragraph of text that follows it.
3. Move the insertion point to the beginning of the document and then create an odd page footer that includes the following:
   a. Insert the current date at the left margin. (Choose the date option that displays the month spelled out, such as *January 1, 2024*.)
   b. Using the Pictures button in the Insert group on the Header & Footer tab, insert the **RobotWalking.jpg** image file in the middle of the footer. Change the height of the robot image to 0.5 inch and the text wrapping to Behind Text. If necessary, drag the robot image below the footer pane border.
   c. At the right margin, type Page, press the spacebar, and then insert a plain page number at the current position.
4. Create an even page footer that includes the following:
   a. At the left margin, type Page, press the spacebar, and then insert a plain page number at the current position.
   b. Insert the **RobotWalking.jpg** image file in the middle of the footer and apply the same formatting as you did to the image in the odd page footer.
   c. Insert the current date at the right margin in the same format you chose for the odd page footer.
5. Save, preview, and then close **3-Robots.docx**.

Assessment 2

Insert a Header and Footer in a Report on All Pages Except the First Page

1. Open **Volcanoes.docx** and then save it with the name **3-Volcanoes**.
2. Create a header for all pages except the first page and type Volcano Report at the right margin of the Header pane. (Make sure the First Page Header pane is blank.)
3. Create a footer for all pages except the first page and insert the Banded predesigned footer in the Footer pane. (Make sure the First Page Footer pane is blank.)
4. Save, preview, and then close **3-Volcanoes.docx**.

Assessment 3

Insert a Section Break and Format and Print Sections

1. Open **CompViruses.docx** and then save it with the name **3-CompViruses**.
2. Insert a section break that begins a new page at the beginning of the title *CHAPTER 2 SECURITY RISKS*.
3. Move the insertion point to the beginning of the document and then create a footer for the first section in the document with *Chapter 1* at the left margin, the page number in the middle, and your first and last names at the right margin.
4. Edit the footer for the second section to Chapter 2 instead of Chapter 1. ***Hint: Make sure you break the link.***
5. Print only the pages in section 2.
6. Save, preview, and then close **3-CompViruses.docx**.

Assessment 4

Insert Footnotes in a Designing Newsletters Document

1. Open **DesignNwsltr.docx** and then save it with the name **3-DesignNwsltr**.
2. Create the first footnote shown in Figure 3.10 at the end of the first paragraph in the *Applying Guidelines* section.
3. Create the second footnote shown in the figure at the end of the last paragraph in the *Applying Guidelines* section.
4. Create the third footnote shown in the figure at the end of the only paragraph in the *Choosing Paper Size and Type* section.
5. Create the fourth footnote shown in the figure at the end of the only paragraph in the *Choosing Paper Weight* section.
6. Save and then preview **3-DesignNwsltr.docx**.
7. Select the entire document and then change the font to Constantia.
8. Select all the footnotes and then change the font to Constantia. ***Note: Pressing Ctrl + A will select all the footnotes in the document.***
9. Delete the second footnote (*Maddock*).
10. Save, preview, and then close **3-DesignNwsltr.docx**.

Figure 3.10 Assessment 4

James Haberman, "Designing a Newsletter," *Desktop Designs* (2024): 23-29.

Arlita Maddock, "Guidelines for a Better Newsletter," *Desktop Publisher* (2023): 32-38.

Monica Alverso, "Paper Styles for Newsletters," *Design Technologies* (2024): 45-51.

Keith Sutton, "Choosing Paper Styles," *Design Techniques* (2024): 8-11.

Assessment 5

Insert Sources and Citations in a Privacy Rights Document

1. Open **PrivRights.docx** and then save it with the name **3-PrivRights-MLA**.
2. Make sure that MLA style is selected in the Citations & Bibliography group on the References tab.
3. With the insertion point positioned at the beginning of the document, type your name, press the Enter key, type your instructor's name, press the Enter key, type the title of your course, press the Enter key, and then type the current date.
4. Set the text in the document to 12-point Cambria and then make this the default font for the document. ***Hint: Do this with the Set As Default button at the Font dialog box.***

5. Insert a header that displays your last name and the page number at the right margin.
6. Select and then delete the text *(Hartley)* that appears in the second paragraph.
7. With the insertion point positioned between the word *policy* and the period that ends the third sentence in the second paragraph, press the spacebar and then insert the source information for a journal article written by Kenneth Hartley using the following information:

Author	Kenneth Hartley
Title	Privacy Laws
Journal Name	Business World
Year	2024
Pages	33-46
Volume	XII

8. Select and then delete the text *(Ferraro)* that appears in the second paragraph.
9. With the insertion point positioned between the word *place* and the period that ends the fourth sentence in the second paragraph, press the spacebar and then insert the following source information for a book:

Author	Ramona Ferraro
Title	Business Employee Rights
Year	2024
City	Tallahassee
Publisher	Everglades Publishing House

10. Select and then delete the text *(Aldrich)* that appears in the last paragraph.
11. With the insertion point positioned between the word *limit"* and the period that ends the second sentence in the last paragraph, press the spacebar and then insert the following information for an article in a periodical:

Author	Kelly Aldrich
Title	What Rights Do Employees Have?
Periodical Title	Great Plains Times
Year	2024
Month	May
Day	6
Pages	18-22

12. Insert page number 20 in the Kelly Aldrich citation using the Edit Citation dialog box.
13. Edit the Kenneth Hartley source title to read *Small Business Privacy Laws* in the *Master List* section of the Source Manager dialog box. (Update both the Master List and the Current List.)
14. Insert a works cited page on a separate page at the end of the document.
15. Create a new source in the document using the Source Manager dialog box and include the following source information for a website:

Author	Harold Davidson
Name of Web Page	Small Business Policies and Procedures
Year	2023
Month	December
Day	12
Year Accessed	2024
Month Accessed	February
Day Accessed	23
URL	https://ppi-edu.net/policies

16. Insert a citation for Harold Davidson at the end of the last sentence in the first paragraph.
17. Update the works cited page.

18. Format the works cited page to meet MLA requirements with the following changes:
    a. Select the *Works Cited* heading and all the entries and then click the *No Spacing* style.
    b. Change the spacing to 2.0.
    c. Format the works cited entries with a hanging indent.
    d. Center the title *Works Cited*.
19. Save and then preview **3-PrivRights-MLA.docx**.
20. Save the document with the name **3-PrivRights-APA**.
21. Change the document and works cited page from MLA style to APA style. Make sure you change the title of the sources list to *References*. Select the references in the list and then change the line spacing to double spacing.
22. Save, preview, and then close **3-PrivRights-APA.docx**.

Visual Benchmark

Format a Report in MLA Style

1. Open **SecurityDefenses.docx** and then save it with the name **3-SecurityDefenses**.
2. Format the document so it displays as shown in Figure 3.11 with the following specifications:
    a. Change the document font to 12-point Cambria and then set 12-point Cambria as the default.
    b. Use the information from the works cited page when inserting citations into the document. The Hollingsworth citation is for a journal article, the Montoya citation is for a book, and the Gillespie citation is for a website.
    c. Format the works cited page to meet MLA requirements.
3. Save, preview, and then close **3-SecurityDefenses.docx**.

Figure 3.11 Visual Benchmark

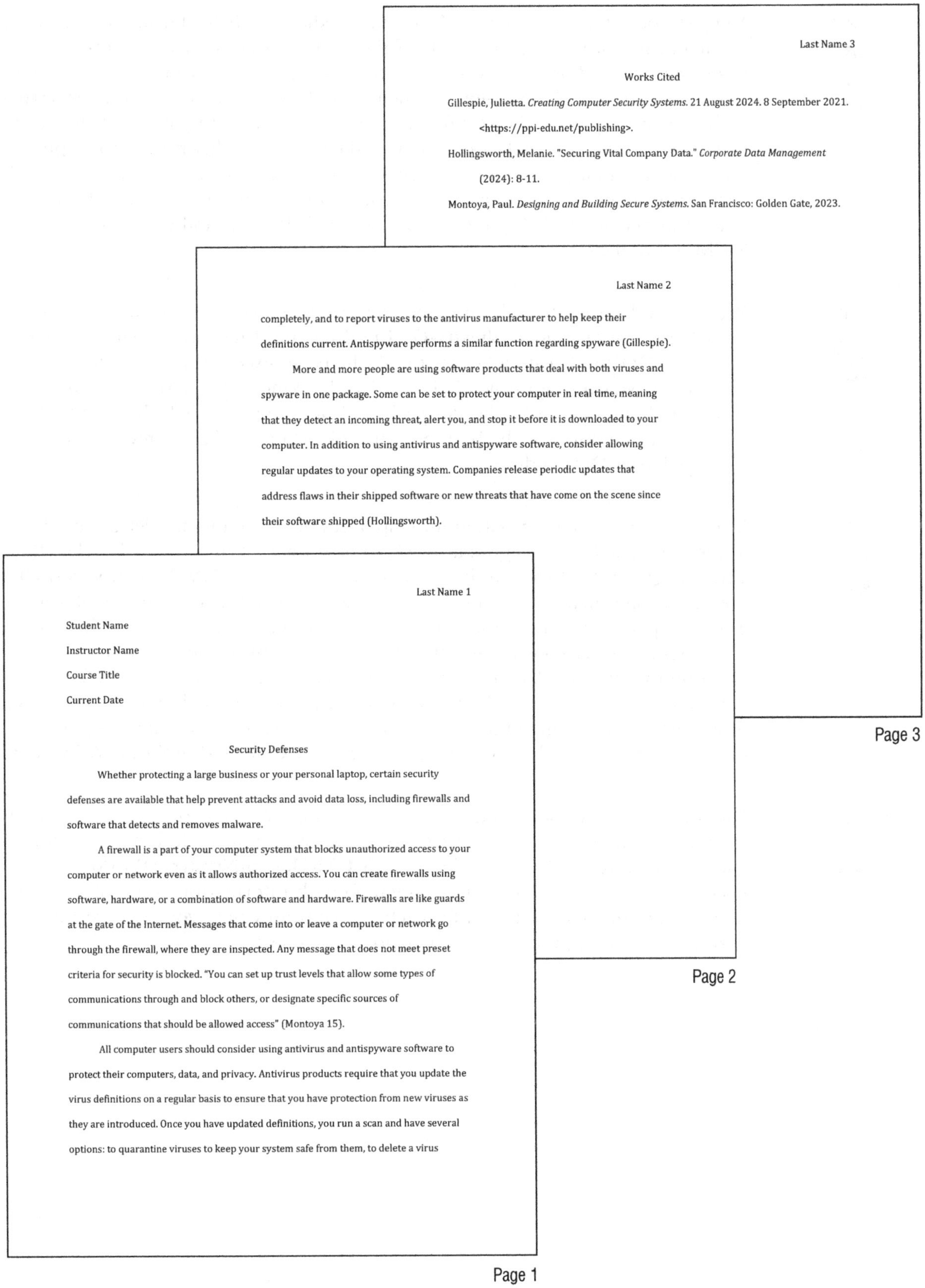

Last Name 3

Works Cited

Gillespie, Julietta. *Creating Computer Security Systems.* 21 August 2024. 8 September 2021. <https://ppi-edu.net/publishing>.

Hollingsworth, Melanie. "Securing Vital Company Data." *Corporate Data Management* (2024): 8-11.

Montoya, Paul. *Designing and Building Secure Systems.* San Francisco: Golden Gate, 2023.

Page 3

Last Name 2

completely, and to report viruses to the antivirus manufacturer to help keep their definitions current. Antispyware performs a similar function regarding spyware (Gillespie).

More and more people are using software products that deal with both viruses and spyware in one package. Some can be set to protect your computer in real time, meaning that they detect an incoming threat, alert you, and stop it before it is downloaded to your computer. In addition to using antivirus and antispyware software, consider allowing regular updates to your operating system. Companies release periodic updates that address flaws in their shipped software or new threats that have come on the scene since their software shipped (Hollingsworth).

Page 2

Last Name 1

Student Name

Instructor Name

Course Title

Current Date

Security Defenses

Whether protecting a large business or your personal laptop, certain security defenses are available that help prevent attacks and avoid data loss, including firewalls and software that detects and removes malware.

A firewall is a part of your computer system that blocks unauthorized access to your computer or network even as it allows authorized access. You can create firewalls using software, hardware, or a combination of software and hardware. Firewalls are like guards at the gate of the Internet. Messages that come into or leave a computer or network go through the firewall, where they are inspected. Any message that does not meet preset criteria for security is blocked. "You can set up trust levels that allow some types of communications through and block others, or designate specific sources of communications that should be allowed access" (Montoya 15).

All computer users should consider using antivirus and antispyware software to protect their computers, data, and privacy. Antivirus products require that you update the virus definitions on a regular basis to ensure that you have protection from new viruses as they are introduced. Once you have updated definitions, you run a scan and have several options: to quarantine viruses to keep your system safe from them, to delete a virus

Page 1

Case Study

Part 1

You just opened a new company, Chrysalis Media, that helps businesses creatively communicate with customers. Some of the media design services you offer are business letterhead, logos, flyers, newsletters, signage, and business cards. Create a company letterhead document by opening a blank document and then inserting the **CMHdr.png** image file as a first page header. Change the height of the image to 1.4" and change the header position from the top to 0.3". Insert the **CMFtr.png** image file as a first page footer. If necessary, make adjustments to the header and/or footer to improve the appearance of each on the page Save the completed letterhead document with the name **3-CMLtrhd**. Preview and then close **3-CMLtrhd.docx**.

Part 2

You have a document on defining newsletter elements that you want to make available to clients. Open **Nwsltr-Define.docx** and then save it with the name **3-Nwsltr-Define**. Create a header for all the pages except the first page and insert the **CMHdr.png** image file in the Header pane. Change the width of the image to 2" and change the header position from the top to 0.3". Insert a footer with the page number at the bottom center of each page. Save, preview, and then close **3-Nwsltr-Define.docx**.

Part 3

You want to provide information for employees on designing newsletters and have a report on newsletter design that needs to be formatted into the APA style. Open **CM-DesignNwsltr.docx** and then save it with the name **3-CM-DesignNwsltr-APA**. Look at the information in Figure 3.10 (on page 110) and then insert the information as in-text journal article citations in the locations indicated in Steps 2 through 5 in Assessment 4. However, position the insertion point inside the period before inserting the citation. Add a reference page on a separate page at the end of the document. Center the title *References* and change the title to all uppercase letters. Select the entire document and change the font to 12-point Cambria. Apply any other formatting to follow APA guidelines. Save **3-CM-DesignNwsltr-APA.docx**.

Part 4

You want to include some additional information on newsletter guidelines. Using the internet, look for websites that provide information on desktop publishing and/or newsletter design. Include in the **3-CM-DesignNwsltr-APA.docx** report document at least one additional paragraph with information you found on the internet and include a citation for each source from which you have borrowed information. Save, preview, and then close the report.

WORD

CHAPTER 4

Creating Specialized Tables and Navigating in a Document

Performance Objectives

Upon successful completion of Chapter 4, you will be able to:

1 Insert a table of contents
2 Number the table of contents page
3 Navigate using a table of contents
4 Customize, update, or remove a table of contents
5 Assign levels to table of content entries
6 Mark table of contents entries as fields
7 Insert, update, or delete a table of figures
8 Create and customize captions for figures
9 Navigate in a document using the Navigation pane, bookmarks, hyperlinks, and cross-references
10 Insert hyperlinks to a location in the same document, a different document, a file in another program, or an email address

A book, textbook, report, or manuscript often includes sections such as a table of contents and a table of figures. Creating these sections manually can be tedious. However, using Word's automated features, these sections can be created quickly and easily. In this chapter, you will learn how to mark text for a table of contents and a table of figures and how to insert captions. You will also learn how to insert hyperlinks, bookmarks, and cross-references to allow for more efficient navigation within a document.

Data Files

The data files for this chapter are in the WL2C4 folder that you downloaded at the beginning of this course.

Activity 1 Create a Table of Contents for a Computer Interface Report — 2 Parts

You will open a report on computer interfaces, insert a section break, insert the table of contents in the document, and then number the table of contents page. You will also customize and update the table of contents.

Creating a Table of Contents

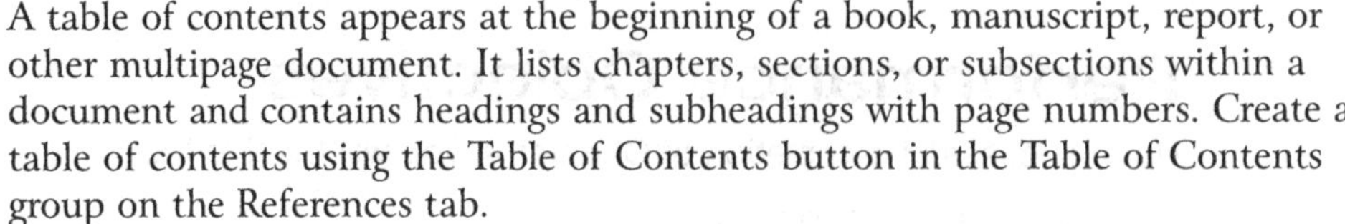

Table of Contents

A table of contents appears at the beginning of a book, manuscript, report, or other multipage document. It lists chapters, sections, or subsections within a document and contains headings and subheadings with page numbers. Create a table of contents using the Table of Contents button in the Table of Contents group on the References tab.

One method for identifying text to be included in a table of contents is to apply built-in heading styles. Apply built-in heading styles with options in the Styles group on the Home tab. Text with the Heading 1 style applied is used for the first level of the table of contents, text with the Heading 2 style applied is used for the second level, and so on.

Inserting a Table of Contents

Quick Steps

Insert Table of Contents

1. Apply heading styles.
2. Click References tab.
3. Click Table of Contents button.
4. Click option at drop-down list.

Inserting a Table of Contents

After applying styles to the headings, insert the table of contents in the document. To do this, position the insertion point at the beginning of the document where the table of contents is to appear, click the References tab, click the Table of Contents button, and then click the specific option at the drop-down list.

Page Number

Quick Steps

Number Table of Contents Page

1. Click Insert tab.
2. Click Page Number button.
3. Click *Format Page Numbers.*
4. Change number format to lowercase roman numerals.
5. Click OK.

Numbering the Table of Contents Page

Generally, the page or pages containing the table of contents are numbered with lowercase roman numerals (*i*, *ii*, *iii*). Format the page numbers as lowercase roman numerals at the Page Number Format dialog box, shown in Figure 4.1. Display this dialog box by clicking the Insert tab, clicking the Page Number button in the Header & Footer group, and then clicking *Format Page Numbers* at the drop-down list.

The first page of text in the main document, which usually comes immediately after the table of contents, should begin with arabic number 1. To change from roman to arabic page numbers within the same document, separate the table of contents from the first page of the document with a section break that begins a new page.

Figure 4.1 Page Number Format Dialog Box

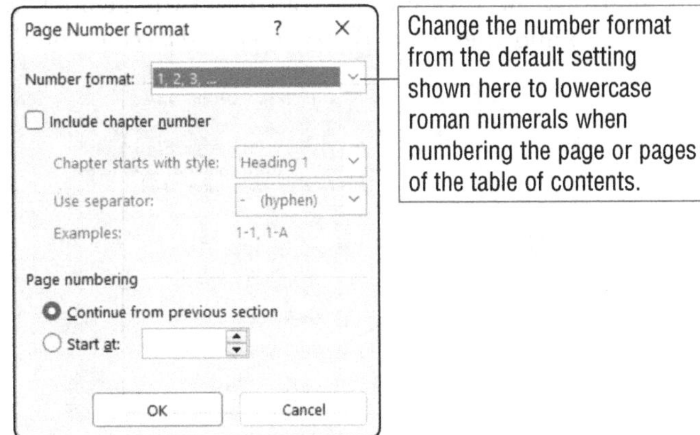

Navigating Using a Table of Contents

Hint You can use a table of contents to navigate quickly in a document and to get an overview of the topics it covers.

When a table of contents is inserted in a document, each entry automatically becomes a hyperlink that can be used to navigate within the document. To navigate in a document using the table of contents, click in the table of contents to select it. Position the pointer over an entry and a ScreenTip displays with the path and file name as well as the text *Ctrl+Click to follow link*. Press and hold down the Ctrl key, click the left mouse button, and then release the Ctrl key to go directly to the page where the content is located.

Activity 1a Inserting a Table of Contents — Part 1 of 2

1. Open **AIReport.docx** and then save it with the name **4-AIReport**. (This document contains headings with heading styles applied.)
2. Position the insertion point immediately left of the first *N* in *NATURAL INTERFACE* and then insert a section break by completing the following steps:
   a. Click the Layout tab.
   b. Click the Breaks button in the Page Setup group.
   c. Click the *Next Page* option in the *Section Breaks* section.
3. With the insertion point positioned immediately left of the *N* (and below the section break), insert page numbers and change the beginning number to *1* by completing the following steps:
   a. Click the Insert tab.
   b. Click the Page Number button in the Header & Footer group, point to *Bottom of Page*, and then click *Plain Number 2*.

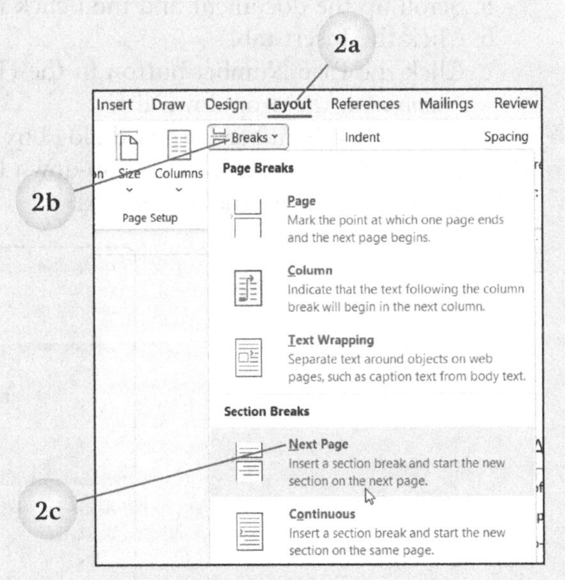

c. Click the Page Number button in the Header & Footer group on the Header & Footer tab and then click *Format Page Numbers* at the drop-down list.

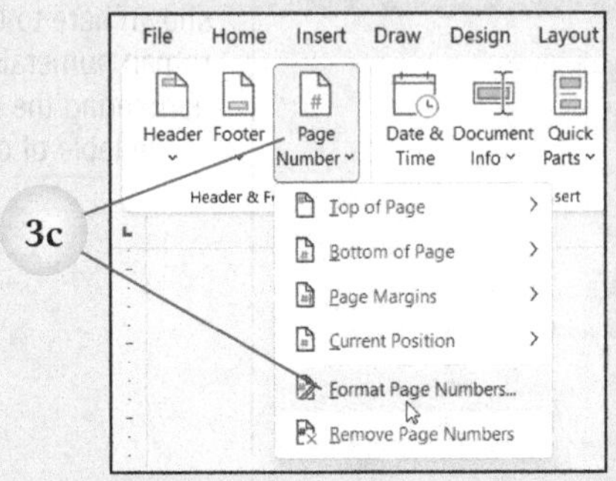

Page Number Format
Number format: 1, 2, 3, ...
Include chapter number
Chapter starts with style: Heading 1
Use separator: - (hyphen)
Examples: 1-1, 1-A
Page numbering
Continue from previous section
Start at: 1
OK
Cancel
3d
3e

d. At the Page Number Format dialog box, click *Start at* in the *Page numbering* section. (This inserts *1* in the *Start at* measurement box.)

e. Click OK to close the Page Number Format dialog box.

f. Click the Close Header and Footer button.

4. Insert a table of contents at the beginning of the document by completing the following steps:
   a. Press Ctrl + Home to move the insertion point to the beginning of the document.
   b. Click the References tab.
   c. Click the Table of Contents button in the Table of Contents group and then click the *Automatic Table 1* option in the *Built-In* section of the drop-down list.

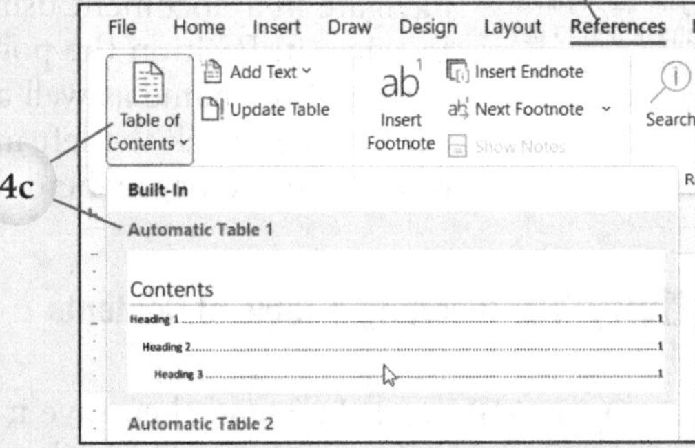

5. Modify the page number on the table of contents page by completing the following steps:
   a. Scroll up the document and then click in the heading *Contents*.
   b. Click the Insert tab.
   c. Click the Page Number button in the Header & Footer group and then click *Format Page Numbers* at the drop-down list.
   d. At the Page Number Format dialog box, click the *Number format* option box arrow and then click *i, ii, iii, …* at the drop-down list.
   e. Click OK to close the dialog box.

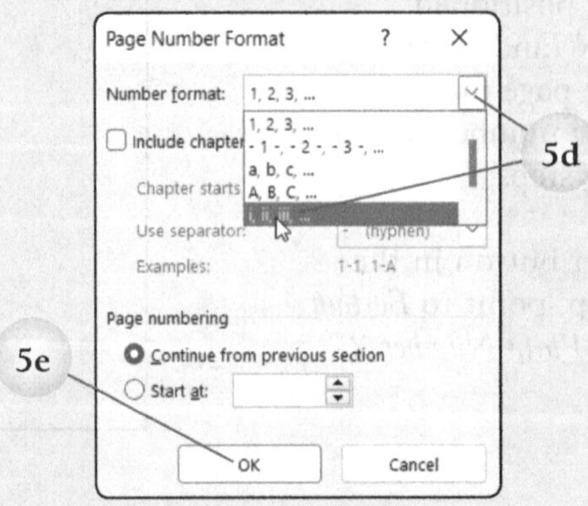

6. Navigate in the document using the table of contents by completing the following steps:
   a. Click in the table of contents.
   b. Position the pointer on the entry *Virtual Reality*, press and hold down the Ctrl key, click the left mouse button, and then release the Ctrl key. (This moves the insertion point to the beginning of the heading *Virtual Reality* in the document.)
   c. Press Ctrl + Home to move the insertion point to the beginning of the document.
7. Save and then preview **4-AIReport.docx**.

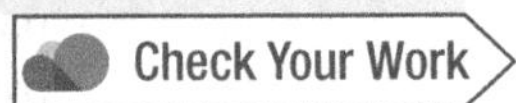

Customizing and Updating a Table of Contents

Customizing a Table of Contents

Customize an existing table of contents in a document with options at the Table of Contents dialog box, shown in Figure 4.2. Display this dialog box by clicking the Table of Contents button on the References tab and then clicking *Custom Table of Contents* at the drop-down list.

At the Table of Contents dialog box, a sample table of contents appears in the *Print Preview* section. Change the table of contents format by clicking the *Formats* option box arrow in the *General* section. At the drop-down list, click a format. When a different format is selected, that format displays in the *Print Preview* section.

Page numbers in a table of contents will display after the text or aligned at the right margin, depending on what option is selected. Page number alignment can also be specified with the *Right align page numbers* option. The possible number of levels in the contents list that appears in a table of contents depends on the number of heading levels in the document. Control the number of levels that display with the *Show levels* measurement box in the *General* section. Tab leaders help guide readers' eyes from the table of contents heading to the page number. The default tab leader is a period or dotted line leader. To choose a different leader, click the *Tab leader* option box arrow and then click to select a dotted line, dashed line, or solid underline at the drop-down list.

Figure 4.2 Table of Contents Dialog Box

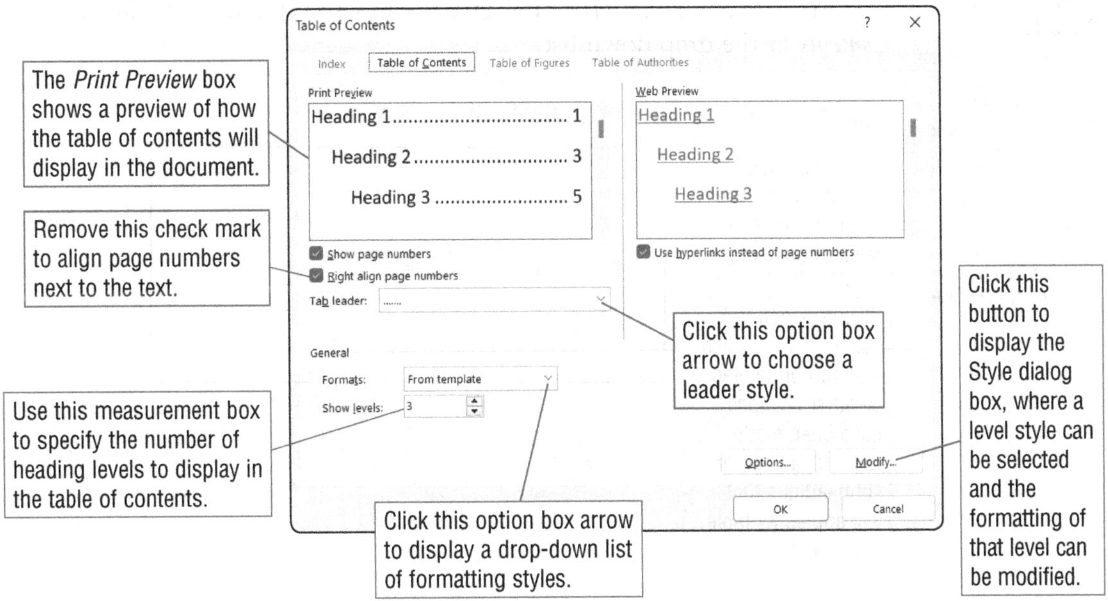

Word automatically formats the entries in a table of contents as hyperlinks and inserts page numbers. Each hyperlink can be used to move to a specific location in the document.

The *Use hyperlinks instead of page numbers* check box in the *Web Preview* section of the Table of Contents dialog box contains a check mark by default. With this option active, if the document is posted to the web, readers will only need to click the hyperlink to view specific content in the document. If the document is viewed in a web browser or the table of contents is used to navigate in the document, page numbers are not necessary and can be removed from the table of contents by removing the check mark from the *Show page numbers* check box at the Table of Contents dialog box.

If changes are made to the options at the Table of Contents dialog box, clicking OK will cause a message to display asking if the selected table of contents should be replaced. At this message, click Yes.

Updating a Table of Contents

Update Table

Quick Steps

Update Table of Contents

1. Click in table of contents.
2. Click References tab.
3. Click Update Table button, click Update Table tab, or press F9.
4. Click *Update page numbers only* or *Update entire table*.
5. Click OK.

Remove Table of Contents

1. Click References tab.
2. Click Table of Contents button.
3. Click *Remove Table of Contents*.

OR

1. Click in table of contents.
2. Click Table of Contents tab.
3. Click *Remove Table of Contents*.

If headings or other text in a document is deleted, moved, or edited after the table of contents is inserted, the table of contents will need to be updated. To do this, click in the current table of contents and then click the Update Table button in the Table of Contents group, click the Update Table tab, or press the F9 function key (the Update Field key). At the Update Table of Contents dialog box, shown in Figure 4.3, click *Update page numbers only* if changes were made that only affect page numbers or click *Update entire table* if changes were made to the headings or subheadings in the document. Click OK or press the Enter key to close the dialog box.

Removing a Table of Contents

Remove a table of contents from a document by clicking the Table of Contents button on the References tab and then clicking *Remove Table of Contents* at the drop-down list. Another way to remove a table of contents is to click in the table of contents, click the Table of Contents tab in the upper left corner of the table of contents (immediately left of the Update Table tab), and then click *Remove Table of Contents* at the drop-down list.

Figure 4.3 Update Table of Contents Dialog Box

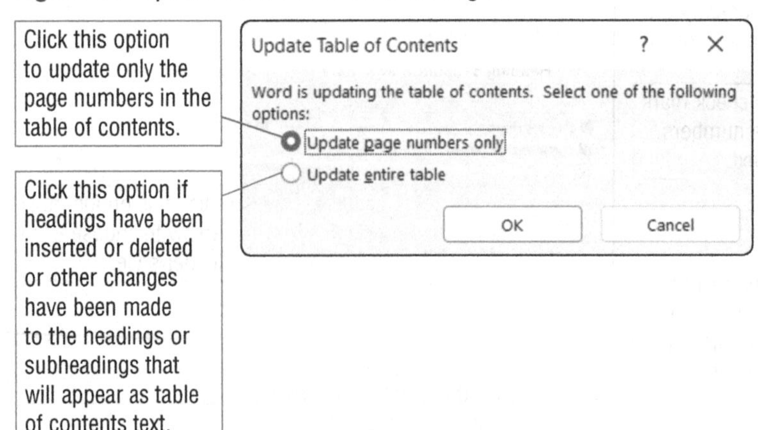
Click this option to update only the page numbers in the table of contents.
Click this option if headings have been inserted or deleted or other changes have been made to the headings or subheadings that will appear as table of contents text.
Update Table of Contents
?
Word is updating the table of contents. Select one of the following options:
Update page numbers only
Update entire table
OK
Cancel

Activity 1b Customizing and Updating a Table of Contents

Part 2 of 2

1. With **4-AIReport.docx** open and the insertion point positioned at the beginning of the document, apply a different formatting style to the table of contents by completing the following steps:
   a. Click the References tab, click the Table of Contents button, and then click *Custom Table of Contents* at the drop-down list.
   b. At the Table of Contents dialog box with the Table of Contents tab selected, click the *Formats* option box arrow in the *General* section and then click *Formal* at the drop-down list.
   c. Click the *Tab leader* option box arrow and then click the solid line option (bottom option) at the drop-down list.
   d. Click the *Show levels* measurement box down arrow to change the number to *2*.
   e. Click OK to close the dialog box.
   f. At the message asking if you want to replace the selected table of contents, click the Yes button.

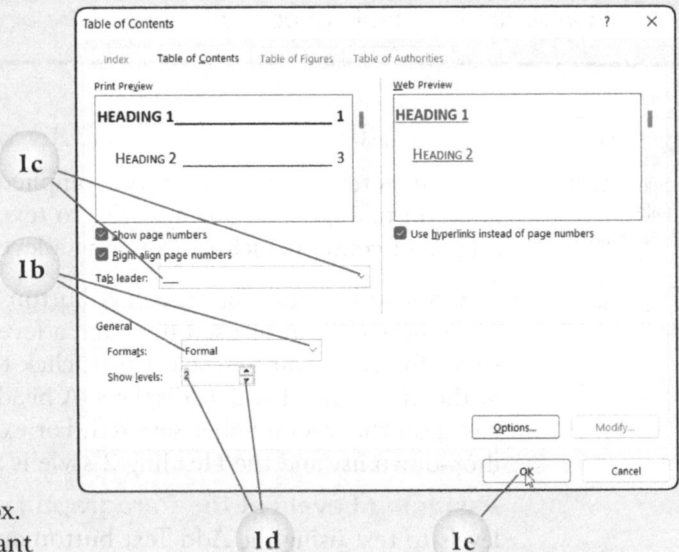

2. Use the table of contents to move the insertion point to the beginning of the heading *Audio Perception*.
3. Press Ctrl + Enter to insert a page break.
4. Update the table of contents by completing the following steps:
   a. Press Ctrl + Home and then click in the table of contents.
   b. Click the Update Table tab.
   c. At the Update Table of Contents dialog box, make sure *Update page numbers only* is selected and then click OK.

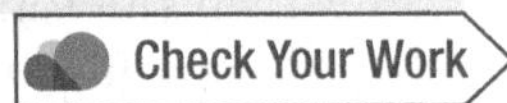

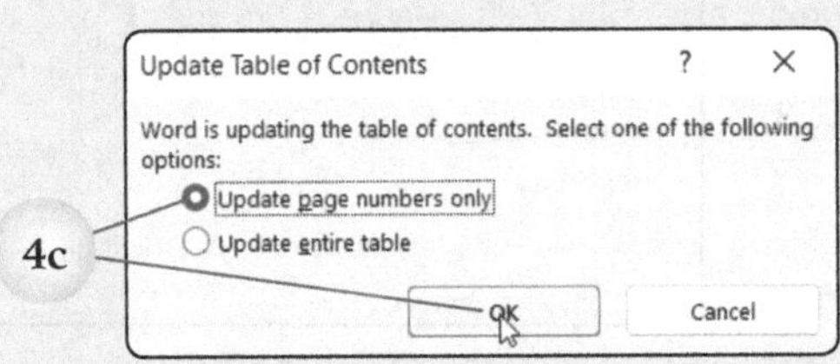

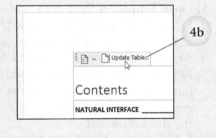

5. Save, preview, and then close **4-AIReport.docx**.

Check Your Work

Activity 2 Assign Levels, Mark Text, and Insert a Table of Contents in Company Documents

3 Parts

You will open documents that contain employee pay and evaluation information, mark text as table of contents fields, and then insert a table of contents. You will also insert a file containing additional information on employee classifications and then update the table of contents.

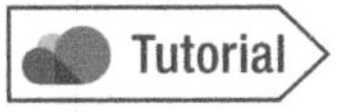

Assigning Levels for Table of Contents Entries

Assigning Levels for a Table of Contents

Word uses text with heading styles applied to create a table of contents. In addition to applying heading styles to text, other methods for identifying text for a table of contents include assigning a level to text and marking text as a field.

Assigning Levels The Add Text button in the Table of Contents group on the References tab can be used to assign a level to text, which also applies a heading style. To use the button, select text, click the button, and then click a specific level at the drop-down list that displays. A heading style is applied to the selected text based on the level number selected. For example, click the Level 2 option at the drop-down list and the Heading 2 style is applied to the selected text.

Assigning Levels at the Paragraph Dialog Box Applying styles or assigning levels to text using the Add Text button applies specific formatting. The *Outline level* option box at the Paragraph dialog box can be used to assign a level to text for a table of contents that does not apply a style. To use this option, select text, display the Paragraph dialog box, click the *Outline level* option box arrow, and then click the specific level at the drop-down list.

Activity 2a Assigning Levels to Text

Part 1 of 3

1. Open **EmployeeEval.docx** and then save it with the name **4-EmployeeEval.**
2. Select the title *EMPLOYEE MANUAL* at the beginning of the second page.
3. Assign a level to the title by clicking the References tab, clicking the Add Text button in the Table of Contents group, and then clicking *Level 1* at the drop-down list.

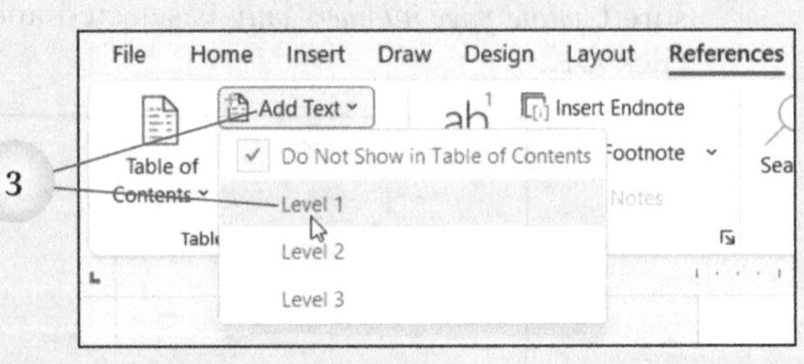

4. Select the heading *Evaluation* and then assign a level by completing the following steps:
   a. Click the Home tab.
   b. Click the Paragraph group dialog box launcher.
   c. At the Paragraph dialog box with the Indents and Spacing tab selected, click the *Outline level* option box arrow and then click *Level 2* at the drop-down list.
   d. Click OK.

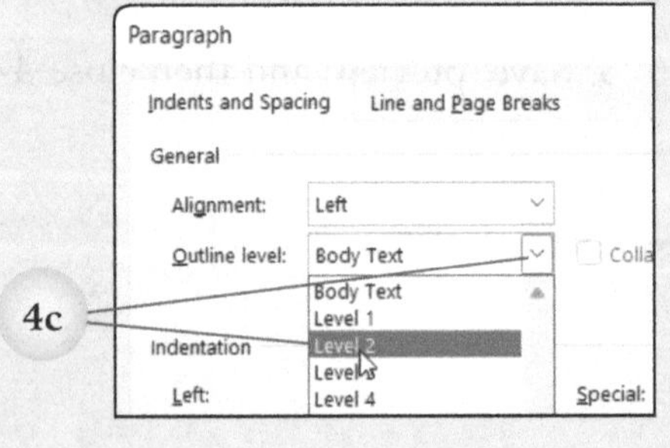

5. Complete steps similar to those in Step 4 to assign Level 3 to the subheadings *Performance Standards*, *Performance Evaluation*, and *Employee Records*.
6. Insert a page break at the beginning of the subheading *Employee Records*. (This heading and the text that follows should display on page 3.)
7. Move the insertion point to the beginning of the document (on the blank page) and then insert insert the Automatic Table 1 table of contents.
8. Save, preview, and then close **4-EmployeeEval.docx**.

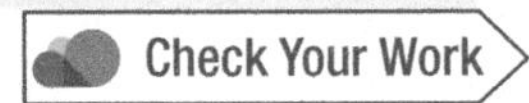

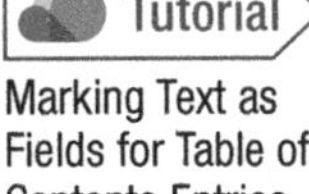

Marking Text as Fields for Table of Contents Entries

Marking Text as Fields Another method for identifying titles and/or headings for a table of contents without applying style formatting is to mark each title or heading as a field entry. To do this, select the text to be included in the table of contents and then press Alt + Shift + O. This displays the Mark Table of Contents Entry dialog box, shown in Figure 4.4. In the dialog box, the selected text displays in the *Entry* text box. Specify the text level using the *Level* measurement box and then click the Mark button. This turns on the display of nonprinting characters in the document and also inserts a field code immediately after the selected text.

For example, when the title is selected in Activity 2a, the following code is inserted immediately after the title *COMPENSATION*: { TC "COMPENSATION" \f C \l "1" }. The Mark Table of Contents Entry dialog box also remains open. To mark the next entry for the table of contents, select the text and then click the Title bar of the Mark Table of Contents Entry dialog box. Specify the level and then click the Mark button. Continue in this manner until all the table of contents entries have been marked.

The *Table identifier* option box at the Mark Table of Contents Entry dialog box has a default setting of *C*. (For a table of figures discussed later in this chapter, the table identifier is *F*.) To create more than one table of contents for a document, mark text with a specific table identifer and then use that identifer when inserting the table of contents.

If the table of contents entries are marked as fields, the *Table entry fields* option will need to be activated when inserting the table of contents. To do this, display the Table of Contents dialog box and then click the Options button. At the Table of Contents Options dialog box, shown in Figure 4.5, click the *Table entry fields* check box to insert a check mark and then click OK.

Figure 4.4 Mark Table of Contents Entry Dialog Box

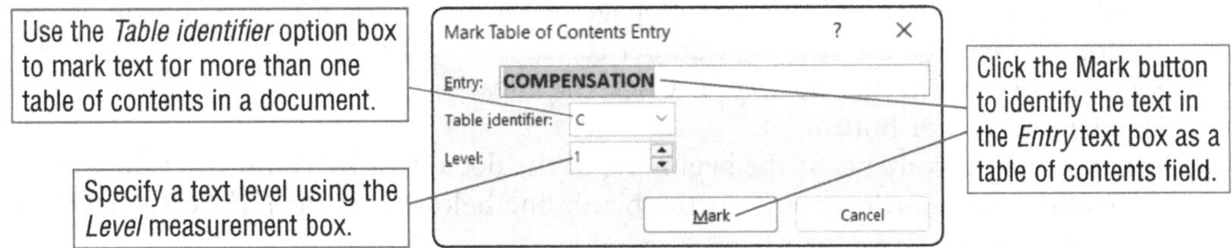

Figure 4.5 Table of Contents Options Dialog Box

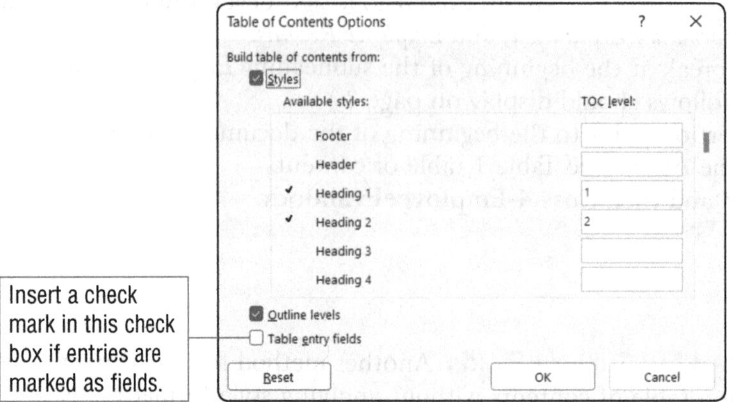

Activity 2b Marking Headings as Fields

Part 2 of 3

1. Open **EmployeeComp.docx** and then save it with the name **4-EmployeeComp**.
2. Mark the titles and headings as fields for insertion in a table of contents by completing the following steps:
   a. Select the title *COMPENSATION* (on the second page).
   b. Press Alt + Shift + O.
   c. At the Mark Table of Contents Entry dialog box, make sure the *Level* measurement box is set at *1* and then click the Mark button. (This turns on the display of nonprinting characters.)
   d. Click in the document and then select the heading *Rate of Pay*.
   e. Click the dialog box Title bar.
   f. Click the *Level* measurement box up arrow in the Mark Table of Contents Entry dialog box to display *2*.
   g. Click the Mark button.
   h. Mark the headings *Direct Deposit Options* and *Pay Progression* as level 2.
   i. Click the Close button to close the Mark Table of Contents Entry dialog box.

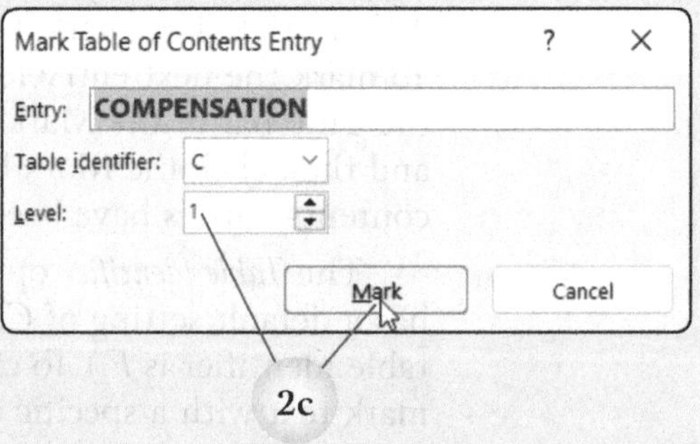

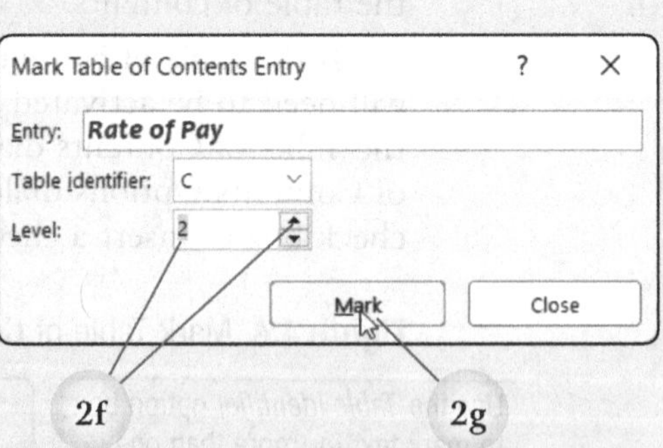

3. Position the insertion point at the beginning of the title *COMPENSATION*. Insert a page number at the bottom center of each page of the section and change the starting number to *1*. ***Hint: Refer to Activity 1a, Step 3.*** Click the Close Header and Footer button.
4. Insert a table of contents at the beginning of the document by completing the following steps:
   a. Position the insertion point on the blank line below the title *TABLE OF CONTENTS* on the first page.
   b. Click the References tab.
   c. Click the Table of Contents button and then click *Custom Table of Contents* at the drop-down list.
   d. At the Table of Contents dialog box, click the Options button.

e. At the Table of Contents Options dialog box, click the *Table entry fields* check box to insert a check mark.
f. Click OK to close the Table of Contents Options dialog box.
g. Click OK to close the Table of Contents dialog box.

5. Insert a lowercase roman numeral page number on the table of contents page. ***Hint: Refer to Activity 1a, Step 5.***
6. Click the Show/Hide ¶ button in the Paragraph group on the Home tab to turn off the display of nonprinting characters.
7. Save and then preview **4-EmployeeComp.docx**.

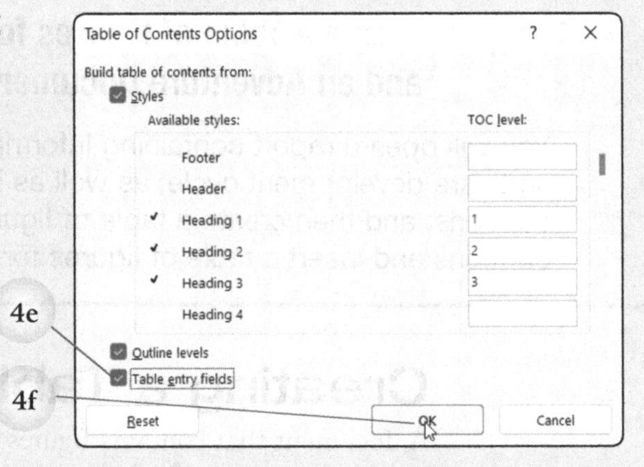

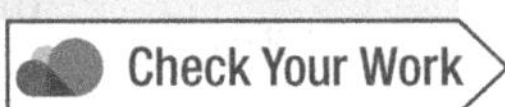

If additional information is inserted in a document with headings marked as fields, the table of contents can be easily updated. To do this, insert the text and then mark the text with options at the Mark Table of Contents Entry dialog box. Click in the table of contents and then click the Update Table tab. At the Update Table of Contents dialog box, click the *Update entire table* option and then click OK.

Activity 2c Updating an Entire Table of Contents

Part 3 of 3

1. With **4-EmployeeComp.docx** open, move the insertion point to the end of the document and then insert a file in the document by completing the following steps:
   a. Click the Insert tab.
   b. Click the Object button arrow in the Text group and then click *Text from File* at the drop-down list.
   c. At the Insert File dialog box, navigate to your WL2C4 folder and then double-click ***PosClass.docx***. (This document contains a title that has already been marked as a level 1 field.)

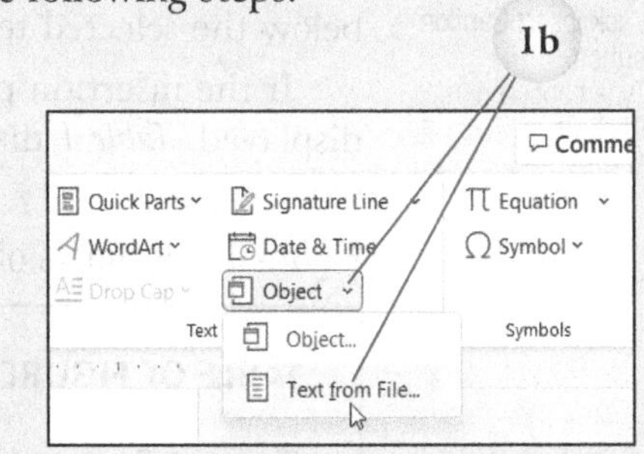

2. Update the table of contents by completing the following steps:
   a. Select the entire table of contents (excluding the title).
   b. Click the References tab.
   c. Click the Update Table button in the Table of Contents group.
   d. At the Update Table of Contents dialog box, click the *Update entire table* option.
   e. Click OK.
3. Save, preview, and then close **4-EmployeeComp.docx**.

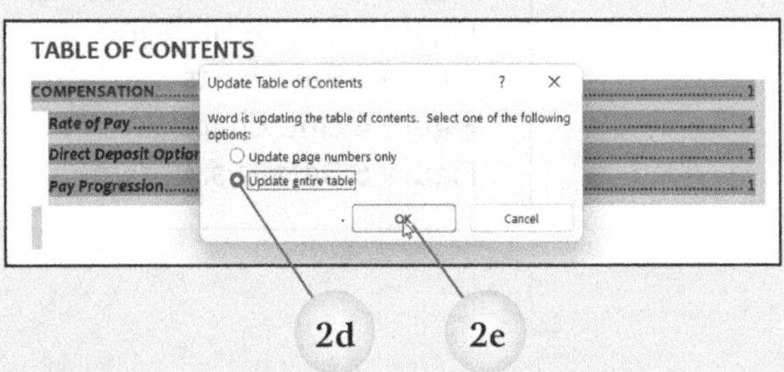

Check Your Work

Activity 3 Create a Table of Figures for a Technology Report and an Adventure Document

3 Parts

You will open a report containing information on software, output devices, and the software development cycle, as well as images and a SmartArt diagram; insert captions; and then create a table of figures. You will also create and customize captions and insert a table of figures for an adventure document.

Creating a Table of Figures

Insert Caption

Insert Table of Figures

A document that contains figures should include a table of figures so readers can quickly locate specific figures, images, tables, equations, and charts. Figure 4.6 shows an example of a table of figures. Create a table of figures by marking text or images with captions and then using the caption names to create the table. The Captions group on the References tab includes the Insert Caption button for creating captions and the Insert Table of Figures button for inserting a table of figures in a document.

Creating a Caption

Creating and Customizing Captions

Quick Steps

Create Caption

1. Select text or image.
2. Click References tab.
3. Click Insert Caption button.
4. Type caption name.
5. Click OK.

A caption is text that describes an item such as a figure, image, table, equation, or chart. The caption generally displays below the item. Create a caption by selecting the figure text or image, clicking the References tab, and then clicking the Insert Caption button in the Captions group. This displays the Caption dialog box, shown in Figure 4.7. At the dialog box, *Figure 1* displays in the *Caption* text box and the insertion point is positioned after *Figure 1*. Type a name for the figure and then press the Enter key. Word inserts *Figure 1* followed by the typed caption below the selected text or image.

If the insertion point is positioned in a table when the Caption dialog box is displayed, *Table 1* displays in the *Caption* text box instead of *Figure 1*.

Figure 4.6 Example of Table of Figures

TABLE OF FIGURES

Figure 4.7 Caption Dialog Box

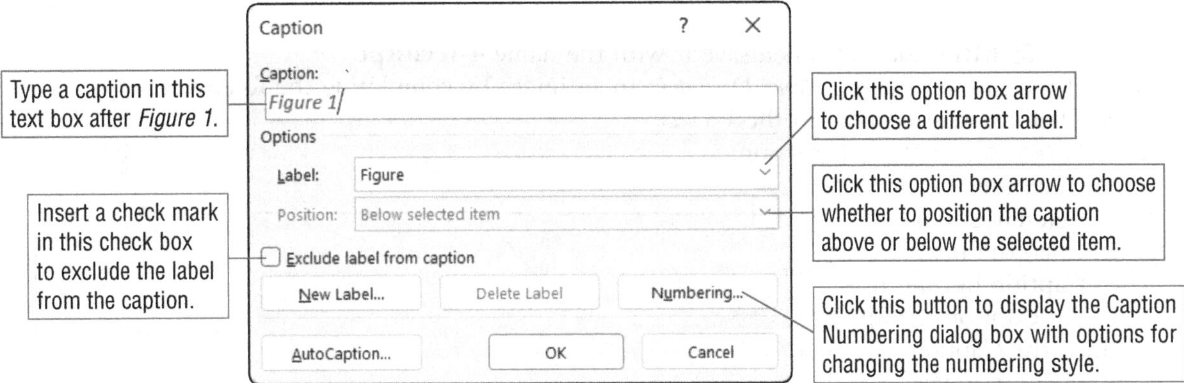

Inserting and Updating a Table of Figures

Quick Steps

Insert Table of Figures

1. Click References tab.
2. Click Insert Table of Figures button.
3. Select format.
4. Click OK.

Inserting a Table of Figures

After marking figures, images, tables, equations, and charts with captions in a document, insert the table of figures. A table of figures generally displays at the beginning of the document after the table of contents and on a separate page. To insert the table of figures, click the Insert Table of Figures button in the Captions group on the References tab. At the Table of Figures dialog box, shown in Figure 4.8, make any necessary changes and then click OK.

The options at the Table of Figures dialog box are similar to the options at the Table of Contents dialog box. They include choosing a format for the table of figures from the *Formats* option box, changing the alignment of the page numbers, and adding leaders before page numbers.

Figure 4.8 Table of Figures Dialog Box

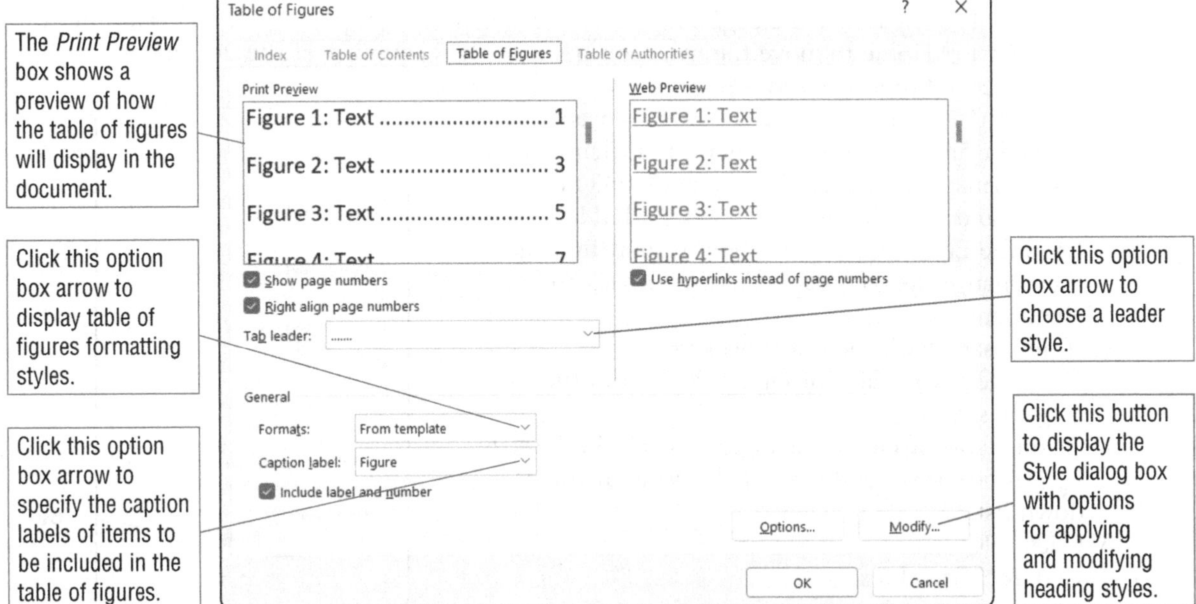

Activity 3a Creating a Table of Figures

Part 1 of 3

1. Open **TechRpt.docx** and then save it with the name **4-TechRpt**.
2. Add the caption *Figure 1 Word Document* to an image by completing the following steps:
   a. Click the screen image in the *Word Processing Software* section.
   b. Click the References tab.
   c. Click the Insert Caption button in the Captions group.
   d. At the Caption dialog box with the insertion point positioned after *Figure 1* in the *Caption* text box, press the spacebar and then type Word Document.
   e. Click OK or press the Enter key.
   f. Press Ctrl + E to center the caption in the text box.

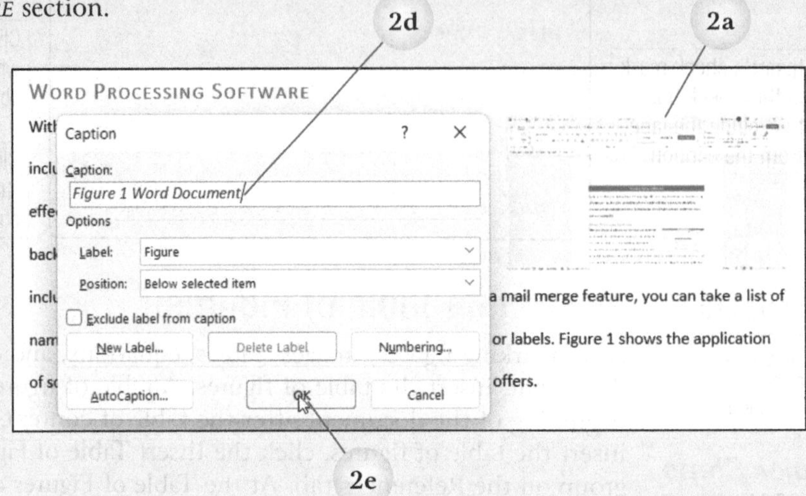

3. Complete steps similar to those in Step 2 to create and center the caption *Figure 2 Excel Worksheet* for the image in the *Spreadsheet Software* section.
4. Complete steps similar to those in Step 2 to create and center the caption *Figure 3 Monitor* for the image in the *Monitor* section.
5. Complete steps similar to those in Step 2 to create and center the caption *Figure 4 Software Life Cycle* for the SmartArt graphic in the *Developing Software* section.
6. Insert a table of figures at the beginning of the document by completing the following steps:
   a. Press Ctrl + Home to move the insertion point to the beginning of the document.
   b. Press Ctrl + Enter to insert a page break.
   c. Press Ctrl + Home to move the insertion point back to the beginning of the document and then turn on bold formatting, change the paragraph alignment to center, and type the title TABLE OF FIGURES.
   d. Press the Enter key, turn off bold formatting, and then change the paragraph alignment back to left alignment.
   e. If necessary, click the References tab.
   f. Click the Insert Table of Figures button in the Captions group.
   g. At the Table of Figures dialog box, click the *Formats* option box arrow and then click *Formal* at the drop-down list.
   h. Click OK.
7. Save **4-TechRpt.docx**.

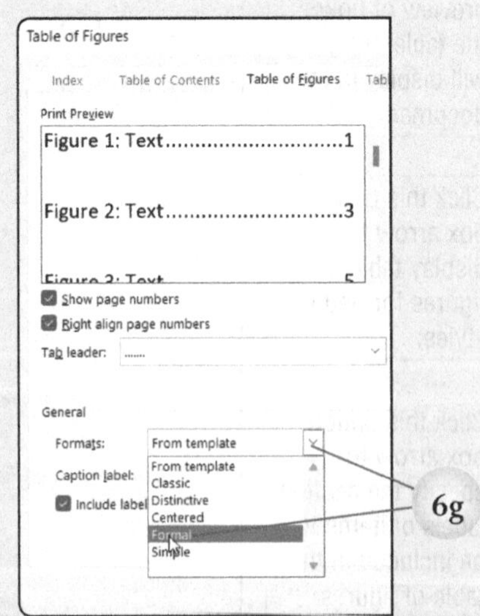

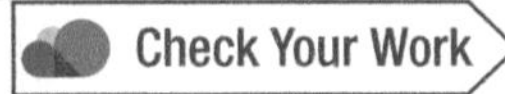

Updating or Deleting a Table of Figures

Quick Steps

Update Table of Figures
1. Click in table of figures.
2. Click References tab.
3. Click Update Table button or press F9.
4. Click OK.

Delete Table of Figures
1. Select entire table.
2. Press Delete key.

If changes are made to a document after a table of figures is inserted, update the table. To do this, click in the table of figures and then click the Update Table button in the Captions group on the References tab or press the F9 function key. At the Update Table of Figures dialog box, click *Update page numbers only* if changes were made only to the page numbers or click *Update entire table* if changes were made to the caption text. Click OK or press the Enter key to close the dialog box. To delete a table of figures, select the entire table using the mouse or keyboard and then press the Delete key.

Activity 3b Updating a Table of Figures — Part 2 of 3

1. With **4-TechRpt.docx** open, insert an image of a laser printer by completing the following steps:
   a. Move the insertion point to the beginning of the second paragraph of text in the *PRINTERS* section.
   b. Click the Insert tab, click the Pictures button in the Illustrations group, and then click *This Device* at the drop-down list.
   c. At the Insert Picture dialog box, navigate to your WL2C4 folder and then double-click the image file ***LaserPrinter.png***.
   d. Change the height of the image to 1.5".
   e. Change to square text wrapping.
2. Add the caption *Figure 4 Laser Printer* to the printer image and then center the caption.
3. Click in the table of figures.
4. Press the F9 function key.
5. At the Update Table of Figures dialog box, click the *Update entire table* option and then click OK.
6. Save, preview, and then close **4-TechRpt.docx**.

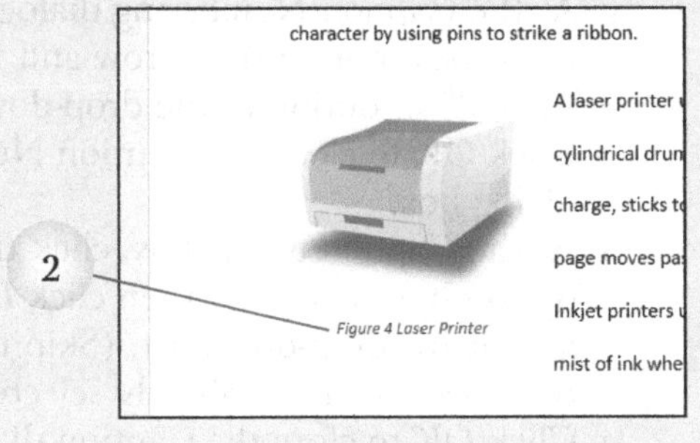

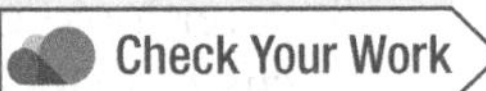

Check Your Work

Customizing a Caption

The Caption dialog box contains a number of options for customizing captions. These are shown in Figure 4.7 (on page 127). Click the *Label* option box arrow to specify the caption label. The default is *Figure*; it can be changed to *Equation* or *Table*. The caption is positioned below the selected item by default. Use the *Position* option to change the default position of the caption so it is above the selected item. A caption contains a label, such as *Figure*, *Table*, or *Equation*. To insert only a caption number and not a caption label, insert a check mark in the *Exclude label from caption* check box.

Click the New Label button and the Label dialog box displays. At this dialog box, type a custom label for the caption. Word automatically inserts an arabic number (*1, 2, 3,* and so on) after each caption label. To change the caption numbering style, click the Numbering button. At the Caption Numbering dialog box, click the *Format* option box arrow and then click a numbering style at the drop-down list. For example, caption numbering can be changed to uppercase or lowercase letters or to roman numerals.

If items such as tables are inserted in a document on a regular basis, captions can be inserted automatically with these items. To do this, click the AutoCaption button. At the AutoCaption dialog box, insert a check mark before the item (such as *Microsoft Word Table*) in the *Add caption when inserting* list box and then click OK. Each time a table is inserted in a document, Word inserts a caption above it.

Activity 3c Creating and Customizing Captions and Inserting a Table of Figures — Part 3 of 3

1. Open **BEA-ZA-Advs.docx** and then save it with the name **4-BEA-ZA-Advs**.
2. Insert a custom caption for the first table by completing the following steps:
   a. Click in any cell in the table.
   b. Click the References tab.
   c. Click the Insert Caption button in the Captions group.
   d. At the Caption dialog box, press the spacebar and then type Antarctic Zenith Adventures in the *Caption* text box.
   e. Remove the label (*Figure*) from the caption by clicking the *Exclude label from caption* check box to insert a check mark.
   f. Click the Numbering button.
   g. At the Caption Numbering dialog box, click the *Format* option box arrow and then click the *A, B, C, …* option at the drop-down list.
   h. Click OK to close the Caption Numbering dialog box.
   i. At the Caption dialog box, click the *Position* option box arrow and then click *Below selected item* at the drop-down list. (Skip this step if *Below selected item* is already selected.)
   j. Click OK to close the Caption dialog box.

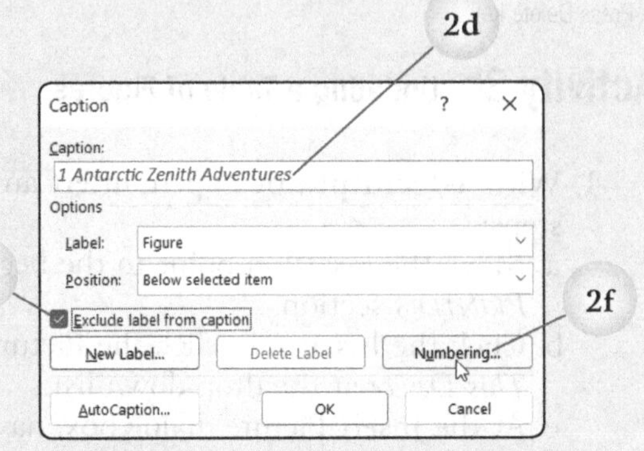

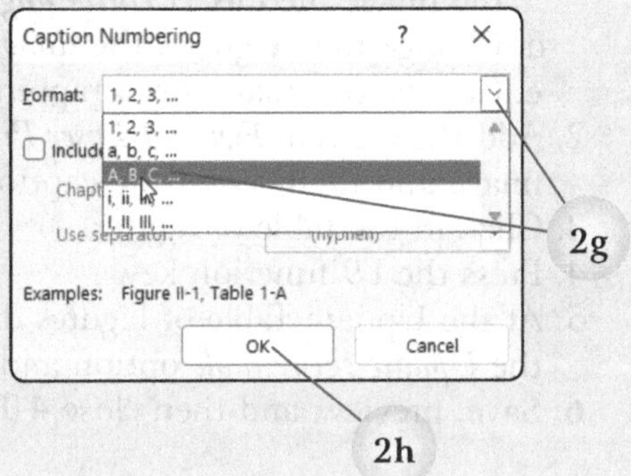

3. After looking at the caption, you decide to add a custom label and change the numbering. Do this by completing the following steps:
   a. Select the caption *A Antarctic Zenith Adventures*.
   b. Click the Insert Caption button.
   c. At the Caption dialog box, click the *Exclude label from caption* check box to remove the check mark.
   d. Click the New Label button.
   e. At the New Label dialog box, type Adventure and then click OK.
   f. Click OK to close the Caption dialog box.

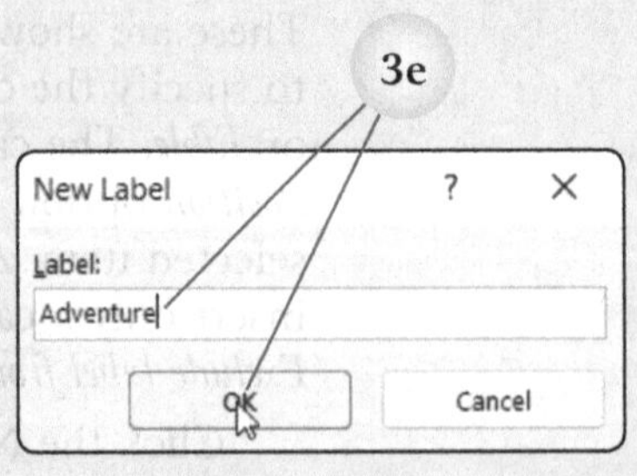

4. Format the caption by completing the following steps:
   a. Select the caption *Adventure 1 Antarctic Zenith Adventures*.
   b. Click the Home tab.
   c. Click the Font Color button arrow.
   d. Click the *Dark Blue* option (ninth color in the *Standard Colors* section).
   e. Click the Bold button.

5. Insert a custom caption for the second table by completing the following steps:
   a. Click in the second table.
   b. Click the References tab and then click the Insert Caption button.
   c. At the Caption dialog box, press the spacebar and then type Bicycle Adventures.
   d. Make sure *Below selected item* appears in the *Position* option box and then click OK to close the Caption dialog box.
6. Select the caption *Adventure 2 Bicycle Adventures,* apply the Dark Blue font color, and then apply bold formatting.
7. Insert a table of figures by completing the following steps:
   a. Press Ctrl + Home and then press Ctrl + Enter to insert a page break.
   b. Press Ctrl + Home to move the insertion point above the page break.
   c. Turn on bold formatting, type TABLES, turn off bold formatting, and then press the Enter key.
   d. Click the References tab and then click the Insert Table of Figures button in the Captions group.
   e. At the Table of Figures dialog box, click OK.
8. Save, preview, and then close **4-BEA-ZA-Advs.docx**.

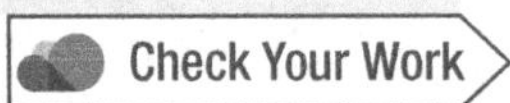

Activity 4 Navigate in a Computer Security and Viruses Report — 6 Parts

You will open a report on computer security and computer viruses, navigate using the Navigation pane, and then insert and navigate using bookmarks, hyperlinks, and cross-references.

Navigating in a Document

Word provides a number of features for navigating in a document. Navigate in a document using the Navigation pane or using bookmarks, hyperlinks, or cross-references.

Navigating Using the Navigation Pane

Quick Steps

Display Navigation Pane
1. Click View tab.
2. Click *Navigation Pane* check box.

Navigating Using the Navigation Pane

The Navigation pane can be used to navigate in a document by clicking the View tab and then clicking the *Navigation Pane* check box in the Show group to insert a check mark. The Navigation pane displays at the left side of the screen and includes a search text box and three tabs.

Click the first tab, Headings, and titles and headings with certain styles applied display in the Navigation pane. Click a title or heading and the insertion point moves to it. Click the Pages tab and a thumbnail of each page displays in the pane. Click a thumbnail to move the insertion point to that specific page. Click the Results tab to browse the current search results in the document.

Close the Navigation pane by clicking the *Navigation Pane* check box in the Show group on the View tab to remove the check mark. Another option is to click the Close button in the upper right corner of the pane.

Activity 4a Navigating Using the Navigation Pane

Part 1 of 6

1. Open **Security.docx** and then save it with the name **4-Security**.
2. Since this document has heading styles applied, you can easily navigate in it with the Navigation pane by completing the following steps:
   a. Click the View tab.
   b. Click the *Navigation Pane* check box in the Show group to insert a check mark. (This displays the Navigation pane at the left side of the screen.)
   c. With the Headings tab active, click the heading *CHAPTER 2: INFORMATION THEFT* in the Navigation pane.
   d. Click *CHAPTER 3: COMPUTER VIRUSES* in the Navigation pane.
   e. Click *Systems Failure* in the Navigation pane.

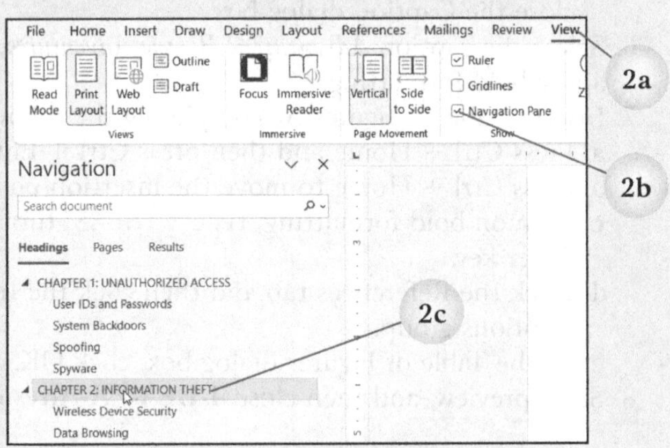

3. Navigate in the document using thumbnails by completing the following steps:
   a. Click the Pages tab in the Navigation pane. (This displays thumbnails of the pages in the pane.)
   b. Click the page 1 thumbnail in the Navigation pane. (You may need to scroll up the Navigation pane to display this thumbnail.)
   c. Click the page 3 thumbnail in the Navigation pane.
4. Close the Navigation pane by clicking the Close button in the upper right corner.
5. Save **4-Security.docx**.

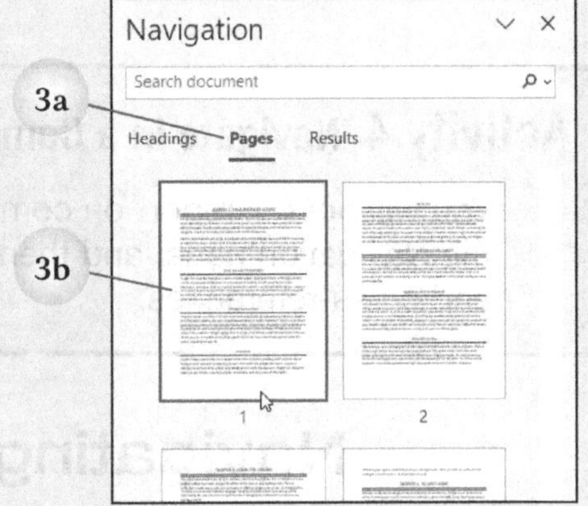

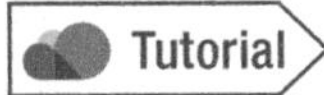

Inserting and Navigating with Bookmarks

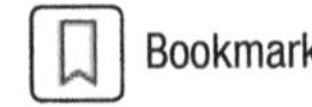

Quick Steps

Insert Bookmark

1. Position insertion point at specific location.
2. Click Insert tab.
3. Click Bookmark button.
4. Type name for bookmark.
5. Click Add button.

Inserting and Navigating with Bookmarks

When working in a long document, marking a place in it with a bookmark may be useful for moving the insertion point to that specific location. Create bookmarks for locations in a document at the Bookmark dialog box.

To create a bookmark, position the insertion point at the specific location, click the Insert tab, and then click the Bookmark button in the Links group. This displays the Bookmark dialog box, as shown in Figure 4.9. Type a name for the bookmark in the *Bookmark name* text box and then click the Add button. Repeat these steps as many times as needed to insert additional bookmarks.

Give each bookmark a unique name. A bookmark name must begin with a letter and can contain numbers but not spaces. To separate words in a bookmark name, use the underscore character.

By default, the bookmarks inserted in a document are not visible. Turn on the display of bookmarks at the Word Options dialog box with *Advanced* selected. Display this dialog box by clicking the File tab and then clicking *Options*. At the Word Options dialog box, click *Advanced* in the left panel. Click the *Show bookmarks*

Figure 4.9 Bookmark Dialog Box

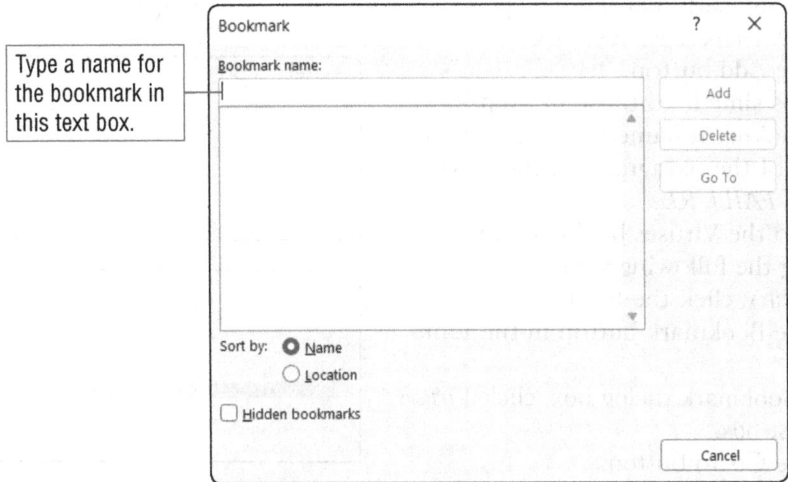

check box in the *Show document content* section to insert a check mark. Complete similar steps to turn off the display of bookmarks. A bookmark displays in the document as an I-beam marker.

Hint Bookmark brackets do not print.

A bookmark can be created for selected text. To do this, first select the text and then complete the steps to create a bookmark. A bookmark created with selected text displays a left bracket ([) indicating the beginning of the selected text and a right bracket (]) indicating the end of the selected text.

Quick Steps

Navigate with Bookmarks

1. Click Insert tab.
2. Click Bookmark button.
3. Double-click bookmark name.

Navigate in a document by moving the insertion point to a specific bookmark. To do this, display the Bookmark dialog box and then double-click the bookmark name or click the bookmark name and then click the Go To button. When Word stops at the location of the bookmark, click the Close button to close the dialog box. When moving to a bookmark created with selected text, Word moves the insertion point to the bookmark and then selects the text. Delete a bookmark in the Bookmark dialog box by clicking the bookmark name in the list box and then clicking the Delete button.

Activity 4b Inserting and Navigating with Bookmarks

Part 2 of 6

1. With **4-Security.docx** open, turn on the display of bookmarks by completing the following steps:
   a. Click the File tab and then click *Options*.
   b. At the Word Options dialog box, click *Advanced* in the left panel.
   c. Scroll down the dialog box and then click the *Show bookmarks* check box in the *Show document content* section to insert a check mark.
   d. Click OK to close the dialog box.
2. Insert a bookmark by completing the following steps:
   a. Move the insertion point to the beginning of the paragraph in the section *TYPES OF VIRUSES* (the paragraph that begins *Security experts categorize*).
   b. Click the Insert tab.
   c. Click the Bookmark button in the Links group.

d. At the Bookmark dialog box, type Viruses in the *Bookmark name* text box.
e. Click the Add button.

3. Using steps similar to those in Step 2, insert a bookmark named *Electrical* at the beginning of the paragraph in the section *SYSTEMS FAILURE*.
4. Navigate to the Viruses bookmark by completing the following steps:
   a. If necessary, click the Insert tab.
   b. Click the Bookmark button in the Links group.
   c. At the Bookmark dialog box, click *Viruses* in the list box.
   d. Click the Go To button.
5. With the Bookmark dialog box open, delete the Electrical bookmark by clicking *Electrical* in the list box and then clicking the Delete button.
6. Click the Close button to close the Bookmark dialog box.
7. Save **4-Security.docx**.

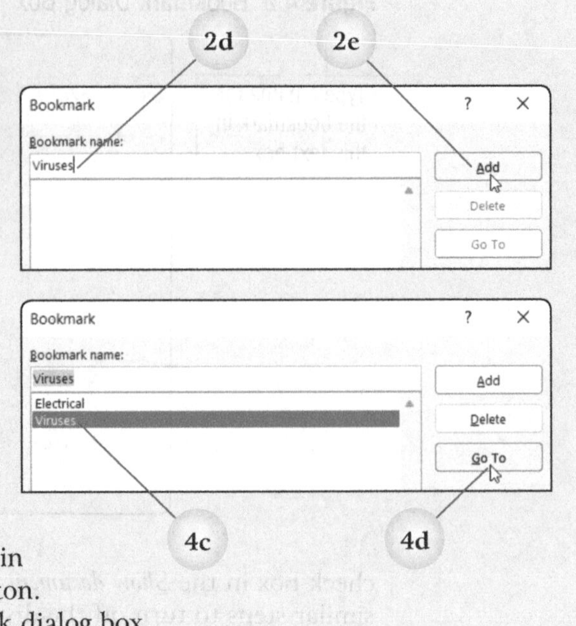

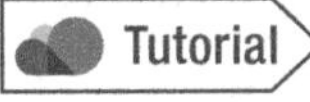

Inserting and Editing a Hyperlink

Inserting Hyperlinks

Hyperlinks can serve a number of purposes in a document. A hyperlink can be used to navigate to a specific location in a document, to display a different document, to open a file in a different program, to create a new document, and to link to an email address.

Insert a hyperlink by clicking the Link button in the Links group on the Insert tab. This displays the Insert Hyperlink dialog box, as shown in Figure 4.10. This dialog box can also be displayed by pressing Ctrl + K. At the Insert Hyperlink dialog box, identify what to link to and where to find the link. Click the ScreenTip button to customize the ScreenTip for the hyperlink.

Quick Steps

Insert Hyperlink

1. Click Insert tab.
2. Click Link button.
3. Make changes at Insert Hyperlink dialog box.
4. Click OK.

Figure 4.10 Insert Hyperlink Dialog Box

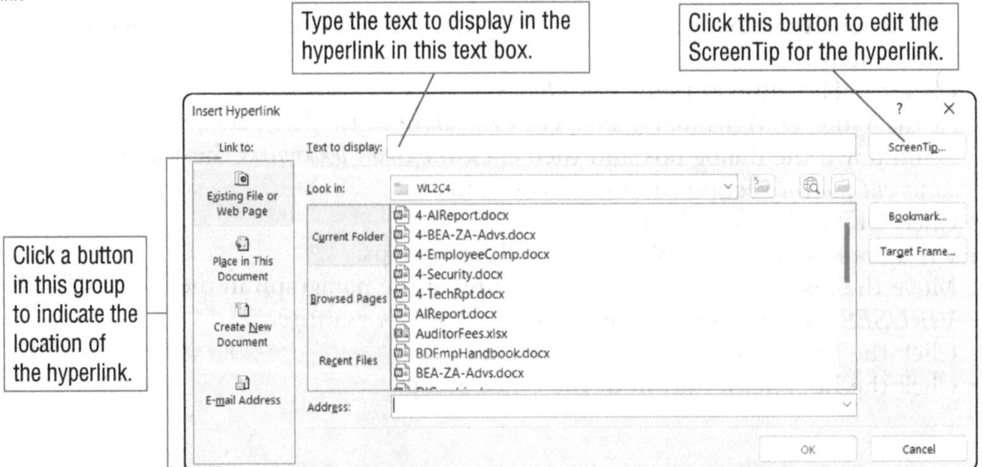

Linking to a Place in the Document To create a hyperlink to another location in the document, first mark the location by applying a heading style to the text or inserting a bookmark. To hyperlink to that heading or bookmark, display the Insert Hyperlink dialog box and then click the Place in This Document button in the *Link to* section. This displays text with heading styles applied and bookmarks in the *Select a place in this document* list box. Click the heading style or bookmark name and the heading or bookmark name displays in the *Text to display* text box. Leave the text as displayed or select the text and then type the text that will appear in the document.

Navigating Using Hyperlinks Navigate to a hyperlink by hovering the pointer over the hyperlink text, pressing and holding down the Ctrl key, clicking the left mouse button, and then releasing the Ctrl key. When hovering the pointer over the hyperlink text, a ScreenTip displays with the name of the heading or bookmark. To display specific information in the ScreenTip, click the ScreenTip button in the Insert Hyperlink dialog box, type the text in the Set Hyperlink ScreenTip dialog box, and then click OK.

Activity 4c Inserting and Navigating with Hyperlinks — Part 3 of 6

1. With **4-Security.docx** open, insert a hyperlink to a bookmark in the document by completing the following steps:
   a. Position the insertion point at the immediate right of the period that ends the first paragraph of text in the section *CHAPTER 4: SECURITY RISKS* (on page 4).
   b. Press the spacebar.
   c. If necessary, click the Insert tab.
   d. Click the Link button in the Links group.
   e. At the Insert Hyperlink dialog box, click the Place in This Document button in the *Link to* section.
   f. Scroll down the *Select a place in this document* list box and then click *Viruses,* which displays below *Bookmarks* in the list box.
   g. Select the text in the *Text to display* text box and then type Click to view types of viruses.
   h. Click the ScreenTip button in the upper right corner of the dialog box.
   i. At the Set Hyperlink ScreenTip dialog box, type View types of viruses and then click OK.
   j. Click OK to close the Insert Hyperlink dialog box.
2. Navigate to the hyperlinked location by hovering the pointer over the Click to view types of viruses hyperlink, pressing and holding down the Ctrl key, clicking the left mouse button, and then releasing the Ctrl key.

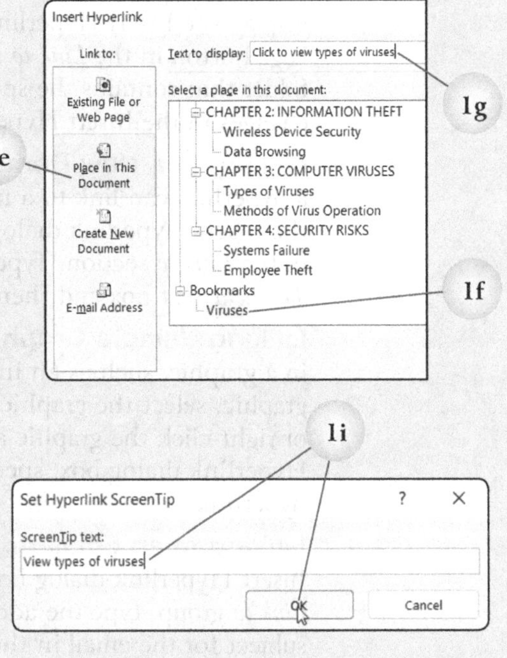

3. Insert a hyperlink to a heading in the document by completing the following steps:
   a. Press Ctrl + Home to move the insertion point to the beginning of the document.
   b. Move the insertion point to the immediate right of the period that ends the second paragraph in the document and then press the spacebar.
   c. Click the Link button on the Insert tab.
   d. At the Insert Hyperlink dialog box with the Place in This Document button active in the *Link to* section, click the *Methods of Virus Operation* heading in the *Select a place in this document* list box.
   e. Click OK to close the Insert Hyperlink dialog box.
4. Navigate to the hyperlinked heading by hovering the pointer over the Methods of Virus Operation hyperlink, pressing and holding down the Ctrl key, clicking the left mouse button, and then releasing the Ctrl key.
5. Save **4-Security.docx**.

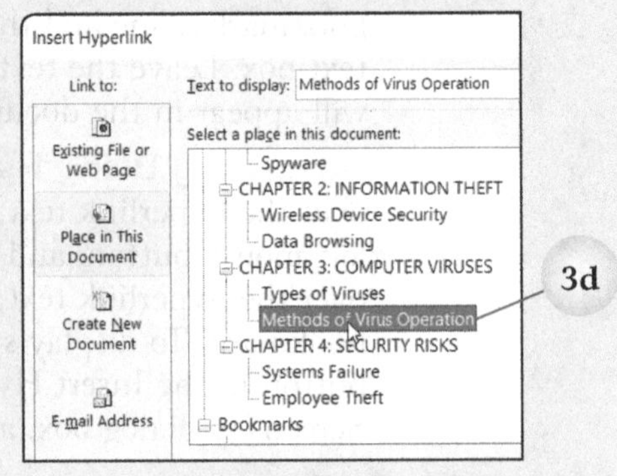

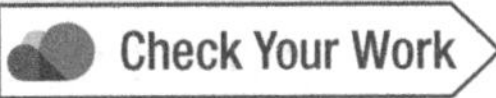

Linking to a File in Another Application A hyperlink can be inserted in a document that links to another Word document, an Excel worksheet, or a PowerPoint presentation. To link a Word document to a file in another application, display the Insert Hyperlink dialog box and then click the Existing File or Web Page button in the *Link to* section. Use the *Look in* option box to navigate to the folder that contains the specific file and then click the file name. Make other changes in the Insert Hyperlink dialog box as needed and then click OK.

Linking to a New Document In addition to linking to an existing document, a hyperlink can link to a new document. To insert this kind of hyperlink, display the Insert Hyperlink dialog box and then click the Create New Document button in the *Link to* section. Type a name for the new document in the *Name of new document* text box and then specify if the document will be edited now or later.

Linking Using a Graphic A hyperlink to a file or website can be inserted in a graphic, such as an image, table, or text box. To create a hyperlink with a graphic, select the graphic, click the Insert tab, and then click the Link button or right-click the graphic and then click *Link* at the shortcut menu. At the Insert Hyperlink dialog box, specify where to link to and what text to display in the hyperlink.

Linking to an Email Address Insert a hyperlink to an email address at the Insert Hyperlink dialog box. To do this, click the E-Mail Address button in the *Link to* group, type the address in the *E-mail address* text box, and then type a subject for the email in the *Subject* text box. Click in the *Text to display* text box and then type the text to display in the document. To use this feature, the email address must be set up in Outlook.

Activity 4d Inserting a Hyperlink to Another Program, to a New Document, and Using a Graphic

Part 4 of 6

1. The **4-Security.docx** document contains information used by Northland Security Systems. The company also has a PowerPoint presentation that contains similar information. Link the document with the presentation by completing the following steps:
   a. Move the insertion point to the immediate right of the period that ends the first paragraph in the section *CHAPTER 3: COMPUTER VIRUSES* and then press the spacebar.
   b. If necessary, click the Insert tab.
   c. Click the Link button in the Links group.
   d. At the Insert Hyperlink dialog box, click the Existing File or Web Page button in the *Link to* section.
   e. Click the *Look in* option box arrow. At the drop-down list that displays, navigate to your WL2C4 folder and then click the folder.
   f. Click the ***NSSPres.pptx*** PowerPoint file in the list box.
   g. Select the text in the *Text to display* text box and then type Computer Virus Presentation.
   h. Click OK to close the Insert Hyperlink dialog box.

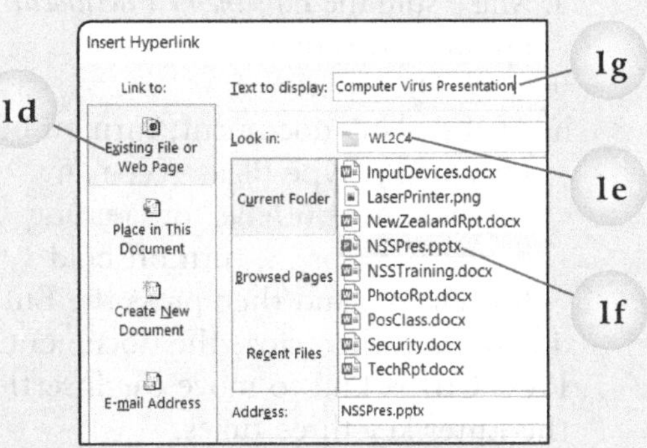

2. View the PowerPoint presentation by completing the following steps:
   a. Position the pointer over the Computer Virus Presentation hyperlink, press and hold down the Ctrl key, click the left mouse button, and then release the Ctrl key.
   b. At the PowerPoint presentation, click the Slide Show button in the view area on the Status bar.
   c. Click the left mouse button to advance each slide.
   d. Click the left mouse button at the black screen that displays the message *End of slide show, click to exit*.
   e. Close the presentation and PowerPoint by clicking the Close button (which contains an *X*) in the upper right corner of the screen.
3. Insert a hyperlink with a graphic by completing the following steps:
   a. Press Ctrl + End to move the insertion point to the end of the document.
   b. Click the compass image to select it.
   c. Click the Link button on the Insert tab.
   d. At the Insert Hyperlink dialog box, make sure the Existing File or Web Page button is active in the *Link to* section.
   e. Navigate to your WL2C4 folder and then double-click ***NSSTraining.docx***. (This selects the document name and closes the dialog box.)
   f. Click outside the compass image to deselect it.
4. Navigate to **NSSTraining.docx** by hovering the pointer over the compass image, pressing and holding down the Ctrl key, clicking the left mouse button, and then releasing the Ctrl key.
5. Close the document by clicking the File tab and then clicking the *Close* option.

6. Insert a hyperlink to a new document by completing the following steps:
   a. Move the insertion point to the immediate right of the period that ends the paragraph in the section *USER IDS AND PASSWORDS* and then press the spacebar.
   b. Click the Link button on the Insert tab.
   c. Click the Create New Document button in the *Link to* section.
   d. In the *Name of new document* text box, type 4-PasswordSuggestions.
   e. Edit the text in the *Text to display* text box so it displays as *Password Suggestions*.
   f. Make sure the *Edit the new document now* option is selected.
   g. Click OK.
   h. At the blank document, turn on bold formatting, type Please type any suggestions you have for creating secure passwords:, turn off bold formatting, and then press the Enter key.
   i. Save and then close the document.
7. Press Ctrl + End to move the insertion point to the end of the document and then press the Enter key three times.
8. Insert a hyperlink to your email address or your instructor's email address by completing the following steps:
   a. Click the Link button.
   b. At the Insert Hyperlink dialog box, click the E-mail Address button in the *Link to* section.
   c. Type your email address or your instructor's email address in the *E-mail address* text box.
   d. Select the current text in the *Text to display* text box and then type Click to send an email.
   e. Click OK to close the dialog box.

   Optional:* *If you have Outlook set up, press and hold down the Ctrl key, click the Click to send an email hyperlink, release the Ctrl key, and then send a message indicating that you have completed inserting hyperlinks in 4-Security.docx.
9. Save **4-Security.docx**.

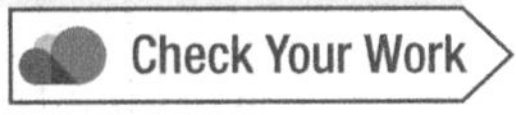

Editing a Hyperlink

The hyperlink or the hyperlink destination can be edited with options at the Edit Hyperlink dialog box. The Edit Hyperlink dialog box contains the same options as the Insert Hyperlink dialog box. Display the Edit Hyperlink dialog box by clicking the hyperlinked text and then clicking the Link button on the Insert tab or by right-clicking the hyperlinked text and then clicking *Edit Hyperlink* at the shortcut menu. Like the hyperlink, the hyperlinked text can be edited. For example, a different font, font size, text color, or text effect can be applied to the hyperlinked text. Remove a hyperlink from a document by right-clicking the hyperlinked text and then clicking *Remove Hyperlink* at the shortcut menu.

Activity 4e Editing and Removing a Hyperlink

Part 5 of 6

1. With **4-Security.docx** open, edit a hyperlink by completing the following steps:
   a. Display the hyperlink at the end of the paragraph below the title *CHAPTER 3: COMPUTER VIRUSES.*
   b. Right-click the Computer Virus Presentation hyperlink and then click *Edit Hyperlink* at the shortcut menu.

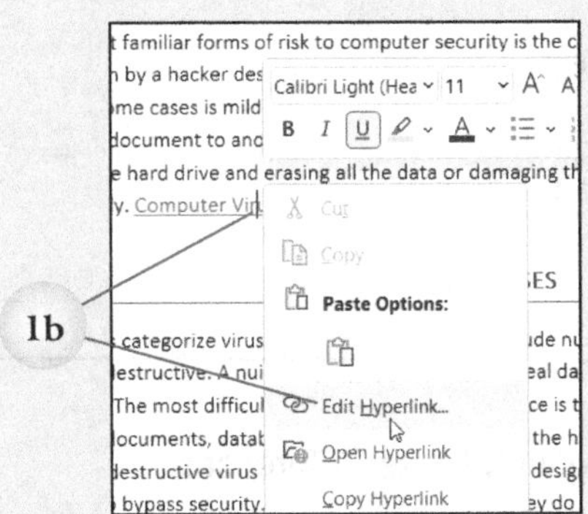

   c. At the Edit Hyperlink dialog box, select the text in the *Text to display* text box and then type Click to view a presentation on computer viruses.
   d. Click the ScreenTip button in the upper right corner of the dialog box.
   e. At the Set Hyperlink ScreenTip dialog box, type View the Computer Viruses PowerPoint presentation and then click OK.
   f. Click OK to close the Edit Hyperlink dialog box.
2. Remove a hyperlink by completing the following steps:
   a. Press Ctrl + Home to move the insertion point to the beginning of the document.
   b. Right-click the Methods of Virus Operation hyperlink at the end of the second paragraph below the title *CHAPTER 1: UNAUTHORIZED ACCESS.*
   c. At the shortcut menu, click the *Remove Hyperlink* option.
   d. Select and then delete the text *Methods of Virus Operation.*
3. Save **4-Security.docx.**

Creating a Cross-Reference

Quick Steps

Insert Cross-Reference

1. Type text or position insertion point.
2. Click Insert tab.
3. Click Cross-reference button.
4. Identify reference type, location, and text.
5. Click Insert.
6. Click Close.

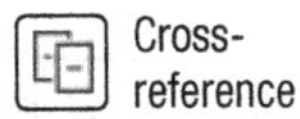

Creating a Cross-Reference

A cross-reference in a Word document refers readers to another location within the document. Providing cross-references is useful in a long document or a document containing related items or sections of information. References to items such as headings, figures, and tables are helpful to readers. For example, a cross-reference can be inserted that refers readers to a location with more information about the topic, to a specific table, or to a specific page. Cross-references are inserted in a document as hyperlinks.

To insert a cross-reference, type introductory text or position the insertion point at a specific location, click the Insert tab, and then click the Cross-reference button in the Links group. This displays the Cross-reference dialog box, similar to the one shown in Figure 4.11. At the Cross-reference dialog box, identify the type of reference, the location to reference, and the specific text to reference.

The reference identified in the Cross-reference dialog box displays immediately after the introductory text. To move to the specified reference, press and hold down the Ctrl key, position the pointer over the text (the pointer turns into a hand), click the left mouse button, and then release the Ctrl key.

Figure 4.11 Cross-Reference Dialog Box

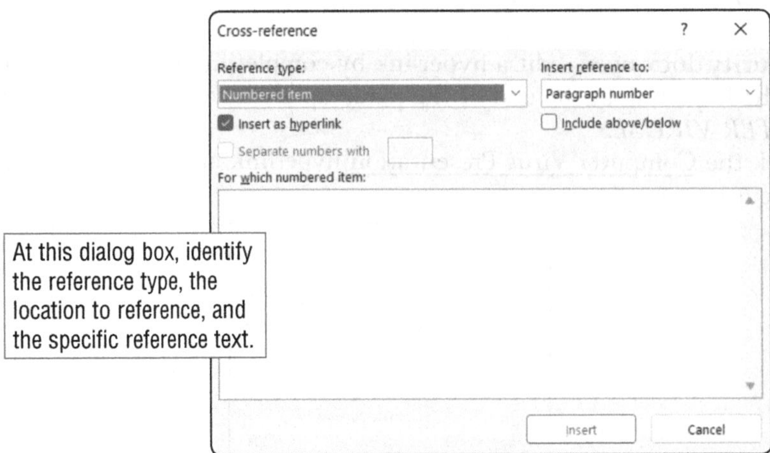

Activity 4f Inserting and Navigating with Cross-References

Part 6 of 6

1. With **4-Security.docx** open, insert a cross-reference in the document by completing the following steps:
   a. Move the insertion point immediately right of the period that ends the paragraph in the section *TYPES OF VIRUSES*.
   b. Press the spacebar and then type (For more information, refer to.
   c. Press the spacebar.
   d. If necessary, click the Insert tab.
   e. Click the Cross-reference button in the Links group.
   f. At the Cross-reference dialog box, click the *Reference type* option box arrow and then click *Heading* at the drop-down list.
   g. Click *Spyware* in the *For which heading* list box.
   h. Click the Insert button.
   i. Click the Close button to close the dialog box.
   j. At the document, type a period followed by a right parenthesis.

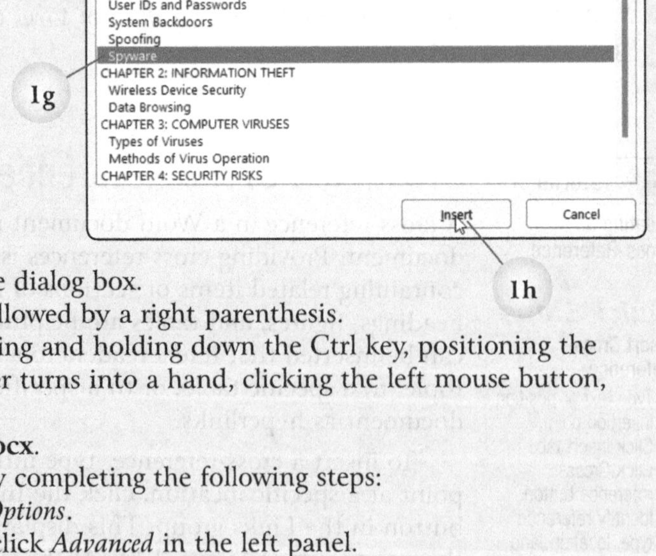

2. Move to the referenced text by pressing and holding down the Ctrl key, positioning the pointer over *Spyware* until the pointer turns into a hand, clicking the left mouse button, and then releasing the Ctrl key.
3. Save and then preview **4-Security.docx**.
4. Turn off the display of bookmarks by completing the following steps:
   a. Click the File tab and then click *Options*.
   b. At the Word Options dialog box, click *Advanced* in the left panel.
   c. Click the *Show bookmarks* check box in the *Show document content* section to remove the check mark.
   d. Click OK to close the dialog box.
5. Close **4-Security.docx**.

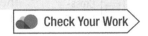

Check Your Work

Chapter Summary

- Create a table of contents using the Table of Contents button in the Table of Contents group on the References tab. Creating a table of contents involves two steps: applying the appropriate styles to mark text that will be included and inserting the table of contents in the document.
- Identify the text to be included in a table of contents by applying a heading style, assigning a level, or marking text as a field entry.
- To insert a table of contents, position the insertion point where the table is to appear, click the References tab, click the Table of Contents button, and then click an option at the drop-down list.
- Generally, the pages containing the table of contents are numbered with lowercase roman numerals. Change the format of the page number at the Page Number Format dialog box.
- To separate the table of contents from the first page of the document, insert a section break that begins a new page.
- The headings in a table of contents are hyperlinks that connect to the headings where they appear in a document and can be used to navigate in a document.
- Customize a table of contents with options at the Table of Contents dialog box. Display this dialog box by clicking the Table of Contents button on the References tab and then clicking *Custom Table of Contents* at the drop-down list.
- If changes are made to a document after the table of contents is inserted, update the table of contents by clicking in the current table of contents and then clicking the Update Table button in the Table of Contents group on the References tab or by pressing the F9 function key.
- Remove a table of contents by clicking the Table of Contents button on the References tab and then clicking *Remove Table of Contents* at the drop-down list.
- To identify titles and/or headings for a table of contents without applying a style, mark each as a field entry at the Mark Table of Contents Entry dialog box. Display this dialog box by pressing Alt + Shift + O.
- When table of contents entries are marked as fields, the *Table entry fields* option needs to be activated when inserting a table of contents. Do this at the Table of Contents Options dialog box.
- Create a table of figures by marking specific text or images with captions and then using the caption names to create the table. Create a caption by selecting the figure text or image and then clicking the Insert Caption button in the Captions group on the References tab. This displays the Caption dialog box, where the figure name is typed.
- Insert a table of figures in a document by clicking the Insert Table of Figures button in the Captions group on the References tab. A table of figures generally appears at the beginning of the document after the table of contents on a separate page.
- Update a table of figures by clicking in the table of figures and then clicking the Update Table button in the Captions group on the References tab or by pressing the F9 function key. At the Update Table of Figures dialog box, specify if just page numbers are updated or the entire table.

- Customize a caption with options at the Captions dialog box. Display this dialog box by clicking the Insert Caption button in the Captions group on the References tab.
- To navigate in a document using the Navigation pane, click the View tab and then click the *Navigation Pane* check box in the Show group. The Navigation pane includes a search text box and three tabs: Headings, Pages, and Results.
- Navigate in a document using bookmarks, which move the insertion point to specific locations. Create bookmarks with options at the Bookmark dialog box.
- Insert hyperlinks in a document with options at the Insert Hyperlink dialog box. Insert a hyperlink to a location in the current document, to display a different document, to open a file in a different program, to create a new document, or to link to an email address. A graphic can also be used to link to a file or website. Edit the hyperlink or the hyperlink destination with options at the Edit Hyperlink dialog box.
- Create a cross-reference to another location within the same document with options at the Cross-reference dialog box.

Commands Review

FEATURE	RIBBON TAB, GROUP	BUTTON, OPTION	KEYBOARD SHORTCUT
Bookmark dialog box	Insert, Links		
Caption dialog box	References, Captions		
Cross-reference dialog box	Insert, Links		
Insert Hyperlink dialog box	Insert, Links		Ctrl + K
Mark Table of Contents Entry dialog box			Alt + Shift + O
Navigation pane	View, Show	*Navigation Pane*	
Remove table of contents	References, Table of Contents	, *Remove Table of Contents*	
Table of Contents dialog box	References, Table of Contents	, *Custom Table of Contents*	
Table of Contents Options dialog box	References, Table of Contents	, *Custom Table of Contents*, Options button	
Table of Figures dialog box	References, Captions		
update table of contents	References, Table of Contents		F9

Review and Assessment

CHAPTER 4

Skills Assessment

Assessment 1

Create and Update a Table of Contents for a Photography Report

1. Open **PhotoRpt.docx** and then save it with the name **4-PhotoRpt**.
2. Move the insertion point to the beginning of the heading *Photography* and then insert a section break that begins a new page.
3. With the insertion point positioned below the section break, insert a page number at the bottom center of each page and change the beginning number to *1*.
4. Press Ctrl + Home to move the insertion point to the beginning of the document (on the blank page) and then create a table of contents with the *Automatic Table 1* option at the Table of Contents button drop-down list.
5. Display the Table of Contents dialog box, change the *Formats* option to *Distinctive*, and make sure a *3* displays in the *Show levels* measurement box.
6. Change the page number format of the table of contents page to lowercase roman numerals.
7. Save and then preview the document.
8. Insert a page break at the beginning of the heading *Camera Basics*.
9. Update the table of contents.
10. Save, preview, and then close **4-PhotoRpt.docx**.

Assessment 2

Insert Captions and a Table of Figures in a Report

1. Open **InputDevices.docx** and then save it with the name **4-InputDevices**.
2. Insert a caption for each of the three images in the document that uses *Figure* as the label, uses an arabic number (1, 2, 3) as the figure number, and displays centered below the image. Use *Keyboard* for the first figure caption, *Mouse* for the second, and *Laptop* for the third.
3. Move the insertion point to the beginning of the title *Computer Input Devices* and then insert a section break that begins a new page.
4. Press Ctrl + Home, type Table of Figures, press the Enter key, and then insert a table of figures with the Formal format applied.
5. Apply the Heading 1 style to the title *Table of Figures*.
6. Move the insertion point to the title *Computer Input Devices*. Insert a page number at the bottom center of each page and change the starting number to *1*.
7. Move the insertion point to the title *Table of Figures* and then change the page numbering style to lowercase roman numerals.
8. Insert a page break at the beginning of the heading *Trackball*.
9. Update the table of figures.
10. Save, preview, and then close **4-InputDevices.docx**.

Assessment 3 — Format and Navigate in a Corporate Report

1. Open **DIReport.docx** and then save it with the name **4-DIReport**.
2. Turn on the display of bookmarks.
3. Move the insertion point to the end of the third paragraph (the paragraph that begins *The audit committee selects*) and then insert a bookmark named *Audit*.
4. Move the insertion point to the end of the first paragraph in the section *FEES TO INDEPENDENT AUDITOR*, following the *(Excel worksheet)* text, and then insert a bookmark named *Audit_Fees*.
5. Move the insertion point to the end of the last paragraph and then insert a bookmark named *Compensation*.
6. Navigate in the document using the bookmarks.
7. Move the insertion point to the end of the first paragraph in the section *COMMITTEE RESPONSIBILITIES*, press the spacebar, and then insert a hyperlink to the Audit_Fees bookmark.
8. Select the text *(Excel worksheet)* at the end of the first paragraph in the section *FEES TO INDEPENDENT AUDITOR* and then insert a hyperlink to the Excel file **AuditorFees.xlsx**.
9. Move the insertion point to the end of the document, click the image, and then insert a hyperlink to the Word document **DIGraphic.docx**. At the Insert Hyperlink dialog box, create a ScreenTip with the text *Click to view a long-term incentives graphic*.
10. Press and hold down the Ctrl key, click the *(Excel worksheet)* hyperlink, and then release the Ctrl key.
11. Close the Excel program without saving the file.
12. Press and hold down the Ctrl key, click the image to display the Word document containing the graphic, and then release the Ctrl key. Close the graphic document.
13. Save, preview, and then close **4-DIReport.docx**.

Assessment 4 — Customize a Table of Contents

1. Open **DIInformation.docx** and then save it with the name **4-DIInformation**.
2. By default, an automatic table of contents is created using text with the Heading 1, Heading 2, and Heading 3 styles applied. The **4-DIInformation.docx** document contains text with Heading 4 applied. Display the Table of Contents Options dialog box and determine how to specify that the table of contents should include text with the Heading 4 style applied. Replace the existing table of contents.
3. Save, preview, and then close **4-DIInformation.docx**.

Visual Benchmark

Create a Table of Contents and a Table of Figures

1. Open **NewZealandRpt.docx** and then save it with the name **4-NewZealandRpt**.
2. Format the document so it appears as shown in Figure 4.12 with the following specifications:
   a. Insert the captions for the figures as shown (see Page 3 of the figure). (You will need to expand the figure text box for the *Women Voting* figure so the figure text displays on one line.)

b. Insert the table of figures as shown (see Page 2 of the figure) using the *From template* format option with period leaders. Apply the Heading 1 style to the *FIGURES* heading.
c. Insert the table of contents as shown (see Page 1 of the figure) using the *From template* format option with period leaders. Apply the Heading 1 style to the *TABLE OF CONTENTS* heading.
d. Insert page numbers at the right margins as shown (see Pages 2, 3, and 4 of the figure).

3. Save, preview, and then close **4-NewZealandRpt.docx**.

Figure 4.12 Visual Benchmark

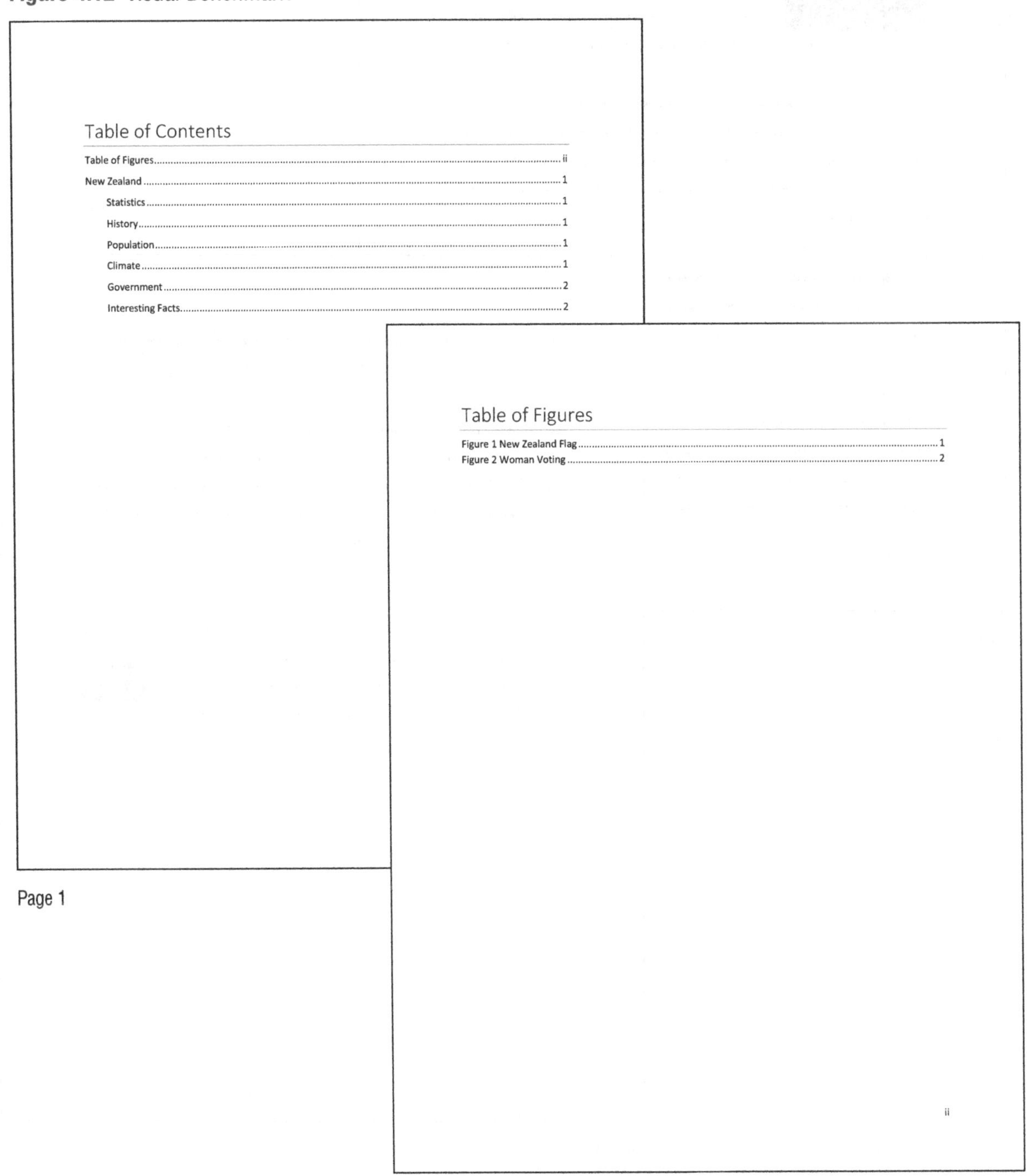
Table of Contents

Table of Figures.....ii
New Zealand.....1
Statistics.....1
History.....1
Population.....1
Climate.....1
Government.....2
Interesting Facts.....2

Page 1

Table of Figures

Figure 1 New Zealand Flag.....1
Figure 2 Woman Voting.....2

ii

Page 2

Continues

Figure 4.12 Visual Benchmark—*Continued*

New Zealand

Statistics

New Zealand is a country in the southwestern section of the Pacific Ocean. The country consists of two main islands—the North Island and South Island. In addition to these two main islands, New Zealand contains more

Figure 1 New Zealand Flag

than 700 smaller islands and covers a total area of 103,500 squares miles. The country is approximately 1,200 miles east of Australia and 600 miles south of the islands of Fiji, Tonga, and New Caledonia. Wellington is the capital of New Zealand and Auckland is the most populous city.

History

Polynesians began settling in the islands between 1280 and 1350 A.D. and developed the Māori culture. In 1642, Abel Tasman, a Dutch explorer, is the first European to visit New Zealand. New Zealand became a colony within the British Empire in 1841 when representatives of the United Kingdom and Māori chiefs signed the Treaty of Waitangi. In 1907, New Zealand became a dominion of the British Empire and then gained full independence in 1947.

Population

Today, approximately five million people live in New Zealand, w

descent. Indigenous Māori are the largest minority population f

official languages in New Zealand are English, Māori, and New Z

Climate

Annual temperatures in New Zealand range from 10 degrees Ce

to 16 degrees Centigrade (61 degrees Fahrenheit) in the north.

83 days out of the year. The rainfall is high with the northern ar

rain in winter than in summer and the southern part having the

generally falls during the months of June through October. Mos

Page 3

Central Plateau in the north and the Southern Alps in the south. The coastal area of the country rarely receives snowfall.

Government

New Zealand has a parliamentary government based on the British model. The House of Representatives (Parliament) is the legislative power and members serve a three-year term. The political party that commands the majority in the House forms the government and, generally, the leader of the governing party becomes the prime minister. The British monarch is the formal head of state, and the monarch appoints a governor-general to represent the monarch. The governor-general has minimal authority but retains some residual powers to protect the constitution.

Interesting Facts

An interesting fact about New Zealand is that in 1893 it was the first country to approve the right for women to vote. Other interesting facts are that over thirty percent of the country is a national reserve, the country has more sheep than people, it has the most southerly capital in the world, and it is the last country in the world inhabited by humans.

Figure 2 Woman Voting

2

Page 4

Case Study

Part 1

You work in the Human Resources Department at Brennan Distributors and are responsible for preparing an employee handbook. Open **BDEmpHandbook.docx** and then save it with the name **4-BDEmpHandbook**. Apply the following specifications to the document:

- Insert a page break before the centered titles *Employee Categories*, *Probationary Periods*, *Employee Performance*, *Position Classification*, and *Compensation*.
- Apply the Heading 1 style to the centered titles and the Heading 2 style to the headings.
- Apply a style set of your choosing.
- Apply a theme that makes the handbook easy to read.
- Insert a table of contents.
- Insert appropriate page numbering. ***Hint: Insert a* Next Page *section break at the beginning of the title* Introduction**.
- Add any other elements that will improve the appearance of the document.

Save **4-BDEmpHandbook.docx**.

Part 2

After looking at the handbook document, you decide to add captions to the tables. With **4-BDEmpHandbook.docx** open, make the following changes to the document:

- Position the insertion point in the first table and then use the caption feature to create the caption *Table 1: Employee Categories* above the table.
- Position the insertion point in the second table and then create the caption *Table 2: Employee Appointments*.
- Insert a table of figures with the title Table of Figures on the page following the table of contents. (Apply the Heading 1 style to the heading *Table of Figures* and then update the table of contents to include a reference to the table of figures.)
- Check the page breaks in the document. If a heading displays at the bottom of a page and the paragraph of text that follows displays at the top of the next page, format the heading so it stays with the paragraph. ***Hint: Do this at the Paragraph dialog box with the Line and Page Breaks tab selected***.
- If necessary, update the table of contents and the table of figures.

Save, preview, and then close **4-BDEmpHandbook.docx**.

Part 3

Send an email to your instructor detailing the steps you followed to create the table captions. Attach **4-BDEmpHandbook.docx** to the email.

WORD LEVEL 2

Unit 1 Performance Assessment

Data Files

The data files for this unit work are in the WL2U1 folder that you downloaded at the beginning of this course.

Assessing Proficiency

In this unit, you have learned to apply advanced character formatting; insert symbols and special characters; find and replace formatting, special characters, styles, and using wildcard characters; manage, inspect, and proof documents; and insert custom headers, footers, and references. You have also learned to create a table of contents and a table of figures and to navigate in a document with the Navigation pane as well as bookmarks, hyperlinks, and cross-references.

Assessment 1

Apply Character Spacing and OpenType Features

1. Open **CVTakeoutMenu.docx** and then save it with the name **U1-CVTakeoutMenu**.
2. Select the title *Take Out Menu*, change the character spacing to Expanded by 1.5 points, turn on kerning, apply Stylistic Set 5, and use contextual alternates.
3. Select the heading *Soups*, change the font size to 22 points, change the character spacing to Expanded, turn on kerning, and apply Stylistic Set 5.
4. Apply the same formatting applied to the heading *Soups* in Step 3 to the other headings (*Salads*, *Main Dishes*, and *Desserts*).
5. Select the last sentence in the document (the sentence that begins *Enjoy the tastes*) and then turn on kerning and apply Stylistic Set 5.
6. Save, preview, and then close **U1-CVTakeoutMenu.docx**.

Assessment 2

Find and Replace Formatting and Use a Wildcard Character

1. Open **Agreement.docx** and then save it with the name **U1-Agreement**.
2. Find text set in the *+Headings* font and replace the font with Corbel.
3. Find text set in the *+Body* font and replace the font with Candara.
4. Using a wildcard character, find all occurrences of *Pin?h?rst?Mad?s?n Builders* and replace them with *Pinehurst-Madison Builders*. (Make sure you remove the formatting option from the *Find what* and *Replace with* text boxes.)

5. Using a wildcard character, find all occurrences of *?erry L?w?ndowsk?* and replace them with *Gerry Lewandowski*.
6. Save, preview, and then close **U1-Agreement.docx**.

Assessment 3

Sort Text

1. Open **SHSSort.docx** and then save it with the name **U1-SHSSort**.
2. Select the five clinic names, addresses, and telephone numbers below the heading *SUMMIT HEALTH SERVICES* and then sort the text alphabetically in ascending order by clinic name.
3. Sort the three columns of text below the heading *EXECUTIVE TEAM* by the extension number in ascending order.
4. Sort the text in the table in the *First Half Expenses* column numerically in descending order.
5. Save, preview, and then close **U1-SHSSort.docx**.

Assessment 4

Insert Document Properties and Inspect a Health Plan Document

1. Open **KLHPlan.docx** and then save it with the name **U1-KLHPlan**.
2. Display the Properties dialog box, type the following in the specified text boxes, and then close the dialog box:

Title	Key Life Health Plan
Subject	Company Health Plan
Author	(Insert your first and last names)
Category	Health Plan
Keywords	health, plan, network
Comments	This document describes highlights of the Key Life Health Plan.

3. Save the document and then print only the document properties.
4. Inspect the document and remove any hidden text.
5. Check the accessibility of the document. Type the alternate text Key Life Logo for the image (a key with *KEY LIFE* on the key) and the alternate text KLHP SmartArt including Compassion, Quality, and Commitment for the SmartArt diagram.
6. Save, preview, and then close **U1-KLHPlan.docx**.

Assessment 5

Proof and Insert Custom Footers for a Document

1. Open **NZ-Australia.docx** and then save it with the name **U1-NZ-Australia**.
2. Display the Word Options dialog box with *Proofing* selected in the left panel, remove the check mark in the *Ignore words in UPPERCASE* check box, insert a check mark in the *Show readability statistics* check box, and then close the dialog box.
3. Using the Editor, complete a spelling and grammar check on the document. (Proper names, except the country names, are spelled correctly.)
4. Create an odd page footer and type New Zealand and Australia at the left margin and insert the page number at the right margin. Create an even page footer and insert the page number at the left margin and type New Zealand and Australia at the right margin.
5. Display the Word Options dialog box with *Proofing* selected in the left panel, insert a check mark in the *Ignore words in UPPERCASE* check box, remove the check mark in the *Show readability statistics* check box, and then close the dialog box.
6. Save, preview, and then close **U1-NZ-Australia.docx**.

Assessment 6

Insert Footnotes in a Leadership Report

1. Open **LeadershipRpt.docx** and then save it with the name **U1-LeadershipRpt**.
2. Insert the first footnote shown in Figure U1.1 at the end of the second paragraph in the section *Basic Leadership Skills*.
3. Insert the second footnote shown in the figure at the end of the fourth paragraph in the section *Basic Leadership Skills*.
4. Insert the third footnote shown in the figure at the end of the second paragraph in the section *Essential Leadership Skills*.
5. Insert the fourth footnote shown in the figure at the end of the last paragraph in the document.
6. Save and then preview **U1-LeadershipRpt.docx**.
7. Select the entire document and then change the font to Constantia.
8. Select all the footnotes and then change the font to Constantia.
9. Delete the third footnote.
10. Save, preview, and then close **U1-LeadershipRpt.docx**.

Figure U1.1 Assessment 6

Laurie Fellers, *Effective Coaching Techniques* (Dallas: Cornwall & Lewis, 2024), 67-72.

Joel Moriarity, "Motivating Employees," *Leaderhip Development* (2024): 3-6.

Jin Loh, *Incentive Management Techniques* (Los Angeles: Monroe-Ackerman, 2024), 89-93.

Andrea Rushton, *Guide to Managing Employees* (Minneapolis: Aurora, 2024), 26-43.

Assessment 7

Create Citations and Prepare a Works Cited Page for a Report

1. Open **DesignWebsite.docx** and then save it with the name **U1-DesignWebsite**.
2. Format the title page to meet Modern Language Association (MLA) style requirements with the following changes:
   a. Make sure that MLA style is selected in the Citations & Bibliography group on the References tab.
   b. With the insertion point positioned at the beginning of the document, type your name, press the Enter key, type your instructor's name, press the Enter key, type the title of your course, press the Enter key, type the current date, and then press the Enter key. Type the title Designing a Website and then center the title.
   c. The text in the document is set in 12-point Cambria. Make this the default font for the document.
   d. Insert a header that displays your last name and the page number at the right margin.

3. Select and then delete the text *(Mercado)* in the second paragraph of text. With the insertion point positioned between the word *users* and the period that ends the sentence, press the spacebar and then insert the source information from a journal article using the following information:

Author	Claudia Mercado
Title	Connecting a Web Page
Journal Name	Connections
Year	2024
Pages	12-21
Volume	4

4. Select and then delete the text *(Holmes)* in the second paragraph of text. With the insertion point positioned between the word *routing* and the period that ends the sentence, press the spacebar and then insert the source information from a website using the following information:

Author	Brent Holmes
Name of Web Page	Hosting Your Web Page
Year	2023
Month	September
Day	20
Year Accessed	(type current year)
Month Accessed	(type current month)
Day Accessed	(type current day)
URL	https://ppi-edu.net/webhosting

5. Select and then delete the text *(Vukovich)* in the last paragraph of text. With the insertion point positioned between the word *hyperlinks"* and the period that ends the sentence, press the spacebar and then insert the source information from a book using the following information:

Author	Ivan Vukovich
Title	Computer Technology in the Business Environment
Year	2024
City	San Francisco
Publisher	Gold Coast

6. Insert the page number *20* in the citation by Ivan Vukovich using the Edit Citation dialog box.
7. Edit the Ivan Vukovich source by changing the last name to *Vulkovich* in the *Master List* section of the Source Manager dialog box. Click Yes at the message asking about updating the source in both the *Master List* and the *Current List* sections.
8. Create a new source in the document using the Source Manager dialog box and include the following source information for a journal article:

Author	Sonia Jaquez
Title	Organizing a Web Page
Journal Name	Design Techniques
Year	2024
Pages	32-44
Volume	9

9. Type the following sentence at the end of the last paragraph in the document: Browsers look for pages with these names first when a specific file at a website is requested, and index pages display by default if no other page is specified.
10. Insert a citation for Sonia Jaquez at the end of the sentence you just typed.
11. Insert a citation for Claudia Mercado following the second sentence in the first paragraph of the document.

12. Insert a works cited page at the end of the document on a separate page.
13. Format the works cited page as follows to meet MLA requirements:
    a. Select the *Works Cited* title and all the entries and then click the *No Spacing* style.
    b. Change the line spacing to double spacing.
    c. Center the title *Works Cited*.
    d. Format the works cited entries with a hanging indent. ***Hint: Use Ctrl + T to create a hanging indent***.
14. Save and then preview **U1-DesignWebsite.docx**.
15. Change the document and works cited page from MLA style to APA style. Change the title *Works Cited* to *References*. Select the references in the list and then change the line spacing to double spacing with 0 points of spacing after paragraphs.
16. Save, preview, and then close **U1-DesignWebsite.docx**.

Assessment 8

Create Captions and Insert a Table of Figures in a Report

1. Open **SoftwareCareers.docx** and then save it with the name **U1-SoftwareCareers**.
2. Click in the first table and then insert the caption *Table 1 Software Development Careers* above the table. (Change the paragraph spacing after the caption to 3 points.)
3. Click in the second table and then insert the caption *Table 2 Application Development Careers* above the table. (Change the paragraph spacing after the caption to 3 points.)
4. Move the insertion point to the beginning of the heading *SOFTWARE DEVELOPMENT CAREERS* and then insert a next page section break.
5. With the insertion point below the section break, insert a page number at the bottom center of each page and change the starting page number to *1*.
6. Move the insertion point to the beginning of the document and then insert the *Automatic Table 1* table of contents.
7. Press Ctrl + Enter to insert a page break.
8. Type Tables, press the Enter key, and then insert a table of figures using the Formal format.
9. Apply the Heading 1 style to the title *Tables*.
10. Move the insertion point to the beginning of the document and then apply the Heading 1 style to the title CONTENTS.
11. With the insertion point at the beginning of the document, change the number format to lowercase roman numerals.
12. Update the entire table of contents.
13. Save, preview, and then close **U1-SoftwareCareers.docx**.

Writing Activities

Activity 1

Prepare an APA Guidelines Document

You work for a psychiatric medical facility and many of the psychiatrists and psychiatric nurses you work with submit papers to journals that require formatting in APA style. Your supervisor has asked you to prepare a document that describes the APA guidelines and provides the steps for formatting a Word document in APA style. Find a website that provides information on APA style and include the hyperlink in your document. (Consider websites for writing labs at colleges and universities.) Apply formatting to enhance the appearance of the document. Save the document with the name **U1-APA**. Preview and then close **U1-APA.docx**.

Activity 2

Create a Rental Form Template

You work in a real estate management company that manages rental houses. You decide to automate the standard rental form that is normally filled in by hand. Open **LeaseAgreement.docx** and then save the document with the name **U1-LeaseAgreement**. Look at the lease agreement document and determine how to automate it so it can be filled in using the Find and Replace feature in Word. Change the current *Lessor* and *Lessee* names to *LESSOR* and *LESSEE*. Save the document as a template named **LeaseForm.dotx** in your WL2U1 folder. Use File Explorer to open a document based on the **LeaseForm.dotx** template. Find and replace the following text (use your judgment about which occurrences should be changed and which should not):

DAY	22nd
MONTH	February
YEAR	2024
RENT	$1,250
DEPOSIT	$700
LESSOR	Samantha Herrera
LESSEE	Daniel Miller

Save the document with the name **U1-Lease1** and then close **U1-Lease1.docx**. Use File Explorer to open a document based on the **LeaseForm.dotx** template and then create another rental document. You determine the text to replace with the standard text. Save the completed rental document with the name **U1-Lease2**. Preview and then close **U1-Lease2.docx**.

Internet Research

Create a Job Search Report

Use a search engine to locate companies that offer jobs in a field in which you are interested in working. Locate at least three websites that identify employment opportunities and then create a report in Word that includes the following information about each site:

- Name and URL
- A brief description
- Employment opportunities available

Create a hyperlink from your report to each site and include any additional information pertinent to the site. Apply formatting to enhance the document. Save the document with the name **U1-JobSearch**. Preview and then close **U1-JobSearch.docx**.

WORD

LEVEL 2

Unit 2

Editing and Formatting Documents

WORD

CHAPTER 5

Customizing Objects, Using the Draw Feature, and Creating Charts

Performance Objectives

Upon successful completion of Chapter 5, you will be able to:

1 Insert, format, and customize images and text boxes
2 Group and ungroup objects
3 Edit points and wrap points in a shape
4 Link and unlink text boxes
5 Insert, format, and customize icons
6 Insert, format, and customize 3D models
7 Customize a document with options on the Draw tab
8 Insert and format charts

Objects such as images, shapes, text boxes, icons, and 3D models can be inserted in a Word document and then formatted with a variety of options. Use buttons on the object format tab and task pane to customize an object. An object can also be formatted with options at the Layout dialog box. The Draw tab contains options for drawing in a document, creating shapes, editing text, and selecting and highlighting text. In this chapter, you will learn how to customize objects, draw in a document, and how to present text visually in a chart and apply formatting to the chart.

Data Files

The data files for this chapter are in the WL2C5 folder that you downloaded at the beginning of this course.

Activity 1 Customize the Layout of an Adventure Agency Flyer — 3 Parts

You will open an adventure agency flyer describing sites and activities for adventures in Maui and improve the attractiveness of the layout by inserting and customizing images and a text box.

Customizing Objects

Word provides a number of methods for formatting and customizing objects, such as images, photographs, shapes and text boxes. Format images with buttons on the Picture Format tab and further customize images with options at the Format Picture task pane and the Layout dialog box. Use buttons on the Shape Format tab to format and customize shapes and text boxes and further customize shapes and text boxes with options at the Format Shape task pane and the Layout dialog box.

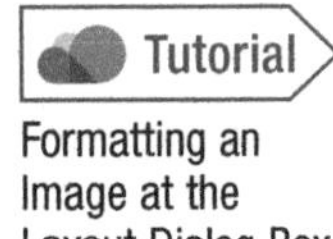

Formatting an Image at the Layout Dialog Box

Customizing Image Layout

Customize the layout of images with options at the Layout dialog box. Display the Layout dialog box by clicking the Size group dialog box launcher on the Picture Format tab. The Layout dialog box contains three tabs. Click the Position tab and the dialog box displays as shown in Figure 5.1.

Use options at the Layout dialog box with the Position tab selected to specify horizontal and vertical layout options. In the *Horizontal* section, choose the *Alignment* option to specify left, center, or right alignment relative to the margin, page, column, or character. Choose the *Book layout* option to align the image with

Figure 5.1 Layout Dialog Box with the Position Tab Selected

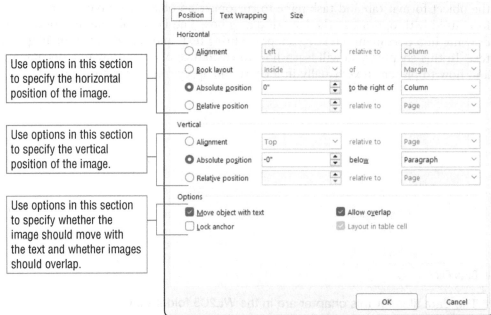

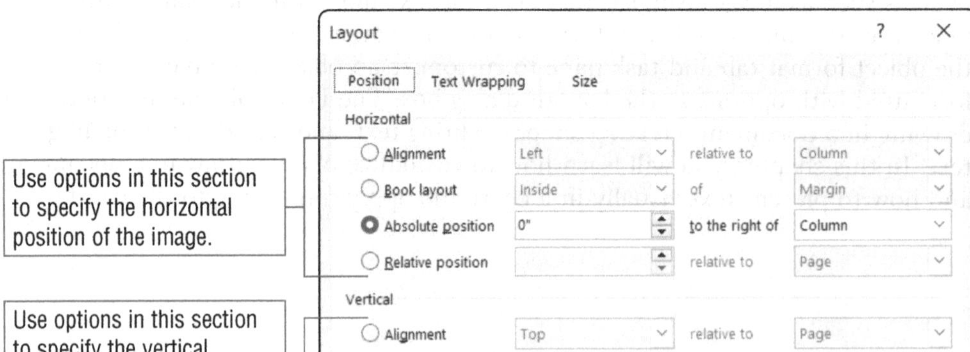

the inside or outside margin of the page. Use the *Absolute position* measurement box to align the image horizontally with the specified amount of space between the left edge of the image and the left edge of the page, column, left margin, or character. The *Relative position* measurement box uses a percentage to position an image relative to a specific location. For example, enter *50%* in the *Relative position* measurement box to align relative to the left margin and the image is positioned half way (50%) between the left edge of the page and the left margin.

In the *Vertical* section of the dialog box, use the *Alignment* option to align the image at the top, bottom, center, inside, or outside relative to the page, margin, or line. Use the *Absolute position* measurement box to align the image vertically with the specified amount of space relative to a specific location and use the *Relative position* measurement box to specify a percentage.

In the *Options* section, attach (anchor) the image to a paragraph so that the image and paragraph move together. Choose the *Move object with text* option to move the image up or down on the page with the paragraph to which it is anchored. Keep the image anchored in the same place on the page by choosing the *Lock anchor* option. Choose the *Allow overlap* option to overlap images with the same wrapping style.

Use options at the Layout dialog box with the Text Wrapping tab selected to specify the wrapping style for the image. Specify which sides of the image the text is to wrap around and the amounts of space between the text and the top, bottom, left, and right edges of the image.

Click the Size tab at the Layout dialog box to display options for specifying the height and width of the image relative to the margin, page, top margin, bottom margin, inside margin, or outside margin. Use the *Rotation* measurement box to rotate the image by degrees and use options in the *Scale* section to change the percentage of the height and width scales. By default, the *Lock aspect ratio* check box contains a check mark, which means that if a change is made to the height measurement of an image, the width measurement automatically changes to maintain the proportional relationship between the height and width. Change the width measurement and the height measurement automatically changes.

To change the height measurement of an image without changing the width or to change the width measurement without changing the height, remove the check mark from the *Lock aspect ratio* check box. To reset the image size, click the Reset button in the lower right corner of the dialog box.

Activity 1a Inserting and Customizing the Layout of an Image

Part 1 of 3

1. Open **BEAMaui.docx** and then save it with the name **5-BEAMaui**.
2. Insert an image by completing the following steps:
   a. Click the Insert tab.
   b. Click the Pictures button in the Illustrations group and then click *This Device* at the drop-down list.
   c. At the Insert Picture dialog box, navigate to your WL2C5 folder and then double-click the ***HawaiiBanner.png*** image file.
3. Select the current measurement in the *Shape Height* measurement box in the Size group on the Picture Format tab, type 2, and then press the Enter key.

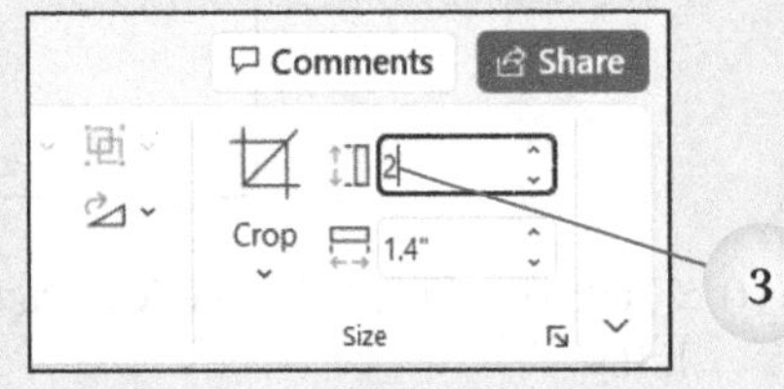

4. Click the *Beveled Matte, White* style in the Picture Styles group (second style from the left).

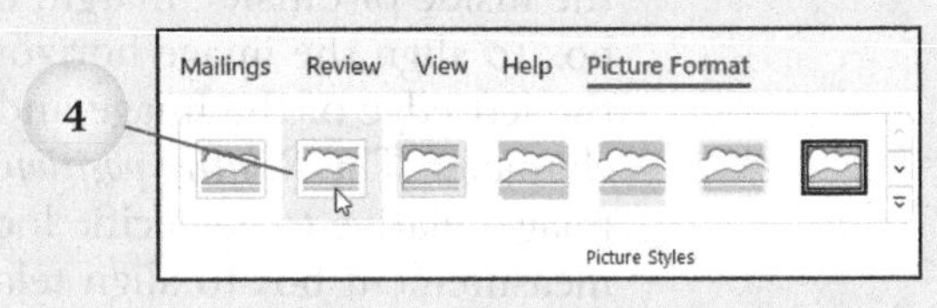

5. Click the Corrections button in the Adjust group and then click the *Brightness: –20% Contrast: +20%* option (second column, fourth row in the *Brightness/Contrast* section).
6. After looking at the image, you decide to reset it. Do this by clicking the Reset Picture button arrow in the Adjust group and then clicking *Reset Picture & Size* at the drop-down list.

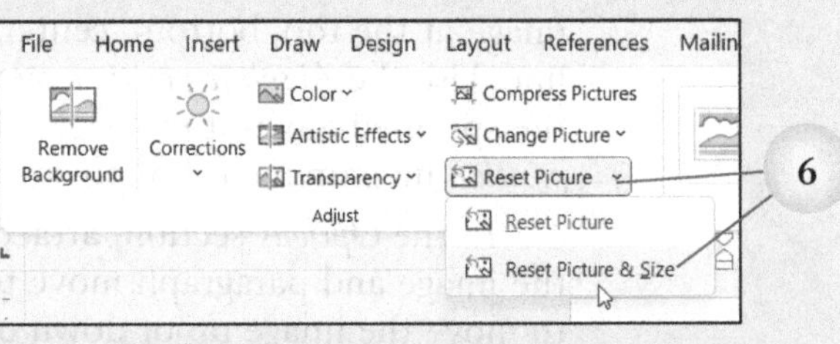

7. Select the current measurement in the *Shape Height* measurement box, type 1.3, and then press the Enter key.

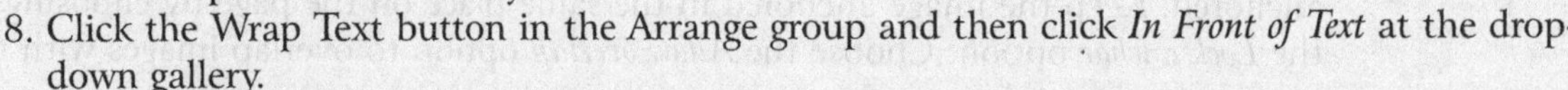

8. Click the Wrap Text button in the Arrange group and then click *In Front of Text* at the drop-down gallery.
9. Position the image precisely on the page by completing the following steps:
   a. With the image selected, click the Size group dialog box launcher.
   b. At the Layout dialog box, click the Position tab.
   c. Make sure the *Absolute position* option in the *Horizontal* section is selected.
   d. Press the Tab key two times and then type 6.2 in the *Absolute position* measurement box.
   e. Click the *to the right of* option box arrow and then click *Page* at the drop-down list.
   f. If necessary, click the *Absolute position* option in the *Vertical* section.
   g. Select the current measurement in the *Absolute position* measurement box and then type 2.
   h. Click the *below* option box arrow and then click *Page* at the drop-down list.
   i. Click OK to close the Layout dialog box.

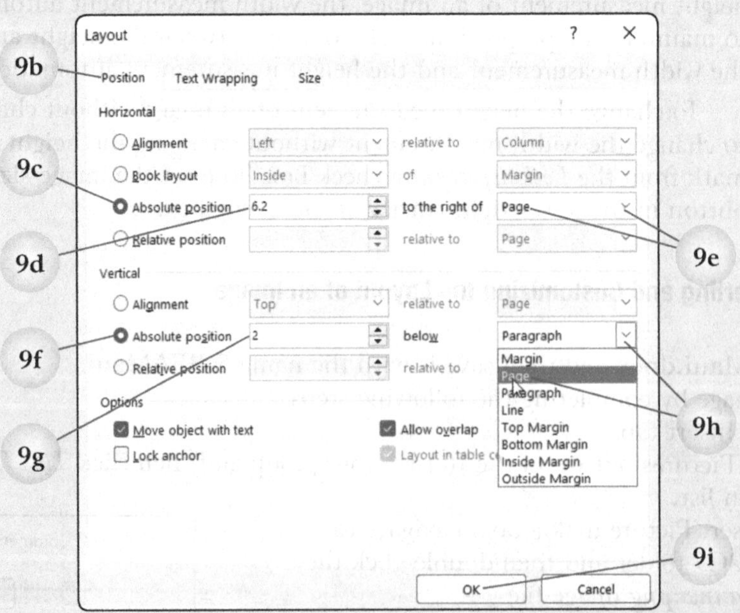

10. Click the *Drop Shadow Rectangle* style in the Picture Styles group (fourth style from the left).

11. Click the Color button in the Adjust group and then click the *Blue, Accent color 5 Dark* option (sixth column, second row in the *Recolor* section).
12. Compress the image by clicking the Compress Pictures button in the Adjust group and then clicking OK at the Compress Pictures dialog box.
13. Click outside the image to deselect it.
14. Save **5-BEAMaui.docx**.

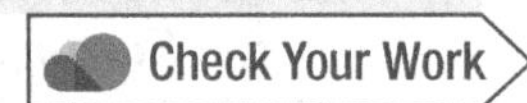

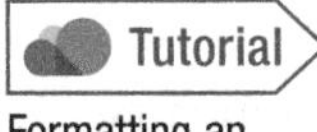

Formatting an Image at the Format Picture Task Pane

Applying Formatting at the Format Picture Task Pane

Options for formatting an image are available at the Format Picture task pane, shown in Figure 5.2. Display this task pane by clicking the Picture Styles group task pane launcher on the Picture Format tab.

The options in the Format Picture task pane vary depending on the icon selected. The formatting options may need to be expanded within the icons. For example, click *Shadow* in the task pane with the Effects icon selected to display options for applying shadow effects to an image. Many of the options available at the Format Picture task pane are also available on the Picture Format tab. The task pane is a central location for formatting options and also includes some additional advanced formatting options.

Applying Artistic Effects to Images

Apply an artistic effect to a selected image with the Artistic Effects button in the Adjust group on the Picture Format tab. Click this button and a drop-down gallery displays with effect options. Hover the pointer over an option in the drop-down gallery to see the effect applied to the selected image. An artistic effect can also be applied to an image with options at the Format Picture task pane with the Effects icon selected.

Figure 5.2 Format Picture Task Pane

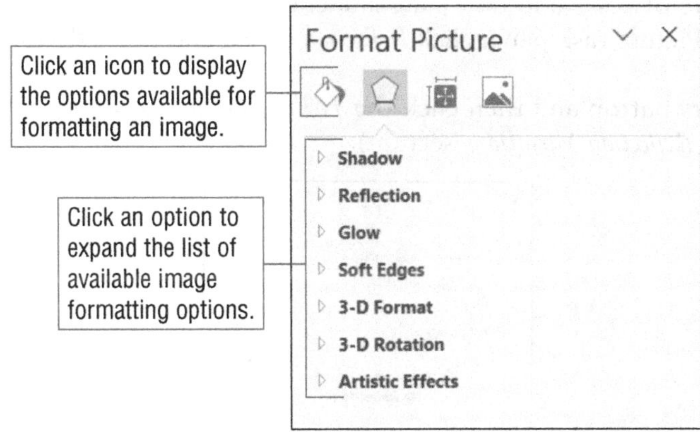

Activity 1b Inserting and Customizing a Photograph

1. With **5-BEAMaui.docx** open, press Ctrl + End to move the insertion point to the end of the document and then insert a photograph by completing the following steps:
   a. Click the Insert tab, click the Pictures button in the Illustrations group, and then click *This Device* at the drop-down list.
   b. At the Insert Picture dialog box, navigate to your WL2C5 folder and then double-click the ***Surfing.png*** image file.
2. With the surfing photograph selected, click the Picture Effects button in the Picture Styles group, point to *Bevel*, and then click the *Round* option (first column, first row in the *Bevel* section).
3. Click the Artistic Effects button in the Adjust group and then click the *Cutout* option (first column, bottom row).

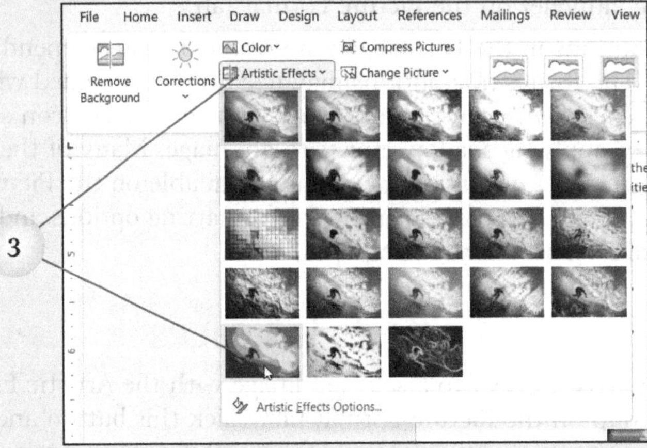

4. After looking at the formatting, you decide to remove it from the image by clicking the Reset Picture button in the Adjust group.
5. Select the current measurement in the *Shape Height* measurement box, type 1.4, and then press the Enter key.
6. Format the photograph by completing the following steps:
   a. Click the Picture Styles group task pane launcher.
   b. At the Format Picture task pane, click *Reflection* to expand the reflection options in the task pane.
   c. Click the Presets button and then click the *Tight Reflection: Touching* option (first column, first row in the *Reflection Variations* section).

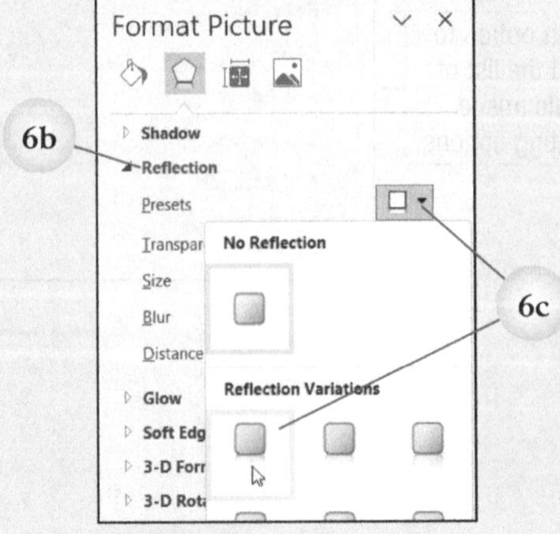

d. Decrease the size percentage of the reflection by selecting the current percentage in the *Size* measurement box and then typing 20%.
e. Click *Artistic Effects* in the task pane to expand the artistic effect options.
f. Click the Artistic Effects button and then click the *Paint Brush* option (third column, second row).
g. Close the task pane by clicking the Close button in the upper right corner.

7. Click the Wrap Text button in the Arrange group on the Picture Format tab and then click *Tight* at the drop-down list.
8. Position the photograph precisely on the page by completing the following steps:
   a. With the photograph selected, click the Position button in the Arrange group and then click *More Layout Options* at the bottom of the drop-down gallery.
   b. At the Layout dialog box with the Position tab selected, select the current measurement in the *Absolute position* measurement box in the *Horizontal* section and then type 5.3.
   c. Click the *to the right of* option box arrow and then click *Page* at the drop-down list.
   d. Click the *Absolute position* option in the *Vertical* section.
   e. Select the current measurement in the *Absolute position* measurement box and then type 6.8.
   f. Click the *below* option box arrow and then click *Page* at the drop-down list.
   g. Click OK to close the Layout dialog box.
9. Click outside the photograph to deselect it.
10. Save **5-BEAMaui.docx**.

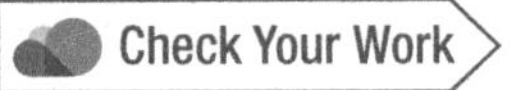

Customizing Colors, Text Boxes, and Shapes

When an object such as a text box or shape is inserted in a document, the Shape Format tab is active. Use options on this tab or the Format Shape task pane to apply custom colors at the Colors dialog box and apply formatting to customize a text box or shape.

Customizing Colors Apply color to text and objects with options at a Colors dialog box. The Colors dialog box contains two tabs—Standard and Custom. With the Standard tab active, colors display in a honeycomb. Choose a color by clicking the specific color in the honeycomb. Click the Custom tab and the dialog box displays a color box along with measurement boxes for specifying the red, green, and blue (RGB) values for a color ranging from 1 to 255. In addition to RGB values, colors can be represented by hue, saturation, and lightness (HSL). Change to HSL values by clicking the *Color model* option box arrow and then clicking *HSL* at the drop-down list. The *Hex* text box is available for entering a hexidecimal (six-digit) code representing a specific color. A hex code compresses the RGB values into one six-digit code that is a representation of color values in binary code. Hex codes are an integral part of HTML and web design for representing color formats digitally. The bar to the right of the color bar is a luminance scale. Drag the slider bar along the scale to make a color lighter or darker. Use the *Transparency* measurement box at the Colors dialog box to specify a percentage of color transparency.

Customizing a Text Box Click the Shape Styles group task pane launcher and the Format Shape task pane displays with three icons: Fill & Line, Effects, and Layout & Properties. Click the WordArt Styles group task pane launcher and the Format Shape task pane displays but with different icons. The task pane displays with *Text Options* selected and with three icons: Text Fill & Outline, Text Effects, and Layout & Properties.

Activity 1c Inserting and Customizing a Text Box

1. With **5-BEAMaui.docx** open, insert a text box by completing the following steps:
   a. Click the Insert tab, click the Text Box button in the Text group, and then click the *Draw Text Box* option at the drop-down list.
   b. Click above the heading *MAUI SITES* and then type Hawaii, the Aloha State.
2. Select the text box by clicking its border. (This changes the text box border from a dashed line to a solid line.)
3. Press Ctrl + E to center the text in the text box.
4. Click the Text Direction button in the Text group on the Shapre Format tab and then click *Rotate all text 270°* at the drop-down list.

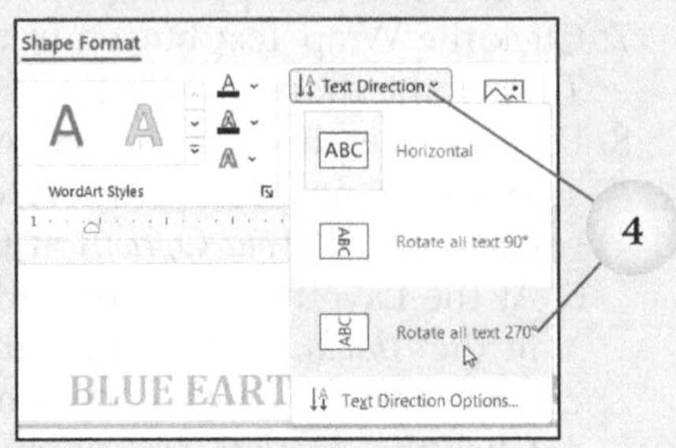

5. Select the current measurement in the *Shape Height* measurement box, type 5.7, and then press the Enter key.
6. Select the current measurement in the *Shape Width* measurement box, type 0.8, and then press the Enter key.
7. Format the text box by completing the following steps:
   a. Click the Shape Styles group task pane launcher.
   b. At the Format Shape task pane with the Fill & Line icon selected, click *Fill* to expand the options.
   c. Click the Fill Color button (displays at the right of the *Color* option) and then click the *More Colors* option.
   d. At the Colors dialog box, click the Custom tab.
   e. Select the number in the *Hex* text box and then type #8AB4F2.
   f. Select the percentage number in the *Transparency* text box, type 50, and then press the Enter key.
   g. Click the Effects icon and then click *Shadow* to expand the options.
   h. Click the Presets button and then click the *Offset: Bottom* option (second column, first row in the *Outer* section).

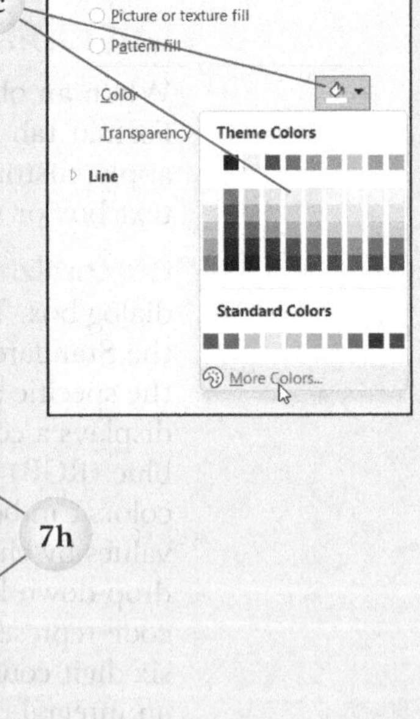

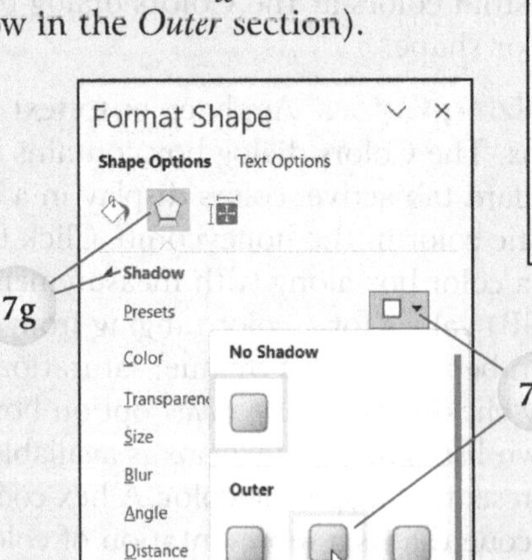

   i. Select the current point size in the *Distance* measurement box, type 5, and then press the Enter key.
   j. Close the Format Shape task pane by clicking the Close button in the upper right corner.

8. Click the More WordArt Styles button in the WordArt Styles group and then click the option in the fourth column, second row (white fill, blue outline).
9. Position the text box precisely on the page by completing the following steps:
   a. With the text box selected, click the Size group dialog box launcher.
   b. At the Layout dialog box, click the Position tab.
   c. Select the current measurement in the *Absolute position* measurement box in the *Horizontal* section and then type 1.
   d. Click the *to the right of* option box arrow and then click *Page* at the drop-down list.
   e. Select the current measurement in the *Absolute position* measurement box in the *Vertical* section and then type 2.7.
   f. Click the *below* option box arrow and then click *Page* at the drop-down list.
   g. Click OK to close the Layout dialog box.
10. Click the Home tab, click the *Font Size* option arrow, and then click *36* at the drop-down gallery.
11. Click outside the text box to deselect it.
12. Save, preview, and then close **5-BEAMaui.docx**.

Activity 2 Customize Shapes and Link and Unlink Text Boxes in a Financial Services Flyer — 4 Parts

You will open a promotional flyer for a financial services group and customize the design. To do this, you will format, group, customize, ungroup, and edit points of a shape. You will also edit wrap points around an image and link and unlink text boxes.

Customizing Shapes Like a text box, a shape can be customized with buttons and options on the Shape Format tab or with options at the Format Shape task pane. Customize or format one shape or select multiple shapes and then customize and apply formatting to all the selected shapes. Display the Format Shape task pane for a shape by clicking the Shape Styles group task pane launcher. When a shape is selected, the WordArt Styles group task pane launcher is dimmed and unavailable.

Grouping and Ungrouping Objects

Quick Steps

Group Objects

1. Select objects.
2. Click Picture Format tab (or Shape Format tab).
3. Click Group button.
4. Click *Group*.

Grouping and Ungrouping Objects Objects in a document, such as images, text boxes, or shapes, can be grouped so that they can be sized, moved, or formatted as one object. Text wrapping other than *In Line with Text* must be applied to each object to be grouped. To group objects, select the objects, click the Picture Format tab (or Shape Format tab), click the Group button in the Arrange group, and then click *Group* at the drop-down list. With the objects grouped, move, size, or apply formatting to all the objects in the group at once.

To select objects, click the first object, press and hold down the Shift key, click each remaining object to be included in the group, and then release the Shift key. Another method for grouping objects is to click the Select button in the Editing group on the Home tab, click the *Select Objects* option, and then use the mouse to draw a border around all the objects. Turn off selecting objects by clicking the Select button and then clicking the *Select Objects* option.

Hint Group multiple objects to work with them as if they are a single object.

Hint A group can be created within a group.

Grouped objects can be sized, moved, and formatted as one object. However, an object within a group of objects can be sized, moved, or formatted individually. To do this, click the specific object and then make the changes to the individual object.

To ungroup grouped objects, click the group to select it and then click the Picture Format tab (or Shape Format tab). Click the Group button in the Arrange group and then click the *Ungroup* option at the drop-down list.

Activity 2a Customizing and Formatting Shapes

Part 1 of 4

1. Open **Leland.docx** and then save it with the name **5-Leland.**
2. Rotate the middle arrow shape by completing the following steps:
   a. Scroll down the document and then click the middle arrow shape to select it (on the first page).
   b. Click the Shape Format tab.
   c. Click the Rotate button in the Arrange group and then click *Flip Horizontal* at the drop-down list.

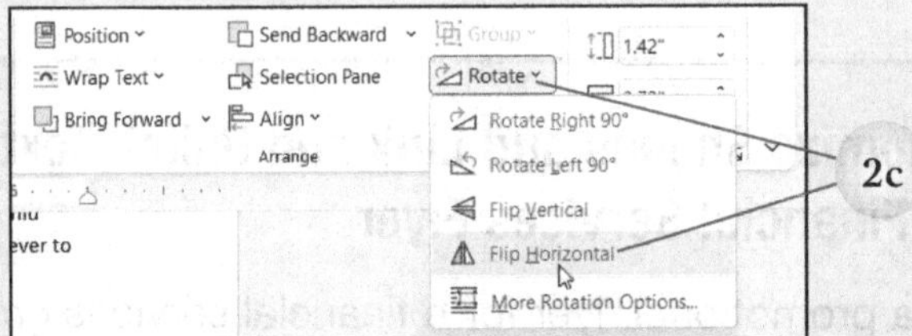

3. Align and format the arrow shapes by completing the following steps:
   a. With the middle arrow shape selected, press and hold down the Shift key.
   b. Click the top arrow shape, click the bottom arrow shape, and then release the Shift key.
   c. With all three arrow shapes selected, click the Align button in the Arrange group and then click *Align Left* at the drop-down list.
   d. Click the Shape Styles group task pane launcher.
   e. At the Format Shape task pane with the Fill & Line icon selected, click *Fill*, if necessary, to expand the fill options.
   f. Click the *Gradient fill* option.
   g. Click the Preset gradients button and then click the *Top Spotlight - Accent 2* option (second column, second row).

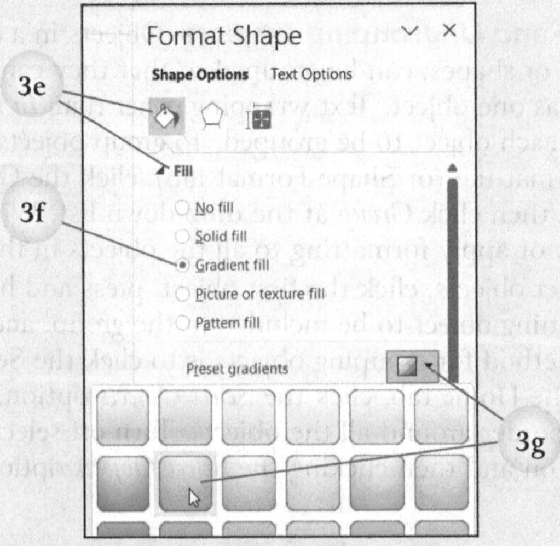

h. Scroll down the task pane and then click *Line* to expand the line options.

i. If necessary, scroll down the task pane and then click the *No line* option.

j. Click the Effects icon (at the top of the task pane).

k. If necessary, click *Shadow* to expand the shadow options.

l. Click the Presets button and then click the *Inside: Top Right* option (third column, first row in the *Inner* section).

m. Close the Format Shape task pane.

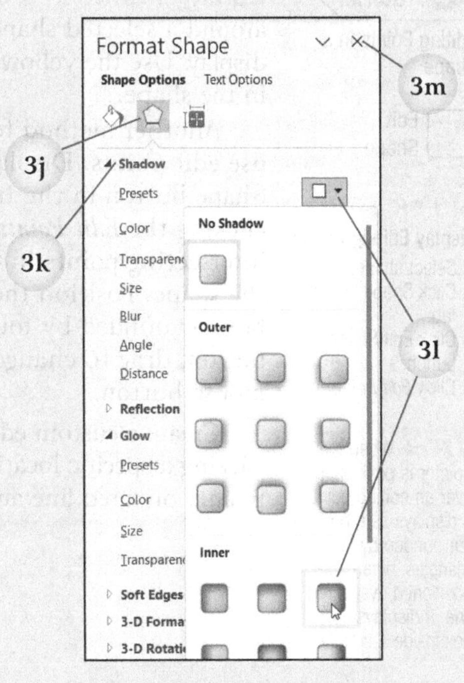

4. With the three arrow shapes still selected, group the shapes, size and move the group, and then ungroup the shapes by completing the following steps:

a. Click the Group button in the Arrange group and then click *Group* at the drop-down list.

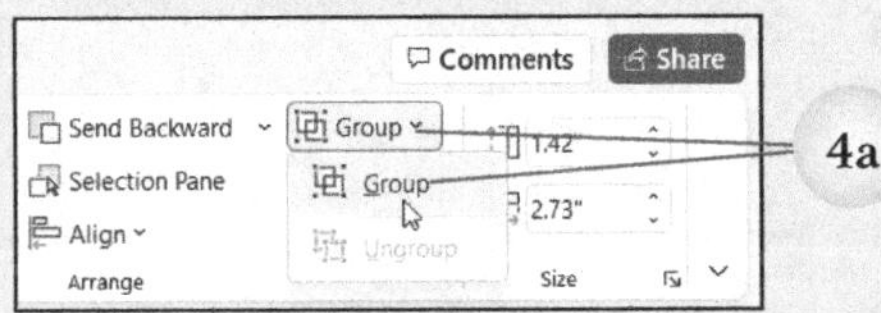

b. Click in the *Shape Height* measurement box and then type 6 in the Size group.

c. Click in the *Shape Width* measurement box in the Size group, type 3.7, and then press the Enter key.

d. Click the Position button in the Arrange group and then click the *Position in Bottom Center with Square Text Wrapping* option (second column, third row in the *With Text Wrapping* section).

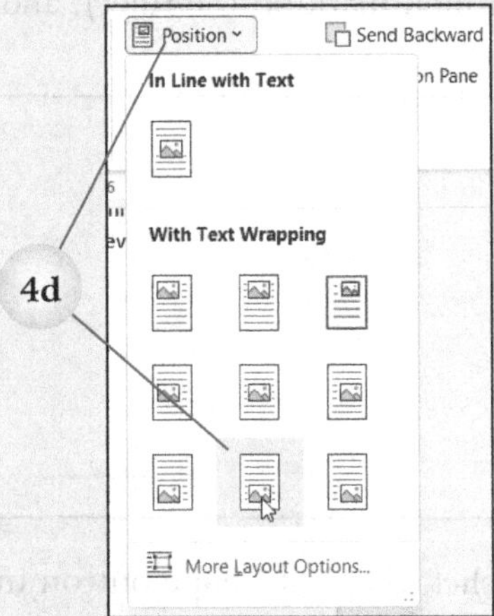

e. Click the Group button and then click *Ungroup* at the drop-down list.

f. Click outside the arrow shapes to deselect the shapes.

5. Delete the bottom arrow shape of the three arrow shapes by clicking the shape (make sure the border displays as a solid line) and then pressing the Delete key.

6. Save **5-Leland.docx**.

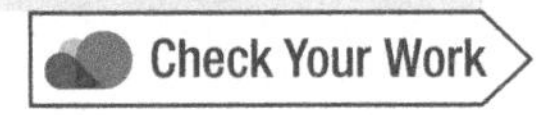

Editing Points in a Shape

Edit Shape

Quick Steps

Display Editing Points

1. Select shape.
2. Click Shape Format tab.
3. Click Edit Shape button.
4. Click *Edit Points*.

Hint When the pointer is positioned over an editing point, it displays as a box surrounded by four triangles; when positioned over a red line, it displays as a box inside a cross.

Editing Points in a Shape Sizing handles are small white circles that display around a selected shape. Depending on the shape, small yellow circles might also display. Use the yellow circles to change the width or height of a specific element in the shape.

Another method for customizing specific elements is to display and then use edit points. Display edit points by selecting the shape, clicking the Edit Shape button in the Insert Shapes group on the Shape Format tab, and then clicking the *Edit Points* option. Edit points display as small black squares at the intersecting points in the shape. A red line also displays between edit points in the shape. Position the pointer on an edit point and the pointer displays as a box surrounded by four triangles (✥). Click and hold down the left mouse button, drag to change the specific element in the shape, and then release the mouse button.

Create a custom editing point by pressing and holding down the Ctrl key, clicking a specific location on a red line, and then releasing the Ctrl key. Position the pointer on a red line and the pointer displays as a box inside a cross (✥).

Activity 2b Editing Points in a Shape

Part 2 of 4

1. With **5-Leland.docx** open, press Ctrl + End to move the insertion point to the end of the document (page 2).
2. Click the shape on the second page to select the shape.
3. With the shape selected, edit points by completing the following steps:
   a. Position the pointer on the top yellow circle, click and hold down the left mouse button, drag to the right approximately one-half inch (use the horizontal ruler as a guide and drag to approximately the 2.5-inch mark on the ruler), and then release the mouse button.

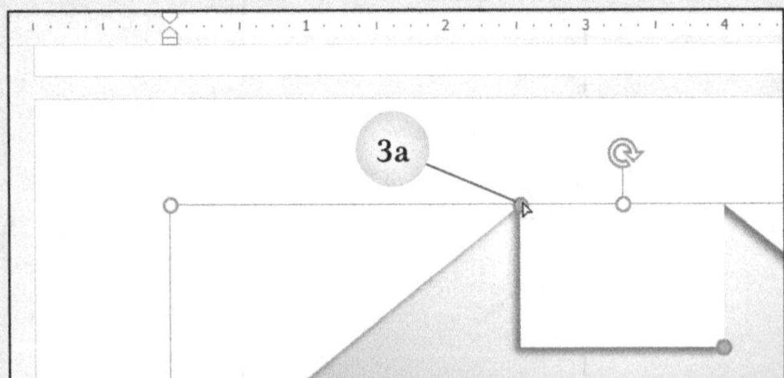

   b. Click the Shape Format tab, click the Edit Shape button in the Insert Shapes group, and then click *Edit Points* at the drop-down list.

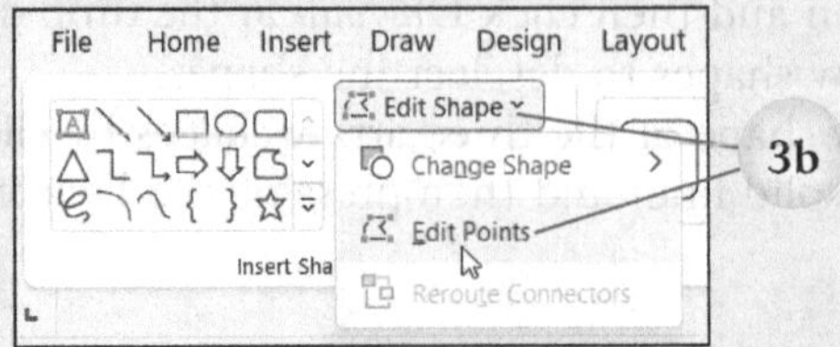

c. Position the pointer on the edit point that displays at the tip of the arrow at the right side of the shape. Click and hold down the left mouse button, drag to the left approximately 1 inch (use the horizontal ruler as a guide), and then release the mouse button. (The shape will move when you release the mouse button.)

d. Position the pointer on the edit point that displays at the tip of the arrow at the left side of the shape. Click and hold down the left mouse button, drag to the right approximately 1 inch (use the horizontal ruler as a guide), and then release the mouse button. (The shape will move when you release the mouse button.)

4. Reposition the shape by clicking the Position button in the Arrange group and then clicking the *Position in Top Center with Square Text Wrapping* option (second column, first row in the *With Text Wrapping* section).
5. Insert and format text in the shape by completing the following steps:
   a. With the shape selected, type Free seminar!, press the Enter key, and then type 1-888-555-4588.
   b. Click the border of the shape to change the border to a solid line.
   c. Click the Text Fill button arrow in the WordArt Styles group and then click the *Orange, Accent 2, Darker 50%* color option (sixth column, bottom row in the *Theme Colors* section).
   d. Click the Home tab and then click the Bold button in the Font group.
   e. Click the *Font Size* option box arrow and then click *24* at the drop-down gallery.
6. Press Ctrl + Home to move the insertion point to the beginning of the document.
7. Save **5-Leland.docx**.

3c

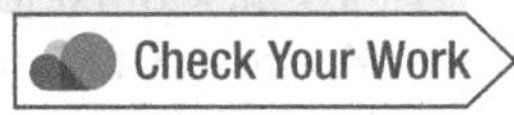

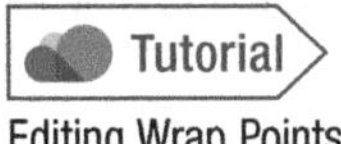

Editing Wrap Points in an Object

Quick Steps

Display Wrap Points for Object

1. Select object.
2. Click Picture Format tab (or Shape Format tab).
3. Click Wrap Text button.
4. Click *Edit Wrap Points.*

Editing Wrap Points in an Object When an object such as an image or shape is inserted in a document, a series of wrap points are defined around the object. These wrap points display in a manner similar to the editing points around an object. The difference between editing points and wrap points is that editing points change the shape of specific elements in an object while wrap points wrap text closer to or farther away from an object.

To display wrap points in a shape, select the shape, click the Shape Format tab, click the Wrap Text button in the Arrange group, and then click the *Edit Wrap Points* option. Display wrap points for an image in a similar manner except click the Wrap Text button on the Picture Format tab. Use wrap points to change how text or other data wraps around an object by dragging specific wrap points.

When wrap points are displayed in an object, red lines appear between wrap points. Create a custom wrap point by positioning the pointer on a location on a red line, pressing and holding down the left mouse button, dragging to a specific position, and then releasing the mouse button. Remove a wrap point by pressing and holding down the Ctrl key, clicking the wrap point, and then releasing the Ctrl key.

Activity 2c Editing Wrap Points in a Shape

Part 3 of 4

1. With **5-Leland.docx** open, click the border of the banner shape in the paragraph of text below the title.
2. Edit wrap points in the shape by completing the following steps:
   a. Click the Shape Format tab.
   b. Click the Wrap Text button in the Arrange group and then click *Edit Wrap Points* at the drop-down list.
   c. Drag the wrap point at the left side of the shape into the shape, as shown below.

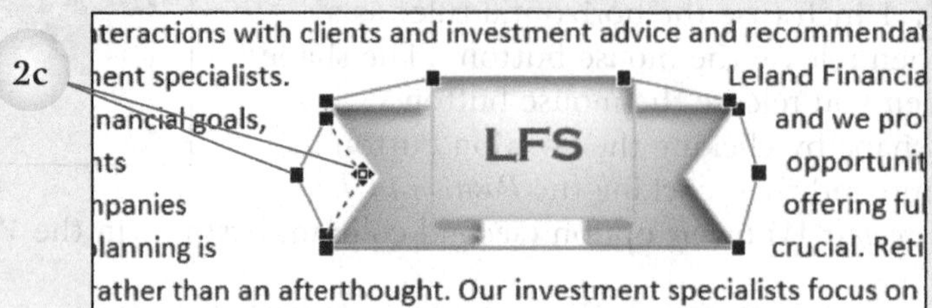

   d. Drag the wrap point at the right side of the shape into the shape, as shown below.

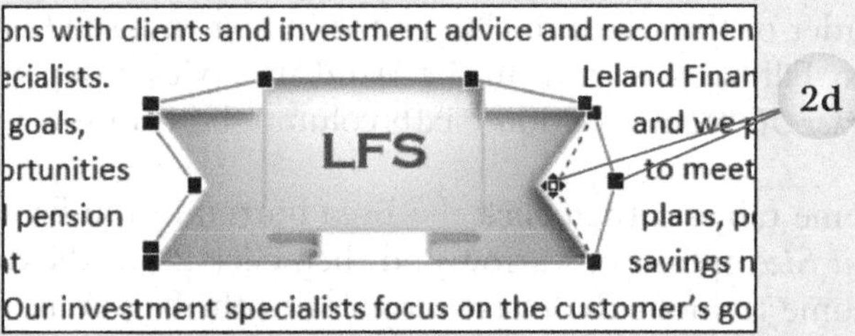

3. Click outside the shape to remove the wrap points.
4. Save **5-Leland.docx**.

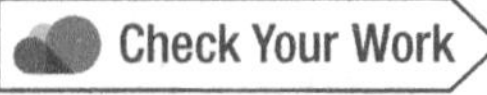

Linking and Unlinking Text Boxes

Quick Steps

Link Text Boxes
1. Select text box.
2. Click Shape Format tab.
3. Click Create Link button.
4. Click in another text box.

Hint Link text boxes to flow text in columns across multiple pages.

Inserting a Text Box on a Shape Not only can text be typed directly in a shape, but a text box can be drawn on a shape. When a text box is drawn on a shape, it is actually added as a layer on top of the shape. To format or move the text box with the shape, select or group the shape with the text box.

Linking and Unlinking Text Boxes Linking text boxes allows the text in them to flow from one box to another. To do this, draw the text boxes and then click in the first text box. Click the Create Link button in the Text group on the Shape Format tab and the pointer displays with a pouring jug icon ( ) attached. Click an empty text box to link it with the selected text box. Type text in the first text box and the text will flow to the linked text box.

More than two text boxes can be linked. To link several text boxes, click the first text box, click the Create Link button on the Shape Format tab, and then click in the second text box. Select the second text box, click the Create Link button, and then click the third text box. Continue in this manner until all the text boxes are linked.

To break a link between two boxes, select the first text box in the link and then click the Break Link button in the Text group. When a link is broken, all the text is placed in the first text box.

Activity 2d Linking and Unlinking Text Boxes

1. With **5-Leland.docx** open, scroll down the document to display the first arrow shape on the first page.
2. Insert, size, and format a text box by completing the following steps:
   a. Click the Insert tab.
   b. Click the Text Box button in the Text group and then click *Draw Text Box* at the drop-down list.
   c. Click in the document near the first shape.
   d. With the text box selected, click in the *Shape Height* measurement box and then type 0.73.
   e. Click in the *Shape Width* measurement box and then type 2.
   f. Click the Shape Fill button arrow in the Shape Styles group and then click *No Fill* at the drop-down list.
   g. Drag the text box so it is positioned on the first arrow (see the image at the right).
   h. Copy the text box to the second arrow shape by pressing and holding down the Ctrl key, clicking the text box border and holding down the left mouse button, dragging the copy of the text box so that it is positioned on top of the second arrow shape, and then releasing the mouse button and the Ctrl key.

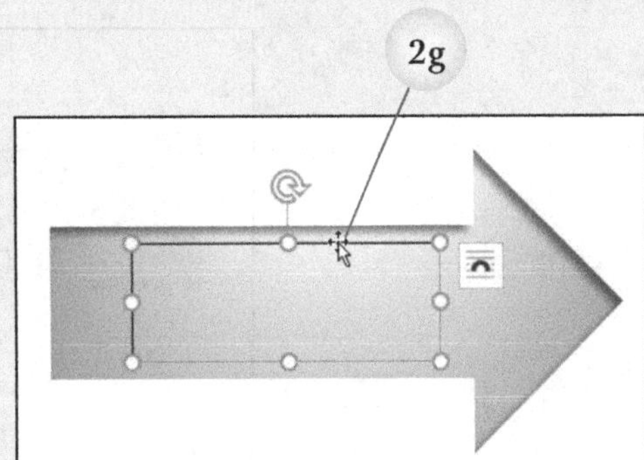

3. Link the text boxes by completing the following steps:
   a. Click the border of the text box on the first arrow shape to select the text box.
   b. Click the Create Link button in the Text group on the Shape Format tab.
   c. Click in the text box on the second arrow shape.

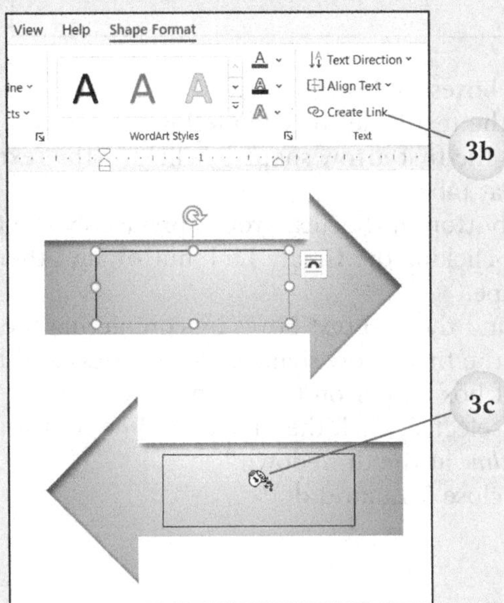

4. Insert text in the text box on the first arrow shape by completing the following steps:
   a. Click in the text box on the first arrow shape.
   b. Click the Home tab, change the font size to 12 points, apply the Orange, Accent 2, Darker 50% font color (sixth column, bottom row in the *Theme Colors* section), and then apply bold formatting.
   c. Click the Center button in the Paragraph group.
   d. Click the Line and Paragraph Spacing button in the Paragraph group and then click *Remove Space After Paragraph*.
   e. Click the Line and Paragraph Spacing button and then click *1.0*.
   f. Type Let Leland Financial Services help you plan for retirement and provide you with information to determine your financial direction. (The text will flow to the text box on the second arrow shape.)

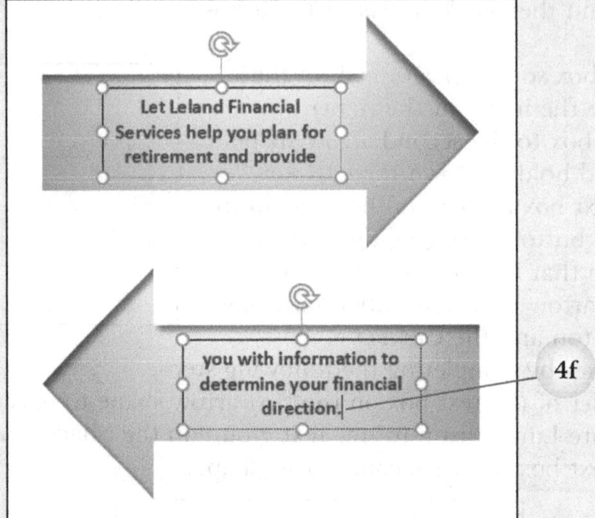

   g. Click outside the text boxes to deselect them.
5. Break the link between the text boxes by completing the following steps:
   a. Select the text box on the first arrow shape by clicking the text box border.
   b. Click the Shape Format tab.
   c. Click the Break Link button in the Text group (previously the Create Link button).
6. Relink the text boxes by clicking the Create Link button and then clicking in the text box on the second arrow shape.
7. Remove the outline around the two text boxes by completing the following steps:
   a. With the text box on the first arrow shape selected, press and hold down the Shift key and then click the text box border on the second arrow shape.
   b. With both text boxes selected, click the Shape Outline button in the Shape Styles group and then click *No Outline* at the drop-down list.
8. Save, preview, and then close **5-Leland.docx**.

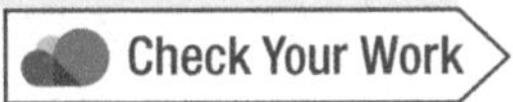

Activity 3 Insert an Icon and 3D Model in an Award Certificate — 3 Parts

You will open an award certificate document and then insert and customize a football icon and a 3D model of a lion.

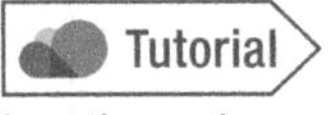

Inserting and Customizing Icons

Quick Steps

Insert Icon

1. Click Insert tab.
2. Click Icons button.
3. Double-click icon.

Hint Insert multiple icons at the same time by clicking each icon at the Insert Icons window and then clicking the Insert button.

Inserting and Customizing Icons

Use the Icons button in the Illustrations group on the Insert tab to insert an icon in a Word document. An icon is a graphical representation of something, such as an animal, weather, an emotion, or an element from nature. Click the Icons button on the Insert tab and the Icons window opens, as shown in Figure 5.3. At this window, scroll down the list box to view the various icons or click a category to display a specific category of icons. To insert an icon in a document, double-click the icon in the list box or click the icon and then click the Insert button.

When an icon is inserted and selected in a document, the Graphics Format tab is active, as shown in Figure 5.4. Use options on this tab to apply a graphic style, fill, outline, and effect; type alternate text for the icon; position, align, group, rotate, and size the icon; and apply text wrapping.

Icons, like other images, can be formatted with options at the Layout dialog box and with options at a task pane. Display the Layout dialog box by clicking the Size group dialog box launcher. Click the Graphics Styles group task pane launcher to display the Format Graphic task pane. The task pane contains the Fill & Line, Effects, Layout & Properties, and Picture icons. Use options at the Format Graphic task pane to format an icon in a manner similar to formatting an image, shape, or text box.

Figure 5.3 Icons Window

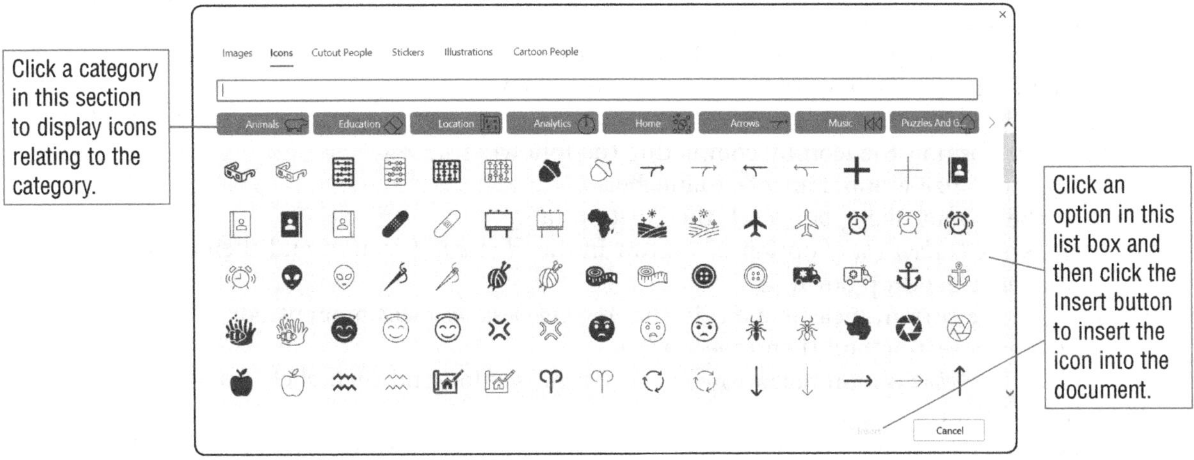

Figure 5.4 Graphics Format Tab

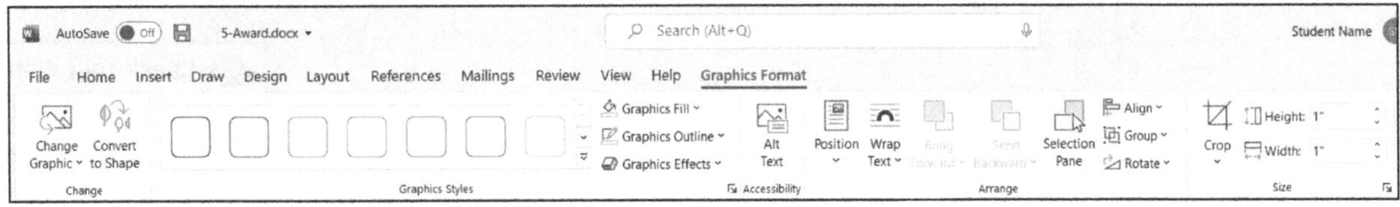

Activity 3a **Inserting and Customizing an Icon** Part 1 of 3

1. Open **Award.docx** and then save it with the name **5-Award.**
2. Insert an icon by completing the following steps:
   a. Click the Insert tab.
   b. Click the Icons button in the Illustrations group.
   c. At the Icons window, type football in the search text box.
   d. When football icons display, double-click the football icon shown at the right.

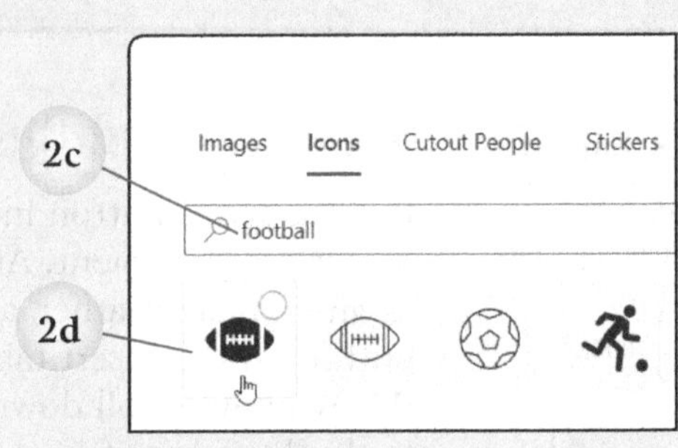

3. Increase the height of the football icon by clicking in the *Height* measurement box in the Size group, typing 2.7, and then pressing the Enter key.

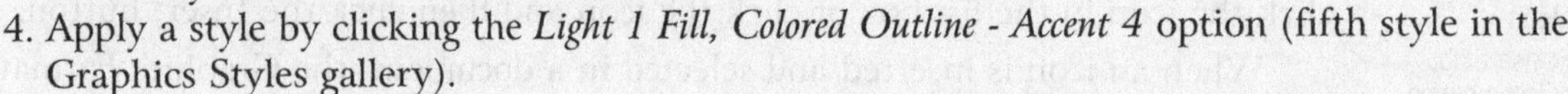

4. Apply a style by clicking the *Light 1 Fill, Colored Outline - Accent 4* option (fifth style in the Graphics Styles gallery).

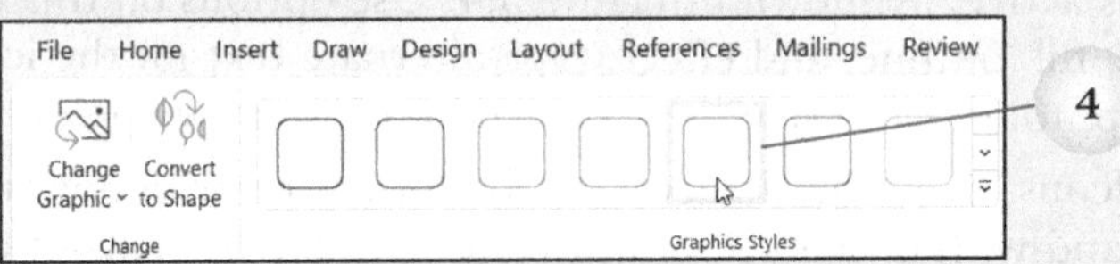

5. Change the width of the icon lines by completing the following steps:
   a. Click the Graphics Styles group task pane launcher.
   b. At the Format Graphic task pane, click *Line*, if necessary, to expand the line options.
   c. Click the *Width* measurement box up arrow two times. (This changes the width to *1.5 pt.*)
   d. Click the Close button in the upper right corner of the task pane.
6. Change text wrapping by clicking the Wrap Text button and then clicking *Behind Text* at the drop-down gallery.

Line
No line
Solid line
Gradient line
Color
Transparency 0%
Width 1.5 pt
Sketched style
5b
5c

7. Precisely position the icon by completing the following steps:
   a. Click the Size group dialog box launcher.
   b. At the Layout dialog box, click the Position tab.
   c. Click the *to the right of* option box arrow in the *Horizontal* section and then click *Left Margin* at the drop-down list.
   d. Select the current measurement in the *Absolute position* measurement box in the *Horizontal* section and then type 4.15.
   e. Click the *below* option box arrow in the *Vertical* section and then click *Top Margin* at the drop-down list.
   f. Select the current measurement in the *Absolute position* measurement box in the *Vertical* section and then type 1.65.
   g. Click OK to close the Layout dialog box.
8. Save **5-Award.docx.**

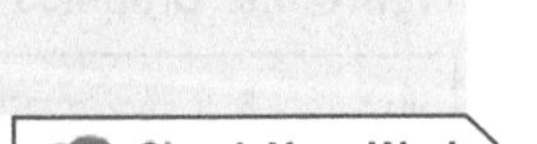

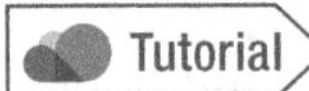

Inserting and Customizing 3D Models

 3D Models

Quick Steps

Insert 3D Model

1. Click Insert tab.
2. Click 3D Models button.
3. Click 3D model category.
4. Double-click 3D model.

Hint *3D* is an abbreviation for *three-dimensional*. It describes an object that has width, height, and depth.

 Pan & Zoom

Inserting and Customizing 3D Models

Word supports inserting 3D models into a document. A 3D model is a graphic file of an image shown in three dimensions. The model can be rotated or tilted to allow viewing from various angles or to display a specific portion or feature. Microsoft's 3D model gallery includes a collection of free 3D models that can be inserted in a document. Access these models by clicking the 3D Models button in the Illustrations group on the Insert tab. At the Online 3D Models window, as shown in Figure 5.5, click a category to view all the 3D models within the category or type one or more keywords in the search text box and then press the Enter key. Some 3D models include animation. These are identified with a "runner" badge (an icon of a runner in the lower left corner of the model). Insert a 3D model in a document by double-clicking the model or clicking the model and then clicking the Insert button.

When a 3D model is inserted in a document, the 3D Model tab is active. If the model is animated, the Play 3D group is available on the 3D Model tab. Click the Play button to play the animation and click the Scenes button to display a drop-down list of preset animations called *scenes*. Use buttons in the Adjust group to insert a different 3D model or to reset the selected model to its original size and position. The 3D Model Views group includes a gallery of preset views for the model. Click the Alt Text button in the Accessibility group and the Alt Text task pane displays where a description of the model can be added. Use options in the Arrange group to position the model, apply text wrapping, send the model forward or backward, and align the model. Change the height and width of the model with options in the Size group.

The Size group also contains the Pan & Zoom button. Click this button and a button (a magnifying glass with a plus symbol inside) displays at the right of the selected model. Position the pointer on this button, click and hold down the left mouse button, and then drag up to increase the size of the model (pan in) or drag down to decrease the size (pan out). To turn off the pan feature, click the Pan & Zoom button to deactivate it.

When a 3D model is selected, a Layout Options button displays outside the upper right corner. Click the Layout Options button and a side menu displays with text wrapping options. Click a text wrapping option and then click the side menu Close button.

Figure 5.5 Online 3D Models Window

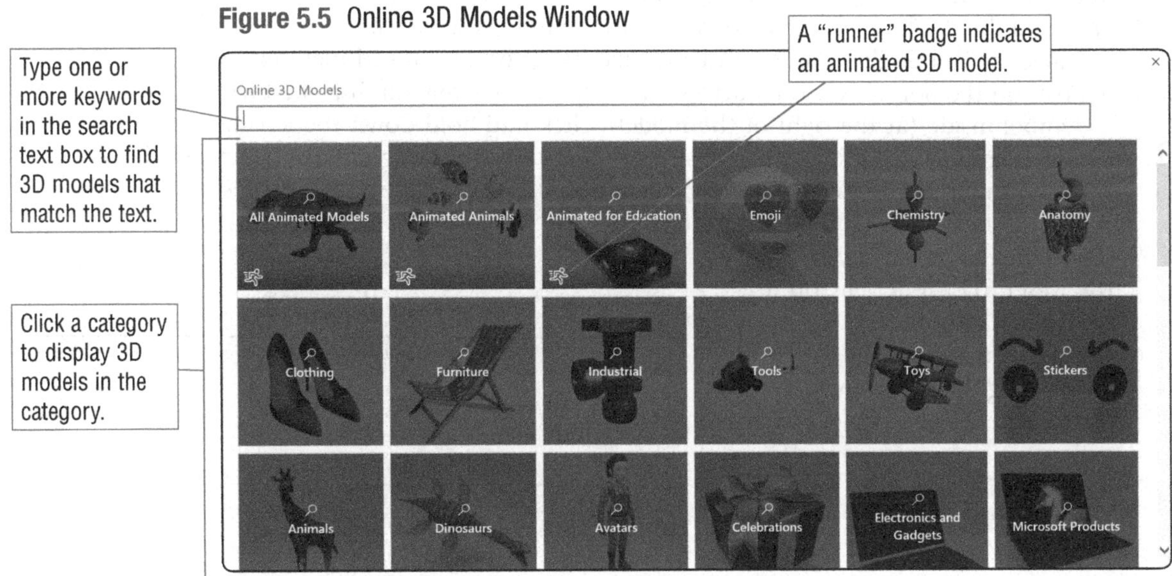

Use the 3D control in the middle of a selected 3D model to rotate or tilt the model. To use the 3D control, position the pointer on the control, click and hold down the left mouse button, and then drag with the mouse to rotate or tilt the model.

Advanced layout options are available at the Layout dialog box. Click the Size group dialog box launcher to display the dialog box. Use options at the Layout dialog box to specify the size, text wrapping, and position of the 3D model.

A 3D model saved to the computer's hard drive can be inserted in a document. Click the 3D Models button arrow and a drop-down list displays with the options *This Device* and *Stock 3D Models*. Click the *Stock 3D Models* option and the Online 3D Models window opens. Click the *This Device* option and the Insert 3D Model dialog box displays. At this dialog box, navigate to the folder containing the 3D model and then double-click the model to insert it in the document.

Activity 3b Inserting and Customizing a 3D Model

Part 2 of 3

1. With **5-Award.docx** open, press Ctrl + End to move the insertion point to the end of the document.
2. Insert a 3D model from the 3D model gallery by completing the following steps:
   a. Click the Insert tab.
   b. Click the 3D Models button in the Illustrations group.
   c. At the Online 3D Models window, type lion in the search text box and then press the Enter key.
   d. Double-click the lion model shown at the right.
   Note: If you do not have access to the Online 3D Models window, open Award3D.docx from your WL2C5 folder. This document contains the 3D lion model.

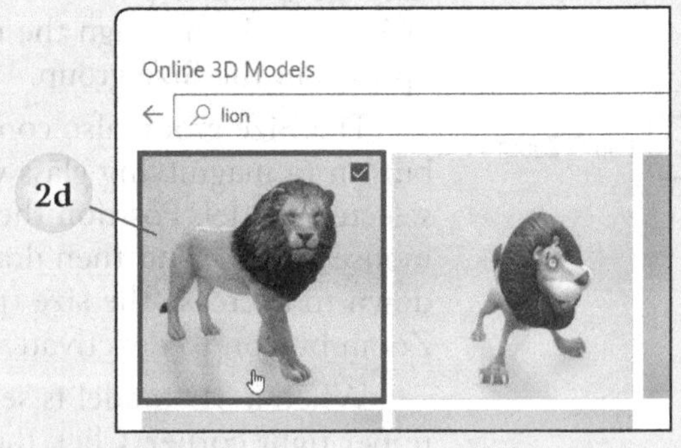

3. Experiment using the 3D control, which displays in the middle of the lion model, by positioning the pointer on the 3D control, clicking and holding down the left mouse button, and then dragging with the mouse to rotate the model.
4. Pan in and out of the model by completing the following steps:
   a. Click the Pan & Zoom button in the Size group on the 3D Model tab.
   b. Position the pointer on the button that displays as a magnifying glass with a plus symbol inside (at the right of the model), click and hold down the left mouse button, and then drag up to increase the size of the model and drag down to decrease the size. Make sure the lion displays within the placeholders after decreasing the size.
   c. Click the Pan & Zoom button to deactivate it.
5. Reset the lion model by clicking the Reset 3D Model button in the Adjust group.
6. Change the view of the model by clicking the *Left* view (second option) in the 3D Model Views gallery.

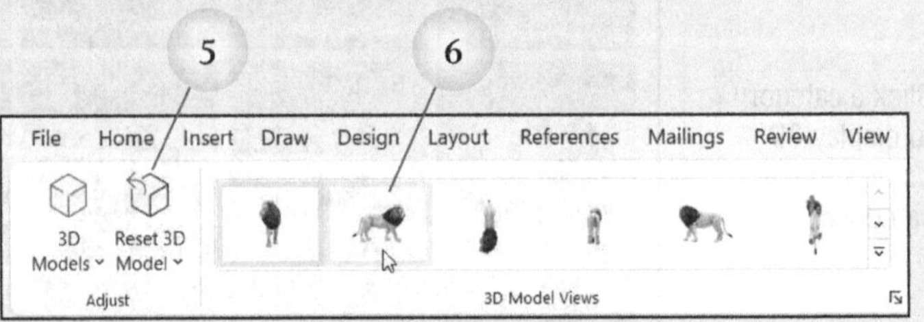

7. Using the 3D control, rotate the model so that it displays as shown at the right.
8. Change the height of the model by clicking in the *Height* measurement box, typing 3.7, and then pressing the Enter key.
9. Precisely position the lion model by completing the following steps:
   a. Click the Size group dialog box launcher.
   b. At the Layout dialog box, click the Position tab.
   c. Click the *to the right of* option box arrow in the *Horizontal* section and then click *Left Margin* at the drop-down list.
   d. Select the current measurement in the *Absolute position* measurement box in the *Horizontal* section and then type -0.2. (Hint: Use the hyphen key to create the minus symbol before typing *0.2*.)
   e. Click the *below* option box arrow in the *Vertical* section and then click *Page* at the drop-down list.
   f. Select the current measurement in the *Absolute position* measurement box in the *Vertical* section and then type 4.2.
   g. Click OK to close the Layout dialog box.
10. Check for alternative text for the lion model by completing the following steps:
    a. Click the Alt Text button in the Accessibility group.
    b. Notice that the description box in the Alt Text task pane contains the word *Lion*.

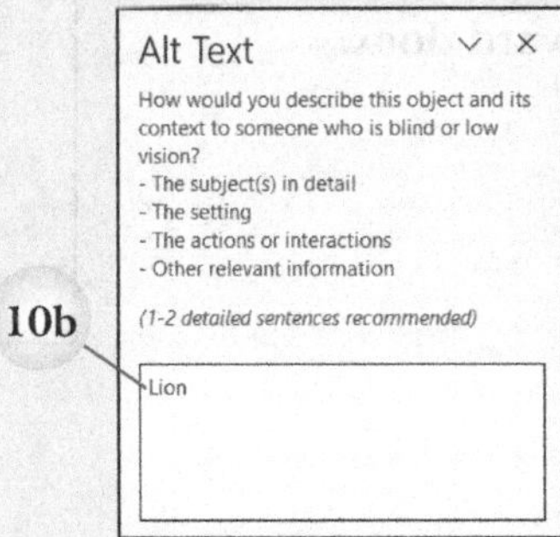

    c. Close the Alt Text task pane.
11. Save **5-Award.docx**.

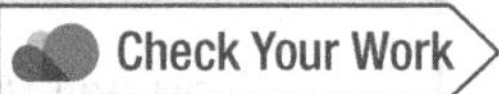

Options for formatting and customizing a 3D model are available at the Format 3D Model task pane. Display the task pane by clicking the 3D Model Views group task pane launcher. The task pane displays with four icons: Fill & Line, Effects, Layout & Properties, and 3D Model. The options in the task pane vary depending on the icon selected.

The task pane opens with the 3D Model icon selected and contains options for specifying a rotation and camera view. Click the Fill & Line icon to display options for formatting the border line and fill of the 3D model. Use options at the task pane with the Effects icon selected to apply formatting effects, such as shadow, reflection, glow, and soft edges, and to format and rotate the model. Click the Layout & Properties icon and the options in the task pane are dimmed and unavailable.

Activity 3c Formatting a 3D Model with Task Pane Options

Part 3 of 3

1. With **5-Award.docx** open, make sure the lion model is selected and the 3D Model tab is active.
2. Display the Format 3D Model task pane by clicking the 3D Model Views group task pane launcher.
3. Format the lion model by completing the following steps:
   a. With the 3D Model icon selected in the task pane, click *Model Rotation*, if necessary, to expand the options.
   b. Select the current degree measurement in the *X Rotation* measurement box and then type 3.5.
   c. Select the current degree measurement in the *Y Rotation* measurement box and then type 45.
   d. Select the current degree measurement in the *Z Rotation* measurement box and then type 2.7.
   e. Click the Effects icon in the task pane.
   f. Click *Shadow* to expand the shadow options, if necessary.
   g. Click the Presets button and then click the *Offset: Center* option (second column, second row in the *Outer* section).
   h. Close the Format 3D Model task pane.
4. Save, preview, and then close **5-Award.docx**.

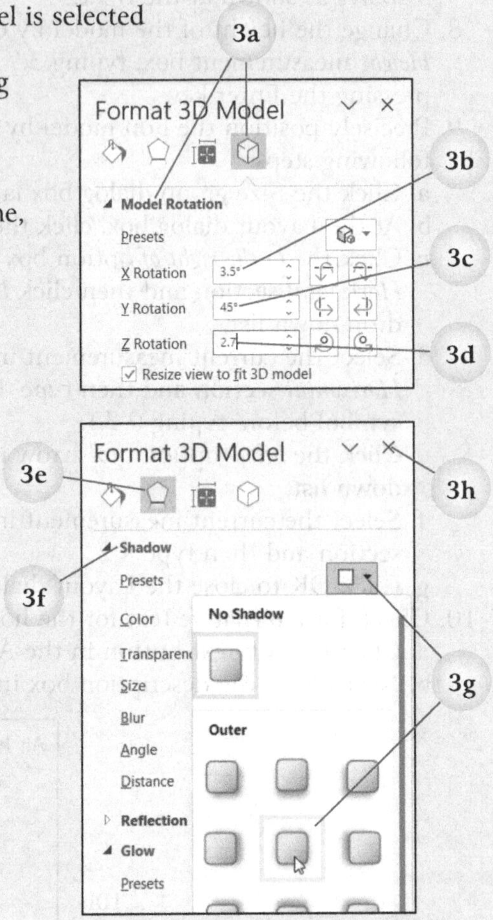

Check Your Work

Activity 4 Use Options on the Draw Tab in a Produce Flyer

3 Parts

You will use options on the Draw tab to draw, select, convert, and format ink drawings, highlight text, and use editing features to edit a document.

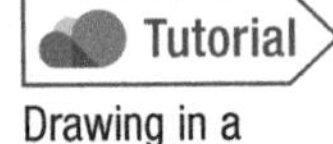

Drawing in a Document

Drawing in a Document

The Draw tab shown in Figure 5.6, contains buttons for drawing in a document, converting shapes, editing text, and selecting and highlighting text. If this tab is not visible, display the tab by right-clicking the ribbon and then clicking *Customize the Ribbon*. At the Word Options dialog box with *Customize Ribbon* selected in the left panel, click the *Draw* check box in the right list box to insert a check mark and then click OK. The Draw tab should display between the Insert and Design tabs. Use options on the Draw tab to draw using a mouse, finger, or digital pen.

Figure 5.6 Draw Tab

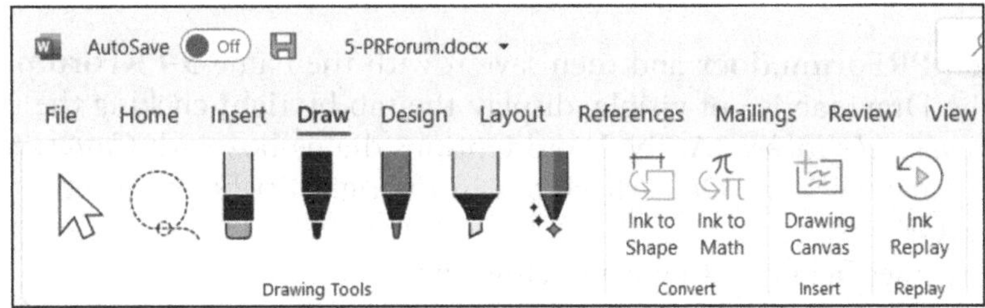

Using Pens to Draw and Highlight

The Drawing Tools group on the Draw tab contains buttons for selecting and erasing ink drawings as well as pens for drawing in a document, a highlighter pen for highlighting text, and an Action Pen for editing a document. Click a pen or highlighter button to select it and then use the mouse, a finger, or digital pen to draw in the document. A pen button stays active until a different button is selected. Click an active pen button and a drop-down list displays with options for changing the size, thickness, and color of the pen. Add additional pens to the Draw tab by right-clicking a pen and then clicking *Add Another Pen* at the shortcut menu. To remove a pen from the Draw tab, right-click the pen and then click *Delete Pen* at the shortcut menu.

Use the Highlighter pen to highlight specific text in a document. Click the Highlighter pen to activate it and then draw over text. The Highlighter pen button drop-down list contains the *Snap to Text* option. Click this option to turn it on and drawing with the Highlighter pen causes the highlighting to snap to the text. If this option is not turned on, drawing with the Highlighter pen is more freeform. Remove highlighting from text by drawing across the text again with the Highlighter pen active.

Selecting and Erasing Ink Drawings

Lasso

Select an object such as an ink drawing or shape with the Select button in the Drawing Tools groups. Use the Lasso button to select ink drawings. To do this, click the Lasso button and then draw around the ink drawings.

Use the Eraser pen to erase ink drawn in the document. Click the Eraser button to activate it and then click the button again to display a drop-down list with options for specifying the width of the eraser. Choose the *Point Eraser* option at the drop-down list to precisely erase parts of an ink drawing.

Replaying Ink Drawings

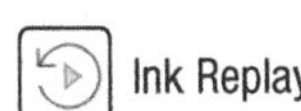

Use the Ink Replay button in the Replay group on the Draw tab to show a replay of the most recent ink drawings. Click the Replay button and a replay bar displays along the bottom of the screen and any ink drawing is played in the document. Use buttons on the replay bar to rewind or play the ink drawings again. Remove the replay bar by clicking the Close button in the upper right corner of the bar or by clicking in the document outside the replay bar.

Activity 4a Using Pens to Draw and Highlight Text in a Document

Part 1 of 3

1. Open **PRForum.docx** and then save it with the name **5-PRForum**.
2. If the Draw tab is not visible, display the tab by right-clicking the ribbon and then clicking *Customize the Ribbon*. At the Word Options dialog box with *Customize Ribbon* selected in the left panel, click the *Draw* check box in the right list box to insert a check mark and then click OK.
3. Draw lines below text by completing the following steps:
   a. Click the Draw tab to make it active.
   b. Click the left pen button (the first pen button after the Eraser button) to activate it.
   c. Click the left pen button again to display the drop-down list.
   d. Click the *1 mm* option in the *Thickness* section.
   e. Click the *Indigo* color in the *Colors* section (first column, second row).
   f. Using the mouse, draw a line below the text ***Date:*** *Wednesday, May 15, 2024*.
   g. Using the mouse, draw a line below the text *9:00 a.m. to 2:30 p.m.*

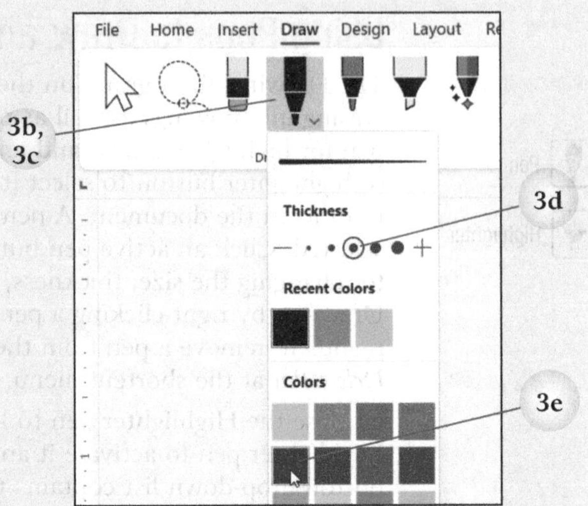

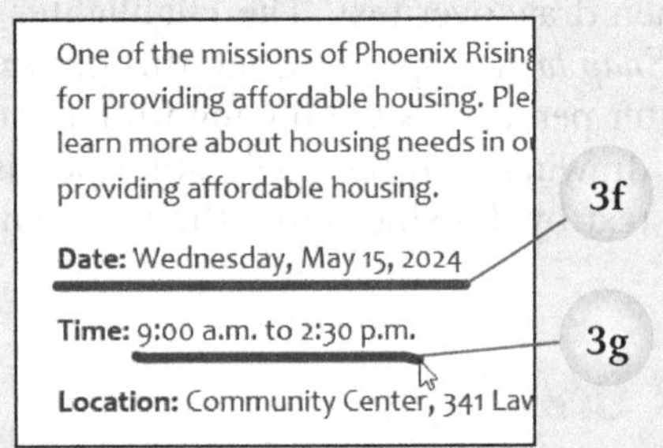

4. Replay the ink drawings you just made by clicking the Ink Replay button on the Draw tab.
5. Click in the document to remove the replay bar.
6. Erase the line below *9:00 a.m. to 2:30 p.m.* by completing the following steps:
   a. Click the Eraser button in the Drawing Tools group to activate it.
   b. Click the button again to display the drop-down list.
   c. At the drop-down list make sure *Eraser* is selected in the *Types* section.
   d. Click anywhere on the line below *9:00 a.m. to 2:30 p.m.*
7. Erase a portion of the line below ***Date:*** *Wednesday, May 15, 2024* by completing the following steps:
   a. Click the Eraser button and then click the *Point Eraser* option in the *Types* section.
   b. Using the mouse, remove the portion of the line below **Date:** by drawing along that portion of the line.

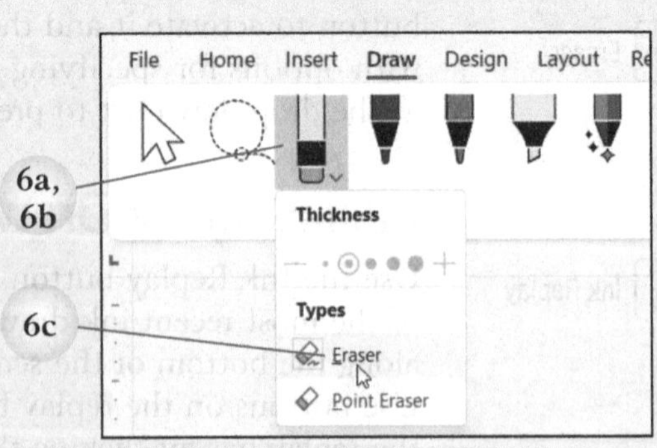

8. Highlight text by completing the following steps:
   a. Click the Highlighter button in the Drawing Tools group.
   b. Click the Highlighter button again to display the drop-down list.
   c. Click the *6 mm* option in the *Thickness* section.
   d. Click the *Pink* color in the *Colors* section (fourth column, first row).
   e. Click the *Snap to Text* option to insert a check mark before the option.
   f. Using the mouse, drag through the text *"With better understanding comes possibilities for solutions."*
   g. Using the mouse, drag through the text *"Opening doors to all."*
9. Remove highlighting by dragging through the text *"With better understanding comes possibilities for solutions."*
10. Save **5-PRForum.docx**.

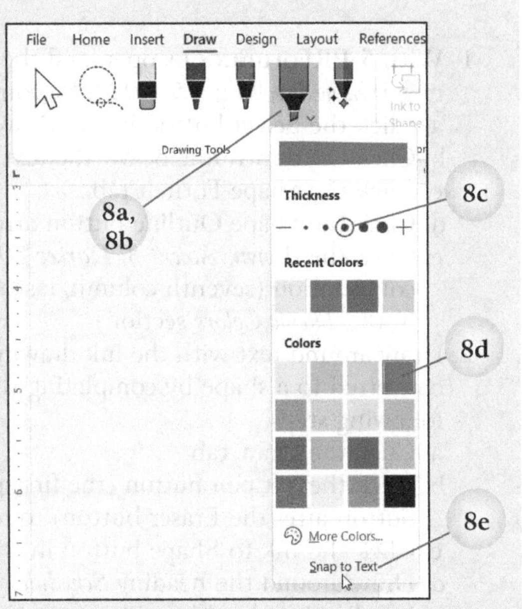

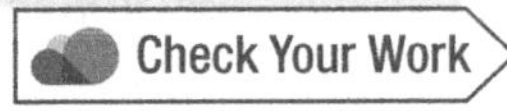

Converting an Ink Drawing

The Ink to Shape button will convert an ink drawing to a shape. To convert an ink drawing to a shape, choose a pen, click the Ink to Shape button to activate it, and then draw a shape in the document. The ink drawing is converted to the shape most similar to the ink drawing. For example, draw a box around text in a document and the ink drawing is converted to a square or rectangle. Draw a circle around text and the ink drawing is converted to a circle or oval.

Formatting an Ink Drawing and Converted Shape

Select an ink drawing and the Shape Format tab displays on the ribbon. Click this tab and options display for formatting the drawing. Some of the options on the Shape Format tab are dimmed and unavailable. If an ink drawing is converted to a shape and the shape is selected, most of the options on the Shape Format tab are available.

Activity 4b Formatting and Converting an Ink Drawing

Part 2 of 3

1. With **5-PRForum.docx** open and the Draw tab active, format the ink drawing below the text *Wednesday, May 15, 2024,* by completing the following steps:
   a. Click the Select button in the Drawing Tools group.
   b. Click the drawn line below the text *Wednesday, May 15, 2024* to select the line.
   c. Click the Shape Format tab.
   d. Click the Shape Outline button arrow.
   e. Click the *Brown, Accent 3, Darker 50%* color option (seventh column, last row in the *Theme Colors* section).
2. Draw around text with the ink drawing converted to a shape by completing the following steps:
   a. Click the Draw tab.
   b. Click the left pen button (the first pen button after the Eraser button) to activate it.
   c. Click the Ink to Shape button in the Convert group.
   d. Draw around the heading *Schedule of Events*. (When you release the mouse button, the ink drawing should convert to an oval shape. If this does not happen, undo the ink drawing and then try again.)

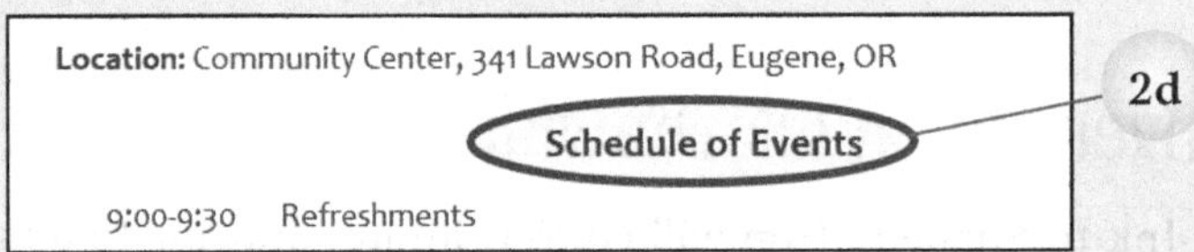

3. Format the converted shape by completing the following steps:
   a. Click the Select button in the Drawing Tools group.
   b. Click the shape around the heading *Schedule of Events*.
   c. Click the Shape Format tab.
   d. Click the Shape Outline button and then click the *Brown, Accent 3, Darker 50%* color option (seventh column, last row in the *Theme Colors* section).
   e. Click the Shape Effects button arrow, point to *Shadow*, and then click the *Offset: Bottom* option (second column, first row in the *Outer* section).
4. Save **5-PRForum.docx**.

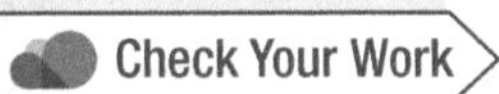

Editing with the Action Pen

Action Pen

Edit text in a document with the Action Pen on the Draw tab. Natural gestures can be used when editing with the Action Pen. Click the Action Pen button to select it and then click the button again to display a drop-down list with the options *Tracked Changes* and *Ink Gesture Help*. (You will learn about tracked changes in Chapter 8.) To see the gestures available for editing, click the *Ink Gesture Help* option and the Help task pane displays with a list of gestures and the result when using the gesture. For example, scribble through text to delete it, circle text to select it, and draw a line up or down to split or join text.

Activity 4c Editing a Document with the Action Pen

Part 3 of 3

1. With **5-PRForum.docx** open and the Draw tab active, click the left pen button.
2. Click the Action Pen button.
3. Click the Action Pen button again and then click *Ink Gesture Help* at the drop-down list. (This displays the Help task pane with information on gestures to use for editing.)

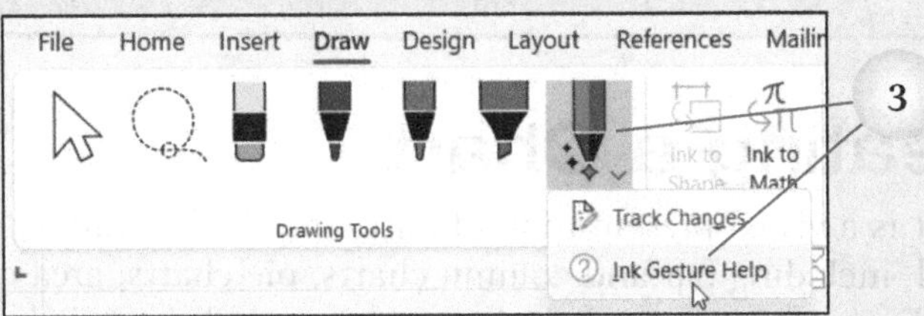

4. Using the mouse, scribble through the words *Reliable and* in the title. (This deletes the words.)

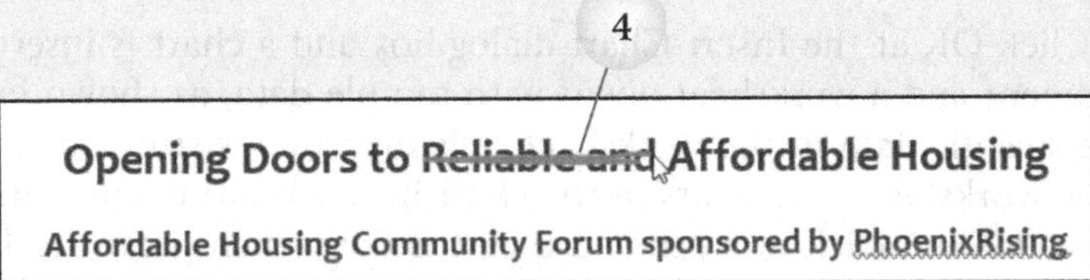

5. Using the mouse, draw a line down between the letters *x* and *R* in *PhoenixRising* in the subtitle. (This inserts a space between the two letters.)
6. Using the mouse, draw a line up in the space between *Home* and *lessness* in the text after the *10:00 to 11:30* time to join the text.
7. Close the Help task pane.
8. Click the Select button in the Drawing Tools group on the Draw tab.
9. Click the Home tab.
10. Save, preview, and then close **5-PRForum.docx**.

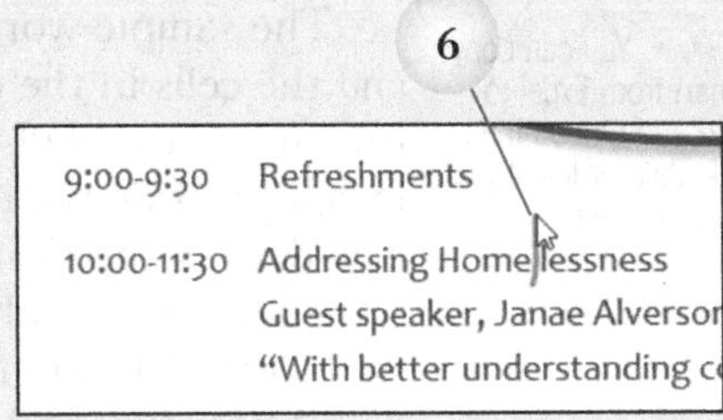

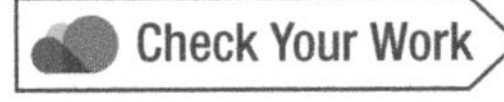

Activity 5 Create and Format a Column Chart and a Pie Chart

5 Parts

You will use the Chart feature to create and format a column chart and then create and format a pie chart.

Creating a Chart

Chart

Creating a Chart

A chart is a visual presentation of data. In Word, a variety of charts can be created, including bar and column charts, pie charts, area charts, and many more. To create a chart, click the Insert tab and then click the Chart button in the Illustrations group. This displays the Insert Chart dialog box, as shown in Figure 5.7. At this dialog box, choose the chart type in the list at the left side, click the chart style, and then click OK.

Quick Steps

Insert Chart

1. Click Insert tab.
2. Click Chart button.
3. Enter data in worksheet.
4. Close Excel.

Click OK at the Insert Chart dialog box and a chart is inserted in the document and a worksheet opens with sample data, as shown in Figure 5.8. Type specific data in the worksheet cells over the existing data. As data is typed in the worksheet, it appears in the chart in the Word document. To type data in the worksheet, click in a cell and type the data; then press the Tab key to make the next cell active, press Shift + Tab to make the previous cell active, or press the Enter key to make the cell below active.

Hint You can copy a chart from Excel to Word and embed it as static data or link it to the worksheet.

The sample worksheet contains a data range of four columns and five rows and the cells in the data range display with a light fill color. More columns and rows may be added to the range as needed to create the chart. Simply type data in cells outside the data range and the data range expands and incorporates the new data in the chart. This occurs because the table AutoExpansion feature is turned on by default. If data is typed in a cell outside the data range, an AutoCorrect Options button displays in the lower right corner of the cell. Use this button to turn off AutoExpansion.

Figure 5.7 Insert Chart Dialog Box

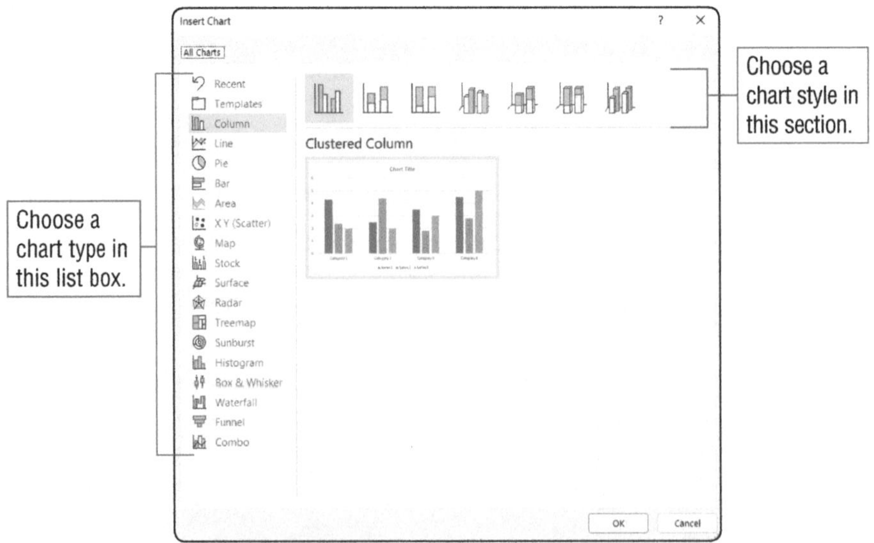

Figure 5.8 Sample Chart

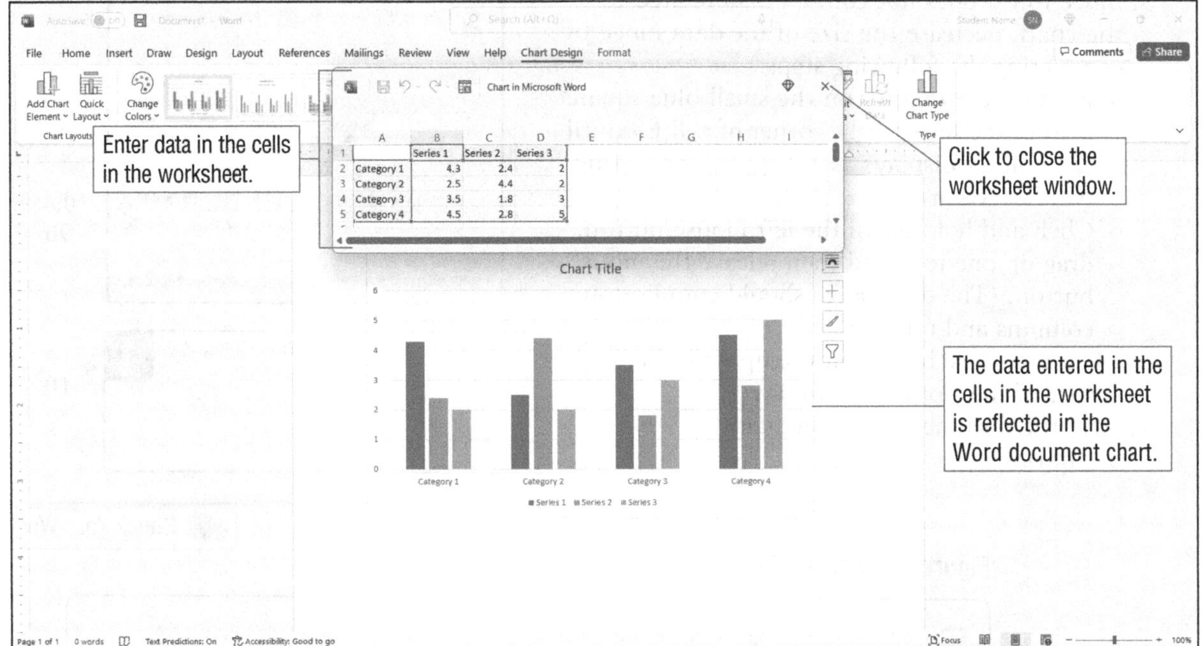

If data is not typed in all four columns and five rows, decrease the size of the data range. To do this, position the pointer on the small blue square icon in the lower right corner of cell E5 until the pointer displays as a diagonally pointing two-headed arrow; then drag up to decrease the number of rows in the range and/or drag left to decrease the number of columns.

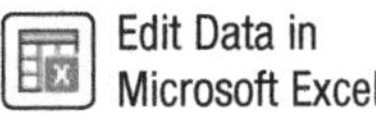

Chart data can also be entered in Excel by clicking the Edit Data in Microsoft Excel button that displays in the worksheet window. When all the data is typed, click the Close button in the upper right corner of the worksheet. The worksheet window closes, the Word document window expands, and the chart displays in the document.

Activity 5a Creating a Column Chart

Part 1 of 5

1. At a blank document, click the Insert tab and then click the Chart button in the Illustrations group.
2. At the Insert Chart dialog box, click OK.
3. If necessary, drag the bottom border of the worksheet window down to display row 5 of the worksheet.
4. Click in cell B1 in the worksheet and then type Sales 2022.
5. Press the Tab key and then type Sales 2023 in cell C1.
6. Press the Tab key and then type Sales 2024 in cell D1.
7. Press the Tab key. (This makes cell A2 active.)
8. Continue typing the remaining data in cells, including dollar signs as shown in Figure 5.9. After typing the last entry, click in cell A1.

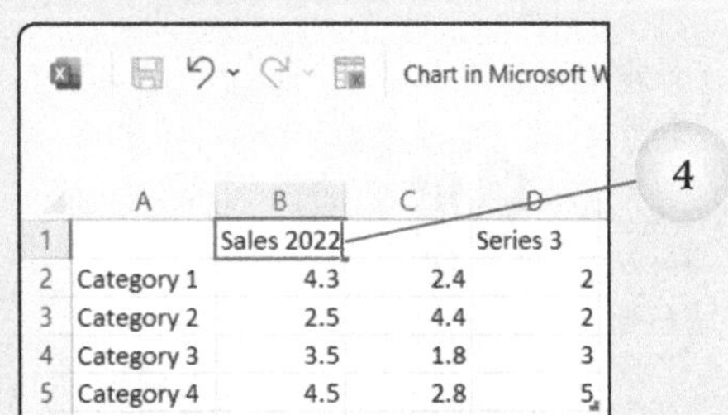

9. Since row 5 does not contain data related to the chart, decrease the size of the data range by completing the following steps:
   a. Position the pointer on the small blue square icon in the lower right corner of cell E5 until the pointer displays as a diagonally pointing two-headed arrow.
   b. Click and hold down the left mouse button, drag up one row, and then release the mouse button. (The data range should contain four columns and four rows.)
10. Click the Close button in the upper right corner of the worksheet window.
11. Save the document with the name **5-Charts**.

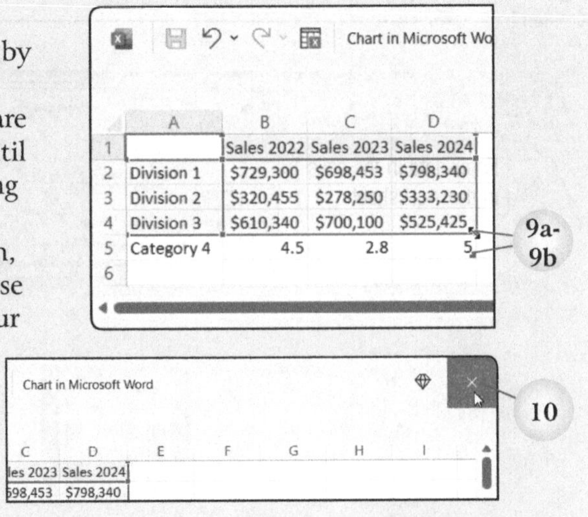

Check Your Work

Figure 5.9 Activity 5a

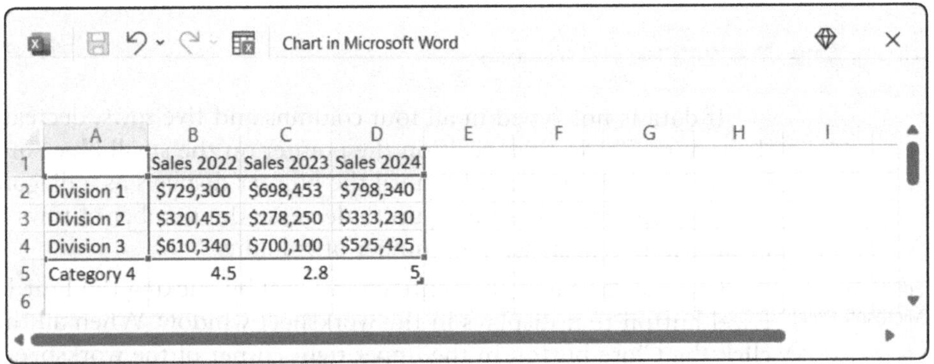

	A	B	C	D
1		Sales 2022	Sales 2023	Sales 2024
2	Division 1	$729,300	$698,453	$798,340
3	Division 2	$320,455	$278,250	$333,230
4	Division 3	$610,340	$700,100	$525,425
5	Category 4	4.5	2.8	5
6				

Formatting a Chart with Chart Buttons

Formatting with Chart Buttons

When a chart is inserted in a document, four buttons display at the right of the chart border, as shown in Figure 5.10. These buttons contain options for applying formatting to the chart.

Figure 5.10 Chart Buttons

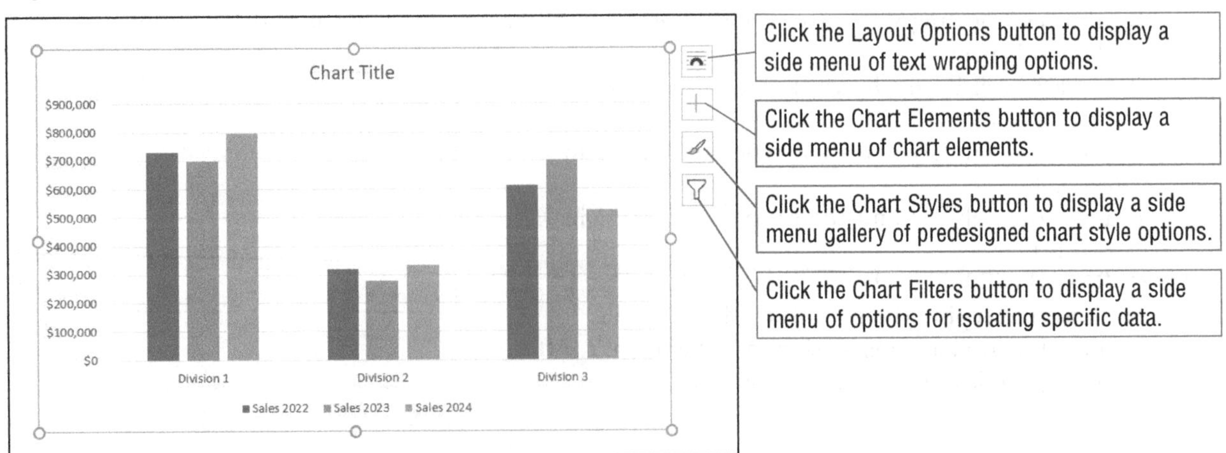

Click the top button, Layout Options, and a side menu displays with text wrapping options. Click the next button, Chart Elements, and a side menu displays with chart elements, such as axis title, chart title, data labels, data table, gridlines, and legend. Elements with check marks inserted in the check boxes are included in the chart. To include other elements, insert check marks in the check boxes for them.

Click the Chart Styles button at the right of the chart and a side menu gallery of styles displays. Scroll down the gallery and hover the pointer over an option and the style formatting is applied to the chart. In addition to providing options for chart styles, the Chart Styles button side menu gallery provides options for chart colors. Click the Chart Styles button, click the Color tab at the right of the Style tab, and then click a color option at the color palette that displays. Hover the pointer over a color option to view how the color change affects the elements in the chart.

Hint Use a pie chart if the data series you want to plot has seven categories or less and the categories represent parts of a whole.

Use the bottom button, Chart Filters, to isolate specific data in the chart. Click the button and a side menu displays. Specify the series or categories to display in the chart. To do this, remove the check marks in the check boxes for those elements that should not appear in the chart. After removing any check marks, click the Apply button in the lower left corner of the side menu. Click the Names tab at the Chart Filters button side menu and options display for turning on and off the display of column and row names.

Activity 5b Formatting with Chart Buttons

Part 2 of 5

1. With **5-Charts.docx** open, make sure the chart is selected.
2. Click the Layout Options button outside the upper right corner of the chart and then click the *Square* option in the side menu (first option in the *With Text Wrapping* section).
3. Remove and add chart elements by completing the following steps:
   a. Click the Chart Elements button below the Layout Options button outside the upper right side of the chart.
   b. At the side menu, click the *Chart Title* check box to remove the check mark.
   c. Click the *Data Table* check box to insert a check mark.

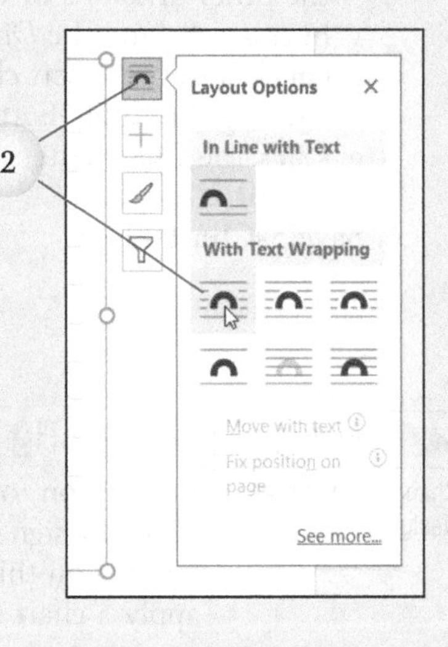

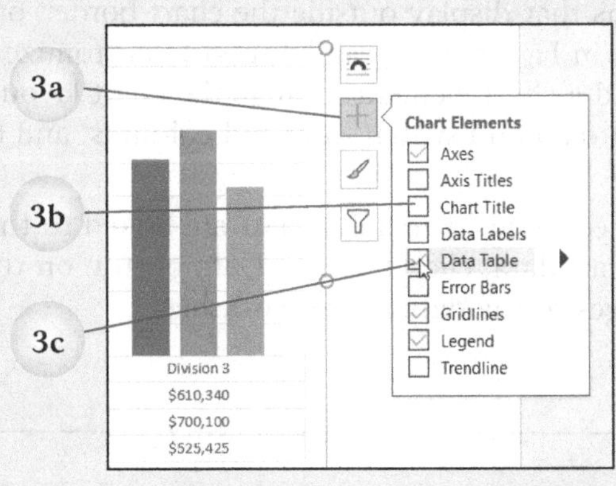

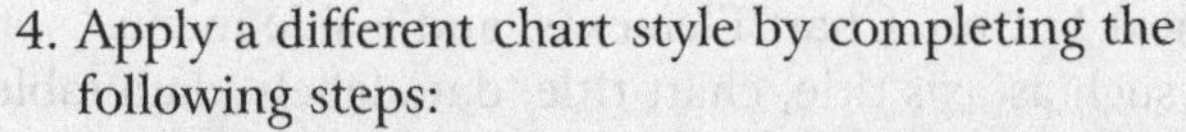

4. Apply a different chart style by completing the following steps:
   a. Click the Chart Styles button below the Chart Elements button.
   b. At the side menu gallery, click the *Style 3* option (third option in the gallery).
   c. Click the Color tab at the top of the side menu and then click the *Colorful Palette 4* option at the drop-down gallery (fourth row in the *Colorful* section).
   d. Click the Chart Styles button to close the side menu.

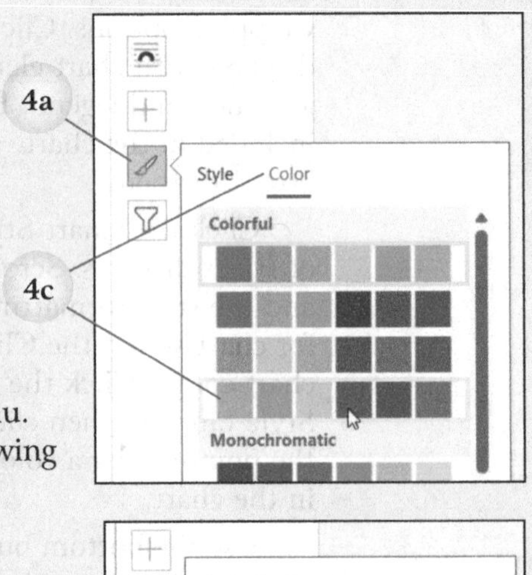

5. Display only Division 1 sales by completing the following steps:
   a. Click the Chart Filters button below the Chart Styles button.
   b. Click the *Division 2* check box in the *Categories* section to remove the check mark.
   c. Click the *Division 3* check box in the *Categories* section to remove the check mark.
   d. Click the Apply button in the lower left corner of the side menu.
   e. Click the Chart Filters button to close the side menu.
   f. After viewing only Division 1 sales, redisplay the other divisions by clicking the Chart Filters button, clicking the *Division 2* and *Division 3* check boxes to insert check marks, and then clicking the Apply button.
   g. Click the Chart Filters button to close the side menu.
6. Save **5-Charts.docx**.

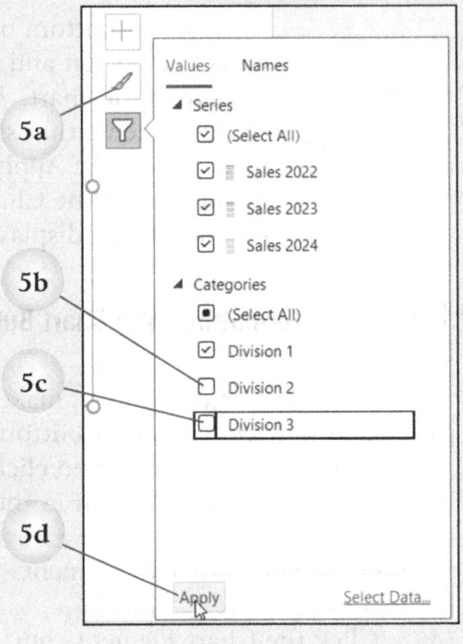

Changing the Chart Design

Changing the Chart Design

In addition to the buttons that display outside the chart border, options on the Chart Design tab, shown in Figure 5.11, can be used to customize a chart. Use options on this tab to add a chart element, change the chart layout and colors, apply a chart style, select data and switch rows and columns, and change the chart type.

The cells in a worksheet used to create a chart are linked to the chart in the document. To edit the chart data, click the Edit Data button on the Chart Design tab and then make changes to the data in the worksheet.

Figure 5.11 Chart Design Tab

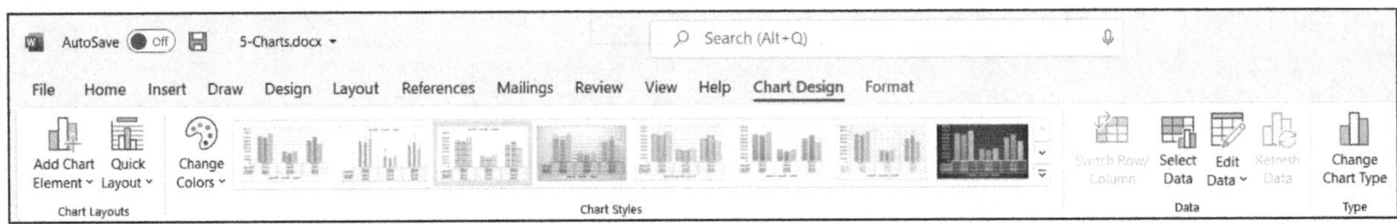

Activity 5c Changing the Chart Design

Part 3 of 5

1. With **5-Charts.docx** open, make sure the chart is selected and the Chart Design tab is active.
2. Change to a different layout by clicking the Quick Layout button in the Chart Layouts group and then clicking the *Layout 3* option (third column, first row in the drop-down gallery).
3. Click the *Style 7* chart style in the Chart Styles group (seventh option from the left).
4. Click the Add Chart Element button in the Chart Layouts group, point to *Chart Title* at the drop-down list, and then click *Centered Overlay* at the side menu.

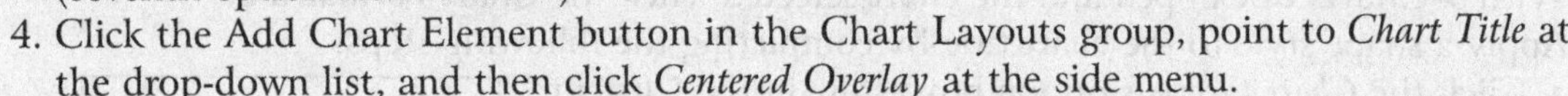

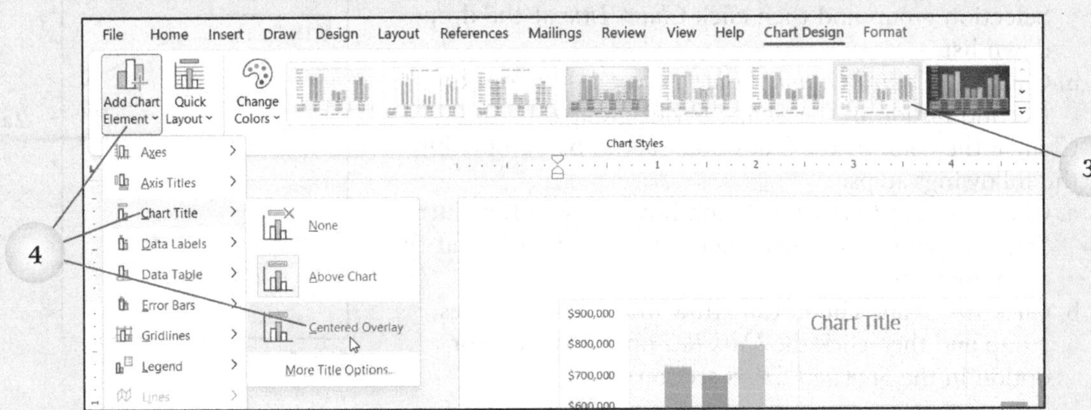

5. Type Regional Sales as the chart title.
6. Click the chart border to deselect the chart title.
7. Edit the data by completing the following steps:
   a. Click the Edit Data button in the Data group.
   b. Click in cell C3 in the worksheet.
   c. Type 375250. (Typing this text replaces the original amount, *$278,250*.)
   d. Click the Close button in the upper right corner of the worksheet.
8. Save **5-Charts.docx**.

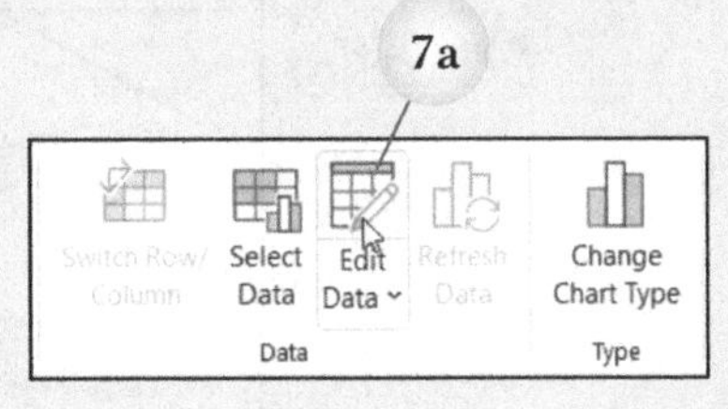

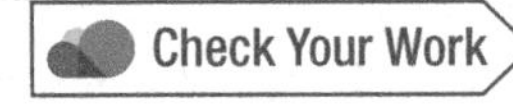

Changing Chart Formatting

Changing Chart Formatting

Use options and buttons on the Chart Format tab, shown in Figure 5.12, to format and customize a chart and chart elements. To format or modify a specific element in a chart, select the element. Do this by clicking the element or by clicking the *Chart Elements* option box in the Current Selection group and then clicking the element at the drop-down list. Use other options on the Chart Format tab to apply a shape style and WordArt style and to arrange and size the chart or chart element.

Figure 5.12 Chart Format tab

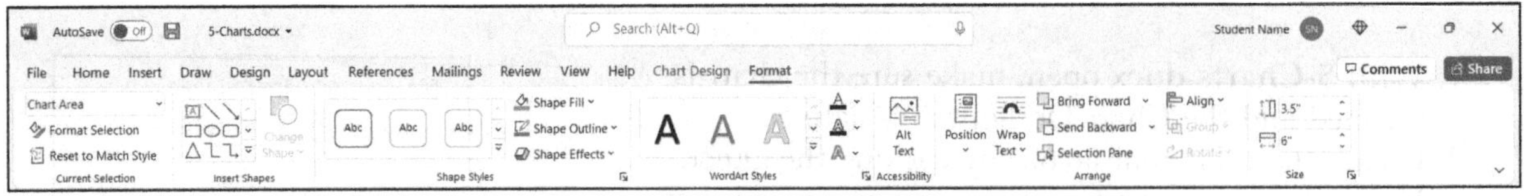

Activity 5d Formatting a Chart and Chart Elements

Part 4 of 5

1. With **5-Charts.docx** open and the chart selected, click the Chart Format tab.
2. Apply a shape style to the chart title by completing the following steps:
   a. Click the *Chart Elements* option box arrow in the Current Selection group and then click *Chart Title* at the drop-down list.
   b. Click the *Colored Outline - Blue, Accent 1* style option (second option in the Shape Styles group).
3. Change the color of the Sales 2024 series by completing the followings steps:
   a. Click the *Chart Elements* option box arrow in the Current Selection group and then click *Series "Sales 2024"* at the drop-down list.
   b. Click the Shape Fill button arrow in the Shape Styles group and then click the *Dark Red* option (first color option in the *Standard Colors* section).

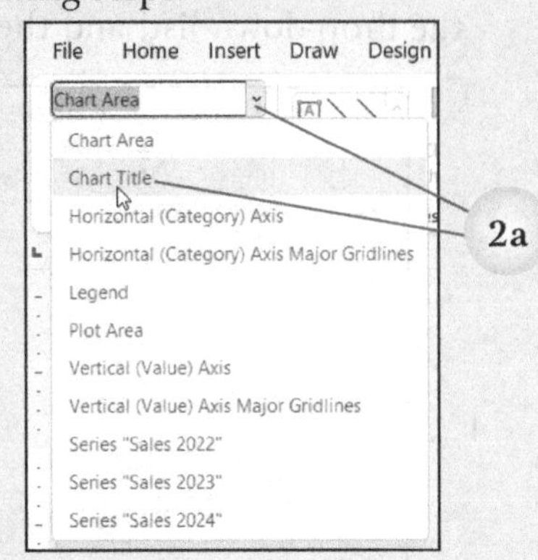

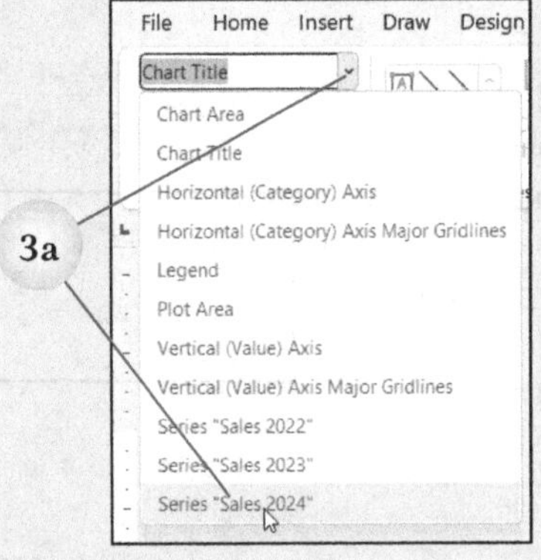

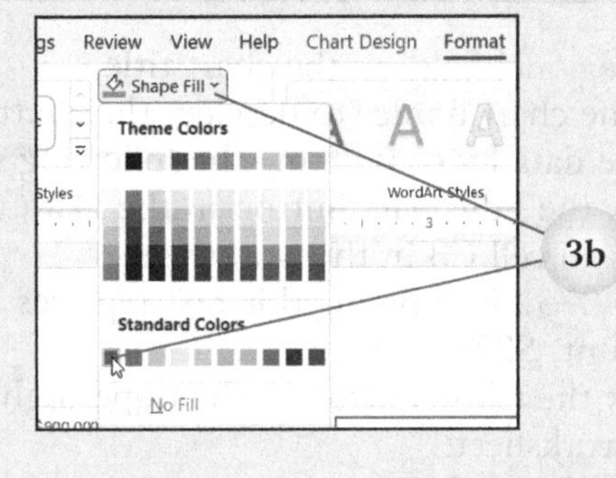

4. Apply a WordArt style to all the text in the chart by completing the following steps:
   a. Click the *Chart Elements* option box arrow.
   b. Click *Chart Area* at the drop-down list.
   c. Click the first WordArt style in the WordArt Styles group (black fill, shadow).

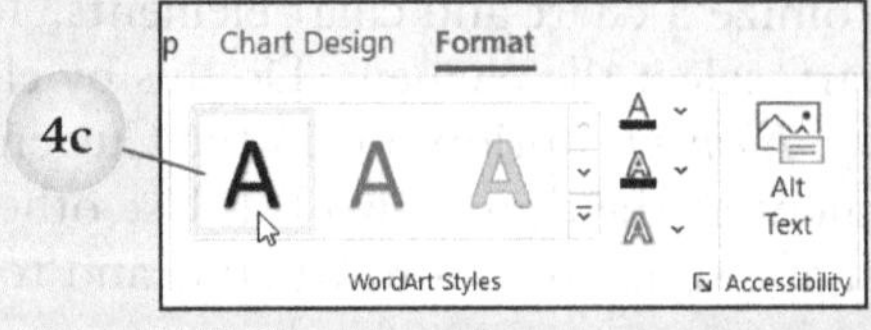

5. Change the size of the chart by completing the following steps:
   a. Click in the *Shape Height* measurement box and then type 3.
   b. Click in the *Shape Width* measurement box, type 5.5, and then press the Enter key.
6. With the chart selected (not a chart element), change its position by clicking the Position button in the Arrange group and then clicking the *Position in Top Center with Square Text Wrapping* option (second column, first row in the *With Text Wrapping* section).
7. Save and then preview **5-Charts.docx**.

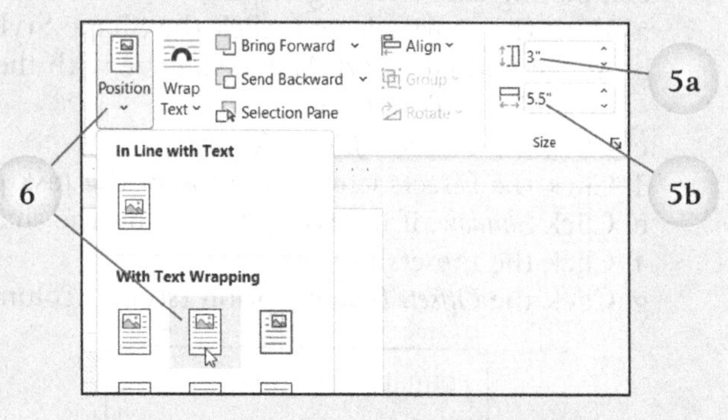

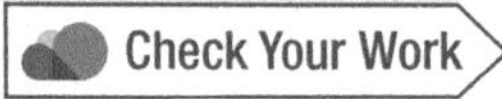

Formatting a Chart with Task Pane Options

Additional formatting options are available at various task panes. Display a task pane by clicking the Format Selection button in the Current Selection group on the Chart Format tab or a group task pane launcher. The Shape Styles and WordArt Styles groups on the Chart Format tab contain task pane launchers. Which task pane opens at the right side of the screen depends on which chart or chart element is selected.

Activity 5e Creating and Formatting a Pie Chart — Part 5 of 5

1. With **5-Charts.docx** open, press Ctrl + End (which deselects the chart) and then press the Enter key 12 times to move the insertion point below the chart.
2. Click the Insert tab and then click the Chart button in the Illustrations group.
3. At the Insert Chart dialog box, click *Pie* in the left panel and then click OK.
4. Type the data in the worksheet cells, including the percentage symbols as shown in Figure 5.13 (on page 193). After typing the last entry, click in cell A1.
5. Click the Close button in the upper right corner of the worksheet.
6. Click in the title *Percentage* and then type Investments.
7. Add data labels to the pie chart by completing the following steps:
   a. Click the Add Chart Element button in the Chart Layouts group on the Chart Design tab.
   b. Point to *Data Labels* at the drop-down list and then click *Inside End* at the side menu.
8. Click on the chart border to select the chart (not a chart element).
9. Click the Chart Format tab.

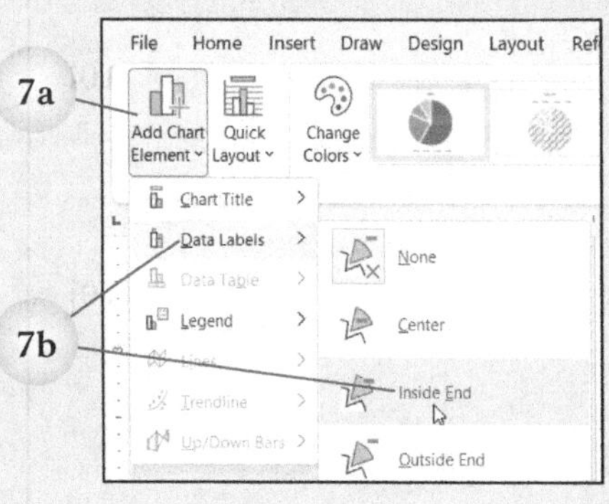

10. Apply formatting to the chart with options at the Format Chart Area task pane by completing the following steps:
   a. With the chart selected, click the Shape Styles group task pane launcher.
   b. At the Format Chart Area task pane with the Fill & Line icon selected, click *Fill* to expand the fill options.
   c. Click the *Gradient fill* option.
   d. Click the Effects icon at the top of the task pane.
   e. Click *Shadow*, if necessary, to expand the shadow options.
   f. Click the Presets button.
   g. Click the *Offset: Bottom* option (second column, first row in the *Outer* section).

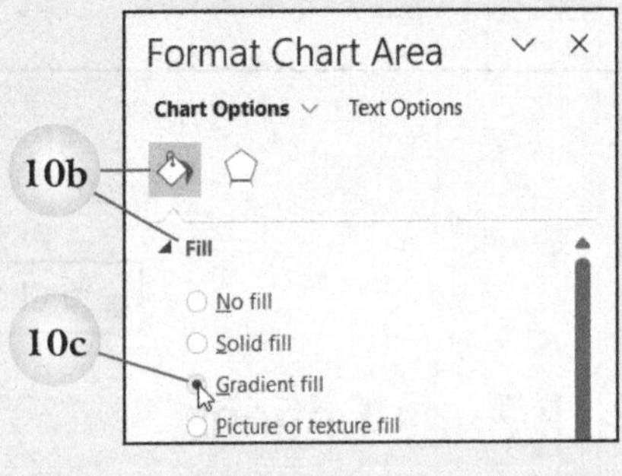

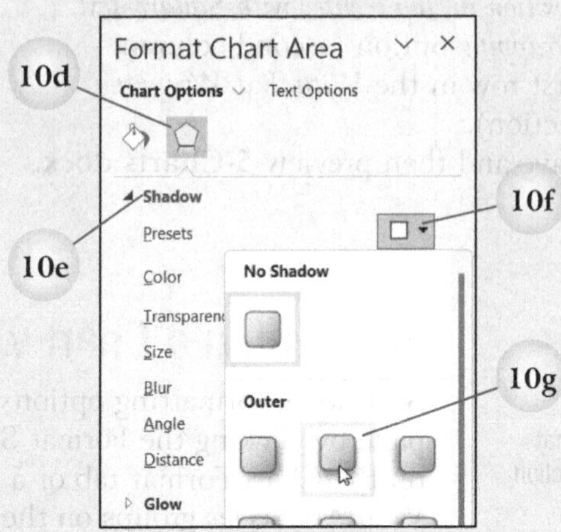

   h. Click the Text Options tab at the top of the task pane.
   i. Click *Text Outline*, if necessary, to expand the options.
   j. Click the *Solid line* option.
   k. Click the Color button and then click the *Blue, Accent 1, Darker 50%* option (fifth column, bottom row in the *Theme Colors* section).

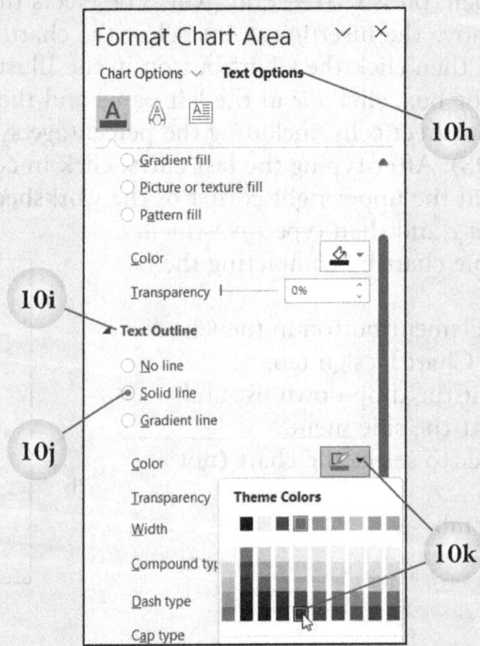

11. Format the pie chart by completing the following steps:
    a. Click in a blank area in any piece of the pie. (This selects all the pieces of the pie. Notice that the name of the task pane has changed to *Format Data Series*.)
    b. Click the Effects icon at the top of the task pane.
    c. Click *3-D Format* to expand the options.
    d. Click the Top bevel button and then click the *Soft Round* option at the drop-down gallery (second column, second row in the *Bevel* section).
    e. Close the task pane by clicking the Close button in the upper right corner.
12. Click the chart border to select the chart (not a chart element).
13. Change the size of the chart by completing the following steps:
    a. Click in the *Shape Height* measurement box and then type 3.
    b. Click in the *Shape Width* measurement box, type 5.5, and then press the Enter key.
14. Change the position of the chart by clicking the Position button in the Arrange group and then clicking the *Position in Bottom Center with Square Text Wrapping* option (second column, third row in the *With Text Wrapping* section).
15. Save, preview, and then close **5-Charts.docx**.

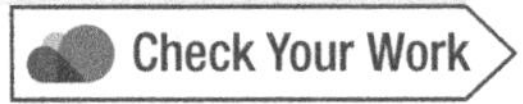

Figure 5.13 Activity 5e

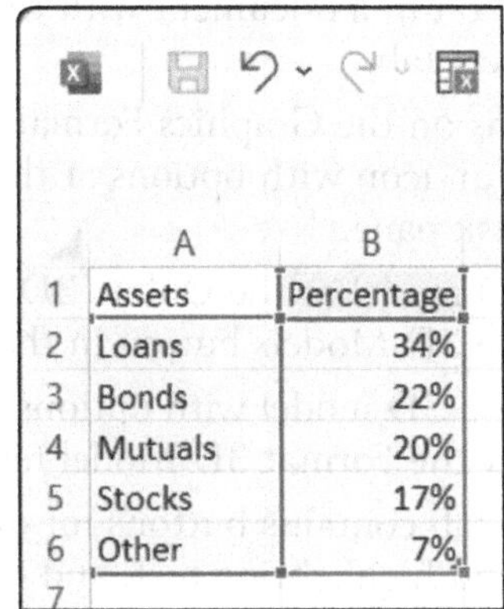

	A	B
1	Assets	Percentage
2	Loans	34%
3	Bonds	22%
4	Mutuals	20%
5	Stocks	17%
6	Other	7%
7		

Chapter Summary

- Customize the layout of images with options at the Layout dialog box. Display this dialog box by clicking the Size group dialog box launcher on the Picture Format tab.
- The Layout dialog box contains three tabs. Click the Position tab to specify the position of the image in the document, click the Text Wrapping tab to specify a wrapping style for the image, and click the Size tab to display options for specifying the height and width of the image.
- Format an image with options at the Format Picture task pane. Display this task pane by clicking the Picture Styles group task pane launcher on the Picture Format tab.
- Apply artistic effects to a selected image with the Artistic Effects button in the Adjust group on the Picture Format tab or with options at the Format Picture task pane with the Effects icon selected.
- Customize colors with options at the Colors dialog box with the Custom tab selected.
- Use the small yellow circles that display around certain selected shapes to change the width and height of a specific element in a shape.
- Use edit points to customize specific elements in a selected shape. Display edit points around a shape by clicking the Edit Shape button in the Insert Shapes group on the Shape Format tab and then clicking *Edit Points*.
- Display wrap points in a selected shape by clicking the Wrap Text button in the Arrange group on the Picture Format tab or the Shape Format tab and then clicking *Edit Wrap Points*. Use wrap points to wrap text closer to or father away from an object.
- Link text boxes with the Create Link button in the Text group on the Shape Format tab. Break a link with the Break Link button in the Text group.
- Insert an icon in a document with the Icons button in the Illustrations group on the Insert tab.
- Use options on the Graphics Format tab to customize an icon. Further customize an icon with options at the Layout dialog box and the Format Graphic task pane.
- Insert a 3D model at the Online 3D Models window. Display the window by clicking the 3D Models button in the Illustrations group on the Insert tab.
- Customize a 3D model with options on the 3D Model tab, at the Layout dialog box, and at the Format 3D Model task pane.
- The Draw tab contains buttons for drawing in a document, converting shapes, selecting and highlighting text, and editing text.
- The Drawing Tools group on the Draw tab contains buttons for selecting and erasing ink drawings and pens for drawing in a document and highlighting and editing text in a document.
- Click a pen button on the Draw tab to activate the pen and then click the button again to display a drop-down list with options for changing the size, thickness, and color of the pen.
- Use the Highlighter pen on the Draw tab to highlight text in a document. Click the Highlighter button to activate it and then click the button again to display a drop-down list with option for changing the size, thickness, and highlighting color as well as a feature to snap the highlighting to text.

- Use the Select button on the Draw tab to select an ink drawing and use the Lasso button to select multiple ink drawings. Use the Eraser pen to erase an ink drawing.
- Replay ink drawings in a document with the Ink Replay button in the Replay group on the Draw tab.
- Convert an ink drawing to a shape by activating a pen, clicking the Ink to Shape button, and then drawing in the document. The shape converts to the shape most similar to the ink drawing.
- Format an ink drawing or an ink drawing converted to a shape with options on the Shape Format tab.
- Edit text in a document with the Action Pen on the Draw tab. Click the Action pen button to activate it, click the button again to display the drop-down list, and then click *Ink Gesture Help* to display the Help task pane with information about editing gestures
- To present data visually, create a chart with the Chart button in the Illustrations group on the Insert tab. Choose a chart type at the Insert Chart dialog box and then enter chart data in a worksheet.
- Four buttons display at the right of a selected chart. Use the Layout Options button to apply text wrapping, the Chart Elements button to add or remove chart elements, the Chart Styles button to apply a predesigned chart style, and the Chart Filters button to isolate specific data in the chart.
- Modify a chart design with options and buttons on the Chart Design tab.
- The cells in a worksheet used to create a chart are linked to the chart in the document. To edit the chart data, click the Edit Data button in the Data group on the Chart Design tab and then make changes to the data in the worksheet.
- Customize the format of a chart and chart elements with options and buttons on the Chart Format tab. Select the chart or a specific chart element and then apply a style to a shape, apply a WordArt style to the text, and arrange and size the chart.
- Apply formatting to a chart with options in task panes. Display a task pane by clicking the Format Selection button in the Current Selection group on the Chart Format tab or a group task pane launcher. The options in the task pane vary depending on the chart or chart element selected.

Commands Review

FEATURE	RIBBON TAB, GROUP/OPTION	BUTTON, OPTION
edit points	Shape Format, Insert Shapes	, *Edit Points*
Format 3D Model task pane	3D Model, 3D Model Views	
Format Graphic task pane	Graphics Format, Graphics Styles	
Format Picture task pane	Picture Format, Picture Styles	
Format Shape task pane	Shape Format, Shape Styles	
group objects	Picture Format, Arrange OR Shape Format, Arrange	, *Group*
Icons window	Insert, Illustrations	
Insert Chart dialog box	Insert, Illustrations	
Layout dialog box	3D Model, Size OR Shape Format, Size OR Graphics Format, Size OR Picture Format, Size	
link text boxes	Shape Format, Text	
Online 3D Models window	Insert, Illustrations	
text box	Insert, Text	, *Draw Text Box*
ungroup objects	Picture Format, Arrange OR Shape Format, Arrange	, *Ungroup*
unlink text boxes	Shape Format, Text	
wrap points	Picture Format, Arrange OR Shape Format, Arrange	, *Edit Wrap Points*

Review and Assessment

CHAPTER 5

Skills Assessment

Assessment 1

Insert and Customize an Image and Text Box in a Timeline Document

1. Open **Au-Timeline.docx** and then save it with the name **5-Au-Timeline**.
2. Move the insertion point to the text that begins *1985*.
3. Display the Insert Picture dialog box, navigate to your WL2C5 folder, and then double-click the ***Uluru.png*** image file.
4. Customize the image so it appears as shown in Figure 5.14 by completing the following steps:
   a. Change the width of the image to 3 inches.
   b. Change the text wrapping to Square.
   c. Display the Layout dialog box with the Position tab selected.
   d. Precisely position the image on the page with an absolute horizontal measurement of 4.5 inches to the right of the left margin and an absolute vertical measurement of 5 inches below the page.
   e. Display the Format Picture task pane with the Effects icon active.
   f. Click *Shadow* to expand the shadow options.
   g. Apply the Offset: Top Left shadow effect (last option in the *Outer* section).
   h. Change the shadow color to Dark Blue (ninth option in the *Standard Colors* section). (Do this with the Color button in the *Shadow* section of the Format Picture task pane.)
   i. Click *Artistic Effects* to expand the options and then apply the Paint Brush artistic effect (third column, second row in the drop-down gallery). (Do this with the Artistic Effects button in the *Artistic Effects* section of the task pane.)
   j. Close the Format Picture task pane.
5. Insert the years *1908* and *1967* in text boxes as shown in Figure 5.14 with the following specifications:
   a. Insert a text box above the arrow line.
   b. Change the font size to 9 points, turn on bold formatting, and then type 1908 in the text box.
   c. Use the Text Direction button to rotate the text in the text box 270 degrees.
   d. Remove the outline from the text box. (Do this with the Shape Outline button in the Shape Styles group.)
   e. Change the text wrapping to Behind Text.
   f. Drag the text box so it is positioned as shown in Figure 5.14.
   g. Complete similar steps to create the text box with the year *1967* and position the text box as shown in the figure.
6. Save, preview, and then close **5-Au-Timeline.docx**.

Figure 5.14 Assessment 1

Australian History: 1900–2000 Timeline

1908: Female citizens in all Australian states gain the right to vote

1914–1918: World War I, over 330,000 Australians serve during the war

1917: Trans-Australian railway opens

1927: Federal parliament moves from Melbourne to Canberra

1939–1945: World War II, over 1,000,000 Australians serve during the war

1956: Olympic Games held in Melbourne

1960: Australia grants citizenship to Aboriginal people

1962: Aboriginal people gain the right to vote in federal elections

1967: Aboriginal people gain the right to vote in all Australian states

1972: "White Australia" immigration policy abandoned

1973: Sydney Opera House completed

1985: Uluru (Ayers Rock) and Kata Tjuta (The Olgas) returned to Aboriginal people

1993: Aboriginal lands recognized by government

1999: Referendum rejects prototype republic

2000: Olympic Games held in Sydney

Voting Rights Timeline

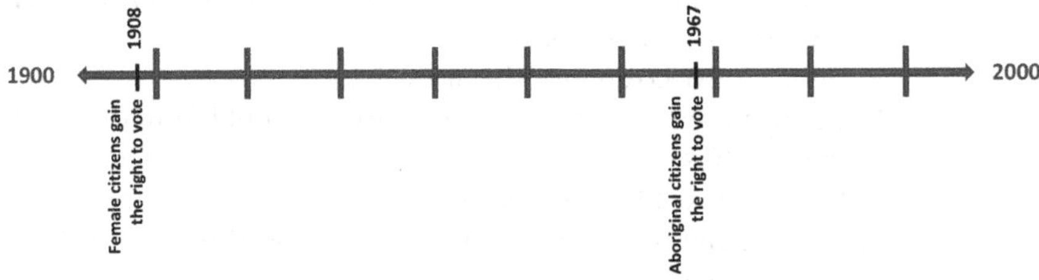

Assessment 2

Format a Shape and Edit Points and Wrap Points

1. Open **CedarMeadows.docx** and then save it with the name **5-CedarMeadows**.
2. Select the shape in the document, display the Format Shape task pane (click the Shape Styles group task pane launcher on the Shape Format tab), and then apply the following formatting:
   a. Apply the Bottom Spotlight - Accent 5 gradient fill (fifth column, fourth row).
   b. Apply the Inside: Bottom shadow effect (second column, third row in the *Inner* section).
   c. Close the Format Shape task pane.
3. Display editing points around the shape and then adjust the points so the shape displays in a manner similar to what is shown in Figure 5.15. (Click outside the shape after adjusting the editing points.)
4. Select the shape, display the wrap points, and then adjust the wrap points so text wraps around the shape in a manner similar to what is shown in Figure 5.15. (Click outside the shape after adjusting the wrap points.)
5. Save, preview, and then close **5-CedarMeadows.docx**.

Figure 5.15 Assessment 2

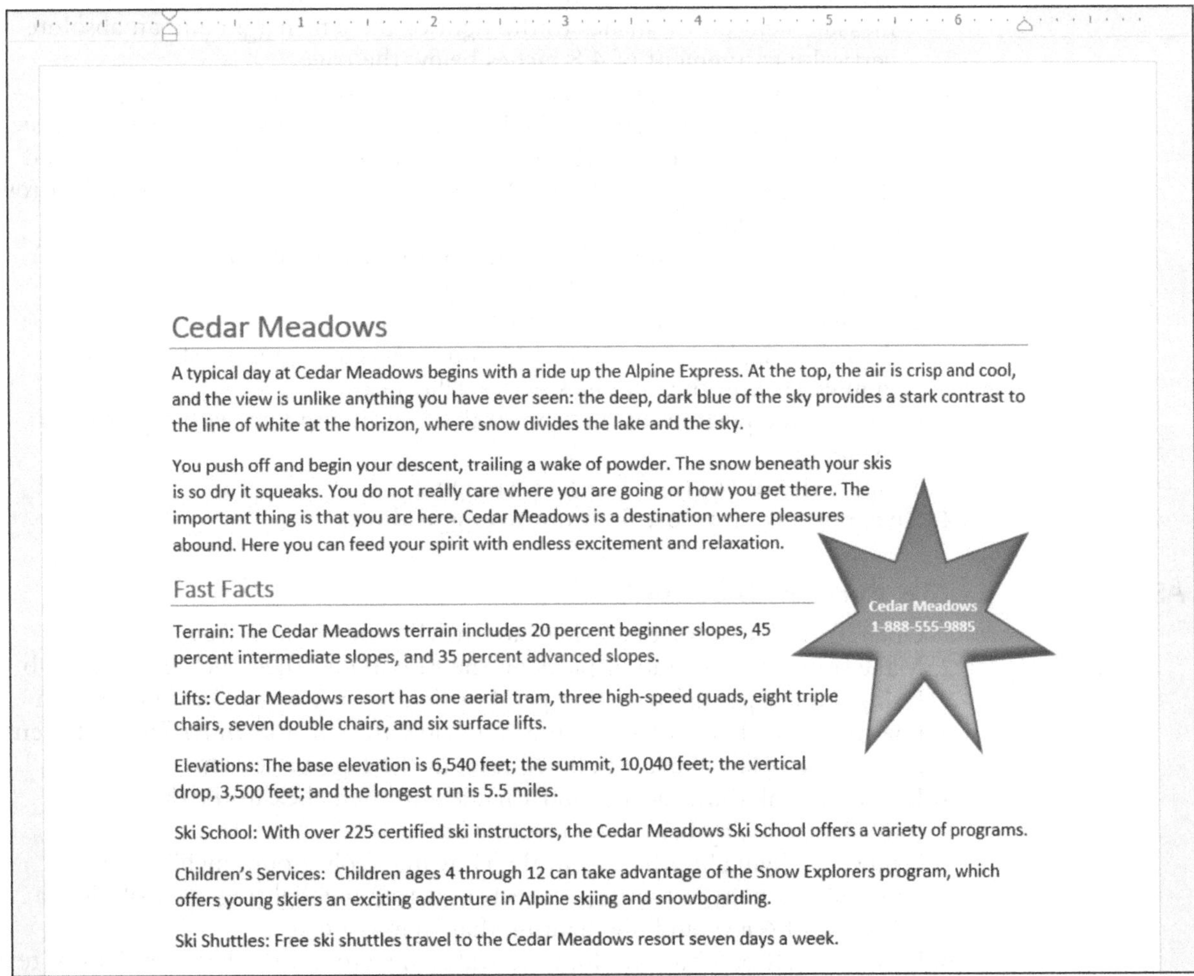

Assessment 3

Link Text Boxes

1. Open **ProtectIssues.docx** and then save it with the name **5-ProtectIssues**.
2. Select the text box at the left and link it to the text box at the right.
3. With the insertion point positioned in the text box at the left, insert the file named **ProIssues.docx**. ***Hint: Click the Insert tab, click the Object button arrow, and then click the*** **Text from File** ***option***.
4. Adjust the columns so all the text fits in the two columns by changing the height of both text boxes to 8.4 inches and the width of both to 3.1 inches.
5. Save, preview, and then close **5-ProtectIssues.docx**.

Assessment 4

Customize a 3D Model

1. Open **Announcement.docx** and then save it with the name **5-Announcement**.
2. Select the 3D model (a red square with a cross) and then apply the following formatting:
   a. Apply the Above Front Right 3D model view. (You will need to click the More 3D Model Views button in the 3D Model Views group to display additional views. The Above Front Right view is in the fifth column, second row.)
   b. Change the height of the model to 2.7 inches.
   c. Apply Tight text wrapping.
   d. Precisely position the model on the page with an absolute horizontal measurement of 4.7 inches to the right of the left margin and an absolute vertical measurement of 4.8 inches below the page.
   e. Display the Format 3D Model task pane and then apply the Perspective: Upper Right shadow effect. (To do this, click the Effects icon, click *Shadow* to expand the options, click the Presets button in the *Shadow* section, and then click the *Perspective: Upper Right* option, in the second column, first row in the *Perspective* section.)
3. Select the icon in the upper left corner of the document (a cross in a circle) and then apply the following formatting:
   a. Change the height of the icon to 1.7 inches.
   b. Apply the Light 1 Fill, Colored Outline - Accent 4 graphic style (fifth graphic style in the Graphics Styles gallery).
   c. Change the position of the icon to Position in Top Left with Square Text Wrapping.
   d. Apply the In Front of Text text wrapping.
4. Save, preview, and close **5-Announcement.docx**.

Assessment 5

Draw in a Travel Document

1. Open **TravelTips.docx** and then save it with the name **5-TravelTips**.
2. Make sure the Draw tab displays on the ribbon and then click the Draw tab.
3. Using the left pen button (first pen button after the Eraser button), draw a line with a thickness of *1 mm* in green below the subtitle *Travel Tips* and then draw a line below the last bulleted item in the *Baggage* section.
4. Replay the ink drawings you must made and then click in the document (outside the replay bar) to remove the bar.
5. Using the Highlighter button in the Drawing Tools group, highlight the first bulleted item in the *Baggage* section with a highlighting color of blue, a thickness of *6 mm*, and highlighting that snaps to text.
6. Using the left pen button, draw an oval shape around the last two lines of text that converts to a precise oval shape.

7. Erase the drawn line below the subtitle, *Travel Tips*.
8. Click the Select button in the Drawing Tools group and then make the Home tab active.
9. Save, preview, and then close **5-TravelTips.docx**.

Assessment

Create and Format a Column Chart and a Pie Chart

1. At a blank document, use the data in Figure 5.16 to create a column chart (using the default chart style at the Insert Chart dialog box) with the following specifications:
    a. Use the Chart Elements button outside the upper right border of the chart to add a data table and remove the legend.
    b. Apply the Style 4 chart style.
    c. Change the chart title to *Units Sold First Quarter*.
    d. Apply the first WordArt style to the chart area.
    e. Change the chart height to 4 inches.
    f. Change the position of the chart to Position in Top Center with Square Text Wrapping.
2. Move the insertion point to the end of the document, press the Enter key two times, and then create a pie chart (using the default pie chart style at the Insert Chart dialog box) with the data shown in Figure 5.17 and with the following specifications:
    a. Apply the Style 3 chart style.
    b. Move the data labels to the inside end of the pie pieces. ***Hint: Click the Chart Elements button that displays outside the upper right corner of the chart, click the arrow at the right of* Data Labels, *and then click* Inside End.**
    c. Change the chart title to *Expense Distribution*.

Figure 5.16 Assessment 6, Step 1, Data for Column Chart

Salesperson	January	February	March
Barnett	55	60	42
Carson	20	24	31
Fanning	15	30	13
Han	52	62	58
Mahoney	49	52	39

Figure 5.17 Assessment 6, Step 2, Data for Pie Chart

Category	Percentage
Salaries	67%
Travel	15%
Equipment	11%
Supplies	7%

d. Apply the Colored Outline - Orange, Accent 2 shape style to the title (third shape style).
e. Change the chart height to 3 inches and the width to 5.5 inches.
f. Change the position of the chart to Position in Bottom Center with Square Text Wrapping.

3. Save the document with the name **5-ColumnPieCharts**.
4. Preview and then close **5-ColumnPieCharts.docx**.

Assessment 7 Insert a Horizontal Line in a Footer

1. Open a blank document and then insert a horizontal line by clicking the Borders button arrow in the Paragraph group on the Home tab and then clicking *Horizontal Line* at the drop-down list. Click the horizontal line to select it and then right-click the line. Click *Picture* at the shortcut menu and the Format Horizontal Line dialog box displays. Look at the formatting options that are available at the dialog box and then click the Cancel button to close the dialog box. Close the document without saving it.
2. Open **KECharityEvents.docx** and then save it with the name **5-KECharityEvents**.
3. Keep the Step 6 text at the bottom of the first page together with the paragraph that follows it.
4. Create a footer that contains a horizontal line in the standard green color (sixth color option in the *Standard Colors* section) with a height of 3 points.
5. Save, preview, and then close **5-KECharityEvents.docx**.

Visual Benchmark

Create a Company Chart

1. Open **Blueline.docx** and then save it with the name **5-Blueline**.
2. Select the gears icon and then customize the icon so it appears as shown in Figure 5.18 with the following specifications:
   - Flip the gears icon horizontally.
   - Apply the Colored Fill - Accent 1, Dark 1 Outline graphic style (second column, third row in the Graphics Styles group gallery).
   - Apply text wrapping that moves the icon behind text.
   - Size and move the gears icon so it is positioned as shown in Figure 5.18.
3. Create the column chart shown in Figure 5.18 with the following specifications:
   - Choose the 3-D Clustered Column Chart at the Insert Chart dialog box.
   - Use the information shown in the chart in the figure to create the data for the chart. (You will need to decrease the size of the data range by one column.)
   - Add a data table to the chart.
   - Change the color of the 2024 series to Dark Blue.
   - Make any other changes so your chart appears similar to the chart in the figure.
4. Save, preview, and then close **5-Blueline.docx**.

Figure 5.18 Visual Benchmark

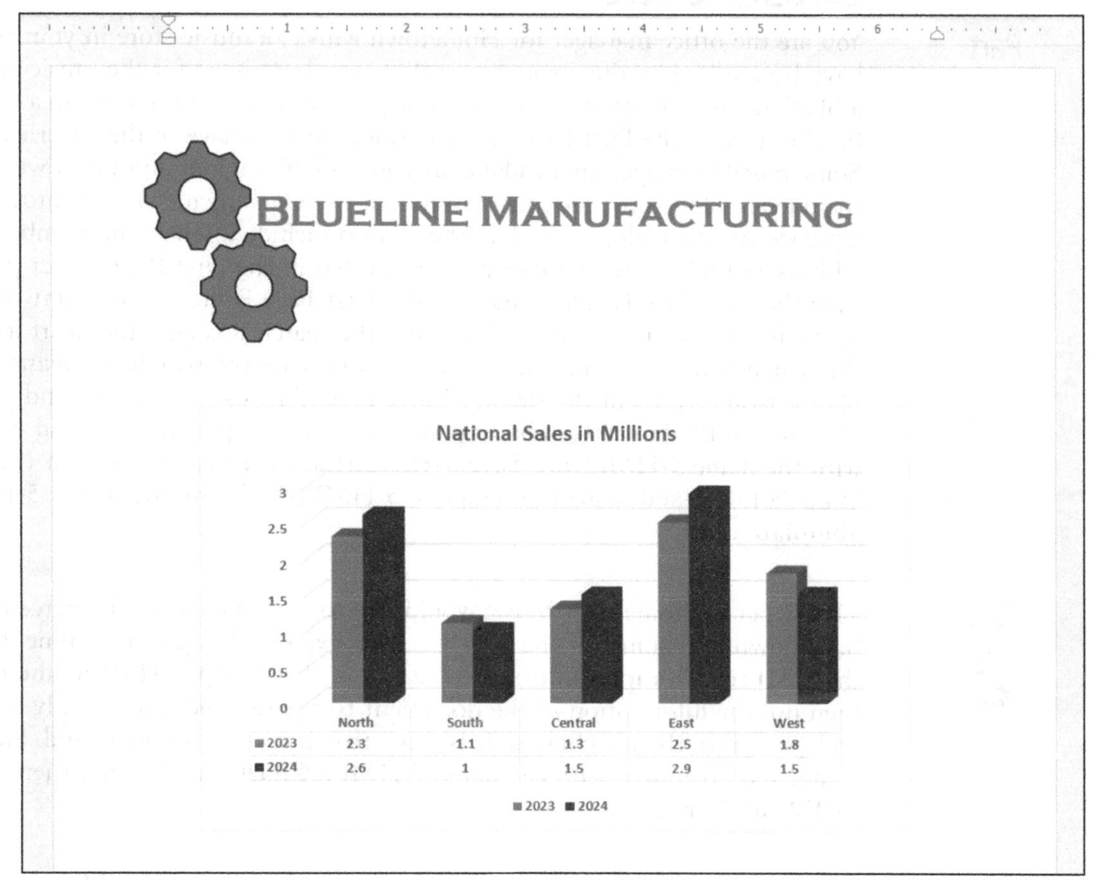

Case Study

Part 1

You are the office manager for Hometown Music, a music store in your town. You have been asked by the owner to create a new letterhead for the music store. Open a blank document, create a custom first page header, and then create a letterhead for the store in the First Page Header pane. Use an image in the letterhead. Some possible images are available in your WL2C5 folder and begin with *Music*. Include an address for the music store and use your town, state (or province), and zip code (postal code) in the letterhead; also include a telephone number. (The address and telephone number can be inserted in the First Page Footer pane rather than the First Page Header pane.) In the First Page Footer pane, insert three icons in the footer, including the eye icon (use the search text *eye*), the heart icon (use the search text *heart*), and the music note icon (use the search text *music note*). (These icons represent the saying "I love music.") Customize, size, and position the icons in the First Page Footer pane. Save the completed letterhead document with the name **5-HMLtrhd**. Save **5-HMLtrhd.docx** as a template in your WL2C5 folder and name the template **5-HMLtrhd-Template**. Close **5-HMLtrhd-Template.dotx**.

Part 2

The owner of Hometown Music would like to have a chart of the percentage breakdown of income for the year. Use File Explorer to open a document based on the **HMLtrhd-Template.dotx** you created in Part 1. Open **HMIncome.docx** and then use the information in the document to create a pie chart. Apply formatting and customize the pie chart so it is attractive and easy to understand. Save the completed document with the name **5-HMPieChart**. Preview and then close **5-HMPieChart.docx**.

Part 3

You have created an invitation for an upcoming piano recital at Hometown Music. You inserted a 3D model in the invitation and need to customize it so it has more visual impact. Open **HMPianoRecital.docx** and then save it with the name **5-HMPianoRecital**. Select the grand piano 3D model, rotate the image so that the keyboard is facing to the right, increase the size, apply a text wrapping option, and move the piano image into the lower left corner of the invitation. Save, preview, and then close **5-HMPianoRecital.docx**.

Part 4

The owner would like to have a flyer describing Hometown Music's instrument rental program that can be distributed at recitals and at local schools. Open **HMRentals.docx**, look at the information, and then create a flyer that includes some of the information in the document. Include visual interest in the flyer by inserting a photograph, picture, icon, and/or 3D model. Format the flyer so it appears similar to other Hometown Music documents you have created. Save the completed flyer with the name **5-HMRentalFlyer**. Preview and then close **5-HMRentalFlyer.docx**.

WORD

CHAPTER 6

Merging Documents

Performance Objectives

Upon successful completion of Chapter 6, you will be able to:

1. Create a data source file
2. Create a main document and merge it with a data source file
3. Preview a merge and check for errors before merging documents
4. Create an envelope, a label, and a directory main document and then merge it with a data source file
5. Edit a data source file
6. Select specific records for merging
7. Use the Mail Merge wizard to merge a letter main document with a data source file

Word includes a Mail Merge feature for creating customized letters, envelopes, labels, directories, and email messages. The Mail Merge feature is useful when the same letter is to be sent to a number of people and an envelope needs to be created for each letter. Use Mail Merge to create a main document that contains a letter, an envelope, or other data and then merge it with a data source file. In this chapter, you will use Mail Merge to create letters, envelopes, labels, and directories.

Data Files

The data files for this chapter are in the WL2C6 folder that you downloaded at the beginning of this course.

Activity 1 Merge Letters to Customers — 3 Parts

You will create a data source file and a letter document and then merge the main document with the records in the data source file.

Completing a Merge

Start Mail Merge

Select Recipients

Use Word's mail merge feature to create multiple documents—such as letters, envelopes, and directories—with fixed or standard text along with variable text (text that changes with each document). Use buttons and options on the Mailings tab to complete a merge. A merge generally takes two files: the data source file and the main document. The main document contains the standard text along with fields identifying where variable information is inserted during the merge. The data source file contains the variable information that will be inserted in the main document.

Use the Start Mail Merge button in the Start Mail Merge group on the Mailings tab to identify the type of main document to be created and use the Select Recipients button to create a data source file or specify an existing data source file. The Mail Merge wizard is also available to provide guidance on the merge process.

Tutorial

Creating a Data Source File

Quick Steps

Create Data Source File

1. Click Mailings tab.
2. Click Select Recipients button.
3. Click *Type a New List* at drop-down list.
4. Type data in predesigned or custom fields.
5. Click OK.

Creating a Data Source File

Before creating a data source file, determine what type of correspondence will be created and what type of information is needed to insert in the correspondence. Word provides predesigned field names when creating the data source file. Use these field names if they represent the specific data. Variable information in a data source file is saved as a record. A record contains all the information for one unit (for example, a person, family, customer, client, or business). A series of fields makes one record and a series of records makes a data source file.

Create a data source file by clicking the Select Recipients button in the Start Mail Merge group on the Mailings tab and then clicking *Type a New List* at the drop-down list. At the New Address List dialog box, shown in Figure 6.1, use the predesigned fields offered by Word or edit the fields by clicking the Customize Columns button. At the Customize Address List dialog box, insert new fields or

Figure 6.1 New Address List Dialog Box

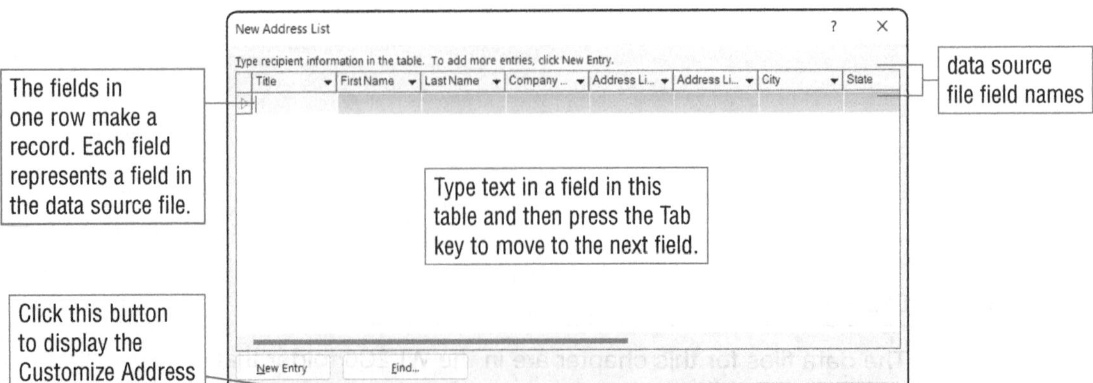
New Address List
Type recipient information in the table. To add more entries, click New Entry.
Title
First Name
Last Name
Company ...
Address Li...
Address Li...
City
State
New Entry
Find...
Delete Entry
Customize Columns...
OK
Cancel
The fields in one row make a record. Each field represents a field in the data source file.
data source file field names
Type text in a field in this table and then press the Tab key to move to the next field.
Click this button to display the Customize Address List dialog box.

delete existing fields and then click OK. With the fields established, type the required data. Note that fields in the main document correspond to the column headings in the data source file. When all the records have been entered, click OK. At the Save Address List dialog box, navigate to the desired folder, type a name for the data source file, and then click OK. Word saves a data source file as an Access database. Having Access on the computer is not required to complete a merge with a data source file.

Activity 1a Creating a Data Source File

Part 1 of 3

1. At a blank document, click the Mailings tab.
2. Click the Start Mail Merge button in the Start Mail Merge group and then click *Letters* at the drop-down list.
3. Click the Select Recipients button in the Start Mail Merge group and then click *Type a New List* at the drop-down list.

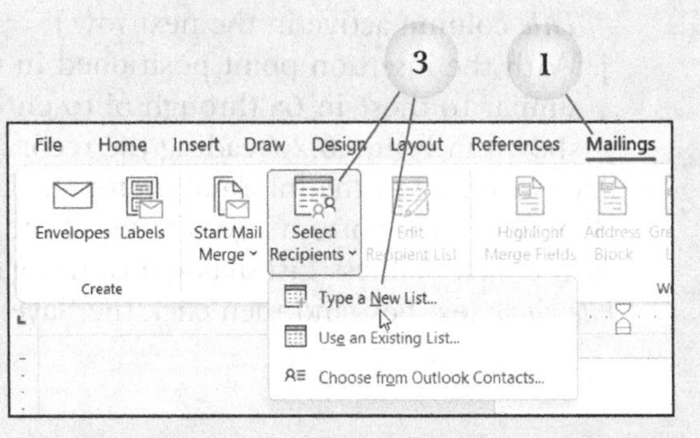

4. At the New Address List dialog box, Word provides a number of predesigned fields. Delete the fields you do not need by completing the following steps:
   a. Click the Customize Columns button.
   b. At the Customize Address List dialog box, click *Company Name* to select it and then click the Delete button.
   c. At the message that displays, click Yes.
   d. Complete steps similar to those in 4b and 4c to delete the following fields:
      Country or Region
      Home Phone
      Work Phone
      E-mail Address

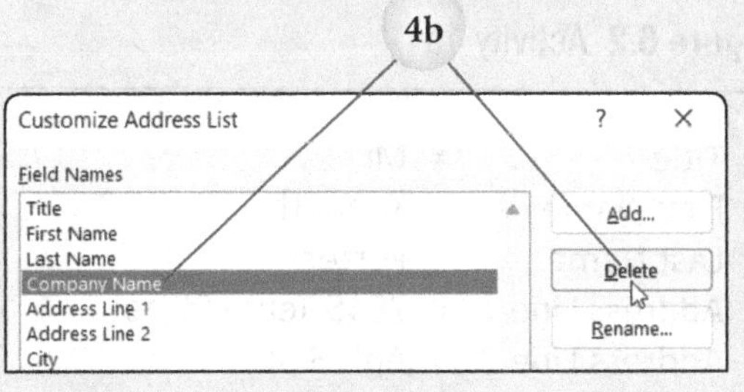

5. Insert a custom field by completing the following steps:
   a. With the *ZIP Code* field selected in the *Field Names* list box in the Customize Address List dialog box, click the Add button.
   b. At the Add Field dialog box, type Fund and then click OK.
   c. Click OK to close the Customize Address List dialog box.

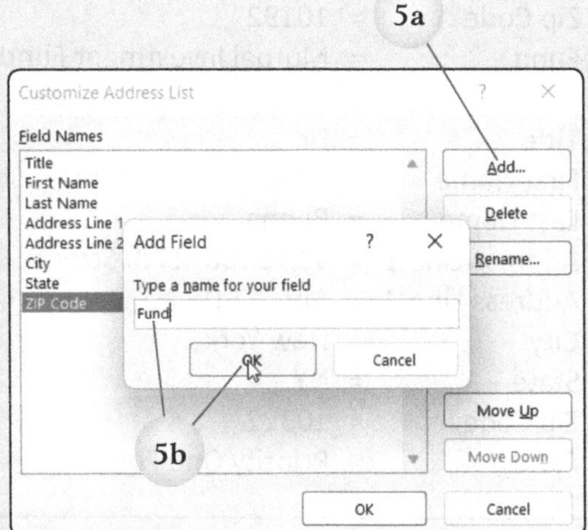

6. At the New Address List dialog box, enter the information for the first client shown in Figure 6.2 by completing the following steps:
   a. Type Mr. in the field in the *Title* column and then press the Tab key. (This moves the insertion point to the field in the *First Name* column. Pressing Shift + Tab will move the insertion point to the previous field. When typing text, do not press the spacebar after the last word in the field, and proofread all the entries to ensure the data is accurate.)
   b. Type Kenneth and then press the Tab key.
   c. Type Porter and then press the Tab key.

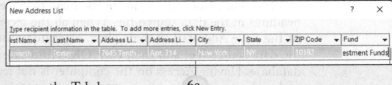

d. Type 7645 Tenth Street and then press the Tab key.
e. Type Apt. 314 and then press the Tab key.
f. Type New York and then press the Tab key.
g. Type NY and then press the Tab key.
h. Type 10192 and then press the Tab key.
i. Type Mutual Investment Fund and then press the Tab key. (This makes the field in the *Title* column active in the next row.)
j. With the insertion point positioned in the field in the *Title* column, complete steps similar to those in 6a through 6i to enter the information for the three other clients shown in Figure 6.2 (reading the records from left to right in each row).

7. After entering all the information for the last client in Figure 6.2 (Ms. Wanda Houston), click OK in the bottom right corner of the New Address List dialog box.
8. At the Save Address List dialog box, navigate to your WL2C6 folder, type 6-MFDS in the *File name* text box, and then click the Save button.

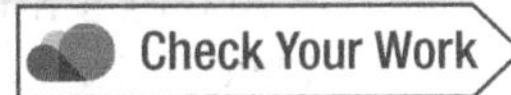

Figure 6.2 Activity 1a

Title	= Mr.	Title	= Ms.
First Name	= Kenneth	First Name	= Carolyn
Last Name	= Porter	Last Name	= Renquist
Address Line 1	= 7645 Tenth Street	Address Line 1	= 13255 Meridian Street
Address Line 2	= Apt. 314	Address Line 2	= (leave this blank)
City	= New York	City	= New York
State	= NY	State	= NY
Zip Code	= 10192	Zip Code	= 10435
Fund	= Mutual Investment Fund	Fund	= Quality Care Fund
Title	= Dr.	Title	= Ms.
First Name	= Amil	First Name	= Wanda
Last Name	= Ranna	Last Name	= Houston
Address Line 1	= 433 South 17th Street	Address Line 1	= 566 North 22nd Avenue
Address Line 2	= Apt. 17-D	Address Line 2	= (leave this blank)
City	= New York	City	= New York
State	= NY	State	= NY
Zip Code	= 10322	Zip Code	= 10634
Fund	= Priority One Fund	Fund	= Quality Care Fund

Creating a Main Document

Creating a Main Document

After creating and typing the records in the data source file, type the main document. Insert fields to identify where variable information will be added when the document is merged with the data source file. Use buttons in the Write & Insert Fields group to insert fields in the main document.

Quick Steps

Create Main Document

1. Click Mailings tab.
2. Click Start Mail Merge button.
3. Click document type at drop-down list.
4. Type main document text and insert fields as needed.

Address Block

Greeting Line

Insert Merge Field

Insert all the fields required for the inside address of a letter with the Address Block button in the Write & Insert Fields group. Click this button and the Insert Address Block dialog box displays with a preview of how the fields will be inserted in the document to create the inside address; the dialog box also contains buttons and options for customizing the fields. Click OK and the *«AddressBlock»* field is inserted in the document. The *«AddressBlock»* field is an example of a composite field, which groups a number of fields (such as *Title*, *First Name*, *Last Name*, *Address Line 1*, and so on).

Click the Greeting Line button and the Insert Greeting Line dialog box displays with options for customizing how the fields are inserted in the document to create the greeting line. Click OK at the dialog box and the *«GreetingLine»* composite field is inserted in the document.

To insert an individual field from the data source file, click the Insert Merge Field button. This displays the Insert Merge Field dialog box with a list of the fields from the data source file. Click the Insert Merge Field button arrow and a drop-down list displays containing the fields in the data source file.

A field or composite field is inserted in the main document surrounded by chevrons (« and »). The chevrons distinguish fields in the main document and do not display in the merged document. Formatting can be applied to merged data by formatting the merge field in the main document.

Activity 1b Creating a Main Document

Part 2 of 3

1. At the blank document, create the letter shown in Figure 6.3. Begin by clicking the *No Spacing* style in the styles gallery on the Home tab.
2. Press the Enter key six times and then type February 21, 2024.
3. Press the Enter key four times and then insert the *«AddressBlock»* composite field by completing the following steps:
   a. Click the Mailings tab and then click the Address Block button in the Write & Insert Fields group.
   b. At the Insert Address Block dialog box, click OK.
   c. Press the Enter key two times.
4. Insert the *«GreetingLine»* composite field by completing the following steps:
   a. Click the Greeting Line button in the Write & Insert Fields group.
   b. At the Insert Greeting Line dialog box, click the option box arrow for the option box containing the comma (the box at the right of the box containing *Mr. Randall*).
   c. At the drop-down list, click the colon.

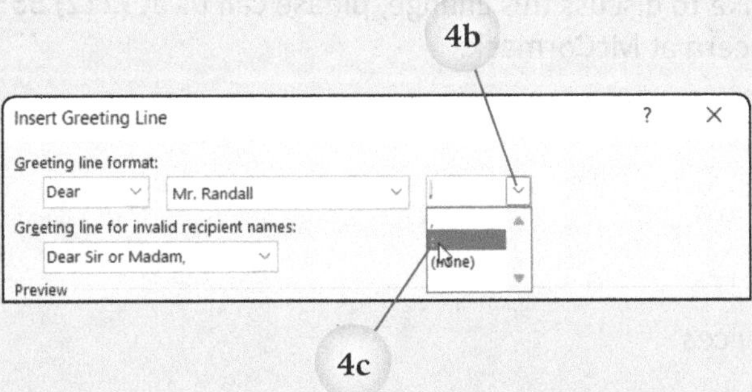

   d. Click OK to close the Insert Greeting Line dialog box.
   e. Press the Enter key two times.

5. Type the letter shown in Figure 6.3 to the point where *«Fund»* appears and then insert the *«Fund»* field by clicking the Insert Merge Field button arrow in the Write & Insert Fields group and then clicking *Fund* at the drop-down list.
6. Type the letter to the point where the *«Title»* field appears and then insert the *«Title»* field by clicking the Insert Merge Field button arrow and then clicking *Title* at the drop-down list.
7. Press the spacebar and then insert the *«Last_Name»* field by clicking the Insert Merge Field button arrow and then clicking *Last_Name* at the drop-down list.
8. Type the remainder of the letter shown in Figure 6.3. (Insert your initials instead of *XX* at the end of the letter.)
9. Save the document with the name **6-MFMD.**

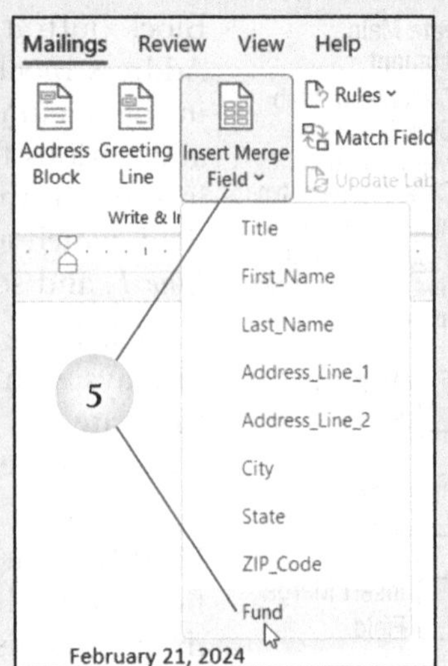

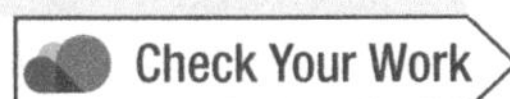

Figure 6.3 Activity 1b

February 21, 2024

«AddressBlock»

«GreetingLine»

McCormack Funds is lowering its expense charges beginning May 1, 2024. The reduction in expense charges means that more of your account investment performance in the «Fund» is returned to you, «Title» «Last_Name». The reductions are worth your attention because most of our competitors' fees have gone up.

Lowering expense charges is noteworthy because before the reduction, McCormack expense deductions were already among the lowest, far below most mutual funds and variable annuity accounts with similar objectives. At the same time, services for you, our client, will continue to expand. If you would like to discuss this change, please call us at (212) 555-2277. Your financial future is our main concern at McCormack.

Sincerely,

Jodie Langley
Director, Financial Services

XX
6-MFMD.docx

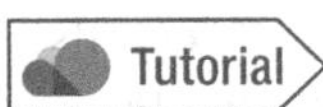

Previewing and Merging Documents

Preview Results

First Record

Previous Record

Next Record

Last Record

Find Recipient

Previewing a Merge

To view how the main document will appear when merged with the first record in the data source file, click the Preview Results button in the Preview Results group on the Mailings tab. View the main document merged with other records by using the navigation buttons in the Preview Results group. This group contains the First Record, Previous Record, Next Record, and Last Record buttons and the *Go to Record* text box. Click the button that will display the main document merged with the specific record. Viewing the merged document before printing is helpful to ensure that the merged data is correct. To use the *Go to Record* text box, click in the text box, type the number of the record, and then press the Enter key. Turn off the preview feature by clicking the Preview Results button.

The Preview Results group on the Mailings tab also includes a Find Recipient button. To search for and preview merged documents with specific entries, click the Preview Results button and then click the Find Recipient button. At the Find Entry dialog box, type the specific field entry in the *Find* text box and then click the Find Next button. Continue clicking the Find Next button until Word displays a message indicating that there are no more entries that contain the typed text.

Checking for Errors

Check for Errors

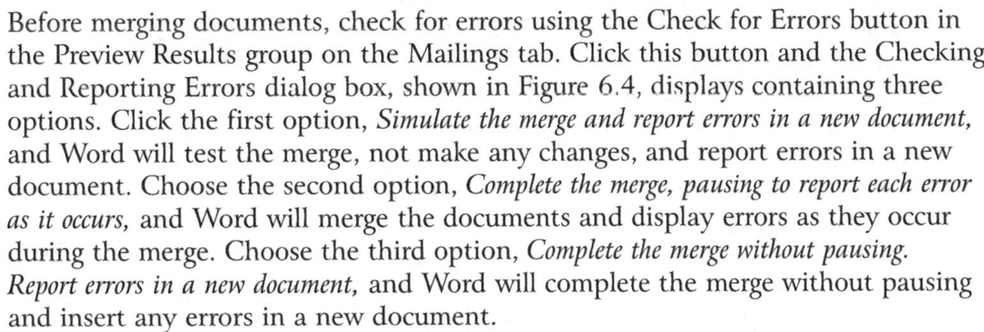

Before merging documents, check for errors using the Check for Errors button in the Preview Results group on the Mailings tab. Click this button and the Checking and Reporting Errors dialog box, shown in Figure 6.4, displays containing three options. Click the first option, *Simulate the merge and report errors in a new document,* and Word will test the merge, not make any changes, and report errors in a new document. Choose the second option, *Complete the merge, pausing to report each error as it occurs,* and Word will merge the documents and display errors as they occur during the merge. Choose the third option, *Complete the merge without pausing. Report errors in a new document,* and Word will complete the merge without pausing and insert any errors in a new document.

Merging Documents

Finish & Merge

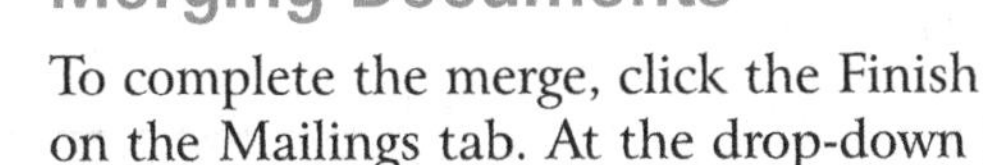

To complete the merge, click the Finish & Merge button in the Finish group on the Mailings tab. At the drop-down list, merge the records and create a new document, send the merged documents directly to the printer, or send the merged documents by email.

Figure 6.4 Checking and Reporting Errors Dialog Box

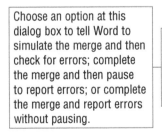

Choose an option at this dialog box to tell Word to simulate the merge and then check for errors; complete the merge and then pause to report errors; or complete the merge and report errors without pausing.

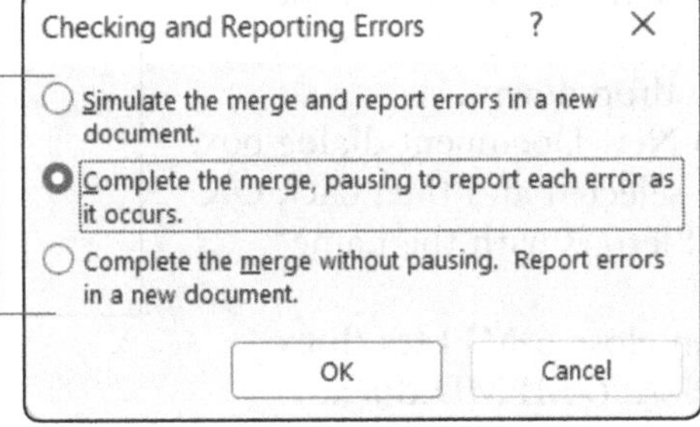

Quick Steps

Merge Documents

1. Click Finish & Merge button.
2. Click *Edit Individual Documents* at drop-down list.
3. Make sure *All* is selected in Merge to New Document dialog box.
4. Click OK.

Hint Press Alt + Shift + N to display the Merge to New Document dialog box and press Alt + Shift + M to display the Merge to Printer dialog box.

To merge the documents and create a new document with the merged records, click the Finish & Merge button and then click *Edit Individual Documents* at the drop-down list. At the Merge to New Document dialog box, make sure *All* is selected in the *Merge records* section and then click OK. This merges the records in the data source file with the main document and inserts the merged documents in a new document.

Identify specific records to be merged with options at the Merge to New Document dialog box. Display this dialog box by clicking the Finish & Merge button on the Mailings tab and then clicking the *Edit Individual Documents* option at the drop-down list. Click the *All* option in the Merge to New Document dialog box to merge all the records in the data source file and click the *Current record* option to merge only the current record. To merge specific adjacent records, click in the *From* text box, type the beginning record number, press the Tab key, and then type the ending record number in the *To* text box.

Activity 1c Merging the Main Document with the Data Source File — Part 3 of 3

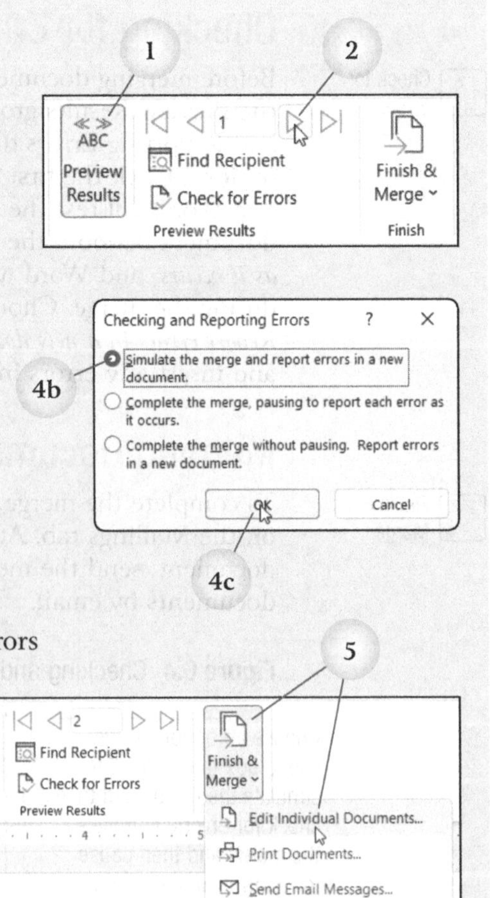

1. With **6-MFMD.docx** open, preview the main document merged with the first record in the data source file by clicking the Preview Results button on the Mailings tab.
2. Click the Next Record button to view the main document merged with the second record in the data source file.
3. Click the Preview Results button to turn off the preview feature.
4. Automatically check for errors by completing the following steps:
   a. Click the Check for Errors button in the Preview Results group on the Mailings tab.
   b. At the Checking and Reporting Errors dialog box, click the first option, *Simulate the merge and report errors in a new document*.
   c. Click OK.
   d. If a new document displays with any errors, print the document, close it without saving it, and then correct the errors. If a message displays that no errors were found, click OK.
5. Click the Finish & Merge button in the Finish group and then click *Edit Individual Documents* at the drop-down list.
6. At the Merge to New Document dialog box, make sure *All* is selected and then click OK.
7. Save the merged letters with the name **6-MFLtrs**.
8. Preview and then close **6-MFLtrs.docx**.
9. Save and then close **6-MFMD.docx**.

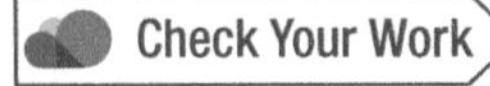
Check Your Work

Activity 2 Merge Envelopes — 1 Part

You will use Mail Merge to prepare envelopes with customer names and addresses.

Merging with Other Main Documents

In addition to being merged with a letter, a data source file can be merged with an envelope, a label, or a directory main document. Create an envelope main document with the *Envelopes* option at the Start Mail Merge button drop-down list and create a label main document with the *Labels* option. Create a directory, which merges fields to the same page, with the *Directory* option at the Start Mail Merge button drop-down list.

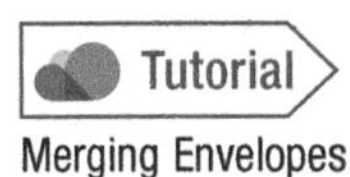

Merging Envelopes

Merging Envelopes

To send out a letter created as a main document and then merged with a data source file will likely require creating properly addressed envelopes. To prepare an envelope main document that is merged with a data source file, click the Mailings tab, click the Start Mail Merge button, and then click *Envelopes* at the drop-down list. This displays the Envelope Options dialog box, as shown in Figure 6.5. At this dialog box, specify the envelope size, make any other changes, and then click OK.

The next step in the envelope merge process is to create the data source file or identify an existing data source file. To identify an existing data source file, click the Select Recipients button in the Start Mail Merge group and then click *Use an Existing List* at the drop-down list. At the Select Data Source dialog box, navigate to the folder containing the data source file and then double-click the file.

With the data source file attached to the envelope main document, the next step is to insert the appropriate fields. Click in the envelope in the approximate location the recipient's address will appear and a box with a dashed gray border displays. Click the Address Block button in the Write & Insert Fields group and then click OK at the Insert Address Block dialog box.

Figure 6.5 Envelope Options Dialog Box

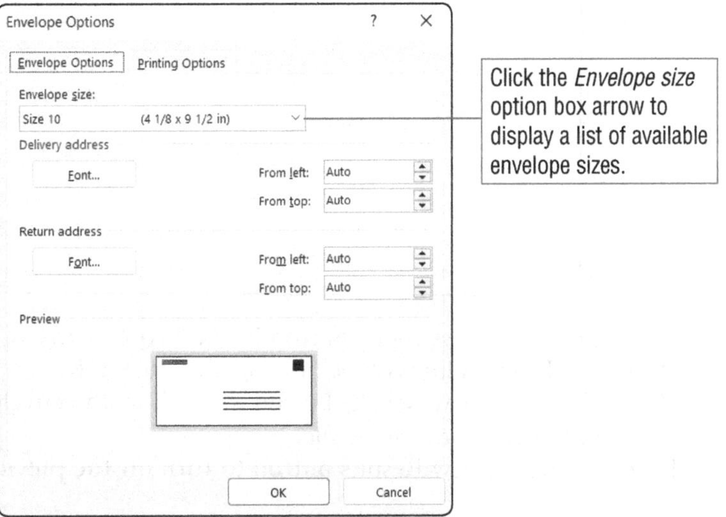

Activity 2 Merging Envelopes

Part 1 of 1

1. At a blank document, click the Mailings tab.
2. Click the Start Mail Merge button in the Start Mail Merge group and then click *Envelopes* at the drop-down list.

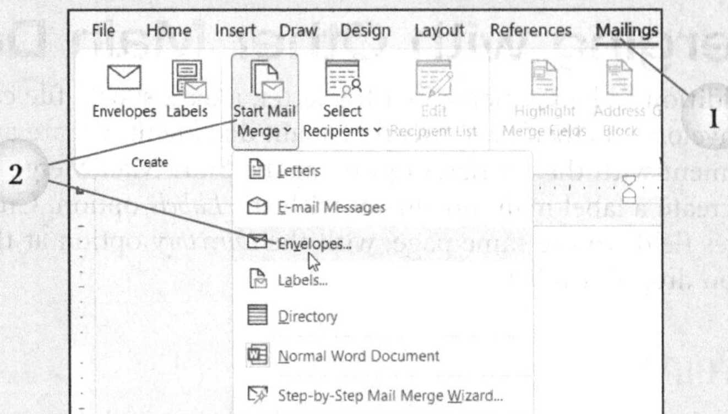

3. At the Envelope Options dialog box, make sure the envelope size is Size 10 and then click OK.
4. Click the Select Recipients button in the Start Mail Merge group and then click *Use an Existing List* at the drop-down list.
5. At the Select Data Source dialog box, navigate to your WL2C6 folder and then double-click the data source file named ***6-MFDS.mdb***. (Notice the Access icon that displays before the 6-MFDS.mdb file identifying it as an Access database file.)

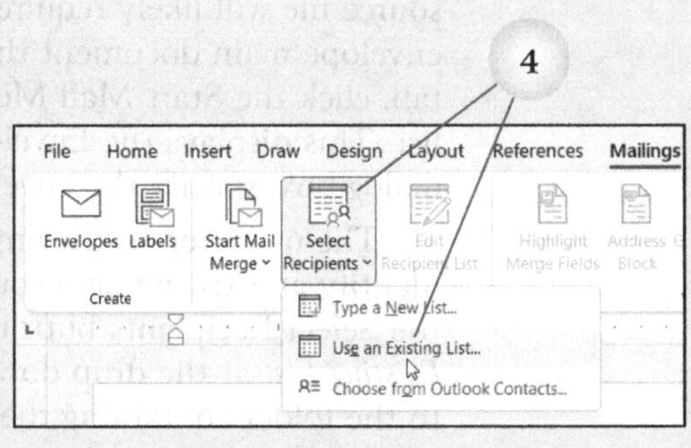

6. Click in the approximate location in the envelope document where the recipient's address will appear. (This causes a box with a dashed gray border to display. If you do not see this box, try clicking in a different location on the envelope.)

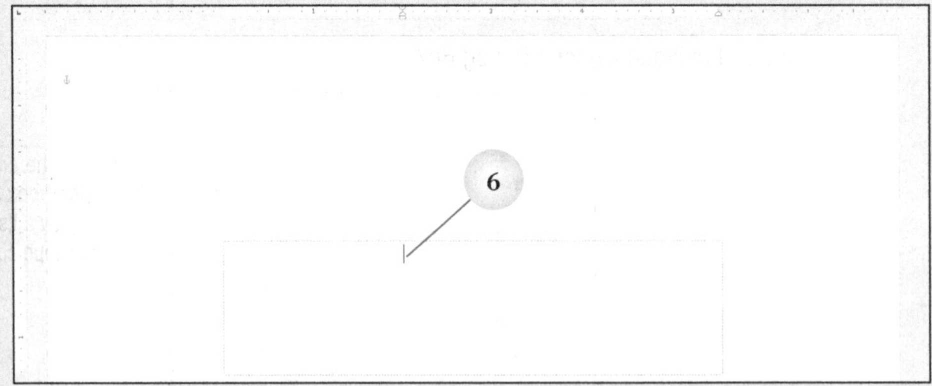

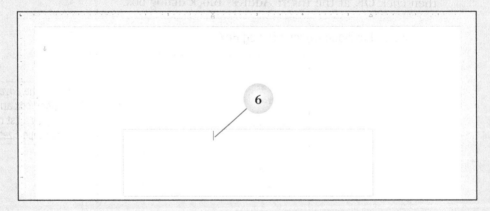

7. Click the Address Block button in the Write & Insert Fields group.
8. At the Insert Address Block dialog box, click OK.
9. Click the Preview Results button to see how the envelope appears merged with the first record in the data source file.
10. Click the Preview Results button to turn off the preview feature.

11. Click the Finish & Merge button in the Finish group and then click *Edit Individual Documents* at the drop-down list.
12. At the Merge to New Document dialog box, specify that you want only the first two records to merge by completing the following steps:
    a. Click in the *From* text box and then type 1.
    b. Click in the *To* text box and then type 2.
    c. Click OK. (This merges only the first two records and then opens a document with two merged envelopes.)
13. Save the merged envelopes with the name **6-MFEnvs**.
14. Preview and then close **6-MFEnvs.docx**.
15. Save the envelope main document with the name **6-EnvMD**.
16. Close **6-EnvMD.docx**.

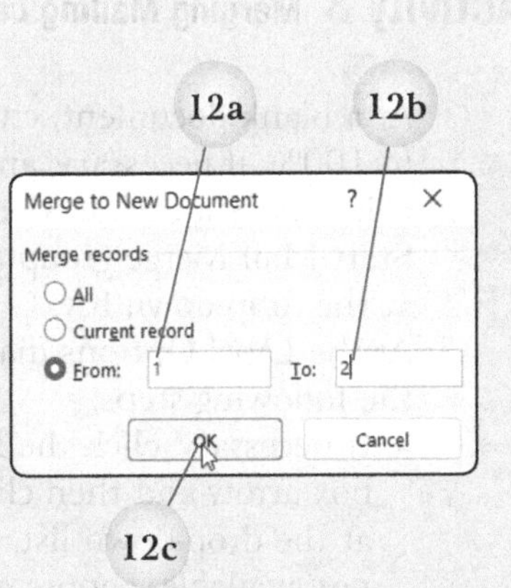

Activity 3 Merge Mailing Labels — 1 Part

You will use Mail Merge to prepare mailing labels with customer names and addresses.

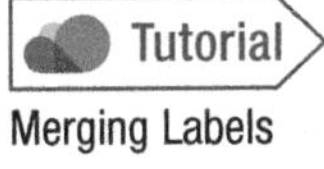

Merging Labels

Merging Labels

Mailing labels for records in a data source file are created in much the same way that envelopes are created. Click the Start Mail Merge button and then click *Labels* at the drop-down list. This displays the Label Options dialog box, as shown in Figure 6.6. Make sure the desired label is selected and then click OK to close the dialog box. The next step is to create the data source file or identify an existing data source file. With the data source file attached to the label main document, insert the appropriate fields and then complete the merge.

Figure 6.6 Label Options Dialog Box

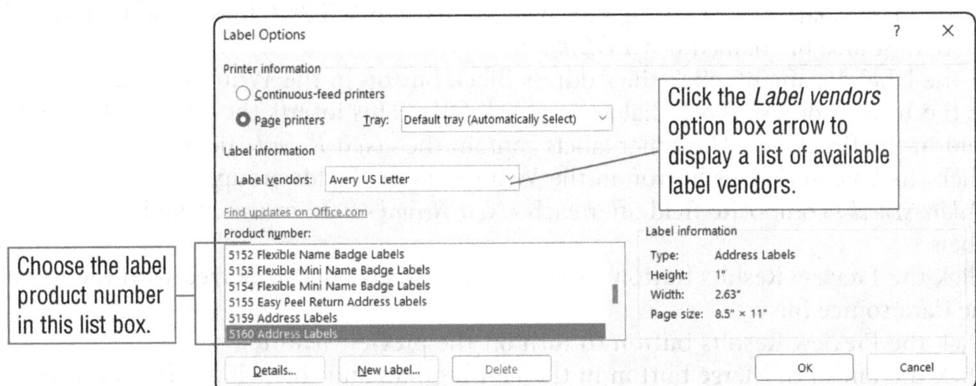

Activity 3 Merging Mailing Labels

1. At a blank document, change the document zoom to 100%, if necessary, and then click the Mailings tab.
2. Click the Start Mail Merge button in the Start Mail Merge group and then click *Labels* at the drop-down list.
3. At the Label Options dialog box, complete the following steps:
   a. If necessary, click the *Label vendors* option box arrow and then click *Avery US Letter* at the drop-down list. (If this option is not available, choose a vendor that offers labels that print on a full page.)
   b. Scroll in the *Product number* list box and then, if necessary, click *5160 Address Labels*. (If this option is not available, choose a label number that prints labels in two or three columns down a full page.)
   c. Click OK to close the dialog box.

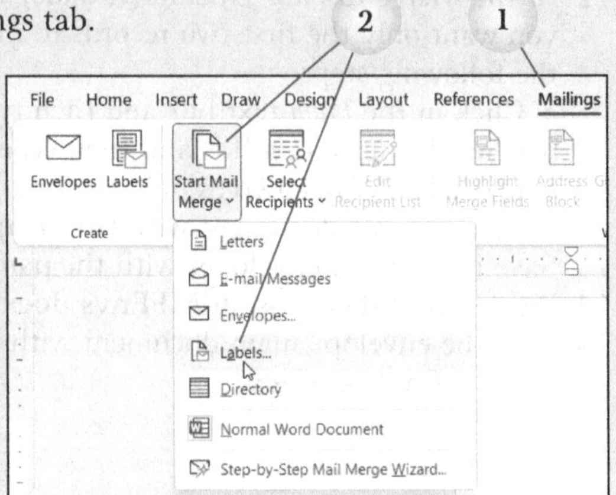

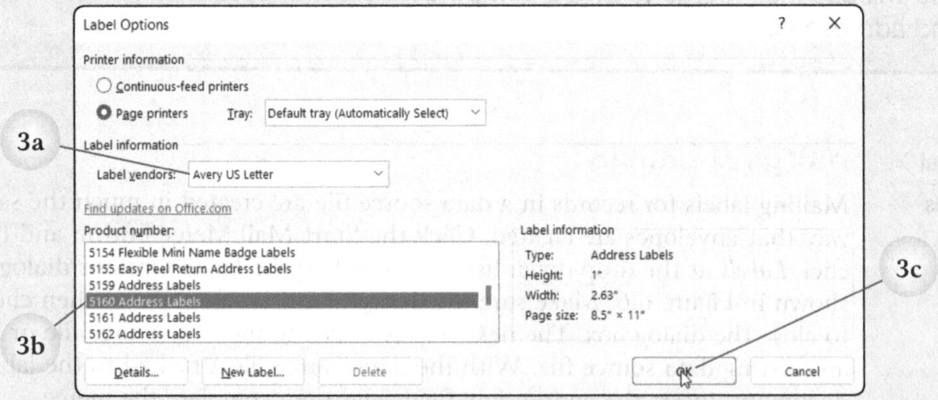

4. Click the Select Recipients button in the Start Mail Merge group and then click *Use an Existing List* at the drop-down list.
5. At the Select Data Source dialog box, navigate to your WL2C6 folder and then double-click the data source file named ***6-MFDS.mdb***.
6. At the label document, click the Address Block button in the Write & Insert Fields group.
7. At the Insert Address Block dialog box, click OK. (This inserts the *«AddressBlock»* composite field in the first label. The other labels contain the *«Next Record»* field.)
8. Click the Update Labels button in the Write & Insert Fields group. (This adds the *«AddressBlock»* composite field after each *«Next Record»* field in the second and subsequent labels.)
9. Click the Preview Results button to see how the labels appear merged with the records in the data source file.
10. Click the Preview Results button to turn off the preview feature.
11. Click the Finish & Merge button in the Finish group and then click *Edit Individual Documents* at the drop-down list.
12. At the Merge to New Document dialog box, make sure *All* is selected and then click OK.

13. Format the labels by completing the following steps:
    a. Click the Table Layout tab.
    b. Click the Select button in the Table group and then click the *Select Table* option.
    c. Click the Align Center Left button in the Alignment group.
    d. Click the Home tab and then click the Paragraph group dialog box launcher.
    e. At the Paragraph dialog box, click the *Before* measurement box up arrow to change the measurement to 0 points.
    f. Click the *After* measurement box up arrow to change the measurement to 0 points.
    g. Click the *Inside* measurement box up arrow three times to change the measurement to 0.3 inch.
    h. Click OK.
14. Save the merged labels with the name **6-MFLabels**.
15. Preview and then close **6-MFLabels.docx**.
16. Save the label main document with the name **6-LabelsMD**.
17. Close **6-LabelsMD.docx**.

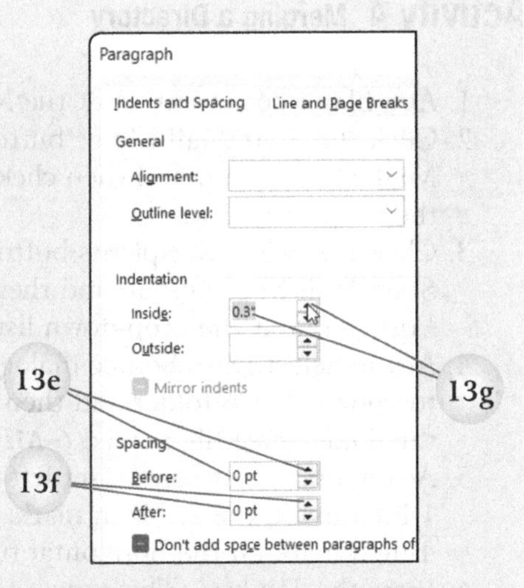

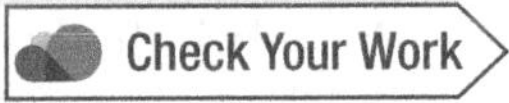

Activity 4 Merge a Directory

1 Part

You will use Mail Merge to prepare a directory list containing customer names and types of financial investment funds.

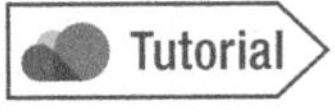

Merging a Directory

Merging a Directory

When merging letters, envelopes, or mailing labels, a new form is created for each record. For example, if the data source file merged with the letter contains eight records, eight letters are created, each on a separate page. In some situations, merged information should remain on the same page. This is useful, for example, when creating a list such as a directory or address list.

Begin creating a merged directory by clicking the Start Mail Merge button and then clicking *Directory* at the drop-down list. Create or identify an existing data source file and then insert the necessary fields in the directory document. To display the merged data in columns, set tabs for all the columns.

Activity 4 Merging a Directory

1. At a blank document, click the Mailings tab.
2. Click the Start Mail Merge button in the Start Mail Merge group and then click *Directory* at the drop-down list.
3. Click the Select Recipients button in the Start Mail Merge group and then click *Use an Existing List* at the drop-down list.
4. At the Select Data Source dialog box, navigate to your WL2C6 folder and then double-click the data source file named ***6-MFDS.mdb***.
5. At the document screen, set left tabs at the 1-inch mark, the 2.5-inch mark, and the 4-inch mark on the horizontal ruler.
6. Press the Tab key. (This moves the insertion point to the tab set at the 1-inch mark.)
7. Click the Insert Merge Field button arrow and then click *Last_Name* at the drop-down list.
8. Press the Tab key to move the insertion point to the tab set at the 2.5-inch mark.
9. Click the Insert Merge Field button arrow and then click *First_Name* at the drop-down list.
10. Press the Tab key to move the insertion point to the tab set at the 4-inch mark.
11. Click the Insert Merge Field button arrow and then click *Fund* at the drop-down list.
12. Press the Enter key.
13. Click the Finish & Merge button in the Finish group and then click *Edit Individual Documents* at the drop-down list.
14. At the Merge to New Document dialog box, make sure *All* is selected and then click OK. (This merges the fields in the document.)
15. Press Ctrl + Home, press the Enter key, and then press the Up Arrow key.
16. Press the Tab key, turn on bold formatting, and then type Last Name.
17. Press the Tab key and then type First Name.
18. Press the Tab key and then type Fund.

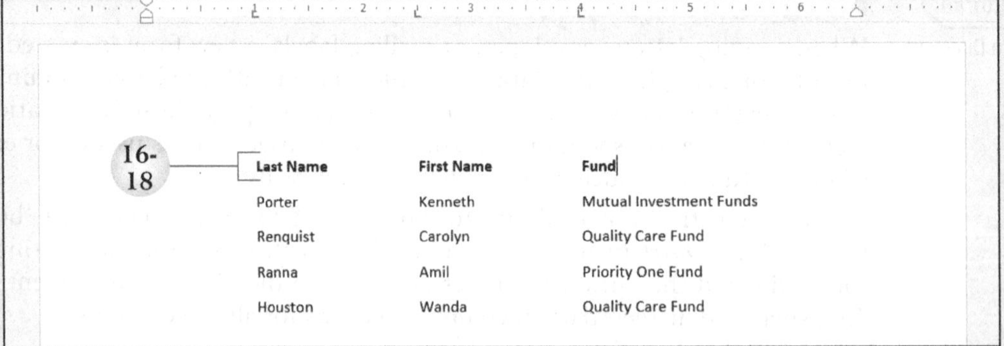

Last Name	First Name	Fund
Porter	Kenneth	Mutual Investment Funds
Renquist	Carolyn	Quality Care Fund
Ranna	Amil	Priority One Fund
Houston	Wanda	Quality Care Fund

19. Save the directory document with the name **6-Directory**.
20. Preview and then close **6-Directory.docx**.
21. Save the directory main document with the name **6-DirectoryMD** and then close the document.

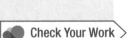

Activity 5 Select Records and Merge Mailing Labels **1 Part**

You will use Mail Merge to prepare mailing labels with the names and addresses of customers living in Baltimore.

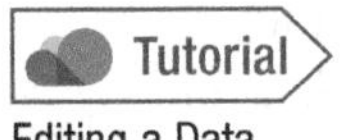

Editing a Data Source File

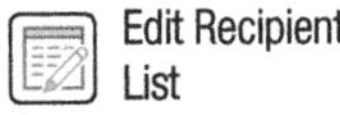

Edit Recipient List

Editing a Data Source File

Edit a main document in the normal manner. Open the document, make the required changes, and then save the document. Since a data source file is actually an Access database file, it cannot be opened in the normal manner. Open a data source file for editing using the Edit Recipient List button in the Start Mail Merge group on the Mailings tab. Click the Edit Recipient List button and the Mail Merge Recipients dialog box displays, as shown in Figure 6.7. Select or edit records at this dialog box.

Selecting Specific Records

Each record in the Mail Merge Recipients dialog box contains a check mark before the first field. To select specific records for merging, remove the check marks from those records that should not be included in a merge. This way, only certain records in the data source file will be merged with the main document.

Figure 6.7 Mail Merge Recipients Dialog Box

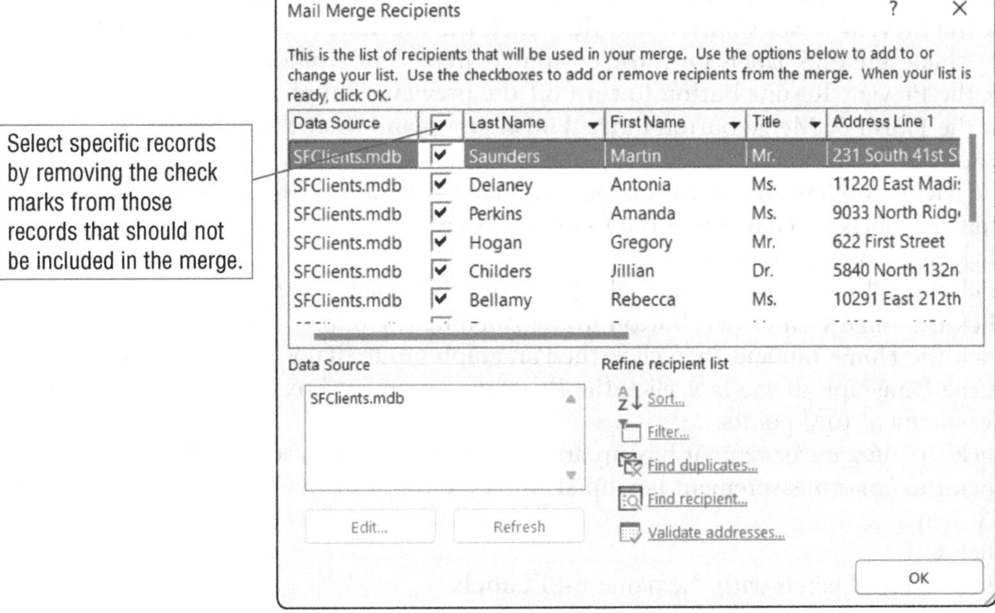

Activity 5 Selecting Records and Merging Mailing Labels

Part 1 of 1

1. At a blank document, create mailing labels for customers living in Baltimore. Begin by clicking the Mailings tab.
2. Click the Start Mail Merge button in the Start Mail Merge group and then click *Labels* at the drop-down list.
3. At the Label Options dialog box, make sure *Avery US Letter* displays in the *Label vendors* option box and *5160 Address Labels* is selected in the *Product number* list box and then click OK.
4. Click the Select Recipients button in the Start Mail Merge group and then click *Use an Existing List* at the drop-down list.
5. At the Select Data Source dialog box, navigate to your WL2C6 folder and then double-click the data source file named ***SFClients.mdb***.
6. Click the Edit Recipient List button in the Start Mail Merge group.
7. At the Mail Merge Recipients dialog box, complete the following steps:
   a. Click the check box immediately left of the *Last Name* field column heading to remove the check mark. (This removes all the check marks from the check boxes.)
   b. Insert check marks by clicking the check box immediately left of each of the following last names: *Saunders*, *Perkins*, *Dutton*, *Fernandez*, and *Stahl*. (These are the customers who live in Baltimore.)
   c. Click OK to close the dialog box.

7a

Mail Merge Recipients

This is the list of recipients that will be used in your merge. Use the
change your list. Use the checkboxes to add or remove recipients f
ready, click OK.

Data Source		Last Name	First Name
SFClients.mdb		Saunders	Martin
SFClients.mdb		Delaney	Antonia

8. At the label document, click the Address Block button in the Write & Insert Fields group.
9. At the Insert Address Block dialog box, click OK.
10. Click the Update Labels button in the Write & Insert Fields group.
11. Click the Preview Results button and then click the Previous Record button to display each label. Make sure only labels for those customers living in Baltimore display.
12. Click the Preview Results button to turn off the preview feature.
13. Click the Finish & Merge button in the Finish group and then click *Edit Individual Documents* at the drop-down list.
14. At the Merge to New Document dialog box, make sure *All* is selected and then click OK.
15. Format the labels by completing the following steps:
    a. Click the Table Layout tab.
    b. Click the Select button in the Table group and then click *Select Table*.
    c. Click the Align Center Left button in the Alignment group.
    d. Click the Home tab and then click the Paragraph group dialog box launcher.
    e. At the Paragraph dialog box, click the *Before* measurement box up arrow to change the measurement to 0 points.
    f. Click the *After* measurement box up arrow to change the measurement to 0 points.
    g. Click the *Inside* measurement box up arrow three times to change the measurement to 0.3 inch.
    h. Click OK.
16. Save the merged labels with the name **6-SFLabels**.
17. Preview and then close **6-SFLabels.docx**.
18. Save the labels main document with the name **6-SFLabelsMD** and then close the document.

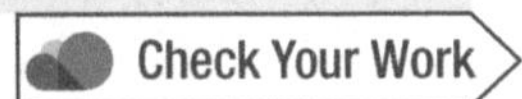

Activity 6 Edit Records in a Data Source File 1 Part

You will edit records in a data source file and then use Mail Merge to prepare a directory with the edited records that contains customer names, telephone numbers, and cell phone numbers.

Editing Records

Quick Steps

Edit Data Source File

1. Open main document.
2. Click Mailings tab.
3. Click Edit Recipient List button.
4. Click data source file name in *Data Source* list box.
5. Click Edit button.
6. Make changes at Edit Data Source dialog box.
7. Click OK.
8. Click OK.

A data source file may need editing on a periodic basis to add or delete customer names, update fields, insert new fields, or delete existing fields. To edit a data source file, click the Edit Recipient List button in the Start Mail Merge group. At the Mail Merge Recipients dialog box, click the data source file name in the *Data Source* list box and then click the Edit button below the list box. This displays the Edit Data Source dialog box, as shown in Figure 6.8. At this dialog box, add a new entry, delete an entry, find a particular entry, and customize columns.

Figure 6.8 Edit Data Source Dialog Box

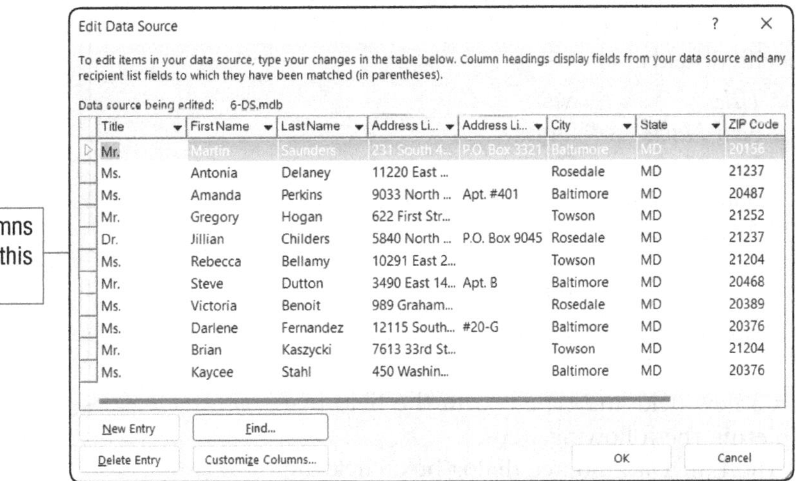

Activity 6 Editing Records in a Data Source File Part 1 of 1

1. Make a copy of the **SFClients.mdb** data source file by completing the following steps:
   a. Display the Open dialog box and make WL2C6 the active folder.
   b. If necessary, change the file type option to *All Files*.
   c. Right-click the ***SFClients.mdb*** data source file and then click *Copy* at the shortcut menu.
   d. Position the pointer in a white portion of the Open dialog box Content pane (outside any file name), click the right mouse button, and then click *Paste* at the shortcut menu. (This inserts a copy of the file in the dialog box Content pane and names the file **SFClients - Copy.mdb**.)
   e. Right-click ***SFClients - Copy.mdb*** and then click *Rename* at the shortcut menu.
   f. Type 6-DS and then press the Enter key.
   g. Close the Open dialog box.

2. At a blank document, click the Mailings tab.
3. Click the Select Recipients button and then click *Use an Existing List* from the drop-down list.
4. At the Select Data Source dialog box, navigate to your WL2C6 folder and then double-click the data source file named ***6-DS.mdb***.
5. Click the Edit Recipient List button in the Start Mail Merge group.
6. At the Mail Merge Recipients dialog box, click *6-DS.mdb* in the *Data Source* list box and then click the Edit button.
7. Delete the record for Steve Dutton by completing the following steps:
    a. Click the square at the beginning of the row for *Mr. Steve Dutton*.
    b. Click the Delete Entry button.
    c. At the message asking if you want to delete the entry, click Yes.
8. Insert a new record by completing the following steps:
    a. Click the New Entry button in the dialog box.
    b. Type the following text in the new record in the specified fields:

Title	Ms.
First Name	Jennae
Last Name	Davis
Address Line 1	3120 South 21st
Address Line 2	(none)
City	Rosedale
State	MD
ZIP Code	20389
Home Phone	410-555-5774

9. Insert a new field and type text in the field by completing the following steps:
    a. At the Edit Data Source dialog box, click the Customize Columns button.
    b. At the message asking if you want to save the changes made to the data source file, click Yes.
    c. At the Customize Address List dialog box, click *ZIP Code* in the *Field Names* list box. (You will insert a new field below this field.)
    d. Click the Add button.
    e. At the Add Field dialog box, type Cell Phone and then click OK.
    f. You decide that you want the *Cell Phone* field to display after the *Home Phone* field. To move the *Cell Phone* field, make sure it is selected and then click the Move Down button.
    g. Click OK to close the Customize Address List dialog box.

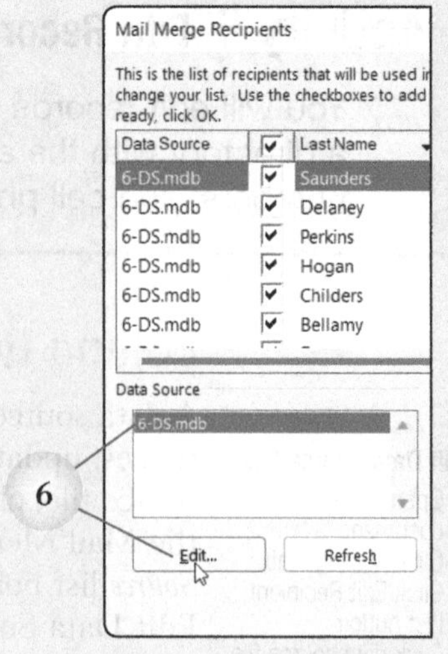

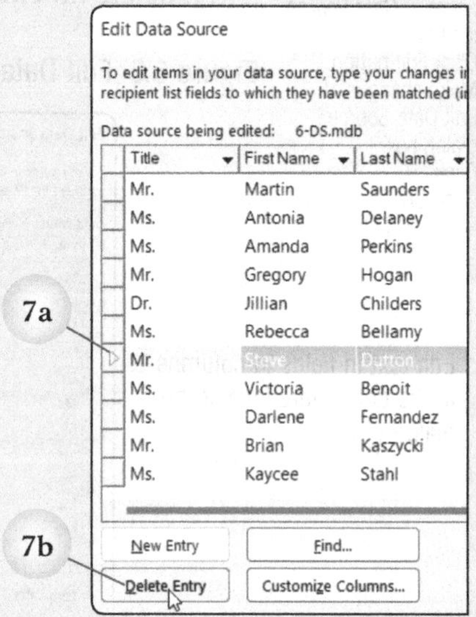

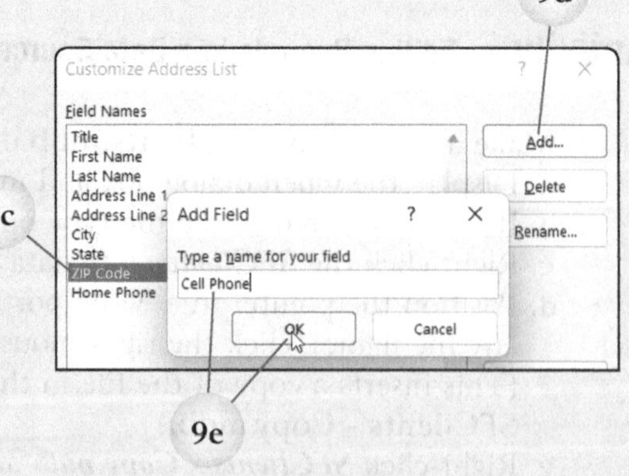

h. At the Edit Data Source dialog box, scroll right to display the *Cell Phone* field (the last field in the file) and then type the following cell phone numbers. (After typing each cell phone number except the last number, press the Down Arrow key to make the next field below active.)

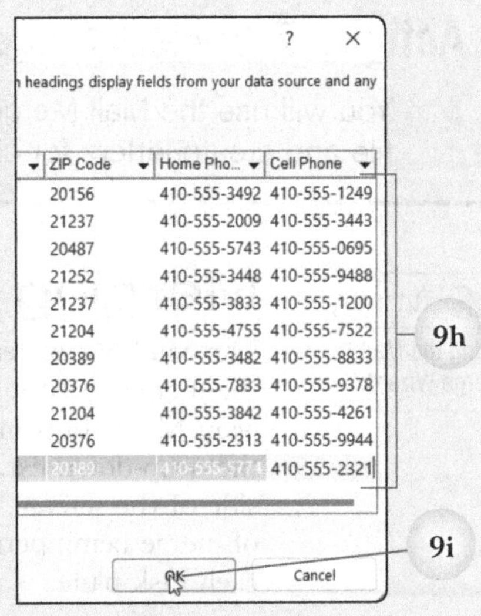

Record 1 410-555-1249
Record 2 410-555-3443
Record 3 410-555-0695
Record 4 410-555-9488
Record 5 410-555-1200
Record 6 410-555-7522
Record 7 410-555-8833
Record 8 410-555-9378
Record 9 410-555-4261
Record 10 410-555-9944
Record 11 410-555-2321

i. Click OK to close the Edit Data Source dialog box.
j. At the message asking if you want to update the recipient list and save changes, click Yes.
k. At the Mail Merge Recipients dialog box, click OK.

10. Create a directory by completing the following steps:
    a. Click the Start Mail Merge button and then click *Directory* at the drop-down list.
    b. At the blank document, set left tabs on the horizontal ruler at the 1-inch mark, the 3-inch mark, and the 4.5-inch mark.
    c. Press the Tab key. (This moves the insertion point to the first tab set at the 1-inch mark.)
    d. Click the Insert Merge Field button arrow and then click *Last_Name* at the drop-down list.
    e. Type a comma and then press the spacebar.
    f. Click the Insert Merge Field button arrow and then click *First_Name* at the drop-down list.
    g. Press the Tab key, click the Insert Merge Field button arrow, and then click *Home_Phone* at the drop-down list.
    h. Press the Tab key, click the Insert Merge Field button arrow, and then click *Cell_Phone* at the drop-down list.
    i. Press the Enter key.
    j. Click the Finish & Merge button and then click *Edit Individual Documents* at the drop-down list.
    k. At the Merge to New Document dialog box, make sure *All* is selected and then click OK.
11. Press Ctrl + Home, press the Enter key, and then press the Up Arrow key.
12. Press the Tab key, turn on bold formatting, and then type Name.
13. Press the Tab key and then type Home Phone.
14. Press the Tab key and then type Cell Phone.

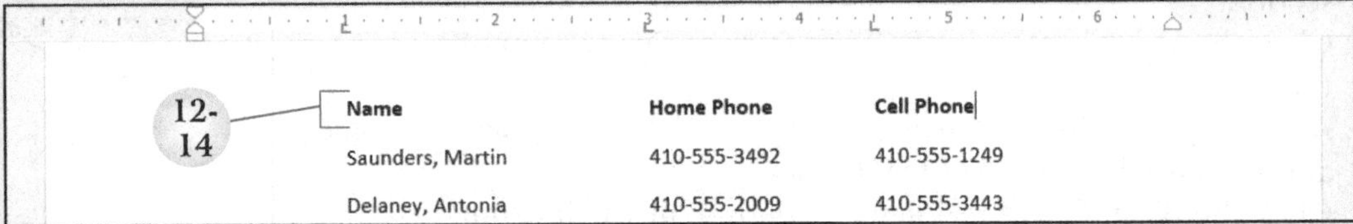

15. Save the directory document with the name **6-Directory-Act6**.
16. Preview and then close **6-Directory-Act6.docx**.
17. Save the directory main document with the name **6-Directory-Act6-MD** and then close the document.

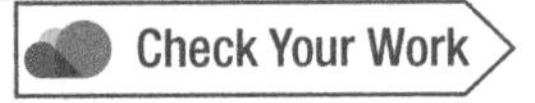

Activity 7 Use Mail Merge Wizard — 1 Part

You will use the Mail Merge wizard to merge a main document with a data source file and create letters for clients of Sorenson Funds.

Using the Mail Merge Wizard

Merging Using the Mail Merge Wizard

The Mail Merge feature includes a Mail Merge wizard with steps for completing the merge process. To access the wizard, click the Mailings tab, click the Start Mail Merge button, and then click the *Step-by-Step Mail Merge Wizard* option at the drop-down list. The first of six Mail Merge task panes displays at the right side of the screen. The options in each task pane may vary depending on the type of merge being performed. Generally, one of the following steps is completed at each task pane:

- Step 1: Select the type of document to be created, such as a letter, email message, envelope, label, or directory.
- Step 2: Specify what is to be used to create the main document: the current document, a template, or an existing document.
- Step 3: Specify whether a new list will be created or an existing list or Outlook contacts list will be used.
- Step 4: Use the items in this task pane to help prepare the main document by performing tasks such as inserting fields.
- Step 5: Preview the merged documents.
- Step 6: Complete the merge.

Activity 7 Preparing Form Letters Using the Mail Merge Wizard — Part 1 of 1

1. At a blank document, click the Mailings tab, click the Start Mail Merge button in the Start Mail Merge group, and then click *Step-by-Step Mail Merge Wizard* at the drop-down list.
2. At the first Mail Merge task pane, make sure *Letters* is selected in the *Select document type* section and then click the Next: Starting document hyperlink at the bottom of the task pane.
3. At the second Mail Merge task pane, click the *Start from existing document* option in the *Select starting document* section.
4. Click the Open button in the *Start from existing* section of the task pane.
5. At the Open dialog box, navigate to your WL2C6 folder and then double-click ***SFLtrMD.docx***.
6. Click the Next: Select recipients hyperlink at the bottom of the task pane.

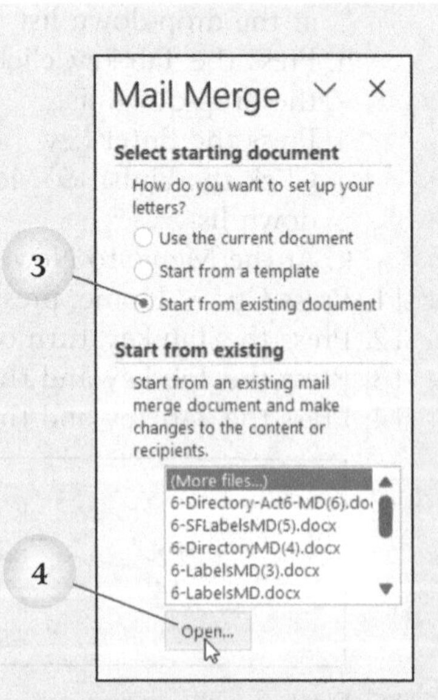

7. At the third Mail Merge task pane, click the Browse hyperlink in the *Use an existing list* section of the task pane.
8. At the Select Data Source dialog box, navigate to your WL2C6 folder and then double-click the ***SFClients.mdb*** data source file.
9. At the Mail Merge Recipients dialog box, click OK.
10. Click the Next: Write your letter hyperlink at the bottom of the task pane.
11. At the fourth Mail Merge task pane, enter fields in the form letter by completing the following steps:
    a. Position the insertion point a double space above the first paragraph of text in the letter.
    b. Click the Address block hyperlink in the *Write your letter* section of the task pane.
    c. At the Insert Address Block dialog box, click OK.
    d. Press the Enter key two times and then click the Greeting line hyperlink in the *Write your letter* section of the task pane.
    e. At the Insert Greeting Line dialog box, click the option box arrow at the right of the option box containing the comma (the box at the right of the box containing *Mr. Randall*).
    f. At the drop-down list, click the colon.
    g. Click OK to close the Insert Greeting Line dialog box.
12. Click the Next: Preview your letters hyperlink at the bottom of the task pane.
13. At the fifth Mail Merge task pane, look over the letter in the document window and make sure the information is merged properly. If you want to see the letters for the other recipients, click the Next button (the button containing two right-pointing arrows) in the Mail Merge task pane.
14. Click the Preview Results button in the Preview Results group to turn off the preview feature.
15. Click the Next: Complete the merge hyperlink at the bottom of the task pane.
16. At the sixth Mail Merge task pane, click the Edit individual letters hyperlink in the *Merge* section of the task pane.
17. At the Merge to New Document dialog box, make sure *All* is selected and then click OK.
18. Save the merged letters document with the name **6-SFLtrs**.
19. Preview and then close **6-SFLtrs.docx**.
20. Save the main document with the name **6-SFLtrsMD** and then close the document.

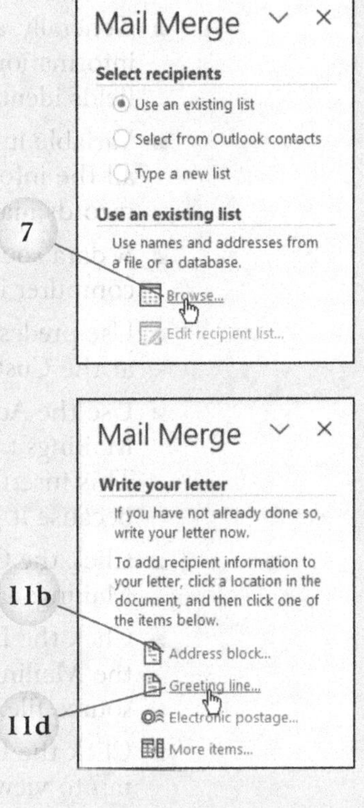

Chapter Summary

- Generally, a merge takes two files: the data source file containing the variable information and the main document containing the standard text along with fields identifying where variable information is inserted during the merge process.
- Variable information in a data source file is saved as a record. A record contains all the information for one unit. A series of fields makes a record and a series of records makes a data source file.
- A data source file is saved as an Access database, but having Access on the computer is not required to complete a merge with a data source file.
- Use predesigned fields when creating a data source file or create custom fields at the Customize Address List dialog box.
- Use the Address Block button in the Write & Insert Fields group on the Mailings tab to insert all the fields required for the inside address of a letter. This inserts the *«AddressBlock»* field, which is considered a composite field because it groups a number of fields.
- Click the Greeting Line button in the Write & Insert Fields group on the Mailings tab to insert the *«GreetingLine»* composite field in the document.
- Click the Insert Merge Field button arrow in the Write & Insert Fields group on the Mailings tab to display a drop-down list of the fields contained in the data source file.
- Click the Preview Results button in the Preview Results group on the Mailings tab to view the main document merged with the first record in the data source file. Use the navigation buttons in the Preview Results group on the Mailings tab to display the main document merged with specific records.
- Before merging documents, check for errors by clicking the Check for Errors button in the Preview Results group on the Mailings tab. This displays the Checking and Reporting Errors dialog box with three options for checking errors.
- Click the Finish & Merge button in the Finish group on the Mailings tab to complete the merge.
- A data source file can be merged with a letter, envelope, label, or directory main document.
- To begin preparing envelopes for merging, click the Mailings tab, click the Start Mail Merge button, and then click *Envelopes* at the drop-down list. Click *Labels* at the drop-down list to begin preparing labels for merging.
- Create a directory when merging records in a data source file on the same page. Begin preparing a directory for merging by clicking the Mailings tab, clicking the Start Mail Merge button, and then clicking *Directory* at the drop-down list.
- Select specific records for merging by inserting or removing check marks from the records in the Mail Merge Recipients dialog box. Display this dialog box by clicking the Edit Recipient List button in the Start Mail Merge group on the Mailings tab.
- Edit specific records in a data source file at the Edit Data Source dialog box. Display this dialog box by clicking the Edit Recipient List button on the Mailings tab, clicking the data source file name in the *Data Source* list box, and then clicking the Edit button.
- Word includes a Mail Merge wizard that provides guidance through the process of creating letters, envelopes, labels, directories, and email messages with personalized information.

Commands Review

FEATURE	RIBBON TAB, GROUP	BUTTON, OPTION
Address Block field	Mailings, Write & Insert Fields	
Checking and Reporting Errors dialog box	Mailings, Preview Results	
directory main document	Mailings, Start Mail Merge	, *Directory*
envelope main document	Mailings, Start Mail Merge	, *Envelopes*
finish merge	Mailings, Finish	
Greeting Line field	Mailings, Write & Insert Fields	
insert merge fields	Mailings, Write & Insert Fields	
label main document	Mailings, Start Mail Merge	, *Labels*
letter main document	Mailings, Start Mail Merge	, *Letters*
Mail Merge Recipients dialog box	Mailings, Start Mail Merge	
Mail Merge wizard	Mailings, Start Mail Merge	, *Step-by-Step Mail Merge Wizard*
New Address List dialog box	Mailings, Start Mail Merge	, *Type a New List*
preview merge results	Mailings, Preview Results	« » ABC

Review and Assessment

CHAPTER 6

Skills Assessment

Assessment 1 — Create a Data Source File

1. At a blank document, display the New Address List dialog box and then display the Customize Address List dialog box. (To do this, click the Mailings tab, click the Select Recipients button, click the *Type a New List* option, and then click the Customize Columns button.)
2. At the Customize Address List dialog box, delete the following fields—*Company Name*, *Country or Region*, *Work Phone*, and *E-mail Address*—and then add a custom field named *Cell Phone*. (Position the *Cell Phone* field after the *Home Phone* field.)
3. Close the Customize Address List dialog box and then type the following information in the New Address List dialog box as the first record:

Title	Mr.
First Name	Tony
Last Name	Benedetti
Address Line 1	1315 Cordova Road
Address Line 2	Apt. 402
City	Santa Fe
State	NM
ZIP Code	87505
Home Phone	(505) 555-0489
Cell Phone	(505) 555-0551

4. Type the following information as the second record:

Title	Ms.
First Name	Theresa
Last Name	Dusek
Address Line 1	12044 Ridgeway Drive
Address Line 2	(leave blank)
City	Santa Fe
State	NM
ZIP Code	87504
Home Phone	(505) 555-1120
Cell Phone	(505) 555-6890

5. Type the following information as the third record:

Title	Ms.
First Name	Mary
Last Name	Arguello
Address Line 1	2554 Country Drive
Address Line 2	#105
City	Santa Fe
State	NM
ZIP Code	87504
Home Phone	(505) 555-7663
Cell Phone	(505) 555-5472

6. Type the following information as the fourth record:

Title	Mr.
First Name	Preston
Last Name	Miller
Address Line 1	120 Second Street
Address Line 2	(leave blank)
City	Santa Fe
State	NM
ZIP Code	87505
Home Phone	(505) 555-3551
Cell Phone	(505) 555-9630

7. Save the data source file with the name **6-CCDS**.
8. Close the blank document without saving changes.

Assessment 2 Create a Letter Main Document and Merge with a Data Source File

1. Open **CCVolunteerLtr.docx** and then save it with the name **6-CCMD**.
2. Select the **6-CCDS.mdb** data source file you created in Assessment 1.
3. Move the insertion point to the beginning of the first paragraph of text in the body of the letter, insert the *«AddressBlock»* field, and then press the Enter key two times.
4. Insert the *«GreetingLine»* field specifying a colon rather than a comma as the greeting line format and then press the Enter key two times.
5. Move the insertion point one space to the right of the period that ends the second paragraph of text in the body of the letter and then type the following text inserting the *«Title»*, *«Last_Name»*, *«Home_Phone»*, and *«Cell_Phone»* fields where indicated:

   Currently, *«Title» «Last_Name»*, our records indicate your home telephone number is *«Home_Phone»* and your cell phone number is *«Cell_Phone»*. If this information is not accurate, please contact our office with the correct numbers.

6. Merge the main document with all the records in the data source file.
7. Save the merged letters document with the name **6-CCLetters**.
8. Preview and then close **6-CCLetters.docx**.
9. Save and then close **6-CCMD.docx**.

Assessment 3 — Create an Envelope Main Document and Merge with a Data Source File

1. Create an envelope main document using the Size 10 envelope size.
2. Select **6-CCDS.mdb** as the data source file.
3. Insert the *«AddressBlock»* field in the appropriate location in the envelope document.
4. Merge the envelope main document with all the records in the data source file.
5. Save the merged envelopes document with the name **6-CCEnvs**.
6. Preview and then close the envelopes document.
7. Save the envelope main document with the name **6-CCEnvsMD** and then close the document.

Assessment 4 — Create a Label Main Document and Merge with a Data Source File

1. Create a label main document using the option *Avery US Letter 5160 Address Labels*.
2. Select **6-CCDS.mdb** as the data source file.
3. Insert the *«AddressBlock»* field.
4. Update the labels.
5. Merge the label main document with all the records in the data source file.
6. Save the merged labels document with the name **6-CCLabels**.
7. Preview and then close the labels document.
8. Save the label main document with the name **6-CCLabelsMD** and then close the document.

Assessment 5 — Edit a Data Source File

1. Open **6-CCMD.docx**. (At the message asking if you want to continue, click Yes.) Save the main document with the name **6-CCMD-A5**.
2. Edit the **6-CCDS.mdb** data source file by making the following changes:
   a. Change the address for Ms. Theresa Dusek from *12044 Ridgeway Drive* to *1390 Fourth Avenue*.
   b. Delete the record for Ms. Mary Arguello.
   c. Insert a new record with the following information:
      Mr. Cesar Rivera
      3201 East Third Street
      Santa Fe, NM 87505
      Home Phone: (505) 555-6675
      Cell Phone: (505) 555-3528
3. Merge the main document with all the records in the data source file.
4. Save the merged letters document with the name **6-CCLtrsEdited**.
5. Preview and then close **6-CCLtrsEdited.docx**.
6. Save and then close **6-CCMD-A5.docx**.

Visual Benchmark

Prepare and Merge Letters

1. Open **FPLtrhd.docx** and then save it with the name **6-FPMD**.
2. Look at the information in Figure 6.9 and Figure 6.10 and then use Mail Merge to prepare four letters. (When creating the main document, as shown in Figure 6.10, insert the appropriate fields where you see the text *Title*; *First Name*; *Last Name*; *Street Address*; and *City*, *State ZIP*. Insert the appropriate fields where you see the text *Title* and *Last Name* in the first paragraph of text.) Create the data source file with customized field names using the information in Figure 6.9 and then save the file with the name **6-FPDS**.
3. Merge the **6-FPMD.docx** main document with the **6-FPDS.mdb** data source file and then save the merged letters document with the name **6-FPLtrs**.
4. Preview and then close **6-FPLtrs.docx**.
5. Save and then close **6-FPMD.docx**.

Figure 6.9 Visual Benchmark Data Source Records

Mr. Chris Gallagher
17034 234th Avenue
Newport, VT 05855

Ms. Heather Segarra
4103 Thompson Drive
Newport, VT 05855

Mr. Gene Goodrich
831 Cromwell Lane
Newport, VT 05855

Ms. Sonya Kraus
15933 Ninth Street
Newport, VT 05855

Figure 6.10 Visual Benchmark Main Document

FRONTLINE
PHOTOGRAPHY

Current Date

Title First Name Last Name
Street Address
City, State ZIP

Dear Title Last Name:

We have enjoyed being a part of the Newport business community for the past two years. Our success has been thanks to you, Title Last Name, and all our other loyal customers. Thank you for shopping at our store for all your photography equipment and supply needs.

To show our appreciation for your business, we are enclosing a coupon for 20 percent off any item in our store, including our incredibly low-priced clearance items. Through the end of the month, all camera accessories are on sale. Use your coupon and take advantage of additional savings on items such as camera lenses, tripods, cleaning supplies, and camera bags.

To accommodate our customers' schedules, we have extended our weekend hours. Our store will be open Saturdays until 7:00 p.m. and Sundays, until 5:00 p.m. Come by and let our sales associates find the right camera and accessories for you.

Sincerely,

Student Name

XX
6-FPMD.docx

Enclosure

559 Tenth Street, Suite A, Newport, VT 05855
802.555.4411 ◉ https://ppi-edu.net/frontline

Case Study

Part 1

You are the office manager for Freestyle Extreme, a sporting goods store that specializes in snowboarding and snow skiing equipment and supplies. The store has two branches: one on the east side of town and the other on the west side. One of your job responsibilities is to send letters to customers letting them know about sales, new equipment, and upcoming events. Next month, both stores are having a sale and all snowboarding and snow skiing supplies will be 15 percent off the last marked price.

Create a data source file that contains the following customer information: first name, last name, address, city, state, zip code, and branch. Add six customers to the data source file. Indicate that three usually shop at the East branch and three usually shop at the West branch.

Create a letter as a main document that includes information about the upcoming sale. The letter should contain at least two paragraphs and in addition to the information on the sale, it might include information about the store, snowboarding, and/or snow skiing.

Save the data source file with the name **6-FEDS**, save the main document with the name **6-FEMD**, and save the merged document with the name **6-FELtrs**. Create envelopes for the six merged letters and name the merged envelope document **6-FEEnvs**. Save the envelope main document with the name **6-FEEnvsMD**. Preview and then close the merged letters document and the merged envelopes document.

Part 2

A well-known extreme snowboarder will be visiting both branches of Freestyle Extreme to meet with customers and sign autographs. Use the Help feature to learn how to insert an *If...Then...Else...* merge field in a document and then create a letter that includes the name of the extreme snowboarder (you determine the name), the times of the visits to the two branches (1:00 p.m. to 4:30 p.m.), and any additional information that might interest customers. Also include in the letter an *If...Then...Else...* merge field that will insert *Wednesday, September 25* if the customer's branch is *East* and *Thursday, September 26* if the customer's branch is *West*. Add visual interest to the letter by inserting an image, WordArt, or other feature that will attract readers' attention. Save the letter main document with the name **6-SnowMD**. Merge the letter main document with the **6-FEDS.mdb** data source file. Save the merged letters document with the name **6-SnowLtrs**. Preview and then close the merged letters document.

Part 3

The owner of Freestyle Extreme wants to try selling short skis known as "snow blades" or "skiboards." He has asked you to research these skis and identify one type and model to sell only at the West branch of the store. If the model sells well, the owner will consider selling it at the East branch at a future time. Prepare a main document letter that describes the new snow blade or skiboard that the West branch is going to sell. Include information about pricing and tell customers that they can save 40 percent if they purchase the new item within the next week. Merge the letter main document with the **6-FEDS.mdb** data source file and include only those customers that shop at the West branch. Save the merged letters document with the name **6-SBLtrs**. Preview and then close the merged letters document. Save the letter main document with the name **6-SBMD**. Save and then close the main document.

WORD

Managing Building Blocks and Fields

CHAPTER 7

Performance Objectives

Upon successful completion of Chapter 7, you will be able to:

1 Insert and sort building blocks
2 Save content as building blocks in specific galleries
3 Edit building block properties
4 Insert and modify custom building blocks
5 Create a building block gallery and save building blocks in a different template
6 Delete building blocks
7 Insert document property placeholders from Quick Parts
8 Insert and update fields from Quick Parts

Word contains a number of predesigned blocks of text and formatting referred to as *building blocks*. Building blocks are available in galleries throughout Word, most of them on the Insert tab, where they can be quickly and easily inserted into any document. You have been inserting building blocks such as predesigned headers, footers, page numbers, text boxes, cover pages, and so on. Predesigned building blocks can be customized to meet specific needs, or a new building block can be created and then saved in a gallery. In this chapter, you will learn how to build a document using building blocks; how to create, save, and edit your own building blocks; and how to create a button on the Quick Access Toolbar for faster access to a gallery. You will also learn how to insert fields in a document and to format and customize fields.

Data Files

The data files for this chapter are in the WL2C7 folder that you downloaded at the beginning of this course.

Activity 1 Build a Document with Predesigned Building Blocks **1 Part**

You will open a document on home safety and then add elements to it by sorting and then inserting predesigned building blocks.

Managing Building Blocks

Word includes a variety of tools for inserting data such as text, fields, objects, and other items to help build a document. To view some of the tools available, click the Quick Parts button in the Text group on the Insert tab. This displays a drop-down list of choices for inserting document properties, fields, and building blocks. Word provides a number of predesigned building blocks that can be inserted in a document or custom building blocks can be created. Building blocks are pieces of predesigned document content that can be used over and over again to build a document.

Inserting a Building Block

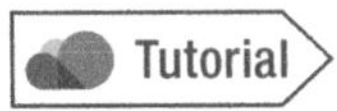

Inserting and Sorting Building Blocks

Quick Steps

Insert Building Block

1. Click Insert tab.
2. Click Quick Parts button.
3. Click *Building Blocks Organizer*.
4. Click building block.
5. Click Insert button.
6. Click Close.

To insert a building block into a document, click the Insert tab, click the Quick Parts button in the Text group, and then click *Building Blocks Organizer* at the drop-down list. This displays the Building Blocks Organizer dialog box, shown in Figure 7.1. The dialog box contains columns of information about each building block, including its name, the gallery that contains it, the template in which it is stored, its behavior, and a brief description of it.

The Building Blocks Organizer dialog box is a central location for viewing all the predesigned building blocks available in Word. Some of the building blocks were used in previous chapters when a predesigned header or footer, cover page, page number, or watermark was inserted in a document. Other galleries in the Building Blocks Organizer dialog box contain predesigned building blocks such as bibliographies, equations, tables of contents, tables, and text boxes. The Building Blocks Organizer dialog box provides a convenient location for viewing and inserting building blocks.

Sorting Building Blocks

Quick Steps

Sort Building Blocks

1. Click Insert tab.
2. Click Quick Parts button.
3. Click *Building Blocks Organizer*.
4. Click column heading.

The Building Blocks Organizer dialog box displays the building blocks in the list box sorted by the *Gallery* column. The building blocks can be sorted by another column by clicking that column heading. For example, to sort the building blocks alphabetically by name, click the *Name* column heading.

Figure 7.1 Building Blocks Organizer Dialog Box

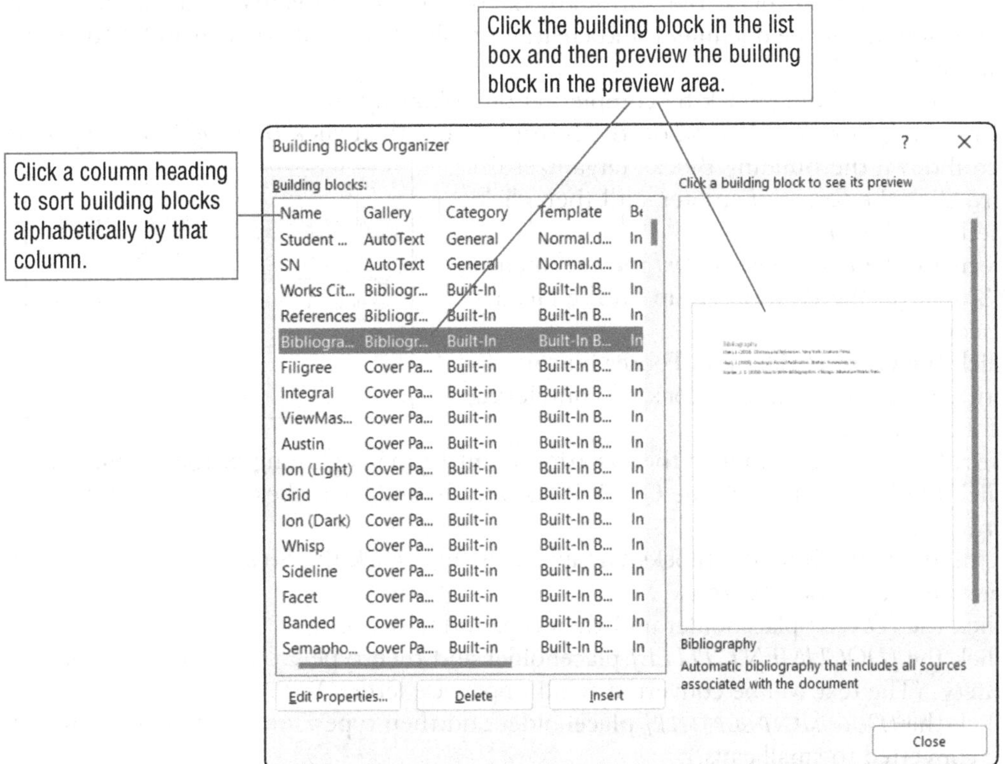

Activity 1 Sorting and Inserting Predesigned Building Blocks

Part 1 of 1

1. Open **HomeSafety.docx** and then save it with the name **7-HomeSafety**.
2. Sort the building blocks and then insert a table of contents building block by completing the following steps:
   a. Press Ctrl + Home to move the insertion point to the beginning of the document, press Ctrl + Enter to insert a page break, and then press Ctrl + Home again.
   b. Click the Insert tab, click the Quick Parts button in the Text group, and then click *Building Blocks Organizer* at the drop-down list.
   c. At the Building Blocks Organizer dialog box, notice the arrangement of building blocks in the list box. (The building blocks are most likely organized alphabetically by the *Gallery* column.)
   d. Click the *Name* column heading. (This sorts the building blocks alphabetically by name. However, some blank building blocks may display at the beginning of the list box.)
   e. Scroll down the list box and then click *Automatic Table 1*. (You may see only a portion of the name. Click the name and the full name as well as a description display in the dialog box below the preview of the table of contents building block.)

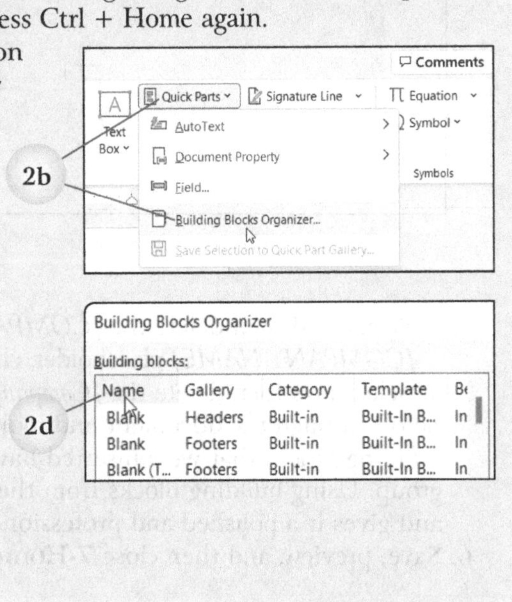

f. Click the Insert button at the bottom of the dialog box. (This inserts a contents page at the beginning of the document and creates a table of contents that includes the headings with styles applied.)

3. Insert a footer building block by completing the following steps:
   a. Click the Quick Parts button on the Insert tab and then click *Building Blocks Organizer*.
   b. Scroll down the Building Blocks Organizer list box, click the *Sempahore* footer, and then click the Insert button.
   c. Decrease the *Footer from Bottom* measurement to 0.3 inch (in the Position group on the Header & Footer tab).
   d. Click the Close Header and Footer button.
4. Insert a cover page building block by completing the following steps:
   a. Press Ctrl + Home to move the insertion point to the beginning of the document.
   b. Click the Insert tab, click the Quick Parts button, and then click *Building Blocks Organizer*.
   c. Scroll down the Building Blocks Organizer list box, click the *Semaphore* cover page, and then click the Insert button.
   d. Click the *[DATE]* placeholder and then type today's date.
   e. Click the *[DOCUMENT TITLE]* placeholder and then type Citizens for Consumer Safety. (The text will be converted to all uppercase letters.)
   f. Click the *[DOCUMENT SUBTITLE]* placeholder and then type Home Safety. (The text will be converted to small caps.)
   g. Select the name above the *[COMPANY NAME]* placeholder and then type your first and last names.

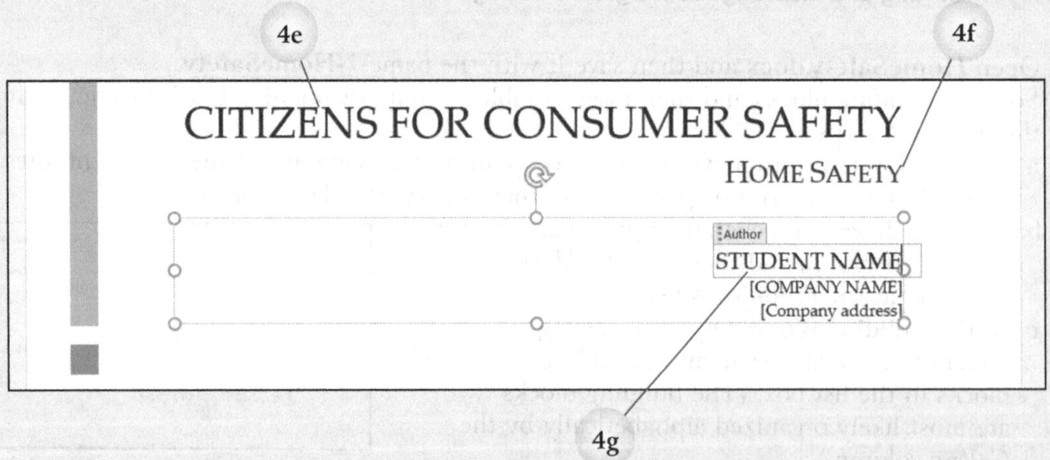

   h. Select and then delete the *[COMPANY NAME]* placeholder. (To do this, click in the *[COMPANY NAME]* placeholder, click the placeholder tab, and then press the Delete key.)
   i. Select and then delete the *[Company address]* placeholder.
5. Scroll through the document and look at each page. The Semaphore footer and cover page building blocks that were inserted have similar formatting and are part of the Semaphore group. Using building blocks from the same group provides consistency in the document and gives it a polished and professional appearance.
6. Save, preview, and then close **7-HomeSafety.docx**.

Activity 2 Create a Letter Document Using Custom Building Blocks 3 Parts

You will create custom building blocks and then use them to prepare a business letter.

Saving Content as a Building Block

Quick Steps

Save Content in Text Box Gallery

1. Select content.
2. Click Insert tab.
3. Click Text Box button.
4. Click *Save Selection to Text Box Gallery*.

Save Content in Header Gallery

1. Select content.
2. Click Insert tab.
3. Click Header button.
4. Click *Save Selection to Header Gallery*.

Save Content in Footer Gallery

1. Select content.
2. Click Insert tab.
3. Click Footer button.
4. Click *Save Selection to Footer Gallery*.

Hint When selecting content to save as a building block, turn on the display of nonprinting characters by clicking the Show/Hide ¶ button in the Paragraph group on the Home tab.

Saving Content as a Building Block

Consider saving data that is typed and formatted on a regular basis as a building block. Saving commonly created data as a building block saves time and reduces errors that might occur each time the data is typed or formatting is applied. The data can be saved as a building block in a specific gallery, such as the Text Box, Header, or Footer gallery, or saved in the AutoText gallery or Quick Part gallery.

Saving Content in a Specific Gallery To save content in a specific gallery, use the button for the gallery. For example, to save a text box in the Text Box gallery, use the Text Box button. To do this, select the text box, click the Insert tab, click the Text Box button, and then click the *Save Selection to Text Box Gallery* option at the drop-down gallery. At the Create New Building Block dialog box as shown in Figure 7.2, type a name for the text box building block, type a description of it, and then click OK.

To save content in the Header gallery, select the content, click the Insert tab, click the Header button, and then click the *Save Selection to Header Gallery* option at the drop-down gallery. This displays the Create New Building Block dialog box, as shown in Figure 7.2 (except *Headers* displays in the *Gallery* option box). Complete similar steps to save content in the Footer gallery and Cover Page gallery.

When data is saved as a building block, it is available in the Building Blocks Organizer dialog box. If content is saved as a building block in a specific gallery, the building block is available at both the Building Blocks Organizer dialog box and the gallery. For example, if a building block is saved in the Footer gallery, it is available when the Footer button on the Insert tab is clicked.

Figure 7.2 Create New Building Block Dialog Box

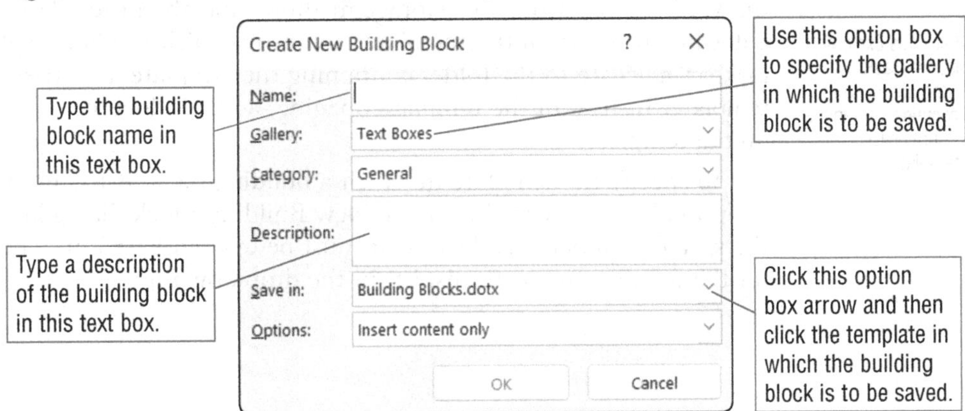

Quick Steps

Save Content in AutoText Gallery

1. Select content.
2. Click Insert tab.
3. Click Quick Parts button.
4. Point to *AutoText*.
5. Click *Save Selection to AutoText Gallery*.

Saving Content in the AutoText Gallery Content can be saved as a building block in the AutoText gallery. The building block can be inserted into a document by clicking the Insert tab, clicking the Quick Parts button, pointing to *AutoText*, and then clicking the AutoText building block at the side menu. To save content in the AutoText gallery, type and format the content and then select it. Click the Insert tab, click the Quick Parts button, point to *AutoText*, and then click the *Save Selection to AutoText Gallery* option at the side menu or use the keyboard shortcut Alt + F3. At the Create New Building Block dialog box, type a name for the building block, type a description of it, and then click OK.

Quick Steps

Save Content in Quick Part Gallery

1. Select content.
2. Click Insert tab.
3. Click Quick Parts button.
4. Click *Save Selection to Quick Part Gallery*.

Saving Content in the Quick Part Gallery Not only can content be saved in the AutoText gallery, but selected content can also be saved in the Quick Part gallery. To do this, select the content, click the Insert tab, click the Quick Parts button, and then click the *Save Selection to Quick Part Gallery* option at the drop-down gallery. This displays the Create New Building Block dialog box with *Quick Parts* specified in the *Gallery* option box and *Building Blocks.dotx* specified in the *Save in* option box. Type a name for the building block, type a description of it, and then click OK.

Quick Steps

Save as Template

1. Click File tab.
2. Click *Save As* option.
3. Click *Browse* option.
4. Click *Save as type* option.
5. Click *Word Template (*dotx)*.
6. Type name for template.
7. Click Save button.

Saving Building Blocks in a Specific Template By default, building block content is saved in one of two templates: *Building Blocks.dotx* or *Normal.dotm*. The template location depends on the gallery selected at the Create New Building Block dialog box. A building block saved in either of these templates is available each time a document is opened in Word. In a public environment, such as a school, saving to one of these templates may not be possible. To create a new personal template, display the Save As dialog box and then change the *Save as type* option to *Word Template (*.dotx)*. Choosing this option automatically selects the Custom Office Templates folder. Type a name for the template and then click the Save button; the template is saved in the Custom Office Templates folder.

Quick Steps

Open Document Based on Template

1. Click File tab.
2. Click *New* option.
3. Click *Personal* option.
4. Click template thumbnail.

OR

1. Click File Explorer icon on taskbar.
2. Navigate to folder containing template.
3. Double-click template.

To open a document based on a personal template, click the File tab and then click the *New* option. At the New backstage area, click the *Personal* option above the search text box. This displays thumbnails of the templates saved in the Custom Office Templates folder. Click the thumbnail of a specific template and a blank document opens based on the selected template.

Another option for opening a document based on a template is to save a template to a location other than the Custom Office Templates folder, such as the WL2C7 folder on your storage medium, and then use File Explorer to open a document based on the template. To do this, click the File Explorer icon on the taskbar, navigate to the folder containing the template, and then double-click the template. Instead of the template opening, a blank document opens that is based on the template.

To specify the template in which a building block is to be saved, click the *Save in* option box arrow in the Create New Building Block dialog box and then click the specific template. A document must be opened based on a personal template for the template name to display in the drop-down list.

Activity 2a Saving a Template and Saving Content in the Text Box, Footer, AutoText, and Quick Part Galleries

Part 1 of 3

1. Press Ctrl + N to display a blank document and then save the document as a template by completing the following steps:
   a. Press the F12 function key to display the Save As dialog box.
   b. At the Save As dialog box, type 7-QEATemplate in the *File name* text box.
   c. Click the *Save as type* option box and then click *Word Template (*.dotx)* at the drop-down list.
   d. Navigate to your WL2C7 folder.
   e. Click the Save button.
2. Close **7-QEATemplate.dotx**.
3. Open a document based on the template by completing the following steps:
   a. Click the File Explorer icon on the taskbar. (The taskbar displays along the bottom of the screen.)
   b. Navigate to your WL2C7 folder.
   c. Double-click ***7-QEATemplate.dotx***.
4. Insert the document named **QEAContent.docx** into the current document. (Do this by clicking the Object button arrow in the Text group on the Insert tab and then clicking *Text from File* at the drop-down list. This document is in your WL2C7 folder.)
5. Save the text box as a building block in the Text Box gallery by completing the following steps:
   a. Select the text box by clicking in it and then clicking its border.
   b. With the Insert tab active, click the Text Box button and then click *Save Selection to Text Box Gallery* at the drop-down list.
   c. At the Create New Building Block dialog box, type QEATextBox in the *Name* text box.
   d. Click the *Save in* option box arrow and then click *7-QEATemplate.dotx* at the drop-down list.
   e. Click OK to close the Create New Building Block dialog box.

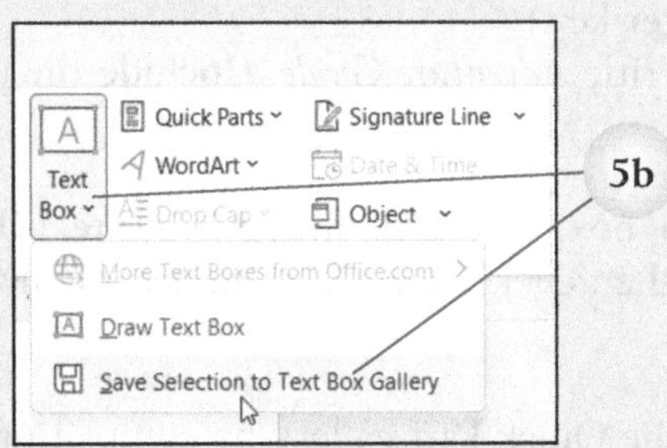

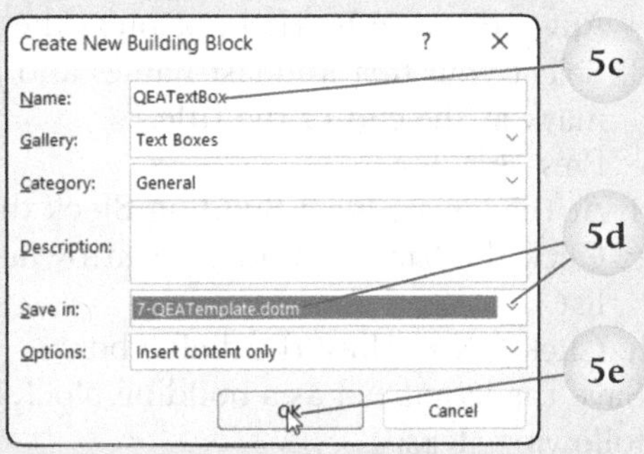

6. Save content as a building block in the Footer gallery by completing the following steps:
   a. Select the text *"Making your extreme adventure dreams a reality"* below the text box. (Be sure to select the paragraph mark at the end of the text. If necessary, click the Show/Hide ¶ button in the Paragraph group on the Home tab to display the paragraph mark.)
   b. Click the Footer button in the Header & Footer group on the Insert tab and then click *Save Selection to Footer Gallery* at the drop-down list.
   c. At the Create New Building Block dialog box, type QEAFooter in the *Name* text box.
   d. Click the *Save in* option box and then click *7-QEATemplate.dotx* at the drop-down list.
   e. Click OK to close the Create New Building Block dialog box.

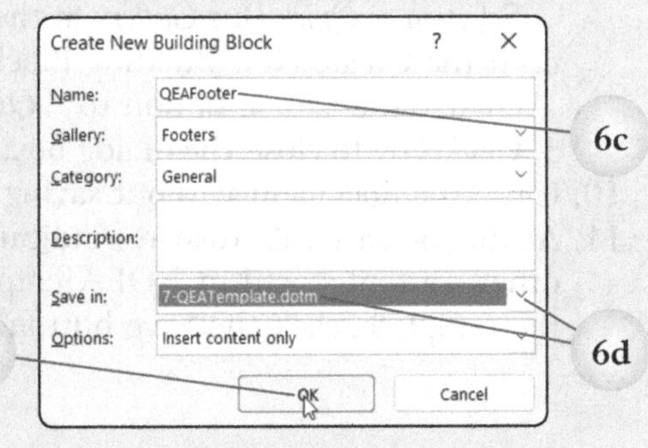

7. Save the company name *Southern Adventure Tours* and the address below it as a building block in the AutoText gallery by completing the following steps:
   a. Select the company name and address (the two lines below the company name). (Be sure to include the paragraph mark at the end of the last line of the address.)
   b. Click the Quick Parts button in the Text group on the Insert tab, point to *AutoText*, and then click *Save Selection to AutoText Gallery* at the side menu.

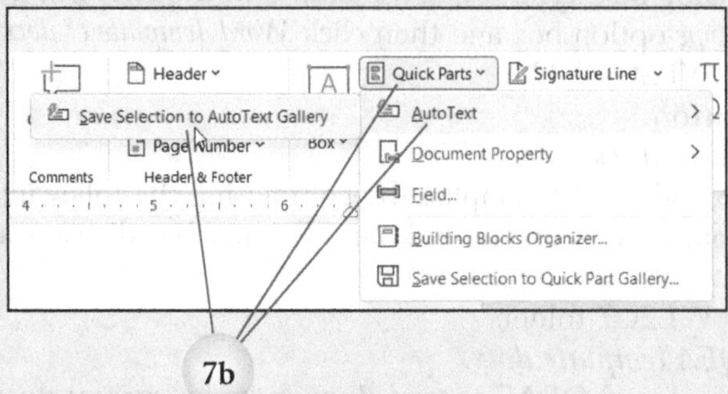

   c. At the Create New Building Block dialog box, type SAT in the *Name* text box.
   d. Click the *Save in* option box arrow and then click *7-QEATemplate.dotx* at the drop-down list.
   e. Click OK to close the dialog box.
8. Type your name and company title and then save the text as a building block in the AutoText gallery by completing the following steps:
   a. Move the insertion point two lines below the address for Southern Adventure Tours.
   b. Type your first and last names and then press the spacebar.
   c. Press the Down Arrow key to move the insertion point to the next line and then type Adventure Guide. (Do not press the Enter key.)
   d. Select your first and last names and the title *Adventure Guide*. (Include the paragraph mark at the end of the title.)
   e. Press Alt + F3.
   f. At the Create New Building Block dialog box, type Title in the *Name* text box.
   g. Click the *Save in* option box arrow and then click *7-QEATemplate.dotx* at the drop-down list.
   h. Click OK to close the dialog box.
9. Save the letterhead as a building block in the Quick Part gallery by completing the following steps:
   a. Select the letterhead text (the company name *QUEST EXTREME ADVENTURES*, the address and telephone number below the name, and the paragraph mark at the end of the address and telephone number).
   b. Click the Quick Parts button in the Text group on the Insert tab and then click *Save Selection to Quick Part Gallery* at the drop-down list.
   c. At the Create New Building Block dialog box, type QEA in the *Name* text box and then change the *Save in* option to *7-QEATemplate.dotx*.
   d. Click OK to close the dialog box.
10. Close the document without saving it.
11. At the message that displays indicating that you have modified styles, building blocks, or other content stored in 7-QEATemplate.dotx and asking if you want to save the changes to the template, click the Save button.

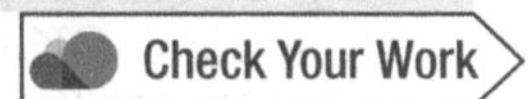

Editing Building Block Properties

Quick Steps

Edit Building Block

1. Click Insert tab.
2. Click Quick Parts button.
3. Click *Building Blocks Organizer*.
4. Click building block.
5. Click Edit Properties button.
6. Make changes.
7. Click OK.

OR

1. Click button.
2. Right-click custom building block.
3. Click *Edit Properties*.
4. Make changes.
5. Click OK.

Editing Building Block Properties

Changes can be made to the properties of a building block with options at the Modify Building Block dialog box. This dialog box contains the same options as the Create New Building Block dialog box.

Display the Modify Building Block dialog box by opening the Building Blocks Organizer dialog box, clicking the specific building block in the list box, and then clicking the Edit Properties button. The dialog box can also be displayed for a building block in the Quick Parts button drop-down gallery. To do this, click the Quick Parts button, right-click the building block in the drop-down gallery, and then click *Edit Properties* at the shortcut menu. Make changes to the Modify Building Block dialog box and then click OK. At the confirmation message, click Yes.

The dialog box can also be displayed for a custom building block in a button drop-down gallery by clicking the button, right-clicking the custom building block, and then clicking the *Edit Properties* option at the shortcut menu. For example, to modify a custom text box building block, click the Insert tab, click the Text Box button, and then scroll down the drop-down gallery to display the custom text box building block. Right-click the custom text box building block and then click *Edit Properties* at the shortcut menu.

Activity 2b Editing Building Block Properties

Part 2 of 3

1. Open a blank document based on your template **7-QEATemplate.dotx** by completing the following steps:
   a. Click the File Explorer icon on the taskbar.
   b. Navigate to your WL2C7 folder.
   c. Double-click ***7-QEATemplate.dotx***.
2. Edit the SAT building block by completing the following steps:
   a. Click the Insert tab, click the Quick Parts button, and then click *Building Blocks Organizer* at the drop-down list.
   b. At the Building Blocks Organizer dialog box, click the *Gallery* heading to sort the building blocks by gallery. (This displays the AutoText galleries at the beginning of the list.)
   c. Using the horizontal scroll bar at the bottom of the *Building blocks* list box, scroll to the right and notice that the SAT building block does not contain a description.
   d. Click the *SAT* building block in the list box.
   e. Click the Edit Properties button at the bottom of the dialog box.

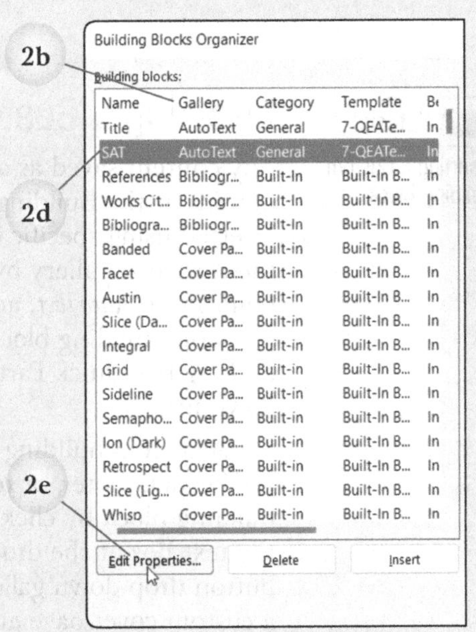

f. At the Modify Building Block dialog box, click in the *Name* text box and then type Address at the end of the name.

g. Click in the *Description* text box and then type Inserts the Southern Adventure Tours name and address.

h. Click OK to close the dialog box.

i. At the message asking if you want to redefine the building block entry, click Yes.

j. Close the Building Blocks Organizer dialog box.

3. Edit the letterhead building block by completing the following steps:

   a. Click the Quick Parts button, right-click the *QEA* letterhead building block, and then click *Edit Properties* at the shortcut menu.

   b. At the Modify Building Block dialog box, click in the *Name* text box and then type Letterhead at the end of the name.

   c. Click in the *Description* text box and then type Inserts the Quest Extreme Adventures letterhead including the company name and address.

   d. Click OK to close the dialog box.

   e. At the message asking if you want to redefine the building block entry, click Yes.

4. Close the document.

5. At the message that displays, click the Save button.

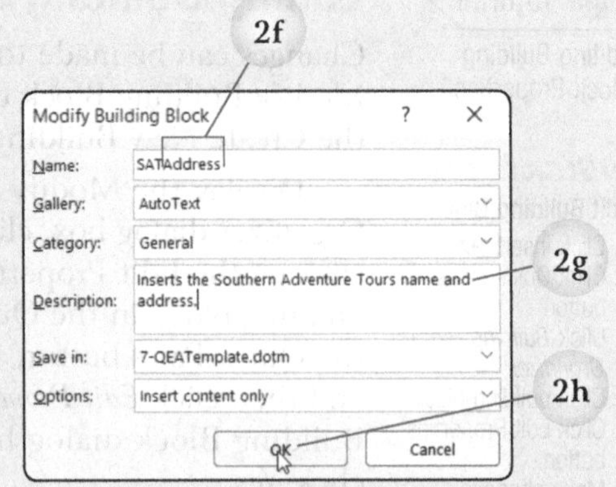

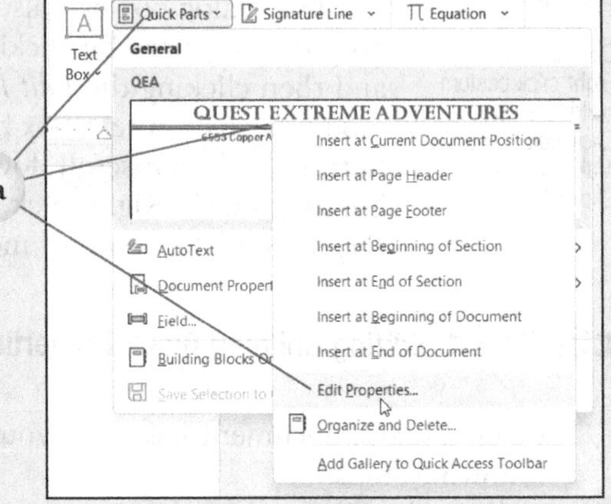

Check Your Work

Inserting a Custom Building Block

Inserting a Custom Building Block

Any content saved as a building block can be inserted in a document using options at the Building Blocks Organizer dialog box. Some content can also be inserted using specific drop-down galleries. Insert a custom building block saved to the AutoText gallery by clicking the Insert tab, clicking the Quick Parts button, pointing to *AutoText*, and then clicking the building block at the side menu. Insert a custom building block saved to the Quick Part gallery by clicking the Insert tab, clicking the Quick Parts button, and then clicking the building block at the drop-down list.

A custom building block can also be inserted from a specific gallery such as the header, footer, or text box gallery. For example, insert a custom text box building block by clicking the Text Box button on the Insert tab and then clicking the text box at the drop-down gallery. Insert a custom header at the Header button drop-down gallery, a custom footer at the Footer button drop-down gallery, a custom cover page at the Cover Page button drop-down gallery, and so on.

Use the button drop-down gallery to specify where the custom building block content should be inserted in a document. To do this, display the button drop-down gallery, right-click the custom building block, and then click the location at the shortcut menu. For example, click the Insert tab, click the Quick Parts button, and then right-click the *QEALetterhead* building block and a shortcut menu displays, as shown in Figure 7.3.

Figure 7.3 Quick Parts Button Drop-Down Gallery Shortcut Menu

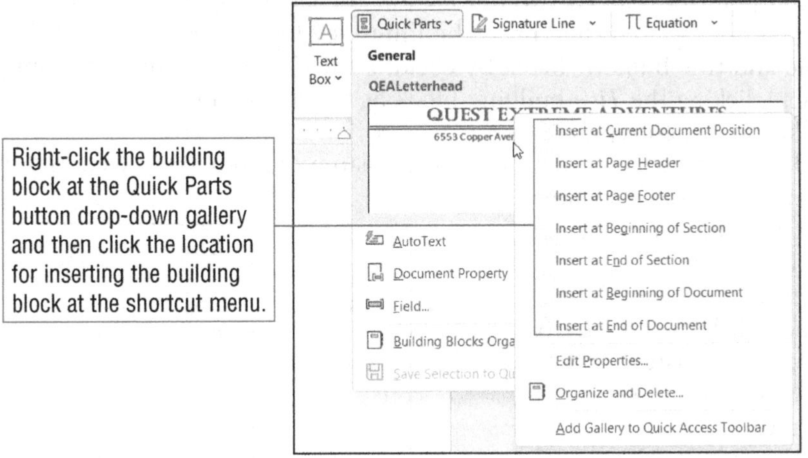

Activity 2c Inserting Custom Building Blocks

Part 3 of 3

1. Open File Explorer, navigate to your WL2C7 folder, and then double-click *7-QEATemplate.dotx*.
2. At the blank document, click the *No Spacing* style in the Styles group on the Home tab.
3. Change the font to Candara.
4. Insert the letterhead building block as a header by completing the following steps:
   a. Click the Insert tab.
   b. Click the Quick Parts button, right-click the *QEALetterhead* building block, and then click the *Insert at Page Header* option at the shortcut menu.

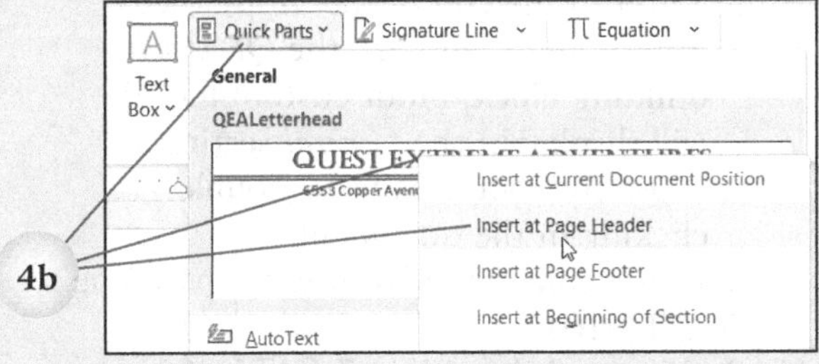

5. Press the Enter key two times, type the current date, and then press the Enter key five times.
6. Type Mr. Geraldo Vargas and then press the Enter key.
7. Insert the Southern Adventure Tours name and address building block by clicking the Quick Parts button, pointing to *AutoText*, and then clicking the *SATAddress* building block at the side menu.

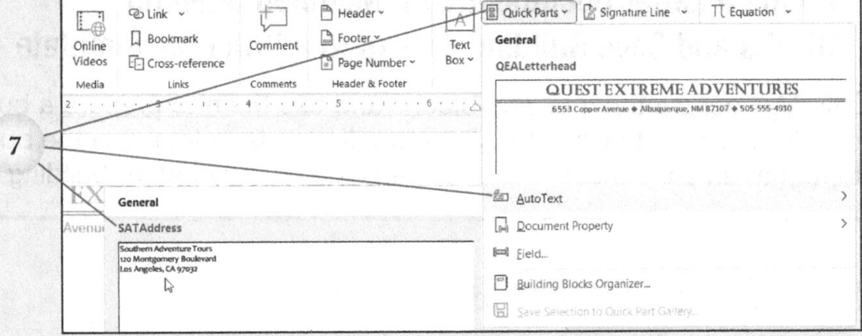

8. Press the Enter key and then insert a letter document by completing the following steps:
   a. Click the Object button arrow in the Text group on the Insert tab and then click *Text from File* at the drop-down list.
   b. At the Insert File dialog box, navigate to your WL2C7 folder and then double-click *SATLetter01.docx*.

9. With the insertion point positioned two lines below the last paragraph of text in the body of the letter, type Sincerely, and then press the Enter key four times.
10. Insert your name and title building block by clicking the Quick Parts button, pointing to *AutoText*, and then clicking the *Title* building block at the side menu.
11. Press the Enter key and then type 7-SATLtr01.docx.
12. Press the Enter key five times and then insert the custom text box you saved as a building block by completing the following steps:
    a. Click the Text Box button in the Text group on the Insert tab.
    b. Scroll to the end of the drop-down gallery and then click the *QEATextBox* building block. (Your custom text box will display in the *General* section of the drop-down gallery.)
    c. Click in the document to deselect the text box.
13. Insert the custom footer you created by completing the following steps:
    a. Click the Insert tab.
    b. Click the Footer button in the Header & Footer group.
    c. Scroll to the end of the drop-down gallery and then click the *QEAFooter* building block. (Your custom footer will display in the *General* section.)
    d. Close the footer pane by double-clicking in the document.
14. Save the completed letter with the name **7-SATLtr01**.
15. Preview and then close **7-SATLtr01.docx**.

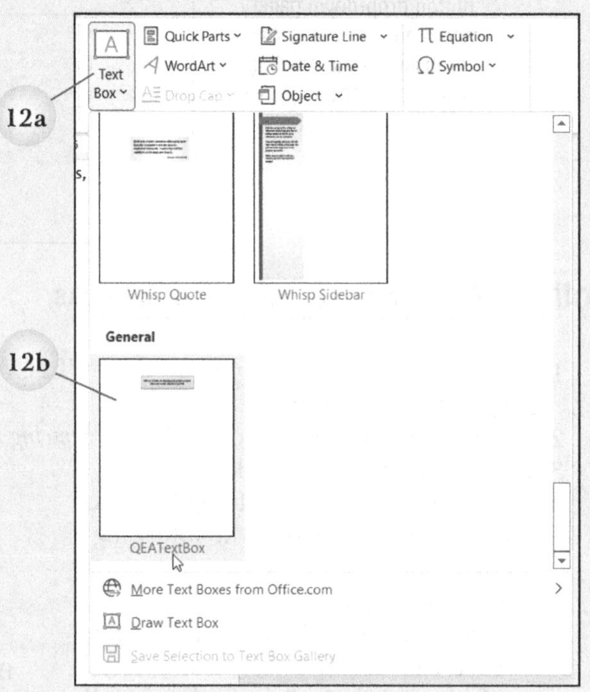

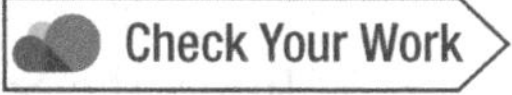

Activity 3 Create a Letter Document with Modified Building Blocks and Save Building Blocks to a Different Template — 3 Parts

You will modify your custom building blocks and use them to prepare a business letter. You will also save building blocks to a different template, use the building blocks to format an announcement, and then delete your custom building blocks.

Modifying and Deleting Building Blocks

Modifying a Custom Building Block

A building block can be inserted in a document, corrections or changes can be made to the building block, and then the building block can be saved with the same name or a different name. Save a building block with the same name when updating the building block to reflect any changes. Save the building block with a new name when using an existing building block as the foundation for creating a new building block.

To save a modified building block with the same name, insert the building block into the document and then make modifications. Select the building block data and then specify the gallery. At the Create New Building Block dialog box, type the original name and description and then click OK. At the confirmation message that displays, click Yes.

Adding a Building Block Gallery as a Button on the Quick Access Toolbar

Adding a Building Block Gallery as a Button on the Quick Access Toolbar

To make building blocks more accessible, add a building block gallery as a button on the Quick Access Toolbar. By default, the Quick Access Toolbar does not display. Turn on the display by clicking the Ribbon Display Options button (small button with down arrow) that displays at the right side of the ribbon and then click *Show Quick Access Toolbar* at the drop-down list.

Quick Steps

Add Building Block Gallery as Button on Quick Access Toolbar

1. Click specific button.
2. Right-click building block.
3. Click *Add Gallery to Quick Access Toolbar*.

To add a building block gallery as a button on the Quick Access Toolbar, display the toolbar, right-click a building block, and then click *Add Gallery to Quick Access Toolbar*. For example, to add the *Quick Part* gallery to the Quick Access Toolbar, click the Quick Parts button on the Insert tab, right-click a building block at the drop-down gallery, and then click *Add Gallery to Quick Access Toolbar*.

To remove a button from the Quick Access Toolbar, right-click the button and then click *Remove from Quick Access Toolbar* at the shortcut menu. Removing a button containing a building block gallery does not delete the building block. To turn off the display of the Quick Access Toolbar, click the Ribbon Display Options button and then click *Hide Quick Access Toolbar* at the drop-down list.

Activity 3a Modifying Building Blocks and Adding Custom Building Blocks as Buttons on the Quick Access Toolbar

Part 1 of 3

1. Open File Explorer, navigate to your WL2C7 folder, and then double-click *7-QEATemplate.dotx*.
2. Modify your name and title building block to reflect a title change by completing the following steps:
   a. At the blank document, click the Insert tab, click the Quick Parts button, point to *AutoText*, and then click the *Title* building block at the side menu.
   b. Edit your title so it displays as *Senior Adventure Guide*.
   c. Select your name and title, click the Quick Parts button, point to *AutoText*, and then click the *Save Selection to AutoText Gallery* option.
   d. At the Create New Building Block dialog box, type Title in the *Name* text box.
   e. Click the *Save in* option box arrow and then click *7-QEATemplate.dotx* at the drop-down list.
   f. Click OK.
   g. At the message asking if you want to redefine the building block entry, click Yes.
   h. With your name and title selected, press the Delete key to remove them from the document.

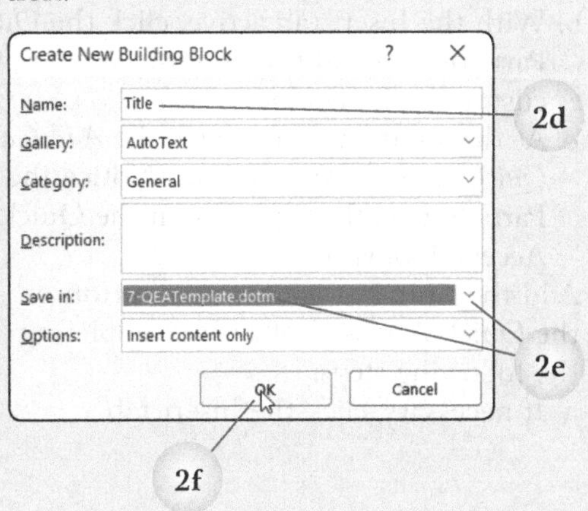

3. Since most of the correspondence you send to Southern Adventure Tours is addressed to Geraldo Vargas, you decide to include his name at the beginning of the company name and address by completing the following steps:
   a. With the Insert tab active, click the Quick Parts button, point to *AutoText*, and then click the *SATAddress* building block at the side menu.
   b. Type Mr. Geraldo Vargas above the name of the cruise line.

      3b

      Mr. Geraldo Vargas
      Southern Adventure Tours
      120 Montgomery Boulevard
      Los Angeles, CA 97032

   c. Select the name, company name, and address.
   d. Click the Quick Parts button, point to *AutoText*, and then click the *Save Selection to AutoText Gallery* option.
   e. At the Create New Building Block dialog box, type SATAddress (the original name) in the *Name* text box.
   f. Click the *Save in* option box arrow and then click *7-QEATemplate.dotx* at the drop-down list.
   g. Click OK.
   h. At the message asking if you want to redefine the building block entry, click Yes.
4. Press Ctrl + End and then add the QEAFooter building block in the Quick Part gallery by completing the following steps:
   a. Click the Footer button on the Insert tab, scroll down the drop-down gallery, and then click the *QEAFooter* custom building block.
   b. Press the Down Arrow key to move the insertion point to the blank line below the text in the footer and then press the Backspace key to delete the extra space below the footer text.
   c. Press Ctrl + A to select the footer.
   d. Click the Insert tab, click the Quick Parts button, and then click *Save Selection to Quick Part Gallery*.
   e. At the Create New Building Block dialog box, type QEAFooter in the *Name* text box.
   f. Click the *Save in* option box arrow and then click *7-QEATemplate.dotx* at the drop-down list.
   g. Click OK to close the Create New Building Block dialog box. (You now have the footer saved in the Footer gallery and the Quick Part gallery.)
   h. Double-click in the document.

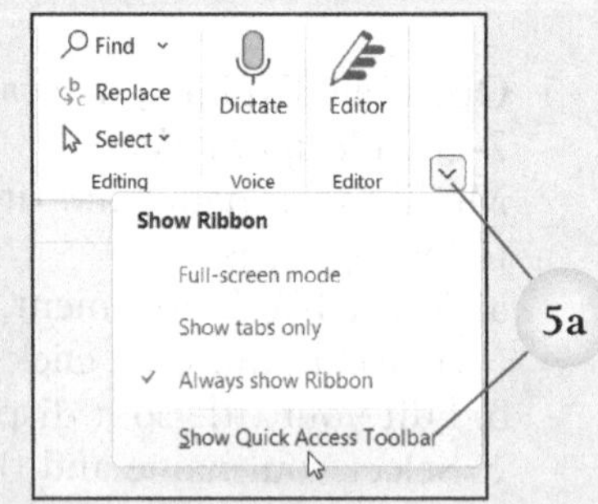

5. Add the Quick Part gallery as a button on the Quick Access Toolbar by completing the following steps:
   a. If the Quick Access Toolbar does not display, turn it on by clicking the Ribbon Display Options button at the right side of the ribbon and then clicking *Show Quick Access Toolbar* at the drop-down list.
   b. With the Insert tab active, click the Quick Parts button and then right-click one of your custom building blocks.
   c. At the shortcut menu, click the *Add Gallery to Quick Access Toolbar* option. (Notice the Quick Parts button that appears on the Quick Access Toolbar.)

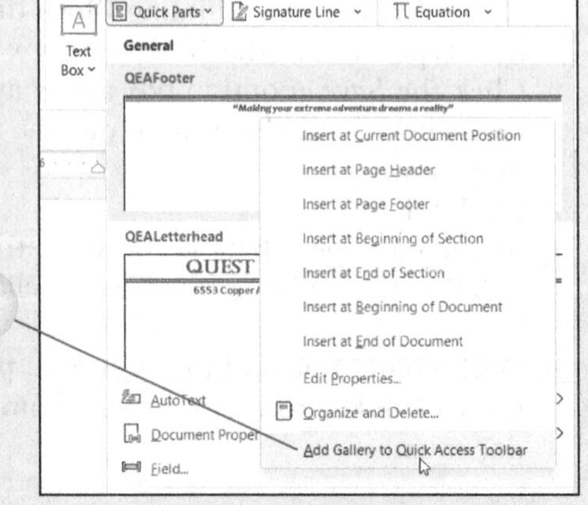

6. Add the AutoText gallery as a button on the Quick Access Toolbar by completing the following steps:
   a. If necessary, click the Insert tab.

b. Click the Quick Parts button, point to *AutoText*, and then right-click one of your custom building blocks.
c. At the shortcut menu, click the *Add Gallery to Quick Access Toolbar* option. (Notice the AutoText button that appears on the Quick Access Toolbar.)

7. Close the document without saving it. At the message that displays indicating you have modified styles, building blocks, and other content, click the Save button.
8. Create a business letter by completing the following steps:
   a. Use File Explorer to open a blank document based on **7-QEATemplate.dotx** in your WL2C7 folder.
   b. Click the *No Spacing* style in the Styles group on the Home tab.
   c. Change the font to Candara.
   d. Insert the QEALetterhead building block as a page header.
   e. Press the Enter key two times, type today's date, and then press the Enter key four times.
   f. Insert the building block that includes the name Geraldo Vargas and the company name and address by clicking the AutoText button on the Quick Access Toolbar and then clicking the *SATAddress* building block at the drop-down list.
   g. Press the Enter key and then insert the file named **SATLetter02.docx** in your WL2C7 folder. ***Hint: Do this with the Object button arrow in the Text group on the Insert tab.***
   h. Type Sincerely, and then press the Enter key four times.
   i. Click the AutoText button on the Quick Access Toolbar and then click the *Title* building block.
   j. Press the Enter key and then type 7-SATLtr02.docx.
   k. Insert the footer building block by clicking the Quick Parts button on the Quick Access Toolbar, right-clicking *QEAFooter*, and then clicking *Insert at Page Footer* at the shortcut menu.

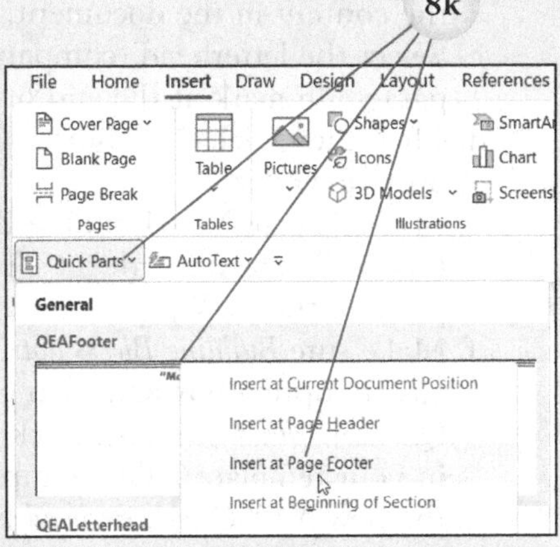

9. Save the completed letter with the name **7-SATLtr02**.
10. Preview and then close **7-SATLtr02.docx**.
11. Use File Explorer to open a blank document based on your template **7-QEATemplate.dotx**.
12. Click the AutoText button on the Quick Access Toolbar, press the Print Screen button on your keyboard, and then click in the document to remove the drop-down list.
13. At the blank document, click the Paste button. (This pastes the screen capture in your document.)
14. Save the document with the name **7-ScreenCapture**.
15. Preview and then close **7-ScreenCapture.docx**.
16. Remove the Quick Parts button you added to the Quick Access Toolbar by right-clicking the Quick Parts button and then clicking *Remove from Quick Access Toolbar* at the shortcut menu. Complete similar steps to remove the AutoText button from the Quick Access Toolbar. (The buttons will display dimmed if no documents are open.)
17. If necessary, turn off the display of the Quick Access Toolbar by clicking the Ribbon Display Options button and then clicking *Hide Quick Access Toolbar* at the drop-down list.

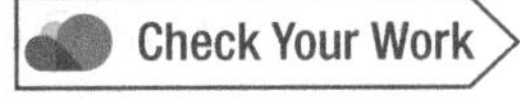
Check Your Work

Saving Building Blocks in a Different Template

Building blocks saved to a personal template are available only when a document is opened based on the template. To make building blocks available for all documents, save them in the Building Block.dotx template or Normal.dotm template. Use the *Save in* option at the Create New Building Block or Modify Building Block dialog box to save building blocks to one of these two templates.

If an existing building block in a personal template is modified and saved in the Normal.dotm or Building Block.dotx template, the building block is no longer available in the personal template. It is available only in documents based on the default template Normal.dotm. To keep a building block in a personal template and also make it available for other documents, insert the building block content in the document, select the content, and then create a new building block.

Activity 3b Saving Building Blocks in a Different Template — Part 2 of 3

1. Use File Explorer to open a blank document based on your template **7-QEATemplate.dotx**.
2. Create a new QEALetterhead building block and save it in the Building Blocks.dotx template so it is available for all documents by completing the following steps:
   a. Click the Insert tab.
   b. Click the Quick Parts button and then click the *QEALetterhead* building block to insert the content in the document.
   c. Select the letterhead (company name, address, and telephone number, including the paragraph mark at the end of the line containing the address and telephone number).
   d. Click the Quick Parts button and then click *Save Selection to Quick Part Gallery* at the drop-down list.
   e. At the Create New Building Block dialog box, type XXX-QEALetterhead. (Type your initials in place of the *XXX*.)
   f. Make sure *Building Blocks.dotx* displays in the *Save in* option box and then click OK. (The *QEALetterhead* building block is still available in your template 7-QEATemplate.dotx, and the new *XXX-QEALetterhead* building block is available in all documents, including documents based on your 7-QEATemplate.dotx template.)
   g. Delete the selected letterhead text.

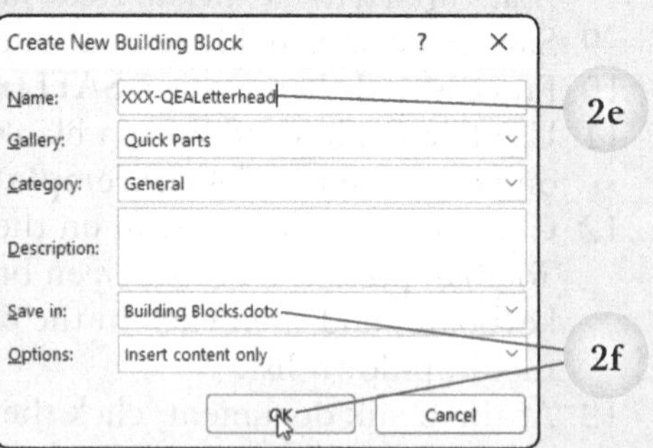

3. Create a new *QEAFooter* building block and then save it in the Building Blocks.dotx template so it is available for all documents by completing the following steps:
   a. Click the Quick Parts button and then click the *QEAFooter* building block to insert the content in the document.
   b. Select the footer text *"Making your extreme adventure dreams a reality"* (including the paragraph mark at the end of the text).
   c. Click the Quick Parts button and then click *Save Selection to Quick Part Gallery* at the drop-down list.
   d. At the Create New Building Block dialog box, type XXX-QEAFooter. (Type your initials in place of the *XXX*.)
   e. Make sure *Building Blocks.dotx* displays in the *Save in* option box and then click OK.
4. Close the document without saving it.

5. Open **QEAContent.docx**.
6. Create a new *QEATextBox* building block and save it in the *Building Blocks.dotx* template so it is available for all documents by completing the following steps:
   a. Select the text box by clicking the text box and then clicking the text box border.
   b. Click the Insert tab, click the Text Box button, and then click *Save Selection to Text Box Gallery* at the drop-down list.
   c. At the Create New Building Block dialog box, type XXX-QEATextBox. (Type your initials in place of the *XXX*.)
   d. Make sure *Building Blocks.dotx* displays in the *Save in* option box and then click OK.
7. Close **QEAContent.docx**.
8. Insert in a document the building blocks you created by completing the following steps:
   a. Open **SATAnnounce.docx** and then save it with the name **7-SATAnnounce**.
   b. Insert the *XXX-QEALetterhead* building block as a header by clicking the Insert tab, clicking the Quick Parts button, right-clicking *XXX-QEALetterhead* (where your initials display in place of the *XXX*), and then clicking *Insert at Page Header* at the shortcut menu.

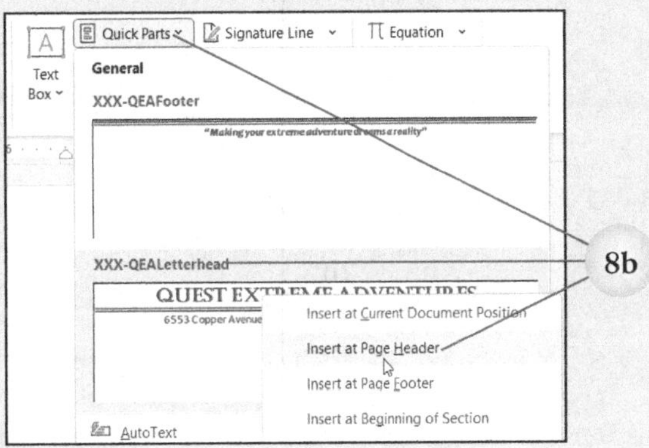

   c. Insert the *XXX-QEAFooter* building block by clicking the Quick Parts button, right-clicking *XXX-QEAFooter* (where your initials display in place of the *XXX*), and then clicking *Insert at Page Footer* at the shortcut menu.
   d. Press Ctrl + End to move the insertion point to the end of the document.
   e. Insert the *XXX-QEATextBox* building block by clicking the Text Box button, scrolling down the drop-down gallery, and then clicking *XXX-QEATextBox* (where your initials display in place of the *XXX*).
   f. Horizontally align the text box by clicking the Align button in the Arrange group on the Shape Format tab and then clicking *Distribute Horizontally* at the drop-down list.

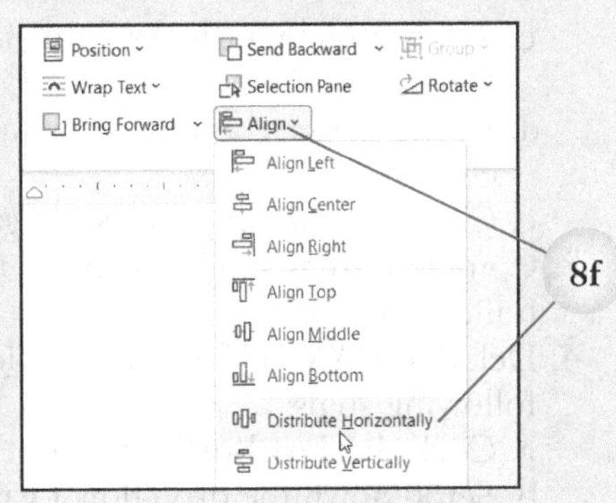

9. Save, preview, and then close **7-SATAnnounce.docx**.

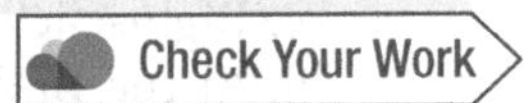

Quick Steps

Delete Building Block

1. Display Building Blocks Organizer dialog box.
2. Click building block.
3. Click Delete button.
4. Click Yes.

OR

1. Display button drop-down gallery.
2. Right-click building block.
3. Click *Organize and Delete* option.
4. Click Delete button.
5. Click Yes.

Deleting a Building Block

A custom building block that is no longer needed can be deleted by displaying the Building Blocks Organizer dialog box, clicking the building block, and then clicking the Delete button. At the confirmation message box, click Yes.

Another method for deleting a custom building block is to right-click the building block at the drop-down gallery and then click the *Organize and Delete* option at the shortcut menu. This displays the Building Blocks Organizer dialog box with the building block selected. Click the Delete button and then click Yes at the confirmation message box.

Activity 3c Deleting Building Blocks

1. Press Ctrl + N to open a blank document.
2. Delete the *XXX-QEALetterhead* building block by completing the following steps:
   a. Click the Insert tab and then click the Quick Parts button in the Text group.
   b. Right-click the *XXX-QEALetterhead* building block and then click *Organize and Delete* at the shortcut menu.

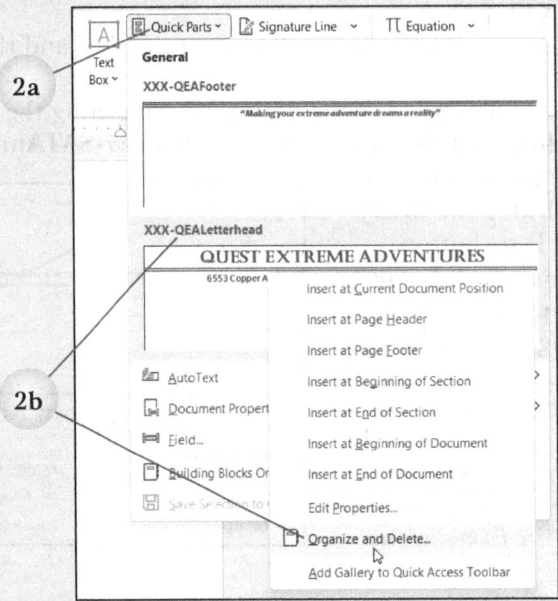

   c. At the Building Blocks Organizer dialog box with the building block selected, click the Delete button.
   d. At the message asking if you are sure you want to delete the selected building block, click Yes.
   e. Close the Building Blocks Organizer dialog box.
3. Complete steps similar to those in Steps 2a through 2e to delete the *XXXQEAFooter* building block.
4. Delete the *XXX-QEATextBox* building block (in the Text Box gallery) by completing the following steps:
   a. Click the Text Box button in the Text group on the Insert tab.
   b. Scroll down the drop-down gallery to display your custom text box.
   c. Right-click your text box and then click *Organize and Delete* at the shortcut menu.
   d. At the Building Blocks Organizer dialog box with the building block selected, click the Delete button.
   e. At the message asking if you are sure you want to delete the selected building block, click Yes.
   f. Close the Building Blocks Organizer dialog box.
5. Close the document without saving it.

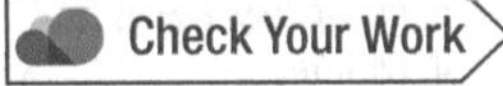

Activity 4 Insert Document Properties and Fields in a Testing Agreement Document — 2 Parts

You will open a testing agreement document and then insert and update document properties and fields.

Inserting a Document Property Placeholder

Inserting a Document Property Placeholder

Click the Quick Parts button on the Insert tab and then point to *Document Property* at the drop-down list and a side menu displays with document property options. Click an option at this side menu and a document property placeholder is inserted in the document. Text can be typed in the placeholder.

If a document property placeholder is inserted in multiple locations in a document, updating one occurrence of the placeholder will automatically update all occurrences of that placeholder in the document. For example, in Activity 4a, a Company document property placeholder is inserted in six locations in a document. The content of the first occurrence of the placeholder will be changed and the remaining placeholders will update to reflect the change.

Click the File tab and then click the *Info* option and the Info backstage area displays containing information about the document. Document properties display at the right side of the Info backstage area, including information such as the document size, number of pages, title, and comments.

Activity 4a Inserting Document Property Placeholders — Part 1 of 2

1. Open **TestAgrmnt.docx** and then save it with the name **7-TestAgrmnt.**
2. Select the first occurrence of *FP* in the document (in the first line of text after the title) and then insert a document property placeholder by completing the following steps:
   a. Click the Insert tab, click the Quick Parts button in the Text group, point to *Document Property*, and then click *Company* at the side menu.
   b. Type Frontier Productions in the company placeholder.
   c. Press the Right Arrow key to move the insertion point outside the company placeholder.

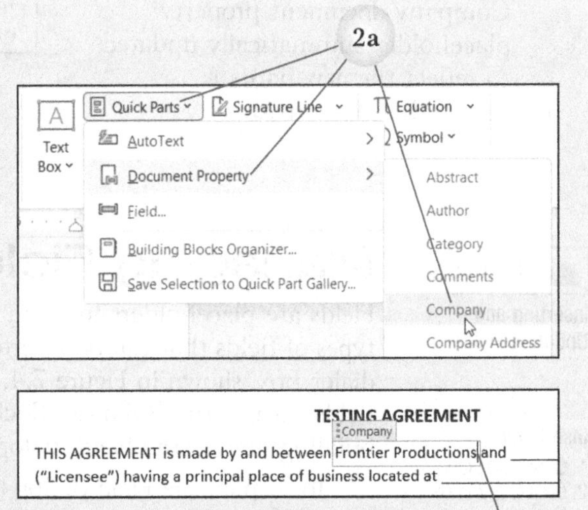

3. Select each remaining occurrence of *FP* in the document (it appears five more times) and insert the company document property placeholder. (The company name, *Frontier Productions,* will automatically be inserted in the placeholder.)

4. Press Ctrl + End to move the insertion point to the end of the document and then insert a comments document property placeholder by completing the following steps:
   a. Click the Quick Parts button, point to *Document Property*, and then click *Comments* at the side menu.
   b. Type First Draft in the comments placeholder.
   c. Press the Right Arrow key.
   d. Press Shift + Enter.
5. Click the File tab, click the *Info* option, and notice that the comment typed in the comments document property placeholder displays at the right side of the Info backstage area. Click the Back button to display the document.

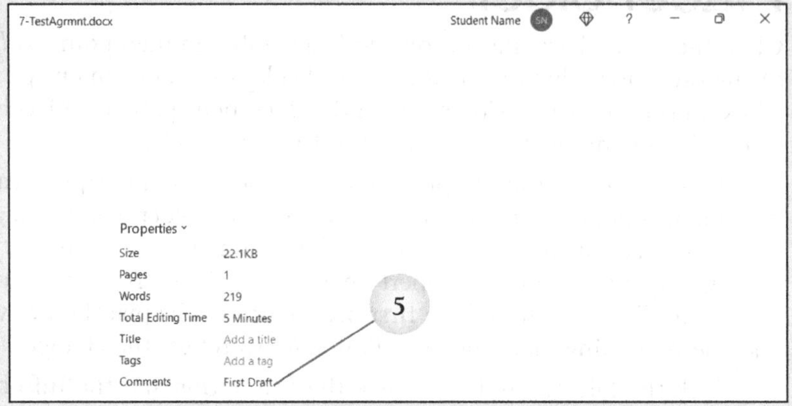

6. Save and then preview **7-TestAgrmnt.docx**.
7. Click in the first occurrence of the company name *Frontier Productions* and then click the company placeholder tab. (This selects the company placeholder.)
8. Type Frontier Video Productions.
9. Press the Right Arrow key. (Notice that the other occurrences of the Company document property placeholder automatically updated to reflect the new name.)
10. Save **7-TestAgrmnt.docx**.

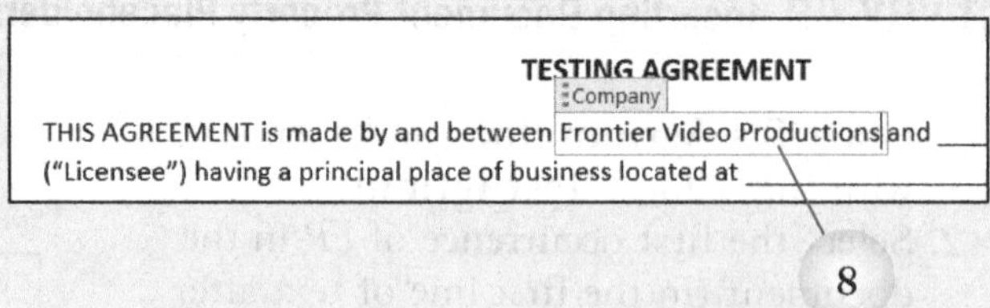

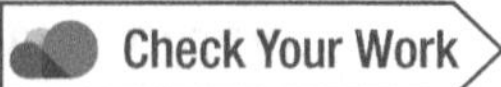

Inserting and Updating Fields

Quick Steps

Insert Field
1. Click Insert tab.
2. Click Quick Parts button.
3. Click *Field* at drop-down list.
4. Click field.
5. Click OK.

Managing Fields

Fields are placeholders for data that varies. Word provides buttons for many of the types of fields that can be inserted in a document as well as options at the Field dialog box, shown in Figure 7.4. This dialog box contains a list of all the available fields. Just as the Building Blocks Organizer dialog box is a central location for building blocks, the Field dialog box is a central location for fields.

To display the Field dialog box, click the Insert tab, click the Quick Parts button in the Text group, and then click *Field* at the drop-down list. At the Field dialog box, click a field in the *Field names* list box and then click OK.

Figure 7.4 Field Dialog Box

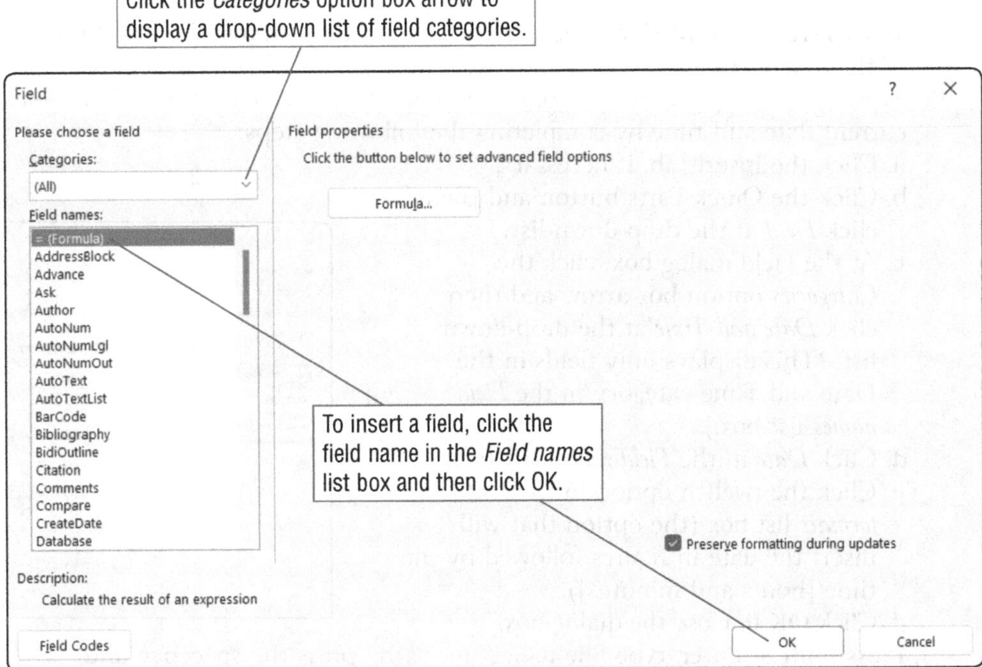

Choosing Field Categories

All the available fields display in the *Field names* list box at the Field dialog box. Narrow the list of fields to a specific category by clicking the *Categories* option box arrow and then clicking a specific category at the drop-down list. For example, to display only date and time fields, click the *Date and Time* category at the drop-down list.

Creating Custom Field Formats

Click a field in the *Field names* list box and a description of the field displays below the list box. Field properties related to the selected field also display in the dialog box. Custom field formats can be created for some fields. For example, click the *NumWords* field in the *Field names* list box and custom formatting options display in the *Format* list box and the *Numeric format* list box.

By default, the *Preserve formatting during updates* check box contains a check mark. With this option active, the custom formatting specified for a field will be preserved if the field is updated.

Updating Fields

Quick Steps

Update Field

1. Click field.
2. Click Update tab.

OR

1. Click field.
2. Press F9.

OR

1. Right-click field.
2. Click *Update Field*.

Some fields, such as the date and time field, update automatically when a document is opened. Other fields can be updated manually. A field can be updated manually by clicking the field and then clicking the Update tab; by clicking the field and then pressing the F9 function key; and by right-clicking the field and then clicking *Update Field* at the shortcut menu. Update all the fields in a document (except headers, footers, and text boxes) by pressing Ctrl + A to select the document and then pressing the F9 function key.

Activity 4b Inserting and Formatting Fields

Part 2 of 2

1. With **7-TestAgrmnt.docx** open, press Ctrl + End to move the insertion point to the end of the document.
2. Type Current date and time:, press the spacebar, and then insert a field that inserts the current date and time by completing the following steps:
   a. Click the Insert tab, if necessary.
   b. Click the Quick Parts button and then click *Field* at the drop-down list.
   c. At the Field dialog box, click the *Categories* option box arrow and then click *Date and Time* at the drop-down list. (This displays only fields in the Date and Time category in the *Field names* list box.)
   d. Click *Date* in the *Field names* list box.
   e. Click the twelfth option in the *Date formats* list box (the option that will insert the date in figures followed by the time [hours and minutes]).
   f. Click OK to close the dialog box.

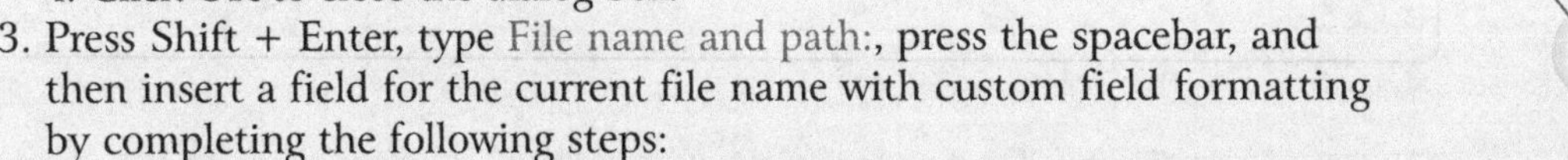

3. Press Shift + Enter, type File name and path:, press the spacebar, and then insert a field for the current file name with custom field formatting by completing the following steps:
   a. With the Insert tab active, click the Quick Parts button and then click *Field* at the drop-down list.
   b. At the Field dialog box, click the *Categories* option box arrow and then click *Document Information* at the drop-down list.
   c. Click *FileName* in the *Field names* list box.
   d. Click the *Uppercase* option in the *Format* list box.
   e. Click the *Add path to filename* check box to insert a check mark.

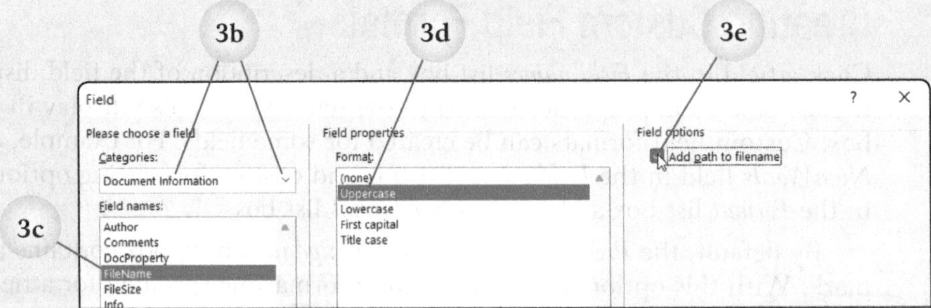

   f. Click OK to close the dialog box. (The current file name is inserted in the document in uppercase letters and includes the path to the file name.)
4. Insert a header and then insert a custom field in the header by completing the following steps:
   a. Click the Header button in the Header & Footer group and then click *Edit Header* at the drop-down list.
   b. In the Header pane, press the Tab key two times. (This moves the insertion point to the right tab at the right margin.)
   c. Click the Quick Parts button in the Insert group on the Header & Footer tab and then click *Field* at the drop-down list.

d. At the Field dialog box, click the *Categories* option box arrow and then click *Date and Time* at the drop-down list.
e. Click in the *Date formats* text box and then type MMMM yyyy. (This tells Word to insert the month as text followed by the four-digit year.)
f. Click OK to close the dialog box.
g. Double-click in the document.

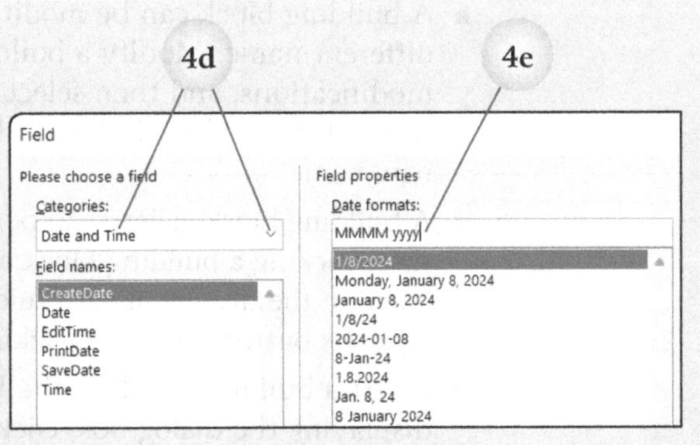

5. Update the time in the date and time field at the end of the document by clicking the date and time and then clicking the Update tab.
6. Save, preview, and then close **7-TestAgrmnt.docx**. (If a message displays asking if you want to save the changes to the template, click the Don't Save button.)

Chapter Summary

- Word provides a number of predesigned building blocks that can be used to help build a document.
- Insert building blocks at the Building Blocks Organizer dialog box. Display the dialog box by clicking the Quick Parts button in the Text group on the Insert tab and then clicking *Building Blocks Organizer* at the drop-down list.
- Sort building blocks at the Building Blocks Organizer dialog box by clicking the column heading.
- Content can be saved as building blocks in specific galleries, such as the Text Box, Header, Footer, and Cover Page galleries.
- Save content to the AutoText gallery by selecting the content, clicking the Insert tab, clicking the Quick Parts button, pointing to *AutoText*, and then clicking the *Save Selection to AutoText Gallery* option.
- Save content to the Quick Part gallery by selecting the content, clicking the Insert tab, clicking the Quick Parts button, and then clicking *Save Selection to Quick Part Gallery*.
- Building block content is saved, by default, to the *Building Blocks.dotx* template or the *Normal.dotm* template. The template location depends on the gallery selected at the Create New Building Block dialog box. A personal template can be created and saved to the Custom Office Templates folder and then building blocks can be saved to the personal template using the *Save in* option at the Create New Building Block dialog box.
- Open a personal template saved to the Custom Office Templates folder at the New backstage area with the *Personal* option selected.
- A personal template can be created and saved to a specific location other than the Custom Office Templates folder and then File Explorer can be used to open a document based on the template.
- Edit building block properties with options at the Modify Building Block dialog box. Display this dialog box by displaying the Building Blocks Organizer dialog box, clicking the specific building block in the list box, and then clicking the Edit Properties button.

- A building block can be modified and then saved with the same name or a different name. Modify a building block by inserting the building block, making modifications, and then select the building block data and specify the gallery. At the Create New Building Block dialog box, type the original name or type a new name.
- A building block gallery can be added as a button on the Quick Access Toolbar by right-clicking a building block and then clicking *Add Gallery to Quick Access Toolbar*. Turn on the display of the Quick Access Toolbar by clicking the Ribbon Display Options button and then clicking *Show Quick Access Toolbar* at the drop-down list.
- Insert a building block at the Building Blocks Organizer dialog box by displaying the dialog box, clicking the building block in the *Building blocks* list box, and then clicking the Insert button.
- Insert a custom building block saved to the AutoText gallery by clicking the Insert tab, clicking the Quick Parts button, pointing to *AutoText*, and then clicking the building block at the side menu.
- Insert a custom building block saved to the Quick Part gallery by clicking the Insert tab, clicking the Quick Parts button, and then clicking the building block at the drop-down list.
- Insert a custom building block from a specific drop-down gallery using a button by clicking the specific button (such as the Text Box, Header, Footer, or Cover Page button), scrolling down the drop-down gallery, and then clicking the custom building block at the gallery.
- Delete a building block at the Building Blocks Organizer dialog box by clicking the building block, clicking the Delete button, and then clicking Yes at the confirmation message.
- Insert a document property placeholder by clicking the Insert tab, clicking the Quick Parts button, pointing to *Document Property*, and then clicking the document property placeholder at the side menu.
- Fields are placeholders for data that varies. They can be inserted with options at the Field dialog box, which is a central location for all the fields provided by Word. Display the Field dialog box by clicking the Quick Parts button and then clicking *Field* at the drop-down list.
- A custom field format can be created for some fields by clicking the field in the *Field names* list box at the Field dialog box and then customizing formatting options.
- Some fields in a document update automatically when a document is opened. Other fields can be manually updated by clicking the field and then clicking the Update tab, by clicking the field and then pressing the F9 function key, or by right-clicking the field and then clicking *Update Field* at the shortcut menu.

Commands Review

FEATURE	RIBBON TAB, GROUP	BUTTON, OPTION	KEYBOARD SHORTCUT
Building Blocks Organizer dialog box	Insert, Text	*Building Blocks Organizer*	
Create New Building Block dialog box	Insert, Text	*Save Selection to Quick Part Gallery*	Alt + F3
Document Property side menu	Insert, Text	*Document Property*	
Field dialog box	Insert, Text	*Field*	

Review and Assessment

CHAPTER 7

Skills Assessment

Assessment 1

Create Building Blocks

1. Press Ctrl + N to open a blank document and then save the blank document as a template in your WL2C7 folder with the name **7-WLTemplate**. (Make sure to change the *Save as type* option at the Save As dialog box to *Word Template.dotx*.)
2. Close **7-WLTemplate.dotx**.
3. Use File Explorer to open a document based on **7-WLTemplate.dotx** in your WL2C7 folder.
4. Insert **WLFooter.docx** into the document. ***Hint: Use the Object button arrow on the Insert tab.***
5. Select the line of text containing the address and telephone number (including the nonprinting paragraph mark that ends the line). Save the selected text in a custom building block in the Footer gallery; name the building block *WLFooter* and save it in **7-WLTemplate.dotx**. ***Hint: Use the Footer button to save the content to the Footer gallery.***
6. Select the entire document, press the Delete key, and then insert **WLHeading.docx** into the current document. ***Hint: Use the Object button arrow on the Insert tab.***
7. Select the two lines of text (including the paragraph mark at the end of the second line). Save the selected text in a custom building block in the Quick Part gallery; name the building block *WLHeading* and save it in **7-WLTemplate.dotx**.
8. Select the entire document, press the Delete key, and then insert **WLFees.docx** into the current document. ***Hint: Use the Object button arrow on the Insert tab.***
9. Select the paragraph of text (including the paragraph mark at the end of the paragraph), save the selected text in a custom building block in the AutoText gallery and name the building block *WLFeesPara* and save it in **7-WLTemplate.dotx**.
10. Close the document without saving it. At the message asking if you want to save changes to the template, click the Save button.

Assessment 2

Use Building Blocks to Prepare an Agreement

1. Use File Explorer to open a blank document based on **7-WLTemplate.dotx** in your WL2C7 folder.
2. At the blank document, create an agreement with the following specifications:
   a. Insert the *WLHeading* custom building block in the Quick Part gallery.
   b. Press the Enter key and then insert the *WLFeesPara* custom building block in the AutoText gallery.
   c. Insert **WLRepAgrmnt.docx**. ***Hint: Use the Object button arrow on the Insert tab.***
   d. Insert the *WLFooter* custom building block. ***Hint: Do this with the Footer button.***

3. Click the Close Header and Footer button.
4. Save the completed agreement with the name **7-WLRepAgrmnt**.
5. Preview and then close **7-WLRepAgrmnt.docx**.
6. Use File Explorer to open a document based on **7-WLTemplate.dotx**.
7. Click the Insert tab, click the Quick Parts button, and then point to *AutoText*.
8. Press the Print Screen button on your keyboard and then click in the document.
9. At the blank document, click the Paste button.
10. Preview the document and then close it without saving it.

Assessment 3

Format a Report on the Writing Process

1. Open **WritingProcess.docx** and then save it with the name **7-WritingProcess**.
2. With the insertion point positioned at the beginning of the document, insert the *Automatic Table 2* table of contents building block.
3. Insert the *Banded* header building block, click the *[DOCUMENT TITLE]* placeholder and then type writing process.
4. Insert the *Banded* footer building block and then make the document active.
5. Press Ctrl + End to move the insertion point to the end of the document and then insert a field that will insert the file name (without any formatting).
6. Press Shift + Enter and then insert a field that will insert the current date and time (you choose the format).
7. Save, preview, and then close **7-WritingProcess.docx**.

Assessment 4

Insert an Equation Building Block

1. The Building Blocks Organizer dialog box contains a number of predesigned equations that you can insert in a document. At a blank document, display the Building Blocks Organizer dialog box and then insert one of the predesigned equations.
2. Select the equation and then click the Equation tab. Notice the groups of commands available for editing an equation.
3. Type the steps you followed to insert the equation and then type a list of the groups available on the Equation tab.
4. Save the document with the name **7-Equation**.
5. Preview and then close **7-Equation.docx**.

Visual Benchmark

Create an Agreement with Building Blocks and AutoCorrect Text

1. Use File Explorer to open a document based on **7-WLTemplate.dotx**.
2. Create the document shown in Figure 7.5 with the following specifications:
   a. Insert **WLAgreement.docx** into the open document.
   b. Display the AutoCorrect dialog box with the AutoCorrect tab selected and then create AutoCorrect entries for the text *Woodland Legal Services* (use *wls*) and *Till-Harris Management* (use *thm*).
   c. Press Ctrl + Home, press the Enter key, and then type the first two paragraphs of text shown in Figure 7.5 using the AutoCorrect entries you created.
   d. Move the insertion point to the beginning of the document and then insert the *WLHeading* building block and insert the *WLFooter* building block as a footer.
   e. Justify the six paragraphs of text in the document.

3. Save the completed document with the name **7-THMAgrmnt**.
4. Preview and then close **7-THMAgrmnt.docx**.
5. Display the AutoCorrect dialog box, delete the *wls* and *thm* entries, and then close the dialog box.

Figure 7.5 Visual Benchmark

REPRESENTATION AGREEMENT

Carlos Sawyer, Attorney at Law

This agreement is made between Carlos Sawyer of Woodland Legal Services and Till-Harris Management for legal services to be provided by Woodland Legal Services.

Legal Representation: Woodland Legal Services will perform the legal services required by Till-Harris Management, keep Till-Harris Management informed of progress and developments, and respond promptly to Till-Harris Management's inquiries and communications.

Attorney's Fees and Costs: Till-Harris Management will pay Woodland Legal Services for attorney's fees for legal services provided under this agreement at the hourly rate of the individuals providing the services. Under this agreement, Till-Harris Management will pay all costs incurred by Woodland Legal Services for representation of Till-Harris Management. Costs will be advanced by Woodland Legal Services and then billed to Till-Harris Management unless the costs can be met from deposits.

Deposit for Fees: Till-Harris Management will pay to Woodland Legal Services an initial deposit of $5,000, to be received by Woodland Legal Services on or before November 1. Twenty percent of the deposit is nonrefundable and will be applied against attorney's fees. The refundable portion will be deposited by Woodland Legal Services in an interest-bearing trust account. Till-Harris Management authorizes Woodland Legal Services to withdraw the principal from the trust account to pay attorney's fees in excess of the nonrefundable portion.

Statement and Payments: Woodland Legal Services will send Till-Harris Management monthly statements indicating attorney's fees and costs incurred, amounts applied from deposits, and current balance owed. If no attorney's fees or costs are incurred for a month, the statement may be held and combined with that for the following month. Any balance will be paid in full within 30 days after the statement is mailed.

Effective Date of Agreement: The effective date of this agreement will be the date when it is executed by both parties.

Client: ______________________________ Date: _______________

Attorney: ____________________________ Date: _______________

7110 FIFTH STREET ◆ SUITE 200 ◆ OMAHA NE 68207 ◆ 402-555-7110

Case Study

Part 1

You have been hired as the office manager for Highland Construction Company. The address of the company is 9025 Palmer Park Boulevard, Colorado Springs, CO 80904 and the telephone number is (719) 555-4575. You are responsible for designing business documents that have a consistent visual style and formatting. You decide that your first task is to create a letterhead document. Press Ctrl + N to open a blank document and then save the document as a template with the name **7-HCCTemplate.dotx** in your WL2C7 folder. Close the template document. Use File Explorer to open a document based on **7-HCCTemplate.dotx**. At the blank document based on the template, create a letterhead that includes the company name, address, and telephone number, along with an image and/or any other elements to add visual interest. Select the letterhead text and element(s) and then create a building block in the Quick Part gallery named **HCCLtrhd** that is saved in **7-HCCTemplate.dotx**. Create the following additional building blocks for your company. (You decide on the names and save the building blocks in **7-HCCTemplate.dotx**.)

- Create a building block footer that contains a border line (in a color matching the colors in the letterhead) and the company slogan:
  Colorado Business Since 1985
- Create the following complimentary close building block:
  Sincerely,

  Your Name
  Office Manager
- Create the following company name and address building block:
  Mr. Eric Rashad
  Roswell Industries
  1020 Wasatch Street
  Colorado Springs, CO 80902
- Create the following company name and address building block:
  Ms. Claudia Sanborn
  S & S Supplies
  537 Constitution Avenue
  Colorado Springs, CO 80911

Select and then delete the contents of the document. Close the document without saving it. At the message asking if you want to save changes to the template, click the Save button.

Part 2

Use File Explorer to open a document based on **7-HCCTemplate.dotx**. Apply the No Spacing style and then create a letter to Eric Rashad by inserting the Highland Construction Company letterhead (the *HCCLtrhd* building block). Press the Enter key, type today's date, press the Enter key four times, and then insert the *Eric Rashad* building block. Press the Enter key, type an appropriate salutation (such as *Dear Mr. Rashad:*), insert the file named **HCCLetter.docx**, and then insert your complimentary close building block. Finally, insert the footer building block you created for the company. Check the letter and modify the spacing as needed.

Save the letter with the name **7-RashadLtr**. Preview and then close the letter. Complete similar steps to create a letter to Claudia Sanborn. Save the completed letter with the name **7-SanbornLtr**. Preview and then close the letter.

Part 3

Use File Explorer to open a document based on **7-HCCTemplate.dotx**. Insert the Highland Construction Company letterhead building block you created in Part 1, type the title *Company Services*, and then insert a SmartArt graphic of your choosing that contains the following text:

Residential Construction
Commercial Construction
Design Consultation
Site Preparation

Apply a heading style to the *Company Services* title, insert the company footer building block, and then save the document with the name **7-CoServices**. Preview and then close **7-CoServices.docx**.

WORD

Managing Shared Documents

CHAPTER 8

Performance Objectives

Upon successful completion of Chapter 8, you will be able to:

1. Insert, edit, show, reply to, print, resolve, and delete comments
2. Navigate between comments
3. Distinguish comments from different users
4. Edit a document using the Track Changes feature
5. Display changes, show markups, display tracked changed information, and change user information
6. Lock the Track Changes feature and customize tracked changes options
7. Navigate to and accept/reject changes
8. Restrict and enforce formatting and editing in a document and protect a document with a password
9. Protect a document by marking it as final, encrypting it, restricting editing, and adding a digital signature
10. Open a document in different views
11. Share a document electronically
12. Manage document versions

In a workplace environment, you may need to share documents with coworkers and associates. You may be part of a workgroup, which is a networked collection of computers that share files, printers, and other resources. As a member of a workgroup, you can collaborate with other members and distribute documents for their review and/or revision. Workgroup activities include inserting and managing comments and tracking the changes made to a document. Managing shared document might also include restricting the formatting and editing changes users can make to a document and protecting a document with a password. In this chapter, you will learn how to manage shared documents as well as how to open a document in different views, share a document electronically, and manage document versions.

Data Files

The data files for this chapter are in the WL2C8 folder that you downloaded at the beginning of this course.

Activity 1 Insert Comments in a New Employees Document — 3 Parts

You will open a report containing company information for new employees and then insert and edit comments from multiple users.

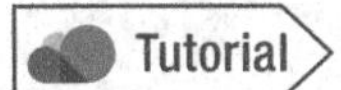

Inserting Comments

Quick Steps

Insert Comment

1. Select text.
2. Click Review tab.
3. Click New Comment button.
4. Type comment.

New Comment

Comments

Show Comments

Hint If your computer has a sound card and microphone, you can record voice comments.

Hint Ctrl + Enter is the keyboard shortcut to post a comment.

Inserting and Managing Comments

Use Word's comment feature to provide feedback on and suggest changes to a document that someone else has written. Similarly, get feedback on a document by distributing it electronically to others and having them insert comments in it or reply to comments. *Note: The functionality of the Comments feature is dependent on the version of Word you are using. Some of the information and steps in the textbook may vary from what you see on your screen.*

Inserting Comments

Insert a comment with the New Comment button in the Comments group on the Review tab or with the Comments button at the right side of the ribbon. Click the New Comment button on the Review tab and a comment box displays at the right side of the screen as shown in Figure 8.1. Type the comment in the comment box and then click the Post comment button. Click the Comments button at the right side of the ribbon and the Comments task pane displays. Click the New button in the task pane, type the comment, and then click the Post comment button.

Showing Comments

For a comment to display in a document, the *Display for Review* option box in the Tracking group needs to display either *Simple Markup* or *All Markup.* With either of the options displayed, the Show Comments button in the Comments group is active. If the *Display for Review* option box displays *No Markup* or *Original*, the Show Comments button is inactive and the comments do not display. To specify an option, click the *Display for Review* option box and then click either *Simple Markup* or *All Markup* at the drop-down list. If the Show Comments button is active, clicking the button will turn off the display of comments.

Figure 8.1 Sample Comment Box

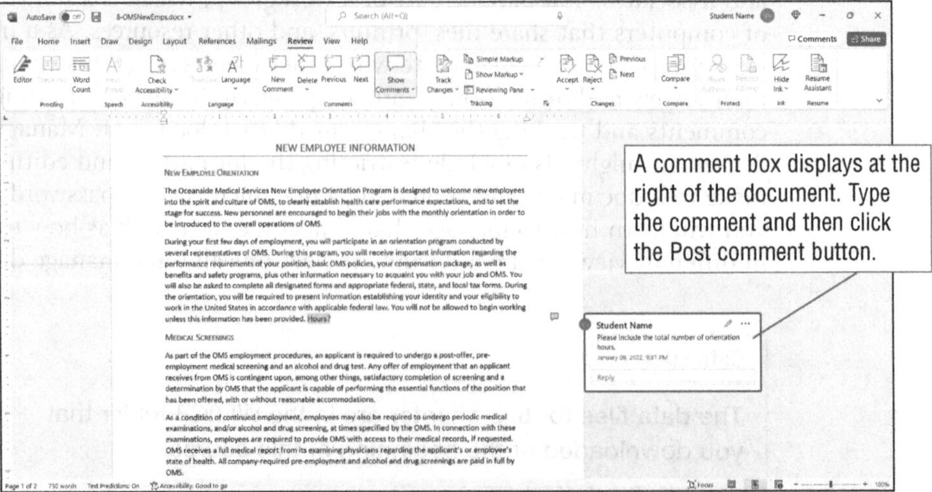

Activity 1a Inserting Comments

1. Open **OMSNewEmps.docx** and then save it with the name **8-OMSNewEmps.**
2. Insert a comment using the New Comment button on the Review tab by completing the following steps:
   a. Position the insertion point at the end of the second paragraph in the *New Employee Orientation* section.
   b. Press the spacebar and then type Hours?.
   c. Select *Hours?*.
   d. Click the Review tab.
   e. Make sure *Simple Markup* displays in the *Display for Review* option box. If not, click the *Display for Review* option box arrow and then click *Simple Markup* at the drop-down list.
   f. Click the New Comment button in the Comments group.
   g. Type Please include the total number of orientation hours. in the comment box.
   h. Click the Post comment button (right-pointing white arrow with blue background). (If your comment does not contain a Post comment button, click in the document to post the comment.)

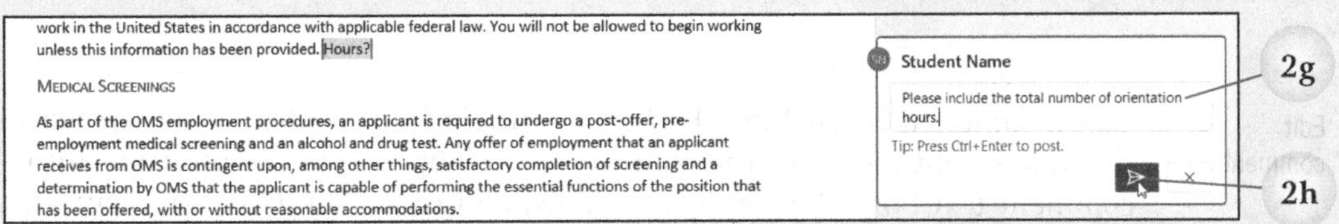

3. Insert a comment in the Comments task pane by completing the following steps:
   a. Move the insertion point to the end of the third (last) paragraph in the *Medical Screenings* section.
   b. Click the Comments button at the right side of the ribbon.

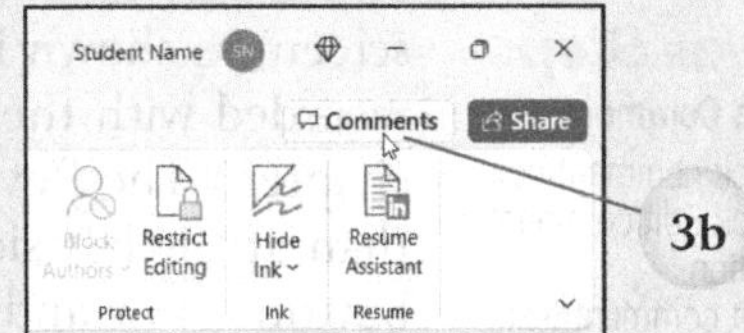

   c. Click the New button in the Comments task pane. (If a Comments task pane does not display, click the *New* option at the Comments button drop-down list.)

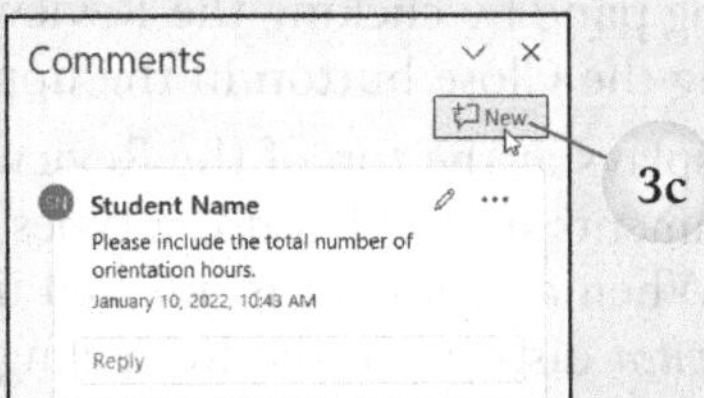

   d. Type Specify the locations where drug tests are administered. in the comment box. (Since you did not select any text before clicking the New button, Word selects the word immediately left of the insertion point.)
   e. Click the Post comment button. (If a Post comment button does not display, click in the document to post the comment.)
   f. Click in the document.

4. Insert another comment in the Comments task pane by completing the following steps:
   a. Move the insertion point to the end of the paragraph text in the *Introductory Period* section.
   b. Press the spacebar once, type Maximum?, and then select *Maximum?*.
   c. Click the New button in the Comments task pane.
   d. Type Please include in this section the maximum length of the probationary period. in the comment box.
   e. Click the Post comment button. (If a Post comment button does not display, click in the document to post the comment.)
   f. Click in the document.
   g. Close the Comments task pane by clicking the Close button in the upper right corner of the task pane.
5. Save **8-OMSNewEmps.docx**.

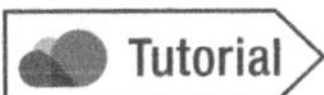

Managing Comments

Previous

Next

Navigating between Comments

When working in a long document with many comments, use the Previous and Next buttons in the Comments group on the Review tab to move easily from comment to comment. Click the Next button to move the insertion point to the next comment in the document or click the Previous button to move the insertion point to the previous comment.

Editing Comments

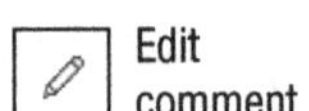

Edit comment

Reviewing Pane

Quick Steps

Edit a Comment
1. Click comment box.
2. Click Edit comment button.
3. Edit comment text.
4. Click Post comment button in comment box.

OR
1. Click Reviewing Pane button.
2. Click in the comment text.
3. Edit comment text.

Edit a comment by clicking the Edit comment button (display as a pencil) in the upper right corner of the comment box. This moves the insertion into the comment text box. Make edits as needed and then click Post comment button (displays as a white check mark on a blue background) in the comment box.

A comment can also be edited in the Reviewing pane. Turn on the display of the Reviewing pane by clicking the Reviewing Pane button in the Tracking group on the Review tab. The Reviewing pane usually displays at the left side of the screen, as shown in Figure 8.2 and displays both inserted comments and changes recorded with the Track Changes feature. (Track Changes is covered later in this chapter.) The Reviewing pane might display along the bottom of the screen, rather than at the left side. To specify where the pane displays, click the Reviewing Pane button arrow and then click *Reviewing Pane Vertical* or *Reviewing Pane Horizontal*. Close the Reviewing pane by clicking the Reviewing Pane button in the Tracking group or by clicking the Close button in the upper right corner of the pane.

A summary displays at the top of the Reviewing pane and provides counts of the number of comments inserted and the types of changes that have been made to the document. When a comment is inserted in a document, the reviewer's name followed by *Commented* displays in the Reviewing pane. Edit a comment in the Reviewing pane by clicking in the comment text and then making the changes.

Figure 8.2 Vertical Reviewing Pane

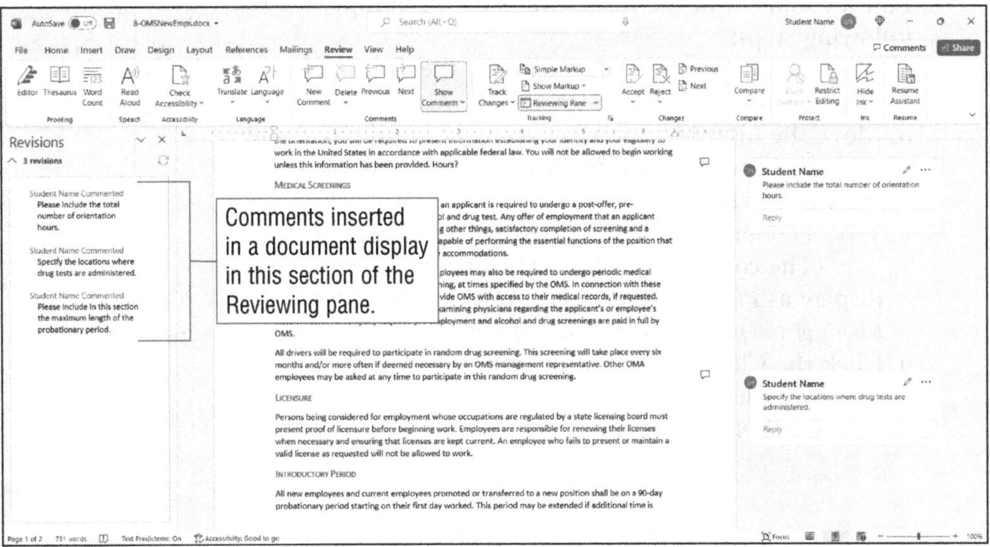

Activity 1b Editing Comments

Part 2 of 3

1. With **8-OMSNewEmps.docx** open, navigate from one comment to another by completing the following steps:
   a. Press Ctrl + Home to move the insertion point to the beginning of the document.
   b. If necessary, click the Review tab.
   c. Click the Next button in the Comments group. (This selects the first comment box.)
   d. Click the Next button to select the second comment box.
   e. Click the Next button to select the third comment box.
   f. Click the Previous button to select the second comment box.
2. Edit the second comment by completing the following steps:
   a. Click the Edit comment button (displays as a pencil) in the upper right corner of the comment box. (If an Edit comment button does not display, click in the comment text box.)

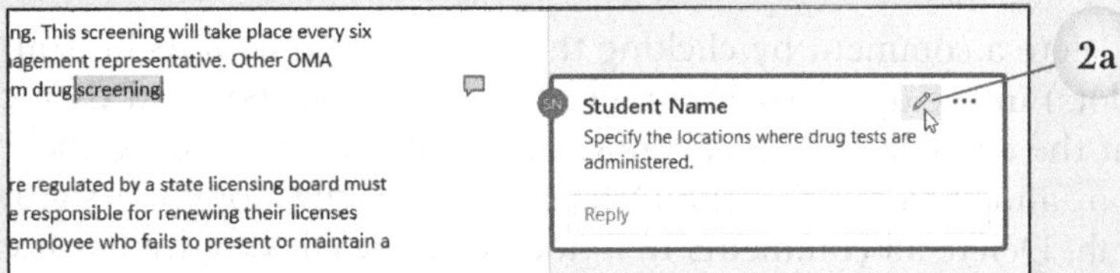

   b. Select the comment text and then type Specify the locations within OMS where drug tests are administered as well as any off-site locations.
   c. Click the Post comment button (white check mark on blue background) in the comment box. (If a Post comment button does not display, click in the document to post the comment.)

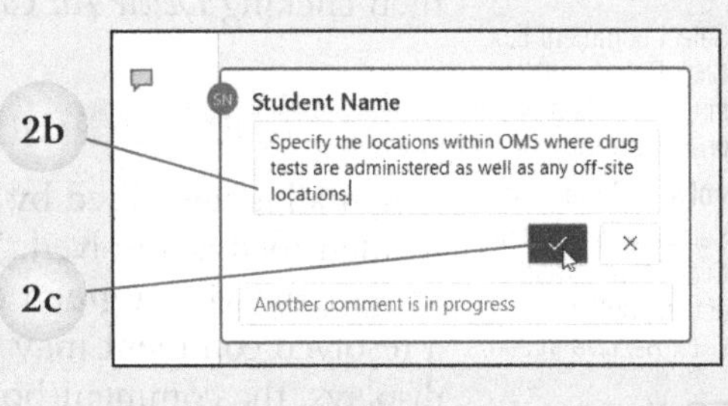

3. Edit a comment in the Reviewing pane by completing the following steps:
   a. Click the Reviewing Pane button in the Tracking group on the Review tab.
   b. Move the insertion point between the word *period* and the period puncutation mark in the third comment in the Reviewing pane.
   c. Type a comma, press the spacebar and then type if any. (The comment in the Reviewing pane should now display as *Please include in this section the maximum length of the probationary period, if any.*)
   d. Click the Close button in the upper right corner of the Reviewing pane.
4. Save **8-OMSNewEmps.docx.**

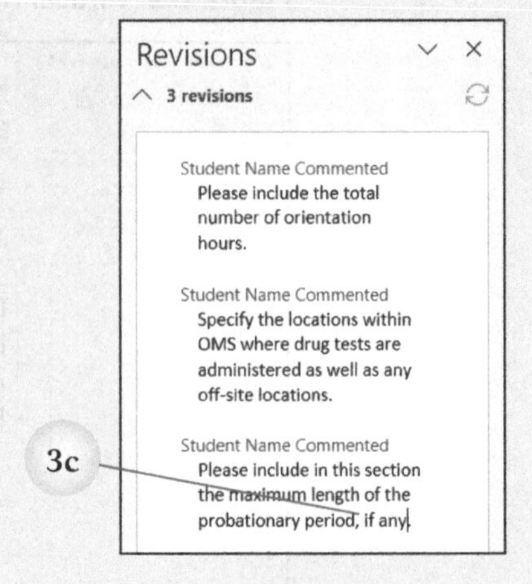

Replying to Comments

Quick Steps

Reply to Comment
1. Click in *Reply* text box.
2. Type reply.
3. Click Post reply button.

Print Document with Comments
1. Click File tab.
2. Click *Print* option.
3. Click first gallery in *Settings* category.
4. If necessary, click *Print Markup* to insert check mark.
5. Click Print button.

Print Only Comments
1. Click File tab.
2. Click *Print* option.
3. Click first gallery in *Settings* category.
4. Click *List of Markup*.
5. Click Print button.

Delete a Comment
1. Select comment box.
2. Click More thread actions button.
3. Click *Delete thread*.

OR
1. Select comment box.
2. Click Delete button in Comments group on Review tab.

Resolve a Comment
1. Select comment box.
2. Click More thread actions button.
3. Click *Resolve thread*.

More thread actions

During the review of a document, a reply can be made to a comment. To reply to a comment, click in the *Reply* text box in the comment box, type the reply, and then click the Post reply button (right-pointing white arrow on blue background).

Printing Comments

A document containing comments can be printed one of three ways: the document and the comments, the document without the comments, or only the comments. By default, a document will print with the comments. To print the document without the comments, display the Print backstage area and then click the first gallery in the *Settings* category (the gallery that contains the text *Print All Pages*). At the drop-down list, click the *Print Markup* option to remove the check mark, and then click the Print button. To print only the comments, display the Print backstage area, click the first gallery in the *Settings* category, and then click the *List of Markup* option at the drop-down list.

Deleting Comments

Delete a comment by clicking the More thread actions button (button with three dots) in the upper right corner of the comment box and then clicking *Delete thread* at the drop-down list. A comment can also be deleted by clicking the comment box and then clicking the Delete button in the Comments group on the Review tab. Delete all comments in a document by clicking the Delete button arrow and then clicking *Delete All Comments in Document* at the drop-down list.

Resolving Comments

When all issues raised by a comment have been addressed, the comment thread can by identified as resolved. When a comment is resolved, the comment box is reduced to an icon with a green check mark. (Depending on the version you are using, a resolved comment may display in a dimmed manner.) If the Comments task pane displays, the comment box displays in the task pane with *Resolved* at the top of the box preceded by a check mark. To resolve a comment, click the More thread actions button in the comment box and then click *Resolve thread* at the drop-down list. (Or, depending on your version, you may need to just click the Resolve button.) To delete all resolved comments, click the Delete button arrow in the Comments group and then click *Delete All Resolved Comments* at the drop-down list.

Distinguishing Comments from Different Users

More than one user can insert comments in the same document. Word uses different colors to distinguish comments inserted by different users, generally displaying the first user's comments in red and the second user's comments in blue. (These colors may vary.)

Change user name and initials at the Word Options dialog box with *General* selected, as shown in Figure 8.3. To change the user name, select the name that displays in the *User name* text box and then type the new name. Complete similar steps to change the user initials in the *Initials* text box. A check mark may need to be inserted in the *Always use these values regardless of sign in to Office* check box.

Figure 8.3 Word Options Dialog Box with *General* Selected

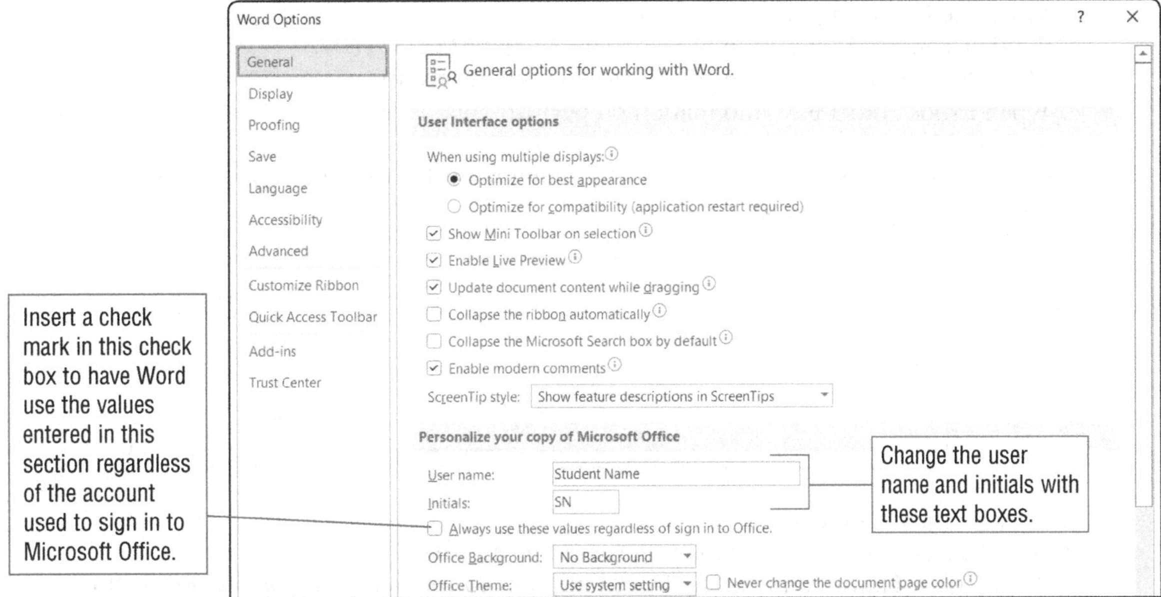

Activity 1c Changing User Information and Inserting, Resolving, and Deleting Comments Part 3 of 3

1. With **8-OMSNewEmps.docx** open, change the user information by completing the following steps:
   a. Click the File tab.
   b. Click *Options*.

c. At the Word Options dialog box, make sure *General* is selected in the left panel.

d. Make a note of the current name and initials in the *Personalize your copy of Microsoft Office* section.

e. Select the name displayed in the *User name* text box and then type Taylor Stanton.

f. Select the initials displayed in the *Initials* text box and then type TS.

g. Click the *Always use these values regardless of sign in to Office* check box to insert a check mark.

h. Click OK to close the Word Options dialog box.

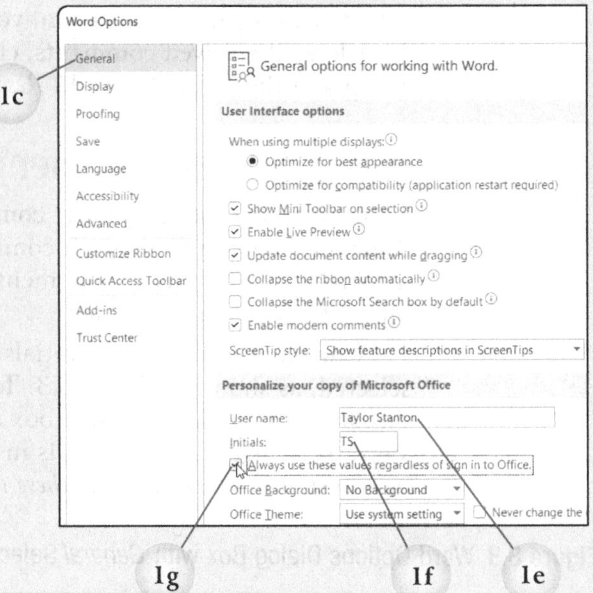

2. Insert a comment by completing the following steps:
   a. Move the insertion point to the end of the first paragraph of text in the section *Performance Review*.
   b. Click the New Comment button in the Comments group.
   c. Type Provide additional information on performance evaluation documentation. in the comment box.
   d. Click the Post comment button. (If a Post comment button does not display, click in the document to post the comment.)

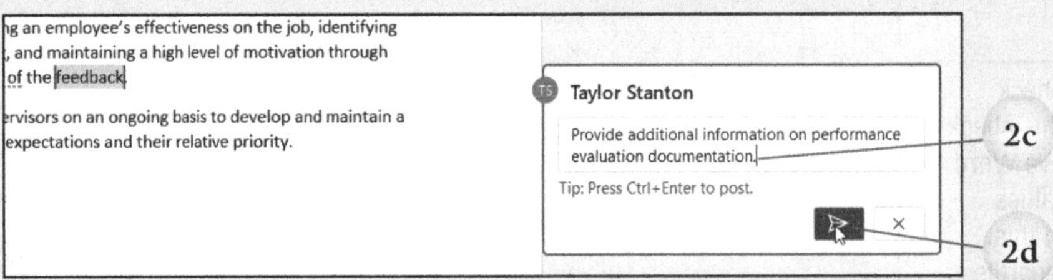

   e. Click in the document.

3. Respond to a comment by completing the following steps:
   a. Press Ctrl + Home to move the insertion point to the beginning of the document.
   b. Click the Next button in the Comments group. (This selects the first comment box.)
   c. Click in the *Reply* text box in the comment box.
   d. Type Check with Barb on the total number of orientation hours.
   e. Click the Post reply button. (If a Post reply button does not display, click in the document to post the reply.)

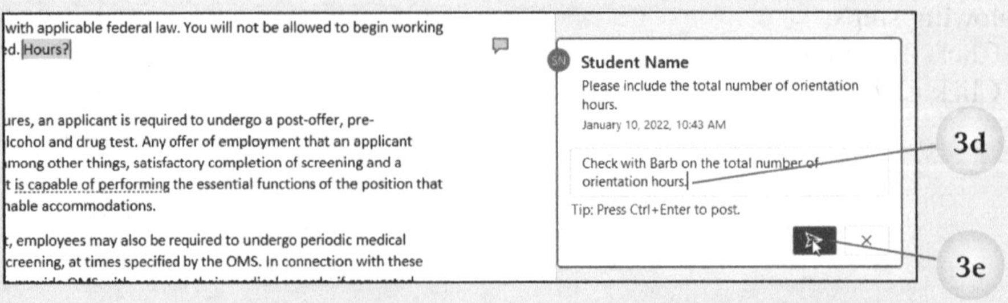

f. Click in the document.

4. Print only the comments by completing the following steps:
   a. Click the File tab and then click the *Print* option.
   b. At the Print backstage area, click the first gallery in the *Settings* category and then click *List of Markup* in the *Document Info* section of the drop-down list.
   c. Click the Print button.

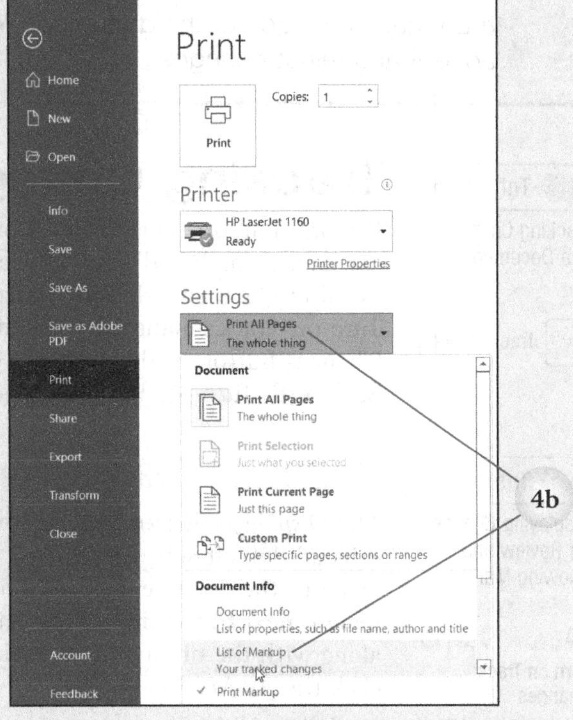

5. Resolve and delete a comment by completing the following steps:
   a. Press Ctrl + Home.
   b. Click the Next button. (This selects the first comment box.)
   c. Click the More thread actions button.
   d. Click *Resolve thread* at the drop-down list. (The comment is reduced to an icon with a green check mark.) (Depending on your version, you may need to click the Resolve button and the resolved comment will display dimmed.)
   e. Click the Next button again.
   f. Click the Next button again. (This selects the third comment box.)
   g. Click the Delete button in the Comments group.

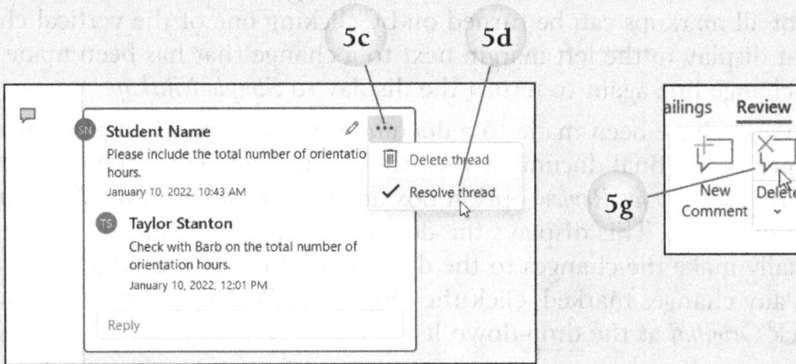

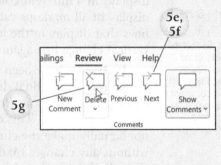

6. Print only the comments by completing Step 4.
7. Change the user information back to the default settings by completing the following steps:
   a. Click the File tab and then click *Options*.
   b. At the Word Options dialog box with *General* selected, select *Taylor Stanton* in the *User name* text box and then type the original name.
   c. Select the initials *TS* in the *Initials* text box and then type the original initials.
   d. Click the *Always use these values regardless of sign in to Office* check box to remove the check mark.
   e. Click OK to close the dialog box.
8. Save and then close **8-OMSNewEmps.docx**.

Activity 2 Track Changes in a Building Construction Agreement 4 Parts

You will open a building construction agreement, turn on Track Changes, and then make changes to the document. You will also customize Track Changes and accept and reject changes.

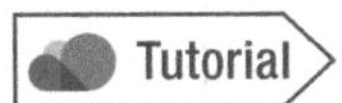

Tracking Changes in a Document

 Track Changes

Tracking Changes in a Document

If more than one person in a workgroup needs to review and edit a document, consider using Word's Track Changes feature. When Track Changes is turned on, Word tracks each deletion, insertion, and formatting change made in a document. Turn on Track Changes by clicking the Review tab and then clicking the Track Changes button in the Tracking group or by using the keyboard shortcut Ctrl + Shift + E. Turn off Track Changes by completing the same steps.

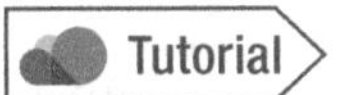

Displaying Changes for Review and Showing Markup

Quick Steps

Turn on Track Changes

1. Click Review tab.
2. Click Track Changes button.

OR

Press Ctrl + Shift + E.

Hint Each of the four options at the *Display for Review* option drop-down list displays a document at various stages in the editing process.

Displaying Changes for Review

The *Display for Review* option box in the Tracking group on the Review tab has an original default setting of *Simple Markup*. With this setting applied, each change made to the document displays in it and a vertical change line displays in the left margin next to the line of text in which the change was made. To see the changes along with the original text, click the *Display for Review* option box arrow and then click the *All Markup* option.

With *All Markup* selected, all the changes display in the document along with the original text. For example, if text is deleted, it stays in the document but displays in a different color and with strikethrough characters through it. The display of all markups can be turned on by clicking one of the vertical change lines that display in the left margin next to a change that has been made. Click a vertical change line again to return the display to *Simple Markup*.

If changes have been made to a document with Track Changes turned on, the appearance of the final document with the changes applied can be previewed by clicking the *Display for Review* option box arrow and then clicking *No Markup* at the drop-down list. This displays the document with the changes made, but does not actually make the changes to the document. To view the original document without any changes marked, click the *Display for Review* option box arrow and then click *Original* at the drop-down list.

Showing Markups

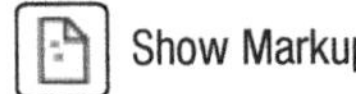

With the display of all markups turned on, specify what tracking information displays in the body of the document with options at the Balloons side menu. To show all the changes in balloons in the right margin, click the Show Markup button, point to *Balloons*, and then click *Show Revisions in Balloons* at the side menu. Click *Show All Revisions Inline* to display all the changes in the document with vertical change lines in the left margin next to the affected lines of text. Click the *Show Only Formatting in Balloons* option at the side menu and insertions and deletions display in the text while formatting changes display in balloons in the right margin.

Activity 2a Tracking Changes in a Document

Part 1 of 4

1. Open **Agreement.docx** and then save it with the name **8-Agreement.docx**.
2. Turn on Track Changes by clicking the Review tab and then clicking the Track Changes button in the Tracking group.

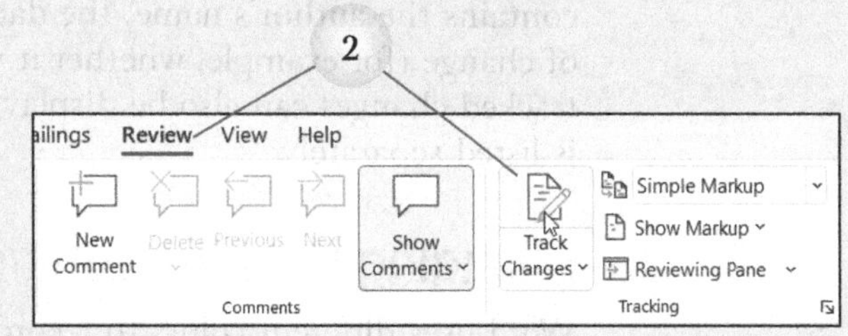

3. Type the word BUILDING between the words *THIS* and *AGREEMENT* in the first paragraph of the document.

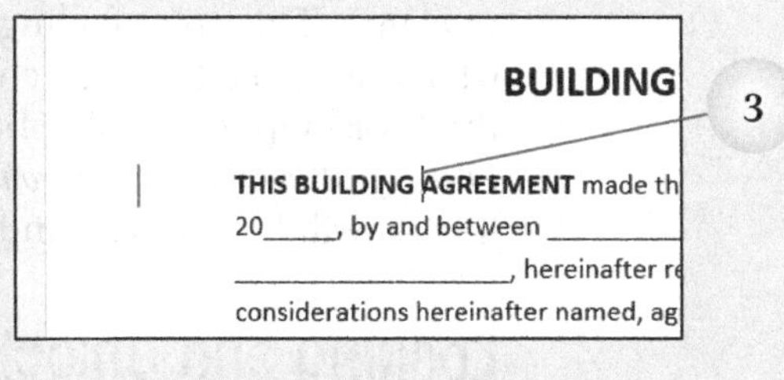

4. Show all markups by clicking the *Display for Review* option box arrow in the Tracking group and then clicking *All Markup* at the drop-down list. (Notice that the text *BUILDING* is underlined and displays in red in the document [the color may vary].)

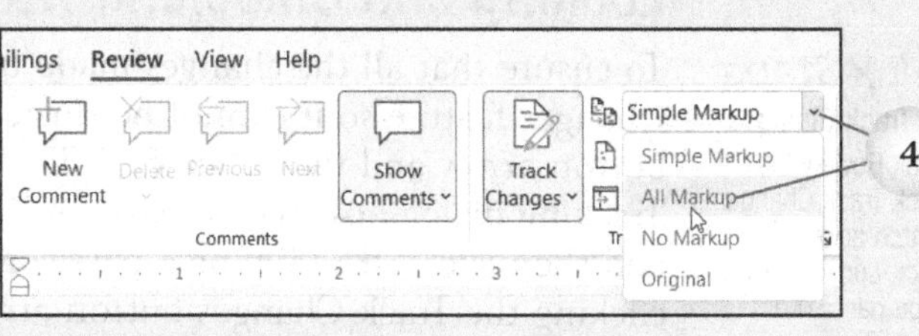

5. Click the Show Markup button, point to *Balloons*, and then click the *Show Only Formatting in Balloons* option. (Depending on your version, the option may display as *Show Only Comments and Formatting in Balloons*.)
6. Select and then delete *thirty (30)* in the second paragraph. (The deleted text displays in the document with strikethrough characters through it.)
7. Type sixty (60).

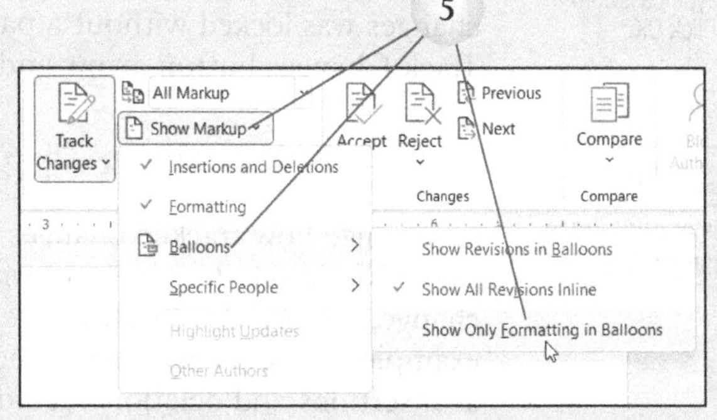

8. Move a paragraph of text by completing the following steps:
   a. Select the paragraph that begins *Supervision of Work* (including the paragraph mark that ends the paragraph).
   b. Press Ctrl + X to cut the text. (The text stays in the document and displays in red with strikethrough characters through it.)
   c. Position the insertion point immediately before the word *Start* (in the paragraph that begins *Start of Construction and Completion:*).
   d. Press Ctrl + V to paste the cut text in the new location. The inserted text displays in green and has a double underline below it. Notice that the text in the original location changes to green and has double-strikethrough characters through it.)
9. Turn off Track Changes by clicking the Track Changes button in the Tracking group.
10. Display revisions in balloons by clicking the Show Markup button, pointing to *Balloons*, and then clicking *Show Revisions in Balloons* at the side menu.
11. After looking at the revisions in balloons, click the Show Markup button, point to *Balloons*, and then click *Show All Revisions Inline* at the side menu.
12. Save **8-Agreement.docx**.

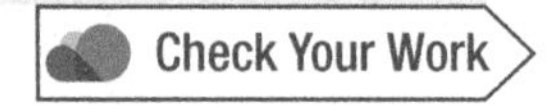

Displaying Information about Tracked Changes

Display information about a specific tracked change by hovering the pointer over it. After approximately one second, a box displays above the change that contains the author's name, the date and time the change was made, and the type of change (for example, whether it was a deletion or insertion). Information on tracked changes can also be displayed in the Reviewing pane, where each change is listed separately.

Changing User Information

Word uses different colors to record the changes made by different people (up to eight). This color coding allows anyone looking at the document to identify which users made which changes. How to change the user name and initials at the Word Options dialog box was covered earlier in the chapter (see the section *Distinguishing Comments from Different Users*). In Activity 2b, the user name and initials will be changed and then additional tracked changes will be made.

Locking and Unlocking Track Changes

Quick Steps

Lock Track Changes

1. Click Review tab.
2. Click Track Changes button arrow.
3. Click *Lock Tracking*.
4. Type password.
5. Press Tab.
6. Type password.
7. Click OK.

To ensure that all the changes made to a document will be tracked, lock the Track Changes feature so it cannot be turned off. To do this, click the Track Changes button arrow and then click *Lock Tracking* at the drop-down list. At the Lock Tracking dialog box, type a password, press the Tab key, type the password again, and then click OK. (Typing a password is optional.) Unlock Track Changes by clicking the Track Changes button arrow and then clicking *Lock Tracking*. At the Unlock Tracking dialog box, type the password and then click OK. If track changes was locked without a password, unlock track changes by clicking the Track Changes button arrow and then clicking *Lock Tracking* at the drop-down list.

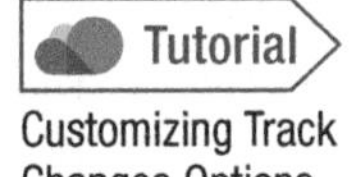

Customizing Track Changes Options

Customizing Track Changes Options

Customize how tracked changes display in a document with options at the Show Markup button drop-down list. To show only one particular type of tracked change, remove the check marks before all the options except the specific one. For example, to view only formatting changes and not other types of changes, such as insertions and deletions, remove the check mark before each option except *Formatting*. Another method of customizing the tracked changes display is to use options at the Track Changes Options dialog box, shown in Figure 8.4. Display this dialog box by clicking the Tracking group dialog box launcher.

Figure 8.4 Track Changes Options Dialog Box

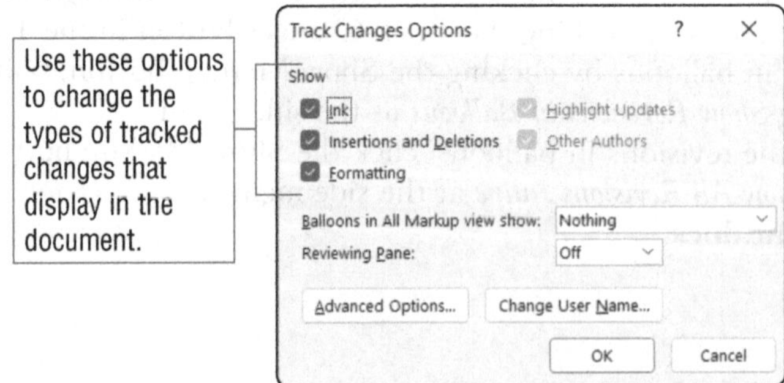

If the changes made by multiple reviewers have been tracked in a document, the changes made by a particular reviewer can be displayed. To do this, click the Show Markup button, point to *Specific People* at the drop-down list, and then click the *All Reviewers* check box to remove the check mark. Click the Show Markup button, point to *Reviewers*, and then click the check box of the specific reviewer.

Printing Markups

A document, by default, will print with all markups including comments, tracked changes, and changes to headers, footers, text boxes, footnotes and endnotes. To print a document without markups, display the Print backstage area, click the first gallery in the *Settings* category (contains the text *Print All Pages*) and then click the *Print Markup* option to remove the check mark. To print only the markups, display the Print backstage area, click the first gallery in the *Settings* category, and then click the *List of Markup* option at the drop-down list.

Activity 2b Changing User Information, Tracking Changes, and Locking Track Changes — Part 2 of 4

1. With **8-Agreement.docx** open, change the user information by completing the following steps:
   a. Click the File tab and then click *Options*.
   b. At the Word Options dialog box with *General* selected, select the current name in the *User name* text box and then type Julia Moore.
   c. Select the initials in the *Initials* text box and then type JM.
   d. Click the *Always use these values regardless of sign in to Office* check box to insert a check mark.
   e. Click OK to close the dialog box.
2. Make additional changes to the contract and track the changes by completing the following steps:
   a. Click the Track Changes button in the Tracking group to turn on tracking.
   b. Select the title *BUILDING CONSTRUCTION AGREEMENT* and then change the font size to 14 points.
   c. Delete the text *at their option* (located in the second sentence in the second paragraph).
   d. Delete the text *and Completion* (in the heading in the fourth paragraph).

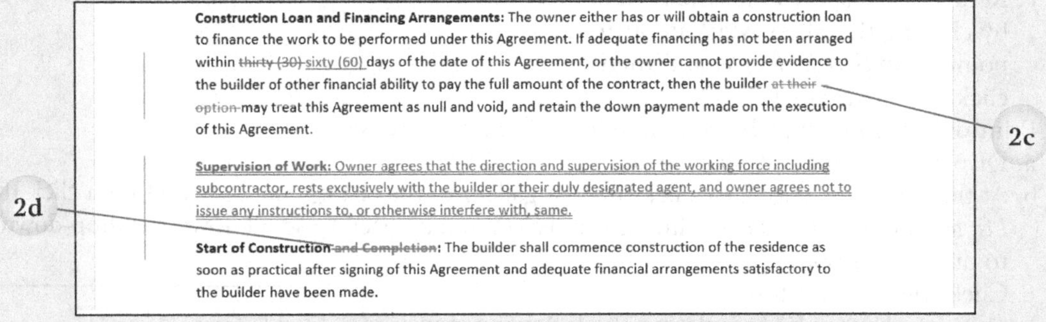
Construction Loan and Financing Arrangements: The owner either has or will obtain a construction loan to finance the work to be performed under this Agreement. If adequate financing has not been arranged within ~~thirty (30)~~ sixty (60) days of the date of this Agreement, or the owner cannot provide evidence to the builder of other financial ability to pay the full amount of the contract, then the builder ~~at their option~~ may treat this Agreement as null and void, and retain the down payment made on the execution of this Agreement.

Supervision of Work: Owner agrees that the direction and supervision of the working force including subcontractor, rests exclusively with the builder or their duly designated agent, and owner agrees not to issue any instructions to, or otherwise interfere with, same.

Start of Construction ~~and Completion~~: The builder shall commence construction of the residence as soon as practical after signing of this Agreement and adequate financial arrangements satisfactory to the builder have been made.

   e. Delete *thirty (30)* in the paragraph that begins *Builder's Right to Terminate the Contract:* (located on the second page).
   f. Type sixty (60).
   g. Select the text *IN WITNESS WHEREOF* (located near the bottom of the document) and then apply bold formatting.

3. Click the Review tab and then click the Track Changes button to turn off Track Changes.
4. Click the Reviewing Pane button to turn on the display of the Reviewing pane and then use the vertical scroll bar at the right of the Reviewing pane to review the changes.
5. View the changes in balloons by clicking the Show Markup button, pointing to *Balloons*, and then clicking *Show Revisions in Balloons*.
6. Click the Reviewing Pane button to turn off the display of the pane.
7. Scroll through the document and view the changes in the balloons.
8. Click the Show Markup button, point to *Balloons*, and then click *Show All Revisions Inline* at the side menu.
9. Change the user information back to the original information by completing the following steps:
   a. Click the File tab and then click *Options*.
   b. At the Word Options dialog box, select *Julia Moore* in the *User name* text box and then type the original name.
   c. Select the initials *JM* in the *Initials* text box and then type the original initials.
   d. Click the *Always use these values regardless of sign in to Office* check box to remove the check mark.
   e. Click OK to close the dialog box.
10. Display only those changes made by Julia Moore by completing the following steps:
   a. Click the Show Markup button in the Tracking group and then point to *Specific People* at the drop-down list.
   b. Click *All Reviewers* at the side menu.
   c. Click the Show Markup button, point to *Specific People*, and then click *Julia Moore*.
   d. Scroll through the document and notice that only changes made by Julia Moore display.
   e. Return the display to all the reviewers by clicking the Show Markup button, pointing to *Specific People*, and then clicking *All Reviewers*.
11. Print only the markups by completing the following steps:
   a. Display the Print backstage area.
   b. At the Print backstage area, click the first gallery in the *Settings* category and then click the *List of Markup* option at the drop-down list. (You may need to scroll down the drop-down list to display this option.)
   c. Click the Print button.
12. Lock track changes by completing the following steps:
   a. Click the Track Changes button arrow and then click *Lock Tracking* at the drop-down list.

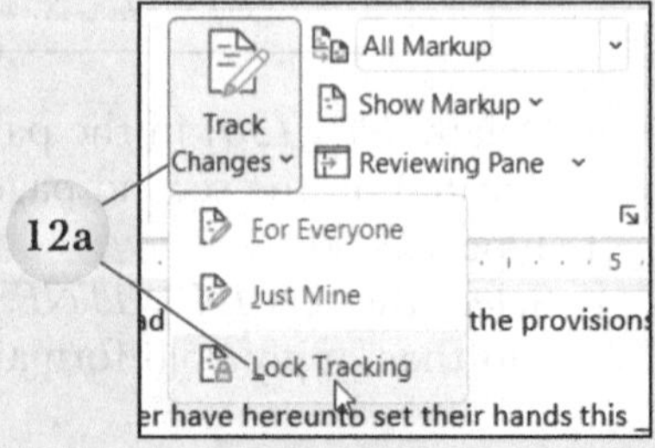

b. At the Lock Tracking dialog box, type agreement in the *Enter password (optional)* text box, press the Tab key, and then type agreement again in the *Reenter to confirm* text box.

c. Click OK.

13. Save **8-Agreement.docx**.

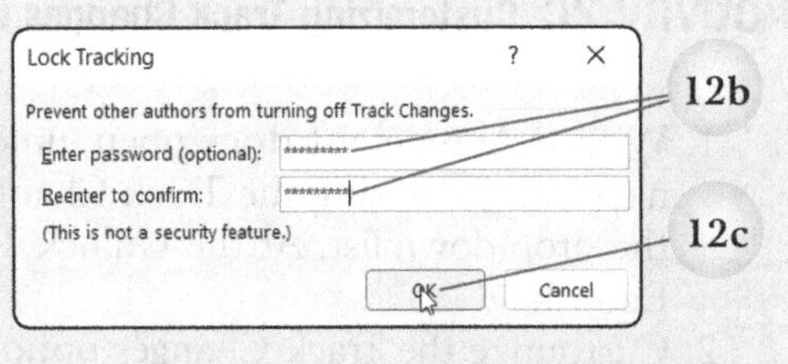

Customizing Advanced Track Changes Options

Customizing Advanced Track Changes Options

How tracked changes display in a document is determined by default settings. For example, with all the markups showing, inserted text displays in red with an underline below it and deleted text displays in red with strikethrough characters through it (these colors may vary). Moved text displays in the original location in green with double-strikethrough characters through it and in the new location in green with double-underlining below it.

Customize these options, along with others, at the Advanced Track Changes Options dialog box, shown in Figure 8.5. Use options at this dialog box to customize the display of markup text, moved text, table cell highlighting, formatting, and balloons. Display the dialog box by clicking the Tracking group dialog box launcher. At the Track Changes Options dialog box, click the Advanced Options button.

Figure 8.5 Advanced Track Changes Options Dialog Box

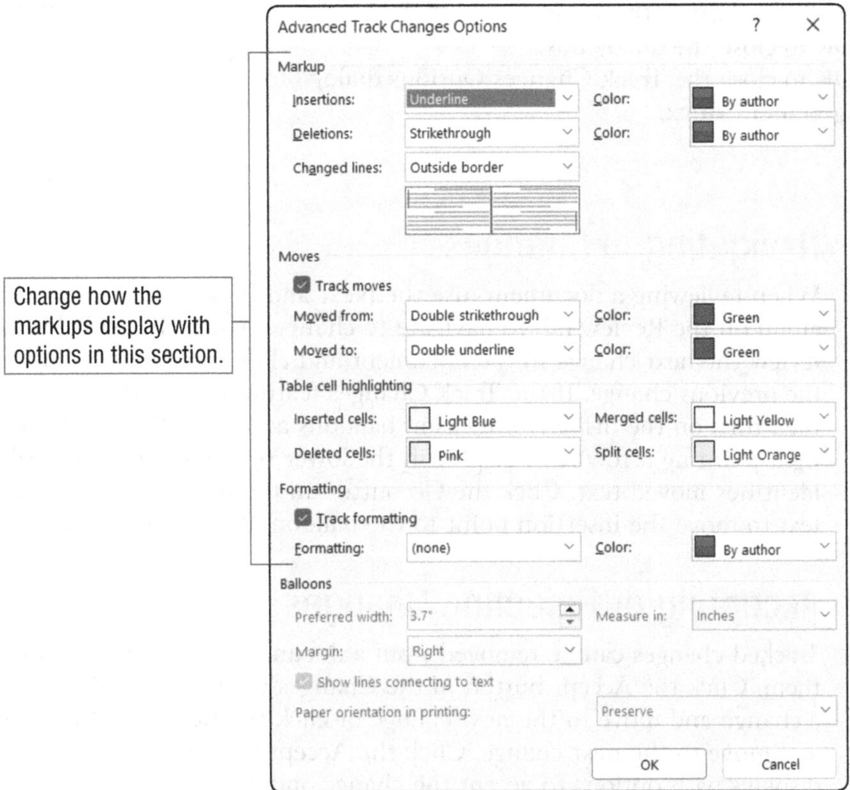

Activity 2c Customizing Track Changes Options

Part 3 of 4

1. With **8-Agreement.docx** open, unlock track changes by clicking the Review tab (if necessary), clicking the Track Changes button arrow, and then clicking *Lock Tracking* at the drop-down list. At the Unlock Tracking dialog box, type agreement and then press the Enter key.
2. Customize the Track Changes options by completing the following steps:
   a. If necessary, click the Review tab.
   b. Click the Tracking group dialog box launcher.
   c. Click the Advanced Options button at the Track Changes Options dialog box.
   d. At the Advanced Track Changes Options dialog box, click the *Insertions* option box arrow and then click *Double underline* at the drop-down list.
   e. Click the *Insertions Color* option box arrow and then click *Green* at the drop-down list. (You will need to scroll down the list to display this color.)
   f. Click the *Moved from Color* option box arrow and then click *Dark Blue* at the drop-down list.
   g. Click the *Moved to Color* option box arrow and then click *Violet* at the drop-down list. (You will need to scroll down the list to display this color.)
   h. Click OK to close the dialog box.
   i. Click OK to close the Track Changes Options dialog box.
3. Save **8-Agreement.docx**.

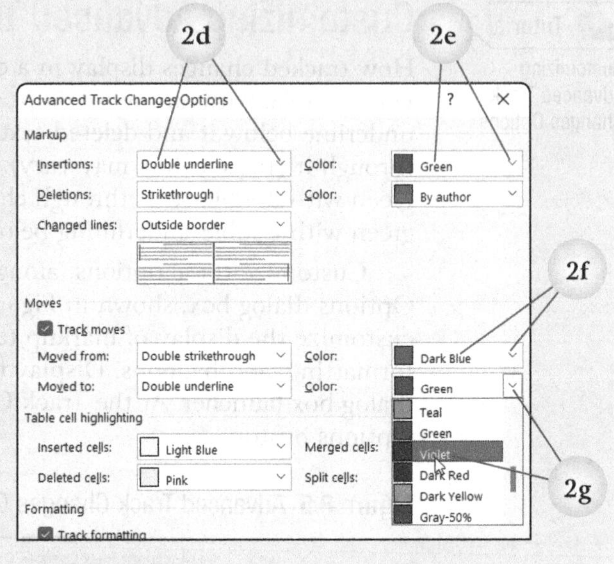

Check Your Work

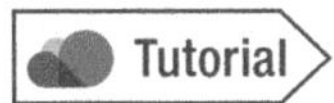

Navigating, Accepting, and Rejecting Tracked Changes

Navigating to Changes

When reviewing a document, use the Next and Previous buttons in the Changes group on the Review tab to navigate to changes. Click the Next button to review the next change in the document and click the Previous button to review the previous change. If the Track Changes feature is turned on, move text and then turn on the display of revision balloons and a small Go button (a blue right-pointing arrow) will display in the lower right corner of any balloon that identifies moved text. Click the Go button in the balloon identifying the original text to move the insertion point to the balloon identifying the moved text.

Accepting or Rejecting Changes

Tracked changes can be removed from a document only by accepting or rejecting them. Click the Accept button in the Changes group on the Review tab to accept a change and move to the next change or click the Reject button to reject a change and move to the next change. Click the Accept button arrow and a drop-down list displays with options to accept the change and move to the next change, accept the change, accept all the changes showing, and accept all the changes and stop tracking. Similar options are available at the Reject button drop-down list.

Activity 2d Accepting or Rejecting Changes

1. With **8-Agreement.docx** open, show all the tracked changes *except* formatting changes by completing the following steps:
   a. Click the Show Markup button in the Tracking group and then click *Formatting* at the drop-down list. (This removes the check mark before the option.)
   b. Scroll through the document and notice that the vertical change lines in the left margin next to the two formatting changes have been removed.
   c. Click the Show Markup button and then click *Formatting* at the drop-down list. (This inserts a check mark before the option.)
2. Navigate to review tracked changes by completing the following steps:
   a. Press Ctrl + Home to move the insertion point to the beginning of the document.
   b. Click the Next button in the Changes group to select the first change.
   c. Click the Next button again to select the second change.
   d. Click the Previous button to select the first change.
3. Navigate between the original and new locations of the moved text by completing the following steps:
   a. Press Ctrl + Home to move the insertion point to the beginning of the document.
   b. Click the Show Markup button, point to *Balloons*, and then click *Show Revisions in Balloons*.
   c. Click the Go button (a blue right-pointing arrow) in the lower right corner of the Moved balloon. (This selects the text in the *Moved up* balloon.)
   d. Click the Go button in the lower right corner of the *Moved up* balloon. (This selects the moved text in the document.)
   e. Click the Show Markup button, point to *Balloons*, and then click *Show All Revisions Inline*.

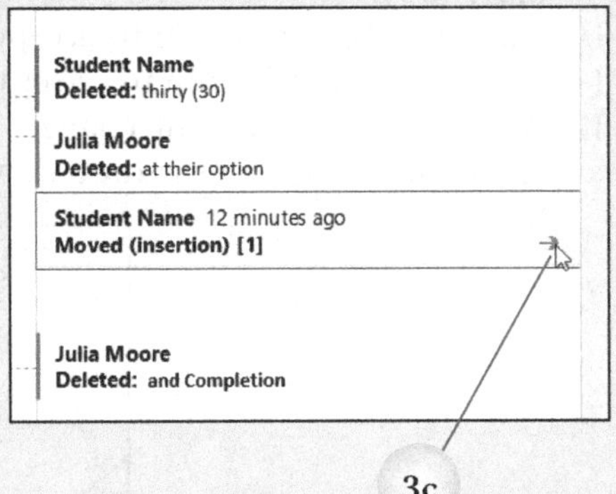

4. Press Ctrl + Home to move the insertion point to the beginning of the document.
5. Display and then accept only formatting changes by completing the following steps:
   a. Click the Tracking group dialog box launcher.
   b. At the Track Changes Options dialog box, click the *Ink* check box to remove the check mark.
   c. Click the *Insertions and Deletions* check box to remove the check mark.
   d. Make sure the *Formatting* check box contains a check mark. If it does not, click the *Formatting* check box to insert a check mark.
   e. Click OK to close the Track Changes Options dialog box.

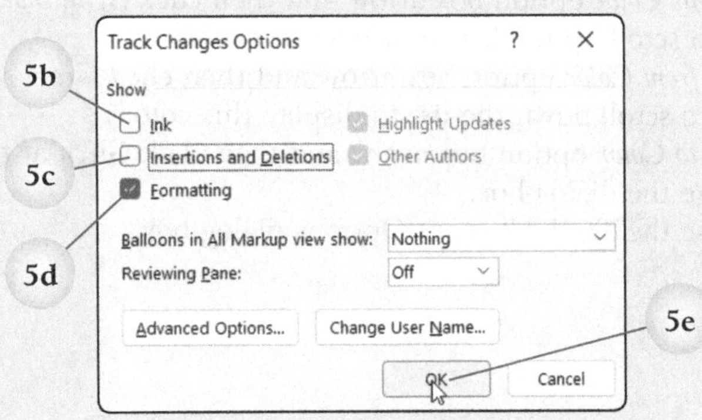

f. Click the Accept button arrow and then click *Accept All Changes Shown* at the drop-down list. (This accepts only the formatting changes in the document because those are the only changes showing.)

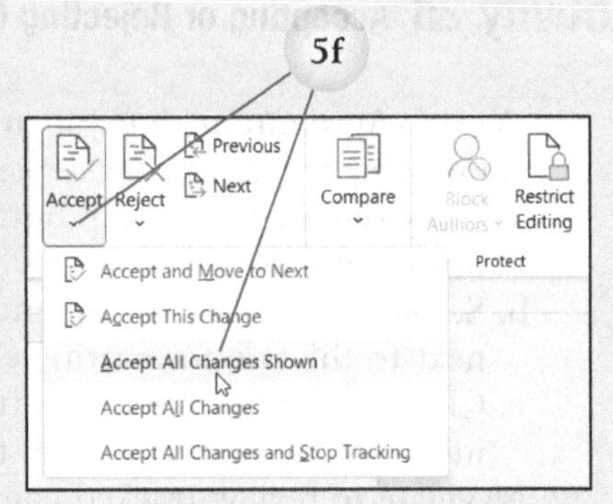

6. Redisplay all the changes by completing the following steps:
   a. Click the Tracking group dialog box launcher.
   b. Click the *Ink* check box to insert a check mark.
   c. Click the *Insertions and Deletions* check box to insert a check mark.
   d. Click OK to close the Track Changes Options dialog box.
7. Press Ctrl + Home to move the insertion point to the beginning of the document.
8. Reject the change that inserts the word *BUILDING* by clicking the Next button in the Changes group and then clicking the Reject button. (This rejects the change and moves to the next revision in the document.)

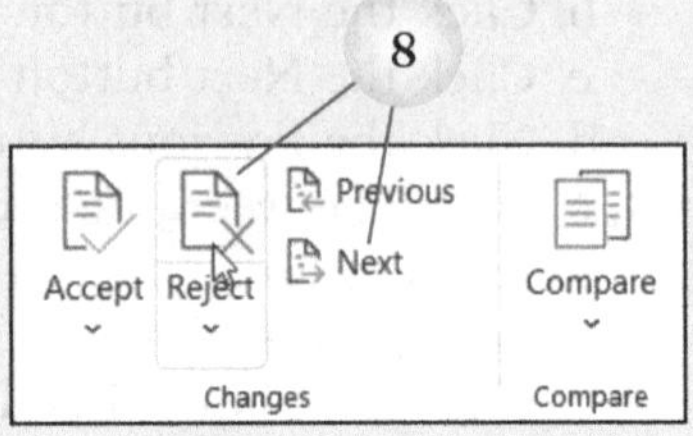

9. Click the Accept button to accept the change that deletes *thirty (30)*.
10. Click the Accept button to accept the change that inserts *sixty (60)*.
11. Click the Reject button to reject the change that deletes the words *at their option*.
12. Accept all the remaining changes by clicking the Accept button arrow and then clicking *Accept All Changes* at the drop-down list.

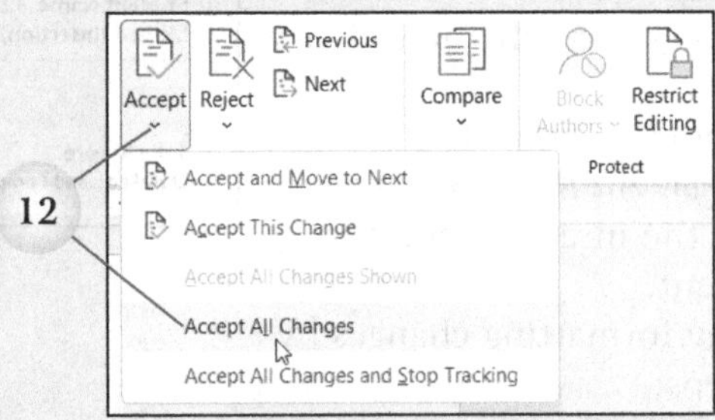

13. Return the track changes options to the default settings by completing the following steps:
    a. If necessary, click the Review tab.
    b. Click the Tracking group dialog box launcher.
    c. At the Track Changes Options dialog box, click the Advanced Options button.
    d. At the Advanced Track Changes Options dialog box, click the *Insertions* option box arrow and then click *Underline* at the drop-down list.
    e. Click the *Insertions Color* option box arrow and then click *By author* at the drop-down list. (You will need to scroll up the list to display this option.)
    f. Click the *Moved from Color* option box arrow and then click *Green* at the drop-down list. (You may need to scroll down the list to display this color.)
    g. Click the *Moved to Color* option box arrow and then click *Green* at the drop-down list.
    h. Click OK to close the dialog box.
    i. Click OK to close the Track Changes Options dialog box.

14. Check to make sure all the tracked changes are accepted or rejected by completing the following steps:
    a. Click the Reviewing Pane button in the Tracking group.
    b. Check the information at the top of the Reviewing pane and make sure that each option is followed by a 0. (You may need to click the up arrow at the right of *0 revisions* to show all the options.)
    c. Close the Reviewing pane.
15. Save, preview, and then close **8-Agreement.docx**.

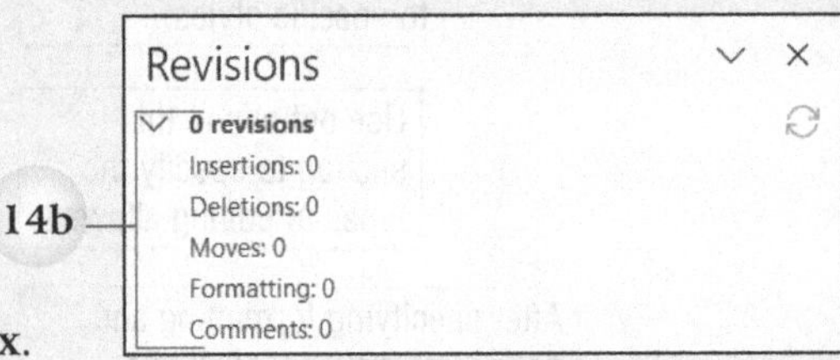

Activity 3 Restrict Formatting and Editing in a Company Report — 4 Parts

You will open a company report document, restrict formatting and editing in the document, enforce protection, and protect the document with a password.

Restricting Formatting and Editing

Restricting a Document

Within an organization, copies of a document may be distributed among members of a group. In some situations, the document may need to be protected and the changes that can be made to it need to be limited. If a document contains sensitive, restricted, or private information, consider protecting it by saving it as a read-only document or securing it with a password.

Use options in the Restrict Editing task pane to limit what formatting and editing users can perform on a document. Limiting formatting and editing is especially useful in a workgroup environment, in which a number of people review and edit the same document.

For example, suppose a company's annual report is being prepared and it contains information from a variety of departments, such as Finance, Human Resources, and Sales and Marketing. Access to the report can be restricted so only certain employees are allowed to edit specific parts of the document. For instance, the part of the report pertaining to finance can be restricted to allow only someone in the Finance Department to make edits. Similarly, the part of the report on employees can be restricted so only someone in Human Resources can make edits. By limiting options for editing, the integrity of the document can be protected.

Restrict Editing

To protect a document, display the Restrict Editing task pane, shown in Figure 8.6, by clicking the Review tab and then clicking the Restrict Editing button in the Protect group. Use options in the *Formatting restrictions* section to limit formatting to specific styles and use options in the *Editing restrictions* section to specify the types of editing allowed in the document.

Figure 8.6 Restrict Editing Task Pane

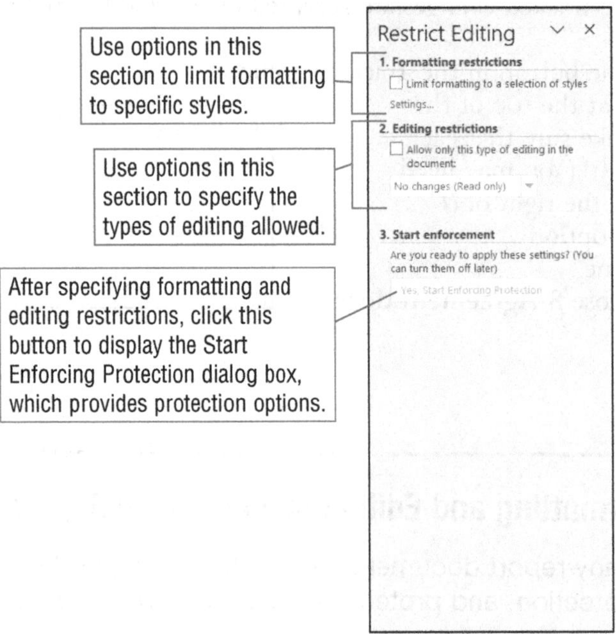
Use options in this section to limit formatting to specific styles.
Use options in this section to specify the types of editing allowed.
After specifying formatting and editing restrictions, click this button to display the Start Enforcing Protection dialog box, which provides protection options.
Restrict Editing
1. Formatting restrictions
Limit formatting to a selection of styles
Settings...
2. Editing restrictions
Allow only this type of editing in the document:
No changes (Read only)
3. Start enforcement
Are you ready to apply these settings? (You can turn them off later)
Yes, Start Enforcing Protection

The Protect group on the Review tab contains a Block Authors button when a document is saved to a Microsoft SharePoint site that supports workspaces. If the button is active, select the portion of the document to block from editing and then click the Block Authors button. To unblock authors, click in the locked section of the document and then click the Block Authors button.

Applying Formatting Restrictions

Quick Steps

Display Formatting Restrictions Dialog Box

1. Click Review tab.
2. Click Restrict Editing button.
3. Click Settings hyperlink.

Use options in the *Formatting restrictions* section of the Restrict Editing task pane to lock specific styles used in a document, thus allowing the use of only those styles and prohibiting users from making other formatting changes. Click the Settings hyperlink in the *Formatting restrictions* section and the Formatting Restrictions dialog box displays, as shown in Figure 8.7.

Insert a check mark in the *Limit formatting to a selection of styles* check box and the styles become available in the *Checked styles are currently allowed* list box. In this list box, insert check marks in the check boxes preceding the styles that are allowed and remove check marks from the check boxes preceding the styles that are not allowed. Limit formatting to a minimum number of styles by clicking the Recommended Minimum button. This allows formatting with styles that Word uses for certain features, such as bulleted and numbered lists. Click the None button to remove all the check marks and prevent all the styles from being used in the document. Click the All button to insert check marks in all the check boxes and allow all the styles to be used in the document.

Use options in the *Formatting* section of the dialog box to allow or not allow AutoFormat to make changes in a document. Also use options in this section of the dialog box to allow or not allow users to switch themes or style sets.

Figure 8.7 Formatting Restrictions Dialog Box

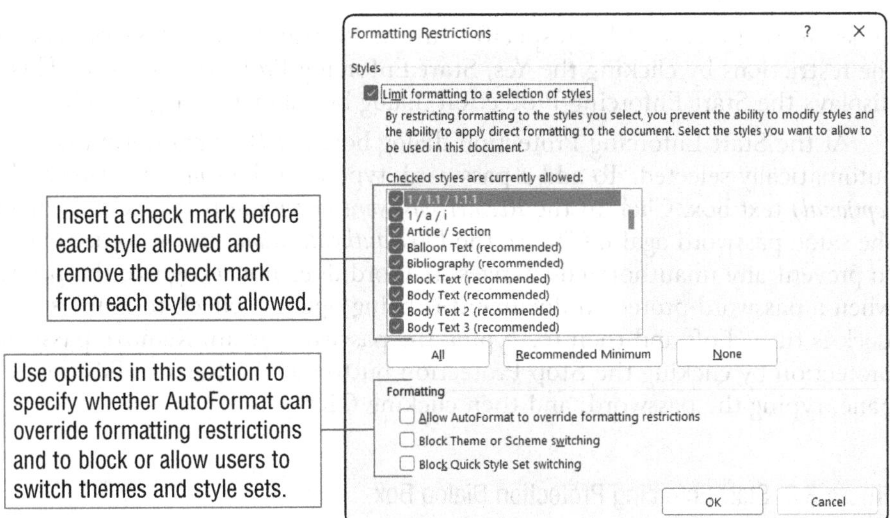

Activity 3a Restricting Formatting of a Document

Part 1 of 4

1. Open **TECRpt.docx** and then save it with the name **8-TECRpt**.
2. Restrict formatting to the Heading 1 and Heading 2 styles by completing the following steps:
   a. Click the Review tab.
   b. Click the Restrict Editing button in the Protect group.

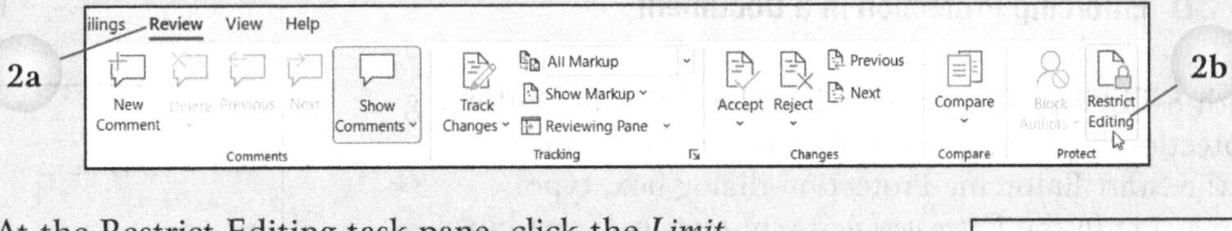

   c. At the Restrict Editing task pane, click the *Limit formatting to a selection of styles* check box to insert a check mark. (Skip this step if the check box already contains a check mark.)
   d. Click the Settings hyperlink.

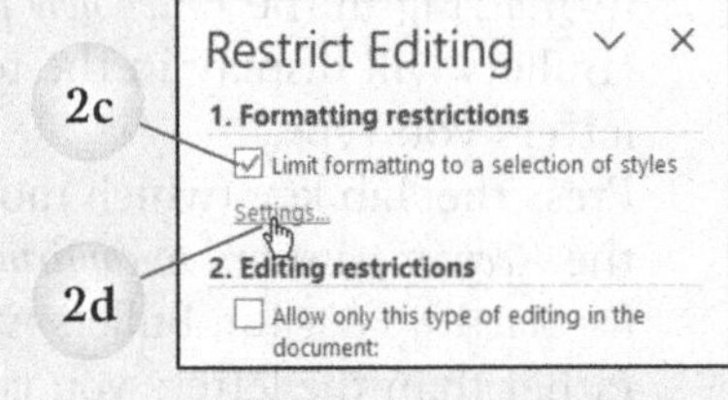

   e. At the Formatting Restrictions dialog box, click the None button.
   f. Scroll down the *Checked styles are currently allowed* list box and then click to insert check marks in the *Heading 1* and *Heading 2* check boxes.
   g. Click OK.
   h. At the message stating that the document may contain formatting or styles that are not allowed and asking about removing them, click Yes.
3. Save **8-TECRpt.docx**.

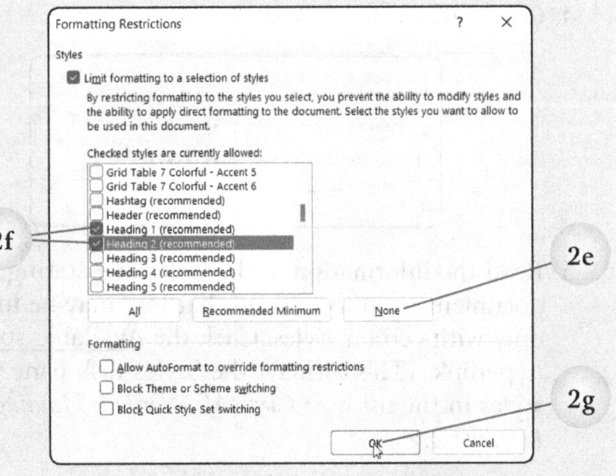

Check Your Work

Enforcing Protection

Quick Steps

Display Start Enforcing Protection Dialog Box

1. Click Review tab.
2. Click Restrict Editing button.
3. Specify formatting and/or editing options.
4. Click Yes, Start Enforcing Protection button.

When restrictions have been specified in the Restrict Editing task pane, enforce the restrictions by clicking the Yes, Start Enforcing Protection button. This displays the Start Enforcing Protection dialog box shown in Figure 8.8.

At the Start Enforcing Protection dialog box, the *Password* option is automatically selected. To add a password, type it in the *Enter new password (optional)* text box. Click in the *Reenter password to confirm* text box and then type the same password again. Choose the *User authentication* option to use encryption to prevent any unauthorized changes. If Word does not recognize the password when a password-protected document is being opened, check to make sure Caps Lock is turned off and then try typing the password again. Remove password protection by clicking the Stop Protection button at the Restrict Editing task pane, typing the password, and then clicking OK.

Figure 8.8 Start Enforcing Protection Dialog Box

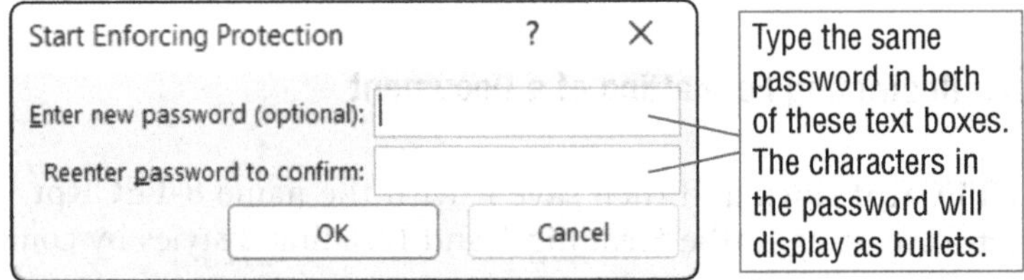

Activity 3b Enforcing Protection in a Document

Part 2 of 4

1. With **8-TECRpt.docx** open, click the Yes, Start Enforcing Protection button (in the middle of the task pane).
2. At the Start Enforcing Protection dialog box, type formatting in the *Enter new password (optional)* text box. (Bullets will display in the text box, rather than the letters you type.)
3. Press the Tab key (which moves the insertion point to the *Reenter password to confirm* text box) and then type formatting. (Again, bullets will display in the text box, rather than the letters you type.)
4. Click OK to close the dialog box.

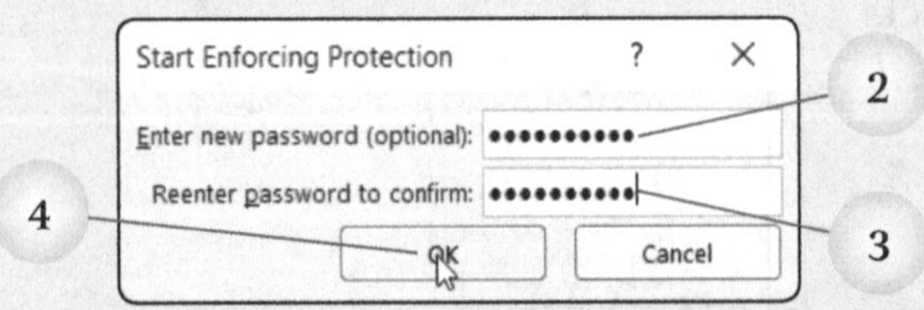

5. Read the information in the task pane stating that the document is protected and that text may be formatted only with certain styles. Click the Available styles hyperlink. (This displays the Styles task pane with four styles in the list box: *Clear All*, *Normal*, *Heading 1*, and *Heading 2*.)

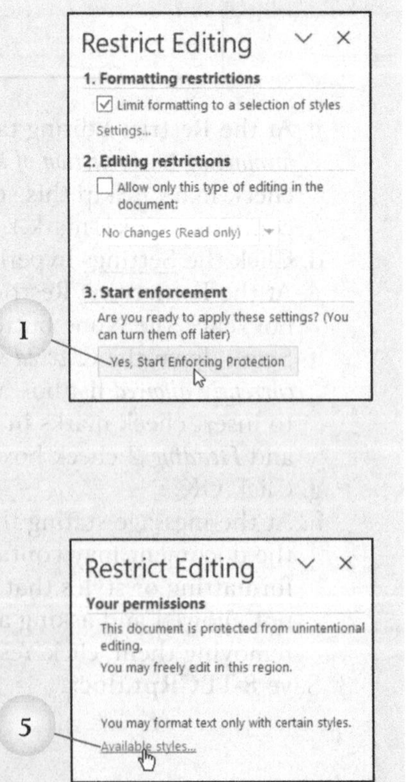

6. Close the Styles task pane.
7. Apply the Heading 1 style to the title *TANDEM ENERGY CORPORATION* and apply the Heading 2 style to the following headings: *Overview, Research and Development, Manufacturing,* and *Sales and Marketing.*
8. Apply the Lines (Simple) style set. (This style set is in the Document Formatting group on the Design tab.)
9. At the message stating that some of the styles could not be updated, click OK.
10. Save the document.
11. Remove the password protection from the document by completing the following steps:
    a. Click the Stop Protection button at the bottom of the Restrict Editing task pane.
    b. At the Unprotect Document dialog box, type formatting in the *Password* text box.
    c. Click OK.
12. Save **8-TECRpt.docx**.

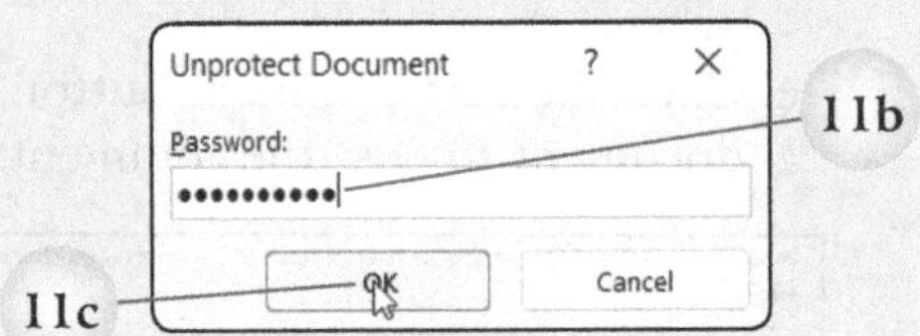

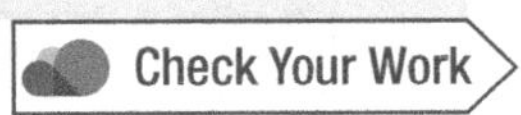

Applying Editing Restrictions

Use the *Editing restrictions* option in the Restrict Editing task pane to limit the types of changes users can make to a document. Insert a check mark in the *Allow only this type of editing in the document* check box and the drop-down list below the option becomes active. Click the option box arrow and the following options become available: *Tracked changes, Comments, Filling in forms,* and *No changes (Read only).*

To restrict users from making changes to a document, choose the *No changes (Read only)* option. Choose the *Tracked changes* option to allow users to make tracked changes in a document and choose the *Comments* option to allow users to insert comments in a document. These two options are useful in a workgroup environment, in which a document is routed to various individuals for review. Choose the *Filling in forms* option and users will be able to fill in the fields in a form, but not make any other changes.

Activity 3c Restricting Editing of and Enforcing Protection in a Document — Part 3 of 4

1. With **8-TECRpt.docx** open, restrict editing to inserting comments by completing the following steps:
    a. Make sure the Restrict Editing task pane displays.
    b. Click the *Allow only this type of editing in the document* check box to insert a check mark.
    c. Click the option box arrow below *Allow only this type of editing in the document* and then click *Comments* at the drop-down list.
2. Click the Yes, Start Enforcing Protection button at the bottom of the task pane.
3. At the Start Enforcing Protection dialog box, click OK. (Adding a password is optional.)
4. Read the information in the task pane stating that the document is protected and that editing is restricted to inserting comments.

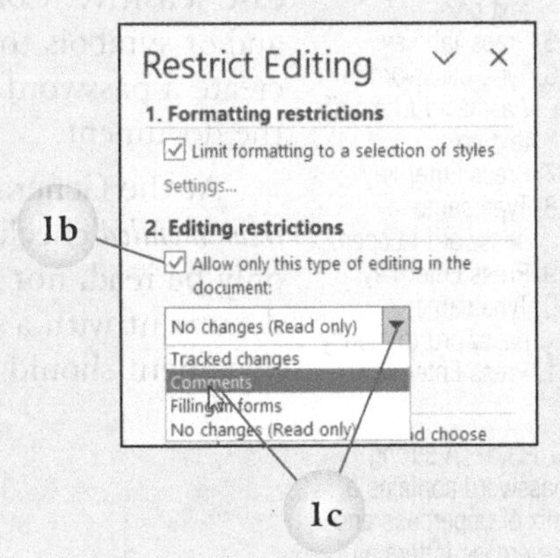

5. Click each ribbon tab and notice the buttons and options that are dimmed and unavailable.
6. Insert a comment by completing the following steps:
   a. Move the insertion point immediately to the right of the period that ends the last sentence in the second paragraph of the *Overview* section.
   b. Click the Review tab, if necessary; click the Show Markup button in the Tracking group; point to *Balloons*; and then click the *Show All Revisions Inline* option if necessary.
   c. Click the New Comment button in the Comments group on the Review tab.
   d. Type the following comment text: Include additional information on the impact of this purchase.
   e. Click the Post comment button. (If a Post comment button does not display, click in the document to post the comment.)

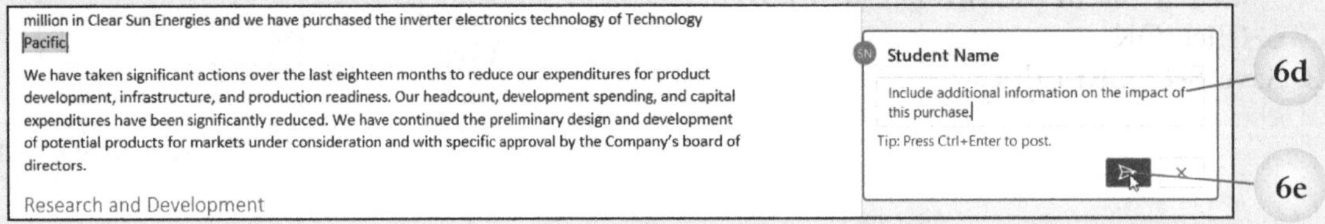

   f. Click the Stop Protection button at the bottom of the Restrict Editing task pane.
   g. Close the Restrict Editing task pane.
7. Save **8-TECRpt.docx**.

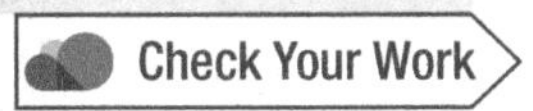

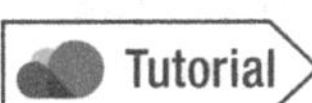

Protecting a Document with a Password

Quick Steps

Protect Document with Password

1. Press F12.
2. Click Tools button.
3. Click *General Options*.
4. Type password in *Password to open* text box.
5. Press Tab key.
6. Type password in *Password to modify* text box.
7. Press Enter key.
8. Type same password to open.
9. Press Enter key.
10. Type same password to modify.
11. Press Enter key.

Hint A strong password contains a mix of uppercase and lowercase letters as well as numbers and symbols.

Protecting a Document with a Password

In addition to protecting a document with a password using options at the Start Enforcing Protection dialog box, a document can be protected with a password using options at the General Options dialog box, shown in Figure 8.9. Display this dialog box by pressing the F12 function key to display the Save As dialog box, clicking the Tools button at the bottom of the dialog box next to the Save button, and then clicking *General Options* at the drop-down list.

Use options at the General Options dialog box to assign a password to open the document, modify the document, or both. To insert a password to open the document, click in the *Password to open* text box and then type the password. A password can contain up to 15 characters, should be at least 8 characters, and is case sensitive. Consider combining uppercase letters, lowercase letters, numbers, and/or symbols to make a password secure. Use the *Password to modify* option to create a password that someone must enter before being allowed to make edits to the document.

At the General Options dialog box, insert a check mark in the *Read-only recommended* check box to save a document as a read-only file. A read-only file can only be read, not modified. If changes are made, they must be saved into a new document with a new name. Use this option if the contents of the original document should not be changed.

Figure 8.9 General Options Dialog Box

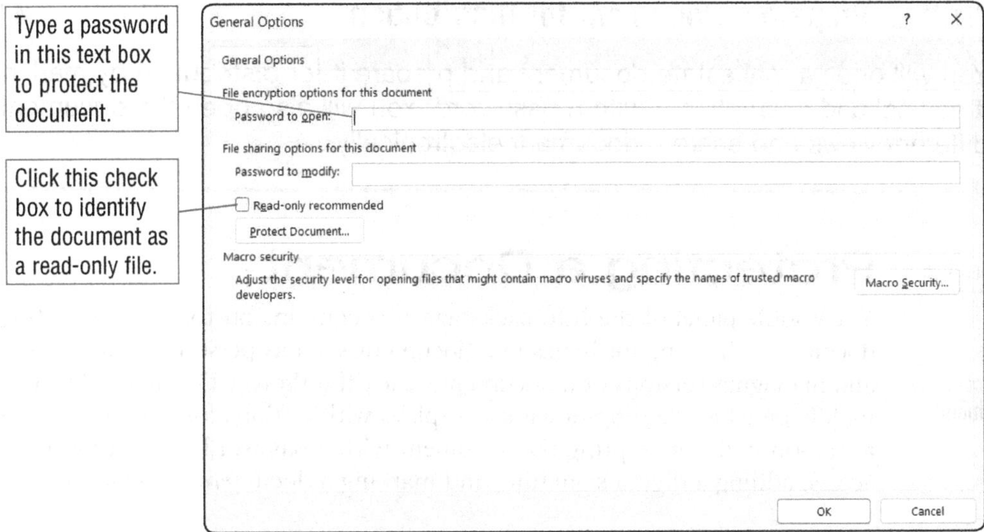

Activity 3d Protecting a Document with a Password

Part 4 of 4

1. With **8-TECRpt.docx** open, save the document and protect it with a password by completing the following steps:
   a. Press the F12 function key to display the Save As dialog box.
   b. Click the Tools button near the bottom of the dialog box (next to the Save button) and then click *General Options* at the drop-down list.
   c. At the General Options dialog box, type your first name in the *Password to open* text box. (If your name is longer than 15 characters, abbreviate it. You will not see your name; Word inserts bullets in place of the letters.)
   d. After typing your name, press the Enter key.
   e. At the Confirm Password dialog box, type your name again in the *Reenter password to open* text box. (Be sure to type it exactly as you did in the *Password to open* text box, including the same uppercase and lowercase letters.) Press the Enter key.
   f. Click the Save button at the Save As dialog box.

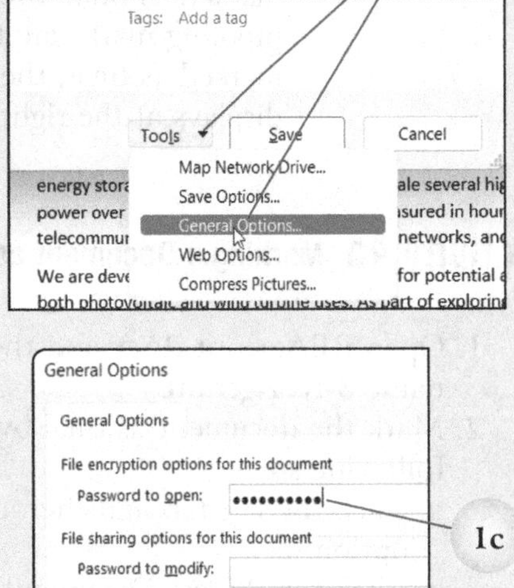

2. Close **8-TECRpt.docx**.
3. Open **8-TECRpt.docx** and type your password when prompted in the *Enter password to open file* text box and then press the Enter key.

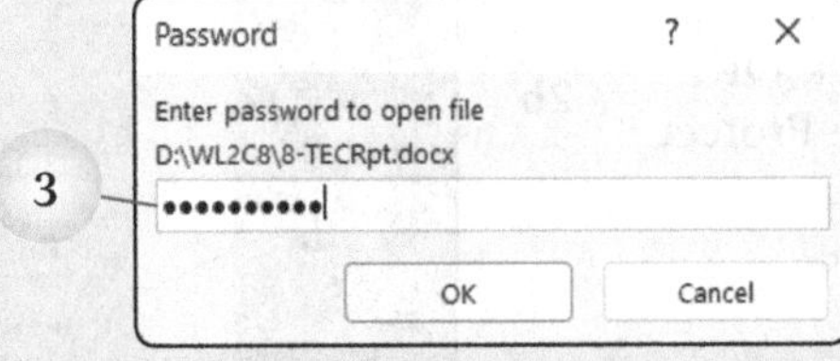

4. Close the document.

Check Your Work

Activity 4 Prepare a Document for Distribution — 4 Parts

You will open a real estate document and prepare it for distribution by marking it as final and encrypting it with a password. You will also open the document in different views and share a document electronically.

Protecting a Document

Protect Document

Protecting a Document

The middle panel of the Info backstage area contains buttons for protecting a document, checking for issues in a document such as personal data and accessibility, and managing versions of a document. Click the Protect Document button in the middle panel and a drop-down list displays with options for opening a document as a read-only file, encrypting the document with a password, restricting editing and access, adding a digital signature, and marking a document as final.

Marking a Document as Final

Click the *Mark as Final* option at the Protect Document button drop-down list to save the document as a read-only document. Click this option and a message displays stating that the document will be marked and then saved. At this message, click OK. This displays another message stating that the document is the final version of the document. The message further states that when a document is marked as final, the status property is set to *Final*; typing, editing commands, and proofing marks are turned off. At this message, click OK. After a document is marked as final, the message *This document has been marked as final to discourage editing* displays at the right of the Protect Document button at the Info backstage area.

Activity 4a Marking a Document as Final — Part 1 of 4

1. Open **REAgrmnt.docx** and then save it with the name **8-REAgrmnt.**
2. Mark the document as final by completing the following steps:
   a. Click the File tab and then click the *Info* option.
   b. Click the Protect Document button at the Info backstage area and then click *Mark as Final* at the drop-down list.
   c. At the message stating that the document will be marked and saved, click OK.
   d. At the next message that displays, click OK. Notice the message at the right of the Protect Document button.
   e. Click the Back button to return to the document.

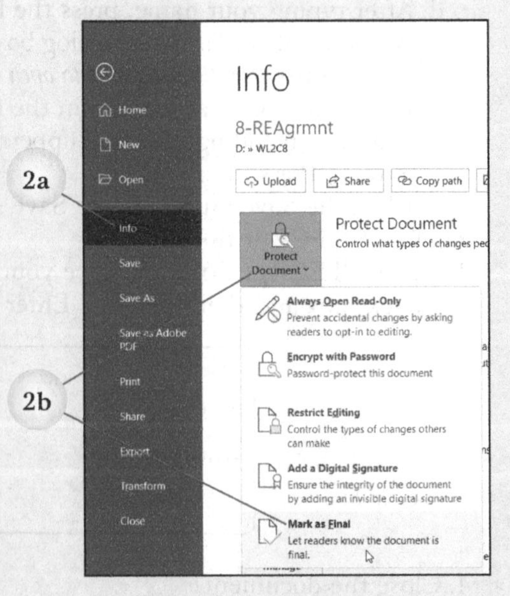

3. In the document window, notice the message bar at the top of the screen and then close the document.
4. Open **8-REAgrmnt.docx** and then click the Edit Anyway button on the yellow message bar.

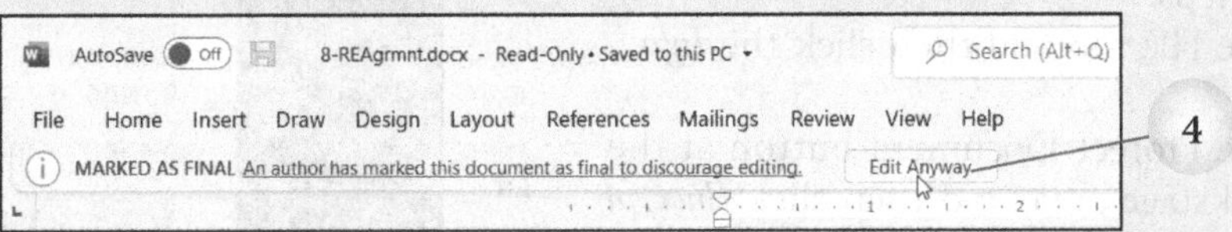

5. Save **8-REAgrmnt.docx**.

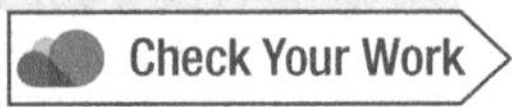

Opening as Read-Only

Click the *Always Open Read-Only* option at the Protect Document button drop-down list to identify a document that should be read and not edited. When a document is opened with this read-only option selected, a message displays indicating that the author of the document would like it to be opened as read-only, unless it needs editing. At this message, click Yes to open the document as read-only or click No if the document needs editing.

Encrypting a Document

Quick Steps

Encrypt Document

1. Click File tab.
2. Click *Info* option.
3. Click Protect Document button.
4. Click *Encrypt with Password.*
5. Type password and then press Enter key.
6. Type password again and then press Enter key.

Word provides a number of methods for protecting a document with a password. As previously discussed in this chapter, a document can be protected with a password using options at the Start Enforcing Protection dialog box and the General Options dialog box.

In addition to these two methods, a document can be protected with a password by clicking the Protect Document button at the Info backstage area and then clicking the *Encrypt with Password* option at the drop-down list. At the Encrypt Document dialog box, type a password in the text box (the text will display as bullets) and then press the Enter key or click OK. At the Confirm Password dialog box, type the password again (the text will display as bullets) and then press the Enter key or click OK. When a password is applied to a document, the message *A password is required to open this document* displays at the right of the Protect Document button.

Restricting Editing

Click the Protect Document button at the Info backstage area and then click the *Restrict Editing* option at the drop-down list and the document displays with the Restrict Editing task pane open. This is the same task pane discussed previously in this chapter.

Adding a Digital Signature

Use the *Add a Digital Signature* option at the Protect Document button drop-down list to insert an invisible digital signature in a document. A digital signature is an electronic stamp that verifies the authenticity of the document. Before a digital signature can be added, it must be obtained. A digital signature can be obtained from a commercial certification authority.

Activity 4b Encrypting a Document with a Password

Part 2 of 4

1. With **8-REAgrmnt.docx** open, encrypt the document with a password by completing the following steps:
   a. Click the File tab and then click the *Info* option.
   b. Click the Protect Document button at the Info backstage area, and then click *Encrypt with Password* at the drop-down list.
   c. At the Encrypt Document dialog box, type your initials in uppercase letters in the *Password* text box. (The text will display as bullets.)

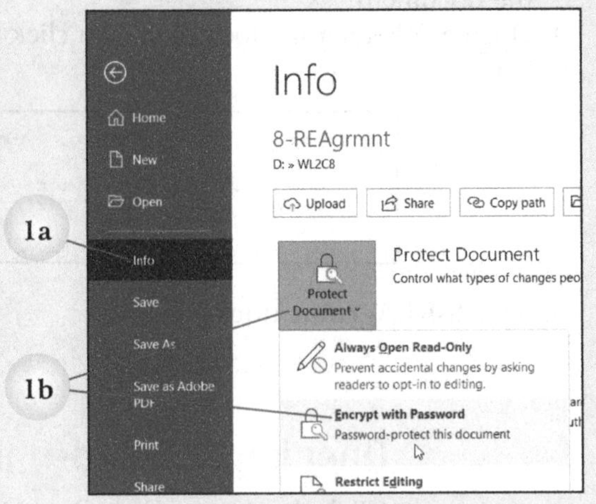

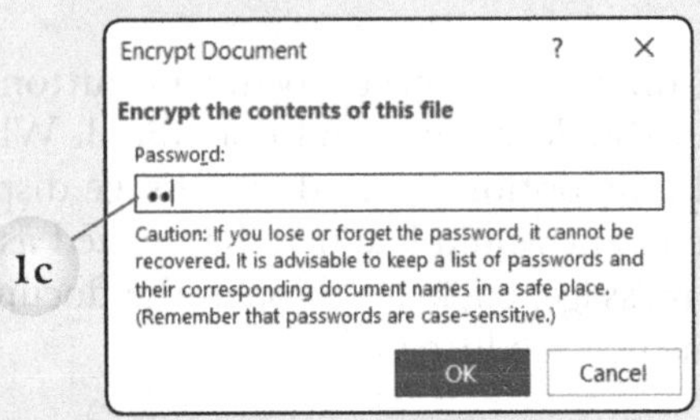

   d. Press the Enter key.
   e. At the Confirm Password dialog box, type your initials again in uppercase letters in the *Reenter password* text box (the text will display as bullets) and then press the Enter key.
2. Click the Back button to return to the document.
3. Save and then close the document.
4. Open **8-REAgrmnt.docx**.
5. At the Password dialog box, type your initials in uppercase letters in the *Enter password to open file* text box and then press the Enter key.
6. Save **8-REAgrmnt.docx**.
7. Remove the password from the document by completing the following steps:
   a. Click the File tab and then click the *Info* option.
   b. Click the Protect Document button and then click *Encrypt with Password*.
   c. Delete the circles in the *Password* text box.
   d. Click OK.
   e. Click the Back button to return to the document.
8. Save and then close **8-REAgrmnt.docx**.

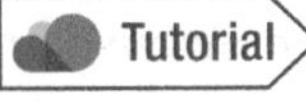

Opening a Document in Different Views

Opening a Document in Different Views

Use the Open button at the Open dialog box to open a document in different views. At the Open dialog box, click the Open button arrow and a drop-down list of options displays. Click the *Open Read-Only* option and the document opens in Read-Only mode. In Read-Only mode, changes can be made to the document, but the document cannot be saved with the same name.

Quick Steps

Open Document in Different Views

1. Display Open dialog box.
2. Click document name.
3. Click Open button arrow.
4. Click option at drop-down list.

Click the *Open as Copy* option and a copy of the document opens with the text *Copy (1)* before the document name in the Title bar. Click the *Open in Protected View* option and the document opens with the text *(Protected View)* after the document name in the Title bar. A message bar displays above the document indicating that the file was opened in Protected view. To edit the document, click the Enable Editing button in the message bar. Open a document with the *Open and Repair* option and Word will open a new version of the document and attempt to resolve any issues.

Activity 4c Opening a Document in Different Views

Part 3 of 4

1. Open a document as a read-only document by completing the following steps:
   a. Press Ctrl + F12 to display the Open dialog box and then navigate to your WL2C8 folder.
   b. Click the document name ***8-REAgrmnt.docx***. (Click only one time.)
   c. Click the Open button arrow (in the bottom right corner of the dialog box) and then click *Open Read-Only* at the drop-down list.
   d. The document opens as a read-only document. Notice that *Read-Only* displays after the name of the document in the Title bar.
   e. Close the document.

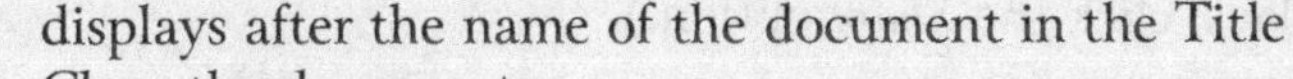

2. Open a document in protected view by completing the following steps:
   a. Press Ctrl + F12 to display the Open dialog box.
   b. Click the document name ***PremProduce.docx***.
   c. Click the Open button arrow and then click *Open in Protected View* at the drop-down list.
   d. Notice the message bar stating that the file was opened in Protected view.
   e. Click each tab and notice that most of the formatting options are dimmed.
   f. Click in the document and then click the Enable Editing button in the message bar. This removes *Protected View* after the document name in the Title bar and makes available the options on the tabs.

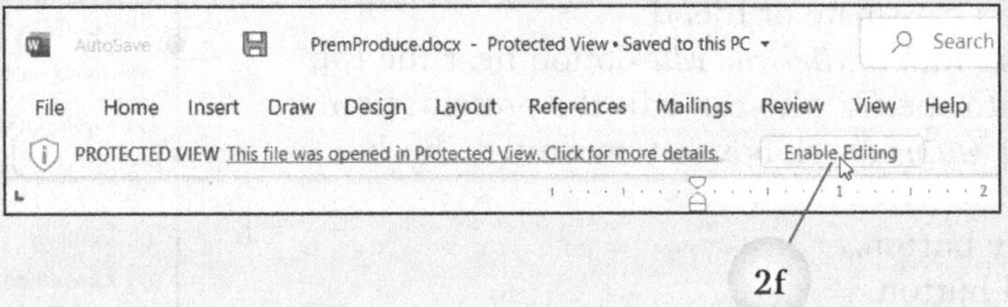

3. Close the document.

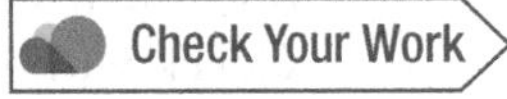

Sharing a Document Electronically

When collaborating with others in a workplace environment, being able to share files electronically may be useful. To share a document electronically with others, the document must be saved to a OneDrive account or a shared location such as a website. Share a document saved to a OneDrive account or other shared location by clicking the Share button in the upper right corner of the screen; clicking the File tab and then clicking the *Share* option; or by clicking the File tab, clicking the *Info* option, and then clicking the Share button below the document name.

At the Share window or task pane that displays, follow the instructions to send a link and invite others to view the document by typing in the email addresses of people to be invited. By default, anyone who is invited to view the document can also make edits to it. This option can be changed so that people can only view, but not edit, the document.

Activity 4d Sharing a Document Electronically

Part 4 of 4

Note: To complete this optional activity, you need to be connected to the internet and have a OneDrive account. Depending on your version of Word, the activity steps may vary. Activity 4d assumes that a Share window will display. If a Share task pane displays, check with your instructor to determine the steps to follow to share your document.

1. Open **8-REAgrmnt.docx**.
2. Save **8-REAgrmnt.docx** to your OneDrive account folder with the name **8-REAgrmnt-Shared** by completing the following steps:
   a. Click the File tab and then click the *Save As* option.
   b. Double-click the OneDrive account in the middle panel.
   c. At the Save As dialog box with the OneDrive account folder active, type 8-REAgrmnt-Shared in the *File name* text box and then click the Save button.
3. With **8-REAgrmnt-Shared.docx** open, click the Share button at the right side of the ribbon. (If a drop-down list displays, click the *Share* option.)

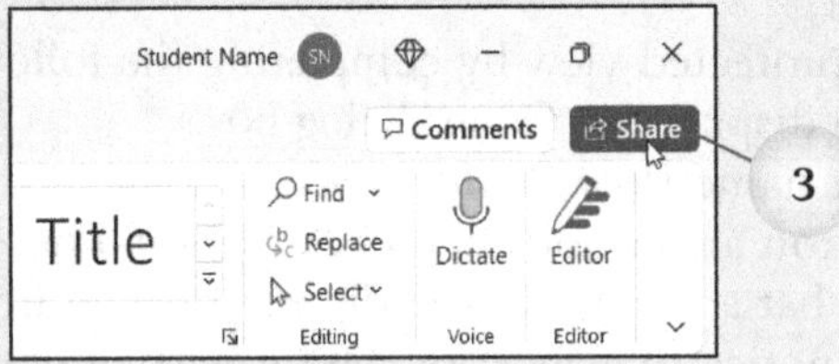

4. Click in the text box containing *To: Name, group or email* text box (displays above the blue line) in the Share window, type the email address for your instructor and/or the email of a classmate or friend.
5. Click the *Anyone with the link can edit* option near the top of the window to specify who can edit the presentation.
6. Click the *Allow editing* check box to remove the check mark.
7. Click the Apply button.
8. Click the Send button.
9. At the message that displays stating the link to the document was sent, click the Close button.
10. Check with your instructor, classmate, and/or friend to determine if he or she was able to open the email containing the link to your document.
11. Close **8-REAgrmnt-Shared.docx** saved to your OneDrive account folder.

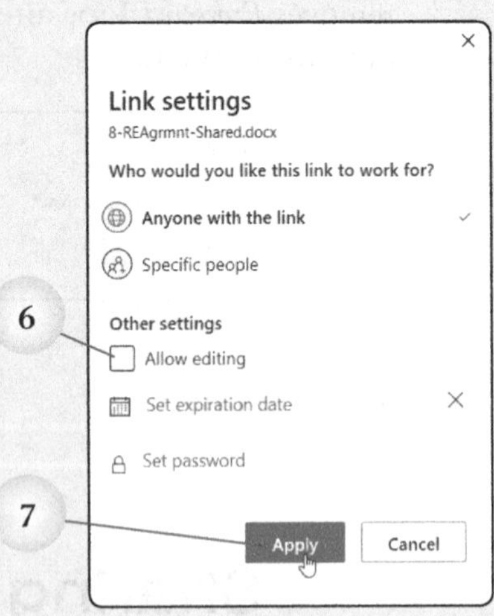

Activity 5 Manage Versions of a Document — 1 Part

You will decrease the autorecovery time to 1 minute, open a document containing an advertising flyer for a produce market, and make changes to it without saving the file. You will then review autorecovered versions of the document created automatically by Word.

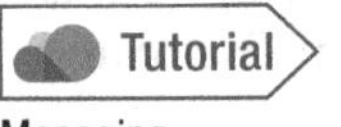

Managing Document Versions

Manage Document

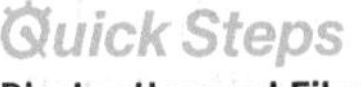

Display Unsaved Files Folder

1. Click File tab.
2. Click *Info* option.
3. Click Manage Document button.
4. Click *Recover Unsaved Documents*.

OR

1. Click File tab.
2. Click *Open* option.
3. Click Recover Unsaved Documents button.

Managing Document Versions

When working in an open document, Word automatically saves it every 10 minutes. This automatic backup feature can be very helpful if the document is closed accidentally without saving it or the power to the computer is disrupted. As backups of the open document are automatically saved, they are listed at the right of the Manage Document button at the Info backstage area, as shown in Figure 8.10. Each autorecovered document displays with *Today* followed by the time and *(autorecovery)*. When the document is saved and then closed, the autorecover backup documents are deleted.

To open an autorecover backup document, click the File tab, click the *Info* option, and then click the autorecover document. An autorecover document can also be opened by right-clicking the autorecover document at the Info backstage area and then clicking the *Open Version* option. When an autorecover document is opened, a message bar displays. What displays on the message bar depends on the Microsoft 365 update being used. The message bar may display a Save As button, a message indicating that a newer version is available, a Compare button, or a Compare and Restore button. Use the Restore button to save the original document and use the Compare button to compare the current version of the document with the autorecover document. If the hyperlink A new version is available displays on the message bar, click the hyperlink to display a message

Figure 8.10 Autorecover Documents at the Info Backstage Area

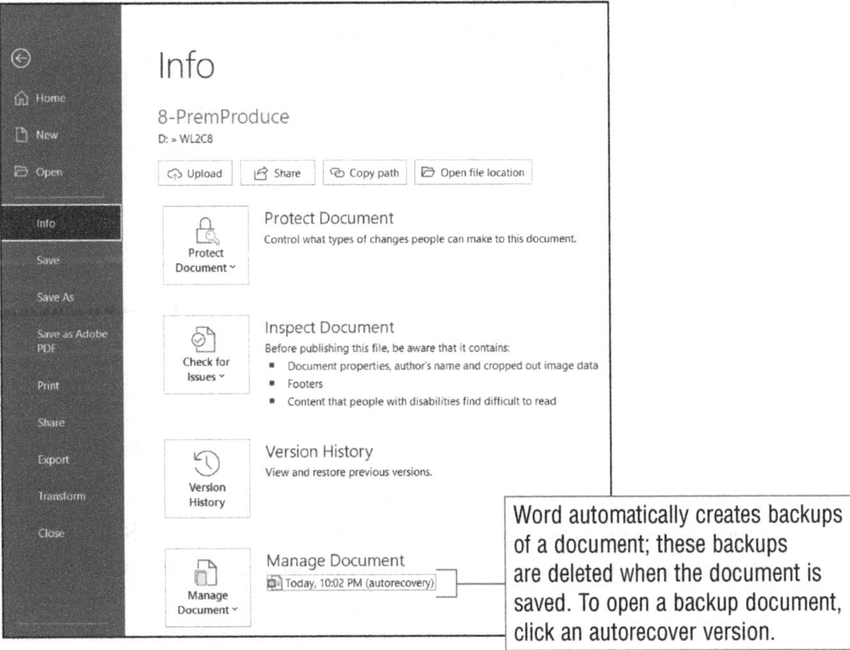

indicating that if you upload your file (to a OneDrive account, for example), Office will automatically save versions of your file as you work.

When a document is saved, the autorecover backup documents are deleted. However, if a document is closed without being saved (after 10 minutes) or the power is disrupted, Word keeps the autorecover backup files in the UnsavedFiles folder on the hard drive. Access this folder by clicking the Manage Document button at the Info backstage area and then clicking *Recover Unsaved Documents*. At the Open dialog box, double-click the backup file to be opened. The UnsavedFiles folder can also be displayed by clicking the File tab, clicking the *Open* option, and then clicking the Recover Unsaved Documents button below the *Recent* option list. Files in the UnsavedFiles folder are kept for four days after a document is created. After that, they are automatically deleted.

Delete an autorecover backup file by displaying the Info backstage area, right-clicking the autorecover file (at the right of the Manage Document button), and then clicking *Delete This Version* at the shortcut menu. At the confirmation message, click the Yes button. To delete all unsaved files from the UnsavedFiles folder, display a blank document, click the File tab, click the *Info* option, click the Manage Document button, and then click the *Delete All Unsaved Documents* option at the drop-down list. At the confirmation message, click Yes.

As mentioned previously, Word automatically saves a backup of an unsaved document every 10 minutes. To change this default setting, click the File tab and then click *Options*. At the Word Options dialog box, click *Save* in the left panel. Notice that the *Save AutoRecover information every* measurement box is set at 10 minutes. To change this number, click the measurement box up arrow to increase the number of minutes between autorecovers or click the down arrow to decrease the number of minutes.

Quick Steps

Delete Autorecover Backup File
1. Click File tab.
2. Click *Info* option.
3. Right-click autorecover backup file.
4. Click *Delete This Version* at shortcut menu.

Delete All Unsaved Files
1. Click File tab.
2. Click *Info* option.
3. Click Manage Document button.
4. Click *Delete All Unsaved Documents*.
5. Click Yes.

Change AutoRecover Time
1. Click File tab.
2. Click *Options*.
3. Click *Save*.
4. Type minutes in *Save AutoRecover information every* measurement box.
5. Click OK.

Activity 5 Opening and Deleting an Autorecover Document

Part 1 of 1

1. At a blank screen, decrease the autorecover time to 1 minute by completing the following steps:
   a. Click the File tab and then click *Options*.
   b. At the Word Options dialog box, click *Save* in the left panel.
   c. Click the *Save AutoRecover information every* measurement box down arrow until *1* displays.

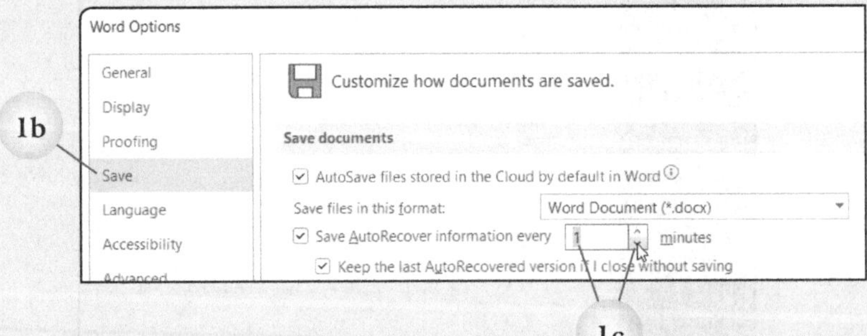

   d. Click OK to close the dialog box.
2. Open **PremProduce.docx** and save it with the name **8-PremProduce**.
3. Press Ctrl + End to move the insertion point to the end of the document and then type your first and last names.

4. Leave the document open for more than one minute without making any further changes. After at least one minute has passed, click the File tab and then click the *Info* option. Check to see if an autorecover document displays at the right of the Manage Document button. (If not, click the Back button to return to the document and wait a few more minutes.)

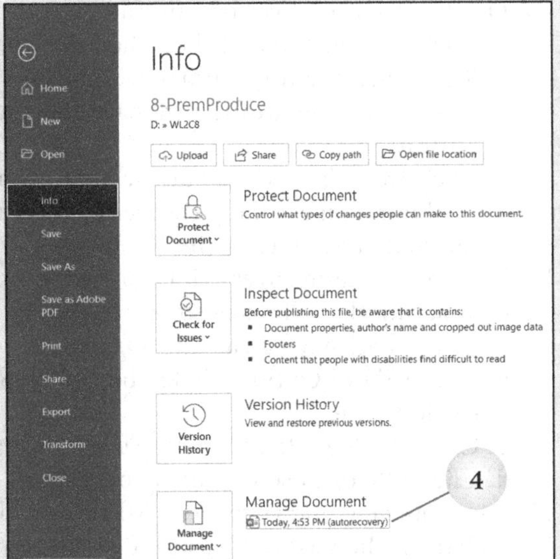

5. When an autorecover document displays at the Info backstage area, click the Back button to return to the document.
6. Select the SmartArt graphic at the end of the document, and then delete it.
7. Click the File tab, click the *Info* option, and then click the autorecover document at the right of the Manage Document button. If more than one autorecover document displays, click the one at the top of the list (the most recent autorecover document). This opens the autorecover document as a read-only file. Notice that the autorecover document contains the SmartArt graphic.

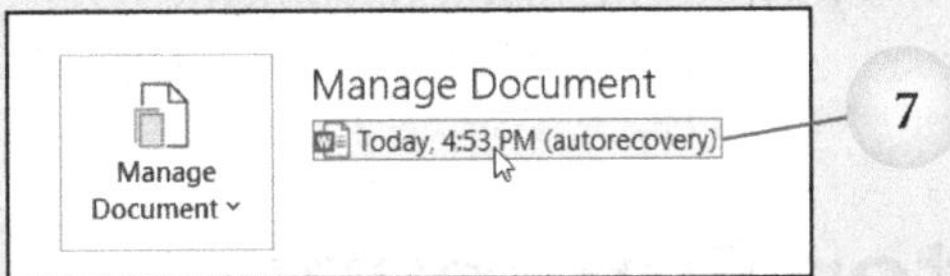

8. Instead of saving the autorecover document, close it without saving it.
9. Check to see what versions of previous documents Word has saved by completing the following steps:
   a. At the Info backstage area, click the Manage Document button and then click *Recover Unsaved Documents* at the drop-down list.
   b. At the Open dialog box, check the documents that display in the content pane.
   c. Click the Cancel button to close the Open dialog box.

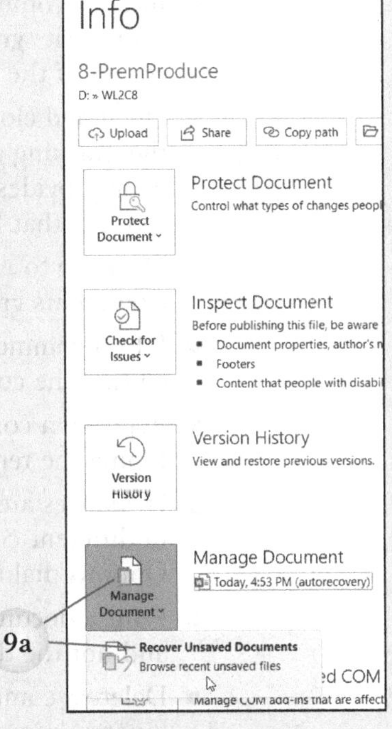

10. Delete an autorecover backup file by completing the following steps:
    a. Click the File tab and then click the *Info* option.
    b. Right-click the first autorecover backup file name at the right of the Manage Document button.
    c. Click *Delete This Version* at the shortcut menu.
    d. At the message asking whether to delete the selected version, click the Yes button.
11. Return the autorecovery time to 10 minutes by completing the following steps:
    a. At the backstage area, click *Options*.
    b. At the Word Options dialog box, click *Save* in the left panel.
    c. Click the *Save AutoRecover information every* measurement box up arrow until *10* displays.
    d. Click OK to close the dialog box.
12. Save, preview, and then close **8-PremProduce.docx**.
13. Delete all the unsaved backup files by completing the following steps:
    a. Press Ctrl + N to display a blank document.
    b. Click the File tab and then click the *Info* option.
    c. Click the Manage Document button and then click *Delete All Unsaved Documents*.
    d. At the message that displays, click Yes.
14. Click the Back button to return to the blank document.

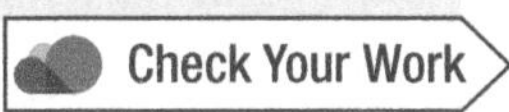

Chapter Summary

- Insert a comment in a document with the New Comment button in the Comments group on the Review tab or the Comment button in the upper right corner of the screen. A comment box opens and displays in the right margin.
- Open and close the Reviewing pane by clicking the Reviewing Pane button in the Tracking group on the Review tab. The summary section of the Reviewing pane provides counts of the number of comments inserted and the types of changes that have been made to the document.
- Navigate to review comments using the Previous and Next buttons in the Comments group on the Review tab.
- Edit a comment with the Edit comment button in the comment box. After editing the comment, click the Post comment button in the comment box.
- Reply to a comment by clicking in the *Reply* text box in the comment box, typing the reply, and then clicking the Post reply button.
- If changes are made to a document by different users, the changes display in different colors. The user name and initials can be changed at the Word Options dialog box with *General* selected.
- Print a document with or without the comments or print only the comments and not the document.
- Delete a comment with the *Delete thread* option at the More thread actions button drop-down list or with the Delete button in the Comments group on the Review tab.

- Use the Track Changes feature when more than one person is reviewing and editing a document. Turn on Track Changes by clicking the Track Changes button in the Tracking group on the Review tab.
- The *Display for Review* option box in the Tracking group on the Review tab has a default setting of *Simple Markup*, which shows changes in the document and a vertical change line at the left margin where the change was made. This setting can be changed to *All Markup*, showing all changes in the document along with the original text or *No Markup*, showing the document with all the changes applied.
- With the *Display for Review* option box set at *All Markup*, specify what tracking information displays in the document with options at the Balloons side menu. Display this side menu by clicking the Show Markup button in the Tracking group on the Review tab and then pointing to *Balloons*.
- Display information about tracked changes—such as the author's name, date and time, and type of change—by hovering the pointer over a change. After approximately one second, a box displays with the information. Another method for displaying information about tracked changes is to display the Reviewing pane.
- To ensure that all changes made to a document are tracked, lock the Track Changes feature by clicking the Track Changes button arrow in the Tracking group on the Review tab, clicking *Lock Tracking*, and then typing a password at the Lock Tracking dialog box.
- Customize what tracked changes display in a document with options at the Show Markup button drop-down list. At the drop-down list, remove check marks from those options that should not display and specify what reviewer changes should display.
- Change Track Changes default settings with options at the Advanced Track Changes Options dialog box. Display this dialog box by clicking the Tracking group dialog box launcher and then clicking the Advanced Options button at the Track Changes Options dialog box.
- When reviewing a document, move to the next change by clicking the Next button in the Changes group on the Review tab and move to the previous change by clicking the Previous button.
- Use the Accept and Reject buttons in the Changes group on the Review tab to accept and reject changes made in a document.
- Restrict formatting and editing in a document and apply a password to protect it with options in the Restrict Editing task pane. Display this task pane by clicking the Review tab and then clicking the Restrict Editing button in the Protect group.
- Apply formatting restrictions in a document by specifying what styles are and are not allowed at the Formatting Restrictions dialog box. Display this dialog box by clicking the Settings hyperlink in the *Formatting restrictions* section of the Restrict Editing task pane.
- Enforce restrictions to a document by clicking the Yes, Start Enforcing Protection button at the Restrict Editing task pane and then entering a password at the Start Enforcing Protection dialog box.
- Apply editing restrictions in a document using options in the *Editing restrictions* section of the Restrict Editing task pane.

- Mark a document as final, which saves it as a read-only document, by clicking the Protect Document button at the Info backstage area and then clicking *Mark as Final* at the drop-down list. Typing, editing commands, and proofing marks are turned off when a document is marked as final.
- Protect a document with a password by clicking the Protect Document button at the Info backstage area, clicking the *Encrypt with Password* option, and then specifying a password at the Encrypt Document dialog box.
- Another method for displaying the Restrict Editing task pane is to click the Protect Document button at the Info backstage area and then click *Restrict Editing* at the drop-down list.
- Open a document in different views with options at the Open button drop-down list at the Open dialog box.
- Share a document that has been saved to a OneDrive account or a shared location such as a website with options at the Share window or Share task pane. Use options at the Share window or task pane to identify who will receive the shared document and to specify whether or not the shared document can be viewed only or viewed and edited.
- By default, Word automatically saves a backup of an unsaved document every 10 minutes. A list of autorecover backup documents of an open document displays at the right of the Manage Document button at the Info backstage area. To open an autorecover backup document, click the File tab, click the Info option, and then click the autorecover document.
- When a document is saved, Word automatically deletes the autorecover backup documents. However, if a document is closed without saving it or the power to the computer is disrupted, Word keeps a backup document in the UnsavedFiles folder on the hard drive. Access this folder by clicking the Manage Document button at the Info backstage area and then clicking *Recover Unsaved Documents* at the drop-down list.
- Delete an autorecover backup file by displaying the Info backstage area, right-clicking the autorecover backup file, and then clicking *Delete This Version* at the shortcut menu.
- Delete all the unsaved documents from the UnsavedFiles folder by displaying a blank document, clicking the File tab, clicking the Manage Document button, and then clicking *Delete All Unsaved Documents*. At the message that displays, click Yes.
- Change the 10-minute autorecover default setting with the *Save AutoRecover information every* measurement at the Word Options dialog box with *Save* selected in the left panel.

Commands Review

FEATURE	RIBBON TAB, GROUP	BUTTON, OPTION	KEYBOARD SHORTCUT
accept changes	Review, Changes		
Advanced Track Changes Options dialog box	Review, Tracking	, Advanced Options	
balloons	Review, Tracking	, *Balloons*	
delete comment	Review, Comments		
display for review	Review, Tracking		
Encrypt Document dialog box	File, *Info*	, *Encrypt with Password*	
Formatting Restrictions dialog box	Review, Protect	, *Settings*	
new comment	Review, Comments		
next comment	Review, Comments		
next revision	Review, Changes		
previous comment	Review, Comments		
previous revision	Review, Changes		
reject changes	Review, Changes		
Restrict Editing task pane	Review, Protect		
Reviewing pane	Review, Tracking		
Share window			
show markup	Review, Tracking		
Track Changes	Review, Tracking		Ctrl + Shift + E
Track Changes Options dialog box	Review, Tracking		
UnsavedFiles folder	File, *Info*	, *Recover Unsaved Documents*	

CHAPTER 8

Review and Assessment

Skills Assessment

Assessment 1

Insert Comments in a Country Report

1. Open **SingaporeRpt.docx** and then save it with the name **8-SingaporeRpt**.
2. Delete the only comment in the document.
3. Position the insertion point at the end of the first paragraph below the title *Singapore* and then insert a comment and type the following comment text: Please provide an image of the flag of the Republic of Singapore.
4. Position the insertion point at the end of the second paragraph below the heading *History* and then insert a comment and type the following comment text: Provide more information on the British East India company.
5. Position the insertion point at the end of the last paragraph below the heading *History* and insert a comment and type the following comment text: Describe the current government of the Republic of Singapore.
6. Save the document and then print only the comments.
7. Close **8-SingaporeRpt.docx**.

Assessment 2

Track Changes in a Building Agreement Document

1. Open **BuildAgrmnt.docx** and then save it with the name **8-BuildAgrmnt**.
2. Turn on Track Changes and then make the following changes:
   a. Select and then bold the text *THIS AGREEMENT* at the beginning of the first paragraph below the title.
   b. Select and then delete the text *and Financing* that displays at the beginning of the second paragraph (the text in bold).
   c. Type either has or between *owner* and *will* in the first sentence in the *Construction Loan Arrangements* paragraph.
   d. Turn off Track Changes.
3. Display the Word Options dialog box with *General* selected and then change the user name to *Sandra Payne* and the initials to *SP*. Insert a check mark in the *Always use these values regardless of sign in to Office* check box.
4. Turn on Track Changes and then make the following changes:
   a. Select and then delete the last sentence in the *Changes and Alterations* paragraph (the sentence that begins *Where such change results*.)
   b. Move the *Exclusions* paragraph above the *Changes and Alterations* paragraph.
   c. Turn off Track Changes.
5. Display the Word Options dialog box with *General* selected. Change the user name back to the original name and the initials back to the original initials. Also remove the check mark from the *Always use these values regardless of sign in to Office* check box.
6. Preview the document with tracked changes displayed inline.
7. Accept all the changes in the document *except* the change deleting the last sentence in the *Changes and Alterations* paragraph; reject this change.
8. Save, preview, and then close **8-BuildAgrmnt.docx**.

Assessment 3

Restrict Formatting and Editing of a Writing Report

1. Open **WritingProcess.docx** and then save it with the name **8-WritingProcess**.
2. Display the Restrict Editing task pane and then restrict formatting to the Heading 2 and Heading 3 styles. (At the message asking about removing formatting or styles that are not allowed, click No.)
3. Enforce the protection and include the password *writing*.
4. Click the Available styles hyperlink.
5. Apply the Heading 2 style to the two titles *THE WRITING PROCESS* and *REFERENCES*.
6. Apply the Heading 3 style to the seven remaining headings in the document. (The Heading 3 style may not display until the Heading 2 style is applied to the first title.)
7. Close the Styles task pane and then close the Restrict Editing task pane.
8. Save, preview, and then close **8-WritingProcess.docx**.

Assessment 4

Insert Comments in a Software Life Cycle Document

1. Open **SoftwareCycle.docx** and then save it with the name **8-SoftwareCycle**.
2. Display the Restrict Editing task pane, restrict editing to comments only, and then start enforcing the protection. Do not include a password.
3. At the end of the first paragraph in the document, type the comment Create a SmartArt graphic that illustrates the software life cycle.
4. At the end of the paragraph in the *Design* section, type the comment Include the problem-solving steps.
5. At the end of the paragraph in the *Testing* section, type the comment Describe a typical beta testing cycle.
6. Print only the comments.
7. Close the Restrict Editing task pane.
8. Save, preview, and then close **8-SoftwareCycle.docx**.

Assessment 5

Track Changes in a Table

1. Open **SalesTable.docx** and then save it with the name **8-SalesTable**.
2. Make the Review tab active and then change the *Display for Review* option box setting to *All Markup*.
3. Display the Advanced Track Changes Options dialog box, look at the options for customizing tracked changes in a table, and then make the following changes:
   a. Change the color for inserted cells to Light Purple.
   b. Change the color for deleted cells to Light Green.
4. Turn on Track Changes and then make the following changes:
   a. Insert a new row at the beginning of the table.
   b. Merge the cells in the new row. (At the message stating that the action will not be marked as a change, click OK.)
   c. Type Clearline Manufacturing in the merged cell.
   d. Delete the *Fanning, Andrew* row.
   e. Insert a new row below *Barnet, Jacqueline* and then type Montano, Neil in the first cell, $530,678 in the second cell, and $550,377 in the third cell.
   f. Turn off Track Changes.
5. Save and then preview the document.
6. Accept all the changes.
7. Display the Advanced Track Changes Options dialog box and then return the color of the inserted cells to Light Blue and the color of the deleted cells to Pink.
8. Save, preview, and then close **8-SalesTable.docx**.

Visual Benchmark

Track Changes in an Employee Performance Document

1. Open **NSSEmpPerf.docx** and then save it with the name **8-NSSEmpPerf**.
2. Turn on Track Changes and then make the changes shown in Figure 8.11. (Make the editing changes before moving the *Employment Records* section after the *Performance Evaluation* section.)
3. Turn off Track Changes and then print only the list of markups. ***Hint: Do this by displaying the Print backstage area, clicking the first gallery in the Settings category, and then clicking the*** **List of Markup** ***option***.
4. Accept all the changes to the document.
5. Save, preview, and then close **8-NSSEmpPerf.docx**.

Figure 8.11 Visual Benchmark

N
Northland Security Systems
3200 North 22nd Street ✦ Springfield ✦ IL ✦ 62102

EMPLOYEE PERFORMANCE

Work Performance Standards

Some work performance standards are written statements of the results expected of an employee when his or her job elements are satisfactorily performed under existing working conditions. Each employee in a permanent position must be provided with a current set of work performance standards for his or her position.

Employment Records

Your personnel file is maintained in the human resources department at the main office of Northland Security Systems. The human resources department maintains a file with copies of the documentation in your specific department. Your file includes personnel action documents, mandatory employment forms, your performance evaluations, and documentation of disciplinary action. Your file may include letters of commendation, training certificates, or other work-related documents that your supervisor has requested to be included in your file.

Performance Evaluation

If you are serving a six-month probationary period, your supervisor will evaluate your performance at the end of the second and fifth months. If you are completing a one-year probationary period, your evaluations will be conducted at the end of the third, seventh, and eleventh month. You will receive a copy of each performance report. Once you have attained permanent employee status, your performance will be evaluated annually during the month prior to your pay progression date. Each evaluation will include a discussion between you and your supervisor to review and clarify goals and methods to achieve them. The evaluation will also include a report of your progress on the job. Evaluations will be made with reference to established work performance standards.

and/or behavior

cap

working

(full-time equivalent)

written

1-888-555-2200 ✦ https://ppi-edu.net/nss

Case Study

Part 1

You work for Premier Associates, a career development company that provides career placement, transition, and outplacement for clients. Some of the company's materials need formatting to reflect the company's brand. Open **PALtrhd.docx** and look at the first page header and first page footer. Notice the colors and shapes used in the header and footer and then close the document. Open **PAResume.docx** and then save it with the name **8-PAResume**. This document has been reviewed by your supervisor, who made her edits as tracked changes. Accept the editing changes to the document and turn off tracked changes. Look at the one comment in the document, make the change mentioned in the comment and then delete the comment. Format the document so it is attractive and easy to read. Consider using the **PAHead.png** image as a header and **PAFoot.png** as a footer. Add any additional information to the header or footer that you think is needed. Save, preview, and then close **8-PAResume.docx**.

Part 2

Your supervisor has given you another document that she has edited and wants you to format. Open **PAResumeStyles.docx** and then save it with the name **8-PAResumeStyles**. Accept or reject the edits made by your supervisor and then turn off tracked changes. (The document contains two edits that should be rejected.) Make the change suggested by her comment. Apply formatting to the document similar to what you applied to **8-PAResume.docx**. Save, preview, and then close **8-PAResumeStyles.docx**.

Part 3

Your company provides a sample chonological resume to clients. Your supervisor wants you to open the sample resume and apply formatting to the resume so it has the look and branding of the other Premier Associates documents. Open **PAChronoResume.docx** and then save it with the name **8-PAChronoResume**. Apply formatting so the document has the look of other Premier Associates documents. Save, preview, and then close **8-PAChronoResume.docx**.

Part 4

Your supervisor has asked you to search for a resume template and then download and print it to make it available for clients. Display the New backstage area and search for resumes. Download a resume that looks interesting to you. Apply formatting to the resume so it has the look of the other Premier Associates documents. Save the resume with the name **8-PAWordResume**. Preview and then close **8-PAWordResume.docx**.

WORD LEVEL 2

Unit 2 Performance Assessment

Data Files

The data files for this unit work are in the WL2U2 folder that you downloaded at the beginning of this course.

Assessing Proficiency

In this unit, you have learned to customize objects, create and format charts, merge documents, apply and customize building blocks, and insert and update fields. You have also learned to insert and manage comments, track changes, and restrict and protect documents.

Assessment 1 Insert and Format Objects

1. Open **HMConcert.docx** and then save it with the name **U2-HMConcert**.
2. The border is a drawn image that is positioned in the First Page Header pane. Double-click in the header, select the border image, apply the following formatting, and then close the First Page Header pane:
   - Apply the Light Gray, Background 2, Darker 10% shape fill (third column, second row in the *Theme Colors* section).
   - Apply the Offset: Center shape shadow effect (second column, second row in the *Outer* section).
3. Select the image of the music notes and then apply the following formatting:
   - Change the height of the image to 2.5 inches.
   - Precisely position the image on the page with an absolute horizontal measurement of 0.6 inch to the right of the left margin and an absolute vertical measurement of 0.65 inch below the page.
4. Click in the table cell immediately left of the telephone number 253.555.4500 (you may want to turn on the display of table gridlines), insert the telephone icon ☎ (use the search word *telephone* at the Icons window), and then apply the following formatting:
   - Change the height of the image to 0.3 inch.
   - Apply the Light 1 Fill, Colored Outline - Accent 3 graphic style (fourth style in the Graphic Styles gallery).

5. Click in the table cell immediately left of the email address, insert the envelope icon ✉ (use the search word *envelope* at the Icons window), and then apply the same formatting to the envelope icon that you applied to the telephone icon.
6. Save, preview, and then close **U2-HMConcert.docx**.

Assessment 2 Customize a 3D Model

1. Open **OpenHouse.docx** and then save it with the name **U2-OpenHouse**. (This document contains a 3D model of a person in a spacesuit.)
2. Select the 3D model of the person in a spacesuit and then apply the following formatting:
   - Apply the Above Front Right 3D model view (fifth column, second row in the 3D Model Views drop-down gallery).
   - Increase the height of the image to 4.4 inches.
   - Precisely position the model on the page with an absolute horizontal measurement of 5.2 inches to the right of the left margin and an absolute vertical measurement of 2.7 inches below the page.
3. Save, preview, and then close **U2-OpenHouse.docx**.

Assessment 3 Create and Format a Column Chart

1. At a blank document, use the data in Figure U2.1 to create a column chart with the following specifications:
   a. Choose the 3-D Clustered Column chart type.
   b. Apply the Layout 3 quick layout.
   c. Apply the Style 5 chart style.
   d. Change the chart title to *Yearly Sales*.
   e. Insert a data table with legend keys.
   f. Select the chart area, apply the Subtle Effect - Green, Accent 6 shape style (last column, fourth row in the *Theme Styles* section), and then apply the Offset: Bottom shadow shape effect (second column, first row in the *Outer* section).
   g. Select the series *Second Half* and then apply the standard dark red shape fill (first option in the *Standard Colors* section).
   h. Change the chart height to 4 inches and the chart width to 6.25 inches.
   i. Use the Position button in the Arrange group to position the chart in the middle center of the page with square text wrapping.
2. Save the document with the name **U2-SalesChart** and then preview the document.

Figure U2.1 Assessment 3

Salesperson	First Half	Second Half
Bratton	$235,500	$285,450
Daniels	$300,570	$250,700
Hughes	$170,200	$180,210
Marez	$308,520	$346,400

3. With the chart selected, display the Excel worksheet and then edit the data in the worksheet by changing the following:
   a. Change the amount in cell C2 from *$285,450* to *$302,500.*
   b. Change the amount in cell C4 from *$180,210* to *$190,150.*
4. Save, preview, and then close **U2-SalesChart.docx**.

Assessment 4 Create and Format a Pie Chart

1. At a blank document, use the data in Figure U2.2 to create a pie chart with the following specifications:
   a. Apply the Layout 6 quick layout.
   b. Apply the Style 3 chart style.
   c. Change the chart title to *District Expenditures*.
   d. Move the legend to the left side of the chart.
   e. Select the chart area, apply the Gold, Accent 4, Lighter 80% shape fill (eighth column, second row in the *Theme Colors* section), and then apply the Glow: 11 point; Gray, Accent color 3 glow shape effect (third column, third row in the *Glow Variations* section).
   f. Select the legend and apply the Blue color shape outline (eighth option in the *Standard Colors* section).
   g. Move the data labels to the inside ends of the pie pieces.
   h. Use the Position button to center the chart at the top of the page with square text wrapping.
2. Save the document with the name **U2-ExpendChart**.
3. Preview and then close **U2-ExpendChart.docx**.

Figure U2.2 Assessment 4

	Percentage
Basic Education	42%
Special Needs	20%
Support Services	19%
Vocational	11%
Compensatory	8%

Assessment 5

Merge and Preview Letters

1. Look at the information shown in Figure U2.3 and Figure U2.4. Use the Mail Merge feature to prepare six letters using the information shown in the figures. When creating the letter main document, open **SoundLtrhd.docx** and then save it with the name **U2-SoundMD**. (Change the punctuation in the greeting line from a comma to a colon.) Create the data source file with the text shown in Figure U2.3 and name the file **U2-SoundDS**. (When creating the data source, customize the columns to accommodate the text in the figure.)
2. Type the text in the main document as shown in Figure U2.4. Insert the *Title* and *Last_Name* fields in the last paragraph as indicated.
3. Merge the document with the **U2-SoundDS.mdb** data source file.
4. Save the merged letters document with the name **U2-SoundLtrs**.
5. Preview and then close **U2-SoundLtrs.docx**.
6. Save and then close the main document.

Figure U2.3 Assessment 5

Mr. Antonio Mercado 3241 Court G Tampa, FL 33623	Ms. Kristina Vukovich 1120 South Monroe Tampa, FL 33655
Ms. Alexandria Remick 909 Wheeler South Tampa, FL 33620	Mr. Minh Vu 9302 Lawndale Southwest Tampa, FL 33623
Mr. Curtis Iverson 10139 93rd Court South Tampa, FL 33654	Ms. Holly Bernard 8904 Emerson Road Tampa, FL 33620

Figure U2.4 Assessment 5

December 16, 2024

«AddressBlock»

«GreetingLine»

Sound Medical is switching hospital care in Tampa to Bayshore Hospital beginning January 1, 2025. As mentioned in last month's letter, Bayshore Hospital was selected because it meets our requirements for high-quality, patient-centered care that is also affordable and accessible. Our physicians look forward to caring for you in this new environment.

Over the past month, staff members at Sound Medical have been working to make this transition as smooth as possible. Surgeries planned after January 1 are being scheduled at Bayshore Hospital. Mothers delivering babies after January 1 are receiving information about delivery room tours and prenatal classes available at Bayshore Hospital. Your Sound Medical doctor will have privileges at Bayshore Hospital and will continue to care for you if you need to be hospitalized.

You are a very important part of our patient family, «Title» «Last_Name», and we hope this information is helpful. If you have any additional questions or concerns, please call our health coordinator at (813) 555-9886 between 8:00 a.m. and 4:30 p.m.

Sincerely,

Jody Tiemann
District Administrator

XX
U2-SoundMD.docx

Assessment 6

Merge and Preview Envelopes

1. Use the Mail Merge feature to prepare Size 10 envelopes for the letters created in Assessment 5.
2. Specify **U2-SoundDS.mdb** as the data source document.
3. Save the merged envelopes document with the name **U2-SoundEnvs**.
4. Preview and then close **U2-SoundEnvs.docx**.
5. Save the envelope main document with the name **U2-SoundEnvMD**.
6. Close **U2-SoundEnvMD.docx**.

Assessment 7

Create and Insert Custom Building Blocks

1. Using the Open dialog box in Word, open the template **CPTemplate.dotx** and then save it as a template with the name **U2-CPTemplate**.
2. This template contains three custom building blocks for Capital Properties. Add two more custom building blocks with the following specifications:
   a. Select the heading *Attorney's Fees* and the paragraph of text below the heading and then save the selected text in a custom building block in the Quick Part gallery with the name *Fees*.
   b. Select the image (the horizontal line and house with *Est. 1990*) and then save the image as a custom building block in the Footer gallery with the name *CPFooter*.
3. Select and then delete the entire document.
4. Save and then close **U2-CPTemplate.dotx**.
5. Use File Explorer to open a blank document based on **U2-CPTemplate.dotx**.
6. Build a real estate agreement by completing the following steps:
   a. Insert the *CPHeader* building block located in the Header gallery. Close the Header pane.
   b. Insert the *CPFooter* building block located in the Footer gallery. Close the Footer pane.
   c. Insert the *REAgreement* building block located in the Quick Part gallery.
7. Save the document with the name **U2-CPAgreement**.
8. Preview and then close **U2-CPAgreement.docx**.
9. Use File Explorer to open a blank document based on **U2-CPTemplate.dotx**.
10. Build a lease agreement by completing the following steps:
    a. Insert the *CPHeader* building block located in the Header gallery. Close the Header pane.
    b. Insert the *CPFooter* building block located in the Footer gallery. Close the Footer pane.
    c. Insert the *LeaseAgreement* building block located in the Quick Part gallery.
    d. Move the insertion point to the beginning of the heading *Use of Premises* and then insert the *Fees* building block in the Quick Part gallery. (If necessary, press the Enter key to start a new paragraph at the *Use of Premises* heading.)
11. Save the document with the name **U2-CPLease**.
12. Preview and then close **U2-CPLease.docx**.

Assessment 8

Insert Comments and Track Changes in an Orientation Document

1. Open **Orientation.docx** and then save it with the name **U2-Orientation**.
2. Move the insertion point to end of the first paragraph below the title and then insert a comment and type the following comment text: Specify that the orientation is required.
3. Move the insertion point to the end of the first paragraph in the *Medical Screenings* section and then insert a comment and type the following comment text: Provide specific information on the required medical screening.
4. Click the *Display for Review* option box arrow and then click *All Markup* at the drop-down list, if necessary.
5. Turn on Track Changes and then make the following changes:
   a. Move the insertion point to the beginning of the word *designed* in the first sentence in the first paragraph, type (VIS) and then press the spacebar.
   b. Select and then delete the words *As part of the employment procedures* and the comma and space that follow the words that display at the beginning of the first paragraph in the *Medical Screenings* section.
   c. Turn off Track Changes.
6. Display the Word Options dialog box with *General* selected and then type Trudy Holmes as the user name and TH as the user initials. (Make sure you insert a check mark in the *Always use these values regardless of sign in to Office* check box.)
7. Turn on Track Changes and then make the following changes:
   a. Select and then apply italic formatting to the words *New Employee Orientation Program* that display in the first paragraph below the title.
   b. Select and then delete the second paragraph in the *Identification Badges* section (located on page 2).
   c. Turn off Track Changes.
8. Print the document with markups.
9. Display the Word Options dialog box with *General* selected and then change the user name back to the original name and the initials back to the original initials. (Remove the check mark from the *Always use these values regardless of sign in to Office* check box.)
10. Accept all the changes in the document *except* reject the change deleting the last paragraph in the *Identification Badges* section. (Leave the comments in the document.)
11. Save, preview, and then close **U2-Orientation.docx**.

Assessment 9

Restrict Formatting in a Report

1. Open **CompPioneers.docx** and then save it with the name **U2-CompPioneers**.
2. Display the Restrict Editing task pane and then restrict formatting to the Heading 1 and Heading 2 styles. (At the message that displays asking if you want to remove formatting or styles that are not allowed, click No.)
3. Enforce the protection and include the password *report*.
4. Click the Available styles hyperlink in the Restrict Editing task pane.
5. Apply the Heading 1 style to the title of the report (*PIONEERS OF COMPUTING*) and apply the Heading 2 style to the two headings in the report (*Konrad Zuse* and *William Hewlett and David Packard*).
6. Close the Styles task pane.
7. Close the Restrict Editing task pane.
8. Save, preview, and then close **U2-CompPioneers.docx**.

Writing Activities

Activity 1

Create Building Blocks and Compose a Letter

You are the executive assistant to the vice president of Clearline Manufacturing. You are responsible for preparing company documents and decide to create building blocks to increase the efficiency of and consistency in the documents. Press Ctrl + N to open a blank document and then save the document as a template named **U2-CMTemplate.dotx** in your WL2U2 folder. Create the following building blocks in the template:

- Create a letterhead that includes the company name and any other enhancements to improve the appearance. Save the letterhead as a building block in the Header gallery.
- Create a building block footer that inserts the company address and telephone number. (You determine the address and telephone number.) Include a visual element in the footer, such as a border. Save the footer building block in the Footer gallery.
- You send documents to the board of directors and decide to include the board members' names and addresses as building blocks. Save each board member's name and address as a building block in the Quick Part gallery.

Ms. Nancy Logan
12301 132nd Avenue East
Warminster, PA 18974

Mr. Dion Jarvis
567 Federal Street
Philadelphia, PA 19093

Dr. Tanner Svoboda
9823 South 112th Street
Norristown, PA 18974

- Create a complimentary close building block that includes *Sincerely yours,* your name, and the title *Executive Assistant*. Save the building block in the Quick Part gallery.

Delete the contents of **U2-CMTemplate.dotx** and then save the template. (This saves the building blocks you created in the template.)

At a blank document, write the body of a letter to a member of the board of directors and include at least the following information:

- Explain that the director of the Human Resources Department has created a new employee handbook and that it will be made available to all new employees. Also mention that the attorney for Clearline Manufacturing has reviewed the handbook and approved its content.
- Open **CMHandbook.docx** and then use the headings to summarize the contents of the handbook in a paragraph in the letter. Explain in the letter that a draft of the handbook is enclosed.
- Include any additional information you feel the directors may want to know.

Save the body of the letter as a separate document named **U2-CMLtr** and then close **U2-CMLtr.docx**. Use File Explorer to open a blank document based on **U2-CMTemplate.dotx** and then create a letter to Nancy Logan with the following specifications:

- Insert the letterhead building block you created for Clearline Manufacturing.
- Insert the footer building block.
- Insert the building block containing Nancy Logan's name and address.
- Insert into the document the file named **U2-CMLtr.docx**.

- Insert the complimentary close building block.
- Insert any other text or make any changes to complete the letter.

Save the completed letter with the name **U2-CMLtrNL**. Preview and then close **U2-CMLtrNL.docx**. Complete similar steps to create a letter to Dion Jarvis. Save the letter with the name **U2-CMLtrDJ**. Close the letter. Complete similar steps to create a letter to Tanner Svoboda. Save the letter with the name **U2-CMLtrTS**. Preview and then close **U2-CMLtrTS.docx**.

Activity 2

Create a Slogan Building Block

You decide to create a building block for the company slogan and save it in **U2-CMTemplate.dotx**. Open **U2-CMTemplate.dotx** from your WL2U2 folder. In the template, create a text box with the slogan *Where innovation and production come together.* inside the text box. Enhance the appearance of the text box by applying formatting similar to that applied to the company letterhead. After creating the text box, select it and then save it in the Text Box gallery with the name **CMSlogan**. After saving the text box as a building block, delete the text box and then save and close **U2-CMTemplate.dotx**. Use File Explorer to open a document based on **U2-CMTemplate.dotx**. Insert the letterhead header building block and the footer building block you created in Activity 1 and then insert the text box building block you created in this activity. Save the document with the name **U2-CMDocument**. Preview and then close **U2-CMDocument.docx**.

Internet Research

Create a Population Chart

Use a search engine to determine the population of the country in which you currently live for the years 1980, 1990, 2000, 2010, and 2020. Create a line chart with the information you find. Apply formatting to the chart to make the data easy to interpret and to improve the visual interest of the chart. Save the document with the name **U2-Population**. Preview and then close **U2-Population.docx**.

Job Study

Format a Guidelines Report

As a staff member of an electronics retailer, you are required to maintain cutting-edge technology skills, including being well versed in the use of new software applications, such as those in Microsoft 365. Recently, your supervisor asked you to develop and distribute a set of strategies for reading technical and computer manuals that staff members will use as they learn new applications. Use the concepts and techniques you learned in this textbook to edit the guidelines report as follows:

1. Open **Strategies.docx** and then save it with the name **U2-Strategies**.
2. Turn on Track Changes and then make the following changes:
   a. Change all the occurrences of *computer manuals* to *technical and computer manuals*.
   b. Format the document with appropriate heading styles.
   c. Turn off Track Changes.
   d. Insert at least two comments about the content and/or formatting of the document.
   e. Print the list of markups.
   f. Accept all the tracked changes.
3. Insert a table of contents.
4. Number the pages in the document.
5. Insert a cover page.
6. Save, preview, and then close **U2-Strategies.docx**.

INDEX

D

E

F

G

H

I

K

P

Q

R

S

Interior Photo Credits

All screen captures provided by the authors.

Preface

Page x: © LightField Studios/Shutterstock.com; **Page xii:** © Neyman Kseniya/Shutterstock.com; **Page xiv:** © Cameron Prins/Shutterstock.com; **Page xvii:** laptop © Kite_rin/Shutterstock.com, tablet © guteksk7/Shutterstock.com; **Page xviii:** © KucherAV/Shutterstock.com; **Page xix:** © Prostock-studio/Shutterstock.com

Chapter 2

Page 71: rainbow: publicdomainvectors.org

Chapter 4

Page 129: printer: publicdomainvectors.org; **Page 146:** flag: publicdomainvectors.org, voting icon: publicdomainvectors.org

Chapter 5

Page 196: photo © Kelly Rutkosky

Chapter 8

Page 305: compass: publicdomainvectors.org